W9-AEB-662

the AMERICANA ANNUAL

1990

AN ENCYCLOPEDIA OF THE EVENTS OF 1989

YEARBOOK OF THE ENCYCLOPEDIA AMERICANA

This annual has been prepared as a yearbook for general encyclopedias. It is also published as *Encyclopedia Year Book*.

Library of Congress Catalog Card Number: 23-10041

ISBN: 0-7172-0221-6
ISSN: 0196-0180

Printed and manufactured in the United States of America

Grolier Enterprises, Inc. offers a varied selection of both adult and children's book racks. For details on ordering, please write:

Grolier Enterprises, Inc.
Sherman Turnpike
Danbury, CT 06816
Attn: Premium Department

Contents

Feature Articles of the Year

The Alphabetical Section

Entries on the continents, major nations of the world, U.S. states, Canadian provinces, and chief cities will be found under their own alphabetical headings.

AP/Wide World

The Year in Review

The passage of each year is accompanied by changes in governments and international relationships, but few years have brought the fundamental shifts evidenced in the Communist-bloc countries of Eastern Europe in 1989.

Poland, Hungary, Czechoslovakia, and East Germany all peacefully established new governments with non-Communist themes, after more than four decades of Marxist rule. The new order was symbolized by the November opening of the Berlin Wall. The Soviet Union, continuing to pursue its own liberalization, gave its allied states wide latitude in carrying out reforms, in marked contrast to the brutal repressions of 1956 in Hungary and of 1968 in Czechoslovakia. Tragically, Romania had to endure additional violence in 1989, before a swift revolution ended the 24-year reign of a hard-line Communist dictator. The sad spectacle of a Communist regime's repression also was played out in China when Red Army troops shot down hundreds of prodemocracy demonstrators in Tiananmen Square.

Strife was evident in other parts of the world. Soviet troops withdrew from Afghanistan and Vietnamese troops left Cambodia, but civil war continued in both countries. Despite the start of peace talks in 1989, El Salvador erupted in the fiercest fighting of the decade-long civil war there. In the Philippines, President Corazon Aquino barely survived a coup attempt.

Indian voters turned out Prime Minister Rajiv Gandhi. In Japan, the death of Emperor Hirohito ended a 62-year era; the Japanese government, rocked by scandals within the ruling Liberal Democratic Party, had three prime ministers in 1989. Latin America's ABC powers (Argentina, Brazil, and Chile) all went to the polls. The Namibian election leading to independence from South Africa was judged free and fair by UN observers. Within South Africa, new President Frederik de Klerk took less of a hard line on apartheid.

U.S. President George Bush took military action to oust Panamanian Gen. Manuel Antonio Noriega. Bush met with Soviet President Mikhail Gorbachev, and also dealt with the myriad changes in Eastern Europe in his first year of office. At home, the Bush administration launched a war on drugs and pushed through legislation to bail out the troubled savings and loan industry. The U.S. Congress was preoccupied with ethics issues that led to the resignation of House Speaker Jim Wright. The Supreme Court, meanwhile, upheld a Missouri law restricting abortion.

Natural disasters were brought home to the United States in 1989 as Hurricane Hugo slammed into the U.S. Virgin Islands, Puerto Rico, and the Carolina mainland. A major earthquake also rumbled across northern California.

The environment suffered with a crude oil spill in Alaska's pristine waters and the continued conflagration in South America's tropical rain forests. An international ban on the sale of ivory promised to preserve Africa's elephant herds.

In science, a claim that cold fusion had been achieved was disputed. While a cure to AIDS remained elusive, tests of AZT offered hope that the drug could slow the disease.

In sports, baseball's Pete Rose was banned as a result of alleged gambling; A. Bartlett Giamatti, the major league's new commissioner, died of a heart attack. Basketball great Kareem Abdul Jabbar and tennis ace Chris Evert retired gracefully from their respective courts.

The movie *Batman* was a huge hit that fueled weeks of batmania. The biggest movie news, however, was the Time-Warner merger and the purchase of Columbia Pictures by Japan's Sony Corp. It was a year that rocked with reunion tours of The Who and the Rolling Stones, among other groups; the biggest "new" musical was *Jerome Robbins' Broadway*. The entertainment world mourned the passing of the composer Irving Berlin, comedienne Lucille Ball, pianist Vladimir Horowitz, and actor Sir Laurence Olivier.

THE EDITORS

"Peacefully and prudently, with their eyes open to danger, but not giving up what is right and necessary, the Poles gradually pave the way for historic transformation. We are joined along this way, albeit to various extents, by others: Hungarians and Russians, the Ukrainians and people of the Baltic Republics, Armenians and Georgians, and . . . the East Germans. We wish them luck and rejoice at each success they achieve. We are certain that others will also take our road, since there is no other choice." These were some of the words Poland's Solidarity leader Lech Walesa, *page 6,* *spoke at a joint meeting of the U.S. Congress in November. Vice-President Dan Quayle* (left) *and Speaker of the House Thomas Foley welcomed Walesa enthusiastically.*

January

1 Israel's Finance Minister Shimon Peres unveils an economic austerity plan, including budget reductions of $550 million.

4 Two U.S. Navy F-14 fighters shoot down two Libyan MiG-23 fighters in a clash over the Mediterranean Sea off the Libyan coast. The United States states that its jets fired in "self-defense." Libya claims its aircraft were victims of premeditated attack. Relations between Libya and the United States already were tense over U.S. charges that Libya recently had built a chemical-weapons factory.

7 Crown Prince Akihito becomes emperor of Japan following the death of his father, Emperor Hirohito.

11 In Paris representatives of 149 nations condemn the use of chemical weapons.

Less than two weeks before leaving the U.S. presidency, Ronald Reagan delivers a farewell address to the nation.

16 Thirty-five nations, including the United States and the USSR, issue a new East-West agreement to protect human rights.

17 In Stockton, CA, a gunman armed with a semiautomatic rifle and two pistols opens fire on a group of schoolchildren, killing five before committing suicide.

18 The U.S. Supreme Court upholds the constitutionality of the federal system, effective since Nov. 1, 1987, for sentencing convicted criminals.

19 Calm returns to the predominantly black Overton section of Miami, FL, following three nights of rioting. The shooting of a black motorcyclist by an Hispanic police officer sparked the unrest.

Ante Markovic is named premier of Yugoslavia, succeeding Branko Mikulic who resigned Dec. 30, 1988.

20 George Herbert Walker Bush is sworn in as 41st president of the United States; J. Danforth Quayle takes the oath as vice-president.

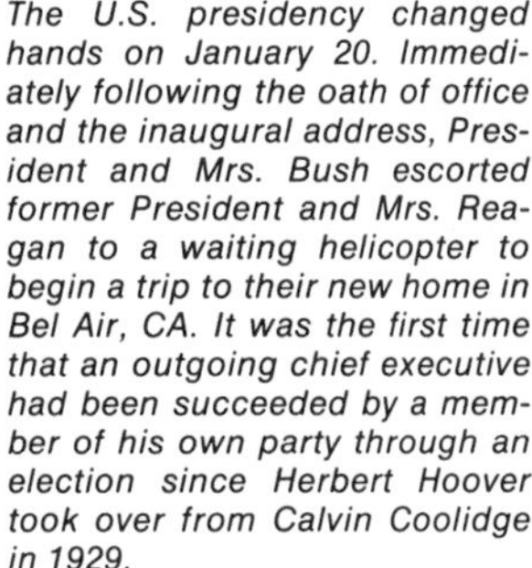
The U.S. presidency changed hands on January 20. Immediately following the oath of office and the inaugural address, President and Mrs. Bush escorted former President and Mrs. Reagan to a waiting helicopter to begin a trip to their new home in Bel Air, CA. It was the first time that an outgoing chief executive had been succeeded by a member of his own party through an election since Herbert Hoover took over from Calvin Coolidge in 1929.

22 In professional football's Super Bowl XXIII, the San Francisco 49ers defeat the Cincinnati Bengals, 20–16.

23 An earthquake strikes the central Asian republic of Tadzhikistan, the USSR, killing more than 250 persons.

The U.S. Supreme Court invalidates a Richmond, VA, law that channels 30% of public works funds to minority-owned construction companies.

Surrealist painter Salvador Dali, 84, dies in Figueras, Spain.

24 Convicted murderer Ted Bundy is executed at the Florida State Prison.

27 Political extremist Lyndon H. LaRouche, Jr., is sentenced to 15 years in prison for scheming to defraud the Internal Revenue Service and defaulting on more than $30 million in loans from supporters.

30 Canada's Prime Minister Brian Mulroney announces a reorganization of his cabinet.

February

2 Carlos Andres Pérez is sworn in as president of Venezuela.

In Washington, President Bush confers with Japanese Prime Minister Noboru Takeshita.

South Africa's President P. W. Botha, who recently suffered a stroke, resigns as leader of the ruling National Party but agrees to remain president for the time being. Education Minister Frederik W. de Klerk is selected as the party's new leader.

3 Gen. Andrés Rodríguez, the second-ranking officer in Paraguay's armed forces, takes the oath as Paraguay's president. Earlier, Alfredo Stroessner, who had led the nation from 1954, had been overthrown as president and commander in chief of the armed forces.

© C. Carrion/Sygma

Gen. Andrés Rodríguez, who in early February led a coup that overthrew Paraguay's longtime President Alfredo Stroessner, held a news conference February 6 to announce that presidential and congressional elections were scheduled for May 1, 1989.

4 Soviet Foreign Minister Eduard A. Shevardnadze concludes a three-day visit to China.

6 President Bush reveals a program to rescue the U.S. thrift industry.

7 The U.S. Congress votes to reject planned salary increases for federal legislators, federal judges, and top members of the executive branch.

9 President Bush outlines his budget priorities in a televised address to a joint session of Congress.

10 In his first trip outside the United States as president, George Bush confers with Canada's Prime Minister Mulroney in Ottawa.
Ronald H. Brown is elected chairman of the Democratic National Committee, becoming the first black to head a major U.S. political party.

13 Michael Manley takes the oath as prime minister of Jamaica. His social democratic People's National Party had defeated the right-of-center Jamaica Labour Party of Prime Minister Edward Seaga in national elections on February 9.

14 Concluding a two-day summit meeting in Tesoro Beach, El Salvador, the presidents of five Central American nations announce an agreement under which Nicaraguan rebel bases in Honduras would be closed in return for free elections in Nicaragua.

India's Supreme Court orders the Union Carbide Corporation to pay $470 million in compensation to victims of a toxic gas leak

Japan's Emperor Hirohito, who died January 7, was buried following daylong ceremonies February 24. Court musicians, right, played a funeral melody as the palanquin containing the emperor's coffin was carried by 51 members of the Imperial Household Agency upon its arrival at the Shinjuku Imperial Gardens for the Shinto and state rites.

AP/Wide World

from its pesticide plant in Bhopal, India, in December 1984. More than 2,000 persons were killed in the disaster.

Iran's Ayatollah Ruhollah Khomeini declares that the author and publisher of a novel offensive to Islam have been "sentenced to death." Salman Rushdie, author of *The Satanic Verses,* published by Viking Penguin, indicates that he is taking the threat "very seriously indeed."

15 The Soviet Union completes its troop withdrawal from Afghanistan.

17 Leaders of Algeria, Libya, Mauritania, Morocco, and Tunisia sign a treaty creating the Arab Maghreb Union (UMA), a North African common market. On February 16 the leaders of Egypt, Iraq, Jordan, and North Yemen had signed an agreement creating another regional common market, the Arab Cooperation Council (ACC).

The United States vetoes a UN Security Council resolution condemning Israel's treatment of Palestinians in the occupied territories.

24 The U.S. Federal Reserve Board increases the discount rate from 6.5% to 7%.

26 During a ten-day tour of the Middle East, Soviet Foreign Minister Eduard Shevardnadze confers with Iran's Ayatollah Ruhollah Khomeini.

27 En route home from the funeral of Japan's Emperor Hirohito, President Bush stops off in Seoul, South Korea, and addresses the National Assembly. Earlier the president had conferred with Deng Xiaoping and other Chinese leaders during three days in China.

The Yugoslav government sends troops to Kosovo province, an area torn by ethnic disturbances, in an effort to restore calm.

March

3 Robert C. McFarlane, former national security adviser in the Reagan administration, is sentenced to two years' probation and fined $20,000 for withholding information from Congress regarding the Iran-contra affair.

4 In Canada, Ed Broadbent resigns as national leader of the New Democratic Party.

5 Calm is restored in several cities of Venezuela following several days of rioting and looting brought on by government-imposed increases in transportation fares and gasoline prices. Some 250 persons were killed in the unrest.

7 Martial law is imposed in the Tibetan capital of Lhasa following three days of disturbances between anti-Chinese demonstrators and police in which at least one dozen persons were killed.

9 Eastern Airlines, which was hit by a strike by machinists on March 4, files for bankruptcy under Chapter 11.

15 Israel turns the Sinai beach resort of Taba over to Egypt.

17 The U.S. Senate confirms the nomination of U.S. Rep. John Cheney (R-WY) as U.S. secretary of defense. The nomination of former U.S. Sen. John Tower (R-TX) for the post had been rejected by the Senate on March 9.

The U.S. Food and Drug Administration announces that it is ending a five-day quarantine of grapes and berries imported from Chile. The quarantine had been imposed after U.S. government investigators discovered traces of cyanide in two Chilean grapes.

18 The space shuttle *Discovery* completes a five-day mission.

19 Alfredo Cristiani, 41-year-old candidate of the right-wing Nationalist Republican Alliance (ARENA), is elected president of El Salvador.

21 The U.S. Supreme Court upholds federal drug-testing programs for employees in jobs involving public safety and health.

22 Republican members of the U.S. House of Representatives elect Rep. Newt Gingrich (GA) to the post of House Republican whip, succeeding former Rep. Dick Cheney.

Alvin (Pete) Rozelle announces his resignation as commissioner of the National Football League, a post he has held since 1960.

24 The oil tanker Exxon *Valdez* runs aground on a reef in the Gulf of Alaska, causing a massive oil spill.

26 For the first time since 1917, multicandidate parliamentary elections are held throughout the Soviet Union.

28 In Iran, Ayatollah Hosein Ali Montazeri resigns as designated successor to Ayatollah Ruhollah Khomeini, the nation's supreme religious leader.

A New York State Supreme Court justice rules that the San Diego Yacht Club must forfeit the America's Cup, yachting's most prestigious trophy, to New Zealand because it defeated its challenger unfairly. (The U.S. *Stars & Stripes,* a catamaran, had defeated the *New Zealand* in two races in September 1988.)

29 *Rain Man* is given an Academy Award as the year's best picture.

Alfredo Cristiani, 41-year-old candidate of El Salvador's right-wing Nationalist Republican Alliance (ARENA), staged a successful campaign for the presidency. By capturing 53.82% of the vote on March 19, he was able to avoid a runoff election.

© Bocxe/Sipa

April

3 The University of Michigan captures the men's National Collegiate Athletic Association Division I basketball title by defeating Seton Hall, 80–79.

4 In Havana, Cuba's President Fidel Castro and Soviet President Gorbachev sign a Cuba-USSR friendship treaty.

Richard M. Daley (D), 46-year-old Cook County, IL, prosecutor, is elected mayor of Chicago.

5 In Poland, talks between representatives of the government and the opposition conclude with agreements on political and economic reform, including free elections and the legalization of the Solidarity trade union.

Vietnam declares that it would remove all of its troops from Cambodia by Sept. 30, 1989.

6 Soviet President Gorbachev and British Prime Minister Margaret Thatcher engage in "lively" and "frank" discussions in London.

President Bush meets with Israel's Prime Minister Yitzhak Shamir at the White House. The president had conferred with Egypt's President Hosni Mubarak earlier in the month.

7 A Soviet nuclear submarine catches fire and sinks in international waters off Norway, killing 42 of 69 crew members.

9 Soviet troops clash with nationalist demonstrators in Tbilisi, the capital of the Soviet republic of Georgia. Nineteen persons are killed in the unrest.

Nick Faldo wins the Masters golf tournament.

11 Los Angeles Mayor Tom Bradley is reelected to a fifth term.

12 Officials charge that a drug gang, seeking demonic protection from police, is responsible for the murders of at least 12 persons, including a 21-year-old University of Texas student, in Matamoros, Mexico. Five suspects are arrested in the case.

The White House announces the nomination of former astronaut Richard H. Truly as administrator of the National Aeronautics and Space Administration.

13 A U.S. federal jury convicts George H. Kaub and Eugene R. Sullivan, who were vice-presidents of Teledyne Electronics of Newbury Park, CA, of conspiring to defraud the government. The two are acquitted of a bribery charge. The case was the first criminal trial to stem from the three-year-old Pentagon procurement scandal.

15 Ninety-five persons are killed and at least 200 are injured as soccer fans surge forward in a crowded stadium in Sheffield, England.

18 In Beijing, Chinese students march in a prodemocracy demonstration. The death of former Communist Party leader Hu Yaobang on April 15 precipitated the march.

President Bush signs legislation appropriating $49.75 million in humanitarian aid for the Nicaraguan contra rebels.

19 An explosion inside a gun turret on the battleship U.S.S. *Iowa* kills 47 American sailors.

In Jordan, riots, caused by increased prices, spread to several southern towns. At the time, King Hussein is meeting with President Bush and other U.S. officials in Washington.

Roberto Garcia Alvadora, 53-year-old attorney general of El Salvador, is killed by a bomb explosion on his car's roof.

25 In a "serious and important milestone in *perestroika* (restructuring)," 110 members of the Soviet Communist Party's Central Committee and the Central Auditing Commission resign in a purge.

British policemen assisted the injured after several thousand late-arriving soccer fans surged into overcrowded stands at Hillsborough Stadium in Sheffield, England, April 15. Ninety-five persons, including many teenagers, were killed in the tragedy.

© Leo Mason/Sygma

26 Comedienne Lucille Ball dies at the age of 77.

27 In an effort to reduce spending, Canada cancels plans to purchase a fleet of nuclear-powered submarines and announces the closing of seven military bases.

30 In New York City, President Bush participates in ceremonies commemorating the bicentennial of George Washington's inauguration as president.

Meeting in Deidesheim, West Germany, British Prime Minister Thatcher and West German Chancellor Helmut Kohl differ on disarmament strategy for the North Atlantic Treaty Organization.

May

1 Gen. Andrés Rodríguez is elected president of Paraguay.

2 In the Netherlands, the seven-year-old coalition government of Prime Minister Ruud Lubbers falls.

3 John N. Turner announces that he would resign as leader of Canada's Liberal Party following the selection of a successor.

4 Former U.S. National Security Council staff member Oliver L. North is convicted of three of 12 counts for his role in the Iran-contra affair.

President Bush and Canada's Prime Minister Brian Mulroney confer at the White House.

U.S. Surgeon General C. Everett Koop announces his resignation, effective July 13.

6 Pope John Paul II concludes a nine-day trip to Africa.

8 The U.S. space shuttle *Atlantis* and its five-member crew complete a five-day mission, including deploying the Magellan spacecraft on a 15-month trip to Venus.

10 Charging foreign interference, Panama's government annuls the presidential elections held on May 7. Opposition presidential and vice-presidential candidates are attacked physically by paramilitary squads.

11 Soviet President Gorbachev informs visiting U.S. Secretary of State James Baker that the USSR plans to reduce its nuclear arsenal in Europe.

14 Carlos Saúl Menem, a Peronist, is elected president of Argentina.

16 Sheik Hassan Khaled, the religious leader of Lebanon's Sunni Muslims, is assassinated in West Beirut.

17 Milan Pancevski is chosen as leader of Yugoslavia's Communist Party. On May 15, Janez Drnovsek took office as the nation's president for one year.

18 Soviet President Gorbachev concludes a four-day visit to China, during which Sino-Soviet relations were restored. A massive pro-democracy demonstration by students in Beijing on May 17 overshadowed the summit.

20 President Bush and France's President François Mitterrand meet in Kennebunkport, ME.

25 In the Soviet Union, the Congress of People's Deputies, the nation's first national assembly in some 70 years in which most members were elected in competitive balloting, opens and elects Mikhail S. Gorbachev to the newly enhanced position of president.

The Calgary Flames capture the National Hockey League's Stanley Cup by defeating the Montreal Canadiens in the play-off finals.

Addressing the Soviet Congress of People's Deputies on May 25, human-rights activist Andrei Sakharov urged President Gorbachev to self-assess his years in power. Some 2,250 deputies, including many chosen in direct elections, attended the session.

© Robert B. Tonsing/Picture Group

© Peter Turnley/Black Star

Massive student-led prodemocracy protests, including one outside the gate of the Forbidden City, above, *were held in China during April and May. Thousands of armed Chinese troops crushed the demonstrations in early June.*

26 Rep. Tony Coelho (D-CA) announces that he would resign from the U.S. House of Representatives rather than put his party and colleagues through an investigation of his personal finances.

A four-day meeting of the Arab League ends in Casablanca, Morocco. During the summit, Egypt was readmitted to the league and the Palestine Liberation Organization's plan to pursue peace with Israel was supported. The league failed, however, to persuade Syria to withdraw its 40,000 troops from Lebanon.

28 Emerson Fittipaldi of Brazil wins the Indianapolis 500.

29 A state of emergency is declared in Argentina, following a week of looting and rioting in several cities.

30 A two-day meeting of the North Atlantic Treaty Organization ends in Brussels, Belgium. The participants expressed support for President Bush's plan for far-reaching reductions in conventional forces in Europe and reached a compromise regarding the divisive issue of East-West negotiations on SNF (short-range nuclear forces) weapons.

31 Jim Wright announces his resignation as speaker of the U.S. House and that he would "offer to resign his House seat sometime before the end of June." On April 17, the House Committee of Standards of Official Conduct had charged the Texas Democrat with violating House rules regarding the acceptance of gifts and outside income.

June

2 Japan's Foreign Minister Sosuke Uno is chosen as the nation's prime minister, succeeding Noboru Takeshita, who resigned as the result of a scandal.

3 Iran's Ayatollah Ruhollah Khomeini dies.

A Soviet gas pipeline explodes, demolishing part of the trans-Siberian railway. An estimated 400 persons are killed in the disaster.

4 Thousands of Chinese troops move into the center of Beijing to quell prodemocracy demonstrations. Scores of students and workers are killed in the action.

5 President Bush suspends U.S. military sales to China in response to the "violent and bloody" crackdown against the prodemocracy movement.

6 Thomas S. Foley (D-WA) is elected speaker of the U.S. House of Representatives.

7 Pakistan's Prime Minister Benazir Bhutto addresses a joint session of the U.S. Congress.

9 The United States vetoes a UN Security Council resolution condemning Israel's policies in the occupied territories.

In El Salvador, José Antonio Rodriguez Porth, the minister of the presidency, is assassinated.

10 The Chinese government reports the arrest of 400 participants in the democracy movement.

13 In Bonn, West Germany, Chancellor Helmut Kohl and Soviet President Gorbachev sign a declaration pledging closer Soviet-West German ties.

The Detroit Pistons capture the National Basketball Association championship by defeating the Los Angeles Lakers, four games to zero, in the play-off finals.

14 Democratic members of the U.S. House of Representatives elect Rep. Richard A. Gephardt (MO) as majority leader and William H. Gray III (PA) as whip.

The U.S. House of Representatives fails to override President Bush's veto of a bill to increase the nation's minimum wage to $4.55 per hour.

18 Elections for the European Parliament are completed. Parties to the left of center win a majority of the parliamentary seats.

20 Ali Akbar Hashemi Rafsanjani, the speaker of Iran's parliament, meets with President Gorbachev in Moscow.

21 The U.S. Supreme Court rules that no laws can prohibit protesters from burning the U.S. flag.

22 Leaders of the Angolan government and rebel forces agree to a cease-fire in their 14-year-old war.

24 China's Communist Party dismisses General Secretary Zhao Ziyang from all his posts. Jiang Zemin, 62-year-old Communist Party leader in Shanghai, is named party chief.

26 The U.S. Supreme Court upholds the execution of murderers who are mentally retarded as well as of those who were as young as 16 when they committed their crimes.

27 A U.S. federal appeals court overturns the 1988 ethics conviction of Lyn Nofziger, former adviser to President Reagan.

30 Sudan's Prime Minister Sadiq al-Mahdi is ousted in a military coup.

Chris Niedenthal/"Time" Magazine

In parliamentary elections in Poland, June 4, voters overwhelmingly supported candidates backed by the Solidarity trade union.

July

1 In Greece, Communists and conservatives join to form a new government; Tzannis Tzannetakis of the conservative New Democratic Party is named prime minister. No party had won a majority in June 18 parliamentary elections.

3 The U.S. Supreme Court upholds, 5-4, a restrictive Missouri abortion law.

5 U.S. District Judge Gerhard Gesell fines Oliver North $150,000, sentences him to 1,200 hours of community service, and places him on probation for two years for his crimes in the Iran-contra case.

6 During a three-day visit to France, Soviet President Gorbachev addresses the Council of Europe in Strasbourg.

8 Carlos Saúl Menem is inaugurated president of Argentina as an economic crisis forces the resignation of Raúl Alfonsín five months before the expiration of his term.

South Africa's government announces that President P. W. Botha and Nelson Mandela, the imprisoned leader of the African National Congress, had met for 45 minutes on July 5.

Leaders of the Warsaw Pact conclude their annual summit meeting in Bucharest, Romania.

9 West Germany's Boris Becker and Steffi Graf win the men's and women's singles tennis titles, respectively, at Wimbledon.

11 Sir Laurence Olivier dies at the age of 82.

12 Charles J. Haughey is elected prime minister of Ireland for a fourth time after agreeing to lead his Fianna Fail Party into a governing coalition. Elections on July 15 were inconclusive.

13 Cuba announces the execution of four Cuban Army officers convicted of drug smuggling and other crimes.

President Bush concludes an official visit to Hungary. The president had been in Poland, July 9–11.

14 In France, celebrations marking the bicentennial of the French Revolution come to a high point.

Leaders from the seven major industrial democracies—(left to right) European Community President Jacques Delors, Italy's Prime Minister Ciriaco de Mita, West Germany's Chancellor Helmut Kohl, U.S. President Bush, host, French President François Mitterrand, Britain's Prime Minister Margaret Thatcher, Canada's Prime Minister Brian Mulroney, and Japan's Premier Sousuke Uno—line up in front of the new Louvre Pyramid addition in Paris during opening ceremonies for the 15th annual economic summit, July 14-16. The summit, which coincided with the celebration of the 200th anniversary of the French Revolution, had a heightened degree of pomp and ceremony.

16 The leaders of the seven major industrial democracies end their 15th annual economic summit taking a strong position on protecting the environment and backing U.S. debt restructuring efforts in the Third World.

19 A United Airlines DC-10 crashes in a cornfield just short of the airport runway in Sioux City, IA, after a complete hydraulic control failure. At least 112 of the 296 persons aboard are killed.

20 President Bush calls for a stepped-up U.S. space effort aimed at building an orbiting space station, establishing a base on the moon, and sending a manned mission to Mars.

23 The Japanese Socialist Party stuns the long-dominant Liberal Democratic Party by winning control of the upper house of the Diet, Japan's parliament, with 46 seats to the LDP's 36 seats.

Giulio Andreotti is sworn in as prime minister of Italy's 49th government since World War II. Prime Minister Ciriaco DeMita had resigned on May 19 after 13 months in office.

24 British Prime Minister Margaret Thatcher reorganizes her cabinet. John Major succeeds Sir Geoffrey Howe as foreign secretary.

26 A two-week strike by Siberian coal miners that threatened the stability of the Gorbachev regime winds down after the government makes concessions.

31 Lebanese extremists report their execution of U.S. hostage Marine Lt. Col. William R. Higgins in retaliation for the abduction of Sheik Abdul Karim Obeid, a pro-Iranian Shiite Muslim, from southern Lebanon by Israeli commandos on July 28.

© Eric Sampers/Gamma-Liaison

American Greg LeMond comes from behind on the last day of the Tour de France, July 23, to wheel to victory in the world's premier bicycle race. It was LeMond's second win in the 2,020-mi (3 232-km) race and the culmination of a comeback from near-fatal injuries he received in a 1987 hunting accident.

August

2 Following a two-and-a-half-year undercover operation by the U.S. Federal Bureau of Investigation, 46 futures traders in Chicago are arrested on such charges as racketeering, mail fraud, and skimming clients' profits.

3 In Iran, Hojatolislam Ali Akbar Hashemi Rafsanjani is sworn in as president. He succeeds Ali Khamenei, who became Iran's religious leader following the death of Ayatollah Ruhollah Khomeini.

6 Jaime Paz Zamora is inaugurated as president of Bolivia after he forms a power-sharing alliance with former military dictator Hugo Banzer Suarez.

7 Meeting in Tela, Honduras, the presidents of five Central American countries issue a call to dismantle Nicaraguan contra rebel camps in Honduras.

8 In New Zealand, Geoffrey Palmer is sworn in as prime minister, succeeding David Lange, who resigned.

9 In Japan, Toshiki Kaifu, a former education minister, replaces Sousuke Uno as premier. Uno had resigned in the wake of a sex scandal and a recent defeat for the ruling Liberal Democratic Party in the upper house of parliament.

President Bush signs legislation establishing a record $166 billion bailout of the U.S. savings and loan industry.

13 War in Lebanon escalates as Syrian troops and their Lebanese Muslim allies attack Christian strongholds.

The U.S. space shuttle *Columbia* with a five-man crew returns to earth after completing a secret military mission.

The wreckage of a small plane carrying U.S. Rep. Mickey Leland (D-TX) and 15 others, including eight Americans, is found in western Ethiopia.

© Eslami Rad/Gamma-Liaison

Ali Rafsanjani swept into power as Iran's president, August 3, after winning an election with only token opposition the previous week. A former speaker of Iran's parliament, he was viewed as a shrewd politician.

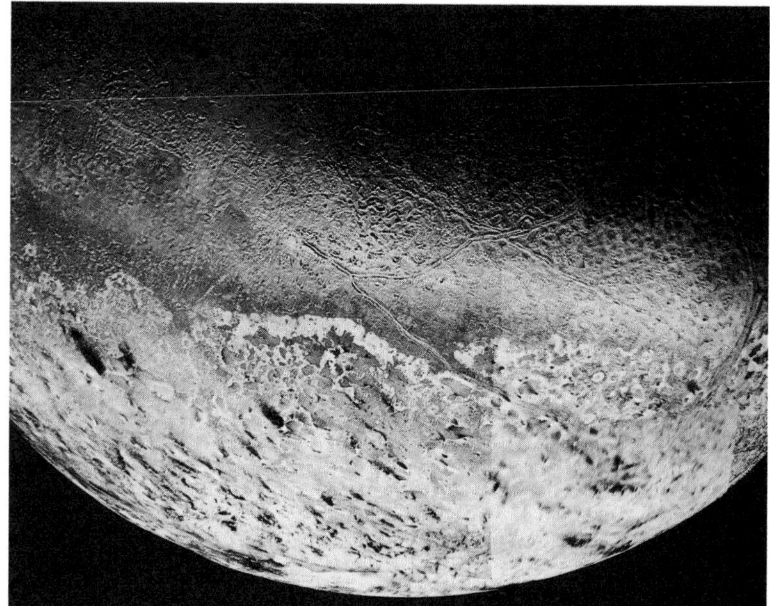
NASA

The close flyby of Neptune by the "Voyager 2" spacecraft led to the discovery of at least six new satellites where only Triton and Nereid had been known. The spacecraft sent back stunning and scientifically vital photographs, including this August 25 view of Neptune's largest moon, Triton, facing the planet.

14 Frederik de Klerk takes power as acting president of South Africa following the resignation of President P. W. Botha.

17 Researchers report that the drug AZT is effective in delaying the onslaught of AIDS for those who are infected with the disease but have not shown its symptoms.

18 In Colombia, leading presidential candidate Luís Carlos Galán is assassinated at a campaign rally by Medellín drug cartel henchmen, triggering a government effort to crack down on the entrenched drug lords.

24 Solidarity official Tadeusz Mazowiecki is confirmed as premier of Poland. On July 29, Gen. Wojciech Jaruzelski resigned as Communist Party leader to devote himself to the post of president.

Major League Baseball Commissioner A. Bartlett Giamatti announces an agreement under which Cincinnati Reds Manager Pete Rose is banned from baseball. Rose, who with Giamatti signed the agreement, had been under investigation for betting on the game.

25 Following a 12-year journey, the U.S. *Voyager 2* spacecraft passes within about 3,000 mi (4 828 km) of Neptune.

Rep. Barney Frank (D-MA) acknowledges having hired a male prostitute as his personal aide.

30 In Paris, a 19-nation peace conference on Cambodia ends without any resolution to the roles competing Cambodian factions will play in the country's future.

September

1 In Panama, the inauguration of Francisco Rodriguez as president is called a sham by opposition leaders and international observers. Rodriguez, 51, a friend of military strongman Gen. Manuel Noriega, was appointed by a government council; results of the May presidential election had been thrown out by a government tribunal. The United States refuses to recognize the new government.

5 In a nationally televised speech, President Bush unveils his plan for a $7.9 billion war on drugs. Leading Democrats call the plan inadequate.

6 In South African elections the ruling National Party retains a slim majority in parliament, but loses ground to the liberal New Democratic Party and the far-right Conservative Party. Meanwhile, a national strike in protest of apartheid shuts down commerce and industry, and police clash with blacks and mixed-race youths in what antiapartheid leaders call a massacre. Estimates run as high as 25 persons killed and 100 injured.

A reputed financier for Colombia's Medellín drug cartel, Eduardo Martinez Romero, is extradited to the United States. Martinez, indicted on money-laundering charges, was arrested by Colombian authorities in a crackdown in response to the cartel's reputed murder of presidential candidate Luís Carlos Galan in August.

10 West German Boris Becker defeats the top-seeded Ivan Lendl to win the U.S. Open tennis tournament. Fellow West German Steffi Graf had defeated Martina Navratilova for the women's title on September 9.

11 Hungary opens its borders with Austria, allowing thousands of East Germans to migrate to the West. About 10,500 East Germans were to cross into Austria within the first 36 hours, the largest exodus since the construction of the Berlin Wall in 1961.

14 Public services in Quebec are disrupted as 225,000 provincial employees strike. Meanwhile, Quebec Premier Robert Bourassa refuses to grant amnesty to nurses who walked out September 11, but who since had returned to work.

A lone gunman armed with a semiautomatic assault rifle kills seven coworkers at a Louisville, KY, printing plant and wounds 15 others before turning the gun on himself.

18 India signs a conditional agreement with Sri Lanka to withdraw its troops from the island nation by December 31. India intervened in a civil war in Sri Lanka, sending peacekeeping forces to its neighbor in 1987.

Hungary and Israel restore diplomatic relations, which had been suspended over the 1967 Arab-Israeli war.

19 A French DC-10 en route from the Congo to Paris explodes in midair, killing the 171 people aboard. A bomb, rather than a catastrophic failure, is suspected.

A New York Appeals Court returns yachting's America's Cup trophy to the San Diego Yacht Club. In March 1989 the New Zealand challenger had argued successfully in a lower court that the San Diego club had no right to the trophy, because the club used a catamaran to defend the trophy.

20 Frederik W. de Klerk is sworn in for a five-year term as president of South Africa. He was chosen by the electoral college of Parliament, which is controlled by the ruling National Party de Klerk heads.

Soviet President Mikhail S. Gorbachev purges three of the 12 voting members of the Politburo, the Communist Party's policy-making body.

21 After devastating a number of Caribbean islands, Hurricane *Hugo* slams into South Carolina before heading north. At least 28 deaths and billions of dollars in property damage are caused by the storm.

The 44th session of the UN General Assembly opens.

22 Ten members of a British military band are killed in an explosion in Deal, Kent, with the Irish Republican Army taking responsibility.

Songwriter Irving Berlin dies at the age of 101.

25 In an address to the United Nations, President Bush offers to cut U.S. chemical weapons by 80% if the USSR will reduce its stockpile to U.S. levels.

© Juhan Kuus/Sipa

F. W. de Klerk, 53-year-old leader of South Africa's National Party and the nation's former education minister, took office as president on September 20. The ruling NP had won a slim majority in elections September 6.

© Walker/Gamma-Liaison

At the University of Virginia in Williamsburg, September 27–28, President Bush and the nation's governors asserted that it is time "to re-orient the education system and marshall widespread support for the needed reform."

26 Vietnam announces the last of its troops have left Cambodia after a ten-year occupation. However, Prince Norodom Sihanouk, former Cambodian ruler, claims Vietnamese troops remain in the country.

28 Former Philippine President Ferdinand E. Marcos dies in Hawaii.

October

1 In China, a celebration of the 40th anniversary of Communist rule is held in Tiananmen Square but most diplomats, mindful of the government's suppression of a student prodemocracy movement in the same square in June, boycott the event.

2 The 1989–90 session of the U.S. Supreme Court opens with the justices adding 22 cases to the docket, including three cases involving abortion issues.

3 Rebel officers of the Panama Defense Force seize Gen. Manuel Antonio Noriega in an aborted coup, but later surrender to troops loyal to the military strongman.

4 Canadian Transportation Minister Benoit Bouchard announces that service on the government-owned passenger railroad will be cut back by 51%, starting Jan. 15, 1990. Routes in the Maritime and Prairie provinces, along with Quebec and Ontario, will be affected most.

6 As thousands of its citizens continue to stream across borders to the West, the German Democratic Republic (East Germany) begins celebrations marking its 40th anniversary. Soviet President Gorbachev is among the guests at the festivities.

Israel rejects a plan put forward by Egyptian President Hosni Mubarak for Palestinian elections in the occupied West Bank and Gaza Strip.

Ramon Hnatyshyn is nominated as the 24th governor-general of Canada.

7 Hungary veers away from Marxist doctrine, changing the name of the Hungarian Socialist Workers' (Communist) Party to the Hungarian Socialist Party.

11 In a defeat for antiabortion activists the Florida legislature votes down restrictions on abortion that had been proposed by Gov. Bob Martinez (R).

12 The U.S. House of Representatives approves a new bill prohibiting desecration of the nation's flag. The U.S. Senate had approved a version of the bill the previous week.

13 The Dow Jones Industrial Average plunges 190 points, its biggest single-day fall since the October 1987 crash.

16 In Norway, Jan Syse, heading a center-right coalition of three minority parties, is sworn in to succeed Socialist Party leader Gro Harlem Brundtland as premier.

17 A major earthquake rocks northern California, causing at least 67 deaths and property damage of at least $6 billion.

Egypt's President Hosni Mubarak concludes a series of talks with Libya's leader Col. Muammar el-Qaddafi.

18 Longtime East German leader Erich Honecker is ousted and replaced by Egon Krenz, 52-year-old member of the Politburo.

In China, a series of earthquakes and aftershocks over two days, centered west of Beijing, causes extensive damage.

20 Rep. Robert Garcia (D-NY) and his wife Jane Lee Garcia are convicted of extortion and conspiracy in the Wedtech case.

23 The space shuttle *Atlantis* returns to Earth after launching the *Galileo* spacecraft on a six-year exploration mission to Jupiter.

Commemorating the 1956 uprising against Soviet domination, Hungary proclaims itself a free republic.

In a speech to the Supreme Soviet, Foreign Minister Eduard Shevardnadze calls his country's intervention in Afghanistan in 1979 an illegal act.

24 The biennial Commonwealth heads of government meeting ends in Kuala Lumpur, Malaysia.

26 Great Britain's Prime Minister Margaret Thatcher reorganizes her cabinet, following the resignation of Chancellor of the Exchequer Nigel Lawson.

28 The Oakland Athletics win baseball's World Series, defeating the San Francisco Giants four games to zero.

29 In South Africa, 70,000 people turn out for a rally of the outlawed African National Congress (ANC) Party to welcome home ANC leaders recently released after long terms in prison.

In Spain, the Socialist Workers Party of Prime Minister Felipe González wins a one-seat majority in elections to the Cortes (parliament).

31 Turkey's parliament elects Turgut Ozal, premier since 1983, to a seven-year term as president.

November

1 Nicaragua President Daniel Ortega ends a cease-fire with contra forces, citing renewed contra activity.

In a compromise with President Bush, Congress approves a measure that will raise the minimum wage to $4.25 an hour by April 1991. Under the compromise, a subminimum training wage is allowed for teenagers during the first three months of employment.

5 For the second time in five months, elections in Greece fail to produce a majority government.

7 In off-year elections, Virginia's Lt. Gov. L. Douglas Wilder (D) is elected to the state's top office, becoming the first black elected governor in U.S. history; David N. Dinkins (D) is the first black to be elected mayor of New York City; Rep. James J. Florio (D) is chosen governor of New Jersey; Seattle elects Councilman Norm Rice (D) as the first black to hold the mayor's office in that city; and Detroit returns incumbent Mayor Coleman Young (D) for a fifth term.

David Dinkins (D) took 51% of the vote to be elected New York City's 106th mayor on November 7. The 62-year-old Manhattan borough president had based his campaign on his long experience in city government and on a promise to promote racial harmony in a city that many perceived was riven with racial tension.

9 East Germany opens all borders, including the notorious Berlin Wall, allowing its citizens to travel and emigrate freely.

11 In El Salvador, hopes raised by peace talks between the government and rebels are dashed as the country erupts in the fiercest urban fighting in ten years of civil war.

In an election for an assembly to lead Namibia to independence from South Africa, the leftist liberation group South West Africa People's Organization (SWAPO) wins a majority but not the two-thirds vote required to control the writing of the new constitution.

16 Six Jesuit priests, their housekeeper, and her daughter are massacred in El Salvador by uniformed men suspected to be government soldiers.

17 In Bulgaria, the new Communist Party leader Petar T. Mladenov is named president, and expresses support for free elections. On November 10, Todor Zhivkov, party head since 1954 and president since 1971, resigned from both posts.

21 In Greece, the three major political parties form a coalition government, with Xenophan Zolatos as premier, after two separate elections failed to provide enough support for a majority-party government.

22 The first session of the 101st Congress adjourns.

24 Elias Hrawi, a moderate Maronite Christian, is elected president of Lebanon, succeeding René Moawad, another Christian moderate, who was assassinated by a car bomb on November 22, just 17 days after taking office.

26 In Uruguay, Luís Alberto Lacalle of the National Party is elected president.

27 In Honduras, Rafael Leonardo Callejas claims victory in a close presidential race.

30 For the first time since 1949, opposition candidates are allowed to participate legally in elections in Taiwan.

December

2 In India, V. P. Singh is sworn in as prime minister. In November elections, Singh led a coalition of parties in defeating the Congress(I) Party of incumbent Prime Minister Rajiv Gandhi.

In the first meeting between the top leader of the Soviet Union and a pope, Mikhail Gorbachev confers with Pope John Paul II at the Vatican on December 1. Gorbachev promised increased religious freedom for Soviet citizens. John Paul II offered his blessing for the president's plans for Soviet reforms.

© Sygma

Audrey McLaughlin, a member of Canada's Parliament from the Yukon, is elected leader of Canada's New Democratic Party.

3 U.S. President George Bush and Soviet President Mikhail Gorbachev conclude a two-day summit meeting in Malta.

7 In the Philippines, a military coup attempt that came close to toppling President Corazon Aquino winds down. Two U.S. jet fighters had provided air cover for Philippine government forces during the aborted coup.

9 A U.S. presidential delegation visits China—the first publicized, official U.S. contact since China's suppression of the prodemocracy demonstrations in June.

East Germany's Socialist Unity (Communist) Party elects Gregor Gysi to succeed Egon Krenz as the nation's leader.

12 Concluding a three-day summit meeting in San José, Costa Rica, the presidents of five Central American nations agree to a new plan for peace in the region.

14 In Chile, Christian Democrat Patricio Aylwin wins election as president to displace the military rule of Gen. Augusto Pinochet.

17 In Brazil, Francisco Collor de Mello, a free-market advocate, defeats socialist Luis da Silva in a runoff election for president. The two had been the top vote-getters of 21 candidates in Brazil's first presidential election in 29 years in November.

19 A bomb is removed from the headquarters of the National Association for the Advancement of Colored People in Jacksonville, FL. The device is similar to bombs that killed Alabama federal appellate judge Robert S. Vance and Savannah, GA, alderman and attorney Robert E. Robinson earlier in December. A bomb also had been removed from the federal court building in Atlanta on December 18.

West Germany's Chancellor Helmut Kohl and East Germany's Premier Hans Modrow meet in East Germany.

20 U.S. forces based in Panama are joined by some 12,000 additional troops from the United States in an effort to depose Panama's Gen. Manuel Antonio Noriega.

The Lithuanian Communist Party declares itself independent of the Soviet Communist Party.

22 Author Samuel Beckett, winner of the Nobel Prize for literature, dies in Paris.

25 In Romania, Communist dictator Nicolae Ceauşescu and his wife, Elena, are executed by the army, which sided with a revolution against Ceauşescu's oppressive 24-year rule. The couple was charged with genocide, including a massacre by security forces in Timisoara on December 17 that sparked the revolution, undermining state power, destroying the nation's economic and spiritual values, and having hidden funds abroad.

27 At least 35 people die in heavy flooding in northeastern Brazil. An estimated 200,000 are left homeless.

28 The first major earthquake ever to hit a populated area of Australia leaves at least ten dead and causes extensive property damage in the city of Newcastle.

29 In Czechoslovakia, writer and human-rights activist Václav Havel is elected interim president. Alexander Dubček, the leader of the 1968 Prague liberation movement that was put down by the Soviets, had been named chairman of parliament on December 28.

30 President Bush acknowledges that U.S. troops erred when they searched the residence of the Nicaraguan ambassador in Panama City on December 29. The search led Nicaragua's President Daniel Ortega to expel 20 U.S. diplomats from Managua.

31 South Korea's former President Chun Doo Hwan appears before the National Assembly to testify about his eight years of martial rule.

AP/Wide World

As an American GI keeps a close watch on the Vatican embassy in Panama City, a helicopter eases in for a landing. U.S. forces ringed the embassy after Panamanian strongman Gen. Manuel Antonio Noriega, the target of the U.S. military incursion, was granted temporary asylum there on Christmas Eve.

COMMUNISM IN FLUX

THE DEMOCRATIC REVOLUTION

by Robert A. Senser

The year 1989 was one of change and drama for the world Communist movement. Addressing the opening of the Soviet parliament on May 25, Mikhail Gorbachev, who would be elected to the revamped Soviet presidency, declared that reform of the Soviet system "is trying to break loose, so is the political process. . . ."

© Sergei Guneyev/"Time" Magazine

"So you've been over into Russia," a famous financier of the time, Bernard Baruch, remarked to a famous journalist of the time, Lincoln Steffens. "I have been over into the future," Steffens responded, "and it works."

Steffens' comment, made just after a visit to Moscow in 1919, typified a widespread conviction—or fear—that the Russian Revolution had created a force that history had fated to sweep the world. A slogan posted at a Soviet-Finnish border crossing once proclaimed: "We are living in an age in which all roads lead to communism." The signposts of history have changed, however, and seldom more radically than in 1989. They now are pointing toward democracy and away from dictatorships of all kinds, but especially the Communist version. "Democracy is emerging as the dominant ideal that has captured imaginations everywhere," Zbigniew Brzezinski, a Columbia University professor and former U.S. national security adviser, in May told a conference sponsored by the National Endowment for Democracy in Washington, DC. The title of the conference was "The Democratic Revolution."

In his new book, *The Grand Failure: the Birth and Death of Communism in the Twentieth Century,* Brzezinski describes what he calls "the accelerating velocity of communism's historical disintegration," caused above all "by the failure of the Soviet experience." Yet at the time he finished his book in August 1988, neither Brzezinski nor anyone else realized how fast the disintegration would proceed.

About the Author. Freelance writer Robert A. Senser spent much of 1989 researching and writing a book on the current worldwide movement toward democracy and away from totalitarianism. During a writing career spanning 40 years, he served during the 1950s and 1960s as editor of *Work,* published by the Catholic Council on Working Life in Chicago, was a labor and political officer in the U.S. Foreign Service for 22 years, and now is a consultant on human-rights issues for the Asian-American Free Labor Institute in Washington, DC.

Surprise after Surprise. Anyone predicting the surprising events of 1989—that Chinese students and workers by the thousands would demonstrate for democracy, that the Berlin Wall would come tumbling down, that Solidarity would win a parliamentary election in Poland and put a non-Communist into office as prime minister, that Hungary, East Germany, Czechoslovakia, Bulgaria, and even Romania would see sharp upheavals in their Communist structures, that the changes would come almost without violence (except in Romania), and that the Soviet Union would do nothing to stop the crumbling of the East bloc—would have been dismissed as a writer of science fiction or a candidate for psychiatric care.

The military strength of Communist countries long hid a debilitating reality—the loss of faith in Marxism-Leninism within the countries. Unlike tanks and troops, the gradual disillusionment with the official ideology could not be measured, but it quietly contributed to communism's erosion as a system of power. The depth of the erosion, Brzezinski predicted, would make communism "largely irrelevant to the human condition" in another decade or so. The upheavals of 1989 seemed certain to shorten that timetable of imbalance.

People vs. People's Republics. Apart from the Soviet withdrawal from Afghanistan, the setbacks in the Communist world came not because of military reversals, but because of a "revolution from below," in the words of a speaker at an East Berlin rally. Citizens of key Communist countries officially designated as "People's Republics" or as "Democratic'' massively disavowed the Marxist-Leninist rationale that the Communist Party is the voice of the people and the sole source of legitimate authority.

In the People's Republic of Poland rising discontent in the population forced the regime to respond in a way that Communist governments almost never do: by holding elections. The outcome of voting for Parliament in June humiliated the party. A slate sponsored by the Solidarity labor movement, which only two months earlier had regained its legal status, captured all but one of the 261 parliamentary seats it was allowed to contest. Top party leaders lost even though they ran unopposed. Only election rules guaranteeing the Communist Party a majority in the Lower House, combined with its control of the police and military, allowed the discredited leadership to continue in power. However, Tadeusz Mazowiecki, a 62-year-old Solidarity activist, was installed as Poland's premier in late summer. It was the first time that a ruling Communist Party had permitted a non-Communist to head a government.

A 30-ft (9-m) replica of the Statue of Liberty served as an inspiration for prodemocracy demonstrators in Beijing's Tiananmen Square in the spring. In June the Chinese Army squelched the movement, killing hundreds and injuring many others.

In the People's Republic of China spring brought the Communist Party the greatest challenge of its 40-year ironfisted rule. For seven weeks in Beijing's historic Tiananmen Square thousands and then hundreds of thousands of demonstrators chanted slogans for democracy. There they erected a symbol for their ideas, a 30-ft (9-m) Statue of Liberty, and defiantly faced it toward the giant portrait of the late Chairman Mao. After the demonstrations spread to other cities, the regime's leadership on June 3–4 sent the People's Liberation Army against the people, killing uncounted hundreds. Across the globe, television screens carried live pictures of a Communist regime's need to rely on tanks to maintain power.

Events in Poland got little coverage on China's TV broadcasts. The news from other East European countries was deemed more fitting for Chinese consumption, but not for

Photos, © J. Langevin/Sygma

© Sichov/Sygma

long. Within an action-filled period of seven weeks in October and November the top leaders of four Communist nations—Hungary, East Germany, Bulgaria, and Czechoslovakia—all had to resign. Then in December even Romania's longtime dictator Nicolae Ceauşescu and his wife had to flee, only to be captured and executed by a secret military tribunal.

In that cascade of changes, the most important ones came in the German Democratic Republic (East Germany), ruled by Erich Honecker, 77, for 18 years of hard-line communism. His country was so regimented that in his last few months of power he even banned several Moscow publications, lest information about Soviet President Gorbachev's reforms contaminate East Germany. Two kinds of mass protest led to his resignation in October: the exodus of 200,000 East Germans to West Germany and the nationwide demonstrations of people chanting slogans like "We want to stay!" and "Gorby! Gorby!" Honecker's successor, Egon Krenz, promised free elections and unexpectedly opened the Berlin Wall, but was forced out of office in seven weeks. An interim government, with a coalition cabinet of 28 members, including 11 non-Communists, scheduled parliamentary elections for May. In East Germany and elsewhere the tactic of making a series of concessions in the name of democracy raised questions of whether the reforms signified genuine democratic change.

© Eric Bouvet/Gamma-Liaison

As the borders between East and West Germany were opened in November, thousands celebrated in the square at the historic Brandenburg Gate. A piece of the Berlin Wall, which had divided East and West Berlin since 1961, was cherished.

Criteria for Democracy. Fang Lizhi, the astrophysicist who has become known as China's Andrei Sakharov, has pointed out that in China slogans about democracy have "often been nothing more than a poker chip" that one political faction uses against another in what is only "a game of power." The tactic is not peculiar to China, nor is the problem of how to tell whether a political change is a real step toward democracy.

© Tom Haley/Sipa

Fang Lizhi, China's leading dissident, took refuge in the U.S. embassy in Beijing following the suppression of the prodemocracy movement. The Chinese media called him the instigator of the spring demonstrations.

Jacek Kuron, an intellectual and leading adviser to Solidarity who was elected to the Polish Parliament in June 1989, provided a guide at the National Endowment for Democracy conference in May. The opposite of pluralistic democracy, totalitarianism, Kuron said, is a system that in its pristine form "commands all social life." In principle, the totalitarian system's hold on power "is so total that if citizens gather of their own accord and freely discuss a matter so simple as roof repairs on a block of apartments, that is already a challenge to the central authority." That monopoly—the monopoly on organization—is the most important, Kuron said. The next in importance is a monopoly on information—"every printed word, not to mention the electronic media, is centrally steered by central authority." The third monopoly, flowing from the previous two, is one of decision-making, "meaning all decisions are made by central authority."

The crucial test for democracy, then, is whether a nation has a flourishing "civil society," a term popular in Europe to describe the network of free institutions that exist between the state on the one hand and the individual and family on the other. Does the government encourage or at least tolerate those independent institutions, such as a free press, private enterprise, free trade unions? In the case of a dictatorship, is it loosening the central authority's monopolies on organization, information, and decision-making?

Dominant Role of Party. In Marxist-Leninist doctrine that system of central control bears a rather polite label—the "leading role" or "vanguard role" of the Communist Party—for the party's dominance of society. China demonstrated the extreme lengths to which a ruling Communist Party can go to maintain that dominance. The Chinese regime showed its true character by suppressing violently a movement seeking limited autonomy in Tibet in March and then, more drastically and publicly in June, by its violent crackdown on prodemocracy forces. What infuriated and frightened the old-line party leaders was that students and workers dared not only to organize huge demonstrations but also to form their own independent organizations outside of party control in Beijing, Shanghai, and a half dozen other cities.

Deng Xiaoping, Mao Zedong's successor as China's supreme leader, made known that China would not allow itself to succumb to the "Polish disease," the presence within a Communist body politic of autonomous organizations. The Chinese Party had, only months after taking power in 1949, set up its own organizational branches for students and workers, and wanted no interference with that monopoly. The organization for workers, the All-China Federation of Trade Unions, the largest organization in the country, kept 93 million members under tight control.

At the other end of the scale, Poland's Communist Party made history in 1989 by gradually relinquishing the party's leading role. Even during its years of trying to destroy Solidarity completely, the Communist regime had to tolerate the gradual proliferation of almost every kind of independent group, as well as the spread of pluralistic political ideas by another autonomous force, the Catholic Church. These "enclaves of civil society," in the words of Polish intellectual Leszek Kolakowski, prevented the achievement of "totalitarian excellence . . . despite all of the efforts of the party and its state." The only significant organization that the regime vowed not to recognize, after declaring martial law in December 1981, was the Independent Self-Governing Trade Union-Solidarity, or *NSZZ Solidarnosc* for short in Polish. The anti-Solidarity campaign, ended in April 1989 with unparalleled breakthroughs—the regime's agreement to recognize freedom of association (for Solidarity and other organizations as well), to guarantee press freedom, and to hold parliamentary elections under quasi-democratic rules.

Under pressure from prodemocracy movements, three of Poland's neighbors—East Germany, Hungary, and Czechoslovakia—made the wrenching decision to abolish the Communist Party's leading role, at least on paper. Czechoslovakia's 350-member parliament did so grudgingly, late in November, two days after almost half the country participated in a two-hour general strike. At year's end, the parties in Bulgaria and Romania were ready to follow suit. The practical effect of such high-level policy decisions remained to be seen. Simply allowing multiparty participation in elections would not guarantee progress toward democracy. East Germany long has had four minor opposition parties, but the ruling Communist Party maintained its despotic dominance not only through security forces but through workplace organizations that gave it control over the economy and over the work force.

© D. Aubert/Sygma

Lech Walesa was particularly proud to cast his ballot in Poland's parliamentary elections in June. Solidarity, the independent trade union he heads, was the overwhelming victor.

Reforms in the USSR. Unlike the "revolution from below" elsewhere, the changes under way in the Soviet Union were initiated from the top. President Mikhail Gorbachev launched *perestroika* to end economic stagnation and to achieve "a thorough renewal of every aspect of Soviet life," but only within the framework of a one-party socialist system.

© Josef Polleross/JB Pictures

Hungary's Foreign Minister Gyula Horn (right) *invites Austria's Foreign Minister Alois Mock to help dismantle part of the 150-mi (240-km) fence separating the two nations. Hungary was the first Eastern-bloc nation to open its border with the West.*

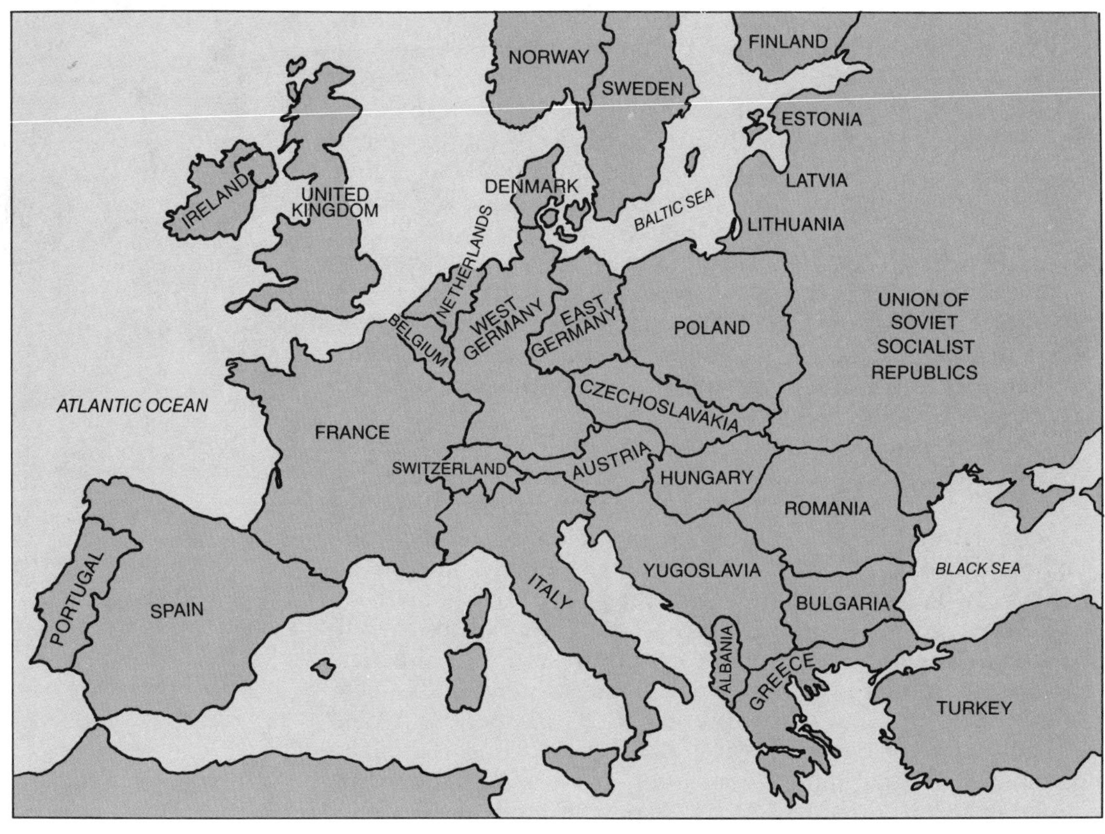

> ***"And the task before us, therefore, is to consolidate the fruits of this peaceful revolution and provide the architecture for continued peaceful change, to end the division of Europe and Germany, to make Europe whole and free."***
>
> **George Bush**
> **Brussels, Belgium,**
> **Dec. 4, 1989**

Even within that circumscribed framework, "Soviet society is in a state of ferment," Walter Laqueur of the Institute of Contemporary History in London writes in his 1989 book *The Long Road to Freedom: Russia and Glasnost*. Week after week the fermentation bubbled anew. Russian Orthodox priests conducted a religious service in the Kremlin's Uspensky Cathedral, the first such service since 1918. The Baltic states pressed vigorously for independence. Moscow journals printed long-suppressed works by exiled author Aleksandr Solzhenitsyn, including his 1974 essay, "Live Not by Lies." Coal miners went on strike and won concessions after their representatives negotiated personally with a Soviet Politburo member. A meeting of 2,000 lawyers voted to form a bar association, the first ever in the Soviet Union. Over the opposition of the scientific establishment, Nobel Peace Prize laureate Andrei Sakharov became a representative of the prestigious Academy of Sciences in the newly established legislative body, the Congress of People's Deputies. The U.S. Defense Department established a network of seismic monitoring stations within the Soviet Union. And so on.

The most celebrated change of 1989 came in March, just four years after Mikhail Gorbachev's election as Communist Party general secretary. In the freest Soviet elections in 72 years, some 150 million voters broke tradition by ousting several dozen Communist Party bosses in races for 1,500 seats in the Congress of People's Deputies. In the huge all-Moscow

© F. Hibon/Sygma

© D. Hudson/Sygma

© Yan Morvan/Sygma

Democratic Openings: *In March a Russian woman votes in the Soviet Union's first nationwide multicandidate parliamentary elections since 1917. There is dancing in the streets of Prague as Czechoslovakia takes steps late in the year toward a freer society. A new Czech government, with non-Communists holding the majority of the positions, took office in December. In Hungary a massive prodemocracy march occurs along the Danube River in Budapest. The Hungarian Communist Party renamed itself the Socialist Party in October.*

The year also witnessed nationalistic demonstrations and unrest in the Soviet republics. In Lithuania, right, thousands gathered in the capital of Vilnius to celebrate Independence Day, a period of independence prior to Soviet annexation in 1940.

© Peter Turnley/Black Star

constituency, Boris Yeltsin, expelled as Moscow party boss in November 1987 and from the Politburo in February 1988, won a landslide victory (89% of the vote) against a party-slated candidate. Afterward, Gorbachev hailed the results as "people's power" in action. However, since party domination of the two organs had been assured in advance (for example, one third of the Congress' 2,250 members were not elected but chosen by organizations almost entirely under party control), the election was not a model of democracy in action. Nor was the process whereby the Congress chose the 542 members of a smaller legislative body, the Supreme Soviet. But an unprecedented openness marked the proceedings of both bodies. Delegate after delegate criticized party policies, the KGB (the secret police), and even Gorbachev—and found their criticisms broadcast on national television. Arguments and shouts sparked the sessions so often that Gorbachev said apologetically from the chair: "We are still learning democracy—all of us."

Boris Yeltsin, the populist former party boss of Moscow, was elected easily to an at-large seat in the Soviet parliament. He later warned against giving Mikhail Gorbachev excessive power and toured the United States.

© F. Hibon/Sygma

A telling lesson came from Sakharov himself. In his speeches, the last given the day before he died in December, Sakharov charged that Gorbachev's reforms did not go far enough in instituting political democracy, since they left the party-state apparatus largely intact and gave "virtually unlimited power" to Gorbachev as the newly elected chairman of the Supreme Soviet (president), on top of his role as head of the Communist Party. In a speech to the People's Congress in June, Sakharov said: "The concentration of that much power in the hands of one man is extremely dangerous, even if he is the author of *perestroika*. . . . What happens when someone else fills this post?'' Sakharov urged that a future session of the Congress make basic reforms in the Soviet Union's constitution to decentralize power. First on his list was repeal of Article 6, which states that the Communist Party is ''the leading and guiding force of Soviet society and the nucleus of its political system.''

Gorbachev, on the contrary, repeatedly reaffirmed a declaration in his book *Perestroika:* ''No, the party's leading role cannot weaken.'' However, the biggest obstacle to Gorbachev's reform program was the party establishment itself, with its 18 million party officials who run the stagnating state/party/military/industrial complex. His dilemma was that if he moved too fast, he risked strengthening a dump-Gorbachev movement in the party, and if he moved too slowly, he risked strengthening popular resentment because expectations of an improved standard of living have not been forthcoming in the Soviet Union.

The popular demand for an end to the party's monopoly of organization could not be stilled, partly because Gorbachev's *glasnost* weakened its monopoly on information. In July the media publicized the nationwide strike of nearly 500,000 miners—their defiance of their own party-controlled labor organization but also their demands for the formation of a union ''like Solidarity'' and the repeal of Article 6. They got only economic concessions, but their voices reached millions in the Soviet Union and beyond. Then in December, two Baltic republics of the Soviet Union, Latvia and Lithuania, defied President Gorbachev and amended their constitutions to eliminate clauses guaranteeing the Communist Party's monopoly.

Ironically, as Gorbachev defended the Communist Party's continuing preeminence at home, he has been in effect a collaborator in the decline of the once-powerful neighboring par-

Alexander Dubcek, leader of Czechoslovakia's reform movement of 1968 that led to an invasion by Warsaw Pact forces, waves to an overflowing crowd in Prague's Wenceslas Square in late November. At year's end he was elected chairman of the national Parliament.

The 24-year rule of Romanian dictator Nicolae Ceaușescu, below, *ended rapidly in late December as young Army members supported a popular uprising,* right. *Ceaușescu and his wife, the nation's deputy leader, were executed by a military tribunal.*

Photos, AP/Wide World

ties. Erich Honecker would have loved it if Gorbachev had been more like the late Leonid Brezhnev, who ordered Warsaw Pact troops into Czechoslovakia in 1968 when a new government there decided to pursue "socialism with a human face." It was more than a coincidence that in November, as Czechs were holding daily demonstrations in Prague, the official Communist newspaper *Pravda* in Moscow published an article by Gorbachev saying his goal is to provide the socialist system "with a human face."

Among the Communist countries unaffected by such democratic trends in 1989 was North Korea, where Kim Il Sung, 77, revered as the "Great Leader," was grooming as his successor his son, Kim Jong Il, the "Dear Leader." As Henry Kissinger has pointed out, one of the attractions that Marxism-Leninism has for some rulers is the rationale it provides for maintaining power. Successful as President Kim Il Sung has been in dominating his own country, he is a severe and embarrassing liability to world communism, since his regime stands out as a living but anachronistic model of institutionalized human-rights violations. Despite their reform efforts, Gorbachev and others of similar persuasion still defend communism as a viable system.

Debate on U.S. Policy. In February, President Bush told a joint session of Congress that "around the globe, we must continue to be freedom's best friend." That world outlook was in keeping with Reagan administration policies, which columnist and former Reagan administration official Jeane J. Kirkpatrick credits with giving "new life to the idea of freedom in our time" and thereby helping "to precipitate the explosion of democracy and democratic institution-building throughout the world." The very success of those policies in opposing communism, however, has fueled a controversy challenging the need for continuing an activist U.S. prodemocracy role. In a public-television debate Patrick Buchanan, a conservative columnist and former White House aide, denounced "this mission democracy thing" as "messianic globaloney." By way of example, he cited the case of Chile, which the United States has prodded down the road toward democracy. "My view is," Buchanan said, "let the Chileans solve their own problems."

In a celebrated essay, "The End of History?", published in the summer issue of *The National Interest,* Francis Fukuyama, a State Department policy analyst, speculated that history now has reached "the end point of mankind's ideological evolution and the universalization of Western liberal democracy." For many readers, the essay was an erudite justification for declaring victory and narrowing U.S. concerns, a belief reinforced by Fukuyama's statement that "it matters very little what strange thoughts occur to people in Albania or Burkina Faso." From other platforms, some liberals also argued for a more isolationist foreign policy. De facto allies for this policy came from among middle-of-the-road Democrats and Republicans in Congress who feel that, with the Soviet military threat perceived as past, the nation must turn inward, expanding domestic programs and curtailing those for security and foreign assistance.

Champions of a continuing prodemocracy activism—also a mixed lot of conservatives, liberals, and centrists—still remained strong and vocal. For them, the changes in the Soviet bloc do not justify losing interest in the cause of freedom in the world. Morton Kondracke, a prodemocracy advocate, argued in *The New Republic* that "the main idea behind fighting communism in the first place [was] to secure liberty for everyone, not just ourselves." Journalist and commentator Kondracke cited an example of the prodemocracy activism he favors: "To save Hong Kong from losing its freedom when it reverts to Chinese control in 1997 may require intense diplomatic pressure, the use of economic and political sanctions, or even the threat of force."

Besides, even in countries that experienced dramatic breakthroughs in 1989, the future of democracy is by no means assured. After successfully struggling for political freedom, long-suffering populations, in Poland, for example, might lose faith in democratic reforms if the devastated Polish economy does not deliver material results soon. In a talk at the National Endowment for Democracy conference in May, Leszek Kolakowski of the universities of Oxford and Chicago pointed out that "rage and aggressivity" can flare up when expectations of economic returns are disappointed. Widespread feelings of frustration among people living in misery, he said, create "fertile ground for successful demagogy of totalitarian movements and for the temptation to 'solve' social problems by means of a military dictatorship." In other words, the gains for freedom in 1989 are not irreversible. "Freedom," Kolakowski said, "is always vulnerable and its cause never safe."

See also articles on the individual countries within the Alphabetical Section.

"The progress of democracy seems irresistible, because it is the most uniform, the most ancient, and the most permanent tendency which is to be found in history."

Alexis de Tocqueville

"A democracy is the most difficult kind of government to operate. It represents the last flowering, really, of the human experience."

John F. Kennedy

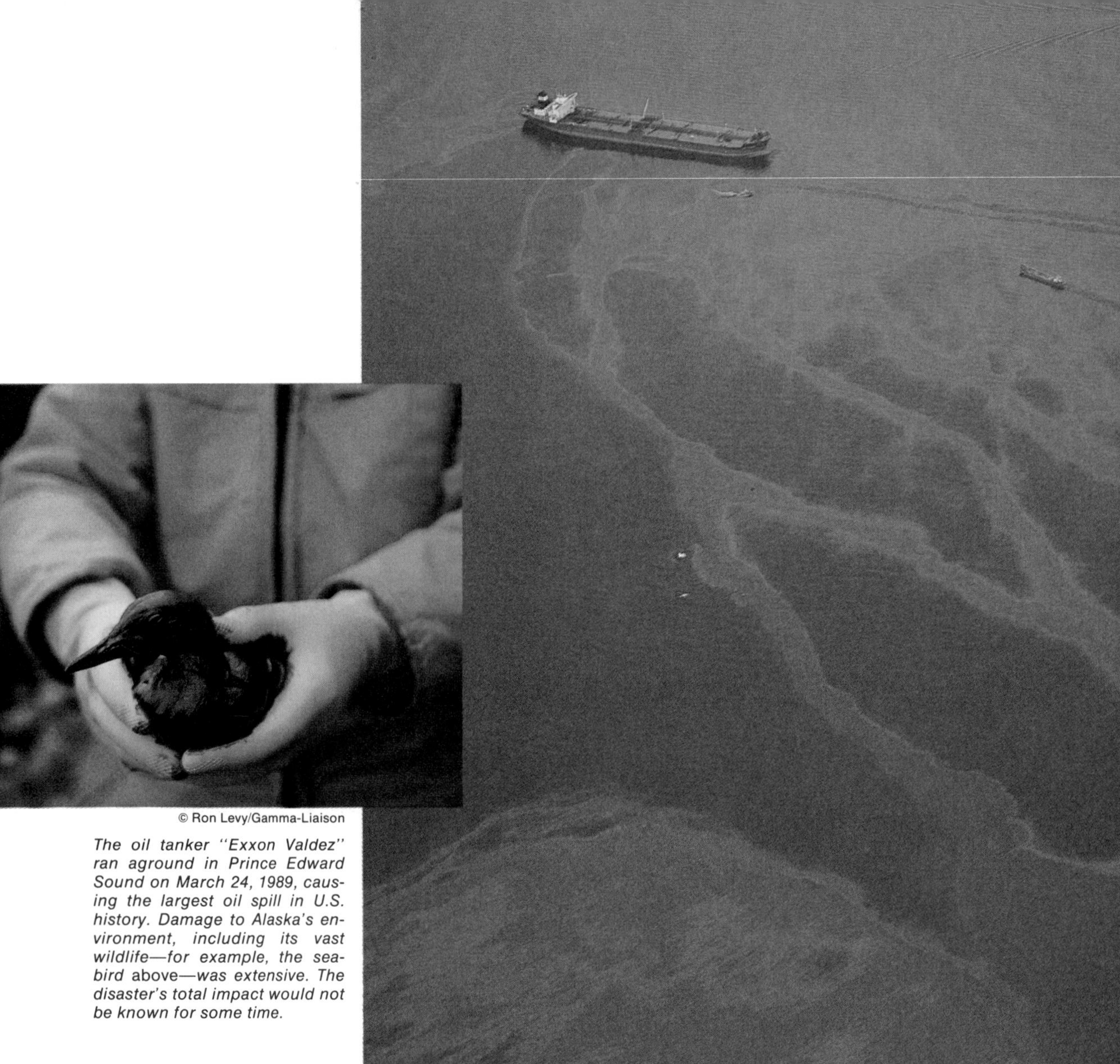

© Ron Levy/Gamma-Liaison

The oil tanker "Exxon Valdez" ran aground in Prince Edward Sound on March 24, 1989, causing the largest oil spill in U.S. history. Damage to Alaska's environment, including its vast wildlife—for example, the seabird above—was extensive. The disaster's total impact would not be known for some time.

© Erik Hill, "Anchorage Daily News"/Gamma-Liaison

THE EXXON VALDEZ
The Largest Oil Spill in U.S. History

By Paul A. Witteman

About the Author. Paul A. Witteman is San Francisco Bureau Chief of *Time* magazine. He traveled to Valdez and Prince William Sound three times in 1989 so that he could report on the *Exxon Valdez* oil spill. He also has served as the magazine's Bureau Chief in Detroit and has reported from Tehran on the Iranian revolution.

Shortly after midnight on the 24th of March 1989, the captain of the oil tanker *Exxon Valdez* radioed the Coast Guard Vessel Traffic Control station in Valdez, AK, that his ship had gone aground in Prince William Sound. Capt. Joseph Hazelwood, 42, reported in a matter-of-fact tone to the Coast Guard duty officer, "We should be on your radar there. We've fetched up hard aground north of Goose Island off Bligh Reef. And evidently we're leaking some oil and we're going to be here for awhile . . ."

Thus began the drama surrounding the largest oil spill in U.S. history, an event that many believe helped to cause the reawakening of the environmental movement in the United States. The 987-ft (301-m) *Exxon Valdez* continued to leak oil for two days, a total of 260,000 barrels in all. The cleanup lasted six months before being shut down officially for the winter by Exxon. The impact on the environment and wildlife would last for years and perhaps decades.

Other Spills. The *Exxon Valdez* spill was the first and worst of the year, but 1989 was notable in that there were other spills, all of which pointed out the vulnerability of the environment to contamination and man's frailty in preventing such mishaps. On June 23 the *World Prodigy,* a tanker of Greek registry, struck a rock off Brenton Reef near Newport, RI, and spilled more than 14,000 barrels of light oil into Rhode Island Sound. Several hours later the *Rachel B,* a tanker registered in Panama, struck a barge in the Houston ship channel and spilled almost 6,000 barrels of oil into the inland waterway. The following day, a Uruguayan tanker, *Presidente Rivera,* fetched hard aground in the Delaware River near Claymont, DE, and spilled about 20,000 barrels of industrial fuel into an area where it threatened marine life in Delaware Bay.

Coming hard on the heels of the *Valdez* accident, the spills galvanized the U.S. Congress to hasten its debate of new laws to protect the environment. In addition, the Petroleum Industry Response Organization (PIRO), a consortium of the nation's oil companies, proposed in June the establishment of a new organization with a $250 million budget over its first five years to react to future spills. PIRO would create five regional response centers ready to act speedily to limit the spread of future spills, and fund a research and development project to discover new ways to treat spills.

"I think it's quite clear right now that our area is faced with destruction of our entire way of life."

Valdez Mayor
John Devens
March 27, 1989

Exxon "will meet our obligations to all those who have suffered damage from the spill."

Exxon Chairman
L. G. Rawl
April 3, 1989

The Circumstances of the *Exxon Valdez* Spill. While dramatic, the triple spills in June were ultimately less serious than the *Exxon Valdez* disaster. As bad as it was, however, the Alaska spill could have been much worse. The *Exxon Valdez,* one of the newest and most modern ships in the Exxon tanker fleet, had 1.26 million barrels of Prudhoe Bay crude oil on board when she ran onto the reef. It was only because of alert and careful work by crews working for Marine Pollution Control, a veteran oil spill company, that the remaining 1 million barrels were removed successfully from the damaged vessel and transferred to other Exxon tankers that were able to moor at her side.

The only thing that was clear in the first moonlit hours after the grounding was that absolutely nobody was ready for it. The chronology of the spill itself made that difficult to understand. When the *Exxon Valdez* set sail from the Alyeska Marine Terminal across the harbor from the town of Valdez at 9 P.M. on March 23, skies were crystal clear and the wind was calm. The ship was guided south, through the narrows and out into the sound proper by licensed harbor pilot Capt. William

Murphy. The pilot left the ship off Rocky Point at 11:24 P.M., and Captain Hazelwood immediately informed the Coast Guard that he would be veering off course to avoid some icebergs that had separated off Columbia Glacier and posed a threat to the ship.

Twenty-five minutes later Hazelwood returned to his cabin and left command of the ship to Third Mate Gregory Cousins, who was not certified to handle the ship inside the confinement of the sound. For reasons that are not entirely clear to investigators, Cousins did not initiate course changes soon enough to bring the ship back into the outbound shipping channel and out of harm's way. By the time Captain Hazelwood was summoned back to the bridge by his third mate with the terse message, "We are in trouble," the ship had begun to grind across the rocks of the reef. Eight of the ship's 13 cargo tanks were pierced and 50% of the hull was damaged before the *Exxon Valdez* came precariously to rest, impaled on the rocks. At that point Captain Hazelwood slowed, then stopped the engines. Within the hour he had to turn them back on and increase power to "full answering speed" in order to keep the ship from slipping off the reef and sinking. By 1:30 in the morning, however, the tide in Prince William Sound had become low and Hazelwood again turned off the engines and deployed his anchor. By midmorning state police officers tested the captain for alcohol and found his blood-alcohol level above the legal requirements for operating a ship. Subsequent investigations disclosed that Hazelwood had a documented drinking problem. He had been arrested several times for drunk driving, had been treated for alcoholism at a clinic, and was seen drinking in various Valdez bars the afternoon his ship sailed. He later was fired by Exxon and charged by the state of Alaska with three felonies and three misdemeanors for his role in the spill. For his part, Hazelwood later claimed that he was exempt from prosecution, since he had been first to report the spill, but a judge refused in November to halt the case against Hazelwood.

AP/Wide World

As a result of the disaster, Joseph Hazelwood, the 42-year-old captain of the "Exxon Valdez," lost his job and faced criminal charges. He had worked for Exxon since 1968.

But while Hazelwood was being tested for alcohol content, oil was escaping unimpeded. The Alyeska Pipeline Service Company, which operates the marine terminal and the 800-mi-(1 287-km)-long pipeline that brings crude oil down from the Arctic fields, had primary responsibility to defend against the spill. The state requires Alyeska to maintain an oil spill contingency plan that insures the company would be able to respond to a large spill within four hours, surrounding oil with booms. A slick that is surrounded is easier to control and skim up. The problem regarding the *Exxon Valdez* was that the large barge Alyeska kept for such a purpose was laid up and could not be deployed until 15 precious hours had elapsed. Moreover, it did not have sufficient booms to surround the ship. The contingency plan also called for the applications of dispersants, which separate the oil into small particles that are consumed more easily by bacteria in the water. There was not enough available, nor was there sufficient equipment with which to apply it. Another option was to burn the oil on the water. A test burn was conducted on a small patch of oil, eliminating 350 barrels, but the wind picked up, spreading the slick and making further burning impossible. Three days after the spill, storm winds up to 70 knots further spread the oil and made the use of dispersants an academic question for the remainder of the cleanup.

Consequences. The spill continued to move south, coating the rocky shorelines of Smith, Naked, Knight, Green, Montague, Latouche, and numerous smaller islands with a thick, black residue. When the oil was mixed with seawater during wave action, it became a frothy, chocolate-colored substance that scientists called mousse. The oil began to coat shore-nesting birds by the thousands and sea otters. Eventually, the carcasses of more than 34,000 birds, such as murres and cormorants, were recovered. Biologists for the U.S. Fish and Wildlife Service believed that the body count represented only 5 to 10% of the victims. The toll among sea otters was equally severe. The oil coated their fur, reducing their natural insulation, and many of them died of exposure. Approximately 1,000 sea-otter carcasses were found. Of the 300 or so animals that were brought in to hastily set up treatment centers, 200 eventually were returned safely to their home territories.

Although the number of deaths of bald eagles was smaller at 139, the fact that the raptor is the nation's symbol made their deaths all the more significant. Many eagles, which scavenge on beaches, ate the carcasses of other oiled animals and died of internal poisoning. There were smaller numbers of marine mammals that fell victim to the oil. Scientists found a total of 15 harbor seals, 14 stellar sea lions, and two northern fur seals dead in the area impacted by the oil. But officials with the National Marine Fisheries Services were quick to

© Al Grillo/Picture Group

The sea otter was a particular victim of the disaster as oil coated its fur, reducing its natural insulation. Some 1,000 of the marine animals, native to the northern Pacific, died as a consequence of the spill.

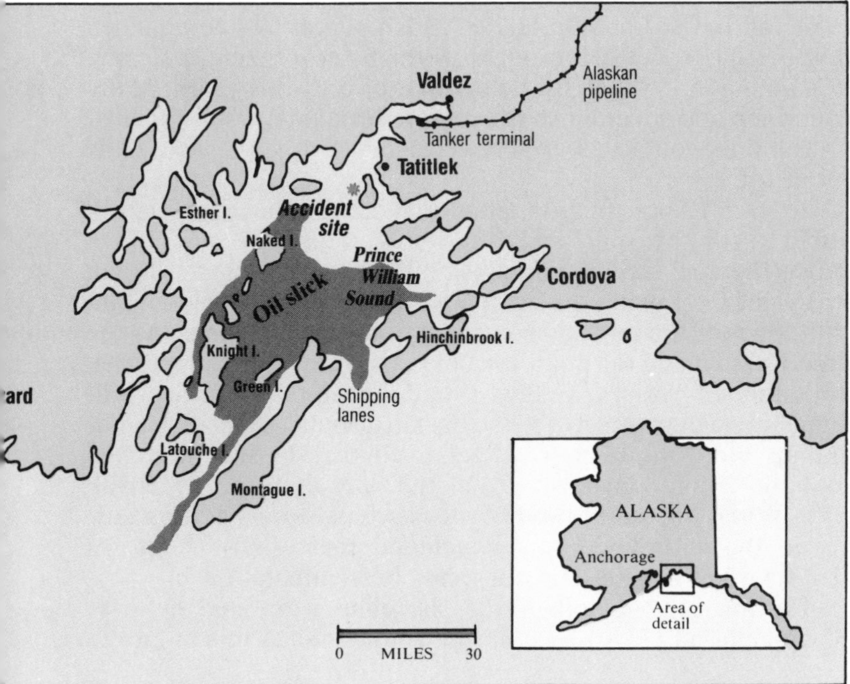

The oil industry in Alaska began to flourish in the late 1970s, following completion of the trans-Alaska pipeline, which runs from Prudhoe Bay to the ice-free port of Valdez. The "Exxon Valdez" plowed into a reef 25 mi (40 km) from Valdez. Within one week, its oil had spread over 900 sq mi (2 300 km²).

© B. Nation/Sygma

Volunteers used pure dishwashing detergent to clean oil-soaked birds before releasing them in areas not affected by the spill.

point out that the deaths may not have been related to the spill. Researchers also were investigating the reported deaths of some gray and minke whales.

It was more difficult to determine the fate of some ground mammals because of search restrictions placed on the interior of some of the islands affected by their owners, the local Alaska Native Corporation. As a result, islands were searched only to the high water line. But scientists expected some river otters, mink, Sitka black-tailed deer, and bear to suffer from ingesting oil-contaminated organisms and plants. Along the Alaska Peninsula where fox and coyote scavenge on shorelines, there also were possibilities of casualties.

The Cleanup. Exxon was slow off the mark in organizing its cleanup efforts. In early days before large amounts of equipment were massed for an all-out assault, workers spent days futilely washing individual rocks. Local fishermen, based in Prince William Sound towns and villages like Cordova and Tatitlek, quickly and effectively threw their own boats into the battle. The members of the Prince William Sound Aquaculture Association constructed handmade booms of logs to surround salmon hatcheries at Main Bay, Sawmill Bay, and on Esther Island, which is the largest salmon hatchery in the world. The oil was held out of all the hatcheries and when the salmon fry were released in May, most were expected to survive until maturity.

Nonetheless, fishing in the sound and out in the Gulf of Alaska was affected seriously. The state Department of Fish and Game closed the Prince William Sound herring season in April. The year before, herring fishing yielded 10,000 tons and brought fishermen $12.2 million. The salmon season did take place but was limited by the state because of localized contamination. The salmon fishery in 1989 brought fishermen a total of $44 million, down dramatically from the $76 million in 1988 and the $67 million in 1987. Fish processors complained that the quality of fish brought to them for freezing, packing, or canning in 1989 fell far below that of previous years. Many fishermen and several fish processors brought lawsuits against Exxon that would seek to recover damages for 1989 as well as for future losses.

In early April, Exxon Chairman L. G. Rawl apologized publicly for the spill, and Interior Secretary Manuel Lujan called the spill the oil industry's "Three Mile Island." Lujan was right in drawing the comparison to the 1979 accident and shutdown of the nuclear-power plant in Pennsylvania. At the time Lujan made his point the spill covered 1,000 sq mi (2 590 km^2) and still was expanding. It had flowed out of Prince William Sound into the Gulf of Alaska, around Kodiak Island, and up into Cook Inlet. The leading edge of the spill stretched past the Trinity Islands and all the way down to Stepovak Bay. When the state, the U.S. Coast Guard, and Exxon surveyed the shoreline, they concluded that almost 1,100 mi (1 770 km) of the Alaskan coast had been affected.

Fortunately, not all of the shoreline was oiled heavily. Forty-eight mi (77 km) within the sound and 11 mi (18 km) in

© Sygma

The smaller tanker "Exxon Baton Rouge," right, was brought in to pump the unspilled oil from the hold of the "Exxon Valdez." The damaged ship continued leaking even as its remaining cargo was removed.

the Seward area near the Kenai Fjords National Park were heavily oiled. Ninety-nine mi (159 km) in both areas were oiled moderately. The rest of the shoreline was either lightly or very lightly oiled, which consisted mainly of oil tarballs that washed up sporadically on beaches. Exxon set out to clean all of that coastline, but geared its heaviest efforts in Prince William Sound where the majority of heavy oiling occurred.

Two weeks after the spill Exxon had just 350 workers out cleaning up in the sound. A month after that, the number had increased to several thousand and at the peak of the cleanup in the summer month of July, there were 11,300 people involved in the effort, twice as many people as there were full-time residents of Prince William Sound communities. Exxon amassed a flotilla of 1,400 boats large and small. There were hotel ships, barges, an oil platform that served as a dormitory, and converted U.S. Navy landing ships. There was even a 425-ft- (130-m)-long Soviet skimmer, brought in from Siberia. The *Vaydaghubsky,* the largest skimmer in the world, experi-

AP/Wide World

The "Vaydaghubsky," a 425-ft- (130-m)-long Soviet skimmer, went to Alaskan waters from Siberia to aid in the cleanup.

© J. L. Atlan/Sygma

© Michael Baytoff/Black Star

The Cleanup Effort: Loose floating oil in the areas of Knight and Eleanor islands was corralled by booms deployed by boats. Exxon workers, right, *flushed the coast with water from high-pressure hoses.*

enced equipment malfunctions periodically and was not as effective as had been hoped. Exxon faced the daunting task of providing 200 tons of food a week to workers and disposing of 1.4 million gal (5.3 million l) of human waste weekly. The only human fatality of the cleanup was suffered by a worker in the galley of one of Exxon's ships who was crushed when riding a dumbwaiter.

The oil spill was treated in three ways. Loose floating oil was corraled by booms deployed by boats. The most effective booms used were called curtain booms since they hung below the surface, preventing the oil from escaping. While several boats held the boom in place, a skimmer would suck the oil up along a conveyor belt and into a holding tank. Oil that made its way onto the coastline was more difficult to retrieve. Exxon either flushed the beaches with seawater or with water heated to 140°F (60°C) and delivered out high-pressure hoses. The second treatment was the most effective at moving the oil back out into the sea, but it also killed small tidal animals like snails and mussels in the process. Once the oil was flushed into the water, it was boomed and skimmed. On steep, difficult-to-reach beaches, Exxon used a sprinkler system on the end of a 100-ft- (30-m)-long, adjustable mechanical arm that could be operated from on board ship. This device became known as the omni-sweep.

On the most heavily polluted beaches, oil seeped down through sediment to bedrock. In some cases bedrock was 3 ft (.9 m) below the surface. The buried oil was impossible to remove by flushing. With each change of the tide from low to high, the pressure of the water brought much of that buried oil to the surface. This required Exxon cleanup crews to flush some beaches as many as seven times. More effective was the application of Inipol, a fertilizer. When applied to the cobbled beaches by power spray, Inipol encouraged the quick growth of organisms that ate the oil and caused it to degrade harmlessly. Exxon applied Inipol to almost 70 mi (113 km) of oiled coastline. The state of Alaska was less sure that Inipol was the cure-all Exxon believed it to be.

The state and Exxon disagreed about much concerning the cleanup. Alaska fought the use of dispersants, specifically one called Corexit. The chemicals in Corexit are themselves toxic and the state contended that they would do as much damage as good. They also asserted that Exxon did not have the ability to control the spread of the Corexit. As a result, it was not used. Another weapon that never was used was a large incinerator barge brought to Alaska by Exxon to burn oil-contaminated waste such as driftwood and absorbent booms. Exxon had been told by the state that burning was the preferred means of eliminating those wastes, but the permit process dragged on for four months. As a result, the $5 million spent by Exxon on the effort went for naught without a single piece of waste being burned.

When Exxon announced that it would shut down cleanup operations on September 15, it brought howls of protest from the state. Pointing to weather data compiled by the National Oceanic and Atmospheric Administration, Exxon said that increases in wind speed and the reduction in time between major storms made it dangerous for crews to be on the water. The Coast Guard, which was functioning as the coordinator for the federal government, agreed with that assessment. The state disagreed and on the day that the last workers filed off boats in Valdez and onto buses and planes to return home, Gov. Steve Cowper announced Alaska's own winter cleanup. The winter program involved volunteers from local communities in the sound and on the Alaska Peninsula and would cost $21 million. In addition, approximately $2 million was allocated to provide mental-health services to those residents who had trouble coping with the loss of livelihood they suffered at the hands of the spill.

© Jim Lukoski/JB Pictures

The rebirth of the environmental movement among the general public was a by-product of the March 24, 1989, oil disaster.

For its part, Exxon announced a scaled-back winter program, which involved monitoring the affected areas by boat and plane. The company moved its headquarters staff from a brand-new 20,000 sq ft (1 858 m²) building in Valdez back to Anchorage. The company also said that it had signed a one-year lease on the building and would be back in the spring. The company also sued Alaska, charging that the state had hindered cleanup by prohibiting the use of oil-dispersing chemicals.

Whether Exxon would find any more oil at that point was anyone's guess. Exxon said that it had picked up 61,000 barrels by the time the cleanup ended in September. Some experts felt that an additional 25% of the spill had evaporated in the early days, leaving 134,000 barrels unaccounted for. Although most experts and officials were reluctant to admit it publicly, most said that they believed that oil was ultimately so diluted in ocean water that it was impossible to find or recover. But the lesson of the *Exxon Valdez* was clear. The United States should have better contingency plans to deal with oil spills. If not, the tragedy of the *Exxon Valdez* would be likely to happen over and over again.

ABORTION
The Continuing Controversy

By Mary H. Cooper

The year 1989 was a watershed for the debate throughout the United States over abortion rights. With its summer decision to allow the states greater leeway in regulating abortion, the U.S. Supreme Court reopened a controversy that it had closed 16 years earlier. Although the nation's highest court stopped short of overturning its landmark 1973 *Roe v. Wade* decision establishing a constitutionally protected right for women to terminate unwanted pregnancies, it took a significant step in that direction with the July 3 ruling. By returning to the state legislatures greater power to restrict access to abortion, the court also returned the issue of abortion rights to the political realm, unleashing a wave of activity at the national, state, and grass-roots level not seen in the United States since the early 1970s.

About the Author. Mary H. Cooper is a staff writer for *Editorial Research Reports,* a news service published by Congressional Quarterly in Washington, DC. A specialist in international economics, Ms. Cooper is the author of *The Business of Drugs, An Economic Study of the Narcotics Industry,* published in early 1990. Ms. Cooper has been observing the abortion controversy from her vantage point on the Washington scene.

In some respects, little changed on the abortion front during the 1980s. More than 1.5 million abortions were performed each year in the United States, a number that remained constant during the decade. Lack of appropriate sex education and lack of access to efficient methods of birth control frequently are cited as explanations for the high incidence of abortion, the most common surgical procedure among women after operations related to childbirth. Whatever the reason,

the United States has the highest abortion rate—one abortion for every 2.5 live births—in the industrial world.

What changed in the 1980s and placed abortion back on the political agenda was the growth of the antiabortion movement. Bolstered by the conservative shift in public opinion that began with Ronald Reagan's election to the presidency in 1980, opponents of abortion rights worked throughout the decade to introduce restrictions on abortion in the state legislatures. The same conservative tilt was seen in the appointment to the Supreme Court of justices opposed to abortion. By 1989 the stage was set for the first major challenge to *Roe v. Wade*.

In all, the Supreme Court had four abortion-related cases on its 1989 docket. In its July decision in *Webster v. Reproductive Health Services,* the Supreme Court upheld a Missouri statute banning abortions in public hospitals. Another case, *Turnock v. Ragsdale,* involved a challenge to Illinois state regulations requiring abortion clinics to be built, equipped, and staffed according to the same stringent standards required of full-service hospital operating rooms. Because the vast majority of abortion clinics are small and could not have met the Illinois standards, the Supreme Court could have forced most clinics out of business if it had upheld the Illinois statute. Challengers to the law said it violated women's constitutional right to obtain abortions during the first trimester without restrictions and thus could have been used as a vehicle for overturning *Roe v. Wade*. In a major victory for abortion-rights supporters, however, that case was settled out of court in November. Also in November, the Supreme Court heard arguments for the other two abortion-related cases—*Hodgson v. Minnesota* and *Ohio v. Akron Center for Reproductive Health*. Both cases, scheduled to be decided in 1990, involve

A much-discussed July 3, 1989, decision by the U.S. Supreme Court upholding a Missouri law banning abortions in public hospitals led to a marked increase in the number of demonstrations by pro-lifers as well as by pro-choicers, those opposing and those favoring abortion.

© Ralf-Finn Hestoft/Picture Group

© Ken Hawkins/Sygma

With judicial and legislative actions on the abortion issue under consideration in the United States, adherents on both sides of the issue resort to such techniques as petitions and demonstrations, including sit-ins, to vocalize their views. Above: Members of an Illinois pro-choice alliance sign a petition to keep abortion legal, while antiabortionists in Atlanta stage a protest at an abortion clinic.

state laws requiring that parents be notified before minors may obtain abortions.

By galvanizing forces on both sides of the abortion issue, the Supreme Court's July decision had the greatest political impact of any decision handed down in 1989. The ruling injected renewed energy into the so-called "pro-life," or antiabortion, forces who had spent 16 years building an extensive grass-roots organization whose activities included support for restrictive regulations governing abortion at the state level and picketing of family-planning clinics where abortions are performed. Advocacy groups and membership organizations, including the National Conference of Catholic Bishops, also stepped up their campaign against abortions in 1989. The July decision also shook "pro-choice," or abortion-rights, advocates out of the complacency into which they had been lulled by *Roe v. Wade*. Advocates of both sides of the abortion debate took to the streets in public demonstrations in attempts to win support.

The outcome of that struggle was far from clear by year's end. The *Webster* ruling was a clear victory for antiabortion forces, who long had sought to restore power to the states to regulate abortion. The National Right to Life Committee pegged its hopes of more restrictive abortion regulations on several states that held special legislative sessions in the fall in response to the Supreme Court ruling. Pennsylvania, whose legislature is among the country's most antagonistic to abortion, became the first state to take advantage of the ruling by passing a law that was signed by Gov. Robert P. Casey in November. The measure imposes a 24-hour waiting period before a woman can obtain an abortion and requires that married women notify their husbands before going through with the procedure. The other provisions of the new law that many observers said contradicted the principles embodied in *Roe v. Wade* are the prohibition of most abortions after 24 weeks of pregnancy and a ban on all abortions performed because of the fetus' sex. The law also carries stiff penalties—up to seven years in prison and $15,000 in fines—for doctors who violate the sex-selection ban.

Following Pennsylvania's lead, the Michigan legislature passed a law requiring minors to obtain parental consent before having an abortion, while other states also were considering new abortion restrictions. For its part, the Louisiana legislature responded to the *Webster* ruling by directing its district attorneys to begin enforcing an 1855 criminal statute against abortion that the state never repealed. The statute, which is the strictest antiabortion law in the nation and since 1973 has had an injunction against it, bans abortions under any circumstances and imposes up to ten years' imprisonment for doctors who perform them. Louisiana is one of about 30 states that have antiabortion laws still on the books that were declared unenforceable after *Roe v. Wade*.

"Now, a woman's access to abortion will become hostage to geography as states enact a patchwork of laws and regulations aimed at blocking abortions."
Faye Wattleton
President,
Planned Parenthood Federation of America
July 3, 1989

But the tide turned as the year wore on, as abortion-rights advocates won important victories for their cause. The Florida legislature, for example, rejected a series of regulations Republican Gov. Bob Martinez had proposed in the wake of the *Webster* decision. Texas Gov. Bill Clements (R) also stunned antiabortion supporters by refusing to allow abortion restrictions to be discussed in any of the state's year-end special legislative sessions. Abortion-rights supporters promised to file suit to block major portions of the Pennsylvania abortion-control statute before they were to take effect in January 1990.

"By upholding the Missouri statute, the [Supreme] Court appears to have begun to restore to the people the ability to protect the unborn. We continue to believe that **Roe v. Wade** ***was incorrectly decided and should now be reversed."***
President George Bush
July 3, 1989

Another disappointment for antiabortion supporters was the out-of-court settlement reached by Illinois Attorney General Neil Hartigan (D) in *Turnock v. Ragsdale,* one of the three abortion-related cases that had been scheduled for Supreme Court action in 1989. Then in November, voters elected pro-choice candidates L. Douglas Wilder of Virginia and James J. Florio of New Jersey, both Democrats, to the governorship of those states following campaigns that hinged largely on this issue. In a California special election, voters elected Lucy Killea, a pro-choice Catholic, to the state Senate after a Catholic bishop denied her Communion because of her position on abortion.

Although the abortion debate was most heated at the state level, it received renewed attention at the national level as well, as congressional backers of abortion rights sparred with the Bush administration over the use of federal funds to pay for abortions through the medicaid program. In the first federal legislative victory for pro-choice forces in the 1980s, the House reversed its previous position by rejecting language in the 1990 spending bill for the District of Columbia barring the city from using its own tax dollars to fund abortions for poor women. Both the House and Senate approved less restrictive language in the fiscal 1990 appropriations for the Departments of Labor, Health and Human Services (HHS), and Education—the main legislative vehicles for abortion-related policy—

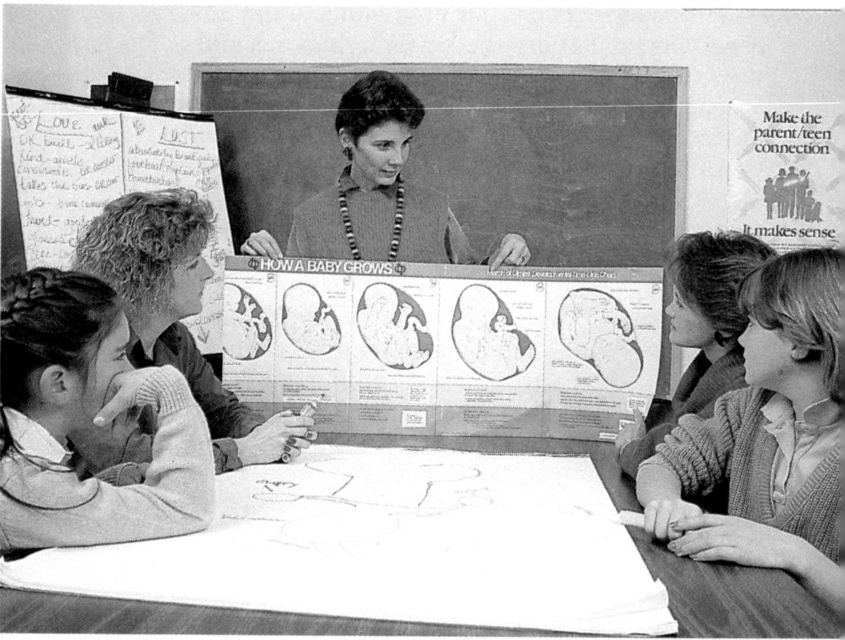

Proper sex education is seen as a way to counter the large number of abortions occurring annually in the United States.

© David R. Frazier/Photo Researchers

than they had in previous years. Since 1976, when Congress adopted the so-called Hyde amendment, medicaid funds could not be used to pay for any abortions "except where the life of the mother would be endangered if the fetus were carried to term." In 1989, Congress voted to allow federal funding of abortions in cases of rape or incest as well.

But the Bush administration prevented the lawmakers' more liberal stance on abortion rights from becoming law. The president has become more outspoken in his opposition to abortion since he took office in January 1989, and his administration in October asked the Supreme Court to overrule *Roe v. Wade*. Bush vetoed the appropriations bills as well as the District of Columbia's spending bill and foreign operations legislation that would have funded a United Nations family-planning program in China, whose government has been accused of sanctioning forced abortions as part of its population-control campaign. Congressional supporters of abortion rights failed to muster the two-thirds consensus needed to override the presidential vetoes but pledged to continue their quest for more liberal abortion policy when Congress reconvened in January 1990. As a sign of their commitment, pro-choice legislators introduced a measure just before adjournment that would write into law the principles embodied in *Roe v. Wade* and override the Supreme Court's *Webster* ruling by making abortion legal in all states.

Political strategists on both sides of the abortion debate were gearing up for the 1990 elections. As the events of 1989 demonstrated, the American public has not yet reached a clear consensus on the issue. Public-opinion polls repeatedly have shown the public's ambivalence toward abortion. They generally suggest that Americans support a woman's right to choose whether or not to have children, but at the same time want abortion to be restricted under some circumstances. According to a poll conducted in November by the National Abortion Rights Action League, 60% of adults support laws already on the books in 24 states that restrict teenagers' access to abortion by requiring the consent or notification of one or both parents or by forcing them to observe a waiting period to reconsider their decision. On the basis of these surveys, the National Right to Life lobby is focusing its efforts at the state level on specific legislative goals aimed at restricting access to abortion. Among these are stricter parental-notification requirements for minors seeking abortions, waiting periods aimed at encouraging women to reconsider their decision to terminate pregnancy, a ban on abortions used as a means of birth control or selecting the sex of children, and a requirement that a woman notify the fetus' father before proceeding with an abortion.

Although the focus of the abortion debate moved from the judicial to the political sphere in 1989, the Supreme Court by year's end had not issued rulings on two pending cases on the subject, both addressing the parental-consent arrangement. In accordance with standards set in the wake of *Roe v. Wade,* most states allow a waiver of these restrictions by a process known as judicial bypass. This means that a pregnant teenager can obtain permission to have an abortion without telling her parents if she can convince a judge either that she is mature enough to make the decision regarding the procedure on her own or that her welfare would be endangered if she informed her parents.

© Fred S. Prouser/Gamma-Liaison

Public attention on the abortion question focused on Pennsylvania's capitol in Harrisburg in the fall as the state enacted a significant antiabortion law.

But laws passed in Ohio and Minnesota, whose constitutionality must be decided by the nation's Supreme Court, would eliminate the judicial bypass or make it harder to obtain. The Ohio legislation at issue in *Ohio v. Akron Center for Reproductive Health* requires a teenager seeking an abortion to present to the judge "clear and convincing" evidence in the bypass procedure. If the teenager fails to meet this stricter standard, her attending physician must inform one of her parents 24 hours before performing the abortion. The 1981 Minnesota statute at issue in the case of *Hodgson v. Minnesota* dispenses with the judicial bypass altogether by requiring that both biological parents of a minor be informed 48 hours before the abortion is performed.

The outcome of the deliberations on both the judicial bypass question and ultimately all women's access to abortion hinges on the vote of Justice Sandra Day O'Connor, since the rest of the nine-member court is divided on the question of abortion rights. The court's first female justice has avoided addressing the basic principle at stake in the abortion debate, whether or not to let stand the right of women to obtain an abortion as embodied in the 1973 *Roe v. Wade* ruling. In hearing arguments in the two cases in November, Justice O'Connor expressed concern over the parental notification requirements in the two laws under review. If she formally objects to them when the Supreme Court finally rules on the abortion laws in 1990, she may be forced finally to clarify her position on abortion rights in general.

The Bay Area EARTHQUAKE

Oct. 17, 1989, 5:04 p.m.

By Paul Witteman

Tuesday, Oct. 17, 1989, promised to be a festive day in the San Francisco Bay area. The sky was clear, the wind was still, and temperatures climbed into the mid-70s. It was perfect Indian summer weather for the first-ever "Bay Bridge" World Series between the Oakland Athletics and San Francisco Giants. Game three of the best of seven series was to commence at San Francisco's Candlestick Park at 5:25 P.M., Pacific time. By 5:00 traffic in and out of the metropolitan area had thinned considerably as those fans without tickets left work early to watch the game on TV.

The commuter ferries to Larkspur and Sausalito, scheduled to depart at 5:20 and 5:30, were loading passengers in the shadow of the historic ferry building that dates back to 1898. Andy Rubini, the bar manager at the venerable Tadich Grill in the heart of San Francisco's financial district, was pouring a glass of wine for a customer. Noel Murphy, an employee of NCR, had just driven onto the upper deck of the 8.4-mi (14-km) Bay Bridge on his way from the East Bay into San Francisco.

At 5:04 the ground began to shake, gently at first, then more severely. For the next 15 seconds a massive earthquake, centered in the Santa Cruz mountains some 70 mi (113 km) south of the city, shattered the late afternoon calm. It registered 7.1 on the sliding Richter scale and was the largest quake in California since the temblor on April 17, 1906, that registered 8.3, killing an estimated 2,500 persons and leaving 250,000 homeless. This time at least 67 persons were killed as a result of the earthquake, 3,700 suffered injuries, and 12,000 were displaced.

About the Author. *Time* magazine's San Francisco Bureau Chief Paul Witteman was on the telephone in his office on the 19th floor of Two Embarcadero, overlooking the Bay Bridge, when the Oct. 17, 1989, earthquake struck.

A young boy, page 50, *is fascinated by some of the ground rumbled by the massive earthquake that struck northern California on Oct. 17, 1989. The quake ruptured gas mains, releasing natural gas into the air and causing several fires, including a powerful blaze in San Francisco's affluent Marina District overlooking the Golden Gate Bridge,* below left.

AP/Wide World

Destructive Force. Noel Murphy thought his tires had gone flat and he pulled over to the side of the Bay Bridge. When he looked back toward Oakland he saw a sea of humanity rushing toward him. "It was total panic," he said. "People were yelling, 'run to land'." For good reason: A 50-ft (15-m) section of the upper deck of the bridge was wrenched from its supports and fell to the deck below, killing a woman on her way home. The lower deck held, preventing a further collapse into the waters of the bay 210 ft (64 m) below. Meanwhile, the ferrymen quickly cast off the lines of their boats as the docks shook and the flagpole on the ferry building swayed out of control. At the Tadich Grill, Rubini prevented a panicked customer from running into the street, saving her from falling glass from the shattered windows of a bank building across the street.

AP/Wide World

Around the corner on Front Street, the third story of an office building that first saw service in 1908 as a warehouse for chocolate candy blew out, cascading a waterfall of bricks to the sidewalk below. Miraculously, no one was hit by the falling debris. On Sixth and Bluxome, however, an entire wall of a four-story building bowed out, then crashed down on cars holding people who were waiting for friends and family to leave work. Six were crushed to death. But the biggest toll was exacted on a 1.25-mi (2-km) stretch of the Nimitz Freeway in West Oakland that is a key connector to the Bay Bridge. The harmonic tremors destroyed the structural integrity of the double-decked highway. The upper deck pancaked down onto the lower deck, squashing some cars to a height of 12 inches (30 cm), and killing 42 people.

A potentially greater disaster was averted at Candlestick Park where almost 62,000 people sat awaiting the start of the World Series game. When the temblor began, many confused the sound and shaking with crowd reaction. But as the light stanchions swayed, and the rest of the country watching the World Series broadcast saw television screens go blank, the crowd realized that a quake had occurred. There was no panic in the ballpark, however. As players, fans, and dignitaries left

© Paul Miller/Sygma

Some 62,000 fans jamming San Francisco's Candlestick Park for game three of the World Series remained calm as the quake struck. The safety of family members was the prime concern of the players. A 1.25-mi (2-km) stretch of the upper level of the Nimitz Freeway, right, collapsed, crushing cars and killing 42.

© Michael K. Nichols/Magnum Photos

Some 60 homes in the Marina District, an area of Mediterranean-style houses built on a landfill in the early 1900s, were destroyed, left. *Northern Californians were most anxious to learn the latest details.*

© Richards/Sipa

the stadium, the smoke of a major fire in the city showed a suddenly subdued crowd that the quake was a large one.

The fire in the city's tony Marina District was caused, as were many of the fires in the 1906 quake, by a ruptured gas main. Within minutes the San Francisco Fire Department sounded a general alarm and a city block of houses and apartment buildings along Divisadero Avenue were burning out of control. On a normal evening the wind would be blowing through the neighborhood at 20 mph (32 km/hr). The fact that it was calm helped to prevent the fire from spreading. Another factor was the quick action of Assistant Fire Chief Frank Blackburn. With all water mains out, he set up a link from the city's fireboat that pumped 6,000 gallons (22 712 l) per minute on the blaze. Nonetheless the fire was not extinguished for ten hours.

Closer to the earthquake's epicenter, property damage was awesome. Highway 17, the main artery that connects San José to the shore city of Santa Cruz, was closed by landslides. The business districts of Santa Cruz and Watsonville were rendered largely unusable. At the Pacific Garden Mall in Santa Cruz many of the old brick buildings tumbled to the ground and the front of Ford's Department Store collapsed, pinning two people. Three people died in the rubble. The historic bandstand by the beach collapsed but the beautiful old roller coaster next to the Pacific Ocean survived. In downtown Watsonville, however, damage to stores was so severe that the shopping district eventually may be abandoned.

Slightly north of the epicenter, damage was not as dramatic but still was substantial. On the Stanford University campus in Palo Alto, 30 buildings were declared structurally damaged by the quake at a total cost estimated by school officials of $160 million. The San Francisco Public Library saw 250,000 volumes crash to the floor and still had not reopened by December.

Rescue and relief efforts began at once. After declaring seven counties of California disaster areas, thereby subject to federal aid, on October 18, President Bush inspected the devastation two days later.

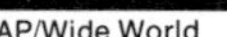

AP/Wide World

© Gripp/Sipa

Rescue and Rebuilding. Rescue efforts the night of the quake centered around the Nimitz Freeway in Oakland. Residents of the West Oakland neighborhood pitched in with highway patrolmen and workers from the California Department of Transportation in a desperate search for survivors. For many rescue workers the searching went too slowly. They believed there were still victims who needed help quickly. On Saturday morning, 89 hours after the quake, their premonitions proved true. Buck Helm, 57, a longshoreman, was found miraculously and removed from the wreckage of the Nimitz. Although doctors held out hope for a full recovery, Helm died suddenly of respiratory failure 32 days after his rescue.

The collapse of the Nimitz Freeway and the Bay Bridge were the most visible of the damage that officials estimated to be at least $6 billion. The Nimitz was not expected to be rebuilt until the spring of 1992. In San Francisco, another double-decker highway, the Embarcadero Freeway, remained closed to all traffic and a debate raged over whether it ever would be returned to service.

Reopening the Bay Bridge, however, was the priority mission of the California Department of Transportation. Cranes mounted on barges lifted off the 50-ft (15-m) section of roadway for repair. Heavier bolts were used to replace those that had sheared off as the bridge moved 11 inches (28 cm) during the quake. One month after the quake, California Gov. George Deukmejian led 11,000 walkers out onto a repaired and freshly painted Bay Bridge. Singer Tony Bennett joined them and sang his signature song, ''I Left My Heart in San Francisco.'' On November 17, at one minute before midnight, the bridge reopened to normal traffic.

The reopening of the Bay Bridge symbolized the area's quick recovery, but many faced spending Christmas and the foreseeable future without housing. Many of the thousands who were made homeless by the quake set up housekeeping in tents reminiscent of life during the Great Depression. Six weeks after the quake many still were living in those tents. Some elderly Marina residents on fixed incomes never will be able to rebuild homes that were underinsured. Some of the damage also was psychological. Many people fortunate enough not to lose loved ones or property nonetheless suffered from what doctors call posttraumatic stress disorder. Anger, loss of appetite, and in extreme cases, suicidal tendencies were principal symptoms. "People's sense of invulnerability has been punctured," said Dr. Daniel Weiss, a psychologist at the University of California at San Francisco Medical School. Rescuers of victims also were expected to suffer from reliving the gruesome ordeal.

Nor was there any long-term comfort to be drawn from the predictions of geologists and seismologists. All were in agreement that the Loma Prieta quake, as the 1989 temblor was named, was not "The Big One" predicted for California within the next 50 years. While scientists agreed that a quake registering 8.0 or better is a certainty, none would forecast where it might take place. Earthquake prediction is at best an uncertain science, and the forces of nature never rest. In the two weeks after the quake there were more than 3,000 aftershocks along the San Andreas Fault in the vicinity of the first shock. The massive "plates" that make up the substructure of the surface of the earth continue to grind together in the depths unreachable by man's most sophisticated measuring instruments. The quake of 1989 provided a warning that residents of California must be better prepared for the next one. The state government immediately began to allocate funds for preparation. Most of the 30 million citizens who live in California also made preparations. Many wondered, however, if any preparation would be adequate when the megaquake does strike.

To the relief of Oakland-San Francisco commuters, the Bay Bridge reopened to traffic four and one-half weeks after the quake. At the reopening, California Gov. George Deukmejian declared, "We are back."

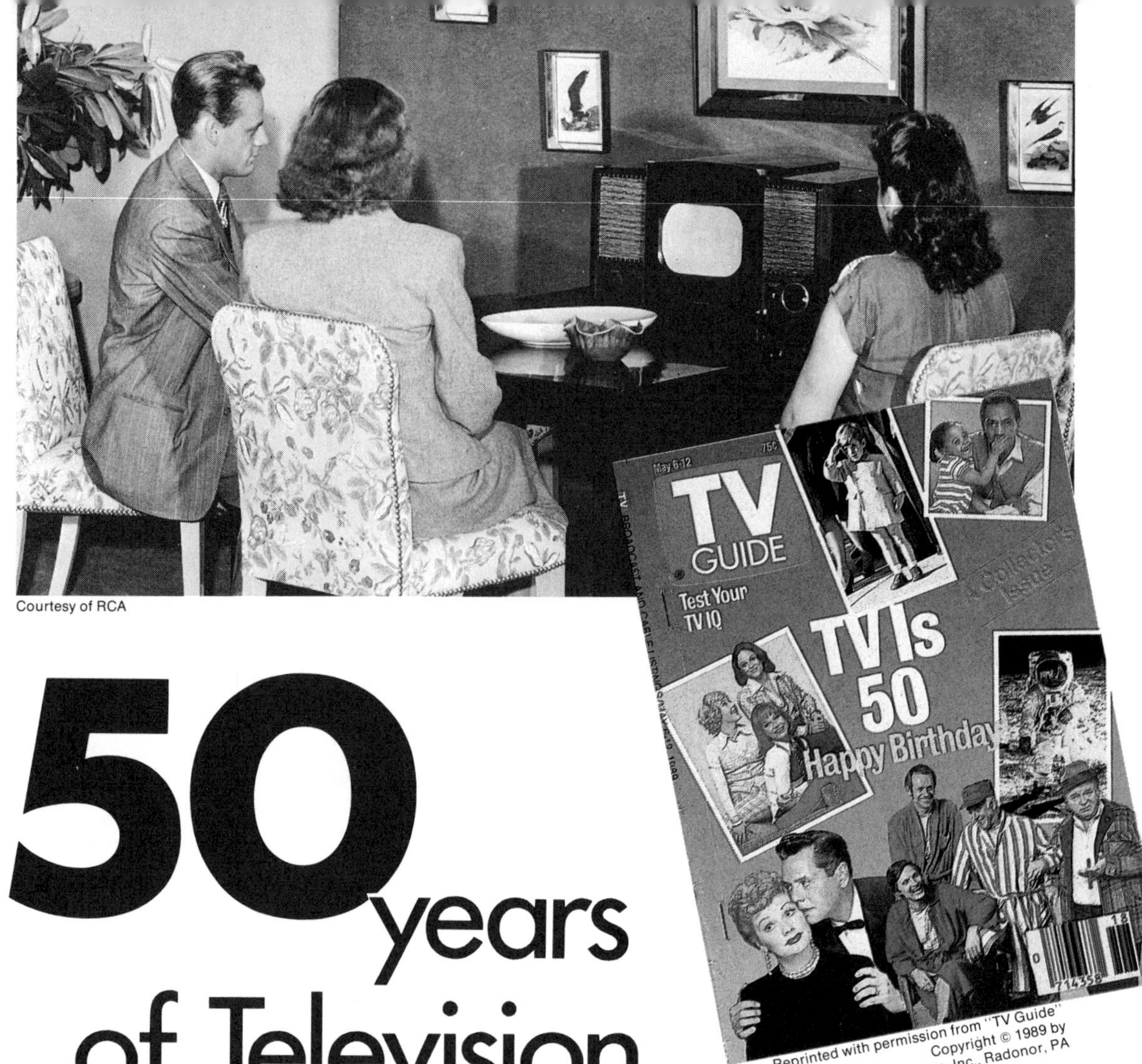

Courtesy of RCA

Reprinted with permission from "TV Guide" Copyright © 1989 by News America Publications, Inc., Radonor, PA

50 years of Television

By Jeffrey H. Hacker

About the Author. Jeffrey H. Hacker, a free-lance writer and editor, has been a contributor to and editor of this annual for some ten years. In the mid-1980s, Mr. Hacker was editor of an extensive study of the broadcasting industry, published by Knowledge Industry Publications in White Plains, NY. He is the author of four books for young adults—*Government Subsidy to Industry* (1982), *Franklin D. Roosevelt* (1983), *Carl Sandburg* (1984), and *The New China* (1986).

The first flickering images hit the airwaves on April 30, 1939. The occasion was opening day of the New York World's Fair—christened "The World of Tomorrow"—in Flushing, Queens. Before a bulky iconoscope camera, President Franklin D. Roosevelt gave a short speech declaring open the fair and kicking off a new age in mass communication. It was the first public broadcast of an electronic medium called television.

Aired by the Radio Corporation of America (RCA), Roosevelt's speech was seen on only a handful of primitive receivers. The new "picture radio," as many called it, had only just been offered for sale, and fewer than 100 sets had been sold. During the six months of the 1939 World's Fair, millions of curiosity seekers pressed into the RCA pavilion for a glimpse of the tiny glowing boxes. The screens ranged from five to 12 inches (13 to 30 cm), with a cabinet-lid mirror to reflect the image for viewers.

© S. Proctor/The Stock Market

Introduced publicly at the 1939 New York World's Fair, television was marketed initially as a way of bringing the family together. By the late 1980s, American households averaged 1.9 sets, and the typical family was spending seven hours daily watching television.

What began as a curiosity has become an integral part of the American way of life. In the 50 years since its formal debut, television has emerged as a primary entertainment medium, chronicler of history, wellspring of popular culture, and force of political and social change. By the early 1980s, 98% of U.S. households were equipped with at least one TV set, a majority with two or three. By 1989, the average American family was spending no less than seven hours and five minutes per day watching television—the average individual about 30.5 hours per week. Few technological innovations, if any, have exerted as great an influence on as many people.

Adding Sight to Sound. Television's 50th anniversary was celebrated with a variety of special events during the spring of 1989. Among them were an extensive exhibition at the Smithsonian Institution's National Museum of American History titled "American Television: From the Fair to the Family, 1939–89"; commemorative editions of *TV Guide, People Weekly,* and other magazines; and, of course, an aerial bombardment of broadcast specials. Nobody loves a birthday party—for Bob Hope, *Sesame Street,* or itself—more than television.

In reality, the birth of the tube cannot be traced to a particular day or event. Unlike the light bulb or telephone, TV was not invented by a single individual at a specific time and place. Rather, it was developed, improved, tested, and refined over a period of more than five decades.

The earliest device for the electrical transmission of pictures was invented by the German scientist Paul Gottlieb Nipkow in 1884. Nipkow's invention was a perforated disk used to scan a pictorial image. Mechanically rotated, the disk could break down the image into tiny fragments of light, which were converted into electrical impulses by a photoelectric cell and transmitted over short distances. The receiver was a similar disk, synchronized with the transmitter and illuminated by a light source controlled by the signal.

© Photofest

With all of early television broadcast live, careful supervision from the control booth was a must. Television technology has advanced tremendously in the last 50 years.

As improvements in mechanical scanning were pursued, key advances were made in instrumentation: a three-element vacuum tube to amplify weak currents, an improved photoelectric cell, and a new kind of neon light for the receiver. It was during the 1920s, however, that the major advances were made. In 1928 the American engineer Philo T. Farnsworth introduced a working electronic scanning system. And in 1929, after several years of development, the Russian emigré Vladimir K. Zworykin demonstrated the first completely electronic TV system with a camera tube (iconoscope) in the transmitter and a cathode-ray tube (kinescope) in the receiver.

During the 1930s, electronic television was adopted in Great Britain, France, Germany, Italy, the Soviet Union, and Japan. The first regular broadcasts were begun in 1936 by the British Broadcasting Company (BBC), which carried the coronation procession of King George VI the following May.

In the United States, meanwhile, RCA in 1936 installed experimental televisions in 150 New York homes and a transmitter on the Empire State Building for a trial broadcast; Felix the Cat was used as a guinea pig. Then on April 20, 1939, ten

© Photofest

Advertising always has been a force on television, with spending for TV commercials increasing from $171 million in 1950 to an estimated $32 billion in 1989. In the late 1940s, Betty Furness, a former actress and future consumer-affairs advocate, became a TV spokeswoman for Westinghouse. When the company sponsored all CBS's television coverage at both the Democratic and Republican conventions in 1952, she enjoyed more airtime than the nominees.

days before the opening of the World's Fair, RCA's David Sarnoff took to the airwaves for an informal public introduction. "Now we add sight to sound," he declared.

Following President Roosevelt's official launching, RCA began broadcasting every day from a small studio at Radio City in Manhattan. Beaming primarily to the fairgrounds, it carried a selection of cartoons *(Donald's Cousin Gus)*, travelogues *(Jasper National Park, Washington—Shrine of Patriotism)*, and cooking lessons. It also dispatched cameras around New York City and the fair to capture local events. Other "firsts" in 1939 included the first televised sporting event (a college baseball game between Columbia and Princeton on May 17) and the first broadcast of a major league baseball game (between the Cincinnati Reds and Brooklyn Dodgers on August 26).

On Dec. 7, 1941, the Columbia Broadcasting System (CBS) presented the first television newscast, reporting the events at Pearl Harbor, HI. The onset of World War II, however, put a temporary halt to the spread of the medium.

Postwar Boom. After being grounded from 1942 to 1945, the fledgling U.S. television industry took off in the years following World War II. The number of commercial stations rose from nine in 1945 to 100 in 1950 and 458 in 1955. The cities of New York and Los Angeles had seven stations each; dozens of other metropolitan areas boasted two or more stations. By mid-1954, some 90% of the United States could receive television transmission. Meanwhile, NBC set up the first network in 1945, linking stations in Philadelphia, New York City, and Schenectady (NY). NBC soon was joined by CBS, the American Broadcasting Companies (ABC), and the DuMont Television Network (which disbanded in 1955). Regularly scheduled network broadcasts began in 1946.

With programming filling the airwaves, the manufacture and sale of TV receivers boomed. By 1948 production reached about 1 million sets annually, skyrocketing to 7.4 million in 1950. Consumers had more than 100 brands (all of them American) to choose from. As television was finding its way into

In the early days of television, the popularity of Milton Berle, "Uncle Miltie," encouraged the sale of TV sets to working-class families. For the children of the late 1940s and 1950s, television meant "Howdy Doody Time." Starring Bob Smith as Buffalo Bob, the "Howdy Doody" show ran from 1947 to 1960. Ed Sullivan's variety program, a Sunday night tradition (1948–71), frequently made entertainment history by presenting emerging new stars as well as performers at the height of their careers. On Feb. 9, 1964, four young Englishmen, the Beatles, made their U.S. debut on the show.

© Photofest

© Photofest

© Warnecke & Lautenberger/CBS Photo

Program Favorites: *"The Dick Van Dyke Show" introduced Mary Tyler Moore to TV land. "Bonanza," starring Lorne Greene as head of the Cartwrights and Dan Blocker as one of his sons, was the first TV Western to be shown in color. The British import "Upstairs, Downstairs" was a subseries of Public Broadcasting Service's Masterpiece Theatre. The antics of Ralph Kramden (Jackie Gleason) and Ed Norton (Art Carney) of "The Honeymooners" have become part of TV's culture.*

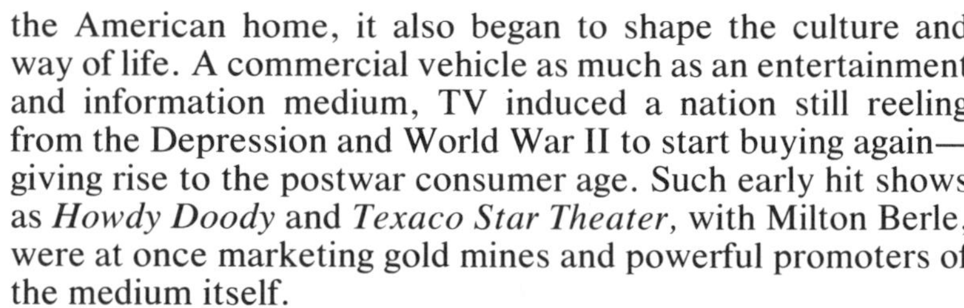

the American home, it also began to shape the culture and way of life. A commercial vehicle as much as an entertainment and information medium, TV induced a nation still reeling from the Depression and World War II to start buying again—giving rise to the postwar consumer age. Such early hit shows as *Howdy Doody* and *Texaco Star Theater,* with Milton Berle, were at once marketing gold mines and powerful promoters of the medium itself.

The Golden Age. With the assembly lines and studios in full production, television took the United States by storm as the 1940s gave way to the 1950s. When the new decade began, only 3.8 million U.S. homes—9.0%—were equipped with a set. When *I Love Lucy* premiered in 1951, the figure had reached 10.3 million—23.5%. And by 1960, some 45.8 million U.S. households—87.1%—could tune in to the Kennedy-Nixon debates.

Known as TV's Golden Age, the 1950s gave birth to programs and stars that would live forever in American folklore (if not syndication reruns): *I Love Lucy* with Lucille Ball; *The Honeymooners* with Jackie Gleason; *Your Show of Shows* with Sid Caesar; *The Ed Sullivan Show; The Red Skelton*

Courtesy of Viacom

Globe Photos

LTV International (photo below); Courtesy of Viacom (photo right)

Show; Gunsmoke with James Arness; *American Bandstand* with Dick Clark; *The Mickey Mouse Club; Father Knows Best; Leave It to Beaver; The Today Show* (still broadcast); and such news legends as Edward R. Murrow, Walter Cronkite, Chet Huntley, and David Brinkley. And it was all broadcast live, even commercials. Cues were missed and lines forgotten, but it was classic.

As the mythology grew, so, too, did the power of the industry. Madison Avenue was among those cast under television's spell. Spending on TV advertising soared from $171 million in 1950 to more than $1.6 billion in 1960 ($3.6 billion in 1970, $11.4 billion in 1980, and a projected $32 billion in 1989). As television became America's dominant leisure-time activity, other media industries suddenly were playing second fiddle. Movie attendance plummeted from 4.3 billion in 1945 to

Presenting morning news and talk, "The Today Show" celebrated its 35th birthday in 1987. Johnny Carson and his straight man Ed McMahon have dominated late-night viewing since 1962. The residents of "Sesame Street," for example, Big Bird and David, have been teaching preschoolers since 1969. With Alex Trebek as quizmaster, "Jeopardy" has become one of the highest-rated shows in syndicated television history. "The Cosby Show," which premiered in 1984, has made Bill Cosby America's favorite dad. "Roots," a dramatization of Alex Haley's novel with LeVar Burton as Kunta Kinte, had one of the largest audiences in TV history.

Courtesy of The National Broadcasting Company, Inc.

© James H. Karales/Peter Arnold Inc.

© NBC Photo by Chris Haston

Merv Griffin Enterprises (photo below)

Photo by R. M. Lewis, Jr., Courtesy of The National Broadcasting Company, Inc.

© 1977 Warner Brothers Inc., All Rights Reserved

Courtesy of The National Broadcasting Company, Inc.

The first NBC peacock symbolized the arrival of color television during the mid-1960s. NBC was the first network to televise all of its programs in color in 1966. CBS followed in 1967, ABC in 1968.

less than 2.4 billion in 1955. The big-time radio days of *Fibber McGee* and *Amos 'n' Andy* became a thing of the past. Bookstores reported a decline in sales, and libraries reported a drop in circulation. According to TV historian Erik Barnouw, "Even jukebox receipts were down."

All the while, television technology continued to evolve. Screens got bigger, consoles got smaller. Black-and-white portables were introduced in 1956. A color system was approved by the Federal Communications Commission (FCC) as early as 1953, though widespread use would wait another decade. Perhaps the major development was the invention of videotape, by which studio programming could be recorded, edited, and aired more easily and more cheaply than film. Adopted by the industry in the late 1950s, videotape meant the demise of live broadcasting. Programs got slicker, production costs got out of hand, and on Sept. 25, 1959, *The Mickey Mouse Club* was canceled. The Golden Age was over.

Medium and Message. A mature, technically sophisticated, and nearly universal communications medium, television in the 1960s extended its reach, quickened its reflexes, and flexed its muscles. With the advent of satellite transmissions and portable transmitters, it gave instantaneous access to the once inaccessible. Media guru Marshall McLuhan heralded a new "global village" and saw a message in the medium. To some the message was violence, erosion of culture, and sheer mindlessness. To hundreds of millions of viewers around the world, it was a chance to witness history—and shape it.

The assassination of President John F. Kennedy in November 1963 had more than 750 million people glued to their screens over four days. From that point on, television became the primary source of news for the American people. Coverage of the civil-rights movement hastened reform. On-the-spot reporting of the Vietnam War helped turn the tide of public opinion. And on July 20, 1969, a camera aboard Apollo 11 allowed 700 million viewers worldwide—the biggest single television audience ever—to see the first men walk on the moon.

The satellite dish antenna has improved television reception in rural areas. The world of sports has been revolutionized by television coverage, including the arrival of the instant replay in 1963. Five of the ten most popular programs of all time were football Super Bowl games.

© Frank P. Rossotto/The Stock Market

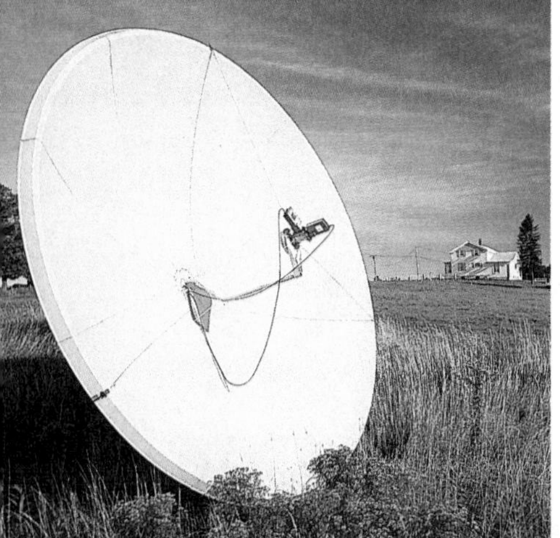

© Ken Regan/Camera 5

© Brent Jones

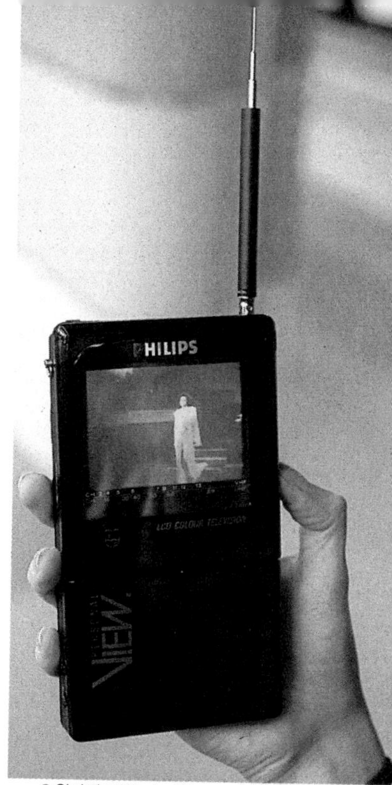

© Christian Vioujard/Gamma-Liaison

Large outdoor television screens now are utilized so that the widest audience possible can view breaking news events. Pocket-size black-and-white sets became available during 1984; color versions followed.

For the industry itself, the biggest change was color. In development for decades, color TV began to catch on as prices declined and quality improved. The transition began in 1965, when black-and-white sales reached their peak of 8.4 million units and color sales jumped to 2.8 million units. By December 1966, more color TVs were being sold than black-and-white TVs. The introduction of solid-state color sets in 1967 and a steady increase in color programming further boosted sales. By the early 1970s, about one half of U.S. households were equipped with a color TV (more than 90% today), and nearly every new program was broadcast in color.

Another noteworthy development of the 1960s was the spread of public television. The term "educational television" had been coined in the early 1950s for stations licensed to nonprofit institutions, such as schools, community groups, and state government departments. The terminology was changed to "public televison" in 1967, when Congress formed the Corporation for Public Broadcasting (CPB) and set as a goal the availability of noncommercial television and radio to every citizen. The CPB underwrites production, pays for satellite connections, and awards grants to local stations—of which there are now more than 300. In 1969 the Public Broadcasting Service (PBS) was formed to handle scheduling and distribution of programs.

New Electronic Media. Inevitably, the common consumer TV set underwent further improvement and innovation. Miniaturization was one trend, giantism another. Following black-and-white portables in the mid-1950s, the first battery-powered transistorized set was offered to the public in 1960. Hi-fi stereo sound and a black-and-white pocket TV were introduced in 1984, followed a few years later by color pocket sets and wristband sets. Meanwhile, giant "projection screen" TVs (several feet in diagonal) came into vogue during the late

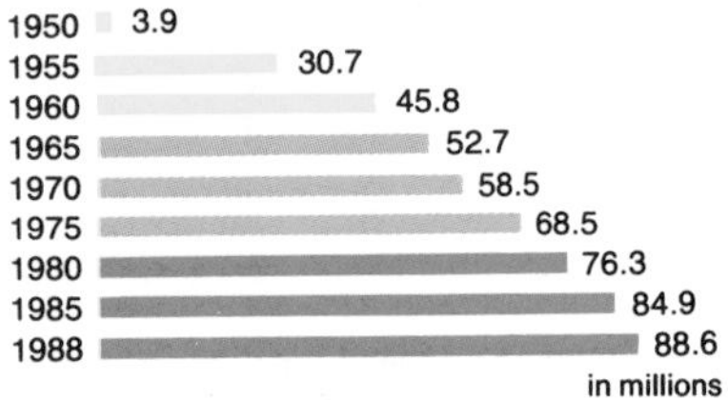

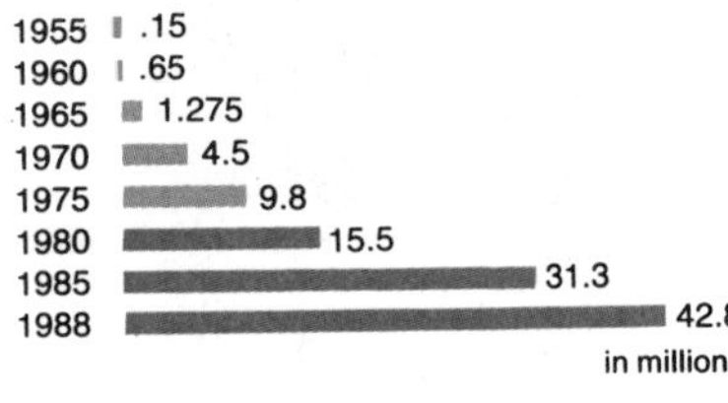

All-news programming, for example, the Cable News Network (CNN), below, is a prime feature of today's cable television.

© Randy Taylor/Sygma

1970s, followed by 25- and 35-inch (64-cm and 89-cm), high-resolution "monitors" in the 1980s. Only one U.S. manufacturer, Zenith, was still in business.

These were the least of the changes. Long dominated by network broadcasting, the U.S. television industry was being revolutionized by a handful of new electronic media. The emergence of cable and pay TV, videocassette recorders (VCRs), and other systems opened a new era in audiovisual entertainment and information delivery. Each requires the use of a conventional television, but each brings to it some new capability, type of programming, or expanded viewing option.

Unlike conventional broadcasting, cable television transmits signals via cable rather than through the air. Although it dates back to the 1940s, cable TV as we know it today emerged in the mid-1970s with the advent of satellite distribution capability and increased system channel-capacity. As of 1989, half of all U.S. homes were "wired" for cable, giving access to approximately 120 million viewers. For a monthly subscription fee ($15-$25), the viewer may get access to literally dozens of nonbroadcast channels. The term "narrowcasting" is used to describe the specialized programming—such as news, sports, music, and weather—on individual cable stations.

For an extra monthly premium, the subscriber also can receive one or more special pay-TV channels. Among these are Home Box Office (HBO), Showtime, and Cinemax, which carry feature movies, plays, concerts, and some original programming. Yet another option is pay-per-view, by which the viewer selects a first-run movie, sporting event, or live concert and pushes the appropriate button on a remote-control unit (or cable box). A central computer delivers the order to the screen for a single viewing and records a $3-$5 charge.

The VCR, a separate device hooked up to the television, can perform three basic functions: record programs from the TV and play them back at a more convenient time; play prerecorded tapes (such as movies and "how to" items) that are rented or purchased by the viewer; and, with the addition of a hand-held video camera, allow immediate viewing of color home videos. As of early 1989, more than 60% of U.S. homes had VCRs. In 1988 alone, Americans purchased 65 million prerecorded cassettes and rented more than 2 billion.

The cable and VCR explosions have rocked network broadcasting in much the same way that television damaged motion pictures. In just ten years, ABC, CBS, and NBC have seen their combined share of prime-time audiences drop from 92% to 68%. And as the networks have lost their grip on viewers, they also have lost their hold on affiliated stations. The number of independent TV stations in the United States nearly has quadrupled during the 1980s, sparking a surge in syndicated programming—and further erosion of the network share.

The Future. For TV audiences, the next 50 years promise even greater innovation and more freedom of choice. The most immediate prospect, touted as the entertainment break-

© Christopher Springmann/The Stock Market

When connected to a television, a VCR (videocassette recorder), below, can record programs from the TV for replay at another time, play prerecorded tapes, and, with the addition of a hand-held video camera, left, allow immediate viewing of color home videos. Manufacturers' shipments of VCRs exceeded 12 million in 1987.

through of the 1990s, is high-definition television (HDTV). Offering larger screens, twice the sharpness of current sets, richer color, and compact-disc (CD) sound quality, HDTV receivers are expected to represent a $1.5 billion market by the year 2000. Although Japan planned to introduce three HDTV channels, broadcast from its own satellite, in 1990, the United States is far behind in HDTV development. Accordingly, in 1989 the U.S. electronics industry asked for $1.35 billion in federal assistance to help it compete against Japanese and European HDTV manufacturers.

In another potentially far-reaching move, the FCC in 1989 recommended to Congress that it lift regulations barring telephone companies from providing video services. According to experts, such a move would make network and cable TV obsolete. Fiber-optic cables, which can carry thousands of channels, could be attached to telephone lines and linked to a central computer bank. The result would be a universal system by which subscribers could run their errands—such as shopping, banking, or making plane reservations—and choose from a myriad of programs at the touch of a button.

Farther down the road, scientists foresee such innovations as computerized "imaging" systems, by which viewers could see themselves in store or catalog clothes without leaving their armchairs; edit-yourself systems, with which viewers could reshoot endings to their favorite movies; and even hologram systems, in which tiny, three-dimensional figures might act out a scene or play a ball game on the living-room floor.

Science fiction? Of course. But consider how today's television might have looked to visitors at the 1939 New York World's Fair. In light of the astonishing developments since Franklin Roosevelt first went on the air a half-century ago—coast-to-coast networks, color transmission, instant satellite relays, pay-per-view cable, home videotaping—television's world of tomorrow may not be far off.

© Adam Scull/Globe Photos

THE IDEAL CITY

By Dennis Judd

What are Americans looking for when they consider an urban place in which to live? Is there an "ideal" city or urban setting?

The answer is a resounding yes, according to an article in the Feb. 6, 1989, issue of *Newsweek* magazine. *Newsweek* observed that "Americans are finding the road to the good life leads not to the steel jungle or the rural backwater, but to the midsize city that combines the best of both worlds." Indeed, the only city on their list of ten "hot cities" in the United States with a population of more than 500,000 people is Columbus, OH.

But wait! This list looks all wrong, if we consider *MONEY* magazine's third annual ranking published in September 1989. Though Danbury, CT, is second on its list, eight of the top-ten places are in or immediately adjacent to some of the nation's largest metropolitan areas. Seattle ranks first and San Francisco third, with Boston and Boston's north shore sixth and seventh.

The problem of finding an ideal city or urban setting is made more complicated still if other rankings are consulted. *Places Rated Almanac,* for instance, reveals a list of top-ten urban areas different in some ways from the other two. Seattle, WA, leads its list, with San Francisco number two. Among the ten

In judging Seattle, WA, Number 1, "MONEY" took note of the area's "unparalleled scenic beauty and cyclical economy now in full throttle." The city also was judged Number 1 by the 1989 "Places Rated Almanac."

© Seattle—King County News Bureau

© St. Paul Convention and Visitors Bureau

"Newsweek" magazine noted that its "hottest" city, St. Paul, underwent "a decade worth of development" without losing its unique character.

leading urban places there are six metropolitan areas anchored by large and older cities. These kind of urban areas are notably absent from *Newsweek*'s "hot" cities.

Since the late 1960s, a multitude of city and urban-area rankings have been compiled. Academic specialists have built a minor industry debating the various rankings and proposing their own. In most cases, after pages of complicated mathematics, the authors usually conclude that there is little or no correlation between their own rankings and lists published by other researchers.

Despite the considerable confusion about how to rank cities, the overall intent is similar: Almost everyone is interested in measuring "quality of life" or "livability;" sometimes there is an explicit attempt to find the "ideal" city and urban setting. But measuring "quality of life" or precisely defining an "ideal" place to live is an inherently vexing enterprise. People have fundamentally different ideas about how to measure these elusive qualities. Just how elusive they are may be appreciated by a consideration of why the various rankings turn out so differently.

MONEY Magazine's Poll

According to *MONEY* magazine's third annual survey, published in September 1989, "the best places [urban areas] to live in the USA" are:

	Population[1]
1. Seattle, WA	1.8
2. Danbury, CT	.162
3. San Francisco, CA	1.6
4. Denver, CO	1.6
5. Nashua, NH	.173
6. Boston, MA	2.8
7. Boston's North Shore, MA	.26
8. Central New Jersey	.99
9. Minneapolis/ St. Paul, MN	2.4
10. Pittsburgh, PA	2.1

in millions[1]

Newsweek's Poll

The results of *Newsweek* magazine's survey, published in its Feb. 6, 1989, issue, judged America's top-ten "hot cities" as:

	Population
1. St. Paul, MN	261,036
2. Birmingham, AL	272,841
3. Portland, OR	353,931
4. Fort Worth, TX	438,333
5. Orlando, FL	149,527
6. Sacramento, CA	331,211
7. Providence, RI	157,002
8. Charlotte, NC	342,146
9. Columbus, OH	566,915
10. Albuquerque, NM	374,106

Places Rated Almanac

The 1989 edition of *Places Rated Almanac*, published by Prentice Hall Travel, rated the ten leading U.S. urban areas as:

	Population[1]
1. Seattle, WA	1.8
2. San Francisco, CA	1.6
3. Pittsburgh, PA	2.1
4. Washington, DC	3.7
5. San Diego, CA	2.3
6. Boston, MA	2.8
7. New York, NY	16.8
8. Anaheim-Santa Ana, CA	2.3
Louisville, KY-IN (tie)	.969
10. Nassau-Suffolk, NY	2.7

in millions[1]

© Stuart Cohen/Comstock

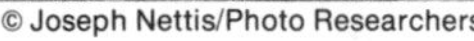

© Joseph Nettis/Photo Researchers

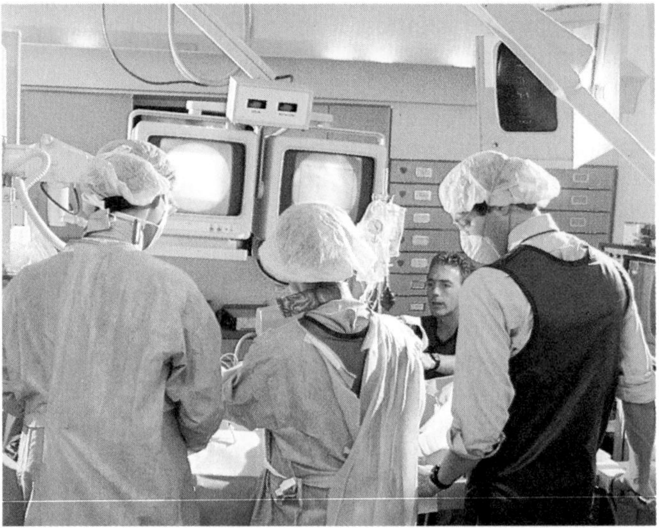

© Howard Sochurek

Rating the "Quality of Life." Let us consider the different methods employed. For its list, *Newsweek* asked its reporters to rank the "best places to live and work in America today." This method is almost completely subjective, but perhaps not much more so than the procedure used by *MONEY* magazine. *MONEY* asked a "representative sample" of 251 of its subscribers to indicate the relative importance of 50 different regional characteristics. Their readers said that the most important of these were the availability of affordable homes, the opportunity to gain equity in a house, and the availability of hospitals and doctors. On the basis of the findings, the magazine fit statistics on America's metropolitan areas to the subscribers' preferences. One problem is that *MONEY* subscribers are hardly representative of the U.S. population: Their median household income in 1989 was $42,500, compared with a U.S. median of less than $30,000. It is very likely that affluent people have different tastes and needs than peo-

About the Author. Dennis Judd is professor and chair in the department of political science, University of Missouri-St. Louis. He has written extensively on urban politics and public policy. Two recent books include *The Development of American Public Policy* and *The Politics of American Cities* (third edition). He is coeditor of the *Urban Affairs Quarterly*.

© Al Stephenson/Picture Group

© Comstock

© Joan Marcus

ple with lower incomes. Likewise, there is an upper-income bias in the *Newsweek* study, unless the magazine's editors are paid very poorly indeed.

Rather than relying on people's opinions, the *Places Rated* authors used 55 different variables grouped into nine categories to arrive at an overall "quality of life" score for a metropolitan area. The nine categories include measures of climate, housing, health care and environment, crime, transportation, education, the arts, recreation, and economic factors. It might seem that adding up so many variables might yield an "objective" ranking of urban areas, but such an attempt at objectivity is fraught with endless difficulties.

The first problem is to decide those aspects of quality of life which are most important to people. In the absence of reliable surveys assessing people's own opinions (which are prohibitively expensive to conduct), researchers are guided by their own sense of what is important. In the case of *Places Rated*

Whatever the poll and whoever the pollster, such items as affordable housing, low crime rate, the availability of hospitals and doctors, good public transportation, fine school system, and cultural and recreational opportunities are considerations in searching for the "ideal city."

Almanac, the authors decided for themselves how to "weight" different factors. For example, in measuring the crime rate for a metropolitan area, they counted the rate of violent crime as ten times as important as property crime. In rating an area's recreational opportunities, such diverse facilities as restaurants, zoos, sports teams, golf courses, movie theaters, theme parks, bowling alleys, auto racing, pari-mutuel betting, and the proximity of coastlines and inland water all were awarded points toward a final score. By a similar procedure, urban areas were ranked separately on nine categories, then the scores for each of these were summed. Thus climate and the arts each were considered as important as an area's economic performance. It is not hard to see why the place rankings that result from this exercise strike many people as arbitrary.

All rankings have a built-in bias for either small or large metropolitan areas and cities. *MONEY* magazine's survey generally favored smaller, wealthier areas not only because of its sample of readers, but also in this way: The percentage of adults registered to vote in an urban area was adopted as a measure of "civic pride." But voting registration is always highest among affluent, well-educated whites. "Civic pride" actually measured, in this case, population composition.

Many of the indicators used by *Places Rated Almanac* seem manifestly to favor large urban areas. For example, a metropolitan area's rankings go up if there are more physicians, hospitals, medical schools, and specialized medical centers (proportionate to the area's population); the education rating goes up if there are lots of colleges and college opportunities for high-school students; an area's score goes up in the arts if there are more symphonies, performing arts facilities, public libraries, and museums. Large urban areas tend to do well on these characteristics, although they also tend to score lower on such factors as crime rates, commuting to work, and air quality. It is probably impossible to avoid a bias one way or the other, since the good and the bad in large urban areas tend to go together. Large urban areas and big cities tend to have more amenities, such as professional sports teams, symphony orchestras, and theme parks—there is "more to do." But they usually also have higher crime rates and their highways are more crowded. This is why no ranking, no matter what measures it employs or how many people are consulted, ever can be the last word.

A major portion of William H. Whyte's book "City," published by Doubleday in 1988, is concerned with "the design and management of urban spaces."

Courtesy of Doubleday

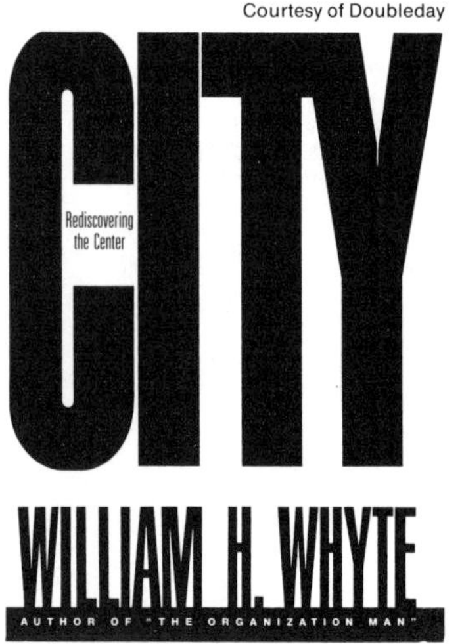

As noted by one urban scholar, even "whether residents of different cities have the same preferences must be questioned." It is probable that the citizens of St. Louis, MO, have different views about quality of life than the citizens of Los Angeles or Omaha. Transplant California sun addicts to Minneapolis and they may feel deprived no matter how much they make or how much there is to do in that city. Likewise, move Minnesotans to Malibu Beach and one can be sure that many of them will miss the change of seasons.

As noted by the eminent urban scholar William H. Whyte, who likes big cities, "the time to worry is when street people begin to leave a place. Like canaries in a coal mine, street

© Peter Yates/Picture Group

Enclosed malls where the public can shop, be entertained, dine, and even have their blood pressure checked have become a part of all suburbs and cities of various sizes. Urbanologist William H. Whyte and some, not all, Americans consider the food vendor, below, the heart of city life.

© Thomas Wear/Comstock

people are an index of the health of a place. This is not reflected in the kind of city ratings lately so popular: the ten best quality-of-life cities in the U.S., the 20 happiest communities, and so on. Cities like New York go to the bottom, the top going to communities that could also qualify as the highest on any blandness index. . . .

"It might be in order to come up with a city index of enjoyability—the number of street entertainers, food vendors, people in conversation, the number smiling. A silly index, perhaps, but there is a simple point to be made. Street people are not just a problem; they are the heart of the street life of the center and its liveliness is the test of the city itself." In today's America, Whyte's vision of the ideal city is apparently not shared widely. What Americans consider "ideal" in a city or urban area, perhaps, might be discovered better by what they do and where they move to than by any attempt to rank the "best" or the "worst" places.

Change, the Suburbs, and Center Cities. Americans always have evinced an ambivalent attitude toward their cities. From the flood tide of foreign immigrants to America's cities from the 1830s to the 1920s, to the movement of millions of blacks and Hispanics to the cities after World War II, American cities have seemed to be places of constant change, chaos, and frequent ethnic and racial conflict. Poor people, and minorities, still are concentrated in America's older cities, and the suburbs surrounding these cities tend to hold people who are more affluent, are white and better educated, and have higher

Heritage Village from Peter Cris Associates, Inc.

Suburbs across the United States now include common interest developments—complexes that offer living quarters, shopping, recreational areas, and, at times, self-government. Heritage Village in Southbury, CT, above, *is intended only for those over 55 years of age.*

status jobs. For decades, many Americans who could afford to have "voted with their feet" for the suburbs.

But what are American suburbs like? They have changed from the bedroom communities that proliferated in the 1950s, with their look-alike frame houses, the tree in the front yard, and barbecue in the back. They have been replaced, often enough, with almost self-contained condominium "communities." Perhaps the fullest and most recent expression of this trend is to be found in "common interest developments (CIDs)," which have mushroomed across America. CIDs are complexes that include living spaces—condominiums, community apartments, and sometimes single-family units—often together with shopping areas, small parks, community swimming pools, and community centers. CIDs provide their own police protection and have their own self-government so that they are, in essence, private municipalities. In exchange for such a privatized, controlled environment, the residents receive a sense of safety and exclusion that would not be available anywhere else. But there is a price—they must abide by various covenants, conditions, and restrictions. Restrictions may dictate the color of paint on a house, the pets that are allowed, the minimum or maximum ages of tenants and homeowners, whether children are allowed, and even may stipulate fines for speeding, parking, or failure to cut the grass. Is this becoming the suburb of tomorrow, and is this the "ideal city" of the future?

Center cities have moved in a similar direction. According to N. Christine Boyer, a leading critic of urban planning, "consumption is the economic role of many of our center cities today, consequently they are becoming places of enter-

© Thomas Wear/Comstock

Large cities in the United States now feature their own common interest developments. In such CIDs, the entire environment is separated from the city street. The Waterside complex, above, *is situated on the East River in downtown New York City.*

tainment and pure play.'' In place of the urban streets of yesteryear, with their harsh sounds and ethnic and racial diversity, users of today's cities often drive to an enclosed mall where they may spend hours in a climate-controlled environment patrolled by private police forces, where ''undesirable'' characters and activities are prohibited—no pawn shops, beer halls, or seedy secondhand stores here. Then they may drive to a domed stadium and watch a ball game, or to a theme park where they rub shoulders with other tourists from the suburbs.

Many new residential developments within the cities have taken a form similar to the CIDs in the suburbs. Clusters of condominiums and apartments are separated off from the street, with a private keyed entrance to a small common garden, foyer, or underground private parking garage. The entire environment is separated from the city street.

Americans always have moved, and continue to do so. In an affluent, mobile society it is natural that cities will become viewed as nearly interchangeable, and classified according to their ''livability'' or ''quality of life.'' This is not to say that Americans do not seek ''community.'' They do; indeed, their restless search for community may explain why the majority of Americans (according to various studies) want to live somewhere else. They feel that they can find community elsewhere. So off they go, perhaps guided by someone's list of ''top-ten'' places. But it is doubtful that ''community'' can be found in segregated homogeneous environments, like CIDs. And the constant search for the ''ideal city'' means that few will find it, for where they already are rarely measures up to an abstract ideal.

200 Years of Presidential Inaugurations

"I do solemnly swear (or affirm) that I will faithfully execute the office of president of the United States, and will to the best of my ability, preserve, protect, and defend the Constitution of the United States."

By Bernard A. Weisberger

About the Author. Bernard A. Weisberger is a historian and free-lance writer whose numerous books include *The Impact of Our Past: A History of the United States*. Dr. Weisberger taught American history for 30 years at such institutions as the University of Chicago and the University of Rochester. A member of the Society of American Historians, he also has written for television.

The year 1989 actually saw two presidential inauguration celebrations in the United States. On the West Front of the U.S. Capitol in Washington, DC, on January 20, George Herbert Walker Bush took the oath as the 41st president. At Federal Hall in New York City, the nation's first capital, on Sunday, April 30, ceremonies were held to mark the 200th anniversary of George Washington's swearing-in as the first president. There was plenty in both occasions to gratify what a surprised 1789 observer called "the public curiosity" about "a ceremony so very common and familiar" as the administration of an oath—even though the oath has the distinction of being written into the U.S. Constitution itself.

© Zoltnik/Sipa Press

© R. Maiman/Sygma

Had George Washington come back to life to watch the New York reenactment he probably would not have been surprised by the parade to the replica of Federal Hall nor by the fireworks set off the preceding evening. He even might have enjoyed watching a costumed actor, William Sommerfield, reread his short (1,425-word) inaugural address. But there is no telling what he would have made of the giant closed-circuit television screen on which President Bush was watched as he spoke from behind a bullet-proof screen on the dais.

Before a crowd of some 300,000 at the West Front of the Capitol at 12:03, Jan. 20, 1989, George Herbert Walker Bush took the oath as 41st president of the United States, opposite page. *Mrs. Bush held a family Bible and the one used by George Washington in 1789. Later the new president and first lady enjoyed the inaugural galas,* below. *On April 30 at Federal Hall in New York City, ceremonies were held commemorating the 200th anniversary of the first presidential inauguration. Actor William Sommerfield,* above, *portrayed George Washington. Marchers dressed in Revolutionary War uniforms led the parade.*

AP/Wide World

Symbolic Meaning. Although the details of the democratic ritual of inauguration have changed in two centuries, there always has been clear recognition that every step in the installation of the people's chief executive has symbolic meaning. George Washington, for example, arrived at the ceremony in an elegant carriage—to impress viewers with the dignity of the new office. But he also wore a plain brown suit, made in America, to show that he was not putting on monarchical airs. And, at a time when the country still was divided sharply over the very idea of a strong national government, he delivered a speech (not constitutionally required) that was nonpartisan. He was using the occasion to set a tone and a precedent.

Each of the 39 men inaugurated since likewise has used the moment to make a defining statement—either by action or speech or both. Some of these launchings made history. Most are long forgotten. But the highlights, taken together, form a kaleidoscopic survey of the growth, crises, lasting values, and changing outlooks of the American people.

There is, for example, that matter of democratic style. Thomas Jefferson, wanting to emphasize the "simplicity of republican government," walked from his boardinghouse to the uncompleted Capitol to take his oath (the first in the District of Columbia) in 1801. In 1829, Andrew Jackson, hero of the "common man," nearly was smothered by boisterous, drunken admirers at a White House reception open to all. Woodrow Wilson refused to hold inaugural parties on Jeffersonian grounds. Jimmy Carter reechoed the Jeffersonian note in 1977 by walking in his inaugural parade up Pennsylvania Avenue. Incoming and outgoing presidents have at different times worn knee breeches and formal cutaways; Carter, Ronald Reagan (1985), and Bush insisted on business suits.

Bettmann Archive

Library of Congress

Library of Congress

Inaugural Moments: *New York Chancellor Robert R. Livingston administered the oath to the first U.S. chief executive on the balcony of Federal Hall. The dome of the Capitol was unfinished as Abraham Lincoln rode to his first inauguration in President James Buchanan's open carriage. President and Mrs. James Garfield attended but did not dance at the Grand Inaugural Ball in the new National Museum in 1881.*

Historical Highlights. Inaugurations have taken place in fair weather and foul. Seven had snowy settings, especially since the 20th Amendment set the date at January 20, beginning in 1937. But man-made storms, too, have darkened the proceedings. James Madison's second inauguration (1813) was the first to be held in a Washington at war. A year and a half after it, the British burned the Capitol. When Abraham Lincoln spoke from the East Front of the Capitol—scene of 36 inaugurations —on March 4, 1861, the Union was breaking up. Soldiers lined the base of the steps and Pinkerton detectives guarded him on the platform. Four years later, with Washington a great base camp for Northern armies, troops again protected Lincoln, but failed to detain a suspicious-looking onlooker named John Wilkes Booth. Uniforms again predominated among onlookers on Jan. 20, 1945, when Franklin Roosevelt took his unprecedented fourth-term oath at the White House. He eliminated the Capitol ceremonies and parade partly to spare his health and partly to emphasize the call for sacrifice on the World War II home front. And there have been the tragic and sudden "inaugurations" in which the oath was taken by a vice-president succeeding one who died in office, for example, Lyndon Johnson in the cabin of Air Force One in 1963.

As for the speeches, some have been short, like that of Washington at his second inaugural, a mere 135 words. Some have been long, like William Henry Harrison's two-hour, record-setting performance on a raw day in 1841. It literally gave him his death of cold. And some—whether crafted by the president or speechwriters under his direction—have contributed unforgettable phrases to the language. Lincoln's second inaugural gave us "with malice towards none, with charity for all." Franklin D. Roosevelt's assertion to a depression-smitten land that "the only thing we have to fear is fear

Library of Congress

At 2:47 A.M. on Aug. 3, 1923, in his family's Vermont farmhouse, Calvin Coolidge was sworn in following the sudden death of Warren Harding. Coolidge's father, a notary public, administered the oath before a kerosene lamp. The inauguration of Benjamin Harrison, below, as 23d president marked the centenary of the establishment of the federal government. On March 4, 1933, Franklin D. Roosevelt told Depression-weary Americans that "the only thing we have to fear is fear itself—nameless, unreasoning, unjustified terror." Following the Capitol ceremonies on Jan. 20, 1977, Jimmy Carter and Mrs. Carter walked down Pennsylvania Avenue to the White House.

UPI/Bettmann Newsphotos

Library of Congress

Courtesy, Jimmy Carter Library

itself" is now classic. John F. Kennedy's exhortation, "Ask not what your country can do for you, but what you can do for your country," inspired a whole generation of young volunteers. President Bush spoke of a "new breeze" blowing democratically in the world, urged conciliation between Republicans and Democrats, Congress and the White House, and cheered for civic activism.

The Future. Whatever the festivities, the weather, or the dress code, the inauguration is that moment when the nation's and, in fact, the world's attention is focused on the incoming chief executive. For a very brief time, the new president stands with a clean record and a reservoir of public goodwill.

Given the facts of television and White House life, the actual ceremony probably will tend more and more toward the stage-managed and image-conscious. Some say that media advisers are turning the presidency into something a bit too monarchical for comfort. But not yet worrisomely so. The presidential crown is lifted every four years. It can be placed on the head of any U.S.-born citizen over 35 years of age, with no other qualifications. And while it may or may not lie uneasily on that head, it definitely will do so only temporarily. That undoubtedly would have satisfied George Washington, who set that precedent, too.

AP/Wide World

People, Places, and Things

Anniversaries and Milestones. *President Bush used the 20th anniversary of the Apollo II mission—the "giant leap" that first put man on the moon—as a launching pad to call for a stepped-up space program. Vice-President Quayle* (left) *and the Apollo II astronauts* (r-l)*—Collins, Aldrin, and Armstrong—joined in the ceremonies. In a more down-to-earth milestone, the nation's heart was captured when the Bushes' springer spaniel Millie gave birth to six puppies.*

© David Valdez/The White House

© Kolczinski/Gamma-Liaison

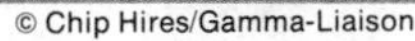

© Chip Hires/Gamma-Liaison

© Tom Ives/Sygma

Different Worlds. *The 50th anniversary of the start of World War II, Sept. 1, 1989, found Poland's Communist President Wojciech Jaruzelski, Prime Minister Tadeusz Mazowiecki—the country's first non-Communist leader since the war—and Solidarity leader Lech Walesa on the same stage,* left. *Having left the world behind for 130 days in an isolation experiment, Italian interior designer Stefania Follini, 27, emerged from a cave in Carlsbad, NM, on May 23,* above. *Creating new worlds in Florida, the Disney-MGM Studios Park and the Disney water-theme park, Typhoon Lagoon, opened separately near Disney World.*

© Abolafia/Gamma-Liaison

Heroes and Fantasy. *Nintendo,* right, *the computer game that promises such absorbing fantasy as a quest through a medieval landscape or a brawl with world heavyweight champion Mike Tyson, was the hottest toy in 1989. Estimates placed 20 million Nintendo joysticks in American homes, and spinoffs for Nintendo characters included cartoon shows and appearances on lunch boxes. Just as Nintendo took over the computer screens, Batman mania swept down on American movie screens in a summer blockbuster movie starring Michael Keaton and Jack Nicholson. A well-orchestrated merchandising campaign was launched simultaneously with the movie. Meanwhile, the premier cat-man, animal trainer Gunther Gebel-Williams, 54, announced his retirement after 21 years in the center ring with the Ringling Brothers and Barnum & Bailey Circus.*

© James Wilson/Woodfin Camp & Associates

© Scott McKiernan/Black Star

© Nina Berman/Sipa

© Ronald C. Modra/"Sports Illustrated"

Headliners. *During Little League's 50th-anniversary year, an underdog team from Trumbull, CT, upset a team from Kaohsiung, Taiwan, 5-2, in the World Series, becoming the first U.S. team to win the crown in six years. Hotel queen Leona Helmsley,* below left, *was convicted of 33 counts of tax evasion, fraud, and conspiracy but acquitted of eight additional counts. The charges stemmed from the allegedly fraudulent billing of personal items to business accounts. After spending 25 months in jail for refusing to reveal the whereabouts of her daughter, Dr. Elizabeth Morgan was released in September. Dr. Morgan, who was hiding the child from a father Morgan accused of abuse, was freed after Congress passed a law setting a 12-month cap on the amount of time a person can be jailed for civil contempt.*

© R. Maiman/Sygma

© P.F. Gero/Sygma

Photos, © Raghu Rai/Magnum

Despair and Hope. *Tibetans in exile in Dharmsala, India,* (above) *protest the renewed Chinese crackdown in their homeland. A series of independence demonstrations in 1989, in the Tibetan capital of Lhasa, drew harsh reprisals from Chinese troops stationed in the mountain kingdom. In October the exiled community had a happier reason to gather—to celebrate the awarding of the 1989 Nobel Peace Prize to the Dalai Lama, their spiritual leader.*

The Alphabetical Section

After a nearly 40-year effort to free Tibet from Chinese domination, the struggle continues for the Dalai Lama (*below*), the mountain kingdom's spiritual leader. And the world was reminded of his nonviolent campaign to preserve the cultural heritage of his people when he was awarded the 1989 Nobel Peace Prize. The Dalai Lama thanked the selection committee for recognizing his beliefs in "love, compassion, and a sense of universal respect," but he protested any personal honors. "My case is nothing special. I am a simple Buddhist monk—no more, no less," he said.

Tibet's spiritual leader in exile, the Dalai Lama, meditates on a visit to his homeland. Born Tenzin Gyatso on July 6, 1935, he was installed as the 14th Dalai Lama, spiritual leader of Tibet, when he was five years old. The Dalai Lama tried to maintain Tibet's Buddhist culture when the Chinese took over the country in 1950, but he fled to India, along with 100,000 of his followers, after an abortive uprising in 1959. Taught exclusively by Buddhist monks, he is the author of several books on Buddhism. His autobiography is scheduled to be published in 1990.

ACCIDENTS AND DISASTERS

AVIATION

Jan. 8—At least 32 are killed and 80 injured when a British airliner crashes near Kegworth, England.

Jan. 31—A military refueling jet crashes upon takeoff at Dyess Air Force Base, Abilene, TX, killing 17.

Feb. 8—A U.S. charter jet crashes in the Azores while trying to land, killing all 144 on board.

Feb. 24—Part of the outer fuselage of a United Airlines jet rips away from the plane; the plane lands safely in Honolulu, HI. Nine passengers are killed.

March 10—Twenty-four are killed when an Air Ontario jet crashes near Dryden, Ontario, shortly after takeoff.

March 12—An Air Force helicopter crashes near Tucson, AZ, killing all 15 aboard.

March 20—A Marine Corps helicopter participating in a joint military exercise in South Korea crashes near Pohang. At least 21 Marines are killed.

June 7—A Surinamese jet crashes while trying to land in dense fog at Paramaribo, killing 169 persons.

July 19—A United Airlines DC-10 jet crashes on attempting to land at Sioux City, IA, killing 112 persons.

July 27—At least 82 are killed, including four on the ground, when a Korean Air DC-10 crashes in heavy fog while landing at Tripoli airport in Libya.

Aug. 25—A Pakistani airliner disappears in bad weather in northeastern Pakistan; 54 are feared dead.

Sept. 3—A Brazilian jetliner crashes in the Amazon jungle, killing 13 of the 54 persons aboard.

Sept. 3—A Cuban Airlines jet crashes near the airport at Havana, Cuba; at least 139 are killed.

Sept. 8—A Norwegian charter plane crashes off the coast of Denmark, killing all 55 aboard.

Sept. 15—An Indonesian plane disappears over the jungles of eastern Indonesia; 22 are feared dead.

Sept. 19—A French jetliner bound for Paris from Congo crashes in a West African desert; all 170 aboard are killed. Terrorism is suspected.

Oct. 18—A Soviet military transport plane catches fire and crashes in the Caspian Sea, killing 57.

Oct. 21—A Honduran jetliner crashes as it prepares to land at Tegucigalpa, killing 131.

Oct. 26—A China Airlines jet crashes shortly after takeoff from Hualien, Taiwan, killing all 54 aboard.

Oct. 28—A commuter plane crashes into a valley on the island of Molokai, HI, killing all 20 aboard.

Oct. 29—Five persons are killed when a Navy jet trainer crash lands on the deck of the aircraft carrier *Lexington* in the Gulf of Mexico.

Nov. 21—Thirty-four are killed when a transport plane crashes in Siberia, USSR.

Nov. 27—A Colombian jet explodes shortly after takeoff from Bogota on a domestic flight, killing 110.

FIRES AND EXPLOSIONS

March 19—Seven are killed when an explosion ignites an oil platform in the Gulf of Mexico near New Orleans, LA, and the fire spreads to a nearby platform.

April 19—Explosions of unknown cause rock a gun turret on the U.S. battleship *Iowa* during a firing exercise off the coast of Puerto Rico, killing 47 servicemen.

May 9—Six sailors are killed when leaking fuel ignites in the boiler room of the *White Plains,* a U.S. navy combat supply ship in the South China Sea.

Sept. 13—An explosion of methane gas in a coal mine in Wheatcroft, KY, kills ten miners.

Oct. 23—An explosion and resulting fire at a Phillips Petroleum plant in Pasadena, TX, destroys the plant and leaves at least 18 workers dead.

Nov. 17—A fire breaks out in a coal mine in eastern Serbia, Yugoslavia, killing at least 90 miners.

Dec. 24—Sixteen persons are killed in a fire in a high-rise retirement center in Johnson City, TN.

LAND AND SEA TRANSPORTATION

Jan. 1—At least 59 are killed when a ferry sinks in Amatique Bay, Guatemala, after it runs out of fuel.

Jan. 15—A crowded express train crashes into a mail train near Tongi, Bangladesh, killing at least 110.

Jan. 17—A train slams into a crowded bus at Ahungalle, Sri Lanka, killing 51 persons.

Jan. 28—Forty-eight children are killed when a bus falls into a culvert during a storm in Ivory Coast.

March 4—Two passenger trains collide at a switching point south of London, England, leaving nine dead.

March 8—An overloaded boat carrying Vietnamese refugees to Japan collides with a Japanese tanker in the South China Sea, killing 130 of the refugees.

April 7—A Soviet nuclear submarine sinks off the coast of Norway; 42 crew members are killed.

June 3—A natural gas pipeline explosion near the trans-Siberian railway causes two passenger trains to burst into flames; at least 400 are killed.

July 6—A Palestinian bus passenger wrenches the steering wheel from the driver and sends the bus over a cliff in Israel, leaving 16 dead in an act of terrorism.

July 16—A passenger ferry capsizes in the Jamuna River near Dhaka, Bangladesh, leaving at least 60 dead.

Aug. 9—A train plunges into a river in northwestern Mexico, killing at least 112 and injuring 205.

Aug. 20—A pleasure vessel on a night cruise on the Thames in London, England, is sunk by a barge; 51 passengers are killed.

Sept. 6—An oil tanker collides with a Soviet fishing trawler in the Baltic Sea, killing all 15 crew members of the trawler.

Sept. 10—At least 150 are killed when a Romanian river cruiser collides with a Bulgarian tugboat on the Danube River northeast of Bucharest.

Sept. 21—Nineteen students are killed when a school bus falls into a rain-filled gravel pit in Alton, TX, after being struck by a truck.

Nov. 4—A U.S.-owned oil-drilling ship capsizes in the Gulf of Thailand during a typhoon, leaving 97 dead.

STORMS, FLOODS, AND EARTHQUAKES

Jan. 23—An earthquake strikes the Republic of Tadzhikistan, USSR, triggering a huge landslide which buries three villages and leaves 1,000 dead.

April 26—A tornado strikes central Bangladesh, killing at least 1,000 persons and injuring 12,000.

May 27—A cyclone rips through Bangladesh and eastern India, killing at least 84 persons.

June 4—Torrential rains cause floods and landslides in central Sri Lanka, destroying entire villages and leaving 171 persons dead.

Sept. 16–21—Hurricane *Hugo* sweeps through the Caribbean, killing 33 persons, and makes landfall on the South Carolina coast, leaving at least 29 dead in Georgia and the Carolinas and causing billions of dollars in damage.

Oct. 17—An earthquake measuring 7.1 on the Richter scale strikes northern California, causing a highway to collapse and leaving 67 persons dead.

Oct. 18—Twenty-nine are left dead when a strong earthquake hits two provinces in northern China.

Oct. 29—Two major earthquakes, measuring 6 and 4.8 on the Richter scale, respectively, leave at least 30 dead and 250 injured in Algeria.

Nov. 15—Tornadoes sweep through northern Alabama, killing 18 and causing $100 million in damage.

Nov. 16—Seven children are killed in Newburgh, NY, when a hurricane-force wind blows in a cafeteria wall at an elementary school.

Dec. 26—Heavy rains flood much of northeastern Brazil, killing at least 35 and leaving 200,000 homeless.

Dec. 27—At least ten persons are killed in the first earthquake ever to strike Australia. Measuring 5.5 on the Richter scale, the quake devastates the city of Newcastle in New South Wales.

MISCELLANEOUS

April 1—A section of a concrete highway bridge over the Hatchie River in Covington, TN, collapses, killing seven persons.

April 15—A huge crowd of soccer fans in Sheffield, England, surges forward into a barrier at the edge of the playing field; 95 are crushed to death.

Aug. 13—A hot-air balloon collides with another and crashes during a sightseeing trip in central Australia, leaving all 13 aboard dead.

ADVERTISING

Outcries about sex and violence on television in 1989 established an environment where, for the first time, a network TV show was canceled because of lack of advertising support. But despite the conservative atmosphere, an advertising breakthrough also was achieved: Lexis Pharmaceuticals became the first drug manufacturer to try brand-specific consumer advertising for a prescription product (its N.E.E. 1/35 birth-control pill) without any objection from the U.S. Food and Drug Administration.

Controversies. Reflecting what some have termed "the new puritanism," public and religious outrage about the sexual content of TV programming spilled over to affect TV advertisers as well. A Michigan housewife achieved major public-relations impact by sending letters to advertisers asking them to stop running commercials during Fox Broadcasting Company's *Married . . . With Children*. Christian Leaders for Responsible Television (CLeaR-TV), a fundamentalist group that monitors TV shows and their advertisers, called for a boycott of Clorox Company and Mennen Company, based on their advertising schedules. While the boycott had no impact on sales, which actually increased, CLeaR-TV was more successful when it objected to PepsiCo's use of singer Madonna in commercials based on her "Like a Prayer" music video. CLeaR-TV said that the video misused Christian symbols; the commercial was short-lived.

The environment became such that several major advertisers pulled commercials from controversial network TV shows. In late April, ABC became the first network ever to pull a program for lack of advertiser support.

Tobacco advertising continued to take the heat, including calls in Congress to ban attempts by cigarette companies to work their products promotionally into movies. But the tobacco industry launched a major two-day, $500,000 newspaper ad campaign in January in support of smokers' rights. Toward year's end, Philip Morris launched a controversial two-year, $60 million corporate image ad campaign making no mention of smoking, but celebrating the 200th anniversary of the Bill of Rights. Critics were irate that the National Archives had accepted $600,000 from Philip Morris as part of the plan to film the document.

New Media Vehicles. Controversy extended into the development of new media opportunities for advertisers. Whittle Communications came up with "Channel One," an ad-supported news and information network for high schools. Despite rejections of the idea from state education offices in California and New York and opposition from the National Parent-Teacher Association, "Channel One" was proceeding as planned.

The search for new media in which to place advertising continued unabated and with new ingenuity in 1989. "900-number" telephone lines were explored as ways to sell investment or weather information sponsored by an advertiser. While advertising sponsorship of videotaped movies continued to grow, PepsiCo became the first advertiser to run ads in a video game: In one basketball-based sports game, a Pepsi sign even appears as a billboard on the electronically represented basketball court.

Ad Volume. While there was a search for new ad-carrying media, the traditional media did fairly well. The McCann-Erickson ad agency predicted that U.S. ad spending in 1989 would increase 6.9% to $126.2 billion, with all national advertising expected to increase 7.6% to $70.6 billion and all local advertising to be up 6% to $55.6 billion. Despite erosion in audience size, network TV continued to take in record amounts of money. The 1989–90 network TV upfront market closed at $3.8 billion for ABC, NBC, and CBS—$4.1 billion if Fox Broadcasting is included. The previous year's $3.2 billion had set a record.

Creative. The struggle by advertisers to get their messages seen led to new approaches. One of the most talked-about ad campaigns of 1989 was for Eveready's Energizer battery, in which a mechanical bunny running on the battery leaves the battery commercial and then reappears to disrupt what at first seems to be a separate commercial. Another technique, tried for Nissan's Infiniti luxury car, shows only scenes of nature and philosophical discussions about the nature of luxury.

Advertisers continued to lure big names to do the unexpected, on both sides of the camera. Film director Martin Scorsese directed his first TV spot, for Armani fragrances for men. Singer Tina Turner appeared for Plymouth cars. Disney animated characters were licensed to appear in commercials introducing Chevrolet's new Lumina. And Henry Bloch, company spokesman for H.&R. Bloch, appeared in Subaru commercials to talk about the value of that car company's rebates.

Acquisitions. European-based ad agencies continued to buy out their U.S. counterparts in 1989. Great Britain's WPP Group, which acquired the JWT Group in 1987, was successful in 1989 in snagging another blue-chip U.S.-based international ad agency, Ogilvy & Mather. On a smaller scale, Great Britain's Gold Greenles Trott bought its second U.S. agency, as did France's RSCG. The Paris-based Eurocom, in a highly unusual deal, took over control of Della Femina, McNamee WCRS, the U.S. agency known for the Isuzu "Liar" ad campaign, when the British owner, WCRS, decided to concentrate on media buying and assumed full ownership of Europe's largest media buying firm.

STEWART ALTER, *"Adweek"*

© Vlastimir Shone/Gamma-Liaison

After a costly ten-year campaign to eradicate the "mujahidin" resistance in Afghanistan, the last of a contingent of Soviet troops that once numbered 120,000 returned to their homes in the Soviet Union early in 1989.

AFGHANISTAN

On Dec. 27, 1979, the Soviet 40th Army, confident of swift victory, struck south from Central Asia into neighboring Afghanistan. On Feb. 15, 1989, after nearly ten years of bloody combat, its commanding officer, Lt. Gen. Boris Gromov, marched onto the "friendship" bridge connecting Afghanistan with the USSR, paused under its center span for a silent soliloquy, then trudged on north. The last of the 120,000-strong "limited contingent" of Soviet troops, defeated by the impoverished but unbending Afghans, had come home.

Behind Lieutenant General Gromov lay a devastated nation still at war, nearly one tenth of its people dead and half the survivors displaced as refugees, its economy in shambles, and its future clouded. There was a belief that the discredited, Soviet-installed regime called the Republic of Afghanistan (RA) would collapse swiftly, and that the nation then could look forward to the hard but peaceful task of reconstruction. That prediction—like so many about Afghanistan—proved wrong, and at year's end the nation's agony continued.

Military Developments. As the last Soviet troops withdrew, the desertion rate among RA troops at first skyrocketed; in late February, 2,000 defected to the resistance in Takhar province alone. Two helicopter crews flew to Pakistan. As instability increased, the regime began arming members of the ruling People's Democratic Party of Afghanistan (PDPA) and created an elite 16,000-man presidential guard. To help the RA survive, departing Soviet forces left behind mammoth arms dumps and, as 1989 wore on, augmented these with $250 million to $300 million worth of new arms per month. From March to mid-July, Soviets supplied 550 Scud surface-to-surface missiles with a 200-mi (320-km) range, 160 T-55 and T-62 tanks, 615 armored personnel carriers, and 1,600 five-ton trucks. During six weeks in July and August, some 400 Scuds were fired from Kabul at *mujahidin* forces.

U.S. arms supplies to the *mujahidin* (holy warrior) resistance forces had been scaled back starting in September 1988. Nevertheless, the *mujahidin* reportedly launched 280 210-mm rockets at Afghan cities during July and August 1989, occasionally shutting down airfields and often inflicting civilian casualties. The original *mujahidin* strategy had been to surround and slowly strangle major cities held by the government. Under pressure from their Pakistani supporters, however, several groups launched a joint frontal assault on Jalalabad, a provincial capital near the Pakistan border. The goal was to provide a seat for the newly formed Afghan Interim Government (AIG), still located in Pakistan. Untrained for such operations, short of ammunition, and split by political infighting, the *mujahidin* attack fell just short of success. A key element in their defeat was the execution of some captured government troops, an act that may have deterred other RA soldiers from deserting en masse.

The setback at Jalalabad slowed *mujahidin* activities, but by summer's end they were again on the offensive, surrounding and isolating the country's second-biggest city, Kandahar, in southern Afghanistan. In September the RA tried to relieve the city with a 1,300-truck, 200-tank convoy carrying a six-month supply of food and arms. After a four-week running battle, only 100 trucks had succeeded in reaching Kandahar by a circuitous route through the desert; of the remainder, 410 last were seen retreating northward, still loaded. The rest were destroyed. Meanwhile, the U.S. arms supply program accelerated and included such new weaponry as mine-clearing devices, special rounds for cratering airstrips, cluster shells, and 120-mm Spanish mortars. These arms improved *mujahidin* siege capabilities.

Political Developments. The most striking political development of the year was the survival of the RA under President Najib (also known as Najibullah). In January predictions of the government's collapse were voiced not only in the West but in Moscow. Widely perceived as a Soviet puppet, detested as the former chief of the secret police, and supported only by the faction-ridden PDPA, Najib seemed doomed to quick extinction. As late as April, a Soviet official said that the Najib regime could not last six months; the PDPA, he added, though boasting of 230,000 members, actually had only about 30,000 who were committed.

On February 19, Najib declared a state of national emergency, suspended most civil liberties, and appointed a 20-man Supreme Defense Council, made up mostly of ranking military and police officers with himself at its head. A day later he dismissed the crypto-Communist cabinet of Prime Minister Hassan Sharq, replacing it with one whose membership was 75% known PDPA members.

To improve the PDPA's image, Najib tried to change its name to the Liberal Democratic Party of Afghanistan but had to yield to the party's conservatives. He intensified efforts to portray the regime and its members as deeply religious and not at all socialist. Party activities ceased to be covered in official media, and government officials, including Najib, no longer were called "comrade" but "esteemed." Najib referred to the *mujahidin* in respectful terms as "the armed opposition," and in March made a sweeping offer of aid from Kabul to anyone who would pledge allegiance to the RA. This campaign's most noted success was with the Ismaili sect in northern Afghanistan, which accepted the offer and guaranteed to keep communications routes free of *mujahidin* attacks. Only a few other communities accepted Najib's proposal, however, and of those who did, few could be called reliable RA allies.

By early summer, Najib's growing confidence was reflected in his changed view of the *mujahidin*. No longer calling them the "armed opposition," he said they were "terrorists."

© Alfred/Sipa

© Nickelsberg/Gamma-Liaison

President Najib held tenuous control of a Soviet-backed regime in Afghanistan in the face of continued pressure from "mujahidin" forces, left, who launched a major offensive against the city of Jalalabad after the Soviet withdrawal.

With the embarrassment of Soviet occupation troops removed, he now tried to turn the psychological tables by alleging that the Pakistanis and Saudi volunteers providing aid to the *mujahidin* were the alien elements against whom all Afghans should fight. Although Najib did not improve his own popularity with the message, it did have some effect on the *mujahidin*. Willing to die to expel the hated Soviets, they were less enthusiastic about risking their lives for the AIG.

Toward summer's end, Najib's position again appeared to be weakening. The lavish bestowal of military promotions and medals and the claim that entire military units were reenlisting voluntarily were indirect evidence of regime insecurity. In August the former chief of Najib's personal guard, General Zarif, defected, claiming that the regime was weakening. He was the highest ranking defector of the war thus far.

Kabul still claimed to control 26 of 31 provincial capitals, but the resistance reportedly held some 200 of the 220 district and subdistrict centers and virtually the entire countryside. As winter closed in, the regime's long-term prospects for survival remained bleak, as did the chances for peace. The Afghan people lent silent confirmation to such judgments by continuing to seek refuge in Pakistan. Although the regime claimed success in enticing refugees home, United Nations (UN) observers stated that refugees leaving Afghanistan still were far outpacing the returnee influx.

AIG Disunity. Throughout 1989, the *mujahidin* were unable to take advantage of the apparent political instability of Najib's government because the AIG resistance government was even weaker. The hastily patched together AIG, made up of the leaders of seven Pakistan-based groups belonging to the Sunni branch of Islam, was a nonrepresentative collection of hostile politicians whose main role had been to act as conduits for weapons needed by the *mujahidin* in the field. Internally divided, their efforts to reach a common ground with eight smaller Shiite exile groups based in Iran also were unsuccessful. Many Afghans at home and abroad held the AIG in low regard and viewed it as nothing more than a tool of the Pakistani intelligence service. Among its severest critics were the *mujahidin* field commanders.

The most disruptive of the AIG leaders was the unscrupulous Gulbuddin Hekmatyar, chief of the Islamic fundamentalist Hezbe Islami (Islamic Party). In early July his ambush and murder in northern Afghanistan of 12 key Jamiat Islami (Islamic Society) *mujahidin* officers caused cancellation of a major Jamiat antigovernment offensive planned for late 1989. Then, over the objections of other AIG leaders, Hekmatyar also allegedly tried to collaborate with the Khalqi (Masses) faction of the PDPA to stage a coup against Najib. The rumored plot apparently failed, further discrediting Hekmatyar. Despite the support of influential Pakistani patrons, he was driven from the AIG and by September had taken refuge among his forces in Afghanistan.

Another major political difficulty for the resistance was the behavior of Saudi Arabian volunteers from the Wahabi sect, whose fanaticism led them to execute all RA prisoners. This policy stiffened the resolve of government troops to fight to the death. Although most *mujahidin* disliked and distrusted the Wahabis, Saudi Arabia's importance as a source of support ruled out any action against the unwanted volunteers.

Economy. During the winter of 1988–89, there were severe shortages of food and fuel in Kabul. In January prices had trebled over their July 1988 levels. Citizens of the capital trekked into the *mujahidin*-controlled countryside to buy food, then had to pay bribes of up to 50% of their purchases to police upon returning home. A UN airlift of 32 tons of food and medicine for the poor was halted in early February when Egyptian airline pilots refused, for security reasons, to continue the flights.

Under the austere conditions, the population of Kabul, which had swollen to more than 2 million by 1987, began to decline. In July 1989 one journalist estimated that the city held only 1.5 million people; that same month, the Soviet paper *Pravda* said the population had dropped to 900,000.

The price to the USSR of supporting the government continued to be high, especially with the arms resupply, but was less than the estimated 5 billion ruble (about $7.8 billion) annual cost of the occupation. In partial fulfillment of its $600 million obligation to the UN for Afghan reconstruction, Moscow also claimed to have delivered $165 million worth of consumer goods. Meanwhile, the USSR lost the annual $300 million worth of Afghan natural gas that had been imported into the Central Asian network; with the departure of Soviet technicians, the wells were capped and they remained closed in 1989. The share of Afghan

AFGHANISTAN • Information Highlights

Official Name: Republic of Afghanistan.
Location: Central Asia.
Area: 250,000 sq mi (647 500 km^2).
Population: (mid-1989 est.): 14,800,000.
Chief Cities (March 1982): Kabul, the capital, 1,127,417; Kandahar, 198,161; Herat, 155,858.
Government: Najibullah, general secretary, People's Democratic Party (appointed May 1986) and president; Mohammed Hassan Sharq, prime minister (named May 1988). *Legislature*—bicameral National Assembly.
Monetary Unit: Afghani (50.6 afghanis equal U.S.$1, July 1989).
Gross Domestic Product (1988 U.S.$): $3,100,-000,000.
Foreign Trade (1988 U.S.$): *Imports*, $599,000,000; *exports*, $403,000,000.

© P. Robert/Sygma

© A. Tannenbaum/Sygma

Kabul in 1989 featured such contrasting images as everyday life in a bustling marketplace and armed women awaiting the possibility of an attack from the "mujahidin."

trade with the USSR remained at about 60% of overall foreign trade. Agreements running through 1990 were signed in February 1989, and the direct border trade in the northern areas continued. The Afghans exchanged such products as fruit, nuts, and cotton for Soviet fuel, machinery, and vehicles.

Diplomatic and Foreign Affairs. During 1989, the RA was less an initiator of foreign policy moves than their object. Starting at the end of 1988 and continuing into January 1989, Soviet Ambassador and Deputy Foreign Minister Yuli M. Vorontsov held talks in Saudi Arabia and Pakistan with *mujahidin* leaders about a possible future transition government in Kabul. At *mujahidin* insistence there was no RA participation in these talks, which soon foundered because of continued Soviet insistence that the PDPA be represented in any future government. Another Soviet topic of discussion with the *mujahidin* was the fate of some 311 to 313 Soviet servicemen missing in action. An unknown number of Soviets were being held prisoner by the *mujahidin,* and others actually were fighting on the resistance side. Inasmuch as these Soviet POWs served as tacit hostages for the 7,500 *mujahidin* prisoners held by the RA, the *mujahidin* had little incentive to repatriate them.

Pakistan's President Benazir Bhutto discussed Afghanistan in talks with President Bush on her trip to the United States in June. The two leaders agreed to continue support to the *mujahidin* while seeking a peaceful settlement of the Afghan conflict. India, Pakistan's rival in the region, continued to be the only non-Communist government offering support to the RA. That support appeared to be only financial and diplomatic, despite Pakistani claims that the Indians had supplied 600 combat pilots to the RA.

Believing that the RA could endure for an additional 12 to 18 months, the United States settled in for a long-term program of both military and humanitarian aid. In September, obviously unhappy with the AIG's political squabbling, Washington decided to give that aid directly to *mujahidin* field commanders, bypassing the AIG politicians. The AIG's international stock remained low. Having failed to establish itself within Afghanistan, it received diplomatic recognition only from Saudi Arabia, Bahrain, Malaysia, and the Sudan.

ANTHONY ARNOLD
Hoover Institution, Stanford

© Barry Iverson/"Time" Magazine

The $200 million Basilica of Our Lady of Peace, the largest church in Christendom, was dedicated in Yamoussoukro, the administrative capital of the Ivory Coast. It was part of a building boom organized by President Felix Houphouët-Boigny.

AFRICA

Historians well may look back on 1989 as a watershed year in sub-Saharan Africa. It was a year of exceptional promise in resolving a number of Africa's chronic conflicts. It was a year of modest promise in the economic area as well, as signs of economic recovery began to appear in a number of countries. It was also a year in which portentous political and economic changes outside of Africa—above all, in Western and Eastern Europe—in all likelihood eventually would have a major influence on Africa's political and economic future.

Namibian Promise. The biggest news of the year was the move toward independence for Namibia. An agreement on a timetable for Namibian independence was signed by South African officials in New York in late 1988. Despite an unfortunate incident in April in which 1,700 armed guerrillas from the South West African People's Organization (SWAPO)—the main insurgent group fighting for Namibian independence—crossed into Namibia from Angola and clashed with the South African army, the goal of achieving independence in 1990 moved forward as planned. Elections took place in November for the constituent assembly which would write a constitution. As expected, SWAPO won the majority of seats.

South Africa. A second important and promising change appeared to begin in South Africa, after President P. W. Botha suffered a stroke in January and F. W. de Klerk took over as chief of the ruling Nationalist Party (NP). Botha formally resigned as president in August and de Klerk replaced him. De Klerk was confirmed as president in national elections held in September in which the NP won a slim majority in parliament. And he appeared to take a more conciliatory approach to dealing with antiapartheid groups than his predecessor. He permitted demonstrations against apartheid in October, after police violently put down several demonstrations before the September elections. He met with such antiapartheid leaders as Bishop Desmond Tutu and the Rev. Alan Boeseak and released several well-known officials of the banned African National Congress (ANC), including Oscar Mpeta and Walter Sizulu, who had spent the last 25 years in prison. But ANC leader and antiapartheid symbol Nelson Mandela was not released and the ANC remained banned. Thus it was unclear how far the new president would be willing to go in making more changes in apartheid.

Angola. A third change involved the conflict in Angola. Cuban troops began to pull out in 1989 and were due to be gone completely by 1991. Their South African adversaries already had pulled out. But the conflict between the Angolan government and UNITA, the insurgency group led by Jonas Savimbi, continued into 1989. In June 1989, Angolan President José Eduardo dos Santos and Savimbi met in Gbadolite, Zaire, with 18 African heads of state. With Zairian President Mobutu Sese Seko mediating, they agreed to a cease-fire as well as starting a process of national reconciliation. That process came to a halt when Savimbi complained that he had not agreed to go into exile as claimed by the Angolan government. Savimbi refused to attend further scheduled meetings between UNITA and the Angolan government. Both Savimbi and President Mobutu paid visits to Washington, DC, in October and, after talking with U.S. President George Bush, both agreed to try again to negotiate for peace in Angola. Savimbi's political future remained uncertain, however.

In other parts of Africa there were preliminary signs of a resolution of long-standing conflicts, including in Mozambique, where the government in Maputo indicated for the first time a willingness to talk to Renamo, the insurgent group operating in that country. The Ethiopian government, under military pressure from an increasingly bold and successful insurgency in Eritrea, sent representatives to Atlanta, GA, to participate in talks with the Eritrean People's Liberation Front (EPLF), the largest political and military movement challenging Ethiopian rule in Eritrea. Former President Jimmy Carter acted as a mediator at the Atlanta talks. Little but procedure was discussed. Further talks were held later in Nairobi, however.

Sudan. A coup in late June deposed the democratically elected government of Sadiq al-Mahdi, as an obscure brigadier general named Hassan Ahmed al-Bashir took power. The coup also ended rumors that peace talks were about to begin with the Sudanese People's Liberation Army, led by Col. Joseph Garang and representing a diverse group of southern Sudanese peoples who long have felt discriminated against by the Arabic-speaking Muslim northerners. The imposition of Islamic Sharia law on the entire country, including the Christian and animist south, had provoked fighting.

Two countries long plagued by internal conflict—Chad and Uganda—appeared to be making progress toward internal peace and economic recovery in 1989. Several countries also had held, or were moving toward, local and national elections. Ghana held local elections, and Nigeria showed every indication of sticking to its timetable for national elections and a return to civilian rule by 1992.

Economy. On the economic front, an increasing number of African governments committed themselves to economic reform programs. At the beginning of 1989, approximately 30 countries of sub-Saharan Africa had entered into stabilization programs with the International Monetary Fund (IMF), designed to reduce deficits in their balance of payments, or had structural adjustment programs with the World Bank, intended to increase the efficiency of resource use. As programs of economic restructuring spread throughout the region during the mid- to late-1980s, structural adjustment became an issue of high politics in one African country after another. Government austerity programs, rising unemployment, increasing costs of living, and other painful changes were the source of much controversy and dispute.

The controversy over the impact of structural adjustment in Africa was highlighted by two 1989 reports. The World Bank, in its report on *Africa's Adjustment and Growth in the 1980s,* argued that the positive results of economic reforms were becoming evident, specifically, that countries with strong reform programs had experienced improved agricultural production, improved export volumes, and growth in their gross domestic products. The Economic Commission for Africa (ECA), a United Nations regional commission, published its own study of economic reforms in Africa, entitled *African Alternative Framework to Structural Adjustment Programmes for Socio-Economic Recovery and Transformation,* that took a contrary view. The ECA study challenged the World Bank's findings and argued on the basis of somewhat less well-grounded statistical analyses that countries undertaking strong reform programs had experienced the worst economic problems since the beginning of the 1980s.

The disagreement between the World Bank and the ECA did not reflect well-considered judgments on the success or failure of economic restructuring in sub-Saharan Africa. It was far too soon to reach definitive conclusions on a restructuring experiment which only really had been under way intensively since the middle of the decade. Rather, the dispute between the two international agencies reflected the frustration felt by many Africans—on the slowness of their economies to recover and grow, and the extensive involvement of international institutions like the IMF and the World Bank in their business. The controversy over structural adjustment promised to continue until there was clear evidence that reforms were either effective or were incapable of achieving their goals in Africa.

A Kenyan official inspects some confiscated elephant tusks. In an attempt to protect the African elephant, all trading in ivory was banned by the 103-nation Convention of International Trade in Endangered Species.

© William Campbell/"Time" Magazine

On the issue of African debt, there was some progress toward greater debt relief for low-income African countries in 1989. Many small African countries were among the most heavily burdened debtors in the world. If they paid their foreign debts fully each year, they would be spending an average of one third of export earnings on debt service. Most African debtors judged that fully repaying their debts would wreak unacceptable havoc on their economies, forcing them to cut back too far on essential imports. Since the late 1970s, they had sought debt reschedulings and there had been nearly 100 debt reschedulings for sub-Saharan African countries since the beginning of the 1980s. Some countries had had repeated reschedulings with Zaire holding the record of 11.

While reducing the immediate burden of servicing foreign debts, however, debt reschedulings did not resolve the long-run problem of how these countries eventually would repay their loans and support healthy growth rates at the same time. African officials and economic experts emphasized this problem at a 1989 conference on African debt in Cairo. The intractability of the African debt problem was recognized increasingly by major creditor governments, as well as by international financial institutions. A number of European governments had cancelled some debts. In July 1989, President Bush also announced that the United States would cancel $1 billion in debt owed by low-income African countries. Several other proposals on debt relief were floated by the World Bank, including setting up a fund to finance the buy-back of foreign commercial debts at deep discounts by African governments. These were small but useful steps, with others likely to follow.

The long-held goal of economic integration among African economies, formalized in the Lagos Plan of Action signed at the Organization of African Unity meeting in 1980, was still a dream in 1989. The largest of the eight groups in economic integration in sub-Saharan Africa—the 16-member Economic Community of West African States (ECOWAS)—met in July and member governments signalled their unhappiness at the lack of progress toward integration. Yet, the lack of progress was their own fault. The governments still affirmed their commitment to integration but were unwilling to take risky steps to bring that integration about.

Economic integration was seen by many Africans as a strategy for fostering long-term growth and industrial development. However, the World Bank published in late November a study on long-term development strategies in Africa that did not emphasize economic integration as a key to achieving long-term development. The report seemed likely to stir up even more controversy.

Another economic problem involved the future amount of economic assistance to be provided African governments from the World Bank and the governments of developed countries. The loan window of the bank, the International Development Association (IDA)—a major source of economic aid for Africa in recent years—was to be replenished, beginning in 1990. But because of U.S. reluctance, it looked like IDA would be replenished at a lower real level than it had been at in the previous three years. With less money and more claims on that money, aid from the World Bank to Africa could drop. And with budgetary problems in the United States, the USSR, Great Britain, and other developed countries, there was little hope that any drop would be made up by other developed countries, except perhaps Japan. However, Japanese interests in and knowledge of African countries remained limited, and it was not clear how much the Japanese would be willing to increase aid in the region.

International Relations. There were two portentous trends in world affairs in 1989 which promised to affect Africans into the next century, although their specific impact remained uncertain. First was the much discussed "end of the Cold War" in Africa. While it was still too early to declare a termination of political competition between the United States and the USSR in Africa, the two superpowers were cooperating much more than in the past. This superpower cooperation was shown in the negotiations for Namibian independence and the withdrawal of Cuban troops from Angola. It also was increasingly clear that Africa was a low-priority region in the foreign-policy agendas of both countries. What the increase in U.S.-Soviet cooperation means for Africa—whether it be fewer destructive conflicts, a sharing of power, or simply a turning away by both nations—remained unclear in 1989.

A more immediate event with possible repercussions for Africa was the unification of the European Common Market (EC) in 1992. The EC planned to eliminate all internal barriers to the free movements of goods, services, capital, and persons. In the short term, it appeared that the unification might not mean very much to Africa since most African countries exported primary products to Europe, products which would be affected minimally by the completion of the European market. But in the long run, the impact of "Europe 1992" was less certain. What would it mean for those many countries whose currencies were linked to the French franc and supported by the French treasury if the Europeans moved toward monetary union? What would happen to potential investment in Africa with a more open, dynamic, and attractive European market just to the north? Africans had reason to be concerned about the future of their relationships with Europe as well as with the superpowers.

CAROL LANCASTER, *Georgetown University*

AGRICULTURE

World agricultural yields continued upward under improving technology. Rice and soybean production achieved record highs. Yet world supplies of major crops remained tight after a drawdown in 1988, keeping prices high for coarse grains, rice, wheat, and cotton.

Specialized v. Sustainable Agriculture. Modern agriculture received competing cues in 1989. On one side were markets and farm subsidies that encouraged specialized production, such as the intensive animal confinement operations in Asia, supplied by specialized grain farms of the United States. In Europe such a specialized system could displace traditional agricultural patterns as the European Community (EC) moved to integrate its internal markets by 1992.

On the other side, a less specialized "sustainable" agriculture became a priority goal in 1989. For decades, modern agriculture was praised for its "miracle" of increasing global food supplies faster than the burgeoning world population. Meanwhile critics of this high-output system pointed out that, while it fed the world, modern agriculture also produced undesirable side effects. Fertilizers and pesticides polluted the earth's surface and the drinking water and the products of chemically dependent agriculture were not always safe to eat. Lakes and rivers had become silted, and the air poisoned. Furthermore, the industrial products the system depends on were increasingly expensive and ultimately nonrenewable. The critics of conventional agriculture concluded that such a profligate agriculture was not sustainable. They proposed an alternative agriculture that would, for example, use crop rotation rather than chemicals for enriching soils and discouraging pests.

In 1989 a number of mainstream agricultural leaders—among them the managers of Europe's Common Agricultural Program, and a prestigious committee of the U.S. National Research Council whose report was endorsed by U.S. Secretary of Agriculture Clayton Yeutter—embraced the principle of sustainable agriculture. The conservative American Farm Bureau also supported the search for alternatives, as did leaders in agricultural science and economics. These mainstream leaders prudently noticed the political successes of Europe's "green" parties, along with taking note of vigorous new U.S. state laws protecting the groundwaters. Mainstream leaders also had gained some confidence that sustainable agriculture, using new practices and technology, could produce adequate food, perhaps while accumulating fewer costly surpluses.

U.S. Programs. By 1989 a total of 31 million acres (12.6 million ha) had been entered under the conservation reserve program that retired marginal croplands under ten-year contracts. In responding to the 1988 drought, Congress included disaster payments to producers of nontraditional crops. Congress also displayed more than usual interest in utilizing agricultural products to improve the environment, such as creating biodegradable bags and methanol fuel. In 1989, Congress also began an evaluation of existing programs in planning for a new farm bill in 1990. There was general satisfaction with the existing programs since government costs had declined to less than half the amount spent in 1986.

As U.S. government farm programs became more flexible, U.S. agriculture also proved to be flexible but resilient. The domestic catfish industry grew again at an annual rate of 30% and markets were found for its product. Iowa pork producers worked for higher efficiency to protect their markets from North Carolina's intensive "hog factories." In addition, U.S. agriculture recovered well from the 1988 drought. Farm receipts were at a record high and net

AP/Wide World

The home computer has become common on the typical farm. Jim Badtke, left, *of Union Grove, WI, uses his computer to maintain his cows' production records.*

It was a good year for farm-equipment sales in the United States, as farmers purchased tractors and other items at a pace not seen in ten years. Accordingly, Ford New Holland, Inc., a Ford Motor Company subsidiary, doubled production of its 400-hp Versatile tractor, right. *A four-wheel-drive vehicle, it is used for plowing, planting, and fertilizing.*

Courtesy, Ford New Holland, Inc.

farm income was up sharply from 1988, thanks to good prices.

U.S. Exports. American farmers applauded the government's aggressive trade stance, which opened more markets in Asia. But feelings were mixed when U.S. negotiators achieved a tentative multilateral agreement (under GATT) to begin to phase down worldwide governmental support of agriculture. Farm groups powerful in Congress feared that the government might enact farm policy under international agreements rather than by congressional legislation. In the meantime, U.S. agricultural exports increased in value, particularly exports to Asian markets. Beef exports to Japan, South Korea, and Taiwan increased sharply, and poultry exports—two thirds of which went to Asia—rose 30% from 1988. U.S. grain exports to Asia increased in value because of higher prices, despite drought-reduced volume. Exports of cotton and hides for industrial use declined, because rising labor costs slowed some manufacturers in Taiwan, South Korea, and Japan. Soybean exports tumbled because of inadequate domestic production, along with competition from Brazil and China, and from the growing popularity of Canada's rapeseed.

Food Exporters. Canada, Australia, New Zealand, and the United States were major exporters to Pacific Rim nations in 1989. These food exporters were all strong competitors for Asia's enlarging food markets, after weathering the loss of European agricultural markets earlier.

Wheat production in Canada, Australia, and the United States rose by 25% in 1989, rebuilding stocks depleted by the 1988 North American drought. All the food exporters geared up for increased meat production. Australia, the world's largest beef exporter, sought investment capital for an even larger presence in the Asian meat market. New Zealand, the world's largest exporter of lamb and mutton, moved to increase its beef production, and also to increase wool output to take advantage of new wool-processing technology that enhances the future of this fiber. Australia also made a major commitment to supply oranges to the Japanese market.

Some exporters lowered their own trade barriers in 1989. New Zealand and Australia nearly finished implementing their bilateral Closer Economic Relations Agreement, and the United States and Canada began to implement a new free-trade agreement.

Canadian farmers were early beneficiaries of the U.S.-Canada free-trade agreement, achieving $2.4 billion in agricultural exports to the United States during 1989, mainly in live cattle and hogs. Canada also benefited as the United States became the world's largest importer of oats, a new health food. The United States in return was expecting to find new Canadian markets for horticultural produce, wine, and poultry.

Asia. South Korea, Taiwan, and Japan continued to experience similar dilemmas in managing their successful agricultures. Farmers demanded protection from agricultural imports, but the countries were also under pressure from the United States—their major customer—to lower agricultural barriers. In response to U.S. pressures, Taiwan's government agreed to permit beef imports, but backed down when farmers protested, and then angered Australia by allowing imports only of specialized cuts produced in the United States. Japan's Liberal Democratic Party suffered election losses due in part to allowing more U.S. agricultural imports. U.S. rice producers, acting under tough U.S. trade law, filed a formal request for retaliation against Japan for barring U.S. rice imports.

Industrialization in Asian nations drained resources from agriculture in 1989. Rural areas in South Korea, Taiwan, and Japan faced labor shortages and poor future prospects for manpower because of the rapidly aging rural populations. All were searching for ways to reduce the need for added labor with larger farm size and mechanization. Taiwan's total agricultural output actually declined. Poultry production turned downward in Japan, and South Korea's small farmers continued to dispose of beef cattle that the government earlier had persuaded them to buy. All three governments continued to support the price of rice, the main source of small farmers' incomes, well above the world level. Thailand remained the world's principal rice exporter, as that nation also moved toward a more varied economy.

China's rural development, which had plateaued in recent years, probably was slowed by political instability following the demonstrations in Tiananmen Square in the spring. Grain production fell below modest targets and rice output declined due to lower price incentives and some adverse weather. Because of short supplies and urban discontent, the Chinese government, in deciding among competing uses for scarce foreign exchange, gave highest priority to paying for imports of food grains. However, China's agricultural imports declined overall. China, which usually exported cotton, suffered a decline in stocks for domestic use.

Europe. The European Community (EC), blessed with agricultural prosperity and abundance in 1989, took steps toward reducing its agricultural budget while also preparing to integrate fully its internal agricultural markets by 1992. Wheat acreage and production increased slightly, although total grain production declined slightly because of dry weather. There was increased consumption of coarse grains by animals and also by humans, who suddenly were consuming large quantities of oats. EC grain exports also increased sharply, to a record 33 million tons, as a result of higher world prices and lessened competition due to the 1988 North American drought. The EC displaced Canada in becoming the second-largest wheat exporter. Its share of the international wheat trade increased from 16% to 21%; the EC also experienced record exports of barley and corn. The European Community's Agricultural Council accepted a proposal from its Commission to freeze support prices and reduce storage subsidies. But farm groups, who usually had their way in agricultural policies, argued that the price freeze, as administered, turned out to be a price cut. EC farm-program costs actually declined slightly from the $31 billion of 1988. Many steps were being taken to integrate Europe's internal markets by 1992. These steps included standardizing regulations, including those affecting plant and animal health, food labeling and packaging, and also repealing nontariff barriers to internal trade.

Meanwhile, several nonmembers of the Community, loosely associated in the European Free Trade Association, also were reexamining their farm programs and health regulations with the prospect of increasing trade. These nations included Sweden, Norway, Finland, Austria, and Switzerland.

The Soviet Union. The Soviet agricultural system was caught in the maelstrom of the Mikhail Gorbachev revolution. Gorbachev's government was anxious to increase domestic food production as a means to domestic tranquility and as a way to save foreign exchange. Yet it purchased feed grain in order to provide more meat and it continued to finance consumer food subsidies through deficit spending. The commitment to increased meat in diets suggested that the Soviet Union would continue to be a major market for U.S meat and feed grains. The proportion of U.S. wheat sales was expected to decline slightly; wheat made up about half of all 1988 U.S. exports to the Soviet Union. In 1989, Soviet agricultural development was aimed at speeding the adoption of new technology, decentralizing management, building roads and rural housing, and improving the storage and processing of commodities. While the Gorbachev government also encouraged a shift to individual family farms and small voluntary cooperatives, local bureaucracies struggled to retain the traditional collectives and state farms. A sense of crisis resulted from the feeling that if proposed reforms did not occur, agriculture would stagnate and resulting food shortages would threaten political stability.

The Chernobyl nuclear reactor disaster of 1986 shaped up as an enduring disaster for Soviet agriculture. One fifth of the arable land in Byelorussia still was not farmable in 1989. The government was hard-pressed to dispose of contaminated products or find secondary uses for them.

Latin America. General political and economic conditions impeded agricultural growth in Latin America. Brazil, Latin America's largest agricultural producer, also was its largest debtor, and the nation's economic conditions continued to deteriorate in 1989. Under the government's austerity programs, agricultural subsidies were cut, especially for wheat and sugarcane. Coffee and cocoa production stagnated. Reduced world coffee prices created hardship for the Andean countries, strengthening the hand of a large and profitable cocaine industry. In Argentina, wheat producers recovered from 1988 drought, but the country had difficulty capitalizing on higher world wheat prices because of extremely unstable exchange rates.

Africa. Food production recovered in many African countries that earlier had required food aid. Famine continued to be evident in Sudan and Somalia due mainly to civil conflict in both countries. The Sahel of sub-Saharan Africa, which includes parts of eight nations, remained the only region in the world where population growth had outpaced seriously food production during the previous two decades. Increased population had led to increased cultivation and overgrazing, turning land into desert. Some

Sahel countries were obliged to use scarce foreign exchange to import rice and corn at prices more than 30% higher than in 1988.

See also FOOD.

DON F. HADWIGER, *Iowa State University*

ALABAMA

During most of 1989, Alabama was preoccupied with alleged corruption of public figures. But attention was diverted to Huntsville, AL, on November 15, when a devastating tornado struck. The tornado left 18 dead, hundreds injured, and caused more than $100 million in damage.

Public Misconduct. The most famous name to come out of investigations of alleged misconduct was that of Gerald Wallace, 68, brother of former Gov. George C. Wallace. Gerald Wallace was indicted by a federal grand jury for failing to pay in excess of $165,000 in income taxes due for 1984 and 1985. His initial plea, on July 19, was innocent. However, on October 11 he pleaded guilty to the charges. He was required to pay all taxes and penalties due and was expected to receive probation.

Later in October the Republican whip of the U.S. House of Representatives, Newt Gingrich of Georgia, requested that U.S. Rep. William Dickinson, the dean of the Alabama congressional delegation and a fellow Republican, be investigated by the House ethics committee for an alleged influence-peddling agreement with a prominent Montgomery businessman.

On May 5, Fayette County Sheriff Hubert M. Norris (D) resigned after being linked with bootlegging. On May 15 three Democratic state representatives from the Bessemer area were indicted by a federal grand jury for allegedly accepting shares from former legislator Hugh Boles in a proposed dog track in return for their help in getting the proposal (ultimately unsuccessful) through the legislature. Boles was convicted in August. The others were to be tried later. On September 13, Bessemer Mayor Ed Porter was indicted on similar charges.

On October 6 three more Jefferson County legislators were indicted for allegedly accepting money from a mineworkers' union local for the legislators' support of a bill to stimulate the mining of more Alabama coal by restricting use of foreign coal in utility steam plants.

Legislative Activity. The Democrat-controlled Alabama legislature, meeting in regular session in February, opposed Republican Gov. Guy Hunt's tax-reform program. However, the legislature increased hazardous-waste dumping fees from $14 to $30 per ton over a three-year period. This was aimed at slowing business at the chemical-waste landfill at Emelle—the largest hazardous-waste-disposal facility in the country. Lawmakers also prohibited the import of hazardous waste from states that do not have a cooperative agreement with Alabama or do not offer some way of disposing of such wastes themselves.

The legislature quit work on May 11, having passed the $732.4 million general fund and $2.4 billion education budgets well before final adjournment. This was in marked contrast to 1988, when it had taken two special legislative sessions to pass the basic appropriations bills.

Political Struggles. Democratic versus Republican sparring continued in the off-year. On April 4, Democratic Secretary of State Glen Browder was elected to the U.S. House of Representatives to fill the vacancy created by the death of Rep. Bill Nichols, also a Democrat. Republicans enjoyed increased success in 1989, particularly in persuading eight Democratic state legislators to switch parties. Meanwhile, the Democratic Party faced a challenge from the Alabama Democratic Conference (ADC), its black wing, which objected to a rule adopted on April 15, making 24 appointive state executive committee seats that had been controlled by the ADC into elective positions. A rival black political organization, the New South Coalition, supported the rules change.

On the issue of the Confederate flag flying over Alabama's Capitol, blacks were united, however. On January 10, Thomas Reed, state president of the National Association for the Advancement of Colored People (NAACP), and 13 black legislators were convicted of attempting to remove the flag physically. Challenges against the Confederate flag in the state House of Representatives on February 21 and in federal district court on March 1 proved futile, although appeals were continuing. The swearing in of three black Dallas County commissioners in Selma on January 16, the day set aside to honor the late Dr. Martin Luther King, Jr., was a special symbolic moment for the black political movement in Alabama.

WILLIAM H. STEWART
The University of Alabama

ALABAMA • Information Highlights

Area: 51,705 sq mi (133 915 km^2).
Population (July 1, 1988): 4,102,000.
Chief Cities (July 1, 1986 est.): Montgomery, the capital, 194,290; Birmingham, 277,510; Mobile, 203,260; Huntsville, 163,420.
Government (1989): *Chief officers*—governor, Guy Hunt (R); lt. gov. Jim Folsom, Jr. (D). *Legislature*—Senate, 35 members; House of Representatives, 105 members.
State Finances (fiscal year 1988): *Revenue*, $8,022,000,000; *expenditure*, $6,877,000,000.
Personal Income (1988): $52,720,000,000; per capita, $12,851.
Labor Force (June 1989: *Civilian labor force*, 1,931,700; *unemployed*, 144,300 (7.5% of total force).
Education: *Enrollment* (fall 1987)—public elementary schools, 521,000; public secondary, 208,000; colleges and universities, 183,348. *Public school expenditures* (1987–88), $1,899,500,000 ($2,612 per pupil).

ALASKA

The major issue for Alaska in 1989 was clearly the grounding of the *Exxon Valdez* on Bligh Reef in Prince William Sound on March 24, and the subsequent spill of 11 million gallons (41.6 million l) of oil into waters touching hundreds of miles of the state's coastline. Besides the immediate impact and future damage to the environment, fish, and wildlife, the event also affected Alaska's politics and economics. (*See* feature article, page 36.)

Government and Politics. While Gov. Steve Cowper (D) announced in March he would not seek reelection in 1990, he realized one of his major priorities in 1989 with the revision of the Economic Limit Factor (ELF), that eliminated many tax breaks for oil companies. The ELF was a tax formula designed to encourage oil production by reducing the tax levied on oil produced in marginal fields. Governor Cowper and others had maintained that the ELF formula was applied to Prudhoe Bay and Kuparek fields before they became marginal producers, thereby costing the state millions of dollars in lost revenues. A perception of an inadequate response to the oil spill by the industry may have overcome opposition in the state Senate to an ELF revision, and the measure passed during the 1989 legislative session.

Another legislative issue that stirred controversy in 1989 was a proposal to guarantee educational funding for grades K-12 by using a portion of the earnings from the Alaska Permanent Fund. Debate and opposition from all sides of the political spectrum accompanied this proposal and its future was uncertain.

Economy. The economic impact of the oil spill was hard to gauge. Fears that tourism would be hurt thus far appear unfounded.

While a direct relationship between salmon prices and the oil spill was not demonstrated, record runs of fish in areas outside the waters of the Sound have been offset by the declining market price for Alaska salmon.

ALASKA • Information Highlights

Area: 591,004 sq mi (1 530 700 km^2).
Population (July 1, 1988): 524,000.
Chief Cities (1980 census): Juneau, the capital, 19,528; Anchorage (July 1, 1986 est.), 235,000; Fairbanks, 22,645; Sitka, 7,803.
Government (1989): *Chief Officers*—governor, Steve Cowper (D); lt. gov., Stephen McAlpine (D). *Legislature*—Senate, 20 members; House of Representatives, 40 members.
State Finances (fiscal year 1988): *Revenue,* \$5,592,000,000; *expenditure,* \$4,198,000,000.
Personal Income (1988): \$10,006,000,000; per capita, \$19,079.
Labor Force (June 1989): *Civilian labor force,* 246,400; *unemployed,* 17,300 (7.0% of total force).
Education: *Enrollment* (fall 1987)—public elementary schools, 77,000; public secondary, 29,000; colleges and universities, 26,937. *Public school expenditures* (1987–88), \$661,307,000 (\$6,538 per pupil).

Exxon has honored claims from fishing boat owners on losses incurred as a result of the spill. But workers in the fishing industry have not been compensated for lost wages. In view of the potential of contaminated fish, there also are concerns about the economic future and the health of Alaskans living in several subsistence villages dependent upon fishing.

The spill also has altered unemployment demographics in Alaska. Many workers moved to the affected areas of Valdez and Seward for short-term employment as cleanup workers. This migration eased the strain on other Alaskan cities with high unemployment rates. As the cleanup wound down, however, there was the danger that high unemployment rates could overwhelm Valdez and Seward. Workers who left permanent positions for high-paying cleanup jobs were finding their former jobs filled when the cleanup work ran out.

While oil prices rose dramatically following the spill, the state's revenue picture did not improve to any great extent. Revenues continued to decline, putting increased pressure on municipalities and small villages across the state. This economic pressure was demonstrated in the recent attempts by large municipalities to sell their public utilities to save money.

Other Events. Illegal drift-net fishing by foreign vessels in Alaskan waters created an international stir in 1989. In the southeastern portion of the state, a Canadian fishing vessel was seized by the Coast Guard in the summer for illegal fishing in Alaskan waters.

A federal jury in Anchorage on May 23 convicted lobbyist Lewis Dischner and his business associate Carl Mathieson on charges of extortion, racketeering, and fraud in a political corruption case. The trial focused on Dischner's and Mathieson's alleged role in the corruption of local officials, and in influence peddling to acquire contracts during the heavy construction phase on the North Slope in the early 1980s.

Redoubt Volcano, located 115 mi (185 km) southwest of Anchorage, erupted in December for the first time since 1966, spewing volcanic ash miles into the air.

CARL E. SHEPRO, *University of Alaska*

ALBANIA

In 1989, Albania remained an oasis of calm and stability in the midst of the whirlwind of political and economic liberalization that was sweeping through Eastern Europe.

Domestic Affairs. Albania continued to be dominated by the policies and personality of Enver Hoxha, the Communist dictator who had ruled the country for more than four decades before his death in 1985. His heirs, led by Head of State Ramiz Alia, remained committed to xenophobic self-reliance and fanatical

© Marvine Howe/NYT Pictures

In Albania where private cars are banned, a mostly empty city square in Tiranë reflects the startling contrast between this rigidly controlled Communist state and the liberalization so evident in many Soviet-bloc countries of Eastern Europe.

Marxist orthodoxy, including unyielding atheism. In February the UN Commission on Human Rights cited Albania's regime for its severe repression of religious freedom. Prison sentences of up to ten years have been meted out for such religious observances as praying, owning religious symbols, and making the sign of the cross.

The ruling Albanian Workers' (Communist) Party officially continued to resist and denigrate Soviet-style *glasnost* and *perestroika,* but there were a few signs of ideological loosening. Party spokesmen publicly encouraged "debate and deep scientific criticism" to help eradicate complacency and inefficiency in carrying out the nation's tasks. More Albanian athletic and cultural groups have been permitted to travel abroad. In an effort to earn much-needed hard currency, the regime also has begun to admit limited and carefully monitored numbers of foreign tourists. About 10,000 were expected in 1989.

Economy. Albania continued to bear the label of "the poorest country in Europe." In December 1988, Niko Gjyzari, chairman of the State Planning Commission, announced that the 1988 production goals for mining and nonferrous metallurgy had been exceeded, but those for agriculture, electricity production, and oil and chrome production had not been met. The draft economic plan for 1989 emphasized the improvement of consumer-goods production, slated to increase by 8.8% over the 1988 level. Labor productivity was to rise by 3%, agricultural productivity by 16.9%, and exports by 19.6%. In March 1989, Albania joined Bulgaria, Greece, Romania, Turkey, and Yugoslavia in the first Balkan economic summit in Ankara. The participants agreed to ease trade and travel barriers and facilitate economic contacts in the region and to create a Balkan Chamber of Commerce. Biannual follow-up meetings were planned.

Foreign Affairs. Albania maintained its hard line in foreign affairs, too. It refused to send an official representative to the public memorial ceremonies in Budapest on June 16 for Imre Nagy, the executed leader of the crushed Hungarian revolution of 1956. Later in the year, it upgraded its diplomatic relations to ambassadorial level with Bulgaria, Czechoslovakia, and East Germany—Communist states that so far had resisted *perestroika.*

Albania's relations with neighboring Yugoslavia suffered from the continuing violence between Serbian security forces and the 1.7 million ethnic Albanians in Yugoslavia's Kosovo Autonomous Province. In February and March thousands of ethnic Albanian miners and students staged strikes and sit-ins protesting Serbia's attempt to control the internal affairs of Kosovo. Dozens of ethnic Albanian leaders were arrested, and there were scores of deaths on both sides. Yugoslavia charged that Albania was stirring up separatist elements in Kosovo in hopes of incorporating the province into a "Greater Albania." Albanian Foreign Minister Reis Malile denied that Albania had

ALBANIA • Information Highlights

Official Name: People's Socialist Republic of Albania.
Location: Southern Europe, Balkan peninsula.
Area: 11,100 sq mi (28 750 km^2).
Population (mid-1989 est.): 3,200,000.
Chief City (mid-1987): Tiranë, the capital, 225,700.
Government: *Head of state,* Ramiz Alia, chairman of the Presidium (took office November 1982) and first secretary of the Albanian Workers' Party (April 1985). *Head of government,* Adil Carçani, chairman, Council of Ministers—premier (took office January 1982). *Legislature* (unicameral)—People's Assembly, 250 members.
Monetary Unit: Lek (6 leks equals U.S.$1, July 1989).
Gross National Product (1986 est. U.S.$): $2,700,000,000–$2,900,000,000.

any territorial claims on Yugoslavia or posed any threat to its internal security but vowed that it would continue to protest against Yugoslav treatment of its Albanian minority as "second-class citizens."

JOSEPH FREDERICK ZACEK
State University of New York at Albany

ALBERTA

During 1989, Alberta showed positive signs of recovery from almost a decade of stagnation.

Weather, Agriculture, Forestry. Part of the economic improvement was due to changes in weather, especially in southern Alberta, which for the previous few years had bordered on drought conditions. In 1989 all parts of the province received adequate rainfall to ensure bountiful grain crops, although a damp autumn made harvesting difficult and caused some grade deterioration. Rain came in sufficient quantity and at the right time to prevent serious problems from forest fires. Tornadoes created minor property damage but no loss of life. Announcement of several proposed new pulp plants created a feeling of optimism in a province where unemployment is about the same as that of eastern Canada, but also created apprehension about threats to the environment, especially to the river and lake systems. Concern over such hazards never has been more vocal.

Economy and Business. After some stagnant years, urban commercial construction was making a steady if unspectacular comeback, although there still was a surplus of office space. Urban and suburban residential construction showed healthy growth. Rising and stabilizing prices of oil have increased exploration and developmental activity. Demands for natural gas increased.

A decade marked by the collapse of financial companies culminated in a 14-month investigation by lawyer William Code of the 1987 failure of Principal Group, Ltd., an Edmonton-based financial conglomerate. Code blamed Principal's founder Donald Cormie, a 67-year-old former law instructor, for the collapse, although no charges have been brought against him. He also placed part of the responsibility on the provincial government for not being a firmer watchdog. The provincial government did take steps to reimburse partially investors in the conglomerate.

Politics. For Alberta, 1989 was marked by both provincial and municipal elections. In the March 20 provincial voting, the Progressive Conservative (PC) government of Premier Don Getty was returned with a reduced majority. The mildly socialistic New Democrats, led by Ray Martin, remained as the official opposition and the Liberals under new leader Laurence Decore, mayor of Edmonton, doubled their provincial parliamentary representation from four to eight seats. Calgary Mayor Ralph Klein was a successful PC candidate and subsequently joined the cabinet. Both Decore and Klein resigned from their municipal posts. Premier Getty, who lost his Edmonton seat, was forced to run in a May 9 by-election. He easily won in the rural riding of Stettler.

In the October municipal elections, political feminism came of age in Alberta. Edmonton chose its first woman mayor, Jan Reimer, and six of the 12 aldermen from female candidates. St. Albert and Fort McMurray also elected women as mayors, and other women gained seats on councils or school boards.

The elections were unique in that voters also were asked to choose a nominee for appointment by the federal government to a vacant Senate seat. The surprising choice was Lt. Gen. Stanley Waters (ret.), member of the fringe Reform Party.

Professional Sports. Alberta's honor in the world of sports was maintained by the Calgary Flames, who captured hockey's 1989 Stanley Cup.

JOHN W. CHALMERS
Historical Association of Alberta

ALBERTA • Information Highlights

Area: 255,286 sq mi (661 190 km²)
Population (June 1989): 2,423,200.
Chief Cities (1986 census): Edmonton, the capital, 573,982; Calgary, 636,104; Lethbridge, 58,841.
Government (1989): *Chief Officers*—lt. gov., Helen Hunley; premier, Don Getty (Progressive Conservative). *Legislature*—Legislative Assembly, 79 members.
Provincial Finances (1989–90 fiscal year budget): *Revenues,* $10,200,000,000; *expenditures,* $11,700,000,000.
Personal Income (average weekly earnings, June 1989): $485.42.
Labor Force (August 1989, seasonally adjusted): *Employed* workers, 15 years of age and over, 1,226,000; *Unemployed,* 7.1%.
Education (1989–90): *Enrollment*—elementary and secondary schools, 489,300 pupils; postsecondary—universities, 46,450; community colleges, 25,500.
(All monetary figures are in Canadian dollars.)

ALGERIA

Constitutional reforms, a new prime minister, a profusion of new political parties, and a new regional union all changed Algeria's political landscape as the country still was adjusting to the trauma of the October 1988 riots that resulted in a brief state of emergency. Yet a split between President Chadli Benjedid and Prime Minister Kasdi Merbah in September revealed the tensions generated by the process of economic and political change.

Politics. President Chadli Benjedid, reelected to a third five-year term in December 1988, orchestrated the process of reform. No

ALGERIA • Information Highlights

Official Name: Democratic and Popular Republic of Algeria.
Location: North Africa.
Area: 919,591 sq mi (2 381 740 km²).
Population (mid-1989 est.): 24,900,000.
Chief Cities (Jan. 1, 1983): Algiers, the capital, 1,721,607; Oran, 663,504; Constantine, 448,578.
Government: *Head of state,* Chadli Benjedid, president (took office Feb. 1979). *Head of government,* Mouloud Hamrouche, prime minister (appointed Sept. 16, 1989).
Monetary Unit: Dinar (7.686 dinars equal U.S.$1, July 1989).
Gross Domestic Product (1986 est. U.S.$): $59,000,000,000.
Foreign Trade (1987 U.S.$): *Imports,* $7,029,000,000; *exports,* $8,186,000,000.

sooner elected as the only candidate under the terms of the 1976 constitution, Benjedid presented Algerians with a revised constitution to be adopted in February. The new document omitted any reference to socialism or the National Charter, the erstwhile official guide for the country. It established the right to form "associations of a political character," thus ending the National Liberation Front's (FLN) single-party status. Benjedid explained to the electorate that the constitution must be ideologically neutral to render Algeria a "state of law." Both Islamists who disliked the predominantly secular nature of the constitution and some elements of the FLN urged a negative vote, but 74.4% of the voters approved it on February 23.

Long-bottled-up political activity erupted throughout the country under the new law. By September five new parties had been granted official status by the ministry of the interior. These were the Social Democratic Party (PSD), the Socialist Vanguard Party (PAGS), which emerged from 34 years of clandestine existence, the fundamentalist Islamic Safeguard Party (FIS), the Berber-oriented Rally for Culture and Democracy (RCD), and the National Party for Solidarity and Development (PNSD), a coalition of diverse reformists. Other parties also filed for recognition. Throughout this burst of political energy, the FLN sought to stand above the fray as the party of government. The Central Committee decided in September to postpone the promised Extraordinary Congress from October until November while Benjedid urged the party to open itself up to new currents of dialogue and to "the youth."

The strain of channeling the movement for change through existing institutions like the People's National Assembly (all of whose members represent the FLN) came to a head in September when Benjedid dismissed Prime Minister Kasdi Merbah. The threat of constitutional crisis loomed momentarily as Merbah questioned the president's right to disband the government, but he stepped aside to allow Benjedid's close aide, Mouloud Hamrouche, to form a new cabinet. Only five ministers retained their jobs and three others switched portfolios, including Sid Ahmed Ghozali, the influential finance minister who became foreign minister in the cabinet named on September 16.

Foreign Policy. Algeria joined Morocco, Tunisia, Libya, and Mauritania to form the Union of the Arab Maghreb (UMA) in February. The treaty establishing this regional economic grouping calls for a presidential council, the chairmanship of which is to rotate every six months, a foreign ministerial council, a monitoring committee to implement decisions, and a secretariat to handle day-to-day affairs. The goal of the UMA is to institutionalize cooperation politically and culturally. The main UMA objective, however, is aimed at working toward a common market and multilateral joint economic ventures. Prior to the treaty ceremonies, Benjedid paid his first state visit to Morocco, a fruit of the diplomatic rapprochement initiated in 1988. Despite signature of an agreement to build a gas pipeline from Algeria through Morocco, the détente between the two states appeared strained by the end of the year as their long dispute over self-determination for Western Sahara remained unresolved.

Lengthy negotiations with France culminated in two agreements in January. Algeria agreed to a lower price for its natural-gas shipments to France while the latter extended a $1.1 billion aid and credit package to its former dependency. French President Mitterrand visited Algeria in March to express support for Benjedid's program of democratization. Algeria exercised diplomatic muscle in the secret negotiations that led to a settlement of the Libyan-Chadian dispute signed in Algiers at the end of August.

Economy and Culture. Strikes occurred in numerous sectors as workers questioned the government's economic strategy and performance.

Two of the country's most eminent writers, novelist Mouloud Mammeri and Kateb Yacine, died in 1989, depriving Algeria of two eloquent voices for democracy just as the country embarked upon its pluralist experiment.

ROBERT MORTIMER, *Haverford College*

ANGOLA

The first tentative steps toward a cease-fire between government forces of the Popular Movement for the Liberation of Angola (MPLA) and rebels of the Union for the Total Independence of Angola (UNITA) were taken in December of 1988, with the signing of the so-called New York Accords by Angola, Cuba, and South Africa. There was cautious optimism that this might, in time, lead to direct political negotiations and ultimately to genuine national reconciliation. In January 1989, the

AP/Wide World

Angolan rebel leader Jonas Savimbi, head of the Union for the Total Independence of Angola (UNITA), agreed in October to a new round of talks with the Soviet-backed Angolan government in an attempt to break the impasse to achieving an end to Angola's 14-year civil war.

first group of an estimated 50,000 Cuban troops in Angola left the country as part of a 27-month phased withdrawal.

Cease-Fire Discussions. The first face-to-face discussions between the government of Angolan President José Eduardo dos Santos and representatives of UNITA took place at a meeting of more than a dozen African heads of state on June 22 in Zaire. The summit, perhaps the largest ever held by African leaders to discuss a single issue, had been orchestrated by the president of Zaire, Mobutu Sese Seko, and was part of a larger international effort to bring about a solution to the 14-year-old civil war. In addition to Seko, other African leaders, including Zambia President Kenneth B. Kaunda and Mali President Moussa Traoré played a crucial role in bringing about a cease-fire agreement. Unfortunately, the cease-fire was ignored as both sides continued limited operations. There were three more negotiating sessions in July and August, but the Angolan government launched a major offensive against a UNITA stronghold on August 18. While agreeing to a cease-fire was in itself an important first step, ways to monitor it remained unresolved. Far more problematic, however, were the institutional changes and power-sharing arrangements which would be necessary to integrate the two factions in a government of national unity and reconciliation.

On August 22 a follow-up summit of African leaders took place in Harare, Zimbabwe, without UNITA. The Harare summit found that UNITA should recognize the existing constitution of Angola and integrate its cadres into existing government institutions, and that UNITA's Jonas Savimbi should agree to a temporary retirement from politics. All three points had been rejected previously by UNITA. Savimbi declined to attend a meeting called in September to sign yet another cease-fire agreement. In October, after renewed efforts by the African heads of state, as well as by the United States and South Africa, the MPLA government and UNITA agreed to a new round of discussions.

Great obstacles in negotiations remained at year's end, but the fact that the Soviet Union was considering gradual disengagement from southern Africa, while the Bush administration publicly had committed itself to continuing support for UNITA, suggested a shift in the balance of power which might force the government to negotiate as soon as possible rather than risk losing advantage by waiting.

Economic Changes. Meanwhile, in an apparent shift of economic policy, the Angolan government began to move away from socialist policies toward a free-market economy after the country was admitted to the International Monetary Fund on July 20. The government also increased its efforts to attract foreign investment and devalued its currency, the kwanza.

PATRICK O'MEARA AND
N. BRIAN WINCHESTER
Indiana University

ANGOLA • Information Highlights

Official Name: People's Republic of Angola.
Location: Western Africa.
Area: 481,351 sq mi (1 246 700 km²).
Population: (mid-1989 est.): 8,500,000.
Chief City (1982 est.): Luanda, the capital, 1,200,000.
Government: *Head of state and government,* José Eduardo dos Santos, president (took office 1979). *Legislature*—People's Assembly.
Gross Domestic Product (1987 est. U.S. $): $4,700,-000,000.

ANTHROPOLOGY

In 1989 anthropologists challenged traditional views of hunter-gatherers; a fossil discovery sparked debate over whether Neanderthals could talk; and investigations continued into the origin of modern humans.

Hunter-Gatherers. Modern groups of hunter-gatherers, particularly those living in Africa, often are seen by anthropologists as "living fossils" who have lived in virtual isolation and exist much as people did 10,000 or more years ago, before agriculture began. Thus, hunter-gatherers are used in attempts to reconstruct prehistoric human behavior as much as 2 million years ago.

But after reviewing much of the research on hunter-gatherers published since the late 1950s, Thomas N. Headland of the Summer Institute of Linguistics in Dallas and Lawrence A. Reid of the University of Hawaii concluded that these groups provide, at best, a limited glimpse of prehistoric behavior patterns. Most hunter-gatherers have interacted with neighboring groups for thousands of years, the researchers said. In many cases, hunter-gatherer groups have cultivated foods, raised livestock, and engaged in active trading long before their first contacts with Europeans in the 16th century.

Other investigators, however, contended that hunter-gatherers often maintain their basic social organization—including a division of labor between the sexes, lack of a political hierarchy, and food sharing—through long periods of contact with outsiders. In their view, careful study of hunter-gatherer societies still may shed light on the evolution of human culture.

Neanderthal Speech. A team of investigators, led by Baruch Arensburg of Tel Aviv University in Israel, reported finding a small, U-shaped bone in the neck of a Neanderthal skeleton that, they assert, demonstrates Neanderthals could talk in much the same way as people do today. The Neanderthal skeleton, unearthed at an Israeli cave, yielded a hyoid bone, which lies between the root of the tongue and the larynx, or voice box. The hyoid anchors muscles connected to the jaw, larynx, and tongue. No other hyoid bones have been found for Neanderthals or for any other ancient hominids—members of the evolutionary family that includes modern humans.

The shape and size of the Neanderthal hyoid bone and the position of marks left by muscle attachments closely match those observed in modern humans, according to Arensburg. This suggests that evolutionary change in vocal mechanisms occurs slowly, he said. Arensburg argues that human ancestors living at least 1 million years ago probably possessed the ability to talk much as people do now.

Other scientists held that a single hyoid bone reveals little about speech capabilities, which probably were limited among Neanderthals. On the basis of a computer model of a Neanderthal vocal tract constructed several years ago, Philip Lieberman of Brown University in Providence, RI, argued that Neanderthals could not pronounce sounds for the vowels "i" or "u." He also said their voices would have been highly nasal and subject to many errors in pronunciation.

Modern Human Origins. Scientists using a recently developed dating technique said anatomically modern humans inhabited an Israeli cave about 100,000 years ago. This is consistent with a recent report that modern humans lived at a nearby Israeli cave more than 90,000 years ago. Christopher B. Stringer and his coworkers at the British Museum in London, who obtained the new date from two previously excavated animal teeth, said the evidence supports the theory that modern humans originated in Africa and spread throughout the world, replacing groups such as the Neanderthals. But modern humans and Neanderthals occupied the same small area of the Near East for 60,000 years, the researchers added, and the relationship, if any, between the two groups remains unknown.

Proponents of an opposing theory arguing for at least some interbreeding between Neanderthals and modern humans, and the evolution of the latter group in areas outside of Africa, also presented new evidence. Researchers at the University of Tennessee in Knoxville studied a Neanderthal skull from the Near East and concluded there were anatomical similarities to modern humans in the region between 145,000 and 100,000 years ago. The similarities are strong enough to suggest genetic ties between the groups, the researchers said.

BRUCE BOWER, *"Science News"*

ARCHAEOLOGY

Varied archaeological discoveries in 1989 included everything from the wreckage of the World War II Nazi battleship, the *Bismark,* to the remains of what is believed to be the world's oldest beer brewery, dating back 5,400 years.

Eastern Hemisphere

Bismark. The World War II battleship *Bismark* was discovered sitting upright in more than 15,000 ft (4 572 m) of water about 600 mi (965.6 km) off the coast of France. Researchers led by Robert Ballard, the explorer who directed the expedition that found the sunken ocean liner *Titanic* in 1986, said the *Bismark* is preserved remarkably. Inspection of its remains with a deep-sea robot equipped with sonar, video, and still cameras suggested the most powerful Nazi battleship was scuttled by

© Sygma

Significant archaeological finds of 1989 included large amounts of gold bricks and coins, left, *from the SS "Central America" which sank off South Carolina in 1857, and a 2,000-year-old jug that probably was used to anoint the kings of Judah.*

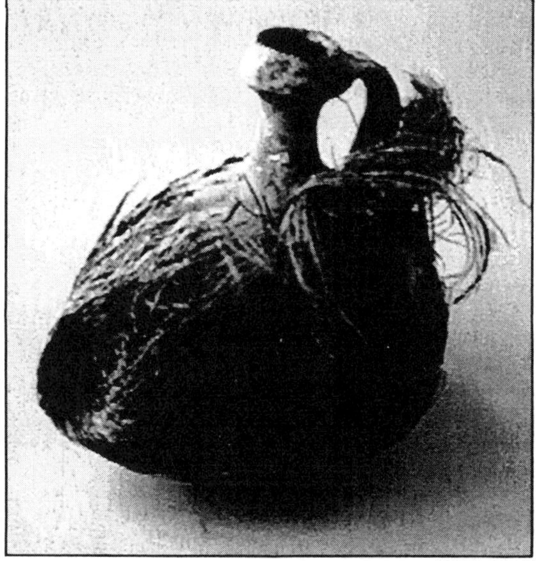

AP/Wide World

its own crew rather than sunk by British naval forces in a celebrated battle that took place on May 27, 1941. Ships that make it to the ocean floor in one piece, such as the *Bismark,* usually have been scuttled, Ballard said.

Mesopotamian City. One of the world's oldest cities was found in a desert in southern Iraq. Archaeologists said it was built 4,000 years ago in Mesopotamia to honor the ancient Babylonian god of death. Unlike other Mesopotamian cities under excavation, the new site was not reoccupied after its destruction in 1720 B.C. Called Mashkan-shapir, the walled city first was settled in 2050 B.C. and later became an important trade center. Clay fragments inscribed with cuneiform writing established the construction date of the city wall as 1843 B.C. Investigators also found the remains of a large palace, a religious quarter, a cemetery, several canals, and two harbors.

Early Cultivation. A microscopic analysis of stone blades found at prehistoric sites in the Middle East indicated they were used to harvest cereals for food between 12,000 and 6,000 years ago. Some kind of small-scale cultivation of cereals also may have occurred 12,000 years ago. The evidence supported the theory that agriculture originated gradually over several thousand years, rather than in a sudden revolution as some archaeologists have proposed. Polish and wear on the stone blades were similar to that observed on experimental stone blades used to harvest wild and cultivated cereals.

Ancient Oil. The discovery of a 2,000-year-old jug containing oil was announced by Israeli archaeologists. Chemical analysis of the still-fluid oil found it came from no plant that exists today. The scientists concluded that the oil probably was manufactured from the sap of the ancient persimmon plant. Persimmon oil, also known as balsam oil around the time of Christ, was used to anoint the kings of Judah as part of a ceremony marking their ascension to the throne. The single-handled jug is 5 inches (12.7 cm) in diameter and contained about 3 cubic inches (49 cm^3) of oil when it was found in a cave near the Dead Sea. It was wrapped in palm leaves and buried in a pit 3 ft (10 m) deep, suggesting it was a valued object that had been hidden carefully.

Egyptian Finds. An ancient Egyptian city on the banks of the Nile River, dating to about 5,400 years ago, yielded the remains of what may be the world's oldest beer brewery. Archaeologists found four large vats sitting on a raised platform that apparently had been heated slowly with fires. Analysis of a black residue on the inside of the various vats revealed it was the remains of a prehistoric beer made with wheat and a sugary syrup, probably date juice.

Another team of researchers discovered a well-preserved, 2,000-year-old mummy in an Egyptian cemetery. The mummy, which dates to a time of transition between Egyptian religion and Roman Christianity, lay in a finely carved hardwood coffin. An elaborately decorated gold death mask portraying a young woman covered its head and a plaster breastplate reached down to the mid-thigh.

Elizabethan Theater. A team of archaeologists working on the site of a razed building in south London discovered the foundations of the Rose Theater, the only Elizabethan theater unearthed in the city. The Rose was smaller than had been thought, about 70 ft (21 m) in diameter, with a seating capacity of approximately 2,000 when it was built in 1587. Shakespeare's first play, *Henry VI,* was performed on its stage in 1592. Preservationist groups are attempting to have the site listed as a national historic monument, although a development company intends to build high-rise offices over the archaeological remains.

Western Hemisphere

Nasca Site. Excavations at Cahuachi, a site long thought to have been a major city in Peru's Nasca culture that flourished from about 1 A.D. to 700 A.D., indicated it was a "now you see it, now you don't" metropolis. The layout of the site and the nature of pottery and other artifacts that were uncovered suggested the more than 40 mound-shaped dwellings at Cahuachi were used as temples, housing for priests, and storage facilities, not as domestic residences. Investigators said Cahuachi apparently was a sacred site inhabited mostly by priests and their assistants, springing to life during periodic pilgrimages to the spot by thousands of Nasca worshipers. Religious objects were traded in Cahuachi's expansive plazas, and elaborate ritual ceremonies were held in tribute to the priests and the gods they represented.

Maya Settlement. A coral island off the coast of Belize yielded evidence of shared cultural influences and widespread trading among Maya settlements more than 200 years after the collapse of the "classic" Maya civilization about 900 A.D. Archaeologists identified the remains of 49 structures at the island site. Large quantities of ceramics were unearthed that share the same designs, forms, and colors as a well-documented pottery tradition at a Maya site in Belize extending from 1150 A.D. to 1300 A.D. Researchers said the general style of potterymaking at the inland site probably was borrowed by the island potters.

Other items found at the island site, such as gray obsidian and jade, indicated extensive trading took place with mainland settlements. The coral island site may have been a trading port for larger Maya outposts.

Colonial Almshouse. The remains of what was probably New York City's first homeless shelter and workhouse for the poor, known as the Almshouse of 1735, were unearthed behind City Hall. An 8 sq ft (.7 m^2) excavation turned up foundation stones, a builder's trench, and plaster from an 18th-century structure. What may have been the cellar of the Almshouse is strewn with a pile of bricks. A human arm bone also was found among the bricks, suggesting the quick or violent destruction of the building. Other artifacts from the site include darning pins, brass needles, buttons, and a piece of lead-glazed yellow slipware with iron-oxide stripes that was made in the 1700s.

Shipwrecks. A ship from the early 1600s, possibly a Spanish galleon, was found off southwest Florida in 1,500 ft (457 m) of water. Much of the 120-ft (36.6-m)-long wooden vessel and her cargo is intact, according to the private ocean salvage group that made the discovery. A remote-controlled underwater vehicle videotaped dozens of large jars on the deck, as well as the ship's brass and silver bell, which was brought to the surface. The ship lies in the route used by the Spanish galleons as they returned, laden with gold, silver, and other valuables, from the New World to Spain.

Another salvage team, which found a shipwreck 200 mi (322 km) off the South Carolina coast in 1986, returned to the site and recovered large amounts of gold bars, bricks, and coins from the vessel. The wreck is that of the SS *Central America,* which sank in 1857 carrying fortunes made in the California Gold Rush to New York banks. An estimated three tons of gold were on the ship, which now lies in 8,000 ft (2 438 m) of water.

Tiwanaku Capital. The Tiwanaku civilization dominated a large area of South America for more than 1,000 years until its collapse about 1200 A.D. It is thought to have influenced importantly the Inca civilization. Excavations at a pyramid in the Tiwanaku empire's capital, located just south of La Paz, Bolivia, yielded nearly 50 hand-sized copper alloy clamps cut into adjoining pieces of stone to hold them together. Similar clamps have been found in ancient Greek and Egyptian stonework, but this is the only evidence of metal clamping in the Americas.

At several points along the base of another pyramid, which is largely covered by sediment, researchers uncovered the bones of dozens of dismembered human bodies. The bones were not cut or broken, suggesting the bodies were taken apart after death. The cause of death has not been determined.

BRUCE BOWER, *"Science News"*

ARCHITECTURE

While 1989 saw little of a predicted downturn in construction that would have limited seriously architects' ability to design new projects, architects found that their ever-growing numbers were leading them to compete for work ever more aggressively. American Institute of Architects (AIA) president Benjamin Brewer pointed out that the situation was bound to get much worse: Twice as many U.S. students were enrolled in the architectural schools as there were architects, proving, if nothing else, that the popular interest in architecture never had been higher. U.S. architects looked abroad for new work, including in Japan, which recently had opened its doors to their services. At home, architects competed in an ever-tighter marketplace. The new level of marketing acumen exhibited by architects was reflected in more sophisticated architectural brochures and advertisements that now rival the promotional materials of the companies that market consumer goods.

Designs. It could be argued that architects' competitive efforts to draw attention to themselves were reflected in the buildings they designed in 1989. Critic, author, and teacher Witold Rybczynski held that architects were using freely historic styles to make their buildings more individual and assertive without understanding how historic styles were meant originally to contribute to harmony. Rybczynski cited such historic examples of unity as Bath, England's crescents of similar townhouses, and recent examples such as Seaside, FL (where stringent controls on style, siting, and building size prevailed) as displaying an understanding of what classical "good manners" were meant to accomplish. Nonetheless, architects took issue with design controls in 1989. There was a widespread consensus that the United States' first major-scale design control ordinance, in San Francisco, was not leading always to the distinguished designs intended, but producing instead bland buildings that appeared to be designed by committee compromise.

New Buildings. Among the most controversial and, to some, the most assertive single building unveiled in 1989 was the addition to the Louvre in Paris by architect I. M. Pei that, although hiding much of the new space under the existing courtyard, included four clear-glass-sheathed pyramids sticking up in front of the historic façades. While defying stylistic categorization, the pyramids' shapes could be seen to have historic precedent. But critics pointed out that, while three of the pyramids, meant to bring light to spaces below, were of a respectfully small scale, the fourth, meant to serve as the Louvre's new main entrance, was almost as high as the original complex itself.

One architect who clearly bucked the trends toward Post-Modern styles was Paul Rudolph, whose idiosyncratic work (including Boston Government Service Center and Yale's school of architecture) made him well-known during the 1960s before he largely disappeared from view in the United States. Massive office and apartment buildings unveiled in Hong Kong, Singapore, and Jakarta (Indonesia) during the year proved he had been working all along to further his own special view of buildings. The new buildings appear to be composed of prefabricated units inserted into partially exposed structural frames.

Another notable building opening during the year, and reflecting divergent styles, was the massive Convention and Trade Center in Seattle by TRA & HNTB, Architects, in association with Dandjieva & Koenig. It was clearly in

The shoe box-shaped Morton H. Meyerson Symphony Center, the first symphony hall to be designed by I. M. Pei, 72, opened in Dallas in the fall. Another Pei project, an addition to the Louvre in Paris, also was unveiled in 1989.

© 1989 Nathaniel Liberman

American Institute of Architects

1989 Honor Award Winners

Martin May House Museum, Grand Rapids, MI; Tilton + Lewis Associates, Inc., Architects; restored 1909 Frank Lloyd Wright Prairie Style house "radiates with the energy and enthusiasm of Wright himself and feels more like a private house than a museum"

Reid House, Johns Island, SC; Clark & Menefee Architects; "a noble little farmhouse" with "a poignant quality, as though it were a proud remnant from a past civilization"

Seneca Lake Pier and Pavilion, Watkins Glen, NY; Chad Floyd, of Centerbrook, Architect; "a charming architectural gateway linking the past to the present"

Miller Park Plaza, Chattanooga, TN; Derthick, Henley & Wilkerson/Koetter, Kim & Associates, Architects; the first component of a five-block plaza, the glass pavilion is "a public meeting place that brings new vitality to this once lifeless block"

Central Housing Office Building, University of California, Irvine; Eric Owen Moss, Architect; "challenges our perceptions of form and materials . . . creating a building of powerful intensity"

Headquarters Library of the Clayton County Library System, Jonesboro, GA; Scogin Elam and Bray Architects; built close to both the Atlanta airport and a busy highway, "this startling building defies the notion that libraries are stuffy places"

Desert View Elementary School, Sunland Park, NM; Perkins & Will, Architect; "comfortable and durable, this building incorporates many elements of local architecture . . . with its expansive corridors, child-size scale, and brightly lit interiors, this school supports the idea that learning is a joy"

Delaware Aqueduct, Minisink, NY/Lackawaxen, PA; Beyer Blinder Belle, Architect; built in 1847, the earliest surviving work of John A. Roebling, this newly reopened suspension bridge retains the integrity of the original structure "through meticulous research and uncompromising craftsmanship"

Hansen House, Wilmette, IL; Hammond Beeby Babka, Inc., Architect; "understated, yet elegant, formal, and inviting, this handsome house is imaginative without upstaging its older neighbors"

Kings Point Pool Addition, Long Island, NY; Tod Wiliams Billie Tsien & Associates, Architect; "a building that is sculptural as well as functional; a place to exercise the soul as well as the body"

Folger Shakespeare Library, Washington, DC; Hartman-Cox Architects; new reading room's "classically inspired forms reinforce the historic significance of the library's collections, while the . . . freshness and vitality reflect the enduring importance of scholarly explorations in the modern world"

Martha's Vineyard Residence, MA; Steven Holl Architects; likened by the architect to an Indian dwelling built of whale skin and skeleton, "this taut, trim, jaunty structure is very much at home [at the seaside]"

the Modernist style with an artfully manipulated and segmented bulk concealing its true size. Ellerbee Beckett, a large, highly successful firm not noted for taking chances, was a surprising source of avant-garde architectural proposals, seemingly in the disjointed Deconstructivist style. The firm's plans for the Consolidated Terminal at Kennedy Airport in New York resembled a sloping steel plane emerging from the ground and about to take off.

Awards. The year's AIA gold medalist, Joseph Esherick, long has been noted for designs that fit into their contexts. Among these designs are the popular retail center, The Cannery, a remodeled industrial building in San Francisco that inspired a multitude of similar reuses of older buildings across the country. Indeed, many of the institute's 1989 honor awards for outstanding projects went to either restorations of existing buildings or projects meant to revitalize downtowns. A library on a highway was described by architects Scogin Elam and Bray as "a filling station for information" (*see* list above).

Other architects working in the most fashionable styles showed that they could use their talents to benefit down-to-earth concerns. Hammond Beeby and Babka produced a Post-Modern, "Wild-West" camp-retreat in Connecticut to provide a morale boost to children suffering from cancer. A city hall for Escondido, CA, by Pacific Associates demonstrated how "Mediterranean-Deco" could create senses of communal pride and familiarity for a California community that was lacking in them. While Keven Roche, John Dinkeloo & Associates tried to carry through the theme of the 1920s by replacing brick-and-slate buildings in New York City's Central Park Zoo, the project was praised much more roundly for freeing the animals from cages into more open communal environments meant to resemble original habitats.

That architects could help in the quest for housing for low- and moderate-income people —a notion often disputed by those who felt that architects only help to drive the costs of construction up—was proven by the results of an awards program sponsored by *Architectural Record* magazine. Of 103 entries submitted by U.S. architects, a dozen winners showed that housing built with high-level design guidance can be both more affordable and more liveable than housing built without it. While the Farmers Home Administration reportedly objected to John Mutlow Architects' angular, pastel-stucco units, thinking they looked like middle-income housing, the architects were able to produce the farm-worker housing in Saticoy, CA, for $33 per square foot. Architects/builders, the Mad Housers, built prefabricated wood sheds for the homeless in Atlanta, putting each unit up in approximately 17 minutes, a pace they used as a weapon in laying claim to vacant land belonging to both the city and private owners. Not all of the efforts to provide affordable housing were included in the awards programs. Architects Turner Associates and nonprofit developer, So Others Might Eat, helped Washington, DC, move toward housing its homeless in a former single-room-occupancy hotel. Architects across the country were involved in similar projects.

CHARLES K. HOYT, *"Architectural Record"*

© Raphael Woolmann/Gamma-Liaison

New President Carlos Saúl Menem rides in an inaugural parade that marks Argentina's first transfer of power from one democratically elected government to another in more than 60 years.

ARGENTINA

In 1989, Argentina elected a new president, restored relations with Britain on the consular level, and began to set its economic house in order.

Government and Politics. The principal candidates in the presidential election of May 14 were the Peronist (Justicialist) Carlos Saúl Menem (*see* BIOGRAPHY) and Eduardo Angeloz, candidate of the Radical Civic Union (UCR), the party of outgoing President Raúl Alfonsín. The predominant campaign issue, and Angeloz' main handicap, was the disastrous decline of the Argentine economy under UCR rule. Menem, who promised a "productive revolution" that would increase both output and consumption, won the election, 47% to 37%, with support from the unions, as well as the urban and rural poor. Peronists also won working majorities in both houses of congress.

Before Menem took office food riots forced the Alfonsín government to declare a state of siege on May 30. Reinforcements were rushed to police forces in the capital and other major cities to help put down the disturbances, in which 16 people lost their lives and about 3,000 were injured. Most of the rioters were from working-class and shantytown populations that were affected by falling real wages and hourly price increases. (Prices inflated by 70% in May alone.) To avert a worsening of the situation, the government distributed basic foodstuffs in impoverished areas and joined the Peronists in an 11-point communiqué defending constitutional order. A delegation of Radicals and Peronists headed for Washington in search of relief. Alfonsín agreed to an early resignation so that Menem could begin trying to deal with the economic crisis as soon as possible. Menem's assumption of office marked the first occasion in more than 60 years when one regularly elected president peacefully succeeded another in Argentina.

Economy. During the final months of Alfonsín's tenure the economy deteriorated rapidly. Both the World Bank and the International Monetary Fund (IMF) suspended payments on existing loans and refused further funding. A change of economy ministers failed to alter the situation. In May interest arrears on the $60 billion foreign debt approached $4 billion. Most banks and exchange houses were closed during the last ten days of the month, awaiting the establishment of a new exchange rate. A fixed rate of 175 australs to the dollar was accompanied by withdrawal limits and interest rates on savings deposits of up to 300% monthly. Hyperinflation reached 115% in June and was projected at an annual rate of 12,000%. Currency reserves were depleted and tax revenues covered only a third of public expenditures.

Unexpectedly, international bankers were encouraged by the incoming Peronist administration's economic stabilization plan. It attacked the root causes of Argentina's malaise, calling for a balanced budget through sharply higher fees for services—electricity, gasoline, water, and natural gas—provided by the state, a three-month wage and price freeze, heavy cuts in government spending, and privatization of most state-owned companies. Official subsidies to private companies would be eliminated, the central bank would be given autonomy, and foreign investment would receive treatment equal to domestic. The program was endorsed by industry, commerce, and labor. Interest rates on savings fell to 13% with Menem's inauguration (July 8), and five days later he devalued the currency by almost 54%, to 650 australs to the dollar. Inflation peaked at 197% in July. Talks formally resumed with the IMF for a standby credit of $1.5 billion, on July 26. A symbolic payment of $40 million toward back interest due international lending agencies was made in August. By September the inflation rate had plummeted to 6% and a 180-day emergency plan was passed by congress allowing Menem to halt all direct subsidies, cut in half the tax breaks provided certain industries, and adopt needed economic measures by executive decree.

Pressure for higher wages built up and a work-to-rule protest, lasting 48 hours, started on September 12 among engineers on the state-owned railway system. The privatization of state-owned enterprises was opposed adamantly by the General Labor Federation (CGT), under the leadership of erstwhile Menem supporter Saúl Ubaldini. He opposed Menem's neo-liberal economic plan, an austerity feature of which held wage increases to the rate of inflation and ended subsidies to labor. A CGT demand on August 30 for a hike in the $30 monthly minimum wage preceded the mid-October convention of the CGT in which Ubaldini was replaced by Güerino Andreoni. He represented unions operating in the private sector. Some 75,000 drivers of privately owned buses in Buenos Aires and other cities went on strike for a week in November. They called for a monthly increase of 52,000 australs in their basic monthly wage of 36,000 australs. To end the deadlock, government mediators ruled that wage increases could surpass government guidelines of 15% wage hikes for the final three months of 1989, but the higher labor costs could not be passed on to the public by the bus owners.

A law passed by congress September 1 expedited the privatization of more than 30 state-run enterprises. It was revealed on November 19 that the state-owned railways would be sold to company workers. The national airline was to go on sale before 1989 ended. Also, Menem ordered the state oil company to sell oil leases and exploitation rights to foreign buyers, including Texaco and Exxon. Telephone service was slated for early transfer. Menem appealed in November to creditor banks to invest in his country. As Argentina owed the banks $40 billion, plus an estimated $5.3 billion in back interest, they refused to talk about debt reduction until the Menem government had made a "good faith" payment on the arrears. A tax-reform package prepared with assistance from the IMF was to be ready in December. It would raise tax revenues from 16% to 24% of gross domestic product (GDP) in 1990.

Presidential Pardon. Menem's most controversial act was pardoning (October 7) 277 military men and civilians for their roles in human-rights abuses during the 1970s and the mismanagement of the Falklands War with Great Britain in 1982. An additional 174 officers were pardoned for various military uprisings against the Alfonsín government in 1987–88. Among the beneficiaries were 64 former guerrilla activists. Menem defended his controversial decree by saying it would reduce military-civilian tensions. While the pardon was pending, 30,000 people marched through downtown Buenos Aires in protest against it.

Foreign Relations. Argentina and Great Britain agreed on October 19 to resume consular ties and to lift trade and financial barriers in existence since the 1982 war. Air and sea links would be restored between Buenos Aires and London. Britain would permit entry of Argentine commercial vessels into a 150-mi (241-km) exclusion zone around the disputed Malvinas (Falkland) Islands without prior permission. Also, Britain would expedite cooperation between Argentina and the European Community. Argentina formally ended its state of hostility with Britain. Future disputes between the two countries were to be resolved peacefully. A working group was established to monitor military issues. The reestablishment of direct diplomatic relations was expected to follow a resumption of peace talks in February 1990. Argentine claims to the Malvinas were not discussed during the October parley.

As a consequence of Menem's disposition to normalize relations with Great Britain, the United States resumed military sales to Argentina, and joint naval exercises between Argentine and U.S. squadrons were held in the South Atlantic in September.

Argentina was said to be linked with Iraq in a joint venture to develop a medium-range missile. (Egypt reportedly dropped out of the project.) Some observers worried that Iraq could use the missile to launch chemical weapons and eventually nuclear warheads.

LARRY L. PIPPIN, *University of the Pacific*

ARGENTINA • Information Highlights

Official Name: Argentine Republic.
Location: Southern South America.
Area: 1,068,297 sq mi (2 766 890 km²).
Population (mid-1989 est.): 31,900,000.
Chief Cities (1980 census): Buenos Aires, the capital, 2,922,829; Cordoba, 970,570; Rosario, 794,127.
Government: *Head of state and government,* Carlos Saúl Menem, president (took office July 8, 1989). *Legislature*—Senate and Chamber of Deputies.
Monetary Unit: Austral (655.0 australs equal U.S.$1, Dec. 6, 1989).
Gross National Product (1987 U.S.$): $74,300,-000,000.
Economic Indexes (1988): *Consumer Prices* (1980 = 100), all items, 2,626,430; food, 2,630,301. *Industrial Production* (1987, 1980 = 100), 93.
Foreign Trade (1988 U.S.$): *Imports,* $5,322,000,000; *exports,* $9,137,000,000.

AP/Wide World

Arizona Gov. Rose Mofford, a Democrat, holds up a bill she signed that reinstates Martin Luther King Day as a state holiday in Arizona. Former Gov. Evan Mecham, a Republican, created a great controversy when he had rescinded the holiday in 1987.

ARIZONA

Arizona remained a state in turmoil in 1989, as an impeached governor sought to return to office, the economy continued in a major slump, and disputes in the Navajo nation escalated into violence.

Politics and Legislation. Former Gov. Evan Mecham unsuccessfully challenged in court his 1988 impeachment by the state House of Representatives on charges of obstruction of justice and misuse of a state protocol fund, but he also announced he would run for office again. Meanwhile, Republican Jane Dee Hull was elected the first woman speaker of the Arizona House, as the legislature grappled with a chronic budget shortfall of several hundred million dollars. The legislature also made plans to revise the state's tax code early in 1990 and voted to create an official state holiday to honor Dr. Martin Luther King, Jr. The measure, which Mecham had opposed, was passed in a special session on September 21.

Economy. Arizona's economy remained in a major slump. Only the copper industry, buoyed by high world prices and a reduced labor force, did well. Bankruptcy filings continued to set new records, retail and office vacancies reached unprecedented levels, and banks saw increases in nonperforming loans of more than 70%. In September the U.S. Department of Housing and Urban Development ordered its appraisers to lower their evaluations in Maricopa County (Phoenix) saying ". . . there is an oversupply of housing, with marketing time exceeding six months and values declining."

The most spectacular economic debacle involved the bankruptcy filing of Charles Keating, Jr.'s American Continental Corporation on April 13. Keating long had been active in right-wing politics, with particular emphasis on banning sexually explicit material. Keating's downfall led his antiporn group, Citizens for Decency Through Law, to change its name to the Children's Legal Foundation. Federal regulators on September 15 brought civil-racketeering charges against Keating in conjunction with the collapse of American Continental's Lincoln Savings and Loan in California.

Navajo Turmoil. There was turmoil on the Navajo reservation over the leadership of Peter MacDonald, who had been chairman of the tribe—except for one four-year term out of office—since 1971. On February 17 the Tribal Council voted to suspend MacDonald pending resolution of charges he had accepted massive

ARIZONA • Information Highlights

Area: 114,000 sq mi (295 260 km^2).
Population (July 1, 1988): 3,489,000.
Chief Cities (July 1, 1986 est.): Phoenix, the capital, 894,070; Tucson, 358,850; Mesa, 251,430; Tempe, 136,480; Glendale, 125,820.
Government (1989): *Chief Officers*—governor, Rose Mofford (D); secretary of state, Jim Shumway (D). *Legislature*—Senate, 30 members; House of Representatives, 60 members.
State Finances (fiscal year 1988): *Revenue,* $6,883,000,000; *expenditure,* $6,319,000,000.
Personal Income (1988): $52,233,000,000; per capita, $14,970.
Labor Force (June 1989): *Civilian labor force,* 1,729,000; *unemployed,* 98,400 (5.7% of total force).
Education: *Enrollment* (fall 1987)—public elementary schools, 413,000; public secondary, 160,000; colleges and universities, 237,233. *Public school expenditures* (1987–88), $1,929,000,000 ($3,408 per pupil).

kickbacks in tribal business dealings. The allegations had been made before a U.S. Senate Select Committee on Indian Affairs that met in January to investigate charges of corruption in tribal governments.

On July 20 a crowd of between 200 and 300 MacDonald loyalists, some armed with clubs, gathered to break into the tribe's offices and oust the interim government. Navajo police officers on the scene were threatened with citizen's arrest. In an ensuing melee, shots were fired. When it was over, two MacDonald supporters lay dead, and between nine and 11 others, including three policemen, were injured. In the aftermath each side blamed the other, but MacDonald said there would be more violence unless he were reinstated. This led the interim tribal government to hire a former member of the U.S. Army's antiterrorist Delta Force to provide security and training for the tribal police.

PETER GOUDINOFF
The University of Arizona

ARKANSAS

Politics dominated the Arkansas scene in 1989. The General Assembly convened for its 77th session, considered some 2,000 proposals, and passed more than 600 bills.

Legislative Session. Key items among the legislation passed included a state version of the federal "taxpayers' bill of rights" to bring the state's procedures for collecting personal income tax in line with federal regulations, and a bill to require individuals to undergo an eye examination before renewing their drivers' licenses. The state minimum wage was increased to equal the federal minimum, and a new juvenile-justice system was established.

A number of bills passed that related to education. Kindergarten was made mandatory for five-year-olds; a minimum teacher's salary was set at $16,000; a literacy corps was established to teach adults to read; and an "accountability office," without funding, was created to issue annual performance reports on every school. School districts whose students performed below standards on national tests were required to merge with districts that have met the standards, and parents whose children failed minimum competency at the third-, sixth-, or eighth-grade levels were required to attend a conference with school officials. Parents or guardians who knowingly contributed to their child(ren)'s excessive absences could be fined a maximum of $500 per complaint.

Considerable discussion was directed toward what the Assembly failed to accomplish in 1989. A proposed one-cent sales-tax increase to raise more than $200 million in new revenue failed to be enacted. Another major tax proposal, a seven cents-per-gallon levy on retail gasoline sales, also was defeated, as was a bill to set criteria for establishing school-based health clinics.

Special Sessions and Politics. Action by the Assembly became embroiled in controversy when legislators ignored a ruling by the state's attorney general and passed a series of revenue bills by less than the three-fourths majority mandated by the state constitution. Members of the state Supreme Court refused to rule on the matter because of possible conflict of interest (the legislature appropriates funds for the court), and Gov. Bill Clinton was forced to appoint a special commission to decide the issue. That body ruled the Assembly's action unconstitutional, and legislators were convened in a special session in June to reenact the original proposals.

The governor also called two other special sessions—one to deal primarily with funding for a school-desegregation settlement in Pulaski County, the other to focus on a "war on drugs" program. The latter failed when the Assembly did not fund the program.

The state's three-term Democratic Congressman Tommy F. Robinson from the 2d District switched to the Republican Party and announced his candidacy for governor in 1990.

Economy. Arkansas' economic outlook improved despite millions of dollars in damage to the agricultural industry. A winter snowstorm damaged the poultry industry, a freeze severely reduced fruit production, and an extended rainy season hampered soybean and cotton farmers. A number of savings and loan associations, including the state's largest, went into receivership.

Tyson Foods, Inc., the nation's largest chicken processor, based in Springdale, AR, acquired Holly Farms Corp. in June for about $1.29 billion, after a long and tangled takeover battle.

C. FRED WILLIAMS
University of Arkansas at Little Rock

ARKANSAS • Information Highlights

Area: 53,187 sq mi (137 754 km²).
Population (July 1, 1988): 2,395,000.
Chief Cities (1980 census): Little Rock, the capital (July 1, 1986 est.), 181,030; Fort Smith, 71,626; North Little Rock, 64,288; Pine Bluff, 56,636.
Government (1989): *Chief Officers*—governor, Bill Clinton (D); lt. gov., Winston Bryant (D). *General Assembly*—Senate, 35 members; House of Representatives, 100 members.
State Finances (fiscal year 1988): *Revenue,* $3,958,000,000; *expenditure,* $3,570,000,000.
Personal Income (1988): $29,263,000,000; per capita, $12,219.
Labor Force (June 1989): *Civilian labor force,* 1,195,900; *unemployed,* 100,300 (8.4% of total force).
Education: *Enrollment* (fall 1987)—public elementary schools, 307,000; public secondary, 130,000; colleges and universities, 79,273. *Public school expenditures* (1987–88), $1,071,671,000 ($2,481 per pupil).

AP/Wide World

Col. John Williams (right), *chief of the U.S. team verifying Soviet compliance with the U.S.-USSR ban on intermediate-range weapons, presents Soviet Maj. Igor Kirichenko with a document certifying that the last Soviet SS-23 was destroyed in October 1989.*

ARMS CONTROL AND DISARMAMENT

Coincident with the remarkable changes occurring in the Communist world (*see* feature article, page 24) were substantial changes in the areas of arms control and disarmament, particularly between the Soviet Union and the United States.

Unilateral Reductions in the USSR. Late in the year the official Communist Party newspaper, *Pravda,* announced that the Soviet Union had, in 1989, unilaterally reduced certain of its military forces by significant numbers, following a plan established by President Mikhail Gorbachev. According to *Pravda* 235,000 troops and officers were released from active duty, along with the retirement of some 7,000 tanks, nearly 3,000 artillery pieces, and 735 aircraft.

While Western analysts were uncertain if the Soviet numbers were correct, they generally did agree that the USSR had begun an impressive reduction of its deployed military forces in Eastern Europe. Whether the Soviets would continue—as Gorbachev indicated—to reduce also the military forces located inside the Soviet Union remained an unanswered question.

Although American military officials and political observers expressed their pleasure over the Soviet actions, some noted that the highly visible activity might not decrease by much the potential Soviet military threat to the NATO countries. What concerned them was that the apparent reduction in capability might be gained back in terms of the modernization and restructuring of the forces that remained. This concern was expressed by the senior Republican on the House Armed Services Committee, William Dickson of Alabama, who said, "Make no mistake, the more armor the Soviets pull out of Europe, the better. . . . However, the threat may not decrease if the result is a 'leaner and meaner' Red Army." Another expression of both optimism and caution regarding the Soviet actions was issued by Congressman Les Aspin (D-WI), chairman of the House Armed Services Committee. He said late in the year, "Soviet military withdrawals from Eastern Europe are occurring on schedule, if not quite as advertised. That's very important. But we don't see as much evidence that they're actually reducing forces in the western Soviet Union as promised, and that's important too."

Bilateral Reductions. On March 9, 1989, the Conventional Armed Forces negotiations began in Vienna. The focus was upon troop strength and conventional weapons such as tanks and artillery pieces. Naval forces, chemical weapons, and tactical nuclear weapons were excluded. Nations in attendance were the 16 members of the North Atlantic Treaty Organization (NATO) and the seven members of the Warsaw Pact. Much of the impetus for the negotiations came from President Gorbachev's "New Thinking"—suggestions that Soviet foreign and military policies be reorganized in accord with the demands of a changing world. This stems from long-standing U.S. insistence that the Soviets prune their forces in Eastern Europe down to a level where they could defend against a NATO attack, but not threaten an attack against NATO. Also important are concerns held by both the Western and the Communist nations about the fiscal drains on their national economies caused by the maintenance of large standing armies.

The U.S. conventional arms proposal, offered by President Bush, consisted of the following points—a ceiling of 20,000 tanks, 28,000 armored troop carriers, and 24,000 artillery pieces each for NATO and for the Warsaw countries; reduction in the number of U.S. and Soviet troops stationed outside their respective national boundaries to 275,000 each; and a 15% reduction in combat aircraft and helicopters on both sides. A 1992–93 deadline would be set for these reductions to take place. At year's end the negotiators were busy attempting to meld together into an acceptable disarmament package the U.S. proposals, those from the NATO nations, and the suggestions from the Warsaw Pact countries.

Chemical Weapons. Diplomats from more than 140 nations signed a declaration condemning the use of chemical weapons. The declaration, issued at a special UN conference in Paris in January, also called for a greater worldwide effort to complete a treaty that bans the development, production, and possession of chemical weapons. Current international law—the Geneva Protocol of 1925, which has been ratified by more than 100 countries—only bans the use of chemical weapons.

On September 25, President Bush addressed the United Nations General Assembly and proposed that the United States and the Soviet Union join in cutting back their stockpiles of chemical weapons by 80% as an initial step toward entering into an international ban on chemical weapons. The next day, Soviet Foreign Minister Eduard A. Shevardnadze welcomed the president's plan, but then went further and urged that the United States join the USSR in stopping the production of binary agents, which comprise the most advanced arms in both nations' chemical arsenal. (Binary chemical agents are inert when stored separately, but produce a lethal compound when mixed together.) After several months of hesitation, Bush appeared to agree with the Soviet position when he and Gorbachev met at the Malta summit in early December. The United States and the USSR also agreed to a Memorandum of Understanding calling for the exchange of data concerning the chemical weapons production and storage facilities of each nation, and a verification experiment to validate that the data furnished by each side is accurate. The latter proposal, patterned after the on-site inspection provisions of the Intermediate Nuclear Forces Treaty negotiated by former President Ronald Reagan and President Gorbachev in 1988, requires both nations to open up some of their chemical weapons facilities to the other nation's inspectors.

START. Another round of the Strategic Arms Reduction Talks (START) negotiations began in June in Geneva with the United States and the USSR edging closer to agreement. By the fall both sides had agreed to the principle of equal reductions in their strategic offensive forces, phased into place over a seven-year period. Agreement also was reached on the proposal that neither nation could possess more than a total of 1,600 strategic nuclear weapons delivery systems, such as ICBMs, SIBMs, and strategic bombers; and that these delivery systems could carry no more than 6,000 warheads. Heavy ICBMs were limited to no more than ten warheads each, with 154 such missiles being allowed.

Although the details remain to be worked out, U.S. and USSR officials agreed that each would verify the compliance of the other to the START terms by various types of on-site inspections. These include visual observation of the destruction of excess weapons, continuous monitoring of the "perimeter and portals of critical production facilities," short-notice inspection of weapons deployment and storage sites, and inspections of sites where a party considers that secret production, storage, repair, or deployment may be occurring.

Some disagreement remained over the linkage between strategic offensive weapons limitation and the building of space defense weapons, such as the U.S. Strategic Defense Initiative. But the announcement by the Soviets that the Krasnoyarsk radar site, long contended by the United States to be a violation of the 1972 ABM Treaty, was in fact a violation, and that it would be corrected, helped allay U.S. concerns.

Open Skies. In December the 16 members of the NATO alliance endorsed President Bush's proposal that unarmed Warsaw Pact aircraft be permitted to fly over NATO territory in search of suspicious military activity. Reciprocal action by the Soviet Union was expected to follow during 1990.

Nuclear Weapons Proliferation. Worldwide interest in the arms control and disarmament activity of the two military superpowers overshadowed a persistent arms problem for which there appears to be no immediate solution. The problem is that to the five countries which first obtained nuclear weapons—the United States, the USSR, Great Britain, France, and China—must be added several nations which may be building such forces clandestinely. In addition to India, which detonated a "peaceful nuclear explosive" in 1974, and Israel, which many observers believe has possessed a stockpile of atomic bombs for more than a decade, there is Pakistan. Although Pakistani Prime Minister Benazir Bhutto assured the United States that her nation does not possess, nor does it intend to make, atomic weapons, President Bush noted that while Pakistan is not thought to possess such weapons now, "Pakistan has continued its efforts to develop its unsafeguarded nuclear program." Another potential candidate for nuclear weapons status is the Republic of South Africa.

ROBERT M. LAWRENCE
Colorado State University

ART

Auction prices soared upward in an ever expanding market during 1989, while museums, in general, continued their retreat from blockbuster exhibitions and concentrated more on scholarly shows. Although there were no major new museum openings, renovations were completed and multimillion-dollar museum projects were begun or announced.

The accelerating market can be explained by the greater number of buyers from all over the world and the participation of the newly rich playing in a dwindling market of top quality works. Although the market is international, it is clear that Americans are the major sellers of art today and the Japanese are the major buyers. Buyers have become increasingly anonymous as bids are made over the telephone and buying art now is perceived as an investor's game as well as a collector's game. Art exhibitions, higher art prices, and the building and expanding of museums probably will increase over the years ahead. There even has been speculation that the price of a single painting could reach $100 million.

The interrelationship between shows, auctions, and expanding museums becomes obvious when it is noted that retrospectives push auction prices up and spiraling auction prices create a greater interest in art and a larger viewing public. This in turn generates a need to build and expand museums. Art exhibitions, in some sense, have become a new art form. Not only are the shows well-researched, they are packaged beautifully as well. However, higher auction prices and greater numbers at museum exhibitions will not necessarily create a more discriminating viewer.

Auctions. The highest priced painting for 1989, and the second-highest priced painting ever, was Pablo Picasso's 1905 "Pierrette's Wedding," which brought $51.3 million at the November 30 sale at the Drouot auction house in Paris. It was purchased by Tomonori Tsurumaki, a Japanese real-estate developer. In Sotheby's May 9 sale, Picasso's "Yo Picasso" sold for $47.85 million, followed later by "Au Lapin Agile," which sold for $40.7 million. Two other Picassos sold for $26.4 million and $18.7 million.

The top price paid for an old master painting was at the May 31 sale at Christie's when the hammer fell at $35.2 million for "The Halberdier," an oil painting by the 16th-century Mannerist painter, Jacopo da Carucci, known as Pontormo. Purchased by George Goldner for the Getty Museum in Malibu, CA, the price more than tripled the previous record at auctions for old master paintings. The portrait, a fashionable young condottiere—in short, a dandy—whose identity as Cosimo I de Medici is in question—had been at the Frick Collection in New York since the late 1960s. Sales of other old master paintings broke records but none came close to the Pontormo. The most popular paintings selling for $4 million and below were 17th-century Dutch paintings, genre paintings, and still life paintings—especially flower paintings.

© Sotheby's

At a May 9 auction at New York City's Sotheby's, an unidentified buyer purchased "Yo Picasso," Pablo Picasso's 1901 blue-period portrait, for $47.85 million.

The highlight of 19th-century European painting sales was a landscape by Theodore Gericault entitled "Landscape with Aqueduct," acquired at Sotheby's June 1 sale for the Metropolitan Museum at a price of $2.42 million. The painting fetched twice its presale estimate, but it was a superb acquisition for the Metropolitan Museum because Gericault is not well represented there.

The 19th-century American art market continued to do well. Two records were set with the sale of Frederick Edwin Church's painting "Home by the Lake," a Catskill mountain scene which sold for $8.25 million at Sotheby's May 2 auction, and Frederick Remington's sculpture, "Coming Through the Rye," which sold for $4.4 million at Sotheby's May 23 sale. Prices also rose for painter Martin Johnson Heade and the American Impressionists.

The Impressionist and modern art market remained the top market for paintings in 1989 even though no painting brought the $53.9 million recorded by Van Gogh's "Irises" in 1987. Of the 12 Impressionist and Post-Impressionist paintings that were sold for more than $10 million, two were by Manet (his "Rue Mosnier, Paris, Decorated with Flags on June 30, 1878," purchased for $26.4 million by the Getty Museum at Christie's November 14 sale, broke records for the artist); three by Renoir; two by Monet; one by Cézanne; two by Gauguin (his Tahitian landscapes with figures, entitled

"Mata Mau," sold for $24.2 million); and two by Van Gogh.

With the exception of Picasso's paintings, modern paintings did not match the Impressionist and Post-Impressionist paintings in price. However, records were broken by individual artists. Names include Édouard Vuillard ($7.7 million), Maurice de Vlaminck ($7.5 million), Piet Mondrian ($9.6 million), Joan Miró ($9.4 million), Giorgio de Chirico ($5.3 million), and the sculptor Constantin Brancusi ($8.25 million).

In the contemporary art market, the top auction price went to Willem de Kooning's "Interchange," for $20.7 million (a record for de Kooning) at Sotheby's November 8 sale. Coming in second was Jackson Pollock's "Number 8, 1950" for $11.35 million. This was followed by Francis Bacon's "TriptYch, May-June" which sold for $4.07 million, and Franz Kline's "Scudera" for $2.86 million. One important factor in the record-breaking prices was increased participation by Japanese and European buyers and their great demand for "blue-chip" paintings, or those considered to be of long-term value—the major works by the biggest names of the 1950s, 1960s, as well as the 1980s. These artists include Alexander Calder, Roy Lichtenstein, Robert Rauchenberg, Andy Warhol, Tom Wesselman, Cy Twomley, Jean-Michel Basquait, Eric Fischel, David Salle, Julien Schnabel, and Ed Ruschia.

Undervalued markets, such as antiquities and Chinese art, continued to rise. One of the reasons for the rising Chinese art market is that the Chinese are buying back their own works of art. Jade and 18th-century Qing porcelain made for the court were in demand. In painting, a record was set with the sale of a 14th-century handscroll for $1.87 million.

The Latin American art market also rose. The top lot in Christie's May 17 sale was Fernando Botero's "Princess Margareta After Velasquez," selling for $400,000, followed by Rufino Tamayo's "Hombre Asombrado de la Aviacion" at $385,000.

Exhibitions. Major museum exhibitions of 1989 were quite varied, ranging over Chinese, Islamic, old master, 19th-century American, Impressionist, Post-Impressionist, modern, and contemporary styles. The emphasis was on scholarship and educational value as opposed to showmanship. It was a quality year for museum exhibitions.

Continued interest in China was reflected in a major show entitled "Masterworks of the Ming and Qing: Painting from the Forbidden City," which started in Honolulu, moved to Atlanta, Cleveland, and Minneapolis, and

Topkapi Saray Library, Istanbul
Courtesy, Los Angeles County Museum of Art

Exhibits of note in 1989 included one of Islamic works shown in Washington and Los Angeles and a Goya show in Boston and New York. The former featured "Prince Baysunghur Seated in a Garden" (1429), left, *and the latter, "The Duke of Osuna and His Family,"* below.

Scala/Art Resource

Collection of the Nelson-Atkins Museum of Art

"Palisades," left, *was part of the Thomas Hart Benton centennial exhibit that opened at the Nelson-Atkins Museum of Art in Kansas City, MO, in April. "Nature Abhors a Vacuum,"* below, *an acrylic on canvas, was on view at the much-discussed Helen Frankenthaler retrospective that opened at New York's Museum of Modern Art in June.*

ended up at New York's Metropolitan Museum in the fall.

Islamic art was represented splendidly by the exhibition "Timur and the Princely Vision: Persian Art and Culture in the 15th Century," which traveled from the Sackler Gallery at the Smithsonian to the Los Angeles County Museum of Art in the fall.

Old master European painting was represented handsomely by four outstanding painters—two Spaniards, one Italian, and one Dutchman. One of the most beautiful shows was the silverly toned exhibition of works by Francesco Goya, including both his extraordinary prints and drawings, as well as his enormous portraits, entitled "Goya and the Spirit of Enlightenment." Organized by the Prado in Madrid, the show started at the Boston Museum of Fine Arts in the winter and traveled to the Metropolitan Museum in the spring. Another Spanish painter, Diego Velasquez, court painter to Philip II in the 17th century, was represented by 38 works mainly from the Prado. Exhibited at the Metropolitan in the fall, the show was the first concentrated display of the artist's greatest paintings. Also at the Metropolitan Museum from November 1989 to January 1990 were 125 works by the 18th-century Venetian painter Canaletto, the first comprehensive U.S. exhibition of this painter. Finally, works of the 17th-century Dutch portrait painter Franz Hals were displayed with 60 paintings and oil sketches at the National Gallery of Art in the fall. The first major U.S. exhibit for Hals, the show would travel to London in 1990.

Photo by Steven Sloman/Courtesy, Andre Emmerich Gallery

American 19th-century and early 20th-century paintings by such diverse talents as Frederick Edwin Church, Mary Cassatt, and Thomas Hart Benton were exhibited. Hudson River landscape painter Church was represented by 50 easel paintings—including his large-scale masterpieces, "Niagara," "The Heart of the Andes," and "Icebergs"—in a show curated by Franklin Kelly of the Corcoran that opened at the National Gallery in October. Also, opening at the National Gallery in June were 115 works by Mary Cassatt which included preliminary drawings, early states, and color variations of final states of her color

Salvador Dali (1904–89)

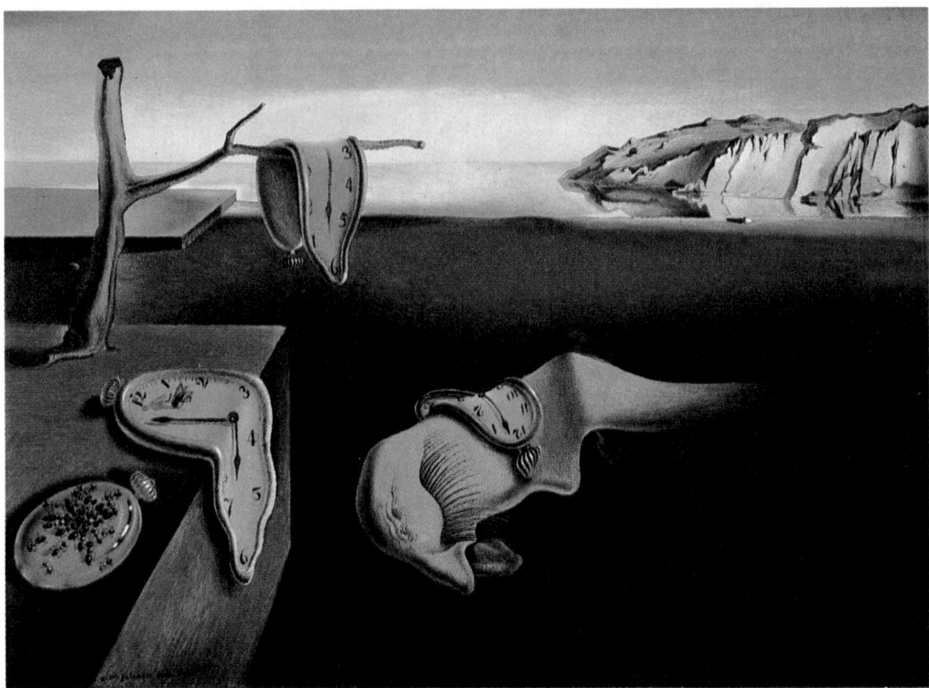

Collection, The Museum of Modern Art, New York, Given anonymously

Spain's Salvador Dali, a pioneer of European surrealism, died in Figueras, Spain, Jan. 23, 1989. "The Persistence of Memory" (above), *completed in 1931, is one of his best-known works.*

AP/Wide World

One of the most celebrated and controversial artists of the 20th century, Salvador Dali was recognized as much for his outrageous personality as for his influential and often brilliant paintings. Dali, a pioneer of European surrealism in the late 1920s and 1930s, died Jan. 23, 1989, at the age of 84. His paintings of exotic and bizarre images, drawn, he believed, from the unconscious, were rendered with a meticulous attention to detail that made even the most fantastic scenes appear convincingly real. Although Dali's early brilliance tended to give way to increasingly commercial work in later years, his penchant for self-promotion enhanced the popularity of his art. A 1980 retrospective organized by Paris' Pompidou Center attested to Dali's popularity and the diversity of his work. The show featured 168 paintings, 219 drawings, 38 objects, some 200 documents, as well as a "Dali environment."

Background. Salvador Dali was born in Figueras, Spain, on May 11, 1904. The young Dali showed a talent for art early on, and began study at the National School of Fine Arts in Madrid at the age of 17. Due to a similar talent for getting into trouble, he was expelled five years later.

After experimenting with various artistic styles, Dali traveled to Paris in 1928, and soon joined the surrealist movement. The surrealists rejected logic, looking instead for inspiration in madness and dream images. Dali discovered that with this style, he could combine his interest in picturing subconscious ideas and hallucinations with the exacting techniques he preferred. A 1929 film he produced in collaboration with the director Luis Buñuel, *Un Chien Andalou,* attempted to reach the unconscious mind through graphic images of violence. Although the violence of the film caused public protests, Dali's paintings won wider and wider acceptance. His best-known work, *The Persistence of Memory* (1931), became almost universally recognized.

After his first one-man show in New York in 1933, Dali became a familiar figure in U.S. art circles, as well as one of the world's richest and most popular artists. Always experimenting and never loyal to one idea or movement, he announced in 1938 that he would begin painting in the style of the 16th-century Italian mannerists. Feeling betrayed, the surrealists formally ejected him from their movement in the early 1940s.

Dali, undaunted, continued producing works in what he dubbed the "paranoic-critical system," claiming that he trained himself to hallucinate and then paint the images he saw. He also launched a career in the United States, where he moved in 1940, undertaking numerous commercial projects.

A Catholic, Dali turned to religion for artistic inspiration in the late 1940s. Many of his later works were depictions of religious themes. Despite the popularity of such paintings as *Sacrament of the Last Supper* (1955), critics decried them as "bland" and "saccharine." Manipulative advisers and his own greed combined to cause a tangle of problems in his later years. Many of his copyrights were sold, defrauding him of much income, and he was said to have signed thousands of sheets of blank paper, giving rise to false lithographs on which collectors have spent millions.

Dali's wife Gala, whom he had married in 1935, died in 1982. Two years later, the flamboyant and eccentric artist was burned severely in an electrical fire, and after that was wheelchair-bound. He was buried in the inner court of the Dali Museum which had opened at the artist's birthplace in Figueras in 1974.

prints. The Cassatt show traveled to Boston in September and to the Williams College Museum in November. Regionalist painter and teacher of Jackson Pollack, Thomas Hart Benton, was featured in a centennial exhibition of 85 canvases that opened at the Nelson-Atkins Museum in April, traveled to the Detroit Institute of Art in the summer, and went on to the Whitney Museum in New York in November. Its final destination was the Los Angeles County Museum of Art in 1990.

Impressionist, Post-Impressionist, and modern art held its own with shows of scholarly merit such as: "Cézanne: the Early Years 1859–1872" at the National Gallery; "Masterpieces of Impressionism and Post-Impressionism" at the Philadelphia Museum of Art; and "Picasso and Braque: Pioneering Cubism" at the Museum of Modern Art (MoMA).

One of the most talked-about contemporary painting exhibitions was the Helen Frankenthaler retrospective that included 40 paintings from 1952 until the present. Organized by E. A. Carmean, Jr., director of the Modern Art Museum of Fort Worth, it opened at New York's MoMA in June, traveled to Fort Worth in November, and would continue on to the Los Angeles County Museum of Art in 1990. Also opening at the Modern in New York in February was Andy Warhol's retrospective that included paintings from the last three decades—the most comprehensive Warhol show since a 1988 Stockholm retrospective. Curated by Kynaston McShine, the show also traveled to the Art Institute of Chicago. Another major show, of 60 works by British Expressionist painter Francis Bacon, considered to be one of the artistic giants of his time, opened at the Hirshhorn. The first U.S. overview in 25 years for this painter, the show would travel to the Los Angeles County Museum in 1990.

Two widely different but interesting contemporary group shows were on view in New York at the Guggenheim and the Whitney. In February the Guggenheim offered "Refigured Painting: The German Image 1960–80," a comprehensive examination of the last three decades of German painting. "Image World: Art and Media Culture" opened at the Whitney Museum in November. Demonstrating the influence of the mass media on contemporary art, 100 works, including paintings, photographs, and videos from Warhol in the 1960s to Barbara Kruger and Jeff Koons in the 1980s, were shown.

Museums. Although 1989 did not see the completion of a major new museum, there were expansions and the announcements of upcoming multimillion-dollar museum projects, as well as donations of money and paintings. One relatively modest but beautiful completion was the 17-acre (7-ha) Henry Moore Sculpture Gar-

Displayed in New York and Chicago, an Andy Warhol retrospective was one of the year's more popular art exhibits, expecially among pop-art fans.

The Museum of Modern Art, New York

den, adjacent to the Nelson-Atkins Museum in Kansas City, which opened in June. Twelve monumental bronzes were placed in a $2.5 million park designed by architects Daniel Urban Kiley and Jacquelin T. Robertson.

Completed projects included the Chrysler Museum in Norfolk, VA, which reopened in February after doubling its museum space in a $13.5 million renovation. In September the Phillips Collection in Washington opened with the completion of its two-year, $7.8 million renovated wing.

A major new museum project is the $55 million Seattle Museum, a five-story postmodern structure to be designed by Venturi, Rauch and Scott Brown of Philadelphia and scheduled to open in 1991. (The Seattle Museum also received a sizable National Endowment for the Humanities [NEH] grant for installation of its Asian collection.) Robert Venturi also will design an $11 million, 33,000-sq-ft (3 066-m^2) addition to the La Jolla Museum of Contemporary Art, scheduled for completion in 1992. The Guggenheim Museum in New York began construction of its controversial $18 million tower addition to the 1959 Frank Lloyd Wright building. The 28,000-sq-ft (2 600-m^2) annex, scheduled to be completed in the fall of 1991, was designed by Gwathmey, Siegel and Associates. In Fort Worth a planned $8 million two-part addition to the Kimball Museum is to be designed by Romaldo Giurgola. The original museum was designed by Louis Kahn in 1972, a mentor to Giurgola.

Gifts to museums in 1989 included $20 million to the Dallas Museum of Fine Arts for expansion from Nancy Hamon, a Dallas philanthropist. The Metropolitan Museum of Art received $15 million from Walter H. Annenberg, the publisher. He also gave $5 million to the National Gallery of Art in Washington and $5 million to the Philadelphia Museum of Art. Iris Canton, a trustee of the Brooklyn Museum, and her husband Gerald, gave $3.5 million to complete the Brooklyn Museum's 460-seat state-of-the-art auditorium, scheduled for the spring of 1990.

A few museums acquired major new works and even entire art collections in 1989, despite the change in tax laws which no longer allows the donor to use his gift as a tax deduction. James Michener gave his collection of 350 works of art to the Huntington Art Gallery at the University of Texas. Estimated to be worth $12 million, it includes paintings by Thomas Hart Benton, Philip Guston, Franz Kline, and Morris Louis. Michener also has given his $18 million collection of Japanese prints to the Honolulu Academy of Arts. The National Gallery of Art in Washington was the recipient of Pamela Harriman's gift of Vincent Van Gogh's painting, "Roses." Another Van Gogh painting, "Portrait of Joseph Rolin," was acquired by the MoMA in New York from a Swiss collector in an exchange of seven works.

One of the more notable personnel changes in American museums in 1989 was the appointment of George Goldner, curator of European drawings at the Getty Museum, as curator of painting at the museum. In New York, Thomas Krens, the Guggenheim's new director, assembled a new team of contemporary art curators. The international trio included Germano Celant, who is Italian, Carmen Gimenez, who is Spanish, and Mark Rosenthal, an American. Rosenthal, who would work part-time, was curator of 20th-century art at the Philadelphia Museum of Art.

MARGARET BROWN HALSEY
New York City Technical College

ASIA

In recent years, the stability and peace of Asia has been based, in part, on the foundation of a moderate and outward-looking government in China. In 1989 that assumption was suddenly, severely shaken. During the spring massive protest demonstrations, demanding democracy and an end to official corruption, broke out in major cities throughout China. In early June the government cracked down, driving demonstrators from Tiananmen Square and reportedly killing thousands.

Beijing Spring. Student protests had been taking place with increasing frequency in China in recent years, but the outburst in the spring of 1989 far surpassed earlier ones in size and scope. They began in April, following the death of popular former party leader Hu Yaobang, and culminated in a hunger strike in Beijing's Tiananmen Square during the visit of Soviet President Mikhail Gorbachev in May.

What worried leading Chinese figures like Deng Xiaoping was not simply the size of the demonstrations, but that demonstrators also included much of the urban population, which had been angered by official corruption and rapid rise in the price of consumer goods. First declaring martial law on May 19, the regime sent troops and tanks into the square on June 4, crushing the movement. Party General Secretary Zhao Ziyang was charged with encouraging the protests and removed from office.

In the months following the crackdown, Chinese leaders tried to reassure foreign countries and observers that Beijing's program of economic modernization would continue. During the summer, Jiang Zemin, former mayor of Shanghai and a supporter of the reform program, was appointed the new party chief. But foreign confidence in the prospects for the future stability of China was shaken severely, and a number of countries sharply reduced their economic and cultural relations with the People's Republic of China. Beijing has contributed to its own image problem by arresting thousands suspected of taking part in the demonstrations, and by reemphasizing ideological training as part of the educational curriculum.

The Indochina Tangle. The protests overshadowed another 1989 event of potential significance—the visit of Mikhail Gorbachev to Beijing, marking the first summit meeting between the leaders of China and the USSR since the outbreak of the Sino-Soviet dispute nearly 30 years earlier. The meeting apparently did not end the deep-seated rivalry between the two countries, although it is clear from the increase in economic contacts that relations have improved substantially. There also was some unfulfilled optimism that the talks would lead to a settlement of the conflict in Cambodia, where Moscow's and Beijing's support of rival groups has hampered a settlement.

Concern over the rival Cambodian groups increased after Vietnam pledged in the spring to end its ten-year occupation of the country. Among the rival factions competing for power were the regime Vietnam leaves behind in the capital of Phnom Penh, followers of the former ruler Prince Sihanouk, and the Khmer Rouge —the Communist force that governed Cambodia from 1975 to 1979 in a reign of terror. An international peace conference held in Paris in August could not overcome the mutual distrust among the various factions and adjourned without result, leading to widespread fears that the struggle would intensify in future months. Some blamed China for refusing to abandon its support for the hated Khmer Rouge.

Turmoil in Sri Lanka. Elsewhere in Asia, the year 1989 was relatively peaceful, except in Sri Lanka, where the long-festering civil war between Tamils in the north and the majority Sinhalese continued. In 1987 troops from neighboring India were brought in to curb the rebellion and create conditions for a settlement, but the bloodshed has not come to an end, despite conciliatory efforts by Sri Lankan President Ranasinghe Premadasa to reach a compromise.

Democratic Changeover in India. Since the assassination of Indira Gandhi, her son Prime Minister Rajiv Gandhi had attempted to govern a nation severely split by religious and ethnic rivalries and economic problems. In 1989 discontent was fueled by continued grinding poverty and a bribery scandal involving government officials. V. P. Singh, a onetime Gandhi cabinet member, was able to forge a union of disparate political parties. The opposition coalition defeated Gandhi's Congress(I) party in national elections, and Singh was sworn in as prime minister.

Government Shakeup in Tokyo. Outside China, it was a relatively quiet year in East Asia, except in Japan, where the ruling Liberal Democratic Party (LDP) suffered a major defeat in elections for the upper house of parliament. The LDP has ruled Japan without interruption for four decades, but a series of scandals involving bribery and sexual misconduct, combined with an unpopular consumption tax, forced the resignation of two successive prime ministers. The ruling party's problems also raised the possibility of a victory for the minority Japanese Socialist Party (JSP) in elections for the more-powerful lower house scheduled for early in 1990.

The possibility of a JSP-dominated government worried the Bush administration, since the Socialists long have called for changes in the defense relationship with the United States. However, in late August, the party approved a policy switch to maintain the U.S. treaty for the time being.

WILLIAM J. DUIKER
The Pennsylvania State University

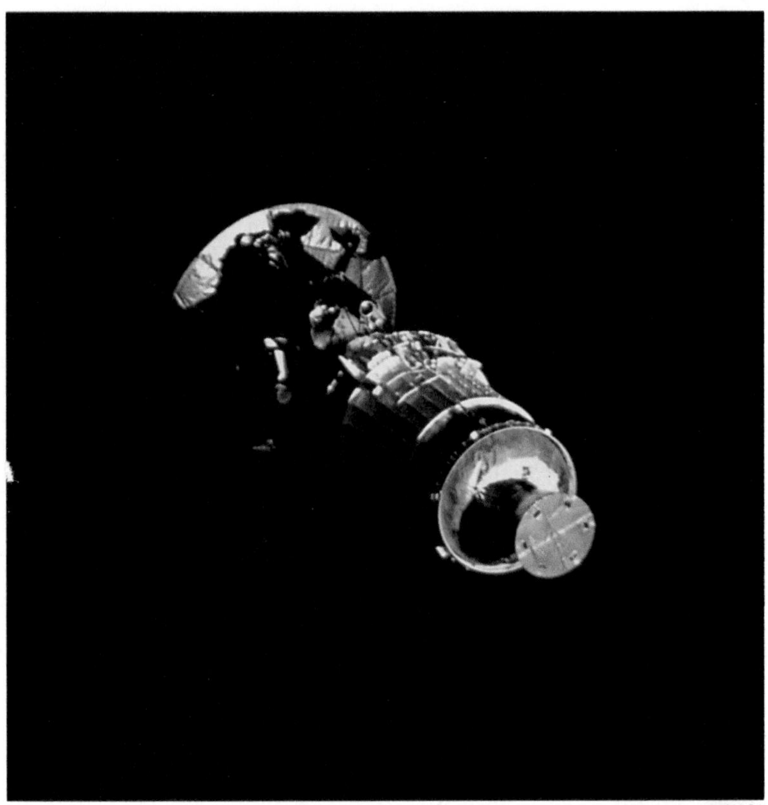

En route to planet Jupiter, the Galileo spacecraft was deployed from the space shuttle "Atlantis" into the blackness of space on Oct. 18, 1989.

NASA

ASTRONOMY

It almost seemed as if astronomy took a year off in 1989 in anticipation of unimagined riches from the scheduled 1990 launch of the Hubble Space Telescope. Except for the stunning pictures returned by *Voyager 2* of Neptune, its rings, and its satellites, there were few profound discoveries or breakthroughs in understanding the cosmos.

That conclusion is underscored by the fact that two of the most widely reported findings in the popular press turned out to be wrong! Despite media hoopla, there still was no unequivocal evidence that so-called brown dwarfs exist, those putative planet-size objects that never became massive enough to ignite their atomic fires to become stars. And the isolated gas cloud announced as a galaxy in the process of condensing—the long-sought "primordial" galaxy, a key to understanding cosmic evolution—seems to have been a bungled interpretation of radio signals from a very ordinary dwarf galaxy near our own.

Target Earth. What the media largely overlooked was the steadily mounting evidence that our planet may be more vulnerable to a catastrophic impact with a giant meteorite or cometary nucleus than previously believed. On March 22, 1989, the Earth dodged a cosmic bullet by a whisker when a piece of space debris, perhaps one-quarter mile (.4 km) in diameter, whizzed past at only twice the moon's distance. Had this celestial "boulder" hit, it would have blasted a crater some 5 mi (8 km) in diameter and released energy equivalent to 2 billion tons of TNT—an explosive force 20 times greater than the eruption of the Krakatau volcano in 1883, which claimed 36,000 lives.

And a piece of space debris one-quarter mile in diameter is a tiny object by solar-system standards. The probable scar from a much larger object was announced in 1989, seen on images returned by a weather satellite. According to several lines of evidence, a 200-mi- (322-km-) wide circular crater centered near Prague, Czechoslovakia, was caused by the impact of an enormous meteorite at least 100 million years ago. If astronomers and geologists can verify its origin, it will be the largest of the 100 or so meteorite craters known on Earth. The consequence of another such impact, with its accompanying changes in living conditions, would be similar to the event 65 million years ago that seems to have caused the extinction of the dinosaurs.

But there is also good news. Even more catastrophic for Earth than the impact of a large meteorite would be the passage of a star through the solar system. Reassuringly, a recent study of the orbits of the major planets indicates that since the solar system's formation 4.5 billion years ago, no star with more than 10% of the sun's mass likely has passed through it. Also, no body with more than three times the mass of the planet Jupiter has crossed Earth's orbit.

An Active Sun. Since 1987, when the last minimum phase in the sun's activity cycle occurred, storms on the solar surface have developed at an unprecedented rate. This flurry is expected to continue until 1990, when the peak of the 11-year cycle is anticipated. In 1989 several giant solar flares—enormous ejections of high-energy charged particles—produced dramatic displays of the northern lights over enormous areas of our planet. On March 13 a flare-induced geomagnetic storm caused a surge on the Quebec, Canada, power grid and knocked out electricity across the province. Canada took a second hit in August from what was perhaps the largest flare ever observed, causing the computers on Toronto's stock exchange to crash and halt trading for a total of three hours.

Supernova 1987A. It is unlikely that any object in the universe has been scrutinized as thoroughly as the exploding supernova that first was observed on Feb. 23, 1987. The rate at which it since has dimmed confirmed theoretical predictions that the star's energy source for the first 600 days after its core collapsed was the radioactive decay of the isotopes nickel-56 and cobalt-56.

Supernovae are responsible for enriching interstellar space with chemical elements. From this dust and gas new stars are born. The death of a star promotes the birth of new ones. The first studies of what elements Supernova 1987A contributed to its parent galaxy—the Large Magellanic Cloud, a companion to our own—agrees with theoretical calculations.

Ever since the explosion first was observed, the "holy grail" sought by astronomers was the stellar corpse of the supernova—a remnant pulsar, a spinning neutron star a million times smaller than the one that blew up. But no one anticipated what was found on Jan. 18, 1989—a pulsar flashing 1,968 times a second, far faster than any detected previously. Since each flash presumably marks one rotation of the pulsar, its equator is moving at a good fraction of the speed of light and the star is at the brink of breaking apart. No conventional model explains the existence of such an object.

Astronomy Space Probes. In 1989 the United States launched two planetary spacecraft, the first in 11 years, from the space shuttle *Atlantis*. On May 4, *Magellan* was sent on its 15-month-long voyage to Venus, where it will use sophisticated radar instrumentation to map areas as small at 800 ft (244 m) across on the planet's cloud-shrouded surface. And on October 18, after a legal battle with antinuclear activists, but a go-ahead from President Bush, the long-delayed, plutonium-powered, $1.2 billion Galileo probe was fired toward Jupiter. In 1995 it will enter into orbit around the solar system's largest planet and begin taking high-resolution pictures of its clouds and its retinue of moons. Galileo also will deploy a parachute-probe into Jupiter's atmosphere.

As these new planetary missions began, the most successful one to date ended in August, when *Voyager 2* took close-up photographs of Neptune and its environs (*see* page 469). Thus concluded a 12-year, 4.4 billion mi (7.1 billion km) journey that already had carried the resilient spacecraft past Jupiter, Saturn, and Uranus.

The stunning performance of *Voyager 2* stood in marked contrast to the flawed mission of the Soviet Union's Phobos 2 probe to Mars and its largest moon, Phobos. The mission came to an end on March 27, when an onboard computer failed, causing the spacecraft to tumble and lose radio contact with Earth. Nevertheless, Phobos 2 did manage to make the first temperature map of Mars' surface, which should allow scientists to determine its composition. Also, the craft's instruments determined that the rocks on Mars' satellite Phobos are water-poor, a characteristic similar to certain meteorites that have fallen on Earth. Since meteorites have been linked to the asteroids—tiny planetlike bodies mainly between the orbits of Mars and Jupiter—the long-held notion that Phobos and Mars' other satellite, Deimos, merely are captured asteroids has been strengthened further.

The star-mapping satellite Hipparcos failed to reach its intended orbit, but there is hope that it will accomplish most of its goals. This European Space Agency mission was designed to provide the most precise catalogue of positions, distances, and motions for hundreds of thousands of stars—data fundamental to many areas of astronomical research. Hipparcos' ultimate success depends on its longevity, and that rests on how well its energy-producing solar panels survive degradation by Earth's radiation belts.

Observatories. On March 22 the most efficient and cost-effective telescope ever built for ground-based astronomy made its maiden observations. Called the New Technology Telescope (NTT) because of its avant-garde design, this instrument collects light with a mirror 11.5 ft (3.5 m) in diameter and focuses it so precisely that a tennis ball 25 mi (40 km) away could be seen. Operated in the Chilean Andes by the European Southern Observatory, the NTT will be used as a test bed for designs to be incorporated into that organization's 52.5-ft (16-m) Very Large Telescope, which is scheduled to become fully operational in 1998.

Seven months after the 300-ft (91-m) radio telescope at Green Bank, WV, collapsed in November 1988, Sen. Robert Byrd (D-WV) announced that $75 million had been allocated for its replacement.

LEIF J. ROBINSON, *Sky & Telescope*

On a visit to Canberra in April 1989, U.S. Vice-President Dan Quayle (left) *conferred with Australia's Prime Minister Robert J. Hawke to reaffirm the strong bond between the two countries.*

© Gamma-Liaison

AUSTRALIA

As 1988's bicentennial euphoria faded, Australians were confronted in 1989 by a barrage of headlines on crime and corruption, business failures, stock-market volatility, and a large foreign-trade deficit.

The Economy. In 1989, Australia had a current account deficit in foreign trade of A$20 billion or 6% of the gross domestic product (GDP) for the year. The inflation rate was at 8%, well ahead of the rate of Australia's international trading partners. Bankruptcies were at a record level. The gap between the country's rich and the poor remained wide. Observers blamed such underlying problems as stagnant productivity, rising costs, and declining competitiveness in the international marketplace for Australia's economic woes. Dismayed at the drift of the economy, Australia's leading welfare lobbyist, on resigning his position, criticized "lotusland expectations," and questioned whether—in a nation with a growing foreign debt exceeding A$100 billion—middle-class Australians could expect to maintain "the standard of living they now enjoy, without fundamental improvements in productivity."

The economic news in 1989 was not all bad. Many of Australia's leading companies showed strong growth in profits, with many benefiting from a restructuring of work practices and wages. The businesses in trouble were those with heavy debt, aggravated by a high interest rate.

Australia's premier rural exports, wool and wheat, had a difficult year. Wool was hit by lower world prices, with total revenue for the product declining by A$2 billion. Unfavorable weather in some regions hurt the wheat crop. However, agriculture in general enjoyed a bountiful year.

On August 24 the 1,600 pilots flying for Australia's domestic-airline industry resigned, demanding higher wages. The government—reportedly concerned that a large wage hike would spur other workers to demand similar increases—used Royal Australian Air Force planes and pilots and allowed foreign carriers to set up domestic service in Australia to help maintain a limited schedule of services.

Just as tourism was becoming Australia's number one source of foreign exchange at A$6.2 billion per year, its meteoric rise faltered. The downturn in foreign visitors was aggravated by service disruption of the domestic airline. Many tourist areas and resorts that recently had thrived, now were languishing. At the same time more Australians than ever were traveling abroad.

Record mortgage rates cooled real-estate markets and housing starts showed a marked decline. However, the commercial building boom in the major cities was slower to fade. In Melbourne, office construction in 1989 was topping off a building spree. In Brisbane, plans advanced for Australia's tallest office skyscraper, the A$600 million, 78-story Brisbane Central Tower.

Immigration. The rate of immigration to Australia continued at about 150,000 for the year. At the same time 20,000 persons left the country. Advocates of limiting immigration argued that the levels were too high in view of the environmental impact. The government policy continued to support keeping immigration at the 1989 level, but with preferred treatment to those able to contribute directly to Australia's economic growth.

Education and Budget. In a move to end full funding of universities and colleges by the government, a new system was adopted under which students contribute A$1,800 a year toward higher education, payable on a deferred basis. The move brought widespread student protests. At the secondary school level, efforts were made to revise the curriculum, bringing it more in line with practical objectives.

The 1989–90 federal budget increased by 5.7% to A$86.7 billion; tax revenue was estimated to be up by 9.7% to A$91.36 billion. Some nontax receipts were expected to fall 4.7% to A$4.5 billion. After subtracting a A$3 billion overseas deficit, the budget would post a A$9 billion surplus, up from A$6 billion in 1988.

Politics. In its seventh year in power, the Labor government of Prime Minister Robert J. Hawke prepared for a tough campaign for general elections in 1990. Despite Australia's economic problems, the media continued to support the Australian Labor Party (ALP). Public-opinion polls showed the ALP behind the opposition Liberal and National parties but only by 1% to 3%.

In preparation for the upcoming election, both major opposition parties changed their leaderships. The Liberals dropped John Howard in favor of former party leader Andrew Peacock, a polished campaigner. The Nationals replaced Ian Sinclair with 38-year-old political newcomer Charles Blunt. The opposition's thrust was to regain middle-class support by promising to ease the financial squeeze on the family. An Economic Action Plan proposed by the opposition promised to cut government expenditures and lower taxes.

French Premier Michel Rocard reaches out to touch a large example of Australia's sheep-wool industry on a visit to the country. World wool prices were down during 1989.

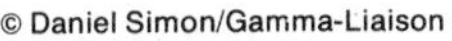
© Daniel Simon/Gamma-Liaison

AUSTRALIA • Information Highlights

Official Name: Commonwealth of Australia.
Location: Southwestern Pacific Ocean.
Area: 2,967,896 sq mi (7 686 850 km^2).
Population (mid-1989 est.): 16,800,000.
Chief Cities (June 30, 1986, provisional): Canberra, the capital, 285,800; Sydney, 3,430,600; Melbourne, 2,942,000; Brisbane, 1,171,300.
Government: *Head of state,* Elizabeth II, queen; represented by Bill Hayden, governor-general (took office February 1989). *Head of government,* Robert Hawke, prime minister (took office March 11, 1983). *Legislature*—Parliament: Senate and House of Representatives.
Monetary Unit: Australian dollar (1.2804 A$ equal U.S.$1, Nov. 6, 1989).
Gross National Product (1987 U.S.$): $202,200,-000,000.
Economic Indexes (June 1989): *Consumer Prices* (1980 = 100), all items, 201.3; food, 194.8. *Industrial Production* (Dec. 1988, 1980 = 100), 115.
Foreign Trade (1988 U.S.$): *Imports,* $33,245,-000,000; *exports,* $32,734,000,000.

The ALP was to campaign on tax cuts the government initiated in mid-1989, environmental issues, and Aboriginal land claims. The ALP attempted to accommodate many of the requests from Australia's environmental "Green" movement in 1989. Plans for a major pulp mill in the forest of Tasmania were dropped, and permission was withdrawn to allow mining in Kakadu National Park in the Northern Territory.

The resilience of the ALP was demonstrated in state government elections. Despite a 10% drop in support, Western Australia's labor government retained power with a smaller majority. The votes the ALP lost went to minor parties rather than the Liberal and National coalition. South Australia's labor government also retained power. In Tasmania, Labor allied itself with five independent "Green" candidates and formed a government at the expense of the Liberals. The ALP-Green coalition marked the first time the environmentalists were to have a role in governing Tasmania. In Queensland in December, the ALP ousted the Nationals, who had been in power for 32 years.

Crime and Corruption. An 18-month investigation of corruption in Queensland by a special commission of inquiry led to charges against state police officers, judges, and politicians. Many of the findings were linked to the National Party.

A national public inquiry into the deaths of Aborigines in police custody called into question the practice of jailing Aborigines for relatively minor offenses.

Foreign Affairs. Prime Minister Hawke confirmed Australia's close economic and military ties to the United States, in meetings with U.S. Vice-President Quayle in Canberra in April and with President Bush in Washington in June.

R. M. YOUNGER
Author, "Australia and the Australians"

AUSTRIA

Economically 1989 was a good year for Austria, and the nation continued to be a vital host for the transit of refugees from Eastern Europe. After long consideration the government applied for membership in the European Community (EC).

Government. Provincial elections in Carinthia, Salzburg, and Tyrol on March 12 brought substantial gains to the Freedom Party led by Jörg Haider. The Socialists lost their majority in Carinthia and Salzburg and the People's Party share of the vote in Tyrol fell from 64% to 48%. These elections led indirectly to a cabinet reshuffle involving four members of the People's Party in the federal coalition government headed by Franz Vranitzky, a Socialist. On April 17, Alois Mock resigned as vice-chancellor but retained his post as foreign minister. At the People's Party Congress on May 19–20 he resigned as leader of the party and was succeeded as vice-chancellor and party chairman by Agricultural Minister Josef Riegler.

Foreign Affairs. On January 19 the Conference on Security and Cooperation in Europe concluded its 26-month review of the Helsinki human-rights pact of 1975 in Vienna. Chancellor Vranitzky paid visits to Egypt in January; in mid-February to Hungary; in April to Luxembourg for celebrations marking its 150th anniversary as a state, where he consulted with Soviet Prime Minister Nikolai Ryzhkov; May 2–8 to the United States where he met with President Bush and Secretary of State James Baker; and in mid-September to Denmark. Austria's application for membership in the EC was one of the chief topics of discussion during those meetings. President Kurt Waldheim made an official visit to the United Arab Emirates March 20–22.

On July 17, Austria formally applied for membership in the EC with "the understanding that her internationally recognized status of permanent neutrality, based on the Federal Constitutional Law of Oct. 26, 1955, shall be maintained." The application was endorsed by large majorities in both houses of parliament and had broad popular support. Austria's insistence on maintaining its status of neutrality may prove a stumbling block for EC membership. In this regard Ireland's position may be of help. Ireland, a member of the EC, has not joined the other 11 EC states in the NATO alliance. The USSR has opposed Austria's joining the EC. Serious negotiations in regard to Austria's membership are not likely to begin until the proposed EC common internal market comes into being at the end of 1992.

On May 2, Hungary began to dismantle the barbed wire fences and electronic alarm system along the 150-mi (240-km) border with Austria, an action welcomed in Vienna. When Hungary on September 10–11 opened its border to permit thousands of East German tourists in Hungary to journey to West Germany, Austria gave important transit aid. Early in the year Austria had been awarded the 1989 Humanitarian Award by the Jewish refugee organization Rav Tov, in recognition of the transit aid given over the years to more than 290,000 Soviet Jews, as well as other Jews.

Economy. On Jan. 1, 1989, a new tax law went into effect. Among other changes, personal income taxes were reduced from a top marginal rate of 62% to 50% and the corporate tax from 55% to 30%. The resulting increase in net income has stimulated investment and private consumption. For 1989 real growth of the gross domestic product (GDP) was estimated to be better than 3%; there was a slight increase in inflation to about 3%; unemployment was down to around 4.5%. The net budget deficit for 1989 was expected to be cut to about 66 billion schillings (about $5 billion) or 4% of the GDP. About 65% of Austrian exports go to EC countries, around half of these to West Germany; roughly 8% to Eastern Europe; and 3.5% to the United States.

Domestic Affairs. Early in April it was revealed that employees at the state-run Lainz hospital in a suburb of Vienna had killed at least 49 patients by lethal injections. The incident became a news sensation and led to widespread criticism of the hospital administration and the state-run national health service.

On March 26, Austrian Airlines inaugurated nonstop service between New York and Vienna with convenient connections to Eastern European countries.

Empress Zita, exiled widow of Charles I, the last emperor-king of Austria-Hungary, died March 14 at the age of 96 in Zizers, Switzerland. She lay in state in St. Stephen's Cathedral before she was buried in the traditional Hapsburg family crypt on April 1.

ERNST C. HELMREICH, *Professor of History Emeritus, Bowdoin College*

AUSTRIA • Information Highlights

Official Name: Republic of Austria.
Location: Central Europe.
Area: 32,375 sq mi (83 850 km²).
Population (mid-1989 est.): 7,600,000.
Chief Cities (1981 census): Vienna, the capital, 1,531,346; Graz, 243,166; Linz, 199,910; Salzburg, 139,426; Innsbruck, 117,287.
Government: *Head of state,* Kurt Waldheim, president (took office July 1986). *Head of government,* Franz Vranitzky, chancellor (took office June 16, 1986). *Legislature*—Federal Assembly: Federal Council and National Council.
Monetary Unit: Schilling (13.00 schillings equal U.S. $1, Oct. 24, 1989).
Gross Domestic Product (1987 U.S.$): $118,100,-000,000.
Economic Indexes (1988): *Consumer Prices* (1980 = 100), all items, 133.4; food, 127.3. *Industrial Production* (1980 = 100), 116.
Foreign Trade (1988 U.S.$): *Imports,* $36,608,-000,000; *exports,* $31,088,000,000.

AUTOMOBILES

U.S. automakers wound up the decade of the 1980s on a downbeat note as production capacity overtook sales demand for the first time in five years. A continued decline in both new-car and truck volume was forecast by nearly all industry executives for the 1990-model year, though there were no signs of a severe recession of the type last experienced in 1982–83.

In the first eight months of 1989, new-car sales, including imports, totalled 6,948,284 units for a decline of 4.4% from the comparable period of 1988. Retail deliveries of light trucks, vans, and utility vehicles—a strong element of the total U.S. market—fell 3.1% to 3,249,001 vehicles.

Though it appeared certain that 1989 would result in final sales of close to 15 million cars and trucks, divided again by two thirds and one third, respectively, only General Motors predicted a similar conclusion for 1990. Ford Motor Company reduced its projection for 1990 to about 14.5 million and Chrysler Corporation to 14.2 million. New-car sales, rather than the truck group, were expected to suffer the principal falloff because of growing competition among all producers in every segment of the market.

A measure of the sales pressure facing domestic and import players alike on the U.S. scene was the heavy "incentivizing" at the dealer and consumer levels, starting in the winter of 1989. American Honda, for the first time in its history, offered sales inducements to purchasers as it increased output at its first Ohio assembly plant and prepared to open a second facility early in the 1990-model run. Several makes, defying escalating cost trends, posted price cuts on 1990 models.

Each of the domestic Big Three manufacturers resorted to frequent production stoppages in the spring and summer quarters to help dealers clear out swelling inventories of unsold cars. GM's share of new-car sales, which exceeded 40% in the early 1980s, receded to 33.5% in the January-August period of 1989. Ford kept its penetration gains in force at the expense of its domestic competitors, reaching 21.8%, but Chrysler tumbled to 9.3% after notching a decade high of 10.2% in 1988.

Importers and their "transplant" cars made in U.S. plants accounted for about 2.5 million new-car sales in the first eight months of 1989, about equal to the 1988 level, but their share of sales climbed to 35.4% from 34.1%. "Transplant" capacity was due to expand in 1990 with the opening of the second Honda plant, as well as the launch of a new Subaru car and Isuzu

WORLD MOTOR VEHICLE DATA, 1988

Country	Passenger Car Production	Truck and Bus Production	Motor Vehicle Registrations
Argentina	135,776	28,386	5,542,000
Australia	314,500	25,000	9,022,700
Austria	7,000	3,500	3,336,022
Belgium	345,327	53,775	3,841,069
Brazil	782,608	286,292	11,937,283
Canada	1,024,807	1,018,317	14,715,000
China	10,500	636,500	4,122,939
Czechoslovakia	175,000	55,000	3,149,442
France	3,223,987	474,478	24,854,000
Germany, East*	217,900	44,290	3,739,199
Germany, West	4,346,283	279,031	30,105,249
Hungary	–	13,043	1,879,002
India	159,841	151,521	2,878,412
Italy	1,884,313	226,706	24,716,000
Japan	8,198,400	4,501,403	49,901,936
Korea, South	872,074	211,581	1,611,275
Mexico	353,900	158,876	7,785,899
The Netherlands	119,786	19,325	5,624,248
Poland	293,475	57,164	4,875,000
Spain	1,497,967	368,497	12,130,484
Sweden	407,117	76,506	3,626,147
USSR	1,330,000	850,000	21,700,000
United Kingdom	1,226,835	318,013	23,017,870
United States	7,110,728	4,079,724	179,044,449**
Yugoslavia	294,138	36,285	3,276,886
Total	34,332,262	13,973,213	515,386,230***

* Includes East Berlin. ** U.S. total does not include Puerto Rico, which has 503,090 vehicles. *** World total includes 394,209,867 cars and 121,176,363 trucks and buses, of which U.S. share is 137, 323,632 cars and 41,720,817 trucks and buses. Other countries with more than one million registrations are: Bulgaria, 1,128,000; Colombia, 1,196,403; Denmark, 1,882,280; Finland, 1,919,719; Greece, 2,107,469; Indonesia, 2,044,000; Malaysia, 1,539,855; New Zealand, 1,750,916; Nigeria, 1,380,000; Norway, 1,926,340; Portugal, 1,683,500; Saudi Arabia, 3,560,698; South Africa, 4,185,277; Switzerland, 3,151,481; Taiwan, 1,727,663; Thailand, 1,486,270; Turkey, 1,812,241; and Venezuela, 2,159,397. Source: Motor Vehicle Manufacturers Association of the United States, Inc.

Courtesy, Ford Motor Company

Ford's popular Probe sports coupe, built by Mazda in Flat Rock, MI, entered its second year in 1989. The GT, left, features an electronically fuel-injected, turbocharged engine.

truck plant in Lafayette, IN. The U.S. assembly lines operated by Toyota, Nissan, Mazda, and Mitsubishi all planned 1990 expansions, moreover, bringing potential capacity of the "transplant" vehicles assembled in the United States to approximately 2 million units per year.

Each of the Big Three domestics was involved with a Japanese transplant facility, mitigating the competitive impact, but the success of the nine-member Japanese auto industry in the U.S. arena nevertheless was viewed with great concern in Detroit as the 1990s decade arrived. For the first time ever, Japan's production of cars surpassed the U.S. total in 1988 by more than one million units.

Ford, whose successful Probe sports coupe is built by Mazda in Flat Rock, MI, announced a joint venture with Nissan to produce minivans in Avon Lake, OH. GM is a partner with three Japanese automakers—Toyota, at a car plant in Fremont, CA; Isuzu, which furnishes two small cars sold by Chevrolet's separate Geo franchise; and Suzuki, at a car and utility-vehicle plant in Ingersoll, Ont.

Chrysler and Mitsubishi run a plant in central Illinois at which three sports coupes are assembled, and the Number 3 automaker has agreed to market a portion of the Sonata compacts being produced by the South Korean Hyundai company at a new facility in Bromont, Que. In turn, Hyundai is closely allied with Chrysler partner Mitsubishi of Japan.

At the Nissan car and truck plant in Smyrna, TN, an organizing bid by the United Auto Workers union was rejected in July by a 2-1 margin of the 2,400 workers.

The 1990 Models. The upscale luxury sedan segment of the market, stronghold of the Big Three, was invaded head-on for the first time by the Toyota Lexus and Nissan Infiniti brands. Sold through separately franchised

The Mustang Is 25

© Cindy Lewis

The 1964½ Ford Mustang

The Ford Mustang celebrated its silver anniversary in 1989. With 25-year sales exceeding 5.7 million, the Mustang has joined the Ford Model T, the Chevrolet Corvette, and the Volkswagen Beetle as one of the four most popular cars ever built. Although its target market originally was young adults with families, the Mustang's appeal has transcended all boundaries. Young singles, established professionals, and as many women as men buy the cars. Hundreds of "Mustang clubs" have been formed during the past 25 years, and a perfectly restored 1965 model is a prize to car enthusiasts. As in its earlier days, the Mustang remains a name at national racetracks.

Ford unveiled the Mustang at the New York World's Fair on April 17, 1964. A new concept in automobile design, the Mustang provided sportiness, performance, and practicality, all in one attractive package. Aimed at car buyers youthful enough to want a new, different design, yet family-oriented enough to need practical features at an affordable price, the new "ponycar" immediately found its audience. Response to the Mustang was overwhelming, and, on introduction day, some dealers were forced to take as many as 15 bids on the same car. Weighing only 2,572 lbs (1 174 kg) and base priced at a reasonable $2,368, the long-hooded car seated four. It was available as a convertible, hardtop, or fastback, and could be equipped with a high-performance V-8 engine.

The Mustang has undergone major redesigns since its inception, and Ford has offered sports, performance, and economy models. The first powerful "ponycar" of the late 1960s and early 1970s gave way in 1974 to Mustang II, a smaller, more economical version with many similarities to the original. It, however, was equipped with a small, four-cylinder engine. In 1978, a completely new, slightly larger and roomier Mustang was introduced. Today, the car again is available with a large, powerful engine.

Courtesy, Mazda Motor of America

The Mazda MX-5 Miata, a two-seater coupe with rear-wheel drive, was unveiled in the summer. With a suggested price of $13,800, it was a big hit.

Courtesy, Toyota Motor Sales U.S.A., Inc.

Toyota invaded the Big Three's upscale luxury sedan line with the Lexus. Six years in development, the LS 400, left, *includes a 4-liter, V8 engine.*

dealers, like the four-year-old Honda Acura upmarket cars, the Lexus and Infiniti V-8 sedans also were designed to capitalize on the sharply higher prices charged by the venerable West German entries—BMW and Mercedes-Benz. The Lexus LS-400 and Infiniti Q45 flagship models were priced at $35,000 to $38,000.

Still another wavemaker from Japan was Mazda's MX-5 Miata two-seater coupe unveiled in the summer for a suggested price of $13,800. The Miata resembled the classic British two-seaters of the 1950s and 1960s and proved to be an instant hit, ironically in the 25th anniversary year of the debut of Ford's Mustang (*see* sidebar). Some Mazda dealers asked buyers for up to $3,000 above retail prices for instant delivery, and the Miata was viewed as evidence of Americans' desire for distinctive sporty roadsters.

Chevrolet's high-powered Corvette ZR-1 also rolled out in 1989, at a $50,000-plus price, to be matched in the summer of 1990 by the Ferrari-like Acura NS-X model.

Facing a veritable onslaught of new rivals in the luxury and sporty brackets, established makes sought to catch up and shorten their model-overhaul lead times. Ford's Lincoln Town Car underwent its first revamping in five years. Chrysler added extended-length editions of the New Yorker, called the Imperial and Fifth Avenue.

Four-door sedans were introduced for the mid-size GM10 series by Chevrolet, Buick, Oldsmobile, and Pontiac. The convertible list also grew in 1989 as GM added the Chevrolet's Geo Metro, Buick Reatta, and Olds Cutlass Supreme softtops. Chevrolet, Olds, and Pontiac uncorked a new front-drive minivan with aero looks.

Among imports, new-model news was highlighted by introduction of a redesigned and enlarged Honda Accord, plus refashioning of sports coupes by Toyota and Nissan. Mazda and Mitsubishi said they were considering upscale sedans to challenge Acura, Infiniti, and Lexus. Subaru unveiled the Legacy compact series, and Mercedes-Benz recast its 500SL twin-seater with a $75,000 price tag. Chrysler agreed to take over distribution of Italy's Alfa Romeo cars, starting in 1990. Set for rollout in late 1990, after a seven-year gestation period, was GM's Saturn sporty compact car with a separate channel of close to 100 dealers across the United States.

President Bush endorsed a plan to mandate production of one million "alternate-fuel" cars a year, beginning in 1993. Automakers were studying methanol, now powering cars in Brazil, or reformulated gasoline as fuel possibilities to meet this requirement.

MAYNARD M. GORDON
Detroit Editor, "Auto Age"

BANGLADESH

Continuing opposition to President H. M. Ershad, unrest in the Chittagong Hills Tract (CHT), and economic problems plagued Bangladesh in 1989.

Politics. Observers felt early in 1989 that President Ershad had been able to outmaneuver the opposition Awami League (AL) and Bangladesh Nationalist Party (BNP) by focusing attention on 1988's flood damage and relief efforts. However, by midyear, the opposition rallied briefly, opposing efforts to alter the constitution by limiting the tenure of the president to two five-year terms and creating the post of an elected vice-president. The AL and BNP felt this measure would institutionalize the presidential system which they oppose, favoring the original 1972 constitution in which parliament is the supreme body of government. The AL challenged the presidential limitation in court, along with several other measures including a 1988 law that makes Islam the state religion. One of these, a provision that would have permitted the creation of High Court benches outside the capital, Dhaka, was struck down by the Supreme Court, handing Ershad his first constitutional defeat.

The opposition continued their attempts to achieve more formal unity, but this was made difficult by differences between the BNP and AL on how to handle a growing group of Islamic fundamentalists and ideological splits among leftist groups. Nonetheless, toward the year's end they were able to call for several strikes which paralyzed major cities.

The ruling Jaitya Party (JP) had unity problems of its own. President Ershad ousted Nurul Islam from the vice-presidency, replacing him with former Prime Minister Moudud Ahmed. Kazi Zafar Ahmed's appointment as prime minister created problems with party stalwarts since he was in the left-wing opposition when Ershad assumed power. Further cabinet reshuffles and a few defections indicated a growing factionalism in the JP.

President Ershad took steps to calm the ongoing armed insurgency in the CHT by Chakma rebels, allegedly aided by India. At issue have been demands for local autonomy, preservation of tribal land rights, and lack of development. These were dealt with in legislation passed in March. Elections to local councils took place in June with an estimated 60% voter turnout despite predictions of massive violence. A major point of contention remained the continued movement of "plains" people into the Chakma tribal lands in the Chittagong Hills.

The Bihari Question. The fate of more than 250,000 Biharis who claim Pakistani citizenship remained in limbo in 1989. Many still were in refugee camps, shunned by Bengalis for their support for Pakistan during the 1971 civil war, and bitter about Ershad's perceived lack of action on their behalf. Pakistan had agreed tentatively to repatriate the Biharis in 1985, and President Mohammad Zia ul-Haq formed a group to raise funds for the purpose. But Zia was killed in 1988, and his successor, Benazir Bhutto, seemed less committed to repatriation. On a visit to Dhaka in October, she refused to meet with Bihari leaders, and was rumored to favor financing their resettlement in Bangladesh.

Economy. The Third Five Year Plan ended with shortfalls in economic performance. Ravaged by 1988's mix of floods, storms, and drought, agricultural production was expected to decrease by 32% in 1989 with a loss of more than $8 million in critical crops such as jute and tea. The industrial base suffered $272 million in damages to 1,200 units. Communications and the distributive infrastructure remained skeletal. A 30% shortfall was expected in investment and 45% in employment generation. While foreign aid rose slightly, obstacles such as requirements for local resource mobilization prevented much of it from being available. Toward the end of the year private investment rose, but not enough to offset losses sustained earlier.

Foreign Relations. Dhaka had problems in its relations with both India and Pakistan. Bangladesh felt that India was not doing enough to support a regional approach necessary to solve issues of water use, flooding, and general environmental degradation, despite the Indian government's expressed desire to cooperate in these efforts. According to some analysts, major portions of Bangladesh could be flooded permanently short of strong measures. Adding to the tension created by the Biharis, relations with Pakistan were strained by Bangladesh's purchase of Thai rice at prices higher than those charged by Islamabad. Relations with the West remained generally stable, with economic assistance overshadowing any political concerns.

ARUNA NAYYAR MICHIE
Kansas State University

BANGLADESH • Information Highlights

Official Name: People's Republic of Bangladesh.
Location: South Asia.
Area: 55,598 sq mi (144 000 km^2).
Population (mid-1989 est.): 114,700,000.
Chief City (1981 census): Dhaka, the capital, 3,430,312.
Government: *Head of state,* Hussain Mohammad Ershad, chief executive (assumed power March 24, 1982) and president (Dec. 1983). *Head of government,* Kazi Zafar Ahmed, prime minister (took office 1989). *Legislature*—Parliament.
Monetary Unit: Taka (32.27 taka equal U.S.$1, July 1989).
Economic Indexes: *Consumer Prices* (Dhaka, June 1988, 1980 = 100), all items, 218.9; food, 225.3.
Foreign Trade (1988 U.S.$): *Imports,* $2,729,000,000; *exports,* $1,347,000,000.

BANKING AND FINANCE

While the savings and loan (S&L) crisis (*see* special report, page 130) preoccupied many in the banking industry for much of 1989, regulators in Washington, DC, still had to look for buyers for several large insolvent banks, Treasury Secretary Nicholas F. Brady pushed to get the industry's leaders to write off large amounts of Third World debt, and all eyes were on the Federal Reserve Board (the Fed), hoping it would drive down interest rates that had been rising for almost 12 months.

It was also a year in which the fortunes of banks diverged strikingly from those of the savings industry, as bankers continued to earn generous profits and S&L executives experienced almost unprecedented huge losses.

But analysts nonetheless warned that the banking industry had weaknesses. Almost 200 institutions failed, underlining the fact that the industry had not ridden itself of the deep problems that began when the oil economy of the Southwest and the agricultural economy of the Midwest plunged into regional depressions in the mid-1980s. Some analysts also cautioned that the industry's newfound fondness for higher levels of real-estate lending made it vulnerable to the same problems that beset the S&L industry.

Regulation. For the Federal Deposit Insurance Corporation (FDIC), the government agency that insures deposits at commercial banks for up to $100,000, 1989 was a year of trying to finish the cleanup of Texas banking. In March the FDIC took control of 20 insolvent banks with assets of more than $15 billion belonging to MCorp of Dallas, and after injecting more than $1 billion of assistance, agreed to sell them to the Banc One Corporation of Columbus, OH.

Not long thereafter, the agency struck a deal for the sale of the last two remaining large insolvent Texas bank holding companies, the $4.2 billion Texas American Bancshares Inc. of Fort Worth, and the National Bancshares Corporation of Texas in San Antonio, at a cost to the government of more than $2 billion. That meant that since the mid-1980s, almost all the major banks in Texas needed some form of outside help, either from the federal government or another banking group, to remain viable.

Also, for the first time, some experts raised questions about the financial health of the FDIC itself, which had shut down more than 800 banks over the previous five years and had seen its assets dwindle from $1.20 per $100 of insured deposits to a dangerously low $.80.

Third World Debt. The huge burden of Third World debt, which most experts agree never will be paid off, took center stage in 1989, as Treasury Secretary Brady proposed that the money center banks take strong measures to write off much of the debt and make new loans available. There is little dispute that the levels of debt are such that just keeping up with interest payments is draining developing countries of their only real means of future prosperity.

Some banks responded with their own method of resolving the problem. Morgan Guaranty, the nation's fourth-largest bank, decided to set aside a whopping $2 billion for possible Third World debt losses. Though it meant a large annual loss for the bank, the action effectively eliminated Morgan's exposure to future losses on Third World loans. Several other big banks followed Morgan's lead, and in the process, some had to look outside the United States for financial help. Manufacturers Hanover, for instance, reached an agreement under which Dai-Ichi Kangyo, the world's largest bank, would invest $1.4 billion in the sixth-largest U.S. bank. In return, Dai-Ichi would get a 4.9% ownership stake in the bank and 60% control of its consumer financing subsidiary, the CIT group.

Federal Reserve Board. The Fed's interest-rate policies were watched almost as closely as the S&L crisis as the economy hovered between modest growth and weakness.

After pushing up interest rates from early 1988 through early 1989 in an effort to stop any resurgence of inflation, the Fed began to change its policy in March 1989. First it simply held rates steady, deciding against any further increases. Then in June and July it began easing credit for the first time in more than a year, as rates fell more than a full percentage point. But a major drop in rates in the fall, which some had hoped for, did not come, as the Fed returned to its neutral stance in August.

Thus interest rates peaked in the spring and began to drift lower. For example, bank certificates of deposit topped out at just above 9.5%, but fell toward 8% in the latter part of 1989. The rising rates did provide a big boost to money market mutual funds, which saw investors flood their coffers with more than $70 billion during the year. At the same time, the higher rates tended to discourage homeowners from taking out home-equity loans, and new investments in individual retirement accounts remained mostly stagnant.

Legislation. After passing legislation to bail out the S&L industry, Congress had little stomach for slogging through another bill. But the Bush administration sent clear signals that it was not about to give up the fight to give banks new powers and modernize the nation's financial system. Most experts believed those who favored reforms would try again in 1990 or 1991. But in the meantime, the regulators took the initiative. In January 1989, the Fed, in its role as regulator of bank holding companies, permitted a number of giant banking organizations to underwrite corporate debt.

NATHANIEL C. NASH
Washington Bureau, "The New York Times"

The Savings and Loan Crisis

For many Americans, savings and loan associations (S&Ls) were hardly a popular topic of conversation as 1989 began. Some perhaps had a small S&L in their community where they kept a few dollars on deposit, and others may have gotten the mortgage for their house from a local thrift. But the image of the small-town mortgage lender was benign and akin to all that was good about America. By the end of the year, however, all had changed; S&Ls had earned a notoriety that few businesses have had in this century.

Massive losses of depositors' money at almost 1,000 institutions around the country would end up costing each U.S. taxpayer the equivalent of $3,000. Almost on a daily basis, the public read about lax regulation, incompetent management, fraud, and insider dealings in the industry.

The crisis even took experts by surprise. By the mid-1980s, most banking specialists knew hundreds of S&Ls were in trouble because of heavy lending in the Southwest just at the time when the Texas oil economy collapsed. But they missed the magnitude of the problem. At most, they were predicting that the cost to shut down the sick thrifts and pay off depositors would range from $5 billion to $15 billion and that a coming recovery in the Southwest's economy would make the task easier.

But by early 1989, Congress, newly elected President Bush, and regulators finally realized that years of lax regulation, a speculation frenzy on Texas real estate, and corrupt, high-flying industry operators had combined to cause the biggest bill on record for a federal bailout. The price tag was to be $159 billion over the next decade and almost $300 billion over the next 30 years, greater than all previous federal bailouts put together.

The numbers simply staggered Congress as the reality of the bailout sunk in. But the speed at which rescue legislation moved on Capitol Hill was accelerated by the realization that every day of delay added $15 million to $20 million to the final cost. Thus on August 9, President Bush signed the Financial Institutions Reform, Recovery and Enforcement Act of 1989, hopefully putting S&Ls on the road to recovery.

How the Crisis Happened. For decades after they were created during the New Deal legislation of the 1930s, S&Ls enjoyed a sleepy, stable, and profitable existence. They would take in customer deposits, paying, say, 5% interest, and make mortgage loans that earned

AP/Wide World

Congressmen and members of the administration attend an Aug. 9, 1989, Rose Garden ceremony as President Bush signs a bill to bail out the savings and loan industry.

perhaps 7%. The two-percentage-point spread covered operating expenses and provided modest profits. But when inflation surged in the 1970s and the government began to deregulate interest rates, life changed dramatically for the S&Ls. While the industry was unable to refinance the 7% mortgages, it found the rates it had to pay on deposits soared up past 10%. The institutions hemorrhaged in a major way and hundreds folded by the early 1980s.

Though a modest respite was granted when rates fell in the early 1980s, the memory of the interest-rate mismatch drove many surviving institutions toward looking for investments that yielded more than fixed-rate 30-year mortgages to cushion the impact of volatile interest rates. Since higher-rate investments tend to indicate more risk, institutions soon found themselves speculating on raw land in Texas, junk bonds, and direct ownership of huge apartment and office complexes. Moreover, the budget cuts under the Reagan administration, plus a general deregulatory attitude that wanted to keep government out of business, created an environment that cast aside much restraint and prudence.

The oil prices collapse in the mid-1980s brought down the Texas economy and Texas real-estate values. The S&L industry began to dive as well. In 1986 the industry's top trade group estimated the total losses at $6 billion. But by the end of 1988 that number had risen to more than $100 billion. And as regulators began to sift through the rubble, they found case after case of fraud, insider dealing, and blatant looting of some institutions.

The Bush Plan. While President Reagan was able to avoid addressing the S&L problem, President Bush could not. Making it almost his first order of business, on Feb. 6, 1989, he announced a sweeping proposal to spend billions to bail out the industry and reorganize its regulation, centralizing power with the Treasury Department and the Federal Deposit Insurance Corporation (FDIC). Power was taken away from the Federal Home Loan Bank Board, which had failed to contain the problem.

Though lawmakers cringed at voting for the biggest federal bailout on record, they had little choice, since federal deposit insurance committed Congress to making good on depositors' money. Otherwise, most agreed, there could be massive runs on the nation's banks.

The final version of the plan approved in August called for spending $159 billion over the next decade to handle failures in the industry. Taxpayers would pay almost 75% of the cost, while the S&L industry would pay the rest. Almost $61 billion would be spent to cover debts incurred when regulators closed more than 200 institutions in 1989, $50 billion to pay for some 500 institutions that would have to be closed from 1989–92, $24 billion to pay for S&Ls that would fail after 1992, and another $24 billion in interest costs on the borrowings.

The Resolution Trust Corporation. The most immediate step was to establish a new agency to take over the sick institutions and begin the process of finding buyers for them and their assets. Thus the bill created the Resolution Trust Corporation (RTC). Run on a day-to-day basis by the top management of the FDIC, the RTC was chartered both to strike deals with would-be investors for entire institutions and to take over troubled real-estate assets and manage them for a time, then selling them to investors.

The agency's broad policies would be set by an oversight board headed by the secretary of the treasury and including the chairman of the Federal Reserve Board, the secretary of housing and urban development, and two private citizens appointed by the president. It would have at its disposal at least $50 billion of borrowed funds for its task.

But the sheer magnitude of the project had many experts warning that the RTC would be almost unmanageable. L. William Seidman, chairman of both the FDIC and the RTC, noted that the trust corporation would acquire institutions with assets of more than $300 billion, including $120 billion of bad assets—an amount that dwarfed the total of all troubled assets the FDIC had dealt with during its entire 56-year history.

And indeed, during the first months of the RTC's existence, bickering between the FDIC and the Treasury, charges that it favored banks over S&Ls in its deals, and pressure from Congress led to a rocky start. FDIC officials at times lamented the new responsibilities granted it under the legislation.

A New Regulatory Structure. But while the FDIC's work load rose, that of the Federal Home Loan Bank Board diminished. The legislation took away the independence of the bank board, placing it under the supervision of the Treasury, and renamed it the Office of Thrift Supervision. In addition, it removed the thrift deposit insurance fund from the bank board's jurisdiction and put it under FDIC control, renaming it the Savings Association Insurance Fund. And realizing that both the bank and S&L deposit insurance funds needed to be bolstered, the law required that both pay higher deposit insurance fees.

But perhaps the most significant regulatory change in the entire bill aimed at preventing a recurrence of the debacle was a hotly contested requirement that the entire S&L industry more than double the amount of cash reserves, often called capital, that owners would have to hold in order to operate as an S&L. Previously, institutions could operate on paper-thin capital levels equal to 1% to 2% of their total assets. Since capital is used as a cushion in hard times to absorb losses, those reserves often were used up quickly, pushing hundreds of S&Ls into insolvency. The Bush plan required that by 1994, the industry have capital between 6% and 8% of assets, depending on certain measurements. If an institution failed to meet those requirements, it quickly could be taken over by regulators and shut down.

Other safeguards were imposed as well. Fines and jail terms for bank fraud were increased greatly. Regulators were given power to take control of a bank or S&L before it became insolvent. And S&Ls had to sell off all their holdings of junk bonds.

But despite this monumental effort, S&L experts had a troubling prediction about the future, warning that the bill did not provide enough money to fix the entire problem and that Congress would have to consider a second bailout by 1992. Members of Congress did not even want to think about or discuss that possibility.

NATHANIEL C. NASH

BELGIUM

During 1989, Belgium's coalition government led by Flemish Christian Democrat Prime Minister Wilfried Martens took steps to reduce the linguistic controversies that disrupted domestic politics in previous months. The economy showed strength, and investments increased as Belgian industries prepared for the single Europe economy projected for 1992.

Politics. A political deal removed Mayor José Happart of Voeren from the spotlight. His refusal to speak Flemish although his commune was in Flanders was a national issue. Deposed by the courts, Happart repeatedly was reinstated as mayor by his local council. But in January, Happart declined to run again, instead accepting a high place on the Walloon Socialist election list for the June balloting for the European Parliament. His twin brother received a similar offer for a seat in the Belgian Chamber. The status of the French language in Voeren was improved. Its use was to be allowed in council meetings, and the French school was permitted to extend its grounds.

The quieting of Happart aided passage in Parliament of measures furthering Martens' program for federation through devolution of central government powers to Brussels, Flanders, and Wallonia. A Brussels regional government was formed. A third of the national budget—funds for education, roads and communications, and scientific research—was transferred to the three regions. A new constitutional court is to handle conflicts resulting from devolution.

In June elections for the European Parliament, both Walloon and Flemish Christian Democrats did well. After the vote, Leo Tindemans resigned as foreign minister to head the latter delegation to the European Parliament.

Foreign Policy. A serious rift arose with Zaire, the former Belgian Congo. In November 1988, Martens traveled to Zaire with an offer to write off some 20% of the Zairian debt to Belgium. This offer was rejected as insufficient by Mobuto Sese Seko, the president of Zaire. He also was offended by Belgian press reports of corruption in his regime and comparison of his personal wealth, rumored to be \$2–5 billion, with the \$7 billion foreign debt of his country. Mobuto stopped payments on loans from Belgium and renounced two friendship treaties with the low country. The 13,000–15,000 citizens of Zaire living in Belgium were told to sell their assets and return home. Mobuto also demanded compensation for Belgian actions taken before the independence of the former colony (claims previously settled) and threatened appeal to the Court of International Justice. Belgium in turn halted new development plans in Zaire.

In July, Belgium's new Foreign Minister Mark Eyskens announced that matters were regularized between the two nations. Belgium would forgive \$115 million of the debt Zaire owed the Belgian government and \$140 million of the commercial debts underwritten by the government.

Within NATO, Martens opposed British and U.S. pressure for quick modernization of short-range Lance nuclear missiles. Instead he supported West German proposals for disarmament talks with the Soviets. Foreign Minister Eyskens was criticized by Socialists for his reluctance to approve initiation by the European Community of Austria's application for membership. Eyskens withdrew his opposition once assured that the import of Austria's neutrality, which Eyskens feared might slow European integration, would be studied.

Economics. The gross national product grew, while inflation rates stayed below 3% and unemployment decreased. Industries operated at 85% of capacity, with higher figures in Flanders. Favorable location and a multilingual public with international tastes are making Belgium an active product test-market for the single Europe economy of 1992.

Other. Former Prime Minister Paul Vanden Boeynants was kidnapped in January and released a month later after payment of a large ransom.

In March, Abdullah al-Ahdal, the Saudi Arabian imam who was spiritual leader of the Belgian Muslim community, was assassinated, along with a Tunisian assistant. The act was considered a reprisal for the imam's moderate posture toward Salman Rushdie's *The Satanic Verses* (*see* BIOGRAPHY).

Ten British soccer fans were acquitted and 15 found guilty of manslaughter in the Heysel Stadium riots of May 1985. The former head of the Belgian Football Union and the security chief at Heysel were found guilty of criminal negligence.

J. E. HELMREICH, *Allegheny College*

BELGIUM • Information Highlights

Official Name: Kingdom of Belgium.
Location: Northwestern Europe.
Area: 11,780 sq mi (30 510 km^2).
Population (mid-1989 est.): 9,900,000.
Chief Cities (Dec. 31, 1987): Brussels, the capital (incl. suburbs), 970,346; Antwerp (including suburbs), 476,044; Ghent, 232,620; Charleroi, 208,938; Liège, 200,312; Bruges, 117,857.
Government: *Head of state,* Baudouin I, king (acceded 1951). *Head of government,* Wilfried Martens, prime minister (formed new government Oct. 1985). *Legislature*—Parliament: Senate and Chamber of Representatives.
Monetary Unit: Franc (39.02 francs equal U.S.\$1, Oct. 18, 1989).
Gross National Product (1988 est. U.S.\$): \$115,000,000,000.
Economic Indexes (1988): *Consumer Prices* (1980 = 100), all items, 146.2; food, 142.7. *Industrial Production* (1980 = 100), 113.
Foreign Trade (1988 with Luxembourg, U.S.\$): *Imports,* \$92,578,000,000; *exports,* \$92,786,000,000.

BIOCHEMISTRY

The 1988–89 period was highlighted by the identification of the biochemical events that control cell division and by continued advances in cancer biochemistry.

Cell Division. Although it has been known for years how cells divide, the biochemical machinery that controls cell division had remained a mystery. Scientists solved part of the mystery in 1989 and made the surprising discovery that the basic control mechanism appears to be the same from yeast to humans. Essentially, the control mechanism involves just two proteins. One is an enzyme, known as p34 kinase, which adds phosphate groups to other proteins. Phosphate additions or removals are one of the major ways by which cells activate or deactivate proteins. The second major protein is cyclin, which activates p34 kinase. It is the activation of p34 kinase that sets in motion the changes (such as coiling and shortening of the chromosomes) preceding actual cell division. Cyclin levels in cells fluctuate. The levels go up —turning on p34 kinase—and then decrease precipitously, turning off the kinase and allowing the cells to complete division. How cyclin levels control the activity of p34 kinase remains unknown. Similarly, which proteins are phosphorylated by this kinase have not been identified precisely, although there are several possibilities.

Oncogenes. Within the past decade, remarkable advances have been made to identify the biochemical events that cause cells to become cancerous. Several dozen genes (oncogenes) have been discovered to contribute to cancer formation when they are abnormal or abnormally activated. Some oncogenes, designated as *dominant,* contribute directly to excessive and abnormal growth of cells; other oncogenes, designated as *recessive,* protect against abnormal growth, and their loss causes cells to become cancerous. A prototype of the latter class is the retinoblastoma gene, which appears to have important but as yet undefined functions in normal cell growth. A loss of both copies of the gene causes tumors to develop in the eye retina as well as in certain other tissues.

Scientists now have discovered a third type of oncogene which appears to turn off the genes that keep cell growth under control. This unexpected activity was found in an oncogene called v-erbA. It is an aberrant form of a normal cellular gene that directs the production of the receptor for the thyroid hormone. A receptor is a protein located either within a cell or in its membrane to which the hormone binds to elicit the response in the cell. In the case of thyroid hormone, the target cell responds by increasing protein synthesis and oxygen consumption. A more recent finding is that thyroid hormone also causes maturation of the newly formed blood cells into their functional form. What the scientists now have found is that v-erbA oncogene causes the production of an abnormal receptor protein which binds to the thyroid hormone. The complex then prevents activation of certain genes that promote the maturation of cells responsive to thyroid hormone, including blood cells. This results in the accumulation of abnormally immature blood cells and possibly other cells.

In another major development in cancer biochemistry, scientists reported that more than one genetic change must occur before cells become cancerous. Dr. Bert Vogelstein and his colleagues at Johns Hopkins University found that colon cancer occurs only after four to six genes are altered. They also have identified the precise genetic events that lead normal colon cells to form a benign polyp and then to go to malignancy. One of the first events is loss of part of chromosome 5—one of 46 chromosomes in human cells—so that a gene, which apparently keeps a cell from growing too rapidly, is deleted. This results in the cell losing control over its growth. In the next few steps —the precise sequence appears unimportant— a gene undergoes alteration which turns on growth, making the cell grow even more rapidly. By this time, the cell has become cancerous. If further genetic changes accumulate, the cancer seems more likely to spread elsewhere in the body.

Dr. John Minna and his colleagues at the National Cancer Institute in Bethesda, MD, reported similar findings in their studies of small cell lung cancer, except that this cancer required ten to 15 gene alterations rather than the four to six alterations in colon cancer. These studies provide hope that it eventually may be possible to control cancer by intervention in just one of the steps.

Gene Transfer. A group of Italian scientists made the surprising discovery that sperm can be used as a vehicle to transport genes. The remarkably simple method involved incubating for 30 minutes mouse sperms with DNA containing a gene for the bacterial enzyme called chloramphenicol acetyltransferase (CAT). They then fertilized the mouse eggs with DNA-incubated sperms and transferred the eggs to mice serving as surrogate mothers. Of the 250 progeny, 30% carried the CAT gene and indeed certain cells of these transgenic mice contained functional CAT enzyme. Interestingly, the next generation inherited the gene in the expected fashion, indicating that the bacterial gene had become part of the genome of these mice. Similar findings were made with sea urchin and frog eggs. Although there are ethical considerations, using sperm to produce transgenic animals might have a major impact on the scientific and commercial uses of transferring genes.

PREM P. BATRA
Wright State University

BIOGRAPHY

A selection of profiles of persons prominent in the news during 1989 appears on pages 134–45. The affiliation of the contributor is listed on pages 591–94; biographies that do not include a contributor's name were prepared by the staff. Included are sketches of:

AKIHITO

On Jan. 7, 1989, Akihito acceded to the Chrysanthemum Throne of Japan as the 125th emperor upon the demise of his father, Hirohito (*see* OBITUARIES, p. 400). The government recognized the new era as *Heisei* (peace and concord), which would be Akihito's reign name. In the new emperor's first audience ceremony on January 9, he spoke of his father's incumbency as an "age of turbulence" spanning six decades. "In succeeding to the throne," he added, "I lay to heart the august virtues of his late majesty and pledge that I shall keep in mind his wish ever to be with the people under any circumstances and that I shall observe the constitution of Japan together with you and discharge my duties in accordance with it."

During nearly 30 years of state visits (often representing his father), tours, and academic exchanges, Akihito became an educated and worldly man. He was prepared to assume the role, under the new constitution, of "symbol of the state and of the unity of the people, with whom resides sovereign power." Akihito represented to the Japanese the importance of the nation's growing international status. In subtle ways, Emperor Akihito and his poised wife, Empress Michiko, have shown a tendency to mix with ordinary Japanese citizens more than in previous imperial practice.

Background. Tsugu Akihito was born in Tokyo on Dec. 23, 1933, the eldest son of Emperor Hirohito and Empress Nagako. He studied at Gakushuin (peers' school) elementary, junior, and senior high schools, spending the wartime period in Karuizawa and in Nikko. In 1945 he returned to Tokyo and soon thereafter began his study of the English language and Western culture under the tutelage of Elizabeth Gray Vining of Philadelphia. He completed his formal education at Gakushuin University in 1956.

Akihito's coming-of-age ceremony and investiture as crown prince were celebrated in 1952. One of his first official duties was to attend the coronation of Queen Elizabeth in London in 1953.

In 1959, Crown Prince Akihito married Michiko Shoda, a commoner. The courtship, conducted on the tennis courts at Karuizawa, and the marriage attracted unusual interest because this was the first instance of an imperial heir marrying outside the traditional nobility. Soon after the wedding, the imperial couple visited some 37 countries on behalf of Emperor Hirohito.

In accordance with the constitution, Akihito acted for his father during Emperor Hirohito's visits to Europe in 1971 and to the United States in 1975, as well as during his father's long illness from September 1987 to 1989.

As his father did, Akihito has shown a scholarly interest in marine biology. A well-known ichthyologist, he has made taxonomic studies of the goby and has published a book and 25 articles on the species. Emperor Akihito also has displayed a keen interest in conservation. His favorite sport is tennis. The emperor and empress have three children: Crown Prince Naruhito, (b. 1960), Prince Fumihito, (b. 1965), and Princess Sayako, (b. 1969).

ARDATH W. BURKS

BHUTTO, Benazir

When Benazir Bhutto was named Pakistan's prime minister on Dec. 2, 1988, culminating more than a decade of political struggle, she became, at age 35, the youngest prime minister in Pakistan's history and the first woman prime minister of a modern Muslim nation.

The national elections which catapulted Benazir Bhutto to power followed two dramatic and unforeseen events in 1988. On May 29, Gen. Zia ul-Haq, who had led a coup against Prime Minister Zulfikar Ali Bhutto, Benazir Bhutto's father, in July 1977, abruptly dismissed his prime minister, Mohammed Khan Junejo, disbanded the National Assembly, and announced that fresh elections would be held. On August 17, President Zia was killed in an air crash. The elections were held November 16 and Bhutto's Pakistan's People's Party (PPP) emerged with a plurality of 93 seats in the National Assembly. Nearly two

Benazir Bhutto

AP/Wide World

weeks later, following hectic coalition-building and extensive discussions, Benazir Bhutto was invited by Acting President Ghulam Ishaq Khan to form a government.

During her first year as prime minister, Benazir Bhutto steered a moderate course. She faced a strong president, an influential military, and an entrenched political opposition. Her major challenge was opposition control of Punjab, Pakistan's largest province, a situation unprecedented in Pakistan's history. In foreign relations, she has continued Pakistan's commitment to the Afghan resistance and friendship with the United States. She also has attempted to improve relations with both India and Iran.

Background. Born June 21, 1953, Benazir Bhutto attended convent schools in Pakistan prior to going abroad in 1969 to study at Radcliffe College in Cambridge, MA. Graduating with a degree in government in 1973, she went to England to study politics, philosophy, and economics at Lady Margaret Hall, Oxford. After graduating in 1976, she remained an additional year to complete a foreign service course, and was elected to the prestigious post of president of the Oxford Union, the first Asian woman so honored.

Benazir Bhutto returned to Pakistan in June 1977, intent on joining her country's foreign service. Days later her father was overthrown. During Zulfikar Ali Bhutto's subsequent imprisonment and trial (for conspiracy to commit murder) and following his execution on April 4, 1979, the leadership of his PPP fell to Benazir and her mother, Begum Nusrat Bhutto.

The future prime minister herself suffered house arrest and imprisonment. In 1984 she was released on medical grounds and went into exile in London. After martial law was terminated on Dec. 30, 1985, and political parties were legalized a few weeks later, Benazir returned to Pakistan in April 1986 and was greeted by tumultuous crowds. She again took up the demand for fresh democratic elections, but had difficulty in maintaining unity among the anti-Zia opposition and in sustaining popular pressure on the government. She again was imprisoned for a few weeks in August 1986.

Ms. Bhutto's arranged marriage, to Asif Ali Zardari, took place on Dec. 17, 1987. Their son Bilawal was born Sept. 21, 1988. Her autobiography, *Daughter of Destiny,* also appeared in 1988.

WILLIAM L. RICHTER

BUSH, Barbara Pierce

Immediately after becoming the 38th first lady of the United States in January 1989, Barbara Bush began putting her own stamp on the office. In so doing, Mrs. Bush quickly gained a popularity all her own. Although she often had been criticized for her matronly appearance (a size 14 figure and undyed, white hair), Mrs. Bush's down-to-earth approach to her new job as well as to life in general made her an ideal role model for many American women. Her acute sense of humor (often directed at herself), extreme devotion to her family, occasional outspokenness, and humanitarian concerns were welcomed attributes. In fact, in critiquing President Bush's first 100 days in office, more than one commentator judged Mrs. Bush to be one of his principal assets.

Barbara Bush long had been dedicated to helping many causes and welcomed her new position as an opportunity to be even more active in the fights against illiteracy, homelessness, and AIDS. As first lady, her deepest commitment, however, would be to eradicating illiteracy, a cause in which she first became interested more than 25 years ago when the Bushes' third son, Neil, was diagnosed as dyslexic. She serves on the boards of several national literacy organizations and has attended more than 500 fund-raisers to combat this problem. In 1984, she authored *C. Fred's Story,* a wry look at the Washington scene from the viewpoint of her late cocker spaniel; all proceeds from sales of the book went to literacy charities. On March 6, 1989, a private grant-awarding foundation called the Barbara Bush Foundation for Literacy was established, with Mrs. Bush as honorary chairwoman. The foundation's aim is to target the family as the key ingredient in increasing literacy. Mrs. Bush also is interested in medical research and often visits children's cancer wards. The Bushes' second child, Robin, a daughter, died of leukemia at age three in 1953. The new first lady intends to encourage increased volunteerism among all Americans.

© Carol T. Powers/The White House

Barbara Bush

The Bushes discuss world news together daily and Mrs. Bush often offers advice, particularly on matters of special concern to her. She has been quoted as saying that her husband does not interfere with her household, and she does not interfere with his office. However, she is said to have considerable influence with the president, which she chooses to exercise discreetly.

Despite suffering from Graves' disease (a thyroid disorder) in early 1989, and undergoing radioactive iodine treatment, Mrs. Bush has shown herself to be an active first lady in several spheres. She accompanied her husband to Japan for Emperor Hirohito's funeral in February, with brief stops in several other countries. She has been active in entertaining White House guests in an informal, comfortable style, and has had one room of the East Wing family quarters redecorated as a playroom for the Bush grandchildren.

Background. Barbara Pierce was born in Rye, NY, on June 8, 1925, the daughter of a publisher of *McCall's* magazine. She had a wealthy upbringing, attending mostly private schools. At the age of 16, she met George Bush at a Christmas dance in Greenwich, CT; the couple became engaged a year later. She dropped out of Smith College to marry the future president on Jan. 6, 1945.

Mrs. Bush chose to make a vocation of being a wife and mother, and put all her energies into raising her family and helping her husband. Bush's career has taken the family through 29 homes in 17 cities, including Beijing, China. In her spare time, the first lady enjoys gardening and needlepoint. The Bushes have five children and 11 grandchildren.

CHENEY, Richard Bruce (Dick)

When President George Bush, trying to recover from the first major defeat of his presidency—the Senate's refusal to confirm former Sen. John G. Tower (R-TX) as secretary of defense—quickly nominated Wyoming Rep. Richard B. Cheney for the post, the praise from both sides of the aisle was close to unanimous. In part this was an indication of the desire by senators in both parties to put the bitterness stirred by Tower's controversial nomination behind them (*see* special report, page 542). But in the main the positive reaction reflected the Senate's judgment on the new 48-year-old nominee, who was confirmed swiftly. Cheney's 20 years of service in both the executive and legislative branches, combined with his Western roots, made him a rare figure in Washington, a politician with an insider's experience and an outsider's point of view.

What made the enthusiasm for Cheney all the more striking was that the Wyoming congressman never has been reluctant to engage in controversy; he had earned a reputation as an effective partisan for the GOP and a vigorous spokesman for conservative positions. Nevertheless, even those who were often his adversaries respected him for his forthrightness, intelligence, and independence. He demonstrated this independence in his first months at the Pentagon by recommending $10 billion in reductions from the defense budget proposed by former President Reagan, championing the B2 Stealth bomber in the face of congressional attack, and publicly criticizing the Commerce Department for easing curbs on the sale of high-powered computers to the Soviet Union.

Background. Arriving in Washington as a congressional fellow in 1968, Cheney took his first government post as a special assistant to Donald Rumsfeld at the Office of Economic Opportunity in the Nixon administration. He followed Rumsfeld to the Nixon White House and later became chief of staff to President Ford. In 1978 he returned to his native Wyoming to run for and win the state's only congressional seat. He was reelected five times, and in December 1988 was elected House Republican whip.

During the Reagan presidency one of his prime concerns was what he regarded as attempts by Congress to interfere in the conduct of foreign policy, an issue that was underlined by the disclosures of the Iran-contra affair in 1986 and 1987. "The Congress has a role in shaping foreign policy," he told *Congressional Quarterly*. "But the president has to be the architect, he has to manage it on a day-to-day basis." While defending Reagan's backing for the contra forces opposing the leftist Nicaraguan government, he contended that the president erred by not confronting Congress over the issue and trying to gain public support for aid to the guerrilla group.

Cheney's health was questioned during his confirmation hearings because he had suffered three heart attacks and had undergone quadruple bypass surgery in August 1988. But his physician reported that he could carry out his new duties without restrictions. Dick Cheney and his wife, Lynne, who is director of the National Endowment for the Humanities, have two children. The defense secretary was born Jan. 30, 1941, in Lincoln, NE. He holds bachelor's and master's degrees from the University of Wyoming.

ROBERT SHOGAN

DALEY, Richard Michael

The second Mayor Daley of Chicago, like his father before him, is a quiet family man and consummate politician who could set his own legacy as mayor of the third-largest city in the United States.

After 13 years of political division in Chicago's City Hall following the death of Mayor Richard J. Daley in 1976, his son Richard M. Daley was given a chance to restore peace in 1989. In a special April mayoral election, Daley was chosen to fill out the unexpired term of the late Harold Washington, the city's first black mayor, who died in office in 1987. Daley's 56% of the vote came from a coalition of white and Hispanic, but few black, voters. He succeeded Eugene Sawyer, a black who served as interim mayor and who was defeated by Daley in the February 1989 Democratic mayoral primary.

AP/Wide World

Richard M. Daley

Critics of the new mayor said he never would have had a chance to be elected if he were not a Daley, a name still held in awe by many Chicago voters who remember his father's 21 years as mayor. The younger Daley displays the same mannerisms, wry sense of humor, and poor speaking style as his father—attributes that bode well with Chicago's rather unsophisticated electorate.

During his initial months as mayor, Daley won praise for his efforts to tackle city budget deficits, curb rising property taxes, end racial factionalism in City Hall, and repair the city's crippled public school system. Such challenges could spell victory or defeat as Daley faces election to a full four-year term in 1991.

Background. Richard Michael Daley was born in Chicago on April 24, 1942. The eldest of four sons, he obtained a bachelor's degree from Providence College and a law degree from DePaul University. After working in the city's attorney office, he served in the Illinois Senate (1973–80). In 1980 he was elected prosecutor of Cook County—a position to which he was reelected in 1984 and 1988. In 1983 he tried for the City Hall spot but lost out to Harold Washington in the Democratic primary.

Mayor Daley and his wife, the former Margaret Corbett, have two daughters and a son. A second son died at the age of three in 1981. The Daleys live in Chicago's working-class neighborhood of Bridgeport and send their children to private schools. They spend weekends in Grand Beach, MI, where the mayor enjoys watching movies and reading mysteries, Westerns, and books on crime.

ROBERT ENSTAD

DINKINS, David Norman

David N. Dinkins, an experienced clubhouse Democratic politician, scored a narrow victory in New York City's mayoral election on Nov. 7, 1989, becoming the first black man to hold the chief executive's job in the largest city of the United States.

Throughout the campaign, the 62-year-old Dinkins, the current Manhattan borough president, sought to project an image of a peacemaker in a city torn by racial and economic strife. That image drew 50% of the vote to the Dinkins camp, 27% of which were white votes, in a city that is 75% white. Some questions that arose during the campaign concerning Dinkins' personal finances were said to have contributed to the close vote. Dinkins had captured the Democratic nomination by defeating three-term Mayor Edward I. Koch in an upset victory in the September primary election. In the November election, Dinkins captured 917,544 votes, beating Republican candidate Rudolph Giuliani, a political newcomer and former U.S. attorney whose campaign focused on his well-publicized record as a tough prosecutor. Giuliani got 870,464 votes or 48%.

As mayor-elect, Dinkins inherited a municipal government with a new city charter that further empowers the mayor. He would have to use those powers wisely. The city must grapple with a $500 million deficit, widespread drug-related violence and social problems, and an AIDS epidemic that is crippling the city's health-care system. (*See* NEW YORK CITY.)

Background. David Norman Dinkins, a native of Trenton, NJ, was born on July 10, 1927. The son of a barber, Dinkins, who served one year in the Marine Corps, is a graduate of Howard University in Washington, DC, where he earned a degree in mathematics. He moved to New York in 1953 where he obtained a degree from Brooklyn Law School.

Dinkins was a protégé of J. Raymond Jones, a political leader who ran a training ground for young black politicians. Dinkins began his political career by hanging candidate posters in subways. After being elected to the New York State Assembly in 1965 and serving one term, he was named a deputy mayor by New York City's Mayor-elect Abraham D. Beame in 1973. Tax problems, however, forced him to withdraw. He paid his back taxes, and was appointed city clerk in 1975. Dinkins was elected Manhattan borough president in 1985 after two unsuccessful bids for that position.

An avid tennis player and Big Band enthusiast, New York's new mayor is married to the former Joyce Burrows, the daughter of a Harlem politician who also served as a Dinkins mentor. The David Dinkins are the parents of two children.

LIONEL BASCOM

FOLEY, Thomas Stephen

Capitol Hill admirers of Rep. Thomas Foley and his centrist approach to politics long have contended that the Democrats would have done much better in recent presidential elections if they had put the Washington congressman at the top of their ticket. The Democrats did not take that advice. However, in June 1989, Foley's Democratic colleagues in the House did elect him House speaker, the highest national office the party holds.

The son of a judge and a lawyer, the 60-year-old Foley is known best in Congress for his judicial temperament. This trait, Democrats believed, was just the right quality to help them escape the quagmire of partisan wrangling and muckraking that dragged down Foley's predecessor as speaker, Jim Wright. (*See* special report, page 542.)

Background. First elected to the House in 1964, Foley has moved slowly but steadily up the congressional ladder, often with the help of circumstances. He was elected head of the Agriculture Committee in 1975 when the House Democratic Caucus ousted the previous chairman because of complaints he was too autocratic. In 1980 he was appointed by then-Speaker Thomas P. O'Neill as Democratic whip after the incumbent was defeated for reelection. That paved the way for Foley to be elected majority leader in 1986 when Wright succeeded O'Neill in the speakership.

On most issues Foley's positions are typical of Northern Democratic liberals. He is against capital punishment, is prochoice on abortion, and was active in framing legislation to cut off aid to the contra guerrillas in Nicaragua. But he also accommodates his conservative district by opposing gun control. He won reelection in 1988 with 77% of the vote.

His main strength as a legislator has been his ability to adjust to difficult realities in order to advance his basic beliefs. Typical was his response to the 1985 Gramm Rudman deficit reduction legislation. Instead of flatly opposing the law, as some House Democrats would have preferred, Foley persuaded liberal and conservative Democrats to agree on a compromise alternative which shielded social programs from the automatic cuts required by the law, while making significant cuts in defense spending.

Foley's inherent caution has kept him from being better known nationally. While he talks freely with journalists on a broad range of subjects, he almost always insists on not being quoted by name.

Born March 6, 1929, in Spokane, WA, Thomas Stephen Foley received his bachelor's degree and law degree from the University of Washington. Before his election to the House, he practiced law, was a deputy prosecuting attorney, taught constitutional law at Gonzaga University, and was assistant attorney general for the state of Washington and special counsel to the U.S. Senate Committee on Interior and Insular Affairs.

His wife Heather, whom he married in 1968, serves as his unpaid administrative assistant. They have no children.

ROBERT SHOGAN

FOSTER, Jodie

The biggest surprise of the 1989 Academy Awards occurred when 26-year-old Jodie Foster took home the best actress Oscar for her performance as a rape victim in *The Accused,* winning over such favorites as Glenn Close and Meryl Streep. It was the second nomination of her career: The first, for best supporting actress, was for another brutal role, that of the drug-addicted 12-year-old prostitute in *Taxi Driver* (1976). Yet if anyone could be expected to pull off an Oscar upset, it was Foster, an actress who continually has challenged people's expectations.

Background. Alicia Christian Foster was born in Los Angeles, CA, on Nov. 19, 1962, the youngest of four children. Her parents, Lucius and Brandy, were divorced shortly before her birth. In order to help pay the bills, Brandy took Jodie's eight-year-old brother Buddy to au-

Jodie Foster

AP/Wide World

dition for TV commercials. At one session the three-year-old Jodie was spotted by an advertising executive, who hired her to appear in a Coppertone ad.

Jodie always had been an alert, inquisitive child who had begun talking at nine months and learned to read at the age of three. Not surprisingly, she was right at home in front of the cameras. Her mother encouraged her and managed her career, and by the age of eight Jodie had acted in nearly 45 commercials. Moving on to more challenging parts, the youngster landed a succession of guest-starring roles on TV series, beginning with *Mayberry, R.F.D.* in May 1969. She made her feature film debut in 1972, starring in Walt Disney's *Napoleon and Samantha,* the story of a girl and boy and their love for a circus lion. Other roles in feature films included the daughter of roller-derby skater Raquel Welch in *Kansas City Bomber* (1972), and Becky Thatcher in *Tom Sawyer* (1973). She made her first big break from family-oriented roles by costarring as a drinking, thieving youth in *Alice Doesn't Live Here Anymore* (1974). She also had her own short-lived TV series that year, *Paper Moon,* based on the film about a con man and his daughter.

Despite her busy schedule, Foster remained a student at the bilingual Lycée Français in Los Angeles. She was graduated at the head of her class in 1980 and continued her education at Yale University, where she studied literature and writing and appeared on the university stage. She made six films during semester breaks and vacations, and was graduated in 1984.

During her freshman year at Yale, Foster unwittingly found herself at the center of one of the biggest news stories of 1981, when John Hinckley, Jr., infatuated with the actress, attempted to assassinate President Ronald Reagan in order to get her attention. Although she has avoided commenting at length about her unwanted celebrity in the matter, Foster stated in an essay written shortly after the incident, "That kind of pain doesn't go away. It's something you never understand, forgive or forget."

Resuming her career full-time and winning the Oscar has helped the actress to put that unfortunate era behind her. The movie *Backtrack,* a love story in which she costarred with Dennis Hopper, was released in 1989.

JEFF ROVIN

GRAF, Stefanie Maria

In 1988, West German tennis star Steffi Graf enjoyed what many experts consider the finest year anyone ever has had in tennis. By winning the Australian Open, the French Open, Wimbledon, and the U.S. Open tournaments, she became only the fifth person in tennis history —and the first since 1970—to win a Grand Slam. In addition, Graf added to her tennis reputation by winning a gold medal at the 1988 Summer Olympics.

Despite not equaling her spectacular achievements of 1988, the 20-year-old star continued in 1989 to compile a record that shows her to be one of tennis' most successful players. In fact, the world's Number 1-ranked women's player won three of the four Grand Slam tournaments in 1989, losing only the French Open to 17-year-old Arantxa Sanchez Vicario of Spain. She also took the Virginia Slims crown in November.

The rise of Steffi Graf to prominence on the world tennis circuit was rapid. After several years on the pro circuit, she won her first Grand Slam event, the French Open, in 1987 at the age of 18. That year she also took over the Number 1 spot from Martina Navratilova. Graf's powerful style, marked by her trademark forehand, often intimidates other players, as does her intense attitude. Calm and unemotional on the court, Graf has been called a "tennis machine." Opponents dread playing her because of this exceptional combination of mental concentration and physical ability, and many consider her virtually unbeatable when at the top of her form.

Background. Stefanie Maria Graf was born June 14, 1969, in Mannheim, West Germany. Her parents, Peter and Heidi, both were semiprofessional tennis players, and Steffi was learning the game by the age of 4. Her father, recognizing her extraordinary talent, gave up his job as co-owner of an automobile dealership to move his family to nearby Brühl and open a tennis school, building Steffi into a player of world-class ability.

After several years of competing nationally and internationally, usually dominating her age group, Graf turned professional at 13. Despite a brief setback caused by a serious tendon injury to the thumb of her right hand, she continued her dramatic rise and was ranked 22d in the world by 1984.

Although she failed to win any major tournaments over the next two years, Graf improved steadily, taking matches from such established champions as Chris Evert and Martina Navratilova. In 1986 she was named West Germany's Sportswoman of the Year. After a few months of rest and training with her father (still her principal coach and manager) in the winter of 1986–87, Graf returned to the world circuit and has dominated women's tennis ever since.

Graf enjoys reading, going to rock concerts, and movies. She lives in Brühl with her family, but spends much time at her condominium in Florida.

GRAY, William H., III

Democratic Rep. William H. Gray III of Pennsylvania hardly could have anticipated the opportunity that presented itself in June 1989 due to the abrupt resignation of California Rep. Tony Coelho, the Democratic House whip, because of conflict of interest charges. Nevertheless, Gray took advantage of that opening with the same political acumen and intensity which in his ten previous years in the House had helped to make the 48-year-old Philadelphia congressman one of the most influential Democrats on Capitol Hill and one of the most prominent black leaders in the country.

Background. Gray launched his political career from the ministry, which has been a natural forcing ground for many black politicians. But what early on separated Gray from Jesse Jackson and other black political figures was Gray's facility for compromise and his skill at building coalitions. In defeating an incumbent black congressman to win his north Philadelphia seat in 1978, Gray had the endorsements of such prominent black leaders as Coretta Scott King, but also the backing of white Philadelphia businessmen, which aroused the suspicions of some militant blacks in his community. But in 1982 he beat back a challenge from the militants in the Democratic primary, which allowed him to consolidate his support in the district.

Meanwhile in the House, Gray used contacts with Democratic colleagues to get himself a choice seat on the House budget committee. Then by carefully steering a path for himself between rival factions of the committee he became the committee's chairman in 1985, and thus the highest-ranking black elected official on the national scene. In his new post he built a reputation as a conciliator by getting his fellow liberal Democrats to accept a lid on social spending while getting conservatives to go along with reductions in defense outlays. He strengthened that reputation following the 1987 stock market crash by his role in forging a budget compromise that won agreement from both the Congress and the White House and also complied with the Gramm-Rudman deficit reduction law.

For all his moderation, Gray never has lost touch with his base support among blacks and liberals. He has been a vigorous opponent of apartheid in South Africa and led the fight to get the House to override President Reagan's veto of the antiapartheid (economic sanctions) act in 1986. He also has pressed for expanding aid to black Africa.

Nor has Gray's talent for compromise stunted his ambition. Within a few hours of Coelho's resignation he was on the phone to congressional allies around the country, who helped him nail down the job. Following reports that he was the subject of a Justice Department probe of irregularities in his office, Gray took the offensive, by denying the charges and denouncing the leaks.

Born in Baton Rouge, LA, Aug. 20, 1941, William H. Gray III was educated at Franklin and Marshall, Drew Theological Seminary, and Princeton Theological Seminary. A former lecturer at several universities, he was an assistant professor at, and director of, St. Peter's College in Jersey City, NJ (1970–74). Since 1972 the congressman has been senior minister at the Bright Hope Baptist Church in Philadelphia, where his father and grandfather also ministered. He and wife, Andrea, have three sons.

ROBERT SHOGAN

HARRIS, Barbara Clementine

The Rev. Barbara C. Harris made religious history when she was consecrated a suffragan (assistant) bishop in the Episcopal Diocese of Massachusetts on Feb. 11, 1989. The event marked the first time a woman was installed in such a position in a church that considers its bishops to be successors to Jesus' apostles.

Bishop Harris' election in September 1988 stirred a furor from conservatives who objected because of her sex, her lack of a seminary degree, and the liberal positions she had taken on issues like homosexual rights as a columnist for *The Witness,* an unofficial Episcopal magazine. Her superior in Massachusetts, Bishop David E. Johnson, said he would not send her into a parish that would find her presence "painful" so long as its members agreed to meet with both bishops.

Background. Barbara Clementine Harris was born in Philadelphia on June 12, 1930, and grew up in the Germantown section. After graduating from a girls high school, she joined the staff of Joseph V. Baker Associates, a black-owned public relations firm.

Harris became president of Baker Associates in 1958 and held that post until she joined the Sun Oil Company's community relations department ten years later. During that period she also became a civil-rights activist, taking part in the 1965 march from Selma to Montgomery, AL, led by the Rev. Martin Luther King, Jr.

Barbara C. Harris

AP/Wide World

In July 1974, Harris led the procession during the unauthorized ordination of 11 women as Episcopal priests in Philadelphia's Church of the Advocate. The Episcopal Church formally approved women priests in 1976, and Harris was ordained in October 1980, after studying for three months at the Episcopal Divinity School in Cambridge, MA.

Following her ordination she left the Sun Oil Company to serve St. Augustine of Hippo Parish in Norristown, PA, and began a four-year chaplaincy in the Philadelphia County prison system. In 1984, Harris became executive director of the unofficial Episcopal Church Publishing Company in Ambler, PA. She started to write a column, "A Luta Continua," a Portuguese phrase meaning "the struggle continues," for *The Witness* and used it to advance her views on social justice.

Although she has criticized the Episcopal Church for not taking stronger stands on social issues, Harris says she feels "bound to work within the structures of the church." At the same time, she says, "I certainly don't want to be one of the boys. I want to offer my peculiar gifts as a black woman."

Harris' three-year marriage ended in divorce in 1965. She has no children.

DARRELL J. TURNER

HERSHISER, Orel Leonard, IV

Ever since Orel Hershiser became a member of the starting pitching rotation for the Los Angeles Dodgers in 1984, his record has reflected the team's performance. He was 11-8 when the team finished fourth in 1984, 19-3 when it won a divisional title in 1985, 14-14 and 16-16 during two off years that followed, and 23-8 during the 1988 World Championship season. When the team fortunes fell again in 1989, Hershiser remained the star pitcher but failed to duplicate his 1988 numbers. He finished the 1989 campaign with a 15-15 record and a 2.31 earned run average (ERA).

"I look at what I think is humanly possible to achieve," said the 6'3" (1.9-m), 192-lb (87-kg) sinkerball specialist. "I see myself allowing three runs or less, keeping the team in the game, and giving it a chance to win. If I play with a real good team, I'll win a lot of games. If I'm on an average team, I'll win an average number of games."

The 31-year-old right-hander conceded that his concentration occasionally was diverted in 1989 by demands on his time following the miracle season of 1988. Hershiser was almost a one-man show that year, pitching 59 consecutive scoreless innings—a record that ended in the first inning of his first 1989 start. He finished the 1988 regular season at 23-8 and with a 2.26 ERA, before winning Most Valuable Player honors in both the National League Championship Series and the World Series. He later was presented with the Cy Young Award, given to the top pitcher in each league. As a result of his excellent year the Dodgers awarded Hershiser, who also was named *Sports Illustrated* Sportsman of the Year for 1988, with a three-year, $7.9 million contract.

A myriad of endorsement offers also followed, yet Hershiser remained a man of grace, modesty, and good humor. He is an intelligent, articulate athlete with a well-deserved reputation as a thinking man's pitcher. (He uses a computer to keep tabs on opposing hitters.) Hershiser is also a devoted family man who is so devoutly religious that he often sings hymns to himself. He also is involved in charity and volunteer work.

Background. Orel Leonard Hershiser IV was born in Buffalo, NY, on Sept. 16, 1958—two weeks before the transplanted Brooklyn Dodgers completed their first season in Los Angeles. He was the oldest of Orel and Millie Hershiser's four children, all of whom parlayed their father's competitive spirit and perfectionist philosophy into proficiency at sports. Katie and Judd earned scholarships in volleyball and golf, respectively, while Gordie became a pitcher in the Dodger farm system.

AP/Wide World

Orel Hershiser

Young Orel IV showed an early affinity for excellence in sports, especially baseball. He was a pitcher-shortstop for his Cherry Hill, NJ, high-school team before enrolling at Bowling Green University in Ohio. He was selected by the Dodgers in the amateur free agent draft of June 1979. The following summer, while playing for the San Antonio Dodgers in the Texas League, he met Jamie Byars at a party. They were married on Feb. 7, 1981. The Hershisers have two children. Orel's autobiography, *Out of the Blue,* written with Jerry B. Jenkins, was a 1989 best-seller.

DAN SCHLOSSBERG

HOFFMAN, Dustin

Dustin Hoffman, winner of the 1989 Academy Award for best actor for his challenging role in *Rain Man,* is considered by many to be the greatest living U.S. actor. Certainly the body of Hoffman's work, as well as the amazing diversity of his roles, supports his claim to the title. Whether he is playing a 121-year-old pioneer in *Little Big Man* (1970), Watergate reporter Carl Bernstein in *All the President's Men* (1976), a suave ladies' man in *Ishtar* (1987), or an autistic savant in *Rain Man* (1988), Hoffman displays both the extraordinary versatility of a character actor and the charisma of a leading man. As a further example of his range as a performer and his devotion to his profession, Hoffman traveled to London's West End to portray Shylock in *The Merchant of Venice* in 1989. The Oscar winner declared that he did not want to die without doing Shakespeare.

Background. Dustin Hoffman was born on Aug. 8, 1937, in Los Angeles, CA, the son of a furniture designer. Hoffman was always shorter than his schoolmates, and thus considered himself "an outsider, an observer." Interested in becoming a professional pianist, he enrolled in Santa Monica City College as a music major. He also took a theater course and, falling in love with acting, left college to study for two years at the Pasadena Playhouse. Upon finishing that course in 1958, he went to New York to find work.

Hoffman struggled for eight years, auditioning while he supported himself with a variety of menial jobs. After landing bit parts on the stage, in films, and on television, he finally graduated to supporting and leading roles in offbeat stage works such as *The Journey of the Fifth Horse* (1966)—for which he won an Obie Award as the best off-Broadway actor of the year—and *Eh?* (1966), in which he portrayed a rebellious factory worker. Hoffman's stage work was noticed by director Mike Nichols and, when casting the part of the naive Benjamin in the film *The Graduate* (1967), Nichols brought Hoffman to Hollywood for a screen test. The film, about a young man who has a love affair with an older woman, then falls in love with her daughter, became a huge hit. It catapulted Hoffman to stardom and earned him an Oscar nomination for best actor.

To avoid being stereotyped, Hoffman next took the decidedly different role of vagrant Ratso Rizzo in *Midnight Cowboy* (1969), another successful film which earned him his second Oscar nomination. A third nomination was awarded him in 1974 for his portrayal of self-destructive comic Lenny Bruce in *Lenny.* He finally won the gold statuette on his fourth nomination, playing a devoted single parent fighting a bitter custody battle with his estranged wife, played by Meryl Streep, in *Kramer vs. Kramer* (1979). Hoffman earned a fifth nomination for *Tootsie* (1982), in which he played a hungry actor who pretends to be a woman in order to get work. He also starred in a Broadway and television production of *Death of a Salesman.*

The 1989 Oscar, his second, was awarded for his portrayal of Raymond in *Rain Man,* a role he researched with his usual dedication. The actor spent months with autistic people, doctors, and researchers before undertaking the part of an autistic man who is taken from the security of a mental institution by his brother, played by Tom Cruise.

Hoffman married ballerina Anne Byrne in 1969, and they had one child together, Jenna; they were divorced in 1979. He married Lisa Gottsegen in 1980, and they have four children.

JEFF ROVIN

JIANG Zemin

Jiang Zemin was appointed general secretary of the Chinese Communist Party in June 1989 in the wake of the suppression of the Chinese prodemocracy movement, following the dismissal of Zhao Ziyang. In November he was named to replace retiring Deng Xiaoping as chairman of the party's Military Affairs Committee. First party secretary in Shanghai since 1988, Jiang had taken the side of the conservative elements as the democracy movement unfolded in his city in May. He fired the editor of a small but influential liberal newspaper, the *World Economic Herald*—a move that was protested widely in Shanghai.

In his new posts, Jiang confronted the task of rebuilding the legitimacy of a party known by most Chinese today for the corruption of its leaders and the ineffectiveness of its attempts to stem inflation and unemployment. Attempting to lend legitimacy to the appointment, Deng Xiaoping spoke of Jiang as a worthy successor to Mao Zedong and himself, though few believed Deng's imprimatur would figure significantly in the actual succession crisis that would follow his death.

Background. Born in Yangzhou, Jiangsu, in July 1926, Jiang Zemin was educated at Shanghai's Communications University, earning a degree in electrical engineering in 1947. He spent several years in Moscow in the early 1950s as an intern at the Stalin Automobile Factory. Returning to China in 1956, he held a series of industrial positions in Manchuria, Shanghai, and Wuhan. In 1971 he joined the central government in Beijing as head of the foreign affairs department in the first ministry of machine building—a position he held for eight years.

Following Deng Xiaoping's return to power, Jiang was promoted to the first in a series of three vice-ministerial positions in 1980. During the next three years he served as vice-minister in the Administrative Commission for Import and Export Affairs, the State Foreign Investment Commission, and the ministry of the electronics industry.

In 1983 he became minister of the electronics industry and after a restructuring of the State Council (or cabinet) the next year, Jiang was appointed deputy head of the leading group for the electronics industry.

At the Twelfth Congress of the Chinese Communist Party in 1982, Jiang was elected to its Central Committee. Five years later he became a member of the Politburo—the party's most powerful decision-making body.

Meanwhile, in 1985, he was appointed mayor of Shanghai, China's largest city, and turned his attention to developing its substantial economic potential and to resolving its very serious problems of aging and inadequate infrastructure. During his three years as mayor, he gained a reputation for his enthusiastic support of the municipality in its competition for scarce resources. In 1988 he was appointed to the position of first party secretary in Shanghai, a policy-making post technically superior to that of mayor.

Although he has a reputation for speaking and reading several foreign languages, Jiang has not traveled extensively abroad. He is married to Wang Yeping; they have a son, who currently is studying in the United States.

JOHN BRYAN STARR

KAIFU, Toshiki

Wracked by a political scandal, Japan's ruling Liberal Democratic Party (LDP) on Aug. 8, 1989, chose Toshiki Kaifu as its party president to finish the unexpired term of Noboru Takeshita. Accordingly, the Diet (parliament) on August 9 elected Kaifu as Japan's 19th postwar prime minister. He was the third LDP party member to hold Japan's top leadership post in 1989, following resignations first by Takeshita and later by Sousuke Uno. In October he was elected president of the LDP.

At age 58, Kaifu became the second-youngest prime minister in Japan's history. Although he had only a narrow political base as a member of the LDP faction led by former State Minister Toshio Komoto, Kaifu also maintained close ties with Takeshita. Kaifu is a political heir of his mentor, the late Prime Minister Takeo Miki, a reformer who also assumed office from a weak power base in a 1974 party crisis involving corruption.

Toshiki Kaifu

AP/Wide World

In one of his first steps in office, possibly taken to bolster his image at home, Prime Minister Kaifu met with U.S. President George Bush in Washington on September 1.

Background. Toshiki Kaifu was born in Ichinomiya on Jan. 2, 1931, the first son of a photo-studio owner. As a teenager during World War II, he had planned to join the air corps, when Japan surrendered. In 1948 he entered Chuo University, and he began the study of law at Waseda in 1952.

A series of coincidences gave Kaifu the nickname "Mr. 29." His university graduation came in the 29th year of the Showa period (1926–88). At age 29, in 1960, Kaifu was elected the youngest member of the Diet, in the 29th general election. Kaifu joked with supporters that, with their help, he would be prime minister in 29 years. Exactly 29 years later he became Japan's leader.

Despite his relative youth, Kaifu has had wide political experience, winning reelection to the Diet ten times. In 1966 he became parliamentary vice-minister of labor. Under Prime Minister Miki in 1974, he was deputy chief cabinet minister. At age 45 he became education minister, the first Showa-born cabinet minister in Japan's history.

Until he became prime minister, Kaifu lived quietly with his wife Sachiyo in an apartment in Tokyo. They have two children, a son and a daughter who works as a secretary in his office. Kaifu neither smokes nor drinks, and he exercises regularly. He has such a reputed fondness for polka-dot bow ties that he is said to own 600. His motto is "Be resolute, and even the devil will run!"

ARDATH W. BURKS

LEMIEUX, Mario

Although Wayne Gretzky of the Los Angeles Kings has gained the reputation as the "Great One" of the National Hockey League (NHL), Mario Lemieux of the Pittsburgh Penguins has begun challenging him as "the best" (the English translation of *le mieux*). During the 1988–89 season, the 23-year-old center amassed a league-leading 199 points to capture his second consecutive Ross (scoring) Trophy. He also finished second to Gretzky in the voting for the Hart (most valuable player) Trophy, a prize he won in 1988.

Lemieux' excellent play during 1988–89 included setting a record for short-handed goals with 13, having a hand in 109 of Pittsburgh's NHL high 118 power play goals, and scoring eight points in a play-off game against Philadelphia. With 41 points in his first 12 games, he had the fastest start of any player in NHL history. While he could not keep up the torrid pace for all 80 regular-season games, his 199 points was the fourth-highest total for a season. Only Gretzky, who has had four 200-plus-point years, including an all-time 215 in 1985–86, ever has done better. But Gretzky turned 28 in 1989. The 6′4″ (1.9 m), 210-lb (95-kg) Lemieux, whose jersey number (66) is the flip side of Gretzky's 99, is four years younger.

Background. Mario Lemieux, who was born in Montreal, Que., to Jean-Guy Lemieux, a construction worker, and his wife Pierrette on Oct. 5, 1965, started skating when he was three. At the age of 15 he joined the Laval Voisins of the Quebec Major Junior Hockey League. The following year he left school to devote himself to hockey. During his three years with the Voisins, he was the most productive player in the league's history. As the team with the worst record during the 1983–84 season, Pittsburgh had the right to pick first in the draft of juniors. Lemieux was their selection, and it was like winning the lottery. Lemieux totaled 100 points during his first year at Pittsburgh and was voted rookie of the year. During his five seasons in the NHL, he has 300 goals and 715 points. Only Gretzky has more points (923). According to Montreal's Larry Robinson, "Wayne and Mario have helped change the NHL into a scorer's league. The game is faster, and it rewards players like Mario who can do inventive things with the puck."

Lemieux, who spoke virtually no English when he entered the NHL, now speaks the language well. But it is never volumes about his game. "Wayne [Gretzky] is the best player," Lemieux has said, acknowledging that his hockey résumé will be incomplete until it includes a Stanley Cup. Despite Lemieux' individual success, the Penguins have made the play-offs only once during Mario's tenure. He, however, has spread the hockey gospel to Pittsburgh. Before Lemieux' arrival, the Penguins were drawing crowds that averaged 6,839. Now the Civic Arena is full to capacity (16,168) for every game.

JIM MATHESON

LI Peng

The rise to power of Li Peng, China's premier since late 1987, can be attributed to his technical expertise, his bureaucratic skills and, perhaps most importantly, to his excellent personal connections to the elder generation of China's political leaders.

China's leaders were divided in their response to student demonstrations in April and May of 1989. Deng Xiaoping denounced the demonstrators as counterrevolutionaries; party head Zhao Ziyang acknowledged their patriotism and advocated a "flexible approach" in dealing with them. Li took Deng's side in the dispute, declaring martial law in Beijing in late May. Demonstrators responded by calling for his and Deng's dismissal.

Following the suppression of the democracy movement in June, Deng announced that Li Peng, together with the new party leader Jiang Zemin, were his choices to succeed him following his imminent retirement.

Background. Li Peng was born in Chengdu, Sichuan, in October 1928. His father, the writer Li Shouxun, was executed in 1930 for his role in the Communist revolution. When young Li was 11 years old he was taken under the wing of the leading Communist revolutionary, Zhou Enlai, and his wife Deng Yingchao. They kept him with them at the Communist liaison office in the wartime capital of Chongqing for two years and, in 1941, sent him to the Institute of Natural Science in the Communist base area in Yan'an.

In 1948, Li was sent to Moscow, enrolling in the Power Institute. He remained in the USSR for seven years, returning to China to head up a series of hydroelectric and telecommunication projects. The patronage of Zhou, by then premier of the State Council, apparently protected Li from criticism during the Cultural Revolution of the 1960s.

Following Deng Xiaoping's return to power in 1978, Li joined the central government as vice-minister (in 1979) and then as minister (in 1981) of the ministry of power industry. After a restructuring of the State Council in 1982, Li became vice-minister of the new ministry of water conservancy and power and was appointed to the Twelfth Central Committee of the Chinese Communist Party.

In 1983, Li became vice-premier, with particular responsibility for energy, transportation, and education. In 1985 he was appointed to the Politburo—the inner circle of party policy-making. He was regarded as a skilled bureaucratic infighter and effective crisis manager, but not as a leader in the formulation of reform policy.

Following the forced resignation of party head Hu Yaobang after student demonstrations late in 1986, Zhao Ziyang was chosen to replace him. Li was chosen to replace Zhao as premier of the State Council.

Li quickly gained the reputation for being a conservative foil to the relatively more liberal Zhao. Li was a consistent advocate of moderately paced reform and central planning. He denied that this approach was the result of his Soviet training. Many saw its roots in his close personal ties to the more cautious members of the elder generation of Chinese political leaders.

Li, who has traveled extensively abroad, is married to Zhu Lin. They had two sons, one of whom no longer is living, and one daughter.

JOHN BRYAN STARR

MAZOWIECKI, Tadeusz

The appointment of Tadeusz Mazowiecki as prime minister of Poland on Aug. 24, 1989, was an event of international historical importance. For the first time, a Communist regime constitutionally was allowing a non-Communist to take over government leadership. After Poland's first relatively free and competitive parliamentary election since World War II—held in June, and won by the Solidarity union movement—the Polish United Workers' (Communist) Party (PZPR) could maintain its majority in the Sejm (parliament) only by alliance with the two traditionally docile adjunct parties, the Peasants and the Democrats. Under the impact of Solidarity's popular mandate, the two parties defected and threw their support to Solidarity.

A Communist-led government then became practically impossible. President Wojciech Jaruzelski, following a period of consultations in which Lech Walesa declined to be a candidate, named Mazowiecki, a close associate of Walesa, as premier-designate on August 19. Mazowiecki was confirmed by the Sejm on August 24 by a vote of 378 to four with 41 abstentions. The choice ultimately was aided by Soviet leader Mikhail Gorbachev, who urged the Polish Communists to accept Mazowiecki and to participate in a coalition government with him.

Background. Tadeusz Mazowiecki was born April 18, 1927, in the small town of Plock. His father was a physician; his brother was killed in a Nazi concentration camp. Mazowiecki was educated as a lawyer, although he has made his livelihood mainly as a journalist and editor.

Mazowiecki has been a lifelong Catholic activist and intellectual with excellent connections to top figures in the hierarchy of the Polish Catholic Church as well as Solidarity. Among his friends have been Pope John Paul II and Cardinal Jozef Glemp, Catholic primate of Poland. In 1958 he founded the liberal Catholic journal *Wiez (Link),* which he edited until 1981.

He first was elected to the Sejm in 1961 but was denied reelection by the Communists in 1970 because of his activities in investigating the official killings of Gdansk shipyard workers. In 1980, Mazowiecki helped Lech Walesa negotiate the agreement bringing Solidarity official recognition. He was imprisoned for a year in 1981–82 when Solidarity was banned and martial law imposed. He later served as editor of the Solidarity weekly, *Tygodnik Solidarnosc.*

Tadeusz Mazowiecki

AP/Wide World

Mazowiecki is a widower with three grown sons. He is a rather shy, unassuming man with a quiet sense of humor who is respected widely among those who know him personally. On taking office, Mazowiecki committed himself publicly to three major objectives: (1) pluralism and diversity in Poland; (2) transformation of the economy from socialism to capitalism; and (3) maintenance of Poland's obligations under the Warsaw Pact.

ALEXANDER J. GROTH

MENEM, Carlos Saúl

Carlos S. Menem, former governor of La Rioja province, became president of Argentina on July 8, 1989. He won the presidency with 47.3% of the votes cast in May 14 elections, in which his Justicialista (Peronist) Party gained effective control of both houses of congress. The inauguration had been scheduled for December 10, but the lame-duck administration of Raúl Alfonsín of the Radical Civic Union was pressured by hyperinflation, widespread food riots, and social unrest into leaving office early. Once Menem had selected his center-right cabinet, he was ready to assume the top post.

An undistinguished speaker, Menem drew the poor and working classes to his cause through his forceful personality, humility, and a flamboyant life-style. The charismatic populist's campaign slogan was, "Follow me!" Menem stumped for a five-year grace period on the $60 billion foreign debt. He focused at times on a restoration of diplomatic relations with the British government, cut off since the 1982 Falklands war, although at other times he suggested that this was unlikely. He offered gradual wage increases to workers, in accordance with hikes in productivity. Menem, more free-enterprise oriented than traditional Peronists, would privatize inefficient, state-owned businesses and would seek increased foreign investment. On other issues, he appeared to favor pardons for the military men charged with rebellion against the Alfonsín government and also those being held for the murders and disappearances of at least 9,000 Argentines during the so-called "Dirty War" (1976–83).

Once in office, President Menem found that his program encountered resistance. Labor unions chafed under an official ban against strikes during the next two years. Businessmen reluctantly agreed on July 14 to a 90-day price freeze that would slow inflation. On September 8 nearly 30,000 people marched through downtown Buenos Aires to protest a possibility of presidential pardons.

Background. Carlos Saúl Menem was born on July 20, 1930, in La Rioja province to Syrian immigrants. While a law student, he became interested in politics. In 1973, Menem reached the governorship of his native province. Following the overthrow of President Isabel Perón by the armed forces in 1976, Menem was jailed for nearly five years. Once the military clique was replaced in 1983 by an elected government, he reentered politics and twice more was elected to the governorship of La Rioja province.

The new president is an avid sportsman and enjoys racing cars and socializing with celebrities. Menem married Zulema Yoma in 1966; they have two college-age children.

LARRY L. PIPPIN

MITCHELL, George John

Sen. George Mitchell (D-ME) was waiting patiently on a long airport line for a flight he seemed certain to miss when someone suggested that he try to get to the head of the line. The senator demurred. "Oh, I couldn't ask for special treatment," he said. Fortunately for Mitchell, an airline employee recognized him and hurried him onto the plane in time for him to keep an important speaking engagement.

AP/Wide World

George Mitchell

That sort of low-keyed style is scarcely typical of other U.S. senators, considered to be members of the world's most exclusive and powerful club. But if Mitchell refuses to push his way to the front of airport lines, his patience and persistence, combined with shrewd partisanship, have helped the Maine senator move to the forefront of the Senate where he took over in 1989 as Democratic majority leader. In part the 56-year-old Mitchell's style reflects the heritage of his native state, whose voters tend to resent flamboyance and pushiness in their politicians. But the ups and downs of his own career also have shaped his cautious but determined approach to politics.

Background. As a protégé of former Maine Sen. Edmund S. Muskie, the dominant Democrat in the state in the 1960s and 1970s, Mitchell at first moved ahead quickly. He was chairman of the Maine Democratic Party (1966–68) and deputy campaign manager of Muskie's bid for the presidency in 1972. But Muskie's highly favored candidacy for the Democratic nomination suddenly collapsed and then Mitchell had troubles of his own. He was defeated in bids to become Democratic national chairman in 1972 and governor of the state of Maine in 1974. Even so, Mitchell's connections to Muskie were later to prove valuable.

Mitchell's fortunes changed again in the late 1970s. After serving as U.S. attorney for Maine (1977–79), he was appointed to the federal bench in 1979. In 1980, when Muskie resigned from the Senate to become President Carter's secretary of state, Mitchell was named to fill that vacancy. In 1982, Senator Mitchell retained the seat with his first victory in a statewide election campaign, getting more than 60% of the vote. He won reelection in 1988 by an even bigger margin.

In the Senate, Mitchell characteristically kept a low profile at first, concentrating on environmental issues of concern to his Down East constituents. But in 1986 he became chairman of the Democratic Senate Campaign Committee and led the charge that won back the Senate for the Democrats after six years of Republican domination.

The esteem in which he was held by his Democratic colleagues was evidenced by his being named to the Senate committee probing the Iran-contra affair. During the hearings, Mitchell's cool, dispassionate style served as an effective counterpoint to the often melodramatic testimony of Marine Col. Oliver North. At one point, when North invoked the name of the Lord in justifying his actions, Mitchell retorted: "God does not take sides in American politics."

Born in Waterville, ME, Aug. 20, 1933, George John Mitchell was graduated from Bowdoin College in 1954. He served in the U.S. Army Counterintelligence Corps in Berlin (1954–56) and earned a law degree from Georgetown University in 1960. The former attorney is divorced and has one child.

ROBERT SHOGAN

POWELL, Colin Luther

U.S. Gen. Colin L. Powell has had a wide-ranging career in recent years, alternating between such prestigious Army posts as commander of the Fifth Corps in West Germany, to such high-level civilian assignments as assistant to President Reagan for national security affairs. In August 1989, President George Bush capitalized on Powell's experience by naming the four-star Army general successor to Adm. William J. Crowe, Jr., as chairman of the Joint Chiefs of Staff.

The appointment was also noteworthy in that Powell, the son of Jamaican immigrants, was the first black and, at 52, the youngest officer to be named to the nation's top military post. After being confirmed by the Senate on September 22, General Powell took office on October 1.

Background. Colin Luther Powell was born on April 5, 1937, in Harlem and grew up in the south Bronx. He received his undergraduate degree in geology from City College of New York in 1958, where he was also the top cadet in the Reserve Officers' Training Corps (ROTC). Upon his graduation, Powell was commissioned a second lieutenant in the U.S. Army. Serving two tours of duty in Vietnam (1962–63 and 1968–69), he was wounded in combat and awarded the Purple Heart, as well as the Bronze Star.

The future general earned a master's degree in business administration from George Washington University in 1971 and later studied at the National War College. He was named a White House Fellow in 1972, and this led to a series of public-policy positions, interspersed with military posts. In 1983 he became the senior military adviser to Secretary of Defense Caspar W. Weinberger. In 1986, Powell was given command of the Fifth Corps. However, National Security Adviser Frank C. Carlucci soon asked him to return to Washington to help reorganize a National Security Council tainted by the Iran-contra scandal. Powell left his command reluctantly, and only at the urging of President Reagan. He served first as Carlucci's deputy and later succeeded him as national security adviser. Powell was back at a military post, heading the U.S. Forces Command at Fort McPherson, GA, when President Bush tapped him for the Joint Chiefs.

Powell is well-regarded in Washington for his handling of public-policy assignments. He has a reputation of being able to work with competing constituencies. And he has solid credentials in foreign affairs, particularly Soviet-American relations. In naming Powell, President Bush bypassed some 30 other four-star generals.

On Aug. 25, 1962, he was married to Alma V. Johnson. They are the parents of one son and two daughters.

RAFSANJANI, Ali Akbar Hashemi

Hojatolislam Rafsanjani, who succeeded the late Ayatollah Khomeini (*see* OBITUARIES) as leader of Iran in 1989, enjoyed Khomeini's confidence as no other of his associates did. In June 1988, Khomeini made him commander in chief of the armed forces, and it was he who persuaded Khomeini the war with Iraq must end. Yet he does not resemble Khomeini in character. He is a pragmatist who knows a good deal about the world outside Iran.

The election manifesto Rafsanjani issued prior to his overwhelming victory in the presidential election of July 28, 1989, stressed the need for modernization and economic development in Iran. Although not a friend to the West, he was considered a more flexible holder of power.

Background. Ali Akbar Hashemi Rafsanjani was born in 1934 near Rafsanjan, in Kerman province in southern Iran. As is usual with Iranian clergy, he takes his surname from his place of birth. He was the eldest of five sons in a prosperous family of nine children; his father owned land and grew pistachio nuts.

Rafsanjani married into a religious family from the same area, and chose to pursue a career in the clergy. He moved in 1949 to the holy city of Qum and in due course attained the title of *hojatolislam,* "authority on Islam," a comparatively modest religious rank one step below ayatollah. His rank is the reason he could not become the heir of Khomeini's power in all its aspects.

In Qum in the 1950s, Rafsanjani became a disciple of Khomeini and also met many of the other future leaders of the Islamic revolution of 1979. Rafsanjani supported Premier Mohammed Mossadegh, nationalizer of the oil industry, in the early 1950s, and from then on worked actively against the rule of Shah Mohammed Reza Pahlavi. He was in Qum in 1963 when riots occurred that led to Khomeini's enforced exile. Rafsanjani himself was imprisoned for subversive activities in 1964, and was jailed on four occasions in all.

During the 1960s, with a colleague, he ran a school that was a cover for political activities, and became Khomeini's chief agent inside Iran. In the 1970s, boom years of the Shah's reign, Rafsanjani made a fortune in real estate in Tehran, traveled in Europe and the United States, and met Palestinian leader Yasir Arafat.

Rafsanjani's rise came with the 1979 revolution, when the Shah fell and Khomeini became Iran's supreme ruler. After that, Rafsanjani progressed in power and showed himself to be an extraordinary operator in the arena of Iranian politics. In 1979 he was one of the founders of the Islamic Republican Party, the dominant group in Iran until 1987. He became speaker of the *Majlis* (parliament), a post he filled through four parliaments, until becoming president. He was also Khomeini's personal agent on the Supreme Defense Council.

ARTHUR CAMPBELL TURNER

ROBBINS, Jerome

Jerome Robbins, the foremost native son of American dance, added another dazzling star to his constellation of accomplishments in the musical theater when

Jerome Robbins

AP/Wide World

Jerome Robbins' Broadway won six Tony Awards in 1989, including one for best musical and one naming Robbins as best director of a musical. His latest blockbuster is a musical assemblage of dances he choreographed for Broadway shows between 1944 and 1964, including numbers from *The King and I* (1951), *West Side Story* (1957), and *Fiddler on the Roof* (1964).

Robbins, a key figure in Broadway musical history, is reputed to be a hard-driving and imperious perfectionist. He has said of himself, "I'm enormously demanding . . . I ask for a great deal, but no more than I give myself." His works are viewed as a seamless blend of classicism and pop culture, with broad audience appeal. Many of his ballets are considered modern classics, and the Broadway musicals he has choreographed and/or directed are among the treasures of the modern musical theater. His 45-year career has garnered him innumerable national and international awards, among them four Tony Awards (prior to 1989), two Academy Awards, and Kennedy Center Honors (1981).

Background. Jerome Rabinowitz was born in New York City on Oct. 11, 1918. His parents, Russian Jewish immigrants, moved to Weehawken, NJ, when he was very young. Robbins' interest in dance, spurred by his older sister, started when he was a teenager.

Robbins entered New York University in 1935, but left school in 1936 to become a dancer. At first he studied an eclectic mix of Spanish, Oriental, and modern dance, and then at the urging of his teacher, took up ballet. Although Robbins made his debut as a Broadway hoofer in 1938, in 1940 he joined the newly formed American Ballet Theatre. He was a soloist there from 1941 to 1944, and a choreographer from 1944 to 1948.

Fancy Free (1944), Robbins' first ballet, was hailed as a turning point in the history of dance—the first substantive ballet in a modern American idiom. Within a year of its successful opening, the work was transformed by Robbins, designer Oliver Smith, and composer Leonard Bernstein into Robbins' first Broadway musical, the hit *On the Town,* with a book by Betty Comden and Adolph Green. Its success led to Robbins' increasing involvement with the legitimate theater.

In 1948, Robbins began his long-term association with the embryonic New York City Ballet as a dancer and choreographer, and in 1969 he became its ballet master. In late 1989, Robbins announced his retirement as co-director of the City Ballet. He planned to pursue other interests, including developing an autobiographical theater piece and writing his memoirs.

GLADYS HANDELMAN

RUSHDIE, Salman

Regarded in literary circles as one of the most important writers of his generation yet unknown to much of the general public, the 41-year-old Indian-born British novelist Salman Rushdie suddenly emerged in early 1989 as the most talked-about writer in the world. His fourth novel, *The Satanic Verses* (1988), was condemned by Muslims everywhere as a blasphemous attack on Mohammed, the Koran, and the Islamic faith. A long and richly imagined work of fiction, alternately fantastic, comic, and philosophical, *The Satanic Verses* had been nominated for (but did not win) the 1988 Booker Prize, Britain's most prestigious literary award. At the same time, it had sparked a violent uproar—including threats, protests, and demonstrations—throughout the Muslim world. India banned the book to avoid sectarian violence, followed soon by Pakistan, South Africa, Saudi Arabia, and Egypt.

Then in mid-February 1989, in a twist more bizarre and nightmarish than even Rushdie might have imagined, the Ayatollah Ruhollah Khomeini, Iran's 88-year-old spiritual leader, announced that Rushdie and "all those involved in [the book's] publication" must be killed for the crime of insulting Islam. As an inducement, Khomeini's disciples put a bounty of more than $5 million on Rushdie's head.

AP/Wide World

Salman Rushdie

Western governments reacted angrily to the threat, but the book industry was at first intimidated. Publishers in France and West Germany initially indicated that they would not publish the book, but later reversed themselves. Some U.S. bookstore chains, fearing violence against their employees and property, removed *The Satanic Verses* from store shelves. Civil libertarians and the literary community, however, soon expressed outrage at the threat against Rushdie and the removal of his book. In Britain, fellow writers presented a petition on Rushdie's behalf to Prime Minister Margaret Thatcher. Rushdie, meanwhile, had fled his house in north London and had gone into hiding under police guard. He issued a statement expressing "profound regret" at any distress the book had caused, but the ayatollah rejected his apology. U.S. chain stores did resume sales, and *The Satanic Verses* became a Number 1 best-seller. Rushdie remained in hiding as the threat continued, even after the ayatollah's death in June.

Background. Ahmed Salman Rushdie was born in Bombay, India, on June 19, 1947 (two months before the British pulled out). His parents were wealthy Kashmiri Muslims who admired English customs—but raised their son as a Muslim. At age 13, Rushdie was sent to England to be educated at the prestigious Rugby public school. Becoming a British citizen in 1964, he attended King's College of Cambridge University, where he studied history (with an emphasis on Islamic subjects) and earned an M.A. degree in 1968. After a brief stay in Pakistan, where his parents had relocated, he returned to London and began writing advertising copy.

Rushdie's first novel, *Grimus* (1974), was a critical and commercial failure. His second, however, *Midnight's Children* (1981), was a dazzling achievement; it won the Booker Prize and sold half a million copies worldwide. *Shame* (1983) cemented Rushdie's reputation as a writer of sweeping, brilliantly executed allegorical novels; it, too, earned a Booker nomination (but did not win). In 1987, Rushdie published *The Jaguar Smile,* an account of his 1986 visit to Nicaragua. He also has written articles for various newspapers.

Sharing Rushdie's fate in 1989 was his second wife, the American author Marianne Wiggins. The death threat against Rushdie sent her into hiding with him and forced her to cancel a promotional tour for her latest work, the novel *John Dollar.* Later in the year, however, the couple separated, and Wiggins indicated that she no longer knew of Rushdie's whereabouts.

BIOTECHNOLOGY

The year 1989 brought further progress in improving the quality and quantity of food, the preserving of endangered species, and the testing for human traits.

Engineered Tomatoes. Most store-bought tomatoes are plastic in consistency and flavorless in taste. These repelling characteristics result from the fruit being picked green, refrigerated while shipped, and then treated with ethylene to bring on the red color. Vine-ripened tomatoes are found to be too soft for shipping. The enzyme responsible for fruit softening is polygalacturonase.

Calgene Inc., a biotechnology company in Davis, CA, took the softening gene and transferred it, in reverse orientation, into a tomato plant. As a result, the tomato plant had two versions of the gene, one normal and the other in reverse orientation. Once inside a chromosome, the reverse gene makes "backward" RNA, which is complementary to the messenger RNA of the normal gene. The two RNAs, being complementary, bind to one another, and thus cannot be translated into the polygalacturonase enzyme. This results in a decrease in the activity of the softening gene by about 90%. Under these conditions, the tomatoes could be left to ripen on the vine, allowing the natural flavor to be developed fully, and then shipped without refrigeration. Field tests were being conducted in 1989 to test the hardiness of the genetically engineered plants.

Testing Human "Test Tube" Embryos. Women who know they carry the gene for a recessive X-chromosome-linked disease (for example, muscular dystrophy, hemophilia, Lesch-Nyhan) realize there is a 50% chance that each of their sons will inherit the affected X chromosome and suffer from the particular disease. A new procedure developed by Dr. A. H. Handyside and his associates in Great Britain provides for the testing of an embryo before a pregnancy is initiated.

An egg is obtained from the woman, fertilized in a test tube, and permitted to develop to the ten-cell stage. At this point, one cell of the embryo is removed and tested for the presence of a male-determining Y chromosome. If there is no Y chromosome, implying the embryo is XX in genotype, the embryo is placed in the woman's womb, where a pregnancy is initiated. It has been found that the loss of one or two cells from an early embryo does not interfere with normal development. This procedure guarantees the birth of a female child who, although having a 50% chance of being a carrier of the gene, will be free of the disease.

Preserving Endangered Species. The Indian desert cat, *Felis sylvestris,* is threatened with extinction. A small group of these exotic cats is housed at the Cincinnati Zoo where, unfortunately, they have failed to breed.

In 1989, Dr. B. L. Dresser of the zoo announced the successful birth of one of these animals. The procedure by which this was achieved involved the test-tube fertilization of an egg, followed by implantation of the developing embryo into the uterus of a domestic cat, *Felis catus*. The domestic cat required hormonal treatment so that its uterus was synchronized with the developmental state of the embryo. The ability to perform test-tube fertilization and then to use females of other species as surrogate mothers greatly improves the chances of preserving endangered species.

Distinguishing Genetically Identical Persons. When a person's body cells (blood, semen, hair) are available, with one exception, an analysis of the DNA in the cells, using DNA-cutting enzymes, will yield a unique DNA "fingerprint" or "profile" of the individual. The one exception is a set of genetically identical individuals (identical twins, identical triplets) whose DNA profiles, as well as all other genetic traits, are indistinguishable. However, Dr. A. M. Francoeur of Miragen, Inc., a biotechnology firm in San Diego, CA, has reported that it is possible to distinguish genetically identical individuals from one another.

Certain individuals form antibodies that attack particular tissues of their own bodies. The actions of these so-called autoantibodies result in autoimmune diseases (for example, rheumatoid arthritis, myasthenia gravis). Unexpectedly, it was found that all people produce a considerable number of autoantibodies that do not cause autoimmune diseases. The benign autoantibodies of any one individual form an array that is unique to that person, including each member of a set of genetically identical brothers or sisters, making it possible to distinguish each one from the others.

Herbicide-Resistant Plants. American farmers spray their fields with chemical herbicides in order to eliminate weeds. One of the more popular herbicides is bromoxynil, which inhibits photosynthesis, thereby resulting in the death of the plant. Unfortunately, many crop plants also are affected adversely by this herbicide.

It has been known for some time that the soil bacterium *Klebsiella ozaenae* produces the enzyme nitrilase, which breaks down bromoxynil to a nontoxic compound. Using recombinant DNA techniques, Dr. D. M. Stalker and associates at the Calgene biotechnology company transferred the bacterial gene that codes for nitrilase to tobacco plants. It was found that the plants were resistant to bromoxynil and that the resistance trait was inherited in subsequent generations. Experiments were planned to transfer the nitrilase-specifying gene to food-producing plants in order to make them resistant to the herbicide bromoxynil.

LOUIS LEVINE, *City College of New York*

BOLIVIA

Bolivia's developing democracy survived a formidable challenge in 1989 in a peaceful transfer of power from octogenarian four-term president Victor Paz Estenssoro to Jaime Paz Zamora, a second cousin of the outgoing president and a former vice-president of the country.

Paz Zamora was, by any measure, an anomalous choice. A onetime fiery leftist revolutionary who had served time in jail and in exile for his activities, he finished third in presidential elections on May 7, garnering 19.6% of the vote, behind former military dictator Hugo Banzer Suarez, who finished with 22.7%, and Gonzalo Sanchez de Losada of the governing Nationalist Revolutionary Movement (MNR) with 23%.

Since no candidate in the ten-man race received a majority of the vote, the selection of the next president fell to the national congress. Unexpectedly, Banzer, who had forged an alliance with the MNR during Paz Estenssoro's presidency, threw his support to Paz Zamora and on August 5, the latter was chosen president, receiving 97 of the 157 votes in the two houses of the Bolivian congress.

NEP Upheld. Also uncharacteristically, Paz Zamora pledged to continue the conservative fiscal and monetary policies of Paz Estenssoro. The former president's New Economic Policy (NEP), adopted in 1985, had rescued Bolivia from a disastrous runaway inflation that topped 24,000% a year.

The NEP espoused free-market principles, drastically cutting the size of the government bureaucracy and closing some of the country's largest state-owned tin mines, paring the work force of Comibol, the state mining company, from 30,000 to 9,000 in less than two years. The economic hardship brought on by the NEP stirred strong popular protest and fomented numerous nationwide strikes. But the policy produced visible results. Inflation during the first half of 1989 was less than 3%, and a revamped tax-collection system sharply reduced the government's chronic fiscal deficit.

Power Sharing. To win the presidency, Paz Zamora agreed to share power with Banzer's conservative National Democratic Action (ADN) party. Banzer's running mate in the May election, Luís Ossio Sanjines, was named vice-president and ten of the 17 cabinet posts were allotted to the ADN.

Paz Zamora also made statements intended to reassure foreign investors and international creditor banks. He promised "stability with growth," pledged fiscal discipline and a free currency exchange rate, and said he would allow prices and interest rates to be determined by market forces. The Bolivian economy, after falling into a severe recession in the first two years of the NEP austerity program, resumed modest economic growth in 1987 and continued it through 1988 and early 1989. The government has projected a 3.5% growth rate for all of 1989.

BOLIVIA • Information Highlights

Official Name: Republic of Bolivia.
Location: West-central South America.
Area: 424,162 sq mi (1 098 580 km²).
Population (mid-1989 est.): 7,100,000.
Chief Cities (mid-1987 est.): Sucre, the legal capital, 92,917; La Paz, the actual capital, 1,013,688; Santa Cruz de la Sierra, 577,803; Cochabamba, 360,446.
Government: *Head of state and government,* Jaime Paz Zamora, president (took office Aug. 5, 1989). *Legislature*—Congress: Senate and Chamber of Deputies.
Monetary Unit: Boliviano (2.610 bolivianos equal U.S.$1, May 1989).
Gross National Product (1987 U.S.$): $4,600,000,000.
Economic Index (1988): *Consumer Prices* (La Paz, 1980 = 100), all items, 9,082,864; food, 9,118,960.
Foreign Trade (1988 U.S.$): *Imports,* $595,000,000; *exports,* $598,000,000.

Drug Threat. Aside from maintaining economic growth and fiscal stability, Paz Zamora's principal challenge will be to confront Bolivia's thriving trade in illicit drugs. Bolivia, along with Peru, has been the main source of coca leaves, from which coca paste and cocaine are derived. While the coca bush is a mainstay of the Bolivian economy—up to 400,000 farmers are engaged in its cultivation—most cocaine refining and international trafficking in the drug has been centered in Colombia. But the government crackdown on drug cartels there has driven many producers of coca paste into Bolivia. Officials also have noted an increase in the use of the drug within Bolivia, particularly among the young. In September, U.S. President Bush announced a $261 million aid package for Bolivia, Peru, and Colombia, made up principally of weapons, to fight drugs. The following month, the presidents of the three countries invited Bush to a summit meeting on the drug crisis early in 1990.

RICHARD C. SCHROEDER, *Consultant to the Organization of American States*

BRAZIL

On Nov. 15, 1989, Brazilians voted in their first direct presidential election in 29 years. The ballots revealed dissatisfaction with President José Costa Sarney's ruling Brazilian Democratic Movement Party (PMDB) because his government failed to deliver the country from intractable economic and social woes. Fernando Collor de Mello, 40, a former governor of the northeast Alagoas state and founder of the center-right National Reconstruction Party (NRP), captured about 28% of the nearly 90 million votes cast, to finish first among the 22 candidates. However, since Collor's victory fell short of an absolute majority, he had to face

© Bob Strong/Sipa

Fernando Collor de Mello, a former governor known as a "maharaja hunter" for his crackdown on high-living bureaucrats, hugs a supporter during his successful 1989 presidential race. He defeated a Socialist candidate in a runoff race.

the second-place finisher, Luís Inácio (Lula) da Silva, who received more than 16% of the vote, in a December 17 runoff.

Collor, the son of a Rio businessman, captured the runoff by about four percentage points. Despite his privileged background, his appeal to Brazil's rural poor was strong. His first task as president-elect would be to put together a congressional alliance. The inauguration was scheduled for March 15, 1990.

Politics and Government. As governor, Collor was best known as a "maharaja hunter" for slashing the salaries of high-living bureaucrats as part of an anticorruption drive. In his campaign for president, Collor backed up his attacks on official wrongdoing and inefficiency with specific suggestions for reductions in the bloated government. His proposals included: constitutional reform to eliminate the ban on the expropriation of productive land for agrarian reform; administrative reform to pare the 20 ministries to 11 or fewer; patrimonial reform to allow the privatization of state companies; fiscal reform to collect a proportional income tax; and debt reform to withdraw federal backing from external borrowing.

On the other hand, da Silva, 44, a former autoworker and standard-bearer of the Marxist-oriented Workers' Party (PT), promised to redistribute income to the "have nots." Currently, 1% of the population owns half of the wealth. Da Silva also pledged to raise wages, control prices, declare a moratorium on the $110 billion external debt, and expand health and education services. In the November elections, da Silva edged out Leonel Brizola, a former Rio de Janeiro state governor, by just more than one half of one percentage point. In a contest in which 70% of the electorate never had voted for a president before, da Silva ran well with the youth, rural peasants, and urban workers. Of the top five finishers, da Silva's views were the most extreme. Mario Amato, president of the Federation of São Paulo Industries, warned that 800,000 businessmen would leave Brazil if da Silva became president. Da Silva, meanwhile, called the contest "the biggest dispute between labor and capital in history."

Collor and da Silva shared a weakness in that their respective parties jointly control less than 5% of the legislature. Conversely, candidates representing more dominant parties, such as the PMDB and the Liberal Front, marshaled barely 5% of the popular vote.

Municipal elections on Nov. 15, 1988, foreshadowed the decline of Sarney's PMDB. Da Silva's Workers' Party won control of 36 towns and urban centers, including São Paulo, the largest city in Latin America.

Economy. The economy showed signs of veering out of the Sarney administration's control as a gigantic internal debt fed the wide-

BRAZIL • Information Highlights

Official Name: Federative Republic of Brazil.
Location: Eastern South America.
Area: 3,286,473 sq mi (8 511 965 km²).
Population (mid-1989 est.): 147,400,000.
Chief Cities (mid-1987 est.): Brasília, the capital, 1,567,709; São Paulo, 10,063,110; Rio de Janeiro, 5,603,388; Belo Horizonte, 2,114,429.
Government: *Head of state and government,* José Sarney Costa, president (took office April 21, 1985). *Legislature*—National Congress: Senate and Chamber of Deputies.
Monetary Unit: Cruzado (7.507 cruzados equal U.S.$1, Dec. 1, 1989).
Gross National Product (1987 U.S.$): $313,000,-000,000.
Economic Indexes (1988): *Consumer Prices* (São Paulo, 1980 = 100), all items, 363,795; food, 429,302. *Industrial Production* (1980 = 100), 107.
Foreign Trade (1988 U.S.$): *Imports,* $14,604,-000,000; *exports,* $33,787,000,000.

spread fear of hyperinflation. Despite the 1988 commitment to reduce the public-sector deficit to 2% of gross domestic product (GDP), the 1989 deficit was to exceed 6% of GDP. After eight years of low or zero growth, GDP grew by 0.3% in the first eight months of 1989, compared with a negligible 0.04% in all of 1988.

In September 1989 prices soared to a record high of 36% over prices the previous month. Such sharp rises undermined the economy despite government assurances that monetary controls were in force and that foreign exchange reserves were adequate. Prices in 1988 climbed 933.6% and by November 1989 inflation neared a 1,200% annual rate.

On June 14, 1989, the Brazilian government formally jettisoned Sarney's anti-inflation "Summer Plan." The program, adopted in January, froze prices, forbade indexation that ties wages in with prices, and introduced a "new" cruzado—equal to 1,000 old cruzados and equivalent to about one U.S. dollar—as the main currency. Prices, however, were authorized to rise again by late March. In early April labor unrest erupted with a wave of strikes involving approximately 2 million workers demanding that wages be kept in line with inflation.

With the complete repudiation of Sarney's initiative, the government permitted indexation of the economy and daily currency devaluation, in effect linking wages to the inflation rate. Finance Minister Mailson da Nobrega favored wholesale price indexing to keep the rate of inflation "stable," which in Brazil means holding inflation down to a 30% monthly rate.

The booming underground economy remained far from the government's grasp. Of 145 million Brazilians, only about 3 million pay income tax. The so-called "parallel" economy generates an estimated $100 billion each year, equaling almost one third of the $330 billion GDP. The persisting vitality of the black-market system means that Brazil loses both taxes and control over the economy.

Brazilian officials missed a deadline for $812 million in debt payments in the first week of July. Government officials maintained that this lapse did not constitute a moratorium because Brazil needed only "temporary delays" in payment to preserve the $5.5 billion held in reserves. On August 9, da Nobrega announced that foreign creditors had agreed to a delay in debt payments. Cash reserves at this point surpassed the "safe" minimum level of $6 billion —the equivalent needed to purchase four months' worth of imports and thereby forestall fears of instability.

Da Nobrega insisted that Brazil remain a part of the international economy. In addition, he maintained the country also must avoid any shock that would act as a catalyst for runaway inflation. The finance minister considered the greatest danger not to be inflation itself but a possible panic, perhaps leading to an economy that operates only on U.S. dollars rather than the official cruzado.

In September the nation's foreign debt totaled $110 billion, the highest of any Third World nation. Brazilian negotiators again emphasized to foreign creditors that the nonpayment of $1.6 billion in interest was not a moratorium but a pragmatic measure to conserve foreign-exchange reserves.

Foreign Affairs. Disagreements over ecological and trade practices soured Brazil's relations with the United States throughout 1989. Amid mounting worldwide concern over the depletion of the Amazon Jungle, which accounts for more than 30% of the world's rain forest, several U.S. congressmen toured Brazil in March. Afterward, the delegation vowed to campaign against U.S. aid for Amazonian projects that lacked "objective" safeguards for peasants, Indians, and the environment.

In April, Sarney condemned the United States and other countries for leading a "cruel and unjust campaign" against his country. The Brazilian leader claimed that the developed countries had manipulated the rain-forest issue to impede the integration of Latin American countries. He also accused the industrial nations of seeking to "turn ecology into a business" by offering debt-for-nature swaps. Fearing international interference over sovereign territory, Sarney rejected the concept of retiring a portion of Brazil's foreign debt at a discount in return for guarantees of local funding for Amazon preservation.

Trade practices were also an issue between the United States and Brazil in 1989. On May 26, Brazilian officials responded to U.S. complaints of unfair trade practices by arguing that Brazil's import barriers allowed the nation to build up a surplus to help make payments on the huge foreign debt. The United States, after all, was Brazil's largest commercial creditor as well as its largest trading partner. The United States, nonetheless, began investigations under so-called Super 301 provisions in accordance with the U.S. Trade Act which ultimately could lead to retaliatory import duties.

In September, Paulo Tarso Flecha de Lima, Brazil's most senior diplomat, met with U.S. Special Trade Representative Carla Hills to mend relations between the two countries. Part of the bilateral tension sprang from U.S. licensing restraints on certain high-tech exports. Washington feared that these high-tech components could aid Brazil in developing nuclear weaponry. In October the United States and Brazil announced the end of a four-year dispute over Brazil's treatment of foreign computers and electronics in its protected market. Hills terminated the trade investigation and praised Brazil for its constructive approach.

George W. Grayson
College of William and Mary

BRITISH COLUMBIA

Renewed migration into British Columbia (B.C.) at levels not seen since 1980 was only one of the indicators of continuing economic growth and optimism in 1989. In contrast, the political scene remained uncertain as speculation continued about the future of Premier William Vander Zalm of the Social Credit Party.

Public Policy. The buoyant economy increased government revenue and reduced the general-fund deficit shown for 1988–89 to C$329,500,000.

A six-year "Access to All" program was announced, making advanced education and university degree courses more readily available outside of Victoria and Vancouver. A new School Act implemented a reorganization of the public school system that included the introduction of ungraded primary classes.

Responses to mounting public concern for effective environmental protection and efficient management of forest resources included increased fines and penalties for polluters and the formation of a ten-member forestry resources commission. A government task force recommended formation of a permanent "round table" of advisers to the cabinet on sustainable development, and public reviews of property taxation and tree farm licenses were initiated.

The government announced a minimum wage increase from C$4.50 to C$5.00, beginning with a 25¢ raise in October, with a second 25¢ increase in April 1990.

The Economy. Falling commodity prices and the rise in the value of the Canadian dollar undermined some of the economic growth experienced between 1987 and 1989, but continued momentum resulted in a 21% increase in capital investment during the year, and retail sales grew by more than 10%. Unemployment was at its lowest level since 1982, but remained above the national average. During 1988, British Columbia enjoyed the highest rate of job creation in Canada. The long-promised Vancouver Island natural-gas pipeline came closer to fruition when the provincial government gave approval for Pacific Coast Energy Corporation to begin construction. In June a new Crown corporation, the B.C. Trade Development Corporation, began assistance in the marketing and export of B.C. products. A breakdown in negotiations between the B.C. Nurses' Union and the province's 144 hospitals and health centers produced a 13-day strike, finally resolved through binding arbitration.

Party Politics. Discussion about the leadership of Premier Vander Zalm was stimulated by a September 20 by-election defeat in the Social-Credit stronghold of Cariboo, the fifth by-election loss since the premier took office in 1986. On the same day, Minister of Tourism and Provincial Secretary William Reid also resigned from the cabinet as a result of allegations surrounding the allocation of funds for a recycling project. Divisions with the government party publicly erupted in October when four backbenchers announced their intention to sit as independent Social-Credit members.

Judicial News. The B.C. Supreme Court ruled that the current provincial electoral boundaries were unconstitutional, and subsequent legislation set a January 1990 deadline for implementation of a new 75-seat electoral map. The B.C. Supreme Court and County Court systems were to merge.

NORMAN J. RUFF, *University of Victoria*

BRITISH COLUMBIA • Information Highlights

Area: 365,946 sq mi (947 800 km²).
Population (June 1989): 3,044,200.
Chief Cities (1986 census): Victoria, the capital, 66,303; Vancouver, 431,147; Prince George, 67,621; Kamloops, 61,773; Kelowna, 61,213.
Government (1989): *Chief Officers*—lt. gov., David C. Lam; premier, William Vander Zalm (Social Credit Party). *Legislature*—Legislative Assembly, 69 members.
Provincial Finances (1989–90 fiscal year budget): *Revenues,* $13,500,000,000; *expenditures,* $13,500,000,000.
Personal Income (average weekly earnings, June 1989): $497.77.
Labor Force (August 1989, seasonally adjusted): *Employed* workers, 15 years of age and over, 1,436,000; *Unemployed,* 8.8%.
Education (1989–90): *Enrollment*—elementary and secondary schools, 551,600 pupils; postsecondary—universities, 39,900; community colleges, 26,500.
(All monetary figures are in Canadian dollars.)

BULGARIA

Bulgaria's President Todor I. Zhivkov, the Communist Party stalwart, abruptly stepped down on Nov. 10, 1989. Although Zhivkov publicly made attempts to quell opposition, Bulgarian officials said privately that he stepped down in an apparent attempt to avoid the fate of fellow party leaders in East Germany and Hungary whose power vanished in the face of demands for democratic reforms. He was succeeded as party general secretary by Petar T. Mladenov, who also replaced Zhivkov as head of state and indicated in December that the Communist Party would give up its monopoly on power and that free elections soon would be held.

The Political Scene. Throughout the year, Bulgaria had been buffeted by demands for liberalization of its Communist regime and violent resistance to its attempt to assimilate forcibly its large ethnic Turkish minority.

Although formally approving the sweeping political and economic changes taking place in the Soviet Union, Poland, and Hungary, Bulgaria's Communist Party had done little to emulate them. A planned comprehensive restructuring of the party and state apparatus had

AP/Wide World

Bulgaria's Foreign Minister Petar Mladenov, 53, a full member of the Politburo since 1977, succeeded Todor Zhivkov as the nation's Communist Party chief in November.

been aborted in late 1987. Opposition groups proliferated in the country. Led by such organizations as the Democratic League for Human Rights, the Discussion Club for *Glasnost* and *Perestroika,* and Podkrepa, the first independent trade union, they grew increasingly bolder in their demands for reforms. In February, Zhivkov, the 78-year-old party general secretary, attributed such activities to foreign provocation. Police and military forces were deployed throughout the country, and leading dissenters were harassed, imprisoned, and deported. However, neither force nor belated governmental assurances of toleration for free association and a new passport law promising the right of free travel for all citizens succeeded in quieting popular unrest.

Criticism from abroad and the growing chaos in fellow hard-lining East Germany split the Bulgarian Communist Party leadership. In October, Zhivkov admitted the need for serious political changes and promised to tackle the problem at the Central Committee meeting scheduled for November. Taking advantage of a 35-nation international conference in Sofia, on November 3, demonstrators numbering between 4,000 and 9,000 marched in the capital shouting "Democracy!" and "*Glasnost*!" Zhivkov stepped down seven days later. In December, he was expelled formally from the Bulgarian Communist Party.

The regime's response to the need to modernize Bulgaria's stagnating economy had been ineffective. In January it announced a 15% cut in military spending over the following two years. In March it sent a representative to the economic conference of six Balkan nations in Ankara, agreeing to help improve economic contacts and diminish regional trade barriers. In May, acknowledging problems in food production and processing, Zhivkov announced a land-reform program that would break up the collective farms and permit individual farmers to lease land for periods of five to 75 years.

BULGARIA • Information Highlights

Official Name: People's Republic of Bulgaria.
Location: Southeastern Europe.
Area: 42,823 sq mi (110 910 km^2).
Population (mid-1989 est.): 9,000,000.
Chief Cities (April 1985): Sofia, the capital, 1,114,759; Plovdiv, 342,131; Varna, 302,211.
Government: *Head of state,* Petar T. Mladenov, president and general secretary of the Communist Party (took office 1989). *Head of government,* Georgi Atanasov, chairman of the Council of Ministers (took office March 1986).
Monetary Unit: Lev (1.73 leva equal U.S.$1, July 1989).
Gross National Product (1988 U.S.$): $67,600,-000,000.
Economic Index: *Industrial Production* (November 1988, 1980 = 100), 139.
Foreign Trade (1988 U.S.$): *Imports,* $16,582,-000,000; *exports,* $17,223,000,000.

Ethnic Turks. The government's five-year-old campaign to assimilate forcibly Bulgaria's 1.5 million ethnic Turkish minority also came to a head in 1989. In March there were widespread, violent clashes between the ethnic Turks and security forces, with perhaps 100 killed and hundreds expelled. The government then decided to grant exit visas to all ethnic Turks who wished to emigrate to Turkey, which agreed to accept them. Some 300,000 fled to Turkey between May and July. Unable to handle such a flood, Turkey closed its border on August 31, stranding additional hundreds of thousands of would-be emigrants in Bulgaria. The exodus created a severe labor shortage in Bulgaria. In Turkey, thousands demanded a military invasion of Bulgaria. World opinion condemned Bulgaria, and the United States withdrew its ambassador, in protest.

JOSEPH FREDERICK ZACEK
State University of New York at Albany

BURMA

The military regime of Saw Maung that took power in September 1988 changed Burma's name to the Union of Myanmar in 1989. Political and economic realities proved much more intractable. A nine-man cabinet, backed by the 19-member (18 military, 1 civilian) State Law and Order of Restoration Council (SLORC), was governing. It was a regime discredited by the massacre of thousands in 1988, the flight of thousands of students to insurgent-held border areas and neighboring Thailand, and a level of repression unknown before in Burma.

The SLORC promised to hold elections, perhaps as early as May 1990, but the military is unlikely to give up power it has held since the 1962 coup of Gen. U Ne Win. Most commentators assume that the general, who retired officially in 1988, continued to govern indirectly. SLORC attempted to defuse opposition by permitting the formation of political parties and by announcing a draft election law. By the February deadline, 233 political parties had registered. The formation of these parties may have been accelerated more by the promise of a petrol quota and a telephone line for each party than by ideological considerations. Parties affiliating with the government-favored National Unity Party (NUP) enjoyed other benefits. The fragmented political parties had few rights, however. Under martial law no more than four persons are legally able to gather and only one state-run newspaper is allowed to operate. The chief opposition party, the National League for Democracy (NLD), enrolled an estimated 3 million members but then faced heightened harassment and arrests.

Aung San Suu Kyi, 44, the wife of a British professor and mother of two sons, is leader of the NLD and daughter of assassinated nationalist hero Aung San. She returned to Burma in 1988 to care for her mother (who died in January 1989) and became a charismatic leader of the prodemocracy forces. The government attacked the popular leader as an outsider allied to Communists. It also drafted election law provisions that may disqualify her as a candidate. She ignored the government's actions and became increasingly outspoken, rallying enormous crowds in defiance of martial law. In late July she was put under house arrest. Thousands of others, primarily from the NLD, also were arrested.

On August 2 more than 17,000 jailed criminals were released, though diplomats speculate the general amnesty was simply to make room for new political prisoners. The arrests, the massive army presence, and the martial-law regulations kept the August 8 anniversary of the government's 1988 crackdown under control. On October 20 the regime barred anyone being detained from running in the 1990 election. Thus, Aung San Suu Kyi and hundreds of other NLD members would be disqualified unless released before December nominations.

BURMA • Information Highlights

Official Name: Union of Myanmar.
Location: Southeast Asia.
Area: 261,969 sq mi (678 500 km^2).
Population (mid-1989 est.): 40,900,000.
Chief Cities (1983 est.): Yangon (Rangoon), the capital, 2,458,712; Mandalay, 532,895.
Government: *Head of government,* Gen. Saw Maung (took power Sept. 18, 1988). *Legislature* (unicameral)—National Assembly.
Monetary Unit: Kyat (6.708 kyats equal U.S.$1, July 1989).
Gross Domestic Product (1988 U.S.$): $9,300,000,000.
Economic Index (Rangoon, 1988): *Consumer Prices* (1980 = 100), all items, 196.4; food, 197.8.
Foreign Trade (1988 U.S.$): *Imports,* $244,000,000; *exports,* $138,000,000.

Insurgencies. Burma's 40-year insurgencies are the oldest in Asia. Nearly half of the country's territory is controlled by ethnic rebel groups. Many of these absorbed thousands of student refugees but reports indicated major army victories against the largest group, the Karens. Students were being rounded up in the cities to serve as army porters through areas mined by rebels. The 50-year-old Burmese Communist Party (BCP) fell victim to internal rebellion when its aging Burmese leaders were overthrown by younger, more ethnically diverse members. The BCP was dissolved and a Burma National Democratic Alliance Army calling for multiparty democracy was formed.

Economic and Cultural Conditions. To counter economic deterioration, the regime vigorously courted capitalist investment. Though most governments had cut off foreign aid, Malaysia, Japan, Thailand, and China established trade. Environmentalists deplored the fact that logging and fishing concessions sold to Thailand threaten to accelerate deforestation, while others noted that most of the revenues were going for military equipment and 200-300% increases in military and civil service salaries. A $5 billion external debt further crippled prospects for economic recovery. While the country has extensive oil reserves, a July refinery bombing exacerbated already critical gas shortages that sent gasoline prices to $17 per gallon on the black market.

Further decline was reflected in the fact that Burma, once the largest rice exporter in Asia, faces the prospect of famine. Rice prices rose 900% in two years. In July the government was forced to sell low-quality rice on the market at one third the official rate.

Universities had been closed since June 1988, though elementary and secondary schools reopened in late 1989. The easing of passport restrictions led many critics to leave the country. Some feared a "brain drain" of Burmese talent. Limited tourism was permitted after being stopped for several months.

Foreign Relations. The government reversed nearly three decades of xenophobia by opting for foreign investment and claiming to favor a capitalist multiparty government. But it sent mixed signals abroad. It held its first news conference for foreign journalists in 27 years but forbade civil servants to speak to them. It launched agreements that clearly favored foreign governments, while accusing unnamed embassies and foreign media of trying to subvert the government. Various nations appealed to the regime to respect human rights.

LINDA K. RICHTER
Kansas State University

BUSINESS AND CORPORATE AFFAIRS

The U.S. business world was a battleground in 1989. Competition in the usual sense was intensified by foreign goods competing in the U.S. market, which forced companies everywhere to cut prices and expenses to the bone. Making the atmosphere even more frantic was the almost constant threat of takeovers. It was not just a market of goods and services; it was a marketplace in which companies themselves continued to be gobbled up, even against the efforts of their managements.

Economic Instability. Vast economic uncertainties added to the unease. While profits turned in a respectable if not outstanding year and the economy remained on a fairly even course—the gross national product showed a year-to-year gain of 2.5% through most of the year—there was almost no relief from repeated dire forecasts, some of them engendered by a belief that an economy in its seventh year of expansion simply had to be facing a downturn. Fears of inflation and high interest rates alternated with recession forecasts, but as the year wore on inflation and interest rates retreated again. For the year, increases in both the consumer price index and the gross national product price deflator, a broader measure of prices, averaged just over 4%. The prime interest rate, at 11.5% early in the year, was down to 10.5% and falling as the year ended.

As if there were not enough instability, the stock market continued to perform erratically. After having recovered almost fully from the collapse of October 1987, it plunged again—by 190 points—on Friday, October 13. On the very next business day it regained almost half the loss, typifying the unpredictable, somewhat ragged atmosphere of the business, financial, and economic world throughout the year.

Various other thorny issues plagued the business scene. The U.S. dollar's value in international trade remained erratic. The specter of trade protectionism persisted, with American companies incensed over Japanese trade restrictions. The savings and loan debacle left the federal government with a bailout bill of at least $160 billion and the task of closing down hundreds of financial institutions. (*See* special report, page 130.)

Disasters also played a role in the financial scene. The ire of environmentalists was raised again when the supertanker *Exxon Valdez* went aground off Alaska, spoiling hundreds of miles of coast, costing the company more than $1.2 billion in cleanup costs, and inviting suits from various groups—the most important of them being a still dissatisfied State of Alaska. (*See* feature article, page 36.)

Companies in Trouble. While corporate profits early in the year were strong by most measures, they were losing momentum, and they continued to do so for the rest of the year. The companies making up the Standard & Poor's 500-stock index, which had an earnings gain of 36% in 1988, fell to a gain of 22% in the year's first quarter and to just 4% in the second three-month period. The erosion continued for the rest of the year, leaving after-tax profits at less than $160 billion, or about 5% below those of 1988. In fact, many large companies fell into the red. Control Data reported a quarterly loss in the hundreds of millions of dollars. Wang Laboratories suffered a fiscal 1989 loss of $424.3 million. Unisys Corp., another computer concern, which saw its earnings tumble 67% in the second quarter, said late in the year that it would lay off thousands of workers. Eastman Kodak Co. said it would cut its work force by 4,500 and sell or consolidate about 20 ailing businesses.

© Melinda Berge/Bruce Coleman Inc.

The Japanese acquired more assets in the United States in 1989. In October the Mitsubishi Estate Co. purchased a 51% interest in New York City's Rockefeller Center.

Price competition was that tough, and it showed up everywhere. Sears, the retailing giant, abandoned its highly publicized policy of repeated sales in favor of everyday low prices; it shut down 800 stores for 42 hours to cut price tags by up to 50% on most products. Wall Street securities firms, competing viciously for commissions in a shrinking market, laid off thousands of workers, bringing to at least 20,000 the total number of workers dropped since the big collapse of 1987. Some brokerage houses began cutting paychecks, too. Carmakers tried to keep sales moving with price rebates of as much as $2,000 a car on previously announced price increases, and by cutting interest rates far below the market. Chrysler even offered a two-year no-interest car loan.

Competing with Japan. With competition intense, American companies complained throughout the year about the Japanese. They contended that some Japanese products—and products from other Asian Pacific nations, as well—were sold below cost in the United States, a practice referred to as "dumping." The dumping of cheap foreign goods, such as computer memory chips—to give a recent example—forced smaller American companies out of the market. Yet Japan, despite repeated requests from the United States, continued to restrict imports of American goods.

The Japanese denied the charges, claiming that the United States blamed them for its own internal problems associated with lagging productivity, a focus on short-term results, and excessive consumer, business, and government debt. Nevertheless, the Japanese worried that their investments in the United States were probably offensive to Americans. With dollars accumulated from their huge trade surplus with Americans—in 1988, for example, the United States imported $90 billion of Japanese goods but sold them only $37 billion—the Japanese had billions to invest. While the British still remained the biggest owners of U.S. assets, the Japanese were moving up, having surpassed the Dutch in 1988. They particularly liked real estate. In the fall, Mitsubishi Estate Co. paid $846 million for a 51% share of the Rockefeller Group, the primary owner of the 19-building Rockefeller Center in midtown Manhattan, including Radio City Music Hall. Almost simultaneously, Japan's Mori Building Development purchased 85% of Houston's Four Oaks Place, an office complex, for $300 million.

Employee Stock Ownership. Whatever its negative implications, competition was good for consumers and good for restraining inflation, too. The developing globalization of business helped in that regard also, and so did the unusual stability of worker paychecks. Strikes were relatively few, and wage demands by organized labor continued to give way to an increased emphasis on job security and benefits. Management, however, took an increasingly strong stand against extension of medical and health-care benefits, and even sought cutbacks, prodded by the ever-rising costs of such programs. With the U.S. unemployment rate just above 5% of the work force, unusually low by recent standards, companies sought other ways in which to keep good employees. One of the most popular was the employee stock ownership plan, or ESOP.

ESOPs were nothing new, but the extent of their usage was, and for a reason not originally intended. Created in the 1950s by attorney Louis Kelso, ESOPs were meant to motivate and reward workers through share ownership and a sense of participation. Their acceptance, slow at first, became significant in the 1980s, and by 1989 about 10 million workers were enrolled in various ESOPs, three times the number of a decade earlier. By 1989 nearly 10,000 companies offered stock plans, including 1,500 in which workers owned most of the shares. In 1989, ESOPs received a boost from unexpected sources. Management saw in them a way to put stock in friendly hands, those of their workers. Conversely, corporate raiders saw in ESOPs an aid to financial takeovers. In the latter instance, borrowing costs would be reduced because of tax breaks afforded those who set aside stock for employees.

In this way, a concept of the 1950s was wed to one common to the 1980s. To shore up their defenses against raids, J. C. Penney, Ralston Purina, and Texaco poured a total of $1.75 billion into their company ESOPs. Procter & Gamble said it would spend $1 billion to bring its ESOP to 20% ownership from 14%. Polaroid defended itself from an unwelcome suitor by raising employee ownership to 14% of the company.

Buyouts and Mergers. If many workers slowly but surely were becoming moderately rich, some corporate raiders and investors were instantly propelling themselves into the superwealthy class. Financier and raider Carl Icahn for a while sought to control Texaco. While he abandoned the idea before the year was out, he managed to walk away with a profit of $340 million, after pressuring management to vote a $2 billion payout to shareholders. The takeover technique was stunningly simple for those with access to billion-dollar lines of credit. That is where junk bonds continued to play their role, inducing institutional investors to lend money for extremely high rates of interest. But in 1989, the annual rate of removal was $162 billion for the first three months. The risky loans would be repaid in part from the sale of the acquired company's assets. As with so many creative financing concepts, this too was developed to a damaging extreme. It was in fact a year in which conventional business stories were crowded from the media by tales of junk bonds, leveraged buyouts, and friendly and unfriendly takeovers.

As the year began, Drexel Burnham Lambert, the securities house that junk bonds built into a giant, pleaded guilty to six felony counts involving mail, wire, and securities fraud and agreed to a $650 million fine, $350 million of which was to be compensation to victims, and $300 million to the government. The company

AP/Wide World

Mergers and buyouts continued in 1989. Time Inc.'s acquisition of Warner Communications was a headliner. Time's J. Richard Munro (left) *and Warner's Steven J. Ross were named cochairmen and chief executive officers of the merged corporation.*

also agreed to cooperate in a government investigation of Michael Milken, the individual within the company credited with doing the most to create the $180 billion market. Milken would be tried later.

It was a bad time for other financiers, too. Hours before the Drexel deal was announced, Paul Bilzerian, a 38-year-old corporate raider who had won control of Singer Company, was accused of fraud, conspiracy, and other charges from earlier attempts to take over companies. He would go to jail. Later in the year, five executives of Princeton/Newport Partners were convicted of 63 felony counts stemming from illegal stock-trading schemes and were fined $3.8 million. Their conviction involved the first use against brokers of the Racketeer Influenced and Corrupt Organization Act, known familiarly as the RICO Act. It also would be used in another case involving the indictment of 46 Chicago commodity traders who were charged with defrauding customers, evading taxes, and racketeering.

Meanwhile, some leveraged buyouts, with a volume that soared from just $250 million in 1980 to more than $45 billion in 1988, were in trouble. Perhaps more significant for the country, leveraged buyouts, or taking a company private, involved the retirement of stock. In the five years 1984 to 1988, about $365 billion of equities thus were removed, but in 1989 the annual rate doubled early in the year. In place of stock, companies were financed by high-interest debt, which some financial people thought would be impossible to repay. Management of Freuhauf Corp., which had revenues of $2.7 billion in 1986, borrowed $1.5 billion to repurchase its stock from shareholders, then was forced to sell one division after another until almost nothing was left in 1989. RJR Nabisco went private in December 1988 and then lost $309 million in the second quarter of 1989, after selling off $2.5 billion in businesses. Among other big names that went private were R. H. Macy, Beatrice, TWA, and Safeway Stores.

More conventional mergers were also in the news, in part because industries were attempting to produce more formidable competition in world markets. This was true, for example, in pharmaceuticals. Bristol-Myers, a $6 billion-a-year company, and Squibb, with sales of $2.6 billion, agreed to an $11.2 billion stock swap. SmithKline Beckman approved a merger with British Beecham Group, traditionally strong in Europe. Dow Chemical agreed to merge its Merrell Dow Pharmaceuticals with Marion Laboratories.

The communications-entertainment industry also was in ferment. After months of legal hassling, Time Inc. and Warner Communications merged to create Time Warner. Sony Corp. of Japan acquired Columbia Picture Entertainment for $3.4 billion.

The airline industry had troubles all its own. Eastern Airlines personnel struck through most of the year, and the company declared Chapter 11 bankruptcy to get its financial affairs in order. Among other things, its reemergence left it without its Boston-New York-Washington shuttle, purchased for more than $365 million by real-estate man Donald Trump. (*See also* special report, page 524.)

Trump also bid more than $7.5 billion for American Airlines, withdrawing the bid when share prices fell on October 13. Financially plagued United Airlines remained unsold at the end of 1989, after several deals failed—including a $6.79 billion buyout proposed by UA's pilot union that fell through when the union could not raise enough capital. The growing concentration in the industry became a matter for concern—American, United, Delta, Northwest, and Continental controlled 70% of the passenger business.

JOHN CUNNIFF, *The Associated Press*

CALIFORNIA

A severe earthquake, a somewhat lower level of political conflict, and the apparent failure of an initiative plan to reduce car insurance premiums marked 1989 in California.

Earthquake. An earthquake, centered near Santa Cruz and measuring 7.1 on the Richter scale, struck the San Francisco Bay area on October 17, killing at least 67 people and causing more than $6 billion in property damage. In a special session, the legislature approved Gov. George Deukmejian's request for a ¼-cent sales tax over 13 months to provide for earthquake relief. The tax increase was expected to raise $800 million, a figure some Bay-area legislators called inadequate. (*See* feature article, page 50.)

Legislature. In 1989 conservative Republican Governor Deukmejian and the liberal leaders of the state legislature tried a cooperative approach. With fewer confrontations, some political deadlocks were broken and a series of major policy proposals received bipartisan support. The governor signed a $49.3 billion budget—an 8.7% increase over 1988. But he still used his veto 276 times and cut $646 million from the 1989–90 budget, mostly in health and social service areas. This led to futile protests from officials in numerous counties, who administer several of the state-funded programs.

A seven-year stalemate among special interest groups and political leaders ended with the passage of a new workers' compensation act in 1989. The act overhauled an outmoded system and provided for larger benefits. In another important bill, the legislature placed control of solid-waste disposal under a powerful state board.

After a sniper killed five children in a Stockton schoolyard with an AK-47 semiautomatic assault rifle, the legislature banned the sale of 55 types of assault weapons.

CALIFORNIA • Information Highlights

Area: 158,706 sq mi (411 049 km²).
Population (July 1, 1988): 28,314,000.
Chief Cities (July 1, 1986 est.): Sacramento, the capital, 323,550; Los Angeles, 3,259,000; San Diego, 1,015,000; San Francisco, 749,000; San Jose, 712,080; Long Beach, 396,280; Oakland, 356,960.
Government (1989): *Chief Officers*—governor, George Deukmejian (R); lt. gov., Leo McCarthy (D). *Legislature*—Senate, 40 members; Assembly, 80 members.
State Finances (fiscal year 1988): *Revenue*, $73,229,000,000; *expenditure*, $66,003,000,000.
Personal Income (1988): $530,968,000,000; per capita, $18,753.
Labor Force (June 1989): *Civilian labor force*, 14,355,900; *unemployed*, 785,900 (5.5% of total force).
Education: *Enrollment* (fall 1987)—public elementary schools, 3,172,000; public secondary, 1,317,000; colleges and universities, 1,788,012. *Public school expenditures* (1987–88), $17,482,-953,000 ($3,916 per pupil).

The legislature also voted to place on the state ballot in June 1990 a proposed constitutional amendment to govern the behavior of its membership. All committee meetings would have to be open to the public, except when personnel matters are discussed. The proposal would limit the gifts a legislator can accept, prohibit honoraria, and bar lobbying within the first year of leaving office. It also would create a board to set legislators' salaries.

Another law enacted in 1989 required retailers and utilities to make deliveries and/or provide service within an agreed-upon four-hour period or be liable for damages in small claims court. The legal blood-alcohol level for an intoxicated driver was lowered from .10% to .08%. Toilets in new buildings were limited to using 1.6 gallons of water per flush—about 55% of the amount used by a standard toilet.

Political Corruption. After a four-year investigation of the relationship between lobbyists and state legislators by the Federal Bureau of Investigation (FBI), state Sen. Joseph B. Montoya of Whittier was indicted on federal charges of extortion, racketeering, and money laundering. More indictments were expected.

Politics and Balloting. Governor Deukmejian appointed Los Angeles Appellate Court Judge Joyce Luther Kennard to a vacancy on the state supreme court—making her only the second woman named to the high court. U.S. Rep. Tony Coelho of Modesto, the House majority whip and prominent Democratic fundraiser, resigned in June so as to avoid a prolonged investigation of his personal finances. His seat was filled in a special election by Democratic State Assemblyman Gary Condit.

Voters narrowly rejected a proposal to build a new stadium for the San Francisco Giants to replace windswept Candlestick Park, prompting speculation about the major league team's future in the city. Despite their perceived liberal views toward homosexual relationships, San Francisco voters turned down a proposal to give homosexual couples and unmarried heterosexuals some of the same rights as married couples.

The initiative to reduce auto-insurance premiums by 20%, passed by voters in 1988, failed to live up to its promise in 1989. Hearings on rates could take years and there still was the possibility insurance companies could be granted increases.

CHARLES R. ADRIAN
University of California, Riverside

CAMBODIA

The withdrawal of Vietnamese forces and peace talks in Paris aimed at ending civil war were the landmark events of 1989 in Cambodia.

Politics. The Paris conference in July and August brought together the main Cambodian

AP/Wide World

At Paris peace talks on Cambodia, Khmer Rouge leader Khieu Samphan (right) confers with an aide as Cambodian Premier Hun Sen (left) and an unidentified government delegation member look on. Several Cambodian factions vied for power when Vietnam ended its occupation of the country in 1989. The peace conference adjourned without reaching an agreement.

factions. Those vying for power were: current Prime Minister Hun Sen, who was installed by the Vietnamese; Prince Norodom Sihanouk, a former king who has run the country off and on since 1941; the Communist Khmer Rouge; and the Khmer People's National Liberation Front, headed by former Premier Son Sann. The most powerful of these groups appeared to be the Phnom Penh regime led by Hun Sen, whose government reportedly has an army of about 45,000 troops. In 1989 it began to allow the people a limited amount of political and economic freedom in an attempt to gain cooperation.

Hun Sen and his Vietnamese backers showed little interest in sharing power with any other Cambodian group except the one led by Prince Sihanouk, who could provide an aura of legitimacy for Hun Sen's regime. Prince Sihanouk still had the greatest claim to legitimacy in the eyes of most foreign governments. His support also was probably strong among Cambodia's rural people, judging by the response of refugees whom he visited along the Thai border. Sihanouk reportedly had a small army of about 15,000 troops.

A third group that continued to vie for power was the Khmer Rouge, who slaughtered more than 1 million of their fellow countrymen when they ruled Cambodia from 1975 to 1979. With an army of about 30,000 troops supplied by China and quartered on Thai territory, they represented the main military challenge to Hun Sen's regime. A fourth group, led by former premier Son Sann, was too divided and corrupt to wield much influence.

Economics. According to foreign journalists who visited Cambodia, food supplies had improved, in part because Hun Sen was allowing farmers a limited right to hold land, and there was some private marketing of produce. But Cambodia has been devastated by years of war, and although it is one of the poorest countries in the world, it has been ineligible for aid, because few governments recognize the Hun Sen regime.

CAMBODIA • Information Highlights

Official Name: Cambodia.
Location: Southeast Asia.
Area: 69,900 sq mi (181 040 km²).
Population (mid-1989 est.): 6,800,000.
Chief City (1986 est.): Phnom Penh, the capital, 700,000.
Government: *Head of state,* Heng Samrin (took office 1979). *Head of government,* Hun Sen, prime minister (took office Jan. 1985).
Monetary Unit: Riel (100 riels equal U.S.$1, December 1988).

Foreign aid and investment were essential in order to get the economy moving, but the country's uncertain political future remained a major deterrent to foreign-aid donors. The government has begun to allow a small number of foreign tourists to visit the ancient temples at Angkor Wat. But the redevelopment of tourism, once a major source of income, would depend on the security situation and the cooperation of neighboring Thailand.

Foreign Relations. By the end of September, Vietnam claimed that all of its 200,000 troops had been withdrawn from Cambodia. This was the signal for renewed fighting to begin, because the rainy season, which favors guerrilla forces rather than Hun Sen's more conventionally equipped army, still had two months to run. The three guerrilla groups began to attack Hun Sen's road-bound forces, and some observers believed they might gain control of 10% to 20% of the country.

While the fighting increased, arguments broke out in many capitals over how to resolve the Cambodian conflict. Almost everyone agreed that some kind of coalition government was needed, but there was no consensus on whether to include the Khmer Rouge or not. Unfortunately, most of the factions seemed to believe they could solve Cambodia's problems by using military force rather than diplomacy.

PETER A. POOLE
Author, "Eight Presidents and Indochina"

CANADA

Canadians in 1989 lived with decisions made during the 34th federal election on Nov. 21, 1988. Armed with a parliamentary majority and a mandate for the 1987 Canada-U.S. Trade Agreement, the Mulroney government cut public spending and prepared a new value-added tax, saying in its borrowed slogan that it "opened Canada for business." Resentments heated by regional economic disparities focused on the unratified Meech Lake constitutional amendments, and gained momentum in the West and the East. Meanwhile, a provincial election in Quebec revealed 40% support for independence.

Politics. Winning the Conservative Party's first consecutive majority since 1891 showed some observers that even an unpopular government can survive by appearing decisive and by massive preelection campaign spending of $8 billion in cash and pledges. But now, with the election over, it was time for austerity.

Stanley Hartt, a Montreal lawyer and Mulroney confidant, returned to manage the prime minister's office when Derek Burney became Canada's new ambassador in Washington. A postelection cabinet shuffle filled holes and switched an ambitious Perrin Beatty from national defense to health and welfare. In October the prime minister announced that Ray Hnatyshyn, a former justice minister defeated in the 1988 election, would succeed Jeanne Sauvé as governor-general, Canada's titular head of state under Queen Elizabeth.

Both federal opposition leaders announced their resignations in 1989. Ed Broadbent of the New Democratic Party (NDP), frustrated by his party's failure to win any seats in Quebec, resigned on March 4. When well-known New Democrats such as Stephen Lewis, former Canadian ambassador to the United Nations, and Roy Romanow, a codesigner of Canada's 1982 constitution, failed to enter the leadership race, five less famous members of Parliament (M.P.s) and a schoolteacher declared and toured the country. In October the race heated up with the entry of former British Columbia Premier Dave Barrett. The NDP's leadership convention in Winnipeg in December ended with Audrey McLaughlin, a second-term M.P. from the Yukon, being declared the first woman to head a major national political party in Canada.

Liberal leader John Turner followed Broadbent's example on May 3. Turner's strong showing in the 1988 campaign had persuaded even some of his inveterate party critics that he should stay. The contest to replace Turner was delayed to June 1990, largely to give a better chance to the opponents of his bitter rival, Trudeau-era federalist Jean Chrétien.

A fourth party brought western Canada's sectional resentments home to Parliament on March 13 when a Conservative riding in Alberta elected Deborah Gray as the Reform Party's first M.P. Reform candidate Stan Waters also triumphed on October 16 when Alberta's Conservatives invited voters to choose a nominee for a provincial vacancy in the Senate of Canada, a constitutional innovation which the prime minister refused to countenance.

Government. When Parliament met in April, Governor-General Jeanne Sauvé read a throne speech of Conservative campaign prom-

The 1987 Meech Lake constitutional accord remained unratified in Manitoba and New Brunswick. In Manitoba a seven-member committee held monthlong public hearings on the agreement that recognizes Quebec as a distinct society.

© Dave Bonner

ises that included national day-care, environmental protection, and privatization, but business and editorial concern about Canada's federal deficit—a growing C$30 billion in 1989 —meant that real government policy would be determined by the federal budget. An advance notice of postelection policy came when Employment and Immigration Minister Barbara McDougall announced tighter access to unemployment insurance. Ignoring the Forget Commission of 1987, McDougall proposed to force recipients to work longer before qualifying. At least some of the savings were promised for retraining programs. Some other Canadians got prior notice of budgetary bad news when copies of a promotional leaflet leaked out of the government's printing office. The leak distracted the media and opposition politicians. Attempts to compel Finance Minister Michael Wilson to resign over the breach of secrecy diverted attention from the painful details, which were released officially on April 27.

Tough spending cuts fell chiefly on defense, foreign aid, postage subsidies, VIA Rail, and the publicly owned Canadian Broadcasting Corporation (CBC). Provinces lost part of the federal grants promised for health care and postsecondary education and the proposed day-care plan was shelved. The big emphasis was on new taxes. Besides the usual increases on cigarettes, beer, and liquor, personal income tax rose, and surtax rates increased to 8% for those earning more than C$70,000. A takeback of family allowance and old-age pension payments from beneficiaries earning more than C$50,000 a year cut into the principle of universality in social programs which Mulroney once had called "a sacred trust."

The Sales Tax. The biggest budget news was the Conservatives' long-promised goods and services tax (GST), designed to replace a 13.5% manufacturers' sales tax. The budget promised that the GST would begin in January 1991 at a rate of 9%. While the GST resembled the value-added taxes in most European countries, it was complicated by a long list of exemptions, from food to day-care payments, and by the refusal of the provinces to integrate their sales taxes with the federal levy. Wilson insisted the tax was needed to make Canada competitive in exports and to attack Canada's huge deficit. Special rebates would protect new home buyers and tax credits would compensate the poor.

The GST was not popular. By autumn, when the House of Commons opened its fall session, 79% of Canadians opposed it. Business lobbies condemned the proposal as a bureaucratic mess, while economists and even a few Tory backbenchers argued that the GST would be inflationary. Home builders warned that prices would soar and groups ranging from lawyers to greenhouse operators to musicians demanded exemption. Manufacturers, supposedly the great beneficiaries, had no evidence that the tax change would create new jobs or expand exports.

© Ron Poling/Canapress

Prime Minister Brian Mulroney (lower left) *listens as Finance Minister Michael Wilson explains the details of the leaking of the government's budget to a TV network.*

VIA Rail, Canada's passenger rail system, was another budget victim. Transport Minister Benoit Bouchard announced that, by 1993, public subsidies would fall from C$641 million to C$425 million. Cutting VIA services affected 7,000 rail employees, 115 regional transportation services, and the thousands of poor and disabled passengers most likely to use the services.

The Constitution. In June 1987, Prime Minister Mulroney had persuaded all ten provincial premiers to accept Quebec Premier Robert Bourassa's terms for signing the new constitution. Both opposition party leaders had concurred. The Meech Lake agreement accepted Quebec as a distinct society and extended powers of all the provinces, with federal funding to

CANADA • Information Highlights

Official Name: Canada.
Location: Northern North America.
Area: 3,851,792 sq mi (9 976 140 km²).
Population (mid-1989 est.): 26,300,000.
Chief Cities (1986 census): Ottawa, the capital, 300,763; Montreal, 1,015,420; Toronto, 612,289.
Government: *Head of state,* Elizabeth II, queen; represented by Ray Hnatyshyn, governor-general (took office January 1990). *Head of government,* M. Brian Mulroney, prime minister (took office Sept. 17, 1984). *Legislature*—Parliament: Senate and House of Commons.
Monetary Unit: Canadian dollar (1.1748 dollars equal U.S.$1, Oct. 11, 1989).
Gross National Product (1988 U.S.$): $471,500,-000,000.
Economic Index: *Consumer Prices* (1988, 1980 = 100), all items, 161.8; food, 151.4.
Foreign Trade (1988 U.S.$): *Imports,* $107,204,-000,000; *exports,* $112,340,000,000.

match. In the eyes of critics, including former Prime Minister Pierre Trudeau, Meech Lake weakened Canada's identity and Ottawa's powers and ignored claims of women, multicultural minorities, and aboriginal people.

By the end of 1989, ratification of the Meech Lake agreement by the provincial legislatures by the June 1990 deadline looked unlikely. Three of the supporting premiers had been defeated; opponents of the deal, mainly Trudeau Liberals, had gained power. Resentment at what some Canadians saw as a bribe to Quebec further was fueled in January. The Bourassa government used powers in the 1982 constitution to reverse a Supreme Court ruling that restored language rights to Quebec's English-speaking minority. Amid nationalist demonstrations and the firebombing of the offices of the main English-rights group, Quebec's National Assembly rushed through Bill 178, restricting the use of English on signs inside public and commercial buildings and banning English signs outdoors. Manitoba's new Conservative premier, Gary Filmon, joined Liberal opponents of Meech Lake. So did many New Democrats; candidates for the NDP leadership were unanimous in demanding changes. Yet Bourassa, reelected in Quebec on September 25 in the face of a resurgent separatist movement, dared not make concessions. Quebecers, he told Canadians, had reaffirmed their support for confederation but their commitment was not limitless. Government officials were reduced to reminding poorer provinces opposed to Meech Lake that the financial agreements with Ottawa that kept them afloat might not be honored unless they, in turn, honored the commitments of Meech Lake.

Canada and the World. Elected to a two-year term on the UN Security Council in late 1988, Canada ended its decade-old ban on diplomatic contact with the Palestine Liberation Organization. Canadian troops and a detachment of the Royal Canadian Mounted Police went to Namibia on UN peacekeeping duties. World détente made the government's defense program the chief victim of the 1989 budget. The Navy's C$8 billion nuclear submarine program, tanks for Canada's North Atlantic Treaty Organization (NATO) contingent, and the acquisition of replacement fighters all were canceled. Public protest focused on shutdowns or cutbacks at 14 bases that were the main prop to their respective local economies.

As usual, the relations that mattered most were with the United States. President George Bush and the Canadian prime minister exchanged visits, the former to a frigid Ottawa in February, the latter to Bush's summer retreat at Kennebunkport, ME, in August. Prime Minister Mulroney also presided at the official opening of Canada's new embassy on Washington's Pennsylvania Avenue in May and met with the president at the White House on November 29 to brief Bush on his recent trip to the USSR. Yet neither goodwill nor the Canada-U.S. trade agreement seemed to help in disputes over Canadian trade.

In October in Costa Rica, Mulroney announced that Canada would join the Organization of American States (OAS).

Business. Canadians were pushed into the Free Trade deal in 1987 by warnings of vanishing jobs, brutal U.S. reprisals, and economic disaster. The year brought plenty of evidence of the pace of change, though it was too soon to see whether the Free Trade deal had worked any benefits for Canada.

In January three well-known corporate names disappeared. On the 18th, Carling-O'Keefe and Molson's declared their intention to merge, leaving Canada only two brewing giants. A day later, the sale of a debt-laden Wardair to Pacific Western, owners of Canadian Airlines International, was announced. On the 20th, Imperial Oil, 70% of which is owned by Exxon, acquired Texaco Canada, part of the price of its parent's legal battles. Whatever the corporate benefits, jobs would vanish. Economic nationalists began compiling lists of

---

THE CANADIAN MINISTRY

M. Brian Mulroney, prime minister
Jean Corbeil, minister of labour
John C. Crosbie, minister for international trade
Robert R. de Cotret, president of the Treasury Board
Paul W. Dick, minister of supply and services
Jake Epp, minister of energy, mines, and resources
Tom Hockin, minister of state for small businesses and tourism
Otto J. Jelinek, minister of national revenue
Monique Landry, minister for external relations
Douglas Lewis, minister of justice and attorney general of Canada and leader of the government in the House of Commons
Gilles Loiselle, minister of state for finance
Elmer M. MacKay, minister of public works and minister for the purposes of the Atlantic Opportunities Agency Act
Shirley Martin, minister of state for transport
Marcel Masse, minister of communications
Charles J. Mayer, minister of western economic diversification and minister of state for grains and oilseeds
Donald F. Mazankowski, deputy prime minister, president of Queen's Privy Council for Canada and minister of agriculture
John McDermid, minister of state for privatization and regulatory affairs
Barbara J. McDougall, minister of employment and immigration
William H. McKnight, minister of national defence
Gerald S. Merrithew, minister of veterans affairs
Lowell Murray, leader of the government in the Senate and minister of state for federal-provincial relations
Frank Oberle, minister of state for forestry
Alan Redway, minister of state for housing
Thomas E. Siddon, minister of fisheries and oceans
Monique Vézina, minister of state for employment and immigration, and minister of state for seniors
Gerald Weiner, secretary of state of Canada and minister of state for multiculturalism and citizenship
Michael H. Wilson, minister of finance
William Winegard, minister of state for science and technology

© Dirck Halstead/Gamma-Liaison

Prime Minister Mulroney, accompanied by his family, held "unusually productive" talks with President George Bush at the presidential compound in Kennebunkport, ME, in August.

companies that had closed down in Canada to reopen south of the border though some had gone as far south as Mexico.

It was a mixed year for Canada's business tycoons. Vancouver's Murray Pezim was the big winner when the Supreme Court ruled that LAC Minerals had cheated him out of the huge Hemlo gold deposit. An Alberta inquiry into the collapse of the C$1.2 billion Principal Group resulted in scathing reports on Donald Cormie's behavior toward his 67,000 investors. Robert Campeau's triumphant 1988 acquisition of U.S. retailing giants, including Bloomingdale's, had been a symbol of what Canadians could achieve under free trade but by 1989, Campeau was overextended and lost control of his company to Olympia & York, the property-owning megacorporation of the Toronto-based Reichmann brothers. Edmonton multimillionaire Peter Pocklington, once a Conservative leadership contender, had lost his popularity in 1988 by selling hockey superstar Wayne Gretzky. In 1989 his meat-packing enterprise, Gainers, Canada's second-largest, fell to the Alberta government for nonpayment of debts.

Labor. It was a year for public-sector strikes, particularly among Canada's 242,000 nurses. In British Columbia, nurses at 80 hospitals walked out for 17 days after rejecting a compromise that had been accepted by their leaders. Quebec's 40,000 nurses timed an illegal strike to coincide with the provincial election and forced the embattled Bourassa government to make small concessions—though harsh penalties were exacted in lost pay and seniority and fines for union leaders. The nurses' gains were not matched by striking teachers and other public employees. Private-sector strikes were fewer than usual and most focused on job security as unions struggled to protect their members from the cutthroat free-trade environment.

Environment. An economy heavily based on natural products worried about the weather. The winter was bitter in the West with record lows at the end of January, and temperatures so low in the Yukon that home thermometers went off the scale. However, snow brought moisture and the disastrous drought cycle of the 1980s gave way to green fields and bumper crops. A hot, dry summer fanned forest fires that forced 23,000 Manitobans from their homes and cost the province 7,000 sq mi (18 130 km^2) of forest (compared with a national loss of 5,200 sq mi, 13 648 km^2, in 1988).

A bigger and more predictable environmental disaster was the dramatic fall in Atlantic fish stocks, linked to new technology and years of overfishing by foreign trawler fleets. Cuts in permitted catches destroyed the main industry of coastal communities in the four Atlantic provinces. Combined with the federal cuts to unemployment insurance and economic and regional development agreements, alternative mainstays of the regional economy, 1989 was a brutal year for the frail economy of Atlantic Canada. Wealthier regions, preoccupied by the problem of disposing of mountains of garbage or the relocation of PCBs, barely noticed.

The Law. A series of events and inquiries made Canadians more sensitive to relations between police and minorities. The killing of a black teenager in a stolen car in Mississauga, Ont., ignited black anger and public debate in Ontario. A judicial inquiry in Manitoba pursued the police killing of an Indian leader in Winnipeg. The inquiry also examined the failure for 15 years to solve another murder, of an Indian woman, when many in Flin Flon, the nearby white community, seemed to know the perpetrators. Newfoundland was shocked by delayed revelations of sexual and physical abuse of boys at a Catholic orphanage.

Abortion, an unresolved issue, found a new battleground in the summer when courts upheld the right of an Ontario and a Quebec woman to seek an abortion over the protests of the assumed fathers. A bill that might resolve the issue with a compromise was presented to Parliament in late October and sent to a committee for further study in December. The United Church of Canada continued to be racked with division over its 1988 decision to recognize the ordination of homosexuals.

Montreal Shooting. Fourteen women were killed when a 25-year-old unemployed recluse went on a shooting spree at the University of Montreal engineering school on December 6. The man, who apparently blamed women for his failures, ended by shooting himself. It was the worst mass killing in Canadian history.

People. Canada continued to evolve into a multicultural society as the great majority of immigrants came from Asia, the Caribbean, and other Third World regions. The crushing of the Chinese democracy movement in Beijing in June accelerated the flow of people and money from Hong Kong, particularly to British Columbia and southern Ontario. Some Vancouverites blamed their housing crisis on the influx, and pessimists could find signs of an ethnic backlash in opinion polls demanding that newcomers blend with the majority society. Others worried about the continued decline in the birthrate and the problems of an aging population.

Meanwhile old and young Canadians took advantage of other distractions, including the CBC's All-News channel, which opened in August. Veteran TV personality Patrick Watson was named CBC's new chairman, but the power rested with Gérard Veilleux, a senior official from the Treasury Board. Justice Charles Dubin probed Canada's greatest shame in 1988, the disqualification of Olympic gold medalist Ben Johnson for using steroids. The Dubin inquiry gathered evidence of widespread doping of athletes, much of it linked to a win-at-any-cost morality.

Canada's national hockey team was beaten by the Soviets for the world championship, and the Calgary Flames defeated the Montreal Canadiens for the Stanley Cup. Major league baseball's Toronto Blue Jays, cheered on by large crowds in their newly opened SkyDome, captured their division but lost to Oakland in the championship series.

DESMOND MORTON
Erindale College, University of Toronto

The Economy

By bringing soaring interest rates, fueling inflationary pressure, and creating labor-market tightness, the year 1989 positioned the Canadian economy for a soft landing in 1990. For the first time since September 1984, Statistics Canada's monthly composite leading economic indicator fell during June and July by .1% and .2%, respectively, before recording .1% improvement in August. Even then, six of the ten components making up the August indicator either fell or showed no change. Retail sales, excluding furniture and appliances, and spending on housing showed the biggest drop.

Other signs of sluggishness appeared as the year rolled to the third quarter. For example, despite the first quarter's healthy increase in real personal disposable income, consumption expenditure during the second quarter of 1989 was down to a 1.1% increase as compared with a 4% rise recorded for the second half of 1988. Rising interest rates, increased federal income tax, and rising prices dampened domestic demand. The drop in demand, in turn, was reflected by slow growth of the economy, which expanded at 0.3% in August after adjusting for inflation, up from a 0.2% increase in July and no growth in June. Overall the economy was expected to grow during the third quarter at an annual rate of 2%. Even this performance pales when compared with 1988's growth rate of 4.4%. In fact, in July output of mining, forestry, construction, and fishing declined, while agriculture and utilities posted growth.

In the manufacturing sector the value of shipments was up 0.3% in August. During the first eight months of the year, the value of shipments showed gains only during three months. During the other five months, shipments had declined or remained unchanged. Unfilled orders also were down 0.8% in August, the fourth drop in the previous five months. The rise in housing starts from an annual rate of 197,000 in August to 216,000 in September was an aberration. Rising mortgage rates were expected to discourage new home buyers, leading fourth-quarter starts to drop below 200,000.

In the meantime overall sales started to sag, profit margins were shrinking, and competition was razor-edge. The value of retail sales was down 0.3% in July following a modest gain of 0.2% in June. Falling domestic demand and dwindling exports squeezed the third quarter after-tax earnings of the Canadian corporate sector by 12%. On the international trade front, an overvalued Canadian dollar was the key factor in tipping the trade balance against Canada. Whereas Canadian producers, despite lower tariffs, were having problems in penetrating the U.S. market, American producers were finding it easier to sell goods in the Canadian market. This explains why Canada's surplus in goods and trade with the United States dropped by $1.3 billion in the first eight months of 1989 from a year earlier.

The labor market, however, remained tight. By August the average weekly earnings of workers was up 5% from a year earlier and the unemployment rate stabilized between 7.3% and 7.5%. This showed that despite a sluggish economy the danger of having wage-cost-push inflation did not abate. On the contrary, the consumer price index rose 0.7% in July for year to year increase of 5.4%. Hence the Bank of Canada's persistence in keeping high interest rates to douse inflation could be justified.

R. P. SETH
Mount Saint Vincent University

© Jim Merrithew/Picture Group

The Canadian Museum of Civilization, designed by Douglas Cardinal and spreading across 24 acres (9.7 ha) in Hull, Que., opened in mid-1989. Showcasing artifacts of Canada's cultural heritage, it includes an in-depth History Hall.

The Arts

In 1989 the Canadian government's economy measures to combat the large national debt hit particularly hard at the government-financed Canadian Broadcasting Corporation (CBC), the country's biggest employer of artistic talent. CBC was ordered to cut, within five years, C$140 million from its annual budget of C$1.3 billion, starting with C$20 million in 1989. The cut followed several years of CBC's curtailing programs to keep up with inflation, but the government made no provisions for inflation in the ensuing five years. However, despite its money problems CBC increased its percentage of viewers, dramatically for some programs. Many gave credit for this increase to Ivan Fecan, a former CBC employee who had left for an NBC vice-presidency but later returned in 1987 as CBC's head of network programming. In 1989, CBC took a major step by starting a 24-hour news and information TV service, *CBC Newsworld*.

But a loss to CBC was the retirement of Pierre Juneau, who had been its accomplished president and chairman for seven years. Gérard Veilleux was appointed new CBC president and Patrick Watson was named chairman designate. Canadian artists, whose average income is very low, worried that CBC belt-tightening, inflation, and other factors seriously would weaken their position. Federal Communications Minister Marcel Masse, who strongly supports the artists, was named chairman of a new cabinet committee on culture and national identity.

Visual Arts. The Vancouver Art Gallery rejoiced at the return of a 19th-century watercolor by England's famed J. M. Turner that had been stolen 24 years earlier. The gallery had bought the painting in 1931. When it was stolen in 1965 the gallery did not report the theft because an expert, later discredited, said it was a fake. In 1987 an unidentified man took the painting to Christie's auction room in London for an evaluation. Christie's, knowing it had been in Vancouver, notified the gallery. It took the gallery two years to recover the watercolor, as it had to prove not only that the painting had been stolen, but also that it had entered Britain in the last 50 years, since British authorities control the export of any art that has been in Britain more than 50 years. The painting, "The Custom House, London Bridge," is valued at more than C$300,000.

Performing Arts. In its 29th season at Niagara-on-the-Lake, Ont., the Shaw Festival continued as the sole theater company in the world presenting only plays written during Bernard Shaw's long life (1856–1950). The festival's artistic director, Christopher Newton, directed the opening play, Shaw's *Man and Superman,* starring Michael Ball as John Tanner and Kate Trotter as Ann Whitefield. Shaw's comedy *Getting Married* was directed by Mart Maraden, with Douglas Rain as Reginald Bridgenorth and Susan Wright as his wife Leo. Other plays presented included *Berkeley Square, Once in a Lifetime,* and the musical *Good News*.

In his final year as artistic director of the Stratford (Ont.) Festival, John Neville opened the season with Cole Porter's musical *Kiss Me Kate,* directed and choreographed by Donald Saddler. Shakespeare's *The Merchant of Venice* followed, directed by Michael Langham. An interesting double bill was the pairing of Shakespeare's first tragedy, *Titus Andronicus,* directed by Jeannette Lambermont, with his first comedy, *The Comedy of Errors,* directed by Richard Monette. Actress Lucy Peacock, an outstanding beauty, scored heavily with audiences while starring in four plays. In the double bill she played Lavinia in *Titus Andronicus* and Luciana in *The Comedy of Errors*. She also portrayed Masha in Chekhov's *Three Sisters,* directed by Neville, and Queen of the Fairies in Shakespeare's *Midsummer Night's Dream,* directed by Richard Ouzounian.

At the fifth annual Shakespeare on the Saskatchewan Festival in Saskatoon, Sask., a highly original version of *Romeo and Juliet,* in

The National Film Board at 50

During 1989, Canada's National Film Board (NFB) celebrated its 50th anniversary by receiving its ninth Academy Award—this one for special achievement—by being honored at film festivals worldwide, and by staging North America's first major documentary film festival. The world's oldest active government film production agency, the NFB has made more than 17,000 productions and has won almost 3,000 awards in international competition. NFB films now are translated into 60 languages and distributed in 80 countries.

Background. In the late 1930s, Scottish filmmaker John Grierson was invited to Ottawa by the federal government to study how Canada could improve its filmmaking. He recommended creation of a government-financed national film board, which was to be, in his words, "the eyes of Canada." The NFB was created by act of Parliament, May 2, 1939, with Grierson as its head.

In its earlier years, the NFB presented its films across Canada in a rural circuit of church basements, schools, and auditoriums by traveling projectionists who brought with them projector, generator, and films. In 1941 the NFB produced *Churchill's Island,* about England's wartime battle for survival. It won the NFB's first Academy Award, the first Oscar ever presented for a documentary film. In the same year Grierson hired, for $40 a week and a bed at the YMCA, a fellow Scot, Norman McLaren, who founded the animation department. McLaren's skill at animation and at training others in this art brought the NFB Oscars and world recognition.

At the end of the 1950s, the NFB moved its headquarters to Montreal and soon was making original French-language films. In the 1960s the NFB started making feature length films, notably *Universe,* about space travel, which became required viewing for U.S astronauts. In 1974 the NFB inaugurated Studio D, the world's first all-woman filmmaking unit, under Kathleen Shannon, to produce films reflecting women's perspectives. It has been awarded three Oscars.

As the NFB prepared to begin its second 50 years, two factors were causing a measure of worry. First, despite economies its current budget was not keeping up with inflation. Second, some fear the government may want the NFB to abandon its traditional role of making films independently and instead to work on coproductions with private filmmakers. Thus, in its anniversary year, the NFB took pride in its past while facing uncertainties about its future.

DAVID SAVAGE

modern dress, drew national attention and praise. It was bilingual, with the Montagues of Saskatchewan speaking Shakespeare's English and the Capulets of Quebec speaking classic 17th-century French. Thus Juliet was called "Juliette" and the title was *Romeo and Juliette.* The play was performed in a tent on a bank of the South Saskatchewan River. Codirectors were the festival's artistic head, Gordon McCall of Saskatoon, and Robert LePage of Quebec. In the cast, drawn from Saskatchewan and Quebec, Tom Rooney was Romeo and Celine Bonnier Juliette. To the directors' relief, audiences, although failing to understand some words, had no trouble following the action and emotions, whichever the language. Many viewers saw this bilingual play as symbolic of bilingual Canada, and the feuding Montagues and Capulets as representing the difficulties between the country's two cultures.

Two made-in-Canada musicals appeared in 1989. John Gray, author of the successful play *Billy Bishop Goes to War,* created the unusual *Health, the Musical* about the human body and its problems. Directed by Larry Lillo, it premiered at the Vancouver Playhouse. The hero, Mort, was played by Eric Peterson, and his body parts were Stephen Miller as Bum, Ross Douglas as Snake, and Ian McDonald as Smiley. Previewed first in Toronto, then premiering in Vancouver before touring was *Durante,* a big C$4 million musical based on the life of comedian Jimmy Durante, who wrote most of the play's songs. Lonny Price played Durante, with production by Nicky Fylan.

Film. Canadian filmmakers found money more difficult to obtain due to a federal government tax change. Under the old rule, investors could write off against taxes 100% of any investment in a Canadian film, but the new rule reduced this to 30%. The provincial governments in Ontario and Quebec provided tax incentives to help counteract the federal ruling. But despite some setbacks, Canadian film studios were active, especially in British Columbia, where impetus was given by the opening in North Vancouver of North Shore Studios, Canada's largest filmmaking complex, built at a cost of C$25 million.

In Montreal the exhibition Cités-Cinés built for public display copies of 18 original film sets and showed 180 film clips relating to these sets. Also in Montreal, Vancouver filmmaker Nettie Wild's Philippines documentary *A Rustling of Leaves* took the Prix de Public at the National Salute to the Documentary festival. Quebec director Denys Arcand won the Jury Prize at the Cannes Film Festival with *Jésus de Montréal.* And Vancouver filmmaker Mike Collier's *Land Above the Trees,* about the alpine areas of western Canada, won first place in the nature and wildlife class at Chicago's Film and Video Festival.

DAVID SAVAGE, *Free-lance Writer*

CARIBBEAN

For the second consecutive year, a devastating hurricane roared through parts of the Caribbean, leaving death and massive destruction in its wake, and then slammed into the North American mainland with similar results.

In 1988, Hurricane *Gilbert* hit Hispaniola and wreaked havoc in Jamaica before coming ashore in Mexico's Yucatán peninsula. In 1989, Hurricane *Hugo* tore through the eastern Caribbean, killing dozens of people and leaving thousands homeless in the smaller islands of the lesser Antilles, especially Montserrat and Guadeloupe. The storm then passed directly over the U.S. Virgin Islands and Puerto Rico, causing more damage than any other hurricane in recent history, and it then made a destructive landfall in Georgia and the Carolinas.

In the aftermath of *Hugo* widespread looting broke out in St. Croix in the U.S. Virgin Islands, leading to the dispatch of 1,200 U.S. Army troops and military policemen to restore order. Puerto Rico was even harder hit by the storm, suffering 18 deaths, 4,700 injuries, and an estimated $1 billion in property damage. San Juan, the capital, was without power and water for days, and entire towns were destroyed almost completely. The island, however, remained relatively calm as it began the cleanup, although 5,000 people remained homeless as long as two months (*see* PUERTO RICO).

Photos, © Chris Brown/Sipa

Hurricane "Hugo" hit Puerto Rico and the U.S. Virgin Islands in September, causing much damage. On St. Croix armed residents tried to protect against looting.

Economic Integration. Natural disasters aside, 1989 was a year noted for definitive moves toward economic integration in the English-speaking islands of the Caribbean. Meeting in St. George's, Grenada, in July, the leaders of the islands agreed to create a full-scale common market by the middle of 1993.

The Caribbean leaders also decided to create an interisland stock market and a regional parliament. One member country, the Bahamas, said it would remain within the existing regional political association, the Caribbean Community (CARICOM), but would delay entry into a common market until definitive trading rules are established. The 11 countries that are set to participate in common-market arrangements are Antigua-Barbuda, Barbados, Belize, Dominica, Grenada, Guyana, Jamaica, St. Kitts-Nevis, St. Lucia, St. Vincent and the Grenadines, and Trinidad and Tobago, plus the British colony of Montserrat.

The framework of a common market was established in the Treaty of Chaguaramas, signed in 1973, but never was implemented fully. In a summit meeting in 1988, the Caribbean countries agreed to begin removing tariffs and other nontariff barriers within the region. The new agreement sets a target date of July 1991 for the abolition of intraregional tariffs. Free movement of people among the countries is to begin by December 1990 and the regional stock market is to be in operation by 1993.

CARICOM members began drafting a common external tariff schedule in September. The unified tariff structure is expected to take effect at the beginning of 1991. It will provide some protection for the emerging industries of the region, but low duty rates will be applied to imports that do not compete with existing CARICOM producers. Agricultural imports, such as fertilizer and pesticides, also will receive favorable duty treatment in order to stimulate agricultural development within the 13-member CARICOM group.

Legislation sponsored by the Bush administration to expand and extend the U.S. Caribbean Basin Initiative (CBI) was introduced in Congress at midyear, but failed to win approval by the end of 1989. The CBI provides duty-free entry to the United States for a variety of goods from the Caribbean and Central America. The administration had sought to add favorable trade treatment for several products not currently included in the program. But as the bill, known as CBI-2, moved through the House of Representatives most of the liberalizing provisions, including lower duty rates for imports of leather footwear, petroleum and petroleum products, and canned tuna fish, were stripped out of the legislation. White House sources said that the administration mainly was concentrating on making the CBI a permanent part of U.S. trade policy. The program is scheduled to expire in 1995.

The ongoing debt crisis and a near-stagnant export sector continued to plague the Caribbean through 1989. The region had an unfavorable trade balance with the United States, as U.S. imports during the first half of the year grew to $4.4 billion and region exports to the United States remained relatively unchanged at $3.4 billion. Agricultural exports showed significant declines, particularly sugar and coffee.

A minor assist came in September when the United States announced an increase in its global sugar-import quota, the third increase in the past year. But the United States also extended the sugar-quota year, diluting the impact of the quota rise. The 12-month quota of the Dominican Republic of 204,290 short tons was raised to 333,035 tons for a 21-month period, permitting the country to export about 1% more sugar to the United States. The Jamaican quota went from 12,770 tons for 12 months to 20,815 tons for 21 months.

During the year, Caribbean policymakers also wrestled with the possible effects of the creation of a more unified common market in Europe in 1992. The Caribbean countries currently receive special trade preferences from the European Community under a series of pacts known as the Lomé accords. In negotiations under way in 1989 for a fourth Lomé agreement, the Community has offered to continue the preferences on such important tropical products as bananas and sugar. The Caribbean countries, nonetheless, worry that a unified European common market may turn the Economic Community into a "Fortress Europe," from which the Caribbean exports will be excluded or severely restricted. European leaders have disclaimed any such intent and say special consideration will continue to be given to developing countries in the Caribbean, Africa, and the Pacific. A conference on the implications of "Europe 1992" was held in Barbados in early November, sponsored by the London-based West India Committee in cooperation with the CARICOM secretariat.

Drugs. International drug trafficking was a concern of Caribbean leaders, as trade in illicit substances has grown rapidly, and the use of drugs, such as cocaine and marijuana, heretofore negligible, has sprung up in such countries as Jamaica and Belize.

The new Jamaican Prime Minister, Michael Manley, proposed the creation of an international antinarcotics task force. Taking note of the Manley proposal, the U.S. Senate passed a resolution endorsing the idea, saying that "the Manley plan is the first operative proposal to use multilateral force against the drug cartels in Latin America made by a government leader in the Western Hemisphere."

In October a meeting of Caribbean security officials, police chiefs, military advisers, and government lawyers agreed to intensify regional cooperation in the detection and seizure of drugs concealed in some of the region's legitimate exports to the United States. Some of the measures agreed on were not disclosed publicly because of their sensitivity, but one agreement included intensification of security operations at major Caribbean seaports, including improved training for port personnel and the use of dogs to search for drugs.

See also CUBA, DRUGS AND ALCOHOL ABUSE, HAITI, JAMAICA, NATIONS OF THE WORLD (page 574).

RICHARD C. SCHROEDER, *Consultant to the Organization of American States*

© Bill Gentile/Sipa

U.S. President George Bush met with other hemispheric leaders at a two-day summit of the Organization of American States in Costa Rica in late October. The leaders also honored Costa Rica President Oscar Arias, right with wife, *for his efforts to bring peace to Central America.*

CENTRAL AMERICA

During six of Ronald Reagan's eight years as president, his administration had devoted endless rhetoric, obsessive effort, and billions of dollars in military and humanitarian aid to bring about certain changes in Central America. Yet, when George Bush succeeded him in 1989, few of those goals had been realized. The Sandinistas controlled Nicaragua; civil war consumed El Salvador; Hondurans still were haunted by the presence of U.S. troops and Nicaraguan rebels on their soil; the military still embarrassed and choked Guatemala. One change came late in 1989 when U.S. military action in Panama forced Gen. Manuel Antonio Noriega out of power.

All the states faced heavy debts in 1989. Everywhere economies suffered from soft prices in export crops, and with few exceptions the land remained almost totally in the hands of the few. Even progress had its downside; better roads were bringing about the gradual extermination of lush rain forests, and Central Americans were being warned that industrialization was destroying the environment even before benefits could be realized.

While immediate results were not yet apparent, the Central American policy of President Bush differed significantly from the policy of Ronald Reagan. The failures of Reagan's unilateral approach to intervention and opposition in the U.S. Congress demanded a policy change in Washington. Not too coincidentally, as the Reagan program's failures became more apparent, the leadership in hemispheric affairs was taken over by the Organization of American States (OAS) and Latin American chief executives led by Costa Rica's President Oscar Arias Sánchez. Bush could not ignore this framework.

In a celebration of democracy, the OAS late in October met in San José, Costa Rica, for a two-day hemispheric summit, the first meeting of the heads of state since 1967. Arias, winner of the 1987 Nobel Peace Prize, was in the last year of his term of office, and his colleagues wanted to honor his leadership in Central America's peace process. Additionally, 1989 marked the centennial of free, popular elections in Costa Rica. Pointedly, the presidents of Haiti, Chile, Panama, and Cuba were not invited to the summit. Canada was represented and announced its intention to join the OAS. The occasion was a pageant; no one expected substantive discussions, and none resulted. But President Bush's attendance, in spite of the presence of Nicaragua's President Daniel Ortega, demonstrated that the Reagan policies had been superseded by a willingness to work with the other nations of the region to solve some seemingly perpetual problems.

Some of Bush's verbal attacks upon Ortega were inappropriate, but Ortega committed blunders of his own. During the celebration he announced that, since the Nicaraguan contras were ambushing and killing his government troops, he would put an end to a cease-fire in the country's civil war. While the facts were on Ortega's side, many of the heads of state were appalled by the timing of the announcement, and Bush, in particular, chided the Nicaraguan leader. Ortega then recanted a bit, leaving unclear the future of the cease-fire.

Central American leaders had begun taking matters in their own hands at a meeting in Esquipulas, Guatemala, in 1986, when they committed their nations to peace and cooperation and affirmed their opposition to "external interference of any kind." Ever since then, the presidents of Costa Rica, El Salvador, Guatemala, Honduras, and Nicaragua have met at least once a year for peace talks, their particular concern being a truce and elections in Nicaragua.

In August 1989 the presidents agreed upon a plan to disband the contras in Nicaragua, leaving details up to an international commission. After fierce fighting erupted in El Salvador, the five Central American leaders met again in mid-December and signed another regional peace agreement. The accord equated the leftist guerrilla movement in El Salvador with the contra movement in Nicaragua and called for an expanded role for the United Nations in ending both conflicts.

Central American governments in 1989 also saw some hope for relief from another of their perpetual problems—the crushing debt burden —in a plan presented by U.S. Treasury Secretary Nicholas F. Brady. The Reagan administration had offered only more lending as an answer to heavy interest payments. Brady, apparently with the concurrence of the Japanese government, proposed a lowering of interest rates, pressure on the commercial banks to write down some of the loans, and new terms of credit to nations taking steps to reform their economies.

Belize

Politics and the Economy. The general elections of Sept. 4, 1989, proved to be as close as predicted, but the defeat of the ruling party still surprised many foreigners. Public interest was high in a country where the electorate is well educated, and the democratic process is observed carefully. Belize City has five independent weekly newspapers, two privately owned TV stations, and four cable systems, which served to keep the public informed during the campaign. A total of 72% of the registered voters cast their ballots; 29,986 or 50.2% voted for the People's United Party (PUP) and 28,900 or 48.4% for the incumbent United Democratic Party (UDP). Both parties are relatively centrist; the major issues seemed to be personalities and the economy.

Defeated in his bid for a second five-year term as prime minister was former physics professor Manuel Esquivel, who, however, did retain his seat in parliament. The victor, George Price of the PUP, also had preceded Esquivel as head of the government. In the campaign, the UDP had claimed four years of a surplus trade balance, but this was disputed by PUP. In any event, the economy was stable. The GNP increased 6% in 1988, inflation was under control, unemployment remained low, and even some tax rates recently had been reduced.

Once a British colony, the republic still utilizes British law. The literacy rate exceeds 90%. About one half the population of 170,000 speaks English, and one third speaks Spanish. Many citizens also are descendants of the ancient Maya and speak a variety of dialects and languages.

Antiquities. The preservation of Mayan antiquities was a priority for Belize in 1989. Corporate and private donors began the program by buying land and restricting it from development. The Belize and Massachusetts Audubon societies are attempting to sequester 110,000 acres (44 534 ha) of rain forest as a preserve with controls over logging and chicle tapping. Hundreds of sites of ancient Mayan communities are believed hidden within forests that cover 70% of the land. The nation hopes to move fast enough to save many undiscovered treasures from the insatiable demands of looters as well as jungle decay. The tensions arising from fear of a resurgent Guatemalan claim to sovereignty over Belize, or a renewed boundary dispute, receded in 1989, replaced by growing cooperation between Belize and Guatemala for archaeological preservation. The states planned a peace park with Mexico at a location where the three nations meet.

Costa Rica

The Economy. The nation continued to be troubled by the mistakes in economic policy of a decade ago. During the period from 1979–82, Costa Rica built up a broad and costly social program serving everyone in the land. Money for the program was borrowed at high interest rates at a time when repayment seemed easy because of the high prices paid on export commodities. But energy costs soared and agricul-

CENTRAL AMERICA • Information Highlights

Nation	Population (in Millions)	Area (sq mi)	Area (km²)	Capital	Head of State and Government
Belize	0.2	8,865	22 960	Belmopan	Minita Gordon, governor-general George Price, prime minister
Costa Rica	3.0	19,730	51 100	San José	Oscar Arias Sánchez, president
El Salvador	5.1	8,124	21 040	San Salvador	Alfredo Cristiani, president
Guatemala	8.9	42,042	108 890	Guatemala City	Marco Vinicio Cerezo Arévalo, president
Honduras	5.0	43,278	112 090	Tegucigalpa	Rafael Callejas, president
Nicaragua	3.5	49,998	129 494	Managua	José Daniel Ortega Saavedra, president
Panama	2.4	30,193	78 200	Panama City	Guillermo Endara, president

tural exports sagged. Like many nations, Costa Rica was caught in an impossible squeeze, and the squeeze was made worse by the ambitious welfare program.

The Costa Rican debt became one of the worst per capita national debts in the world. By 1989 it totaled more than $4 billion. The economy was stable but not growing at an acceptable rate compared with the population. The nation continued to rely heavily upon foreign trade for its income—and its debt repayment—but export prices remained low. One way out was to reduce the reliance upon the sale of traditional products such as bananas, sugar, and coffee to major markets, and emphasize the sale of light manufactured items to Third World states. Various tariff breaks and extensive U.S. aid have helped the new export business to flourish. Costa Rica has been trying to obtain foreign investment to assist in the development of electronics, plastics, and pharmaceuticals. Tourism also has been strengthened substantially. Inflation continued at a stiff rate in 1989; unemployment was low.

Debt. Like Mexico, Costa Rica had been singled out for special treatment under the so-called Brady Plan for Third World debtor nations. Costa Rica hoped for easier terms than Mexico's but lacked the larger nation's credit standing. Costa Rica was treated generously by the international lending agencies but wanted to secure better deals from commercial banks in the United States.

In October the nations of the Western Hemisphere celebrated with Costa Rica the centennial of what often is considered the first truly democratic election in Central America. The affair also honored Costa Rica's President Oscar Arias for his efforts to bring regional peace. In a sort of honorific summit most of the heads of state of the hemisphere met for two days in San José. Arias took this occasion to announce that arrangements had been made with the major commercial banks to scale their portion of the nation's debt down about $1 billion, or nearly one third. The banks also reduced the annual interest payment from $150 to $50 million.

Regional Government, Environment, Drugs. The notion of some sort of regional government is brought up regularly by various Central American governments, especially in troubled times. The concept of a common Central American parliament was under consideration in 1989. Typically, Costa Rica's legislature dragged its feet from fear of loss of sovereignty. Just as typically Guatemala suggested proceeding without Costa Rica.

Costa Rica is the home of nearly as many bird species as all the rest of North America, but growing population continued in 1989 to lead to the destruction of rain forests for farm and ranch land. In an effort to reduce the trend the government was acquiring lands from private owners for national parks. Some 25% of the forest land was under government control. With the aid of foundations, the nation hoped to create seven huge parks within five years.

Costa Rica has its share of the world's drug problem. The laws against drug usage are perhaps the toughest in Latin America, however, and local addiction is not believed to be heavy. But much laundering of drug money has taken place in Costa Rica, and several high-ranking officials, including judges, have been linked to illicit gains in the trade.

El Salvador

Politics and Government. In the March election Alfredo Cristiani of the right-wing ARENA Party won 53% of the vote and an absolute majority in an open and fair election, the first time in 60 years that the presidential power has been transferred peacefully from one party to another. Cristiani defeated the Christian Democrats on a platform charging his opponents with corruption, failure to end the nation's civil war, and ruining the economy.

Cristiani, a 41-year-old businessman educated in the United States, was inaugurated June 1, promising a more moderate ARENA and a more open economy in the fashion of Chile's. He also agreed to continue with peace talks even though the hard-line right wing of his party doubtless wanted to put greater pressure on the rebels. The rebels, in turn, showed no signs of weakening as they caused an almost total electric power failure the day of the inauguration.

In July government representatives met with representatives of the rebel group, the Farabundo Martí National Liberation Front (FMNL), and the United States in Mexico. The FMNL admitted to some political killings, but called them mistakes and declared "a new policy." Little of significance came from the talks, but subsequent debate in the U.S. Congress over new aid to El Salvador made it clear that many congressmen had no confidence in either Salvadoran faction.

Many Salvadorans never have known peace. In the late 1970s the nation became polarized over issues of free elections, land redistribution, and other reforms. Violence in the towns accompanied bloody guerrilla warfare in the countryside. The Reagan administration increasingly provided aid to the government, especially during the presidency of José Napoleon Duarte, whose term preceded Cristiani's. In spite of enormous financial assistance the Duarte government accomplished little; peace talks went nowhere, and the war turned into a standoff. Duarte lost credibility at home and in Washington even before he was stricken with cancer. Cristiani's election probably indicated the public's loss of faith in the political center and the reascendancy of the

While a soldier crouches in the background, a mother clutches her baby and runs for cover during fighting in the streets of San Salvador. Many of the casualties in El Salvador's newly intensified civil war were civilians.

© P. Chauvel/Sygma

right wing. But no matter where the presidency lies, the military retains ultimate power.

Violence. Indiscriminate killings seem to have declined since the early 1980s, but torture and selective assassination, especially of students and union leaders, continued to be reported frequently. In the nine years of civil war more than 70,000 people have been killed. Sabotage remained the guerrillas' chief weapon, probably because their numbers had declined in recent years. The remaining forces, however, appeared better led and better motivated.

Late in the year the conflict heated up again. On October 31 a bomb exploded in a union hall, killing, among others, a prominent union leader. Two weeks later, in an apparent response, the guerrillas began the biggest offensive of the entire war, fighting in several provinces simultaneously and enveloping much of the capital city. President Cristiani ordered a state of siege. Hundreds of people, mostly civilians, were killed during the weekend of November 11–12 in San Salvador alone. Assassins in uniform brutally murdered the Jesuit rector of the University of Central America, five other Jesuits, and two laywomen, creating international outrage and demands for an end to U.S. aid. Another response was the murder of a leader of a rightist party. Because of the unlikelihood that the rebels ever could win a struggle against the government's army and air power, the attack upon the capital seemed a desperate measure to justify more talks.

In late November, Jennifer Jean Casolo, an American working for the Christian Education Seminars in El Salvador, was arrested on charges of harboring arms for Salvadoran guerrillas in violation of antiterrorism laws. In mid-December she was freed for lack of evidence and deported to the United States.

Political, social, and economic chaos remained. Almost half the nation's mayors and scores of lesser officials resigned their posts because of threats.

In his inaugural speech President Cristiani had promised a permanent dialogue with the rebels. Talks held at Tela, Honduras in August brought a bit of hope—at least both sides said they wanted the peace talks. But the government insisted on a cease-fire first, and the FMNL wanted that matter negotiated. The government's minister of defense said there was nothing to talk about. More talks continued in October and November, all stalemated over whether reforms must precede a cease-fire. Reforms demanded by the rebels included a purge of the army, prosecution of right-wing death squad members, and numerous broad economic changes—matters that the government likely will not concede.

The Economy. No economy could grow under such conditions; if it were not for U.S. aid—about $3 billion since 1980—El Salvador would face anarchy. Some 35% of the national budget goes to the military, and many elements of the economy declined in 1989. Some modest economic reforms have been made, however. In the 1980s nearly 30% of the nation's arable land was redistributed to about 120,000 families. The owners of the 469 large farms that were expropriated received compensation, but complained it was inadequate. The farms were converted into cooperatives, about half of which failed either because of the war or the ailing economy. President Cristiani also kept his promise of a freer economy by initiating one of Latin America's broadest programs of privatization. Banks and other financial institutions that were nationalized in 1980 were to be put up for bids; other businesses to be included were a large fish processing plant, a $12 million hotel, sugar mills, and coffee mills. In addition, government monopolies in sugar and coffee sales were to be ended.

Guatemala

Unrest. Twice in less than a year elements of the Guatemala military attempted barracks revolts against President Marco Vinicio Cerezo Arévalo, and twice they failed. In each instance the rebelling officers were of junior rank and unable to prevail against the authority of their superiors. The second coup attempt, in May 1989, sought the resignation of the defense minister, who was alleged by the dissidents to be too close to the Christian Democratic Party and too leftist in his sympathies. The younger officers also complained of graft and corruption in the government and charged that the guerrillas, though less numerous, had grown stronger during President Cerezo's administration. Although the rebellions failed, they had repercussions, perhaps the most serious being the declining hope for reform. After the coup, abuses by the army increased dramatically, especially against suspected guerrillas. The Cerezo administration was forced to appease the militant officers, and the press complained that civil-rights violations were the worst in several years.

The Economy. The government also faced a series of economic crises. Cerezo was forced to give pay raises to the army and even purchase two Italian-built military transport planes in the face of high unemployment and heavy national debt. But when public workers sought pay increases they had to go on strike. Some 40,000 teachers and other public employees receiving an average of $2,500 per year, asked for a $75 per month raise. After the strike and subsequent negotiations it appeared that many of the workers might get virtually no increase at all. Sugar workers, making less than $2 a day, struck for an increase with similar results.

Easing the national burden was the unofficial transfer of "foreign aid" from hundreds of thousands of Guatemalans living in the United States. They contributed desperately needed funds amounting to about $430 million per year by government estimates. During the 1989 postal strike nearly two tons of mail backed up in the Miami, FL, post office, awaiting delivery in Guatemala.

Since 1987, Guatemala has developed a new export item—drugs. Aided by financing and training from Mexican dealers, Guatemala became one of the hemisphere's largest growers of opium poppies for heroin production. A farmer can earn more than ten times as much per acre growing poppies than by growing vegetables. It is believed the new farms can meet 60% of the demands of U.S. addicts. Guatemala also was developing a flourishing trade in the transshipment of cocaine to the United States.

Religion. Guatemala at the same time was hosting what is believed to be the fastest-growing religious movement in the world. While Protestant evangelical churches virtually were unknown 30 years ago, today their membership includes about 35% of the population. The churches' 3 million followers are divided among 300 sects with 8,500 congregations. Much of the growth began after the 1976 earthquake and increased greatly during the presidential administration of Gen. Efraín Ríos Montt, himself a minister and a strong candidate in the 1990 presidential election. Religion easily might become an issue in that election.

Honduras

Tragedy and Violence. Tragedy struck Honduras from many directions in 1989. The most dramatic single tragedy occurred in October when a TAN-SAHSA Boeing 727 with 146 people aboard "broke apart" in the air, then smashed into a mountainside 25 mi (40 km) south of Tegucigalpa. Only about 15 passengers survived what was considered the worst air disaster in Central American history. The cause of the accident still was under investigation, but survivors, including the pilot, thought that the roof tore away before the plane struck the mountain. The pilot was trying to land the 21-year-old plane in very windy weather when the crash took place.

A different form of violent tragedy was also on the increase in 1989. The number of political assassinations and killings by police in 1989 appeared to have at least doubled the 1988 record. Police increasingly violated human rights, according to church officials. One hopeful sign came out of the finding by the OAS' Inter-American Court of Human Rights that a unit of the Honduran army was responsible for the killing of two students. The military was ordered to pay $1.4 million to the students' families, the first time the court has assessed monetary damages for human-rights violations.

Hondurans placed much of the blame for renewed violence on the presence of Nicaraguan contras on Honduran soil. About 12,000 former soldiers and their families live in shantytowns in the vicinity of Yamales, having played little part in Nicaragua's civil war since February 1989. Hondurans claimed the contras commit crimes against the local citizens, and several thousand Hondurans have moved from the region. Thousands of other Nicaraguans reside in Honduras away from the official camps. Even the economy is affected; beef exports dropped about two thirds as a result of thefts, and much timber has gone to Nicaraguan housing and fires. Honduras has received about $1 billion in eight years from the United States as a form of compensation.

The Military, Economy, Election. In October the U.S. Congress also began debating a new military appropriation for Honduras. President Bush's request was scaled back considerably, in part because of reports of fraud committed by Honduran generals, and in part because Honduras failed to bring about certain changes in economic policy. Honduras, however, has begun a series of so-called debt-equity swaps, by which the foreign debt is reduced in exchange for the sale of certain government businesses. By late 1989 ten businesses had been privatized and an additional nine were being considered for privatization.

As usual, in the first half of the year about 10,000 U.S. troops conducted joint maneuvers with Honduran forces; the chief task was road construction in the northern department of Yoro. At Palmerola Base the conversion of wooden barracks to metal prefabs also continued.

The presidential election took place on November 26. In a close contest Rafael Callejas claimed victory over Carlos Flores of the ruling Liberal Party with a margin of about two percentage points. The U.S. educated Callejas is an agronomist and a strong advocate of an open-market economy.

© J. B. Diederich/Contact Press Images from Woodfin Camp

Presidential candidate Violeta Barrios de Chamorro, a newspaper publisher, gives some focus to a fragmented Nicaraguan opposition in an election drive against the Sandinistas.

Nicaragua

Sandinistas v. the Contras. The Sandinista problem never long disappears from the agenda of U.S. presidents. That seemed to be the message conveyed to new President George Bush by events in 1989. For two full terms the Reagan administration had tried to rid the hemisphere of the Sandinistas, through economic pressure, diplomacy, and illegal arms sales, all to no avail. President Bush proved more willing than Reagan to accept a multilateral approach, and much of the year was spent in efforts by other Central American nations to bring about a cease-fire and solve the question of the status of the contra forces. Still, little progress took place.

Pressured by other Central American leaders and by the end to U.S. military aid to the contras, the two Nicaraguan factions met at Sapoá in March 1988 and agreed to a truce. In February 1989 an election with international observers was agreed upon for February 1990. In August 1989 the five Central American presidents requested that the United Nations and the OAS establish a commission to verify a peace plan, that the contras accept the plan, and that Nicaragua and Honduras seek a UN force to prevent the contras from using Honduras as a military base. A second Central American summit in mid-December called for an even larger UN role.

Some aspects of the agreements went well. Carrying out its pledge, Nicaragua released nearly 2,000 political prisoners and granted pardons to most of them. But when an international commission visited Honduras and asked an estimated 6,000–10,000 contra troops and their families to disband and leave the country, most did not. A detachment that did return to Nicaragua killed 18 government troops in a pointless ambush. Coming just before the contras were supposed to disband, and just before a hemisphere-wide peace celebration, the action made little sense. Considering the ambush sufficient justification, President Daniel Ortega quickly declared the cease-fire at an end. But then he said he would reconsider, although still blaming the United States for the killings. Neither the contras nor the Sandinistas gained any international stature from this episode. Not clear was the degree of damage the affair might bring to the prospects for an honest election in 1990.

Election, Economy. In August the government and all 21 opposition parties promised to conduct a fair election. The fragmented opposition had little cohesion or power, but in September a number of parties, under the title National Opposition Union (UNO), agreed upon a slate of candidates—Violeta Barrios de Chamorro and Virgilio Godoy for president and vice-president, respectively. De Chamorro is the publisher of the newspaper *La Prensa* and the widow of Pedro Joaquín Chamorro, a longtime opponent of the Somozas. After her husband's assassination in 1978 she had joined the early Sandinista ruling junta, but resigned after less than a year because she feared the abuse of power by the Sandinistas. She since has been a vocal crusader against the government. She is very popular but lacks political experience. The UNO platform called for a free market, open economy, and close economic ties to Japan and the United States. In addition to Washington's public blessing UNO was to get some funding from the $3.5 million appropriated by the United States for the "promotion of democracy in Nicaragua." Registration for the election spread out over several Sundays in October, and an estimated 1.75 million people took part. The major Sandinista advantage was a party membership of about 30,000, but UNO could capitalize on a high level of public discontent with the Sandinistas.

In July the Sandinista regime celebrated its tenth anniversary with less than usual enthusiasm. In 1981, Nicaragua had conducted the most sweeping agricultural reform program in Central America—distributing some 2 million acres (809 370 ha) of land to 68,000 families. In short order illiteracy was reduced from 50% to 13%. And the campesino, or Indian farmer, received a previously unknown degree of respect. But the civil war and the U.S. embargo nullified much of this progress. Thousands of Nicaraguans were killed, wounded, orphaned, or displaced. Many teachers were killed by the contras, and illiteracy rose again to about 25%. The economy became a shambles. Inflation reached nearly incalculable highs; purchasing power often halved in a year. One adult out of five was out of work. Thousands of state workers lost their jobs in 1989, and many food subsidies for the poor had to be dropped. Rebuilding from the havoc of Hurricane Joan in October 1988 continued nonetheless; roads and utilities were provided in some areas lacking them previously, but the rebuilding of homes moved slowly.

The Outlook. While arguments continued over the cease-fire, an equally vexing and perhaps less predictable subject was the status of the contras. After nearly nine years of war the field leadership was finding that it had less and less in common with the Miami-based leadership chosen by the Reagan administration. When military aid from the United States ceased, the commanders in Nicaragua concluded that the politicians comfortably living in Florida had no function and took away their powers; their Miami office was closed. The new, younger officers would not even permit older political advisers to visit Honduran bases. Gradually the U.S. State Department recognized this transition and was supporting Israel Galeano Cornejo, 29, as the military head of the contras. He had been in the field for six years and reportedly had taken part in some 300 skirmishes. This new leadership was on record as not expecting any outside funds or political support. If they should continue the war in spite of truces signed by the old leadership, the peace process may be destroyed.

Panama

Both Presidents Reagan and Bush spent much of their political energy condemning the government of Nicaragua and Panama. In contrast with Nicaragua, where U.S. policy has been to put an end to a regime, the situation in Panama was much more personal—the United States wanted to drive one leader out of office, military strongman and reputed drug trafficker Gen. Manuel Antonio Noriega.

Noriega won a brief respite when a coup attempt by elements of his own army failed in October, as the United States declined to join in the revolt. However, in December a large-scale U.S. military operation toppled the general and sent him into hiding.

Noriega's Rise and Fall. As chief of staff and commanding general of Panama's defense forces since 1981, Noriega had been useful to the Reagan administration. But the relationship had to change when, in 1987, one of the general's deputies confirmed charges of drug trafficking, electoral fraud, and murder. In 1988 a

Panama's Gen. Manuel Antonio Noriega gestures confidently to supporters after an October coup attempt against him failed. His days in power were short-lived, however.

© P. Chauvel/Sygma

© Ron Haviv/AFP

Guillermo Ford, the opposition candidate for vice-president in Panama's May elections, is attacked by a Noriega loyalist. The brutal action became a symbol of the general's theft of the election. Ford took office after Noriega's ouster.

Miami federal grand jury indicted Noriega on drug charges, but had no way to bring him to trial. The United States imposed economic sanctions on Panama that crippled the economy but had little effect on Noriega. Then in May 1989, Noriega brutally stole the apparent presidential victory of the opposition party, despite the close scrutiny of international observers. Noriega remained in power and refused to permit the freely elected president, Guillermo Endara, to assume office in September. Increasingly the Bush administration encouraged dissidents to rise up and overthrow the dictator, but made no promises of military support.

The October revolt by some members of the Panama military failed because of muddled planning, poor intelligence, and even worse communications between the rebels and the United States. The rebel troops briefly held Noriega captive at his military headquarters, but within hours forces loyal to the general were in complete control. Relations between the United States and Noriega continued to decline, with Noriega at one point declaring that a state of war existed between the two countries. Tensions reached the breaking point when an off-duty American officer was killed by Panamanian soldiers.

U.S. Invasion. Early in the morning of December 20, U.S. troops attacked the Panamanian army on a number of fronts. The United States had reinforced its 12,000-troop detachment based in Panama with more than 12,000 additional troops flown in from the United States, along with such equipment as helicopter gunships. The superior U.S. force overwhelmed the Panamanian army, although there was fierce fighting in some areas. A total of 23 American soldiers died in the fighting, along with hundreds of Panamanian soldiers and civilians. Despite the civilian casualties and property damage that left many homeless, the U.S. action to oust Noriega won widespread Panamanian support.

Noriega managed initially to evade capture and there were fears he might lead his paramilitary "Dignity Battalions" in a protracted guerrilla war. Resistance largely evaporated, however, after the general surfaced on Christmas Eve, requesting and receiving asylum at the Vatican embassy. Troops surrounded the embassy and U.S. officials pressed for Noriega's extradition. The general finally surrendered to U.S. authorities in early January and was flown to the United States to stand trial.

Meanwhile the U.S. army oversaw the installation of the Endara government that had won the election in May. In preparation for the eventual withdrawal of American troops, the new government started to build the "Panama Public Force" to replace the disbanded army. The Endara government also was challenged by an economic shambles created by the brief war and the long embargo against Noriega. Bank deposits fell 35% in 1989 and the unemployment rate was upward of 20%. The United States dropped sanctions and U.S. aid and technical assistance began to flow to Panama.

Throughout 1989 the Panama Canal, which handles 14% of U.S. sea trade, continued service under the 1978 treaties governing the operation and defense of the waterway through Dec. 31, 1999. Until then, the canal is to be managed by a nine-member commission. The American chief administrator is slated to be succeeded by a Panamanian in 1990.

THOMAS J. KARNES
Arizona State University

CHEMISTRY

Advances in chemistry in 1989 included the synthesis of new compounds with interesting shapes and surprising properties, a new method for making plastics, and work with small molecular catalysts that mimic some properties of natural enzymes. Also, scientists were startled by claims that nuclear fusion had been observed in simple, room-temperature systems.

Synthesis. The compound *cubane,* first synthesized in 1964, has the molecular shape of a cube, with carbon atoms at each of its eight vertices. Due to its unusual structure, cubane's carbon-carbon bonds are distorted from normal orientations and are strained highly. The compound is of theoretical interest and may have potential as a high-energy fuel.

Late in 1988 Philip Eaton of the University of Chicago, who originally synthesized cubane itself, reported success in introducing a double bond into the structure, to produce *cubene*. Referring to the distortion around the double bond, Eaton described cubene as "the most highly pyramidalized olefin yet known." (Olefins, which are compounds containing double bonds, usually adopt a flat shape.) Despite the fact that cubene quickly reacted to form other compounds, the synthesis confirmed a theoretical prediction that such a compound could exist, however fleetingly.

At the same time other research groups reported further developments in cubane chemistry. Based on X-ray diffraction experiments, the molecular structure of *cubylcubane,* a compound in which two cubanes are joined by a single bond, was reported. Also reported were several new syntheses of compounds related to cubane and cubene.

A number of other notable syntheses of new compounds were reported in 1989. *Propellanes* are paddlewheel-like molecules consisting of flat blade portions joined about a common "shaft." Heretofore they have been constructed with cores of carbon atoms. Chemists at Carnegie Mellon University in Pittsburgh announced the creation of a propellane based on a core of five tin atoms. Two of the tin atoms form the shaft, and the other three are arranged around these to form the triangular blades. The new compound, which has a surprising blue-violet color, may prove useful in constructing advanced materials.

Also in 1989 Harvard chemists reported the total synthesis of *palytoxin,* a highly poisonous compound found in Hawaiian coral. Synthesis of this huge, highly complicated compound took the Harvard team of more than two dozen chemists more than eight years. Chemists at Oxford University, England, announced the synthesis of *gallane,* a compound of gallium and hydrogen that had defied efforts to produce it for almost half a century. The compound, a white solid at low temperatures, appears to have the formula Ga_2H_6 and a structure in which the two gallium atoms are connected through two central hydrogens.

Chemzymes. For the past two years Harvard chemist E. J. Corey and his coworkers have worked to design small, relatively simple organic molecules capable of directing and catalyzing laboratory reactions in much the same way that nature's catalysts, the enzymes (which are large proteins), guide and speed up biochemical reactions in living cells. Corey explained that these efforts now are bearing fruit. Small molecular catalysts, dubbed "chemzymes," have been created for a number of chemical reactions.

Plastics. Many advanced composite materials consist of plastics embedded in fiber networks. A major problem in fabricating these materials, which often have high strength and other desirable characteristics, has been that most plastics are too viscous to flow readily into the fiber network. In 1989, General Electric Company (GE) researchers announced that they had found a way to get around this problem. The first step used by the GE scientists was to develop a procedure that created small rings of the building blocks, or oligimers, used to produce polycarbonate plastic. When melted, these rings yield a liquid that flows easily into the fiber network. Once inside the network, a catalyst opens the rings and allows them to react and form long chains of the plastic. The technique could be a breakthrough in producing composites for automobiles, airplanes, and other products.

New Imaging Technique. Scientists from Israel and the United States described a new analytical technique, called "Coulomb explosion imaging," that is capable of yielding geometrical images of individual molecules. The "explosion" in the technique occurs when a molecule is stripped rapidly of its electrons. This is accomplished by directing a very fast beam of the molecules through a thin metal foil, about 30 angstroms thick, which removes the electrons but allows the nuclei to pass. Upon emerging, the nuclei fly apart as a result of their strong mutual repulsions. Analysis of the paths taken by the nuclei allows scientists to deduce the original structure of the molecule.

Cold Fusion. On March 23, B. Stanley Pons of the University of Utah and Martin Fleischmann of the University of Southampton, England, shocked the scientific world with a claim that they had succeeded in generating a sustained nuclear-fusion reaction in a electrolytic cell at room temperature. This new process was dubbed "cold fusion." The scientists claimed that their apparatus could open the way, possibly, to almost unlimited energy from a simple device. Enthusiasm waned as some scientists reported that they were unable to duplicate the results. (*See also* PHYSICS.)

PAUL G. SEYBOLD, *Wright State University*

Surrounded by his wife, mother, and children, Richard M. Daley greets the crowd following his inauguration as Chicago's mayor. Outgoing Mayor Eugene Sawyer (second row, r) *joins in the applause.*

AP/Wide World

CHICAGO

Chicagoans changed political direction in 1989, bringing back an old name to City Hall, but presenting Mayor Richard M. Daley a full platter of vexing city problems.

Homeowners became angry over soaring property taxes, a result of a declining tax base as the gap between the city's rich and poor has widened. New surveys showed that the gentrification of some neighborhoods had not outpaced the deterioration in other areas.

Education. On the education front, the long-awaited experiment to give parents more input in the education of their children was under way. The new mayor said education would be the top priority of his administration. One of Daley's first acts was to name an interim seven-member school board to carry out the Chicago School Reform Act. The board ousted Schools Superintendent Manfred Byrd, Jr., who had the backing of various black groups and the Rev. Jesse Jackson, and began a nationwide search for a new school head. "This is the third-largest school system, where 78% of the children come from economically disadvantaged situations. It is a major challenge," said School Board President James Compton. Ted Kimbrough, previously superintendent of schools in Compton, CA, was named to the post.

One of the goals of the school reform act was to diffuse the power of the Chicago Board of Education and its bureaucratic administration. In October voters chose among 17,000 candidates for 5,400 seats in local school councils in Chicago. The new school councils were to be given powers to hire and fire principals, approve local school budgets, and develop curricula for a school system that William Bennett, former U.S. secretary of education, called the worst in the nation.

Taxes. For homeowners in the city, 1989 was a year when their property taxes went through the ceiling. Huge rate hikes of more than 50% brought political pressure on aldermen and the new Daley administration to curb any further hikes in property taxes. That will mean searching elsewhere for the revenue-starved city budget. One option pushed by the new city government was to increase the basic parking meter rate from 10¢ to 25¢ per hour.

Politics. On the political front, the election of Richard M. Daley (*see* BIOGRAPHY) as mayor on April 4, 1989, was the end to the brief control that blacks had over city government. One of his most vocal critics, Jesse Jackson, announced he was leaving the city and moving to Washington, DC, as blacks searched for a new political leader.

Police Brutality. Some black leaders reopened the issue of police brutality. They charged that police shootings of and brutality against citizens, particularly blacks, increased dramatically after Daley took office. The mayor moved quickly to lessen any political fallout, appearing before a city council hearing to promise his full help in investigating the charges and announcing an overhaul of the civilian panel that reviews and acts on cases of alleged police brutality.

The brutality charges were denied by David Fogel, head of the city's Office of Professional Standards. Fogel said the number of police shootings has gone down from 136 in 1975, the year his office was established, to 41 during the first eight months of 1989. Of the 41 shootings, nine were fatal, compared with 37 in 1975. In addition, Fogel said the statistics for 1989 showed that blacks filed complaints against black police officers almost as often as they did against white officers.

ROBERT ENSTAD, *"Chicago Tribune"*

Photos, AP/Wide World

To the delight of fellow Christian Democrats, above, Patricio Aylwin calls his presidential victory a sign that "Chile has again taken its destiny in its hands."

CHILE

After more than 16 years under military rule, Chile turned toward democracy in 1989.

The Election. On December 14 the nation elected as its next president Patricio Aylwin, a 71-year-old leader of the Christian Democratic Party, who was backed by an antigovernment coalition of 17 parties of the center and left called the *Concertación por la Democracia*.

Aylwin would assume office in March 1990. In the December presidential race, he received 52.2% of the total vote, defeating the candidate of the government-backed National Renovation Party, Hernán Buchi, who won 29.4%. An independent rightist candidate, Francisco Errazuriz, finished with 15.6%. Buchi had been finance minister in the military government of Gen. Augusto Pinochet.

The opposition coalition also won control of both houses of the Chilean Congress, but no single party gained enough seats to assure control of the legislative process.

The presidential election was made possible when Chileans resoundingly voted "no" in a national plebiscite in October 1988 to a bid by Pinochet, the military dictator, to remain in office for another eight years. The Chilean military, in power since overthrowing Socialist President Salvador Allende in 1973, agreed to abide by the results of the plebiscite.

The full transition back to democracy will be slow and difficult in Chile. Under a national constitution drafted by the military government and adopted in 1980, General Pinochet is entitled to remain as commander of the army until 1997. On December 21, in their first face-to-face meeting following the election, Pinochet informed Aylwin that he intended to exercise the option.

The opposition coalition feared that Pinochet would try to become the power behind the throne from his army headquarters across the street in Santiago from La Moneda, the presidential palace. Aylwin said that he told Pinochet that "it was preferable for the country that he not" stay in the army post, but the general was adamant about retaining command of the army.

Military Influence. In addition to holding on to the reins of the army, Pinochet worked in numerous other ways to ensure a continuing influence of the military in the government. He created several autonomous institutions headed by his appointees, and installed loyalists to the military in important positions throughout the government. Pinochet appointees, for example, control the country's central bank and nine new Supreme Court justices have been appointed to lifetime terms since October 1988.

Mandatory guidelines also have been built into the country's budget process. Seven percent of government spending must go for defense, for instance. Under reforms approved by the Chilean voters on July 30, two thirds of the Congress must approve changes to the laws and the constitution left behind by the military. The most immediate problem for the new civilian government thus would lie in its relationship with the armed forces. Sixteen years of holding power in Chile has accustomed the military to functioning as a dominant force in the political life of the country. Whether the army under Pinochet, or the other uniformed branches, will accept easily civilian authority remained to be seen.

Amnesty. Also at issue was the question of punishment of violators of human rights during the years of military rule. An estimated 3,000 to 5,000 Chileans were killed by security forces since 1973 and thousands more were listed as "disappeared." A 1978 law extended amnesty to all security-related crimes committed during the first five years of the military regime. Aylwin, backed by human-rights groups, said he wants the 1978 law repealed. But Pinochet and other military officers, fearing the kind of retribution that befell Argentine military leaders after civilians won control of that country, are opposed strongly. "My people will not be touched," General Pinochet has declared on several occasions. An open clash over the amnesty issue could jeopardize the fledgling democracy.

Economy. Beyond the military-civilian relationship, economic-policy questions loomed large. On the surface, at least, the Pinochet government achieved a favorable economic record with its policies oriented toward free markets, private initiative, and an open trading system. Compared with other Latin American countries, Chile's inflation rate is relatively low, at about 13% a year. Export earnings nearly doubled since 1985, and the nation's external debt has been stabilized and even slightly reduced through debt-for-equity swaps with foreign lenders.

The economic reality is less rosy than the macroeconomic statistics indicate, however. Gains in the gross national product and in foreign trade have not been distributed broadly. Sharp cutbacks in social spending and severe wage restraints have affected negatively the lower classes and workers, while leaving the upper class relatively untouched.

Aylwin has pledged to continue the economic growth achieved by the Pinochet regime, but to correct the maldistribution of wealth and income that developed under military rule. "There has been a lot of talk about economic progress in Chile," Aylwin said shortly before the election, "but it has not benefited the common Chilean. In the last ten years, the top 20% of the population has increased its portion of the national income from 51% to 60%. The middle class and the workers have become impoverished in these years."

Social Sector. During a visit to Washington in November, Alejandro Foxley, a top economic adviser to Aylwin, said that the new coalition government would retain many of the economic policies espoused by Pinochet, including an open free-market economy, low tariffs, integration into the world market, and preservation of private-property rights. Foxley, a U.S.-trained economist with strong international credentials, was believed to be Aylwin's choice for the post of finance minister. He discounted claims that Pinochet had produced an "economic miracle" during his years in power. "The economy has grown too slowly to provide enough jobs," Foxley asserted. "Unemployment today is 18%, compared with 5% in 1973," the year Pinochet unseated Allende. (Official government figures put the unemployment rate at about 10%.)

"Chile has been underinvested," Foxley charged, saying that the investment rate during the Pinochet years was only 75% of its former level. "The Pinochet policies have been positive in the external sector, but negative domestically," he said. As a result, Foxley declared, Chile must make major investments in the social sector, in such areas as education, job training, and health. But the Chilean government will be hard-pressed to find the funds for social development without incurring a budget deficit, something Foxley said he would resist.

Other problems compound the difficulties that lie ahead, Foxley said. As much as 15% of the country's GDP must go to debt service in the next few years. In addition, copper prices, which have helped buoy the economy in recent years, seemed to be headed downward. Consequently, the Aylwin government will look for help from the outside, perhaps as much as $2 billion in fresh capital over the next four years. Will such help be forthcoming? Foxley hopes for the best. "It is important for everybody," he said, "that the Chilean economy progresses in a climate of freedom, rather than the repressive government of a dictatorship."

RICHARD C. SCHROEDER
Consultant to the Organization of American States

CHILE • Information Highlights

Official Name: Republic of Chile.
Location: Southwestern coast of South America.
Area: 292,259 sq mi (756 950 km²).
Population (mid-1989 est.): 13,000,000.
Chief Cities (July 31, 1985): Santiago, the capital, 4,099,714; Concepción, 280,713.
Government: *Head of state and government,* Gen. Augusto Pinochet Ugarte, president (took power Sept. 1973). *Legislature*—Congress (dissolved Sept. 1973).
Monetary Unit: Peso (280.31 pesos equal U.S.$1, official rate Dec. 26, 1989).
Gross Domestic Product (1988 est. U.S.$): $19,400,000,000.
Economic Index (Santiago, 1988): *Consumer Prices* (1980 = 100), all items, 430.9; food, 402.7.
Foreign Trade (1988 U.S.$): *Imports,* $7,048,000,000; *exports,* $4,924,000,000.

© Peter Turnley/Black Star

Waving banners with slogans, thousands of students and workers demonstrate for democracy in Tiananmen Square in the spring. The Chinese government later retaliated with troops and tanks in a brutal crackdown of the movement.

CHINA, PEOPLE'S REPUBLIC OF

The year 1989 began with China in the vanguard of those nations attempting to reform socialist systems. It ended with China sharing the rear ranks with Albania. The violent assault in June by government forces on prodemocracy demonstrators in Beijing was the pivotal event of the year.

A decade ago, China's leaders made a conscious choice to begin change by reforming their economy. Political reform, which they believed could be unlinked from economic reform, was to be postponed as long as possible. When problems arose as a result of economic reform, hundreds of thousands of students and urban residents took to the streets demanding political changes. Rather than respond to these demands, China's elderly and conservative leaders used military force to suppress the democracy movement and called a temporary halt to further economic reform. International reaction to these events isolated China from the world community and jeopardized plans for expanding international investment and balancing foreign trade.

Background to Discontent. Inflation in 1988 was set officially at 18.5%, but urban residents, who spent nearly two thirds of their monthly outlay on food, found the effective rate to be much higher. Since most urbanites were on incomes set by the state, their real income was declining—in some instances at a rapid rate.

To solve this problem the Chinese Communist Party (CCP) instructed the government to call a temporary halt to economic reform in September 1988. Growth of credit and expansion of the money supply were to be curbed and the runaway rate of industrial growth was to be slowed. While these measures were partially successful in slowing the rate of growth in inflation, the suspension of reforms left the economy bifurcated between a market-controlled sector and a sector still controlled by state planning. Frequently these two sectors were in competition with one another for scarce goods and markets. It was a set of circumstances ideal for the growth of corruption, and cases of bribery, profiteering, and graft were found at every level and in every sector.

Concern over inflation and corruption brought the populace into the streets of every major city in China once demonstrations began in mid-April. The demonstrations were initiated, however, by students, who had concerns of their own. Students last had taken to the streets in December 1986, and it was his failure to respond effectively to the political crisis brought on by these demonstrations that cost Hu Yaobang his position as general secretary of the CCP. It was to mourn Hu's sudden death of a heart attack on April 15 that students in Beijing once again carried out unauthorized street demonstrations.

On both occasions, the cause of the students' discontent was their own immediate circumstances. Having made it through one of the world's most competitive education systems, university students arrive on campus only to discover that the quality of their education is inadequate and their living conditions are deplorable. While in recent years more and more

© J. Langevin/Sygma

Soviet President Gorbachev and his wife tour the Great Wall during a trip to China in May. The arrival of the reform-minded Communist leader encouraged prodemocracy demonstrations. Nevertheless, the trip improved Sino-Soviet relations.

graduates have been able to choose their own jobs, a new regulation was promulgated on April 14 reimplementing a universal state placement system for this year's graduates.

The Demonstrations. On the night of Hu Yaobang's death, posters went up on the campus of Beijing University praising Hu's support of student demonstrators two years earlier and criticizing Deng Xiaoping, China's senior leader, for having dismissed Hu. Four days later, 10,000 students demonstrated in the streets of Beijing, and by then their demands had moved well beyond the campus walls. They wanted an official reassessment of Hu Yaobang, direct talks with government officials, and disclosure of the personal finances of government and CCP leaders.

Deng found his options to quell the demonstrations limited. First, the demonstrators were ostensibly on the streets to mourn a death, and public mourning is a time-honored custom in China. Second, the demonstrations were an almost direct parallel to those that took place 13 years earlier to mourn the death of the much-admired premier, Zhou Enlai (Chou En-lai). The so-called "Gang of Four," then in power, violently suppressed the demonstrations, branded them a counterrevolutionary act, and blamed them on Deng Xiaoping, then just recently reemerged from his post-Cultural Revolution obscurity.

A third limitation on Deng's actions was posed by the imminent celebration of the 70th anniversary of the May Fourth incident—a student demonstration in the streets of Beijing in 1919 protesting Japanese incursions on Chinese sovereignty. Many hold this incident to have given rise to modern Chinese nationalism, and it was out of the ferment that followed it that the Chinese Communist Party was born.

Finally, Deng's options were limited by the imminent arrival of two foreign guests, both representatives of liberalizing authoritarian regimes, although of very different types. Shirley Kuo, finance minister of the government on Taiwan, was to attend a meeting of the Asian Development Bank in Beijing in early May, and Soviet President Mikhail Gorbachev was slated to visit Beijing in mid-May.

Deng's initial ploy was to attempt to intimidate the students into abandoning the streets. Meeting with the Politburo of the CCP on April 25, he denounced the demonstrations as a "conspiracy of unlawful elements." His assessment was read on national television that night and appeared in editorials in the press the next morning. On the following day, 150,000 students marched in defiance of the ban.

Party General Secretary Zhao Ziyang advocated a different strategy. Noting that the students' demands for an end to corruption were in consonance with CCP policy, he argued for a more flexible response to the demonstrations. Until that point many Chinese had blamed Zhao for the numerous negative consequences of economic reform. As a consequence, Zhao had become a relatively unpopular figure. Now, however, his response to the student demonstrators distinguished him from his colleagues, and he was transformed into something of a hero in the eyes of the advocates of democratic reform. Unfortunately, Zhao lacked the political clout that would have enabled him to act as an effective champion of the students' cause—or, as events developed—even to save his own position.

After some 50,000 students took part in demonstrations on May 4, many began to advocate an end to protest and a return to the classroom. Journalists, however, had begun to protest as well. They called for greater press freedom and protested the dismissal of Qin Benli, the outspoken editor of the Shanghai-based *World Economic Herald*.

Gorbachev's arrival in Beijing on May 15 prompted a full-scale revival of demonstrations in Tiananmen Square and the initiation of a hunger strike by more than 2,000 students. The strikers demanded a fully publicized dialogue with government leaders, a formal reassessment of their movement, and a retraction of the critical editorial of April 26 written at Deng's behest. Many, by this time, were calling for the resignations of Deng and Premier Li Peng (*see* BIOGRAPHY).

At this point the demonstrations began to receive worldwide live television coverage, thanks to the facilities that had been put in place in Beijing for the Soviet president's visit. By May 17 more than 1 million people were demonstrating each day, including not only students but also workers, professional people, and government officials.

Crackdown. With Gorbachev's departure, the last of the obstacles that had inhibited a crackdown was removed. Zhao proved unable to outmaneuver his former mentor, Deng Xiaoping, who brought out of retirement a sufficient number of his elderly and conservative colleagues to outvote the moderates in the Politburo, which instructed Li Peng to declare martial law in Beijing and to summon elements of the People's Liberation Army to the capital to clear the streets.

This move encountered stiff resistance on the part of many senior government leaders and military officers, who were reluctant to see the army used in this fashion. More than 100 active duty and retired army officers put their names to a letter to that effect the day after martial law was declared on May 20. The hard-liners' efforts also were thwarted by the people of Beijing themselves, who blocked streets and harangued troops in attempts to dissuade them from moving against student demonstrators in the square.

In the early morning hours of June 4, however, troops opened fire, and by dawn, had brought this episode in China's democracy movement to a bloody halt.

The toll in dead and wounded from this action perhaps never will be determined with complete accuracy. Chinese leaders, in an attempt to limit the adverse consequences of their action, issued statements portraying students and workers as the perpetrators and soldiers as the victims of a "counterrevolutionary rebellion," and minimizing the number of casualties. A careful calculation by *New York Times* correspondent Nicholas Kristof extrapolated from statistics obtained from Beijing hospitals was perhaps the most reliable summary published in the immediate aftermath. He concluded that civilian deaths numbered between 400 and 800, and that perhaps a dozen soldiers and police officers were killed. Although he ventured no estimate as to the number of students among the civilian casualties, he and others agreed that most of those who lost their lives were killed outside of Tiananmen Square.

Arrests and executions began almost as soon as the firing ended and, as was the case with the victims of the event, the number of those targeted was difficult to determine with any degree of accuracy. During the month of June, the Chinese press was filled with stories of arrests, trials, and sentences. A list of 21 student leaders wanted for arrest was published, as was a list of seven leading intellectual dissidents. In early July the press coverage of arrests and executions suddenly terminated. At this point the official tally of those arrested stood at about 2,000. Some 30 executions had been reported, none of them of students or intellectuals. By the end of the summer diplomats based in Beijing estimated that as many as 20,000 may have been arrested or detained nationwide.

Former U.S. President Richard Nixon (right), *whose administration first opened relations with Communist China, confers with Chinese leader Deng Xiaoping in Beijing in November.*

Leadership Changes. At a meeting on June 16, Deng told his colleagues that, whereas Mao had served as the core of the first generation of Chinese Communist revolutionaries and Deng himself had served as the core of the second generation, the third generation was to be led by Jiang Zemin (*see* BIOGRAPHY), member of the Politburo and first party secretary and former mayor of Shanghai. Jiang was appointed as general secretary of the CCP to succeed the ousted Zhao. At its meeting in November the Central Committee received Deng Xiaoping's resignation from his last remaining post as chairman of the Military Affairs Commission. At his suggestion, the post went to Jiang.

The purge of party officials was very narrow. In addition to Zhao, only Politburo member Hu Qili and Hainan Province governor Liang Xiang were dismissed from office for having sympathized with the student demonstrators. Zhao retained his membership on the Central Committee and, although he remained under effective house arrest in Beijing, attempts by hard-liners to have him tried on criminal charges were apparently unsuccessful.

Economic Problems. The events of the spring and summer seriously undermined the already weakened political legitimacy of the party, leaving it ill-equipped to deal effectively with the serious problems plaguing the Chinese economy. By year's end the economy was in recession. Inflation, while slowed somewhat, nonetheless was estimated at more than 25% for the year, and more than 10 million urban workers were unemployed. The one bright spot was the grain harvest, which, while falling short of the record 407 million tons produced in 1984, was likely to come in at about 400 million tons for the year.

The Central Committee adopted an austerity program at its November meeting that set several targets for dealing with the economic crisis. The rate of inflation was to be reduced to less than 10%; the growth of gross national product (GNP) to be slowed from a rate of 11% to about half that figure; growth of the money supply, estimated to be as high as 47% during 1989, to be kept below the rate of overall economic expansion; and the national budget to be balanced. The plan called for a recentralization of economic decision-making, curbing the fast-growing rural collective industrial sector, and limiting private enterprise.

The program bore the familiar imprint of Chen Yun, the economic architect of China's Soviet-influenced development in the 1950s, who reemerged from retirement at the time of the crackdown in June.

China's domestic economic problems were exacerbated by response in the world economy to the events of midyear. As a result of foreign governments' sanctions, some $7 billion in loans were suspended and the sale of military hardware blocked. Moreover, assessments of political risk for investments in China were altered significantly for the worse after June 4, and China's credit rating dropped. A trade deficit of between $8 and $10 billion was projected for the year, which was likely to cause a drawdown of the already dwindling $19 billion in foreign-currency reserves. Some $1.1 billion in foreign-currency earnings were lost in the tourist industry alone.

Foreign Relations. The major foreign policy achievement of the Chinese government in 1989—the normalization of relations with the Soviet Union after a hiatus of nearly 30 years—was overshadowed even as it was being con-

The conservatives of the party were in control as the 40th anniversary of Communist rule was celebrated in October. Jiang Zemin, a Deng protégé who supported the crackdown on demonstrators, had been elevated to the top party post.

© F. Anderson/Gamma-Liaison

CHINA • Information Highlights

Official Name: People's Republic of China.
Location: Central-eastern Asia.
Area: 3,705,390 sq mi (9 596 960 km²).
Population (mid-1989 est.): 1,103,900,000.
Chief Cities (Dec. 31, 1986 est.): Beijing (Peking), the capital, 5,970,000; Shanghai, 7,180,000; Tianjin, 5,460,000.
Government: *General Secretary of the Chinese Communist Party,* Jiang Zemin (chosen June 1989); *Head of government:* Li Peng, premier (took office Nov. 1987); *Head of state:* Yang Shangkun, president (took office March 1988). *Legislature* (unicameral)—National People's Congress.
Monetary Unit: Yuan (3.722 yuan equal U.S.$1, official rate, July 1989).
Gross National Product (1988 U.S.$): $350,000,-000,000.
Foreign Trade (1988 U.S.$): *Imports,* $55,254,-000,000; *exports,* $47,530,000,000.

© Peter Charlesworth/JB Pictures

A Chinese family proudly poses in front of their home, a concrete example of the country's economic progress. But serious problems continued to plague the economy in 1989.

summated, as student demonstrators stole the spotlight from Deng and Gorbachev during the latter's visit to Beijing. Moreover, the unprecedented sequence of events in Eastern Europe in the fall, which transpired with the tacit approval of the Soviet leader, further distanced China's leaders from their newfound Soviet friend.

At least Gorbachev endorsed the Chinese insistence that their treatment of student demonstrators was an internal affair, not subject to international scrutiny. This view was not shared by China's other neighbors and erstwhile friends. In the United States, President George Bush's administration blocked arms sales and, under pressure from Congress to apply broader economic sanctions, announced that it would work to delay consideration of China's loan applications pending before international financial institutions. Congress passed its own package of sanctions on June 30, suspending Overseas Private Investment Corporation support and freezing the liberalization of export controls on dual-use technology for six months. Perhaps most telling among American responses was the granting of refuge in the U.S. embassy in Beijing to dissident astrophysicist Fang Lizhi, his wife Li Shuxian, and their son.

Congress continued to pursue a harder line with the Chinese than did President Bush. Shortly after announcing the suspension of all high-level contacts between the U.S. and the Chinese governments, Bush sent his national security adviser, Gen. Brent Scowcroft, and Deputy Secretary of State Lawrence Eagleburger on a secret mission to China in July. The fact that the trip had been made was revealed only after a second, public visit to Beijing by the two took place in early December. Although Bush insisted that neither visit contributed to a premature normalization of ties, many in Congress faulted the timing of the visits, the seniority of the emissaries, and the failure to extract any concessions from the Chinese authorities. Critics contended that the visits lent unfortunate credence to Deng's comment on June 9 that "as soon as stability has been restored, the foreigners will come knocking on our door again."

Most Western nations imposed sanctions comparable to those imposed by the United States. The Japanese government and business community, however, argued that the history of anti-Japanese sentiment in China and Japan's geographical proximity to China dictated a unique response. The government expressed its disapproval of the violence in Beijing and suspended all aid, including remaining projects in the current seven-year $3.3 billion package and the pending five-year $6 billion package. In mid-August, however, the Japanese were the first to lift government travel restrictions to China and to announce their willingness to consider lifting suspension of aid projects.

Of most apparent concern to Beijing among international reactions to the events of June and beyond was the agreement by the 26-member United Nations Human Rights Subcommission to consider representations concerning human-rights violations by the Chinese government. After deliberation the subcommission voted 15 to nine to place the Chinese case before the 43-member Human Rights Commission during its spring 1990 meeting. Although Beijing angrily rejected the resolution, it could not ignore the fact that it was the first time that human-rights charges had been brought against a permanent member of the UN Security Council.

See also TAIWAN.

JOHN BRYAN STARR, *Yale-China Association*

AP/Wide World

Terry Goddard speaks on behalf of the city, as mayor of Phoenix, AZ, and as president of the National League of Cities, at the organization's convention in November.

CITIES AND URBAN AFFAIRS

In 1989, U.S. city leaders began trying to find local solutions to problems that prior to the Reagan era received attention and dollars from the federal government. At the November 1989 meeting of the National League of Cities, mayors called for federal financial support to help them deal with the drug epidemic, inadequate public education, and the problems of the underclass. But such appeals are not being heard in the White House. In fiscal year 1978 federal grants to state and local governments accounted for 27% of state-local spending. In fiscal 1988, federal assistance accounted for 18%, a one-third loss over ten years. Since 1980 spending for housing assistance has dropped by 75%. Grants for sewage treatment dropped from $5 billion in 1981 to $2.4 billion in 1989. The remaining "urban" aid funding through the Community Development Block Grant program is down to $2.8 billion, from $4 billion in 1981. Most urban leaders hope, at best, to protect what funds they still receive. Cities are no longer a powerful voice in Washington.

Lost Political Clout. As U.S. cities have lost population they also have lost their influence in the White House and in the U.S. Congress. In 1952, for example, voters in New York City cast 48% of that state's presidential vote. By 1988 the city's share had fallen to 31%. This has been the experience for other cities as well: Chicago's share of the popular vote in Illinois dropped from 41% in 1952 to 23% in 1988; for St. Louis the city's share of Missouri's vote fell from 20% to 7%. A similar development has occurred in Congress. The number of U.S. senators and U.S. representatives elected mainly by city voters has declined sharply over the past 30 years. Cities will lose even more influence in the redistricting that will occur after the 1990 census.

Unlike Ronald Reagan, President George Bush does not have a hostile relationship with urban leaders, but urban issues are absent from his agenda. At the 1988 Republican convention, rural, but not urban, development rated a subcommittee in the platform debates. The Democratic convention was not much different. The word "city" was used 23 times in the 1968 Democratic platform, but not at all in the 1988 version. The new substitute, a recognition of the power of the suburbs, was "hometown America."

President Bush promised to establish a task force on urban affairs to "devise strategies for the urban agenda," but such a task force had not been appointed by late 1989. The new Secretary of Housing and Urban Development (HUD), Jack Kemp, has advocated a federal initiative to create 70 enterprise zones, and five bills to create such zones were introduced into Congress during 1989, although no final action was taken. Through the use of corporate tax breaks, investment tax credits, exemptions from capital-gains taxes, and credits for hiring unemployed workers, Kemp believes the zones would leverage investment and economic growth. But the zones also would cost the federal treasury about $1 billion a year in lost revenues.

HUD Scandal Aftermath. Scandals involving federally subsidized housing programs during the Reagan administration derailed any new urban legislation that might have been put forward. Former HUD Secretary Samuel Pierce refused to testify before Congress about his role in interceding to award HUD subsidies to housing projects financed by powerful Republican contributors. Hearings revealed that Republican "consultants," including former Secretary of the Interior James Watt, received $6 million in fees to help procure HUD housing grants.

In such an atmosphere, urban leaders have tried creative new strategies to solve the problems presented by the drug epidemic, AIDS, homelessness, crime, and the underclass. Some states and cities are trying to reduce the rising cost of AIDS treatment by experimenting with home-care and prevention programs. Some local and state governments also are participating in trust funds to build shelters and low-income housing—though these programs are providing a tiny number of homes compared to the magnitude of the problem. Many urban leaders place primary emphasis on local strategies to promote economic growth. Mayors are engaged in bidding wars to lure new businesses, offering low-interest loans, tax exemptions, job-training aid, free land, and other subsidies. According to some experts, however, the cities are giving away too much.

Urban leaders sometimes look to the states for help, but even states that pioneered aid in distressed areas since have retreated. In 1989, Massachusetts dramatically cut the state budget, and California also faced a budget squeeze. In both states, property-tax rollbacks enacted in the 1970s have curtailed revenues. The 50 states were projected to end 1989 with an average budget surplus of only 1.1%, the lowest percentage since 1977. Since a 4% to 5% surplus is considered a needed hedge against brief recessions, urban leaders must rely mainly on their own resources. This will not be easy. According to the National League of Cities, city expenditures were expected to exceed revenues in 1989, after several years of modest budget success.

DENNIS R. JUDD
University of Missouri-St. Louis

COINS AND COIN COLLECTING

In 1989, U.S. coins were struck outside the Mint for the first time since 1792. On June 14 presses were set up at the U.S. Capitol to strike the first $5 gold and $1 silver Bicentennial of Congress commemorative coins. A portion of the proceeds from the sale of the coins was to go to the Capitol Preservation Fund for the restoration of historic public areas of the U.S. Capitol Building in Washington, DC.

The British Royal Mint celebrated the 500th anniversary of the sovereign coin by striking a special series of gold coins. Queen Elizabeth II issued a royal proclamation for the striking of a commemorative frosted gold proof £5 coin, as well as a double sovereign, sovereign, and half sovereign in 22-karat gold. The 1989 commemorative sovereigns recall the majesty of their Tudor ancestor, first struck in 1489.

Courtesy, Krause Publications

Dexter Specimen of the 1804 Dollar

Courtesy, American Numismatic Association

500th Anniversary of Gold Proof Sovereign

Several major Wall Street investment firms entered the rare coin market in 1989, contributing tens of millions of dollars toward the purchase of mostly high-grade, certified U.S. coins. The firms include Kidder, Peabody & Company, Inc., and Shearson Lehman Hutton.

A world's record auction price for a U.S. coin was set July 7 when $900,000 was bid for the Dexter specimen of the 1804 Draped Bust dollar. The previous auction record for a U.S. coin was $725,000, bid for a 1787 Brasher doubloon sold in 1979. The 1804 dollar was sold to the American Rare Coin Fund, a private, limited partnership sponsored by Kidder Peabody.

In a private transaction on May 19, 1989—details of which were not acknowledged officially until September—a U.S. gold piece was sold for $1.35 million. The coin, a proof 1852/1 $20 gold piece, became the first to break the million-dollar price barrier for an individual U.S. numismatic item. The parties involved remained unnamed for security reasons.

The question of U.S. coinage redesign, for the past several years a much-debated issue among hobbyists and legislators, again was presented before lawmakers in 1989. On February 22 a resolution was introduced by Rep. Jim Kolbe (R-AZ) and Rep. Morris Udall (D-AZ), calling for a new circulating U.S. dollar coin and an end to the $1 Federal Reserve note. Supporters of the resolution point to Canada's recent success in enacting similar legislation, and argue that a dollar coin would be more convenient and last longer than its paper counterpart, translating to long-term profits for the Mint. Introduced in 1987, Canada's "Loon" dollar coin has replaced the country's $1 note, withdrawn from circulation in 1989. Opponents point to the failed Susan B. Anthony dollar coin as evidence that public support for such a proposal is lacking.

A resolution introduced early in the 101st Congress called for the modernization of all the portraits presently on U.S. coins. Chief sponsors of the bill included House Banking Committee Chairman Henry B. Gonzales (D-TX), Rep. Charles Rangel (D-NY), and Rep. Lindy Boggs (D-LA). The controversial issue was presented for discussion before the House Banking Subcommittee on Consumer Affairs and Coinage on July 12, shortly after the passage of a similar proposal by the Senate on June 23. The bill remained in subcommittee at year's end; a vote was scheduled for sometime early in 1990.

ANNE O'SHAUGHNESSY
Assistant Editor, "The Numismatist"

COLOMBIA

The assassination on Aug. 18, 1989, of Liberal party presidential candidate Luís Carlos Galán by the Colombian drug gangs hit at the heart of the Colombian elite and plunged the country into a virtual state of civil war. Following the assassination, President Virgilio Barco unleashed special units of Colombian police and army against the two drug cartels based in Medellín and Cali, with the resultant capture and deportation to the United States of several highly placed members of the cartels. In addition, large amounts of real estate and other property belonging to the drug lords were confiscated by the government. The cartels, which had become virtually a state within a state since the mid-1970s, struck back with a series of bombings, assassinations, and other terrorist actions that continued through the end of the year. Despite calls for accommodation by elements in both camps, the war raged on.

The Civil War. Although assassinations of minor government officials had occurred in Colombia before 1989, the drug cartels heretofore had refrained from attacking the Colombian elite directly. The assassination of Galán, however, marked a turning point in relations between the government and the cartels. Galán had been the odds-on favorite to win the presidency in the elections in May 1990 and, perhaps more importantly, was a member in good standing of Colombia's ofttimes coterminous political and social elite. His assassination initiated a breakdown of any tolerance by the government of continued open operation by the cartels in Colombia. Although the cartels fought back, by year's end one of Colombia's leading drug traffickers, José Gonzalo Rodríguez Gacha, had been assassinated, and it appeared that substantial drug manufacturing operations were being transferred to Brazil and leading drug barons were in hiding.

The Barco government also resumed deportations of indicted drug dealers to the United States. The presidential decree ordering such deportations subsequently was declared constitutional by the Colombian Supreme Court. Still, bombs exploded almost daily in the streets and shops of Colombia's major cities. In addition, a right-wing political movement—the National Renovation Movement (MORENA)—made its appearance and immediately made a tacit alliance with the drug lords. MORENA subsequently endorsed the presidential candidacy of Liberal hopeful Hernán Durán.

Despite initial outrage at the Galán assassination, public support for the drug war appeared to be waning by year's end. Opinion surveys indicated a majority of the public favored a dialogue to end the conflict, and a proposal by the drug barons for a commission of conciliation received a great deal of media attention. Although President Barco appeared firm in his resolve to continue the crackdown, he had less than a year left in office, and the decision by the United States to scuttle the International Coffee Agreement in September appeared to many Colombians to indicate a lack of U.S. support for Colombia.

An indication that the government still had to deal with leftist guerrilla groups came on October 4, when Catholic Bishop Jesus Jaramillo Gonsalve was gunned down by elements of the National Liberation Army (ELN). While both the ELN and the Colombian Revolutionary Armed Forces (FARC) remained active, the M-19 guerrilla group agreed to lay down its arms by the end of the year.

Politics. The Galán assassination threw the presidential race into confusion. His probable successors within the Liberal Party were Ernesto Samper, Hernán Durán, and Cesar Gaviria, but none commanded the wide support that Galán had enjoyed. The Conservatives appeared to be supporting former President Misael Pastrana Borrero, while the left-wing Unión Patriótica candidate was Bernardo Jaramillo.

The Economy. The Colombian economy suffered several severe blows during the year. First, the civil war took its toll on production, with agriculture suffering the most. Second, the end of the International Coffee Agreement produced a disastrous drop in coffee prices and an estimated drop of $200 million in exports for the year. Despite these developments, the Colombian economy grew during the year at a projected rate of 3.5%, below the initial projections of 4.5%, but still better than the growth rate of any other Andean nation. Meanwhile it was estimated that drugs, now Colombia's second-largest export, brought in more than $1 billion during the year. The cost of living rose by 20.22% during the first nine months of the year. This was the third-highest increase for the decade. Paradoxically, perhaps, unemployment dropped from 10.1% at the beginning of the year to 8.7% by late September.

ERNEST A. DUFF
Randolph-Macon Woman's College

COLOMBIA • Information Highlights

Official Name: Republic of Colombia.
Location: Northwest South America.
Area: 439,734 sq mi (1 138 910 km²).
Population (mid-1989 est.): 31,200,000.
Chief City (Oct. 15, 1985): Bogotá, the capital, 3,982,941.
Government: *Head of state and government,* Virgilio Barco Vargas, president (took office Aug. 1986). *Legislature*—Parliament; Senate and House of Representatives.
Monetary Unit: Peso (431.00 pesos equal U.S.$1, Nov. 28, 1989).
Gross Domestic Product (1987 U.S. $): $33,000,000,000.
Economic Index (Bogotá, 1988): *Consumer Prices* (1980 = 100), all items, 525.6; food, 575.1.
Foreign Trade (1988 U.S.$): *Imports,* $4,853,000,000; *exports,* $5,037,000,000.

COLORADO

Colorado pulled out of its five-year economic slump in 1989, though its recovery stopped well short of the boom generated by natural resource industries in the 1970s.

Economy. Coloradans were cheered on November 7 when the state Labor Department announced that its seasonally adjusted employment rate dropped to 5% in September. This was the lowest state unemployment figure since February 1984, when slumping oil and real-estate prices sent the Colorado economy into a nosedive that bottomed out with an 8.7% unemployment rate in March 1987.

Not all of the drop in the unemployment statistics was caused by Coloradans finding new jobs, however. Economist Nancy McCallin of the Colorado Legislative Council said part of the reduced unemployment rate reflected a shrinking labor force, caused in part by workers moving to other states. Even so, the September figures did count 9,000 more Coloradans with jobs than at the same time in 1988, for a total of about 1.6 million jobs.

Tax and Bond Issues. Economic issues dominated many of the 1989 municipal and school district elections in the state. On May 16, Denver voters, by a margin of about 63% to 37%, approved building a new international airport on land annexed from neighboring Adams County. Adams County voters had approved the annexation in 1988 and voters in both counties were swayed by arguments that the new airport project would create more jobs.

On November 7, Denver voters said yes again, to a series of ten bond issues totaling $241 million to finance street repairs and other major capital improvements. But voters in suburban Jefferson County narrowly defeated a proposed $179.9 million school-bond issue and also rejected an increase in their school district's operating budget. Voters in Adams County District 12 and Colorado Springs also rejected school-tax increases while Fort Lupton and Longmont voters vetoed sales-tax hikes. Telluride voters killed a property-tax increase that would have been earmarked for public housing but increased the city's lodger's tax.

Boulder voters approved a sales-tax increase to buy more open space and Westminster kept a similar existing sales tax earmarked for open space. Douglas County voters approved both operating budget increases and a capital construction bond issue for their school district. Loveland passed a $36 million school-bond issue. Estes Park, Steamboat Springs, and Ouray voters approved their own civic improvement projects.

Legislation. The Republican-controlled 1989 Colorado General Assembly increased spending for education and toughened laws against air pollution by banning wood-burning in metropolitan Denver on high pollution days. But the legislature adjourned without approving highway-tax increases urged by Democratic Gov. Roy Romer. Romer responded by calling the lawmakers back for a ten-day special session that approved a phased-in package of higher gasoline taxes, vehicle-registration fees, and drivers-license fees that eventually will add $97 million per year for the state highway budget. The legislators also approved $27 million to expand state prisons and passed a bill to help pay for at-home care for AIDS patients.

Airport Project. Hopes for the new airport were both boosted and dampened in the fall. Ground breaking began in September after Denver received $60 million from the federal aviation trust fund as part of the federal financing package for the project. But the city's hopes for raising an additional $1.2 billion in revenue bonds to finance the lion's share of the project were hurt in November when Standard and Poor's issued a negative credit watch on the city's airport bonds because of what the widely watched financial rating service called significant hurdles in the airport-financing package.

State Pride. Economic issues may have been important in 1989, but the year also brought two rare and priceless boosts to state pride—both of them courtesy of the University of Colorado (CU) at Boulder. In October, CU biochemist Thomas Cech won a Nobel Prize for work in molecular biology that revolutionized scientific thinking about the role of RNA.

On the football field, the CU Buffaloes defeated archrival Nebraska, 27-21, in Boulder to cap an undefeated season and a Big Eight championship. The Buffaloes were ranked Number 1 in The Associated Press football poll at season's end and headed for the Orange Bowl in Miami for a showdown with Notre Dame. However, the Buffaloes lost to the Fighting Irish on New Year's night, 21–6.

BOB EWEGEN, *"The Denver Post"*

COLORADO • Information Highlights

Area: 104,091 sq mi (269 596 km^2).
Population (July 1, 1988): 3,301,000.
Chief Cities (July 1, 1986 est.): Denver, the capital, 505,000; Colorado Springs, 272,000; Aurora, 217,990; Lakewood, 122,140.
Government (1989): *Chief Officers*—governor, Roy Romer (D); lt. gov., Michael Callihan (D). *General Assembly*—Senate, 35 members; House of Representatives, 65 members.
State Finances (fiscal year 1988): *Revenue,* $6,527,000,000; *expenditure,* $5,620,000,000.
Personal Income (1988): $54,352,000,000; per capita, $16,463.
Labor Force (June 1989): *Civilian labor force,* 1,651,500; *unemployed,* 110,600 (6.7% of total force).
Education: *Enrollment* (fall 1987)—public elementary schools, 392,000; public secondary, 168,000; colleges and universities, 183,583. *Public school expenditures,* (1987–88), $2,253,720,000 ($4,214 per pupil).

COMMUNICATION TECHNOLOGY

Modern telecommunication is based on integrated solid-state circuitry, microcomputers, software, and photonics (the fusion of light and electricity). In 1989 substantial technical progress was made in each of these areas.

Optical fibers are displacing copper wires and coaxial cables, not only in long-distance telephone lines, but even down to the local "loop" which connects the individual user to the central office. The Integrated Services Digital Network (ISDN) is growing rapidly in the United States and in 20 other countries, bringing the time closer when there will be worldwide, end-to-end connections for voice, data, and visual images.

In the field of microelectronics, essential to the microprocessors which now are an imbedded part of communication technology, 1989 was a year in which it was possible to put 8 million circuit elements on a silicon chip half an inch square (3.2 cm^2), and to build a microcomputer-based system which could handle 100 million instructions per second.

Transmission and Switching Technology. In 1989, AT&T installed the world's highest-capacity commercial lightwave communication system, capable of transmitting 3.4 billion bits (binary pulses) of information per second. In this system, voice, data, and images are encoded digitally and converted to ultrafast pulses of light that then are carried over hair-thin glass fibers. Some 50,000 simultaneous phone calls, or the equivalent capacity in data or picture format, can be carried over a single pair of fibers.

In 1989 the first fiber-optic trans-Pacific undersea cable, TPC-3, went into service between the United States and Japan, transmitting voice, data, and video signals over 8,000 mi (12 874 km). The cable consists of three pairs of hair-thin strands of glass fiber. Each pair can transmit 280 million bits of data per second, or 40,000 simultaneous telephone conversations. TPC-3 is a joint venture of 30 international telecommunication companies. The principal owners are AT&T and Japan's international long-distance company, Kokusai Denshin Denwa (KDD).

Telephone companies were beginning to extend optical fiber cabling and lightwave transmission systems from their central offices to individual homes and offices, replacing copper wire in the "loop." This opens the way to a variety of possible interactive broadband services such as videophone, cable television, high-speed computer connections, high-volume electronic mail, and other potential services requiring wide bands of frequencies at relatively low cost.

The rapid growth of mobile and portable radio telephone service was evidence of a strong demand for communication away from a fixed base. At present, there are about 3 million mobile subscribers in vehicles operating in 300 metropolitan areas in the United States. There also was rapid growth in the number of portable telephones that could operate away from a vehicle, and in the popular cordless telephones which use a low-power radio link as an extension of the drop-wire connected to the central office.

Courtesy, Motorola Inc.

Portable telephones continue to grow in popularity. The Motorola Micro TAC™, above, is the smallest cellular phone on the market; it can slip into a pocket or purse.

The year 1989 was one of further development and commercial introduction of wideband packet-switching technology, in which voice and data signals are converted to digital format and then grouped into "packets," or short bursts of digital bits. These packets are marked with timing and routing data and sent, together with interleaved packets from other customers, over a high-speed transmission line. At the receiving end, the packets are separated out, decoded, and reconstructed into the original messages. Packet switching is several times more efficient than the usual electronic circuit switching.

Increasing usage and technical progress in satellite communications took place in 1989. For both voice and private-line data services, the year's growth rate exceeded 20%. New interest in satellites was stimulated by advances in technology for the 14/12-gigahertz (billions of cycles per second) frequency band (Kμ) and small, low-cost earth stations with very small-aperture terminals (VSATs), using an antenna only 6 ft (1.8 m) in diameter. This system will make satellite communications highly feasible for private networks to be set up by large businesses, government agencies, and entertainment enterprises.

E-mail, electronic mail, electronic messaging, and voice messaging are terms applied to the technique in which messages are sent in digital format between and under the control of computers, then electronically converted to speech or text, or left in the computer as digital data. The message can be stored on magnetic disks for later retrieval (store-and-forward) or sent out to one or hundreds of recipients under the direction of the computers in the information path. The electronic system is highly effective in delivery, since it is not frustrated by the absence of the addressee, the inconvenience of time of day or night, or delays in message handling—common problems for ordinary mail or telephone calling.

Sematech, the industry-government consortium set up to produce semiconductor integrated circuits, began to manufacture a 64-kilobit static random-access chip (SRAM).

A semiconductor chip that stores 4 million bits of information in an area the size of a thumbnail was put into production by IBM. One of the new chips can store the equivalent of 200 pages of typewritten text, representing a four-times improvement over previously available devices. The effect will be to make desktop computers more powerful and versatile.

Bellcore, the laboratory that provides technical research and development support to the regional telephone companies, and AT&T Bell Laboratories jointly created the world's smallest surface-emitting laser. Two million microscopic semiconductor "points of light" were contained in a solid-state structure of 600 alternate layers of gallium arsenide and aluminum arsenide covering an area of about one third of a square inch (2 cm^2).

M. D. FAGEN
Formerly, AT&T Bell Laboratories

COMPUTERS

Ever since microcomputers first were introduced in the late 1970s, potential buyers faced the conundrum of buying now or waiting a year for less expensive but more powerful models. In 1988, for the first time, computer prices rose instead of fell, due to high prices for memory chips. In 1989 things returned to "normal": Prices dropped even on the newest, most powerful models.

Competition among manufacturers of all types of computer hardware and software was strong, with new players entering the market even while some longtime firms, such as Leading Edge, stumbled.

The PC Market. The PC (personal computer) market continued to grow, increasingly at the expense of mainframes and minicomputers, and on a collision course with the workstation market. PCs have the advantage of broadly accepted architectures, huge libraries of applications, lower manufacturing costs, and strong distribution channels.

Portable and laptop computers remained one of the hottest PC markets, growing as much as 50% a year (a growth rate almost twice that of desktop models). Portables are somewhat heavier than laptops, which typically weigh less than 15 lbs (7 kg). One of the lightest machines introduced in 1989 was Atari's Portfolio, which weighed 1 lb (.46 kg), had 128K of memory (expandable to 640K), and was compatible with the IBM PC. Instead of a disk drive, it had credit card-sized program and memory cards.

Powerful New Chips. Intel introduced the 80486 processor, which has 275,000 transistors and works two to four times faster than its predecessor, the 80386. The 80486 is considered to be well-suited to multiprocessing. In this procedure, a task is done more quickly by dividing it among two or more microprocessors. PCs that can do this were expected to be introduced in the near future.

Intel also introduced the i860. It is a RISC (Reduced Instruction Set Computer) design, which eliminates instructions that are used rarely. Instead the chip integrates components such as a floating-point coprocessor that formerly were on separate chips, thereby reducing the time needed for interchip communications. The i860 was the first commercial microprocessor with more than 1 million transistors on a single piece of silicon and the first to handle data in 64-bit chunks.

Network Computing. Connectivity became more than a buzzword in 1989, as firms implemented increasingly complex information networks. Capturing most of the attention were local area networks (LANs), which connect PCs within an organization so that they can share computer data. A LAN consists of computers, printers, and other hardware connected by metallic or fiber-optic cable. Software known as a network operating system controls the operation, enabling a person to access files that reside in computers at other locations. The software may be resident in every device on the network or it can reside on one designated PC called the server.

Industry experts predict that by 1992 the LAN market will amount to more than $10 billion per year, and that more than half of the 60 million PCs installed worldwide will be connected to LANs. The rapid growth has been fueled to a large extent by the increasing need to create, store, and move information easily from one personal computer to others within a corporation. Applications are infinite. For example, hospitals use LANs to connect fetal monitors in a maternity ward. This allows nurses and doctors to monitor vital signs remotely, from a central station, and to store data for review and analysis.

Novell introduced Netware 386, the first network operating system to take advantage of the 80386 and 80486 microprocessors. Support-

In the rapidly changing world of portable and laptop computers, Atari presented the Portfolio, right, weighing just under 1 lb (.46 kg). It includes a built-in word processor and calculator.

Courtesy, Atari Computer

ing up to 250 computers, it can tie together all the major operating systems used by businesses today, allowing users of different types of computers to share data, applications, printers, and other resources.

Another type of network is the wide area network (WAN), which is popular among financial institutions. A bank with automatic teller machines in convenient locations across a city connects those machines to a central computer via a WAN. MasterCard International has a worldwide network called Banknet that is used for credit card authorization, electronic funds transfer, and other applications.

A low-cost alternative to private WANs are public data networks, also known as value-added networks (VANs). In 1989, New York Telephone introduced Nynex InfoLook, a VAN that permits PC users to dial a local number and be connected with a wide range of information services.

At the other end of the scale is a proposed National Research Network that would link supercomputers at laboratories around the nation. Such a network would enable thousands of scientists in academia and industry to use their desktop computers to access the supercomputers as well as equipment such as telescopes, particle accelerators, and wind tunnels, even if they were thousands of miles from the apparatus.

Supercomputers. The number of companies marketing supercomputers grew to more than two dozen, even while some firms, such as Control Data Corporation, withdrew from the business. Fierce competition meant that supercomputers that would have cost $5 million in the mid-1980s sold for less than $1 million by the end of 1989.

Japanese firms increasingly challenged U.S. supremacy in this market. "We're in a very serious race," said Sheryl Handler, president of Thinking Machines, a firm best known for its Connection Machine, a supercomputer that has 64,000 processors connected in parallel. A computational problem is divided into parts, with portions assigned to multiple processors operating simultaneously. The processors calculate subtotals and return them to a central processor for combining. Parallel processing received increased attention among computer designers, who believed it could offer greater speed than the serial operation used in most current supercomputers.

During 1989, Cray Research Corporation, the world's leader in supercomputers, split its operations, creating two rival companies. The firm simultaneously had been developing two supercomputer designs: the Cray-3 and the C-90 (a successor to the firm's Y-MP line), which currently are the world's fastest supercomputers. Cray Research will concentrate on existing models and the C-90 while the new Cray Computer Corporation will develop the Cray-3, a machine powered by gallium arsenide.

Piracy Crackdown. The illegal copying of software continued to be a leading concern, costing the microcomputer software industry billions of dollars in lost sales each year. The problem was particularly acute with business software because many publishers had agreed to user demands to eliminate protection mechanisms for such software. In 1989 alone, the Software Publishers Association, the principal trade group of the PC software industry, filed more than two dozen lawsuits citing copyright infringement. Settlements were reached in the majority of the cases, with cash payments—one in excess of $250,000—earmarked for use in fighting similar cases.

JENNY TESAR
Free-lance Science Writer

AP/Wide World

A severe tornado struck Hamden, CT, on July 10, injuring about 100 people, destroying some 400 structures, and leaving many homeless. The tornado, part of a violent storm system that hit 27 towns in Connecticut as well as portions of the surrounding states of New York and New Jersey, hit hardest in the Hamden area, near New Haven.

CONNECTICUT

The 1989 session of Connecticut's General Assembly approved $694 million of increases in taxes and fees to balance a $6.82 billion budget for the 1989–90 fiscal year. The new budget was an 8.4% increase in state spending over the prior fiscal year.

The tax package was built around increasing the sales tax from 7.5% to 8%, maintaining Connecticut's position of having one of the highest sales taxes in the nation. In addition to the tax increases adopted to balance the new budget, the legislature also enacted other tax increases of about $247 million to remedy a deficit in the budget for fiscal 1988–89. A softening of the state's economy and a decline of expected revenues, especially from the sales tax, was the reason given for increasing taxes and licensing fees.

CONNECTICUT • Information Highlights

Area: 5,018 sq mi (12 997 km²).
Population (July 1, 1988): 3,233,000.
Chief Cities (July 1, 1986 est.): Hartford, the capital, 137,980; Bridgeport, 141,860; New Haven, 123,450; Waterbury, 102,300.
Government (1989): *Chief Officers*—governor, William A. O'Neill (D); lt. gov., Joseph J. Fauliso (D). *General Assembly*—Senate, 36 members; House of Representatives, 151 members.
State Finances (fiscal year 1988): *Revenue,* $8,113,000,000; *expenditure,* $7,518,000,000.
Personal Income (1988): $74,553,000,000; per capita, $23,059.
Labor Force (June 1989): *Civilian labor force,* 1,819,300; *unemployed,* 61,100 (3.4% of total force).
Education: *Enrollment* (fall 1987)—public elementary schools, 326,000; public secondary, 139,000; colleges and universities, 162,382. *Public school expenditures* (1987–88), $2,800,187,000 ($5,992 per pupil).

Legislature. In another significant move, the state legislature approved a parental-medical leave bill that by 1993 will require employers of 75 or more people to offer 16 weeks of unpaid leave every two years to employees who need to care for a newborn or newly adopted child, or seriously ill relative. The three-year phase-in begins July 1, 1990, and will require companies with 250 or more employees to provide 12 weeks of unpaid leave.

Courts. In April a coalition of civil-rights groups sued Gov. William A. O'Neill and nine other state officials in Superior Court, asking the court to order desegregation of public schools in Hartford and its suburbs. The suit was filed on behalf of 17 minority and non-minority children attending Hartford-area schools. Hartford's school census shows more than a 91% minority population.

Also in April, four members of Los Macheteros, a Puerto Rican nationalist group, were convicted in U.S. District Court, Hartford, for their roles in the $7 million robbery at a Wells Fargo depot in West Hartford in 1983. Victor M. Gerena, a Wells Fargo guard, is wanted in connection with the robbery. The trial was the longest ever held in a federal court in Connecticut, lasting more than four years. Government prosecutors claimed the $7 million was stolen to finance the Los Machetero campaign to overthrow the U.S. government in Puerto Rico.

Industry. On June 30, 1989, Emhart Corp., a world leader in manufacturing hardware and machinery, whose Connecticut roots go back to the early 1800s, closed its Farmington headquarters and moved to Towson, MD, the home base of Black & Decker Corp. Black & Decker earlier in 1989 acquired ownership of Emhart for $2.8 billion.

Academia. In September two of Connecticut's private higher-education institutions, Trinity College in Hartford and Wesleyan University in Middletown, installed new presidents. Tom Gerety, 43, became Trinity's 17th president. Before coming to Trinity, he was dean of the College of Law at the University of Cincinnati. William M. Chace, 50, became the 14th president of the 158-year-old Wesleyan. He came to Wesleyan from Stanford University where he taught English and was an administrator.

Politics. In November elections, political newcomer Mary C. Moran (R) upset incumbent Bridgeport Mayor Thomas Bucci (D), and state Sen. John Daniels (D) became New Haven's first black mayor.

Other. On November 9 the Connecticut Criminal Lawyers Association filed suit against the state police, charging that they illegally recorded private telephone conversations made from state police barracks. Lester J. Forst, state police chief, was forced to resign.

Richard Crafts, a pilot from Newtown, was convicted of murdering his wife in 1986 and disposing of the body in a wood chipper. His first trial in 1988 had ended in a mistrial.

John Noel Dempsey, 74, Connecticut's governor from 1961 to 1971, died July 16 of cancer.

ROBERT F. MURPHY, *"The Hartford Courant"*

CONSUMER AFFAIRS

"All the grosser mistakes in economic policy, if not most manifestations of democratic corruption, arise from focusing upon interests of people as producers rather than upon their interests as consumers; that is, from acting on behalf of producer minorities, rather than on behalf of the whole community as sellers of services and buyers of product." This statement, made many years ago by the late Henry Simons, one of the great defenders of free enterprise, continued to apply in 1989.

Consumers are the amateurs in the marketplace while the producers and marketers are the professionals. The sellers are well-organized and make their weight felt in legislative halls, while consumers basically are unorganized and lack the necessary "clout" in those legislative halls. In spite of this imbalance, consumer progress was made in 1989.

A New Car Policy. General Motors, in an attempt to halt customer defections from its Oldsmobile Division—model sales had dropped to less than 700,000 in 1988, from 1 million in 1984—was challenging an industry-wide taboo by permitting dissatisfied buyers to return new cars for full credit. The plan allowed the buyer to return a car within 30 days or 1,500 miles (2 400 km) for credit on another Oldsmobile. No U.S. carmaker ever before had agreed, as a matter of general policy, to take new cars or trucks back from dissatisfied customers. General Motors may expand the policy to other divisions.

Car Safety. Virtually all new cars sold in the United States after 1989 are required to have lap and shoulder safety belts for two passengers in the rear seat. All 1990-model cars were required to have either airbags or automatically fastened seat belts for passengers in the front seat.

Consumer Credit. The Fair Credit and Charge Card Disclosure Act, requiring credit and charge-card issuers to disclose their interest rates and other cost information in a uniform manner, went into effect in 1989. Companies soliciting customers through the mail now must highlight the card's annual percentage rate, whether the rate is variable, and the method for computing the balance on which the rate is applied. The company also must supply information on annual fees, grace periods, and minimum finance charges, as well as the information on fees for ordinary transactions, for late payments, and for exceeding credit limits.

Advertising. The Federal Trade Commission amended its rules on requiring retail stores to provide adequate stocks of items that are advertised for sale. The regulation was amended to exempt grocers from having to keep large quantities of advertised items in stock, as long as their ads explicitly state that supplies are limited. Rain checks are permitted under the new rules but are not required.

Consumer Appointment. After taking office in 1989, President Bush appointed Dr. Bonnie Guiton as special adviser to the president for consumer affairs and director of the U.S. Office of Consumer Affairs. She also serves as chair of the Consumer Affairs Council, an organization of federal agency consumer representatives. Dr. Guiton had been the assistant secretary for vocational and adult education at the U.S. Department of Education.

Free-Trade Agreement. The free-trade agreement between the United States and Canada that went into effect at the beginning of 1989 is of special significance to consumers. The agreement calls for all tariffs between the two countries to be phased out by 1999. U.S. tariffs on computers, office machines, data-processing equipment, motorcycles, whiskey, skis, and ice skates dropped to zero on Jan. 1, 1989, from a previous range of from 2% to as high as 5.8%. Canadian tariffs on the items, ranging from 2% to 12.5%, also dropped to zero.

Inflation. The U.S. Consumer Price Index rose 3.4% during the first nine months of 1989, while the Producer Price Index—frequently referred to as the Wholesale Price Index—rose only 3.2%. Accordingly the fear of renewed high inflation had abated by late 1989.

STEWART M. LEE, *Geneva College*

CRIME

Crime continued to trouble deeply U.S. citizens in 1989. Opinion polls showed that many Americans considered illegal drugs the country's number-one problem. A tragic attack on schoolchildren by a sniper armed with a semiautomatic assault rifle renewed the debate on the need for gun control laws. The murder of a young, successful actress once again showed that the rich and famous are vulnerable to violence. A racially related murder rocked New York City, and the nation's capital, Washington, DC, had to deal with the dubious distinction of being the murder capital as well.

The War on Drugs. America's primary crime issue of 1989 continued to be illicit drugs, especially the use and sale of cocaine. President Bush's first year in office was marked by his appointment of former Secretary of Education William Bennett as "drug czar" and by the unveiling of a $7.9 billion antidrug plan. Bush's "war on drugs" proposal was criticized by opponents as placing too much emphasis upon law enforcement and prisons while spending too little for prevention and treatment programs. Bush's agenda on confronting America's crime problem was complicated further by increased violence by cocaine organized crime "cartels" against Colombian government officials. (*See also* DRUGS AND DRUG ABUSE.)

Crimes of 1989. The crimes that made the nation's headlines in 1989 continued to make crime a top concern for Americans. One of the more tragic stories of the year occurred in Stockton, CA. Patrick Purdy, a 26-year-old unemployed welder, strolled onto the grounds of Cleveland Elementary School armed with a semiautomatic copy of an AK-47, a Chinese assault rifle. Purdy killed five children and wounded 30 others, many of Vietnamese origin, before turning the gun on himself.

One of the most bizarre crime stories of 1989 occurred just outside the United States, in Mexico's Rio Grande Valley. In April, Mexican police found evidence of a drug-smuggling ring that combined its trafficking in narcotics with human sacrifice and "black magic." Adolfo de Jesus Constanzo, a 26-year-old Cuban-American, and his followers allegedly sacrificed humans and participated in occult practices to win satanic protection over their drug-smuggling operation into the United States. Officials recovered 15 bodies from shallow graves, many of them showing evidence of mutilation and torture.

The city of New York was the scene of two highly publicized assaults which drew national attention. In April a crime spree by young black teenagers in Central Park culminated in the brutal attack and rape of a female jogger which left the victim in a coma. The attack became known as "The Wilding," an outing by young people characterized by random, senseless violence. In another incident, a young black male walking through a white neighborhood was shot and killed by youthful residents of the community. The shooting enraged blacks and civil-rights leaders.

Celebrities were also the targets of violent crime. Rebecca Schaeffer, 21, a rising actress and costar of the television series *My Sister Sam,* was shot and killed at her Los Angeles residence by what police described as an "obsessive fan," allegedly John Bardo. Bardo, 19, is said to be an example of an individual whose admiration for a celebrity turns to an obsession, often violent in its intensity. The killing of Schaeffer is the latest in a series of attacks upon celebrities, these attacks becoming more evident since the beginning of the 1980s. Other examples of "obsessive fan" assaults in the 1980s include the shooting of former Beatle John Lennon by Mark David Chapman and the attempted assassination of then-President Ronald Reagan by John Hinckley in a bizarre bid for the affection of actress Jodie Foster.

Serial Murders. In January 1989 one of the most famous serial murderers of the 20th century was executed in Florida's electric chair. Ted Bundy, also suspected of numerous homicides in Washington, Oregon, Utah, and Colorado, was executed for the 1978 slayings of two Florida State University coeds and a 12-year-old girl from Lake City, FL.

Richard Ramirez, the notorious "Night Stalker" serial murderer, was found guilty of 13 counts of murder and sentenced to die in California's electric chair. In 1984 and 1985, Ramirez went on a 14-month rampage, terror-

Richard Ramirez, 29, a Texas drifter judged to be the "Night Stalker" who terrorized southern California in 1984–85, was convicted of 13 murders and 30 other crimes.

AP/Wide World

© A. Weiner/Gamma-Liaison

Mass shootings focused attention on the "assault rifle" in 1989. Gun-control advocates sought to have the weapon banned; the powerful pro-gun lobby fought such action.

izing Los Angeles residents by leaving satanic symbols at murder sites and forcing victims to swear allegiance to the devil.

Law-enforcement officials in the Pacific Northwest turned their attention to another serial murderer in the vicinity of Seattle, an area previously victimized by Bundy. A former law student was named a suspect in the murder of 48 women between 1982 and 1984. After further investigation, however, he was dropped as a suspect in the "Green River Killer" crimes, so named because of the killer's habit of dumping the bodies of his victims in the vicinity of Seattle's Green River.

Law-enforcement agencies are continuing to utilize "personality profiles" in their attempt to identify and arrest America's serial murderers. This technique first was developed by agents of the Federal Bureau of Investigation at the FBI academy in Quantico, VA. "Personality profiles" attempt to combine psychology and the characteristics of a homicide scene to develop a "profile" of the murderer's age, race, motive for the crime, and other factors that may assist in finding a suspect. These profiles are created at the Behavioral Sciences Unit at Quantico and have been instrumental in the apprehension and prosecution of several serial murderers.

Gun Control. Fueled by the shooting in Stockton, CA, as well as drug- and gang-related shootings with semiautomatic weapons, national attention began to focus in 1989 upon the accessibility and ownership of "assault rifles," like the AK-47, the Uzi, and the AR-15. In March the Bush administration and the U.S. Bureau of Alcohol, Tobacco and Firearms announced a temporary ban on the importation of assault rifles. Colt Industries, the American producer of the AR-15, also announced the restriction of sales of this weapon to the general public. California and other states soon attempted to pass legislation prohibiting the sale of assault rifles to local citizens.

Though the National Rifle Association (NRA), a pro-gun lobby, considered the import ban on assault rifles to be a "setback," the 2.8-million-member organization's ability to stifle further gun-control legislation remained largely undaunted. The NRA's success at warding off major gun-control legislation is likely to continue. This is evidenced by the fact that President Bush, a life member of the NRA, has not sought tighter controls on assault rifles and on guns in general beyond the import ban.

A new trend in gun control may be legislation aimed at preventing accidental shooting of children. Two years ago, Florida passed a law making it easier for citizens to own and carry firearms for self-defense. Since that time, the state has experienced a rash of accidental shootings of children by their siblings and playmates. In response to this problem, Florida and other states initiated legislation to enact laws authorizing prison terms for negligent gun owners when their firearms are misused by children.

Crime Rates. After peaking in 1981, crime rates in the United States began a five-year decline. Data released during 1989, however, indicated a continuing rise in the crime rate over more recent years, especially in the area of violent crime. In 1989, *Uniform Crime Reports* showed an increase in violent crimes reported to the police. These increases were recorded for murder and nonnegligent manslaughter (1.8%), forcible rape (.5%), robbery (3.9%), and aggravated assault (5.4%). In 1989, Washington, DC, became the "murder capital" of the nation, with more murders per capita than any U.S. city, and many of these homicides were attributed to drug-related violence.

Research gathered through victimization surveys in the *National Crime Survey (NCS)* also verified an increase in crime. *NCS,* which gathers information from public surveys, found an overall 3.1% increase in crime. Violent crime in general was up 2.0%, while property crime (burglary, larceny, and motor-vehicle theft) remained basically unchanged. One of the largest increases was for aggravated assault, which expanded by 9.7%.

Domestic Violence. One of the crime problems which elicited growing public concern was domestic violence. The issue of battered women was dramatized in the television production *A Cry for Help,* the story of Tracy Thurman. In 1984, Mrs. Thurman was assaulted and stabbed by her husband Buck. When a Torrington, CT, police officer arrived at the scene, Buck continued to assault his wife. As the officer stood by, Buck kicked Tracy Thurman in the head, breaking her neck. Though he subsequently was arrested, the beating left Tracy Thurman paralyzed on the right side of her body and in 1985, she received a $1.9 million settlement from the city of Torrington for violating her constitutional right to equal protection.

The Thurman incident, and the subsequent television drama, illustrated to the American public the problem of domestic abuse and violence. It has been estimated that more than 3 million cases of domestic abuse occur annually. As depicted in the Tracy Thurman scenario, the nation's criminal justice system often has been reluctant and ineffective in dealing with the issue of battered women. As a result of the increased attention, many states have begun to enact special legislation requiring police officers to arrest offenders in cases of probable domestic violence, including Connecticut, which passed a measure known as the Tracy Thurman Law. Some police departments, including the one in Torrington, also have upgraded their training to deal with domestic disputes.

Child Abuse. The 1989 conviction of Joel Steinberg, the "adoptive" father of Lisa Steinberg, in New York, highlighted the national problem of child abuse. Lisa, who died at the age of 6 as a result of abuse, is an example of an estimated 1,200 children who die annually as a result of abuse and neglect. As with the domestic violence directed against women, the criminal justice system often has been accused of improperly handling the more than 1 million cases of child abuse reported every year. Many states, in response to the Steinberg case and other publicized child-abuse incidents, are beginning to introduce legislation to toughen penalties for child abuse.

Another, more recently defined, form of abuse concerns the rising number of infants who are exposed to drugs before birth. More than one in ten women, and one in five at some inner-city hospitals, are giving birth to "drugged" infants. The potential prosecution of mothers for the "child abuse" of unborn babies has become one of the more controversial issues among the nation's court systems.

White-Collar Crime. The year's white-collar crime stories focused upon three investigations involving a governmental agency, defense contracts, and commodity traders. Jack Kemp's first year as the chief of the Department of Housing and Urban Development (HUD) was marked by disclosure of gross mismanagement and alleged fraud under HUD's former secretary, Sam Pierce. An estimated $20 million to $100 million in fraud and losses allegedly oc-

Photos, AP/Wide World

On October 20, U.S. Rep. Robert Garcia (D-NY) and his wife Jane Lee, above, *were convicted of extortion and conspiracy in connection with the Wedtech case. Robert P. Clark,* left, *who authorities believe to be John List, was extradited from Richmond, VA, to New Jersey to face charges that he murdered his mother, wife, and three children. A TV program led to his arrest.*

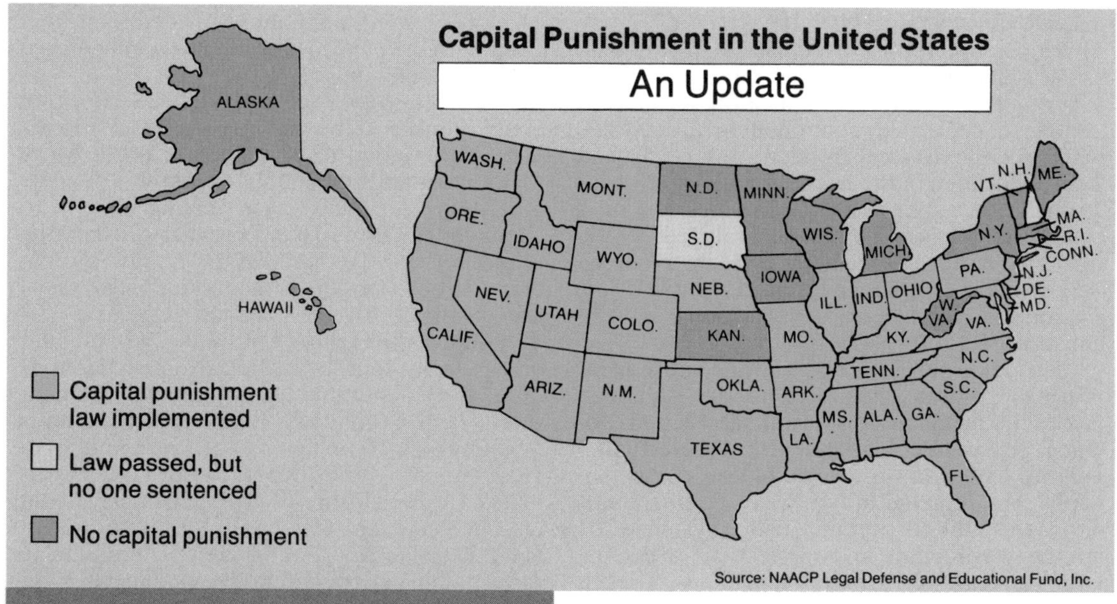

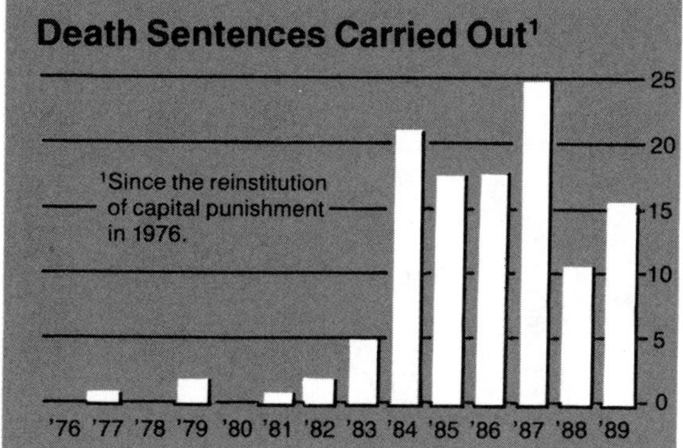

curred during the Pierce administration of HUD.

The FBI and the Naval Investigative Service also announced their probe of the sale of "inside information" concerning government defense contracts. By October, 24 individuals and three corporations had pleaded guilty to, or been convicted of, various crimes ranging from bribery to tax evasion. The FBI also completed an undercover operation at the Chicago commodity exchanges. In August a federal grand jury indicted 46 commodity traders and brokers on charges of cheating customers, dodging taxes, and manipulating prices at the nation's two largest futures exchanges.

Capital Punishment. In one of the more controversial cases of the year, the United States Supreme Court ruled that crime by some juveniles and by mentally retarded persons may be punishable by death. By a 5-to-4 vote, the court ruled that the constitutional amendment on "cruel and unusual punishments" does not forbid the execution of youths who commit crimes at 16 or 17 years of age, nor does it automatically prohibit death sentences for the retarded. Of the estimated 2,200 convicts on death row, 31 committed their crimes as juveniles. Some observers estimate that as many as 30% of death-row inmates may be retarded or mentally impaired.

Forensic Criminology. There was a continued increase in the use of sophisticated crime detection techniques in 1989. The use of DNA (deoxyribonucleic acid) to identify both suspects and victims from samples of human hair, tissue, semen, or blood has gained increased acceptance among the criminal-justice community. Automated Fingerprint Identification Systems (AFIS) also are being used by many state and local law enforcement agencies. AFIS uses computer technology to compare latent fingerprints found at a crime scene with the fingerprint records on file at law-enforcement agencies.

Another form of technology gained notoriety with the arrest of a man identified as John List in Richmond, VA, in June of 1989. List, a suspect in the murder of his mother, wife, and three children, had been a fugitive since 1971. A sculptor, working from an old photograph, created a lifelike bust of what he thought List would look like in 1989. When the bust of List was shown on national television, he quickly was recognized and arrested, although he insisted he was Robert P. Clark. The artificial "aging" of a photograph also can be done via computer technology. The use of artificially aged photographs may prove to be a major advance in the identification of other fugitives. It also may prove valuable in helping to identify the thousands of missing or abducted children whose appearance has changed dramatically from photographs taken prior to their disappearance.

JACK E. ENTER
Georgia State University

CUBA

The July 13 execution of four senior army officers, including Gen. Arnaldo Ochoa Sánchez, former commander of Cuban troops in Angola and one of Cuba's most decorated generals, underscored the serious difficulties that confronted the Castro government in 1989. The problems were revealed further by the arrests and dismissals of scores of other high-ranking officers and government officials.

Purge. Caught up in what looked like a purge of the country's military and political hierarchy were some of the closest lifelong collaborators of President Fidel Castro. Havana conceded that the population was stunned by the June 12 announcement that Ochoa and 13 other officials had been arrested on drug trafficking and corruption charges.

General Ochoa, who led a Cuban force to a victory over South African units that entered Angola in early 1988, recently had been appointed head of Cuba's Western Army, its largest military unit. His 30-year army career included service as chief of the military mission in Ethiopia, where he commanded forces that defeated the Somali army. He later was chief of the Cuban military mission in Nicaragua as well. General Ochoa was awarded the rarely given title of the "Hero of the Cuban Revolution," and was a member of the Communist Party's Central Committee and of the National Assembly, the Cuban parliament.

The 57-year-old general and the other officials were accused of helping Colombia's Medellín cartel to smuggle cocaine to the United States by allowing the Colombians to use Cuban ports and airstrips. While Ochoa was charged with contacting the cartel, other officers were accused of facilitating the movement of six tons of cocaine, making a $3.4 million

AP/Wide World

In January 1989, Cuba marked the 30th anniversary of the Fidel Castro revolution with the president, above, *declaring "socialism or death" for Cuba. Three months later, Soviet President Gorbachev visited the island nation,* below.

© Dirck Halstead/Gamma-Liaison

profit. At the trial, Ochoa, calling his actions foolish and naive, admitted having approached the Colombians to earn dollars for the Cuban tourist industry.

Even before General Ochoa faced the firing squad, Gen. José Abrantes Fernández, for 20 years chief of Castro's personal security force and more recently the minister of the interior, was arrested with six of his closest aides, including two additional generals. They were accused of "negligence," "abuse of authority and improper use of government money and resources." Abrantes, also a member of the Communist Party's Central Committee, was sentenced to 20 years in jail. Among other officials arrested and sentenced to long jail terms were the former transportation minister, Gen. Diocles Torralba González, and Luís Leonardo Domínguez, former head of Cuba's Civil Aviation Institute, who at one time was a protégé of Fidel Castro. All senior officials of the Interior Ministry were either arrested or dismissed. Thousands of lower level officials reportedly were replaced.

The Cuban government treated the Ochoa and Abrantes cases as a matter of grave national concern. "The entire nation realizes that the problems the country faced this summer go far beyond the fate of a handful of corrupt and disloyal individuals," said a page-long editorial in *Granma,* the Communist Party's newspaper. There was speculation on what Fidel Castro—who is involved in virtually every activity in Cuba—knew about drug trafficking by his most trusted collaborators. Many of those arrested were the same officials who directed the Interior Ministry's secret MC Department which Castro created in the early 1980s to circumvent the U.S. economic blockade by obtaining foreign currency through every method possible and whose activities he personally has supervised.

One day after General Ochoa's arrest, Gen. Raul Castro, defense minister and brother of the Cuban president, had broadcast a rambling speech to the armed forces. Stating that the military was facing a "critical situation," he said that those who disagreed with government policies could leave for Hungary or Poland. During the speech, Defense Minister Castro even offered to call his "friend," Gen. Wojciech Jaruzelski, the Polish leader, to get visas for the dissidents.

According to analysts, the most plausible explanation for the purge was that President Castro—who has denied repeated U.S. charges of his government's involvement in the drug trade—tied Ochoa to drug trafficking because the general represented a potential threat to his own authority. General Ochoa was regarded as a hero by thousands of Cuban "Africa Corps" veterans. Ochoa, a graduate of the Soviet Frunze military academy, was supportive of Soviet leader Mikhail Gorbachev's reforms and wanted Cuba to follow the example of Poland and Hungary. But the changes in the Soviet bloc continued to be regarded as a heresy to Marxism by Fidel Castro.

In April, President Gorbachev visited Cuba and was given a lukewarm reception. Addressing the National Assembly, Gorbachev told the Cubans that "those who march along with time and draw the necessary conclusions from change can count on success." The advice fell on deaf ears. In August, Cuba banned the circulation of two Soviet magazines, the weekly *Moscow News* and the monthly *Sputnik,* accusing them of promoting bourgeois democracy and the American way of life and of misinforming Cuban youth. It was the first such action in nearly three decades of close relations between the two countries. Havana also condemned two Hungarian journalists for pointing out human-rights violations in Cuba. Several weeks later, the leading Cuban human-rights advocates were arrested on counterrevolutionary charges.

Economy. According to Havana, the 1989 output of sugar, the country's main export, was 8,124,000 million tons, 800,000 tons higher than in 1988. But relatively low world-market sugar prices reduced the Cuban foreign currency reserve, as did reduced reexports of Soviet oil. In 1988, Cuba had a $2.25 billion trade imbalance and expected to post a similar deficit for 1989, forcing Cuba to delay payments to foreign creditors.

Troop Withdrawals. With hostilities abating in Angola, a Cuban troop withdrawal proceeded on schedule under the December 1988 peace accord. After spending 12 years in Ethiopia to help that country's Marxist government fight Somalia, the last Cuban troops returned home in September. At the height of the war in 1978, more than 20,000 Cuban soldiers fought there.

International Relations. In October, Cuba was elected to the United Nations' Security Council for a two-year term, and six major Latin American countries called for Havana's return to the Organization of American States, from which it was expelled in the early 1960s.

GEORGE VOLSKY, *University of Miami*

CUBA • Information Highlights

Official Name: Republic of Cuba.
Location: Caribbean.
Area: 42,803 sq mi (110 860 km²).
Population (mid-1989 est.): 10,500,000.
Chief Cities (Dec. 31, 1986 est.): Havana, the capital, 2,036,799; Santiago de Cuba, 364,544; Camagüey, 265,588; Holguín, 199,861.
Government: *Head of state and government,* Fidel Castro Ruz, president (took office under a new constitution, Dec. 1976). *Legislature* (unicameral)—National Assembly of People's Power.
Monetary Unit: Peso (0.771 peso equals U.S.$1, June 1989).
Foreign Trade (1988 U.S.$): *Imports,* $7,579,000,000; *exports,* $5,518,000,000.

CYPRUS

In 1989, Cyprus remained an island-nation divided into two geographical parts as it had been since 1974 when Turkey invaded the north, taking over about 37% of the island's territory. In 1983 the Turkish-occupied lands, from which about 200,000 Greek Cypriots had fled, were proclaimed unilaterally as the "Turkish Republic of the North." Besides the Turkish Cypriot natives and numerous Turkish emigrants from the mainland, there were thousands of Turkish troops stationed there.

The rest of the island was in the hands of the majority Greek Cypriots who controlled the internationally recognized government of the Republic of Cyprus under the presidency of George Vassiliou. That government refused to recognize the "Turkish Republic of the North" or Turkish-Cypriot leader Rauf Denktas' presidential title. Great Britain, from which Cyprus had become independent in 1960, retained sovereign rights over several military bases; and the United Nations kept a peacekeeping force on the island to reduce possible intercommunal clashes.

The Cyprus Question. The basic problem remained now to reconcile the majority Greek Cypriots with the minority Turkish Cypriots so that the island could be reunited in some fashion. Under the auspices of the UN, Vassiliou and Denktas in 1988 had resumed the intercommunal talks which had collapsed in 1985. A June 1, 1989, target date for the draft of an agreement, however, proved totally unrealistic. Vassiliou presented a plan early in 1989 for a federal, demilitarized republic. But Denktas wanted a structure that basically would retain the Turkish Cypriot state, something that was opposed strenuously by the Cypriot government.

Vassiliou traveled to numerous meetings with world leaders in 1989. He met with U.S. President George Bush on October 4, and praised the president's view that the current situation of Cyprus could not be considered permanent.

CYPRUS • Information Highlights

Official Name: Republic of Cyprus.
Location: Eastern Mediterranean.
Area: 3,571 sq mi (9 250 km²).
Population (mid-1989 est.): 700,000.
Chief Cities (1982 est.): Nicosia, the capital, 149,100; Limassol, 107,200.
Government: *Head of state and government,* George Vassiliou, president (took office Feb. 1988). *Legislature*—House of Representatives.
Monetary Unit: Pound (0.492 pound equals U.S.$1, July 1989).
Gross Domestic Product (1987 U.S.$): $3,700,-000,000.
Economic Index (1988): *Consumer Prices* (1980 = 100), all items, 148.4; food, 157.2.
Foreign Trade (1988 U.S.$): *Imports,* $1,859,000,000; *exports,* $731,000,000.

Cyprus and Lebanon. The Republic of Cyprus served as an important conduit for news from Lebanon. Many Lebanese refugees traveled through Cyprus and some were given temporary residency rights there. But the Vassiliou government avoided taking sides in the Lebanese conflict.

Protests Against Occupation. During 1989 there were several exceptionally vocal protests against the Turkish occupation in the north. In March thousands of Greek Cypriot women of the Women Walk Home Movement crossed the line forcibly onto Turkish-held territory at two places and stayed there for a few hours. In July at the 15th anniversary of the Turkish invasion a number of Greek Cypriot refugees from the north tried to push across the separation line to stage a walk home; and in November thousands of Greek Cypriots staged antioccupation demonstrations to coincide with the sixth anniversary of the proclamation of the "Turkish Republic of the North."

The Rare Mosaics. Four extremely rare 6th-century Christian mosaics stolen from the Panagia Kanakaria church in northern Cyprus after the Turkish invasion were put on sale by an Indianapolis, IN, art dealer who claimed a proper purchase. The Vassiliou government and the autocephalous Greek Orthodox Church of Cyprus argued in a U.S. court case that the priceless works had been removed illegally and were illegally on the market. A federal judge ruled in favor of the church and ordered the mosaics returned. Archbishop Chrysostomos, primate of the Greek Orthodox Church in Cyprus, praised the court's decision, saying it would have an impact not only in Cyprus but in the selling of looted treasures taken elsewhere.

GEORGE J. MARCOPOULOS, *Tufts University*

CZECHOSLOVAKIA

The democratization process that gained momentum in Hungary and Poland in 1989 further compounded the problems plaguing the hard-line Communist regime of Czechoslovakia. Encouraged by the successes attained by democratic forces in the two neighboring countries, a number of new Czech and Slovak citizens' groups emerged in 1989 to join earlier civic movements, such as the Charter 77, in criticizing the regime's abuses and demanding respect for human rights, freedom, and justice. For the first time since 1948, even members of two of Czechoslovakia's Communist-controlled "non-Communist" parties began to question their parties' subservience to the Communist Party and to demand more democracy.

The Gathering Democratic Force. The historic Wenceslas Square of Prague, where the Czech student Jan Palach set himself on fire in

© Chip Hires/Gamma-Liaison

Demonstrations against Czechoslovakia's Communist regime, including the above candlelight vigil in Prague's historic Wenceslas Square, became very common during 1989.

CZECHOSLOVAKIA • Information Highlights
Official Name: Czechoslovak Socialist Republic.
Location: East-central Europe.
Area: 49,371 sq mi (127 870 km^2).
Population (mid-1989 est.): 15,600,000.
Chief Cities (Jan. 1, 1987 est.): Prague, the capital, 1,200,266; Bratislava, 424,378; Brno, 385,965.
Government: *Head of state,* Václav Havel, interim president (elected Dec. 29, 1989). *Head of government,* Marian Calfa, premier (took office Dec. 10, 1989). *Communist party,* chairman, Ladislav Adamec (elected December 1989). *Legislature*—Federal Assembly.
Monetary Unit: Koruna (10.0 koruny equal U.S.$1, July 1989).
Economic Indexes (1988): *Consumer Prices* (1980 = 100), all items, 111.3; food, 114.0. *Industrial Production* (1986, 1980 = 100), 124.
Foreign Trade (1988 U.S.$): *Imports,* $24,251,-000,000; *exports,* $23,059,000,000.

January 1969 to protest the 1968 Soviet invasion that crushed the Czechoslovak reform movement, became in 1989 increasingly a favorite gathering place for citizens protesting the Prague regime's callous disregard of human rights. In January many thousands of people commemorated there the 20th anniversary of Palach's sacrifice by demanding freedom and democracy and calling for the resignation of hard-line Communist leader Miloš Jakeš. On May 1, traditionally a day of celebration and parades for the Communist world, democratic forces staged their own anti-Communist counter-parade to celebrate the European Labor Day. In August a massive anti-Communist demonstration was held on the 21st anniversary of the Soviet invasion. In October in defiance of the government's express prohibition, dissident groups organized their own celebration of the 71st anniversary of the 1918 founding of the Czechoslovak Republic. Demonstrations also began to spread to many other cities.

Nervous and fearful that things would get out of hand, the Prague regime responded with customary methods ranging from harassment, trials, and incarceration of the most outspoken dissidents to brutal police repression of peaceful demonstrations. But worldwide condemnation of such gross violations of Czechoslovakia's commitments under international human-rights agreements seemed at least to make the repressive measures somewhat less frequent and less consistent than in earlier years.

Sensing the regime's growing weakness and uncertainty and encouraged by the huge anti-Communist demonstrations that erupted in neighboring East Germany in the wake of the exodus of thousands of East Germans to West Germany, Czech dissident groups organized in November and early December a succession of massive demonstrations to force the government to comply with their demands. The final sequence of events that led to the collapse of the Communist dictatorship began on November 17 when a procession of Prague students, honoring students who had been executed by the Nazis 50 years previously, was attacked viciously by helmeted police as soon as the demonstrators started calling for democracy and human rights. Shocked and angered by such a wanton display of brutality, various dissident groups formed a Civic Forum as a united organ of all democratic forces to negotiate with the government for the elimination of the Communist monopoly of power and the creation of a new pluralistic, truly democratic system. Backed by demonstrations of hundreds of thousands of irate citizens, climaxing on November 27 with the general strike of the overwhelming majority of Czechoslovakia's labor forces, the democratic movement finally prevailed.

A Pluralistic Democracy. After more than four decades of Communist rule, and without a shot being fired, Czechoslovakia became once again a pluralistic, multiparty democracy. Following several days of tough bargaining, and some abortive Communist attempts to evade the inevitable by making only minor concessions, a new government of "national understanding" was sworn in on December 10. Ten of its members, including Premier Marian Calfa and the minister of defense, were Communist Party members, but two of the Communists were allied with, and backed by, the Civic Forum. Seven cabinet members, including the ministers of foreign affairs, finances, labor, and social welfare, were representatives of the Civic Forum and its Slovak counterpart, Public Against Violence. Two ministers were members of the Socialist Party and two were members of the People's Party, both of which already had abandoned their earlier status of subservience to the Communist Party. The delicate issue of who should control the police was resolved by placing law enforcement under the supervision of a committee of three cabinet members chaired by First Deputy Premier Jan Cărnogurský, a Catholic activist who had been released from jail only two weeks previously.

AP/Wide World

On December 10, Václav Havel announced the formation of Czechoslovakia's new government of "national understanding." The playwright later became interim president.

Upon swearing in the new government, the Communist president of the republic, Gustav Husák, resigned and the Federal Assembly elected the main spokesman of the Civic Forum, the well-known playwright Václav Havel, to be interim president of the republic to serve until free elections can be held in 1990. Alexander Dubček, the leader of the Prague reform movement in 1968, was elected chairman of the Federal Assembly. Yielding to the demands of the Civic Forum, the Federal Assembly also approved constitutional amendments that deleted articles providing for the leading role of the Communist Party and for Marxism-Leninism to be state ideology.

The leadership of the Communist Party also underwent a thorough reorganization. Of the 13 members of its top body, the Presidium of the Central Committee, only three had served in the previous Presidium and no one in the new group was considered to be a hard-liner. A little-known functionary, Karel Urbánek, considered to be a moderate, became the party's new general secretary, replacing Miloš Jakeš, who also was stripped of his party membership. A reformist group under the label of Democratic Forum of Communism was formed within the Communist Party and called for a prompt convening of an extraordinary party congress to democratize Czechoslovakia's communism. In yet another reorganization of the party leadership in late December, former Premier Ladislav Adamec, considered to be a moderate, was elected as the party's new chairman, and the former leader of the Communist youth organization and an outspoken critic of the party's past policies, Vasil Mohorita, became the new first secretary.

The Economy. The major task of the new government for years to come will be to improve the performance of the country's economy, which as borne out by the mid-1989 official statistical report, continued to be sluggish. According to the government's statistical report for the first half of 1989, per capita income rose by less than 2% over the first half of 1988, gross output of centrally planned industry by 1.1%, construction by 0.7%, labor productivity in industry by 1.4%, retail trade by 3.2%, foreign trade by 4.3%, industrial wages by 1.3%, and the monetary income of the population by 2.4%. But industrial production costs, the lowering of which was one of the government's primary concerns, were reduced only by 0.7%.

Construction firms failed to meet the planned targets by 31.5% and only 33.9% of the apartments scheduled to be built in 1989 were completed in the first half of the year. The share of new products in total industrial output remained a negligible 4.6% and the number of products of high technical level, which was one of the most important goals of the restructuring of Czechoslovakia's economy, actually decreased. Somewhat better results were attained in agricultural production, where the output of milk and eggs increased and a very good grain harvest of some 11 million tons was expected.

International Relations. After years of protracted on-again off-again negotiations, an agreement was reached in April between Czechoslovakia and the Vatican about the appointment of three bishops for ten vacant bishoprics. In July, Czechoslovakia signed an agreement with East Germany for the badly needed protection of the environment. In December the new premier and foreign minister traveled to Moscow to negotiate with the Soviet government about the withdrawal of Soviet troops stationed in Czechoslovakia following the Soviet invasion of August 1968.

EDWARD TABORSKY
University of Texas at Austin

Leningrad's famed Kirov Ballet, appearing in New York in 1989 after a 25-year absence as well as in other U.S. cities, performed a 19th-century tale, "Le Corsaire," with ballerina Tatyana Terekhova playing a maiden captured by pirates.

DANCE

A kaleidoscopic view of dance prevailed in 1989. Disparate companies and contrasting events came to the fore. Important changes in major American dance troupes were signaled by a large number of resignations, retirements, and deaths.

Milestones. A public that reached beyond the regular dance goer was saddened deeply by the death, at the age of 58, of Alvin Ailey, the founder and director of the popular Alvin Ailey American Dance Theater. Judith Jamison, who had been a star in the troupe, was named the new director.

Mikhail Baryshnikov announced in June that he would resign in a year as artistic director of American Ballet Theatre to pursue other career projects, including acting. (He had performed in a Broadway play, *Metamorphosis,* in the spring.) But in September, Baryshnikov suddenly left the company after a dispute with its new executive director over the removal of his assistant. His abrupt departure left Ballet Theatre without an artistic director during its 50th anniversary season. Jane Hermann, the executive director, was empowered by the company's board to direct Ballet Theatre in the interim.

Lincoln Kirstein, who cofounded the New York City Ballet and the School of American Ballet with the late George Balanchine, retired at 82 as the company's general director and the school's president. The choreographer Jerome Robbins (*see* BIOGRAPHY), declaring that at the age of 71 he wished to work on a variety of theater and dance projects, resigned as coartistic director of the City Ballet. Since 1983 he had shared the title of Ballet Master in Chief with Peter Martins. Robbins' and Kirstein's departure meant that Martins became the sole director of the City Ballet with increased authority. Suzanne Farrell, 44, and Patricia McBride, 46, the company's two senior ballerinas, also retired.

The Dance Season. Artistically, the dance season was unusually varied. Tap dancing made a big comeback through the revue *Black and Blue.* A brilliant French company specializing in 17th- and 18th-century dance made its U.S. debut. Soviet visitors ranged from the celebrated Kirov Ballet, paying its first visit to New York since 1964, to the unknown Donetsk Ballet, rescued by American benefactors after its original producers could not finance a scheduled tour. Premieres and revivals were plentiful although only a few stood out. Yet the excellent quality of American and foreign dancers was especially high.

The Kirov Ballet from Leningrad, which also performed in Washington, San Francisco, and Costa Mesa, CA, presented major productions: *Le Corsaire,* a 19th-century tale about pirates and their captives, succeeded largely as a colorful spectacle; *Giselle* had the purity that the company's uneven *Sleeping Beauty* did not; *Potemkin,* a new work about a well-known sailors' mutiny in 1905, was staged by the Kirov's director, Oleg Vinogradov, and finished with the performers running up an aisle. As a theater piece, *Potemkin* seemed dated in its experiments and disappointed those who expected the Kirov to be a purely classical company. The troupe, however, was more successful than expected in the first two Balanchine ballets in its repertory, *Scotch Symphony* and *Theme and Variations.* The 23-year-old Zhanna Ayupova was the Kirov's new ballerina. Other dancers who stood out were Tatyana Terekhova, Lyubov Kunakova, Altynai Assylmuratova, Faruk Ruzimatov, and Konstantin Zaklinsky.

Vadim Pisarev, an astounding virtuoso, was the star of the Donetsk Ballet from the Ukraine, which made headlines after it was stranded by its original producers in Baltimore. The Howard Gilman Foundation and ICM Productions took the troupe to New York, Washington, and Philadelphia. Although not a first-rank company, it presented an especially fine staging of *Giselle*.

Other Soviet troupes visiting the United States were the Moiseyev Dance Company, a group headed by the Bolshoi ballerina Natalya Bessmertnova, a troupe led by the Bolshoi stars Yekaterina Maksimova and Vladimir Vasiliev, and a touring group of senior students from the Bolshoi Ballet School.

Visiting companies from Western Europe included two outstanding troupes. Ris et Danceries, a French Baroque dance ensemble, appeared in Lully's 17th-century opera *Atys* at the Brooklyn Academy of Music and independently in *Caprice* at the Jacob's Pillow Dance Festival in Lee, MA, and the American Dance Festival in Durham, NC. The dancers were cited for their refinement and vibrancy.

Brilliant dancing studded the season of the London Festival Ballet, which returned to the United States for the first time since 1978. Now directed by Peter Schaufuss, the company revived Sir Frederick Ashton's 1955 version of Prokofiev's *Romeo and Juliet,* which was acclaimed as a masterpiece. *Napoli* and a mixed bill introduced superb young dancers like Trinidad Sevillano, Patrick Armand, Leanne Benjamin, Matz Skoog, Christine Camillo, and Maximiliano Guerra.

Among the many international dance troupes that performed in the United States during 1989 was the Moiseyev Dance Company, a Ukrainian group from the Soviet Union.

AP/Wide World

Ballet visitors from abroad also included the Basel Ballet and the Frankfurt Ballet, with William Forsythe's experimental *Impressing the Czar*. Poland sent its folk groups, Slansk and Mazowsz.

The New York City Ballet, dancing at a new peak, presented sophisticated premieres by Peter Martins: *Mozart Serenade, Beethoven Romance,* and *Echo*.

Eliot Feld clearly was inspired in his new works for the Feld Ballet: *Asia,* an inventive gloss on oriental styles; *Kore; Love Song Waltzes; Petipa Notwithstanding;* and *Shadow's Breath*.

American Ballet Theatre presented the premieres of Clark Tippet's *Some Assembly Required* and *Rigaudon,* both of which confirmed the choreographer's developing talent. Twyla Tharp scored a big hit by restaging *In the Upper Room* for the company but was less successful with new works, *Quartet, Everlast,* and *Bum's Rush*.

Baryshnikov's new staging of *Swan Lake* for Ballet Theatre was criticized for its stylistic and dramatic confusion. Odette, the Swan Queen, and the corps wore long Romantic tutus that concealed the choreography and Odile, Odette's evil counterpart, now was nameless and dressed in white, not black. Andris Liepa, a Bolshoi dancer on leave to appear with Ballet Theatre, excelled as Siegfried.

The Joffrey Ballet staged a superb version of Bronislava Nijinska's *Les Noces* from 1923. Gerald Arpino commented on vaudeville entertainingly in *The Pantages and the Palace Present "Two a Day."* Dance Theatre of Harlem succeeded with a rare Nijinska revival, the 1952 *Rondo Capriccioso*. Notable premieres in modern dance included *The Stab,* a powerful hallucinatory piece by Susana Tambutti from Argentina as part of a Latin American series at the American Dance Festival. Paul Taylor created *Speaking in Tongues* and *Minikin Fair*. Merce Cunningham presented the premieres of *Field and Figures, Five Stone Wind,* and *Cargo X*. Trisha Brown collaborated with Robert Rauschenberg in *Astral Convertible*.

Martha Graham did a new version of her *American Document* from 1938 and revived *Steps in the Street* from the 1936 *Chronicle*. In Boston, Mark Morris' company performed his idiosyncratic version of Purcell's *Dido and Aeneas*.

Susanne Linke's profound interpretation of solos of despair was a highlight of the Next Wave Festival at the Brooklyn Academy, which also featured Maguy Marin's satirical theater piece on the French Revolution, *Hey What's All This to Me!?*.

Edward Villella won the Capezio Award, and Alexandra Danilova was awarded the Kennedy Center Honors.

ANNA KISSELGOFF
"The New York Times"

DELAWARE

Public life in Delaware settled down to the search for solutions to difficult problems in 1989. Continuity was the theme at swearing-in ceremonies as most major political leaders retained their offices in 1988 elections. Political newcomers included Dennis Greenhouse, executive of New Castle County, and Lt. Gov. Dale Wolf. Both began new four-year terms.

Legislative Session. Shortly after the 1988 elections the Delaware General Assembly took steps to improve its own operations. An Institute for Delaware Legislators was held at the University of Delaware. Needs for more space and augmented research support were discussed. Following the institute a unique joint seminar with the Maryland General Assembly was held in Annapolis. These sessions fortified the resolve of Delaware's legislators to move ahead with plans to expand Legislative Hall in Dover by adding two new wings.

The legislature also became the focal point for heated debates. Major legislative proposals included a measure to allow banks and trust companies to sell insurance. Opposition from the state's insurance agents kept it from being passed in the 1989 session, however. Another heated legislative controversy centered on a proposal to establish a statewide paramedics program for Delaware. Currently emergency medical teams supplementing ambulance service only are available in New Castle County and the city of Dover. While receiving massive public support, this legislation floundered on the lack of agreement on the sharing of funding between state and local government.

Drug abuse also received much attention in Delaware. Substantial increases were provided in the funding for drug-abuse enforcement and treatment programs. One bill providing for the use of a "whipping post" for drug offenders received national publicity, but was not taken seriously by many legislators. Another bill to allow police to bring dogs into schools to sniff for drugs was passed by the legislature, but vetoed by Gov. Michael N. Castle. The legislature passed a 2% increase in the hotel-lodging tax. Additional revenue from this source would be used to pay the local share of costs for augmenting ocean beaches which had lost much of their sand in recent storms. It also would be used to assist local tourism promotion efforts.

Economy. Governor Castle led a group of business and governmental leaders on a trade mission to Canada. The mission focused particular attention on trade with Ontario and emphasized the possible expansion of Canadian banks in Delaware. Speaker of the House Terry Spence and Sen. Andrew Knox traveled to Poland, the Soviet Union, and Czechoslovakia. The members of the later trade mission discussed with their hosts new efforts to establish small businesses in Eastern Europe and solidified ties between the region and Delawareans for future business, cultural, and educational exchanges.

DELAWARE • Information Highlights

Area: 2,045 sq mi (5 295 km^2).
Population (July 1, 1988): 660,000.
Chief Cities (1980 census): Dover, the capital, 23,512; Wilmington, 70,195; Newark, 25,247; Elsmere, 6,493.
Government (1989): *Chief Officers*—governor, Michael N. Castle (R); lt. gov., Dale E. Wolf (R). *General Assembly*—Senate, 21 members; House of Representatives, 41 members.
State Finances (fiscal year 1988): *Revenue,* $2,090,000,000: *expenditure,* $2,025,000,000.
Personal Income (1988): $11,659,000,000; per capita, $17,699.
Labor Force (June 1989): *Civilian labor force,* 363,100; *unemployed,* 13,900 (3.8% of total force).
Education: *Enrollment* (fall 1987)—public elementary schools, 67,000; public secondary, 29,000; colleges and universities, 36,650. *Public school expenditures* (1987–88), $451,245,000 ($4,781 per pupil).

Delaware continued to be a regional and national leader in low unemployment and high growth in personal income. The state's average 1988 unemployment rate of 3.2% was the lowest in the region and the fifth lowest in the nation. The average rate for the first eight months of 1989 was 3.5%. In 1988, Delaware's per capita income rose 6.8% to $17,699. This was the ninth highest per capita income in the nation.

As the year came to an end, Delawareans seemed to be more aware than ever that continued economic growth and prosperity had real costs. An oil tanker spill in the Delaware River, flooding due to rapid runoff in highly populated areas, as well as repeated reports of low levels of air and water quality focused attention on the need for serious, long-term solutions for environmental problems. As the 1990s open, safeguarding the environment would be one of the state's highest priorities.

JEROME R. LEWIS
University of Delaware

DENMARK

In a country where short-lived and shifting government coalitions have been the rule since World War II, September 1989 marked a milestone for Denmark that many would have thought impossible—the seventh anniversary of a center-right government, under Prime Minister Poul Schlüter. His coalition cabinet, consisting of Conservatives, Liberals, and Radical Liberals, had proved surprisingly viable.

Politics and the Economy. Political strife, which is seemingly endemic among Denmark's various parties, started early in 1989 with the election for a new speaker of the Folketing (parliament). Svend Jakobsen, a Social Democrat, had served as speaker for many years but

© Blue C/Gamma-Liaison

During a June tour of Scandinavia, Pope John Paul II, head of the Roman Catholic Church, visited Denmark, braving Copenhagen's rainy weather with Queen Margrethe (left).

had announced his retirement. The Social Democrats, the majority party, nominated former Prime Minister Anker Jørgensen, but the Conservatives succeeded in getting Erik Ninn-Hansen, a former minister of justice and long-time member of parliament, elected speaker.

Parliament also had difficulty in agreeing on a defense budget, but a compromise finally was reached in March under which current military expenditures would remain virtually unchanged but would be adjusted for inflation during the next three years. There was more disagreement on tax reform. The Social Democrats felt that their differences with the Conservatives over a reformed tax structure were so deep that a parliamentary election would have to be held in January 1990 to settle matters.

The ruling parties and the Social Democrats also differed on how to improve the sluggish economy. Svend Auken, the leader of the Social Democrats, in late April submitted a comprehensive economic plan. The most significant economic problems were a high rate of unemployment and a large foreign debt. Exports, on the other hand, have been growing steadily and continued to increase in 1989, helping to reduce the deficit on the balance of payments. However, to continue cooperation with the other European Community nations, Denmark faced the possibility of readjusting wages and salaries, prices, and interest rates, down to the level prevailing in West Germany.

DENMARK • Information Highlights

Official Name: Kingdom of Denmark.
Location: Northwest Europe.
Area: 16,629 sq mi (43 070 km^2).
Population (mid-1989 est.): 5,100,000.
Chief Cities (Jan. 1, 1986 est.): Copenhagen, the capital, 1,351,999 (incl. suburbs); Århus, 195,152; Odense, 137,286.
Government: *Head of state,* Margrethe II, queen (acceded Jan. 1972). *Head of government,* Poul Schlüter, prime minister (took office Sept. 1982). *Legislature* (unicameral)—Folketing.
Monetary Unit: Krone (7.192 kroner equal U.S.$1, Oct. 24, 1989).
Gross Domestic Product (1987 U.S.$): $101,300,-000,000.
Economic Indexes (1988): *Consumer Prices* (1980 = 100), all items, 165.0; food, 158.0. *Industrial Production* (1980 = 100), 127.
Foreign Trade (1988 U.S.$): *Imports,* $26,514,-000,000; *exports,* $27,879,000,000.

Home Rule. The Faroe Islands, Denmark's archipelago in the North Sea, which enjoys extensive home rule, had an election on Nov. 8, 1988, for a new Assembly, in which the Social Democrats lost one seat and the Conservatives gained a seat. Negotiations to form a new cabinet lasted two months and resulted in Jógvan Sundstein, the chairman of the Faroe Islands' Conservative Party, becoming head of the local government. Greenland on January 17 marked the tenth anniversary of its own home rule.

Papal Visit. Pope John Paul II, in a stop on his extensive world travels, visited Denmark in early June, calling on Queen Margrethe at her castle of Fredensborg in Zealand.

Bridging the Great Belt. After a century of discussion, a new bridge across the Great Belt, the waterway between the islands of Fyen and Zealand, passed the planning stage. At 11.2 mi (18 km), the bridge will be one of the longest in the world. Installation of railroad tracks is slated for 1993, while a highway is scheduled for 1996. The intention to use exclusively Danish materials and workers during construction raised strong protests from various European engineering and construction firms, who contended excluding them violates rules for membership in the European Community.

ERIK J. FRIIS
The Scandinavian-American Bulletin

© Nigel Dickson

Across the United States, citizens have come together to combat drug use and drug dealers in their neighborhoods. Above, a group in Detroit boards up a former crack house.

DRUGS AND ALCOHOL

The United States' "war" against illegal drugs intensified during 1989. But the government's fight against the importation, sale, and use of cocaine, heroin, and marijuana claimed few victories. The federal government stepped up its antidrug trafficking efforts at home and in South America and national polls indicated that overall drug use had declined. However, billion-dollar drug cartels based in Latin America continued to flood the country with illegal drugs. Drug-related violence soared and deaths and illnesses attributable to drug abuse rose at alarming rates.

President George Bush called drugs "the gravest domestic threat facing our nation today" in a nationally televised speech in September. Crack, the smokable form of cocaine, the president said, was "turning our cities into battle zones and murdering our children." In that speech the president called for an expanded federal antidrug strategy that concentrated on stepping up law-enforcement activity against drug traffickers. The program, which would cost some $7.9 billion in fiscal year 1990, was based on recommendations made by William J. Bennett, whom President Bush had named as the nation's first drug-policy director in February.

The American public—according to at least three national polls conducted during the year—ranked drug abuse as the nation's top problem. "There is a real sense of a clear and present danger," said Geoffrey Garin of Garin-Hart Strategic Research Group, a polling firm. "And the concern goes from border to border, and coast to coast. . . ."

The Spread of Drugs. The devastating effects of drug abuse were most visible in many of the nation's poor urban neighborhoods, which experienced rapidly growing rates of drug-related crimes as well as increasing numbers of drug addicts, including an alarming number of young pregnant mothers and teenage girls. The main culprit was the relatively inexpensive crack, which over the past few years has replaced heroin as the most abused drug among poor and working-class families. In New York City health officials estimated that the number of cocaine addicts tripled—from 182,000 to some 600,000—from 1986 to 1989. The number of murders in the city rose by 10.4% from 1987 to 1988, with drugs contributing to about 40% of homicides, according to police estimates.

The story was similar in Washington, DC, where drug-related violence was "out of control," according to William Bennett. Police made some 46,000 drug-related arrests in a 30-month period ending in March in the nation's capital, where the annual number of homicides rose nearly 150% from 1985 to 1989. In Hartford, CT, police arrested 576 persons on drug charges in 1986; in 1988 drug arrests topped 1,500.

In Oakland, CA, doctors estimated that about half of the patients crowding inner-city hospital emergency rooms were drug users. In the city's psychiatric emergency rooms as many as 90% of those admitted were suffering mentally from the effects of crack usage. "This place was turned into a zoo by crack and everything that goes with it," said Dr. Robert Daily, former chief of Oakland's General Hospital.

The social problems of drugs were not confined to the nation's inner cities. Unprecedented amounts of crack and other drugs were being distributed in small cities, towns, suburbs, and even rural areas across the country. Crack could be obtained easily virtually anywhere in the country.

The International Scene. There were some tactical victories in the war against drugs in 1989. Law-enforcement agencies confiscated unprecedented amounts of illegal drugs and arrested several international drug kingpins. In February, for example, FBI agents and New York City police arrested 19 people, confiscated $3 million, and seized more than 800 lbs (363 kg) of heroin worth about $1 billion in a raid in Queens, NY, following an 18-month investigation of a major Southeast Asian heroin network. In a six-day period in October, federal agents and local police confiscated a total of more than 58,000 lbs (26 308 kg) of cocaine in a suburban Los Angeles warehouse and in Harlingen, TX, near the Mexican border. Among the major suspected drug figures arrested in 1989 were Miguel Angel Felix Gallardo of Mexico City, the alleged head of an international cocaine smuggling ring, and José Abello Silva, a Colombian suspected of being a major transporter of cocaine for the infamous Medellín cartel, which was responsible for a wave of drug-related violence in Colombia in 1989.

Meanwhile, supplies of illegal drugs appeared to be abundant and growing. The U.S. marijuana crop increased by nearly 40% in 1988, according to government statistics. Internationally, as listed in the State Department's annual report on drug production, there was a 7.2% increase in the annual production of cocaine in South America; a 22% increase in the worldwide marijuana crop; a 15% increase in the global opium crop; and an 11% increase in worldwide production of hashish. Those statistics, said Secretary of State James A. Baker, showed that the war against drug production "is clearly not being won," and may be "slipping backwards."

International consumption of drugs also increased, primarily in Latin America, parts of the Middle East, and in Western Europe. For example, in the last decade growing numbers of Egyptians became regular users of cocaine, hashish, opium, and heroin. Egyptian officials reported that some 2 million persons were regular drug users, including some 30,000 heroin addicts. Demand for cocaine was rising throughout Western Europe, a situation that caused widespread concern. "Europe is where the United States was eight or ten years ago in terms of cocaine," said Miguel Solans Soteras, the head of Spain's National Drug Program. "It's still the drug of yuppies, of successful artists, and sportsmen. The worst lies ahead."

Possible Decline In Use. Positive news in the U.S. war on drugs involved drug consumption. National surveys released in 1989 indicated that, in general, drug use among Americans declined in 1988. The annual survey of high-school seniors done for the federal government by the University of Michigan's Institute for Social Research found that 7.9% of the seniors interviewed reported using cocaine at least once during the preceding 12 months. That compared with 10.1% the previous year and 13.1% in 1985. As for marijuana, 33.1% of the seniors reported using the drug once during the previous 12 months—a marked decline from 1979's 50.8% figure.

Other surveys, however, indicated a continued strong demand for cocaine, especially among the poor, who typically used crack. A survey released in August by the Department of Health and Human Services, for example, reported that while the number of Americans using all illegal drugs declined 37% from 1985 to 1988, the number of those who used cocaine rose by one third. A substantial number of cocaine users, the survey said, were young and unemployed.

"It's a two-tier system," said David Musto of Yale University Medical School, one of the nation's top drug experts. "You have a fundamental change of attitudes among the middle class and a growing bewilderment that anybody still uses drugs. But then you have the world of the inner city where there isn't the education, the jobs, or the other kinds of things that give people a reason to stop using drugs."

There were signs, however, that residents of some urban neighborhoods with a high drug trade were fed up with the situation and were, in many cases, fighting back. Neighborhood groups in Detroit, Chicago, Los Angeles, and other major cities held vigils in front of "crack houses," successfully brought suit against landlords of empty buildings where crack was sold, cleaned up neighborhoods, formed liaisons with police departments, and engaged in a host of other tactics in their local battles against drugs. Generally, police chiefs welcomed the help, but worried about those who cross the line from community activism to vigilantism.

Alcohol. The American war against drugs did not include a drug that is linked to a variety of serious—and in some cases deadly—health and social problems: alcohol. Despite the fact that per capita consumption of alcohol decreased, health officials reported that more Americans than ever were entering alcohol treatment programs. There was also concern about widespread alcohol abuse among high-school and college students and about the dangers of drunken driving. In 1988 nearly 24,000 people were killed and some 560,000 were injured in alcohol-related accidents.

The good news about alcohol use was that the "New Temperance" trend that began in the early 1980s has continued. According to *Impact,* an alcohol-industry publication, alcohol consumption declined steadily since 1980. Beer consumption was down 7% from 1980 to 1987; wine use decreased 14%, and consumption of distilled spirits dropped 23%.

One very visible sign of the new temperance was a new federal government regulation ordering all containers of beer, wine, or distilled spirits to carry a warning label. The regulation, mandated in 1988, went into effect in November 1989. The labels said drinking alcohol "may cause health problems," and warned of the dangers of drinking during pregnancy and while operating machinery or driving a car.

MARC LEEPSON, *Free-lance Writer*

ECUADOR

In 1989, Ecuador completed its tenth troubled year of democratic rule. President Rodrigo Borja began his term auspiciously in August 1988 with the support of a rare working majority in the unicameral congress, based around his own *Izquierda Democrática* (Democratic Left) (ID) party and two smaller left-of-center parties. Mindful of his country's long history of instability, Borja also was careful to reassure the military and business leaders of his moderation. And in March 1989, the government made progress toward resolving the threat of insurgency when it reached an accord with the guerrilla movement *Alfaro Vive Carajo!* (AVC) in which the AVC agreed to lay down arms and eschew violence, while the government committed itself to a "national dialogue" and recognized the AVC's right to participate in democratic politics. However, a smaller guerrilla group, the *Montonera Patria Libre,* occupied a military museum, abducted a judge, and refused to give up its armed struggle with the government.

The Economy. Working against Borja were Ecuador's severe economic problems—an $11 billion foreign debt, 57% inflation, negative net foreign exchange reserves, and weak economic growth. To combat these problems, he adopted an economic stabilization program that included greatly reduced government subsidies, temporary import restrictions, new sales taxes, and slower growth of the money supply. Some of these measures, such as subsidy reductions that doubled the price of gasoline, worsened the already desperate situation of the country's poorer citizens. The simultaneous decree of a token 15.8% minimum wage increase did not stop the country's small but militant labor unions from protesting the economic austerity measures in a series of strikes culminating in two general strikes called by the United Federation of Workers (FUT) in June and July. The president restored order by declaring a state of siege and using force to prevent paralysis of the transportation network and the hoarding or illegal export of foodstuffs.

Despite this harsh treatment of labor organizations by a social democratic administration, business leaders remained dissatisfied. Early in the year a group of 20 powerful business groups presented President Borja with a list of changes they sought in the government's economic policies, including further devaluation of the sucre to maintain parity in the face of inflation and a lowering of tariffs to stimulate the export sector. The international business community was even less satisfied, as Ecuador had fallen $2 billion behind in its interest payments on the foreign debt since 1987, a shortfall that earned Ecuador the reputation as one of Latin America's least reliable debtors. This situation led Citibank to seize $80 million of Ecuador's assets in May. The conflict was resolved in August, when Ecuador agreed to resume interest payments in exchange for new lending.

The business community's pessimism toward the economy appeared to be justified. While oil exports, the source of half of the country's foreign exchange, held steady, Ecuador's second largest export, shrimp, fell to about one quarter of its 1988 volume, and the collapse of the International Coffee Agreement in September cost Ecuador an estimated $100 million. Overall, the final economic performance was expected to be worse in 1989 than the previous year: Gross domestic product would grow less than 2%, if at all; inflation would be higher, perhaps approaching 100%; and net foreign-exchange reserves still would be negative.

Government Support. Some members of the governing coalition were anxious to disassociate themselves from a government pursuing unpopular policies with no results. The small Broad Leftist Front (FADI) withdrew its support from the government by early February to protest the government's "anti-popular" economic policies. In July the ID's main coalition partner, the Christian democratic *Democracía Popular* (DP), ended its participation in the cabinet when its only minister resigned. DP leader Osvaldo Hurtado pledged to continue his party's support for the government's legislative program, but his ability to deliver on that promise was in doubt. Without DP support, the Borja government would lose its congressional majority and very likely face a hostile opposition with the power to block the government's initiatives and legislate over the president's head. Borja's predecessors dealt with such stalemates by refusing to recognize acts of Congress that they found inconvenient. As 1989 drew to a close, Ecuador appeared to be heading quickly down the same path to constitutional crisis.

MICHAEL COPPEDGE
Johns Hopkins University

ECUADOR • Information Highlights

Official Name: Republic of Ecuador.
Location: Northwest South America.
Area: 109,483 sq mi (283 560 km²).
Population (mid-1989 est.): 10,500,000.
Chief Cities (mid-1986 est.): Quito, the capital, 1,093,278; Guayaquil, 1,509,108; Cuenca, 193,012.
Government: *Head of state and government,* Rodrigo Borja Cevallos, president (took office August 1988). *Legislature* (unicameral)—Chamber of Representatives.
Monetary Unit: Sucre (583.5 sucres equal U.S.$1, financial rate, Oct. 16, 1989).
Gross Domestic Product (1988 est. U.S.$): $9,400,-000,000.
Economic Index (1988): *Consumer Prices* (1980 = 100), all items, 730.8; food, 972.5.
Foreign Trade (1988 U.S.$): *Imports,* $1,714,000,000; *exports,* $2,165,000,000.

EDUCATION

Concerns of policymakers and a surge of changes by educators converged in 1989 to create a new stage in the recent reforms of precollegiate public education.

Reform Activity. Throughout the decade of the 1980s, and especially since a federal commission's 1983 report, *A Nation at Risk,* states had been increasing their concern about and control over school improvement. Most states turned to competency testing as a leverage in the early 1980s; most then mandated higher graduation standards and/or longer time in school. Policies began to focus on both improving the quality of teachers and on meeting the specific needs of students considered most at risk of not completing high school or acquiring the necessary skills for the workplace. By the year 2000, it was predicted, one third of total school enrollment could be at risk of school failure.

During this period of escalating state activity, the federal government remained relatively dormant. Taking its place as the bellwether for school reform was the nation's business community which, by 1989, had come to general agreement on the mismatch between the education young people were receiving and the economy's needs. Needing to increase constantly the technical skills of workers but faced with a future labor pool of ill-prepared workers, business leaders called for radical changes. A select group attending a seminar on education sponsored by the Center on Education and the Economy at Teachers College of Columbia University in September 1989 rejected incremental changes; some said a "revolution" was in order.

One change advocated by the business community would give teachers and administrators greater autonomy over their schools. As in the contemporary workplace, decentralized decision making was seen as a way to increase classroom performance. During 1989 this form of "restructuring" became better understood and more widespread. At least 27 states reported major efforts under way to provide greater authority at the school site, many of them initiated at the state level. The Re:Learn Project, for example, got under way in 1989 in six states, providing a better meshing of state regulations with the efforts of schools participating in the reform concepts of the Coalition of Essential Schools. These changes involved different uses of time and school schedules, reduction in pupil/teacher ratios, and more teacher control over the curriculum.

However, some school districts forged ahead with innovative restructuring plans of their own. Miami/Dade County, FL, for example, added onto its successful school-site management activities with an open invitation to groups, inside or outside the school system, to compete for grants to run schools of their own. An $800 million bond issue approved in Dade County for schools assured a rapid increase in the number of schools, and Superintendent Joseph Fernandez and the school board said they would welcome innovative ideas for "Saturn" schools—those to be run under grants. Fernandez, named chancellor of the New York City schools in fall 1989, predicted his ideas would be portable to the nation's largest school system.

Superintendent Tom Payzant of San Diego, CA, announced a similar school-site management plan, emphasizing that a goal of restructuring would be to eliminate "failure" in that city's schools. Other large school systems announcing restructuring plans during 1989 were Boston, Memphis, and the District of Columbia; Chicago spent the year preparing for the election of boards at each school in October, a radical restructuring of the governance structure for the school system, the country's third-largest. The boards would have authority to hire and fire principals, as well as make decisions regarding staff, budgets, and schedules.

Both the National Education Association, under a new president, Keith Geiger, and the American Federation of Teachers (AFT), headed by Albert Shanker, continued their push for greater local school autonomy. Shanker further urged, at an AFT meeting in July, that groups of teachers willing to form schools-within-schools or restructure whole schools—and who could produce much higher student achievements within a few years—be given large cash incentives for taking risks with change.

Another focus of the business community, greater investment in early childhood care and education, became a centerpiece of policy statements by influential state groups. Congress continued to try to work out church-state issues over a substantive increase in federal child-care programs, but the philosophy behind early childhood education was set by the states. The Council of Chief State School Officers and the National Association of State Boards of Education both issued statements on early childhood education that adopted the "developmental" approach. This emphasizes programs geared to the natural development of young children, rather than those focusing on premature school readiness. Developmental programs should continue into the early grades of school, they said. The groups also proposed much better training for early childhood educators, greater efforts for parent participation, and culturally sensitive services to families of young children. Adopted late in 1988, the philosophies in these statements began to be reflected in state policies in 1989.

While Congress fashioned amendments to the Carl Perkins Vocational Education Act, the business community began to define better what it meant by different skills in the workplace. Basic skills are essential; however, the new concern is for critical thinking and problem-solving skills, group decision making, and an ability to take responsibility for production as a whole. The Academy for Educational Development released a report assessing high school vocational academies across the country, finding them a highly successful way of giving the business community an important, contributing role in school change while providing students with marketable skills. The academies are schools-within-schools that provide sequential vocational training tied to the local job market. This idea of teaching needed skills within the context of specific job opportunities also was reflected in the federal vocational program amendments that encourage better transitions between the last two years of high school and a two-year postsecondary program.

Such attention to the noncollege-bound was encouraged by the final report of the William T. Grant Foundation Commission on Work, Family and Citizenship. It recommended much better transitions to the workplace for the approximately 20 million 16- to 24-year-olds, whose financial footing has eroded considerably from that of young people in the early 1970s. The incomes of families in this age group declined by 27% between 1973 and 1986, the report said.

Business' concern about those entering the job market is based on reality, the report noted, because of the decline in youth ages 15 to 24 from 43 million to 34 million between 1980 and 1996.

Minority Enrollment. The U.S. Office of Education released in 1989 both bad and good news about minority enrollments. Using comparable state data for the first time, it found that the rate of dropout from high school among blacks was declining sharply—from 27.4% in 1968 to 14.9% in 1988. White students reduced their dropout rate by about 2%—to 12.7%. However, the rate for Hispanics increased slightly during those years; it was 35.8% in 1988. One third of Hispanics who dropped out of school had completed less than six years of schooling, according to the report. Yet the Grant Commission pointed out that Hispanic youth are the fastest-growing group of young people in the country—by 1996 they will represent 13% of the total.

Curricula. As with vocational education, 1989 was a time for evaluating and acting upon reform of the school curriculum in general. History texts had been criticized soundly for several years, and continued to be in 1989, but curriculum reform entered new arenas, with greater attention to mathematics education (*see* special report, page 210).

The American Association for the Advancement of Science called for new goals for science education, rather than specific changes, goals that would develop in all students an "openness, curiosity, and healthy skepticism." It recommended two basic and major changes from traditional science instruction—an emphasis on connections rather than boundaries between traditional subject-matter categories (such as biology and chemistry) and an emphasis on ideas and thinking rather than specialized vocabulary or memorization.

The recommendations on math and science were timely. In 1989 the National Assessment of Educational Progress released a report comparing the performance of U.S. 13-year-olds with those in four other countries (South Korea, Spain, Great Britain, and Ireland) and four Canadian provinces. The United States was last in overall math achievement, and, though most U.S. 13-year-olds knew everyday science facts, only 42% could use scientific procedures and analyze data.

Such reports and the concern that educational reform was moving too slowly led to a growing consensus in 1989 about national standards for public education. In fact, the idea, barely mentioned in the reform movement before because of its threat to local control of education, erupted quickly into an action that will dominate public education for years to come. First, the annual Gallup Poll on the public's attitudes toward national standards found an overwhelming endorsement of such standards, though not if drawn up at the federal level. A few days after the release of the poll, the Commission on Workforce Quality and Labor Market Efficiency, a blue-ribbon panel appointed by the U.S. Department of Labor, called for presidential leadership in the development of specific national education goals and

U.S. Public and Private Schools

	1989–90	1988–89
Enrollment		
Kindergarten through Grade 8	32,915,000	32,425,000
High school	12,680,000	13,012,000
Higher education	13,087,000	12,849,000
Total	58,682,000	58,286,000
Number of Teachers		
Elementary and secondary	2,692,000	2,649,000
Higher	755,000	741,000
Total	3,447,000	3,390,000
Graduates		
Public and private high school	2,603,000	2,781,000
Bachelor's degrees	1,006,000	994,000
First professional degrees	72,000	72,000
Master's degrees	301,000	293,000
Doctor's degrees	34,000	34,000
Expenditures		
Public elementary-secondary school	$195,500,000,000	$183,400,000,000
Private elementary-secondary	16,700,000,000	15,700,000,000
Public higher	91,900,000,000	85,500,000,000
Private higher	49,000,000,000	45,800,000,000
Total	$353,100,000,000	$330,400,000,000

$3461\overline{)7958273}$ $\sqrt{105625}$ 65% of 250

A New Focus on Mathematics

$3x-2=x+3+x$ $\frac{a^2+4a-21}{5a^2+35a}$

Several reports issued in the late 1980s focused attention on the teaching of mathematics in the United States and indicated a need for reform in the math curriculum and in the methods of teaching the subject.

The results of the Second International Mathematics Study, conducted in 1981–82 and released in 1987, showed that the math performance of American students ranked quite low in both the eighth and 12th grades when compared with the achievements of their European and Asian peers. Another study, *The Mathematics Report Card,* the results of the 1986 National Assessment of Educational Progress, reinforced those findings, showing that the math skills of eighth graders in the United States were at about the level expected of fifth graders. Eleventh graders barely were at the level expected of eighth graders.

Analyses of the content of the math curriculum find that U.S. teachers spend a great deal of time in repetitive practice of basic computational skills to the exclusion of work with geometry, measurement, and basic data analysis. Accordingly, achievements studies show that U.S. students are competitive in computation but fall behind in the applications of other concepts and general problem solving. Studies of student attitudes about mathematics indicate that Americans view mathematics as a genetic-based ability, *not* one which can be altered by diligent study. Most other societies view mathematics as a discipline requiring hard work.

In 1989 the National Council of Teachers of Mathematics released its recommendations for improving school mathematics. The report, *Curriculum and Evaluation Standards for School Mathematics,* envisions the goals of school mathematics to be: learning to value mathematics, becoming more confident in one's own math abilities, becoming a mathematical problem solver, learning to communicate mathematically, and learning to reason mathematically. The program of study outlined to accomplish these goals is conceptually based and envisions students learning mathematics not by rote but by being involved actively in its study. The necessary changes in the teaching of mathematics would involve more student work in small groups on projects that would span a period of days. There also would be more observing, speaking, and writing assignments so that students would gain skills in the communication of mathematics. The biggest change would be to learn mathematics by "doing," rather than by being "told."

Several individuals took exception with the recommendations of the council's report. The major points of debate concerned the amount of practice and drill required to gain proficiency in math, the amount of proficiency in addition, subtraction, multiplication, and division needed for later progress in the study of algebra and other areas of higher mathematics, and the proper role of the hand-held calculator in the mathematics classroom. The sides of the debate separate along the lines of rote versus meaningful learning of mathematics. The former group views mathematics as a subject with a fixed set of rules to be mastered; the latter sees mathematics as a rapidly changing subject. The latter opinion also is bolstered by the growing role calculators and computers are playing in expanding the knowledge about and applications of mathematics.

As school programs move to respond to the calls for change, several topics, including collecting and analyzing data, looking for relationships in data with patterns, studying three-dimensional settings in geometry, estimation skills, and problem-solving strategies, are being emphasized. Topics being deemphasized include excessive practice with paper-and-pencil computation, e.g., long division and fractions, graphing functions by plotting points, and factoring in algebra.

Reforming the manner in which mathematics achievement is assessed also is under way. New approaches employ more open-ended exercises, rather than multiple-choice or short-answer items. The use of the hand-held calculator in testing situations is being encouraged. As assessment becomes more integrated with teaching, methods of evaluating a student's thinking and problem-solving strategies will take on a greater role in the evaluation of mathematical abilities than previously.

JOHN A. DOSSEY

timetables. And less than two weeks later the National Governors' Association annual report on education said it was time to set national education goals.

Thus the way was paved for President Bush's education summit meeting with governors at Charlottesville, VA, in late September to agree on the areas for the development of national goals. These include early childhood education; student performance, especially in math and science; the dropout rate and performance especially of at-risk students; adult literacy; training for a competitive workforce; the supply of qualified teachers and up-to-date technology; and safe, disciplined, drug-free schools. The federal government pledged to work on deregulation of its education programs in exchange for higher expectations and student performance among the states. Little reference was made to additional funding, except for a possible increase in Head Start funds.

Meanwhile, major steps also were taken in the area of teacher standards and administrator preparation that also would influence education for a long time to come. The National Board for Professional Teaching Standards released its initial standards that will be used to certify teachers in 29 teaching fields. The voluntary program expected to issue its first certificates in 1993. At the first National Forum sponsored by the board, created in 1986 following a recommendation of the Carnegie Corporation's Forum on Education and the Economy, the board indicated that its work also would influence teacher training and school restructuring.

A corollary National Policy Board for Educational Administration, backed by ten national professional education associations, called for major reforms in the preparation of school administrators. It recommended raising entrance standards, recruitment of minorities and women for preparation programs, a national certification exam for administrators, and in-resident graduate training. Its agenda ran into strong criticism at a meeting of deans, administrators, and others concerned with administrator training, but it signaled renewed attention to the development of leadership for public schools.

Future Trends. Other major trends that became evident for the last decade of the century:

• Growing attention to adolescents' unique needs. The Carnegie Council on Adolescent Development released an 18-month study on middle schools that called for smaller units in schools for adolescents, interdisciplinary teaching, higher expectations, more emphasis on experiential and service learning, and closer links with health and social services. Grants were awarded by the Edna McConnell Clark Foundation to stimulate innovative ideas on educating this age group.

• Concern about the exploitation of young people for commercial purposes. A proposal by Whittle Communications to provide equipment and 12 minutes daily of new television programming, accompanied by advertisements, was tried out in six schools in 1989 and slated for nationwide implementation in 1990. This and similar moves were criticized by some education groups and state agencies but supported by others.

• Collaboration of education and social services. With the implementation of the Family Support Act in 1990, public schools will be drawn into much more collaboration with welfare and training agencies seeking to move welfare recipients into independence.

• Growth in the interest in youth service. At least eight bills were introduced in Congress supporting an expansion of youth services from several points. The National Governor's Association also established policies on youth services.

• Growing attention to the need for more and rehabilitated school facilities. A national survey found that one fourth of school buildings in use are unfit and that continued cuts in maintenance budgets would worsen the situation. The estimate for new or renovated facilities was $84 billion, with an additional $41 billion for maintenance and repairs.

• Expansion of state-sponsored school choice plans. Thirteen states were allowing some kind of choice initiative at the local level in 1989, and ten were interdistrict choice plans. The Bush administration considers choice a cornerstone of its education policy.

Higher Education. At the higher education level two issues continued to dominate policy-making and discussion. One was the assessment of the quality of undergraduate learning. The National Governors' Association reported that 28 states now had policies on the assessment of student outcomes. On the issue of minority enrollment, 21 states were developing strategies to increase their participation and completion rates in higher education.

Adult Literacy. Another education issue, new to national agendas, is that of adult literacy. Considered a "stepchild" of the education system, with low funding, part-time teachers, and poor results, adult education has not received much attention. However, with 70% of the workforce of the year 2000 already in the job pool, the issue of upgrading workers' skills has become a major concern. The first comprehensive overview of the problem was issued by the Southport Institute for the Study of Public Policy and recommended a broad range of federal initiatives. These would create a cadre of trained adult educators, expand funding, tie adult education more closely to workplace needs, fund research and expanded use of technology, and create an assessment system.

ANNE C. LEWIS
Education Policy Writer

© El Tayeb/Sipa

Egyptian President Hosni Mubarak (center) *made progress during the year in his efforts toward rapprochement with the Arab world, meeting with Jordan's King Hussein* (right) *and Palestine Liberation Organization Chairman Yasir Arafat* (left) *in March to coordinate their approaches to the Arab-Israeli peace process. Two months later, Egypt was reinstated into the 21-member Arab League from which it had been expelled following the 1979 signing of a separate peace treaty with Israel.*

EGYPT

Egypt continued to be plagued by economic crises and political dissent, especially from Islamic fundamentalists, during 1989. The arrest of several hundred by the authorities led to charges of abuses. President Hosni Mubarak scored greater successes in foreign relations than he did in his domestic policies through his role as a Middle East peacemaker.

Economic Affairs. With population growth at 2.8%, an increase of 1.5 million people yearly, the total was estimated to have reached 55 million by 1989. Consequently, Egypt became the world's largest importer of wheat flour for bread, the nation's basic food. About half the food supply had to be imported at a cost of $5 billion a year, adding to the $44 billion foreign debt. Although the average family size has dropped to 4.5 from 7 children in recent years, resources still are strained. Egypt has become dependent increasingly on U.S. aid, which reached $2.3 billion during 1989, but officials failed to cut the $2.8 million budget deficit and turned to the World Bank and International Monetary Fund (IMF) for assistance. Financial specialists pressured the government to make major economic changes, including cuts in food subsidies, to reach a balanced budget.

Despite the escalating financial crisis, Egypt attracted more private Arab investment than any other nation in 1988–89. Plans were expanded to relieve the population pressure on Cairo and Alexandria, the two largest cities in the Arab world, with 14 million and 5 million inhabitants, respectively, by constructing a new satellite city of Cairo called "Tenth of Ramadan." This was to be one of nine satellite cities (not suburbs) to diminish pressure in the two major urban centers.

Political Affairs. Deteriorating economic conditions, rising food prices, and cuts in subsidies of basic commodities fueled continuing unrest across the political spectrum. Arrests and trials of Muslim fundamentalists continued, including the detention of the well-known blind theologian Sheik Omar Abdel Rahman, thought to be a spiritual leader of the movement. Known collectively as Jihad or Holy War, fundamentalist movements were suspected of instigating major riots in Fayoum south of Cairo during Ramadan, the month of daytime fasting, in April. Using emergency legislation from the time of former President Anwar el-Sadat's assassination, the authorities seized and imprisoned some 1,500 of the fundamentalists in April. Another 300 were jailed after disturbances in Assyut in December.

In August security officials arrested several dozen members of an underground Shiite Muslim group trained in Iran and Syria to attack American and Israeli targets in Cairo and to overthrow Mubarak's government. At the other end of the political spectrum, scores of Communists and trade union leaders were arrested and tried for antigovernment agitation. At the giant Helwan steel mills south of Cairo, employing some 26,000 workers, the police smashed a strike by employees protesting dismissal of their elected representatives on the government-owned company's board of directors. The Egyptian Organization for Human Rights and Amnesty International charged that prisoners were subjected to ill treatment.

In a move that perplexed many Egyptians, the pro-U.S. defense minister, Field Marshal Abdel Halim Abu Ghazala, was demoted from his post in April to a presidential assistant. Abu Ghazala, a hero of three wars with Israel, had been considered the second most powerful person in Egypt after President Mubarak. He had been instrumental in building Egypt's 450,000-man military machine with a $1.5 billion budget into a semiautonomous institution.

EGYPT • Information Highlights

Official Name: Arab Republic of Egypt.
Location: Northeastern Africa.
Area: 386,660 sq mi (1 001 450 km^2).
Population (mid-1989 est.): 54,800,000.
Capital: Cairo.
Government: *Head of state,* Mohammed Hosni Mubarak, president (took office Oct. 1981). *Head of government,* Atef Sedki, prime minister (took office November 1986). *Legislature* (unicameral)—People's Assembly.
Monetary Unit: Pound (0.7 pounds equal U.S.$1, July 1989).
Gross National Product (1987 U.S.$): $25,600,-000,000.
Economic Index (May 1988): *Consumer Prices* (1980 = 100), all items, 325.2; food, 352.9.
Foreign Trade (1988 U.S.$): *Imports,* $23,298,000,-000; *exports,* $5,849,000,000.

In the election during June for 153 places in the Shura or Consultative Council, Mubarak's National Democratic Party won all but one seat, ending hopes that the council might develop into an open senate-like forum of the legislature alongside the People's Assembly.

Foreign Affairs. During 1989, Egypt was reinstated fully in the 21-member Arab League and participated in its summit conference at Casablanca, Morocco, during May. The league had suspended Egypt for making peace with Israel in 1979. President Mubarak acquired the role of an Arab leader with his proposals calling for the right of the Palestinians to choose their own form of government, for a peaceful resolution of the conflict with Israel, and for departure of all foreign troops from Lebanon.

In February, Egypt joined Iraq, Jordan, and Yemen at a conference in Baghdad to form an economic bloc, the Arab Cooperation Council. Following the Casablanca Arab League summit, Libyan President Qaddafi initiated steps to renew relations with Egypt. The border between the two countries had been closed since their five-day war in July 1977. In October, Qaddafi and Mubarak met in Egypt for parleys ending their 12-year feud, and in December Egypt and Syria restored relations after a 12-year break.

Throughout the year Mubarak conducted talks with leaders of various Arab states and with the Palestine Liberation Organization (PLO) on the Arab-Israel conflict. During visits to the United States and with Israeli Defense Minister Yitzhak Rabin in Cairo, Mubarak offered proposals to ease tensions in relations between Israel and the Palestinians. In addition to his ten-point plan to break the impasse, he offered to host negotiations between the antagonists in Cairo. Relations with Israel were eased greatly when it turned over to Egypt the last remnant of the Sinai peninsula at Taba during March following international arbitration.

See also MIDDLE EAST.

DON PERETZ
State University of New York, Binghamton

ENERGY

In 1989 the energy world was in turn startled, hopeful, and skeptical about reports in February that chemists had achieved a sustained hydrogen fusion reaction at room temperature with relatively simple components. (*See* PHYSICS.) The energy world also was rocked by the news that on March 24, a huge oil tanker, the *Exxon Valdez,* had gone aground and ruptured in Prince William Sound off the coast of Alaska. The accident spilled some 260,000 barrels of oil and touched off a national —and international—protest about the environmental consequences of the spill. (*See* feature article, page 36.)

Fossil Fuels. Continued, though lessening, discord was evident among the members of the Organization of Petroleum Exporting Countries (OPEC), as a decade of uncertainty—marked by falling revenues and fluctuating prices—seemed to have come to an end. Prices rose nearly 50% during the first few months of 1989, breaking the $20 per barrel barrier in March, and hovered in this range throughout the year. At an OPEC meeting in September, the daily production ceiling was raised from 19.5 to 20.5 million barrels, and in November the ceiling went to 22 million barrels, still lower than the estimated actual output of more than 23 million barrels.

Oil production in the United States continued to decline, dropping by approximately 1 million barrels per day to 7.5 million barrels. Actual consumption in the United States, however, continued to rise, and was at some 18 million barrels a day in 1989, up 1 million barrels since 1988 and close to the 1978 record of 18.8 million barrels. With imports up some 20% over a year ago, 1989 had the dubious distinction of being the first year since 1977 that imported oil supplied more than half the United States petroleum. Prices to U.S. consumers of home heating oil rose in some areas by more than 50% near the year's end, prompting the Justice Department to investigate possible price collusion.

Estimates of the world's fossil fuel reserves —oil, coal, and natural gas—continued to rise, contrary to the conventional wisdom of the 1970s that these supplies were dwindling. Since 1987, estimates of recoverable oil reserves have increased 30%, to 890 billion barrels, or enough for more than 45 years (compared with 1979's projection of 28.2 years). Likewise, coal reserve estimates have increased some 80% during that period, to nearly 1.1 trillion tons.

Recoverable reserve estimates of natural gas have been doubling every ten years with the latest estimate approximately 4,000 trillion cubic feet (113 trillion m^3), or enough for nearly 60 years. Once considered a worthless by-product of oil production, natural gas continued to take on increased prominence in the

U.S. energy picture. Since 1986, gas consumption has increased 11%, from 16.6 trillion cubic feet (470 billion m^3) to 18.5 trillion cubic feet (524 billion m^3). The American Gas Association estimates usage in 1990 will exceed the 1972 record of 22.7 trillion cubic feet (643 billion m^3). Prices, too, continued to increase, attracting more interest in expanding exploration and recovery operations in the United States and in the Arctic.

The increased reserve estimates and the increased consumption continued to concern environmentalists who had hoped that higher cost and scarcer supply would curb consumption of fossil fuels, the major source of carbon dioxide and other gases believed to be responsible for the alleged global warming trend. The World Energy Conference, at its September convention in Montreal, warned that carbon dioxide emissions could rise by 70% by 2020.

Electricity. Demand for electricity in the United States continued growing almost unchecked—demand in the Northeast region increased by more than 6% and in the mid-Atlantic states by more than 4%. This led energy experts to warn that brownouts (voltage reductions) and blackouts—some caused by excessive demands taxing and burning out supply components like transformers and cable—will become more frequent.

Utilities continued their scramble to head off this bleak scenario. High construction costs coupled with regulatory uncertainty have caused utilities virtually to stop building new large-scale generators. Instead, every utility in the country is stepping up its efforts to encourage conservation and energy efficiency, and in 1989 the industry spent some $1 billion to save 21,000 megawatts—roughly the equivalent of 21 large coal or nuclear plants.

Nuclear Energy. Nuclear power continued producing a substantial share of the country's electricity requirements in 1989—approximately 20%, second only to coal. By year's end, there were 111 plants licensed in the United States and more than 410 worldwide, providing more than 17% of the world's electricity.

One of the country's most controversial nuclear plants, Seabrook in New Hampshire, received its low-power operating license on May 18 and began its first atomic chain reaction June 13. The plant ended its testing in September. At year's end its operators were awaiting approval of a full-power license, pending resolution of emergency planning issues. In Massachusetts the Pilgrim plant, idled since 1986 because of maintenance and management problems, restarted and reached full power in the fall. The troubled Rancho Seco plant in Sacramento, CA, became the first nuclear plant ordered by voters in a referendum to shut down, and it has been removed permanently from service. In New York the fate of the controversial Shoreham plant on Long Island was sealed after state and utility officials reached an agreement to decommission the plant. Shortly after this decision, the Nuclear Regulatory Commission granted the plant a full-power operating license, but the die already had been cast. U.S. Department of Energy (DOE) officials, concerned about the insufficient supply of electricity on Long Island, have requested that the plant not be dismantled immediately as had been planned. The matter remained in negotiation at year's end.

The DOE also was embattled over the issue of nuclear-weapons-plant cleanup. Additional disclosures in 1989 confirmed 1988 charges that several nuclear-weapons facilities—which the DOE oversees—had been polluting the environment for more than 30 years. Energy Secretary James Watkins criticized the DOE for its past inaction in dealing with the problem. In June the DOE agreed to an at least $73 million settlement to cover medical monitoring of residents who lived near a uranium-processing plant in Fernald, OH, that had been cited as one of the worst offenders. In August, Watkins proposed a five-year, $19.5 billion plan to bring nuclear-weapons plants into compliance with federal environmental and employee safety statutes. Congress did not act on the proposal during the year.

A 1989 report of the U.S. National Research Council claimed that American fusion researchers were falling behind their European and Japanese counterparts in the race to achieve economically feasible controlled nuclear-fusion reactions. The report attributed the lag to budget cuts for fusion research at the DOE. The annual fusion research budget stood at $350 million in 1989, down 50% since 1979. Controlled fusion reaction remains an elusive goal, even after 50 years of research, and some physicists say that the goal may not be achieved for another 50 years. A fusion reaction produces energy by fusing, or joining together, atomic nuclei rather than splitting them apart, as conventional fission reactors do.

Solar Technology. In 1989 scientists at Boeing announced an efficiency breakthrough in photovoltaic technology with a cell that operates at 37% efficiency, substantially higher than 1988's record of 31% produced at Sandia National Laboratories in Albuquerque, NM. This compares with 34% efficiency for fossil-fuel burning plants, and opens the door to future widespread use of the sun for generating electricity. However, the solar-power industry has been sent reeling by federal cutbacks in solar-power research and development funds. The government spent $35.5 million in solar-power research in 1989, compared with $155 million in 1981, and the Bush administration has proposed further cutbacks.

ANTHONY J. CASTAGNO, *Energy Specialist*

ENGINEERING, CIVIL

It was a productive year for civil engineering as 1989 saw the completion of the world's tallest offshore oil platform and the resuscitation of Cleveland's Cuyahoga River, which was so polluted in 1972 that it caught on fire. It was also the year when robotics, automatic vehicle identification, and super-tall skyscrapers moved still closer to reality. But the harsher realities of 1989 were the continuing infrastructure woes and the apparent contribution of drugs to construction site accidents, leaving civil engineers to ponder a future of both promise and challenge.

The Projects. One of the biggest stories of 1989 was the completion of a 75,000-ton, 1,600-ft (488-m) tall offshore oil platform known as Bullwinkle, which was named the year's outstanding civil engineering achievement by the American Society of Civil Engineers. Taller than Chicago's Sears Tower, it is anchored in water 1,300 ft (396 m) deep in the Gulf of Mexico. Able to withstand hurricane force winds and 72-ft (22-m) waves, Bullwinkle will reach full production in 1992.

In Chicago, more improvements were made to O'Hare International Airport. A $2.1 billion project included the installation of navigational aids, the redesign of taxiways and runways, and the addition of a people mover. In Cleveland, the completion and full operation of the $320 million Southerly Wastewater Treatment Center made the Cuyahoga River clean enough for fishing and swimming. During its 16-year construction, the plant was kept in continuous operation. The plant—the largest in Ohio and one of the ten largest in the United States—has a capacity of 735 million gallons (2.8 billion liters) per day and serves 600,000 people in and around Cleveland.

The hemisphere's longest rail tunnel, stretching 9.1 mi (14.6 km) under the Selkirk Mountains of British Columbia, was completed in 1989. Construction recalled the building of the transcontinental railroad as contractors started at opposite ends and worked toward each other. When they met, they were just inches out of alignment. At the center of the tunnel is a 1,500-ft (457-m) vertical shaft that rises to the surface. A fan blows air down the shaft to clear fumes from the tunnel.

The pace of rehabilitation hardly slowed as engineers continued to improve and refurbish existing structures. In Arizona, steps were taken to rehabilitate two historic dams without draining their reservoirs. The height of the Theodore Roosevelt Dam—the tallest masonry dam in the world—will be raised by 77 ft (23 m); a new generating turbine also will be added. Meanwhile, the Stewart Mountain Dam will be strengthened with 60 posttensioned cables. Both dams are part of the Salt River Project originally authorized in 1908.

The National Park Service began a multiphase rehabilitation program for the Lincoln and Jefferson Memorials in Washington, DC. Stone deterioration, differential settlement, and water intrusion are problems that the $10 million program will address.

Sports stadiums, too, enjoyed their share of improvements. The massive SkyDome opened in Toronto. Enclosed by a 282-ft (86-m) high retractable roof, the $500 million multipurpose complex features such amenities as a 350-room hotel and a theater. And fans can view plays on

Bullwinkle, a 75,000-ton, 1,600-ft- (488-m)-tall offshore oil platform, is transported for anchoring in the Gulf of Mexico. The structure, completed in 1989, was judged the year's outstanding achievement in civil engineering.

Courtesy, "Civil Engineering Magazine," published by the American Society of Civil Engineers

a video display that is 33 ft (10 m) high and 110 ft (34 m) long. Luxury boxes and a new press box were added to the grandstand of Boston's Fenway Park. It was the first time the grandstand was altered since 1912. Renovations began as well at New York's Madison Square Garden, where $100 million was being spent for luxury boxes and general upgrading.

Nostalgia played a part in civil engineering in 1989 as well. A historic Waddell A-frame truss bridge—one of two left in the United States—was resurrected from the scrap heap and now spans a ravine in a Missouri park. And in Kansas City, construction began on a 4,200-ft (1 280-m) long wooden roller coaster; it features a 95-ft (29-m) drop and two complete circles in a 120-ft (37-m) helix. The project's engineer said that demand for all-wood roller coasters has returned.

Transportation. The bad news continued for transportation infrastructure. The National Council on Public Works Improvement gave a grade of "C+" to the U.S. urban highways. Mass transit fared worse, receiving a grade of "C−." However, a major public transportation project has helped revive the city of Buffalo. A $535 million rail line was completed in 1989, consisting of 14 stations. It is only 6.4 mi (10.3 km) long, but it is still the largest such project in western New York State since construction of the Erie Canal.

Some cities are experimenting with automated people movers. They are designed to carry from ten to 100 passengers at speeds ranging from eight to 50 mph (13 to 80 km/hr). They ride on rubber tires, steel wheels, or cushions of air. They are associated more with airports, but Detroit, Jacksonville, and Miami all have operating systems. The Miami people mover carries 11,000 people a day to points downtown. Although it was supposed to carry 30,000 passengers, the system has relieved downtown congestion and led to the refurbishing of some downtown areas. Extensions are planned.

At the 1989 Transportation Research Board meeting, engineers reported on a "Smart Streets" demonstration project under way in Los Angeles to combat highway congestion. Sensors embedded in a stretch of highway will report to computers in cars, warning drivers of traffic tie-ups and suggesting alternate routes. Studies on new pavements, new materials, and new tests also continued throughout the year, as transportation engineers sought to lengthen the life of existing highways. In New York City, meanwhile, a symbol of urban infrastructure decay was removed: The Westside Highway, abandoned since the 1970s when it collapsed under the weight of traffic, was dismantled and relocated to the bottom of the ocean, its remains forming a reef off Long Island.

Construction Safety. The University of Michigan released a study in 1989 that said one in ten workers at a construction site has a drug problem. Substance abuse, said the study, especially abuse involving alcohol, has a considerable role in workplace injury and costs the U.S. economy $10 billion a year. The study was not good news for an industry that already has a reputation for inherently unsafe conditions. Lawmakers continued to point out that although tragedies such as the L'Ambiance Plaza collapse in Bridgeport, CT, in 1987—in which 28 workers were killed—get more attention, it is less-publicized incidents such as trench collapses where most deaths occur. The U.S. Occupational Safety and Health Administration (OSHA) reported that 23.1 construction workers out of every 100,000 die each year, adding up to 1,000 deaths annually.

Both the government and individual firms took steps in 1989 to improve on-site safety. Federal legislators proposed a bill that would require contractors to notify OSHA within 24 hours of a single serious injury. The bill also would establish more stringent penalties for safety violations. Some contracting firms have beefed up on-site inspection of their projects and have instituted mandatory safety seminars for their employees. Others even have begun treatment programs for employees who are substance-dependent.

The Future. If building engineers are right, the horizon of the future could be dotted with superskyscrapers, buildings that would dwarf Chicago's Sears Tower. The year 1989 saw a proposal for a 125-story needle whose largest floor would be only 18,000 sq ft (1 672 m^2). Planned for construction in Chicago, it would top the Sears Tower by 400 ft (122 m). Some engineers say that 142-story buildings—skyscrapers one third of a mile (.5 km) high—are likely in the near future.

Also a likelihood in the future of civil engineering is the use of robots. Both in the United States and abroad, researchers have reported robotic advances. There already are robots that can paint, drive bolts and studs, and distribute concrete. Eventually, robots should replace human beings on dangerous jobs.

Meanwhile, computers are playing an ever larger role in civil engineering, from planning and engineering to mapping topography. Designers and engineers in Boston are using computer-aided drawings to help them rebuild the city's Central Artery. Planners are beginning to use geographic information systems to help them map out solutions to transportation problems. And computers are being used to design structures that will be located on other planets. NASA managers and engineers long have pondered lunar habitat designs, and now civil engineers are contributing ideas. The idea of moonbases is not that farfetched: There are plans to have one completed by the end of the century.

DOMENIC PREZIOSI, *Free-lance Writer*

Oil that gushed from a supply ship after it smashed off the Antarctic coast in January 1989 was only a fraction of the later spillage of the tanker disaster in Alaska's Prince William Sound, but it defiled a pristine ecosystem.

ENVIRONMENT

Though a series of large oil spills defiled waters from the Arctic to Antarctica during 1989, new reports showed that many air pollutants pose far bigger threats to the global environment—including its surface waters.

The Ozone Hole. The stratospheric ozone layer high above Earth's surface protects life on the planet by screening out much of the harmful ultraviolet energy radiated by the sun. Every September to November since the late 1970s, however, that layer has thinned over Antarctica, creating what is now referred to as a hole. Again in October 1989, that hole reached record proportions. The 1989 opening was predicted to be relatively weak. When the hole matched 1987's as the largest ever, National Aeronautics and Space Administration (NASA) scientists concluded that the ozone over Antarctica was thinning faster than had been anticipated, and that the processes governing hole formation remained poorly understood.

In April, University of Chicago scientists reported finding that 1988's ozone hole—while not a huge one—allowed twice the normal amount of ultraviolet radiation to filter through. Data reported in September by Texas A & M University researchers suggested such holes already may be a threat to the polar ecosystem. Experiments with the phytoplankton, which feed—directly or indirectly—virtually all other polar life, showed that a mere 16% elevation in ultraviolet levels reduced the photosynthetic capacity of the one-celled plants by 35% to 75%.

A January thinning in ozone over the Arctic was reported in the July 13 issue of the British journal *Nature*. The University of Wyoming scientists who discovered it believe it may signal the beginning of a small seasonal hole there.

Controlling CFCs. The release of chlorofluorocarbons (CFCs) used widely in refrigeration, foam products, and solvents continued to contribute about two thirds of the ozone-destroying chlorine in Earth's atmosphere. The Montreal Protocol, an international treaty limiting production of CFCs and related chemicals, took effect July 1, 1989. It required that ratifying nations cut in half their CFC production by the year 2000.

The worsening health of Earth's ozone layer, however, prompted leaders from 81 nations, meeting in Helsinki, Finland, in May, to approve unanimously a revision of the Montreal Protocol. Rather than just cut back CFCs, they now plan to ban the chemicals by 2000.

Ozone in Smog. Ozone in the stratosphere benefits life by filtering out biologically damaging ultraviolet light but it can cause respiratory harm if breathed by plants or animals at ground level. In 1989 roughly half the U.S. population lived in regions exceeding the Environmental Protection Agency's (EPA's) outdoor smog-ozone standard of 120 parts per billion (ppb) in air. Data released in June by the EPA suggested that ozone levels already present in the smog of many cities may be sufficient to cause irreversible lung damage.

New data also showed that, contrary to what had been assumed generally, one cannot easily avoid exposure to this toxic pollutant, formed when hydrocarbons and nitrogen oxides react in the presence of summer sunlight. While ground-level ozone generally is called "urban" smog, Jennifer Logan, a Harvard University atmospheric chemist, reported in June that the magnitude and duration of ozone episodes in rural regions of the eastern United States typically rival, or exceed, those in cities.

Though most pollution analysts had assumed indoor levels of smog ozone were trivial, a Bell Communications Research (Bellcore) scientist showed they can exceed 70% of outdoor levels, depending on how much outdoor air a building's ventilation pulls in. While Charles J. Weschler recorded the high indoor-ozone concentrations in Bellcore's office and research facilities, he noted that homes and schools with open windows can have ventilation rates—and indoor ozone levels—comparable to those he found at Bellcore.

Acid Rain. Of the lakes in New York's Adirondack Mountains, 80% showed signs of having acidified over the past 50 years, according to a March report by ecologists at the Institute of Ecosystem Studies in Millbrook, NY. High-altitude lakes tended to suffer most, they found, not only because they receive more acid rain, but also because the geological conditions around them are less able to neutralize these burning waters.

Such Northeast U.S. lakes and streams are unlikely to get much worse over the next 50 years, however, because much of the damage already has been done, a September EPA study reported. Moreover, the study found that this damage may prove difficult to reverse. While no Southeast waterways yet have become acidified chronically, EPA's computer modeling analyses showed that many are losing their ability to neutralize the acids in rain, and within 50 years will be vulnerable to acute acidifying of the type that sometimes has killed fish.

Fish kills are not the best measure of acidic air pollution's effects on aquatic life, however, according to the Canadian government's Freshwater Institute in Winnipeg. A study it published in May concluded that many, if not most, of the 6,351 Northeastern U.S. lakes identified by the U.S. EPA as being acid-sensitive—owing to their soft water—already have lost some of their species diversity. For example, high-altitude lakes in the Adirondacks, Catskills, and Poconos may have lost almost 70% of their leeches, almost half their insects (especially mayflies and dragonflies), half their mollusks (such as clams), and up to one third of their algae. Losing these species not only jeopardizes the survival of many more valued ones, such as sport fish, the Canadian researchers said, but also the overall health of their ecosystem.

Tropical rain forests continue to be torched indiscriminately to clear land in a conflagration that is causing global damage and concern among environmentalists.

Lead. Childhood exposures to lead have been associated with a range of adverse effects —from impaired hearing to diminished intelligence. In January scientists at the University of Cincinnati reported finding that children who have been exposed to even low levels of this toxic heavy metal can develop trouble balancing. Some children were affected so badly they had trouble climbing stairs. Measured in 6-

year-old children, the balancing difficulties appeared due largely to exposures received at 2, an age when hand-to-mouth exploration of their environment can lead to ingestion of lead-tainted dirt, dust, and paint. Lead also can stunt the growth of children, apparently by suppressing their appetite, the Cincinnati researchers reported six months later.

Toxic Air Pollutants. Major U.S. industries released 2.4 billion lbs (1.09 billion kg) of toxic air pollutants into the air in 1987, the most recent year for which data is available. Described in EPA's first national "Toxic Release Inventory," these emissions involved 320 chemicals, including 60 carcinogens and a number of neurotoxins. Chemical companies were the biggest contributors, emitting four times more than the next biggest polluters.

"[The] EPA has opposed legislation that would tighten emissions from chemical plants because it regarded these emissions as relatively small," said U.S. Rep. Henry A. Waxman (D-CA), chairman of the House subcommittee on health and the environment. But he pointed out that the new figures—provided by the polluters—indicate the chemical industry's toxic air emissions are ten times higher than has been reported previously.

Benzene ranked 21st, in tonnage, on the Toxic Release Inventory. And on August 31, EPA issued regulations—some 15 years in the making—to limit public exposure to industrial releases of benzene. Expected to cost more than $1 billion, these new rules would control 90% of the industrial air emissions of this leukemia-causing chemical.

The new controls did not address the gasoline vapors emitted as vehicles are fueled or driven. They account for 80% of outdoor benzene concentrations. The new controls also did not address benzene emitted in and around the home by such activities as cigarette smoking and the use of latex paints or household solvents. The EPA's Lance Wallace published a study in July showing that these nonindustrial —and unregulated—sources likely caused 99% of the 960 benzene-induced leukemia cases each year in the United States. The data also suggest benzene may be the most prominent cancer-causing chemical the general U.S. population is exposed to.

Oil Spills. To many, 1989 was the year of the oil spill. Though the grounding of the *Exxon Valdez* supertanker in Alaska's Prince William Sound gained the most news coverage, another potentially significant polar spill preceded it. On January 28, the *Bahía Paraíso,* an Argentine supply vessel, hit rocks off Antarctica's Palmer Station. The 30-ft (9.14-m) hole ripped into its hull spilled 200,000 gallons (757 000 l) of diesel oil and jet fuel just 1.5 mi (2.4 km) from a National Science Foundation center for the study of the pristine polar ecosystems. Preliminary reports said the spill killed many krill (shrimp-like organisms that feed everything from fish to whales) and seabirds, including penguins.

This catastrophe was dwarfed, however, by the Alaskan spill on March 24—the largest in U.S. history (*see* feature article, page 36). Three other major spills occurred in U.S. coastal waters over a 12-hour period on June 23 and 24, releasing an estimated 840,000 gallons (3.18 million l) of oil products. Unlike the polar spills, each of these was contained quickly without many immediate wildlife casualties.

Though all five of the spills were large, together they totaled only about 2% of the volume of oil pollution typically released into the oceanic environment each year.

Toxic Food Contaminants. A February 27 report by the Natural Resources Defense Council (NRDC) in Washington, DC, initiated a national food scare that centered on use of one agricultural chemical—Alar, a growth regulator that keeps apples from falling off trees before they redden. Using U.S. government data, NRDC's two-year study calculated that levels of pesticides present on fruits and vegetables eventually may cause an estimated 5,500 cancers among U.S. residents who were preschoolers in 1989. Because of the high proportion of fruit in a preschooler's diet, it estimated that half one's lifetime cancer risk from it generally occurs by age 6. Alar, and the

Food stores picked up on consumer concerns over the safety of the growth regulator Alar and the discovery of two grapes from Chile laced with a small amount of cyanide.

chemical it breaks down to in the body, together accounted for 90% or more of that cancer risk, NRDC said.

The public responded by avoiding apples and apple products. By early June, Alar's manufacturer sealed the pesticide's fate by agreeing to halt sales of it for use on foods.

On September 1 the Food and Drug Administration (FDA) released results of its survey showing minute quantities of extremely toxic dioxins and furans in almost half the milk from the cardboard cartons it sampled. During 1988–89, a host of studies have shown that the routine chlorine bleaching of wood pulp added these chemicals to a range of consumer paper products—from coffee filters and newspaper to facial tissues and paper plates. Papermaking changes, prompted by dioxin concerns, should remove most if not all of these contaminants from milk within five years, FDA said.

Endangered Species. One quarter of the world's plant and animal species could disappear within the next 25 to 50 years, the Washington, DC-based World Resources Institute (WRI) said in an October analysis. Tropical rain forest destruction is the single largest cause, it found. Many of the species lost could be plants with important medicinal properties, wild versions of crops, domestic livestock having genetic properties that could improve modern agriculture, or merely insects and plants that serve as the food for more prized species—from birds to mammals. Yet despite the value that most biologists place on these disappearing resources, WRI found that annual U.S. funding for species conservation in developing countries—where most losses are occurring—totaled only $37.5 million, "less than 1% of what Americans spend every year to go to the movies."

On October 23, WRI joined forces with the United Nations Environment Programme and World Conservation Union to initiate a plan to conserve the diversity of species. They pledged to meet with national and local leaders on every continent to identify the issues fostering species losses so that effective countering strategies can be proposed at a UN meeting in 1992.

One effective species-conservation strategy for animals threatened by poaching has been to limit trade in them. In October 1989, 76 of the nations that have ratified the Convention on International Trade in Endangered Species (CITES)—a treaty to conserve species diversity—voted to ban trade in the African elephant and its ivory as of January 1990. Recommended by CITES' Ivory Trade Review Group in June, the move reflected its assessment that all other efforts to control elephant poaching for ivory had failed. WRI noted that the elephants were being killed at a rate of one every ten minutes—threatening their extinction within ten years.

JANET RALOFF, *"Science News"*

ESPIONAGE

During 1989 espionage moved into a new phase because of the decline of the Cold War. The United States and the Soviet Union ceased to consider one another enemies, and so their spy services apparently ceased to be confrontational. Nevertheless, spies were active inside the superpowers as well as in many other nations.

Changes at the KGB. Soviet restructuring policies *(perestroika)* have transformed the KGB (Russian civil intelligence). Vladimir Kryuchkov, director of the KGB, announced in May that radical reforms would end old abuses. He also said the KGB should be controlled by the Soviet legislature instead of remaining a semi-independent organ of the Kremlin. One suggestion was to divide the KGB into two new departments, one restricted to the USSR, the other for operations abroad. "The KGB Today," a documentary portraying it as essentially a crime-fighting organization, was released in Moscow.

Critics both inside and outside the Soviet Union contended that certain harmful practices remained, such as mass wiretapping. Nobody denied, however, that KGB mass coercion of the Soviet people was a thing of the past.

MI5 in the Light. Another celebrated spy organization bowed to winds of change. In September London sources said that the MI5 (British domestic intelligence) would be opened to greater scrutiny. The identity of the head of the MI5 previously had been hidden for security reasons. Now it has become known that he was Patrick Walker. A National Services Act imposed more oversight on the MI5 by setting new guidelines for agents in most intelligence operations on British soil.

American Spies. U.S. servicemen were charged with spying for the Soviets in West Berlin. Some classified documents were found in the apartment of Air Force Captain John Hirsch. Army Spec. 4 Michael Peri went AWOL (absent without leave) and was thought to have defected to the Soviet Union until he reappeared in March. He admitted giving U.S. secrets to East Germans. Frank Nesbitt, a military communications expert, was accused of trying to pass information to Soviet agents. He claimed he had hoped to be a double agent for U.S. intelligence.

Former Navy technician Craig Kunkle was seized in a sting operation in Virginia. Ronald Wolf, who had been an Air Force linguist, fell to a similar operation in Dallas. Warrant Officer James W. Hall III, arrested in 1988, was sentenced in May to a 40-year jail term. Richard Miller, the only FBI agent ever convicted of espionage, had the verdict set aside in April on a technicality involving lie-detector testing. He was released from prison in late October and a new trial was scheduled.

© S. Allen/Gamma-Liaison

Under investigation as a spy, Felix S. Bloch, who had served as a high-level U.S. diplomat, found that everywhere he went, newsmen and government agents followed.

Glenn Souther, a Navy analyst who defected to Moscow in 1986, died there in June. The KGB termed his death a suicide.

Embassy Suspect. On June 22 the U.S. State Department suspended Felix S. Bloch, who had been attached to the U.S. embassy in Vienna. He was suspected of spying for the Russians. Sources declared that he was photographed in Paris passing a briefcase to a Soviet agent. The agent was said to be Reino Gikman, dubbed "the phony Finn" by the media. Bloch agreed he was in Paris when the briefcase incident allegedly took place. He refused to confirm or deny the espionage allegations.

Since no charges were filed against Bloch at the time, a bizarre spectacle followed. FBI agents kept him under tight surveillance around the clock because the bureau feared he might try to escape to Moscow. Reporters followed him every time he left his house. A circus atmosphere prevailed until the public lost interest. As there was no break in the case, the stalemate continued.

Soviet Bugs. One suspicion of Bloch concerned the bugged American embassy in Moscow. Bloch allegedly knew from secret reports that a marine guard had confessed to spying for the Russians. If so, he could have warned embassy officials in time for them to remove some of the listening devices from the embassy.

U.S. Secretary of State James Baker recommended in October that the unfinished embassy in Moscow, which was found to contain numerous listening devices, be torn down completely and rebuilt. The plan still required the approval of the president and Congress. Baker also charged that the Russians had bugged the U.S. consulate in Leningrad.

Retaliatory Measures. Spy expulsions continued in the East and West. In February, Italian authorities broke a KGB spy ring by arresting two of its agents in Rome. In March the United States expelled a Soviet military attaché. The USSR expelled a U.S. military attaché. In May, British authorities announced that eight Soviet diplomats were being expelled for "impermissible activities." Moscow then expelled eight Britons.

German Hackers. West German authorities revealed in March that a group of hackers had broken into computer systems involving Europe, Japan, and the United States. Exposure of the hackers began in 1986 when astronomer and computer security expert Clifford Stoll noticed a data-bank discrepancy in the computer network at Lawrence Berkeley Laboratory in Berkeley, CA. Those arrested were charged with stealing communications secrets and passing them to the Russians. One of the accused, Karl Koch, committed suicide.

Two Ambiguities. Romanian authorities arrested Mircea Racanu in January and accused him of espionage. Racanu had lived in both Washington, DC, and Moscow. The case was ambiguous because the Romanian government refused to reveal whether he would be tried as a spy for the United States or for the Soviet Union.

Iranian authorities stated in April that a number of military officers had been arrested for spying for the United States. U.S. authorities denied the charge, and some observers judged the case to be camouflage for a power struggle in Tehran.

Death of a Spymaster. Sir William Stephenson died in Jamaica on February 2. During World War II, Stephenson was Winston Churchill's spymaster in the United States. Stephenson worked surreptitiously with Washington agents before the United States got into the war. During the war, he cooperated with William Donovan, head of the U.S. Office of Strategic Services, when they were called "the quiet Canadian" (Stephenson) and "Wild Bill" (Donovan).

Knighted by King George VI and given the Medal for Merit by President Franklin Roosevelt, Stephenson retired to Jamaica after the war. He served until his death as an adviser to several governments on international policies and industrial systems, drawing on his experiences during the war.

VINCENT BURANELLI
Coauthor, "Spy/Counterspy"

ETHIOPIA

In 1989 the Ethiopian government lost control of Tigre region to northern rebels. With a number of military defeats suffered by the government an abortive military coup took place. As a result of the increasing military pressure Ethiopia agreed to begin negotiations with northern rebels aimed at resolving the outstanding disputes.

Civil War. Ethiopia lost control of Tigre region in February. In December 1988, 20,000 soldiers were routed while trying to reopen a road to Asmara in Eritrea. Three thousand soldiers were killed as the local populace gave its support to the rebels. By February 1989, Ethiopia withdrew all its troops from Tigre. The retreat was followed up by rebel attacks in Gondar and Wollo regions in which numerous towns were taken. With tens of thousands of losses in these major battles and with the Tigrean People's Liberation Front (TPLF—who demand the removal of the regime of President Mengistu Haile-Mariam) in control of Tigre and the Eritrean People's Liberation Front (EPLF—who demand secession) controlling 90% of Eritrea, the Ethiopian military was humiliated.

Coup Attempt. Anger by senior military officers at President Mengistu's approach to the secessionist wars led to an attempted coup in May. While Mengistu, a Marxist-Leninist, was on a visit to East Germany, a number of generals tried to take over the government. Mengistu rushed back to the country. Nine generals involved in the coup were executed. Industry Minister Fanta Belai was arrested, as were 400 officers, virtually the entire staff of the defense ministry.

Peace Talks. As a direct result of the failed coup and the string of victories by the TPLF and EPLF, the Ethiopian parliament in June endorsed unconditional peace talks with the rebels in Eritrea and Tigre. Within three weeks both rebel groups had agreed to peace talks without political conditions. The first round of talks began in Atlanta, GA, September 7 and concluded September 19 with former President Jimmy Carter acting as mediator. The talks were only between the Ethiopian government and the EPLF and were held under the auspices of Carter's International Negotiating Network. There was broad discussion regarding a cease-fire in the war that began in 1961.

Separate peace talks between the government and the TPLF rebels were held late in 1989 in Rome. Some progress reportedly was made on procedural matters. After the talks adjourned in December, however, the TPLF launched a successful offensive that captured two towns and a military base.

International Relations. Mengistu, in a serious effort to limit the effects of reduced Soviet aid and the complete withdrawal of Cuban troops announced in September, asked the U.S. State Department to upgrade diplomatic ties and improve relations. Although the United States did not agree officially to the request, in August, Assistant Secretary of State Herman J. Cohen visited Ethiopia for talks with Mengistu that were intended to begin a thaw in relations. And in late August, Mengistu aided the United States in its search for Rep. Mickey Leland (D-TX) and his official party who were reported missing as they flew to visit a refugee camp in Ethiopia. All were found dead on August 13. President Bush, in a private letter to Mengistu, thanked him for his efforts in seeking Leland's plane.

Domestic Affairs. In September, Ethiopia released 87 political prisoners, including three grandsons of the late Emperor Haile Selassie, and former UN envoy Berhanu Dinka.

In 1989 coffee prices plunged from $1.53 per pound to about 76 cents per pound on the international commodities exchanges. The collapse caused economic dislocation as coffee is Ethiopia's primary export crop, accounting for 60% of its exports.

In August, Amnesty International accused Ethiopia of a "high level of serious human-rights abuses" and said Ethiopia had "one of the poorest records among African states."

A plane that was carrying U.S. Rep. Mickey Leland (D-TX) and his party to an Ethiopian refugee camp was found on a mountainside August 13. There were no survivors.

AP/Wide World

ETHIOPIA • Information Highlights

Official Name: Ethiopia.
Location: Eastern Africa.
Area: 471,776 sq mi (1 221 900 km²).
Population (mid-1989 est.): 49,800,000.
Chief Cities (1984 census): Addis Ababa, the capital, 1,412,577; Asmara, 275,385; Dire Dawa, 98,104.
Government: *Head of state,* Mengistu Haile-Mariam, president (took office Sept. 10, 1987). Legislature —Parliament (National Shengo, established Sept. 9, 1987).
Monetary Unit: Birr (2.07 birr equal U.S.$1, May 1989).
Gross Domestic Product (1987 est. U.S. $): $5,400,000,000.
Economic Index (Addis Ababa, 1987): *Consumer Prices* (1980 = 100), all items, 126.8; food, 123.6.
Foreign Trade (1987 U.S.$): *Imports,* $1,097,000,000; *exports,* $477,000,000.

And in February a virulent strain of meningitis reaches epidemic proportions with some 10,000 people dead in Sidamo region alone. And although rainfall returned to normal in 1989 the UN listed Ethiopia as one of 15 countries that would require exceptional food assistance during the year. In part, this was due to the presence of 850,000 refugees from Somalia and the Sudan.

PETER SCHWAB
State University of New York at Purchase

ETHNIC GROUPS

It was a year of retrenchment for U.S. ethnic relations in 1989—minorities once again found themselves the targets of racist attacks and other forms of harassment, affirmative action policies were challenged successfully in the courts, and minority unemployment rates remained high.

Other developments, however, included black political advances, successful suits against discrimination, and the court's affirmation of Native American jurisdictional rights.

Blacks. For blacks, 1989 proved to be largely a year of setbacks. Survey data indicated that whites and blacks evaluated each other's levels of economic success differently. Black unemployment dipped slightly but remained fairly constant around the 11% to 12% mark. At the same time, a number of affirmative action programs had serious reversals. The U.S. Supreme Court set aside Richmond's 30% minority construction policy, finding that unless clear discrimination was being redressed, such an approach constituted reverse discrimination. Likewise, Georgia's Supreme Court rejected Atlanta's minority contractor program for failing to prove previous discrimination. (*See also* LAW.)

On the other side of the docket, blacks successfully pursued a minority discrimination complaint against General Motors Corp. In addition, black, Hispanic, and female workers, along with older employees, settled a discrimination suit with Nissan Motor Corp., U.S.A.

In 1989 the media reported a significant rise in racial harassment on college campuses throughout the nation. Members of the Ku Klux Klan pleaded guilty to attacks on civil-rights marchers, and Klan members reportedly allied themselves with skinhead youths for attacks on minorities. A former Klan leader was elected in 1989 to the Louisiana House of Representatives. Meanwhile, a black police activist and former law enforcement officer detailed a white police officer's violent reaction to him after an alleged traffic incident in Long Beach, CA.

On the political front, blacks had some big wins in 1989. In Virginia, Democratic Lt. Gov. Douglas Wilder defeated a conservative Republican to become the nation's first elected black governor. David N. Dinkins beat Mayor Edward I. Koch in the Democratic primary and went on to win the top spot in New York City. Seattle Councilman Norman B. Rice won a mayor's race by a wide margin, in a city with a black population of only 10%. Both Tom Bradley in Los Angeles and Coleman Young in Detroit won fifth consecutive terms as their cities' mayor. Meanwhile, Maynard Jackson regained the mayor's post in Atlanta as the man he replaces, Andrew Young, prepared for a run for the Georgia governorship.

Blacks also were appointed to a number of high-level political and government posts. Army Gen. Colin L. Powell was named chairman of the Joint Chiefs of Staff—the nation's top military post. Dr. Louis Sullivan was confirmed as secretary of Health and Human Services. And Ronald Brown was elected chair of the Democratic National Committee.

In a different arena, former major league baseball player and broadcaster Bill White became the first black president of baseball's National League and Art Shell was the first black to be named a head coach in the National Football League. He took over the Los Angeles Raiders.

But blacks also suffered some political setbacks in 1989. Eugene Sawyer, the acting mayor of Chicago since Harold Washington's death in 1987, was defeated by Richard M. Daley, the son of the city's late political boss.

In another development, Lee Atwater, the chair of the Republican National Committee, promised to court black voters, and polls showed that blacks gave significantly higher approval ratings to President Bush than to his predecessor.

The American Council of Education reported that black male college enrollment had declined over the past decade. At the same time, blacks criticized proposed new stringent admission rules for college athletes under Proposition 42 of National Collegiate Athletic Association (NCAA) requirements, contending it

AP/Wide World

© Cynthia Johnson/Gamma-Liaison

Bill White (far left), *a former major league baseball player and broadcaster, in 1989 became president of the National League. U.S. Army Gen. Colin L. Powell was the first black promoted to the nation's highest military post, chairman of the Joint Chiefs of Staff.*

has a racial bias and that it could prevent large numbers of blacks from attending college. *See* SPORTS—*Overview*.

At Howard University, students protested the appointment of Lee Atwater to the school's board of trustees and he resigned within a few days. Meanwhile, President Bush sent to Congress a plan for academic excellence which included an allocation of $10 million for traditionally black colleges.

Hispanic Americans. For Hispanic Americans 1989 was a relatively quiet year, but not without setbacks. In Miami, William Lozano, an Hispanic member of the police force, was convicted of manslaughter for allegedly shooting a black motorcyclist in an incident that sparked a three-day riot and strained black-Hispanic relations. Hispanics were also the targets of Ku Klux Klan and skinhead violence. Unemployment rates for Hispanics varied to some degree, but were generally in the 8% range. Meanwhile the U.S. Census Bureau reported that the nation's Hispanic population had grown by 39% since 1980. There now were 20.1 million Hispanics in the United States. Hispanics, like blacks, were affected by court reversals of affirmative action programs. Hispanic business efforts flourished, however, in such states as Texas. In politics, the National Republican Committee also announced its intention to reach out to Hispanics. And a Republican candidate in Florida, Ileana Ros-Lehtinen, became the first Cuban-American to be elected to the U.S. House of Representatives, winning a seat that had been held by the late Claude Pepper. At the same time, one of the nation's highest-profile Hispanic leaders, Mayor Henry Cisneros of San Antonio, TX, decided in 1989 to leave politics for business.

Native Americans. The plight of Native Americans was aggravated in 1989 by the Peter MacDonald scandal. The leader of the Navajo nation in Arizona, MacDonald was accused of accepting money, a car, and other gifts in exchange for construction contracts. After the tribal council tried to suspend MacDonald, his supporters clashed with Navajo police in a melee that left two dead. However, leaders of the American Indian Movement placed much of the blame for corruption in tribal governments with the Bureau of Indian Affairs, which administers federal programs for Native Americans. In a case involving the Mississippi Choctaw tribe, the U.S. Supreme Court upheld tribal control over child-custody battles. In another important development, Stanford University agreed to return remains of the Ohlone Indians to the tribe's elders for reburial. Canadian Indians, meanwhile, protested that nation's planned reduction in aboriginal education assistance.

Asian Americans. In 1989, Asian Americans anxiously followed news accounts of the pro-democracy demonstrations in China and the subsequent brutal crackdown in Tiananmen Square.

On January 17 a sniper armed with a semiautomatic rifle opened fire on young students of Vietnamese and Cambodian origins in a schoolyard at Stockton, CA. The gunman killed five of the children and wounded 29 before taking his own life.

Many older Japanese-Americans were disheartened by the reluctance of Congress to appropriate funds for World War II internment reparations, approved in 1988.

GRAHAM C. KINLOCH, *Author*
"The Sociology of Minority Group Relations"

EUROPE

At no time since the height of the Cold War in 1948–49 had the affairs of Eastern and Western Europe been so intertwined as in 1989. But, miraculously it seemed to many Europeans, the interrelationship was largely positive as Eastern Europe shifted toward democratization and economic reform. In response to these welcome changes—spearheaded by the Soviet Union, Poland, and Hungary—Western Europe and the United States responded by seeking progress in arms agreements and offering political and economic support to leaders pioneering in changing their ossified societies. To prepare Western Europe itself for a new relationship with a changing Eastern Europe, the leaders of the European Community (EC) sought, with only partial success, to speed up the process of integration by preparing for the achievement of a "single market" without internal barriers by Jan. 1, 1993.

Economic Progress in the West. The economic achievements of the majority of the countries of Western Europe in 1989 created a climate of self-confidence in which new approaches to the disintegrating Communist bloc could be made. The overall growth rate of the EC was expected to reach 3.5% and to continue at that level into 1990. Capital investment increased by 3%. After creating 2 million new jobs in 1988, the EC seemed certain to create a further 2.5 to 3 million jobs in 1989–90. As a result, the unemployment rate dipped from 11% to 10%. West Germany led the growth, its gross national product (GNP) increasing by 4.2% and its trade surplus reaching 9.9 billion marks (about $5.6 billion). West German inflation remained low, at 3%, but the Community's inflation rate rose from 3.6% in 1988 to 4.75% because of price rises in Britain, Italy, and Spain.

Perhaps the most encouraging economic sign was the advance of the more fragile economies of the southern European countries. Since its entry into the EC in 1986, Spain had renewed one third of its capital equipment and created one third of a million jobs annually. The expansion was so great that the Socialist government of Prime Minister Felipe González was forced to raise interest rates and, in spite of union strikes, to limit pay raises. To maintain financial rigor, at the end of his six-month presidency of the EC Council of Ministers, he took Spain into the European Monetary System (EMS), thus guaranteeing that Spain would keep its currency within narrow limits of fluctuation in relation to the other EC currencies.

Italy, in spite of continuing political instability, maintained for the sixth year a growth rate of 3.5%. Even Greece, with per capita income only 40% of the EC average, saw its stabilization plan of 1985 bear fruit in reduced trade deficits and lower inflation, while Community aid through the Integrated Mediterranean Program helped it continue the development of its poorer regions.

Toward 1993. Progress in preparing the "single market" without internal barriers to free movement of capital, goods, services, and people, which the 12 EC governments had agreed to establish by passage of the Single European Act in 1986, was slow. At the summit meeting of the heads of state or government in Rhodes in December 1988, they agreed to speed up their action on the almost 300 legislative proposals that the EC Commission was preparing for implementation of the new market. Negotiations were slowed, however, by the divergence of views between British Prime Minister Margaret Thatcher and Commission President Jacques Delors on the extent to which the Community authorities should be given supranational powers, especially in monetary matters.

When Delors presented proposals for a three-stage movement toward monetary union to the summit meeting in Madrid in June, Thatcher accepted only the first stage, increasing cooperation in economic and monetary policy and providing for the eventual entry of the British pound into the exchange regulation of the EMS. The later stages, providing for creation of a Community bank and a common currency, were to be discussed later at an intergovernmental conference.

Several issues discussed at Madrid were taken up again in Paris in July at the meeting of the heads of state or government of the seven major industrial democracies (Britain, Canada, France, Italy, Japan, United States, West Germany), notably the need for greater environmental protection and for aid to the countries of Eastern Europe seeking greater democratization. The growing stature of the EC Commission was reaffirmed when U.S. President George Bush agreed that Western long-term aid for Poland and Hungary should be coordinated by the Commission, which in September announced EC aid for those two countries of $325 million in 1990.

More Effective Arms Agreements. Following the beginning of destruction of intermediate-range nuclear weapons by the United States and the USSR as agreed by treaty in 1987, the focus of negotiations between the Warsaw Pact and the North Atlantic Treaty Organization (NATO) shifted to reduction of conventional forces in Europe. In December 1988, Soviet President Mikhail Gorbachev announced to the United Nations that the Warsaw Pact unilaterally would cut its forces, Russia alone cutting its defense budget by 14% and its armed forces by 500,000 soldiers. In February the Mutual and Balanced Force Reduction (MBFR) talks, which had dragged on ineffectively since 1973, were wound up. They were replaced by talks on Conventional Armed Forces in Europe

© Pascal/Sipa

At a late May summit meeting in Brussels, marking the 40th anniversary of the North Atlantic Treaty Organization, President George Bush proposed a reduction in East-West conventional forces in Europe.

(CFE), at which the Soviet Union again appeared more willing than the NATO powers to undertake serious disarmament by offering to accept the reduction of the forces of both alliances to 10–15% less than that of NATO and to withdraw battlefield nuclear weapons.

President George Bush, under criticism from his NATO allies for excessive caution in negotiating with Gorbachev, received an enthusiastic reception at the NATO summit meeting in Brussels in May, which had been called to celebrate the 40th anniversary of the founding of the alliance, with a dramatic proposal of his own. Both Soviet and U.S. forces in Europe were to be reduced to 275,000 soldiers, and both blocs would make deep cuts in their numbers of tanks, artillery, and combat aircraft. As demanded by West Germany, talks also would begin on reduction of strategic or long-range nuclear forces. In September at the United Nations, Bush proposed that the Russians and Americans each reduce their chemical weapons to one fifth of the current U.S. arsenal. Soviet Foreign Minister Eduard Shevardnadze responded with the even more striking proposal that the arsenals be eliminated completely and production of chemical weapons stopped.

In a notable agreement at their "informal" summit meeting in Malta in December, Bush and Gorbachev stated that they would try to conclude treaties in 1990 on both long-range nuclear weapons and on conventional arms.

Changing Relationships in the East. The shift in relations between the Soviet Union and its East European allies was even more profound in its effects than that between Western and Eastern Europe. Gorbachev at home, by accelerating his policies of restructuring, openness, and democracy *(perestroika, glasnost, demokratizatsiya)*, was providing an example of how a totalitarian society can be changed from within. By withdrawing Soviet troops from Afghanistan, he broke with the interventionist policies of previous Soviet leaders, and he specifically rejected the Brezhnev Doctrine, giving the USSR the duty to intervene in countries where Communist control was threatened. With the encouragement of the Russian example and the guarantee of freedom from Soviet interference—and indeed at times with clear Russian approval—the reform forces in Eastern Europe made revolutionary advances.

In Poland, the independent trade union Solidarity, which had been outlawed in 1981, was legalized in April. After winning all but one of the seats chosen by open voting in the reorganized Senate and Assembly, a leading Solidarity member, Tadeusz Mazowiecki, was called to form a Solidarity-dominated government in August. In Hungary, after first sanctioning the foundation of opposition political parties and promising free elections to parliament in 1990, the Communist Party renamed itself the Hungarian Socialist Party.

East Germany also experienced change. In October, after scores of thousands of East Germans had fled to West Germany, the leadership of the East German Communist Party was replaced. In November, East Germany opened its borders, including the Berlin Wall. Subsequently, following massive demonstrations in Czechoslovakia, a coalition government with a Communist minority was established. In late December the 24-year dictatorial rule of Nicolae Ceaușescu ended in Romania.

The year 1989 thus brought the most far-reaching changes in Eastern Europe since establishment of Communist rule in 1945–48.

See also feature article, page 24.

R. Roy Willis
University of California, Davis

FAMILY

Family-related issues were in the news in 1989, and the most startling ones resulted in the broadening of the legal definition of a family. Several large cities were exploring domestic partnership laws, and New York began offering city employees the same bereavement benefits upon the death of a companion as of a spouse.

The traditional concept of family also was expanded in 1989 when the New York Court of Appeals ruled that a gay couple who lived together for ten years could be considered a family under New York City's rent control regulations.

Family Size. A U.S. Census Bureau report showed the size of the average U.S. family dipping to 3.17 persons in 1988 from 3.19 in 1987. Reasons for the decline included later marriages and the desire for fewer children. The marriage rate in 1988 was 9.7 per 1,000, down from 1987's rate of 9.9 per 1,000. The decline was attributed to there being fewer people in their twenties, when most people marry. But there were more than 4 million new stepfamilies in the United States in 1987, with about 1,300 new stepfamilies formed every day.

There was a 2% increase in births in the United States in 1988 over 1987, with 15.9 births per 1,000. Late childbirths were a trend: In the 12 months ended June 1988, 33% of U.S. children were born to mothers in their thirties, compared with 19% in 1976.

The estimated number of divorces in the United States increased 2% between 1987 and 1988. The divorce rate for 1988, 4.8 per 1,000, remained unchanged from 1987, with divorce rates lowest in northeastern states and highest in the South and West. The number of one-parent families reached 9.4 million in 1988.

Income. According to congressional data, 1979–87 saw a growing income disparity between the richest and poorest segments of the United States. The poorest one fifth of the population saw a drop of 6.1% in average family income during this period, from $5,439 in 1979 to $5,107 in 1987 (all figures expressed in constant 1987 dollars). Families in the top one fifth in terms of income enjoyed an increase of 11.1%, up from $61,917 to $68,775. The average U.S. family income swelled by 5.6%, from $27,917 to $29,487.

One reason cited for the increasing gap between the haves and have-nots was the increasing number of affluent working couples, with each person earning a relatively high income, while the poorest group held jobs paying poverty-level wages or lower. Another factor was the growing number of one-parent families. In 1980, 2.9% of children under 18 lived with a never-married parent; by 1987 the number had jumped to 6.8%.

Child Care. Congress kept its promise to child-care advocates by considering the Act for Better Child Care Services of 1989, also known as the ABC bill. Although the 1989 session adjourned without final action on the subject, House and Senate leaders indicated that child care would be a top priority in 1990. During 1989 the Senate passed an ABC bill, providing $1.75 billion to the states to subsidize child care for low-income working families, but House members could not agree on the form for federal funding. Substantive and procedural disputes interfered with final House action.

The Family and Medical Leave Bill of 1989 (parental leave bill), which would give unpaid job-protected leave for parents of newborn and seriously ill children in companies with more than 50 workers, was readied for floor action in both the Senate and House. This was the fifth year in a row that such legislation had been considered without reaching a vote.

Children's Health and Welfare. A report by the National Association of Children's Hospitals and Related Institutions gave a thumbs-down diagnosis on U.S. children's health. Concern was expressed about an increase in child abuse and neglect, with estimated deaths ranging from 2,000 to 5,000 each year.

The number of children with AIDS was on the rise, with 10,000 to 20,000 pediatric cases (including AIDS-related complex) likely to be diagnosed by 1991. About 7 million children were not receiving routine medical care, with only 60% of children under 4 getting basic immunizations.

The U.S. infant mortality rate was at an all-time low, but still was higher than in some developing nations. House and Senate budget negotiators agreed to increase spending by $200 million in 1990 to reduce infant mortality.

A congressional study reported that 20% of school-age children and 25% of preschoolers lived in poverty in 1987, making them the largest U.S. poverty group. Black and Hispanic children were found to be two to three times more likely to be poor than were whites. Homelessness among children also increased.

"Empty Nest" Repopulates. A Census Bureau report released in January 1989 revealed that 18 million single adults in the 18–34 age bracket were living with their parents, an increase of one third since 1974. Several reasons have been suggested to explain this trend, among them the high cost of housing, low entry-level salaries, and young adults who are separated or divorced.

Drugs. The structure of many poor urban families has been destroyed by the use of crack, a potent form of cocaine. Many mothers have become addicted, and children as young as 12 are selling drugs. A study by the National Institute of Drug Abuse showed that babies born to addicted mothers show serious effects. Without help, they have difficulty relating to other people and the world around them.

GLADYS HANDELMAN, *Writer and Editor*

© Matteini/Sipa

© Barthelemy/Sipa

Two important fashion trends that emerged in 1989 were reflected in the popularity of fake furs and "animal-like" accessories and of clothing inspired by colorful Indian designs and other themes of the American Southwest.

FASHION

The year 1989 was one of "kinder, gentler" fashion. While there were some designers with an outré outlook, most European and American collections were full of looks designed and detailed elegantly, yet totally wearable.

Coats. Coats were the focal point of designer collections. The variety was overwhelming and lengths ranged from three-quarter to ankle-grazing. Classic styles were shown as well as newer pyramid or trapeze silhouettes. There were fitted princess shapes, slouchy bathrobe wraps, and anoraks and duffel coats in bright-colored shearling and rich woolens. Fabrics ranged from plush luxe cashmere, alpaca, camel hair, and mohair through meltons and broadcloths. There was even a "sueded" matte-finish water-repellent silk popular in the rainwear market.

A considerable amount of fur was shown despite animal-rights groups' pressure. Trims of beaver, Persian lamb, and fox were much in evidence, and coats of the new lightweight sheared furs were the most popular types used in couture fur collections. At Fendi the sensation of the collection was an unlined fur coat designed and treated to reverse so that it could be worn either fur- or skin-side out.

However, conservation groups were heartened by the year's massive trend to fakes. Key designers made fashion news with substantial representations of fake fur coats in their collections. Included were styles in tiger, leopard, and ocelot patterned pile fabrics. Fakes of luxury furs like sable, snow leopard, and lynx also were used by European and U.S. manufacturers.

Fashion Trends. The "fakes phenomenon" permeated fashion at every level. Animal prints remained strong in everything from sportswear items to accessories. Fake ivory and tortoiseshell appeared in jewelry lines and belts, bags, and shoes continued their use of reptile patterned or embossed materials.

Two other trends swept fashion in 1989. First, there was the equestrian look, evident in narrow tapered pants with stirrups or modified jodhpurs, done extravagantly by Calvin Klein in both suede and cashmere. There also were tweed hacking jackets, hunting pink blazers with black velvet collars, plaid vests, shirts with ascots, and bit and spur ornaments on shoes and boots.

Photos, AP/Wide World

Plaids made an exciting fashion statement during the fall season in garments that ranged from sporty trousers to suits to evening wear and that were colorful, stylish, durable, and very wearable.

The other, equally prevalent trend took its inspiration from the U.S. Southwest. Leather frontier jackets dripping with fringe topped jeans or chambray skirts. Brightly colored Navajo patterned blanket cloth was used for coats and jackets, while knit sweaters copied these ethnic designs. Accessories included bolo neckties, silver and turquoise jewelry, and conch belts. Indian-inspired fabrics were used in belts and bags.

The hemline issue became moot with designers showing a range of lengths from above the knee down to the ankle. Karl Lagerfeld at Chanel did away with the hemline dilemma altogether when he showed a tunic-length jacket over ribbed tights.

Suits. The suit took on new importance as jackets—especially at Chanel and Armani—showed a new variety and inventiveness. They appeared in every length from cropped above the waist to below the hips. There were fitted, flared, and flyaway versions as well as slouchy styles. Newest were those that buttoned to the side with soft draping, boxy blazers adorned with crests, smoking jackets, cutaways, and redingotes. Carolina Herrera pushed posh black velvet motorcycle jackets decorated with gold studs.

Sweaters. The cardigan sweater enjoyed a resurgence of popularity in 1989. One of Yves St. Laurent's evening looks featured a lime green cardigan over a silk brocade floor-length side-slit skirt. Bill Blass tied an extra pair of "sleeves" as a scarf from the shoulders of his cashmere cardigans, and Carolina Herrera showed cardigans tied around the hips of easy wool jersey dresses. Creative patterns gave excitement to this classic.

Fabrics. High-voltage brights in tactile fabrics were favored. Tartan plaids found a new popularity and dominated one designer's collection: Isaac Mizrahi used them in everything from sporty flannel trousers to a strapless floor-length cashmere flannel evening dress. For evening, seductive velvet in black or Renaissance shades of moss green, copper, or burgundy was the overwhelming favorite in classic pieces such as sheath dresses, pants, smoking jackets, and easy shirts, while lavish brocades and sheers—often elaborately beaded and embroidered—made glittering evening statements.

Accessories. Vests were the best-selling accessory. Day versions were done in foulard or paisley prints; for evening they were elegant in tapestry or brocade. Next in popularity were big, bold stoles, wraps, ponchos, and serapes in elegant ruffle-edged cashmere knit versions, traditional fringed tweed or mohair styles, and fancy ethnic or folkloric patterns.

The most important jewelry trends included: lookalikes of first lady Barbara Bush's omnipresent three-strand fake pearls; crosses—as necklaces or pins—in simple gold metallic versions or elaborate Maltese or Coptic types, enameled or encrusted with gemstones; shoulder-grazing drop earrings; and, in tribute to *glasnost,* the "Russian" watch with Cyrillic markings and a red star on the face.

Footwear, when not in the equestrian or Western mood, was basic. Flat-heeled slippers or low-heeled pumps in lush dark suedes or highly polished leathers were the choice of most designers. Some featured embroidery on the vamp or had detachable bows or jeweled ornaments. For evening, the same styles were done in plain or patterned velvets, tapestry fabrics, or brocade.

Vests were a major fashion accessory in both men's and women's wardrobes and were popular for both casual attire and to enhance and glamorize evening wear.

© Marcio Madeira/Sipa

Menswear. Menswear for business had a looser, unconstructed yet traditional look in 1989. The look of the "sack" suit of the 1940s was revived in boxy, three-buttoned jackets with easy front-pleated trousers. Vests were important, either matched to suits or as accessories.

Ties were wider and in colorful geometric or Art Deco prints that called for plain shirtings. Footwear focused on classic loafers and wing tips, often done in suede. The trench coat in glazed, brushed, or rubberized cottons and the belted wrap in tactile cashmere-like fabrics were the favored coat styles. Here browns, olive green, and other earth tones were replacing gray and navy in solid, tweed, and plaid patternings.

In men's sportswear rugged outdoor looks flourished. Earth tones were brightened and blended with spice and citrus colorations. Fabrics seen most often were cotton corduroys and twills, denim, moleskin, and flannel in baggy trousers, jodhpurs, or jeans; calfskin, suede, and shearling in bomber jackets and duffel coats; and buffalo checks and frontier plaids for lumberjack shirts and jackets. Other important looks were waterproof hooded anoraks, field coats, or shooting jackets. Bulky pullovers or cardigan sweaters had textured stitching or were knit in multicolored ethnic motifs. Footwear completed the outdoor theme with chukka boots, hiking shoes, and sturdy moccasins.

The Fashion Industry. Beyond design, the fashion industry was undergoing changing times. Major retail store mergers, leveraged buy-outs, and bankruptcies were creating an unsettled atmosphere. (*See* RETAILING.)

In Paris, Yves St. Laurent went public, and the House of Dior precipitated a national uproar when it dismissed Marc Bohan, its French designer for the past 28 years, replacing him with an Italian, Gianfranco Ferre.

ANN M. ELKINS, *"Good Housekeeping"*

FINLAND

The year opened with a political development which reminded many of the game of musical chairs and caused a great deal of surprise throughout Finland. It had been announced that Matti Ahde, the vice-chairman of the Social Democratic Party, had resigned as speaker of Parliament, the second-ranking post in the nation. A few weeks later it became known that Foreign Minister Kalevi Sorsa, also of the Social Democratic Party, had resigned for internal party reasons and had been appointed speaker of the Parliament to succeed Ahde. In addition, the new foreign minister, Pertti Paasio, was installed as the chairman of the Social Democratic Party. Ahde subsequently was offered and accepted the post of head of the soccer pool organization.

Finland in July cemented its relations with Europe's other non-Communist states by becoming a member of the Council of Europe, now numbering 23 states. A joint forum of the democratic states of Europe, with headquarters at Strasbourg, France, the Council of Europe in 1989 celebrated the 40th anniversary of its founding.

Economic Developments. In order to remedy an overheated economy, the Finnish government had fashioned plans for reducing consumption, but they ended largely in failure and a prophesied slump never materialized. A boom in many sectors of the economy continued, leading to Finns living more than ever on credit. The government temporarily increased the sales tax by 0.5%; the Bank of Finland raised its interest rate, also to no avail, since it was announced on March 16 that the bank would retain a liberal loan policy. On March 17 the value of the Finnmark was increased officially by the Bank of Finland by 4%, which, however, in actual practice led to an increase in the Finnmark's purchasing power of 3%.

Diplomacy. Soviet President Mikhail S. Gorbachev made his first visit to Finland in October. He talked with President Mauno Koivisto and other Finnish leaders and declared that the Soviet Union had renounced any political, legal, or moral right to invade its Eastern European neighbors. Gorbachev also spoke favorably of Finnish-Soviet relations and of neutral Finland as a model of stability.

Of special interest to Finland as a Baltic nation was Gorbachev's announcement that four Soviet submarines armed with missiles and stationed in the Baltic Sea would be decommissioned. His speech was regarded by many Finns as the climax of a process of warming relations. (During the 1939 Winter War and World War II, Finland lost 12% of its territory and paid heavy reparations to the Soviets. The Finnish-Soviet Treaty of Friendship, Cooperation and Mutual Assistance—extended in 1955, 1970, and 1983—confirmed Finland's status as a neutral nation and also the country's right to trade with the West).

Yasir Arafat, chairman of the Palestine Liberation Organization, and Pope John Paul II also visited Finland during 1989.

Press and Culture. *Helsingin Sanomat,* Finland's biggest daily newspaper, celebrated its 100th anniversary in the fall. The first issue of *Päivälehti,* the predecessor of *Helsingin Sanomat,* was published on Nov. 16, 1889. A special tribute to the musical life of Finland occurred on July 17 when Esa-Pekka Salonen, a 31-year-old conductor, was named music director of the Los Angeles Philharmonic Orchestra.

ERIK J. FRIIS
"The Scandinavian-American Bulletin"

FINLAND • Information Highlights

Official Name: Republic of Finland.
Location: Northern Europe.
Area: 130,127 sq mi (337 030 km²).
Population (mid-1989 est.): 5,000,000.
Chief Cities (Dec. 31, 1987 est.): Helsinki, the capital, 490,034; Tampere, 170,533.
Government: *Head of state,* Mauno Koivisto, president (took office Jan. 27, 1982). *Head of government,* Harri Holkeri, prime minister (took office April 30, 1987). *Legislature* (unicameral)—Eduskunta.
Monetary Unit: Markka (4.277 markkaa equal U.S.$1, Nov. 6 , 1989).
Gross National Product: (1987 U.S.$): $87,700,000,000.
Economic Indexes (1988): *Consumer Prices* (1980 = 100), all items, 169.5; food, 170.1. *Industrial Production* (1980 = 100), 127.
Foreign Trade (1988 U.S.$): *Imports,* $20,914,000,000; *exports,* $21,662,000,000.

FLORIDA

Florida was the focus of national attention during the Miami riot in January 1989 and during the legislative debate over limiting abortion rights in October. Floridians may have been just as concerned about environmental issues and about new gun-control laws.

Abortion Debate. Gov. Bob Martinez called a special legislative session in October to limit abortions after the U.S. Supreme Court ruled that states could impose additional restrictions. Thousands of demonstrators from both the pro-choice and pro-life camps staged rallies in Tallahassee, but all were peaceful. The legislature, however, refused to act and eight bills that would have limited abortions and regulated abortion clinics were killed in committee.

Riot in Miami. One person was killed and at least a dozen others were injured during three nights of rioting beginning on January 16 in Liberty City, a predominantly black section of Miami. The rioting began when a Hispanic officer shot and killed a black man riding on a motorcycle. The officer involved was convicted of manslaughter in December.

People. Ileana Ros-Lehtinen became the first Cuban-American, the first Republican, and the first woman in Congress from Dade County. The conservative party loyalist rode a tide of Hispanic support to victory August 29 over Democrat Gerald F. Richman in an ethnically charged duel to succeed the late U.S. Rep. Claude Pepper (*see* OBITUARIES).

Alcee Hastings, Florida's first black federal judge, was convicted by the U.S. Senate of lying and conspiring to get $150,000 from de-

Jacksonville Chamber of Commerce

A new addition to the Jacksonville, FL, transportation scene was the automated skyway express, a 1.5-mi (2.4-km) stretch between the Convention Center (background) and Southern Bell. An express (sometimes referred to as a people mover) was also in operation in Miami.

fendants in a trial in return for a lenient sentence. He became the sixth federal official removed from office for an impeachable crime.

James Richardson, an Arcadia fruit picker convicted of poisoning his seven children, was cleared of the crime and released from prison after serving 21 years. Another Florida prisoner in the news was serial killer Theodore Bundy, who was put to death January 24 for the murder of a young girl. However, in the hours before his death he admitted to at least 16 other murders.

Environment. A water emergency was declared in south Florida in September after the rainy season failed to meet needed expectations. While mandatory water-use restrictions had been imposed in various parts of the state by regional water managers, urban areas were spared such curbs because rainfall picked up in October.

Federal and state rules were approved requiring shrimp fishermen to affix trapdoors in their trawling nets to avoid accidental drowning of sea turtles. However, the second annual alligator hunt was staged to thin a population that had skyrocketed since the reptile was placed on the endangered species list.

Transportation. A foul-up in road-building plans forced the delay and elimination of some projects. It culminated with the resignation of the state transportation secretary and an unproductive special legislative session in November to solve the problems. The tolls on Florida's turnpike were doubled to pay for refurbishing plazas along the route.

After five months of free service, a tri-rail system linking West Palm Beach, Fort Lauderdale, and Hialeah, connecting with Miami's Metrorail, did fairly well after fares were charged. Plans for a bullet train linking Tampa, Orlando, and Miami encountered obstacles, including Disney World balking at locating a station at the central Florida tourist mecca.

Legislation. A bill requiring adults to keep loaded guns away from children was passed during a special legislative session. A rash of accidental shootings that claimed the lives of several youngsters prompted the new law. It would impose a $5,000 fine and up to five years in prison for those convicted of breaking it. Bills aimed at cracking down on substance abuse became law. They included automatic suspension of the driver's license of anyone refusing to take a blood, breath, or urine test after being stopped for driving under the influence and drug screening of applicants for sensitive state jobs, such as Highway Patrol troopers and prison guards. A minimum, mandatory three-year prison sentence was established for anyone caught selling drugs within 1,000 ft (305 m) of a school. The legislature also okayed a ban on drilling for oil and gas in Florida's territorial waters.

GREG MELIKOV, *"The Miami Herald"*

FLORIDA • Information Highlights

Area: 58,664 sq mi (151 939 km²).
Population (July 1, 1988): 12,335,000.
Chief Cities (July 1, 1986 est.): Tallahassee, the capital, 119,480; Jacksonville, 610,030; Miami, 373,940; Tampa, 277,580; St. Petersburg, 239,480.
Government (1989): *Chief Officers*—governor, Bob Martinez (R); lt. gov., Bobby Brantley (R). *Legislature*—Senate, 40 members; House of Representatives, 120 members.
State Finances (fiscal year 1988): *Revenue,* $19,362,000,000; *expenditure,* $17,833,000,000.
Personal Income (1988): $204,788,000,000; per capita, $16,603.
Labor Force (June 1989): *Civilian labor force,* 6,380,500; *unemployed,* 386,700 (6.1% of total force).
Education: *Enrollment* (fall 1987)—public elementary schools, 1,172,000; public secondary, 493,000; colleges and universities, 489,964. *Public school expenditures* (1987–88), $6,661,680,000 ($4,001 per pupil).

FOOD

The food industry received both accolades and rebuffs in 1989. Indeed, one new product—the "juice box"—was praised and then banned in some locales. Consumers meanwhile were searching for convenience and good health, but without forgoing junk food.

New Products. In judging a competition for the "most significant food science innovation of the last 50 years," the Institute of Food Technologists awarded third place to the microwave oven and second place to the "safe canning of vegetables." But top honors went to the new "aseptive food container," familiar to young consumers as the "juice box" that transports fresh juice in school lunches without need for refrigeration. Aseptic processing is a "high temperature/short time" treatment in which liquids are sterilized and then placed in sterile containers. Aseptic cartons were banned in Minneapolis, and then in Maine and other jurisdictions, however. Facing mountains of waste with few good options for disposal, some municipalities decided to discourage any further use of nonbiodegradable cartons. The Minneapolis ordinance, similar to others, banned plastic food and beverage packaging with the exception of containers that were degradable, reusable, or recycled. Responding to the problem, the McDonald's Corp. and eight plastics producers announced in October a $16 million program to recycle plastic food containers.

Some new biotechnology products, however, were reducing the need for use of chemicals and elaborate packaging. Coming on-line were a genetically engineered tomato that repelled hungry caterpillars and engineered potatoes that resisted major potato viruses.

Some junk foods too became less "junky" when 13 food manufacturers announced they would reformulate their products to eliminate coconut, palm, and palm kernel oils—three fats more highly saturated than old-time lard.

Diets and Health. Television's Oprah Winfrey's "Optifast" diet, which reduced her weight by a celebrated 67 lbs (30 kg), helped spur new interest in liquid diets (or fasting). Dieters and the enlarging diet industry heard both good news and bad news in 1989. For good news, researchers at the Southern Illinois School of Medicine discovered that dieters usually do not fail to achieve their goals, as earlier studies had suggested; they found many dieters in the general population had lost 20% or more of body weight and had maintained the loss for two years or more. The bad news for the diet industry was that successful dieters ordinarily did not rely on external controls such as wonder drugs or weight-loss clinics. Instead, successful dieters personally had taken responsibility for regulating their weight.

As more people tried to slim down, more were found to have developed eating disorders trending toward bulimia (periodic gorging and purging) and anorexia (inability to consume adequate food). One researcher, Dr. Marilyn Crim, estimated that about 5% of all high school and college women displayed serious manifestations of one of these diseases, and another 20% showed minor symptoms.

In 1989 health-conscious citizens who had learned to monitor their cholesterol levels and who had found ways to bring levels down—such as eating oats—were surprised to hear that there is "good" as well as "bad" cholesterol. As a result of their efforts they were reducing not only "bad" cholesterol, which contributes to heart diseases, but also "good" cholesterol, which might prevent other diseases. Arguments flared among experts over what should be done about cholesterol.

Hunger and Malnutrition. Acute hunger was a product of civil war in Afghanistan and the Sudan. In Kabul, Afghanistan, a long-standing food shortage, evidenced by malnourished children, worsened in January 1989 when Soviet troops pulled out. In the Sudan civil war, food-assistance agencies often were frustrated by warring parties. The U.S. State Department helped relief organizations get food convoys permission to traverse rebel territory. Heroes of the relief effort were U.S. Rep. Mickey Leland (D-TX), who died in a plane crash while trying to help refugees in Ethiopia; and Egil Hagen, who organized the delivery of food shipments for people in the southern Sudan.

Elsewhere food shortages threatened political stability. Food riots occurred in Venezuela as supplies declined and prices rose. As the USSR worked its way through *perestroika,* scarce foods including sugar were rationed. In Poland a new non-Communist government pleaded for food assistance as Polish farmers hoarded grain in anticipation of hyperinflation. The U.S. Congress approved $125 million in food aid to Poland for fiscal year 1990. The United Nations noted that world food aid shipments declined by 25% in 1989.

A U.S. study found that children from low-income neighborhoods perform better on tests after a breakfast at school.

Food Prices. U.S. low-income residents felt the consequences of a 7% increase in food prices during 1989, including sharp rises in prices of red meats, poultry, eggs, fresh vegetables, and processed vegetables. Retail-food prices in Japan remained the highest among all developed Pacific Rim countries. But Japanese and other East Asian diets were shifting away from rice and other grains to the higher-priced meat, dairy products, sugar, and fats and oils. Meanwhile, many consumers in the United States were concerned about chemical sprays used on their fruits and vegetables, particularly the apple ripening agent Alar.

DON F. HADWIGER
Iowa State University

© Peter Turnley/Black Star

As part of the festivities marking the 200th anniversary of the French Revolution, government leaders from throughout the world gathered in Paris at President Mitterrand's invitation to celebrate the Declaration of the Rights of Man.

FRANCE

France in 1989 tried the role of mediator and facilitator on the international scene, sponsoring a number of international conferences and diplomatic initiatives that highlighted its special niche as a secondary world power with global ambitions. President François Mitterrand increasingly left domestic affairs to Prime Minister Michel Rocard while he concentrated on the European Community's (EC) consolidation into a single, borderless market—set for the end of 1992—and pursued other international affairs. For one week in July the world's spotlight was focused on France as the country celebrated the bicentennial of the French Revolution (*see* special report, page 238). Leaders of many of the world's wealthiest and poorest nations were invited to Paris by Mitterrand to celebrate the Declaration of the Rights of Man —and perhaps to rub shoulders in a way that had not occurred since the last North-South summit in Mexico in 1981.

At the annual summit of the world's seven wealthiest nations that followed the Bastille Day festivities, the Western leaders charged the European Community with coordinating Western aid to Poland and Hungary. It was a harbinger of the growing place that changes in Eastern Europe would occupy in French and Western European affairs through 1989.

Politics. The year opened on a pragmatic note, with Socialist Prime Minister Rocard, a centrist, telling the country's political factions, "We must face France's important problems together. This is my most important message for the new year." Rocard had just managed to settle weeks of strikes in the public sector without caving in to wage demands. By pursuing rigorous economic policies, Rocard—who many political observers had doubted still would be in office much into 1989—managed to disarm conservative critics. Even while some fellow Socialists openly questioned the prime minister's commitment to socialist goals, Rocard's political star continued to rise without serious interruption throughout 1989. By year's end Mitterrand, who will be in office until 1995, was hinting that he considered Rocard an eventual successor to the presidency.

In January an insider-trading scandal involving the state-owned Pechiney company briefly rocked the Socialist government with allegations that leaks from finance ministry officials allowed individuals, including one of Mitterrand's best friends, to profit from stock purchases. The individuals purchased large blocks of stock in Triangle Industries, Inc., an American packaging company, shortly before it was bought by Pechiney. What became known as the Pechiney affair started to fade with the resignation of a highly placed aide to Finance Minister Pierre Beregovoy and the indictment of five people, including the president's friend. In response to the scandal, Rocard initiated a strengthening of the Commission on Operations of the Bourse, the French equivalent of the U.S. Securities and Exchange Commission, which was considered widely a weak regulator of stock trading.

In municipal elections across the country in March, the Socialists showed surprising strength by taking away control of a number of major cities from conservative parties. Perhaps the most significant single aspect of the elections, however, was the emergence of the country's Greens, who captured up to 15% of the vote in some cities. Political analysts suggested the Greens' success indicated not only a growing interest in environmental issues, which the Greens champion, but a desire among the electorate to find an alternative outside the French political landscape's traditional left-right split. Another trend of the municipal elections, and the European Parliament elections in May, was the continuing decline in support for the French Communist Party.

In late August, Rocard visited the French South Pacific colony of New Caledonia, site of separatist violence in 1988 but subsequently the scene of one of the prime minister's most important successes. After a Rocard-inspired referendum of French voters in November 1988 approved a plan for more autonomous administration of the colony and for a vote on independence in 1998, the archipelago quieted down. Nationalist leader Jean-Marie Tjibaou, who had helped forge a peace plan during the violence, was gunned down in May 1989 by a radical separatist, but the islands remained calm. In October the Rocard government approved a full amnesty of participants in the May 1988 violence, a move criticized by family members of the French gendarmes and commandos killed in the uprising.

Domestic Affairs. Shortly after school began in September three teenage Muslim girls in the Paris suburb of Creil were expelled for wearing scarves over their heads in class. The girls' families said the teachings of the Koran required the girls to cover their hair in the presence of males outside the family, but school officials said France's strict adherence to school secularity ruled out any outward signs of religious faith. Within days girls in several other French cities had been expelled for the same reason, and the "affair of the veils" was launched.

The intensity of discussion of the issue reflected widespread French concern over integration of more than 3 million Muslims, mostly immigrant workers and their families from north Africa, into mainstream French life. The far-right National Front capitalized on the issue to draw attention to its anti-immigration doctrine, as it had done earlier in the year with controversy over proposed mosques in several French cities. Education Minister Lionel Jospin tried to calm troubled waters by stating veils should be allowed "only as a last resort" to avoid expulsion from school of any child, but critics including members of his own Socialist Party said the decision was a dangerous precedent for allowing "extremist religious thought" into the schools.

FRANCE • Information Highlights

Official Name: French Republic.
Location: Western Europe.
Area: 211,208 sq mi (547 030 km²).
Population (mid-1989 est.): 56,100,000.
Chief City (1982 est.): Paris, the capital, 8,706,963.
Government: *Head of state,* François Mitterrand, president (took office May 1981). *Chief minister,* Michel Rocard, prime minister (took office May 1988). *Legislature*—Parliament: Senate and National Assembly.
Monetary Unit: Franc (6.155 francs equal U.S. $1, Nov. 27, 1989).
Gross National Product (1988 U.S.$): $939,200,000,000.
Economic Indexes (1988): *Consumer Prices* (1980 = 100), all items, 171.8; food, 169.9. *Industrial Production* (1980 = 100), 108.
Foreign Trade (1988 U.S.$): *Imports,* $177,518,000,000; *exports,* $162,988,000,000.

On the cultural scene, a new glass-pyramid entrance to the Louvre museum was inaugurated in April amid both lavish praise and criticism—the kind of excitement the French like to create. Designed by American architect I. M. Pei, the pyramid is one of a large number of major architectural monuments commissioned by Mitterrand—including the Bastille Opera, the Grand Arch at La Défense, the Bercy Finance Ministry—and intended to make him the most "monumental" French leader since Napoleon.

Reform of French spelling, an old proposal that received renewed attention with publication in August of a book by an educator, a psychologist, and a linguist advocating widespread simplification of French orthography, won limited approval from Rocard. The prime minister in October said he opposed any large-scale reform, but asked the newly formed Superior Council of the French Language to study modifications including standardization of double consonants, past participle agreement, hyphen use, and creation of new words. Rocard told the council, meeting for the first time, "We need a French language for our time."

Economy. Despite a definite pickup by the end of 1988 after the recession of the mid-1980s, economists continued to emphasize the fragility of the French economy through 1989. In response to public employees' demands for higher wages, Prime Minister Rocard warned that significant wage increases were out of the question because the economy was "still convalescing."

Exports of goods and services continued to grow but at a slower rate than in 1988, while high consumer demand led to a jump in imports. The result was a year-end trade deficit estimated at $10 billion by the Organization for Economic Cooperation and Development (OECD), a disappointment after 1988's slight improvement over the previous year's trade imbalance of $8.9 billion. Inflation increased slightly to about 3.5% annually, well below rates in Britain and Spain, and within a half percentage point of principal trade partner West Germany—an important point psychologically for the French.

The French economy witnessed a continuing growth in employment that took root in 1987, but not at a sufficient rate to offset new entries into the job market. Consequently unemployment, which some economists had projected finally would drop into single digits sometime during the year, hovered stubbornly around 10%. More disturbing still was the OECD's projection that unemployment likely would increase slightly in 1990 to 10.25%. That is the kind of discouraging portent that has convinced growing numbers of French youth that little more than the unemployment line awaits them unless they develop a skill or continue their education beyond high school. As a result enrollment has surged in French universities—up 11% in 1989—leading to overflowing classrooms, overworked professors, and a national debate on the quality of French university education.

In September, Rocard and Beregovoy presented a 1990 budget that will increase spending by 5.3%, with a good part of that increase to cover interest payments on the national debt. The budget, nevertheless, included several signs of a loosening up of Rocard's "policy of austerity," including creation of 7,800 new public-sector jobs, primarily in education. In addition, Rocard presented his idea of a "growth pact" with public-sector workers. Designed to distribute the fruits of an improving economy—a growth in the gross domestic product (GDP) of about 3.5% as opposed to the 2.5% that had been anticipated—Rocard also planned the pact to assuage the kind of discontent that in 1988 led to extensive strikes. In addition to employment creation and professional training measures, the pact included a bonus of about $150 to every public-sector employee.

Despite these measures, a months-long strike of tax collectors continued into November, with Rocard flatly rejecting the collectors' salary demands as "excessive." The strike affected the collection of value-added taxes and forced the treasury to borrow more funds than anticipated.

Job actions against Peugeot, France's largest private-sector company, began September 4 and continued until October 5. A court order was issued to stop the sit-in.

© Hubert Raguet/Gamma-Liaison

Yet Rocard was not alone in facing worker strikes: Peugeot, the country's largest company, which was brought back from the brink of bankruptcy in 1984 by "miracle-worker" company President Jacques Calvet, was hit in September by a crippling strike that waylaid the production of 60,000 cars before workers returned to assembly lines in October. Workers had seen the company's handsome profits ($1.4 billion in 1988) and a 60% increase in productivity and said they deserved to share in Peugeot's improved fortunes. Calvet insisted, however, that the company's profits were needed for reinvestment in anticipation of what he described as approaching international car wars. Eventually workers halted the strike, receiving only minimal salary adjustments.

Foreign Affairs. A year of high international exposure commenced in January 1989, with a conference on chemical weapons called by President Mitterrand and attended by 149 nations. Mitterrand called the meeting to give renewed impetus to the United Nations Conference on Disarmament in Geneva, which had been trying unsuccessfully for ten years to achieve an international curb on chemical arms. The conference's final statement gave "full support" to UN stewardship in "enabling the international community to exercise vigilance with respect to the prohibition of the use of chemical weapons."

Also in January, French police arrested a leader of the Spanish Basque separatist movement outside the city of Bayonne. The arrest of José Antonio Urrutikoetxea, known as Josu Ternera, struck a formidable blow against the violent Basque separatist organization ETA and pointed out increased French-Spanish cooperation in combating terrorism. The arrest, following numerous expulsions of Spanish Basques to Spain, allowed the government to claim a tough antiterrorist record in the face of right-wing criticisms.

In April, France became directly involved in a worsening Lebanese conflict, dispatching a special envoy and a shipment of humanitarian supplies to shell-blasted Beirut. Mitterrand insisted France was acting as "the friend of all Lebanese," but Syrian-backed Muslims interpreted the initiative as pro-Christian, especially after the envoy made pro-Christian statements. The French effort was forced to make a temporary retreat.

In a move that drew heated criticism from French and Jews internationally, Mitterrand in May received PLO Chairman Yasir Arafat. It was the highest-level meeting ever accorded the Palestinian leader. Mitterrand wanted to acknowledge Arafat's December 1988 decision to recognize Israel and renounce terrorism. But a broader motive was to reestablish a French

(Continued on page 240.)

The French Revolution Bicentennial

As American diva Jessye Norman sang "*Allons enfants de la patrie* . . . " ("Go forth, children of the fatherland . . . ") to a rapt audience of 1 million on and around the Place de la Concorde in Paris, it seemed that on Bastille Day 1989—the bicentennial of July 14, 1789, when a prison symbolizing tyranny fell into the hands of the people—the French finally had come to terms with the French Revolution.

Despite early criticism over the cost of the bicentennial celebration to public coffers and the inconvenience it would cause Parisians, French President François Mitterrand found himself on July 15 basking in general praise for the festivities and was able to say they had brought the French people together.

Still, the year of commemorating the revolution's 200th anniversary left many French citizens with mixed feelings at best. Whereas other Bastille Days had been quiet national holidays reserved for neighborhood dances, a somber military parade down the Champs-Élysées, and fireworks over the Eiffel Tower, the fanfare around the bicentennial only heightened the schism that continues to mark the French over their most famous of revolutions. For many of them, the year was a celebration of the Declaration of the Rights of Man, a document that stands for the principle that every man is his own sovereign. Yet for many others, aware of the guillotine and the massacres of the period of the revolution called the Terror, there was nothing to celebrate in what they considered France's darkest gift to mankind: state-sponsored terrorism.

Yet no one could claim there was a lack of interest in the event. International seminars drawing intellectuals from around the world were held to discuss the French Revolution

© Michel Ginies/Sipa

© Gamma-Liaison

© D. Aubert/Sygma

The 200th anniversary of the French Revolution is celebrated with, clockwise from lower left: *an electric night parade, with the theme the "tribes of the world," attracting upward of 1 million revelers and an estimated 700 million television viewers worldwide; a large ball at the newly completed Paris opera house overlooking the Place de la Bastille; and the more traditional morning military parade with a formation of French fighter jets streaming the tricolor in plumes of smoke over the Arc de Triomphe.*

and its fruits. Some historians theorized that the revolution provided an example for future horrors, such as those under Stalin in the Soviet Union and Pol Pot in Cambodia, while others traced the spread of the principles of human rights and subsequent struggles for freedom following the French Republic's example. Others argued simply that France's absolute monarchy was already well on the evolutionary path of economic and constitutional reforms when the revolution took place, and that it frankly had been unnecessary. More than 1,320 books on the revolution were counted by one French intellectual review.

The bicentennial was celebrated throughout the year—one of the first commemorations a January concert of Republican songs that was disrupted violently by rampaging royalists screaming "Vive le roi!"—and throughout France, although the focus was Paris. And while many Parisians, expecting massive traffic jams and other discomforts that never materialized, abandoned their capital for the July 14 weekend, many others stayed home and joined a polite mob of tourists in the city's center to mark the occasion.

The day began with the traditional morning military parade, which enjoyed more viewers than in recent years. But the day's jewel was an artsy, eclectic, and very French night parade, also down the Champs-Élysées, dubbed the "Opéra Goude" after its artistic director, Jean-Paul Goude, a heretofore little-known French adman. The parade, whose theme was the tribes of the world, featured hundreds of torch-lighted French drummers, African singers atop a huge float of red, white, and blue, and waltzers carrying children—dressed in the attire of various nations—at their waists. There was artificial rain for the British contingent, artificial snow for the Soviets, American breakdancers and cheerleaders, and hundreds of Chinese students—the memory of the recent prodemocracy demonstrations and subsequent crackdown in Tiananmen Square still fresh—ringing the bells on the bicycles they pushed below a banner reading, "We will continue." The glue that held the delay-plagued parade together was Miss Norman's rendition of the *Marseillaise,* the French national anthem, her voice carrying beyond the Paris throngs to a worldwide television audience estimated at 700 million.

President Mitterrand had the good fortune to see his country's turn to host the annual summit of the world's seven wealthiest Western nations coincide with the bicentennial, so he chose the Bastille Day weekend for the summit to assure that for this one weekend, France would become the center of world attention. A minor flap arose when British Prime Minister Margaret Thatcher, one of the seven summit leaders, told French television that France was not the originator of the concept of human rights. Playing the magnanimous host, President Mitterrand acknowledged that France shared parentage with other, notably Anglo-Saxon, nations. Nevertheless, President Mitterrand, who likes to consider his country the "advocate" of the world's poorest nations, used the occasion to fashion an impromptu North-South summit, bringing together the world's wealthy with leaders from much of the Third World.

On August 26, in commemoration of the bicentennial of the Declaration of the Rights of Man, President Mitterrand opened the modernistic Arch at La Défense just west of Paris, atop which will be housed the Foundation of the Arch of Fraternity. The foundation is dedicated to watching over and encouraging reflection on human rights throughout the world.

HOWARD LAFRANCHI

Palestine Liberation Organization (PLO) Chairman Yasir Arafat (left) *met with French President Mitterrand at the Elysée Palace on May 2. Following the 90-minute discussion, Arafat declared that the PLO's charter calling for Israel's destruction had been "superseded."*

role in the affairs of the Middle East, a region to which France has long historical ties, and to forge a preeminent role for France in Europe-Middle East relations.

France's Lebanese initiative was redeployed in August as some of the worst shelling of the civil war was launched from Syrian positions against Beirut's Christian sector. Mitterrand dispatched five emissaries to world capitals, including Washington, Moscow, and the UN headquarters in New York, where an emergency meeting of the Security Council was called. Mitterrand also dispatched French warships to the Lebanese coast, but they returned without incident. The Paris daily *Le Monde* somewhat proudly editorialized on France's "obstinacy" in pursuing a diplomatic initiative concerning a conflict that it said other world powers had abandoned in frustration.

Also in August, Paris was the site of an international conference called to find a solution to the 20-year-long Cambodian conflict. Jointly hosted by France and Indonesia, the month-long peace conference involving 20 nations reflected French desire to play a diplomatic role in another region of the world where it has historical links. The conference, considered by most diplomats and analysts to have taken on an impossible task, began with an astonishing spirit of compromise. By its conclusion in early September, however, Cambodian factions were as far apart as ever, and the conference ended in stalemate and anticipation of renewed warfare in Cambodia.

The largest meeting of Chinese dissidents since the violent repression in June of the student-led democracy movement in Tiananmen Square took place in Paris in late September. The inaugural session of the Federation for Democracy in China, regrouping 167 expatriated Chinese now living in more than a dozen countries, culminated in an election of officers and pledges to pursue democratic reforms for mainland China. The Chinese government harshly criticized France for encouraging what it termed a "meeting of criminals" whose purpose was to undermine a sovereign government.

In July, Mitterrand assumed the rotating presidency of the European Community's Council of Ministers. At the outset of his six-month tenure, Mitterrand indicated he would place emphasis on securing a charter of social legislation for the Community, as well as on developing the 12-nation organization's environmental program and support for European audiovisual production. The French were instrumental in EC ministerial approval of a television programming policy that calls for a majority of programs "where practicable" to be of European origin—a policy that had U.S. officials and movie industry representatives crying "protectionism."

Yet Mitterrand was barely into his EC stint when events in Eastern Europe—first in Poland and Hungary, then in East Germany and Czechoslovakia—began increasingly to dominate Western European affairs. As a result, Mitterrand's emphasis in working with other European leaders on EC affairs shifted squarely to the essential economic issue of European monetary union. Mitterrand and other European leaders, including EC Commission President Jacques Delors, expressed their concern that progress toward a single EC market by the end of 1992 could be sidetracked if momentum toward monetary union was not maintained.

In an October speech to the European Parliament, Mitterrand said the appropriate response to prodemocracy movements in Eastern Europe "that are calling out for our values" was "simple: We must strengthen and accelerate the political construction of Europe." At a pivotal December summit of the European Council in Strasbourg, the French president scored a major victory when the EC leaders approved the calling of an intergovernmental conference for December 1990 to set the guidelines for achieving monetary union.

HOWARD LAFRANCHI, *Paris Bureau "The Christian Science Monitor"*

GARDENING AND HORTICULTURE

U.S. retail garden sales declined by about 10% from 1987 to 1988 but gardening activities remained steady, according to the National Gardening Survey conducted by the Gallup Organization for the National Gardening Association. The drop in retail sales was due to the widespread drought of 1988 and the fact that average summer temperatures in many parts of the United States were the hottest in 50 years.

Award Winners. The All-American Selections (AAS) judging produced ten 1990 AAS Awards in the categories of bedding plants, flowers, and vegetables from the 33 flower trial sites and 24 vegetable trial sites across North America.

Two F_1 petunias, "Polo Salmon" and "Polo Burgundy Star," received the AAS Bedding Plant Award. "Polo Salmon," an F_1 multiflora single petunia, produced 2-inch (5.08-cm) diameter, bright salmon flowers two to seven days earlier than other petunias and demonstrated tolerance to heat, drought, and severe weather. "Polo Burgundy Star," an F_1 multiflora, produced "the best star pattern in the multiflora class." Both were bred by Sluis and Groot, Enkhuizen, the Netherlands.

There were four award winners in the flower category. Achillea millefolium "Summer Pastels," a perennial, produces a varied color mix. Bred by K. Sahin, Zaden, Alphen aan den Rijn, the Netherlands, it thrives in full sun and tolerates hot, dry conditions. Celosia "Pink Castle," a semidwarf plant, was chosen for its unique quality of producing pink flowers previously only available as one color in a mixture. Also heat- and drought-tolerant, it was bred by Takii and Co. Ltd., Kyoto, Japan. Zinnia "Scarlet Splendor," an F_1 bred by W. Atlee Burpee Co., Warminster, PA, requires no staking and is both heat- and drought-tolerant. The most unusual annual to win was "Jolly Joker" pansy, which offers a unique new color combination: a rich velvety purple flower with an orange face. "Jolly Joker," bred by Ernst Benary Seed Growers Ltd., West Germany, also received the European 1990 Fleuroselect Gold Medal.

Two squash introductions received 1990 AAS Awards. "Cream of the Crop," the first creamy F_1 acorn squash to be awarded AAS status, bred by Musser Seed Co., Twin Falls, ID, produces 2- to 3-lb (0.9- to 1.36-kg) squash maturing in 85 days and stores well after harvest. The creamy golden interior has a nutty flavor and is particularly excellent for baking. The other squash, "Sun Drop," bred by Northrup King Co., Gilroy, CA, is the first oval summer squash available in North America. Other vegetables receiving AAS Awards were "Derby," an improved bush type bean, bred by Ferry-Morse Seed Co., Modesto, CA, and

Cream of the Crop squash, *above*

All-American SELECTIONS

Super Cayenne peppers, *right*

"Super Cayenne," an ornamental F_1 pepper that produces fiery peppers, bred by Bruce Christensen, Pan American Seed Co., West Chicago, IL.

The All-American Rose Selections Award (AARS) for 1990 went to only one introduction, "Pleasure," hybridized by William A. Warriner and introduced by Jackson and Perkins Co., Medford, OR. A floribunda type, it develops a 3- to 4-ft (.91- to 1.22-m) tall, upright plant that produces coral pink with salmon flowers. It is rated "good" for disease resistance to rust and powdery mildew.

New Publication. *Perennials for American Gardens* by Ruth Rogers Clausen and Nicholas H. Ekstrom was published by Random House in 1989. The book is a guide to more than 3,000 species, cultivars, and hybrids with up-to-date information about perennials grown in North America.

RALPH L. SNODSMITH
Ornamental Horticulturist

GENETICS

The year 1989 saw continued progress in understanding the roles of genes.

Maternal Inheritance of Blindness. In humans a genetically caused form of blindness, Leber's Optic Atrophy (LOA), results from the progressive degeneration of the optic nerve. Affected individuals are blind by age 20. The disease invariably is inherited from one's mother but, fortunately, does not cause blindness in all individuals carrying the gene.

In 1989, Dr. D. C. Wallace and his colleagues at Emory University School of Medicine in Atlanta reported that LOA is caused by a mutation in one of the genes in an individual's mitochondria. Mitochrondria—some several hundred are located in the cytoplasm of each cell—contain collectively only about 0.3% of a cell's total DNA. Mitochondrial DNA (mtDNA) codes for some of the proteins involved in the energy-related processes of the cell. The mutation that causes LOA results in a decreased level of energy in the cell. This decrease in available energy causes death of optic nerve fibers although most other body cells apparently continue to function normally. At present there is no known cure for this disease.

Unlike chromosomes of the nucleus that are inherited equally from both parents, mitochondria are inherited exclusively from the mother. Therefore, any genetic traits caused by mutation in mtDNA are strictly maternal in inheritance.

Role of Food Source in Speciation. It long has been a tenet of evolutionary theory that different populations of a species must be allopatric (physically isolated from one another) before genetic differentiation of the populations can occur. Now, however, studies on the fruit fly species *Rhagoletis pomonella* have indicated that at least one exception to this concept exists.

This fly uses the fruit of the hawthorn tree both as its food source and egg-laying site. Since the mid-1800s, the fly has been known to infest apple trees as well. Recent studies of the flies, collected from each of the two types of trees in the same locality, found that the two groups differed in gene frequencies to an extent that could not occur if the flies in the area had mated randomly with one another. They also found that the duration of egg-to-adult development time varied with whether the fly was collected from an apple (40 days) or a hawthorn (57 days) tree. In the field, the apple tree matures a few weeks before the hawthorn.

When taken into the laboratory, the two types of flies still can mate with one another, indicating that the speciation process is not yet completed. However, although the flies are sympatric (living in the same locality), the choice of a particular food source (hawthorn or apple) has caused the members of this species to be organized into genetically distinct populations.

Long-Distance Runners. In searching for evidence of genetic involvement in the performance of runners, Dr. J. H. Park and her associates at Vanderbilt University in Nashville studied the chemistry of the untrained wrist muscles of long-distance runners and the wrist muscles of a matched group of nonathletes. It was found that the levels of the two most important energy molecules, adenosine triphosphate and phosphocreatine, were significantly higher in the athletes. Further, it was found that in tests of strength of the untrained wrist muscles of both groups, there was far less buildup of lactic acid, the cause of fatigue, in the athletes. These findings support the belief that genes play a significant role in the achievements of long-distance runners.

Diet Control of Mimicry. Defenseless organisms can escape detection by predators if the shape and color of their bodies resemble (mimic) some object in their environment. Some organisms have more than one deceptive form and it is of great interest to discover the mechanism that "turns on" the appropriate gene complex in a particular situation.

The moth species *Nemoria arizonaria* produces two generations per year, one in early spring and the second during the summer. Caterpillars of the spring brood feed on the male flowers of oak trees and take on the flowers' golden color and fuzzy appearance. Those from the summer brood hatch after the flowers have fallen from the trees, feed on oak leaves, and develop into mimics of oak twigs which are greenish-gray in color and smooth in appearance.

In the laboratory, newly hatched caterpillars from both broods can be made to develop into either type of mimic (flower or twig), depending on the food (flowers or leaves) they are fed. This demonstrates that diet controls which mimic will be formed.

Gene Transfer to Human Cells. A new approach to melanoma cancer treatment involves the use of a patient's own lymphocytes to destroy the malignant cells. Dr. S. A. Rosenberg of the National Cancer Institute and associates, using DNA-recombinant techniques, transferred the bacterial gene for neomycin resistance to lymphocytes taken from a cancer patient. On May 22, 1989, these genetically engineered cells were returned to the patient's bloodstream. Periodic testing of the patient's lymphocytes for neomycin resistance would determine whether the number of surviving gene-altered cells are correlated with any observed regression of the cancerous tumor. This test was the first time a patient received an infusion of his own lymphocytes containing a foreign gene.

LOUIS LEVINE, *City College of New York*

GEOLOGY

There were significant advances in geology in 1989 as earth scientists learned more about dinosaurs, discovered buried mountain ranges, monitored global volcanic and seismic events, and followed a gradual rise in sea level.

Fossils. The oldest known lizard was discovered in Scotland by an amateur fossil collector. The 8-inch (19.2-cm), 340-million-year-old fossil is a lizardlike reptile some 40 million years older than the most ancient previously known reptile. In Colorado, a new species of dinosaur, *Denversaurus,* was identified after its remains—discovered in 1924—were located in collections at the Denver Museum of Natural History. About 20 ft (6 m) long, this plant-eating nodosaur was covered with bony armor plates, and spikes protruded from each shoulder. The specimen was identified previously as another species closely related to the nodosaurs.

The oldest dinosaur egg yet found in the Northern Hemisphere was discovered by paleontologists from Brigham Young University. Collected between the boundary of the Lower Jurassic and upper Lower Cretaceous systems in east-central Utah, the egg is about 150 million years old and may be the egg of an *Allosaurus*. This unusual fossil had been broken in half and would be about 4.5 inches (11.5 cm) by 2 inches (5.1 cm) if reconnected. Cross-sectional CAT (computerized axial tomography) scans revealed an early embryo surrounded by two layers of shell. The extra layer of shell may have developed because the egg was retained too long in the oviduct, perhaps because of stress or some predator that disturbed the dinosaur. The Utah paleontologists also reported new information on "Supersaurus" who, at 120 ft (36.5 m), is one of the longest dinosaurs known. Studies of its 135-million-year-old, 6-ft (1.8-m) hip bones revealed that the bones were hollow, an unexpected characteristic for a large sauropod dinosaur weighing as much as 30 tons. There was speculation that the hollow bone sections served to cut down on body weight and reduce the amount of bone the animal had to produce.

Quarry workers in Virginia uncovered what may be the most extensive dinosaur trackways in eastern North America. The more than 1,000 fossilized footprints provide new insight into the behavior of dinosaurs, revealing how the animals lived and moved. Most of the tracks were made by a three-toed carnivorous dinosaur that stood about 11 ft (3.5 m) tall and lived near the end of the Triassic period about 210 million years ago. About 10% of the tracks were made by a smaller three-toed, bipedal, birdlike dinosaur that reached about 8 ft (2.5 m) in length. Tracks made by a third animal remain a mystery but appear to have been made by a lumbering four-footed reptile that may have looked like a flattened crocodile with horns.

The most complete skeleton ever found of a *Tyrannosaurus rex* was uncovered in Montana; it was expected to give scientists a much clearer idea of the tyrannosaur's anatomy.

Meanwhile, the fossil beak of a bird that stood 6.5 ft (2 m) tall was found in Late Eocene rocks on Seymour Island off the Antarctic Peninsula. About 40 million years old, this huge bird had slender legs with a disproportionately large head and body and is similar to the giant meat-eating birds whose fossils were found in Florida and South America. The Seymour Island fossils suggest that a much milder climate existed in Antarctica during Eocene time.

Rising Sea Levels. Recent research hints that greenhouse gases in the atmosphere may be causing sea levels to rise. One theory assumes that a greenhouse warming could raise sea levels by melting ice caps and glaciers and thereby expanding the oceans. There is evidence that global sea level has risen by one tenth of an inch (.25 cm) per year over the past 100 years, or 10 inches (25.4 cm) per century. This could be a sign of global warming. However, some land masses are rising and some falling because of tectonic forces within the earth. Others are rebounding after huge glaciers melted away at the end of the last ice age about 6,000 years ago.

Volcanoes. The six-year activity of Hawaii's Kilauea Volcano's East Rift continued unabated but damage was minimal because 80% of the lava entered the ocean. In July an underwater volcano erupted off the coast of central Japan, ejecting great clouds of ash and steam and generating hundreds of earthquakes that rocked the Izu Peninsula. The eruption occurred on the ocean floor at a depth of about 330 ft (100.6 m). A September eruption of Nevada del Ruiz in Colombia spewed ash and steam 2,500 ft (762 m) high and hurled porous rocks and ash as far as 3 mi (4.8 km) from the crater. This volcano also had erupted in November 1985, melting parts of its ice cap and triggering floods and mudflows that wiped out a valley and killed 23,000 people. Elsewhere, in August, the U.S. Department of Energy started drilling an $8 million exploratory well in the heart of an active volcanic system in central California. This marked the initial phase of a plan to extract heat energy from buried molten rock in volcanic regions. Information gained from the test hole in the Long Valley Caldera will help determine the feasibility of generating geothermal energy in the area.

Earthquakes. A devastating earthquake struck northern California shortly after 5 P.M. on October 17, resulting in the loss of 67 lives and causing billions of dollars in damage. The quake, which was centered near Hollister, CA, 80 mi (129 km) southeast of San Francisco, measured 7.1 on the Richter scale. As the powerful temblor rolled through the San Francisco Bay area it toppled structures, including a section of the Bay Bridge, and caused a portion of a major highway to collapse during rush hour, killing many commuters. *See also* feature article, page 50.

The second major quake in two months hit the Soviet Union on January 23. The temblor, measuring 7 on the 12 point Soviet earthquake scale, buried several central Asian villages in Tajikistan and killed more than 250 people. However, it was not as destructive as the Dec. 7, 1988, quake that caused 25,000 deaths. In Japan, on February 19, a quake measuring 5.5 on the Richter scale hit Tokyo and much of the northern part of the country. A second quake measuring 6 was felt in Tokyo and Yokohama in April, and a major quake of 7.1 on the Richter scale struck near Honshu Island on November 2. Casualties and damage were minimal in these quakes. More than 30 mild earthquakes hit California's Imperial Valley on March 6, raising concern because the tremors were located near the San Andreas fault. An April 3 quake measuring 4.6 on the Richter scale was centered under Newport Beach about 40 mi (64 km) southeast of Los Angeles. And the San Francisco area woke up to a 4.9 magnitude earthquake in August. Unlike the October 17 earthquake, little damage were reported from these two temblors.

On April 25 a strong 6.8 magnitude quake struck Mexico City and Acapulco, cracking buildings and panicking people who remembered the killer earthquake of 1985. The New Madrid, MO area was the center of an April 27 temblor felt in Arkansas, Missouri, Kentucky, and Tennessee. Measuring 4.7 on the Richter scale, the quake originated in the New Madrid fault zone which stretches from southern Illinois to Arkansas. This seismic zone was also the center of several severe quakes in the winter of 1811 and 1812.

The earth's largest earthquake in at least 12 years rocked the Pacific Ocean floor on May 23. It struck about 500 mi (805 km) southwest of New Zealand along the Macquarie Ridge, along the boundary of the Pacific Plate, and an extension of the Australian Plate. This extremely powerful quake apparently did no damage because of its isolated location.

Plate Tectonics and Earth Structure. The remains of a previously unknown mountain range were discovered by Canadian geophysicists. It is an area of great underground faults and folds similar to those that form the roots of the Appalachian and Rocky Mountains. Stretching more than 621 mi (1 000 km) from Great Bear Lake to the Beaufort Sea, the mountains apparently were created as the result of a collision between North America and an unknown landmass about 1 billion years ago.

Plate movements also were responsible for a collision between the African Plate and the Eurasian Plate in the Mediterranean area. In a smashup that has lasted millions of years, the plates continue to crash together causing the Mediterranean to shrink while certain smaller regions like the Aegean sea gradually are growing. This process occurs where the edge of one plate is subducted, or slips, underneath another. American, Greek, and German geoscientists are monitoring satellite data to measure the motions of the crustal blocks involved in the ongoing tectonic process.

A new insight into the formation of the ocean floor was obtained with the geophysical equivalent of a CAT scan of the East Pacific Rise, an ocean ridge off the coast of Mexico. The new data help geologists to understand the structure of the magma chamber that holds the molten rock that is extruded during seafloor spreading. Seismic waves reveal that a region of hot rock about 3.7 mi (6 km) wide and almost 1 mi (1.6 km) deep underlies the ocean ridge. Submarine eruptions pour lava out of vents in the axis of the ridge. This produces new ocean floor and spreads the existing ocean floor apart.

WILLIAM H. MATTHEWS III
Lamar University

GEORGIA

The successes and failures of politicians kept the interest of Georgians in 1989.

Politics. Former Atlanta Mayor Maynard Jackson defeated City Council member Hosea Williams by a four-to-one landslide vote. Jackson's popularity in the polls had led City Council President Michael Lomax to withdraw from the race two months before the election. Jackson had made history in 1973 by becoming Atlanta's first black mayor to be elected. Meanwhile, the outgoing mayor of Atlanta, Andrew Young, was preparing to run for governor in 1990 in a crowded field that included Lester Maddox, former governor (1967–71), and, for a time, University of Georgia football coach Vince Dooley. Dooley resigned from the coaching post he had held for 25 years to enter the race, but later announced his decision not to run.

U.S. Rep. Newt Gingrich, serving his sixth term, was elected House Republican whip in 1989, but later in the year Rep. Bill Alexander (D-AR) filed a complaint against him, charging him with illegal campaign contributions and with using his official letterhead to solicit business for a travel agency. Earlier in 1989, a business deal of Gingrich's was questioned as a possible violation of House rules, but a formal investigation was not opened.

Georgia Sen. Wyche Fowler (D) was chosen assistant floor leader of the U.S. Senate and was appointed to the powerful Appropriations Committee. And former Republican state Sen. Paul Coverdell was appointed by President Bush to head the Peace Corps.

... Mayor Maynard ... his wife Valerie ... ight returns, Oc- ... s returned over- ... y hall.

Meanwhile, former 4th District U.S. Congressman Pat Swindall was convicted of nine counts of perjury, stemming from testimony about his alleged involvement in a money laundering scheme to obtain an $850,000 loan. Swindall was sentenced to one year in prison.

Legislation. Passage of a $7.5 billion budget was the major activity of the General Assembly. The fiscal 1990 budget, which was increased $1.25 billion over the previous year's budget, included funds for education programs, teacher pay raises, and highway and prison construction. Also passed was a one-cent hike in the state sales tax—the first such hike since 1971. A new system for land-use planning also was approved. Legislation that failed to pass included a proposal from Gov. Joe Frank Harris (D) to raise the gasoline tax, a referendum permitting a state lottery, and a reform plan regulating insurance rates. The legislature also was called into special session in September to resolve a legal problem involving taxation of federal pension benefits.

Business. Atlanta continued to be recognized as a business center. In a national sur- ... y corporate ... ce to locate ... u also re- ... d fastest- ... on—not s ... surveys th ... ould sur- p ... mber of workers hire ... ses.

The manufactu ... d a record $3.1 billion in future ... arily in the paper and wood indust ... -based RJR Nabisco Inc. became the ... keover in history when, for $25 bil ... hlberg Kravis Roberts and Company ... d the food and tobacco giant in early 1989. Just north of Atlanta, an interesting transaction occurred when movie star and native Georgian Kim Basinger purchased the small town of Braselton (pop. 500) for $20 million.

I. M. Pei, Cesar Pelli, and Kevin Roche each contracted to design a landmark skyscraper in the Atlanta area.

Disaster. On November 9 a U.S. Navy fighter jet preparing to land at Dobbins Air Force Base in Smyrna, an Atlanta suburb, crashed into an apartment complex. One person was killed and at least three two-story apartments were destroyed in the accident.

Sports. Atlanta enthusiastically presented itself to the International Olympic Committee for consideration as the location for the 1992 Olympic Games. As the only U.S. representative, Atlanta is in competition with five international cities, including Athens, Greece. If Atlanta is selected, plans call for Olympic athletes to utilize a domed stadium which also would be the new home of the Falcons, the city's professional football team. The dome's biggest booster was Governor Harris, who pushed through legislation that increased the local hotel tax in order to finance the $210 million construction of the "Georgia Dome."

KAY BECK, *Georgia State University*

GEORGIA • Information Highlights

Area: 58,910 sq mi (152 576 km²).
Population (July 1, 1988): 6,342,000.
Chief Cities (July 1, 1986 est.): Atlanta, the capital, 421,910; Columbus, 180,180; Savannah, 146,800.
Government (1989): *Chief Officers*—governor, Joe Frank Harris (D); lt. gov., Zell Miller (D). *General Assembly*—Senate, 56 members; House of Representatives, 180 members.
State Finances (fiscal year 1988): *Revenue,* $10,892,000,000; *expenditure,* $9,763,000,000.
Personal Income (1988): $96,779,000,000; per capita, $15,260.
Labor Force (June 1989): *Civilian labor force,* 3,254,500; *unemployed,* 195,600 (6.0% of total force).
Education: *Enrollment* (fall 1987)—public elementary schools, 795,000; public secondary, 316,000; colleges and universities, 224,066. *Public school expenditures* (1987–88), $3,842,715,000 ($3,562 per pupil).

Scrap text:

...ur goal of $75,000.00.
...i Annual Fund has increased more than 325 per ce...
...five years, and the Phonathon has been a major ...
this increase in support. Last year, for example, ...
...n secured pledges of more than $20,000.00.
...ore than ever, Wingate College needs gifts for
...ions from loyal alumni to carry on the tradition of
...llence. The Alumni Phonathon can provide this support
with your participation.
Be ready for our call in February.

© Orban/Sygma

© Witt/Sipa

With the opening of the Berlin Wall between East and West Germany on November 9, thousands of East Germans crossed into West Berlin, where they formed long lines to pick up "welcome" money of 100 marks (about $54), which West Germany traditionally has given East Germans on their initial visit to the West. By year's end nearly 11 million East Germans had visited West Germany and West Berlin.

GERMANY

With the dismantling of the Berlin Wall, 1989 marked the reemergence of an old question: Would Europe once again have a single state uniting almost 80 million Germans? In 1989 the two once-unified German states—the Federal Republic of Germany (FRG) or West Germany, and the German Democratic Republic (GDR) or East Germany—celebrated the 40th anniversary of their foundings. Both states were the product of the Cold War. Unable to agree with the Soviet Union on a common policy for postwar Germany, the victorious Western allies (the United States, Britain, and France) in May 1949, created the Federal Republic from their zones of military occupation. In October 1949 the German Democratic Republic was formed from the Soviet zone. Forty years later, as the Cold War era in international relations comes to an end, the question as to the future of the two Germanys became a major topic in European and world politics.

After years of steady improvement, relations between the two states sharply worsened because of the flight from July to early November of almost 200,000 East Germans to the West via the GDR's "fraternal Socialist allies" of Hungary, Czechoslovakia, and Poland. The "great escape" attracted worldwide attention and was a great embarrassment to East Germany in its anniversary year. It was also a major factor in the downfall of the GDR's leader, Erich Honecker, who was forced to resign in October after 18 years of rule.

At first the GDR accused the Federal Republic of planning and instigating the flight in order to destabilize the country and force a reunification. The West German government responded by urging the GDR to adopt a program of democratic reforms similar to those in Poland, Hungary, and the Soviet Union.

By the end of the year, East Germany had dropped its attacks on West Germany as its new leadership desperately tried to hold the country together. The GDR then proposed a network of economic, cultural, and political treaties which would bring the two states closer together. But many GDR citizens wanted more—a single German state. In late November, West German Chancellor Helmut Kohl proposed a ten-point plan for reunification, which was attacked sharply by the GDR government and the Soviet Union. In December, Kohl made the first official visit of a West German head of government to East Germany. While he and his GDR counterpart, Hans Modrow, disagreed on reunification, Kohl's announcement of a multibillion-dollar economic aid package met with popular approval.

Most East Germans in 1989 had their own personal reunion with the West. After the intra-German borders and the Berlin Wall were opened in early November, almost 11 million people, over two thirds of the country's population, visited West Germany and West Berlin.

Federal Republic of Germany (West Germany)

In spite of a strong economy and improving East-West relations, 1989 was a difficult year for Chancellor Helmut Kohl and his ruling Christian Democratic Union (CDU). At elections in West Berlin, Frankfurt, and the June European Parliament poll, the CDU lost heavily to the Social Democrats and a new right-wing protest party, the Republicans. There were numerous reasons for voter discontent with the chancellor. The 1988 tax law changes, especially the provision for a withholding tax on interest and dividend payments, were very unpopular with his party's middle-class clientele. Cuts in the health-insurance system upset broader sectors of the population. The extension of the length of compulsory military service from 15 to 18 months did not help Kohl's status among younger voters. A shortage of affordable housing in many large cities cost the government support in urban areas. The housing problem, coupled with the government's generous support of ethnic German settlers from the Soviet Union and Eastern Europe, provided the right-wing Republicans with an effective antiforeigners campaign theme.

In April, Chancellor Kohl attempted to respond to his critics and stem the loss of voters. The withholding tax was repealed. The length of military service was cut back to 15 months. New restrictions on foreigners seeking asylum and cuts in benefits for ethnic German settlers were announced. Some social programs such as family allowances were expanded and a new five-year public housing program—the first since 1986—was passed.

After these changes, Kohl was able to retain the chancellorship. In September he was reelected national chairman of the CDU with more than three quarters of the vote, thus ensuring that he would be the party's top candidate in the 1990 national election.

Unlike the Christian Democrats, the Free Democratic Party (FDP), the junior partner in the governing coalition, did not lose any significant support during 1989. This was largely due to the popularity of Foreign Minister Hans-Dietrich Genscher, the titular head of the party. Genscher in 1989 reached the zenith of his power and influence. In April, capitalizing on Kohl's political weakness, Genscher was able to persuade him to challenge the United States and Great Britain and provoke a crisis in the North Atlantic Treaty Organization (NATO) by calling for negotiations with the Soviet Union over short-range nuclear weapons without any modernization or deployment of the existing Lance missile system. Genscher also played the major role in negotiations with Hungary and Czechoslovakia over the release of the thousands of GDR citizens who had occupied West German embassies.

Although the Social Democrats (SPD), the major opposition party, made only modest gains at local elections throughout 1989, the party was able to overtake the Christian Democrats in national opinion polls and was well-positioned for the 1990 national election. During 1989 the Socialists continued to move toward the center of the political spectrum. Two major questions, however, remained unanswered as the SPD prepared to face the 1990 elections: Who would be its candidate for chancellor and what party would be its possible coalition partner? While Oskar LaFontaine remained more popular among voters than his chief rival, Hans-Jochen Vogel, he lacked the support of the party's rank-and-file membership and its leadership in Bonn that Vogel, the SPD's candidate in 1983, enjoyed. The party also was divided over whether it should form a coalition with the Greens or with the Free Democrats after the election. There was also a possibility of a three-party coalition.

West Germany's peace and environmentalist party, the Greens, made small but steady electoral gains in 1989 at local elections and at the June European Parliament election.

The Economy. In 1989 the economy grew for the seventh straight year. Real growth reached almost 4%, the highest level since 1976. Industrial output reached almost 90% of capacity, a 20-year high. Unemployment dropped to about 7.6%, the lowest figure since 1982. Sharp increases in capital investments for new plants and machinery and a surge in foreign demand

WEST GERMANY • Information Highlights

Official Name: Federal Republic of Germany.
Location: North-central Europe.
Area: 95,977 sq mi (248 580 km²).
Population (mid-1989 est.): 61,500,000.
Chief Cities (Dec. 31, 1986 est.): Bonn, the capital, 291,400; West Berlin, 1,879,200; Hamburg, 1,571,300; Munich, 1,274,700.
Government: *Head of state,* Richard von Weizsäcker, president (took office July 1, 1984). *Head of government,* Helmut Kohl, chancellor (took office Oct. 1982). *Legislature*—Parliament: Bundesrat and Bundestag.
Monetary Unit: Deutsche mark (1.687 D. marks equal U.S.$1, Dec. 27, 1989).
Gross National Product (1988 U.S$): $1,120,000-000,000.
Economic Indexes (1988): *Consumer Prices* (1980 = 100), all items, 122.4; food, 117.2. *Industrial Production* (1980 = 100), 111.
Foreign Trade (1988 U.S.$): *Imports,* $248,880,-000,000; *exports,* $322,524,000,000.

for German products were the major factors in this strong economic performance. In 1989, West Germany retained its position as the world's largest trading nation. Its export surplus reached an all-time high of $75 billion, a 9.4% jump over 1988. Many of West Germany's neighbors, and the United States, want the Federal Republic to stimulate its economy in order to increase imports and reduce the large trade surplus. The robust economy, however, was also partly responsible for a rise in inflation to more than 3%.

Terrorism. After several years of relative inactivity, the terrorist Red Army Faction struck in late November with a firebomb that killed Alfred Herrhausen, the head of West Germany's largest bank and a chief economic adviser to Chancellor Kohl. Herrhausen had been a major spokesman for West Germany's business community and had proposed far-reaching investment plans for the reconstruction of the East German economy. His high visibility as Germany's "master of money" and strong advocacy of German reunification along capitalist lines made him a prime terrorist target.

Foreign Policy. West German-U.S. relations in 1989 were characterized by several major differences over weapons sales to Third World countries and NATO defense strategy. In both cases, however, the problems between the two countries were resolved at least temporarily. During his May visit to the Federal Republic, U.S. President George Bush also left little doubt that the U.S. government considers West Germany to be one of its most important European allies, a "partner in leadership."

In early January the Kohl government sharply rejected U.S. charges, first leaked to the media, that German companies were designing and building a large chemical-weapons plant in Libya. Two weeks later, however, the West German government admitted that the charges were indeed true, and the government began legal action against the offending firms.

Over U.S. government objections, the government in April called for NATO to negotiate with Moscow over short-range missiles and nuclear artillery. The Federal Republic also flatly rejected the proposals of President Bush and Prime Minister Thatcher to modernize the short-range forces before any negotiations with the Soviets. For the first time in the post-World War II era, West Germany was challenging openly the United States on an important NATO policy.

In spite of differences over the reunification question, West Germany's relations with the Soviet Union and other Eastern European countries improved in 1989. In June, Soviet President Mikhail Gorbachev paid his first visit. During his stay two major economic agreements were signed. The pacts solidified West Germany's position as the Soviet Union's largest Western trading partner.

© Regis Bossu/Sygma

West German Chancellor Helmut Kohl, left, *met Polish Prime Minister Tadeusz Mazowiecki during a visit to Poland in November that was cut short by events at the Berlin Wall.*

German Democratic Republic (East Germany)

In 1989 the winds of change from Moscow finally reached East Germany with gale force. By year's end, the exodus of hundreds of thousands of its citizens to the West, the protests of millions who remained, and the revelations of widespread corruption by the ruling party elite brought the GDR to the brink of disintegration. After years of resisting the "new thinking" of Mikhail Gorbachev, Erich Honecker, the GDR's hard-line leader since 1971, stepped down from his posts as the leader of the Socialist Unity Party (SED) and head of state. Honecker's departure followed in the wake of the flight of GDR citizens to the West and massive demonstrations in East Berlin, Leipzig, Dresden, and other cities. Many of the riots and demonstrations broke out shortly before and during the official October 7–8 anniversary celebrations and the visit of Gorbachev.

Honecker's successor, Egon Krenz, was, at 52, the youngest member of the SED Politburo. Krenz had been in charge of the state security apparatus and the party's youth organizations. In an effort to relieve tensions after taking office, Krenz ordered police and security forces not to disrupt peaceful demonstrations and allowed the media to report on the antigovernment protests. He promised a dialogue with nonparty dissident groups, including the New Forum, the most prominent of the new groups.

Following trips to Moscow and Warsaw in November, Krenz dismissed many major party and state officials. However, the leader of the Liberal Democratic Party, one of the four small parties tolerated by the Communists, called for a special session of parliament to seek the resignation of the entire government.

In mid-November a new government with 11 non-Communist members was elected by the parliament. The new prime minister, Hans Modrow, a longtime intra-party critic of the Honecker regime, pledged radical changes, including changing the Communists' monopoly on power. But the massive demonstrations calling for free elections, a genuine multiparty system, the abolition of the secret police, and an uncensored press continued.

In a gamble to stop the flight of its people to the West, the party on November 9 announced that the border between the two states and the two halves of Berlin would be opened. That evening thousands of East Berliners went through the Wall converging on the Brandenburg Gate. The scenes of joy and tumult were broadcast worldwide. Over the first weekend more than 3 million East Germans visited West Germany and most returned.

But the opening of the Wall did not save the Krenz regime. He was unable to shake off his association with the discredited old guard. Forced to beat a steady retreat in the face of continued mass protests and the revelations of widespread corruption in the old Politburo to which he belonged, Krenz lost the support of his party. In early December after only 47 days in power, he and the entire Politburo and Central Committee of the SED resigned. They were replaced by a 25-member commission, which was to administer the party until a new party congress could be convened. Two days later Krenz also stepped down as head of state, and was replaced by Manfred Gerlach, the head of the Liberal Democratic Party.

East Germans were shocked and infuriated to learn, from their newly aggressive media, that some Communist Party leaders had built lavish villas for themselves and their children. Others had set up corporations to sell arms, antiques, and artwork, taken from East German museums, to foreign buyers and then pocket the hard-currency proceeds.

Responding to the uproar over the corruption issue, the government and party expelled nine of the old members of the Politburo. A few days later, seven of the nine were imprisoned. Honecker, who was seriously ill, was placed under house arrest. More than 100 other leading party functionaries also were arrested.

Following the mass resignations, Gregor Gysi, a 41-year-old reformist lawyer, was chosen as the Communists' new leader at a special party congress. He, unlike Krenz, did not assume the presidency. The SED's new leader also called for free elections and supported the constitutional changes that repealed the provision granting the party a "leading role" status. In spite of these changes the party at year's end was in disarray.

The virtual collapse of the party left the remaining authority in the country in the hands of the government, headed by Prime Minister

EAST GERMANY • Information Highlights

Official Name: German Democratic Republic.
Location: North-central Europe.
Area: 41,826 sq mi (108 330 km^2).
Population (mid-1989 est.): 16,600,000.
Chief Cities (mid-1987 est.): East Berlin, the capital, 1,246,872; Leipzig, 549,229; Dresden, 519,524.
Government: *Head of state,* Manfred Gerlach, chairman of the Council of State (took office Dec. 1989). *Head of government,* Hans Modrow, prime minister (took office Nov. 1989). General Secretary of the Socialist Unity (Communist) Party, Gregor Gysi (took office 1989). *Legislature* (unicameral)—Volkskammer (People's Chamber).
Monetary Unit: DDR mark (1.95 DDR marks equal U.S.$1, July 1989).
Gross National Product (1988 U.S.$): $207,200,000,000.
Economic Index (1988): *Industrial Production* (1980 = 100), 134.
Foreign Trade (1987 U.S.$): *Imports,* $28,786,000,000; *exports,* $29,870,000,000.

East Germany's Socialist Unity (Communist) Party met in December for a party congress following the resignation of new party leader Egon Krenz. Liberal lawyer Gregor Gysi was elected by the congress to the post of party chairman.

© Sichov/Sipa

Hans Modrow. At meetings with opposition groups and Protestant church leaders the government agreed to hold new elections on May 6, 1990. The new government dissolved the hated State Security Ministry ("Stasi") and assigned its intelligence responsibilities to organizations reporting directly to the prime minister. Visa requirements for visiting West Germans also were abolished, effective on Christmas Eve.

But many East Germans appeared unwilling to wait, or to give any new government a chance at implementing full-scale reforms. By mid-November unification with West Germany was added as a theme to many demonstrations. At the weekly marches in Leipzig, the nerve center of mass protest, banners and posters proclaiming *Deutschland—Einig Vaterland* (Germany, One Fatherland) appeared in increasing numbers accompanied by dozens of large West German flags. This new theme of the street protests mirrored the unification plans announced by the West German government and the major Bonn opposition parties. Due to agreements that date back to the end of World War II, both countries' allies did not wish to see the reunification process go forward too quickly. In view of this, U.S. Secretary of State James Baker paid a visit to the Democratic Republic in mid-December, and many Western powers asked the Kohl government to tone down its statements on the reunification issue.

Economy. For the fourth consecutive year the GDR's economy failed to meet the growth targets of the most recent five-year plan. Real growth was less than 1% and inflation, as well as widespread shortages of consumer goods, were major problems.

East Germany was burdened by aging industrial plants, shortages of labor and spare parts, and a decrepit infrastructure. The country's roads, railbeds, canals, sewers, and communications system were all in need of modernization. Exports had stagnated as the GDR increasingly competed with East Asian countries such as Taiwan and Korea. Products such as machinery and machine tools, which were competitive on the world markets in the 1960s and 1970s, were difficult to sell even to other Eastern European countries.

The economy also was weakened by huge state subsidies for housing and basic foodstuffs, such as bread and milk. The prices for such items had not increased in 40 years. Subsidies consumed more than one fifth of the country's gross national product. The system of central economic planning and the concentration of the country's 3,500 factories into *Kombinats,* large corporations organized by industrial sector, such as chemicals and steel, were further hindrances to economic development. The *Kombinats* were seen as monopolies which discourage competition and innovation. Following Honecker's departure, GDR economists admitted that the country's hard-currency foreign debt was actually more than $20 billion instead of the previous official figure of about $5.5 billion.

Unlike other Eastern European countries, however, the GDR had received extensive public and private aid, estimated at almost $4 billion annually, from West Germany. These funds had helped to prevent a deterioration of economic conditions to the extent seen in Poland or the Soviet Union. West Germany offered massive public and private investments to modernize the GDR if it moved toward a market economy and pluralist democracy. Many West German firms had begun to scout their prewar locations. A joint FRG-GDR economic commission to guide intensified trade and investment cooperation was established in December.

West Berlin

Voters in the divided city in January surprised political observers by replacing the Christian Democratic-Free Democratic government of Eberhard Diepgen with a new coalition composed of the Social Democrats and the Greens, led by the new Lord Mayor, Walter Momper. It marked the first time the Greens had formed a government with the Social Democrats at the state level since 1986. A majority of the cabinet members in the new government were women, a first in Berlin and German political history.

But an even greater surprise was the success of a new right-wing party, the Republicans, who received almost 8% of the vote—enough to gain admittance to the city's parliament. Led by a former Waffen SS officer, the Republicans campaigned on a strong antiforeigner theme and capitalized on dissatisfaction with the Bonn government's housing and health policies. On the evening following the vote more than 10,000 protesters took to the streets to demonstrate against the new party, calling for its prohibition as a "fascist" organization.

In spite of these problems the city's economy grew by a healthy 3%. Efforts to make West Berlin a major center of research and technology continued. In June, Berlin was selected as the site for a new research program in automation and robot technology.

By year's end, West Berlin's leaders were anticipating that the end of the city's isolation from East Germany and Eastern Europe could allow it to become once again Europe's major economic and cultural center between Paris and Moscow. To that end Mayor Momper held meetings with his East Berlin counterpart to discuss cooperative projects in transportation and economic development.

DAVID P. CONRADT, *University of Florida*

GREAT BRITAIN

The longest-serving British prime minister of the 20th century reached another milestone in 1989, celebrating on May 4 her tenth year in office, but for Margaret Thatcher, it was a tough ride for the remainder of the year. In May political observers were hailing her achievements in her decade as prime minister, particularly in reviving the English economy. Abroad, the former confidante of President Ronald Reagan was enjoying a good relationship with the openly admiring Soviet President Mikhail Gorbachev.

Troubled Times. Thatcher, however, had to endure the "summer of discontent," a somewhat loose reference to a period of industrial unrest that began in the spring and lasted into the autumn, when rail workers, engineers, personnel from the state-owned British Broadcasting Corporation, passport office employees, dockworkers, and ambulance drivers went on strike. Thatcher's Conservative Party floundered in European Parliament elections. She was blamed for being "anti-European" because of her resistance to full membership in the European Monetary System. And in July, she was castigated for a cabinet reshuffle that replaced Sir Geoffrey Howe, foreign secretary for six years, with John Major, a junior minister with no foreign experience.

Thatcher's horizons continued to cloud as doctors claimed her reforms of the National Health Service were preparations for its privatization. A flat-rate community charge, known as the "poll tax," provoked the citizenry's ire, as did the privatization of public utilities. Church leaders pointed to the growing numbers of homeless people on the streets of London and asked if Thatcherism meant selfishness. Before the Conservative Party conference in October, a poll found that 54% of voters felt Thatcher should resign before the next general election. The most serious blow of all came in October when Chancellor of the Exchequer Nigel Lawson resigned over what he viewed as the inappropriately elevated status of Sir Alan Walters, Thatcher's economic adviser.

In November, Thatcher indicated for the first time that the general election in 1992 might be the last she fights as Conservative Party leader. As the press began to speculate on Thatcher as a "lame duck" and Sir Anthony Meyer staged a futile challenge to her leadership, Thatcher changed her mind and said she would lead the Conservative Party into two more general elections.

Foreign Affairs. Thatcher also had a trying year on the world stage. In a visit to London, President George Bush assured her that the "special relationship" that thrived under former President Reagan would continue. But he went on to make it clear that the United States

While George Bush was just embarking on his presidency, there were signs that Margaret Thatcher's decade of service as British prime minister soon may be drawing to a close. The two conferred in London in the summer of 1989.

had many special partnerships with its European allies, reinforcing speculation that Bush sees West Germany, not Britain, as the most important player in Europe.

In March, Iran broke off relations with Britain for the country's protection of British citizen Salman Rushdie. Rushdie's novel *The Satanic Verses* had so inflamed Iran's religious leader Ayatollah Khomeini that he called for Rushdie's death. Though the British government publicly distanced itself from the book, saying it was "offensive" to Muslims, Tehran insisted that by sheltering Rushdie, "Britain once again displayed its animosity toward Iran."

In London in April, Soviet President Gorbachev voiced strong opposition to modernization of the North Atlantic Treaty Organization's (NATO's) short-range nuclear missiles in Europe. "The Soviet Union has just completed its short-range nuclear weapons," rejoined Thatcher. "We have not yet begun ours." Despite the clash, their meeting ended on a friendly note, with Thatcher describing the Soviet president as a "bold leader" and both sides agreeing that Anglo-Soviet relations were the best they had been since the 1940s. When, in May, West Germany's Chancellor Helmut Kohl urged NATO to open negotiations on the reduction of short-range missiles, Thatcher called on President Bush to resist such negoti-

© Nils Jorgenson/Rex Features, London

Visiting London in April, Soviet President Mikhail Gorbachev (right) *is joined by Prince Philip in reviewing the Coldstream Guards at Windsor Castle. President Gorbachev enjoyed a good relationship with British leaders during 1989.*

ations lest they lead to a total elimination of the missiles. At the NATO summit, Bush forged a compromise: NATO would ask for a meeting with the Soviet Union to decrease short-range missiles on both sides to below current NATO levels.

After traveling in September to Tokyo to encourage Japanese trade with England, Thatcher stopped in Moscow to talk with Gorbachev. She told a news conference that she was confident *perestroika* would "go through to success," and she predicted that an agreement to reduce conventional arms soon would be reached. Prospects for a ban on chemical weapons, she said, also were "encouraging."

British officials pressed ahead with plans to cede Hong Kong to China in 1997, despite the Tiananmen Square massacre. Ignoring pressure to issue British passports to Hong Kong residents, Thatcher said Britain would seek ways to ensure the rights of the Hong Kong people after 1997. Despite U.S. opposition, Britain fought for the forced repatriation of Vietnamese who came to Hong Kong seeking asylum. Seven years after the Falklands War, Argentina and Britain opened talks to restore diplomatic relations.

Economy. When Nigel Lawson handed over the keys to No. 11 Downing Street, the official residence of the chancellor of the exchequer, he left behind a monster—high inflation—for his successor, John Major, who was named to the post in another cabinet reshuffle. Lawson's modus operandi for fighting inflation and protecting the value of the pound was to manipulate interest rates. After the 1987 stock market crash, Lawson lowered interest rates and income taxes to stave off a depression. What ensued was a credit binge and a trade deficit that grew to $3.25 billion by July 1989. The deficit triggered a loss of confidence in the English economy and the pound's exchange rate decreased, so Lawson raised interest rates, and continued to raise them. In October, with inflation set to reach 7.5%, the highest among the major industrial nations, the country's domestic interest rate—Britain's version of the U.S. prime rate—stood at 15% and homeowners, faced with substantial increases in mortgage payments, howled in protest.

Opposition politicians and Conservatives alike demanded that England become a full member of the European Monetary System so that the Exchange Rate Mechanism could be used to stabilize the pound. But Thatcher insisted that England would not join the organization until British inflation was lower. Despite Prime Minister Thatcher's objections, EC leaders went ahead in December with plans to create a central bank and a common currency for the 12-nation region.

Meanwhile, a Dun & Bradstreet October survey of British business indicated that the British economy was on the brink of a "major slowdown" in the fourth quarter as businesses lost faith in the government's high interest rate policy, and the Confederation of British Industry reported that manufacturing output expectations were at their lowest since January 1983. The news was not all bad: Unemployment stood at 6% in October, its lowest rate since 1980. And Oxford Economic Forecasting predicted that while there may be a "sharp slowdown" into 1990, "there is little chance of a major recession on anything like the scale of the one seen at the turn of the decade."

Domestic Politics. What a difference a year made for Neil Kinnock and his Labour Party. While in 1988 it seemed a virtual impossibility that Thatcher and the Conservative Party might be toppled in the 1992 general election, a Gallup poll conducted in November 1989 showed that Labour had taken a 10.8% lead over Conservatives. With 47% of those polled saying they would vote for a Labour government, the party's showing was the best in any poll in nine years. Former Conservative cabinet minister Sir Ian Gilmour attributed the Conservative Party's fall from dominance to electorally "poisonous" policies—the poll tax and water and electricity privatization—that Conservatives would "not have touched with a barge poll" if ministers had thought a Labour resurgence possible. Also controversial were the government's attempts to inject a free-market philosophy into the legal profession, broadcasting, and even the brewing and pub trade.

Labour's regained credibility was hard-won. In a revamp of policy, the party abandoned its commitment to unilateral nuclear disarmament. Labour also dropped its traditional opposition to European Community membership and the party vowed to restore recently privatized utilities to public control. Labour's new policies paid off immediately when it won 45 seats to the Conservative Party's 32 in the elections for the European Parliament. To the surprise of many, England's Green Party also made a strong showing, pulling in an astounding 15% of the vote. The two center-left parties, the Social Democrats and the Social and Liberal Democrats, drew only 7% between them.

Northern Ireland. In August a wary, war-worn Northern Ireland marked the 20th anniversary of the deployment of British troops in the province. An end to the sectarianism and violence that engulfs the province seemed further away than ever as tit-for-tat killings continued and the 20-year death toll approached 3,000. In the worst attack on the British mainland since 1982, the Irish Republican Army (IRA) bombed the barracks of the Royal Marines School in Deal, Kent, in September, killing ten and wounding dozens. Attempts by Sinn Fein, the IRA's political wing, to widen its base of support were undermined by IRA attacks on civilians, including the fatal shooting of the infant daughter of a Royal Air Force officer in West Germany.

In a landmark decision, the Lord Chief Justice of England in October quashed the convictions of the "Guildford Four," three Irish men and one English woman who were jailed in 1974 for their alleged role in pub bombings in Guildford and Woolwich that killed seven. The four were cheered by hundreds outside the Old Bailey courthouse after their convictions, based solely on uncorroborated confessions, were ruled "unsafe." An inquiry into the police investigation of the case also was ordered. The Guildford Four's release gave new hope to supporters of the Birmingham Six, Irish Catholics jailed in 1974 for pub bombings in Birmingham that killed 21. The Birmingham Six maintained that their confessions were beaten out of them by police. In November three church leaders, including the Bishop of Birmingham, called for a review of the case.

Calls for a new inquiry into the March 1988 shooting deaths of three Irish Republican Army members by England's Special Air Services (SAS) in Gibraltar were rejected, despite new evidence from Spanish police contradicting the British government's version of events and pressure from the National Council for Civil Liberties and Amnesty International. Journalists and civil rights activists held a protest rally in October on the one-year anniversary of a government broadcasting ban meant to deny "terrorists the oxygen of publicity."

In 1989, Protestant paramilitaries were arrested in Paris for planning an arms deal with South Africa, and three South African diplomats were expelled from Britain. In September the future of the Anglo-Irish agreement looked in peril when it came to light that British police and army intelligence files on Catholic nationalists were being leaked to Protestant extrem-

In September an IRA terrorists' bombing shattered the barracks at the Royal Marine School in Deal, Kent, killing ten recruits for the marching band and injuring dozens.

© Rex Features, London from RDR Productions

ists. Support for the IRA in Northern Ireland's nationalist community has been due in part to suspicion of collusion between Protestant paramilitaries and British security forces.

In November, Peter Brooke, the newly appointed secretary of state for Northern Ireland, unwittingly illustrated the intractable nature of the province's affairs by suggesting that the government might talk to Sinn Fein if the IRA laid down arms. Standing logic on its head, the Rev. Ian Paisley, leader of the Democratic Unionist Party, responded: "What (Brooke) has said means that the IRA can bomb their way to the conference table. I will not talk to Sinn Fein under any circumstances."

The Royal Family. Continuing his attack on post-World War II architecture, Prince Charles published a book, *A Vision of Britain,* in which he compared modern architects to "Frankenstein monsters." And the Prince of Wales did not limit himself to architectural criticism in 1989. A passionate conservationist, he began writing a BBC documentary on environmental issues. He also entered the debate on the teaching of grammar in England, saying standards had fallen so low his own staff could not write or speak properly. "All the letters sent from my office I have to correct myself, because English is taught so bloody badly," he said in a speech. The prince also was lauded for his plans to create a volunteer community army of 100,000 young adults, a scheme that would offer the unemployed work experience.

The prince's wife, Princess Diana, also won high marks for social consciousness in 1989, as she cuddled infants dying of Acquired Immune Deficiency Syndrome (AIDS) in a Harlem, NY, hospital and shook the hands of leprosy sufferers at a rehabilitation center in Jakarta, Indonesia. In what was billed "the wedding of the year," Princess Diana's brother, Charles Althorp, married model Victoria Lockwood.

GREAT BRITAIN • Information Highlights

Official Name: United Kingdom of Great Britain and Northern Ireland.
Location: Island, western Europe.
Area: 94,525 sq mi (244 820 km^2).
Population (mid-1989 est.): 57,300,000.
Chief Cities (mid-1987 est.): London, the capital, 6,770,400; Birmingham, 998,200; Glasgow, 715,600; Leeds, 709,000; Sheffield, 532,300.
Government: *Head of state,* Elizabeth II, queen (acceded Feb. 1952). *Head of government,* Margaret Thatcher, prime minister and First Lord of the Treasury (took office May 1979). *Legislature* —Parliament: House of Lords and House of Commons.
Monetary Unit: Pound (0.6369 pound equals U.S.$1, Nov. 17, 1989).
Gross National Product (1988 U.S.$): $758,400,000,000.
Economic Indexes (1988): *Consumer Prices* (1980 = 100), all items, 159.9; food, 144.7. *Industrial Production* (1980 = 100), 119.
Foreign Trade (1988 U.S.$): *Imports,* $189,471,000,000; *exports,* $145,151,000,000.

Other members of the Royal Family had a more difficult year. In April private letters sent to Princess Anne by Timothy Laurence, a Royal Navy commander and equerry to Queen Elizabeth, were stolen and given to *The Sun,* a tabloid newspaper. In August, Princess Anne and her husband, Mark Phillips, announced their agreement to separate after nearly 16 years of marriage, punctuated by periodic rumors of marital strife.

The subject of media scorn since her marriage to Prince Andrew, the Duchess of York, formerly Sarah Ferguson, was criticized in 1989 for frequent skiing trips that took her away from her infant child, Beatrice, and for her plans to keep some of the royalties from two children's books she published during the year. Normally the royals would turn over all such profits to charity; the Duchess said she would give "a percentage" to charity, a decision she defended during a television interview with Barbara Walters, which aired in the United States. The Duke and Duchess of York were expecting a second child in March 1990.

Tragedy and Hope. The year 1988 ended with the explosion of Pan Am Flight 103 over Lockerbie that killed 270 people, a disaster that led to the tightening of airport security in Britain and elsewhere in Europe. The year 1989 had more tragedies in store. In January, 44 people died in the crash of a British Midland Airways Boeing 737 jet that was en route from London to Belfast. In March, nine people died and another 70 were injured when two passenger trains collided south of London. The tragedy that claimed the most lives occurred in April, when 95 people died and hundreds were injured at the Hillsborough soccer stadium in Sheffield. Just after the start of a Football Association play-off between Liverpool and Nottingham Forest, there was a surge in the overcrowded penned-in stadium area known as the "terraces," filled mostly with Liverpool fans. As fans from behind were allowed to continue to push their way into the terraces, the fans at the front were crushed up against a fence and suffocated. An inquiry criticized police for failing to control the crowds. The disaster also raised questions about the design of English soccer stadiums. And in August, 51 young people drowned when their pleasure boat collided with a barge and sunk on the River Thames in London.

Amid disaster, there were hopeful signs for the future as Britain underwent a "green revolution." The shelves of supermarkets filled with recycled paper and biodegradable washing products, cars were converted to run on unleaded fuel, and Prime Minister Thatcher hosted a conference at which 20 nations agreed on a pact to reduce production of ozone-destroying chemicals by 50% by the year 2000.

SUZANNE CASSIDY
London Bureau, "The New York Times"

The Arts

Nearly four centuries after his death, William Shakespeare continued to be a big story on the British arts scene in 1989. Luminaries such as Ian McKellen, Dame Peggy Ashcroft, and Sir John Gielgud successfully campaigned to prevent the remains of the 16th-century Rose Theatre in London, the site of the first production of Shakespeare's *Henry VI,* from being buried under an office building. In October archaeologists in London unearthed the remains of another of Shakespeare's theaters, the Globe, where at least a dozen of his plays premiered. The year 1989 saw the passing of Laurence Olivier (*see* OBITUARIES, page 404), who many believe was the greatest Shakespearean actor of modern time, and the coming of age of the young man some have dubbed "the new Olivier," Kenneth Branagh, who directed and starred in his own film production of *Henry V.*

Arts funding reached a crisis point as the Royal National Theatre announced that it might have to do away with part of its internationally renowned three-theater repertoire, and England's five orchestras sought recording and overseas touring contracts to subsidize their concerts in Britain. Peter Palumbo, the new Arts Council chairman, pleaded with the government and the nation's wealthy to increase subsidies to the arts.

Theater. Andrew Lloyd Webber opened a new play in April, *Aspects of Love,* a departure from his sweeping musicals but nevertheless a major box-office draw. It was booked until spring 1990 before it even opened. *Miss Saigon,* a Cameron Mackintosh musical, opened in September under the direction of Nicholas Hytner, possibly the most-talked-about director of the year. Tim Albery, another exciting new director, staged a provocative version of *As You Like It* at the Old Vic. New plays included Martin Sherman's *A Madhouse in Goa,* starring Vanessa Redgrave; Keith Waterhouse's *Jeffrey Bernard Is Unwell,* starring Peter O'Toole; and Donald Freed's *Veterans Day,* with Jack Lemmon and Michael Gambon.

As Terry Hands reached the end of his tenure as artistic director at the Royal Shakespeare Company, the company presented Shakespeare's *The Plantagenets* and Henrik Ibsen's *The Master Builder,* both directed by Adrian Noble, a contender for Hands' job. The National Theatre drew eager crowds and critics in March when it opened *Hamlet,* starring Daniel Day-Lewis. After 65 performances, for which he earned mixed reviews, Day-Lewis had to withdraw because of nervous exhaustion. Reviews also were mixed for Dustin Hoffman's Shakespearean debut as Shylock in *The Merchant of Venice* (*see* BIOGRAPHY), but the play's West End run sold out. Other notable plays in 1989 included: Ibsen's *Hedda Gabler;* David Henry Hwang's *M. Butterfly,* a Broadway import starring Anthony Hopkins; Iris Murdoch's *The Black Prince;* and Oscar Wilde's *Salome,* directed by and starring Steven Berkoff.

Music. A report by the Policy Studies Institute showed that professional opera in Britain was attracting record audiences, with total attendances exceeding 1.5 million per year, although ticket prices nearly had doubled since 1981. Despite an anticipated year-end deficit of more than $3.5 million and controversy over expansion of its Covent Garden home, the Royal Opera had a fine year, staging in February the British premiere of *Un re in ascolto,* by contemporary Italian composer Luciano Berio, and in June, Verdi's *Il Trovatore* with Placido

The Cameron Mackintosh musical, "Miss Saigon," about a tragic affair between an American soldier and a Vietnamese girl at the time of the fall of Saigon during 1975, was among London's most-talked-about new theater productions of 1989.

© Richard H. Smith/Dominic Photography

Placido Domingo sang the role of the troubadour in the Royal Opera Company's summer production of Giuseppe Verdi's "Il Trovatore"; Rosalind Plowright portrayed Leonora.

© Catherine Ashmore/Dominic Photography

Domingo. The English National Opera presented a controversial new production of Verdi's *A Masked Ball.*

The London Symphony Orchestra featured Itzhak Perlman in a spring season devoted to the violin concerto. In November the Chamber Orchestra of Europe began a three-year collaboration with the Barbican Center. And outside London, plans were announced for a new Glyndebourne opera house and a "Glyndebourne of the Midlands," an opera house to be built at a cost of nearly $40 million at Compton Verney, Warwickshire.

Fine Arts. Major exhibitions included the works of Leonardo da Vinci at the Hayward Gallery; "100 Years of Russian Art" at the Barbican Art Gallery; "The Art of Photography 1839–1989" at the Royal Academy of Arts; and "Degas' Images of Women" at the new Tate Gallery in Liverpool. The Victoria and Albert Museum (V&A) staged "A Vision of Britain," a personal view of architecture by Prince Charles, and an exhibition of the ceramics of Victorian William de Morgan.

These were high points for the V&A in an otherwise controversial year during which the museum's trustees streamlined the curatorial staff, replacing curators with business people schooled in modern management. Museum professionals in Britain, the United States, and Europe registered their concern for the artistic integrity of the 120-year-old museum; many believed the V&A's change of philosophy could have widespread effects in the museum world.

In April a 1929 ban on 30 D. H. Lawrence nudes was lifted by Britain's Customs and Excise Department. In May a fully restored da Vinci cartoon, *The Virgin and Child with St. Anne and St. John the Baptist,* was returned to public view at the National Gallery, two years after it was damaged by a shotgun blast. And the Design Museum, dedicated to the art of industrial design, opened in July.

Dance. The English National Ballet (formerly the London Festival Ballet) staged a revival of Sir Frederick Ashton's *Romeo and Juliet.* A Royal Ballet highlight was *La Bayadère,* choreographed by Natalia Makarova and starring guest artist Sylvie Guillem. The Royal's sister company and touring wing, the Sadler's Wells Royal Ballet, announced its intention to move from London to Birmingham, England's second-largest city, in August 1990; the company would be known as the Birmingham Royal Ballet. Visiting troupes included the Bolshoi Ballet, the New York City Ballet, the Hungarian State Opera Ballet, the Byelorussian Ballet, and the Paul Taylor Dance Company.

Film and Television. London's Pinewood Studios produced Warner Brothers' biggest film of 1989, *Batman,* a $30 million movie starring Michael Keaton and Jack Nicholson. Peter Greenaway delivered *The Cook, the Thief, His Wife and Her Lover,* a scathing movie regarded by some critics as the finest English film of the year. Other cinematic successes included *Scandal,* starring John Hurt; *For Queen and Country,* starring Denzel Washington; and *High Hopes,* a Mike Leigh film. In October the British Association of Film and Theater Artists presented its Lifetime Achievement award to Julie Andrews.

On television, viewers saw two plays in defense of author Salman Rushdie: *Iranian Nights,* by Tariq Ali and Howard Brenton, and *Blasphemers' Banquet,* by poet Tony Harrison.

SUZANNE CASSIDY
Free-lance Writer, London

Photos, AP/Wide World

Greece's former Premier Andreas Papandreou, left, *and chief rival Constantine Mitsotakis each failed to form a government after two indecisive parliamentary elections.*

GREECE

Greece's politics were turbulent in 1989. Four different men held the office of prime minister in turn: Andreas Papandreou, Tzannis Tzannetakis, Yannis Grivas, and Xenophon Zolotas.

Papandreou's Decline. Prime Minister Andreas Papandreou, who with his party, the Panhellenic Socialist Movement (PASOK), had been in power since 1981, began 1989 under a cloud of numerous allegations of governmental corruption. The most spectacular of these revolved around the activities of the former owner of the Bank of Crete, George Koskotas, who had fled to the United States in 1988 under charges of embezzlement. Imprisoned in Salem, MA, he resisted extradition and issued denunciations accusing various persons of being his accomplices.

In addition, Papandreou's personal life had become a public issue. At age 70, he filed for divorce from his estranged U.S.-born wife of 38 years, Margaret Papandreou, and, having received it, he married his constant companion, Dimitra Liani, 35, on July 13.

Two Parliamentary Elections. In parliamentary elections held on June 18, PASOK won 125 seats of the 300 total. The conservative New Democracy party, headed by Papandreou's longtime rival, Constantine Mitsotakis, won the greatest number of seats, 145, but it fell six seats short of a parliamentary majority. Mitsotakis and his party then agreed to join a three-month interim coalition government with the Communist-controlled Coalition of the Left and Progress, which had won 28 seats under its leader Harilaos Florakis. A highly respected New Democracy deputy, Tzannis Tzannetakis, became prime minister and foreign minister.

The newly elected Parliament opened a probe regarding the allegations of corruption against former Prime Minister Papandreou. A blow to PASOK's prestige came in September when the European Commission, the executive branch of the European Community (EC), fined Greece $4 million in a case concerning fraudulent sales of corn during Papandreou's term. Also in September, Parliament determined that Papandreou should stand trial on charges of criminal misconduct.

Preparing for new parliamentary elections, the Tzannetakis government resigned in October, and a caretaker government was formed with the Supreme Court president Yannis Grivas as prime minister. The elections, held on November 5, once more proved indecisive. New Democracy, led by Mitsotakis, failed again to win a parliamentary majority, although it won 148 seats. PASOK received 128 and the Coalition of the Left and Progress, 21.

After several weeks of negotiations to prevent the calling of the year's third parliamentary election, an all-party government was formed on November 23 consisting of New Democracy, PASOK, and the Left Coalition with 85-year-old Xenophon Zolotas, a prominent economist and former Bank of Greece governor, as the new prime minister. He was unaligned with any political party and was not a deputy in Parliament. The new prime minister presented a policy program to Parliament on November 29; in early December he won an overwhelming vote of confidence by 292 to 1, with 2 abstentions.

Former King's Views. Deposed King Constantine II of the Hellenes, who lost his throne in a 1974 plebiscite, broke a long silence on politics in an interview from London with *The New York Times* published on Dec. 10, 1989. Though he made it clear that he was not asking to return as king, he did say he wanted to go home as a Greek patriot to help his country in any way he could. He expressed his feelings about the need for unity in the country, and he encouraged younger people to enter the political scene. The result was a storm of criticism from Greek political parties of every spectrum who saw him as interfering in an inadmissible way.

Foreign Affairs. Greece continued as a member of the North Atlantic Treaty Organization (NATO), while its relations with its NATO partner Turkey were strained because of the Turkish occupation of northern Cyprus. There were also acrimonious Greek-Turkish controversies over the control of sovereign air and sea rights in the Aegean Sea. Another potential source of antagonism related to the 120,000 Muslims in Greece's Western Thrace who are Greek citizens but speak Turkish.

Because of the unsettled Greek political climate, the United States and Greece did not resolve the question of whether and under what circumstances U.S. bases located in the country might be maintained despite the fact that the arrangement for them already had expired. Similarly, the issue of whether a Palestinian, Mohammed Rashid, should be extradited from Greece to the United States to face charges connected to a 1982 airliner bombing was held in abeyance by Greece.

The Economy. Greece's economy seemed in as great a disarray as its political sphere. There were strikes; the rising inflation rate was four times the average of the other members of the EC. The public-sector deficit was enormous, and there was a very large foreign debt. In December, in an effort to stem the economy's continued decline, the all-party Zolotas government took extraordinary measures. Among these were an additional 5% to 7% rise in taxes on income and business profits as well as a 12% to 33% increase on the rates for services.

GEORGE J. MARCOPOULOS, *Tufts University*

GREECE • Information Highlights

Official Name: Hellenic Republic.
Location: Southwestern Europe.
Area: 50,942 sq mi (131 940 km²).
Population (mid-1989 est.): 10,000,000.
Chief Cities (1981 census): Athens, the capital, 885,737; Salonika, 406,413; Piraeus, 196,389.
Government: *Head of state,* Christos Sartzetakis, president (took office March 1985). *Head of government,* Xenophon Zolotas, prime minister (took office Nov. 1989). *Legislature*—Parliament.
Monetary Unit: Drachma (156.6 drachmas equal U.S.$1, Dec. 26, 1989).
Gross National Product (1986 U.S.$): $46,600,000,000.
Economic Indexes (1988): *Consumer Prices* (1980 = 100), all items, 415.9; food, 395.4. *Industrial Production* (1980 = 100), 111.
Foreign Trade (1987 U.S.$): *Imports,* $13,056,000,000; *exports,* $6,535,000,000.

HAITI

The Haitian military government of Gen. Prosper Avril announced in September that it was scheduling elections for a civilian president on Oct. 17, 1990.

Governments. The nationwide election would be preceded by local and regional contests in April 1990 and by legislative elections in July and August, said a government statement on state-run television. Earlier, after crushing an attempted coup d'état in April 1989, General Avril indicated that his regime was committed to an eventual transition to civilian rule, but not for a considerable time, because "we want to achieve an irreversible democracy."

Haiti has experienced three successful coups and lived under four different rulers from 1986 to 1989. Since the overthrow of long-reigning dictator Jean-Claude Duvalier in February 1986, the country has been plagued by continuing unrest, antigovernment demonstrations, charges of human-rights violations, and an aborted election in November 1987. Avril came to power in a coup in September 1988, ousting Lt. Gen. Henri Namphy, a Duvalier associate who effectively had controlled the Haitian government since the dictator's ouster.

Avril, however, also had close ties to the Duvalier government and opponents claimed that he has enriched himself through graft and corruption, acquiring an elegant mansion in Port-au-Prince, the nation's capital. By late 1989 opinion was divided on whether he would remove himself from the political scene when, and if, elections are held in 1990.

International Aid. Despite the frequent changes of government and continuing civil violence, international financial institutions have provided economic and technical assistance to Haiti, one of the Western Hemisphere's poorest nations, throughout the post-Duvalier period. In 1989 the International Development Association, a part of the World Bank group, authorized $24 million for the improvement of power transmission systems in Port-au-Prince. The World Bank itself granted a $22 million loan to the Haitian Water Authority to replace obsolete facilities and train technicians, while the International Fund for Agricultural Development provided $22.3 million for the renovation of small irrigation networks.

HAITI • Information Highlights

Official Name: Republic of Haiti.
Location: Caribbean.
Area: 10,714 sq mi (27 750 km²).
Population: (mid-1989 est.): 6,400,000.
Chief City (mid-1984 est.): Port-au-Prince, the capital, 738,342 (incl. suburbs).
Government: *Head of state and government,* Lt. Gen. Prosper Avril, provisional president (took power Sept. 18, 1988). *Legislature*—suspended.
Monetary Unit: Gourde (5.0 gourdes equal U.S.$1, June 1989).
Gross Domestic Product (1987 est. U.S.$): $2,200,-000,000.
Economic Index (1988): *Consumer Prices* (1980 = 100), all items, 147.0; food, 134.0.
Foreign Trade (1985 U.S.$): *Imports,* $442,000,000; *exports,* $174,000,000.

Bilateral aid has been harder for Haiti to obtain. The United States canceled most of its aid programs in Haiti after the November 1987 election was annulled. The only U.S. assistance for nearly two years was for an antinarcotics program and for emergency aid following Hurricane *Gilbert* in 1988. In August 1989, however, the U.S. Agency for International Development (AID) announced a partial resumption of U.S. assistance in recognition of the "continuing progress" by the Avril government toward free elections. The AID assistance consisted of $10 million in food aid. The Bush administration, meanwhile, asked the U.S. Congress to provide an additional $41 million for Haiti in the fiscal year beginning October 1.

Even with the resumption of bilateral aid flows, though, a report issued by the Inter-American Development Bank in September delcared that "The short-term outlook for the Haitian economy is fraught with problems." The Bank called for continued trade liberalization and special efforts to expand Haiti's agricultural exports.

RICHARD C. SCHROEDER, *Consultant to the Organization of American States*

HAWAII

A massive oil spill, another midair accident over Hawaiian skies, and the death of a high-profile refugee highlighted 1989 events in Hawaii.

Oil Spill. The Exxon *Houston,* sister ship of the Exxon *Valdez* tanker that ran aground off Alaska in late March 1989, broke free of its moorings during a storm and spilled more than 100,000 gallons (378 540 l) of oil along the leeward coast of Oahu in early April. To the relief of environmentalists and marine wildlife officials, damage to reef and shore was minimal. The Coast Guard pulled the tanker free and the captain was cleared of blame.

Air Disaster. For the second time within a year, a fatal air accident occurred over Hawaiian skies when a United Airlines 747 bound for New Zealand lost a cargo door shortly after takeoff February 24. A 10 by 20 ft (3 by 6 m) hole in the fuselage caused nine passengers to be hurled thousands of feet to their deaths into the Pacific Ocean. The pilot managed to fly the crippled jet back to Honolulu.

A High Profile. Ferdinand Edralin Marcos, 72, his body ravaged by illness, and with criminal indictments pending against him in U.S. courts, died September 28 in Honolulu. The former Philippine president had lived with his wife Imelda in the islands since Marcos was ousted from power in 1986. (*See* PHILIPPINES.)

Economy. With tourism booming for most of 1989 at a 9% pace over the previous year, Hawaii's hotels and restaurants and the service industry enjoyed another record in sales. It also meant a fat surplus in state government coffers of some $500 million, since tourism is Hawaii's major revenue source. Some residents were unhappy despite a refund to taxpayers and the lowest jobless rate in the nation. Native Hawaiians (who comprise only a fraction of total population) complained that they were being left out and drafted a constitution proclaiming sovereignty.

Drift Nets in Fishing. The international campaign to outlaw the use of drift nets, which are called "curtains of death" because of their all-consuming harvesting methods in snaring sealife other than the intended catch, focused on Hawaii. Gov. John Waihee III joined with federal marine agencies in calling for outlawing drift nets from local waters.

Hawaiian Medicine. Sea algae collected in Hawaii proved effective against AIDS viruses in a test-tube environment in laboratory experiments conducted at the National Cancer Institute, but officials cautioned against being overoptimistic about the results. Hawaiians have been using the sea algae for medicinal purposes for centuries.

Housing and Infrastructure Crisis. Local surveys showed that housing is one of the

HAWAII • Information Highlights

Area: 6,471 sq mi (16 759 km²).
Population (July 1, 1988): 1,098,000.
Chief Cities (1980 census): Honolulu, the capital (1986 est.), 372,330; Pearl City, 42,575; Kailua, 35,812; Hilo, 35,269.
Government (1989): *Chief Officers*—governor, John D. Waihee III (D); lt. gov., Benjamin J. Cayetano (D). *Legislature*—Senate, 25 members; House of Representatives, 51 members.
State Finances (fiscal year 1988): *Revenue,* $3,619,000,000; *expenditure,* $2,808,000,000.
Personal Income (1988): $18,399,000,000; per capita, $16,753.
Labor Force (June 1989): *Civilian labor force,* 528,300; *unemployed,* 15,800 (3.0% of total force).
Education: *Enrollment* (fall 1987)—public elementary schools, 116,000; public secondary, 50,000; colleges and universities, 52,291. *Public school expenditures* (1987–88), $599,000,000 ($3,612 per pupil).

major concerns of the more than 1 million state residents, and the National Association of Realtors puts the median price of an island home at $262,500. Other problems facing Hawaii's people, according to a First Hawaiian Bank report, include jammed highways, overtaxed sewers and landfills, and other infrastructure inadequacies brought about by the booming economy. The 1990 legislature may be asked to reintroduce a bill that would give the counties more revenues to cope with their problems. Such a bill failed in the 1989 session.

CHARLES TURNER, *Honolulu*

HONG KONG

During 1989 attention in Hong Kong was focused on the Chinese government's brutal suppression of the democracy movement on the mainland, the departure of professional people from the colony, and the Vietnamese boat people.

Political Affairs. The first draft of the Basic Law—the blueprint for the establishment of a Hong Kong Special Administration Region (SAR) when the area reverts from British to Chinese control in 1997—was approved by the Chinese government on February 21. Further work on the document was delayed for a time by the events on the mainland. Hong Kong citizens strongly supported the student democratic movement in China, with more than 500,000 taking part in a May 21 rally. In reaction to the June 3–4 massacre of the students in Tiananmen Square, the Hong Kong committee working on the Basic Law suspended its efforts until July 20. The Sino-British Joint Liaison Group meeting scheduled for July in London also was postponed until September 27.

In view of the events in China, Hong Kong's executive and legislative councillors decided to speed up the pace of political reform. The present SAR Legislative Council will be expanded from 56 seats to 60 seats in 1991, with 20 of the seats to be elected directly. The Chinese government indicated that after 1997 only one third of the Hong Kong legislators would be elected directly. There also was demand to amend sections of the Basic Law draft, particularly Article 18, which allows China to declare a state of emergency in Hong Kong in times of turmoil. The Tiananmen Square massacre and its aftermath increased insecurity in Hong Kong, aggravating the problem of brain drain through emigration, and reinforcing the pleas of Hong Kong citizens to be allowed to live in Great Britain. In December the British government announced that it would grant full British citizenship to a maximum 50,000 households.

Boat People. Under the refugee screening policy introduced in 1988, nonpolitical refugees from Vietnam are regarded as illegal immigrants subject to jail sentences, deportation, or both. By July 1989 there were more than 51,000 Vietnamese boat people in Hong Kong, with one third of that total arriving in the first half of the year. The government placed some of the refugees on Tai Ah Chau, a barren island without shelter or running water. By 1989, Vietnamese boat people were costing the government nearly $17 million a year and there was increasing resentment from Hong Kong citizens, with increasing demands to deport the refugees. In December, in the first forced repatriation of boat people from Hong Kong, 51 were returned to Hanoi.

AP/Wide World

Hong Kong residents, anxious about future Chinese sovereignty over the colony, were part of a 1989 convention group that sought Canadian immigration information.

Economy. A recent trend for reexports exceeding exports continued in the first half of 1989 due to joint ventures with mainland China. Reaction to the crackdown in China, however, may lead to a slowdown in Hong Kong's domestic economy. An immediate negative impact was registered in the tourist industry, with the average occupancy rate of Hong Kong hotels dropping from 75% in June to 65% in July. In transportation, the first bridge at Lok Ma Chau, linking Hong Kong with the mainland's Guandong Province highway, was completed and the second cross-harbor tunnel between Kwun Tong and Quarry Bay was opened, along with a companion mass transit railway.

DAVID CHUENYAN LAI
University of Victoria, British Columbia

© Joyce Dopkeen/NYT Pictures

Efforts are under way to help alleviate the problem of the homeless in the United States. In Mount Vernon, NY, a transitional housing complex, left, *was dedicated in early 1990. Such projects, which are planned for other locales as well, are financed by low-interest bonds and built on donated land.*

HOUSING

The U.S. housing market weakened somewhat in 1989. The production of both single-family homes and apartment buildings declined, sales of both new and existing homes moved downward, and the rate of increase in home prices slackened. As in earlier years of the 1980s, housing activity was quite uneven across the country. In 1989 the Northeast region was the weakest part of the market while the strongest activity was on the West Coast.

Problems of housing affordability continued to be evident in 1989, further dramatizing a growing gap between the housing "haves" and "have nots" in the United States. Young Americans continued to have a difficult time buying their first homes, a problem illustrated by a falling home-ownership rate in the 25-to-35-year age group. Furthermore, low-income renters continued to have a difficult time finding decent rental housing that they could afford, a problem dramatized by a growing number of homeless families.

Despite the evidence of growing housing problems, no new major housing programs were enacted in 1989. On the other hand, two major pieces of "reform" legislation related to housing became law: the Financial Institutions Reform, Recovery and Enforcement Act of 1989 and the HUD Reform Act of 1989. The first law, commonly referred to as "thrift reform," was designed to strengthen the system of thrift institutions that make up a major part of the housing finance system in the United States. The HUD Reform Act was designed to address a series of problems surrounding various programs operated by the Department of Housing and Urban Development (HUD) and to strengthen the mortgage-insurance programs of the Federal Housing Administration. Late in 1989 the Bush administration also announced a number of housing initiatives, as part of a program dubbed Homeownership and Opportunity for People Everywhere, that could lead to major housing legislation in 1990.

Total Production. Housing production in the United States, measured by starts of new units, fell by 6% in 1989 to 1.40 million units. This was the third consecutive annual decline, and was nearly 25% below the recent high in 1986. However, housing activity remained well above the recession year of 1982 when housing starts fell to 1.06 million units.

Housing production was relatively strong in the early part of 1989 (on a seasonally adjusted basis), but weakened later in the year. The U.S. central bank, the Federal Reserve System (Fed), tightened monetary policy during 1988 and early 1989 in an attempt to slow down an overheating economy and diffuse inflationary pressures. The resulting higher interest rates weakened the housing sector during the second quarter of the year, and this weakness persisted. Economic and financial market conditions at the end of the year presaged another slack housing year for 1990.

Single-Family Housing. The production and sale of single-family homes declined moderately in 1989. About 1 million single-family homes were produced, 6% below the 1988 pace but still quite respectable by historical standards. Sales of new and existing homes totaled about 4.1 million, 3% below 1988. Increases in national median prices of both new and existing homes fell well below the increases of the 1986–88 period. The median new-home price rose by about 6%, while the median price of existing homes rose about 4%. Furthermore, price declines were recorded in some markets, particularly in the Northeast.

The production, sale, and pricing of single-family housing was related strongly to mortgage interest rates. The average rate on 30-year, fixed-rate mortgages climbed to 11¾% by March as the Fed tightened credit, and fell to about 10% by year's end as the agency loosened the credit reins. The positive influence of this decline was limited, however, because conditions did not improve nearly as much in the adjustable-rate home-mortgage market.

During 1988 and early into 1989, the adjustable-rate mortgage (ARM) was the major "lifeline" for the single-family market. Buyers could get ARMs with initial interest rates roughly two and one-half percentage points below the traditional fixed-rate mortgage, and ARMs were accounting for nearly two thirds of all home loans written in the United States. "Discounting" of initial ARM interest rates by lenders, particularly by thrift institutions, was a major factor behind their popularity. However, initial rate discounting was cut back in 1989, partly because of the impending thrift-reform legislation. As a result, the initial rate advantage of an ARM over the standard fixed-rate mortgage fell from two and one-half percentage points to about one and one-fourth percentage points and the ARM share of the home-mortgage market fell from two thirds to one fourth. Also, laws and regulations in place at the end of 1989 will prevent future deep and widespread discounting of initial ARM rates.

Multifamily Housing. The production of residential structures with two or more units weakened in 1989, as starts of both rental housing and condominiums slipped. Starts of new multifamily housing fell to 380,000 units—6% below 1988, 45% below 1985, and about equal to the pace of the 1981–82 recession years. The multifamily rental market was plagued by high vacancy rates. The national rental vacancy rate was around 7½%, down only slightly from the 20-year high posted in 1988, and the rate for structures with five or more units was nearly 11%. The rental vacancy rate showed some improvement in the South, where overbuilding had been most serious, but the vacancy situation worsened in the West and showed little change in the Northeast and Midwest. Completions of new rental units slowed during 1989, reflecting the sharp decline in such starts since 1985, and there was some improvement in the pace at which new units were rented. However, the market remained quite weak.

Regional Housing Markets. The 6% decline in U.S. housing activity in 1989 was concentrated highly in the Northeast. Housing starts fell by nearly 25% from the 1988 level, following a 13% decline during 1988, and the sharpest contraction was in the single-family market. Pronounced weakness was evident in both the New England and Middle Atlantic (New York, New Jersey, and Pennsylvania) areas of the Northeast. The Northeast accounted for only about 13% of national housing activity in 1989, down from more than 16% during the years of 1986–87.

Housing activity in the other regions of the country held relatively close to 1988 levels. The Midwest actually posted a small increase, as economic activity in some of the region's industrialized states maintained relatively good momentum. The region accounted for nearly 20% of national housing activity in 1989, its highest share of the 1980s.

Both the South and West regions posted small declines in housing activity in 1989, but both performed better than the national average. Housing markets in the "oil patch" states (Texas, Louisiana, Oklahoma, and Arkansas) remained quite weak in 1989, but the precipitous decline that occurred during 1986–88 was halted and signs of life developed in both the single-family and multifamily markets. This part of the country accounted for about 5% of total U.S. housing starts in 1989, up slightly from 1988 but still well below shares of nearly 25% as recently as 1983.

The Pacific area, led by California, had the nation's strongest housing performance. The Pacific states accounted for a record 23% of national housing activity, with California accounting for 17%. Strength in the Pacific area was concentrated mainly in single-family housing; the multifamily market was flat.

As 1989 ended, regional disparities in the performance of the U.S. housing market appeared to be narrowing. In particular, activity in the Northeast seemed to be bottoming out, the West South Central area seemed to be crawling upward, the Midwest seemed to be losing its newfound momentum, and the West Coast seemed to be cooling down.

International Developments. A gradual but significant tightening of credit markets occurred worldwide during 1988 and early 1989, and economic slowdowns occurred in many industrialized countries. International housing patterns reflected the prevailing economic and financial market conditions.

• In Canada, housing starts peaked at about 245,000 units in 1987, slid to 220,000 in 1988, and declined another 3% to 4% in 1989. Lower interest rates later in the year caused housing activity to perk up to some degree.

• In the United Kingdom, sharply higher interest rates caused the housing sector to contract substantially in 1989, and housing starts fell by more than 25%. Average home prices declined in this difficult environment.

• In France, the central bank applied moderate credit tightening in 1989. As a result, housing starts should be down by about 5%.

• In Japan, housing starts peaked in mid-1988 and have shown only moderate declines since then.

• In West Germany, economic expansion was quite strong in both 1988 and 1989. As a result, housing activity in 1989 was up moderately from 1988—contrary to the pattern in most other industrialized countries.

KENT W. COLTON and DAVID F. SEIDERS
National Association of Home Builders

HUNGARY

In 1989, Hungary paced the progress of political liberalization in Eastern Europe. In March, Károly Grósz, leader of the Hungarian Socialist Workers' (Communist) Party (HSWP) and a moderate reformer, predicted that his party would not have to face the risk of being ousted from political power by Hungarian voters for another six to eight years. But by June, Grósz himself had lost his position, and by October his old party had abandoned orthodox Marxism-Leninism and was girding for stiff competition in the coming free elections.

Domestic Affairs. In January the Hungarian parliament legalized peaceful public demonstrations and political opposition groups. Quickly, a host of such groups—some old and formerly illegal, some new, ultimately numbering almost 50—came into open existence. Led by the Democratic Forum, the Social Democratic Party, and the Solidarity Trade Union Federation, and cooperating with reform elements within the HSWP led by Imre Pozsgay and Rezsö Nyers, they launched an aggressive campaign for the democratization of Hungary. The HSWP, plagued by a rapidly declining membership, steadily gave ground in what progressively became an avalanche of radical political-economic changes.

In February, after bitter infighting, the HSWP's Central Committee agreed to permit other political parties to challenge it in open elections. In March about 80,000 people massed legally in Budapest to commemorate the revolution of 1848 against Habsburg rule, demanding the departure of Soviet troops, free elections, and the rehabilitation of Imre Nagy, the executed leader of the unsuccessful Hungarian uprising in 1956 against Soviet domination. In April some 600 liberal Communists convened a "reform workshop" and threatened to split the HSWP if a special party congress were not called in the fall to make revolutionary changes.

In May they met again, with specific demands: a guarantee of Hungarian neutrality by the two superpowers, an immediate transition to a multiparty political system and a market-oriented mixed economy, and an official reappraisal of the 1956 upheaval. Also in May, the aged János Kádár, already ousted as party chief in 1988, was removed as party president and expelled from the Central Committee. (He died in July.) Premier Miklos Németh at the same time replaced six key cabinet ministers with reformers, including a new foreign minister, Gyula Horn.

On June 16, in a nine-hour memorial ceremony in Budapest attended by 250,000 Hungarians and many foreign representatives, Nagy and five of his lieutenants were reburied with honors. A week later, the HSWP replaced General Secretary Grósz with a four-member collective party presidency headed by Nyers. In September, after three months of negotiations, the HSWP and leading opposition groups agreed on some basic points, including liberalization of the penal code, legal guarantees of human and civil rights and the rights of all political parties, elections for a new national president with as yet undefined powers, and free multiparty elections for the National Assembly, with no reserved seats for the HSWP, by June 1990.

The long battle for basic party and governmental reform culminated in October. At its special party congress on October 6–9, the beaten HSWP formally accepted the negotiated concessions. In a dramatic move, it also abandoned hard-line Marxist-Leninist ideology and embraced democratic socialism, renaming itself the Hungarian Socialist Party and electing Nyers its president. By November, however, it numbered only about 30,000 members. Disgruntled hard-liners, charging "treason," immediately regrouped in a small, new, militant Communist Party called the János Kádár Society. The National Assembly dutifully set about revising 90% of the old state constitution dating from 1949. The new Hungary, itself renamed a "democratic republic" from a "people's (Communist) republic," was to incorporate "the valvalues of both bourgeois democracy and democratic socialism." On October 23, on the 33d anniversary of the 1956 uprising, now officially declared "a genuine popular movement for national independence," and no longer "a Western-inspired counterrevolution," many thousands massed in Budapest, triumphantly shouting "Russians go home!" and "Gorby! Gorby!" (a shortened form of the name of the Soviet leader, Mikhail Gorbachev). The contradiction in the masses' chants—wishing the Russian troops to depart yet hailing the Russian leader—was only superficial. Hungarians were protesting and rejecting the old Soviet military dominance and suppression symbol-

HUNGARY • Information Highlights

Official Name: Hungarian Republic.
Location: East-central Europe.
Area: 35,919 sq mi (93 030 km^2).
Population (mid-1989 est.): 10,600,000.
Chief Cities (Jan. 1, 1988): Budapest, the capital, 2,104,700; Debrecen, 217,364; Miskolc, 209,807.
Government: *Head of state,* Károly Németh, president of the presidential council (took office June 1987). *Head of government,* Miklos Németh, premier of the council of ministers (took office November 1988). President of the Hungarian Socialist Party, Rezsö Nyers (took office October 1989). *Legislature* (unicameral)—National Assembly.
Monetary Unit: Forint (60.048 forints equal U.S.$1, July 1989).
Economic Indexes (1988): *Consumer Prices* (1980 = 100), all items, 184.2; food, 175.5. *Industrial Production* (1980 = 100), 115.
Foreign Trade (1988 U.S.$): *Imports,* $9,366,000,000; *exports,* $9,971,000,000.

ized by the events of 1956 and applauding the new Soviet attitudes under Gorbachev: openness and restructuring—and permitting the development of opposition in East Europe.

The last major political event of the year was a referendum on November 26 on the timetable of the election of the first president of the republic. It was the first free national vote since World War II. The ruling Socialist Party, whose candidate was to be Imre Pozsgay, proposed an election on Jan. 7, 1990—well before the election of the new National Assembly. Opponents, protesting that this would give the Socialists the advantages of incumbency, insisted on the referendum and won narrowly, forcing postponement of the election.

Foreign Affairs. In the midst of its domestic turmoil, Hungary also found itself in the fall the conduit for the flight of some 30,000 East Germans from their homeland to Austria and thence to West Germany. Hungary's humanitarian handling of that tense situation, as well as its remarkable progress toward democracy, received public acquiescence from Soviet President Gorbachev and praise from U.S. President George Bush. Bush, who visited the country in July, promised Hungary permanent most-favored-nation trade status, and the U.S. Congress enacted a financial aid program.

See also feature article, page 24.

JOSEPH FREDERICK ZACEK
State University of New York at Albany

ICELAND

Iceland's center-left coalition government was strengthened in the fall of 1989 when four parliament members (MPs) of the right-wing Citizens' Party (CP) agreed to support the government, which now held 36 of the 63 seats and a secure majority in both chambers of the parliament. The new cabinet formed as a result included 11 ministers: The former nine remained in control of their respective ministries, while CP representatives assumed responsibility for the ministry of justice and a new ministry of the environment planned for 1990.

Pope John Paul II honored Iceland's small Catholic minority of some 2,000 people with a visit in June as part of his tour of Scandinavia. The pope held ecumenical services together with the bishop of Iceland and other representatives of the state Lutheran Church on the hallowed plains of Thingvellir, the site of the National Assembly of the medieval Icelandic Commonwealth.

In July, Spain's King Juan Carlos and Queen Sofia made an official visit to Iceland, while King Carl Gustav of Sweden unofficially went reindeer hunting in east Iceland in September. Iceland President Vigdis Finnbogadóttir made an official visit to Canada, where her itinerary included attending the 100th anniversary celebrations of the Icelandic Festival in Gimli, Manitoba, a nucleus of the main Icelandic settlement in Canada in the 19th century.

ICELAND • Information Highlights

Official Name: Republic of Iceland.
Location: North Atlantic Ocean.
Area: 39,768 sq mi (103 000 km²).
Population (mid-1989 est.): 300,000.
Chief Cities (Dec. 1, 1987): Reykjavík, the capital, 93,425; Akureyri, 13,856.
Government: *Head of state,* Vigdís Finnbogadóttir, president (took office Aug. 1980). *Head of government,* Steingrímur Hermannsson, prime minister (took office Sept. 1988). *Legislature*—Althing: Upper House and Lower House.
Monetary Unit: Króna (58.130 krónur equal U.S.$1, July 1989).
Gross Domestic Product (1987 U.S.$): $5,300,-000,000.
Foreign Trade (1988 U.S.$): *Imports,* $1,574,000,000; *exports,* $1,424,000,000.

Economy. The Icelandic economy contracted in 1989 for the second year in a row, with gross domestic product decreasing by about 2.5% and foreign currency earnings by 4.5%. Appreciable cuts were announced in fishing quotas for cod, down 25% to 250,000 tons for 1990, after the annual report of the Icelandic Marine Research Institute showed that the average size of the fish being caught had decreased slightly and that recruitment for the years 1985, 1986, and 1987 (which can be expected to provide the major portion of the catch for the next three years) had been below average to very poor. Despite relatively high prices for fish, especially on European markets, the freezing industry was beset with continuing difficulties, and several rural plants closed.

There was a net decrease in the Icelandic population of almost 1%, with some 2,000 more individuals emigrating than immigrating.

The finance sector was the scene of several mergers: Three of Iceland's smaller private banks, the Iceland Bank of Commerce, the Industrial Bank of Iceland, and the People's Bank, agreed to amalgamate and purchased the government's controlling interest in the Fisheries Bank of Iceland in June. The merger was followed by the publicly owned National Bank's purchase of the shares formerly held by the Federation of Icelandic Cooperative Societies in the Icelandic Cooperative Bank.

Whaling. Iceland's controversial research whaling program came to its conclusion in August. There would be no whaling whatsoever in 1990, the year agreed upon by the International Whaling Commission (IWC) to reassess whale stocks and decide whether to extend the moratorium on commercial whaling. Extensive aerial and surface monitoring carried out during the past several years indicated a sizable growth in the number of whales.

KENEVA KUNZ
BBC Foreign Correspondent, Reykjavik

IDAHO

The economy of Idaho outperformed that of the nation as a whole for the first time in the 1980s, pumping a $70 million surplus into the state treasury for the fiscal year ending June 30 and promising legislators more than $100 million in uncommitted cash when they convene at Boise in January 1990, which begins the state's centennial celebration. Although little actual growth could be seen outside the urban areas surrounding Boise, Idaho Falls, and Coeur d'Alene, increases in farm and nonfarm earnings boosted income-tax collections to unexpected levels and per capita income stabilized at 76.5% of the national average after years of slippage. Unexpectedly brisk sales of tickets for a new state lottery also helped bulging coffers. Analysts predicted more people would move into the state in 1990 than move away, another first in many years.

Legislature. Surplus cash and renewed harmony between Democratic Gov. Cecil Andrus and Republican legislative leaders contributed to a smoother legislative session than the acrimonious 1988 session. Legislators appropriated $394.3 million to public schools, up from $356 million a year earlier, and sweetened budgets of many state agencies, including the Department of Health and Welfare, which had grown starved for cash during the earlier years of the decade.

Higher Education. In July, Elisabeth Zinser, 48, assumed the presidency of the University of Idaho, replacing Richard Gibb, who retired after 12 years in the job. Zinser, who a year earlier resigned as president of Gallaudet College after Gallaudet's hearing-impaired students protested the hiring of a president with full hearing capability, came to Idaho from the University of North Carolina at Greensboro.

Judiciary. In August, Governor Andrus filled two vacancies on the Idaho Supreme Court, making every justice on the five-member court an Andrus appointee. Larry Boyle, 46, replaced Robert Huntley, who resigned to return to private practice. Charles McDevitt, 57, succeeded Alan Shepard, who died May 27 of a heart attack at age 66. The appointments silenced Republican criticism of the Andrus court for alleged hostility to the state's death penalty, as both Boyle and McDevitt voiced support for it.

Wilderness. Late in the year two bills designating additional Idaho wilderness areas were pending before the U.S. Congress. The first, a compromise addition of 1.4 million acres (567 000 ha) drafted by Republican U.S. Sen. James McClure and Governor Andrus, awaited floor action in the Senate. A second, Pennsylvania Democrat Rep. Peter Kostmayer's addition of 3.9 million acres (1.58 million ha), had yet to move in the House.

Politics. As 1990 began, popular senior Senator McClure announced that he would not seek a fourth term. U.S. Rep. Larry E. Craig (R) and state Attorney General Jim Jones (R) immediately indicated that they would seek the seat. Possible Democratic candidates for the post included former Gov. John V. Evans, Rep. Richard Stallings, and state Agriculture Director Dick Rush.

JIM FISHER
"Lewiston Morning Tribune"

IDAHO • Information Highlights

Area: 83,564 sq mi (216 432 km²).
Population (July 1, 1988): 1,003,000.
Chief Cities (1980 census): Boise, the capital (July 1, 1986 est.), 108,390; Pocatello, 46,340; Idaho Falls, 39,590.
Government (1989): *Chief Officers*—governor, Cecil Andrus (D); lt. gov., C. L. Otter (R). *Legislature*—Senate, 42 members; House of Representatives, 84 members.
State Finances (fiscal year 1988): *Revenue,* $1,913,000,000; *expenditure,* $1,692,000,000.
Personal Income (1988): $12,698,000,000; per capita, $12,665.
Labor Force (June 1989): *Civilian labor force,* 494,500; *unemployed,* 24,100 (4.9% of total force).
Education: *Enrollment* (fall 1987)—public elementary schools, 153,000; public secondary, 59,000; colleges and universities, 45,567. *Public school expenditures* (1987–88), $554,400,000 ($2,778 per pupil).

ILLINOIS

The Illinois political picture changed dramatically in July 1989 as Gov. James R. Thompson, who has occupied the statehouse in Springfield for 14 years, announced he would not seek an unprecedented fifth term. The state's longest-serving governor said he had had enough and that he would seek other career options when his term expires in January 1991.

Thompson may be remembered more for his political acumen than for any dramatic changes or philosophies he brought to Illinois as governor. A Republican, Thompson's chances at reelection in 1990 were in doubt, and his unsuccessful effort to win the 1988 vice-presidential nod from George Bush had cast a shadow over his political future. It may have been a good time for Thompson to bow out while pundits still recognized him as a good, but not exceptional, governor.

As Thompson bowed out, Illinois Secretary of State Jim Edgar jockeyed into position as the likely Republican candidate for governor, while Illinois Attorney General Neil Hartigan was the early favorite for the Democrats. Other potential gubernatorial candidates from both parties said they would not run.

Economy and Business. Sears Roebuck & Co. decided in June not to abandon Illinois, the state that always has been its home, for new headquarters elsewhere. But the merchandiser will vacate half its offices in Sears Tower in

Sixteen members of the Barrington Hills, IL, police force are jubilant following news that they were one of three winners of the state's $25 million lottery drawing on May 27.

AP/Wide World

Chicago in the early 1990s, and move to a new 786-acre (320-ha) site in suburban Hoffman Estates. Meanwhile, Sears would attempt to raise money by mortgaging the tower. Sears' decision to stay in Illinois came despite efforts from other states to lure the merchandiser and its 6,000 jobs. Illinois matched the generous economic incentives offered by the other suitors. State subsidies of $61.1 million were promised to help Sears move to the suburbs, and costs to the village of Hoffman Estates over the next 23 years may reach as high as $764.5 million. The village, however, hopes to recover most of the monies from taxes on the Sears property.

For Illinois farmers, a mild summer and plentiful rainfall—a welcome relief from the drought of 1988—were expected to yield bumper crops of corn and soybeans.

On the less positive side, the decision of the Defense Department to close two military installations in Illinois—the Fort Sheridan army garrison north of Chicago and Chanute Air Force Base in Rantoul—would mean the loss of thousands of jobs. Fort Sheridan alone has more than 3,200 military and civilian jobs, and an annual payroll of $297 million. No state was hit harder than Illinois by the 87 base closings recommended by the Federal Commission on Base Realignment and Closure as part of efforts to cut costs. While some Illinois congressmen disputed the cost-savings, the commission estimated the annual savings in the closing of Fort Sheridan at $40.8 million.

Crime. The nation's business community was shocked in August with the federal indictments in Chicago of 46 commodities traders. The federal government charged the traders with using a variety of schemes to systematically cheat hundreds of customers in the Chicago futures market, and evade taxes on the profits. U.S. Attorney General Richard Thornburgh said the indictments, which followed a 2½-year Federal Bureau of Investigation (FBI) undercover operation, were part "of an expanding Department of Justice crackdown on white-collar crime, from Wall Street to LaSalle Street [in Chicago] to Main Street with stops in between."

In one of the more bizarre criminal cases in recent Illinois history, the state dropped rape charges against Gary Dotson 12 years after he was accused of raping Cathleen Crowell Webb. Dotson, 32, had been sentenced to 25 to 50 years on the rape charge in 1979. The case got international attention in 1985 when Webb, who lives in New Hampshire, said she made up the entire rape case in 1977 because she believed she was pregnant. In the four years since her recantation the case bounced in and out of court, and Dotson in and out of prison. The rape charge was dismissed after a criminal court judge ordered a new trial for Dotson and the state, without Webb's testimony, had no case left. "As far as I'm concerned, my name has been cleared today," said Dotson, as he was released from custody in August.

ROBERT ENSTAD, *"Chicago Tribune"*

ILLINOIS • Information Highlights

Area: 56,345 sq mi (145 934 km²).
Population (July 1, 1988): 11,614,000.
Chief Cities (July 1, 1986 est.): Springfield, the capital, 100,290; Chicago, 3,009,530; Rockford, 135,760.
Government (1989): *Chief Officers*—governor, James R. Thompson (R); lt. gov., George H. Ryan (R). *General Assembly*—Senate, 59 members; House of Representatives, 118 members.
State Finances (fiscal year 1988): *Revenue,* $20,549,000,000; *expenditure,* $19,212,000,000.
Personal Income (1988): $204,115,000,000; per capita, $17,575.
Labor Force (June 1989): *Civilian labor force,* 6,004,000; *unemployed,* 346,000 (5.8% of total force).
Education: *Enrollment* (fall 1987)—public elementary schools, 1,252,000; public secondary, 560,000; colleges and universities, 686,954. *Public school expenditures* (1987–88), $6,787,935,000 ($3,989 per pupil).

The Gandhi era came to an end in India as the Congress(I) party of Rajiv Gandhi, below, *was defeated in November general elections. Vishwanath Pratap Singh,* right, *of the National Front is congratulated by President Ramaswamy Venkataraman after being sworn in as prime minister on December 2.*

INDIA

In 1989 the political landscape in India underwent a transformation. It culminated in the failure of the Congress(I) party, led by Rajiv Gandhi, to retain its majority in the lower house of the Indian Parliament in November's general election, and in the formation of a new government by a shaky coalition spearheaded by the Janata Dal party, with Vishwanath Pratap Singh as the new prime minister. The economic situation in 1989, as usual, was mixed, but on the whole it was more promising than it had been for some time. Foreign policy was dominated by relations with subcontinent neighbors, with events that included the withdrawal of Indian troops from Sri Lanka and harsh treatment of Nepal because of disagreements on a renewal of trade and transit rights.

Election Politics. Faced by the necessity of improving his fading image and of strengthening the Congress(I), Rajiv Gandhi devoted much of his time during the year to preparation for the general election, which he had to call by January 1990. For Gandhi the year brought a series of reversals. One of the first was his failure to boost his sagging political fortunes by making a good showing in state elections in the southern state of Tamil Nadu on January 21. Although he campaigned vigorously for Congress(I) candidates, his party won only 26 of the 234 seats in the State Assembly.

Many Indians were disillusioned because Gandhi had failed to fulfill his promise to eliminate corruption. A major scandal of 1987, involving charges that members of his government had accepted huge "kickbacks" from Bofors, a Swedish arms manufacturer, was revived in 1989. And a report by the comptroller and auditor general of India seemed to confirm the charges.

Photos, AP/Wide World

Another problem facing Gandhi was the growing alienation of Indian farmers. He tried to win them back by providing financial incentives and by granting more power to villages through a revival of the system of *panchayati raj,* a program of local self-government, development, and administration.

Gandhi made little progress in his professed efforts to reform, unify, and strengthen his party. He failed to keep his promise to hold party elections, which had been postponed repeatedly for many years. During the year defections from the party were frequent.

The opposition parties capitalized on the declining support for Gandhi and his party. The National Front, an alliance of five parties including the Janata Dal, itself a merger of five political groups, worked to unite the opposition against the ruling Congress(I). The Front had a potential successor to Gandhi as prime minister in Vishwanath Pratap Singh, who had been minister of finance and defense in Gandhi's cabinet.

Like all other anti-Congress coalitions, the National Front was a strange assemblage of previously warring parties. Its alliance with the Communist Party of India (Marxist) and the right-wing Hindu fundamentalist Bharatiya Janata Party (BJP), which were opposed bitterly to each other, did not make presenting a united front any easier. The National Front staged a series of well-attended rallies and marches with its biggest rally, held in New Delhi on September 25, drawing several hundred thousand people. The Front also had a hand in a series of strikes, some nationwide, organized by labor unions.

Underlying the political uncertainties and jockeying for power was what a correspondent of *The Christian Science Monitor* described as "a level of social conflict and communal violence not seen since the 1950s." This was a nationwide phenomenon, but it was particularly acute in Assam, Bihar, Jammu and Kashmir, and Punjab.

A Watershed Election. On October 17 the Election Commission, conveying a decision of Prime Minister Gandhi, announced that the nation's ninth general election would be held on November 22 and 24 (soon extended to include November 26). The brief but hectic campaign was the most violent in India's electoral history, with more than 100 people killed and many thousands injured. Gandhi, whose campaign was conducted by personal favorites rather than seasoned political veterans, appealed for a new mandate under the slogan, "Power to the People." He warned that chaos would result if his party was defeated. The opposition, led by the National Front, stressed the long list of charges against Gandhi and the Congress(I) that had led to widespread disillusionment among the voters.

Nearly 6,100 candidates—including more than 1,000 in one state, Uttar Pradesh—contested 525 seats in the lower house of the Indian Parliament, the Lok Sabha (which has a total of 545 members), in 24 of the 25 states (in Assam the voting was postponed until January 1990). Assembly elections were held simultaneously in five states—Uttar Pradesh, Andhra Pradesh, Karnataka, Goa, and Sikkim. On the whole the elections went off peacefully, but in many constituencies the voting was marred by violence and widespread voting fraud so serious that the Election Commission ordered repolling on November 27 in more than 1,100 polling stations, including nearly 100 in Rajiv Gandhi's constituency of Amethi in Uttar Pradesh.

The results were truly astonishing. The Congress(I), which in the last general election in December 1984 had won 415 seats in the Lok Sabha, was reduced to a minority of 192 members. The National Front won even fewer seats —145, with the Janata Dal winning 141 of this total—but the two parties with which it had electoral alliances, the CPI(M) and the BJP, won 118 seats. The upsurge of the BJP, which gained 86 seats (it had two in the sitting Lok Sabha), was a reflection of the growth of Hindu fundamentalism in north India.

Ironically, the Congress(I) actually won more seats than in 1984 in the South of India, where non-Congress governments were in power, and lost heavily in the northern states, the traditional base of its political power. While there was no clear overall winner, there was one clear loser: Rajiv Gandhi. The election was viewed widely as a referendum on his leadership. The results indicated that voters not only were disenchanted with him, but also with almost all incumbents, whatever their party affiliation.

When the results were known, Gandhi submitted his resignation as prime minister, and President Ramaswamy Venkataraman invited V. P. Singh to form a government. Singh was able to form his government by obtaining the political support of the CPI(M), the BJP, and some smaller groups. He was sworn in as prime minister on December 2. The formation of the non-Congress government ushered in a new era of coalition politics and increasing political uncertainty, but it showed that India's democratic system could work under crisis conditions. It also may have marked the end of the Nehru-Gandhi dynasty, which had led the country for more than 37 of the 42 years of independence.

The Economy. According to the annual report of the Reserve Bank of India, the economy staged a substantial recovery in the fiscal year 1988–89 (ending March 31, 1989), with an overall growth rate of nearly 10%. Food-grain production, aided by a good monsoon in 1988, increased by 23% over the 1987–88 figure, reaching a record total of 172.5 million tons. But the report also mentioned a number of "areas of concern." These areas included a widening trade deficit, a decline in foreign exchange reserves, a reduction in the stockpile of food grain, and an inflation rate of 9%.

In its *World Economic Survey, 1989* the United Nations commended India for its "robust performance" and for its role in helping to boost the rate of growth in the developing countries. "Over the past ten years," the *Survey* reported, "there has been a gradual but steady pragmatic evolution in India's development priorities and strategies." The report estimated that the growth rate in 1989—the last year of the nation's seventh Five Year Plan—would be about 6.5%.

The budget for 1989–90, presented by Finance Minister S. B. Chavan to the Lok Sabha on February 28, called for expenditures of $53.5 billion with revenues of $48.7 billion,

AP/Wide World

On August 30 workers from the opposition parties staged a nationwide strike to protest alleged government corruption and demand the resignation of Prime Minister Gandhi. Several persons were killed in the walkout.

leaving a deficit of $4.8 billion. Both estimated expenditures and revenues were greater than in 1988–89—by 11% and 13%, respectively—but the estimated deficit was 8% less than in the previous fiscal year. Requests for defense were slightly lower than in 1988–89, but they amounted to about 26% of the total budget.

In June the Aid India Consortium, organized by the World Bank, agreed on an aid package of $6.7 billion for fiscal year 1989–90. This was an increase of 6.3% over the previous year. The Bank and its affiliate, the International Development Association, also made available $620 million in loans and credits to help finance facilities for oil transportation, including a pipeline of more than 900 mi (1 488 km), and for the training of skilled workers.

Foreign Affairs. During most of the year India was criticized increasingly by neighboring subcontinent states for its military buildup and its alleged bullying tactics, especially in its relations with Nepal. In March separate trade and transit treaties between India and Nepal, in effect since 1978, were up for renewal. India notified Nepal that it wanted a unified treaty. When Nepal did not concur, India allowed the treaties to expire, and immediately imposed an almost complete blockade of the smaller country, leaving only two of the 21 trade and 15 transit border crossings open. The Nepalese economy was hurt badly by India's actions. Relations between the two nations reached the lowest point in many years.

After an almost total impasse for about five months, India and Nepal began direct negotiations to resolve their dispute. In late August India's Foreign Minister P. V. Narasimha Rao visited Katmandu and arranged for Nepal's King Birendra to met Prime Minister Gandhi at the nonaligned summit in Belgrade in September. At this meeting the two top leaders agreed to take steps to end the blockade. By the end of the year the dispute seemed to be well on the way to resolution, but Nepal was left with continuing special economic problems and a great deal of bitter feeling toward India.

India's relations with Sri Lanka had been strained ever since the Indo-Sri Lankan accord of 1987 on the island-nation's civil war and the subsequent dispatch of Indian peacekeeping forces to help persuade, or force, the Tamil militants in the north to accept the terms of the accord. Relations worsened in the middle of the year, and then began to improve. They were most tense in June. On June 1, Sri Lanka President Ranasinghe Premadasa publicly demanded that the Indian forces—then numbering about 45,000 troops—leave his country by the end of July. Gandhi's answer was that the Indian forces were there under the 1987 accord, and could be withdrawn only by mutual agreement. The deadline passed with only a token Indian withdrawal. After prolonged negotiations the two governments announced on September 8 that they had reached an agreement. India promised to withdraw all of its forces by the end of 1989, and to cease military operations immediately. The whole episode created added difficulties for the ruling United National Party in Sri Lanka and for Rajiv Gandhi and the Congress(I) in India.

Relations with Pakistan seemed to improve after Gandhi and Pakistan Prime Minister Benazir Bhutto had long talks during the South Asia Association for Regional Cooperation (SAARC) summit in Islamabad in December

1988. They met again in Islamabad in July, and both leaders agreed to take further steps to improve relations between their countries and to encourage more contacts at various levels. But thereafter relations again deteriorated, in part because Bhutto was under increasing pressure from anti-Indian fundamentalist Muslim groups and others, and Rajiv Gandhi likewise was under growing pressure from anti-Pakistan groups. The five-year dispute over control of the Siachen glacier in the remote and forbidding north of Jammu and Kashmir, in the Karakoram range, flared up more seriously during 1989, with several military clashes and casualties.

India's contacts with the Najibullah regime in Afghanistan also were criticized widely in Pakistan. In early May, Najibullah was welcomed warmly in New Delhi during an official visit, and India continued to give his Communist regime substantial diplomatic and military support.

Sino-Indian relations improved considerably following Gandhi's official visit to China in late December 1988. India was also one of the few non-Communist countries not to condemn publicly the Chinese authorities for the massacre of prodemocracy student protesters in Tiananmen Square on June 4. In October a high-level delegation from China, led by Deputy Prime Minister Wu Xieqian, was welcomed in India. Both countries agreed to try to resolve their border differences by negotiation, but little progress was made toward the resolution of this long-standing dispute.

Two incidents in 1989 created additional strains in U.S.-India relations. On May 25 the United States cited India, along with Japan and Brazil, for "unfair trade practices" under Section 301 of the 1988 Trade and Competitiveness Act. Reaction in India to this move was vehement. President Bush phoned Prime Minister Gandhi to urge him to negotiate to resolve the issue, but Gandhi refused. On June 1, at a press conference in Calcutta, he said: "We will not be dictated to on how to run our country and how to frame our laws." India also strongly protested a U.S. decision to sell 60 F-16 jet fighters to Pakistan, that was announced during an official visit to the United States by Pakistan's Prime Minister Bhutto in early June.

On the whole, however, contacts between India and the United States have become more extensive and overall relations have improved. The United States has become India's largest trading partner (in 1988 India had a $620 million trade surplus with the United States) and the main source of foreign investment. In late June, Dr. Karan Singh, son of the last Hindu maharajah of Kashmir, replaced P. K. Kaul as India's ambassador to the United States.

In July, Gandhi spent several days in Paris, as one of the Third World leaders who was invited to attend the celebrations of the bicentennial of the French Revolution. While there he conferred with several other heads of state. On his return trip he stopped briefly in Moscow to meet with Soviet President Gorbachev and in Islamabad to meet with Bhutto. In September he attended the ninth nonaligned summit in Belgrade, where he conferred with many other Third World leaders and proposed a Planet Protection Fund under the aegis of the United Nations. He planned to attend the Commonwealth summit in Kuala Lumpur in October, but he canceled this trip because of the general election.

INDIA • Information Highlights

Official Name: Republic of India.
Location: South Asia.
Area: 1,269,340 sq mi (3 287 590 km²).
Population (mid-1989 est.): 835,000,000.
Chief Cities (1981 census): New Delhi, the capital, 5,157,270; Bombay, 8,243,405; Calcutta, 3,288,148.
Government: *Head of state,* Ramaswamy Venkataraman, president (took office July 25, 1987). *Head of government,* Vishwanath Pratap Singh, prime minister (took office Dec. 2, 1989). *Legislature*—Parliament: Rajya Sabha (Council of States) and Lok Sabha (House of the People).
Monetary Unit: Rupee (16.978 rupees equal U.S.$1, Dec. 13, 1989).
Gross National Product (1987 U.S.$): $231,000,000,000.
Economic Indexes (1988): *Consumer Prices* (1980 = 100), all items, 201.7. *Industrial Production* (1980 = 100), 178.
Foreign Trade (1988 U.S.$): *Imports,* $18,959,000,000; *exports,* $13,160,000,000.

General. Throughout the year India observed the centennial of the birth of Jawaharlal Nehru, the independence movement leader and the nation's first prime minister, whose 100th birthday fell on November 14. The year also marked the 25th anniversary of Nehru's death on May 27, 1964.

On February 14 the Indian Supreme Court announced a "final" settlement of the claims against the Union Carbide Company arising from the deaths and devastation caused by the leakage of poison gas from the company's petrocide plant in Bhopal in December 1984. Union Carbide agreed to pay a lump sum of $470 million by March 23. At one time the Indian government had demanded $3.3 billion to settle claims by victims of the disaster or their families.

On May 22, India became the sixth country to demonstrate an intermediate ballistic missile capability by successfully launching a surface-to-surface missile named *Agni* (Fire). The feat was hailed widely in India as signaling a new political and technological status for the nation.

Late in the year the city of Bhagalpur and various villages were devastated by heavy Muslim-Hindu fighting. As many as 1,000 persons were believed dead.

NORMAN D. PALMER, *Professor Emeritus*
University of Pennsylvania

INDIANA

In October, Indiana launched its first instant lottery game, ending more than a decade of legislative bickering and a 138-year constitutional ban on gambling. A month later, Gary, IN, voters in a nonbinding referendum endorsed casino gambling, but state approval also was needed and was considered unlikely. Educational funding dominated debate in the 1989 legislative session and necessitated a two-day special session.

Legislature. The legislative impotence predicted as a result of the unprecedented 50-50 Democratic-Republican split in the state House of Representatives failed to materialize in 1989. Democratic and Republican speakers conducted House sessions on alternate days, and cochairpersons directed committees of an equal number of Democrats and Republicans.

Legislation creating a state lottery and allowing parimutuel betting on horse races in counties where it was approved by the county council was passed. Lottery surplus revenue would be applied to unfunded liabilities in the pension funds for teachers, police, and firemen and to Gov. B. Evan Bayh's Build Indiana fund.

Designed to reduce the shock of the 1989 decennial property reassessment, tax legislation provided for increases in the homestead credit from 4% to 6%, then to 5%, from 1989 through 1991, and for deductions from reassessed values before the computation of property taxes in forthcoming years. Legislators also changed the reassessment of residential property and business buildings from the current ten-year cycles to every four years. In an effort to alleviate the heavy excise tax on automobiles, lawmakers approved a bill deducting price increases caused by inflation from a vehicle's taxable value and took additional steps to identify those people who attempt to avoid paying the excise tax by registering their vehicles out of state.

INDIANA • Information Highlights

Area: 36,185 sq mi (93 720 km²).
Population (July 1, 1988): 5,556,000.
Chief Cities (July 1, 1986 est.): Indianapolis, the capital, 719,820; Fort Wayne, 172,900; Gary, 136,790.
Government (1989): *Chief Officers*—governor, Evan Bayh (D); lt. gov., Frank L. O'Bannon (D). *General Assembly*—Senate, 50 members; House of Representatives, 100 members.
State Finances (fiscal year 1988): *Revenue,* $9,744,000,000; *expenditure,* $8,848,000,000.
Personal Income (1988): $82,924,000,000; per capita, $14,924.
Labor Force (June 1989): *Civilian labor force,* 2,992,000; *unemployed,* 99,300 (3.3% of total force).
Education: *Enrollment* (fall 1987)—public elementary schools, 659,000; public secondary, 305,000; colleges and universities, 256,264. *Public school expenditures* (1987–88), $3,190,198,000 ($3,418 per pupil).

Educational reform measures also received major legislative attention. Indiana Statewide Testing for Educational Progress (ISTEP), initiated in 1987 as part of former Gov. Robert D. Orr's "A+" program, revealed higher-than-predicted student test scores. As a result, legislators raised standards, increased funding, and provided for more control by local school corporations. Governor Bayh's educational package, dubbed Excel, received legislative sanction and included an adult literacy program, a merit scholarship program for needy students who show proficiency in mathematics, a requirement for drug education from kindergarten through grade 12, and a published annual school report. An early teacher retirement bill that failed to pass in 1988 received only one negative vote in the 1989 session.

Budget. Educational funding, particularly for public schools, was the primary issue that forced Indiana's 106th General Assembly into a two-day special session. The nearly $18.3 billion compromise budget featured a $3.6 billion state aid package for local schools, providing a 6% increase in aid for each year of the 1989–91 biennium but requiring a 6% increase in local state property taxes. The budget also included expanded Medicaid health benefits for children and pregnant women in an attempt to reduce high infant-mortality rates, funds to establish a statewide services office for the deaf and hearing-impaired, and increased funding for a popular home-care program that provides assistance to the elderly or disabled so that they can remain in their homes instead of entering nursing homes. Because operating expenses for the 1989–91 fiscal years exceed estimated revenues and result in deficit spending, the balance in the state's general fund will be reduced to an estimated $65.4 million by 1991, compared with an approximate $258.8 million balance at the end of June 1989.

Other. Indiana experienced its latest-ever snowfall in May and struggled through record amounts of snow in October. The agricultural economy profited from higher-than-normal summer rainfall that resulted in corn yields significantly above 1988's totals, but threatened foreign takeovers of Cummins Engine and Arvin corporations, two Fortune 500 companies, rocked the industrial community.

The year's political news included the victory of Democrat Jill Long for the 4th District House seat vacated by Dan Coats, who took over Dan Quayle's Senate seat.

LORNA LUTES SYLVESTER, *Indiana University*

INDONESIA

The issue of presidential succession, a papal visit, far-reaching economic reforms, and major diplomatic initiatives were at the forefront of Indonesian affairs in 1989.

© Cynthia Johnson/Gamma-Liaison

Indonesia's Suharto indicated that he might give up the presidency at the end of his fifth term in 1993. He also traveled to the United States and the USSR in 1989.

Politics. In an autobiography published in February, 68-year-old President Suharto wrote that his election to a fifth five-year term the previous March would be "the last one for me." This and other signals of a transfer of power in 1993—along with reports that Suharto might accept the idea of more than one candidate standing for office—touched off widespread debate over his successor, the succession process, and the prospects for political change. In early June, however, Suharto issued a lengthy statement calling for an end to the speculation. Emphasizing the enduring principles of his "Pancasila Democracy," the state ideology, Suharto's statement was interpreted by some as indicating a willingness to stand for another term. Indonesia's armed forces ("Abri") assured the government of their commitment to the constitutional process—but calls for a political transition continued.

East Timor, closed to journalists and foreigners since Indonesia's annexation of it in 1976, was opened in October for a visit by Pope John Paul II. Stopping in the predominantly Catholic province during a five-day trip to Indonesia (the world's most populous Muslim country), the pontiff addressed a crowd of 100,000 in the provincial capital of Dili. As he left, a group of Timorese nationalists rushed the altar, unfurling a pro-independence banner and shouting "Viva il papa!" ("Long live the pope!"). Indonesian police quelled the outburst.

Economy. One of the world's top-ten producers of oil (about 1.2 million barrels per day), Indonesia continued to be hurt by depressed world prices. Its economic growth rate of about 5% in 1988–89 lagged behind that of Thailand, Malaysia, and Singapore, but still represented a healthy increase from the 3.7% recorded a year earlier. Underlying the nation's economic expansion was a continuing program of diversification. With oil revenues of less than $8 billion in 1989 (compared with $14.6 billion in 1985), such non-oil commodities as liquefied natural gas, textiles, manufactured goods, electrical equipment, and food and wood products represented an increasing share of foreign trade. Total Indonesian exports rose to $19.5 billion in 1988 and were expected to exceed $20.3 billion in 1989. Other key policy measures included privatization of state-owned enterprises, deregulation of major industries, and incentives to foreign investors.

Foreign Affairs. President Suharto took steps to forge a new global role for his nation. In February, Indonesia and China announced the normalization of relations, frozen since 1965. In June, Suharto traveled to Washington for talks with President George Bush and other U.S. officials; two months earlier, the U.S. government announced that it would be more than doubling its military assistance to Indonesia, to $7 million, in 1989–90. In September, Suharto made a six-day visit to the Soviet Union, the first by an Indonesian president in 25 years. And the Indonesian government, represented chiefly by Foreign Minister Ali Alatas, played a prominent role in efforts to settle the Cambodian conflict; three days of face-to-face talks among the warring factions were held in Jakarta during February, although without significant progress. Indonesia was also a party to the inconclusive 19-nation peace conference convened in Paris in late July to address the Cambodian conflict.

JEFFREY H. HACKER, *Free-lance Writer*

INDONESIA • Information Highlights

Official Name: Republic of Indonesia.
Location: Southeast Asia.
Area: 741,097 sq mi (1 919 440 km²).
Population (mid-1989 est.): 184,600,000.
Chief Cities (Dec. 31, 1983 est.): Jakarta, the capital, 7,347,800; Surabaya, 2,223,600; Medan, 1,805,500; Bandung, 1,566,700.
Government: *Head of state and government,* Suharto, president (took office for fifth five-year term March 1988). *Legislature* (unicameral)—House of Representatives.
Monetary Unit: Rupiah (1,782.0 rupiahs equal U.S.$1, Dec. 1, 1989).
Gross National Product (1987 U.S.$): $69,000,000,000.
Economic Index (1988): *Consumer Prices* (1980 = 100), all items, 198.6; food, 203.2.
Foreign Trade (1988 U.S.$): *Imports,* $13,392,000,000; *exports,* $19,476,000,000.

INDUSTRIAL PRODUCTION

Industrial countries posted a 3% gain in industrial output in 1989, after a nearly 6% increase in 1988. Much of the slowdown in the rate of gain was due to the moderation in the U.S. increase. The U.S. gain in 1989 was 3.1%, compared with a 5.7% growth in 1988.

The number of jobs in goods-producing industries in the United States was about 26 million at year's end, up 0.6% from the year before. Manufacturing jobs stood at 19.5 million, slightly below the figure for 1988. Mining jobs numbered 738,000, an increase of about 3.5%. The job count in construction was almost 5.4 million, an increase of 3% over 1988. Productivity in U.S. manufacturing, measured by output per hour of all persons, increased 2.7% in 1989, a gain that matched the 1988 gain.

The volume of industrial production accounts for about one third of the gross national product. Although industrial output started out at a good pace in the first half, the rate of gain slackened in the second half of 1989. At year's end, the Federal Reserve Board's (FRB's) index of industrial production stood only 1.2% above the 1988 index. The slowdown was most marked in durable consumer goods, where output was down nearly 3% since 1988.

U.S. Industrial Production

	Percent Change 1987 to 1988	Index (1977=100) 1988 level	Percent Change 1988 to 1989
Total Production	5.7	137.2	3.1
Mining	2.8	103.4	−1.2
Utilities	3.5	114.3	1.2
Manufacturing	6.0	142.7	3.7
Consumer Goods	4.8	133.9	4.0
Business Equipment	9.0	157.6	6.6
Defense and Space Equipment	−1.6	185.8	−3.1
Durable Goods Manufacturing	6.6	141.9	3.2
Lumber and products	5.5	137.3	−0.5
Furniture and fixtures	6.1	162.1	3.8
Clay, glass, and stone products	2.9	122.6	1.3
Primary metals	9.5	89.2	−1.7
Fabricated metal products	8.9	120.9	3.3
Nonelectrical machinery	11.9	170.8	8.4
Electrical machinery	4.9	180.1	0.9
Transportation equipment	2.4	132.1	1.0
Nondurable Goods Manufacturing	5.2	143.9	4.4
Foods	3.6	142.7	3.1
Tobacco products	1.7	105.2	−0.1
Textile mill products	0.4	116.2	5.5
Apparel products	1.7	109.1	1.9
Paper and paper products	4.0	150.3	1.4
Printing and publishing	6.8	184.2	8.4
Chemicals and products	8.5	151.9	5.9
Petroleum and products	2.6	96.0	1.7
Rubber and plastic products	6.6	174.4	3.1
Leather and products	−1.0	59.5	2.3

Source: Board of Governors of the Federal Reserve System

Transportation. The U.S. aerospace industry had a solid year as far as large commercial transport aircraft were concerned, but it was a different story in general aviation. In constant dollar terms, large transport-aircraft shipments were up 24%. Some 450 large commercial civilian aircraft were delivered in 1989, valued at $17.5 billion. As for general aviation, the number of units delivered edged down slightly to 1,110 units, a far cry from the industry's heyday in 1978, when a record 17,100 general aviation aircraft were delivered.

Domestic-car manufacturers saw their output decline 0.8% in 1988 to 6.44 million units, and—faced with strong import competition—they recorded a 2.6% drop for 1989 as well. Imports claimed 32.9% of the U.S. market in 1989, and their share climbed to 37.9% in November. Foreign carmakers in the United States produced 1.1 million units, up sharply from the 461,000 produced in 1985.

Steel. U.S. steel production decreased about 3% in 1989, after rising 12% in 1988 to 99.9 million tons of raw steel. Internationalization of the industry continued, taking the form

AP/Wide World

Responding to an overall poor year for the U.S. auto industry, Chrysler Motors previewed the Voyager III as 1990 began. The model combines two units—a three-passenger front with a 1.6-liter propane-fuel engine and a four-passenger rear with a 2.2-liter, four-cylinder engine. The combined car is only slightly longer than the previous Grand Voyager.

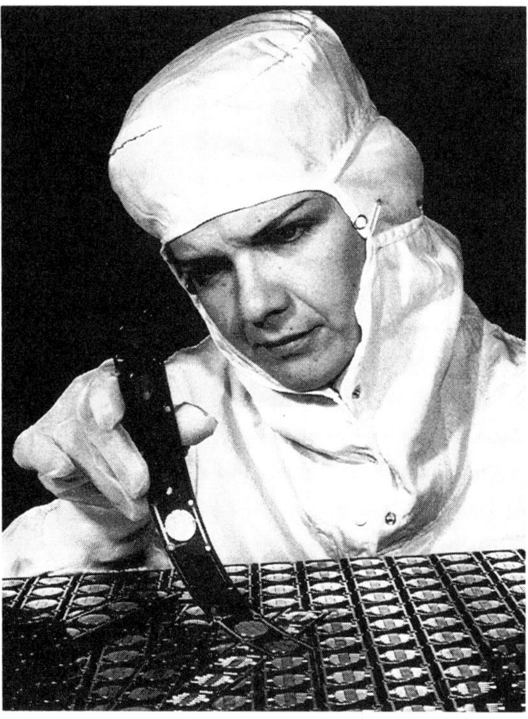

Photos, AP/Wide World

R&D: A technologist, left, *inspects small disks to be used in more intelligent credit cards. With the public becoming more health-conscious, oat products were in demand.*

Employees on Nonagricultural Payrolls
(in thousands)

	1988	1989*	Percent Change
Good-producing industries	25,249	25,630	1.5
Mining	721	719	−0.5
Construction	5,125	5,298	3.4
Manufacturing	19,403	19,615	1.1
Durable goods	11,437	11,528	0.8
Lumber and wood products	765	769	0.5
Furniture and fixtures	530	532	0.4
Stone, clay, and glass products	600	602	0.3
Primary metal industries	744	782	1.1
Fabricated metal products	1,431	1,445	1.0
Machinery, except electrical	2,082	2,146	3.1
Electrical & electronic equip.	2,070	2,038	−1.6
Transportation equipment	2,051	2,049	−0.1
Instruments & related products	749	778	3.9
Miscellaneous mfg. industries	386	392	1.6
Nondurable goods	7,967	8,080	1.4
Food and kindred products	1,636	1,664	1.7
Tobacco manufactures	56	53	−4.3
Textile mill products	729	728	−0.1
Apparel & other textile goods	1,092	1,091	−0.1
Paper & allied products	693	698	0.8
Printing & publishing	1,561	1,607	2.9
Chemicals & allied products	1,065	1,092	2.6
Petroleum & coal products	162	162	0
Rubber & misc. plastics products	829	840	1.3
Leather & leather products	144	141	−2.1

*Preliminary
Source: Bureau of Labor Statistics

of joint ventures between integrated domestic firms and foreign steelmakers. The position of foreign steelmakers accounted for about 25% of domestic integrated steel-mill facilities, with Japan, South Korea, and Brazil making up the major portion of the foreign investment. Domestic steelmakers have fallen behind in technological breakthroughs because their research and development (R&D) outlays lag far behind those of their foreign competitors. While U.S. firms' R&D spending amounts to 0.5% of sales, Japanese steelmakers plow 1.5% of their sales volume into R&D.

More competition to domestic integrated mills in the sheet-steel market came from minimills. Minimills traditionally stuck to lower cost carbon-mill products, especially rod, bar, and light structurals, where they now dominate the market completely. Thanks to a newly developed technology, the thin slab caster, minimills added more than 2 million tons of flat rolled capacity in 1989, still small compared to the overall 40-million-ton flat rolled market in the United States, but destined for further growth.

New Products. Computer offerings grew apace as myriad notebook-sized personal computers were introduced by many manufacturers. Indeed, a palmtop also was introduced that weighs less than 1 lb (.4 kg) and runs on three AAA batteries. Small though they may be, the notepad and smaller machines have the power to run spread-sheet, word-processing, and some other programs.

The electronic still video camera, a device that captures images on electronic sensors instead of film, was offered to consumers who have everything. The camera comes with a playback device, and the package was initially priced at $1,000. Hoping for yet another "revolution" in smoother shaves, the Gillette company introduced a razor blade welded together by lasers; it is to be used in a new permanent "Sensor" razor handle.

Among new products that fizzled in 1989 was the "smokeless" cigarette "Premier" that was test-marketed by R. J. Reynolds beginning in October 1988. As for a runaway success, the Mazda Motor Corp. well may take the prize thanks to its entry in the convertible category that started "Miata mania."

Business Investment. Business spending on new plants and equipment in the U.S. increased 10% in 1989, to $475 billion. It followed a 10.5% increase in 1988. The biggest increase was by airlines, up 31%. Spurred by a brisk demand for large transport aircraft, aircraft manufacturers increased their capital spending by 13.6%. The manufacturing industry as a whole increased investment by 9.4%, a slowdown from the 14% rate of gain in 1988. Steelmakers increased spending by 12.5%, while stone-clay-glass producers raised spending by 7.5%. Nonelectrical machinery manufacturers reduced spending by 0.1%, after an increase of 10.1% in 1988. Electrical-machinery producers cut investment by 2.9%, following a 19.9% increase in 1988. Mining-industry investment dropped 3.5%, but public utilities increased capital spending by 8.8%, following a 4% increase in 1988. Commercial firms raised investment by 11%, after a 9% increase in 1988.

Value of New Construction Put in Place in the United States (Billions of 1982 dollars)

	1988	1989*	Percent Change
Total new construction	352.5	346.7	−1.6
Private construction	284.5	278.1	−2.2
Residential buildings	174.8	168.7	−3.5
Nonresidential buildings	81.2	80.6	−0.7
Industrial	12.5	13.4	7.2
Office	23.4	22.8	−2.6
Hotels and motels	5.7	6.2	8.8
Other commercial	25.1	23.9	−4.8
Religious	2.4	2.4	0
Educational	2.4	2.6	8.0
Hospital and institutional	6.0	6.1	1.6
Miscellaneous buildings[1]	3.6	3.1	−13.9
Telecommunications	7.2	6.3	−12.5
All other private[2]	1.8	2.6	44.4
Public construction	68.0	68.6	0.9
Housing and redevelopment	1.3	1.6	23.1
Industrial	1.2	1.1	−8.3
Educational	9.2	10.3	12.0
Hospital	1.9	1.7	−10.5
Other public buildings[3]	9.4	9.5	1.1
Highways and streets	23.2	22.1	−4.3
Military facilities	2.7	2.8	3.7
Conservation and development	5.8	4.1	−29.3
Sewer systems	7.5	7.6	1.3
Water supply facilities	2.9	3.2	10.3
Miscellaneous public[4]	6.0	4.6	−23.3

Source: Bureau of the Census * preliminary
[1] Includes amusement and recreational buildings, bus and airline terminals, animal hospitals, and shelters, etc. [2] Includes privately owned streets and bridges, parking areas, sewer and water facilities, parks and playgrounds, golf courses, airfields, etc. [3] Includes general administrative buildings, prisons, police and fire stations, courthouses, civic centers, passenger terminals, postal facilities. [4] Includes open amusement and recreational facilities, power generating facilities, transit systems, airfields, open parking facilities, etc.

Construction. Construction activity eased in 1989 as residential, commercial, and office construction declined. Measured in constant dollars, new construction put in place dropped 1.6%. Privately owned housing starts, which reached 1.8 million in 1986, dropped in 1989 for the third year in a row. Successive drops of 10.2% in 1987, 8.2% in 1988, and 6% in 1989 reduced the number of starts to about 1.4 million.

Mining. Mining output registered a 1.2% decline on the FRB index in 1989, after rising 2.7% in 1988. Coal production, including soft coal and anthracite, increased about 2.5% in 1989 from the 950 million tons in 1988. Oil production averaged 7.7 million barrels per day, having dropped for four years in a row. Metal mining registered an advance of 8.5% on the Federal Reserve Board's production index.

International Production. By the end of 1989, U.S. industrial production was only 1.2% higher than in 1988. Considerably smaller than the 4.9% gain posted during 1988, the slower rate of output gain reflected moderation on the part of consumer demand, a slower growth of exports, and a smaller increase in business investment.

Production increases were sluggish also in Canada, up only 0.3%. France showed a 1.2% gain; Italy was up 2.1%. Great Britain posted a decline of 0.4%. Brisk gains were recorded for Australia, where industrial production grew by 10.4% in 1989. Respectable gains were posted for Switzerland, up 5.6%; Japan, up 5.4%; Belgium, up 5.1%; Sweden, up 4.9%; Spain, up 4.4%; West Germany, up 3.3%; and the Netherlands, up 2.9%.

Industrial production in the planned economies apparently stalled in 1989. In the Soviet Union, *perestroika* did very little to improve performance. If anything, the economic reforms that were introduced were confusing to managers and planners accustomed to Brezhnev-era ways of doing business. Severe shortages of consumer goods sparked strikes in coal-mining regions, and weaknesses in the distribution and transportation systems only served to aggravate production bottlenecks.

To alleviate consumers' dissatisfaction, the Soviets shifted defense plants to the production of consumer goods. But such conversion was not proceeding smoothly. Changing a system that for 50 years had emphasized heavy industry into one oriented toward the consumer is disruptive and time-consuming. The increase in industrial production was estimated at 2.3% for 1988. No appreciable increase from that rate was discernible for 1989. Soviet raw-coal output rose 1.6% in 1988, and due to strikes the 1989 output grew even more slowly, if at all. As for petroleum, output edged down 0.1% in 1988, and dropped a little over 1% in 1989, as production in the West Siberian region leveled off and production from other regions contin-

Industrial Production: International Overview

1985 = 100

	1983	1984	1985	1986	1987	1988	1989*
Industrial Countries	91	97	100	101	104	110	114
Australia	90	96	100	105	101	105	112
Austria	90	96	100	101	102	106	112
Belgium	96	99	100	101	104	109	104
Canada	84	91	100	100	106	112	113
Denmark	86	96	100	104	101	102	104
Finland	92	96	100	101	105	110	111
France	97	99	100	100	102	106	112
Germany	93	96	100	102	102	106	111
Ireland	88	97	100	103	115	128	134
Italy	96	99	100	103	107	112	116
Japan	88	96	100	100	103	113	119
Luxembourg	83	94	100	103	103	115	121
Netherlands	92	96	100	100	101	101	105
Norway	89	96	100	103	111	116	132
Spain	97	98	100	102	107	111	118
Sweden	91	98	100	100	105	106	111
Switzerland	92	95	100	104	104	112	116
United Kingdom	95	95	100	102	106	110	109
United States	88	98	100	99	104	110	113

Source: International Monetary Fund
*Preliminary Estimate

ued to fall. As for consumer goods, light-industry output grew by 2.5% in 1988, and a comparable gain was recorded for 1989. However, much of the output continued to be of poor quality, as attested by consumer complaints.

A major bottleneck for the Soviet Union, the world's largest producer of crude oil and natural gas, is its inability to produce enough gasoline to meet rapidly growing demand. The country's refineries are out of date. Only about 5% of the refinery capacity has "cracking" capability compared with about one third of total Western refinery capacity. That means that the Soviet Union's ability to shift refinery output from low-value fuel oil to light products is very limited.

AGO AMBRE
U.S. Department of Commerce

INSURANCE, LIABILITY

Liability insurance was easier to obtain in 1989 than at any time since the insurance crisis of 1984–86. Physicians, municipalities, manufacturers, and other policyholders who had been hit with skyrocketing premiums or outright policy cancellations at mid-decade once again were able to buy protection from lawsuits related to professional malpractice, negligence, and defective products.

The liability crisis sparked a heated debate that pitted property and casualty insurers, which provide liability coverage, against consumer advocates and the legal profession. The insurance industry blamed greedy and litigious plaintiffs—and their attorneys—for forcing liability insurers to raise their premiums to cover the rising cost of high jury awards in cases of personal injury. They cited a tenfold increase in the average size of jury awards over the past 25 years. Consumer groups and lawyers have refused to take responsibility for the premium hikes, however, saying the insurance industry has only itself to blame for any financial difficulties it faced at mid-decade. Imprudent investments and cutthroat competition, they say, are behind the industry's recurrent boom-and-bust cycles.

While the controversy is an old one, the intense publicity surrounding the liability crisis of recent years has brought changes to the insurance market. For one thing, most states have tightened standards pertaining to tort law, the field of jurisprudence that governs personal-injury suits. Although the insurance industry thus far has failed to obtain national tort-reform legislation, more than 40 states have passed laws that benefit the industry, such as caps on monetary awards for pain and suffering, and standards requiring plaintiffs to demonstrate manufacturers' negligence in product-liability suits. Tort reform has reduced the risks to policyholders, allowing insurers to broaden coverage and reduce premiums.

Not all the changes benefited the insurers, however. The industry should have welcomed the boom phase of its traditional cycle. But in 1989, despite broader coverage and rate cuts, insurers found there was less demand for insurance. Outraged by the steep premium increases at mid-decade, consumers struck back. California voters in 1988 approved Proposition 103, mandating insurance-premium rollbacks, an initiative that seems likely to become a model for other states in 1990.

Meanwhile, many former holders of commercial-liability insurance who were squeezed out of the market at mid-decade have devised alternative means to protect themselves from civil suits. Physicians and other high-risk professionals have formed self-insurance pools to cover the costs of damage claims, or set up "captive" insurers to provide liability coverage. Municipalities also have adopted public-liability pools. These alternative insurance providers already have siphoned off more than one third of the industry's business, and their share seems likely to continue to grow in the 1990s.

Manufacturers and municipalities also were turning increasingly to risk management as a way to avoid liability suits in the first place. U.S. manufacturers have stopped making intrauterine devices, light aircraft, and other products that were the focus of product-liability lawsuits during the 1980s. By removing potential causes of lawsuits, such as dangerous playground equipment, municipalities were reducing their exposure to suits and thus their need for liability coverage of any kind.

Falling demand for traditional liability coverage meant falling profitability for the more than 3,000 property and casualty insurers in the United States and the likelihood that the industry faces a shakeout that will force smaller providers out of business.

MARY H. COOPER
"Editorial Research Reports"

Courtesy, Hickory Chair Company

Some leading traditional decorators have begun offering top-notch reproductions of 18th- and 19th-century furnishings to the retail market. The Mark Hampton bedroom pieces, left, *feature a Georgian canopy bed.*

INTERIOR DESIGN

In 1989 and the previous year, the big story in interior design was not a flurry of this or that new fashion; styles had been holding firm for at least half a decade. People had begun talking about business, and the news was that top traditional decorators had branched out and were styling collections for major furniture manufacturers.

Early in the 1980s, several high-style contemporary designers went public in the furniture world, following the example of the late Angelo Donghia, who licensed his own line of furniture to Kroehler Manufacturing Company in the late 1970s. The line did not survive; some say Donghia was simply ahead of his time and others feel that he did not monitor the factory's quality-control standards carefully enough.

In 1984, John Saladino, a contemporary interior designer with a strong Neoclassical bent, worked with Baker Furniture of Grand Rapids, MI, to produce a collection. In 1987, Saladino opened his own New York showroom to sell the sort of pieces he long has designed for clients, furniture he now manufactures himself.

Jay Spectre, a contemporary designer who is inspired by the art deco and moderne styles of the 1920s and 1930s, joined with the Century Furniture Company of Hickory, NC, to produce his first furniture group in 1986. The line expanded rapidly, and in March 1989 the designer opened Jay Spectre at Home, a large department in a Westport, CT, furniture store, displaying all his furniture as well as his linens and tableware. This was the first of a planned chain of in-store boutiques to be located on the East Coast.

And now the great traditional decorators, who depend on antique furniture and accessories for their Anglo-American look, also have climbed on the retail furniture bandwagon. They had seen a growing need for good reproductions of 18th- and 19th-century furnishings in their own practices and in the decorating world at large. Since the mid-1970s, demand far has outstripped supply in the antiques world, and prices became prohibitive for many clients. In addition, it was often impossible to find the right antique, no matter what could be paid.

Into the breach, in the spring of 1988, stepped Mark Hampton, renowned decorator (among his clients are President and Mrs. Bush) and author of a new book of essays on decorating. Now expanded to a group of more than 50 pieces of wood furniture and upholstered seating, the Mark Hampton Collection by the Hickory Chair Company consists of copies and adaptations of antiques that Hampton supplied to the North Carolina manufacturer. The pieces reflect his much-admired traditional style touched with whimsy. And the imprimatur of a known designer is—as with all these collections—a source of reassurance to the often unsure, worried shopper.

Next to enter the market was Hampton's sometime colleague (in the Blair House redecoration in Washington, DC) and rival for top honors in the good-natured celebrity-decorator race, Mario Buatta, working with John Widdicomb Furniture. His line was launched in fall 1988, and although it taps the same rich vein as Hampton's, it is on a slightly grander and more expensive level. Both lines were thriving in 1989.

The latest news on this front came in April 1989 at the High Point, NC, furniture market when McMillen Inc., a distinguished decorating firm founded in 1924, presented the first 31 pieces of its Baker Furniture collection.

ELAINE GREENE
Free-lance Design Reporter

INTERNATIONAL TRADE AND FINANCE

When East Germans freely crossed the Berlin Wall, Nov. 9, 1989, for the first time in 28 years, it not only was of enormous political significance; it also held major economic and financial implications. It hinted that East and West Europe well may move faster than anyone previously imagined toward greater economic unity.

Soviet President Mikhail Gorbachev already had indicated he wanted the Soviet Union admitted to the international financial system in a message to the leaders of the Group of Seven industrial democracies—the United States, Japan, West Germany, France, Britain, Italy, and Canada—meeting in Paris for their annual economic summit on Bastille Day, July 14. "Our *perestroika* [restructuring] is inseparable from a policy aiming at our full participation in the world economy," Gorbachev wrote. "The rest of the world can only gain by the opening of the world economy to a market such as the Soviet Union."

In the West, the major economic, financial, and trade news was less dramatic. One important trend was a further slowing in the United States' economy in the fourth quarter, with economists speculating whether the slump would be deep enough and long enough to be termed a recession. Some economists thought a recession overdue. The recovery that started in December 1982 had become the longest peacetime expansion ever in the United States.

A dash of financial excitement also was provided by the 190.58-point drop in the Dow Jones industrial average of the price of 30 blue chip stocks on Friday, October 13. Some analysts wondered whether there would be a repeat of the 508-point plunge of October 1987. It was a major relief when the average regained 88.12 points on the following Monday.

East-West Economic Relations. It is of some historic interest that the Soviet Union was invited to join in the postwar international economic system in 1944. The USSR participated in the 1944 conference in Bretton Woods, NH, that created the International Monetary Fund (IMF) and the Bank for Reconstruction and Development (the World Bank). The United States offered its wartime ally 13% of the voting shares in these institutions. If the Soviet Union had joined in 1944, it would have been third in the IMF pecking order after the United States and Britain, but then Soviet leader Joseph Stalin declined.

Observers have said it will take at least a few years before the Soviet Union is admitted to the IMF, the World Bank, and the General Agreement on Tariffs and Trade (GATT), the Geneva-based organization that regulates world trade. But the opening of the Berlin Wall puts pressure on U.S. President George Bush and other Western leaders to show support for Gorbachev and his reforms. In fact, at the December Bush-Gorbachev summit, the U.S. president announced his support for observer status for the USSR in GATT. Should the USSR join the IMF and World Bank in the 1990s, under the standard formula for setting the funding quota and voting power of a new member, the Soviets could expect a quota of about 6%. That would give the Soviet Union enough votes to be the number two or three power in the Fund, qualifying for its own seat on the Fund's executive board.

AP/Wide World

U.S. Federal Reserve Board Chairman Alan Greenspan consulted with leading Soviet economists and held a symposium on Western-style banking in Moscow in October.

In September a diplomatic cable first disclosed that the Bush administration might soften its opposition to membership for the Soviet Union and China in GATT. Low-level U.S. officials met with Chinese officials that month to discuss the issue, a process that started in mid-1986 when China first began seeking membership.

Economists in 1989 only were starting to assess the impact the liberalization in Eastern Europe and the Soviet Union would have on the West. In West Germany, for example, the need for housing and other facilities for the more than 200,000 refugees could cost billions. In light of the liberalization, some East Germans feared West German financial power, suspecting that much of their industry might be bought up by West German companies. Developing countries, meanwhile, were concerned that the Soviet bloc might draw from the limited pool of foreign aid available in the West.

At the Paris summit in July, the seven industrial leaders agreed to give assistance to Poland and Hungary, as well as emergency food supplies. They asked the European Community (EC) to coordinate efforts and consider an array of economic issues involving the two countries, including investments and joint ventures. They also allowed Poland to postpone payment of $5 billion due in 1989 on its external debts of $39 billion. West Germany provided more than $1 billion for assistance to Poland, with other EC countries providing smaller amounts.

Monetary Policy and the U.S. Dollar. The Federal Reserve System, the central banking authority of the United States, eased its monetary policy in June in small steps, after seeing a desired slowdown in the economy. The change was made because the Fed did not want to create a recession that would worsen the federal budget deficit and boost unemployment. The Fed acted before the slowdown deepened because it takes at least six months for a shift in monetary policy to influence the level of business activity. However, Michael Boskin, chairman of President Bush's Council of Economic Advisers, indicated he would have liked the Fed to have eased up somewhat faster.

In 1989, Federal Reserve Board Chairman Alan Greenspan disagreed with U.S. Treasury Department efforts to keep the dollar value from rising on the world's foreign-exchange markets. The Treasury and authorities from other Group of Seven nations often intervened in the foreign-exchange markets during 1989, selling dollars to restrain their price. One such sales surge occurred from late April into May, another in September. When the dollar exceeded the value of two West German marks in May, the international authorities reasserted their commitment to coordination to keep the dollar within a certain trading range. West Germany's Bundesbank had taken a surprise poke at the dollar on April 20 when it raised its key interest rate to 4.5% from 4%. Others in the "mark bloc"—Denmark, the Netherlands, and Austria—immediately boosted their interest rates. The action sharply depressed the dollar by making investments in mark financial instruments more attractive. But the dollar bounced back, partially as a result of the suppression of the democracy movement in China. On May 30 the Bank of Japan hiked its key interest rate, the discount rate, by three quarters of a point to 3.25%. The increase in the charge on loans to commercial banks was regarded as both an attempt to weaken the dollar and to restrain inflation within Japan. Despite the coordinated measures by as many as eight central banks, the dollar still fetched 1.96 marks and 146.33 yen at mid-September. But by mid-November, after West Germany again had raised interest rates and the Fed had moved to further reduce U.S. interest rates, the dollar's value slipped to 1.85 marks and 143.17 yen.

Despite the overall strength of the dollar in 1989, the U.S. trade deficit continued to decline modestly. In the first nine months of 1989, the merchandise trade gap averaged $9.1 billion per month, down from a $9.9 billion per month average for the same period in 1988. However, some economists feared that the strong dollar was slowing progress. Martin Feldstein, a former chairman of the Council of Economic Advisers in the Reagan administration, maintained the dollar would have to come down considerably to improve U.S. competitiveness.

Central banks of several industrial nations released a study in September noting that a mix of speculation, investing, and hedging in currencies makes foreign exchange the world's biggest financial market, dwarfing stock and bond markets. The average volume of daily trading on the world foreign-exchange market more than doubled in the previous three years to average $500 billion. Average daily trading in U.S. government securities now might run $125 billion to $150 billion. On the New York Stock Exchange, daily turnover in corporate shares ran about $6.2 billion in 1989. London (U.K.) remained the world's largest currency market, with daily turnover of $187 billion. The United States was second at $128.9 billion. Japan was third at $115.2 billion, and its share of world currency trading has grown since 1986, with London's share falling.

International Stock Markets. Until the October 13 market plunge, most stock shareholders around the world enjoyed a bull market in 1989. During October the overall World Index of stock-market prices maintained by Morgan Stanley Capital International Perspective fell 3.5% when measured in U.S. dollars. While the U.S. average was down 2.5%, the United Kingdom's stock market was down 9.7%, Norway's 11.9%, and Japan's 2.7%. Many other international markets were down substantially in October as well.

Nonetheless, most investors remained in the black. At the end of October and compared to a year earlier, stock prices in the United States were up 31.9% (Dow Jones industrial average). Canadian stocks were up 17.41% (measured in U.S. dollars). Similarly measured, stock prices had climbed 4.49% in Britain and 8.17% in West Germany. In Japan investors defied fears about high price-earnings ratios and had moved a major stock index up 17.87% in yen terms but only 3.11% in dollars. Japanese investors were showing further nervousness in November. In France prices were up 19.51% in dollar terms, and in Hong Kong—undermined by China's problems—up only 1.4%. Prices were up 12.93% on the Netherlands' stock market (in dollar terms).

World Output, International Trade, and Gold. In the non-Communist world, the IMF estimated an expansion in world output in 1989 of 3.1% after removing inflation. The gross national product (GNP) of the United States would grow a real 2.7%, IMF economists reckoned in September. West Germany's output of goods and services was climbing at a handsome 4.6% in inflation-adjusted terms, its strongest performance in 13 years. Japan was anticipating real growth of about 4%, down from around 5% the year before.

According to GATT, world-trade volume grew by about 7% in 1989, compared with an estimated 8.5% growth in 1988. GATT economists explained that there are several reasons for the growth in world commerce outstripping growth in world output by a two to one margin. One reason is the drop by one half in the real cost of petroleum since its peak in 1980, bringing substantial savings to business and households. Further, the number of international joint ventures and mergers was growing alongside a rapidly expanding globalization of financial markets. Another point was that technological innovations are widening the scope of traded goods and services. A third factor was that the share of manufactured goods in world trade, in terms of value, has increased by one third since 1980. Manufactures accounted for 73% of the value of world merchandise trade and about one half of the exports of developing countries. The multilateral trade negotiations under GATT, known as the Uruguay Round, moved ahead. Differences in services, farm products, and other areas had to be solved.

The price of gold slipped below $400 an ounce early in 1989. Ranging in price about $360 an ounce in the summer, it climbed back up to more than $400 an ounce by December. By fall, U.S. inflation fears had subsided, but gold remained weak. Central-bank purchases apparently propped up the price of gold to some extent, with the banks having added 983 tons to their reserves in nine years. With prices still high compared to prices in the early 1970s, gold-mine output has increased, reaching 1,583 tons in 1988.

U.S. GNP and Budget Deficit. The U.S. economy reached something of a milestone in the last quarter of 1988 when the annual gross national product exceeded $5 trillion. The output of goods and services reached that mark only 19 years after it first hit $1 trillion. Since the price level has more than tripled since 1970, however, much of the increase is the result of inflation. Another factor was the growth in the U.S. population from 205 million in 1970 to just short of 250 million at the close of 1989, with the labor force growing even faster as a larger proportion of women joined.

Due to a surge in federal revenues, the U.S. budget deficit declined slightly in fiscal 1989 to $152.1 billion from the previous year's $155.1 billion. The decline in the deficit came even with the addition of billions in outlays to rescue troubled savings and loan associations. The U.S. budget deficit continued to decline as a percentage of national output. It amounted to about 3.2% of gross national product in 1989, less than half of what it was at the peak a few years earlier.

Japanese Investments. A report by Data Resources, Inc., a Lexington, MA, consulting firm, found that Japan would invest $569.9 billion around the world in 1989, some $46 billion more than the United States. Japan was investing $4,549 per capita in plant and equipment, compared with only $2,065 per capita by the United States. The Japan External Trade Organization estimated the country's total overseas direct investment exceeded the $1 trillion level by mid-1988. Japan's stock market has become the world's largest. Its share of world stock market capitalization—the value of all the shares on the world's stock markets measured in dollars—shot up to 45% in 1987–88. The U.S. share was 30%. Measured by their assets, the top ten commercial banks in the world also remained Japanese.

Third World Debt Restructuring. U.S. Treasury Secretary Nicholas F. Brady announced on March 10 a new strategy for encouraging commercial banks in the industrial countries and Third World nations to negotiate the terms of debt reductions. The action, taken soon after rioting in Venezuela over economic austerity measures left 350 people dead, was endorsed by the Paris summit. Under the previous strategy, initiated by former Treasury Secretary James A. Baker III, developing nations were to borrow more money to help them reform their economies. But Brady maintained the United States and other leading industrial democracies should help the debtor nations cut down their $1.3 trillion in external debt and the interest they pay on it.

Mexico provided the first major test of the Brady plan. Banks agreed in July to offer Mexico a 35% reduction on the principal of loans, a corresponding cut in interest to 6.25%, or refinancing amounting to 60% of annual interest, or a mix of the three possibilities. The deal could save Mexico more than $2 billion yearly. The Brady plan also called on the World Bank and the IMF to put up about $12 billion over three years to assist debtor nations. However, at issue at the joint annual meeting of the IMF and World Bank in late September was whether the Fund had adequate financial resources to deal with these debt problems or other imbalances in the international payments of nations. The French managing director of the IMF, Michel Camdessus, called for a 100% boost in the Fund's resources to $113 billion. The United States blocked immediate action, asking whether such a large increase or any increase was needed.

DAVID R. FRANCIS
"The Christian Science Monitor"

IOWA

On July 17, 1989, United Airlines Flight 232, a DC-10 scheduled to fly from Denver to Chicago, lost its number two engine and all hydraulic control. Diverted to the airport in Sioux City, the pilot made a crash landing just short of the main runway. While 112 passengers were killed, 185 survived the crash. And Sioux City residents were lauded for their emergency preparedness and their efforts in saving lives.

The Economy and Agriculture. The May unemployment rate of 3.6% was the lowest of the decade for Iowa. Nonfarm employment was more than 1.2 million workers, also a record for the 1980s. The state revenue picture was the best of the decade, with monthly revenue in May exceeding all previous monthly totals in the state's history. For the first time since 1980, the annual population count increased, by approximately 11,000, although 42 of Iowa's 99 counties still reported a population decline for the year.

In spite of an early drought that rivaled the 1988 dry period, the Iowa corn crop, soybeans, and oats all made a strong comeback in 1989. The harvests of the oat crop and soybeans were first in the nation, while the corn harvest came second only to Illinois. Corn averaged just more than 103 bushels per acre and soybeans 38 bushels per acre.

Politics and Legislation. Republican Gov. Terry Branstad was elected chairman of the National Governors' Association and was among the leaders of the education summit with President Bush in Charlottesville, VA, in late September. The Democratic-controlled Iowa General Assembly enacted 327 laws in a January through May session. Legislators added $35 million to the $2.8 billion budget requested by Governor Branstad. There were no new taxes and no tax increases. And both the temporary three-cent-per-pack cigarette tax and a park-user fee were eliminated.

AP/Wide World

Larry Reed of the Davenport Chamber of Commerce inspects the "Sainte Genevieve" as Iowa moved to revive riverboat gambling. County referenda would decide the issue.

Among the major legislation passed was a schedule to raise the minimum wage in Iowa to $3.85 an hour as of January 1990, with further increases to $4.25 in 1991, and $4.65 in January 1992. The legislature also legalized riverboat gambling effective in April 1991, with a county referendum on the measure required before an application from a locality for gambling is accepted by the state. The road-use fund formula was revised, giving a higher percentage of the fund to cities and less to the counties. Iowa's doctors were given permission to notify the sexual partners of persons who have contracted AIDS. Another law makes marital rape a crime. Iowa landlords were prohibited from discriminating in renting to families with children. To deter illegal dumping, the maximum civil penalty for the practice was increased from $500 to $5,000 per day. Funds were appropriated to add 490 prison beds, thereby easing overcrowding in the state prison system. And laws pertaining to pornography were tightened.

Education. The state's healthy revenue picture allowed for capital improvement programs at the state-supported universities to proceed. An open-enrollment policy was instituted for the public-school districts by the legislature. Under the plan, however, no school district would lose more than 5% of its enrollment during the initial 1990–91 school year. The state school aid formula also was revised, with the new version phasing out so-called phantom students. New state statutes also prohibit corporal punishment in public schools and hazing among college organizations.

RUSSELL M. ROSS, *University of Iowa*

IOWA • Information Highlights

Area: 56,275 sq mi (145 753 km²).
Population (July 1, 1988): 2,834,000.
Chief Cities (July 1, 1986 est.): Des Moines, the capital, 192,060; Cedar Rapids, 108,390; Davenport (July 1, 1984 est.), 102,129.
Government (1989): *Chief Officers*—governor, Terry E. Branstad (R); lt. gov., Jo Ann Zimmerman (D). *General Assembly*—Senate, 50 members; House of Representatives, 100 members.
State Finances (fiscal year 1988): *Revenue,* $5,814,000,000; *expenditure,* $5,316,000,000.
Personal Income (1988): $41,551,000,000; per capita, $14,662.
Labor Force (June 1989): *Civilian labor force,* 1,528,900; *unemployed,* 66,900 (4.4% of total force).
Education: *Enrollment* (fall 1987)—public elementary schools, 328,000; public secondary, 152,000; colleges and universities, 158,230. *Public school expenditures* (1987–88), $1,875,849,000 ($3,961 per pupil).

AP/Wide World

Iran officially celebrated the tenth anniversary of the birth of its Islamic revolution, February 1–11. On the last day, some 1 million people gathered in Tehran to hear President Ali Khamenei's comments on the movement.

IRAN

The year in Iran was split almost precisely into two halves by the death on June 3 of the Ayatollah Khomeini, who had held undisputed sway over the country for the previous decade. Iran was thus in a double sense in the throes of transition: because of the question of succession to Khomeini's leadership; and secondly because it had only been in August 1988 that the eight-year-long war with Iraq had ended in a cease-fire, though no substantive treaty of peace yet had been approached.

The Succession Question. Khomeini's health had been failing obviously for at least a year before he died. The great question in Iranian politics had been who should succeed to his power. Part of the answer was, of course, that no one could succeed to all of it. Khomeini held personally an extraordinary concentration of religious authority and political power, and no one now on the Iranian scene plausibly could claim such wide authority. The year 1989 thus, both before and after the Ayatollah's death, saw a power struggle which was continuing as the year ended. Its ultimate outcome in terms of both personalities and Iranian policies domestic and foreign remained quite uncertain. In 1989, Ali Akbar Hashemi Rafsanjani (*see* BIOGRAPHY) became the victor, but not in any absolute sense.

Eclipse of Montazeri. It was a struggle not only of personalities, but also between holders of different views about what kind of country Iran should be. On the one hand were the mullahs (clergy) and others who wanted the continuance of hard-line Shiite Muslim fundamentalism, which had done little but make Iran grim and poor internally and isolated externally. On the other hand were all those who wanted to moderate such policies: the businessmen, some of the younger clergy, the technocrats, and what was left of the upper classes. The two sides seemed fairly evenly balanced.

Certainly the coming of peace in August 1988 did not bring moderation. It was accompanied by a wave of executions that continued into January, and sporadically afterward. No precise figures were to be had, but even from government admissions it was clear that the numbers of those executed ran well into the thousands. There were said to be drug traffickers, "unreliable" Islamic clergymen, and supporters of the outlawed *mujahidin* or of the equally illegal *Tudeh* (Communist) party. Also, it was said that 43 members of the ministry of information had been rounded up and summarily shot on grounds of having spied for Iraq. More and more, however, informed opinion came to believe that the executions mostly were related to a struggle between the "Khomeinists" and the "Montazerists." The Ayatollah Hussein Ali Montazeri had been elected by the Assembly of Experts in late 1985 as the designated successor to Khomeini's spiritual leadership. In 1988 and early 1989, however, he had made a number of public statements critical of government policies. He was outspoken on the wave of political executions ("This is not how Islamic justice should operate. People will turn to armed opposition against us.") and on unnecessary austerity ("All the present shortages, low earnings, and soaring prices are the natural consequences of your government."). Khomeini himself appeared to be playing a balancing role between the two factions, but the strange episode of his passing a "sentence of death" on the British author Salman Rushdie, author of *The Satanic Verses*, in February suggested that the radical Islamic cause was now in the ascendant.

This was confirmed by Montazeri's forced resignation on March 27 as Khomeini's official spiritual successor. At the same time came the resignations of the deputy foreign minister and the Iranian representative to the United Nations, both of whom were friends and associates of Montazeri and Rafsanjani.

Montazeri had been dismissed, but he had many supporters. There were riots in his hometown and in other places protesting his dismissal. Ahmed Khomeini, the Ayatollah's 44-year-old son, continued the attack with *The Book of Sufferings*, a pamphlet containing Montazeri's recent correspondence with the Ayatollah. This was intended to provide proof of his deviations. The younger Khomeini also rebuked Rafsanjani.

Death of Khomeini. These machinations of Ahmed Khomeini, if intended to augment his own chances of inheriting some or all of his father's power, somehow went astray. After 11 days of extreme illness, the Ayatollah Khomeini died on June 3. His death was, of course, the occasion of great national mourning; and his burial an undignified scene as the immense crowds led to a mishandling of the body. Next day, June 4, the Assembly of Experts, though not unanimously, chose as inheritor of Khomeini's spiritual leadership Hojatolislam Seyyed Ali Khamenei, who was promoted immediately to the status of ayatollah. Khamenei was a good compromise choice. He is low-keyed, very widely respected, and relatively indifferent to power. Though president of Iran since 1981 (reelected in 1985), he had made of the office a largely ceremonial affair. His record is not stained by the wilder excesses of the revolution.

Presidential Election, Constitutional Revision. A commission to revise the constitution had been appointed on April 24, and a presidential election was due to be held in mid-August. In consequence of Khomeini's death, the election of a president was advanced to July 28 and extensive changes in the constitution were approved by referendum on the same day. Despite the confused rivalries of the first half of the year, a smooth transfer of power occurred to Rafsanjani, longtime speaker of the *Majlis* (parliament), adroit politician, and the late Ayatollah's closest confidant and adviser. In his ascension to the presidency he enjoyed the support of all major groups and even of Ahmed Khomeini. Of the 80 original candidates, all except Rafsanjani and Abbas Sheibani, a *Majlis* member, were declared unqualified. The latter was little more than a token candidate. Rafsanjani was elected by 15,551,570 votes to Sheibani's 632,247. The significant constitutional changes also were approved overwhelmingly. Their general effect was to strengthen greatly the presidency. Among other changes, the position of prime minister was abolished, making the president the sole chief executive. The president was empowered to appoint ministers, subject to confirmation by the *Majlis*, and to take control of the economy. He became chairman of the new State Security Council created to formulate and oversee defense policy.

New Cabinet. Rafsanjani was sworn in formally before the *Majlis* on August 17. On August 19 he presented for approval by the *Majlis* the names of 22 proposed members of his cabinet, 12 of whom were new appointees. The cabinet had a much more moderate look than its predecessor. It had been anticipated that Rafsanjani might have some difficulty in having his appointees approved, but in fact he did not. Each was considered individually and voted on, most with comfortable majorities. A number of them had Western educations, six having

On June 4 the Assembly of Experts selected President Ali Khamenei, 50, as Iran's new supreme religious leader.

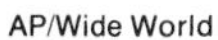
AP/Wide World

IRAN • Information Highlights

Official Name: Islamic Republic of Iran.
Location: Southwest Asia.
Area: 636,293 sq mi (1 648 000 km²).
Population (mid-1989 est.): 53,900,000.
Chief City (1986 census): Tehran, the capital, 5,770,000.
Government: *Head of state and government,* Ali Akbar Hashemi Rafsanjani, president (took office August 1989). *Legislature* (unicameral)—Islamic Consultative Assembly (*Majlis*).
Monetary Unit: Rial (72.049 rials equal U.S.$1, July 1989).
Gross National Product (1988 U.S.$): $93,500,000,000.
Foreign Trade (1986 est. U.S.$): *Imports,* $10,000,000,000; *exports,* $7,800,000,000.

degrees from U.S. universities. Three notable radicals were dropped from the cabinet, the most important the interior minister, Ali Akbar Mohtashemi.

Economy. In his one election speech (July 20, on television), and in his inaugural address (August 17), Rafsanjani stressed economic matters. He said the economy was the country's main concern and outlined plans to improve it. The Iranian economy is indeed in a precarious state. Inflation officially is running at a rate of 25–30% annually, but in reality is much higher. Government attempts to control it, often by brutally enfórced price-fixing regulations, have been quite unsuccessful. The harsh underlying fact is that there was no economic development during the eight years of the war, and private enterprise officially was discouraged. Even if the official attitude has changed, which is only partly true, the new government faces a difficult task in restoring the economy to life again. In an October 23 press conference, a major public relations effort, Rafsanjani did his best to persuade his fellow countrymen that the system would be liberalized. Foreign investment would be welcome and foreign currency would be made available under a scheme of priorities.

The total economic cost of the war to Iran has been estimated at $542 billion. Since Iran's annual foreign-exchange surplus (nearly all from oil) was running at no more than $12 billion, foreign investment would be needed desperately. Iran was beginning to negotiate with West Germany and Japan for loans of up to $15 billion over a period of several years. The United States still was being cold-shouldered. None of these changed attitudes or policies made much difference within 1989. A good deal of reconstruction had been done at the great oil refinery at Abadan (closed since 1980) and on the damaged oil terminal at Kharg Island. But, overall, factories were running at 30% capacity, mostly for lack of raw materials and spare parts. In the area of private life, however, there has been a considerable liberalization. The climate of fear was less oppressive. The *chador* (veil), rigidly imposed on women under Khomeini, was little worn now, at least in the better areas.

Rafsanjani's Limitations. It would be easy to expect too much in the way of liberalization from Rafsanjani. He startled the world on May 5 by suggesting the killing of five American, British, or French citizens in retaliation for every death of a Palestinian. How far he makes this and other pronouncements sincerely, or merely to guard himself against criticisms of being insufficiently radical, remained unclear. He has powerful enemies. The radical majority in the *Majlis* were at present acquiescent in his leadership, but potentially hostile. The clout of former Interior Minister Mohtashemi, a hard-liner who won a parliamentary seat in mid-December, remained to be seen; Ahmed Khomeini and Ali Khamenei were at best rivals. To some extent President Rafsanjani was in a dilemma. He would, no doubt, like to help the Iranian people by reviving Iran's economy and improving relations with the West; but every step likely to do either would offend the radicals, the true believers.

Foreign Relations. Iran remained isolated, apart from its alliance with Syria, and problems caused by its Shiite clients in Lebanon may be causing even that to wear thin. The conflict with Iraq remained in a state of no war, but no peace treaty. Iran's relations with the West, which had been improving, deteriorated because of the *Satanic Verses* affair. On the other hand, there was a warming in relations with Communist countries, and also a marked turning East and away from the Middle East, where revolutionary Iran's ambitions had been frustrated totally. President Ali Khamenei visited China, May 9-14, and North Korea, May 14-17. These two states were among Iran's arms suppliers in the late war. China agreed to double its purchases of Iranian oil and to supply generating equipment. The Korean visit would lead to increased trade. Rafsanjani, not yet president, was in Moscow on June 20 and was welcomed warmly.

ARTHUR CAMPBELL TURNER
University of California, Riverside

IRAQ

Iraq in 1989 inevitably was involved in the long process of transition from war to peace, its eight-year war with Iran having ended with an armistice in August 1988. Iraq, having fought much larger Iran to a draw, increased its international prestige, and the authoritarian Baath Party régime of Saddam Hussein Takriti, president since 1979, seemed able to withstand internal challenges. Some modest advances toward greater political freedom occurred, and economic restrictions were loosened.

Power Struggles. Reports of several attempted coups during the year were denied by the government. When it was announced in May that Defense Minister Adnan Khairallah had been killed in a helicopter crash, the rumor spread that Khairallah had been executed as an ally of Saddam Hussein's son Udai, who had quarreled with his father.

Mystery Explosion. A curious episode was the apparent large explosion on August 17 at a secret defense center near Al Hillah, some 40 mi (64 km) south of Baghdad. Reports in the Western press appeared in early September, based on a number of Middle East sources, that the research establishment had been working on a secret Egyptian-Iraqi missile project, and that the explosion had killed some 700 people, including Egyptian military and civilians. Official Iraqi reports played down but did not completely deny the event. The Iraqi embassy in London on September 7 spoke of gross exaggeration: There was no secret missile project, and 19 people had been killed, all Iraqi nationals.

Political Reforms. Very soon after the cease-fire with Iran, the Iraqi president announced a series of coming political reforms whose seeming purpose was to reward the Iraqi people for surprisingly steady support during a long and costly war. In January, Hussein announced that an *ad hoc* committee was being set up to draft a new constitution; after official scrutiny it would be submitted to a referendum. Political parties would be allowed. Meanwhile, a general election (originally scheduled for August 1988) would be held on April 1. In this election for the 250 seats, 910 candidates, including 62 women, ran. About one quarter of the candidates were Baathists; the rest ran as independents, but they too had to subscribe to basic Baath principles. All election expenses were paid by the government, and there were no political parties. Iraq has not had an election with organized parties since the fall of the monarchy in 1958. The new parliament has a four-year term and is to sit for four months in the year. How important it will be in the Iraqi political process depended on the members and remained to be seen. In fact in recent years power has become more centralized in the office of the president.

IRAQ • Information Highlights

Official Name: Republic of Iraq.
Location: Southwest Asia.
Area: 167,923 sq mi (434 920 km²).
Population (mid-1989 est.): 18,100,000.
Chief City (1985 est.): Baghdad, the capital, 2,200,000.
Government: *Head of state and government,* Saddam Hussein, president (took office July 1979).
Monetary Unit: Dinar (0.311 dinar equals U.S.$1, July 1989).
Gross National Product (1988 U.S.$): $34,000,000,000.
Foreign Trade (1986 est. U.S.$): *Imports,* $9,500,000,000; *exports,* $7,450,000,000.

The Economy. Iraq has a heavy burden of foreign debt and great needs in the reconstruction of war-damaged areas. Its one great economic resource is oil. Rescheduling of foreign debt is being handled with some skill; especially with Western creditors, prospects of future Iraqi business are being made conditional on flexible arrangements for existing debt. New trade pacts have been made with the United States, Britain, and West Germany along such lines. The reconstruction of Basra and Faw, both nearly destroyed during the war, is proceeding fast. Private enterprise is playing a larger role, and the austerities of ordinary life are being eased by a greater supply of consumer goods.

Estimates of Iraqi technological expertise were boosted by reports in December that Iraq had launched a rocket capable of orbiting a satellite.

Egyptian Exodus. The gentle handling of the Iraqi population did not extend to other Arabs who worked in Iraq in very large numbers during the war, the majority being Egyptians. In early October, Iraq reduced the amount of money they were permitted to send home, from half of their earnings to only 10 dinars ($55) a month. There was also much discrimination against Egyptians and violence, even murder, of "guest workers." As a result Egyptians began leaving Iraq at a rate of about 3,000 per day. There was much fury among the Egyptian people at Iraqi behavior, but the Egyptian government, anxious to remain on good terms with Baghdad, did not respond fully to popular feeling.

The Kurds. Another group that felt the heavy hand of the Baghdad government was the rebellious Kurds. In 1989 the Iraqi government seemed determined to crush Kurdish resistance once and for all by creating an empty "security zone" 18.6 mi (30 km) wide along the border with Iran. Enforced deportations of as many as 250,000 Kurds took place in May and June, and their old villages were razed. Earlier, two Kurdish ministers had been dismissed from the government.

Foreign Relations. As the commander of the largest and most experienced army in the Arab Middle East, Saddam Hussein certainly enjoys enhanced regional prestige. A new Arab economic grouping, the Arab Cooperation Council, comprising Iraq, Egypt, Jordan, and North Yemen, was launched at a meeting of the four heads of state in Baghdad on February 16. In Lebanon, Iraq played a spoiling role against its great rival Syria by supporting General Aoun's Maronite group. Negotiations to achieve a definitive peace with Iran rather than a cease-fire made no progress: Iran conceded nothing and gained nothing. (*See* LEBANON, MIDDLE EAST.)

ARTHUR CAMPBELL TURNER
University of California, Riverside

IRELAND

Despite some positive signs, economic problems continued to cause widespread anxiety in Ireland in 1989. The new budget introduced by Finance Minister Albert Reynolds on January 25 lowered the standard tax rate from 35% to 32%—the first such reduction in more than 20 years. At the same time the government raised taxes on both alcohol and cigarettes, and cut back on benefits to mortgage holders. The austere economic measures adopted in 1988, coupled with an amnesty program for delinquent taxpayers, had reduced the budget deficit to 619 million Irish punts (pounds), or about $885 million. But a freeze on hiring and other government measures had a negative impact on services from national health to the National Library.

By late spring the Fianna Fail government of Prime Minister Charles Haughey had managed to hold the inflation rate at 3.5%. In addition, the budget deficit had fallen from 13% to 4.5% of the gross national product. For the first time since the 1960s, Ireland also enjoyed a modest trade surplus. On the downside, unemployment hovered around 18%.

Politics. Even though two years remained in his term of office, Prime Minister Haughey decided to hold an election to gain a larger majority in the Dail (the Irish House of Commons). Claiming that his government had "saved the country from bankruptcy," the taoiseach (prime minister) set the election date for June 18. In an attempt to thwart Fianna Fail's bid for another victory, the principal opposition party, Fine Gael, led by Alan Dukes, entered into an alliance with Des O'Malley's Progressive Democrats, who had broken away from the ruling party in a bitter quarrel in 1985.

The election did not fulfill Haughey's hopes. A number of voters resented the timing of the election and the government's austerity measures. Fianna Fail lost four seats, giving them 77 out of a total of 166 seats. Fine Gael, on the other hand, gained four seats to reach a total of 55. The Progressive Democrats suffered a major reverse, losing eight of their 14 seats. In contrast, the Labour Party made something of a comeback, winning 15 seats, while the Workers' Party gained three seats to bring their number up to seven. Independent candidates won six seats. Given the emphasis on the economy, the Northern Ireland problem played a negligible role in the election.

Haughey tried to form a government on June 29, only to be rejected by a vote of 86–78 in the Dail. It was the first time since the founding of the Irish Republic that the party leader holding the largest number of seats failed to win the endorsement of the national assembly. Stung by this rebuff, Haughey searched hard for a suitable coalition partner. A series of tense negotiations culminated in an alliance with his former adversaries, the Progressive Democrats, who decided to scrap their preelection pledges to Fine Gael. In one of the most remarkable reversals of Irish political life, Des O'Malley agreed to support Haughey for the price of one seat in the cabinet (the ministry for energy), a junior ministry, and reconsideration of the cuts in the national health service. On July 12 the Dail approved the coalition government by 84 to 79 votes with one abstention. Haughey embarked on his fourth term of office confronted by an uneasy partnership, a troubled economy, and the loss of an estimated 40,000 countrymen who would be emigrating overseas in 1989 in search of jobs.

The general election coincided with elections for the European Parliament in Strasbourg, France. In the European contest, the percentage of the Irish vote won by Fianna Fail fell to 31.5%, while Fine Gael managed to win only 21.6%. Labour secured one European Parliament seat, and Roger Garland became the first representative of the Green Party from either Ireland or Great Britain to win a seat at Strasbourg.

To the surprise of many, the British Court of Appeal quashed the convictions of three Irish men and one woman, who had been found guilty of bombing two pubs in Guildford, England, in 1974. Religious leaders and former British government officials, along with many Irish citizens, had protested the 1975 jailing of the so-called "Guildford Four."

Among the political leaders who visited Ireland in 1989 was Soviet President Mikhail Gorbachev, who made a brief stopover at Shannon Airport on April 2 while en route to Cuba. He talked with Prime Minister Haughey for 40 minutes. Daniel Ortega, the president of Nicaragua, also stopped in Dublin during his May tour of European capitals and secured Haughey's support for more economic aid.

L. PERRY CURTIS, JR., *Brown University*

IRELAND • Information Highlights

Official Name: Republic of Ireland.
Location: Island in the eastern North Atlantic Ocean.
Area: 27,135 sq mi (70 280 km²).
Population (mid-1989 est.): 3,500,000.
Chief Cities (1986 census): Dublin, the capital, 920,956 (incl. suburbs); Cork, 173,694; Limerick, 76,557.
Government: *Head of state,* Patrick J. Hillery, president (took office Dec. 1976). *Head of government,* Charles Haughey, prime minister (took office March 1987). *Legislature*—Parliament: House of Representatives (Dail Eireann) and Senate (Seanad Eireann).
Monetary Unit: Pound (0.6944 pound equals U.S.$1, Nov. 8, 1989).
Gross National Product (1988 U.S.$): $30,600,-000,000.
Economic Indexes (1988): *Consumer Prices* (1980 = 100), all items, 195.2; food, 176.7. *Industrial Production* (1980 = 100), 162.
Foreign Trade (1988 U.S.$): *Imports,* $15,563,-000,000; *exports,* $18,738,000,000.

ISRAEL

During 1989, the *intifada* or Palestine Arab uprising in the occupied West Bank and Gaza Strip continued to trouble Israel and aggravated the country's severe economic problems. These conditions helped turn the public against the Labor Party whose leader, Shimon Peres, was serving as minister of finance in 1989, and they were reflected in the outcome of local elections. The stalemate in peacemaking persisted, marked by disagreements between Labor and Likud, the two principal parties in the National Unity Government (NUG), over negotiations with the Palestinians.

Domestic Affairs. By the end of 1989, the unemployment rate reached almost 10%, the projected inflation rate was 22.5%, and an increase in the gross national product (GNP) declined from 1.6% in 1988 to 0.6% by September. Costs incurred by the *intifada* were a major cause of economic troubles. Sales of Israeli products in the occupied territories, Israel's second-largest export market, declined by about one third; maintaining troops in the territories was costly because of the additional number of days per year army reservists were required to serve. A report by the Bank of Israel also blamed government mismanagement and lack of a "well-thought-out long-term economic strategy," government bailouts of public sector and Histadrut (General Labor Federation)-owned enterprises, and the preference of many Israelis to receive unemployment benefits rather than accept low-paying jobs for the slowdown. Such employment was left mostly to Arab laborers from the occupied territories whose number was about the same as the number of unemployed Israeli Jews.

Finance Minister Peres sought to cope with the crisis through major budget cuts imposed in January, several devaluations of the Israeli shekel, and plans for tax cuts and liberalization of capital markets. He sought to combat unemployment through increasing expenditure on a so-called "100 Special Projects" scheme intended to attract foreign and domestic capital in new productive enterprises. However, by October, the Bank of Israel drew attention to a sudden increase in the government deficit, which then reached 10% of GNP. By May, Israel's total foreign debt reached $17.1 billion. To help alleviate the anticipated burden of new immigrants from the Soviet Union, which numbered more than 60,000 in 1989, a 20% increase over 1979, the previous record year, Peres reportedly requested a U.S. loan of $400 million to construct new housing, in addition to $3 billion in aid mostly in the form of grants.

The results of municipal elections held in February reflected growing public disenchantment with the Labor Party and the Histadrut. Likud candidates for mayor won in almost every large city, most of which were controlled by Labor before the election. Although Labor retained its foothold in Haifa, Israel's third-largest city, long a Labor Party redoubt, it lost control in seven other major cities. Orthodox Jewish parties also increased their strength, following the pattern set in the November 1988 Knesset election.

AP/Wide World

Israeli Prime Minister Yitzhak Shamir, leader of the Likud bloc, votes in municipal elections in February. The outcome reflected frustration with Labor Party policies.

Within the Arab sector the percentage of voters was greater than among Jews and new Islamic fundamentalist factions scored surprisingly large gains. Growing unrest among Israeli Arab citizens may have been a response to their difficult economic conditions. According to the National Insurance Institute, 48% of Israeli Arab families lived below the poverty line in 1989. Of some 10,000 Arab academics, 33% were unemployed and the high-school dropout rate was 50%. In Jerusalem, where Arabs in the occupied sector previously had supported Mayor Teddy Kollek, only 3,000 of the approximately 81,000 eligible voted. Consequently, Kollek lost his majority in the City Council despite winning reelection as mayor.

In recent years the Histadrut had experienced a major financial crisis. Several of its factories, holding companies, and other enterprises, among the largest in the country, faced bankruptcy and closure. Many kibbutzim (collective settlements) and moshavim (agricultural cooperatives) had to be rescued from fiscal disaster. Although Finance Minister Peres used government funds to help bail them out, their situation remained critical. In the November Histadrut elections, only 53% of the 1.6 million eligible voters voted, giving the Labor Party 55.5% of the vote. The left-wing Mapam won 9% and Likud, 27%, an increase of 4% over 1985. The outcome disappointed Likud, which expected to increase its strength.

Unrest persisted within the occupied territories, leading to continued altercations between the Arab inhabitants and the Israeli army. In addition to violence, civil resistance in the form of tax strikes and boycotts of Israeli products was organized. Israel maintained that it broke much of the resistance through occupying villages and confiscating property of tax strikers. A new development among the Palestinians was the widespread use of assassination to punish Arabs who collaborated with the Israeli authorities.

Government procedures within the West Bank and Gaza were criticized sharply by Israeli civil-rights organizations and peace groups, as well as by Amnesty International and the U.S. government in the Department of State's annual report to Congress on human-rights practices. The Amnesty report highlighted "severe" and "wide-ranging human-rights abuses" in the territories, calling for a full judicial inquiry into all deaths at the hands of Israeli forces. Israel's response to such charges was that they either were exaggerated, out of context, or rare exceptions to the general practices of its occupation authorities.

Foreign Policy. Pressure built up within the country and from abroad on the NUG to take the initiative in the peace process during the year. In May the government issued a detailed proposal based on the concept of Palestinian elections in the West Bank and Gaza for representatives to negotiate with Israel. The scheme, originally developed by Defense Minister Yitzhak Rabin, later was adapted into a four-point plan of Prime Minister Yitzhak Shamir and issued in May as the "Peace Initiative of the Israel Government."

Principal provisions of the plan called for reaffirmation of the 1978 Camp David peace accords signed by Israel, Egypt, and the United States. It called on the latter two countries to persuade other Arab states to "replace belligerency and boycott with negotiation and cooperation," and to "join direct bilateral negotiations aimed at normalization and peace." Major emphasis was placed on solving the Arab refugee problem with special attention directed at the 300,000 refugee camp residents in the occupied territories. The plan was constructed on a program for "free elections" by Arab residents of the territories "of a delegation that will participate in negotiations on an interim settlement, in which a self-governing administration will be set up." The "interim period" would serve as a "test of cooperation and coexistence," to be followed by further negotiations on a final settlement.

Although the United States accepted the principles of the plan, Arab inhabitants of the territories, backed by the Palestine Liberation Organization (PLO), raised several questions about the election scheme: Would the Palestinian inhabitants of the territories be able to select as their representatives members of the PLO? Would Arab residents of the former Jordanian sector of Jerusalem annexed by Israel be permitted to vote or stand for election? Would international supervision of the election be permitted? Would restrictions be placed on election campaigning by the occupation authorities? Would Israel accept the election results? Would Jewish settlement in the territories be suspended during implementation of the peace process? Would Israel eventually agree to withdraw from the territories as part of a final peace settlement?

Although the "peace initiative" was devised by the NUG, it became the subject of bitter intraparty and interparty dispute. The Labor alignment and Prime Minister Shamir became embroiled in controversy over terms of implementing the plan, on issues such as whether or not Arabs in Jerusalem would be able to participate in the election process, international supervision of the elections, and selection of Arab candidates. Labor favored a broad interpretation; Shamir was a strict constructionist. Several times during the year, it seemed that these disagreements would disrupt the NUG and lead to its dissolution. Within Likud, several militants who opposed elections by Arabs in the territories threatened to topple Shamir from the party leadership. He succeeded in maintaining his position through assuring critics that he favored negative answers to the questions mentioned above. However, to mollify the United States, he stated that a negative response to these questions reflected only the views of Likud, not the NUG.

During the summer, Egyptian President Hosni Mubarak offered a ten-point elaboration intended to clarify the plan and win Palestinian acceptance. Labor members of the NUG cabi-

ISRAEL • Information Highlights

Official Name: State of Israel.
Location: Southwest Asia.
Area: 8,019 sq mi (20 770 km²).
Population (mid-1989 est.): 4,500,000.
Chief Cities (Dec. 31, 1985 est.): Jerusalem, the capital, 457,700 (including East Jerusalem); Tel Aviv-Jaffa, 322,800; Haifa, 224,600.
Government: *Head of state,* Chaim Herzog, president (took office May 1983). *Head of government,* Yitzhak Shamir, prime minister (took office October 1986). *Legislature* (unicameral)—Knesset.
Monetary Unit: Shekel (1.965 shekels equal U.S.$1, Nov. 28, 1989).
Gross National Product (1988 U.S.$): $36,000,-000,000.
Economic Indexes (1988): *Consumer Prices* (1980 = 100), all items, 46,447.3. *Industrial Production* (May 1988, 1980 = 100), 126.
Foreign Trade (1988 U.S.$): *Imports,* $12,873,-000,000; *exports,* $9,585,000,000.

net welcomed Mubarak's suggestions, but Shamir, backed by Likud, totally discounted them. Later, U.S. Secretary of State James Baker added another five points. These included proposals for meetings between Shamir, Mubarak, and the United States to "determine Palestinian representation," Egypt's intervention with the PLO to gain its support, and an understanding that an Israeli and a Palestinian delegation would meet in Cairo for talks restricted to Israel's initiative. The principal obstacle to progress at this point was the dispute over Palestinian representation. Both Labor and Likud adamantly opposed participation by the PLO or its representatives, while the Palestinians continued to insist that the PLO was their sole legitimate representative. By December the impasse over "negotiations for negotiations" persisted.

Despite the controversy over a settlement with the Palestinians, relations with Egypt improved marginally. Taba, the last remnant of Sinai captured by Israel from Egypt in 1967, was returned in March following years of international arbitration. Several African nations renewed relations with Israel, most notably the Marxist government in Ethiopia, which broke its ties after the 1973 war. Improved relations with the Soviet bloc were marked by parleys between the Israeli and Soviet foreign ministers, Russia's abstention on the annual General Assembly resolution to expel Israel from the United Nations, and restoration of full diplomatic ties with Hungary.

DON PERETZ
State University of New York, Binghamton

ITALY

Giulio Andreotti, a Christian Democrat, became Italy's new premier in 1989; however, the year's most exciting event was Mikhail Gorbachev's visit to Italy and the Vatican.

Domestic Affairs. The year started with a government headed—since April 1988—by Ciriaco De Mita, a left-of-center Christian Democrat from southern Italy. His five-party (*pentapartito*) coalition government consisted also of Socialists, Social Democrats, Republicans, and Liberals. Premier De Mita ran into serious trouble at the Christian Democrats' Party Congress in February when that faction-riddled body voted him out of the party secretaryship. This put in jeopardy the weakened De Mita government, because his principal junior partner, Bettino Craxi, leader of the Socialist Party, was eager to take the premiership.

Meanwhile, the major opposition force, Achille Occhetto's Italian Communist Party, began to unveil a new look at its party congress in March. It repudiated the old policy of "democratic centrism" in party management and became less ideological. It also placed emphasis on ecology, feminism, and family issues, hoping thereby to regain some of the losses it had suffered at the polls during the preceding decade. In 1976 the Communist Party had reached its peak, pulling in 34.4% of the popular vote, but in 1988 its share of the vote had fallen to 21.9%.

In May, Occhetto visited the United States, where he met with senior members of Congress but with no Bush administration officials. He repeated assurances that his party was committed to Western security and economic alliances.

By the end of the year, in the wake of the Hungarian Communist Party's decision to change its name to "Socialist," the Italian Communist Party indicated that it probably would change its name, too, at its next congress early in 1990 and also apply for admission to the Socialist International.

On May 19, Premier De Mita offered his resignation, plunging Italy's government into turmoil on the eve of U.S. President George Bush's visit, which was scheduled to begin on May 26. De Mita acted as "caretaker" premier during Bush's visit and until elections for the European Parliament in June might help bring a focus to the Italian political scene.

European Parliament Elections. On June 18, 82% of the Italian voters flocked to the polls to elect their delegation to the European Parliament in Strasbourg, France. Chosen on the basis of proportional representation, Italy's 81 delegates were divided among these groupings: Christian Democrats, 27 seats, an increase of one; Communists, 22, down 5; Socialists, 12, up 3; neo-Fascists, 4, down 1; Liberal/Republicans, 4, down 1; Greens, 5, up 5; Social Democrats, 2, down 1; Regional lists, 2, no change; Extreme Left, 1, no change; Legalize Drugs, 1, up 1; and Federalists, 1, up 1.

The election revealed Italy's political landscape somewhat, though the shifts had to be read on a small scale. The vote weakened further the *pentapartito* coalition. Only Craxi's Socialists made significant gains both in this election (up 3.6 points) and in the 1987 general election (up 0.5 points). However, Craxi had hoped to do considerably better. The Christian Democrats, though still the largest party, could muster only 33% of the popular vote—the lowest share in their party's history. The small Liberal, Republican, Social Democratic, and Radical parties together tallied only 7.1% of the vote. Italy's Greens enjoyed a sudden growth, their two factions getting a total of 6.2% of the vote—another source of concern to Craxi, whose Socialist Party had held the environment portfolio in the outgoing De Mita cabinet. The Communists did manage to improve—by 1 point, to 27.6%—on their 1987 general election result, thus halting their decline.

The Andreotti Government. On July 10, following weeks of bargaining, Giulio Andreotti

AP/Wide World

Italian President Francesco Cossiga, left, *shakes hands with Italy's new Premier Giulio Andreotti, a centrist Christian Democrat heading a five-party coalition, at his swearing-in ceremony in the Quirinal Palace in July.*

received a mandate to form a new government. Andreotti is a five-time Christian Democrat premier who had been foreign minister since 1983. By agreeing to some shifts of portfolios, this centrist Christian Democrat succeeded in remolding the uneasy coalition of the same five parties that had comprised De Mita's government. Premier Andreotti quickly called for budget austerity, a crackdown on tax evaders, and stepped-up preparations for Western Europe's economic integration at the end of 1992.

Economy. The emphasis of Premier Andreotti's new government in July on belt-tightening underscored the nation's concern over the relentless growth of Italy's budget deficit. This is the weakest link in an otherwise robust economy, one of Europe's sturdiest. The budget deficit grew by 3.9% in 1988 and was expected to rise by more than 3% in 1989.

Economists worried that domestic demand was too strong, feeding inflation that had mounted to an annual rate of 7%, the highest in several years. Lowering that figure to below 6% was a high priority, and budget control was the place to start.

The deficit was expected to reach $100 billion in 1989, equal to 11% of the gross national product. (In relative terms, this was about triple the U.S. deficit.) Two thirds of this gap came from obligatory interest payments on Italy's huge national debt of $740 billion. Unless cuts were made or new revenues found, the 1990 budget deficit would exceed $110 billion. Some observers feel that the situation would improve if more Italians reported their income. If that came to pass, it is estimated there would be enough tax revenue to eliminate 75% of the deficit. But many Italians see no reason to hand the government money that they perceive will be poured into a bloated bureaucracy and public services noted for their inefficiency.

Andreotti named as his new treasury minister Guido Carli, a tough and respected former governor of the Bank of Italy. An advocate of privatization of the economy, Carli called for speedy enactment of a package of new taxes and spending cuts worth at least several billion dollars. This could not be accomplished easily,

ITALY • Information Highlights

Official Name: Italian Republic.
Location: Southern Europe.
Area: 116,305 sq mi (301 230 km²).
Population (mid-1989 est.): 57,600,000.
Chief Cities (Dec. 31, 1986): Rome, the capital, 2,815,457; Milan, 1,495,260; Naples, 1,204,211.
Government: *Head of state,* Francesco Cossiga, president (took office July 1985). *Head of government,* Giulio Andreotti, prime minister (sworn in July 10, 1989). *Legislature*—Parliament: Senate and Chamber of Deputies.
Monetary Unit: Lira (1,295.0 lire equal U.S.$1, Dec. 12, 1989).
Economic Indexes (1988): *Consumer Prices* (1980 = 100) all items, 221.7. *Industrial Production* (1980 = 100), 108.
Foreign Trade (1988 U.S.$): *Imports,* $138,665,-000,000; *exports,* $127,114,000,000.

as Carli needed support from Finance Minister Rino Formica, a Socialist who has denounced the spreading "virus of Thatcherism" (the policies of British Prime Minister Margaret Thatcher), and from Budget Minister Paolo Cirino Pomicino, a Christian Democrat. Moreover, Premier Andreotti was being cautious in his support of economic reform. His Socialist rival, Craxi, though promising the new government "complete and loyal support," was ambitious to regain the prime ministership which he had held from 1983 to 1987.

In November, after weeks of wrangling, the Council of Ministers appointed new heads of the parastate sector of the economy. Franco Nobili, a Christian Democrat friend of Andreotti and former head of a private construction group, became the new head of the Institute for Industrial Reconstruction. Gabriele Cagliari, a Socialist chemist and friend of Craxi, became the new head of the state energy combine.

Nationwide, Italy's unemployment ran at about 16.6%, but in hard-scrabble southern Italy it was much higher. Calabria had a 24% unemployment rate, whereas northern and central Italy had an 8% rate. Among young men in southern Italy, the unemployment rate was 50%, and nearly 65% for women. By contrast, only 2% of northern Italian men over age 30 were out of work.

In Palermo, per capita income was $5,825; in the Italian northwest, around Turin, it was $11,145. But the situation in southern Italy was not desperate. Many unemployed youths found part-time jobs.

European Community. Italy has supported European Community (EC) plans to eliminate by 1992 all barriers to Community-wide movement of goods, capital, and labor. Modern, internationally minded companies in northern Italy, such as Fiat and Olivetti, stand to benefit the most. But this may not be true for less competitive industries in southern Italy. Some observers fear, too, that Italy's inefficient bureaucracy and the state sector of the economy will stifle progress.

In September the EC ordered Italy to close the Bagnoli steel plant and three others as the condition for allowing the government to pay part of the companies' huge debt. Italy's restructuring of the steel industry will eliminate 20,000 jobs and reduce production by 1.2 million tons.

Pollution. Air pollution in the industrial cities and the deterioration of architectural treasures continued without much correction in 1989. The phenomenon of a billowing "red tide" of algae that was ruining the Adriatic's northwestern coastline was the most publicized environmental crisis of the summer season.

Terrorism, Mafia, and Bank Scandals. Prosecutors succeeded, after long delays, in convicting a number of Red Brigadesmen and others who had been involved in terrorist acts in the early 1980s. The government also continued its fight against the Mafia in Sicily, as well as against organized crime throughout Italy, but met with only partial success. The Mafia, in addition to its lucrative drug business, infiltrated a number of financial institutions.

Italy's investigation of the 1982 collapse of Milan's Banco Ambrosiano led to indictments in April of 35 former bank officials, but absolved financier Carlo De Benedetti, former deputy chairman of the bank. Chief Vatican banker Archbishop Paul Marcinkus, who has been implicated in the scandal, also was not indicted. Italian courts ruled that Marcinkus was immune to prosecution in Italy.

In September the government began investigating irregularities by directors of Banca Nazionale del Lavoro when it was revealed that its Atlanta, GA, branch had issued $2.6 billion in unauthorized export credits to Iraq.

Foreign Affairs. Italy's foreign policy in 1989 rested on the twin pillars of the North Atlantic Treaty Organization (NATO) alliance and the European Community. In February, Italy's Defense Minister Valerio Zanone claimed that NATO members consistently slighted Italy and other Mediterranean countries, paying more attention to problems of central and northern Europe. He expressed disappointment over the recent naming of a Norwegian general instead of an Italian admiral to a top position in NATO. Nevertheless, Italy's commitment to NATO remained firm.

President Bush, in his trip to Rome in late May, assured Italian leaders that the United States would not reduce its military forces in Europe without consulting its NATO allies first. The president observed Memorial Day by visiting the U.S. military cemetery near Anzio.

Just prior to Bush's visit, Peter Secchia, a Michigan Republican Party leader who had contributed heavily to Bush's presidential campaign, but who possessed no diplomatic experience, was named the new U.S. ambassador to Italy. What some perceived as his penchant for tactless language caused his nomination to be questioned both in the U.S. Senate and in Rome. Italian leftists soon accused Ambassador Secchia of interfering in Italian politics when he reaffirmed U.S. policy of not meeting with Communist leaders.

In October, President Francesco Cossiga paid a visit to President Bush in Washington and was awarded an honorary degree by Columbia University.

Gorbachev Visits Italy. In the wake of explosive changes in Eastern Europe, Soviet President Mikhail Gorbachev visited Italy from November 29 to December 1, en route to his conference at Malta with President Bush. Ordinarily blasé Romans erupted in wild "Gorbymania" as he and his wife toured the city's famous sights. In cordial talks with Premier

Andreotti, Gorbachev sought tangible Italian support for *perestroika* and agreed that semiannual meetings between the Italian and the Soviet foreign ministers should take place. He criticized the West for not discussing naval arms control, and he proposed talks with Italy and the United States regarding American and Soviet naval bases in the Mediterranean.

President Cossiga entertained Gorbachev at a state dinner in the Quirinal Palace, where Gorbachev declared that the "cold war has ended." The next day, in an impressive speech in Rome's Campidoglio, Gorbachev called for a "Helsinki II" conference of 35 European states in 1990 to discuss Europe's common problems, to be held prior to completion of the program for a fully integrated Western Europe, scheduled for 1992.

He also visited Achille Occhetto, leader of the Italian Communist Party, and expressed approval of its changing policies. In a trip to Milan, Gorbachev spoke to Italian industrialists about increasing trade with the Soviet Union. Agreements were signed that set in motion an estimated $3 billion worth of Italian commercial enterprises in the Soviet Union, including an enlarged Fiat auto plant.

The most dramatic point in Gorbachev's visit was his historic, 70-minute conference in the Vatican with Pope John Paul II. It was the first encounter ever between a Soviet Communist leader and a pope. Gorbachev promised that the Supreme Soviet soon would enact a law pledging expanded religious freedom for Soviet citizens. The two men agreed in principle to the establishment of diplomatic relations between the Vatican and the USSR, and the pope expressed support for recent reforms in the Soviet Union. Gorbachev invited the pope to make a return visit in 1990. The pope said that he hoped that "developments would make it possible for him to accept." Much apparently would depend on what happens to the more than four million Eastern Rite Catholics in the western Ukraine whom Joseph Stalin forced into the Orthodox Church before World War II.

CHARLES F. DELZELL
Vanderbilt University

JAMAICA

On Feb. 9, 1989, former Prime Minister Michael Manley's Peoples National Party swept to victory in parliamentary elections, ousting his longtime political opponent, Edward Seaga and the Jamaica Labor Party.

Politics. Manley, Jamaica's prime minister from 1972 to 1980, had vowed during his previous term to bring "democratic socialism" to the island nation. Seaga, a strong advocate of free enterprise, attempted to reverse the thrust of Manley's policies, with some initial success.

JAMAICA • Information Highlights

Official Name: Jamaica.
Location: Caribbean.
Area: 4,243 sq mi (10 990 km^2).
Population (mid-1989 est.): 2,500,000.
Chief City (1982 census): Kingston, the capital, 586,930.
Government: *Head of state,* Elizabeth II, queen, represented by Florizel Glasspole, governor-general (took office June 27, 1973). *Head of government,* Michael Manley, prime minister (took office 1989). *Legislature* (bicameral)—Senate (Upper House) and House of Representatives.
Monetary Unit: Jamaican dollar (5.48 J. dollars equal U.S.$1, June 1989).
Gross Domestic Product (1987 U.S.$): $2,900,000,-000.
Economic Index (1988): *Consumer Prices* (1980 = 100), all items, 283.9; food, 292.3.
Foreign Trade (1988 U.S. $): *Imports,* $1,433,-000,000; *exports,* $821,000,000.

But, as prices for Jamaica's commodity exports dropped during the 1980s, the country slipped into a deep recession and the foreign debt more than doubled from $1.9 billion to $4.0 billion. In an attempt to promote recovery, Seaga adopted economic-austerity measures recommended by the International Monetary Fund (IMF).

The result was a sharp reduction in Jamaican living standards, compounded by the extensive damage and economic hardship caused by Hurricane Gilbert when it pummeled the island in September 1988. The consequent unrest and discontent helped return Manley to office.

In the 1970s, Manley had steered Jamaica on a leftward course, severing relations with the IMF, alienating the United States and much of the foreign business community, and becoming allied with Cuban leader Fidel Castro.

Back in power, Manley said he had changed his political philosophy during his years out of office. In his inaugural address, he asserted that he is now a "mainstream realist." He expressed a desire for "the most constructive possible relations with Washington." He pledged to seek increased trade with and investment from the United States, especially for the tourism sector, Jamaica's principal earner of foreign exchange.

The omens for the future are "moderately favorable" if Manley adheres to the course he has announced, according to a 1989 assessment by the Inter-American Development Bank. "Real GDP growth should recover strongly in 1989," the report said, thanks to a resurgence in tourism and stronger alumina prices. But, the report cautioned, to achieve its goals, the Manley government will have to adhere to the economic conservatism of the Seaga regime. In response, Manley promised to spur privatization of state-owned industries, beginning with Air Jamaica, the government-controlled airline.

RICHARD C. SCHROEDER, *Consultant to the Organization of American States*

JAPAN

Japan's embattled posture in trade negotiation and its role in the economic world in 1989 were hampered severely by a series of political and corruption scandals at home. Between January and August, the Japanese saw no less than three men occupy the post of prime minister. These political upheavals hurt the status of the ruling Liberal-Democratic Party (LDP).

Although Japan's trade surplus, a matter of concern to other nations, dropped almost 3% in 1988, the total reached $77.4 billion. A surplus of more than $50 billion with the United States represented 40% of the American worldwide trade deficit. In April the Finance Ministry announced that Japan's foreign-exchange reserves for the first time surpassed $100 billion. It was probably also the first time any single nation had reached that level since the International Monetary Fund (IMF) was created in 1947 (*see* special report, page 295).

In 1989, Japan began cautiously to assert economic leadership, particularly in the debt crisis strangling the world's poorer nations. At the Paris summit meeting of advanced industrial nations, Prime Minister Sousuke Uno pledged $40 billion for aid to developing countries. Tokyo, however, did insist that Japan should enjoy the same status in the IMF as it holds in the World Bank (second in voting power).

Domestic Affairs

The year marked an important transition in another sense. The death of Emperor Hirohito (*see* OBITUARIES) on January 7 brought to a close the long and tumultuous Showa Era (1926–88). The new emperor, Akihito (*see* BIOGRAPHY), immediately ascended the throne to open the era of *Heisei* (1989–). A measure of Japan's international stature was indicated by the fact that representatives of some 163 countries and 26 international organizations attended Hirohito's funeral.

Party Politics. Already in December 1988 the cabinet of Prime Minister Noboru Takeshita had suffered losses in public support arising out of passage of a sweeping tax reform and from a burgeoning scandal. A rapidly expanding enterprise, the Recruit Cosmos Corp., had paid cash and unlisted stock to businessmen, bureaucrats, and political leaders for favors. Kyodo News Service reported that approval ratings for the Takeshita regime had hit an all-time low (36%).

Late in 1988, Takeshita had reformed his cabinet, a step which still did not offset the resignations of three cabinet ministers: Finance Minister Kiichi Miyazawa, in charge of tax reform; Justice Minister Takashi Hasegawa, in charge of investigation of "money politics"; and Ken Harada, in charge of the Economic Planning Agency (EPA). On January 25 the chairwoman of the Japan Socialist Party (JSP) and leader of the opposition, Takako Doi, called for Takeshita's resignation and a general election.

Takeshita, testifying before a Diet committee on April 11, admitted that his LDP faction had received directly or indirectly more than $1 million from Recruit, but he insisted that contributions were legal under current political funds laws. The major opposition parties were

AP/Wide World

Prime Minister Toshiki Kaifu, the third man in 1989 to hold Japan's top leadership post in a scandal-ridden year for the ruling Liberal Democratic Party (LDP), talks with opposition leader Takako Doi. The first woman to head a political party in Japan, Doi led her Japan Socialist Party to victory over the LDP in 1989 elections for the upper house of parliament.

unanimous in their dissatisfaction with his explanations; they demanded that his predecessor, Yasuhiro Nakasone, also be called to testify under oath. As a sanction, they continued their boycott of Diet deliberations on the fiscal year budget (scheduled to begin April 1).

In mid-April, Kyodo reported that barely 4% of Japanese polled approved of Takeshita and his cabinet. An overwhelming majority had suspicions about his indirect replies in the Diet. On April 25 the prime minister bowed to pressure and announced that he would resign, but only after the Diet passed the budget and after his scheduled trip to Southeast Asia. He would continue to head his LDP faction, which was controlling 25% of the party's Diet members.

One alternative seemed even less viable: As approval of the LDP declined, support for the JSP grew from 11% to only 18% (about the proportion of party seats in the lower house). Moreover, opposition figures as well became enmeshed in the Recruit affair. In February, Democratic Socialist Party (DSP) chairman Saburo Tsukamoto resigned because he had accepted shares of Recruit stock. In May chairman Koshiro Ishida of Komeito, the second-largest opposition party, stepped down after the revelation of shady financial deals.

Big business, usually an ally of the LDP, also was infected by the Recruit virus. In December 1988, Hisashi Shinto, head of the semipublic Nippon Telegraph & Telephone Co. (NTT), resigned. On February 13 two NTT executives and Recruit chairman Hiromasa Ezoe were arrested for accepting and offering bribes. On March 27 all four were indicted.

Selection of a Takeshita successor was complicated further by trouble within the LDP. In February former Prime Minister Nakasone suddenly had cancelled a scheduled trip to the United States. On May 23, after an inconclusive appearance before the Diet, he announced that he would resign from the LDP; he also would relinquish leadership of his party faction, but would retain his seat in the lower house.

The party finally settled on Takeshita's foreign minister, Sousuke Uno, to serve out the party presidential term and on June 2 he was elected by the Diet as prime minister. Less than two months later, the LDP suffered a resounding election defeat and Uno resigned. In fact, earlier the party had lost several elections.

In Fukuoka, a conservative stronghold, a relatively unknown Socialist beat his LDP opponent in February for an upper house seat. On June 25 a woman member of the JSP, Kinuko Ofuchi, defeated the LDP candidate for a seat representing Niigata prefecture. The most ominous sign of LDP trouble was loss of the Tokyo Metropolitan Assembly election, held on July 3. The party gave up 20 of its 63 seats to the JSP, which boosted its representation from 12 to 36 seats. This foreshadowed an even greater LDP defeat in the election for half of the seats in the (upper) House of Councillors.

Election and Aftermath. The main issues in the general election of July 23 included resolution of the Recruit Corp. affair, the recent introduction of a 3% consumption tax, and the government's liberalization of Japan's agricultural market. For the first time since its formation in 1955, the LDP lost control of a Diet chamber. It took only 36 of 69 seats up for election; with 73 seats not at risk, the party's total was 109 seats, well below a simple majority of 127. The JSP parlayed 22 seats up for election into 46 won; with 20 not at risk, the party held 66 seats. The Komeito had 20 seats; the Japan Communist Party (JCP), 14; DSP, 8; others, 35 (total 252).

In the (lower) House of Representatives, the LDP continued to enjoy a majority with 295 of 512 seats. The JSP held 85 seats, followed by the Komeito, DSP, JCP, and independents.

On July 24, Prime Minister Uno announced that he would step down "to take the entire responsibility" for the crushing defeat. In a caucus of LDP Diet members and local representatives on August 8, former Education Minister Toshiki Kaifu (*see* BIOGRAPHY) was nominated to be party president. On August 9 he was elected prime minister. Takako Doi, head of the JSP, was nominated by the upper house, making her the first woman to hold such a lofty political honor.

Kaifu's cabinet reflected a balance among intraparty groups: his own faction (led by former State Minister Toshio Komoto); the Takeshita faction; that of former Foreign Minister Shintaro Abe; and a majority of the former Nakasone faction. Aware of the growing power of female votes, the new prime minister appointed two women to his cabinet: Sumiko Takahara, director of the EPA, and Mayumi Moriyama as director of the Environmental Agency. When Tokuo Yamashita resigned

(Continued on page 297.)

JAPAN • Information Highlights

Official Name: Japan.
Location: East Asia.
Area: 145,882 sq mi (377 835 km²).
Population (mid-1989 est.): 123,200,000.
Chief Cities (March 31, 1988 est.): Tokyo, the capital, 8,155,781; Yokohama, 3,121,601; Osaka, 2,543,520; Nagoya, 2,099,564.
Government: *Head of state,* Akihito, emperor (acceded Jan. 9, 1989). *Head of government,* Toshiki Kaifu, prime minister (took office Aug. 9, 1989). *Legislature*—Diet: House of Councillors and House of Representatives.
Monetary Unit: Yen (143.40 yen equal U.S.$1, Nov. 10, 1989).
Gross National Product (1988 U.S.$): $2,843,000,000,000.
Economic Indexes (1988): *Consumer Prices* (1980 = 100), all items, 116.2; food, 114.4. *Industrial Production* (1980 = 100), 134.
Foreign Trade (1988 U.S.$): *Imports,* $187,494,000,000; *exports,* $264,959,000,000.

The Economic Superpower

The death of Emperor Hirohito in January 1989 and the ascension of Akihito to the Chrysanthemum Throne offered an appropriate moment to look back on Japan's economic "miracle."

Few realize that Japan's prosperity predates both the post-World War II era and Hirohito's 62-year reign. The "miracle" reflects growth reaching back to the late 19th century. In fact, by comparing the economic growth rates of ten nations (including the United States) to Japan's, Columbia University economist James Nakamura found that Japan's performance has been unmatched in the last century. Except for Japan's "take-off" era (1870–1913) and the Pacific War era (1938–53), progress was more rapid for Japan than other nations.

Even the premodern Edo era (1600–1868) was marked by a substantial rise in output. With the population remaining constant, per capita production rose. Further progress followed the modernization process in the Meiji period (1868–1912). Between 1885 and the end of the century, Japan's gross national product (GNP) doubled. The rate of growth increased from 1.2% in 1885 to 4.1% in 1898.

In the late 1930s and early 1940s, the Japanese bore the enormous costs of war. Yet the modern infrastructure survived and a skilled labor force soon reappeared after the surrender.

The mode of Japan's defeat, the way the nation surrendered, the benign nature of the Allied occupation (1945–52), and the style of the peace treaty—all set a tone for the political behavior and economic policy after 1952. The occupation demilitarized Japan and post-treaty governments were free to concentrate on reconstruction and growth.

The U.S. contribution to Japan's revival was impressive. The United States gave money to feed the defeated Japanese, lent technical assistance, and in 1949 helped "rationalize" the economy under the Dodge Plan. Technology flowed to Japan under favorable licensing agreements and Japanese studied American managerial techniques. With U.S. help, the successful Japan Productivity Center also was established. In the early 1950s the Korean conflict brought Japan a windfall: some $3 billion in offshore procurement for the United States and UN war effort.

Since the peace treaty signed in 1952, a conservative coalition has dominated Japan. Early on, the conservatives decided on two gambles. First, they regained sovereignty under the peace treaty by placing Japan under an American strategic umbrella. This decision made the nation dependent on foreign policy. Second, Japan's leaders pledged that, with limited defense expenditures, the nation would set about achieving an unprecedented growth rate. The GNP was to double in a decade. The results were beyond the conservatives' most sanguine hopes.

Japan's electronics industry has contributed significantly to the nation's economic success. A large portion of Japanese-made electronic products is exported.

Since the annual average of real growth needed to double the GNP in the 1960s was 7.2%, public attention focused on that bench mark. Japanese followed GNP statistics just as they watched baseball scores. GNP (in current prices) almost doubled in five years (1955–60), more than doubled again in the following five years (1960–65), and then rose another 2.5 times in the five years from 1965 to 1970. In this last period the annual rate of growth (in real terms) averaged 12.1%.

By 1971 the GNP was estimated at more than $250 billion, with income per capita about $2,000. Japan already had reached the status of the third-largest economy in the world, after the United States and the USSR. Growth became the dominant Japanese religion. Indeed, the Japanese were the originators of supply-side economics. They supported a record savings rate to provide investment funds; they went into advanced technology and plant modernization. Above all, firms invested in human resources, training for a skilled labor force. Lifetime employment (in big corporations), seniority, and a bonus system based on profits made workers powerful constituencies.

The conservative coalition that took credit for the "miracle" was a combine of diverse elements: the Liberal-Democratic Party (LDP), a powerful bureaucracy, business interests, and representatives of agriculture. In ten general elections (1958–83), LDP-led governments won from 41.7% (1976) to 57.8% (1958) of the popular vote for the lower house of the Diet (parliament). Political stability, in turn, helped economic growth.

Japan's growth has had both starts and fits. Two OPEC-driven "oil shocks" (1973–74 and 1979–80) introduced notes of sobriety. Japanese began to talk about "the limits of growth." Private consumption for the Japanese as a proportion of GNP was running at only 52%, compared with 60–61% in the United States and Europe. Many Japanese came to feel they were working hard, only to subsidize exports.

The 1970s' ratio of current-account surplus to GNP remained modest. It moved from 1% (1971) to 2.2% (1973); as the yen's value climbed, the ratio tapered off to 1.7% (1978). The oil shocks had proved effective in reducing Japan's external surplus, which moved temporarily into the red.

In 1974 the GNP growth rate actually dipped below zero. Inflation, a stringent fiscal policy, loss of purchasing power, and a deficit in balance of payments—all contributed to a negative attitude toward growth. Moreover, in the mid-1970s, the Japanese felt a sense of growing crisis because of problems in the environment. By 1982, Japan's oil consumption had fallen to 70% of the 1973 level while inflation-adjusted GNP had grown by 40% over the decade. A turning point came in 1983, ten years after the first oil shock. Oil shortages gave way to glut. There was a resurgence of technological progress. Recovery was led by the electronics industry, followed by production of new ceramics and discoveries in biotechnology. Just as important were developments on the demand side, as both labor unions and consumers welcomed the new technology.

New service industries arose in child care, education, sports, visual media, music, personnel placement, and data processing. Deregulation and privatization, particularly under the administration of Prime Minister Yasuhiro Nakasone (1982–87), eased public deficits and invigorated the private sector. Decentralization spurred the spread of business from the Tokaido industrial zone to outlying areas. The Ina Basin in mountainous Nagano Prefecture, for example, attracted such a vast electronics complex that local residents began referring to the area as the "Silicon Valley of Japan."

The new wave of growth was not without costs. The critical ratio of current-account surplus to GNP rose from 1.8% (1983) to 2.8% (1984) and then to 3.6% (1985). By 1984, Japan's excess of exports over imports amounted to nearly $34 billion, as automobiles, steel, consumer and industrial electronic goods poured across the Pacific. Because of an overvalued dollar, Japan became the second-largest trading partner (after Canada) of the United States. Towering trade and current-account surpluses, however, were bringing Japan into disfavor.

In fiscal 1985 (ended March 30, 1986), the GNP reached $1,626 billion, making Japan the second-largest economic power in the world. By the end of 1985, Japan became the world's largest creditor nation, with assets exceeding liabilities by $120 billion.

In April 1986 a committee chaired by Haruo Maekawa, former governor of the Bank of Japan, unveiled a report on the future of the economy. The Maekawa report noted Japan's important position in the world and the parallel problem of the current-account surplus. The report stated that Japan's policy "should make effective use of the surplus funds now available to promote qualitative improvements in national living standards and harmonious growth of the world's economy." Five specific goals were: (1) expansion of domestic demand, (2) conversion of industrial structure, (3) improvement of market access for imports, (4) stabilization of exchange rates, and (5) promotion of international financial cooperation. Among Japanese, it was agreed that the economy no longer would be export-led; growth was to come from expansion of domestic demand.

Despite the ongoing effects of restructuring the economy, Japan's growth has continued. In fiscal 1988 (ended March 31, 1989), the nominal GNP reached 371.3 trillion yen (about $2,800 billion) with per capita GNP estimated at $19,642, compared with $18,403 in the United States. The growth rate for fiscal 1988 stood at 5.1% (surpassing the official estimate of 4.9%). The rise, however, was generated by about a 5% increase in domestic demand with a drop of about 0.7% in external demand. As a result, the critical ratio of current-account surplus of GNP decreased from 4.5% (fiscal 1986) to 3.5% (fiscal 1987). Nonetheless, by May 1988, Japan's foreign exchange reserves reached an all-time high of $87.24 billion (2.5% of world reserves).

Among advanced industrial nations, Japan has enjoyed a modest inflation rate. In May 1988, the consumer price index stood at 101.4 (May 1985=100). Unemployment also has remained low, the seasonally adjusted rate running between 2.3% and 2.4% between November 1988 and May 1989.

Other social indicators are equally important in plotting the future. Japan's population in mid-1989 was estimated at 123,200,000. Although Japan is settled densely, size is not as significant as population structure. The birth rate of 10.8 per 1,000 is one of the world's lowest; the death rate is also low at 6.5 per 1,000. In 1987 life expectancy in Japan reached 75.2 for men and 80.9 for women, both world-record highs. Demographers have estimated that by the year 2020, one of every four Japanese will be age 65 or older. A "graying Japan" means that the government must shore up the foundation for medical and pension systems. In the short term, this will require cuts in benefits. In the long run, Japan can expand welfare bond issues at the rate of economic growth, without increasing the ratio of debt to GNP.

Japan's leadership, within the famed conservative coalition, also is aging. The high water mark of success for the LDP, the symbol of economic growth, probably came in the dual elections of 1986, when the party won absolute control of the Diet. In 1988–89, the regimes of Nakasone and Noboru Takeshita were caught up in the so-called "Recruit Scandal," involving private transfer of stock to party leaders. The incident led to the LDP's first defeat (in upper house elections, 1989) and brought down the cabinet of Takeshita and his successor, Sousuke Uno (*see* accompanying article). Although the scandal caused only a slight blip in stock market indexes, it, nevertheless, foreshadowed a shift in political leadership.

ARDATH W. BURKS

under fire because of Recruit connections, Moriyama became the first woman to occupy the sensitive post of chief cabinet secretary, spokesperson for the administration.

On October 31, Kaifu was reelected president of the LDP for a two-year term and remained prime minister.

Economy. When Emperor Hirohito fell gravely ill, sober Japanese expected that a period of mourning would interrupt growth of the nation's economy. In fact, on the first working day after the imperial death, January 9, investors on the Tokyo Stock Exchange sent the Nikkei average up to an all-time high of 30,678.39. Nor did political fallout from the Recruit scandal cause more than a few pauses in the pace of Japan's economic growth.

On August 26 the EPA reported that the economy continued on the expansionary track which had lasted 33 months. The January-March quarter showed a rise in inflation-adjusted growth of 2.2%. The result was a real GNP increase of 5.1% for fiscal 1988 (to March 31); the nominal annual GNP for the fiscal year was 371.3 trillion yen (about $2.85 trillion).

The Recruit Corp. investigations interrupted normal Diet proceedings and the government had to adopt emergency measures to meet a budget deadline of April 1. On April 28 the LDP, for the first time in Japan's postwar Diet history, unilaterally passed a budget bill through the lower house session. Opposition and some LDP members boycotted the meeting.

The budget, which went into effect May 27, regardless of upper house action, provided for 60.41 trillion yen (about $483.3 billion) in expenditures. Defense spending was to increase 5.9% to barely more than 1% of GNP. Official development assistance (ODA) was to rise 7.6% over the level of the previous fiscal year.

In December 1988 the Takeshita cabinet had rammed a sweeping tax-reform measure through the Diet as well. In that case, members of the JSP and JCP boycotted the session; Komeito and DSP delegates attended but voted against the bills. The reform provided for cuts in individual and corporate tax rates but imposed a 3% consumption tax on goods and services. Confusion among voters over implementation of the new tax, beginning April 1, may have led to LDP election defeats.

Among advanced industrial nations, Japan was able to boast of a relatively modest inflation rate. The consumer price index stood at 104.2 in June (June 1988=101.2; 1985=100). Nevertheless, for the first time in nine years, the cautious Bank of Japan raised the discount rate beginning May 31 from 2.5% to 3.25% (compared with that of the United States, 7%). In June seasonally adjusted unemployment fell to 2.2%, the lowest rate in seven years.

Foreign Affairs

U.S. Relations. All three men who served as prime minister in 1989 made a point of stressing the importance of Japan-U.S. relations. In February, Takeshita was among the first world leaders to visit U.S. President George Bush in Washington. In Tokyo on February 23, the two met again at the funeral of Emperor Hirohito. Uno met with Bush at a Paris summit. In one of his first official steps, Kaifu visited Bush in Washington on September 1. In all of these meetings, U.S.-Japan trade dominated the conversation.

In fact, the first problem between the two countries arose from an agreement. In November 1988, Tokyo and Washington had signed an understanding concerning coproduction of a new fighter-aircraft called the FSX. Rather than purchase new models of the F-16 outright, the Japanese planned to build the plane in Japan, to subcontract (to Mitsubishi), and to allow 40% of production to American subcontractors (mainly, General Dynamics). Both Prime Minister Takeshita and President Bush approved the plan.

The final pact was signed in April but was subject to congressional approval in the United States. An interagency quarrel in Washington, however, endangered approval of the agreement. The Departments of Defense and State supported the deal but the Office of U.S. Trade Representatives and the Commerce Department opposed it. Public debate in Congress revealed protectionist sentiment, which argued that technological secrets thus would be lost to Japan. Japanese purchase of F-16 aircraft "off the shelf" was preferable, since that would reduce the U.S. trade deficit. Finally, on May 16 the Senate rejected a resolution that would have cancelled the FSX arrangement. The squabble, however, left a bitter taste in Japanese mouths.

An even more serious problem arose out of American trade legislation. In August 1988, President Reagan had signed an omnibus trade bill, aimed at any nation engaged in "unfair trade practice" (section 301). On the recommendation of Trade Representative Carla Hills, President Bush specifically named Japan (along with Brazil and India) as a violator in late May. Specific areas of trade were targeted for negotiation over 18 months. These included supercomputers, lumber products, and intellectual properties (copyrights, patents, and trademarks). Japan objected to discussion tainted with threats of tariff reprisals and appealed to officials at the General Agreement on Tariffs and Trade (GATT). On June 21 in Geneva, GATT officials unanimously criticized the United States for "pursuing multilateral aims with bilateral means." In Tokyo new U.S. Ambassador Michael Armacost defended the 301 clause as "an instrument of fairness."

Soviet Relations. In December 1988, Soviet Foreign Minister Eduard Shevardnadze visited Tokyo, marking the first official contact between the two nations in almost three years. A long-standing territorial dispute that has raged for decades continued to block normal diplomatic relations and a peace treaty. It involved some small islands in the Kuriles (just north of Hokkaido), occupied by Soviet troops but claimed by the Japanese. On August 23 in Moscow a delegation of Japanese businessmen met with their Soviet counterparts to discuss joint development projects in Siberia.

Northeast Asia. On April 16, Chinese Premier Li Peng wound up a five-day visit to Tokyo, obtaining a pledge of continued economic cooperation. In his talks at the Imperial Palace, Li invited Emperor Akihito and Empress Michiko to visit China "at their convenience."

On June 7 the Uno government filed a moderate complaint with Beijing, calling the killing of student demonstrators in Beijing's Tiananmen Square "regrettable." Japan opposed sanctions against Beijing, saying such a move only would serve to isolate the Chinese. With annual investment in China reaching $300 million annually, Japanese firms had much to lose from a closed China. They also did not wish to see $19.3 billion in bilateral trade (1988) eroded by turmoil.

A group of young Japanese sailed from Nagasaki to Seoul in the Republic of (South) Korea, arriving on August 15. The "peace boat" carried those who wished to join their hosts in celebrating the anniversary of Korea's liberation from Japanese annexation. Tokyo has had normal diplomatic relations with Seoul since 1965.

On the other hand, the Democratic People's Republic of (North) Korea has no formal relations with Japan. Kim Yang Gon, a director of the Workers' (Communist) Party, was in Tokyo in January. On an informal visit to the headquarters of the JSP, Gon called for direct negotiations between Tokyo and Pyongyang in order to settle their differences. These included the fate of five Japanese seamen, who were captured in North Korea in the early 1980s from the *Fujisan-maru,* the same ship which a Korean stowaway used to defect to Japan. Return of the defector, Gon said, was a precondition for establishing normal relations with North Korea.

Southeast Asia. Just before he left office, Prime Minister Takeshita went on a nine-day tour of member states of the Association of Southeast Asian Nations (ASEAN). He began his trip in Bangkok, Thailand, proceeded to Kuala Lumpur, Malaysia, and went on to Singapore, Indonesia, and the Philippines. On the tour he pointed out that about 30% of Japan's ODA is earmarked for ASEAN nations, making Japan the largest donor to the regional organization.

On February 17, Japan recognized the government of Gen. Saw Maung in Burma and resumed foreign aid to the regime.

ARDATH W. BURKS, *Rutgers University*

JORDAN

In 1989, Jordan's attempts to solve its financial problems caused some popular unrest, and the country elected a new Parliament on a new territorial basis recognizing that Jordan had severed its connection with the West Bank in 1988.

Financial Crisis. Jordan, long dependent on subsidies from wealthier, oil-producing Arab states, suffered when these were reduced because of the decline in oil prices. In 1989 it had to ask the International Monetary Fund (IMF) for credit while it worked on restructuring its foreign debt, stated to amount to $6.5 billion. At the end of May a new Central Bank governor corrected this figure to $8.1 billion, and revealed that one third of the gold reserve had been cashed in for foreign currency.

Disturbances. A loan agreement made on April 10 between Jordan and the IMF was approved by the Council of Ministers on April 13. In summary form, the IMF was to grant Jordan a standby credit of $125 million over two years, with a like sum available later as Jordan moved to reschedule debt payments. The return obligation on Jordan was to aim at certain reforms: to cut the current budget deficit by four fifths; to reduce inflation from 14% to 7%, to cut imports sharply. Jordan, therefore, moved immediately to cut subsidies on a wide range of goods and services. On April 16 price increases of 15–20% were imposed on gasoline, irrigation water, telephones, transportation, and some household items (though not staples). Sharper increases, 40% up to 100%, applied to tobacco and alcohol products.

Protesting against these measures, some 4,000 youths in the southern town of Maan set fire to vehicles, banks, and other buildings on April 18. On the three succeeding days rioting and random destruction spread to other southern towns, but not to the capital. The rioters appeared to be mostly Bedouin—traditional supporters of the monarchy. King Hussein was in Washington, but the emergency was handled ably by Crown Prince Hassan, brother of the king who returned on April 22. About ten people were killed and some fourscore injured. Firm action by the security forces and the readiness of the monarchy to listen to grievances prevented further trouble. The grievances went beyond the purely economic. Demands were made for the removal of Zaid Rifai, prime minister since April 1985 and a lifelong friend of the king. Other demands, formally voiced in Karak, included amendment of the electoral law, punishment of corrupt officials, more political freedoms, and a freer press.

King Hussein responded on April 27, replacing Premier Zaid Rifai with Field Marshal Sherif Zeid bin Shaker, hitherto a court official and military adviser, and making other cabinet changes. The king mandated the new premier to proceed with reforms, including a return to parliamentary government.

AP/Wide World

Jordanians presented their voting cards to poll workers during Jordan's November general election, the first since 1967 and the first in which women were able to vote.

General Election. The general election held November 8 was for a new 80-seat legislature representing a series of newly defined constituencies, all on the East Bank. It was the first national election since 1967, and the first ever in which women, enfranchised in 1974, were able to vote. There was little in the election results to comfort the monarchy. Muslim fundamentalists and their allies won about one third of the seats. Candidates ran as individuals; parties were banned in Jordan in 1957. The Muslim Brotherhood (allowed to register

JORDAN • Information Highlights

Official Name: Hashemite Kingdom of Jordan.
Location: Southwest Asia.
Area: 35,475 sq mi (91 880 km^2).
Population (mid-1989 est.): 4,000,000.
Chief Cities (Dec. 1986): Amman, the capital, 972,000; Zarqa, 392,220; Irbid, 271,000.
Government: *Head of state,* Hussein I, king (acceded Aug. 1952). *Head of government,* Mudar Badran, prime minister (appointed Dec. 4, 1989). *Legislature*—Parliament: House of Representatives and Senate.
Monetary Unit: Dinar (.62720 dinar equals U.S.$1, Nov. 29, 1989).
Economic Index (1988): *Consumer Prices* (1980 = 100), all items, 133.7; food, 122.1.
Foreign Trade (1988 U.S.$): *Imports,* $2,761,000,000; *exports,* $1,030,000,000.

as a charity) thus enjoyed an enormous advantage, but no overt antimonarchical sentiment surfaced. Following the election, Premier Shaker resigned and was replaced by Mudar Badran, who twice previously held the office. On December 19, Badran announced that his government would lift martial law, imposed after the 1967 Arab-Israeli war.

Foreign Affairs. Hussein continued an active international role. In addition to a Washington visit (April), he was host to Soviet Foreign Minister Eduard Shevardnadze on February 19, and on March 25 he conferred with Egypt's President Hosni Mubarak and PLO leader Yasir Arafat in Ismailia, Egypt. In an action possibly significant for the future, he participated on February 19 in Baghdad, Iraq, in the creation of the Arab Cooperation Council, comprising Egypt, Iraq, Jordan, and North Yemen, a regional economic organization with political and defense potentials.

ARTHUR CAMPBELL TURNER
University of California, Riverside

KANSAS

The Kansas economy was sluggish in 1989 due to a drought that affected the early summer crops and to the depressed oil industry. Issues in the Kansas legislature related to a comprehensive highway improvement program and the need for additional prison facilities.

Agriculture. The 1989 Kansas wheat crop was the smallest since 1966, with production totaling 213.6 million bushels, averaging 24 bushels per acre with 8.9 million acres (3.6 million ha) harvested. Decreased production was due to a lack of rain in 1988 and early 1989 combined with early summer rains that delayed harvest and led to the growth of weeds to the extent that some fields were abandoned.

Kansas continued to lead the nation in sorghum production with an estimated harvest of 227.5 million bushels, up 11% from 1988 with an average of 65 bushels per acre and harvested acreage up 6% during the same period. Corn, soybeans, hay, and oats production also were expected to be up. The number of cattle in Kansas feedlots was down from 1988, corresponding to trends in other beef-producing states. Livestock production, however, was still one of the leading cash producers in the Kansas agricultural economy.

Released in early 1989, figures from the 1987 Census of Agriculture showed a loss of 5,167 farms in Kansas between 1982 and 1987, due to high debt and low land values that forced some farmers into bankruptcy or foreclosure. Farms ranging from 30 to 500 acres (12 to 203 ha) accounted for nearly 45% of the loss. Only "hobby" farms (under 10 acres or 4 ha) and farms of more than 1,000 acres (405 ha) increased.

Legislation. The Kansas legislature met in a record-length session that resulted in the passage of a major highway program and funding for the first new maximum-security prison in the state since 1895. The state was under a federal district court order to reduce the populations at the Kansas State Penitentiary in Lansing and the Kansas State Industrial Reformatory in Hutchinson by July of 1991. The legislature appropriated $65.5 million for approximately 640 maximum-security cells and 256 mental-health prison cells. Construction was to begin in 1990.

A $2.65 billion, eight-year, comprehensive highway improvement plan was passed to upgrade 16% of the state's roads and 20 of the highway bridges. The program would be funded, in part, by the state's largest tax increase ever, with $1.43 billion coming from increased motor fuels and sales taxes and vehicle-registration fees.

The state legislature also passed a $70 million decrease in the state income tax in response to the 1986 changes in the federal income tax. A campaign finance law was passed requiring candidates for county and city offices to follow the same reporting procedures as statewide and legislative office seekers. Funding increases were approved for programs related to nutrition and medical care for mothers and children in poor families. Efforts were made to halt the implementation of a statewide property tax reappraisal plan but no legislation resulted.

Other. U.S. Sen. Nancy Landon Kassebaum announced her intention to seek reelection in 1990 to a third term, reversing the intention expressed in her first campaign to serve only two terms.

The state's only nuclear-power plant, Wolf Creek near Burlington, paid a $50,000 fine to the Nuclear Regulatory Commission for violating cooling system regulations in 1987.

PATRICIA A. MICHAELIS
Kansas State Historical Society

KANSAS • Information Highlights

Area: 82,277 sq mi (213 098 km²).
Population (July 1, 1988): 2,495,000.
Chief Cities (July 1, 1986 est.): Topeka, the capital, 118,580; Wichita, 288,060; Kansas City, 162,070.
Government (1989): *Chief Officers*—governor, Mike Hayden (R); lt. gov., Jack D. Walker (R). *Legislature*—Senate, 40 members; House of Representatives, 125 members.
State Finances (fiscal year 1988): *Revenue,* $4,390,000,000; *expenditure,* $3,814,000,000.
Personal Income (1988): $39,320,000,000; per capita, $15,759.
Labor Force (June 1989): *Civilian labor force,* 1,316,700; *unemployed,* 64,400 (4.9% of total force).
Education: *Enrollment* (fall 1987)—public elementary schools, 299,000; public secondary, 123,000; colleges and universities, 146,439. *Public school expenditures* (1987–88), $1,618,848,000 ($4,051 per pupil).

Photos, AP/Wide World

Ten miners died in a flash fire at the Pyro Mining Company's William Station mine in Wheatcroft, KY, on September 13. Coal company official Charles Schultize, above left, *announces what was the nation's worst mine disaster in five years. Awaiting news of the latest developments, family and friends of the miners keep a vigil near the mine site.*

KENTUCKY

The single most important socioeconomic and political event in Kentucky during 1989 was a ruling on June 8 by the Kentucky Supreme Court that declared the state's entire public-school system unconstitutional. The decision, written by Chief Justice Robert Stephens, found that the Kentucky General Assembly had failed to comply with the constitution, mandating that the legislature "provide an efficient system of common schools throughout the state."

The lengthy decision, stemming from a 1985 lawsuit by 66 poor and rural school districts, focused primarily on three deficiencies that the court found—that overall funding was insufficient to provide an adequate education for all of Kentucky's children, that funds were inequitably distributed, and that the entire system was ineffective in terms of promoting overall student performance. The decision noted that even students in more affluent districts receive an inadequate education when compared with their counterparts in surrounding states or when judged by accepted national standards.

The court emphasized that the sole responsibility in this matter lay with the General Assembly. Legislative leaders responded by establishing, in cooperation with Gov. Wallace Wilkinson, the Education Reform Task Force, which began its work in midsummer. Most observers predicted that the final decisions on legislative reform would not be made prior to an expected 1990 special legislative session. The deadline for complying with the court's decision is July 15, 1990.

Mass Murder. Tragedy struck Kentucky in September when Joseph Wesbecker, a mentally disturbed former employee, marched into Louisville's Standard Gravure Corporation armed with an AK-47-style assault rifle and four other guns and shot 20 people, killing seven (an eighth died later), before taking his own life. The shooting revived the debate over banning semiautomatic weapons, both in Kentucky and across the nation.

Kentucky Lottery. The Kentucky lottery, which was initiated in late 1988 after voters approved a constitutional amendment and the legislature established its framework and basic procedures, sold its first tickets in April 1989. Initial sales exceeded projections considerably. In its first quarter, the lottery recorded $122.6 million in gross sales, with more than $41 million of the proceeds going to the state treasury. In October the lottery experienced its first major snag when a proposed game, Super-

KENTUCKY • Information Highlights

Area: 40,410 sq mi (104 660 km^2).
Population (July 1, 1988): 3,727,000.
Chief Cities (July 1, 1986 est.): Frankfort, the capital (1980 census), 25,973; Louisville, 287,460; Lexington-Fayette, 213,600.
Government (1989): *Chief Officers*—governor, Wallace Wilkinson (D); lt. gov., Brereton Jones (D). *General Assembly*—Senate, 38 members; House of Representatives, 100 members.
State Finances (fiscal year 1988): *Revenue,* $7,352,000,000; *expenditure,* $6,858,000,000.
Personal Income (1988): $47,784,000,000; per capita, $12,822.
Labor Force (June 1989): *Civilian labor force,* 1,763,100; *unemployed,* 128,900 (7.3% of total force).
Education: *Enrollment* (fall 1987)—public elementary schools, 449,000; public secondary, 194,000; colleges and universities, 153,351. *Public school expenditures* (1987–88), $1,993,960,000 ($3,258 per pupil).

sports, involving wagering on National Football League games, was challenged in court by several horse-racing interests. Although the courts ruled in favor of the game, Governor Wilkinson, a former supporter, changed his position and recommended the game's cancellation, which was accepted.

Politics. Two important local elections were decided in November. In Lexington, incumbent mayor Scotty Baesler easily defeated his challenger, Ann Ross, to win a third four-year term. In the most expensive local race in Kentucky history—for Jefferson County judge-executive—former state attorney general Dave Armstrong defeated his Republican opponent, John Heyburn.

Interest also intensified in the 1990 race for the U.S. senate seat held by Republican Sen. Mitch McConnell, who will seek a second term. Early challengers included Harvey Sloane, former Louisville mayor and outgoing Jefferson County judge-executive, and Dr. John Brock, the state superintendent of public instruction.

PAUL BLANCHARD
Eastern Kentucky University

KENYA

After ten years in office, President Daniel arap Moi's power continued to expand, while protections for human rights declined and Kenya's foreign relations deteriorated in 1989.

Domestic Affairs. Following 1988's elections, President Moi expanded his own power by dropping Vice-President Mwai Kibaki, a potential successor. Kibaki was replaced by Dr. Josephat Karanja, whose only political influence came from his relationship with Moi. Karanja immediately sought to oust Arthur Magugu, a political foe against whom he had lost two elections, as the chairman of the ruling Kenya African National Union (KANU) branch in Githunguri. The move backfired when attacks on Karanja came in the form of a parliamentary motion of no-confidence, after which he was replaced as vice-president by Finance Minister George Saitoti.

Moi celebrated his tenth year in office with extensive festivities and the construction of a new Italian marble monument, both of which were paid for by garnishing up to 70% of the salaries of civil servants. In 1989, Moi was firmly in control of the KANU party apparatus, which is far more powerful than parliament. He also has been able to control the powerful Kikuyu politicians by keeping his alliances with them flexible.

Human Rights and Foreign Relations. Moi came under extensive fire from the international community for rampant corruption and extensive violations of human rights. In London, Moi admitted that Kenya's security police torture detained members of dissident organizations. Kenya's preventive detention laws reportedly were used to prevent children from "talking to strangers." Such violations of human rights brought increasing criticism from Kenya's major allies, particularly Britain and the United States.

KENYA • Information Highlights

Official Name: Republic of Kenya.
Location: East Coast of Africa.
Area: 224,961 sq mi (582 650 km^2).
Population (mid-1989 est.): 24,100,000.
Chief Cities (1985 est.): Nairobi, the capital, 1,162,189; Mombasa, 442,369.
Government: *Head of state and government,* Daniel T. arap Moi, president (took office Oct. 1978). *Legislature* (unicameral)—National Assembly, 188 elected members, 12 appointed by the president.
Monetary Unit: Kenya shilling (20.844 shillings equal U.S.$1, July 1989).
Gross Domestic Product (1987 U.S.$): $8,100,000,000.
Economic Index (1988): *Consumer Prices,* (Nairobi, 1980 = 100), all items, 256.7; food, 234.0.
Foreign Trade (1988 U.S.$): *Imports,* $1,993,000,000; *exports,* $1,071,000,000.

Moi's crackdown had other repercussions as well. Scandinavian governments counseled against any increase in foreign investment and, citing long-term political instability, the Kodak Company elected not to locate its regional headquarters in Kenya.

In March, Kenya accused Uganda of conducting an air raid on Lokichoggio near the Sudanese border. Moi also claimed that Uganda was harboring Kenyan dissidents and was working with Sudan and Libya to plot against him. By so doing, Kenya diverted attention from its support for the Sudanese People's Liberation Army. Relations declined still further when Sudan claimed sovereignty over the Elemi Triangle, which was transferred to Kenya in 1938 and now is thought to be rich in gold and oil. Relations with Somalia were no better, as Kenya blamed much of its poaching problem on former members of the Somali army.

In order to protect its tourist industry, Kenya's largest single source of foreign currency, Moi led a successful international movement to halt the trade in ivory by having African elephants officially declared endangered by the Convention on International Trafficking in Endangered Species.

Economic Affairs. In his 1988–89 budget, then Finance Minister Saitoti, a strong advocate of International Monetary Fund policies of structural adjustment, called for the rationalization of import licensing measures, new incentives for investment, and the development of capital markets. The budget also called for a 21% increase in spending and an increase in the growth rate from 4.8% to 5.1%.

WILLIAM CYRUS REED, *Wabash College*

KOREA

The year 1989 saw conflicting indications on two critical issues: whether the democratic trend in South Korean policies since mid-1987 would continue, and whether a significant easing of the tension between North Korea and South Korea was realistically possible.

Republic of Korea (South Korea)

Politics and Government. In 1989 politics in South Korea continued to operate on two levels: between the ruling Democratic Justice Party and opposition parties, which together held a majority of the seats in the National Assembly and had in effect accepted the legitimacy of the existing government; and between the government and a small but militant minority, spearheaded by radical students, that rejected the government's legitimacy and considered it an obstacle to a much-desired unification of the two Koreas.

In the National Assembly, the opposition parties were able to exert considerable influence on the government of President Roh Tae Woo and Premier Kang Young Hoon through debate, hearings, and the exercise of the oversight function. The opposition's wrath was vented less at the existing government than at its predecessor, the administration of the unpopular former President Chun Doo Hwan. Living in self-imposed exile outside Seoul, Chun seemed to be saying late in the year that he would be willing to testify before the Assembly on his conduct of office. The single aspect of Chun's tenure most denounced by the opposition, both the parties and the militants, was the bloody suppression by special forces of a revolt at the southwestern city of Kwangju, a perennial focus of political dissent, in May 1980. This issue was a highly sensitive one for President Roh, since he had been a close military colleague of former President Chun.

Both sections of the opposition claimed to see signs of a reversal of the trend toward political liberalization and democratization that President Roh had done much to launch in mid-1987 in his campaign for the presidency. Roh had promised, at his election in December 1987 to a five-year term, that he would submit his record to a referendum one year after the February 1988 beginning of his term. On March 20, 1989, well past the one-year mark, he announced an indefinite postponement of the referendum, on the grounds it would disrupt the already unstable political situation. The opposition parties accepted this decision with little protest, evidently because Roh probably would have won the referendum if it had been held.

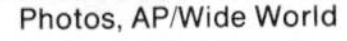

Photos, AP/Wide World

South Korean President Roh Tae Woo (above) of the ruling Democratic Justice Party came under increasing scrutiny from opposition parties fearful that the trend toward democratization begun in 1987 might be reversed. Kim Dae Jung (left), head of the country's largest opposition party, addressed the issue with an announcement that he was launching a campaign to press the government to speed democratic reform.

Even so, Roh had to work hard, not only to cope with the opposition, but to keep his own constituency in line. In March he reshuffled a total of 49 generals. There had been signs that some of the military felt Roh was too indecisive and was letting the political situation get out of hand, and everyone remembered how the army had seized power in 1961 from an ineffective civilian government. In July, Roh reshuffled the cabinet while retaining Premier Kang. The opposition was not happy with this move and was angered further by an indictment brought at the end of August against Kim Dae Jung—the leader of the Party for Peace and Democracy and long a thorn in the side of the establishment—for allegedly having prior knowledge of an illegal visit to North Korea by a member of his party.

The radical opposition, angered by Roh's postponement of the promised referendum, pointed to what it saw as increasingly repressive tendencies of his government. Although the situation was not nearly as bad as it often had been under former President Chun, there was a familiar vicious circle of demonstrations and police heavy-handedness. In March the police were permitted to arm themselves with M-16 rifles and fire at the legs of demonstrators wielding firebombs. Previously, shooting at South Korean demonstrations had been virtually unheard of. In May the perennially volatile city of Kwangju was outraged by the discovery of the body of a radical student who allegedly had been tortured by police. One byproduct of the tension in Kwangju was the closing of the U.S. Cultural Center. Also in May, six policemen were burned to death by radical students in the southeastern city of Pusan.

Two developments later in the year raised hopes for a more rational and productive dialogue, both within South Korea and elsewhere, on the subject of reunification. One was the extraordinary events in Eastern Europe, and especially the opening of the Berlin Wall, with apparent Soviet tolerance. The second was the disenchantment on the part of growing numbers of South Koreans with the violent tactics of the militant students.

Economy. After growing 12.2% in 1988, the South Korean economy's growth slowed in 1989 to 7% to 8%. Among the discernible causes were increased labor costs and unrest, the impact of the appreciating won (up 16% in 1988), and difficulties in some of the export industries, such as shipbuilding, where the government stepped in to bail out two of the largest firms. Independent (noncompany) unions, first allowed in 1987, had tended to grow very confrontational with employers. The police often were quick to crack down, especially where a union was trying to shut down a plant.

To the three largest industries, shipbuilding, steel, and textiles, which had been generating large export earnings, the South Korean business community was working to add a fourth, electronics, again with a heavy emphasis on exports. Rising domestic consumer demand, fueled by rising incomes, tended to impair export performance, however. The large, mostly family-owned companies known as *chaebol* were having difficulty in moving up the technological ladder. They were spending too little on research and development, and other countries, notably Japan, were showing some reluctance to continue transferring technology to South Korea out of concern that they were building up a formidable competitor.

South Korea's trade surplus, which first had appeared only as recently as 1986, fell from $11.5 billion in 1988 to an estimated $8 billion in 1989. The latter figure reflected a deficit with Japan and a surplus (about $5 billion) with the United States. South Korea was trying to hold its surplus with the United States down by, among other things, redirecting exports elsewhere, especially to the countries of the Association of Southeast Asian Nations (ASEAN) and Eastern Europe. On the import side, South Korea had been fairly steadily reducing its tariffs and its nontariff barriers to imports, but not fast enough to satisfy critics, especially in the United States. Although South Korea was the second-largest importer of U.S. agricultural products, the country's farmers objected to the possibility of increased food imports. They were particularly upset about foreign beef, but their cause appeared to be in danger when the South Korean government bowed in November to the General Agreement on Tariffs and Trade (GATT) and agreed to phase out its quotas on beef imports.

Foreign Affairs. As for several years past, South Korea grew increasingly assertive in the international community in 1989. The government had derived more self-confidence from Seoul's successful hosting of the Olympic Games the previous year. One manifestation of this attitude was an increasing interest in membership in the United Nations, which has been

SOUTH KOREA • Information Highlights

Official Name: Republic of Korea.
Location: Northeastern Asia.
Area: 38,023 sq mi (98 480 km²).
Population (mid-1989 est.): 43,100,000.
Chief City (1985 census): Seoul, the capital, 9,639,110.
Government: *Head of state,* Roh Tae Woo, president (formally inaugurated February 1988). *Head of government,* Kang Young Hoon, prime minister (appointed December 1988). *Legislature*—National Assembly.
Monetary Unit: Won (667.4 won equal U.S.$1, July 1989).
Gross National Product (1988 U.S.$): $171,000,-000,000.
Economic Indexes (1988): *Consumer Prices* (1980 = 100), all items, 159.9; food, 162.3. *Industrial Production* (1980 = 100), 268.
Foreign Trade (1988 U.S.$): *Imports,* $51,811,-000,000; *exports,* $60,696,000,000.

blocked by the partition of North and South Korea.

South Korea continued to pursue its so-called Nordpolitik (literally, Northern Policy, or in other words an effort to create links with the Communist countries, including North Korea). There were major successes: the establishment of diplomatic relations with Hungary (February) and Poland (November), and of a Soviet trade office in Seoul (April). The Communist countries were interested not only in trade but in credits and investment from South Korea, and probably also in acquiring U.S. technology via South Korea.

Seoul's official reaction to the June massacre of students demonstrating for democracy in China's Tiananmen Square was a cautious one, presumably out of a desire not to endanger the flourishing "unofficial" trade with China (about $3 billion in 1988) and also an embarrassing memory of the 1980 Kwangju massacre. On the other hand, Seoul refused to return a Chinese major and his wife who defected at Panmunjom in August.

South Korea, which has a large Catholic community, was visited by Pope John Paul II in October. He publicly urged further progress toward democracy and prayed for ultimate unification with the North, both causes popular with most of the South Korean clergy, as well as with the laity.

Relations with the single foreign country most important to South Korea, the United States, presented a mixed picture: generally good at the official level, less so at the unofficial level. On the positive side, U.S. President Bush paid a brief visit to Seoul in February during which he said there were "no plans" to reduce the American military presence; this was confirmed by U.S. Vice-President Quayle during a trip in September. President Roh came to the United States in October and addressed both houses of Congress; he also said that he favored the retention of American forces in his nation, at least as long as they were needed. After protracted negotiations, it was agreed that South Korea would buy 120 F-16 or F-18 fighter aircraft, including 72 to be built in South Korea under license. This acquisition was expected to increase the size of the South Korean air force almost to the level of its North Korean counterpart, and perhaps to facilitate an eventual reduction of the American military presence. An agreement by South Korea to liberalization of imports and foreign investment, reached in May, prevented the country from being named under the "Super 301" section of the 1988 Omnibus Trade Act for unfair trade practices, which could have led to U.S. sanctions. South Korea remained the United States' seventh-largest trading partner. There appeared to be progress on two issues important to Koreans: removal of some conspicuous U.S. military facilities, including a golf course, from an area close to central Seoul; and modification of the structure of the Combined Forces Command in favor of the South Korean component. Seoul agreed to raise its annual financial contribution to the maintenance of U.S. forces in South Korea by 18%, to $340 million, by 1992. Finally, the United States approved the South Korean Nordpolitik in principle and was itself trying to establish a dialogue with Pyongyang.

On the negative side, the main problem was a rapid growth of a chauvinist South Korean nationalism. Among the militant students, who have no memory of the Korean War, nationalism took the form of a strong desire to unify the country at any cost. The militant students also have a strong hostility toward the United States, which they allege had supported oppressive South Korean governments in the past, now was obstructing national unification, and was threatening the South Korean economy by pressing for the reduction of trade barriers (especially with respect to farm products). In October six radical students invaded the residence of U.S. Ambassador Donald Gregg, whose appointment was controversial because he was the second ambassador to Seoul in succession to come from a Central Intelligence Agency background. The increasing anti-American atmosphere, which the Roh government for political reasons was unwilling to condemn publicly, was hard on the morale of U.S. servicemen in South Korea. There was continuing criticism from Americans, especially in Congress, of the South Korean government's occasional heavy-handedness with political dissidents and its seeming lack of enthusiasm about opening its markets to imports from the United States.

Democratic People's Republic of Korea (North Korea)

Although a succession crisis could occur, North Korea continued to be dominated by dictator Kim Il Sung, "the Great Leader," and his son Kim Jong Il, "the Dear Leader."

Domestic Affairs. Apart from the obvious existence of the Kim dictatorship, little is known in the outside world about developments in North Korea. For example, Pyongyang changed premiers in December 1988 (Yon Hyong Muk replaced Li Gun Mo), but the reason is unclear. A careful reassessment by American military intelligence sources puts the total strength of the North Korean armed forces at about 1 million, even higher than had been estimated. It also was believed that Pyongyang might be working on nuclear weapons; the fact that North Korea had joined the International Atomic Energy Agency in 1985 offered no conclusive proof to the contrary, since the government had not allowed the usual inspections of its nuclear facilities.

AP/Wide World

A huge stone statue of Kim Il Sung, considered by North Koreans as their "Great Leader," stands in the capital of Pyongyang. He has been in power since 1948.

NORTH KOREA • Information Highlights

Official Name: Democratic People's Republic of Korea.
Location: Northeastern Asia.
Area: 46,540 sq mi (120 540 km²).
Population (mid-1989 est.): 22,500,000.
Chief Cities (July 1980 est.): Pyongyang, the capital, 1,445,000; Hamhung, 780,000.
Government: *Head of state,* Kim Il Sung, president (nominally since Dec. 1972; actually in power since May 1948). *Head of government,* Yon Hyong Muk, premier (appointed Dec. 1988). *Legislature* (unicameral)—Supreme People's Assembly. The Korea Workers' (Communist) Party: General Secretary, Kim Il Sung.
Gross National Product (1988 U.S.$): $20,000,-000,000.

Foreign Affairs. To a considerable extent, North Korea continued to be isolated from the international community; it was too dictatorial and bellicose for most other countries, even its own allies, the Soviet Union and China. Because of its covert activities abroad, some of which apparently were supervised from an office in Macao, on the South China coast, the United States officially labeled North Korea a terrorist state.

On the other hand, the fact that North Korea was the only important state with which Japan had no official relations made Japanese politicians generally eager to establish contacts (commercial and cultural, in particular) with it. In March 1989, Japanese Premier Noboru Takeshita apologized publicly for the "great suffering" that half a century of harsh Japanese colonial rule had caused the peninsula, including North Korea. Still, the Japanese government refused in December 1988, on humanitarian grounds, to return a North Korean defector.

Although there were no official relations between North Korea and the United States, the latter, with the consent of its South Korean ally, was making contacts that it hoped might help to modify North Korea's bellicose tendencies. There were four meetings between officials of the two sides in Beijing between December 1988 and May 1989. The fact that U.S. Ambassador to China James Lilley previously had served in Seoul appeared likely to facilitate more contacts.

North Korea continued to receive advanced military hardware from its Soviet ally, but the relationship was far from cordial. Relations were somewhat warmer in the case of China. Pyongyang supported the official Chinese crackdown on demonstrators that culminated in the June massacre in Tiananmen Square, and Kim Il Sung visited Beijing briefly and secretly in November, probably to assess the new leadership and the prevailing mood there.

The Two Koreas

As always, the relationship between North Korea and South Korea combined an overall hostility with intermittent attempts at accommodation.

Continuing Confrontation. The cutting edge of the North-South confrontation was the North's armed forces, which were somewhat larger and more powerful and were deployed mostly in tactical, potentially offensive, formations not far north of the misleadingly named Demilitarized Zone.

Another important consideration was that Pyongyang basically refused to recognize the legitimacy of the government in South Korea; it preferred to talk instead with unofficial elements in the South. It seemed possible, however, that this attitude was beginning to change; if so, it was very likely because North Korea's depressed economy was raising the value of enhanced contacts with the relatively prosperous South. Even so, Pyongyang seemed unable to bring itself simply to accept any major proposal by the Roh government, regardless of its content.

Political Contacts. In October 1988, President Roh had proposed a North-South summit and an international conference on the Korean question. Official gestures of this kind undoubtedly were made by Seoul partly because the goal of unification was highly popular with the South Korean public. Pyongyang rejected the October 1988 overture, although Kim Il Sung made the gesture the following April of referring to Roh by his title of president. It appeared that Kim might be trying to give his stamp of approval to a more open policy toward the outside world, including South Korea to some extent, now, rather than leave the initiation to his son, who would have much less influence. In September, Roh once more proposed a summit, plus joint consultative councils in an interim commonwealth embracing the two Koreas. This idea was unacceptable both to Pyongyang and to the South Korean opposition. The North Koreans responded with a call for a summit beginning on Feb. 20, 1990, without preconditions (an unprecedented concession) and with 30 delegates from each side in attendance in addition to the two chiefs of state.

At lower levels, contacts of various kinds were frequent but intermittent. The North suspended contacts twice during 1989, once in response to the annual U.S.-South Korean Team Spirit military exercises, and once in retaliation for the imprisonment in South Korea of Rev. Moon Ik Kwan, who had gone to North Korea in March without official authorization. There were also other arrests of South Koreans, some of them prominent, who had traveled to North Korea without government permission.

Whatever the significance, there were contacts nevertheless. Discussions on resuming talks between the two Korean Red Crosses on humanitarian matters (mainly family visits), which had been in suspense since the end of 1985, were held in the fall. There were tentative suggestions of a meeting between the two premiers. Seoul increasingly was advocating the admission of both Koreas to the United Nations, as a preliminary step toward eventual unification; Pyongyang opposed this idea, on the grounds that it would tend to perpetuate the division of the peninsula.

In October a South Korean court imposed the death penalty on Kim Hyon Hui, who had been convicted of destroying a South Korean airliner with a bomb two years earlier. It appeared likely, however, that she eventually would be pardoned rather than executed, since she apparently had shown sincere remorse.

In November, Pyongyang received its first visit from a U.S. official or former official. He was Gaston Sigur, until recently assistant secretary of state for East Asia and the Pacific. He went to Beijing and Seoul afterward, thus apparently reinforcing the hope that American channels might prove useful in facilitating contacts between the two Koreas.

HAROLD C. HINTON
The George Washington University

LABOR

The labor highlight of the year was the success of Solidarity's nine-year struggle in Poland. The labor movement's leader, Lech Walesa, a shipyard electrician who declined the post of prime minister, won new acclaim worldwide as a force for freedom and free-trade unions.

United States

Contradicting most economic forecasts, unemployment in the United States did not rise during 1989 but edged downward. The civilian unemployment rate was 5.2% in the third quarter, slightly below the 5.5% rate of a year earlier. Once again, the unemployment rate for blacks (11.2%) was more than twice that of whites (4.5%). Most worrisome of all, joblessness among U.S. adult black males actually increased over the year from 9.4% to 9.7%.

The number of employed grew by 2.3 million (*see* table). A record 55% of all adult women held jobs and thereby accounted for almost two thirds of the growth in civilian employment. About four out of five of those women had full-time jobs. Of 51 million married couples, in more than 25 million cases, both husbands and wives worked, and 6.3 million of the working couples had children under 6. In May 7.2 million persons (3.1 million of them women) were working at more than one job. In other words, 6.2% of employed persons were multiple jobholders—the highest rate in over three decades.

Earnings and Costs. Despite a relatively low unemployment rate, big wage increases did not materialize in 1989. In fact, average earnings of production workers decreased in real (inflation-adjusted) terms. Average weekly earnings of nonsupervisory workers in the private sector (excluding agriculture) went up by 3.5% to $339 between September 1988 and 1989 but decreased by 0.8% in real terms. In the case of married couples, weekly income during the second quarter averaged $492 when only the husband had a job; $866 when both husband and wife worked outside the home.

U.S. Employment and Unemployment (Armed Forces excluded)

	1989	1988
Labor Force	124,005,000	121,881,000
Participation rate	66.5%	65.9%
Employed	117,504,000	115,202,000
Unemployed	6,501,000	6,678,000
Unemployment rate	5.2%	5.5%
Adult men	4.5%	4.7%
Adult women	4.7%	4.9%
Teenagers	14.8%	15.3%

N.B.: Figures above, compiled by the Bureau of Labor Statistics, are seasonally adjusted averages for the third quarter of each year. The participation rate is the number of persons in the labor market, whether employed or unemployed, as compared to total population.

Taking into account earnings and all benefits, including vacations, employee compensation costs in the private sector rose by 4.7% in the year that ended in September. Skyrocketing health costs were largely responsible for a 6% increase in the benefit portion of the compensation package.

Health Care. Employer-paid health care, although commonly called a fringe benefit, has become a heavy burden on American business. Costs averaged an estimated $2,700 per employee in 1989—an "albatross around your neck," in the words of Lee A. Iacocca, chairman of Chrysler Corporation. Iacocca is one of a small but growing minority of businessmen who consider the problem serious enough for the United States to take a radical step—adopt some form of national health insurance. Chrysler's health-care outlay averaging $700 per car is twice the average outlay of West German automakers and triple that of Japanese companies; Japanese and German automakers do not feel the pinch because their employees are covered by government insurance. "Other countries put these costs in their taxes," Iacocca said, "but we put them into the price of our products," thereby placing U.S. firms at a competitive disadvantage in the global economy.

One reason for the burden is that persons with health insurance pay part of the health expenses of the 31 million Americans not covered by any health-care plan. Although Congress has considered proposals to extend coverage to the uninsured, it will be especially leery of any such initiative, considering that the outcry against the surtax for catastrophic-health insurance for the elderly prompted the cancelation of that program in November.

Child Care. At the Census Bureau's last count in 1986, there were almost 31 million children under 15 (9.5 million under 5) whose mothers had jobs. Shortly before adjournment, Congress postponed action on a much-debated

The U.S. Minimum Wage

The federal minimum wage was the subject of intense scrutiny and debate during 1989. Although few politicians ruled out the necessity of some sort of increase in the minimum wage, there was wide disagreement on the appropriate level. Many Republican opponents of a substantial increase, including President Bush, felt that raising the wage too much would be inflationary and that it would eliminate entry-level jobs. A central theme of the Bush administration's proposal on the minimum wage was a special six-month training wage for new workers. Proponents of a larger increase felt that the minimum wage had to be a livable wage. Democratic leaders such as U.S. Sen. Edward Kennedy, chairman of the Senate Labor Committee, noted that the minimum wage had lost considerable ground to inflation over the last decade; the wage would be $4.62 per hour if it had kept up with inflation since 1981, the last time the rate was increased.

In June 1989, President Bush vetoed a bill that would have increased the minimum wage base to $4.55 per hour by late 1991, with a two-month training wage. An effort in the House of Representatives to override the veto failed. The issue did not die, however, and in November, Congress worked out a compromise bill to raise the hourly minimum wage from $3.35 to $4.25 by 1991. The legislation, which was signed by the president on November 17, also established a training wage of $3.35 per hour for workers aged 16 through 19 for their first three months in the work force and for an additional three months if they join a sanctioned training program. The new wage would become effective in steps—to $3.80 in April 1990 and to $4.25 in April 1991.

Twelve states already had established their legal minimums at levels higher than the federal standard. In California and Connecticut, for example, it was at $4.25. Areas with tight labor markets also have seen higher pay for jobs that traditionally had low wages. Teenagers employed in fast-food outlets in certain areas, for example, earn as much as $5 or $6 per hour. Still, some 4 million Americans—about two thirds of them women—will benefit from the $3.80 minimum in 1990.

Established in 1938 by the Fair Labor Standards Act at $0.25 per hour to prevent competitive wage cutting during the Depression, the minimum wage has been increased, and its scope expanded, through a half-dozen pieces of legislation. Prior to 1989, the most recent minimum-wage legislation was enacted in the fall of 1977.

Increase Enacted	Effective Date	Rate
1949	Jan. 25, 1950	$0.75
1955	March 1, 1956	$1.00
1961	Sept. 3, 1961	$1.15
	Sept. 3, 1963	$1.25
1966	Feb. 1, 1967	$1.40
	Feb. 1, 1968	$1.60
1974	May 1, 1974	$2.00
	Jan. 1, 1975	$2.10
	Jan. 1, 1976	$2.30
1977	Jan. 1, 1978	$2.65
	Jan. 1, 1979	$2.90
	Jan. 1, 1980	$3.10
	Jan. 1, 1981	$3.35
1989	April 1990	$3.80
	April 1991	$4.25

Photos, AP/Wide World

AFL-CIO President Lane Kirkland (above, l) *congratulates UMW President Richard Trumka after the mineworkers union agreed to rejoin the AFL-CIO. Telephone workers in Pennsylvania,* r, *and elsewhere were picketing in August.*

proposal to improve federal child-care assistance, especially for poor families.

Minimum Wage. Congress and the White House managed to reach agreement in November on another controversial issue: raising the federal minimum wage, which has been frozen at $3.35 per hour since 1981. The minimum would increase to $3.80 in April 1990 and to $4.25 a year later. In a concession to long-standing Republican demands, Congress for the first time established a lower minimum training wage for teenagers at 85% of the adult rate ($3.35 for the first year), but for a period lasting no more than six months. (*See* sidebar.)

Unions. After nearly a half century of self-imposed exile, the United Mineworkers of America in October reaffiliated with the American Federation of Labor and Congress of Industrial Organizations (AFL-CIO), bringing the AFL-CIO's total membership to 14.1 million. Among the few labor groups still outside the AFL-CIO, the most important is the National Education Association, whose membership of nearly 2 million teachers makes it the nation's largest union.

Labor solidarity—at home and abroad—was the dominant theme of the AFL-CIO's 18th constitutional convention, held in Washington in November. On the domestic front, delegates pledged support to strike-weary members, particularly machinists at Eastern Airlines and mine workers at the Pittston Coal Company in Virginia who were engaged in bitter disputes. Marking the first appearance of a U.S. president at an AFL-CIO convention in ten years, George Bush paid tribute to organized labor's long history of support for the worldwide struggle for freedom and democracy. One famous recipient of that support, Lech Walesa, was there to express his warm thanks personally (*see* box) to the delegates. He also returned the favor by videotaping a "support your unions" commercial that the AFL-CIO promptly started using in its nationwide "Say Union Yes" campaign.

Although the size of the AFL-CIO has grown in absolute numbers, union membership continued to dwindle as a proportion of the growing labor force. According to the Census Bureau, only 16.8% of all employed wage and salary workers belonged to unions; 19% when only full-time employees were counted. The media spotlighted a union representation election in July in which assembly-line workers at the Nissan auto plant in Smyrna, TN, rejected the United Auto Workers by a vote of 1,622 to 711, as a major sign of labor's bad times and an omen for the future. The union called the election a "stinging defeat" in its campaign to organize Japanese auto plants in the United States. On the other hand, as some reporters pointed out, it was significant that even 711 had voted for the union, since Nissan carefully had selected 2,400 production workers out of more than 100,000 applicants in an area not noted for union sympathies.

International

As in the United States, unemployment in major foreign industrial countries generally declined slightly in 1989. The U.S. Department of Labor tracks the unemployment trends of seven of those countries and adapts their jobless rates to approximate U.S. concepts. In those comparisons, the rates of all seven countries—Canada, Japan, France, West Germany, Italy, Sweden, and the United Kingdom—edged downward over the year ending in the third quarter. Sweden's rate remained the lowest among the seven at 1.3%, and France's the highest at 10.2%. The United Kingdom enjoyed by far the biggest decrease, 1.8 percentage points, down to 6.2%, its lowest level in nearly ten years.

Canada. Joblessness in Canada continued its gradual slide of recent years, down to a rate of 7.4% in the third quarter (7.8% for women, 7% for men). With about 1 million persons unemployed, and 13.5 million employed, the labor force participation rate reached a record 67.2% in August.

The number of union members—3.9 million—swelled by 2.7% in a year, but continued to shrink as a percentage of the nonagricultural work force—from a record high of 40% in 1983 to 36.6% in 1988 to 36.2% in 1989. The Canadian Labour Congress, with 2.2 million members, accounts for nearly 58% of all Canadian union members. Major collective bargaining settlements in the second quarter of 1989 provided annual wage increases averaging 5%, compared with 4.5% a year earlier.

Japan. A powerful new national labor center, the Japanese Trade Union Confederation, emerged from a unification convention held in Tokyo on November 21. In the last of a recent series of mergers, two large labor centers, Sohyo (the General Council of Trade Unions of Japan) and Rengo (the Japan Private Sector Trade Union Confederation) joined together to form a new organization, known as JTUC-Rengo. With 8 million members from the public and private sectors, it is the third-largest national labor center in the world, after the AFL-CIO in the United States and the British Trades Union Congress. Although union membership has diminished gradually to 26.8% of the labor force, the new unity was expected to expand Japanese labor's influence on both the domestic and international scenes. On July 23, Rengo, then largely limited to the private sector, scored a major victory when 11 out of 12 Rengo-supported candidates won seats in the Upper House elections.

Workaholism has become an issue of increasing concern in Japan. Labor and the government have set a goal of reducing time spent at work, but the program has met with little success so far. Although Japanese workers are entitled to about 15 paid holidays a year, they take only half of them.

Poland. More than seven years after the government suppressed it, Solidarity regained its legal status in April, along with a government agreement to hold quasi-free parliamentary elections. The actions set in motion sweeping reforms in Poland itself and served as a stimulus for fast-paced changes in neighboring countries of Eastern Europe (*see* feature article, page 24). Although Solidarity President Lech Walesa played the prime role in campaigns prior to the June elections, he was careful to maintain Solidarity's separate identity as a trade union. In early 1990, Solidarity would hold its first national congress since relegalization.

Soviet Union. Under traditional Communist doctrine, it is pointless for workers to strike in a "workers' state" such as the Soviet Union. As the party newspaper *Pravda* has phrased the issue, "Who would ever dream of striking against himself?" During the first nine months of the year, however, official Soviet statistics recorded 7 million working days lost through strikes. In July some 500,000 coal miners staged the largest walkout the Soviet Union has seen since the 1920s. Contrary to past practice, the authorities did not react by resorting to force or by sending strike leaders to psychiatric hospitals. Instead they gave de facto recognition to regional strike committees. Negotiations usually bypassed the party-dominated unions. During talks with one important regional strike committee, the chairman of the All-Union Central Council of Trade Unions sat on the government party's side of the table. Although the miners' demand to form their own union was rejected, many of their strike committees have continued functioning. Further, numerous informal worker organizations under various names—workers clubs, independent trade unions, and strike committees—

During a U.S. visit in November, Lech Walesa, president of Poland's Solidarity trade union, received the George Meany Human Rights Award at the AFL-CIO convention.

AP/Wide World

AP/Wide World

After the USSR was hit by a massive strike by some 500,000 coal miners in July, the Supreme Soviet voted to legalize certain, restricted walkouts.

sprang up even outside the mining areas, including the Baltic republics.

In reaction to the labor unrest, the government in October proposed that the Supreme Soviet outlaw strikes completely for 15 months. Instead, the Supreme Soviet adopted a compromise: It banned strikes in key sectors of the economy, such as the defense industry and transport, but for the first time permitted strikes elsewhere under certain restrictions. Significantly, the law also gave strikers the right to choose the body representing them during labor disputes. However, the Soviet Union had no workers' organization remotely approaching Solidarity in 1989. That was also true of Hungary, Czechoslovakia, and East Germany, though there exist in each of these countries the beginnings of free trade-union movements.

Global Cooperation. Many unions in non-Communist nations provided moral and financial support to Solidarity and other struggling trade unions in East European countries. At the same time, spurred by the growth of the global economy, they also intensified their cooperation with each other to deal with multinational corporations. For example, the International Metalworkers Federation, headquartered in Geneva, in April launched a new world trade union council for Electrolux, the Swedish multinational. The council provides a forum for union representatives of Electrolux workers in 19 countries, including nations in Asia and Latin America.

European Community. Employers and unions in the European Community (EC) continued to grapple with the question of how they will be affected by the integrated European market that the EC expects to establish by 1992. While businessmen generally are optimistic about the changes, unions are concerned about the impact on workers. The greater mobility of capital and merchandise within the community could, they fear, cause not only a massive transfer of jobs to countries with low labor costs, such as Portugal and Greece, but also an erosion of living standards in prosperous countries such as West Germany and Denmark.

To reassure workers, EC agencies drafted a "social charter" covering fundamental worker rights that would be respected in all 12 EC countries. Under the leadership of France, the EC Council of Ministers approved the charter in December, over the objection of British Prime Minister Margaret Thatcher. In the process of reaching a consensus, the document was shorn of most specifics, such as setting guidelines for a minimum wage, a ceiling on weekly working hours, and a minimum level of social-security benefits in all 12 countries. One significant specific item that remained concerned child labor: The statutory minimum age proposed for the employment of children was 15. It is 14 under Portuguese law.

Meanwhile, to make the charter more specific, the EC Commission prepared an "action program" of 43 proposals, with 17 of the proposals such as pregnancy leave recommended for adoption in 1990 as community legislation binding on all member states.

International Labor Organization (ILO). In February the ILO governing body elected Michel Hansenne, 49, Belgium's minister for public services and its former minister of labor, as director general of the International Labor Office. He replaced Francis Blanchard, 72, who headed the ILO for 15 years. The ILO is the UN's only agency with labor and management as well as government representation.

ROBERT A. SENSER
Free-Lance Labor Writer

On March 26, Laotians voted in the first national balloting at the central level since the formation of the Lao People's Democratic Republic in 1975. Turnout in the capital, Vientiane, right, *was said to be heavy.*

AP/Wide World

LAOS

In Laos as in many other Communist states, 1989 was a year in which the ruling party loosened its tight political and economic controls in an effort to revive a stagnant economy.

Politics. Elections for the National Congress were held in March, and non-Communist parties were allowed to take part. The media also was given more freedom to report on the election. Nevertheless, the Lao People's Revolutionary Party retained control of the Congress, and Kaysone Phomvihan remained head of the government. The presentation of a revised constitution to the National Congress in 1990 was expected to be the next major step in the gradual opening of the political system.

Economics. The Laotian government has made known its desire to attract foreign investment in order to speed the country's development. Japanese, Swedish, Australian, and other businessmen have expressed interest, and the Australians are building the first bridge that will connect Laos and Thailand across the Mekong River. This should encourage trade with Thailand. But few investment deals actually have been struck, because the government has been slow to put in place a revised constitution and investment laws that would protect the earnings and assets of foreign firms.

Foreign Relations. The year was marked by the resolution of a long-standing border conflict between Laos and Thailand and also by steady improvement in Sino-Lao relations.

According to press reports, Laotian officials have said that they can no longer count on the same level of Soviet aid and that they would be looking to the West for assistance.

Because of the substantial amount of opium poppies grown in Laos, the United States announced in 1989 that Laos would not receive any more U.S. aid until it accepted a UN program to promote crops to replace opium. After an initial angry response to this move, the Laotian government resumed cooperating with the United States in an effort to locate the remains of Americans who are believed to have died in Laos during the Indochina war.

PETER A. POOLE
Author, "Eight Presidents and Indochina"

LAOS • Information Highlights

Official Name: Lao People's Democratic Republic.
Location: Southeast Asia.
Area: 91,430 sq mi (236 800 km²).
Population (mid-1989 est.): 3,900,000.
Chief City: Vientiane, the capital.
Government: *Head of state:* Phoumi Vongvichit, acting president; *Head of government,* Kaysone Phomvihan, chairman. *Legislature* (unicameral)—national Congress of People's Representatives.

LATIN AMERICA

For Latin America, the 1980s were a "lost decade," said Enrique Iglesias, the president of the Inter-American Development Bank. It was a time for declining economic growth, spiraling inflation, mounting foreign-debt problems, and a host of other ills. The region as a whole turned in a stagnant economic performance. A report from the United Nations Economic Commission for Latin America and the Caribbean found that the region's per capita product likely would go down for the second year running.

But more than the state of the economy troubled the hemisphere. The multiple woes of the region were summed up by the agenda of an October summit meeting of 25 heads of state from Latin America, the United States, Canada, Spain, and Portugal. The agenda, drafted by President Oscar Arias of Costa Rica, a Nobel Peace Prize recipient, defined the concerns of Latin America and the Caribbean as the "six Ds:" debt, democracy, drugs, development, deforestation, and disarmament.

Economy. By general consensus, 1989 was a gloomy year for the economies of Latin America. The World Bank, in its *Annual Report* for

1989, declared that "Over the past 18 months, economic growth in Latin America and the Caribbean region has slowed, further delaying the process of restoring per capita output, income, and consumption to average levels that had prevailed during the three-year period 1979–81. Gross domestic product (GDP) per capita declined at an annual rate of 0.6% in 1988 and early 1989. Further, in the first half of 1989, the decline in per capita GDP was accelerating."

The Inter-American Development Bank, in its *Economic and Social Progress in Latin America: 1989 Report,* noted that "the most important development in foreign trade in 1988" was that export earnings reached $102.6 billion (in current dollars), exceeding the previous peak of $100.7 billion reached in 1981. At the same time, the Bank reported that Latin America and the Caribbean attained only a meager 0.6% increase in overall (not per capita) economic output in 1988, that net capital flows and investment declined dramatically, and that high international interest rates and debt problems continued to plague the region.

Privatization. Another consensus that seemed to be developing in Latin America in 1989 was that part of the region's economic problems stemmed from inefficient, government-owned enterprises and that the economies should be opened to greater private-sector participation. Shortly after his inauguration as president of El Salvador in June, for example, Alfredo Cristiani said, "We have to do a lot of privatizing in El Salvador because 60% of the economy is controlled by the government." Mexico was a leader in the privatization movement in 1989 with President Carlos Salinas de Gortari announcing the proposed sale of a majority interest in Telemex, the national telecommunications monopoly, and part of the government's largest airline, Compañía Mexicana de Aviación.

Under a new president, Carlos Saúl Menem, Argentina sharply revised its economic course. A member of the Justicialist Party that vastly increased the state's role in the Argentine economy under the presidency of Juan Perón in the 1940s and 1950s, Menem, nonetheless, said his goal would be "a popular free-market economy." That meant, he said, "private enterprise and free trade, with social justice incorporated." At Menem's urging, the Argentine Congress passed legislation authorizing complete or partial privatization of 30 large state-owned companies, including the national telephone company, the oil company, and the railroads.

Jamaica also was changing direction under a new leader, Michael Manley, formerly a strong statist. During the year, Manley said his goal now was to attract private foreign investment, and he offered to sell Air Jamaica, the state-owned national flag carrier. In Venezuela, the new president, Carlos Andres Pérez, also a former advocate of state involvement in the economy, released a list of government companies slated for sale. Similar privatization programs were under way in Chile, Bolivia, Brazil, Honduras, Costa Rica, and Guyana.

Politics. Underlying the economic reforms in many Latin countries was a realization that democratic institutions were threatened by falling incomes and declining standards of living. On the positive side, Chile elected a new democratic government in December, Bolivia and El Salvador underwent peaceful transfers of power after free and open elections, and in November, Brazil held its first direct presidential election in 29 years.

But Venezuela, seemingly one of the hemisphere's stronger democracies, erupted in bloody rioting in late February as the result of harsh economic austerity measures. Food riots hit Argentina in May and June.

Peru and Colombia also were beset by civil violence. In Colombia, the cause was the government's confrontation with illicit drug cartels. In Peru a murky leftist guerrilla movement, the Sendero Luminoso, waged an increasingly ruthless battle against civilians as well as government troops.

Panama. Although the Organization of American States (OAS) had declared the regime of Panamanian Gen. Manuel Antonio Noriega "devoid of constitutional legitimacy" for ignoring free elections, Latin leaders, nonetheless, condemned the U.S. invasion that ousted the general in December. And the OAS subsequently passed a resolution affirming Panama's right to "self-determination."

Drugs. Growing attention was focused on the problem of illicit drugs, especially cocaine, produced in Latin America. Colombia was the center of action in the war against drugs. Virtual civil war erupted there when drug traffickers assassinated a leading presidential candidate and other public officials. But the drug menace appeared to be spreading throughout the hemisphere and production and internal consumption of drugs became serious problems for countries such as Brazil, Ecuador, Venezuela, Mexico, Guatemala, Peru, and Bolivia.

International control of drug trafficking was discussed at a summit meeting of Latin American presidents in Lima, Peru, in October, and the subject was added to the agenda of the annual General Assembly of the OAS.

International. After protracted negotiations, the Inter-American Development Bank approved a capital increase that would permit additional lending to Latin America of $22.5 billion during the next four years. Reeling under a budget crisis caused by large back-payments owed by member countries, the OAS received a boost in October when Canada announced it would seek membership.

RICHARD C. SCHROEDER, *Consultant to the Organization of American States*

LAW

Although Ronald Reagan left office in 1989, the former president left a legacy at the U.S. Supreme Court that may have a profound impact on the nation for a generation or more. The 1988–89 term marked what legal scholars called the coming of age of the Rehnquist court, and a watershed in the Supreme Court's history. Chief Justice William H. Rehnquist led a narrow majority that delivered a conservative outcome in many of the most important cases.

Conservative themes were sounded in abortion rights, affirmative action, civil rights, and the death penalty. The vote that tipped the balance in many decisions was cast by Justice Anthony W. Kennedy, the last of three Reagan appointees to the high court. In his first full term on the court, Kennedy was part of a reliably conservative 5–4 majority with Chief Justice Rehnquist and Justices Byron R. White, Sandra Day O'Connor, and Antonin Scalia. Justices O'Connor and Scalia are Reagan appointees; Justice White was named to the court by former President John F. Kennedy in 1962.

The four more-liberal members—who often joined in dissent, lamenting what they said was a trend toward less individual rights and reduced concern for race and sex discrimination—were Justices William J. Brennan, Thurgood Marshall, Harry A. Blackmun, and John Paul Stevens.

In the lower courts, national attention focused on the trial of Oliver North, the former White House aide accused of illegal participation in the Iran-contra scandal. There also was a major child-abuse trial in New York City and an AIDS case in Los Angeles that produced an enormous civil damage award for the homosexual lover of the late Rock Hudson. And in Texas, the 12-year-old murder conviction of a man was overturned after a popular documentary movie helped establish his innocence.

In international law, Union Carbide reached a settlement with victims of the 1984 toxic gas spill in Bhopal, India. Iran continued to pursue the United States in international courts for the U.S.S. *Vincennes'* mistaken downing of an Iran Air passenger plane in the Persian Gulf on July 3, 1988.

United States

Supreme Court. In deciding 132 cases in its 1988–89 term, the court split 5–4 in 32 of the cases. Chief Justice Rehnquist, often a lone dissenter in his early days on the court, was in the majority more than 80% of the time. Of more significance than the numbers was the nature of the cases of which the conservatives were in command. They led the way in deciding the outcome of most of the key disputes confronting the justices.

In the most closely watched case of the term—and for that matter the decade—the court voted, 5–4, to give states more power to regulate abortions. The justices stopped short of overturning the 1973 *Roe v. Wade* ruling that established a woman's constitutional right to have an abortion. But the deeply divided court signaled it might be willing to discard, or further weaken, that ruling in the future. The justices agreed to decide three new abortion disputes in its next term. In the 1989 case, the court upheld a Missouri ban on public employees performing, or assisting in, abortions and on abortions taking place in public hospitals. Also upheld was a requirement that doctors test for fetal viability in abortions after the 19th week of pregnancy *(Webster v. Reproductive Health Services). See also* feature article, page 44.

The justices aroused the anger and concern of civil-rights activists in a handful of key cases. The court made it more difficult for minorities and women to prove on-the-job bias with statistics showing that they are underrepresented in an employer's higher-paying jobs *(Wards Cove v. Atonio).* In a rare victory for the civil-rights community, the court made it more difficult for employers to defend themselves against bias when an individual plaintiff alleges intentional discrimination *(Price Waterhouse v. Hopkins).*

The justices allowed white males to challenge, on grounds of "reverse discrimination," affirmative action programs approved years earlier by a judge *(Martin v. Wilks).* The court also threw out a Richmond, VA, ordinance that set aside 30% of public works money for minority-owned businesses. The decision, casting doubt on other affirmative action programs, said the Richmond plan violated the rights of white-owned businesses *(Croson v. City of Richmond).*

The court found that states are shielded from an 1871 law that authorizes monetary damages for violations of civil rights *(Will v. Michigan).* In an interpretation of a related 1866 law, the court protected local governments from being sued when a municipal employee violates someone's rights, unless that violation is part of an official government policy *(Jett v. Dallas Independent School District).* That same 1866 law was also the focus of one of the most closely watched civil-rights cases of the term. The court declined to reverse an earlier precedent, and found that the law's antibias features apply to private contracts, but that the law cannot be used for suing bosses for racial harassment *(Patterson vs. McLean Credit Union).*

In an exception to the conservative trend, the justices touched off a political storm by ruling that burning the U.S. flag in protest is protected by the Constitution's free-speech guarantees *(Texas v. Johnson).* (*See* sidebar.)

Free-speech advocates welcomed a ruling that said obscene telephone dial-up messages may be banned, but not those that are merely indecent *(Sable Communications v. FCC)*. In another case, the court said states may use antiracketeering laws to prosecute adult bookstores charged with selling obscene materials, but may not close down the bookstores before trials are conducted *(Fort Wayne Books v. Indiana)*. The court also limited state power to punish the reporting of lawfully obtained, truthful information that interferes with individual privacy. The justices shielded a Florida newspaper from paying damages to a rape victim whose name it published *(Florida Star v. BJF)*.

Those favoring strict separation of church and state won at least a partial victory when the court barred government-sponsored Christmas nativity scenes and other religious symbols unless the displays are placed in a nonreligious context *(Allegheny County v. Greater Pittsburgh ACLU)*. The court also said states may not tax nonreligious publications while exempting religious ones *(Texas Monthly v. Bullock)*. And the justices barred states from withholding unemployment benefits from those who refuse to work on their Sabbath, even if that day is not based on the doctrine of a religious group *(Frazee v. Illinois)*.

The court rejected several attempts to limit the death penalty or help those on death row. Justices found capital punishment may be meted out to convicted murderers who were as young as 16 when they committed the crime *(Stanford v. Kentucky)*. And the justices permitted the death penalty for mentally retarded killers *(Penry v. Lynaugh)*. The court also held that death row inmates have no constitutional right to a lawyer to assist them in a second round of state court appeals *(Murray v. Giarrantano)*. But the court said personal characteristics of a murder victim, when unrelated to the crime itself, may not be weighed by the jury in choosing the death sentence or life in prison *(South Carolina v. Gathers)*.

In its first rulings on drug testing in the workplace, the court permitted mandatory tests for railroad employees involved in accidents and for U.S. Customs workers seeking drug-enforcement jobs *(Skinner v. Railway Labor Executives* and *National Treasury Employees v. Von Raab)*.

The court refused to expand due-process protections for individuals in a child-abuse case. It said public officials may not be sued in federal court when their alleged gross negligence permits a child to be abused by a parent. The court found that states do not have a constitutional duty to protect people who are not in their custody *(DeShaney v. Winnebago County)*.

The court boosted law-enforcement powers in a pair of cases. It said police may stop and

© Raphael Macia/Photo Researchers

Protecting Old Glory

Affirming the right to burn the U.S. flag in protest was one of the U.S. Supreme Court's most incendiary rulings of 1989.

On June 21 an unusual grouping of liberal and conservative justices formed the 5-4 majority that found a Texas man had not committed a crime by burning the flag, in light of the freedom of expression rights guaranteed under the 1st Amendment of the U.S. Constitution. The decision struck down federal and state laws against the desecration of Old Glory.

The ruling ignited a firestorm of protests. Many Americans, who had pledged allegiance to the flag since childhood, had a strong visceral reaction to anyone mutilating the symbol of the nation. Veterans equated desecrating the flag with desecrating the memory of those who died to protect it. Others contended, however, that the flag was the banner of freedom and such freedom even extended to its desecration. The Supreme Court majority and others who supported the right to burn the flag in protest emphasized that they abhorred the act.

Reaction to the Supreme Court's action was swift, with the U.S. Senate and House overwhelmingly passing resolutions expressing "profound disappointment" and "profound concern," respectively, with the ruling. Meanwhile, President Bush called for a constitutional amendment to prohibit desecration of the flag. Congress instead passed a carefully worded law against the "physical" desecration of the flag, hoping that separating the action from a protester's intention would enable the law to stand in court.

President Bush, fearing the law would be struck down as unconstitutional, allowed it to go into effect in late October without his signature. He continued to push for a constitutional amendment, but the drive was stalled when the proposal received only 51 of a required 67 Senate votes for a two-thirds majority. Almost immediately protesters sought to challenge the constitutionality of the new law by burning the flag at the Capitol.

Mary Sue Davis (extreme right), accompanied by her attorneys, faces the press after a Tennessee Circuit Court judge awarded her custody of seven embryos frozen for in vitro fertilization. The court rejected the efforts of her estranged husband, whose sperm fertilized the eggs, to stop them from being implanted in Ms. Davis' womb. The decision had possible implications for forthcoming abortion cases.

AP/Wide World

question airline passengers whose behavior and appearance suggest they are drug couriers *(U.S. v. Sokolow)*. And the justices allowed the government to freeze the assets of people charged with racketeering even if a defendant is left without enough money to pay a lawyer *(U.S. v. Monsanto)*.

In a case affecting civil action, the court said the Constitution's ban on excessive fines does not limit the size of punitive damage awards in lawsuits *(Browning-Ferris v. Kelco)*. The court also upheld use of a federal racketeering law to sue businesses accused of fraud and said the statute may be invoked based on a single illegal scheme involving more than one criminal act *(H. J. Inc. v. Northwestern Bell)*.

The court also upheld a new system for sentencing convicted criminals, ruling Congress did not infringe on executive or judicial powers in setting up a commission to establish guidelines for the system *(Mistretta v. U.S.)*.

Local Law. The Iran-contra affair that tarnished President Reagan's later years in office reached a courtroom climax with the conviction of Oliver North. The former Marine and White House aide was found guilty of aiding and abetting in obstruction of Congress, destroying or altering government documents, and accepting a gratuity—a security fence around his home. U.S. District Judge Gerhard Gesell of Washington, DC, sentenced North to two years probation and fined him $150,000. North also was ordered to perform 1,200 hours of community service in a local drug program. North contended during his three-month trial that he only acted on behalf of Reagan administration superiors when U.S. arms were sold secretly to Iran and profits were diverted to the Nicaraguan contra rebels.

In a lawsuit in Los Angeles that attracted national attention, the homosexual lover of actor Rock Hudson was awarded $21.75 million by a jury. But the judge in the case reduced the award to Marc Christian to $5.5 million in compensatory and punitive damages. Christian said he suffered extreme emotional distress after discovering that Hudson had concealed from him that the actor was suffering from AIDS (Acquired Immune Deficiency Syndrome). Christian said even the reduced damage award sent a clear message to those with AIDS: They must warn their sex partners they have the disease. Hudson died at age 58 in 1985. The case was considered particularly significant because it was believed to be the first personal injury lawsuit involving sexually transmitted diseases in which a plaintiff was awarded damages without actually contracting a disease.

Domestic violence and child abuse were the focus of a New York City prosecution in which Joel Steinberg was sentenced to 8⅓ to 25 years in prison for killing his illegally adopted daughter, Lisa. A disbarred lawyer, Steinberg was convicted of first-degree manslaughter in the death of the 6-year-old girl in 1987. Hedda Nussbaum, who lived with Steinberg, testified that in their 11 years together she was beaten, brainwashed, deprived of food, and subjected to bizarre punishment and drug use. Lisa was taken unconscious from the apartment where the couple lived, and she died three days later. Prosecutors said they hoped the case would help stem child and drug abuse.

A documentary movie, *The Thin Blue Line*, played a key role in overturning the murder conviction in Texas of Randall Dale Adams. Adams spent more than 12 years in prison and faced execution for the 1976 slaying of police officer Robert Wood. In the film, David Harris, an inmate on death row in Texas for another murder, recanted his testimony against Adams and all but confessed to killing Wood. Adams had been convicted of the crime in 1977 at age 28 and came within three days of execution in 1980 before his sentence was commuted to life in prison. A Texas appeals court threw out his conviction, ruling prosecutors suppressed evidence and used perjured testimony. The Dallas County district attorney's office then dropped the charge against Adams, saying there was insufficient evidence to conduct a new trial. One prosecutor in the office was fired and two others resigned after Adams' conviction was thrown out.

JIM RUBIN, *The Associated Press*

International Law

The Soviet Union and the United States both accepted jurisdiction of the World Court in The Hague in separate cases in 1989. The year also was marked by the death of José Luís Bustamante, the former president of Peru who also had served as a judge and president of the World Court. Bustamante died on January 11 in Lima at the age of 94 after a long illness related to heart problems. He had served on the court from 1967 until 1970.

On March 8, Soviet Deputy Foreign Minister Anatoly L. Admishin announced that the Soviet Union would accept World Court jurisdiction in cases involving the violation of human rights. Admishin said that five major UN conventions would be recognized by the Soviet Union: a 1948 convention condemning genocide, a 1949 convention banning the trafficking of prostitutes and other forms of slavery, a 1952 convention guaranteeing political rights for women, a 1965 convention banning racism, and a 1984 convention outlawing torture. Admishin made his announcement at a meeting of the UN Human Rights Commission in Geneva.

In contrast, the United States has ratified only the 1948 convention. In 1984 the United States withdrew its general recognition of the court's jurisdiction after Nicaragua successfully sued the U.S. government for helping the contras in their failed rebellion against the Sandinista-run Nicaraguan government.

"The Vincennes." In August the United States said World Court jurisdiction would prevail in a case involving the downing of an Iranian passenger airliner by the U.S. Navy warship *Vincennes* in July 1988. Iran had appealed to the World Court in a dispute over the incident. Iran's suit charged that the *Vincennes* had violated an international agreement when the unarmed passenger plane was shot down. Iran demanded compensation for the victims' families. The *Vincennes* shot down the Iran jet after it was picked up by radar over the Persian Gulf. The crew of the ship believed the plane was an attacking Iranian F-14. The incident left 290 people dead, including 250 Iranians. Navy officials later attributed the accident to "combat stress."

After the suit was filed, the U.S. State Department said it was considering whether it would accept the jurisdiction of the World Court, the UN's judicial body, known formally as the International Court of Justice. In July 1989 the State Department said it would pay between $100,000 and $250,000 each to families of the victims. At the same time, the U.S. officials steadfastly maintained that the U.S. government was not obligated to pay any compensation under international law, because the attack had been a "lawful act of self-defense." (Previously, former President Reagan had said that the government would pay families of the victims as a "voluntary humanitarian gesture.") On August 15 the U.S. government agreed to abide by any World Court decisions.

Central America. On August 7, five Central American presidents met in Tela, Honduras, and reached an agreement concerning the dismantling of the Nicaraguan contra rebel camps in Honduras. The five presidents were: José Azcona Hoyo of Honduras, Daniel Ortega of Nicaragua, Oscar Arias of Costa Rica, Vinicio Cerezo of Guatemala, and Alfredo Cristiani of El Salvador. The agreement set a timetable for breaking up the camps and repatriating between 10,000 and 12,000 contras and their families by December 5, but by year's end the goal still had not been achieved.

Presidents Azcona and Ortega said they would seek an out-of-court settlement in a case filed by Nicaragua with the World Court against Honduras. The suit protested Honduras' backing of the contras. Nicaragua said it would withdraw the suit after an international peacekeeping force was in place and the contras had been disbanded.

As the year ended, international-law experts began debating the legal justification for the U.S. invasion of Panama and the arrest of Gen. Manuel Antonio Noriega.

Chad. On August 31, Chad's Foreign Minister Achiek ibn Oumer and Libya's Foreign Minister Jadallah Azzuz al-Talhi signed an accord that may lead to an end of hostilities between their two nations. In 1975, Libya invaded and annexed a 100-mi- (161-km-) wide section of Chad, known as the Aouzou Strip, which was reputed to have rich uranium deposits. Off and on, Chad has fought to reclaim the land, most successfully in 1987 when Libyan troops were routed severely in several skirmishes. The new accord stipulated that if a political solution were not found in a year's time, the Aouzou Strip dispute would be brought before the World Court for judgment.

LIONEL BASCOM
Western Connecticut State University

LEBANON

Lebanon's existence as an independent state, which seemed slightly less precarious than it had been in 1988, was newly threatened in late 1989. The Lebanese parliament's ratification of the "national reconciliation pact," concluded in Taif, Saudi Arabia, in October led to the election of René Moawad as president on November 5 and the formation of a new national government. The assassination of Moawad 17 days later was a blow to peace.

The Taif agreement was the most serious effort to settle the Lebanese conflict to date, as was indicated by the fact that the accord had support from the Arab League, Syria, Iraq, the

United States, the Soviet Union, Britain, France, and the Vatican. This progress was offset by one serious obstacle that threatened to perpetuate the country's fragmentation. Acting Prime Minister Maj. Gen. Michel Aoun refused to recognize both the legitimacy of the national reconciliation pact and parliament's election of René Moawad as the new head of state. He also would not recognize President Elias Hrawi, who was elected November 24—two days after Moawad's death. Some observers believed Aoun was behind the assassination. Whether or not the accusation is true (some blame groups from outside Lebanon), Aoun's actions were divisive and contributed to the breakdown of a ten-week-old cease-fire.

No Central Government. Two rival government claimants had emerged after September 1988 when the Lebanese parliament failed to elect a new president to succeed outgoing President Amin Gemayel. Gemayel appointed Michel Aoun, the army commander, as interim prime minister pending the election of a new president. However, no functioning central government existed for two reasons. First, the Lebanese Forces (LF), the militia controlling much of the Christian enclave, continued to arrogate for itself the functions of the central government, including the levying of taxes. Second, the Muslim and Druze political factions, as well as Syria, refused to recognize Aoun's government. Instead they established a rival government in Syrian-controlled West Beirut. It was headed by Salim al-Hoss, the acting prime minister until Gemayel appointed Aoun. The parliament ceased to meet at all.

Aoun, who hoped to be elected Lebanon's next president, sought to demonstrate that his government was the only legitimate political authority in the country. In order to gain international recognition of his government, Aoun had to demonstrate that he was in control of East Beirut and could bring the militias to heel. In February he launched a military attack on the Lebanese Forces, accusing the militia of usurping the functions of the state and imposing illegal taxes on the people.

The fighting was halted by a cease-fire called by the Maronite Patriarch, Archbishop Nasrullah Sfeir. A broad-based conference of Christian religious and political leaders sided with Aoun and the army. This group called for the restoration of state authority and demanded that the LF withdraw to its barracks, but not be disbanded. Bowing to the Christian leadership's wishes, LF leader Samir Geagea ordered his fighters to give up the remaining checkpoints they controlled. On February 24, Geagea surrendered Beirut Port's fifth wharf to the army and the Lebanese customs authority.

Aoun's "War of Liberation" Against Syria. The subjugation of the Lebanese forces was the first step in Aoun's broader aim of securing the withdrawal of Syrian and Israeli forces from Lebanon. Lacking the power to do that on his own, Aoun's strategy was to produce a regional crisis in order to provoke international attention and pressure that would lead to an eventual evacuation of Syrian troops. Therefore Aoun continued to assert the Lebanese government's authority over all the militias by attempting to close down or take over all ports they controlled. The port within easiest reach of Aoun's forces was one at Jiyeh, controlled by the Druze.

AP/Wide World

Lebanon's refugee problem continues: A stream of refugees fleeing the fierce artillery duels in Beirut arrives at the Israeli-proclaimed security zone in southern Lebanon.

After the Lebanese navy blockaded Jiyeh in March, the Druze militia, commanded by Walid Jumblatt, responded by shelling the Christian enclave. Aoun's forces retaliated by shelling Syrian artillery positions in West Beirut. Syrian guns there and in the mountains responded. On March 14, Aoun, backed by arms and diplomatic support from Syria's archenemy, Iraq, declared a "war of liberation" against Syrian forces occupying Lebanon.

The fighting that erupted in March between Aoun's regular army troops and Muslim militias supported by Syrian troops was among the most intense since Lebanon's civil war began in 1975. The United States and France tried to work out a cease-fire, but Aoun refused to accept this mediation unless Syria began to withdraw. An Arab League mediation team attempted to mediate between Aoun and the Syrians. That effort failed in August after Syria refused to agree to a timetable for withdrawing its troops. Some 930 persons were killed and between 36,000 and 48,000 were injured in the six-month "war of liberation" that ended with a cease-fire on September 23.

If Aoun could show that resisting the Syrians could pay off, Syrian officials feared that the Sunni Muslims in West Beirut would begin to resist the Syrian presence there. An overriding Syrian objective is to prevent the partition of Lebanon, because then Syria's regional enemies—especially Iraq or Israel—could use Lebanon and its defiant Christian enclave as a springboard for activities hostile to Syrian security.

Renewed Concern for Western Hostages. Outside attention to Aoun's anti-Syrian campaign was distracted when Israeli forces abducted Sheikh Abdul Karim Obeid, a pivotal figure in the Iranian-backed Hezbollah, on July 28, in an effort to exchange him for two Israeli soldiers and an airman captured in 1986. In retaliation a Hezbollah affiliate, the Organization for the Oppressed on Earth, announced that it had "executed" U.S. Lt. Col. William Higgins, who had been kidnapped Feb. 17, 1988. Sheikh Obeid had been instrumental in Colonel Higgins' abduction. Another group, the Revolutionary Justice Organization, threatened to kill hostage Joseph Cicippio, a former American University of Beirut administrator, but eventually cooled its threats.

Aoun's war of liberation complicated the hostage problem for both Syria and the United States. Syria could make life difficult for the Iranian-supported terrorist groups that had seized Western hostages by blocking their supply lines from Iran and harassing Hezbollah family members and supporters who live in Syrian-controlled parts of Lebanon. Syria, however, needed Hezbollah's support in its battle against the Iraqi-backed Christians. Thus the Syrians did not want to anger Hezbollah or its sponsor and Syria's ally, Iran. Consequently, Syria's Foreign Minister Farouq al-Shara declared on August 6 that a solution to the hostage crisis "depended on a change in American policies in the area." This was construed to mean that the United States was expected to take a much more sympathetic attitude toward Syria's position in Lebanon. On August 9, however, the United States issued its strongest criticism to date of Syria's participation in the battles that had ravaged Beirut almost without interruption since March. Shortly thereafter the hostage problem reverted to a period of quiet and patient diplomacy. (*See also* TERRORISM.)

The U.S. government's concern for the hostages in Lebanon clearly reduced U.S. ability to take a more active role in defusing the ongoing battle between Aoun's forces and the coalition of Syrian troops and Muslim militias. As the summer wore on, Aoun became increasingly impatient with the U.S. refusal to support his campaign against Syria. On September 2, Aoun accused Washington of "selling" Lebanon to Syria, promoting the country's partition, and allowing U.S. policies to be dictated by concern for the eight U.S. hostages held in Lebanon by pro-Iranian Muslim extremists. Aoun touched a particularly raw nerve when he declared that Christians, too, could take Western hostages if they wanted to. On September 6, U.S. Ambassador John McCarthy and 29 U.S. staff members abruptly evacuated the U.S. embassy and departed Lebanon. This followed a two-day "peaceful siege" of the U.S. embassy building in East Beirut that U.S. officials suspected had been organized and controlled by members of General Aoun's entourage.

LEBANON • Information Highlights

Official Name: Republic of Lebanon.
Location: Southwest Asia.
Area: 4,015 sq mi (10 400 km^2).
Population (mid-1989 est.): 3,300,000.
Chief Cities (1980 est.): Beirut, the capital, 702,000; Tripoli, 175,000.
Government: *President,* Elias Hrawi (took office November 1989); *prime minister,* Salim al-Hoss (took office November 1989). *Legislature* (unicameral) —National Assembly.
Monetary Unit: Lebanese pound (441 pounds equal U.S.$1, Dec. 6, 1989).
Foreign Trade (1985 U.S.$): *Imports,* $2,200,000,000; *exports,* $482,000,000.

Arab League Mediation. As the United States shifted to quiet diplomacy to deal with its hostage problem, the fighting in Beirut increased in ferocity and intensity as Syrian forces, supported by Lebanese and Palestinian allies, tried to break into the Christian enclave. This escalation of the fighting prompted the international attention to the conflict that Aoun had sought. The United States denounced as "irresponsible" the stepped-up Syrian attacks. A UN Security Council emergency session meeting on August 16 called for a cease-fire and urged support for a renewed Arab League mediation effort. France sent five special envoys to Damascus and other Arab capitals as part of a diplomatic initiative to persuade the Arab League to resume its mediation efforts.

The Arab League proposal sought to bridge the gap between Christian concern for security and Muslim insistence on political reforms. This is the impasse that prevented the election of a president to succeed the outgoing Amin Gemayel in 1988. The Muslims demanded that agreement first must be reached on a program of political reforms that would strike a more equitable balance between Lebanon's confessional communities. The power-sharing formula adopted in 1943 when Lebanon became independent gave the Christians political dominance, which, the Muslims argue, is outdated demographically. Muslim leaders and Syria contended that once reforms were agreed upon, the other obstacles to peace could be overcome: the election of a new president, the formation of a new, unified government, the reunification and reconstruction of the army,

Photos, AP/Wide World

Lebanese President René Moawad, left, *was assassinated on November 22, just 17 days after taking office. His successor, Elias Hrawi,* right, *pledged to carry on Moawad's national unity programs, which had international support.*

and the withdrawal of foreign forces from Lebanon.

Aoun and the Christians wanted the same results, but in reverse order. They were unwilling to negotiate political reforms under the pressure of "foreign occupations"—a pointed reference to Syria, but also to Israel. Thus Aoun and the Lebanese Forces demanded an agreement on a timetable for Syrian withdrawal before turning to the subject of political reforms. Previous Arab League efforts had floundered on Syria's refusal to agree to such a timetable.

The Arab League plan presented in August and September was the same as had been presented earlier in the year. It called for a meeting of Lebanon's parliament outside Lebanon to discuss political reforms, army reunification, the withdrawal of foreign troops, and reconstruction. The deputies would return to Lebanon to ratify the constitutional reforms and hold elections for a new president.

On September 30, 62 of the surviving 73 deputies (out of 99 elected in the last elections in 1972) gathered in the Saudi mountain resort of Taif to negotiate a political settlement and an end to the civil war. The Lebanese deputies in Taif were the last vestige of political legality in Lebanon. After nearly three weeks of intense negotiations and arm-twisting by Arab League mediators and diplomatic representatives from the United States, Britain, and France, the deputies agreed on a "charter for national reconciliation" drawn up by the Arab League.

The Pact and the Presidential Elections. The Taif agreement reduced the power of the traditionally Christian president, strengthened the traditionally Muslim prime ministership, and ended the Christians' built-in six-to-five majority in the parliament. Parliamentary seats were to be increased from 99 to 108 and distributed equally between Christians and Muslims. Other government positions also would be divided equally.

The agreement did not include a timetable for the withdrawal of Syrian forces. Muslim deputies and some Christians argued that Syrian forces were all that stood against further chaos in a country that literally was governed by the warring militias which were to be disarmed and disbanded. The charter called for the Syrian troops to assist Lebanese forces in reestablishing control over the country and then, after establishment of a new reform government, to pull back to the Bekaa Valley and other positions nearby. Absent was a timetable for total withdrawal of foreign armed forces.

In order for the agreement formally to take effect, the deputies had to reconvene in Lebanon and ratify it. General Aoun, however, denounced the agreement as a "surrender to the Syrian will." He declared Lebanon's parliament dissolved in an attempt to stop the ratification of the plan and the election of a new president. Hence, ratification took place at a Syrian-controlled airfield at Klaiat in north Lebanon. René Moawad, a Maronite Christian, was elected president November 5 and Salim al-Hoss submitted his resignation as acting prime minister. The new president later named Hoss as prime minister of a new reform government. Aoun declared the ratification and the election of Moawad unconstitutional.

Moawad died November 22, the victim of a large explosion in an abandoned shop as his automobile passed. The parliament moved quickly to fill his spot, and the new president, Elias Hrawi, a Maronite Christian from northern Lebanon, pledged support for the negotiated pact. Aoun, however, remained as defiant as ever. The Syrians, meanwhile, built their troop strength in Lebanon to 50,000 by early December. Aoun commands a following of 15,000 troops. Shelling between Muslim West Beirut and Christian East Beirut began anew in early December, further threatening the fragile peace process.

LEWIS W. SNIDER
Claremont Graduate School

LIBRARIES

Transition seemed to be the theme in 1989 for the library community. The executive directors of both the American Library Association (ALA) and the Canadian Library Association (CLA) resigned. Following the resignation of Thomas J. Galvin, ALA executive director (1985–89), Linda F. Crismond, former county librarian, Los Angeles County Public Library, became the ALA's first female executive director in September. Jane Cooney, the CLA's executive director for three years, resigned and was replaced by Sharon Henry.

There also were changes in the chief positions of two of the nation's largest public libraries: Timothy Healy's appointment as president and chief executive officer of the New York Public Library was announced in February, and in July, Wyman Jones resigned as city librarian of the Los Angeles Public Library.

Intellectual Freedom. Iran's Ayatollah Khomeini's death threat against Salman Rushdie following Rushdie's publication of his novel *Satanic Verses* roused librarians, booksellers, and publishers to stand up in support of the rights of all peoples to write, read, and publish. ALA, the American Booksellers Association, and the Association of American Publishers sponsored a full-page ad in the February 22 edition of *The New York Times* supporting these rights and announcing the availability of the title in bookstores and libraries.

An important legal case, *American Library Association v. Thornburgh,* was decided in 1989. This lawsuit successfully challenged the record-keeping and forfeiture provisions of the Child Protection and Obscenity Enforcement Act, which librarians feared would limit the circulation of nonobscene works involving nudity or adult sexuality which should be available to the public. The federal government appealed the decision in July.

Serial Prices. The rising cost of serials (newspapers and magazines) was a primary concern in 1989, particularly in college and university libraries. The Association of Research Libraries (ARL) conducted a study of serial prices and found that the average annual cost per serial in an ARL library had risen from $21.54 in 1975–76 to $75.18 in 1987–88. ARL began devising ways to combat rising costs.

Fees for Library Services. Most library services traditionally have been free of charge to the user, and ALA policies support the concept of free access to information in libraries. The practice of charging for some services, however, has become more prevalent since the advent of online database searching. In 1989, Arizona State University Libraries successfully defended their right to offer value-added fee-based information services, such as electronically searching for information requested by individuals or businesses, to the off-campus community. Under "FYI," a plan begun at the Los Angeles County Public Library, users can pay the library to compile and deliver information to them; however, information remains free to those who come to the library. Milwaukee Public Library's board of trustees approved a new fee plan as well.

LIBRARY AWARDS FOR 1989

Beta Phi Mu Award for distinguished service to education for librarianship: Charles D. Patterson, professor, School of Library and Information Science, Louisiana State University

Randolph J. Caldecott Medal for the most distinguished picture book for children: Stephen Gammel, *Song And Dance Man* (story by Karen Ackerman)

Melvil Dewey Award for recent creative professional achievement of a high order: Robert R. McClarren, director, North Suburban Library System, Wheeling, IL

Grolier Award for unique contributions to the stimulation and guidance of reading by children and young people: Patricia J. Campbell, consultant, Los Angeles, CA

John W. Lippincott Award for distinguished service to the profession of librarianship: Robert Wedgeworth, dean, School of Library Service, Columbia University

John Newbery Medal for the most distinguished contribution to literature for children: Paul Fleischman, *Joyful Noise: Poems For Two Voices*

Literacy. In their efforts to help people use information, librarians have moved beyond bibliographic instruction (helping people understand the use of indexes and other location tools such as card catalogs and online catalogs) to the concept of information literacy. F. William Summers, 1988–89 ALA president, defined this as "the ability to find, analyze, and use information."

Patricia Berger, 1989–90 ALA president, declared that she would join three previous ALA presidents in stressing the battle against illiteracy during her term. By establishing a new campaign, "1989—Year of the Young Reader," the Library of Congress also recognized the importance of reading. First Lady Barbara Bush served as honorary chairperson of the campaign.

Federal Information Policies. Public access to government information has been limited substantially in recent years by massive increases in the amount of classified government documents, the availability of data in electronic formats (making it very difficult for libraries to obtain), the privatization of federal libraries, and the curtailment of government spending in this area. Nancy Kranich of the New York University Libraries, testifying before a House subcommittee investigating these issues, summarized present government information policy as "nothing less than chaotic."

Publication. Forest Press introduced the 20th edition of the *Dewey Decimal Classification* (DDC), which had been in the works for ten years. The DDC first was devised by Melvil Dewey in 1873 and published in a 44-page book in 1876. The new edition is 3,388 pages long.

CHARLES HARMON
American Library Association

At a two-day summit meeting in Marrakech, Morocco, Libya's leader Col. Muammar el-Qaddafi (second from left) *joined the leaders of Algeria, Mauritania, Morocco, and Tunisia in forming the Union of the Arab Maghreb.*

© Stevens/Sipa

LIBYA

A Libyan campaign to improve relations with neighboring states, begun in 1988, continued during 1989, culminating in the formation of a political union with four other Arab states of North Africa. Libya also entered into an agreement with Chad to resolve a longtime territorial dispute. On the other hand, serious tensions marked Libyan dealings with the United States, which accused the Qaddafi government of building a plant to manufacture chemical weapons. Early in the year, American naval aircraft engaged in combat with Libyan forces for the fourth time since 1981.

Despite the celebration in September of the 20th anniversary of Col. Muammar el-Qaddafi's assumption of power, renewed signs of dissatisfaction with his regime among students, Islamic groups, and other Libyan citizens prompted the reorganization of several government agencies. The government's inability to address continuing economic problems also led to a significant reorientation of segments of the national economy.

Chemical Weapons Controversy. In January the United States demanded that Libya dismantle a factory nearing completion at Rabta, some 25 mi (40 km) southwest of Tripoli, that U.S. officials claimed would be capable of producing such chemical weapons as mustard gas and nerve gas. The Libyan government denied the allegations, asserting that the plant would manufacture only pharmaceutical products. At an international conference on chemical weapons in Paris, the United States raised the specter of Libyan chemical weapons falling into the hands of international terrorists, but failed to rally adequate support for a condemnation of Libya's actions. American relations with several of its allies were strained by the revelation that West German and Japanese firms had supplied equipment and advice for the construction of the Rabta plant and that a Belgian exporter had overseen shipment of machinery and chemicals. Although initially denied, these charges later were verified, resulting in the arrest of the former chairman of a West German chemical company. The revelations also ended the external assistance needed to bring the factory into production.

Early in the crisis over the plant, but apparently not directly related to it, two U.S. Navy fighters from the aircraft carrier U.S.S. *John F. Kennedy* shot down two Libyan MiGs over the Mediterranean Sea. The Navy charged that the January 4 incident occurred when the Libyan pilots continued to pursue the American jets, whose pilots had attempted to evade the MiGs. Libya maintained that its planes were unarmed and only were reconnoitering American naval activity to prevent a possible strike against the Rabta plant. Libya brought the issue before the United Nations Security Council. On January 11 the United States, Great Britain, and France vetoed a resolution deploring the engagement after a U.S. representative produced photographs purportedly showing armaments on the Libyan planes.

Trade Sanctions and U.S. Relations. Despite this fourth military confrontation between the United States and Libya during his administration, President Ronald Reagan, just before leaving office on January 20, amended a series of trade sanctions the United States had imposed on Libya in early 1986. The modifications allowed five American oil companies to resume work in Libya, transfer their operations to foreign subsidiaries, or sell their assets. The changes were aimed at averting a Libyan nationalization of the firms and at eliminating the profits Libya had derived from the sale of the

LIBYA • Information Highlights

Official Name: Socialist People's Libyan Arab Jamahiriya ("state of the masses").
Location: North Africa.
Area: 679,359 sq mi (1 759 540 km²).
Population (mid-1989 est.): 4,100,000.
Chief Cities (1984 census): Tripoli, the capital, 990,697; Benghazi, 485,386.
Government: *Head of state,* Muammar el-Qaddafi (took office 1969). *Legislature*—General People's Congress (met initially Nov. 1976).
Monetary Unit: Dinar (0.298 dinar equals U.S. $1, July 1989).
Gross National Product (1988 est. U.S.$): $20,000,-000,000.
Foreign Trade (1988 est. U.S.$): *Imports,* $5,000,-000,000; *exports,* $6,100,000,000.

companies' oil over the preceding three years when the sanctions were in full effect. Critics of the administration attacked this change in American policy, charging that its announcement on the heels of the recent air battle indicated an inconsistent approach to the Qaddafi government that ultimately accorded first priority to economic considerations.

Later in January, Qaddafi expressed an interest in rectifying relations with the United States and working to secure the release of American hostages in the Middle East. Despite this overture, and the return of the body of an American pilot killed in the 1986 raid on Tripoli, no improvement in relations between the two nations developed. Many issues involving the United States or its allies kept American-Libyan antagonisms alive during 1989. In February a Japanese Red Army terrorist allegedly linked to Libyan agents was convicted by a New Jersey court of plotting to set off bombs in the United States to mark the second anniversary of the attack on Tripoli.

Other International Developments. Qaddafi's rejection of the Palestine Liberation Organization's (PLO) peace initiatives and his support for Syrian-backed rival guerrillas did not further the peace process in the Middle East. Libya's acquisition of several Soviet bombers aroused Israeli concerns. And Great Britain renewed its accusation that Libya was a principal supplier of weapons and explosives to the outlawed Irish Republican Army.

Intervention by Qaddafi did obtain the release of a Belgian hostage in Lebanon in June. Even this seemingly humanitarian gesture drew international criticism, however, in that it came about only after a Belgian decision to unfreeze a $60 million trade credit for Libya.

In February, Libya joined Tunisia, Algeria, Morocco, and Mauritania in forming the Union of the Arab Maghreb to promote economic and political cooperation among the Arab states of North Africa and to lessen Libyan isolation. After the 1988 restoration of diplomatic links with Chad, a country with which Libya long had been at odds, the two states participated in a joint committee to normalize relations. When a July meeting between Qaddafi and Chadian President Hissein Habré in Mali failed to produce an agreement on outstanding issues, the Algerian government assumed a mediating role. In late August the two countries agreed to a mutual withdrawal from disputed territories, an exchange of prisoners of war, and the signing of a treaty of friendship and cooperation. They further resolved to settle the question of sovereignty over the Aouzou Strip by negotiations, specifying that if no progress were made within one year, they would submit the matter to the International Court of Justice in The Hague for binding arbitration.

The Domestic Scene. In contrast to these international diplomatic triumphs, opposition to Qaddafi persisted within Libya. Hundreds reportedly were arrested after an outbreak of antigovernment demonstrations at al-Fatah University in January and February. Islamic groups that had accused the government of paying insufficient attention to religious issues and had demanded more participation in the political process were thought responsible for these disturbances, as well as violent incidents toward the end of the year.

An equally serious cause of disaffection, however, was the deteriorating economic situation. In addition to the problems caused by the decline in petroleum revenues, the inefficient and sometimes corrupt state-operated enterprises were the subject of extensive criticisms. The government inaugurated, at the beginning of the year, a series of reforms transferring some state industries to the private sector and greatly loosening restrictions on imports and exports. In the face of domestic unrest, there also was a major reorganization of the army in 1989.

In a dramatic gesture designed to call attention to the abuses suffered by Libya in the colonial period—and perhaps a bid to distract attention from domestic political and economic disorders—Qaddafi declared a national Day of Mourning on October 26 to commemorate the deportation of thousands of Libyans by the Italian colonial administration. Although the Italian government's position was that all issues pertaining to the colonial era have been closed since Libya became independent in 1951, Italian officials permitted a delegation of Libyans to visit Rome and agreed that future discussions on economic and political ties between the two countries would be conducted with due regard for the colonial past. An international seminar in conjunction with the Day of Mourning issued a call for international consideration of colonial injustices and a system of compensation for formerly colonized states that was well received in many parts of the Third World.

KENNETH J. PERKINS
University of South Carolina

LITERATURE

Overview

The 1989 literary year began with an international uproar surrounding the plight of Indian-born British author Salman Rushdie, who in February was placed under a death threat by Iran's Ayatollah Khomeini for alleged blasphemy of the Islamic faith in Rushdie's book, *The Satanic Verses*. The book, published first in Britain in 1988, earlier had stirred protests and some violence among Muslims in Saudi Arabia, Pakistan, and Egypt. After Khomeini's call for Rushdie's death, the author went into hiding with the aid of British security agents. The literary world vacillated, as B. Dalton and other U.S. booksellers pulled the book from their store shelves for a brief period because they feared for the safety of employees and customers. Publishers in France and West Germany at first indicated they would not publish the book but later decided to do so.

In reaction to a perceived threat to 1st Amendment rights, prominent U.S. authors soon rallied to Rushdie's cause. PEN, the international writers organization, and other literary groups organized public meetings and demonstrations in a show of support. There was a public reading of the book in New York City, as well as protests at Iran's UN mission, and there were similar rallies by writers' unions in Boston, Chicago, Minneapolis, and San Francisco. In London a petition drawn up by British writers on Rushdie's behalf was presented to the prime minister. Soviet writers, at first silent, later called for an end to the death threat, but also condemned the "humiliation and insulting of any religion." Despite the reactions of the literary establishment and the death of Khomeini within a few months, the death threat at year's end still hovered over Rushdie, who remained in hiding.

Literary Prize Winners. The Spanish writer Camilo José Cela won the Nobel Prize in Literature in 1989. The 73-year-old Cela, among the most widely read authors in Spain, was considered a breaker of literary taboos in the post Spanish Civil War years. His first novel, *The Family of Pascal Duarte,* completed in 1942 but banned in Franco's Spain for more than ten years, established him in the naturalist literary tradition. His work—consisting of ten novels, including the critically acclaimed *The Hive;* 20 collections of stories; and essays and travel accounts—is considered experimental but adheres to the Spanish tradition of hilarious grotesqueness. The choice of Cela was seen as somewhat controversial because of his support of the Francoists during the Civil War. Later, however, he became independent and outspoken, and his novels stressing the brutality of ordinary life were seen as exposés of Franco's Spain.

The 1989 Pulitzer Prize in fiction went to Baltimore author Anne Tyler for *Breathing Lessons* (1988). Tyler's eleventh novel, *Breathing Lessons* records a journey, both actual and emotional, exploring a marriage in all its complexity. The Pulitzer Prize for poetry went to former U.S. poet laureate Richard Wilbur for his *New And Collected Poems* (1988).

Other News. The PEN international writers association, a 10,000-member group based in London, voted in 1989 to admit two PEN chapters in the Soviet Union. Soviet participation in the organization has been an issue since 1924, when PEN turned down a Soviet application.

U.S. poet laureate Howard Nemerov, who had assumed that post in September 1988, was given a second term in 1989.

© Poincet/Sygma

Spanish writer Camilo José Cela, the 1989 Nobelist in literature noted for his use of language, is among his country's best-known writers, but may be even better known to many of his countrymen as a journalist and television personality. On a twice-weekly television discussion program, he is renowned for pronouncements on many subjects and noted for his ability to shock, provoke, anger, and entertain. Something of a cult figure in Spain, Cela in his earlier years also was known to dabble in bullfighting, soccer, swimming, and acting.

American Literature

Nineteenth-century authors complained that American literature was impossible—America did not have enough history or culture to write about. Twentieth-century authors complained that no one yet had created the "Great American Novel"—one book that would encapsulate our experience. But as we near the end of the century we see America has too many separate histories and cultures for there to be one American Experience.

Novels. In 1989 novelists wrote not of "America" but of their particular America. E. L. Doctorow's *Billy Bathgate* is of Dutch Schultz' gangster America in the 1930s—a violent, intense world of betrayals and murder rendered with an elegiac lyricism that gives it heroic status—all seen through the eyes of Billy, a young juggler whom the monstrously cruel and unpredictable Schultz finds "capable."

© Fred R. Conrad/NYT Pictures

E. L. Doctorow was, by many accounts, at his best with "Billy Bathgate," a story of the myth of American gangsterism and one of 1989's critically acclaimed novels.

Maxine Hong Kingston's *Tripmaster Monkey* depicts a Chinese America whose inhabitants are American in every way except appearance—Wittman Ah Sing, the main character, comes to terms with his heritage by turning it into a show. In Amy Tan's *Joy Luck Club* the older Chinese-American women do not want to Americanize themselves—their memories are of the families and the land they lost. Tan's young heroine finds the old ways an embarrassing burden until she begins to understand their meaning. Cynthia Kadohata's *The Floating World* centers on a girl growing up in a Japanese family looking for its place in America.

Mary Gordon's *The Other Side* deals with several generations of an Irish-American family, as she explores the burden of the Irish Catholic heritage with its compounding of puritanism and mysticism. Oscar Hijuelos' *The Mambo Kings Play Songs of Love* celebrates Cuban-Americans in New York. The music created in New York is not a nostalgic reconstruction of pre-Castro Cuba—it represents a blending of Cuban vitality and American popular culture.

It is said sometimes that New York is *not* America. But in 1989 several novels depicted New York as an American microcosm. Joyce Johnson's *In the Night Cafe* recreates the rich artistic and literary scene in New York in the 1950s. Wilton Barnhardt's *Emma Who Saved My Life* captures the theater scene of New York in the 1970s. Edward Swift's *The Christopher Park Regulars* is a comic treatment of some eccentric habitués of New York's Greenwich Village.

The novel, however, did not become completely urban and ethnic in 1989. Allan Gurganus' *Oldest Living Confederate Widow Tells All* is a tour-de-force 718-page monologue by 99-year-old Lucy Marsden, who tells a southern saga of adventures and melodrama. It is a much different world from Mary Lee Settle's *Charley Bland,* a portrait of a talented heroine who wants the approval of the bigoted, West Virginia country-club aristocracy of her childhood more than the sophisticated larger world that accepts her and admires her work. Thomas Sanchez' *Mile Zero* deals with a still different South—the zany chaos of Key West with its Haitian refugees, drug dealers, dreamers, and hustlers.

Novels long have contained unacknowledged autobiography. However, Barry Hannah's *Boomerang* not only has intimate vignettes of his boyhood in Mississippi when he was "swift and tiny," and fought with the preacher's kids; it also describes his wives, children, and escapades with friends like Jimmy Buffett and Jim Harrison. Russell Banks' *Affliction* tells of the two sons of an alcoholic, violent father. Banks noted that, "I was trying to understand my own life, and also my father's and grandfather's."

But the novel still is energized by imagination. John Irving's *A Prayer for Owen Meany* invents a tiny messiah-like figure, a New Hampshire boy who can see the future. Katherine Dunn's *Geek Love* creates a family of bizarre freaks, deliberately created by their parents for a carnival. Carl Hiaasen's *Skin Tight* is Florida as if seen by Jonathan Swift—a state seething with corruption and caricature.

Vietnam has not been forgotten, but like the war, its treatment in fiction has not been con-

© Robert Foothorap

© Thomas Victor

Chinese-American newcomer Amy Tan saw her first novel, "Joy Luck Club," become one of the year's biggest best-sellers. Nobel-prize winner Saul Bellow published two novellas, "A Theft" and "The Bellarosa Connection," in 1989.

ventional. In *Buffalo Afternoon* Susan Fromberg Schaeffer, who knew of Vietnam only through stories from veterans, powerfully depicts the war itself through the eyes of a Brooklyn kid named Pete Bravado. Larry Brown's *Dirty Work* and Madison Smartt Bell's *Soldier's Joy* both deal with Vietnam through its aftermath by dramatizing the relationship between two Southern veterans, one black and one white. Brown's Mississippi characters are patients in a veterans hospital. Bell's are from the Tennessee mountains, trying to survive the racism and violence of home.

Despite such classics as Herman Melville's *Billy Budd,* the novella long has been a literary orphan in America. Its awkward length made it too long for most magazines and too short for the usual book. Saul Bellow helped revive the form by publishing *A Theft,* the portrait of a relationship between a strong woman and her lover, and *The Bellarosa Connection,* a tale of a memory expert haunted by his inability to forget. Both novellas first were published not in hardcover but in paperback, a rare occurrence for an accomplished novelist, let alone a Nobel Prize winner such as Bellow. Lynne Sharon Schwartz' novella, *Leaving Brooklyn,* describes the coming of age of a young girl. Jane Smiley's two novellas, *Ordinary Love & Good Will,* published in one volume, concern the fragility of happiness within family relationships.

Short Stories. The American short story in 1989 also revealed a complex, fragmented country. The people in Bob Shacochis' *The Next New World* tend to be on the fringe of America. Ranging down the East Coast and into the Caribbean, his characters are marooned by time, history, or their own fantasies. Ron Hansen's *Nebraska* goes to an American heartland ruled by accident and fate. Bobbie Ann Mason's *Love Life* explores rural lives in Kentucky and Tennessee where the *Phil Donahue Show* and old Protestant values curiously intermingle.

The title story of Rick Bass' *The Watch* tells of an America where a father escapes for awhile from his desperately lonely son to live in a swamp, hunting alligators and swimming with women who have fled their brutal husbands. Bass' America seems to be on a treadmill to oblivion, determined to destroy its own freedom. Lee K. Abbott's *Dreams of Distant Lives* focuses more on domestic collapse and the failure of relationships.

History and Culture. The year 1989 looked like the year of the self. This perhaps represented an apotheosis of narcissism, a renaissance of introspection, or a recognition that only by dealing with personal history can one begin to understand how reality is created. Numerous autobiographies, memoirs, and reminiscences gained attention. Book reviewer Jonathan Yardley's *Our Kind of People* tells of his white Anglo-Saxon Episcopalian background. Journalist Carl Bernstein's *Loyalties* tells of his father, who was a Communist Party member in the 1940s. Columnist Russell Bak-

AMERICAN LITERATURE: MAJOR WORKS | 1989

CULTURE AND CRITICISM

Alter, Robert, *The Pleasures of Reading in an Ideological Age*
Booth, Wayne C., *The Company We Keep: An Ethics of Fiction*
Dawidowicz, Lucy S., *From That Place and Time: A Memoir, 1938–1947*
Dillard, Annie, *The Writing Life*
Ehrenreich, Barbara, *Fear of Falling: The Inner Life of the Middle Class*
Fish, Stanley, *Doing What Comes Naturally: Change, Rhetoric, and the Practice of Theory in Literary and Legal Studies*
Gilbert, Sandra, and Gubar, Susan, *No Man's Land: The Place of the Woman Writer in the Twentieth Century. Volume Two: Sexchanges*
Gould, Stephen Jay, *Wonderful Life*
Kidder, Tracy, *Among Schoolchildren*
Leibowitz, Herbert, *Fabricating Lives: Explorations in American Autobiography*
Morgan, Robin, *The Demon Lover: On The Sexuality of Terrorism*
Naipaul, V.S., *A Turn in the South*
Pinsky, Robert, *Poetry and the World*
Smith, Barbara Herrnstein, *Contingencies of Value: Alternate Perspectives in Critical Theory*
Sontag, Susan, *AIDS and its Metaphors*
Updike, John, *Just Looking: Essays on Art*
Villard, Henry Serrano, and Nagel, James, eds., *Hemingway in Love and War: The Lost Diaries of Agnes von Kurowsky, Her Letters, and Correspondence of Ernest Hemingway*
Waring, Marilyn, *If Women Counted: A New Feminist Economics*
Wilkinson, Alec, *Big Sugar*

HISTORY AND BIOGRAPHY

Abernathy, Ralph David, *And The Walls Came Tumbling Down*
Baker, Russell, *The Good Times*
Bass, Rick, *Oil Notes*
Berg, A. Scott, *Goldwyn: A Biography*
Bernstein, Carl, *Loyalties: A Son's Memoir*
Brady, Frank, *Citizen Welles: A Biography of Orson Welles*
Dorris, Michael, *The Broken Cord*
Drew, Bettina, *Nelson Algren: A Life on the Wild Side*
Duberman, Martin Bauml, *Paul Robeson: A Biography*
Dunne, John Gregory, *Harp*
Evans, Sara M., *Born For Liberty: A History of Women in America*
Friedman, Thomas, *From Beirut to Jerusalem*
Friedrich, Otto, *Glenn Gould: A Life and Variations*
Hoffman, Eva, *Lost In Translation*
Karl, Frederick R., *William Faulkner: American Writer*
Kessner, Thomas, *Fiorello H. La Guardia and the Making of Modern New York*
McNeill, William H., *Arnold J. Toynbee*
Miles, Barry, *Ginsberg: A Biography*
Miller, Donald L., *Lewis Mumford: A Life*
Morris, Roger, *Richard Milhous Nixon*
Novick, Sheldon M., *Honorable Justice: The Life of Oliver Wendell Holmes*
Price, Reynolds, *Clear Pictures: First Loves, First Guides*
Reagan, Maureen, *First Father, First Daughter: A Memoir*
Reagan, Nancy, *My Turn*
Sawyer-Laucanno, Christopher, *An Invisible Spectator: A Biography of Paul Bowles*
Schama, Simon, *Citizens: A Chronicle of the French Revolution*
Stevenson, Anne, *Bitter Fame: A Life of Sylvia Plath*
Updike, John, *Self-Consciousness: Memoirs*
Ward, Geoffrey C., *A First-Class Temperament: The Emergence of Franklin Roosevelt*
Wolff, Tobias, *This Boy's Life*
Woodward, C. Vann, *The Future of the Past: Historical Writings*
Yardley, Jonathan, *Our Kind of People: The Story of an American Family*

NOVELS

Badanes, Jerome, *The Final Opus of Leon Solomon*
Baker, Nicholson, *The Mezzanine*
Banks, Russell, *Affliction*
Barnhardt, Wilton, *Emma Who Saved My Life*
Bausch, Richard, *Mr. Field's Daughter*
Bell, Madison Smartt, *Soldier's Joy*
Bellow, Saul, *The Bellarosa Connection*
Bellow, Saul, *A Theft*
Brown, Larry, *Dirty Work*
Bukowski, Charles, *Hollywood*
Doctorow, E. L., *Billy Bathgate*
Dunn, Katherine, *Geek Love*
Gordon, Mary, *The Other Side in America*
Gurganus, Allan, *Oldest Living Confederate Widow Tells All*
Hannah, Barry, *Boomerang*
Hiaasen, Carl, *Skin Tight*
Hijuelos, Oscar, *The Mambo Kings Play Songs of Love*
Humphrey, William, *No Resting Place*
Kingston, Maxine Hong, *Tripmaster Monkey*
Irving, John, *A Prayer for Owen Meany*
Johnson, Joyce, *In the Night Cafe*
Kadohata, Cynthia, *The Floating World*
Leavitt, David, *Equal Affections*
Leithauser, Brad, *Hence*
McGuane, Thomas, *Keep the Change*
Purdy, James, *Garments the Living Wear*
Reed, Ishmael, *The Terrible Threes*
Sanchez, Thomas, *Mile Zero*
Sarton, May, *The Education of Harriet Hatfield*
Settle, Mary Lee, *Charley Bland*
Schaeffer, Susan Fromberg, *Buffalo Afternoon*
Schwartz, Lynne Sharon, *Leaving Brooklyn*
Smiley, Jane, *Ordinary Love & Good Will*
Swift, Edward, *The Christopher Park Regulars*
Tan, Amy, *The Joy Luck Club*
Theroux, Paul, *My Secret History*
Walker, Alice, *The Temple of My Familiar*
Wiggins, Marianne, *John Dollar*
Young, Al, *Seduction By Light*

POETRY

Applewhite, James, *Lessons in Soaring*
Berryman, John, *Collected Poems, 1937–1971*
Carver, Raymond, *A New Path to the Waterfall*
Ciardi, John, *Echoes*
Dubie, Norman, *Groom Falconer*
Dumas, Henry, *Knees of a Natural Man*
Haxton, Brooks, *Traveling Company*
Moss, Stanley, *The Intelligence of Clouds*
Muske, Carol, *Applause*
Oates, Joyce Carol, *The Time Traveler: Poems 1983–1989*
Rich, Adrienne, *Time's Power: Poems 1985–1988*
Ryan, Michael, *God Hunger*
Seeman, Julianne, *Enough Light to See*
Zweig, Paul, *Selected and Last Poems*

SHORT STORIES

Abbott, Lee K., *Dreams of Distant Lives*
Adams, Alice, *After You've Gone*
Bass, Rick, *The Watch*
Boyle, T. Coraghessan, *If the River Was Whiskey*
Gilchrist, Ellen, *Life Can Be Both Wave and Particle*
Glickfeld, Carol, *Useful Gifts*
Hansen, Ron, *Nebraska*
Mason, Bobbie Ann, *Love Life*
Matthiessen, Peter, *On the River Styx*
Ozick, Cynthia, *The Shawl*
Pesetsky, Bette, *Confessions of a Bad Girl*
Shacochis, Bob, *The Next New World*
Stern, Daniel, *Twice Told Tales*
Wideman, John Edgar, *Fever*

---

er's *The Good Times* celebrates his widowed mother, who insisted on excellence though her family was so poor she had to give up one child for adoption.

Authors known primarily for their fiction wrote important memoirs. Tobias Wolff's *This Boy's Life* is about a childhood of violence and deception. John Gregory Dunne's *Harp* is titled after a derogatory term for Irish Catholics. Reynolds Price's *Clear Pictures* is not only a portrait of the author as a young man, but of the South struggling to come to terms with its complex past. Even John Updike, whose fiction often seemed deeply autobiographical, became explicitly so in *Self-Consciousness*.

© 1989, Jerry Bauer

Thomas L. Friedman in "From Beirut to Jerusalem" recounts his years as a journalist in those cities, reporting on the complex Mideast events that so riveted world attention.

Annie Dillard's *The Writing Life* reveals how she thinks about her own work.

The memoirs of public figures are often combinations of bland anecdotes and pious platitudes. This was not true of 1989's offerings. For instance, Maureen Reagan's *First Father, First Daughter* was candid in its appraisal of her father, Ronald Reagan. Ralph David Abernathy's *And the Walls Came Tumbling Down* created controversy over his depiction of Martin Luther King. Sally Bingham's *Passion and Prejudice* so incensed her family that it became the subject of a court case.

The personal form does not necessarily mean the writer is the central subject of the work. Michael Dorris' *The Broken Cord* is about his adoption, as a single parent, of a son. But it is not so much about Dorris as about the son (who was damaged hopelessly by fetal alcohol syndrome), the culture that is producing these children, and what might be done to change conditions. Rick Bass' *Oil Notes* is about the earth itself as well as his experiences as a petroleum geologist. Eva Hoffman's *Lost in Translation* recounts her childhood in Poland, but it is really about language and culture. Lucy S. Dawidowicz' *From That Place and Time* is a frightening remembrance of her wartime experiences in Europe.

The number, quality, and range of autobiographical writing made Herbert Leibowitz' *Fabricating Lives* particularly appropriate in 1989. He discussed eight American autobiographies from Benjamin Franklin to Richard Wright, concluding that the most important feature is not truth or insight, but style. Like a piece of fiction, memoir or autobiography must create its own world. Even an anthology of memoirs appeared. In *Family Portraits,* Carolyn Anthony collected remembrances of 20 writers, all focusing on a person who particularly influenced them in childhood.

Feminism argues that patriarchal power has defined history, literature, psychology, and politics in masculine terms. In 1989 a number of books addressed the issue, especially Sandra Gilbert's and Susan Gubar's ongoing project, *No Man's Land: The Place of the Woman Writer in the Twentieth Century*. This second volume, subtitled *Sexchanges,* shows how women writers deal with their difficult position. Sara M. Evans' *Born For Liberty* traces the unrecognized contribution women have made to American history. Robin Morgan's *The Demon Lover* is a feminist analysis of political terrorism. Marilyn Waring's *If Women Counted* points out that economic theory has failed to take into account women's economic productivity.

New theories of criticism see all phenomena as illusory, subject to the endless ambiguities of language, power, and culture. Barbara Herrnstein Smith's *Contingencies of Value* argues that virtues, values, and meanings are merely inventions. Stanley Fish's *Doing What Comes Naturally* applies his theory of subjectivity not only to literature but also to legal writings. On the other hand, Robert Alter's *The Pleasures of Reading in an Ideological Age* eloquently defends more traditional criticism. Wayne C. Booth's *The Company We Keep* argues that moral value remains central to the literary experience.

Poetry. John Berryman's *Collected Poems, 1937–1971* brings together the major work of a poet whose stature has grown steadily since his death in 1972. His confessional poems and his long sequence, *The Dream Songs,* strongly influenced the poets of the 1980s.

The unabashed use of autobiography can be seen in James Applewhite's *Lessons in Soaring* where he talks of going back to "Applewhite land," trying to find the house where they "showed movies of relatives I couldn't keep straight." In his brilliant collection, *God Hunger,* Michael Ryan writes of sitting with his friends in a bar with John Cheever: "In a booth for four were mashed five whose egos would have cramped the Astrodome."

Brooks Haxton's *Traveling Company* celebrates life, including a witty five-page ode to a wingnut, "The featherless and nutless one!" Norman Dubie's *Groom Falconer* shows a similar range, from a touching poem on the death of his Great Dane to "The Apocrypha of Jacques Derrida."

JEROME STERN
Florida State University

Children's Literature

The children's book market continued to expand as public recognition of the value of reading to young children grew and classroom trends moved toward incorporating children's literature into reading and language arts curricula.

Paul Fleischman's volume of poetry, *Joyful Noise,* won the prestigious Newbery Medal in 1989. The Caldecott Medal for illustration was presented to *Song and Dance Man*, illustrated by Stephen Gammell and written by Karen Ackerman.

Picture Books. A variety of fresh and visually rich picture books were published in 1989, and fairy tales figured prominently among them. Charlotte Huck's *Princess Furball,* illustrated by Caldecott award-winning book artist Anita Lobel, is a handsome retelling of a Grimm tale about a princess clever enough to reverse her misfortune. Another striking tale, Robert San Souci's *The Talking Eggs* (illustrated by Jerry Pinkney), is a Cinderella variant from the old South about an exploited younger sister whose goodness is rewarded. Besides fairy tales, there were Caldecott winner Paul Goble's *Beyond the Ridge,* a story of a dying Indian woman whose spirit journeys to a better world, and Joyce Maxner's *Nicholas Cricket,* imaginatively illustrated by William Joyce, a particularly fresh fantasy in which the residents of nearby fields and streams revel in music provided by Nick's Bug-A-Wug Cricket band.

Middle Grade Books. Variety in content and form was notable for middle-grade readers in 1989. Entertaining contemporary stories included Jamie Gilson's humorous action story *Hobie Hanson: Greatest Hero of the Mall,* and Juanita Havill's *It Always Happens to Leona,* about a little girl who endures all the trials of being an overlooked middle child. Havill's book has the ring of truth reminiscent of Beverly Cleary's fiction and will appeal to younger middle-grade readers.

One of the year's more unusual titles was *Valentine and Orson,* by Nancy Ekholm Burkert. A distinguished artist long absent from the children's book field, Burkert made a remarkable comeback with this convoluted tale, retold in iambic pentameter couplets, of twin brothers who were separated at birth.

A serious story that pushes readers to think carefully about what it means to be a soldier was Louise Moeri's *The Forty-third War,* about a Central American boy who is kidnapped from his village and forced to become a soldier.

Junior High and Young Adult. For junior high school readers there was Peter Dickinson's *Eva,* a thoughtful and at times riveting novel set in the not-too-distant future that follows the fate of a girl whose brain has been implanted in the body of a chimpanzee after an

Illustrated by Anita Lobel. © Retold by Charlotte Huck, used by permission of Greenwillow Books

Used by permission of Alfred A. Knopf

Used by permission of Harper and Row

SELECTED BOOKS FOR CHILDREN

Picture Books
Brett, Jan, *The Mitten*
Brighton, Catherine, *Nijinsky*
DeFelice, Cynthia C., *The Dancing Skeleton*
Ehlert, Lois, *Eating the Alphabet*
Ernst, Lisa Campbell, *When Bluebell Sang*
Gerrard, Roy, *Rosie and the Rustlers*
Hoban, Tana, *Of Colors and Things*
Howard, Elizabeth Fitzgerald, *Chita's Christmas Tree*
Hughes, Shirley, *The Big Alfie and Annie Rose Storybook*
Martin, Bill, and Archambault, John, *Chicka Chicka Boom Boom*
Munro, Roxie, *The Inside-Outside Book of London*
Pomerantz, Charlotte, *The Chalk Doll*
Rice, Eve, *Peter's Pockets*
Rosen, Michael, *We're Going on a Bear Hunt*
Schotter, Roni, *Captain Snap and the Children of Vinegar Lane*
Steig, William, *Spinky Sulks*
Yorinks, Arthur, *Oh, Brother*
Zemach, Margot, *The Three Little Pigs: An Old Story*

The Middle Grades
Ammon, Richard, *Growing Up Amish*
Beatty, Patricia, *Sarah and Me and the Lady from the Sea*
Byars, Betsy, *Bingo Brown and the Language of Love*
Conrad, Pam, *My Daniel*
DeClements, Barthe, *Five-Finger Discount*
Guy, Rosa, *The Ups and Downs of Carl Davis III*
Hamilton, Virginia, *The Bells of Christmas*
Kherdian, David, *A Song for Uncle Henry*
Kinsey, Warnock, *The Canada Geese Quilt*
Lisle, Janet Taylor, *Afternoon of the Elves*
Lowry, Lois, *Number the Stars*
McBratney, Sam, *The Ghosts of Hungryhouse Lane*
Mayne, William, *Gideon Ahoy!*
Slepian, Jan, *The Broccoli Tapes*
Wallace-Brodeur, Ruth, *Stories from the Big Chair*
Yarbrough, Camille, *The Shimmershine Queens*

Junior High
Avi, *The Man Who Was Poe*
Busselle, Rebecca, *Bathing Ugly*
Cresswell, Helen, *Bagthorpes Liberated*
Dinner, Sherry H., *Nothing To Be Ashamed Of*
Staples, Suzanne Fisher, *Shabanu: Daughter of the Wind*
Yep, Laurence, *The Rainbow People*

accident has destroyed her body. In contrast, the world of the past is the setting for Jan Hudson's *Sweetgrass,* about a young Native American woman who is unhappy that her family considers her not yet ready to marry. Hudson's story is based on careful research and paints a memorable picture of Indian life on the plains. Ephraim Sevela's *We Were Not Like Other People* is an intense story about a Russian Jewish boy separated from his parents by turbulent politics during World War II.

Although autobiography is not commonplace among children's books, Cynthia Rylant brought out *But I'll Be Back Again* in 1989. In the book, the well-known author describes her formative influences, including growing up in the 1960s. Other first-rate nonfiction was found in Rhoda Blumberg's *The Great American Gold Rush* and Jean Fritz' *The Great Little Madison,* books on the California gold rush and the fourth U.S. president.

DENISE MURCKO WILMS
Assistant Editor, "Booklist"

Canadian Literature: English

With Canada facing a huge national debt and other problems, politics understandably inspired many books in 1989.

Nonfiction. The year's most-discussed book was Erik Nielsen's *The House Is Not a Home,* the memoirs of a former key member of Conservative Prime Minister Brian Mulroney's cabinet. While in the House of Commons, Nielsen earned the nickname "Velcro Lips" because he was consistently closemouthed. Readers therefore were surprised when they found he wrote frankly about his personal life and applied the same frankness in his critical comments about some former cabinet colleagues, including Mulroney.

Three books about the 1988 federal election were Graham Fraser's *Playing for Keeps,* Rick Salutin's *Waiting for Democracy,* and Robert Mason's *One Hundred Monkeys.* Other political books included journalist Allan Fotheringham's *Birds of a Feather: Politics and the Press;* Clair Hoy's *Margin of Error: Pollsters and the Manipulation of Canadian Politics;* and Stevie Cameron's *Inside Out: Power, Prestige and Scandal in the Nation's Capital.*

British Columbia's Premier William Vander Zalm and his Social Credit government are treated in *Fantasy Government,* by Stan Persky, and *Inside the Reign of Bill Vander Zalm,* by Gary Mason and Keith Baldry. Joey Smallwood, former premier of Newfoundland, inspired Harold Howard's *Joey.* Former Liberal Prime Minister Pierre Trudeau and Thomas Axworthy coedited *Towards a Just Society: Governing Canada 1968–84,* a collection of essays about the Trudeau era. *Shadow of Heaven* is the first volume of John English's biography of former Prime Minister Lester Pearson.

Attracting much attention was *Dance on the Earth,* the memoirs of famed novelist Margaret Laurence. She completed the book only a short time before her death. Don Bailey contributed *Memories of Margaret,* about his long friendship with Laurence. Another well-known novelist is discussed in Claude Bissell's *Ernest Buckler Remembered.* A living author is treated in Norman Sherry's *The Life of Graham Greene: Volume I.*

Chief: The Fearless Vision of Billy Diamond, by Roy MacGregor, is about the Cree Indian chief who gained for his people a huge land claim settlement from the federal government. Philip Marchand offered *Marshall McLuhan: The Medium and the Messenger,* and A. C. Hamilton presented *Northrop Frye: Anatomy of His Criticism.*

The 75th anniversary of World War I's beginning, and the 50th of World War II's, prompted several books. Desmond Morton and J. L. Granatstein wrote about the first in *Marching to Armageddon: Canadians and the Great War,* and the second in *A Nation Forged in Fire: Canadians in the Second World War.* Other World War II books published in 1989 were Col. C. P. Stacey's *The Canadian Army* and Hal Lawrence's *A Good War,* about the Royal Canadian Navy's small ships. Brian Loring discusses one of World War II's most controversial engagements in *Unauthorized Action: Mountbatten and the Dieppe Raid.*

Poetry. Popular and prolific Irving Layton contributed *Selected Poems, 1945–1989.* Robert Kroetsch's new volume is *The Completed Field Notes. Poetry by Canadian Women,* edited by Rosemary Sullivan, collects works from the 18th to 20th centuries, and George Woodcock edited *The Dry Wells of India,* an anthology of the best poems submitted to his contest in aid of an Indian hospital. Roo Borson's new work is *Intent, or the Weight of the World,* and Des Walsh's is *Love and Savagery.* Lloyd Abbey published *Abbey: Selected Poems 1959 to 1989,* and Paulette Giles contributed *Song to the Rising Sun.*

Fiction. Mordecai Richler broke a lengthy absence in 1989 with a story about bootleggers, *Solomon Gursky Was Here.* The U.S. Central Intelligence Agency's involvement with brainwashing experiments in Montreal in the late 1950s forms the background for William Deverell's exciting thriller *Mindfield.* And Richard Rohmer published another thriller, *The Red Arctic,* about Russians in the far north. Heather Robertson contributed *Igor: A Novel of Intrigue,* based on the Gouzenko spy sensation in Ottawa.

Other noteworthy novels are poet Marilyn Bowering's first, *To All Appearances a Lady;* Jane Rule's *After the Fire;* W. P. Kinsella's *The Miss Hobbema Pageant;* and Larry Zolf's *Scorpions for Sale.* Sandra Birdsell's first novel is *The Missing Child,* and Dennis Jones' *Warsaw Concerto* is a thriller about spies.

Among many short story collections is *The Journey Prize Anthology,* financed by author James Michener and containing what were judged to be the best short stories of the year. Other collections included Barry Dempster's *Writing Home* and Leon Rooke's *How I Saved the Province.*

DAVID SAVAGE, *Free-lance Writer*

Margaret Atwood's seventh novel, "Cat's Eye," a story of a 50-year-old artist who returns to Toronto, her childhood city, and is oppressed by memories, was received well.

AP/Wide World

English Literature

The writing, publishing, and selling of English literature seemed more dangerous in 1989 after the threat to the life of Salman Rushdie, whose *Satanic Verses* brought the condemnation of the Ayatollah Khomeini, leader of Iran, who died in June. The furor over the death threat to the author was kept in the forefront of the public's mind in Britain by two works that tried to crystallize the issues involved: a play, *Iranian Nights* by Tariq Ali and Howard Brenton at the Royal Court Theatre, and then a television "poem" by poet Tony Harrison, *The Blasphemers' Banquet.*

Fiction. Novelists continued their art, nevertheless, making 1989 a bumper year for British fiction with many of the country's established writers producing new work and with several interesting debuts. In the former category were Sybille Bedford's *Jigsaw,* a semiautobiographical account of a writer's youth; Penelope Lively's *Passing On,* in which a dead mother's spirit contrives to dominate the lives of her two children; and another Beryl Bainbridge Liverpool tale, *An Awfully Big Adventure.* Margaret Drabble produced a sequel to her earlier novel, *The Radiant Way,* entitled *A Natural Curiosity,* and Nobel laureate William Golding concluded his seafaring trilogy with the dramatic *Fire Down Below.* Michael Frayn published his first novel in 16 years, *The Trick of It,* an account of a literary marriage.

Two very different literary figures published to wide acclaim in the fall—Anita Brookner, with her ninth novel, *Lewis Percy,* tracing in her deceptively simple way the emotional education of her ineffectual eponymous hero, and Jeanette Winterson with *Sexing the Cherry,* a Gothic farce set among the plagued 17th-century puritans.

From the travel writers Paul Theroux and Colin Thubron came the novels *My Secret History* and *Falling,* respectively. Peter Ackroyd's *First Light* was less well-received than previous publications, with critics preferring the rural settings of Stanley Middleton's *Vacant Places* and Hilary Martell's *Fludd,* a farcical story of Catholic morals in 1950s Lancashire.

Among the less familiar names who produced well-received novels were Paul Sayer with *The Comforts of Madness,* a study of a

© Nigel Parry

Kazuo Ishiguro, 34, a Japanese-born English author, won Britain's prestigious Booker Prize for "The Remains of the Day," an account of the reflections of an English butler.

mental patient, and Lindsay Clarke with *The Chymical Wedding,* involving alchemy and adultery. Highly recommended were Rose Tremain's *Restoration,* a picture of the court of Charles II, and John Banville's *The Book of Evidence,* the prison monologue of a convicted murderer. James Kelman's *A Disaffection,* which told the bleak story of a comprehensive schoolteacher in Scotland, also was acclaimed.

Fictional debuts were made this year by biographer Victoria Glendenning with her story of a philanderer, *The Grown-ups,* and literary journalist Sebastian Faulks with *The Girl at the Lion D'Or,* set in provincial France between the wars and hailed by public and critics alike as a captivating evocation of place, period, and character. Geoff Dyer with his first novel, *The Colour of Memory,* evoked the hectic setting of his native inner London, a subject viewed from a more negative angle in Martin Amis' latest black comedy, *London Fields.*

Another veteran, Anthony Burgess, in addition to a new novel, *Any Old Iron,* which charts the lives of two families through two world wars, produced his first volume of short stories, *The Devil's Modes.* This collection, however, was overshadowed by a new publication from the master of the genre, V. S. Pritchett, whose *A Careless Widow and Other Stories,* portraying subtle fragments of ordinary life, confirmed the reputation of the 89-year-old author.

Among the most adventurous publications of the year was Julian Barnes' experimental *History of the World in 10½ Chapters,* a mixture of fact, fiction, autobiography, and essay that explores accepted limitations. Iris Murdoch's devotees were awarded a new novel, *The Message to the Planet. The Remains of the Day* by Kazuo Ishiguro, an English writer of Japanese origin, gently posed difficult questions about power and dignity in an understated examination of codes of behavior. Britain's most prestigious literary award, the Booker Prize, this year was presented to the latter author.

Nonfiction. History, biography, and memoirs were published in great numbers, some covering the anniversary of the outbreak of World War II. Among many accounts, two were outstanding: *Second World War* by Martin Gilbert, which focused on the leaders, fighters, and ordinary citizens caught up in events, and *The Second World War* by John Keegan, a study in military decision making.

Leading biographies included the second volume of Michael Holroyd's *Bernard Shaw,* which lived up to the high standard of the first, as did the second volume, covering 1957–86, of Alistair Horne's life of Harold Macmillan. Margaret Thatcher, who marked her tenth anniversary as prime minister, was much written about, and Hugo Young's *One of Us* was judged the most perceptive account of her strengths and weaknesses.

The massively researched *Federico García Lorca,* in which the Spanish playwright's tormented life and violent death were portrayed lovingly, was an important achievement of Ian Gibson, A definitive account of the life of Romantic poet William Wordsworth was written by Stephen Gill, and Fiona MacCarthy revealed the explosive character of sculptor Eric Gill.

Among books of literary criticism and philosophy, George Steiner's *Real Presences,* a consideration of the precious and sacred character of the arts, was outstanding. Poet James Fenton found himself as a journalist in Vietnam and the Philippines and summed up his experiences there in *All the Wrong Places.* Catholic journalist John Cornwell brilliantly investigated the death of Pope John Paul I and the Vatican in *A Thief in the Night,* which disproved rumors of foul play but charged neglect. Among the most affecting of nonfiction books was the posthumous publication of essays on travel and people by Bruce Chatwin entitled *What Am I Doing Here?*

Poetry. Ted Hughes, the British poet laureate and a poet of nature, saw his highly acclaimed *Wolfwatching* published during the year. Among other new volumes were *Blue Shoes* by Matthew Sweeney, a young Irish poet; *Perduta Gente* by Peter Reading, reflecting his feelings for the underprivileged in British society; and a first collection by Simon Armitage entitled *Zoom.*

MAUREEN GREEN
Free-lance Writer, London

World Literature*

The most eagerly anticipated, most notable, and in many ways most controversial literary publication outside the Anglo-American orbit in 1989 was undoubtedly Gabriel García Márquez' big new novel, *The General in His Labyrinth,* an earthy, imaginative, and largely affectionate portrait of Latin America's revered hero Simón Bolívar that manages both to demythicize the "Liberator" and add to the myths surrounding his life and person. Hotly debated throughout the Hispanic world, the novel's virtuosic mix of tragedy, epic, and magical realism in portraying its protagonist's ultimate failure to realize his Utopian dream of Latin American unity is sure to provoke worldwide commentary as translations appear.

Latin America. Even without García Márquez' blockbuster, the year would have been a respectable one for literature in Latin America. *Divertimento,* a very early (1949) unpublished work by the late Julio Cortázar, was rescued from oblivion, and it clearly revealed the formal experimentalism and playful narrative style that characterized the Argentine author's later writing. Fellow Argentine Manuel Puig, famed for *Kiss of the Spider Woman,* returned to novel writing after a six-year silence with *The Tropic Night Falls,* the sad and moving account of two sisters fading quietly into the lonely twilight of their lives. *Son of Man* by Augusto Roa Bastos, recounting his native Paraguay's savage 20-year war with Bolivia in 1912–32, had its first U.S. publication. The novelist and playwright Luis Rafael Sánchez presented *The Importance of Being Called Daniel Santos*—a self-proclaimed "Puerto Rican contribution to the formation of the world of popular myth applicable to all of Latin America," as embodied in the story of a celebrated *bolero* singer. Nicaraguan poet and Minister of Culture Ernesto Cardenal evoked his nation's pre-Columbian past in the collection *The Golden UFOs,* subtitled "Indian Poems." From Spain proper came *The Virtues of the Solitary Bird,* Juan Goytisolo's lyric account of the life and vision of Saint John of the Cross.

Translations spread the work of four first-rate Brazilian authors worldwide: *Soulstorm* offered the late prose writer Clarice Lispector's short stories; *This Earth, That Sky* introduced the supple, versatile poetry of the late Manuel Bandeira; *The Republic of Dreams* displayed Nélida Piñon's novelistic craft in all its elegance and intricacy; and *An Invincible Memory* revealed João Ubaldo Ribeiro as a worthy successor to Jorge Amado in composing epics filled with scintillating characters, diverse prose styles, and highly diverting actions.

French and German. It was a lackluster year for French letters, with only the third and final installment of Albert Camus' sensitive, anguished *Notebooks* (1951–59), the octogenarian Julien Green's leisurely historical novel *Stars of the South,* and the late poet-novelist Louis Aragon's often scandalous confessions *To Explain What I Was* rising above the pack.

German letters made a more respectable showing, led by three superb women writers. The 26 stories in Gabriele Wohmann's *Audit* depict a like number of unhappy families and individuals whose lives are foundering not through tragic occurrences but through the sheer banality and tedium of their everyday existence in modern West Germany. Christa Wolf's *Summer Story,* in contrast, finds an antidote to such present-day ennui in the memory of a glorious summer spent with companions exploring the back country of East Germany and the value of genuine friendship. Friederike Mayröcker's *Collected Prose 1949–1975* gathered a quarter century of the Austrian poet's offbeat and often startling short fiction, sketches, impressions, and stylistic experiments. Her compatriot Peter Handke weighed in with the novella *An Experiment in Fatigue* and the full-length drama *The Game of Questions,* an intricate and somewhat Stoppardian "play" on words, Socratic inquiry, role-playing, and the very nature of verbal art. Also of note were the West German Hermann Lenz' short novel *Young and Old,* the late Thomas Bernhard's fragmented lyric novelette *On High,* Hans Magnus Enzensberger's miscellany of poems, dialogues, and essays *Flying Robert,* the East German Stefan Heym's fascinating memoirs *Posthumous Fame,* and the 1946–48 installment of Thomas Mann's voluminous diaries.

Russia and Eastern Europe. The Russian writers enjoyed a reasonably good year, particularly in Western translations. Tatyana Tolstaya made perhaps the biggest splash with her short-story collection *On the Golden Porch,* revealing an exuberant and canny talent eminently worthy of her famous surname. Vladimir Soloukhin's *Scenes from Russian Life* presented eight autobiographical stories by a similarly talented writer little known in the West. Vassily Aksyonov enjoyed the English publication of *two* recent novels: the jazz-influenced satire *Our Golden Ironburg* and the more ambitious but equally wicked *Say Cheese!* In the USSR the highlight of the year—aside from all the *glasnost*-induced first releases of innumerable long-banned writers—was Vladimir Vysotsky's *Collected Poems and Songs,* three large volumes of the erstwhile underground bard's lyric and satiric work.

Eastern Europe also was well represented in 1989. *Temptation,* dissident dramatist Václav Havel's Faust play, emerged from the Czech underground and premiered to great acclaim in New York and Los Angeles. *Life With a Star,* the first Western translation of Czech author Jiri Weil's posthumously published 1964

*Titles translated.

masterpiece, added a remarkably original and understated novel to the growing catalogue of Holocaust literature. Two of Hungary's finest 20th-century poets were published in new English editions: the nimble and versatile Sándor Weöres in *Eternal Moment,* and the hauntingly intense János Pilinszky in *The Desert of Love.* The second and final volume of the iconoclastic Polish novelist Witold Gombrowicz' revealing and influential *Diary* was issued in translation in September. Albania's lone international literary standard-bearer Ismail Kadare saw two more novels released in French: the "epic thriller" *Dossier H* and the historical novel *The Concert,* dealing with events leading up to the break in Albanian-Chinese relations.

Middle East. The few truly notable titles to reach the West from the Middle East in 1989 included three new novels by major Israeli writers. In *For Every Sin* Aharon Appelfeld again explored the breakdown of the communal spirit shared by Holocaust survivors. David Grossman's *See Under: Love* is the tale of a Holocaust survivor, but it is also a challenging and intricately constructed work that interweaves "borrowed" Hebrew adventure stories and an account of the Polish writer Bruno Schulz' death at the hands of the Nazis in 1942, with a Virgilian first-person narrative by an "eternal" indestructible Jew who lived to tell of the death-camp experience. In *His Daughter,* Yoram Kaniuk follows a retired Sabra (Israeli-born) general on his desperate and danger-laden search for his soldier daughter; a hopelessness bordering on nihilism permeates the book, which is ultimately, in the words of one critic, "a condemnation of the Zionist ideal of the Sabra, the 'Jewish Aryan,' utterly self-sufficient, who knows he must fight to defend his people."

From the Arab world came *Leo Africanus* by the Francophone Lebanese author Amin Maalouf, a historical novel chronicling the first 40 years in the life of the 15th-century Andalusian Arab adventurer and scholar whose life brought him in contact with pirates and popes, vagabonds and kings.

Africa and the West Indies. Established African authors and newcomers offered a respectable set of works. Nigerian Nobel laureate Wole Soyinka issued a collection of recent essays titled *Art, Dialogue and Outrage.* The 1988 Kikuyu novel *Matagari* by Kenya's Ngugi wa Thiong'o made its first appearance in English. *To Every Birth Its Blood,* the first novelistic effort by noted South African poet Mongane Serote—finally available after being banned at its scheduled debut in 1981—movingly evokes the 1976 Soweto riots and their aftermath. Serote's compatriot, the poet-painter Breyten Breytenbach, offered the futuristic political novel *Memory of Snow and Dust.* Two newer writers to watch were Nigeria's Ben Okri and Zimbabwe's Charles Mungoshi, who had an impact with the story collections *Stars of the New Curfew* and *The Setting Sun and the Rolling World,* respectively. From Francophone Africa came *Before the Birth of the Moon* by Zaire's V. Y. Mudimbé and *Eve's Sleep* by Algeria's Mohammed Dib. The superb Caribbean poet-playwright Derek Walcott produced a book-length narrative poem titled *Omeros,* recasting Homer's *Odyssey* from the standpoint of the Antillean-African experience.

Asia and India. It was a rich year for Asian literature. From China, several younger writers made their "debuts" in the West. *The August Sleepwalker* introduced the remarkable underground verse of Bei Dao, one of the most gifted poets to emerge from the upheavals of the 1970s and 1980s. The stories in Can Xue's *Dialogues in Paradise* present a world whose mix of realistic detail and nightmarish fantasy may recall several of Latin America's magic realists. Liu Zongren's *6 Tan-yin Alley* hews to a more strictly realistic autobiographical line in its account of daily life in a rundown Beijing neighborhood. Wang Anyi chronicles rural, agrarian life in the 1960s and 1970s in the novels *Baotown* and *The Flow,* the latter filtered through the consciousness of a middle-class, middle-aged woman much like the author herself. The late Ding Ling, often termed China's finest woman writer of the 20th century, was honored posthumously with selected writings in translation titled *I Myself Am a Woman.*

Japan's literary *eminence grise* Yasushi Inoue saw two works released to the West: the powerful novelette *The Hunting Gun* and the story collection *The Counterfeiter.* The Catholic novelist Shûsaku Endô had a similar "double" with the story collection *Foreign Studies* and the three-act play *The Golden Country,* about Christianity's slow progress in 17th-century Japan. The younger novelist Takeshi Kaikô showed a more modern, anguished sensibility in the stories of *Five Thousand Runaways.*

Mistaken Identity, the new novel by Nayantara Sahgal, considered by many to be India's finest woman novelist, explores the social and political upheavals that marked the end of the British raj. Anita Desai, perhaps even more well-known abroad than Sahgal, brought out the novel *Baumgartner's Bombay,* which tracks the peripatetic experiences of a shy, quintessential outsider from Nazi Germany to post-partition India. Several superb recent Hindi tales by Premchand at last were made accessible to the English-reading public in *Deliverance and Other Stories.* And finally, Bhisnam Sahni's bestselling Hindi novel *Tamas* likewise appeared in English translation, bringing to a worldwide audience its devastating account of the murderous 1947 partition riots in the Punjab.

WILLIAM RIGGAN, *"World Literature Today"*

AP/Wide World

Approximately two thirds of Los Angeles' schoolteachers were on the picket lines for ten days in May 1989. A three-year contract calling for a 24% pay increase ended their walkout.

LOS ANGELES

A scandal involving the mayor, a teachers' strike, finding a new Philharmonic director, and continuing problems in building a subway were some of the issues confronting Los Angeles in 1989. The massive earthquake that struck northern California in October had a ripple effect on Los Angeles' residents.

Mayor: Election and Scandal. Tom Bradley, mayor since 1973, was reelected to a fifth term in April in a turnout of only 17% of registered voters, the second lowest in city history. It escaped setting a record only because a single council seat was contested sharply.

The mayor received 52% of the vote in what had been expected to be only token opposition. During the campaign the mayor's relationship to two banks that did business with the city and had paid him fees was questioned. Previously the mayor had a reputation for great integrity but at least four city and three federal investigations were launched in 1989. Bradley, who turned 72 in December, denied any impropriety but City Attorney James K. Hahn filed a lawsuit calling for unspecified civil fines, though arguing that no criminal action was called for. Bradley's popularity dropped; only half of those who had voted for him said they would now. Investigations continued.

Schools: Election, Strike. In the low election turnout in April, union-endorsed candidates became a majority on the Board of Education. On May 25 two thirds of the city teachers ended a ten-day strike from which they gained a three-year contract and a 24% pay raise. This made their income the best among teachers in the area and caused a rush of applicants from other districts to fill Los Angeles vacancies.

Transportation. Metro Rail, the city subway under construction, was two years behind schedule and more than $135 million over budget in 1989, with discrepancies in accounting of at least $100 million. Complaints of poor management and too many cost overruns continued. The cost overruns especially troubled the money-short city council. The city is pledged to pay about 6% of the subway costs, which would run to more than $3.7 billion.

Mayor Bradley's plan to bar trucks from major streets during rush hours faced almost certain defeat or sharp curtailment in the state legislature. The plan was designed both to improve traffic flow and reduce air pollution.

Philharmonic. In a disagreement with the management, André Previn resigned in June as music director of the Los Angeles Philharmonic. After a search, he was succeeded by Esa-Pekka Salonen, 31, of Finland, a frequent guest conductor and the youngest music director in the orchestra's 70-year history.

Water. The city reached agreement with Inyo county concerning groundwater policy in the Owens valley, a matter of dispute for more than 70 years. The legislature also has agreed to help the city buy water to replace the flow from streams which empty into environmentally sensitive Mono Lake, another disputed site.

Crime. Narcotics-driven gang warfare continued without solution, especially in south central Los Angeles. All nine members of one of the county sheriff's four narcotics squads were suspended under the suspicion that they had stolen many thousands of dollars missing from money confiscated in drug raids. The McMartin Preschool child-molestation court case entered its third year, nearly exhausting the supply of juror substitutes. The defense rested in August. Richard Ramirez, 29, was convicted of being the "Night Stalker," and found guilty of 13 murders and 30 other felonies in the mid-1980s. Barry Minkow, 23, was sentenced to 25 years in prison for fraud, conspiracy, and money laundering in running a bogus carpet-cleaning firm. He was ordered to pay back $26 million to cheated investors.

CHARLES R. ADRIAN, *University of California*

LOUISIANA

A roller coaster ride of achievements and setbacks marked Gov. Charles E. "Buddy" Roemer's second year in office. The election to the state House of Representatives of David Duke, a former Ku Klux Klan (KKK) leader and American Nazi Party member, attracted nationwide attention in February just when the Harvard-educated Roemer was trying to change the state's poor image. Duke, who ran as a Republican, won a narrow victory in an almost all-white suburban district near New Orleans. He maintained he was for equal rights for all people but for special privileges for none.

Tax Restructuring. In the spring, state voters turned down a comprehensive tax-restructuring package backed strongly by Roemer. But in the fall, the voters approved key parts of a scaled-down version of the plan, including establishment of a trust fund to finance massive improvements to roads, bridges, and airports.

Roemer's original tax-reform plan would have cut sales and business taxes, raised income taxes, raised the gasoline tax to support transportation improvements, established a statewide property tax, and hiked vehicle license plate fees. The plan was presented as a package, requiring approval or rejection as a whole, but 55% of the 1 million who went to the polls voted no. The measure was supported by middle- and upper-income whites but blacks and blue-collar whites strongly opposed it. Ironically, Roemer contended lower-income groups would have benefited the most by the package. Failure of the tax plan, which had been hammered out in a special legislative session early in the year, left the state facing a massive operating deficit for fiscal 1989–90 and cast doubt on Roemer's political future.

In the legislature's regular session in July a compromise between the governor and lawmakers resulted in the extension of $350 million in sales taxes that had been scheduled to expire. Cuts totaling $180 million balanced a budget that, by year's end, actually showed a surplus because tax revenues proved to be higher than estimated.

AP/Wide World

In February 1989, David Duke, a former Ku Klux Klan leader, was elected narrowly to the Louisiana House of Representatives from the New Orleans suburb of Metairie.

LOUISIANA • Information Highlights

Area: 47,752 sq mi (123 677 km²).
Population (July 1, 1988): 4,408,000.
Chief Cities (July 1, 1986 est.): Baton Rouge, the capital, 241,130; New Orleans, 554,500; Shreveport, 220,380; Houma (1984 est.) 101,998.
Government (1989): *Chief Officers*—governor, Charles E. Roemer (D); lt. gov., Paul Hardy (R). *Legislature*—Senate, 39 members; House of Representatives, 105 members.
State Finances (fiscal year 1988): *Revenue,* $7,845,000,000; *expenditure,* $8,252,000,000.
Personal Income (1988): $54,179,000,000; per capita, $12,292.
Labor Force (June 1989): *Civilian labor force,* 1,940,300; *unemployed,* 185,200 (9.5% of total force).
Education: *Enrollment* (fall 1987)—public elementary schools, 583,000; public secondary, 210,000; colleges and universities, 173,229. *Public school expenditures* (1987-88), $2,237,500,000 ($2,966 per pupil).

Some state officials continued to express concern that Louisiana still had not dealt with its need to restructure tax laws, particularly in light of the constitutional provision that exempts homes assessed at $75,000 or less from paying property taxes.

When voters got a chance to vote on separate parts of a scaled-down tax-reform plan in the fall, they approved a gasoline tax hike to set up the transportation trust fund and a separate plan using oil and gas revenues to set up a fund to help protect Louisiana's rapidly eroding coastal wetlands. The state is losing hundreds of acres of marshland a year to coastal erosion. One of the bigger surprises of the referendum was the approval of an increase in the $3 fee for automobile license plates, which had remained unchanged since 1940.

Voted down were a proposal to create black majority districts for the state's district, appeal, and supreme court judges, and a proposal to allow local governments to raise property taxes without voter approval.

Legislature. Legislative acts in 1989 included tougher penalties for drug offenses and for crimes committed in satanic rituals. The legislature rejected attempts to end both affirmative action and set-aside programs for minorities, and once again killed all attempts to establish a state lottery or legalize casinos in New Orleans.

Prison Overcrowding. Louisiana also had to contend with chronic overcrowding of state prisons and parish jails in 1989. A federal court order set limits on the number of inmates who can be housed in existing state jails, resulting in thousands of inmates being released from the New Orleans parish jails before their times were up. However, New Orleans voters turned down a local proposition to raise taxes to build more jails.

Shrimpers vs. TEDs. An environmental issue of note was the strong opposition by Louisiana shrimpers to turtle excluder devices (TEDs), which are required by the federal government to prevent endangered sea turtles from becoming snared in shrimp nets. Shrimpers vowed to fight the use of the devices, which they said cause the loss of most of their catch. The Coast Guard said it would enforce the law. Meanwhile, U.S. congressmen from Louisiana tried but failed to get the law changed.

JOSEPH W. DARBY III, *"The Times Picayune"*

MAINE

There were strong signals during 1989 that Maine's rates of economic growth were in transition from annual increases averaging 10% to a more moderate 6 to 8%. On election day, November 8, Maine voters approved a nonbinding initiative to ban cruise missile test flights over the state.

The Legislature and the Economy. In response to the fiscal change of pace, Gov. John R. McKernan trimmed his $3 billion 1990–91 budget by some $66 million, a move that set the stage for a protracted battle between the Republican chief executive and a Maine legislature controlled by Democratic majorities in both the House and Senate. As a result of the standoff, the 114th legislative session was pushed ten days beyond its statutory deadline and final debates were marked by bitter partisan acrimony. After adjournment, however, both the governor and lawmakers took pride in the passage of landmark solid-waste-disposal measures that included comprehensive recycling regulations and strict controls over the siting of new landfills.

While the state's fiscal plans took a turn toward the prudent, personal income continued to stay healthy. "Income is up close to 96% of the national average," Sherwood reported, "while unemployment continues low, less than 5% statewide. And Maine's economic base continues to diversify."

President Bush and Tourism. Although there is no precise data available on the ripple effect of presidential visits, the recurrent appearances of George Bush and his family at Walker's Point in Kennebunkport dominated Maine's summer headlines. The president's leisure activities, his accompanying large retinue of staff and national press corps, and the stress that providing first-family security placed on the Kennebunkport municipal budget kept the summer White House on the state's front pages from June through September.

But bumper-to-bumper traffic jams in Kennebunkport's Dock Square were not an accurate indicator of tourist traffic in the rest of the state. Turnpike and motel surveys revealed a lower-than-anticipated volume of summer visitors, with some locations reporting business down as much as 10% from the 1988 season. However, for the first time in its history, Acadia National Park reported its 1 millionth annual visitor before August.

Lobster. For both seasonal vacationers and year-round residents, the summer was a lobster-lovers' bonanza. A market glut drove lobster prices to the lowest level in years, a situation which prompted most of the state's lobstermen to keep their boats in port for almost a week. President Bush responded by meeting with Canadian Prime Minister Brian Mulroney to try to negotiate trade agreements that would hike the low price of Canadian lobsters to U.S. levels, but the conference failed to resolve the international imbalance.

The Future. Yet such economic issues, according to a report issued in September by the Commission on Maine's Future, soon would be overshadowed by other concerns. "As Maine approaches the year 2000," said panel chairwoman Annette Anderson, "the focus of the debate over growth will shift more and more toward environmental considerations." Meanwhile, the Land For Maine's Future Board announced it had purchased 81 waterfront acres (32.8 ha) from the Pittson Company in Eastport for a state park, at a location Pittson once had planned for an oil refinery.

JOHN N. COLE, *Founder, "Maine Times"*

MAINE • Information Highlights

Area: 33,265 sq mi (86 156 km²).
Population (July 1, 1988): 1,205,000.
Chief Cities (1980 census): Augusta, the capital, 21,819; Portland, 61,572; Lewiston, 40,481; Bangor, 31,643.
Government (1989): *Chief Officers*—governor, John R. McKernan, Jr. (R); secretary of state, G. William Diamond (D). *Legislature*—Senate, 33 members; House of Representatives, 151 members.
State Finances (fiscal year 1988): *Revenue,* $2,909,000,000; *expenditure,* $2,500,000,000.
Personal Income (1988): $18,206,000,000; per capita, $15,106.
Labor Force (June 1989): *Civilian labor force,* 619,900; *unemployed,* 23,500 (3.8% of total force).
Education: *Enrollment* (fall 1987)—public elementary schools, 145,000; public secondary, 66,000; colleges and universities, 47,554. *Public school expenditures* (1987-88), $869,406,000 ($4,232 per pupil).

Malaysia's Communist Party leader Chin Peng meets with reporters in Thailand prior to signing an agreement formally ending a 41-year-old insurgency.

AP/Wide World

MALAYSIA

After two years of infighting and legal challenges, the United Malays National Organization (UMNO) made concerted and largely successful efforts in 1989 to shore up internal rifts and regain its stature as Malaysia's dominant political party. The year also saw the election of a new king and strong economic growth.

Domestic Affairs. Amid mounting internal dissension, UMNO, the dominant party in Malaysia's ruling National Front coalition, was declared illegal in February 1988. Recast by Prime Minister Mahathir bin Mohamad as UMNO (Baru), the party by late 1989 appeared to have patched up differences and restored much of its previous dominance. From late 1988 to the fall of 1989, Mahathir's coalition won five out of seven legislative by-elections. Even so, the newly formed opposition alliance, the Muslim Unity Front, could pose a challenge.

The healing process was hastened by the return to the ruling party of former Deputy Prime Minister Musa Hitan in late January 1989, even as Mahathir lay in the hospital, recovering from coronary bypass surgery. In late August, Mahathir informed his cabinet of the appointment of Musa as a United Nations special envoy.

Just days before Musa's announcement of his return to UMNO, Malaysian authorities had released former Democratic Action Party (DAP) deputy chairman Karpal Singh, who had been held since October 1987 under the controversial Internal Security Act (ISA). Soon thereafter, DAP parliamentary opposition leader Lim Kit Siang, the last detainee of the 106 initially held, was released. The act was amended by Parliament in June to remove the power of judicial review in ISA cases.

At a March meeting of the nine Malay sultans in Kuala Lumpur, Sultan Azlan Shah of Perak state was elected Malaysia's ninth king. Under the constitution, the kingship is rotated every five years among the nine state sultans.

In December guerrillas of the Malaysian Communist Party signed two cease-fire agreements, one with Malaysia and one with Thailand. The agreements brought to an end an insurgency, begun in 1948 when the British ruled what was then the colony of Malaya, that had cost thousands of lives.

Economy. As the year progressed, forecasts of more than 7% growth in Malaysia's gross domestic product (GDP) appeared to be on target. The expansion, moreover, was fueled largely by an increase in domestic demand. Although prices for Malaysia's major exports—rubber, timber, cocoa, tin, and petroleum—remained strong and the nation's balance of payments remained in surplus, rapid increases in disposable income and domestic consumption were the driving force. Foreign investments continued to pour in, but domestic investment kept pace.

Nonetheless, competition from other Asian nations could challenge Malaysia's $3 billion electronics industry. Some foreign companies have begun looking elsewhere because of concerns over the government's New Economic Policy (NEP), which sometimes has proved

MALAYSIA • Information Highlights

Official Name: Malaysia.
Location: Southeast Asia.
Area: 127,317 sq mi (329 750 km²).
Population (mid-1989 est.): 17,400,000.
Chief City (1980 census): Kuala Lumpur, the capital, 919,610.
Government: *Head of state,* Sultan Azlan Shah, king (elected March 1989). *Head of government,* Mahathir bin Mohamad, prime minister (took office July 1981). *Legislature*—Parliament: Dewan Negara (Senate) and Dewan Ra'ayat (House of Representatives).
Monetary Unit: Ringgit (Malaysian dollar) (2.663 ringgits equal U.S.$1, July 1989).
Economic Index (1988): *Consumer Prices* (1980 = 100), all items, 130.0; food, 126.4.

troublesome for multinational corporations needing highly skilled labor. Adopted in 1970 to redress racial imbalances, the 20-year program established rules to increase ethnic Malay participation in commerce. Although NEP was set to expire in 1990, a second NEP appeared imminent.

Foreign Affairs. On March 13, Malaysia joined with the five other members of the Association of Southeast Asian Nations (ASEAN) in adopting new restrictions on Vietnamese refugees seeking asylum. Five days earlier, at least 130 Vietnamese boat people were drowned when their fishing vessel collided with a Japanese tanker off the east coast of Malaysia.

Improved ties with Singapore were signaled by an agreement in March to hold joint infantry training in each other's territory.

The biennial Commonwealth Heads of Government conference was held in Malaysia, October 18–24.

JEFFREY H. HACKER, *Free-lance Writer*

MANITOBA

In 1989, Manitoba increased its opposition to proposed changes in Canada's constitution, and investigated police misconduct charges.

The Meech Lake Accord. The 1988 provincial election left Manitoba without a majority government, at a time when the legislature was about to decide on the Meech Lake constitutional accord. For the accord to pass into law, it needed the approval of each provincial legislature by June 1990. Many Manitobans opposed the accord, reflecting the split over official languages which was a major political issue in the province during the 1980s. Other opponents of the accord, mostly Liberals, thought it weakened the federal government.

In October 1988, Premier Gary Filmon introduced the accord in the legislature, and supported it reluctantly. However, before the legislature could debate the accord, the Quebec provincial government overrode English-language privileges in that province. Filmon withdrew the bill from the legislature the next day.

The opposition Liberal leader, Sharon Carstairs, opposed the accord strongly and was able to halt its approval until the minority Progressive Conservative (PC) government agreed to a series of public hearings. Those hearings took up most of early 1989 and showed almost unanimous opposition to the accord. On Oct. 23, 1989, the Meech Lake task force recommended major changes to the accord. The chief change suggested was the removal of the veto power of Quebec (and other provinces). At a federal-provincial conference in November 1989, other opponents appeared, primarily Newfoundland, which lessened the chances of the accord becoming law.

MANITOBA • Information Highlights

Area: 250,946 sq mi (649 950 km^2).
Population (June 1989): 1,083,300.
Chief Cities (1986 census): Winnipeg, the capital, 594,551; Brandon, 38,708; Thompson, 14,701.
Government (1989): *Chief Officers*—lt. gov., George Johnson; premier, Gary Filmon (Progressive Conservative). *Legislature*—Legislative Assembly, 57 members.
Provincial Finances (1989–90 fiscal year budget): *Revenues,* $4,713,000,000; *expenditures,* $4,800,-000,000.
Personal Income (average weekly earnings, June 1989): $446.31.
Labor Force (August 1989, seasonally adjusted): *Employed* workers, 15 years of age and over, 505,000; *Unemployed,* 6.8%.
Education (1989–90): *Enrollment*—elementary and secondary schools, 219,090 pupils; postsecondary—universities, 19,830; community colleges, 3,750.
(All monetary figures are in Canadian dollars.)

Charges Against Police. In another series of public hearings, the Aboriginal Justice Inquiry investigated charges of police cover-ups in the deaths of two Manitobans, J. J. Harper, a native leader, and Helen Betty Osborne. Harper was shot by a police constable in 1988, while Osborne had been murdered in 1974. The inquiry, conducted by two justices, one of them native, attracted wide attention from Canada's native community and strong opposition from several police forces.

In May 1989 the Winnipeg police association temporarily halted the inquiry by saying that the order-in-council setting it up had been passed in English only, and that it was therefore unconstitutional. The appeal court agreed with this position, but the provincial government then reestablished the inquiry by statute in both English and French. Police opposition to the inquiry remained strong, and the officer in charge of Winnipeg's police investigating unit shot himself the morning before he was to testify before the inquiry. The inquiry continued as the year drew to a close.

Liberal Resurgence. In November 1988, Manitoba showed a strong shift away from the Progressive Conservatives of Brian Mulroney, particularly in Winnipeg, where the Liberals picked up five seats, rising from one to five. The federal budget, announced a few months later, made heavy cuts in spending on military bases in Manitoba, and virtually dismantled passenger rail service. Critics tied the antigovernment vote to these fiscal cuts.

Other. The federal government opened up a large site at the junction of Assiniboine and Red rivers, and set up a national historic park. Southern Manitoba recovered somewhat from the drought of 1988, but serious forest fires took place in northern and eastern Manitoba. An estimated 6.7 million acres (2.7 million ha) of timber were destroyed.

MICHAEL KINNEAR
The University of Manitoba

A bridge under construction on Maryland's Route 198 collapsed early on the morning of August 31, injuring at least nine.

AP/Wide World

MARYLAND

The courts reversed convictions against former Gov. Marvin Mandel and five codefendants on charges of racketeering and mail fraud. The convictions in 1977 stemmed from a scheme to arrange additional racing dates for Maryland's Marlboro Race Track in exchange for gifts worth more than $380,000. In the reversal, the court found that the defendants were prosecuted under the wrong criminal statute; it did not deal with the question of guilt or innocence.

Meanwhile, a three-judge panel of the 4th U.S. Circuit Court of Appeals upheld the convictions of former Maryland legislators Clarence M. Mitchell III and Michael B. Mitchell for trying to obstruct a U.S. congressional investigation of the Wedtech Corporation.

Prison Expansion. In an atmosphere of public outrage over crimes committed by inmates who had escaped or been released on furlough, the legislature appropriated more than $50 million to expand and replace the state's jails and prisons. Controls were tightened at the largely autonomous Patuxent Institution—where selected criminals with serious psychiatric problems had been able to win release on parole or furlough through an unusual program of treatment and incentives. In a related matter, three high-level corrections officials resigned from their posts in 1989 after drawing public criticism. Included were State Commissioner of Corrections Fred E. Jordan, Jr., Patuxent Institution Director Norma Gluckstern, and Terrie C. Chavis, the warden of the medium-security Maryland House of Corrections.

Gun Control. In its first year of operation, a new commission approved the sale of 677 types of handguns in Maryland, but disallowed several dozen other types. The commission was set up through 1988 General Assembly legislation. Gun enthusiasts brought the legislation to referendum, but it was upheld by the electorate and would take effect on Jan. 1, 1990.

Education. Maryland public higher education, in the throes of a major reorganization ordered by the state legislature, was shaken by the resignations of several high-level administrators. Peter F. O'Malley, chairman of the Board of Regents for the 11-campus state university system, resigned after clashes with two other officials. John S. Toll, the chancellor of the College Park campus, and Augustus A. White 3d, the newly appointed president of a Baltimore campus, resigned first.

On the public-school level, a new superintendent started a reorganization of the Baltimore city school system; at least 130 administrators were dismissed.

Economy and Other News. Baltimore Federal Financial, the state's third-largest savings and loan institution, joined four other thrifts across the nation taken over by federal regulators the day after President Bush announced a complex, multibillion-dollar plan for bailing out the industry and overhauling the regulatory system.

Agriculture officials estimated at least $10 million in crop losses, as 1989 brought in a severe April frost and unusually wet spring, after three consecutive drought years.

Acquisition of land and demolition of buildings began as the first steps in construction of a $264 million baseball/football stadium complex near the Baltimore harbor.

MARYLAND • Information Highlights

Area: 10,460 sq mi (27 092 km^2).
Population (July 1, 1988): 4,622,000.
Chief Cities (1980 census): Annapolis, the capital, 31,740; Baltimore (July 1, 1986 est.), 752,800; Rockville, 43,811.
Government (1989): *Chief Officers*—governor, Donald Schaefer (D); lt. gov., Melvin A. Steinberg (D). *General Assembly*—Senate, 47 members; House of Delegates, 141 members.
State Finances (fiscal year 1988): *Revenue*, $11,942,000,000; *expenditure*, $9,442,000,000.
Personal Income (1988): $90,071,000,000; per capita $19,487.
Labor Force (June 1989): *Civilian labor force*, 2,566,800; *unemployed*, 111,100 (4.3% of total force).
Education: *Enrollment* (fall 1987)—public elementary schools, 473,000; public secondary, 211,000; colleges and universities, 239,362. *Public school expenditures* (1987–88), $3,060,758,000 ($4,500 per pupil).

The U.S. Nuclear Regulatory Commission repeatedly cited Baltimore Gas and Electric Co. for improper or unsafe practices at its Calvert Cliffs nuclear-power plant, which was closed for most of the year for repairs.

PEGGY CUNNINGHAM, *"The Evening Sun"*

MASSACHUSETTS

In 1988, Gov. Michael S. Dukakis campaigned for the presidency on the slogan, "The Massachusetts miracle," but a major slump in the state's economy in 1989 had some critics talking about "The Massachusetts debacle."

Revenue Shortfall. The first signs that all was not well came early in the year when state revenue projections fell far short of what was required to avoid a huge deficit. The revenue shortfall continued, becoming an embarrassing failure for an administration that had prided itself on competent fiscal management.

In January, Governor Dukakis asked for a $604 million tax hike. Failing to get legislative agreement on taxes, in July, Dukakis called for a $491 million spending cut along with a temporary 15% income-tax increase. Despite the fiscal plans announced in July, major bond companies reduced the state's bond rating—a blow to Dukakis, who long had pointed with pride to the state's favorable rating. These events set off an acrimonious debate about how to make up the growing revenue shortfall. Virtually every branch of the state government was affected. Plans to cut public higher education drew particularly strong opposition. The newly appointed head of the State Board of Regents of Higher Education, former U.S. Sen. Paul Tsongas (D), publicly broke with Dukakis on the issue. Two multibillion-dollar public-works projects—the court-ordered cleanup of Boston harbor and the reconstruction of the Central Artery through Boston—were jeopardized by the state's fiscal problems.

MASSACHUSETTS • Information Highlights

Area: 8,284 sq mi (21 456 km²).
Population (July 1, 1988): 5,889,000.
Chief Cities (July 1, 1986 est.): Boston, the capital, 573,600; Worcester, 157,700; Springfield, 149,410.
Government (1989): *Chief Officer*—governor, Michael S. Dukakis (D); lt. gov., Evelyn F. Murphy (D). *Legislature*—Senate, 40 members; House of Representatives, 160 members.
State Finances (fiscal year 1988): *Revenue,* $14,721,000,000; *expenditure,* $15,387,000,000.
Personal Income (1988): $122,593,000,000; per capita, $20,816.
Labor Force (June 1989): *Civilian labor force,* 3,223,100; *unemployed,* 126,500 (3.9% of total force).
Education: *Enrollment* (fall 1987)—public elementary schools, 565,000; public secondary, 260,000; colleges and universities, 423,916. *Public school expenditures* (1987–88), $3,938,582,000 ($4,753 per pupil).

The state's fiscal crisis was related to a downturn in major sectors of the once-booming economy. Hardest hit was the keystone of the state's past growth—the high-technology industries. Most of the major computer-related companies, such as Wang Laboratories, Digital Equipment Corp., Data General, and Prime Computer, suffered either losses or large declines in profits. Many of the firms were experiencing product development and marketing problems which placed them at a competitive disadvantage with high-tech firms on the West Coast and in Asia. An estimated 10,000 of the 321,000 high-tech workers in the state suffered layoffs. There were also declines in the manufacturing sector. In August the state's only auto-assembly plant, the General Motors Corp. factory in Framingham, was shut down.

The service sector of the economy, the fastest-growing area in recent years, remained in good shape. State unemployment continued to stay well behind the national rate. This led many economists to predict an economic rebound in the near future.

Politics. The main victim of the bad economic news was Governor Dukakis. His popularity in the state, at an all-time high when he accepted the Democratic nomination for president, plummeted steadily throughout the year. By September only one third of registered voters in a statewide poll gave the governor a favorable rating. Some political advisers questioned the wisdom of Dukakis having declared he would not seek another term as governor soon after he was defeated for the presidency. Meanwhile, Dukakis' wife, Kitty, was hospitalized for several weeks for treatment of alcohol addiction. At the start of his presidential campaign she had revealed a long-time addiction to amphetamines.

Dukakis' decision not to run fueled the contest to see who would be his successor. Among Democrats, Lt. Gov. Evelyn Murphy led a wide field of contenders. Republicans have not held the governor's office since January 1975 and their prospects seemed the brightest in many years. Former U.S. Attorney William Weld emerged as the Republican front-runner.

Robert Q. Crane, state treasurer since 1965, announced in October that he would not seek reelection and state House Speaker George Keverian immediately declared for the post. This move in turn may ignite a battle for the powerful House speakership. In other major political departures, U.S. Attorney Frank L. McNamara, Jr., resigned on January 30 after a highly controversial and politically charged two-year term as the top federal law-enforcement officer in New England. His successor was Boston attorney Wayne Budd.

In the fall Massachusetts became the second state to pass a law prohibiting discrimination against homosexuals.

HARVEY BOULAY, *Rogerson House*

AP/Wide World

Louis Sullivan (left), secretary of the U.S. Department of Health and Human Services, and Dr. Anthony S. Fauci, director of the National Institute of Allergy and Infectious Diseases at the department, announced on August 18 that part of a trial for the AIDS drug AZT was being ended early by the government. The incomplete study showed that AZT significantly slowed the disease in some patients. The drug now is available on a prescription basis to any AIDS sufferer.

MEDICINE AND HEALTH

Thanks to improved health care, more exercise, and improved diet, Americans are living longer than ever before. But daunting inequities continue to exist. The National Center for Health Statistics reported a widening gap in life expectancies between blacks and whites. White children born in 1987 (the most recent year for which data have been analyzed) could expect to live an average of 75.6 years; black children could expect to live 69.4 years. The three chief factors in this gap were higher rates among blacks for Acquired Immune Deficiency Syndrome (AIDS), drug abuse, and infant mortality—which is more than twice as high for black infants as for whites.

Pediatrics. The lack of adequate health care for American children was called "a national disgrace" by Dr. Donald Schiff, president of the American Academy of Pediatrics. The infant mortality rate in 1987 was 10.1 per 1,000 live births, ranking the United States 22d among Western industrial nations and behind such places as Singapore and Hong Kong. Schiff pointed out that one of every ten children under age four had not seen a physician within the previous year, and one of every three poor children had not been immunized by age two against measles, mumps, or rubella.

Because many young children had not received the complete basic series of immunizations, some childhood diseases that had leveled off or declined became resurgent. The number of measles cases jumped to a nine-year high during 1989, with the great majority of the cases occurring among young children. Authorities blamed the resurgence on the failure of many parents to get their children immunized. Also, studies have shown that the effectiveness of the measles vaccine may decrease over time. Therefore, the Federal Centers for Disease Control recommended a second dose of vaccine for children who were beginning kindergarten or the first grade.

AIDS. Figures released in late 1989 revealed that more than 65,000 Americans had died of AIDS since the first deaths were recorded in the late 1970s. The disease continued to spread, infecting ever-broadening groups of the population. Data reported in October indicated that the AIDS virus was spreading rapidly among some groups of teenagers. In cities such as New York, as many as 1% of teenagers are believed to be infected. Among this age group, the disease often is transmitted through heterosexual intercourse, and equal numbers of boys and girls are infected.

Although there is still no cure for AIDS, drugs are reducing symptoms and prolonging lives. In September the Food and Drug Administration (FDA) approved distribution of dideoxyinosine (DDI), a still-experimental drug that in early tests appeared to limit multiplication of the AIDS virus. DDI continued to undergo clinical trials, however, to determine its safety, and there was evidence that it causes severe side effects at high doses. This was the first time that the FDA allowed distribution of a drug so early in its testing. The step was taken in response to lobbying by AIDS patients and their advocates.

DDI became the second drug approved to combat the AIDS virus in the United States. Azidothymidine (AZT), the only AIDS drug that actually has been licensed, has been found to prolong and improve the quality of some patients' lives, though other patients do not appear to be helped or cannot take the drug because of severe side effects. AZT was extremely expensive, costing patients with advanced cases of AIDS about $8,000 a year. Protests against the drug's manufacturer, Burroughs Wellcome Company, led to a 20% decrease in the cost.

A study conducted by the National Institute of Allergy and Infectious Diseases found that AZT also can help AIDS sufferers who have not yet developed symptoms of the disease. Subjects of the study who took AZT were half as likely to develop symptoms as subjects who took a placebo. Secretary of Health and Human Services Louis W. Sullivan called the report "a turning point in the battle to change AIDS from a fatal disease to a treatable one." At least 600,000 Americans who are infected with the AIDS virus but still are healthy are likely to benefit from early treatment. Finding and treating these people could cost $5 billion or more a year, however.

Cancer. For the first time in history, the estimated number of newly diagnosed cancer cases in the United States in one year topped 1 million. The projection, made by the American Cancer Society, was coupled with a projected 502,000 cancer deaths for 1989. Leading the list was lung cancer, with 155,000 new cases and 142,000 deaths. Other major categories included colon-rectal cancer, with 151,000 new cases and 61,000 deaths; female breast cancer, with 142,000 new cases and 43,000 deaths; and prostate cancer, with 103,000 new cases and 28,500 deaths.

Melanoma, a potentially fatal form of skin cancer, continued to increase among whites at "an alarming rate," said Dr. Charles M. Balch of the University of Texas. The number of melanomas diagnosed in the United States increased from 14,100 in 1980 to an estimated 27,000 in 1989—a jump of 94%.

Considerable evidence shows that intense exposure to ultraviolet light, which is present in sunlight and in the lights used in tanning salons, plays a central role in the development of melanoma. The young are particularly susceptible, and health professionals urged that special precautions be taken to protect children from damaging exposures to sunlight. A team headed by Dr. Martin A. Weinstock of Brown University found that severe, blistering sunburns during childhood and adolescence were more than twice as likely to lead to skin cancer as severe sunburns later in life.

Researchers reported contradictory findings concerning the possibility of a link between birth-control pills and breast cancer. Dr. Samuel Shapiro of Boston University and his colleagues compared breast cancer incidence in more than 400 women who used birth-control pills with the incidence in more than 400 women who did not. They found that the longer women took the pill, the greater their risk of getting breast cancer. Women who used the pill for ten years or more were four times as likely to get breast cancer as women who did not use the pill. Dr. Clifford R. Kay and others at the Royal College of General Practitioners in Manchester, England, surveyed 46,000 women and found that those who used the pill were more than three times as likely to develop breast cancer in their early 30s as women who did not take the pill. Two studies, one from Sweden, the other from England, found a marked increase in breast cancer among women who began taking the pill as teenagers. But a ten-year Harvard University study of some 118,000 women found that women who did not begin using birth-control pills until they were in their mid-20s did not have a greater incidence of breast cancer.

Birth-control pills contain a synthetic form of estrogen, the female sex hormone. Another synthetic formulation of estrogen is used to treat the symptoms of menopause, a period during which a woman's ovaries cease to make estrogen. Also, some older women are put on lifelong estrogen therapy to help prevent heart disease and osteoporosis. To cut estrogen's long-recognized ability to increase the risk of uterine cancer, the estrogen often is used in combination with progestin, another female hormone. However, according to a study involving 23,000 women by researchers at University Hospital in Uppsala, Sweden, the rate of breast cancer among women taking both estrogen and progestin was four times as high as the rate among women who had no hormone treatments. Women being treated with estrogen alone had double the risk of those receiving no treatments.

Heart Disease. Dr. Thomas Pollare and others at the University of Uppsala reported that diuretics—the so-called "water pills" used to treat high blood pressure—can cause chemical changes that increase people's risk of heart attacks. Hydrochlorothiazide, a type of diuretic, was found to increase blood cholesterol levels and decrease tissue sensitivity to insulin, both factors that make people more susceptible to heart disease.

In addition to diuretics, three other classes of drugs generally are recommended for early treatment of high blood pressure: ACE inhibitors, beta blockers, and calcium channel blockers. The Swedish scientists found that captopril, a type of ACE inhibitor, reduced cholesterol levels and made body tissues more sensitive to insulin, therefore proving captopril's worth as a heart medicine.

People whose treatment for high blood pressure results in either a small or large decrease in blood pressure are more likely to have heart attacks than people whose treatment results in moderate declines. (A drop of between seven and 17 millimeters in the patients' diastolic blood pressure—the lower of two numbers recorded in a blood-pressure measurement—was considered moderate.) Dr. Michael H. Alderman of the Albert Einstein

Medical College of Yeshiva University, who headed the team that reported these findings, suggested that a large reduction in blood pressure may reduce the flow of blood too much in patients with hardening of the arteries, thereby depriving the heart muscles of oxygen and nutrients.

A study directed by Dr. Neil Schulman of Emory University reported that a simple blood test is a very accurate predictor of mortality rates for patients with high blood pressure. The study found that people with elevated levels of creatinine in the blood were five times as likely to die of heart attacks or strokes than people with low creatinine levels. Creatinine is produced during the normal breakdown of muscle tissue, then carried by the blood to the kidneys, which excrete it through the urine. High creatinine levels indicate that the kidneys are not removing the substance from the body. The study noted that creatinine levels were a more reliable predictor of mortality rates for people with high blood pressure than such factors as diabetes, smoking, elevated cholesterol levels, or a history of heart trouble.

Hepatitis B. Although hepatitis B is much more common elsewhere in the world, its incidence in the United States jumped 50% during the 1980s. Some 300,000 Americans became infected annually with the virus. Most experience flu-like symptoms for several days or weeks, then recover. But the disease can cause liver damage, including cancer, and death: 5,000 people die of hepatitis B each year in the United States. About 6% to 10% of the people who get the disease become chronic carriers, capable of transmitting the virus through blood or sexual contact. As a result, the highest-risk groups for the disease are intravenous drug users, heterosexuals with multiple partners, and homosexual men; together, these groups account for 59% of all cases.

Two hepatitis B vaccines are available in the United States, but only about 2.5 million Americans have been vaccinated. Some experts suggest that the vaccine should be included with the shots routinely given to all infants, even though it is relatively expensive.

Pregnant women are screened routinely for evidence of the hepatitis B virus, and newborns of mothers with the disease are recommended for vaccination. A study under the direction of Dr. Adele Franks of the Centers for Disease control found, however, that among refugee families from Southeast Asia, nearly half of the children with the virus did not have an infected mother. The study concluded that the children caught the disease from other children, possibly through biting or scratching.

Alzheimer's Disease. According to a study conducted by researchers at Harvard University Medical School, Alzheimer's disease strikes twice as many elderly people as previously estimated. Alzheimer's is a progressive disease that destroys brain cells, causing memory loss, personality changes, impaired reasoning ability, and other symptoms. The study found that 10.3% of the people over age 65 and 47.2% over age 85 who lived in East Boston had mental problems that most likely were caused by Alzheimer's. If the data is confirmed, that would raise the estimated number of Alzheimer's cases in the United States to 4 million.

Organ Transplants. On November 27 surgeons at the University of Chicago Medical Center transplanted a portion of liver from a live donor, Teresa Smith, into her 21-month-old daughter, Alyssa, who was born with a rare liver disease. Both recovered well after the operation. Although four previous live-donor transplants had been performed, this was the first U.S. operation and the first one performed on a young patient before she became seriously ill. Because livers from cadavers are a rare commodity, liver transplants are performed routinely only on the illest patients, and half of the 700 babies born with liver disease die while waiting for an appropriate donor. The liver is a good candidate for this type of transplant because of its regenerative powers—the 40% portion removed from Mrs. Smith was expected to grow back and Alyssa's transplanted liver would grow as she grows.

An estimated 30,000 organ transplants are performed throughout the world each year. One of the major factors limiting success of the procedure is rejection of a donor organ by the patient's body. To prevent or diminish the rejection phenomenon, an immunosuppressive drug called cyclosporine generally is used. But cyclosporine can cause such side effects as high blood pressure, kidney damage, tremors, and swollen gums.

A team headed by Dr. Thomas E. Starzl of the University of Pittsburgh reported the discovery of a new drug that appeared to be extremely successful in preventing the rejection of transplanted organs. Called FK-506, the drug is derived from a soil fungus. Of the first 45 people taking FK-506, only one experienced a rejection reaction (which was controlled quickly with other drugs). When administered in capsule form, FK-506 seemed to cause few side effects. It also seemed to lower blood-cholesterol levels, offering promise of preventing a form of hardening of the arteries that causes the death of many transplant recipients.

Statistics gathered by the United Network for Organ Sharing, which administers the national transplant network, showed that white males give and receive the majority of transplanted organs in the United States. In 1988, 83.2% of the donors were white, and 62% were male. Whites received 88.9% of the transplanted hearts, 85.9% of livers, 71% of kidneys, and 97.6% of pancreases. Men got 79.2% of the hearts, 60.6% of kidneys, and 56.4% of pancreases. Liver-transplant recipients were divided almost evenly between males and females. The racial disparity is particularly acute in kidney transplants, since blacks are three times as likely as whites to suffer kidney failure, due in large part to high blood pressure and other medical problems that affect blacks more than whites.

Drugs and Medications. A new drug called deprenyl, approved by the Food and Drug Administration (FDA) on June 7, appeared to slow the progress of Parkinson's disease, a degenerative neurological disorder suffered by some 400,000 Americans. Researchers at the California Parkinson's Foundation studied 54 patients in the early stages of the disease. Half the patients took deprenyl while the other half took a placebo, or inactive substance. The deprenyl group averaged 18 months before the onset of severe symptoms, as opposed to ten months in the control group. The drug also seemed to slow the progress of the disease thereafter. It was the first time that a drug appeared to slow the progress of a neurological disease. The re-

Recent Advances in Ophthalmology

As people age, their eyes undergo a variety of changes. Three of the most common changes are presbyopia, dry eyes, and the development of cataracts. Recent advances promise improved methods of preventing or treating each of these disorders.

Presbyopia, a form of farsightedness that generally begins at about age 40, is the most common vision change. The lens of the eye loses its elasticity, making it difficult to focus on objects close at hand. To compensate, people wear reading glasses or bifocal eyeglasses; contact lens users generally wear a distance lens in one eye and a near-vision lens in the other. Several types of bifocal contact lenses are available, but no one type yet has been accepted widely by wearers, and manufacturers are racing to develop products that will satisfy this large market. One design is like a bull's eye, with the distance prescription on the outside and the reading prescription at the center. Another has the distance prescription at the top and the reading prescription at the bottom. In 1989, Allergan Optical, a division of SmithKline Beckman Corporation, introduced Fresnel lenses, which are based on the same principle used in pocket magnifiers and the rearview mirrors of motor homes. Each lens is divided into concentric circles separated by ridged cuts that diffract light waves. The center of the lens focuses on distant objects; the circles on the periphery focus on near objects.

Dry eye disease is a second common eye ailment among people past 40. Afflicting about 10 million Americans, it is caused either by reduced tear production or increased tear evaporation. The result is irritation whenever the person blinks, plus a greater sensitivity to light. Most tear solutions currently on the market provide only limited relief, and prolonged use tends to exacerbate the condition. Researchers at the Eye Research Institute in Boston have developed a new electrolyte-based solution that maintains eye lubrication without undesirable side effects. It was expected to be commercially available by early 1990.

Cataracts, which are a clouding of the lens, afflict more than 1 million people in the United States each year. By age 70, most people have begun to develop cataracts, but the condition can develop at any age. High blood-sugar levels, sunlight, and eye injuries are known to cause cataracts. In 1989 researchers at Johns Hopkins University reported that cigarette smoking increases the risk of prematurely developing nuclear cataracts, a type of cataract that forms in the center of the lens. In a study of 838 men between ages 30 and 94, those who smoked were twice as likely to develop nuclear cataracts before age 70 as those who had quit smoking more than ten years previously. Because the risk decreased when the men stopped smoking, Dr. Sheila K. West, who headed the study, said this "suggests that their lenses may have recovered, that damage to the lens may be reversible."

An epidemiologic study conducted by James McD. Robertson and others at the University of Western Ontario suggests that people who take vitamin C and vitamin E supplements may reduce significantly their risk of getting cataracts. The study compared supplemental vitamin intake and other characteristics of 175 cataract patients over age 55 with 175 adults of similar age and sex who were cataract-free. People who took at least 400 international units (one regular capsule) of vitamin E each day had about 50% less risk of getting cataracts. People taking a minimum of 300 milligrams of vitamin C each day reduced their risk by 70%.

The results of two studies released in 1989 indicated that users of extended-wear contact lenses should remove and clean them daily, despite manufacturers' claims that they can be left in the eye for up to 30 days. Researchers found that extended-wear lens users are ten to 15 times more likely to develop a potentially sight-threatening eye infection, ulcerative keratitis, than are users of daily-wear soft lenses. The risk of infection increases with time.

JENNY TESAR

searchers stressed that their findings were "preliminary and in need of confirmation," saying that a new study involving 800 patients now under way and scheduled to be completed in late 1991 "should provide definitive evidence."

Alpha interferon, a protein manufactured in small quantities in the liver and in large quantities by genetically altered bacteria, has been found effective in combating the virus that causes hepatitis C. Two studies—one at the University of Florida in Gainesville, the other at the National Institute of Diabetes, Digestive, and Kidney Diseases in Bethesda, MD—indicate that interferon stops the virus from destroying liver cells. Hepatitis C, a chronic virus with flu-like symptoms, affects 3% to 7% of the population. Interferon is the first medication that has been found effective against any form of hepatitis. Researchers caution, however, that side effects such as hair loss and diminished white blood cell counts have been observed and that more studies are necessary to assess possible long-term side effects.

A study headed by Dr. Dale P. Sandler of the National Institute of Environmental Health Science found a statistical link between kidney disease and long-term daily use of acetaminophen, a popular painkiller that is the active ingredient in many nonprescription pain pills, including Tylenol, Anacin-3, and Datril. A comparison of 554 adults who had kidney disease and 516 other adults without kidney disease indicated that heavy, prolonged use of acetaminophen appeared to cause a threefold increase in the risk of kidney disease. The study also found that daily users of phenacetin, a chemical relative of acetaminophen, had five times the usual risk of kidney damage. Phenacetin was banned in the United States in 1983 following earlier reports of links to kidney disease and bladder cancer.

A report written by Richard P. Kusserow, inspector general of the Department of Health and Human Services, asserted widespread misuse of prescriptive medications intended for the elderly. Among the problems cited were inadequate training of doctors in geriatric medicine; clinical testing of medications on young adults, even with drugs designed to treat geriatric problems; and misuse by the elderly themselves, such as sharing medications with family members and overusing or underusing drugs. As a result of such problems, people age 60 or older account for 51% of deaths and 39% of hospitalizations from drug reactions, even though they comprise only 17% of the U.S. population.

A study conducted by the National Council on Patient Information found that young patients also jeopardized their health by using medications incorrectly. The study said that in any two-week period, some 13 million people under the age of 18 take medicines prescribed or recommended by a physician; 46% of these people either stop treatment too soon or take incorrect amounts of the drug. The study said that poor communication among health professionals, parents, and children contributed to the problem, as did inadequate monitoring by parents of their children's use of the medicines.

Diet and Exercise. The Centers for Disease Control estimated that 34 million American adults are overweight by 20% or more, giving the nation one of the highest populations of fat people in the world. Although obese people recognize their problem, the majority do not follow the standard recommendations for weight loss: eating fewer calories and increasing physical activity. As a result of their excessive weight, these people experience a disproportionate number of heart attacks and other life-shortening ailments.

Even moderate exercise can improve health dramatically, according to a study conducted by the Institute for Aerobics Research and the Cooper Clinic in Dallas. The researchers looked at the relationship between physical fitness and death rates in more than 13,000 men and women. The people were grouped into five categories, from least to most fit, based on their performance on a treadmill test. Death rates among the least fit (category 1) were more than three times those of the most fit (category 5). The biggest difference in rates occurred between categories 1 and 2. Dr. Steven N. Blair, who headed the study, said that switching from a sedentary life-style to one that included a brisk half-hour walk several times a week would be sufficient to move a person from category 1 to category 2.

A study of 750 women provided the best evidence to date that a diet high in calories, fats, and animal protein increases the risk of breast cancer. The study, headed by Dr. Paolo Toniolo of New York University Medical Center, found that women who consumed more than 2,700 calories a day had almost twice the risk of breast cancer as those who consumed less than 1,900 calories. And the women who ate the most fats and animal proteins were three times as likely to get breast cancer as the women whose diet was low in these foods.

Diets high in fat are related to high blood-cholesterol levels, which in turn increase the risk of heart disease. The Centers for Disease Control reported that an analysis of data gathered during a national health survey indicated that 60 million Americans 20 years and older—36% of adults—have blood cholesterol levels of at least 240 milligrams per 100 milliliters of blood serum, levels sufficiently high to make the individuals "candidates for medical advice and intervention." The rates were roughly equal for whites and blacks, and somewhat higher for men than for women.

JENNY TESAR
Medical and Science Writer

Allergies: Nothing to Sneeze At

Red, watery eyes . . . stuffed-up nose . . . constricted airways . . . hives and itchy rashes. These symptoms of allergies are experienced by some 50 million Americans, making allergies one of the nation's most prevalent health problems. Hay fever, eczema, poison ivy/oak/sumac, as well as reactions to certain foods and insect stings are some of the best-known allergies. Although asthma can be caused by allergies, it also can be nonallergic in origin. For this reason, asthma is discussed separately.

According to the National Institutes of Health, nearly 10% of visits to physicians are prompted by allergies. Each year, people spend millions of dollars for allergy drugs, plus an equal amount for physician services and hospital care. They lose a large number of workdays and school days because of the debilitating effects of allergies.

Nonetheless, there is good news for allergy sufferers. A better understanding of how allergies work, coupled with the development of more effective medications, has improved physicians' ability to control these diseases.

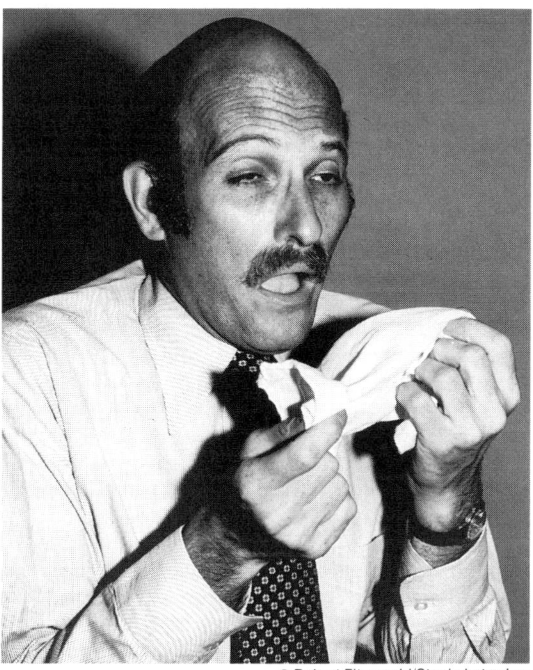

Causes and Detection. Hundreds of substances are potential causes of allergies. Pollens, mold spores, foods, animal saliva, and some drugs, including penicillin and aspirin, are among the most common. Others include insect stings, cosmetics and perfumes, air pollutants such as industrial vapors, chalk dust, and the smoke and carbon generated by fireplaces and stoves, and even Christmas trees.

The majority of allergies first appear during infancy or childhood. Although anyone may acquire an allergy, the odds increase if there are allergies in the family. People who have two allergic parents have a 30 to 60% chance of developing an allergy. Those who have just one allergic parent have a 25 to 40% chance. Grandparents as well as parents can transmit the tendency. But only the tendency, not the specific allergy, is inherited.

When susceptible people are exposed to the substance, called the allergen, the body's immune system recognizes the substance. The body begins to produce excessive amounts of antibodies to fight it—just as if the allergen were a disease-causing bacterium. The antibodies are of a type called immunoglobulin E, or IgE. A different kind of IgE is manufactured for each kind of allergen.

The IgE antibodies attach themselves to the surface of cells called mast cells, which are concentrated in the tissues of the eyes, nose, lungs, intestines, and skin. From the surface of the mast cells, the IgE antibodies capture passing allergen molecules. This in turn causes the mast cells to release histamine and other inflammatory chemicals. It is these chemicals that cause the allergic reaction. The exact type of reaction depends on how the allergen enters the body and how sensitive the person is to it. In people with seasonal hay fever the histamine irritates the mucous membranes in the nose, causing sneezing and itching. A person who is mildly sensitive to the sting of a wasp, bee, or hornet may develop a large swelling at the sting site. A moderately allergic person may experience widespread swellings or hives, faintness, dizziness, vomiting, or abdominal cramps. A highly allergic person may go into shock and die within minutes of being stung.

To determine the cause of a specific allergy, a physician—usually an allergist—interviews and examines the patient to determine the malady's history and symptoms. Skin tests are done to help determine the cause. This involves scratching, pricking, or injecting the skin surface with tiny quantities of suspected substances. If the person is sensitive to one of these, a swollen, red spot develops around the site where the substance was introduced. The greater the reaction, the greater is the person's sensitivity. However, skin sensitivity does not necessarily mean that the nose or lungs are also sensitive to the substance, hence the need for a detailed medical history and a skilled interpretation by the physician.

An alternative to skin tests is blood testing, using a method called RAST (radioallergosorbent testing). With this method a blood sample is taken and analyzed in a laboratory to discover the IgE molecules common to a given allergen. The major advantage of blood testing is that multiple substances can be tested with a single blood sample. However, blood tests are generally more expensive and less sensitive than skin tests.

A simple microscopic examination of the nasal mucus may be done to try to discover if the patient's runny nose is the result of an allergy or another cause, for example, a common cold. The allergist also may have the patient inhale controlled amounts of allergens to see what effect they have on the breathing process. Serious food allergies are detected by giving the patient small amounts of the suspected food substance. The dosage is increased until a definite reaction occurs. To discourage subjective responses, the food extract should be alternated with a placebo. This test should be performed in a hospital environment in case serious reaction occurs. To identify the common skin allergy, contact dermatitis, that is brought about by certain chemicals in cosmetics or other household items, a sticky patch containing possible irritants is placed on the skin. If a rash develops at the patch site within a few days, the test is positive and the allergen is determined.

Treatments. The first defense against allergic reactions is avoidance. Hay fever sufferers should spend more time indoors during pollen season. Windows should be closed, and air conditioners should be used. People who are allergic to cats and dogs should not have such pets. Those who are allergic to nickel should avoid watches and costume jewelry that contain this metal. Those allergic to foods or drugs should avoid them.

A broad range of medications are available today for the treatment of allergies. Some antihistamines are available over the counter; others require a physician's prescription. They block the action of histamine, thereby preventing sneezing, runny nose, and other symptoms. Until recently, however, antihistamines induced drowsiness and dryness of the air passages that often were worse than the disease. In 1985 a nonsedating antihistamine was approved for sale in the United States. Called terfenadine and marketed under the brand name Seldane, the drug is a large molecule that generally does not penetrate the so-called "blood-brain barrier" and therefore does not slow down brain activity or otherwise affect the central nervous system. A similar drug, astemizole or Hismanal, was introduced in 1989. It can be taken less frequently than Seldane.

Decongestants, taken orally or applied in the form of nose drops and sprays, are helpful in reducing the amount of mucus in the nose. These drugs, available over the counter, should be used sparingly, for no more than a few days in a row; overuse can cause chronic irritation and increase mucous discharge.

People with allergies to certain foods, drugs, and insect bites can be treated with an injection of epinephrine (adrenaline). Those so affected can carry a self-injecting dispenser of the hormone for emergency use. Steroid cremes are used to treat reactions to poison ivy/oak/sumac. It should be noted that they can harm the skin.

When allergies are extremely severe and interfere with breathing, they can be treated with bronchodilators. They are available in oral as well as inhaled forms and work by smoothing the muscle of the lungs' air passages. Another treatment for the severe allergy attack are the anti-inflammatory drugs, corticosteroids. If taken regularly, however, such drugs can produce dangerous side effects. Topical corticosteroids, which are sprayed into the nose or inhaled into the lungs and have fewer side effects, have been introduced recently.

Patients with allergies also may try immunotherapy—the so-called allergy shots. Introduced in 1911, immunotherapy remains controversial as physicians debate its effectiveness. In some cases, it provides dramatic relief while in other cases it does not work. In this procedure, the patient is given injections of the allergen to build up his or her natural defenses. At first, doses are very dilute, to avoid provoking an allergic reaction. The dosage is increased until the body has developed a protection against the pollen's action. People treated with shots should see improvement within one or, at most, two years. Experts recommend that shots that are not working should not be continued beyond two years. But if they do work, the patient should continue getting them for three to five years.

As scientists better understand the biochemistry of allergies and isolate factors that cause predisposition to the diseases, they will be able to develop better treatment methods. For instance, in 1989, researchers announced that they had determined the structure of the gene for a protein that binds IgE molecules to mast cells; this should aid the development of drugs that block the binding process.

JENNY TESAR

Asthma

The late 1980s have been classified as a "new era" in the understanding and treatment of asthma, the chronic disease involving a reversible obstruction of the airways, specifically the large and small tubes that carry air into the lungs. Since 10 to 15 million Americans are affected by the disease, since the U.S. annual death rate from the disease doubled to about 4,000 between the mid-1970s and the mid-1980s, and since asthma is the major cause of absenteeism by schoolchildren, such a new era could not come fast enough. Members of minority groups particularly would welcome new discoveries about asthma. A study published in 1989 by the United Hospital Fund found that in New York City blacks are about five times more likely than whites to die from asthma and Hispanic people some three times more likely to die from the disease. Medical experts say this discrepancy results from a lack of access to affordable medical care. Thus a combination of improved education and more accessible medical services could help save lives.

The causes of bronchial asthma long have been debated. Although a study published in 1989 by Dr. Benjamin Burrows of the University of Arizona College of Medicine concluded that virtually all asthma attacks are triggered by allergies, the long-held belief has been that the disease is caused by allergies (extrinsic asthma) as well as nonallergic factors (intrinsic asthma). Most experts believe that about half of the asthma cases in adults and about 90% in schoolchildren are of the extrinsic form. Respiratory-tract infections, colds, flu, and physical exertion have been known to bring about attacks of intrinsic asthma.

The belief that people with asthma should avoid exercise has been challenged recently. Many patients indeed do experience wheezing and other breathing difficulties if they exercise. However, recent research indicates that with proper precautions, such as keeping the air in the lungs moist and warming up before working out, asthmatics can tolerate moderate exercise and avoid exercise-induced asthma. According to Dr. François Haas, author of *The Essential Asthma Book,* the more physically fit subjects "are able to handle their asthma better even when they are not exercising." Swimming is perhaps the best form of exercise for the asthma sufferer.

It also now is accepted that psychological stress does not cause asthma. Rather, it can trigger outbreaks in people who have the disease, either by reducing people's resistance or by increasing their sensitivity to allergens.

© Dan McCoy/Rainbow

Bronchodilators are used commonly to control asthma.

A variety of drugs now are available to asthma sufferers. Cromolyn sodium, which inhibits the release of histamine, is one of the newer and more promising such drugs. For the asthma victim, it is available as an inhalant. As a nasal spray, it can be used to treat hay fever. Cromolyn sodium can be used regularly over a long period of time without dangerous side effects. However, it must be taken before an attack begins to be effective. The drug seems to work particularly well with children.

Many of the patients with more severe asthma are forced to take the more potent steroid pills, such as prednisone. Such drugs can produce dangerous side effects, including cataracts, brittle bones, and diabetes. A 1988 study by the Virginia Mason Clinic in Seattle reported that the side effects of such drugs could be reduced if they were taken with another drug, methotrexate. It later was found that methotrexate, a drug long used to treat rheumatoid arthritis, forms of cancer, and psoriasis, may be used by itself to combat asthma. Unfortunately methotrexate also has its drawbacks, including possible liver damage.

Although many mysteries regarding asthma remain, doctors and experts agree that the disease is more manageable than ever before. According to Dr. Carlos Reed of the Mayo Clinic, "most people with asthma don't need to be disabled, impaired, or even restricted now."

JENNY TESAR

Editor's Note: The reports on allergies and asthma were reviewed by the National Institute of Allergy and Infectious Diseases.

Mental Health

Mental-health researchers in 1989 tested new medication for Alzheimer's disease. Genes that make the neurotransmitter associated with schizophrenia were cloned successfully. Scientists gained a better understanding of how AIDS may affect brain cells. And data from an extensive study showed that depression is a debilitating illness.

Obsessive-Compulsive Spectrum. Investigators at the National Institute of Mental Health (NIMH) showed in 1989 that trichotillomania, a common mental disorder in which a person feels compelled to pull out his or her hair, responds to treatment with the drug clomipramine. Earlier research had shown that the same drug is effective in obsessive-compulsive disorder (OCD), a serious mental illness in which a person feels driven to perform pointless rituals. The latest findings seem to indicate that trichotillomania may be related to OCD and may have a similar biological basis. There may be a whole spectrum of disorders—including severe, compulsive nail biting—that have their origin in malfunctions of the part of the brain involved in OCD. Prior to the recent studies, these problems generally were believed to be based solely on emotional maladjustment.

Schizophrenia. An NIMH-funded investigator reported cloning the genes that make the neurotransmitter dopamine. Also cloned was the gene for one of dopamine's receptors—the area on a nerve cell's surface that permits dopamine to interact chemically with the cell. These achievements will permit scientists for the first time to examine in detail the cellular role played by dopamine, which long has been suspected to be involved in schizophrenia. Such research is essential to understand the biological basis of schizophrenia and to develop more potent and specific antipsychotic medications. Meanwhile, clozapine, an antipsychotic medication, has been approved for use in schizophrenic patients by the Food and Drug Administration (FDA), following the results of a major NIMH-funded study to examine its efficacy and safety. Clozapine will provide a much-needed alternative to standard antipsychotic medications, benefiting many who have not responded to those medications.

Effects of AIDS. The National Institute of Child Health and Human Development (NICHHD) and NIMH investigators have found evidence suggesting that just a portion of the AIDS virus may be enough to impair brain-cell function, and that this impairment may occur without actual cell infection. The stage is set for nerve-cell damage when a portion of the AIDS virus called gp120, which is found floating free in the blood of an infected person, attaches to nerve cells and prevents the cells from taking up a peptide essential to their normal function. This abnormal binding may account for some of the immune dysfunction and neurological deficits seen in AIDS patients.

Anorexia and Bulimia. Using highly accurate magnetic resonance imaging (MRI) of the brain structure, researchers found that eating disorders may cause brain abnormalities. Patients with anorexia nervosa or bulimia have severe brain shrinkage, or "pseudoatrophy" of the brain. (Brain size returns to normal after four to ten months of treatment.) Associated with the brain changes are a number of significant psychiatric and physiological effects, including an increased death rate for both sexes.

Depression. A major new study of 11,242 outpatients in three health-care facilities in different areas of the United States provided the first comprehensive data on the effects of depression on the well-being and functioning of patients under treatment by medical clinicians. The results show that depression is as debilitating an illness as many chronic physical illnesses whose adverse impact on patients' lives is recognized more widely. The study, which was carried out by investigators from the Rand Corporation, may result in greater emphasis being placed on the treatment of depression.

The NIMH Depression/Awareness, Recognition and Treatment (D/ART) program, an ongoing education program for the general public, primary-care providers, and mental-health specialists, continued in its mission to increase the number of people who seek and receive appropriate diagnosis and treatment for depressive disorders, which affect more than 9 million adult Americans during any six-month period. In 1989 an estimated $15 million worth of media time, private support, and volunteer efforts were contributed to this public-private partnership. Through the program, 2 million copies of an NIMH-developed brochure, "Depressive Disorders: What You Need to Know," have been published in English and Spanish and distributed to about 50,000 U.S. physicians, who in turn are distributing them to patients.

Alzheimer's Disease. Clinical studies of a drug called metrifonate indicated that it is safe in patients with Alzheimer's disease and may improve their mental abilities. The research team was conducting a double-blind clinical trial of the drug. Newer drugs called galanin antagonists also appeared promising as treatments for Alzheimer's disease and were being tested in animal models of the disorder. Another investigation has shown that an abnormality in blood platelets identifies a subgroup of Alzheimer's disease patients whose disorder has a relatively early onset and a strong familial component. This form of Alzheimer's disease now is believed to be caused by a gene on chromosome 21. Efforts to locate this defective gene and determine how it causes the disease were under way in 1989.

LEWIS L. JUDD, M.D.
Director, National Institute of Mental Health

AP/Wide World

A Chicagoan emerges from the subway into a February snowstorm that dumped 1 ft (.3 m) of the white stuff over the Midwest. The snow fell after a week of springlike temperatures in Chicago, demonstrating once again the changeability and unpredictability of the weather.

METEOROLOGY

Weather experts continued to worry about holes in the ozone layer and strove to understand, among other things, the physics of tornado formation in 1989. Meanwhile, ordinary people struggled against extreme weather—whether it was hurricanes or droughts. In part to analyze and predict such disasters, scientists worked on improving weather satellites and information-gathering techniques.

Satellites. The Geostationary Operational Environmental Satellite located over the West Coast of the United States (GOES-WEST) failed on January 21 when the last of its tungsten-filament lamps burned out. The burnout, which had been predicted closely by National Aeronautics and Space Administration (NASA) scientists, made the satellite's primary instrument useless, although the rest of the satellite continued to function. The remaining GOES (GOES-EAST) was launched in 1987 and is expected to function for ten years. Until the next GOES is launched, the single satellite will be shifted to the central United States, and be moved slightly east in the spring (to better view hurricane activity in the Atlantic Ocean) and slightly west in the fall (to catch winter storms in the Pacific Ocean).

The next generation of GOES is based on a new design, with an expanded complement of instruments to examine the atmosphere. A number of design problems have pushed back the date for launching the new GOES. One option being considered is to decrease the number of new instruments, decreasing the complexity of preparing the satellite. Assuming no additional delays, launch should occur in mid-1991.

On a brighter note, the Nimbus series of meteorological satellites celebrated 25 years of service. Over that period the Nimbus satellites have been the backbone of the NASA program of Earth observation from space. Their polar orbits have been designed to provide coverage of the entire earth twice a day, once in daylight and once at night. Nimbus applications have extended far beyond exploring the atmosphere. Various sensors have recorded phytoplankton concentrations in the oceans, tracked elk and polar bear activity, and mapped polar ice.

Air Chemistry. The "hole" in the stratospheric ozone over Antarctica was as strong in 1989 as the previous record of 1987; however, the maximum depletion was shorter-lived in 1989. A large disturbance in the usually symmetric flow around Antarctica introduced some ozone-rich air from the surrounding regions and raised the ozone content more quickly than in 1987.

The Airborne Arctic Stratospheric Experiment was carried out in January and February over the Arctic to determine how close that region is to the conditions observed over the Antarctic. Apparently the more asymmetric airflow around the Arctic disperses the trace gases before ozone destruction becomes critical.

Chlorofluorocarbons (CFCs) are the principal culprit in destroying stratospheric ozone, and the international effort to limit their use moved forward in 1989. The previously negotiated Montreal protocol on limiting CFCs went into effect at the beginning of 1989. (*See also* ENVIRONMENT; POLAR RESEARCH.)

Tornado Formation. The origin of the rotary motion around a tornado continues to be an important research topic. A recent study suggests that a systematic change of wind direction with height ("shear") can provide the necessary impetus. The shear causes individual parcels of air to acquire rotary motion around a horizontal axis, then the thunderstorm updraft collects the parcels and turns the axis of rotation into the vertical direction.

A second mechanism discovered earlier for generating horizontally oriented rotation still is considered valid: As parcels travel horizontally along the thunderstorm gust front they experience rising motion to one side (the warm air ahead of the gust front) and sinking motion to the other side (the cold air behind the gust front). The relative importance of each mechanism remains to be determined. In either case, the final spin-up to tornadic strength occurs as the vigorous thunderstorm updraft stretches the parcels vertically, causing them to shrink horizontally and rotate more rapidly to conserve angular momentum.

Climate. The Greenland Ice Sheet Project Two (GISP2) was started, attempting to retrieve the largest ice cores ever taken over the entire depth of the ice sheet covering Greenland. The organizers believe they will be able to date various levels in the cores to within a few years. In addition, they hope that the wider cores will allow them to collect samples of gases which were trapped in minute air bubbles at the time that the ice was formed.

In September the U.S. government announced an initiative on climate change. The seven-agency plan will focus on a variety of climate-related research, including a better understanding of clouds and the development of numerical models that simultaneously predict the behavior of the atmosphere and ocean.

Climatic Conditions. The drought conditions that had persisted over much of the eastern United States eased or were reversed in 1989. The passage of several tropical cyclones or their remnants provided episodes of flooding in the Ohio River valley and the mid-Atlantic states. Drought conditions persisted for much of the year on the eastern slopes of the Rocky Mountains and only slowly improved in the central Mississippi River valley.

Western Europe continued to suffer from drought. The drought in England persisted for 20 months and produced the hottest May in 40 years.

The Asian summer monsoon provided normal or better precipitation amounts in Bangladesh, India, and Sri Lanka. Its arrival broke a particularly dry spell, but then for the second year in a row Bangladesh was hard hit by floods. Further north, several states in India finally received enough rain to fill reservoirs depleted by two years of drought. Eastern and southeastern Asia showed drought conditions throughout the early summer.

Large regions of South America were unusually wet in 1989, with flooding reported in many parts of Brazil and eastern Argentina. Buenos Aires, Rio de Janeiro, and São Paulo all experienced flooding.

The tropical Pacific continued to experience the "La Niña" phase of the El Niño in 1989, with colder-than-average water along the Pacific coast of South America. La Niña was cited as the cause for record warmth in New Zealand, which experienced more than 12 months in a row of the warmest temperatures on record (since 1853). It also was noted as one possible cause of the above-normal tropical cyclone activity in the Atlantic and Caribbean.

Atlantic Hurricanes. The Atlantic hurricane season was more active than average, with 11 named storms, of which seven became hurricanes. In mid-September Hurricane *Hugo* (*see* CARIBBEAN) topped the list, devastating the Lesser Antilles and raking Puerto Rico before going on shore at Charleston, SC, with record damage. Fortunately, predictions of *Hugo's* path proved accurate, allowing excellent disaster preparation and ensuring minimal loss of life. Major damage also had occurred in early August when Hurricane *Dean* hit Bermuda.

Other Weather Highlights. Alaska experienced bitterly cold weather in the second half of January. The temperature in the interior averaged −40° F (−40° C), with lows down to −76° F (−60° C). The high pressure system associated with the cold outbreak set a new record pressure for North America, as well as the third-place world record. Northway Airport, AK, recorded 31.85 inches of mercury (1 079 millibars) on January 31. At the end of January the cold air mass swept into the northern plains. Winds gusted to 114 mph (183 km/h) at Choteau, MT, and the temperature at Valentine, NE, dropped from 70 to 32° F (21 to 0° C) in one hour.

In mid-April a heat wave baked the southwestern United States. In Phoenix, AZ, the temperature exceeded 100° F (38° C) 11 days earlier than ever had been recorded. At the same time an unseasonable cold wave damaged the peach crop in Georgia and spread snow across interior New England.

In early November typhoon Gay sank a number of ships in the Gulf of Thailand with substantial loss of life, then proceeded across southern Thailand and restrengthened in the Bay of Bengal. The rejuvenated storm hit India 1,800 mi (2 897 km) from its origin, the first such storm since 1891. Some 50,000 coastal residents were evacuated from Gay's path, resulting in relatively few casualties.

The month of December set record cold temperatures in more than 20 eastern U.S. cities, climaxed by a devastating ice and snow storm over Florida, Georgia, and the Carolinas.

The tornado season in the United States produced a larger-than-normal number of tornadoes, while the number of deaths for the year (46) was about half the usual number (88). For the second year in a row, November had more than three times the number of tornado deaths of any other month. Outside the United States, a late April twister in Bangladesh destroyed 20 villages, killing more than 1,000 people.

GEORGE J. HUFFMAN, *University of Maryland*

© S. Dorantes/Sygma

Ernesto Ruffo Appel (left) *of the National Action Party was elected governor of the Mexican state of North Baja California on July 2. It was the first time in 60 years that the ruling Institutional Revolutionary Party had lost a gubernatorial contest.*

MEXICO

President Carlos Salinas de Gortari firmly asserted his control over the political system, surprising many by his decisiveness in ordering the arrest of corrupt leaders. In July an opposition party, the National Action Party (PAN), won the governorship of North Baja California state, the first time in more than 60 years that the government has recognized an opposition party gubernatorial victory. On the economic front, Mexico increased its efforts to privatize the economy and received some debt relief through the plan of U.S. Treasury Secretary Nicholas Brady.

Politics. In July, PAN candidate Ernesto Ruffo Appel decisively won the governorship of North Baja California state, located on the U.S. border, leading a PAN ticket which also won the mayoralties of Tijuana and Ensenada, the state's two most important cities. Pro-PAN citizens guarded the polls to prevent the government party, the Institutional Revolutionary Party (PRI), from stealing the election. As the votes were being counted, President Salinas ordered PRI officials not to engage in electoral alchemy, thus ensuring a fair vote count. This was in marked contrast to the 1968 state election PAN had won, only to have the governorship stolen by the PRI and the government it controlled. Much of the pro-PAN vote was a protest against the PRI, which has ruled Mexico since 1929.

In the 1988 national elections in Michoacán, Democratic Revolutionary Party (PDR) leader Cuauhtémoc Cárdenas and his coalition beat Salinas, PRI, and PAN. In state legislative elections that same month, however, Cárdenas was unable to hold together the coalition he used to outpoll Salinas in the presidential election, and the PRI claimed half of the available posts. Some observers, however, believed that the PRI committed fraud and that Cárdenas' PDR had won a majority. The 12 opposition seats were split between the PDR, PAN, and the Authentic Party of the Mexican Revolution.

Salinas Administration. A Harvard-educated intellectual, President Salinas was perceived widely to be a weakling until he dramatically established his authority by using a "hard hand" against corrupt and powerful bosses. In January he used the army to arrest Joaquín Hernández Galicia ("La Quina"), the powerful and corrupt boss of the state petroleum workers' union, and to guard oil trucks from possible union violence. "La Quina" and his union long had been major obstacles to the modernization and efficient operation of PEMEX, the government oil monopoly, which produces 40% of government revenues. He also has been Salinas' political enemy for years. In February, Salinas ordered the arrests of four leading stockbrokers, including a prominent PRI contributor, on charges of fraud. The government also arrested or dismissed a number of corrupt government officials.

In addition, Salinas was wresting control of the 1.1 million-member teachers' union from its corrupt boss, Sen. Carlos Jonguitud Barrios. The union struck in April, demanding a 50% wage increase, but only received a 25% increase, still far above the limits specified in the Plan of Economic Stability and Growth. The wage concession bought teacher allegiance to Salinas' faction, important because the union turns out massive votes for PRI.

Backlash from the political old guard in the PRI and the severity of the economic crisis limited the president's ability to instigate more democratic reforms. Although Salinas named prominent old guard politicians to the internal security posts in his cabinet, most of the key personnel of his administration are technocrats. Without the support of the PRI political machine, however, Salinas would be unable to maintain social peace and carry out his economic strategy. One signal of PRI's continued antidemocratic position was its cancellation of its primary elections in Nuevo León state. Many believed that Salinas had attacked a few very visible corrupt leaders as a symbolic gesture but would do little to change systemic corruption. Similarly, the recognition of the PAN victory may have been little more than a gesture while politics continued as usual. Early in the year Salinas did order the release of 400 political prisoners, who the government previous had denied existed.

Economic Policy. The principal reason for the rise of political opposition has been President Salinas' decision to base his recovery plans on converting the economy from state-owned or controlled enterprises to a market-oriented system in which foreign enterprise would play a significant role. He moved rapidly to privatize much of the economy, ridding government of some of its most inefficient enterprises. The government sold its interests in Mexicana Airlines, and prepared to sell TELMEX (the antiquated telephone company), CONASUPO (a government agency which sold subsidized food and consumer goods), and mines such as the Cananea Copper Company. Observers speculated throughout 1989 about which other government enterprises would be sold next.

The sales represented a major and controversial departure in government policy, which had used government enterprise to further social justice. CONASUPO, for example, was the principal means by which the government subsidized the poor, selling basic commodities below market price and guaranteeing prices to producers. Many feared that privatizing CONASUPO would lead to even higher prices for the 50% of the nation below the poverty line. Also controversial was the government's decision to privatize the bankrupt Cananea mine—the site of a major labor strike instrumental in the coming of the Mexican Revolution. Copper union workers successfully struck in the summer of 1989, getting a promise that they would own 25% of the reorganized company.

MEXICO • Information Highlights

Official Name: United Mexican States.
Location: Southern North America.
Area: 761,602 sq mi (1 972 550 km²).
Population (mid-1989 est.): 86,700,000.
Chief Cities (1980 census): Mexico City (Federal District), the capital (1983 est.), 9,663,360; Guadalajara, 1,626,152; Monterrey, 1,090,009.
Government: *Head of state and government,* Carlos Salinas de Gortari, president (took office Dec. 1988). *Legislature*—National Congress: Senate and Federal Chamber of Deputies.
Monetary Unit: Peso (2,623 pesos equal U.S.$1, floating rate, Nov. 13, 1989).
Gross Domestic Product (1987 U.S.$): $135,900,000,000.
Economic Indexes (1988): *Consumer Prices* (1980 = 100), all items, 9,907.1; food, 9,304.0. *Industrial Production* (1980 = 100), 109.
Foreign Trade (1988 U.S.$): *Imports,* $18,954,000,000; *exports,* $20,658,000,000.

The government also liberalized trade and investment laws in 1989. Tariffs were reduced to an average of 10% with a maximum of 20%. Reversing previous policy which limited foreign ownership of most enterprises, new foreign investment legislation announced in May allowed foreign investors to own up to 100% of most industries. Foreign investment only represented 5% of gross domestic product in 1989, an unusually small percentage for such a large country. A tax amnesty was granted to those willing to bring their capital back to Mexico.

The agricultural sector continued to lag far behind the rest of the economy. Three years of drought, inefficiency, corruption, and insufficient capital investment had damaged agriculture so severely that the government was forced to spend $3 billion to import food. In August, Salinas announced a new agriculture policy to boost spending in rural areas, sell inefficient government-owned agribusinesses, train management personnel, and increase price supports.

Although the nation continued in its seventh year of economic depression, there were encouraging signs. In the first half of the year, the gross domestic product rose 2.4%, industrial production increased 5.2%, and automobile sales rose 45%. The inflation rate dropped to approximately 16% and domestic interest rates declined from 50% to 38%. More than $2 billion of capital was repatriated, indicating growing confidence in the economy.

Economic problems continued, however. There was $84 billion in capital still abroad, an amount that, if brought back to Mexico, would revitalize the economy. Government cash reserves dropped to $4 billion. The underground economy in 1989 constituted about 38% of the gross domestic product, harmful because it indicated a lack of confidence in the government and because it denied needed tax revenues.

As part of the government's effort to raise more revenue and reduce subsidies of state enterprises, the Federal Electric Commission raised its rates 200% for those using 200 or more kilowatts monthly. The new rate structure made electricity 67% more expensive than in the United States.

Debt Reduction. Led by U.S. Treasury Secretary Nicholas Brady, international banks, Mexico, and the United States agreed in July to a plan which might reduce the Mexico foreign debt by 35%. Under the Brady Plan, banks would swap current loans for long-term, fixed 6.5% bonds and provide new loans at below market interest rates, or at a 25% discount. Lenders had not rushed to participate by November, however, even though the Mexican agreement was a test case for the Bush administration's Third World debt reduction strategy. To help Mexico meet its current obligations until the plan becomes effective, international lending institutions advanced $6.9

© S. Dorantes/Sygma

The new Salinas government showed its strength by using the army to arrest Joaquín Hernández Galicia, a corrupt union boss. Several cohorts of Hernández also were apprehended and an arsenal of weapons was taken from his home.

billion in new loans. Debt service absorbed almost 70% of Mexican public spending and 30% of the gross domestic product. At best, the Brady Plan would provide Mexico with some financial breathing room while it gambles on the success of the Salinas economic strategy; at worst, it would increase dramatically government short-term indebtedness.

Social Problems. Mexico City, the world's largest and most polluted city, received special attention during 1989. Japan made a $1 billion loan for antipollution efforts in the city. For three months, beginning in late November, one fifth of the city's automobiles were not allowed to use city streets. Urban crime and violence rose in tandem with the depth of the economic crisis and the inability of the government to hire and retain honest police. The national 40% joblessness and underemployment rate and the rising cost of basic foods strained the capacity of the common people to survive. Many of the poor headed for Mexico City in hopes of finding employment in the service sector, only to find life there equally difficult. Mexico City was particularly hard hit by criminal violence and police corruption.

International drug trafficking and domestic use of illicit drugs increased during 1989. Colombian cocaine traffickers made alliances with Mexican marijuana and heroin traffickers to transship cocaine from bases in Mexico to the United States. During the summer, Mexican police confiscated two and one-half tons of cocaine in South Baja California state. The increased activity was prompted partly because Caribbean transit routes into Florida became more difficult as a result of U.S. interdiction efforts in that region. Mexican and Colombian traffickers established opium poppy farms across the virtually uncontrolled border for use in Mexican processing plants. Inevitably, this increased the domestic supply of illicit drugs, making the drugs cheaper and more readily available.

The government was devoting enormous resources to fight the drug trade in 1989. Some 60% of the national attorney general's budget was spent on antidrug measures and 25% of the Mexican military was assigned to eradication campaigns. Police began a policy of shooting down planes suspected of drug-running. Drug education programs also were stepped up.

U.S. Relations. Mexican President Salinas and U.S. President George Bush fostered improved relations between the two nations. Salinas met with Bush in Washington, DC, in October and addressed a joint session of the U.S. Congress. The two leaders agreed to liberalize trade relations and seek joint solutions to problems. Salinas vowed to push vigorously his nation's attack on drug traffickers, a principal concern of the Bush administration. In August, Miguel Angel Félix Gallardo, one of Mexico's leading drug traffickers, was arrested. Salinas warned, however, that until his nation solves its economic problems, his government would have little interest in trying to prevent Mexicans from migrating to the United States to fill jobs that Americans might not take. During the same October trip, he traveled to New York to encourage business leaders to invest in Mexico.

DONALD J. MABRY
Mississippi State University

MICHIGAN

The Detroit mayor's race, state efforts to revise school financing, and the sale of one of Detroit's oldest businesses were top news stories in Michigan in 1989.

Election and Education. Incumbent Detroit Mayor Coleman A. Young (D) easily won an unprecedented fifth term in the November elections, despite a dip in popularity polls and some personal problems involving a paternity suit earlier in 1989.

After two years of haggling among special interest groups, several task force reports on financing of public schools, and long hours of debate in the state legislature, voters were offered their choice of two separate school financing proposals, but rejected both. One proposal would have raised the sales tax by a half-cent and increased school spending by $421 million a year. The other proposal would have boosted the sales tax by 2 cents to 6 cents and increased school spending by $274 million a year while also offering an average 38% tax break for homeowners and a 23% tax break for businesses. Proponents had acknowledged that neither of the proposals would close the spending gap between rich and poor school districts, one of the original goals of school finance reform, but they argued that the proposals were the best compromises possible.

A local education financing initiative for Detroit public schools had fared better in September. Detroit voters approved a five-mill property tax increase and a $160 million bond issue that school officials said would spark financial and educational recovery for the beleaguered school district that serves 171,000 students. With the added finances, the district planned to restore varsity sports and instrumental music programs, give teachers a 6% pay raise, and institute academic reforms. The overwhelming margin for passage was seen as a vote of confidence for Superintendent John W. Porter, a former Eastern Michigan University president who was selected to head the Detroit school system, succeeding Superintendent Arthur Jefferson. Porter also had served on a state panel that had proposed sweeping changes for Detroit's schools.

MICHIGAN • Information Highlights

Area: 58,527 sq mi (151 586 km²).
Population (July 1, 1988): 9,240,000.
Chief Cities (July 1, 1986 est.): Lansing, the capital, 128,980; Detroit, 1,086,220; Grand Rapids, 186,530; Warren, 149,800; Flint, 145,590; Sterling Heights, 111,960.
Government (1989): *Chief Officers*—governor, James J. Blanchard (D); lt. gov., Martha W. Griffiths (D). *Legislature*—Senate, 38 members; House of Representatives, 110 members.
State Finances (fiscal year 1988): *Revenue*, $21,540,000,000; *expenditure*, $20,380,000,000.
Personal Income (1988): $152,934,000,000; per capita, $16,552.
Labor Force (June 1989): *Civilian labor force*, 4,678,400; *unemployed*, 351,000 (7.5% of total force).
Education: *Enrollment* (fall 1987)—public elementary schools, 1,086,000; public secondary, 520,000; colleges and universities, 535,486. *Public school expenditures* (1987–88), $6,319,477,000 ($4,306 per pupil).

Business and Industry. The Stroh Brewery Co., a family-operated Detroit institution founded in 1850, and the third-largest brewery in the United States, announced in September that it would merge with the Coors Brewing Co., of Golden, CO, for $425 million. Although the merger collapsed before the year ended, it was expected that Stroh would be sold. A new deal between Stroh and Coors, the fourth-largest brewery in the United States, was not ruled out by industry experts.

The cost of clearing a site for a new Chrysler Corp. automobile plant on Detroit's east side continued to soar in 1989. The City Council approved $30.4 million in additional money to cover the unanticipated cost of cleaning up contaminated soil at the site. The increase pushed the taxpayer share of the $1 billion project to more than $264 million.

Opponents of the proposed business operations merger of Detroit's two daily newspapers took their objections to the U.S. Supreme Court in 1989. A joint operating agreement between the Detroit *News* and the Detroit *Free Press* was approved by the U.S. attorney general's office in 1988. The federal Newspaper Preservation Act permits business mergers between competing newspapers, if one of the newspapers is failing and if the two retain separate editorial operations. Although the *Free Press* said it was failing, a group calling itself Michigan Citizens for an Independent Press was opposed to the merger, maintaining that it would decrease press independence. The Supreme Court, discussing the case in November, deadlocked, 4–4, with one abstention, allowing the agreement to take effect.

Police Raises and Bridge Safety. A state arbitrator ordered Detroit in September to increase police pay by 14% over three years—a $48 million settlement that Mayor Young said would plunge the city into financial catastrophe.

A bizarre fatal accident on the Mackinac bridge that links Michigan's two peninsulas prompted concerns over the bridge's safety. A 30-year-old woman from Royal Oak, MI, died after her subcompact car was blown off the bridge in high winds and plunged 150 ft (45.7 m) to the water below. The vehicle was the first ever to fall off the bridge, but there were concerns that the safety railings installed when the bridge was built in 1957 might not be high enough to prevent today's lighter cars from going over them.

CHARLES W. THEISEN
"The Detroit News"

MICROBIOLOGY

The year 1989 brought advances in the knowledge of microbial physiology and evolution, as well as a greater appreciation of the complexities of fighting infectious diseases.

Cellulose-Digesting, Nitrogen-Fixing Bacteria. Photosynthesis produces about 150 billion tons of dry plant material worldwide each year. Approximately half of this material is cellulose, a complex carbohydrate that forms the rigid wall around each plant cell. The remainder of the plant material includes proteins which the plant produces only if nitrogenous chemical compounds are available in the soil.

Cellulose, normally a waste product of agriculture, represents a great storehouse of potential energy for the organisms that can digest it. If the same organisms were capable of forming usable nitrogenous compounds from atmospheric nitrogen (nitrogen-fixation), such organisms could enrich greatly the soil in which they are living.

In late 1988, Dr. S. B. Leschine and colleagues at the University of Massachusetts announced the discovery of bacteria that could both digest cellulose and fix nitrogen. They were found in forest soil. The ability of these bacteria to use the energy obtained from cellulose digestion to transform atmospheric nitrogen into ammonia (the first step in the production of nitrates) could result in a reduced need for artificial fertilizers in many parts of the world.

Hepatitis C Virus. Two viruses cause about 10% of the 150,000 cases of transfusion-caused hepatitis in the United States each year. Based on their antigenic properties, these viruses have been labeled HAV (hepatitis A virus) and HBV (hepatitis B virus).

Dr. M. Houghton and his colleagues at the Chiron Corporation in Emeryville, CA, reported that they had isolated and identified a virus that causes about 85% of the posttransfusion hepatitis cases. The virus produces very little antigen in its hosts and therefore went undetected until a procedure was developed to increase its antigen concentration. This virus has been labeled hepatitis C virus (HCV). A test has been developed for HCV to be used for potential blood donors, which in conjunction with tests for HAV and HBV should reduce drastically the occurrence of transfusion-related hepatitis.

It also should be possible to develop a vaccine against HCV, which together with vaccines against HAV and HBV will protect medical personnel against contracting hepatitis as a result of accidental exposure to infected blood.

Rinderpest Vaccine. Rinderpest is a highly infectious disease of cattle, epidemic in Africa and Asia, accounting for a loss of more than 2 million animals per year. The animals suffer severe hemorrhaging of their gastrointestinal tracts, leading to an almost 100% mortality rate. The disease is caused by a single-stranded RNA virus, belonging to the same group of viruses as the causative agent of human measles and dog distemper. Research has shown that the protein products of the viral genes for hemagglutinin (HA) and for fusion (F) elicit protective immunity in vaccinated animals.

In 1988, Dr. T. Yilma of the University of California, Davis, and his associates made complementary DNA copies of the HA and F genes. Using standard DNA recombinant procedures, they transferred the DNA copies of the genes to the cowpox (vaccinia) virus. Upon injection into cattle, the recombinant vaccinia virus stimulated the animals to produce antibodies against rinderpest virus.

Because of the similarity of the rinderpest virus to both the human measles and dog distemper viruses, tests are planned to see whether the recombinant vaccinia virus also will afford protection against infections by these related viruses.

Hypermutability of the AIDS Virus. How the AIDS (HIV-1) virus manages to evade a person's immune defenses and why it has not been possible to produce an effective vaccine against the virus are questions that appear to have a single answer. HIV-1 is an RNA virus that contains the enzyme reverse transcriptase. This enzyme produces a DNA copy of the virus that becomes incorporated into one of the chromosomes of the infected person's cells.

Studies show that HIV-1 reverse transcriptase has an error rate of 5 to 10 errors per replication of the virus. Under these conditions, the new viral particles formed show tremendous variability and continue to change more rapidly than the immune system's ability to produce specific antibodies against them. This extensive genetic variation of HIV-1 viruses presents a formidable task for the development of a vaccine which, by its very nature, is very specific for a particular viral genome.

Evolutionary Relationships Among Microorganisms. One criterion for the classifying of microorganisms is the presence or absence of subcellular structures (nucleus, mitochondria, endoplasmic reticulum, Golgi apparatus) within their cells. Those possessing these structures are classified as "eukaryotes," whereas those without them are called "prokaryotes." Bacteria, both primitive and advanced, are prokaryotes whereas protozoa, algae, and fungi are eukaryotes. One protozoan species, *Giardia lamblia,* is most interesting. It has a nucleus but lacks mitochondria, endoplasmic reticulum, and Golgi apparatus, thereby sharing characteristics of both eukaryotes and prokaryotes. This protozoan appears to represent an evolutionary link between those two groups.

LOUIS LEVINE, *City College of New York*

MIDDLE EAST

It was not a year of truly major events in the Middle East. There were interesting beginnings in terms of international organization, and steps were taken in diplomacy that could prove truly fruitful later.

United States-Libyan Clash. The year began explosively when on January 4 two U.S. planes shot down two Libyan jets over the Mediterranean. This was the most recent in a considerable series of United States-Libyan clashes, the preceding one having occurred in April 1986 when U.S. aircraft bombed Tripoli and Benghazi. The incident occurred shortly after the United States announced, in an unusual move, that it was considering military action to destroy what was believed to be a chemical-weapons plant at Rabta in Libya. Suspicions were aired that Libya had some connection with Palestinian groups suspected in the destruction of a Pan Am airliner over Lockerbie, Scotland, on Dec. 21, 1988. Another almost concurrent event was the international conference on chemical weapons that convened in Paris on January 7.

The two U.S. planes, F-14 jet fighters, were operating from the aircraft carrier *John F. Kennedy*. Flying some 70 mi (113 km) off Libya's northeast coast, they were in international waters and quite outside the large Gulf of Sirte (or Sidra), claimed by Libya as territorial waters (the same spot where two Libyan jets had been shot down by U.S. F-14s in 1981). U.S. authorities maintained that in the January 4 incident the two Libyan planes had threatened the U.S. jets which, in turn, acted in self-defense.

The Libyan government claimed to be outraged. Libyan leader Col. Muammar el-Qaddafi said that the Libyan people were prepared "to meet the challenge with challenge." The Soviet government accused the United States of "state terrorism" and "political adventurism." An acrimonious debate in the UN Security Council ensued, beginning January 6. The United States, France, and Britain vetoed a draft resolution that condemned the U.S. action and called for an end to U.S. military maneuvers off the Libyan coast.

This portentous event was singularly without any obvious consequences. No more was heard of bombing the supposed chemical plant in Libya. The conference on chemical warfare ended with the passing of staunch resolutions unfortunately doomed to ineffectiveness. If there were a change in Libyan behavior, it was that the country had become somewhat more moderate in 1989.

Diminution of Terrorism. A variety of evidence indicated that some Arab states, such as Libya, Syria, and Iraq—formerly heavy supporters and safe sanctuaries for the most notorious Palestinian terrorist organizations—have

© Eric Bouvet/Gamma-Liaison

The death of the Ayatollah Khomeini in June ended an era in Iran. Hundreds of thousands of emotional mourners viewed his body and attended his funeral in Tehran.

modified their attitudes, at least temporarily. International terrorist activity by Palestinian groups decreased dramatically during the year. No large-scale outrage such as the Lockerbie, Scotland, airplane disaster or the seizure of the cruise ship *Achille Lauro* occurred. Several factors may account for the decline in terrorist activity in 1989: The oil-producing states have fewer surplus resources than they had in the past. State-sponsored terrorism has been very unproductive of actual political results, and has alienated opinion outside the Middle East. Expediency may have suggested a change of course. Pressure from more moderate Middle East states—and perhaps also from the Soviet Union—also has had some effect. Even the fact that the United States has shown several times that it is prepared to take action, especially against Libya, may have had some favorable impact. Another influence has been that the Eastern European states, some of which have provided terrorist training facilities, safe havens, financial channels, and other forms of assistance, are by and large no longer doing so as they undergo political upheavals.

Precisely what was happening was in many cases uncertain, but the general trend was clear. Qaddafi used to afford facilities for hundreds of terrorist training camps in Libya. Now there were believed to be only three. Libyan financial support also has been cut back drastically and, for some organizations, eliminated. In a move believed to be the result of direct Egyptian pressure, Abu Nidal, perhaps the most notorious of Palestinian terrorists, was placed under house arrest in Libya. In Poland, a branch of the Abu Nidal organization was closed down in mid-1988.

Terrorist organizations, indeed, have been handicapped, but they were not about to disappear. Syria's occupying forces still tolerate such groups in Lebanon. Some have created new links with Iran. The PFLP (Popular Front for the Liberation of Palestine) opened offices in Tehran in 1989. Other havens may be found outside the Middle East and outside Europe.

Death of Colonel Higgins. One terrorist incident that caused widespread shock was the murder by hanging on July 31 of the U.S. Marine, Lt. Col. William Higgins. Higgins had been kidnapped in February 1988 in Lebanon. His death was the culminating incident in a sad series of reprisals. On July 28, in the hope of forcing the release of several Israeli soldiers captured in Lebanon by Iranian-backed groups, notably Hezbollah, Israeli commandos in south Lebanon captured Sheik Abdul Karim Obeid, a religious leader and supposedly important figure in Hezbollah. However, some experts disputed his importance.

As a gambit to secure release of the Israelis, Obeid's capture was unsuccessful and roused wide criticism, though not in Israel. Credit for Higgins' death as a reprisal for Obeid's capture was claimed by the "Organization for the Oppressed on Earth" (OOE), a Hezbollah front. (*See* TERRORISM).

Three Major Themes. Between 1987 and 1989 three issues dominated the Middle East picture and, rightly, received more attention than the plethora of lesser issues and events. One was the question of Arab-Israeli relations, particularly in the form of the Palestinian issue. A second was the situation in Lebanon. The third was the Iraqi-Iranian conflict. These three matters of concern still were preeminent, but their relative importance had changed, the Iraqi-Iranian question having lost some urgency with a cessation of actual fighting in 1988.

Palestinian Issue. The *intifada,* or uprising, against Israeli rule in the West Bank and Gaza Strip continued. By December 1989 it had been going on for two years. (The West Bank and Gaza Strip were captured by Israel in the 1967 war and, unlike East Jerusalem and the Golan Heights, have not been incorporated into Israel.) The *intifada* is actually a series of events, strikes, and acts of violence—the latter seemingly not coordinated or directed by the Palestine Liberation Organization (PLO) or, indeed, by any other organization. On the rise in 1989 was the number of killings of Arabs by Arabs, the victims being those accused of collaboration with the occupying power. An Israeli army spokesman said on September 13 that 84 Palestinians accused of collaboration had been murdered since the beginning of the year.

PLO leader Yasir Arafat had acquired some international respectability as a result of his organization's acceptance, late in 1988, of Israel's right to exist, even though the acceptance was hedged carefully and qualified. He visited various European countries in January and was well received. On January 13 in Tunisia he met William Waldegrave, a British junior foreign affairs minister. This was the first such contact between Arafat and a British minister. The PLO in November 1988 had proclaimed the existence of a Palestinian state. This entity had been honored by recognition by more than 80 countries by mid-1989. However, the only major powers to do so were the Soviet Union and China, and Greece was the only European state to do so. On April 11 a meeting of the PLO's central council in Tunis voted unanimously to name Arafat as president of the "State of Palestine" and Farouk Qaddumi as foreign minister. However, dissident Palestinian groups including the PFLP met in Libya in late March to discuss "the creation of an alternative to the PLO."

A notable development, already foreshadowed in 1988 but particularly associated with the new Bush administration, was a cooling in U.S. support for Israel. The first-ever official meetings between U.S. representatives and the PLO had occurred in December 1988 in Tunis. A second round of talks took place in late March 1989, also in Tunis, and there were others later. Israel continued to refuse to have any direct dealings with the PLO, a position hitherto upheld by the United States; but on March 14 U.S. Secretary of State James Baker commented that direct Israeli-PLO negotiations eventually could become inevitable.

The Shamir Plan. Early in 1989 there was no lack of diplomatic activity, mostly on the initiative of the United States, in attempts to further the optimistically named "peace process." Later the focus of attention was on Israeli proposals for elections in the occupied areas, and on reactions to, and variations on, these proposals. These ideas might lead to some results in the long run, but nothing conclusive happened within the year. In April, Washington was host to official visitors from Egypt, Israel, and Jordan. The visit of Egyptian President Hosni Mubarak was significant, as he had briefed himself by previous discussions with Saudis, King Hussein of Jordan, and Arafat.

A somewhat new phase of the affair, which lasted the rest of the year, began during the Washington visit of Israeli Prime Minister Yitzhak Shamir in April. During a meeting with President Bush on April 6 he outlined his four-point Middle East peace plan. The essential point was that elections should be held in the West Bank and Gaza Strip to enable the formation of a non-PLO delegation to participate in negotiations. These talks would bring about an interim settlement; a self-governing administration might be established. This interim settlement would serve as a test of "cooperation and coexistence." Negotiations on a final settlement would follow later. Other points in the Shamir proposal were that Israel, Egypt, and the United States should reaffirm their commitment to the 1979 Camp David agreements, and that the United States and Egypt should call on Arab countries to replace antagonism toward Israel with negotiation and cooperation.

The PLO and Arab leaders in general instantly rejected the plan, but second thoughts prevailed. By late April the PLO was speaking with approval of elections, provided they were "part of a comprehensive settlement," and that Palestinians in exile would be eligible for election. This meant basically that the process had to be designed in the first place to lead to a Palestinian state.

Shamir's plan was approved in the Israeli cabinet on May 14 by 14 votes to six with dissension on both the left and the right. Israeli opinion was divided seriously. The Knesset (the Israeli parliament) approved the plan on May 17 by 43 votes to 15, but with many deputies absent or abstaining. During this debate the prime minister said, "A Palestinian state will not arise and will not be." On May 22, Baker made a speech regarded widely as a landmark because of its "even-handed" tone toward both Arabs and Israelis.

Early in July, Shamir was forced by a group of hard-line cabinet colleagues to modify his plan. These changes made the holding of any elections dependent on an end to the *intifada,* and encouraged Jewish settlement in the territories.

Mubarak played an active diplomatic role in the remainder of the year. The languishing Shamir plan was, in effect, given new life by the Egyptian president on September 10, when he put forward a well-considered ten-point peace proposal. This the U.S. government chose to regard as "complementary" to Shamir's plan, a view curiously echoed by the Soviet Foreign Minister Eduard Shevardnadze, who said that there were "reasonable elements" in both the Israeli and Egyptian election proposals.

Baker attempted to revive the stalled process by advancing a new plan on October 10, whereby the Israelis would begin discussions with a Palestinian group in Cairo under the aegis of the Egyptian government. At year's end it seemed that the next stage would be a three-way U.S.-Egyptian-Israeli meeting in Washington in January 1990 to attempt to iron out incompatibilities in the Egyptian and Israeli negotiating positions.

Lebanon. In Lebanon, perhaps the most significant development has been the degree of interest and activity shown by other regional states in trying to bring to an end an intolerable

Israel's Foreign Minister Moshe Arens (left) *and Egypt's President Hosni Mubarak discussed Middle East peace proposals in New York in September. Palestinian elections in the Israeli-occupied West Bank and Gaza Strip were a key issue.*

AP/Wide World

AP/Wide World

Libya's leader Muammar el-Qaddafi and Syria's President Hafiz al-Assad (left) were among those attending an emergency meeting of the Arab League in Morocco in May.

situation. The Arab League initiatives early in the year came to little, but the cease-fire achieved in September was more successful than any of its predecessors. The meeting in early October, at Taif in Saudi Arabia, of a majority of members of the Lebanese parliament, was an unprecedented and courageous event. The delegates outlined a new political order for Lebanon. They also showed political and personal courage in electing a president and, after his assassination, in electing a successor. Gen. Michel Aoun was blamed widely for standing in the way of the new president's peacefully assuming his duties. Aoun is supported by Iraq.

Though not widely reported, Iran in early October hosted at Tehran a meeting of Lebanese leaders with a different agenda. Iranian leaders wished to see a purely Islamic Lebanon of a strongly religious character. Syria aimed at a secular Lebanon under Syrian tutelage. Aoun, backed by Iraq, as a Maronite Christian struggled against both scenarios, but Iraq's capacity to aid him was limited by geography.

Iraq and Iran. Negotiations to follow up the Iran-Iraq cease-fire of August 1988 by a settlement of issues went on intermittently and fruitlessly throughout the year, generally through intermediaries. Iran insisted that the first necessity was for Iraq to withdraw from those parts of Iranian territory that it occupied. Iraq held that a cease-fire should lead, before anything else, to the reopening of the Shatt Al-Arab to Iraqi navigation. Iraq has not been able to use this waterway, much more vital to it than to Iran, since the beginning of the war. A discouraging aspect of this negotiating stalemate was that the prisoners of war on both sides had not been allowed to return home. Iran was holding more than 70,000 prisoners of war; Iraq 30,000. By the Geneva Convention, of which both states are signatories, all prisoners should be freed as soon as fighting ends. Less than 2,500 had been by late 1989.

Arab League. The most important general meeting of the Arab world in 1989 was the emergency summit meeting in May of the Arab League, held in Casablanca, Morocco. Three topics dominated the meeting: the demonstration of support for Arafat and the PLO; the adoption of a unified stance on Lebanon; and a review of progress on the Gulf War cease-fire. Eighteen of the 22 League members attended. On the Lebanese question, Egypt, Iraq, Jordan, and the PLO pressed for the withdrawal of the 40,000 or so Syrian troops in Lebanon, and their replacement by an Arab peacekeeping force. But in a bitter debate Syria sat tight and the proposal was abandoned. Perhaps the most important outcome of the meeting, however, was that it marked the full welcome of Egypt back into the Arab fold, which ended the period of ostracism which had begun with the Egyptian-Israeli peace treaty of 1979.

New Groupings in the Arab World. The Arab League meeting demonstrated the deep fissures that exist within the Arab world. Developments of 1989 suggested that the future well may lie with smaller regional groups between whose members there are real bonds of interest. One such already existed—the Gulf Cooperation Council, founded in 1981. Two such international organizations came into being, simultaneously, in 1989. Following up on tentative agreements begun in 1988, the five north African Maghreb states—Algeria, Mauritania, Libya, Morocco, and Tunisia—signed a treaty in February which brought into being the Arab Maghreb Union. The five states agreed to formulate common policies on defense, economic issues, and international and cultural issues. On February 16 the heads of state of Egypt, Jordan, Iraq, and North Yemen, meeting in Baghdad, founded a new organization, the Arab Cooperation Council, an economic group which also may develop defense functions. Here again, as at Casablanca, the complete reintegration of Egypt as part of the Arab world was noteworthy. Finally, on December 1, North and South Yemen agreed to merge into a single state.

Iraqi Missiles. Concern at the growing missile armament of Middle East states was increased by the report early in December that Iraq had developed the capacity to put a missile with payload into orbit. The report, however, was greeted with some skepticism.

ARTHUR CAMPBELL TURNER
University of California, Riverside

UPI/Bettmann Newsphotos

In a new era of U.S.-Soviet relations, meetings between top military personnel from each side have become more common. In July, U.S. Adm. William Crowe (left) *conferred with Marshall Sergei Akhromeyev in Chicago.*

MILITARY AFFAIRS

Due to changes in the Communist world (*see* feature article, page 24), 1989 was a watershed year in the more than four decade-long Cold War between the United States and the Soviet Union. The astounding changes that occurred within the Soviet empire, and between the United States and the USSR, also were reflected by remarkable changes in the military policies of both nuclear superpowers.

U.S. Military Climate. An example of the changing military condition is that the U.S. Department of Defense projected a softer image of the Soviet military threat in 1989 than at any time in the past decade. This assessment appeared in *Soviet Military Power,* a yearly publication of the Department of Defense. In the past the publication had contained some of the harshest official assessments of the Soviet threat, and also the associated justification for the United States to augment its military capabilities. However, the 1989 *Soviet Military Power* mirrored the intellectual struggles going on within the Bush administration, and between the administration and nongovernment military analysts, regarding the extent to which the United States can take seriously Soviet statements about military retrenchments.

On the one hand, those who fear that the United States may be misled dangerously by President Mikhail Gorbachev's "new thinking" and "charm offensive," could subscribe to Defense Secretary Dick Cheney's warnings in the report's introduction that the United States ". . . cannot react unilaterally to Soviet initiatives that are not yet implemented or to proposals, which, if implemented, can easily be reversed." On the other hand, those who are more optimistic about the implications for the U.S. military planning that they see in Gorbachev's policies could support the report's statement that, "At present, the Soviets do not seem to anticipate war in Europe in the near future and are stressing political, diplomatic, and economic alternatives to achieve their strategic goals."

Military Exchange Visits. There were other indications of changed United States-USSR military relationships, such as a series of unprecedented and highly publicized exchange visits by the highest ranking military officials of each nation and legislative leaders responsible for reviewing military policy. In June the chairman of the U.S. Joint Chiefs of Staff, Admiral William J. Crowe, Jr., was received by his counterpart, Gen. Mikhail A. Moiseyev, chief of the Soviet General Staff, and taken on an 11-day tour of Soviet military installations. Crowe had the opportunity to climb into the cockpit of the newest Soviet strategic bomber, the Blackjack—a place no American ever had been before. (The 1989 trip was a follow-up to a 1988 visit by senior Soviet military officials to the United States. At that time Admiral Crowe conducted then Soviet Chief of Staff Marshall Sergei F. Akhromeyev on a tour of American military facilities.)

In July, Marshall Akhromeyev, who has become special military adviser to President Gorbachev, returned to Washington to appear before the House Armed Services Committee. In August the House Armed Services Committee toured military areas in the western part of the Soviet Union as guests of the Supreme Soviet's Committee on Defense and State Security.

In early December, on ships anchored at the Mediterranean island of Malta, Presidents Bush and Gorbachev pledged to move their respective bureaucracies forward to 1990 conclusions of the negotiations for treaties on strategic weapons, conventional forces, and chemical weapons. A second summit was scheduled for 1990.

U.S. and USSR Defense Budgets. Another barometer of changing military relations between the United States and the Soviet Union was the cutback in the military budgets of both nations. In Washington the House and Senate agreed upon, and sent to President Bush, a $305 billion military programs bill for the fiscal year which began October 1. For the first time since March 1983, when former President Ronald Reagan called for the creation of the Strategic Defense Initiative (or SDI, otherwise known as Star Wars) to protect the entire United States from Soviet missile attack, the Congress cut back on the program's funding. The total SDI funding was about $3.79 billion, contrasted to the previous fiscal year's price tag of approximately $4.06 billion. As it is, the original plan to protect major American cities with SDI technology has been abandoned and new proposals seek only to protect missile silos.

One budget-trimming measure which has generated a great deal of controversy is the plan to close 86 military bases and reorganize 54 others. In late December 1988 the Department of Defense put together the list of bases to be closed, and Congress approved the list the following April. The plan will take four years to complete—with the first bases slated for closing in January 1990.

In fashioning a defense budget that increasingly is being driven by concerns over the federal budget deficit, Secretary of Defense Cheney received congressional approval to cancel several high-priced weapons systems. Examples are the Air Force F-15E jet interceptor plane and the Army AH-64 helicopter. In what some critics claimed was a concession to pork-barrel politics, the Congress agreed to the purchase of 18 additional F-14 fighter planes, although Cheney had said they were not needed, and money also was provided to continue research and development on the V-22 Osprey, a Marine tilt-rotor craft that can fly like a regular airplane, but also can land and take off like a helicopter. Cheney also had recommended cancellation of that program.

In regard to major weapons programs, Congress provided for the purchase of two more B-2 Stealth bombers, and the initial funding for the production of five more of the aircraft the following year. In December the Air Force announced that 50 MX ICBM missiles would be removed from their silo bases and re-based on trains in the states of Wyoming, Louisiana, Texas, Washington, North Dakota, Arkansas, and Michigan. The Pentagon's logic was that with larger and more accurate missiles the Soviets were endangering the U.S. fixed-base missile force. Those opposing the modernization of the land-based missile force noted that the warming relations with the Soviet Union, and the talk of substantial disarmament, meant that the U.S. missile force would be in less danger than earlier estimates had projected.

For their part, the Soviets announced that for the first time in the history of Communist nations they would make public the amount of money spent upon military activities. This information was in fact made public in the summer. According to the Soviet budget figures the USSR spends $125.5 billion a year on its military forces. Both American and Soviet defense experts quickly noted that this figure substantially understates the actual cost of the Soviet military programs because it fails to account for the fact that the Soviet military pays artificially low prices for the goods and services which it obtains.

Pentagon Leadership Changes. President Bush's initial nominee to be secretary of defense, John Tower, former Republican senator from Texas, encountered insurmountable opposition in the Senate due to allegations of improper conduct (*see* special report, page 541). However, a second nominee, Republican Congressman from Wyoming Dick Cheney (*see* BIOGRAPHY), was confirmed speedily by the Senate. In August, President Bush named Army Gen. Colin L. Powell (*see* BIOGRAPHY) as the chairman of the Joint Chiefs of Staff to succeed Admiral Crowe, who retired on September 30. At 52, Powell became the youngest officer to hold the nation's highest military position, and the first black to do so.

Controversial Weapons. After years of unofficial speculation that the United States was developing a new bomber that would employ advanced technology to avoid radar detection and tracking, the Pentagon presided over the flight test for the Stealth bomber—officially designated the B-2—in the early summer. Controversy immediately enveloped the new plane. Opponents claimed that the Pentagon's planned acquisition of 132 B-2s at a total estimated cost of $70 billion was excessive. Critics also stated the plane would fail in its mission to hunt down and destroy mobile Soviet ICBMs because the Soviets would launch the missiles long before the planes completed their nine-hour flight from the United States to the USSR. Some members of the scientific community suggested that a new type of radar, Over the Horizon Backscatter Radar, might be able to detect the Stealth bombers even though conventional radar could not.

The Drug War. In September, Secretary of Defense Cheney asked his senior military commanders to suggest ways in which U.S. forces could be utilized in the so-called war on drugs. Late in the year a Pentagon official stated that part of the drug-war plan being formulated could involve both an air and a naval blockade of Colombia. Such action would involve an American aircraft-carrier battle group stationed off the coastline of Colombia, thought to be a primary source for large amounts of illegal drugs entering the United States.

On December 20, U.S. military forces invaded Panama in an effort to capture Gen. Manuel Noriega so he could be placed on trial in the United States on drug charges. After several days of fighting the Noriega forces were subdued with a loss of 23 U.S. servicemen. Early in 1990, Noriega gave himself up and was returned to the United States for trial.

ROBERT M. LAWRENCE
Colorado State University

MINNESOTA

A rebounding farm economy, a mixed business outlook, the takeover of Minnesota-based Northwest Airlines, a confrontation between the governor and legislature over taxes, and a stubborn labor dispute were among the major developments of 1989 in Minnesota.

Economy and Agriculture. Crop yields, livestock, and dairy production were up substantially over 1988, although not at record levels. Timely rains offset poor subsoil moisture from the 1988 drought year, but future growing conditions remained touch-and-go. Retail sales were strong, rising in the first half to 5.9% above the national average, but commercial real-estate and financial services were down in the face of a long-term glut of office space, severe loan defaults, and foreclosures. First Banks System, a premier financial institution, forced the resignations of two bank presidents and undertook major restructuring, following large losses.

Despite the mixed business outlook, major development was proceeding. In Bloomington, ground was broken on the $2 billion "Mall of America" which will house 100 new retail businesses in a Disneyland-like setting hailed by its backers as the biggest in the world. In Minneapolis, the nationally recognized Nicollet Mall was undergoing a $23 million facelift and plans were proceeding for a two-tower 53-story development, designed by the I. M. Pei architectural firm, to house First Banks System and IBM.

Airline Takeover. After a bidding war that lasted for three months, a group headed by 41-year-old Alfred Checchi paid $3.65 billion to acquire Northwest Airlines. The new owners made assurances that the change would not adversely affect the Minnesota operations.

Labor Strife. The Boise-Cascade paper mill at International Falls was the target of a wildcat strike protesting the company's use of nonunion workers. Strike-related destruction caused an estimated $1 million in damage. Gov. Rudy Perpich threatened to withdraw a state tax incentive that assisted the company's expansion program.

Politics. Governor Perpich startled fellow Democratic-Farmer-Labor (DFL) Party members in the DFL-controlled state legislature when he vetoed a tax package. In special session the governor and legislature came together on a wide-ranging property-tax reform and reduction package. Perpich, already the longest-serving governor in the state's history, announced—to the consternation of both supporters and opponents—he would seek another four-year term in 1990.

Minneapolis' DFL Mayor Don Fraser, after ten years in office, captured another four-year term. In St. Paul, DFL Mayor George Latimer stepped down after a record-breaking 12 years. City Council President Jim Scheibel was elected to the post.

Sports. The National Football League Minnesota Vikings acquired star running back Herschel Walker from the Dallas Cowboys. Beneath this highly visible excitement was concern over decreasing patronage. The State Fair, the University of Minnesota football team, the new Canterbury Downs racetrack, and the North Stars hockey team also had attendance drops. The racetrack's future was in question because of severe financial problems, but the state welcomed still another sports attraction —the Minnesota Timberwolves of the National Basketball Association (NBA)—at the start of the 1989–90 season.

ARTHUR NAFTALIN, *University of Minnesota*

MINNESOTA • Information Highlights

Area: 84,402 sq mi (218 601 km²).
Population (July 1, 1988): 4,307,000.
Chief Cities (July 1, 1986 est.): St. Paul, the capital, 263,680; Minneapolis, 356,840; Duluth (1980 census), 92,811.
Government (1989): *Chief Officers*—governor, Rudy Perpich (DFL); lt. gov., Marlene Johnson (DFL). *Legislature*—Senate, 67 members; House of Representatives, 134 members.
State Finances (fiscal year 1988): *Revenue*, $11,453,000,000; *expenditure*, $9,648,000,000.
Personal Income (1988): $71,807,000,000; per capita, $16,674.
Labor Force (June 1989): *Civilian labor force*, 2,368,300; *unemployed*, 115,100 (4.9% of total force).
Education: *Enrollment* (fall 1987)—public elementary schools, 497,000; public secondary, 225,000; colleges and universities, 237,212. *Public school expenditures* (1987–88), $2,983,500,000 ($4,166 per pupil).

MISSISSIPPI

Two legislative sessions, quadrennial municipal elections, and a congressional contest that prompted a campaign visit by President Bush held center stage in Mississippi during 1989. Other attention-getters included long-delayed judicial elections, a set of constitutional amendments, and the economy.

The Legislature. While more than 2,500 bills were introduced at the regular 90-day legislative session that began January 3, relatively few noteworthy pieces of legislation were enacted. A bill to reorganize various executive branch agencies was passed, but the measure fell far short of the plan pushed by second-year Gov. Ray Mabus. Other significant items the legislature approved included an equity funding bill designed to reduce disparities in finances among school districts, a tort reform measure shortening the statute of limitations for filing suits, and a bill allowing a Gulfport-based cruise ship to open its casinos while still in state territorial waters. Other gambling measures, including proposals to establish a state

AP/Wide World

U.S. District Judge Walter L. Nixon of Mississippi left the Capitol in November after the Senate voted 89–8 to remove him from the bench on impeachment charges.

lottery and pari-mutuel betting on dog races, were defeated. Controversial bills to allow continued funding of the state's three charity hospitals were vetoed by the governor.

Two measures that were killed in the regular session won approval in a three-day special session that was convened only two weeks after legislators had returned home. Lawmakers authorized the issuance of $78.5 million in bonds to finance repair of state-owned buildings, and they gave the five-member Parole Board full-time status.

Politics. Republicans made substantial gains in the June 6 quadrennial municipal elections, but they continued to comprise only a small percentage of the officeholders in the state's nearly 300 municipalities. Blacks and women also increased their numbers among municipal officials, but they too accounted for a very small share of the total. One city, Tupelo, voted to change its century-old mayor-board of aldermen form of government to the mayor-council form. In many areas of the state, voter turnout was disappointing.

State and national interest was focused on the special election to fill the 5th District vacancy created August 13 when freshman U.S. Rep. Larkin Smith (R, Gulfport) was killed in a small-plane crash. In balloting held October 20, State Sen. Gene Taylor (D, Bay St. Louis) defeated Tom Anderson (R, Gulfport), a longtime aide of U.S. Sen. Trent Lott, by a margin of nearly two to one to give the Democrats control of the district for the first time since 1972.

On June 20 state voters elected circuit and chancery judges for the first time since 1982. Elections had been blocked by a 5th U.S. Circuit Court of Appeals decision requiring that some judicial districts be redrawn to create minority subdistricts to give black candidates a better chance at judicial posts. The elections increased the number of black judges by only one, reviving claims of discrimination.

On June 20 voters also approved two constitutional amendments deleting references to an already unenforceable poll tax and removing the obsolete prohibition against out-of-state corporations operating railroads in Mississippi. A third proposal to provide easier revision of the constitution was rejected.

The Economy. Mississippi's economy continued to expand but at a slower pace than in 1988. The unemployment rate, while down overall, was highly uneven across the state. Tourism along the Gulf Coast improved.

Other Developments. The opening of long-sealed state Sovereignty Commission files in June renewed interest in the state's civil-rights era. In April five savings and loan associations were taken over by federal regulators and a sixth, the state's largest, was taken over in October. In May, U.S. District Judge Walter L. Nixon, Jr., was impeached by the U.S. House of Representatives and in November the Senate voted to remove him from the bench after finding him guilty of two of three articles of impeachment. Approximately half of Mississippi's counties installed the unit system of road administration in October as a result of November 1988 elections.

DANA B. BRAMMER
The University of Mississippi

MISSISSIPPI • Information Highlights

Area: 47,689 sq mi (123 515 km²).
Population (July 1, 1988): 2,620,000.
Chief Cities (1980 census): Jackson, the capital (July 1, 1986 est.), 208,440; Biloxi, 49,311; Meridian, 46,577.
Government (1989): *Chief Officers*—governor, Raymond Mabus, Jr. (D); lt. gov., Brad Dye (D). *Legislature*—Senate, 52 members; House of Representatives, 122 members.
State Finances (fiscal year 1988): *Revenue,* $4,610,000,000; *expenditure,* $4,145,000,000.
Personal Income (1988): $29,123,000,000; per capita, $11,116.
Labor Force (June 1989): *Civilian labor force,* 1,203,400; *unemployed,* 118,300 (9.8% of total force).
Education: *Enrollment* (fall 1987)—public elementary schools, 364,000; public secondary, 141,000; colleges and universities, 105,510. *Public school expenditures* (1987–88), $1,302,241,000 ($2,591 per pupil).

MISSOURI

Major news in Missouri during 1989 focused on the state's 1986 abortion law restricting abortion rights, upheld by the U.S. Supreme Court in July, and the selection of Missouri's U.S. Rep. Richard Gephardt as House majority leader. The controversial abortion statute outlaws use of public facilities or employees to perform or recommend abortions unless the mother's life is in danger and requires testing of the fetus before an abortion can be performed after 20 weeks of pregnancy.

Legislative and Political News. The U.S. Supreme Court threw Missouri into a financial crisis by ruling that states cannot tax federal workers' pensions if state pensions are exempt from income taxes. Missouri, with 65,000 federal retirees, had to refund $151 million, forcing a special session of the General Assembly, which raised sales and corporate income taxes to cover the refunds.

St. Louis Democratic Mayor Vincent Schoemehl won a third term in April, and almost immediately began positioning himself for a run for governor in 1990. Schoemehl's longtime rival on several issues in the metropolitan area, St. Louis County Executive Gene McNary, left Missouri, accepting an appointment as commissioner of the Immigration and Naturalization Service.

U.S. Rep. Richard Gephardt of St. Louis bounced back from his unsuccessful 1988 presidential campaign by becoming House majority leader. With the resignation of Jim Wright as House speaker, Tom Foley moved up to that position, and Gephardt replaced Foley.

Crime. Missouri exercised the death penalty for the first time since 1965, when convicted killer George "Tiny" Mercer was executed by lethal injection at the state penitentiary in Jefferson City. Just months after the execution, the last in the building housing the old gas chamber, the state moved all death-row inmates to a new maximum-security prison in Potosi.

Drug violence increased in Missouri, with both St. Louis and Kansas City fighting the spread of crack and with labs making "crank" amphetamines being found in rural areas. In January, an arson fire in Kansas City that killed six people was attributed to a feud with a neighboring crack house.

A farm couple near Chillicothe, MO, was charged with murdering transients who allegedly worked for the couple in a fraudulent cattle-buying scheme. Five bodies were found on farms where Ray Copeland once had worked, and the investigation was continuing as the year drew to a close. Copeland, 75, and his wife Faye, 68, were charged with three counts of first-degree murder.

Newspapers. St. Louis gained a new daily newspaper and Kansas City lost one. Nearly three years after the demise of the *Globe-Democrat* left St. Louis with only one daily newspaper, Ingersoll Publications launched a flashy tabloid, the *St. Louis Sun,* in September, going head-to-head in the morning with the long-established *St. Louis Post-Dispatch.* In October, the Kansas City Star Company announced that it would merge its afternoon paper, *The Kansas City Star,* and its morning paper, *The Kansas City Times,* into one morning publication, retaining the name of the *Star,* the look of the *Times,* and the features of both papers. The decision to kill the afternoon paper was made after a decade-long loss of 100,000 in circulation.

Public Works. Missouri's two major cities moved at different speeds in expanding downtown convention facilities. St. Louis launched an $80 million expansion of the Cervantes Convention Center. Kansas City got the state General Assembly to approve legislation providing money to help with major local projects, but city officials were unable to agree on a plan for financing the local share of expansion plans for the Bartle Hall convention facility.

STEPHEN BUTTRY
"The Kansas City Times"

MISSOURI • Information Highlights

Area: 69,697 sq mi (180 516 km²).
Population (July 1, 1988): 5,141,000.
Chief Cities (July 1, 1986 est.): Jefferson City, the capital (1980 census), 33,619; Kansas City, 441,170; St. Louis, 426,300; Springfield, 139,360; Independence, 112,950.
Government (1989): *Chief Officers*—governor, John Ashcroft (R); lt. gov., Mel Carahan (D). *General Assembly*—Senate, 34 members; House of Representatives, 163 members.
State Finances (fiscal year 1988): *Revenue,* $8,150,000,000; *expenditure,* $7,408,000,000.
Personal Income (1988): $79,440,000,000; per capita, $15,452.
Labor Force (June 1989): *Civilian labor force,* 2,649,400; *unemployed,* 140,600 (5.3% of total force).
Education: *Enrollment* (fall 1987)—public elementary schools, 557,000; public secondary, 245,000; colleges and universities, 251,778. *Public school expenditures* (1987–88), $2,634,662,000 ($3,641 per pupil).

MONTANA

Montana celebrated its centennial as a state during 1989. The main event among dozens of activities was a week-long, 60-mi (97-km) cattle drive in early September from Roundup to Billings. More than 3,000 riders with 3,300 horses and 200 covered wagons pushed 2,812 cattle through the Bull Mountains and across the prairie. The drive, conceived by two Western cartoonists, was plagued by politics during its planning stages, but area ranchers and Billings organizers cooperated during the final few weeks to make it a success.

Politics and Legislative News. The Montana legislature, meeting in its biennial session, failed to meet a court-mandated deadline for distributing money equally to the state's school districts. A state district judge ordered the legislature to distribute money more evenly between richer school districts—mostly those collecting taxes on minerals—and the poorer districts. The mandate became the focus of a legislative fight over a proposed sales tax, which would have made schools less dependent on property taxes. The sales-tax proposal died at the end of the 90-day session, however, forcing a special summer session. That meeting resulted in a proposal to redistribute existing property-tax money, but by the end of the year, the courts had not decided whether to approve the new formula.

Political news focused on various scandals involving state government department heads. Gov. Stan Stephens' budget director resigned after admitting that he had lied about his education and that he was married to two women; the director of the Department of Family Services resigned after he was caught making threatening telephone calls; and a division manager in the Department of Social and Rehabilitation Services was fired after he was convicted of vandalizing a political opponent's car.

Environment. Yellowstone National Park's elk and bison herds, which migrate into Montana during the winter months, were decimated by a combination of environmental factors and hunters. Suffering from a lack of food and from the stress of the 1988 forest fires in Yellowstone, the herds were ill-prepared for three weeks of subzero temperatures and blizzards in February. In their attempts to flee the cold, the bison moved onto private land outside the park where they became easy prey for hunters.

Religion. The Church Universal and Triumphant, a Christian sect headquartered on a mountain ranch near Livingston, came under fire in 1989 after its security chief was caught using a false name to buy large-caliber assault weapons. The church vice-president admitted in court that he conspired in the case. Local officials also were upset when they discovered that the church was building massive underground bomb shelters on its ranch, some as long as a quarter of a mile (.4 km).

Disaster. An explosion in Helena in February caused millions of dollars worth of damage, but killed no one. A railroad tank car carrying propane gas rolled down a mountain pass and into Helena, where it collided with other rail cars and exploded. The explosion destroyed dozens of buildings throughout the city, including several on the campus of Carroll College, a small private school. The damage shut down classes at the college for several weeks and cut electrical power to most of the city for a day. Much of the damage resulted from subzero cold weather.

ROBERT C. GIBSON
"The Billings Gazette"

AP/Wide World

Horse-drawn covered wagons were part of a massive and colorful cattle drive from Roundup to Billings, MT, staged in celebration of Montana's 100 years of statehood.

MONTANA • Information Highlights

Area: 147,046 sq mi (380 848 km²).
Population (July 1, 1988): 805,000.
Chief Cities (1980 census): Helena, the capital, 23,938; Billings, 66,798; Great Falls, 56,725.
Government (1989): *Chief Officers*—governor, Stan Stephens (R); lt. gov., Allen Kolstad (R). *Legislature*—Senate, 50 members; House of Representatives, 100 members.
State Finances (fiscal year 1988): *Revenue,* $2,026,000,000; *expenditure,* $1,695,000,000.
Personal Income (1988): $10,352,000,000; per capita, $12,866.
Labor Force (June 1989): *Civilian labor force,* 409,500; *unemployed,* 24,500 (6.0% of total force).
Education: *Enrollment* (fall 1987)—public elementary schools, 108,000; public secondary, 44,000; colleges and universities, 35,882. *Public school expenditures* (1987–88), $566,120,000 ($3,878 per pupil).

MOROCCO

The year 1989 was a relatively good year for Morocco. The conflict in the Western Sahara moved from the battlefield to the hallways of the United Nations. Fighting continued but on a much lower scale.

Domestic Affairs. In June 1989, King Hassan II granted amnesty to more than 200 political prisoners but continued to hold such well-known opposition figures as Mohammed Ait Khaddour and Abraham Serfaty.

Heads of major political parties were reelected at their annual congresses in 1989. Mohammed Boucetta was elected secretary-general of the Istiqlal Party for the fourth consecutive time since 1974. Former Prime Minister Maati Bouabid was reelected chairman of the progovernment Constitutional Union which he has headed since its founding in 1983. Abderrahman Bouabid was reelected head of the Socialist Union of Popular Forces (USFP) by the party's political bureau a month following the meeting of the fifth national congress held in April 1989. The government's decentralization policies were proceeding on schedule with new administrative structures proposed for the country's northern region.

The likelihood of another good agricultural season made official predictions of between 3% and 4% in real gross domestic product (GDP) growth in 1989 look realistic. The good economic performance over the previous few years, coupled with the continuing support provided by key international agencies such as the World Bank and the International Monetary Fund (IMF) to the program of economic reform, and the prospect of improved intra-Maghreb (North African) cooperation provided a favorable climate for investment and growth. Banking and industry both looked strong. Tourism was booming, with forecasts of more than 3 million tourist arrivals in 1989. A potential trouble spot was eliminated when miners in the Jerada complex in northeast Morocco decided to return to work in mid-February. The miners had gone on strike in December 1988.

MOROCCO • Information Highlights

Official Name: Kingdom of Morocco.
Location: Northwest Africa.
Area: 172,413 sq mi (446 550 km^2).
Population (mid-1989 est.): 25,600,000.
Chief Cities (mid-1987 est., incl. suburbs): Rabat, the capital, 1,287,000; Casablanca, 2,904,000; Fès, 933,000; Marrakech, 1,425,000.
Government: *Head of state,* Hassan II, king (acceded 1961). *Head of government,* Azzedine Laraki, prime minister (appointed Sept. 30, 1986). *Legislature* (unicameral)—Chamber of Representatives.
Monetary Unit: Dirham (8.702 dirhams equal U.S.$1, June 1989).
Gross Domestic Product (1987 U.S.$): $18,000,-000,000.
Economic Indexes (1988): *Consumer Prices* (1980 = 100), all items, 182.9; food, 183.1. *Industrial Production* (1980 = 100), 136.
Foreign Trade (1988 U.S.$): *Imports,* $4,772,000,000; *exports,* $3,603,000,000.

External debt has risen from $13 billion in 1984 to $22 billion in 1989. For its part the government decided to increase subsidies on flour, sugar, and cooking oil. This went against the earlier conditions for assistance from the IMF and the World Bank, which demanded the elimination of such subsidies by 1990. A major reason for retaining the subsidies was to keep prices down to avoid another outburst of social unrest in the major urban areas.

In May 1989 the text of the proposed law that commits the government to transfer the majority of state enterprises to the private sector was published. The main exceptions included national railways, national water, national electricity, phosphates, mail, telecommunications, and the national airline.

Foreign Affairs. A summit meeting of the five Maghreb heads of state in Marrakech ended on Feb. 17, 1989, with the formation of an Arab Maghreb Union (AMU). It links Mauritania, Morocco, Algeria, Tunisia, and Libya —in a form of association designed to promote and improve economic relations.

At the beginning of March 1989, King Hassan announced that he would ratify a treaty, originally signed in June 1972, defining borders between Morocco and Algeria. An official visit by Algerian President Chadli Benjedid to Morocco in early February followed by the Marrakech summit and the Arab League summit held in Casablanca at the end of May contributed to the consolidation of personal and political relations between the Moroccan and Algerian heads of state. Under such conditions the war in the Western Sahara was beginning to recede as a conflict issue for both parties. With Algerian prodding, the Polisario guerrilla movement was beginning to turn to dialogue and negotiations as the alternative to warfare although the killing continued. Even the hijacking to the Canary Islands on September 19 of a Royal Air Maroc internal civilian flight seemed the work of a lone Sahrawi guerrilla rather than the start of a new, more "terroristic" strategy.

Moroccan-Spanish bilateral relations are potentially the most significant outside the Maghreb region. Spain is the Maghreb's link to Europe with all the implications that this has for Morocco's economic, social, and political development. Key issues concern the future of the Spanish enclaves of Ceuta and Melilla off the Atlantic coast and the treatment of Moroccan workers in transit through Spain from their jobs in Europe. During King Hassan's first state visit to Madrid in September, he and Spain's King Juan Carlos signed several important agreements, including one calling for the building of a bridge across the Strait of Gibraltar, connecting Europe to Africa.

JOHN P. ENTELIS, *Fordham University*

MOTION PICTURES

Woody Allen, often criticized for invading the realm of drama instead of adhering to comedy, returned with an expert fusion of both in his acclaimed *Crimes and Misdemeanors*. Philosophical American movies have been taboo in mainstream entertainment, but Allen broke significant new ground by probing the contemporary American scene with questions customarily reserved for the more esoteric works of Swedish master Ingmar Bergman. Is there a God? If so, is he a merciful or vindictive God? Does evil go unpunished and is good unrewarded? Where are present-day values leading us? Is there really any order to our lives that justifies continued faith? Instead of creating a ponderous film anchored to such weighty questions, the writer-director provided a zesty drama enlivened by hilarious lines and situations. But beneath the laughs *Crimes and Misdemeanors* was also his darkest film.

The central story concerns a renowned ophthalmologist, impressively played by Martin Landau, whose family life is jeopardized when his mistress (Anjelica Huston) threatens to expose their relationship and his financial improprieties. His brother (Jerry Orbach), who has underworld connections, proposes that the woman be eliminated by a hired gunman. In a parallel plot Allen plays a loser as a husband, whose wife (Joanna Gleason) ignores him, and as a serious documentary filmmaker contrasted with his glib brother-in-law (Alan Alda), a successful television producer. Both are wooing the same woman (Mia Farrow). The film's many threads are woven ingeniously by Allen into an exciting and mature example of what cinema can achieve.

Ambitious Work. While there was the customary share of light, blockbuster fare, numerous other creative artists attempted more challenging subjects. At 26, Steven Soderbergh made an impressive debut with *sex, lies, and videotape*, a lauded exploration of what lay behind the facade of ostensibly upwardly mobile characters. His low-budget movie won the *Palme d'Or* at the prestigious Cannes Film Festival, and received rave reviews at home.

Long-festering moral questions concerning the decision to drop two nuclear bombs on Japan in World War II were raised, although somewhat timidly, in *Fat Man and Little Boy*, directed by Roland Joffe (*The Killing Fields*, 1984). The drama, which also attempted to capture the excitement of the race to create atomic weaponry at Los Alamos, NM, afforded Paul Newman an occasion for an impressive portrayal of Gen. Leslie R. Groves, who supervised the project.

Spike Lee, previously praised for his directorial promise, made *Do the Right Thing*, a powerful film about festering racism. Set in a Brooklyn neighborhood that had become Afro-American and Hispanic, the story focuses on an Italian family clinging to its pizzeria and Lee as the deliveryman, with events leading to police brutality and a resulting riot. While not expounding solutions, the film is a provocative cry for resolving racial prejudice.

Other examples of thought-provoking movies included Euzhan Palcy's *A Dry White Season*, a searing drama of repression and the fight against apartheid in South Africa; Norman Jewison's *In Country*, dealing with the effects of the Vietnam War on a Kentucky veteran and on the daughter of a soldier killed in battle; Brian DePalma's *Casualties of War*, which recalls a brutal rape of a Vietnamese woman by GIs and the agonizing decision of a soldier to speak out against the perpetrators; Oliver Stone's *Born on the Fourth of July*, a look at the Vietnam debacle through the eyes of a par-

AP/Wide World

Writer, director, and actor Woody Allen, right, *directs Martin Landau in a scene from his "Crimes and Misdemeanors," a film centering on the dilemma of facing choices which bear life-altering consequences and the capacity of individuals to make moral choices under such circumstances. Landau, in the role of the respected ophthalmologist who becomes involved in the murder of his mistress, portrays the pivotal character through which the film's intentions are revealed most clearly.*

MOTION PICTURES | 1989

THE ADVENTURES OF BARON MUNCHAUSEN. Director, Terry Gilliam; screenplay by Charles McKeown and Mr. Gilliam. With John Neville, Eric Idle, Sarah Polley, Oliver Reed, Jonathan Pryce, Sting, Robin Williams.

ALWAYS. Director, Steven Spielberg; screenplay by Jerry Belson and Diane Thomas. With Richard Dreyfuss, Holly Hunter, Brad Johnson, John Goodman, Audrey Hepburn.

BACK TO THE FUTURE, PART II. Director, Robert Zemeckis; screenplay by Bob Gale. With Michael J. Fox, Christopher Lloyd, Lea Thompson.

BATMAN. Director, Tim Burton; screenplay by Sam Hamm and Warren Skaaren. With Michael Keaton, Jack Nicholson, Kim Basinger.

THE BEAR. Director, Jean-Jacques Annaud; screenplay by Gerard Brach, based on *The Grizzly King* by James Oliver Curwood. With Bart and Douce (trained bears), Jack Wallace, Tceky Karyo, André Lacombe.

BLACK RAIN. Director, Ridley Scott; screenplay by Craig Bolotin and Warren Lewis. With Michael Douglas.

BLAZE. Written and directed by Ron Shelton. With Paul Newman, Lolita Davidovich.

BORN ON THE FOURTH OF JULY. Director, Oliver Stone; screenplay by Mr. Stone and Ron Kovic, based on the book by Mr. Kovic. With Tom Cruise, Willem Dafoe, Kyra Sedgwick.

BREAKING IN. Director, Bill Forsyth; screenplay by John Sayles. With Burt Reynolds.

THE BURBS. Director, Joe Dante; screenplay by Dana Olsen. With Tom Hanks, Bruce Dern, Carrie Fisher.

CASUALTIES OF WAR. Director, Brian De Palma; screenplay by David Rabe. With Michael J. Fox, Sean Penn, Don Harvey, John C. Reilly, John Leguizamo.

COOKIE. Director, Susan Seidelman; screenplay by Nora Ephron and Alice Arlen. With Peter Falk, Dianne Wiest, Emily Lloyd, Brenda Vaccaro, Jerry Lewis.

CRIMES AND MISDEMEANORS. Written and directed by Woody Allen. With Mr. Allen, Martin Landau, Anjelica Huston, Alan Alda, Mia Farrow, Jerry Orbach, Claire Bloom, Joanna Gleason, Sam Waterston, Caroline Aaron, Martin Bergmann.

DAD. Written and directed by Gary David Goldberg, based on the novel by William Wharton. With Jack Lemmon, Ted Danson, Olympia Dukakis.

DEAD POETS SOCIETY. Director, Peter Weir; screenplay by Tom Schulman. With Robin Williams, Robert Sean Leonard, Ethan Hawke, Gale Hansen.

DO THE RIGHT THING. Written and directed by Spike Lee. With Danny Aiello, Ossie Davis, Ruby Dee, Mr. Lee, Rosie Perez, Richard Edson, Giancarlo Esposito, Bill Nunn, John Turturro.

THE DREAM TEAM. Director, Howard Zieff; screenplay by Jon Connolly and David Loucka. With Michael Keaton, Christopher Lloyd, Peter Boyle.

DRIVING MISS DAISY. Director, Bruce Beresford; screenplay by Alfred Uhry from his play. With Morgan Freeman, Jessica Tandy, Dan Aykroyd.

DRUGSTORE COWBOY. Director, Gus Van Sant, Jr.; screenplay by Mr. Van Sant and Daniel Yost, based on the novel by James Fogle. With Matt Dillon.

A DRY WHITE SEASON. Director, Euzhan Palcy; screenplay by Colin Welland and Miss Palcy, based on the novel by André Brink. With Donald Sutherland, Janet Suzman, Zakes Mokae, Jürgen Prochnow, Susan Sarandon, Marlon Brando.

EARTH GIRLS ARE EASY. Director, Julien Temple; screenplay by Julie Brown, Charlie Coffey, and Terrence E. McNally. With Geena Davis, Jeff Goldblum.

84 CHARLIE MOPIC. Written and directed by Patrick Duncan. With Richard Brooks, Nicholas Cascone, Glenn Morshower.

ENEMIES, A LOVE STORY. Director, Paul Mazursky; screenplay by Mr. Mazursky and Roger L. Simon. With Ron Silver, Anjelica Huston, Lena Olin, Alan King.

THE FABULOUS BAKER BOYS. Written and directed by Steve Kloves. With Jeff Bridges, Beau Bridges, Michelle Pfeiffer.

FAMILY BUSINESS. Director, Sidney Lumet; screenplay by Vincent Patrick. With Sean Connery, Dustin Hoffman, Matthew Broderick.

AP/Wide World

Batman and the Joker face off in the persons of Michael Keaton and Jack Nicholson in "Batman," the major box office hit of 1989. The film also featured Kim Basinger.

FAT MAN AND LITTLE BOY. Director, Roland Joffé; screenplay by Bruce Robinson and Mr. Joffé. With Paul Newman, Dwight Schultz, Bonnie Bedelia, Natasha Richardson, Laura Dern, John Cusack.

FIELD OF DREAMS. Written and directed by Phil Alden Robinson, based on the book *Shoeless Joe* by W. P. Kinsella. With Kevin Costner, Amy Madigan, James Earl Jones, Burt Lancaster.

FLETCH LIVES. Director, Michael Ritchie; screenplay by Leon Capetanos. With Chevy Chase, Hal Holbrook, Julianne Phillips.

FRIDAY THE 13TH PART VIII—JASON TAKES MANHATTAN. Written and directed by Rob Hedden. With Kane Hodder.

GHOSTBUSTERS II. Director, Ivan Reitman; screenplay by Harold Ramis and Dan Aykroyd. With Bill Murray, Mr. Aykroyd, Sigourney Weaver, Mr. Ramis, Rick Moranis, Peter MacNicol, Annie Potts, Ernie Hudson.

GLORY. Director, Ed Zwick; screenplay by Mr. Zwick and Kevin Jarre. With Matthew Broderick, Denzel Washington, Morgan Freeman, Cary Elwes, Jane Alexander.

GREAT BALLS OF FIRE. Director, Jim McBride; screenplay by Jack Baran and Mr. McBride. With Dennis Quaid, Winona Ryder.

HARLEM NIGHTS. Written and directed by Eddie Murphy. With Mr. Murphy, Richard Pryor, Redd Foxx, Danny Aiello, Arsenio Hall, Della Reese.

HENRY V. Directed and adapted by Kenneth Branagh, based on the play by William Shakespeare. With Mr. Branagh, Derek Jacobi, Ian Holm, Paul Scofield.

HONEY, I SHRUNK THE KIDS. Director, Joe Johnston; screenplay by Ed Naha and Tom Schulman. With Rick Moranis, Marcia Strassman, Robert Oliveri, Amy O'Neill, Matt Frewer, Kristine Sutherland, Thomas Brown, Jared Rushton.

IMMEDIATE FAMILY. Director, Jonathan Kaplan; screenplay by Barbara Benedek. With Glenn Close, James Woods, Mary Stuart Masterson, Kevin Dillon, Jane Greer.

IN COUNTRY. Director, Norman Jewison; screenplay by Frank Pierson and Cynthia Cidre, based on the novel by Bobbie Ann Mason. With Bruce Willis, Emily Lloyd, Peggy Rea, Joan Allen, Judith Ivey, John Terry.

INDIANA JONES AND THE LAST CRUSADE. Director, Steven Spielberg; screenplay by Jeffrey Boam. With Harrison Ford, Sean Connery, Denholm Elliott, River Phoenix.

JACKNIFE. Director, David Jones; screenplay by Stephen Metcalfe. With Robert De Niro, Kathy Baker, Ed Harris.

JOHNNY HANDSOME. Director, Walter Hill; screenplay by Ken Friedman, based on the novel *The Three Worlds of Johnny Handsome,* by John Godey. With Mickey Rourke, Scott Wilson, Ellen Barkin, Elizabeth McGovern.

THE KARATE KID PART III. Director, John G. Avildsen; screenplay by Robert Mark Kamen. With Ralph Macchio, Noriyuki (Pat) Morita, Thomas Ian Griffith.

LETHAL WEAPON 2. Director, Richard Donner; screenplay by Jeffrey Boam. With Mel Gibson, Danny Glover, Joe Pesci.

THE LITTLE MERMAID. Written and directed by John Musker and Ron Clements. Animation.

LOOK WHO'S TALKING. Written and directed by Amy Heckerling. With John Travolta, Kirstie Alley, Olympia Dukakis, George Segal, Abe Vigoda, and Bruce Willis (as the voice of Mikey).

MAJOR LEAGUE. Written and directed by David Ward. With Tom Berenger, Charlie Sheen, Corbin Bernsen, Margaret Whitton, Rene Russo, Bob Uecker.

MY LEFT FOOT. Director, Jim Sheridan; screenplay by Mr. Sheridan and Shane Connaughton, based on the book by Christy Brown. With Daniel Day Lewis.

MYSTERY TRAIN. Written and directed by Jim Jarmusch. With Masatoshi Nagase, Yonki Kudoh, Screamin' Jay Hawkins, Cinque Lee.

NATIONAL LAMPOON'S CHRISTMAS VACATION. Directed by Jeremiah S. Chechik; screenplay by John Hughes. With Chevy Chase, Beverly D'Angelo, Randy Quaid.

A NIGHTMARE ON ELM STREET 5: THE DREAM CHILD. Director, Stephen Hopkins; screenplay by Leslie Bohem. With Robert Englund, Lisa Wilcox, Joe Seely.

OLD GRINGO. Director, Luis Puenzo; screenplay by Aida Bortnik and Mr. Puenzo, based on the novel by Carlos Fuentes. With Jane Fonda, Gregory Peck, Jimmy Smits.

THE PACKAGE. Director, Andrew Davis; screenplay by John Bishop. With Gene Hackman, Joanna Cassidy, Tommy Lee Jones, John Heard.

PARENTHOOD. Director, Ron Howard; story by Lowell Ganz, Babaloo Mandel, and Mr. Howard. With Steve Martin, Mary Steenburgen, Dianne Wiest, Jason Robards, Rick Moranis, Tom Hulce, Martha Plimpton, Keanu Reeves, Leaf Phoenix.

PARENTS. Director, Bob Balaban; screenplay by Christopher Hawthorne. With Randy Quaid, Mary Beth Hurt, Sandy Dennis, Bryan Madorsky.

PET SEMATARY. Director, Mary Lambert; screenplay by Stephen King, based on his novel. With Fred Gwynne.

POLICE ACADEMY 6: CITY UNDER SIEGE. Director, Peter Bonerz; screenplay by Stephen J. Curwick. With Bubba Smith, David Graf, Michael Winslow, Lance Kinsey, G. W. Bailey.

THE RAINBOW. Director, Ken Russell; screenplay by Mr. Russell and Vivian Russell, based on the book by D. H. Lawrence. With Sammi Davis, Paul McGann, Amanda Donohoe, David Hemmings, Christopher Gable, Glenda Jackson.

ROGER AND ME. Written and directed by Michael Moore. With Mr. Moore. Documentary.

SCANDAL. Director, Michael Caton-Jones; screenplay by Michael Thomas. With John Hurt, Joanne Whalley-Kilmer, Bridget Fonda, Ian McKellen, Leslie Phillips, Britt Ekland.

SCENES FROM THE CLASS STRUGGLE IN BEVERLY HILLS. Director, Paul Bartel; screenplay by Bruce Wagner. With Jacqueline Bisset, Mary Woronov, Robert Beltran, Ray Sharkey, Ed Begley, Jr., Wallace Shawn, Edith Diaz.

SEE NO EVIL, HEAR NO EVIL. Director, Arthur Hiller; screenplay by Earl Barret, Arne Sultan, Eliot Wad, Andrew Kurtzman, and Gene Wilder. With Richard Pryor, Mr. Wilder, Joan Severance, Kevin Spacey.

SEA OF LOVE. Director, Harold Becker; screenplay by Richard Price. With Al Pacino, Ellen Barkin, John Goodman, Barbara Baxley, Jacqueline Brookes.

SEX, LIES, AND VIDEOTAPE. Written and directed by Steven Soderbergh. With James Spader, Andie MacDowell, Peter Gallagher, Laura San Giacomo, Ron Vawter.

SHE-DEVIL. Director, Susan Seidelman; screenplay by Barry Strugatz and Mark R. Burns. With Meryl Streep, Roseanne Barr, Ed Begley, Jr.

SHIRLEY VALENTINE. Director, Lewis Gilbert; screenplay by Willy Russell. With Pauline Collins, Tom Conti.

SLAVES OF NEW YORK. Director, James Ivory; screenplay by Tama Janowitz. With Bernadette Peters, Chris Sarandon, Mary Beth Hurt.

STAR TREK V: THE FINAL FRONTIER. Director, William Shatner; screenplay by David Loughery. With Mr. Shatner, Leonard Nimoy.

STAYING TOGETHER. Director, Lee Grant; screenplay by Monte Merrick. With Sean Astin, Stockard Channing, Melinda Dillon, Jim Haynie, Tim Quill, Dermot Mulroney, Dinah Manoff.

STEEL MAGNOLIAS. Director, Herbert Ross; screenplay by Robert Harling based on his play. With Sally Field, Dolly Parton, Shirley MacLaine, Daryl Hannah, Olympia Dukakis, Julia Roberts.

STORY OF WOMEN. Director, Claude Chabrol; screenplay by Colo Tavernier O'Hagan and Mr. Chabrol, from the book by Francis Szpiner. With Isabelle Huppert.

TRIUMPH OF THE SPIRIT. Director, Robert M. Young; screenplay by Andrzej Krakowski and Laurence Heath. With Willem Dafoe, Edward James Olmos, Robert Loggia.

TRUE BELIEVER. Director, Joseph Ruben; screenplay by Wesley Strick. With James Woods, Robert Downey, Jr.

TURNER AND HOOCH. Director, Roger Spottiswoode; screenplay by Dennis Shryack, Michael Blodgett, Daniel Petrie, Jr., Jim Cash, and Jack Epps, Jr. With Tom Hanks, Mare Winningham, Craig T. Nelson, John McIntire.

VALMONT. Director, Milos Forman; screenplay by Jean-Claude Carrière, based on *Les Liaisons Dangereuses* by Choderlos de Laclos. With Colin Firth, Annette Bening, Meg Tilly.

THE WAR OF THE ROSES. Director, Danny DeVito; screenplay by Michael Leeson and Mr. DeVito. With Kathleen Turner, Michael Douglas, Mr. DeVito.

WE'RE NO ANGELS. Director, Neil Jordan; screenplay by David Mamet. With Robert De Niro, Sean Penn.

WHEN HARRY MET SALLY. . . . Director, Rob Reiner; screenplay by Nora Ephron. With Billy Crystal, Meg Ryan.

WIRED. Director, Larry Peerce; screenplay by Earl Mac Rauch. With Michael Chiklis, Patti D'Arbanville.

YOUNG EINSTEIN. Written and directed by Yahoo Serious. With Yahoo Serious.

"The Bear," directed by Jean-Jacques Annaud, was a beautifully realized outdoor film of 1989 that introduces two talented bears with decidedly anthropomorphic tendencies.

© M. Kosenthiel/Sygma

"The Wizard of Oz" (left) *helped make Judy Garland a star. The musical fantasy was one of ten movies of 1939 filmed in Technicolor. John Wayne's first feature film, "Stagecoach,"* (below) *provided the model for all Westerns to come and set Wayne on the path to becoming a legend.*

THE BIGGIES OF 1939

In 1939, at the height of Hollywood's Golden Age, the studio system was at its peak, and moviegoers filled theaters at the rate of 85 million per week. Advances in filmmaking technology led to newly ambitious movies. Of almost 400 films released that year, an amazing number were milestones. These "biggies" of 50 years ago have attracted new generations of devotees, inspiring books and even other movies.

The film adaptation of Margaret Mitchell's book "Gone With the Wind" (left) *today stands as a classic. Winning eight Oscars at the time, the Civil War saga still enjoys an astonishing popularity 50 years later, as do its late stars, Clark Gable and Vivien Leigh.*

Photos: Movie Still Archives

alyzed veteran; Peter Weir's popular *Dead Poets Society,* with Robin Williams as a teacher who changes the lives of some impressionable young students; Jean-Jacques Annaud's extraordinary family film *The Bear,* an outdoor drama that constitutes a plea for conservation of wildlife, and Michael Moore's satirical documentary *Roger and Me,* lampooning General Motors for the tragedy that befell Flint, MI, when the company closed its plant there. It was also noteworthy that films of substance were rewarded with numerous Oscars in 1989. Barry Levinson's *Rain Man* (1988), which tackled the illness of autism, won for best picture. *See also* PRIZES AND AWARDS.

Several foreign-language movies also were concerned with important topics or themes. Japanese director Shohei Imamura's *Black Rain,* which premiered at the New York Film Festival, examined effects of the atomic attack on Hiroshima. French director Claude Chabrol's *Story of Women,* starring Isabelle Huppert, looked at the hypocrisy of Vichy France that, while collaborating with the Nazis, supposedly struck a blow for morality and family by executing a village woman for performing abortions. Canadian director Denys Arcand's *Jesus of Montreal* commented on current values by dramatizing events that occur when an acting troupe presents a passion play.

Star Performances. The status of Michelle Pfeiffer was boosted with *The Fabulous Baker Boys,* written and directed by Steve Kloves, in which she costarred with Jeff and Beau Bridges. She smoldered as a sexy singer and surprised critics and audiences with her hitherto unknown ability as a vocalist. Ellen Barkin also gained popularity as a siren for her steamy performance opposite Al Pacino in Harold Becker's *Sea of Love.* British actress Emily Lloyd (*Wish You Were Here,* 1987) showed her versatility in two films—Susan Seidelman's *Cookie,* in which she abandoned her British accent for a Brooklyn one as the daughter of a mobster, and *In Country,* in which she went Southern as a Kentucky teenager.

Bruce Willis expanded his horizons as the disturbed veteran in *In Country,* as did Michael J. Fox in his intensely dramatic role in *Casualties of War.* Marlon Brando practically stole *A Dry White Season* with his short but potent portrayal of a civil liberties lawyer. James Spader earned praise for his work in *sex, lies, and videotape,* in which he played a young man who tapes women revealing their sexual experiences. Kevin Costner, whose star has risen in the past few years, was effective once again as a man for whom the seemingly impossible comes true in Phil Alden Robinson's fanciful *Field of Dreams.* Veteran Jack Nicholson, in a class by himself, was immensely entertaining as The Joker in *Batman.* Another veteran film actor, Burt Reynolds, gave a notable performance in *Breaking In.*

Box Office Hits. The big money, as usual, was earned by films that tapped into the public's taste for sheer entertainment. Tim Burton's *Batman* soared to the top, and although results were not complete, it already ranked sixth among the most financially successful films of all time. The summer months of 1989 were crucial for the industry, with a record $2.1 billion spent at the box office. The figure for a similar period in 1988 was $1.7 billion.

Among the other major moneymakers were *Lethal Weapon 2,* teaming Mel Gibson and Danny Glover in another action yarn; *Indiana Jones and the Last Crusade,* with Harrison Ford and Sean Connery; *Ghostbusters II,* a sequel with Dan Aykroyd, Bill Murray, and Sigourney Weaver; *When Harry Met Sally . . . ,* costarring Billy Crystal and Meg Ryan as platonic friends who finally fall in love; *Honey, I Shrunk the Kids,* starring Rick Moranis; *Parenthood,* which gave Steve Martin another opportunity to show his range; *Turner and Hooch,* pairing Tom Hanks with a mess of a dog; and *Star Trek V: The Final Frontier.*

One troubling trend that could be discerned was the increasing difficulty in getting distribution for independently produced films, as opposed to those made by the major studios. A study by *Variety,* the entertainment trade publication, found that 190 independent movies went unreleased in 1988, a rise over 133 in 1987 and 100 in 1986. Numerous independent companies had to close, and the prognosis was not seen as promising in a business where the greatest rewards to producers, distributors, and theater operators come from Hollywood-style mass entertainment, not the sometimes less commercial fare of the independents.

Industry Upheavals. The trend toward mergers and takeovers continued, shaking up the old alignments and creating new entities. Time, Inc., bought Warner Communications, Inc., for $14 billion after sharp infighting with Paramount, which made a counterbid and futilely resorted to court action in its effort to prevent the merger.

More headlines were made when the Sony Corporation of Japan purchased Columbia Pictures for $3.4 billion. Successful producers Jon Peters and Peter Guber agreed to head Columbia for Sony. A suit instituted by Warner claimed the deal violated its contract with Guber and Peters. MGM/UA was also a prospect for a takeover.

The new position of Japan in Hollywood was emphasized earlier by an arrangement that Japan's Victor Company reached with Lawrence Gordon, the producer who has *Die Hard* (1988) and *Field of Dreams* among his credits. Gordon, retaining full artistic control, was to operate as Largo Entertainment, with the Japanese company investing $100 million.

Chaplin Centennial. The 100th anniversary of Charlie Chaplin's birth was the occasion for

The National Film Registry

Under the 1988 National Film Preservation Act, 25 films, all of which had to be at least ten years old, were cited in 1989 for protection as classics and placed on the National Film Registry. Under the law, which provides for the selection of up to 25 films each year, any of the films, if altered through colorization or by other means without the approval of the filmmaker, must carry a notice from the distributor to that effect. The Library of Congress is charged with carrying out the provisions of the law, and the librarian of Congress is empowered to take action against transgressors, but only for failing to label altered films properly, not for making the alterations. The choices were made by a board culled from various sectors of the film community, but the librarian may make changes in the board's selections. The law is a compromise from attempts to stop the practice of coloring black and white films and otherwise editing them to meet television, videocassette, or other needs. Nonetheless, it was opposed by many on the grounds that government should not be involved in deciding what is and is not art.

The 1989 designated films, classified as "culturally, historically, or esthetically significant," were: *The Best Years of Our Lives* (1946), *Casablanca* (1942), *Citizen Kane* (1941), *The Crowd* (1928), *Dr. Strangelove (or, How I Learned to Stop Worrying and Love the Bomb)* (1964), *The General* (1927), *Gone with the Wind* (1939), *The Grapes of Wrath* (1940), *High Noon* (1952), *Intolerance* (1916), *The Learning Tree* (1969), *The Maltese Falcon* (1941), *Mr. Smith Goes to Washington* (1939), *Modern Times* (1936), *Nanook of the North* (1922), *On the Waterfront* (1954), *The Searchers* (1956), *Singin' in the Rain* (1952), *Snow White and the Seven Dwarfs* (1937), *Some Like It Hot* (1959), *Star Wars* (1977), *Sunrise* (1927), *Sunset Boulevard* (1950), *Vertigo* (1958), and *The Wizard of Oz* (1939).

worldwide events to mark the contributions of a seminal figure in cinema, who died in 1977 at the age of 88. The Museum of Modern Art in New York held a major retrospective of his work, as did the National Film Museum in London. The Moscow Film Festival began with the showing of Chaplin's *The Great Dictator,* and CBS/Fox Video issued a Chaplin commemorative series on videocassette. *Remembering Charlie,* a book by Jerome Epstein, longtime producer for the actor and filmmaker, also was published during the year.

WILLIAM WOLF, *New York University*

MOZAMBIQUE

The war against the guerrillas of the Mozambique National Resistance (Renamo) continued in 1989 to be the central problem for the government of Mozambique President Joaquím Chissano.

The Civil War. Renamo forces continued very active in ten of Mozambique's 12 provinces, and despite improvements in the efficiency of the regular army they could strike almost at will, even to the outskirts of major cities. Utilizing the terror tactics that have killed an estimated 900,000 since the beginning of the rebellion, Renamo forced closure of most inland schools and clinics. Travel by road or rail in most areas could be made only with an armed escort.

Chissano's yearlong amnesty program for rebels was only minimally successful since Renamo's rank and file also were held by fear. By midyear, however, there was some indication of the government's willingness to talk to Renamo rebels. Britain, South Africa, and the USSR provided advisers to the Mozambique army, and the Soviet-trained elite Red Berets were used in 1989 in an offensive in Zambézia province. They had some success, but Renamo's bases of operations remained untouched.

The government's problems worsened at midyear when Tanzania removed its 3,000 soldiers that had been assisting in Zambézia. Other nations also provided military assistance. South Africa deployed 1,500 troops to protect Cabora Basa dam, and Zimbabwe's units continued to protect the vital railway to Beira.

Relief Efforts. The United States continued to condemn Renamo and to provide a large portion of the relief supplies. British Prime Minister Thatcher, visiting Mozambique in March, pledged further support. Distribution of relief supplies again was restricted by the size of the country and the breakdown of road communications. Farmers in all areas had ceased planting crops and thousands had fled to larger towns and cities. Since 1987 the numbers of refugees in neighboring states had increased from 1 million to 1.5 million, with an estimated 650,000 in Malawi.

HARRY A. GAILEY, *San José State University*

MOZAMBIQUE • Information Highlights

Official Name: People's Republic of Mozambique.
Location: Southeastern coast of Africa.
Area: 309,494 sq mi (801 590 km^2).
Population (mid-1989 est.): 15,200,000.
Chief City (1987 est.): Maputo, the capital, 1,006,765.
Government: *Head of state,* Joaquím A. Chissano, president (took office November 1986). *Head of government,* Mário da Graça Machungo, prime minister (took office July 1986). *Legislature* (unicameral)—People's Assembly.
Gross National Product (1987 est. U.S.$): $500,000,000.

© Winnie Klotz/Metropolitan Opera

The Metropolitan Opera Company staged Wagner's complete "Ring" cycle. James Morris and Hildegard Behrens, above, *starred in "Die Walküre," the cycle's second opera.*

MUSIC

Return, reunion, remembrance, and renewal were apt expressions for describing some exceptional happenings of the 1989 music year. It was the 20th anniversary of the fabled Woodstock (NY) music festival and the year of concert tours by some of music's most celebrated personalities. In popular music, the British rock group The Who and Diana Ross, a former Supreme, both marked their 25th anniversaries with concert tours, while the Rolling Stones made their first tour in seven years, and Ringo Starr made his first since the 1970 breakup of the Beatles. The classical pianist Van Cliburn also returned to the concert stage. It was the year, too, of the passing of Irving Berlin, of heavy-metal rockers in Moscow, and of new artistic leaders heading major opera companies and orchestras.

Classical

The year 1989 was one of upheaval in classical music, but also a year of great vitality. On one hand, the deaths of the Russian-born American pianist Vladimir Horowitz, the Austrian conductor Herbert von Karajan, and the American composer Virgil Thomson in many ways marked the end of an era. Yet the year also saw the rebirth of Van Cliburn's concert career, with performances in Philadelphia and Moscow marking the end of 11 years of reclusiveness, and the return of José Carreras to the stage after what appears to have been a successful battle with leukemia. The arts festival Pepsico Summerfare in Purchase, NY, closed its doors after a spectacular tenth season, but new concert halls were inaugurated in Tokyo and Dallas, and plans for a new home for the Philadelphia Orchestra were unveiled.

Opera. The dichotomy of upheaval and vitality perhaps was most evident in opera this year. In September the orchestra of the New York City Opera went on strike, and as the dispute raged on, the management cancelled the final weeks of the 1989 season and threatened to cancel part of the 1990 season, too. Wrenching as the cancellation was for operagoers, singers, and musicians, it was, no doubt, particularly upsetting for Christopher Keene, the conductor who succeeded Beverly Sills as the director of the company this season.

At the beginning of 1989, there was an operatic explosion with international reverberations at the new Bastille Opera in Paris when the company's administrator, Pierre Bergé, abruptly dismissed artistic director Daniel Barenboim, charging that Barenboim's plans were too expensive and also "elitist." The Bastille Opera house, built at a cost of $350 million, opened in July with a performance presented as part of the French bicentennial celebration, although its full opera season was not to begin until January 1990. Barenboim at first refused to accept his dismissal; however, it was soon clear that the situation could not be resolved, and within weeks it was announced that Barenboim would succeed Sir Georg Solti as director of the Chicago Symphony, starting in 1991. In May the Bastille Opera announced the appointment of Myung-Whun Chung, a 35-year-old Korean-American conductor, as music director.

Elsewhere there were tempests in the operatic teapot. In London, the New Sadler's Wells Opera Company, which specialized in operetta, was disbanded, the victim of an unwieldy deficit. The Romanian soprano Ileana Cotrubas announced her retirement from the stage and her plan to teach, while Eva Marton, the large-voiced Hungarian soprano, resigned from the Metropolitan Opera roster after a disagreement about casting and scheduling. And the Lyric Opera in Chicago, tired of Luciano Pavarotti's frequent cancellations, announced that it no longer would engage him. Pavarotti said that his cancellations were due to illness, but the company pointed out that he sang elsewhere during the same periods that he claimed to be ailing.

Nonetheless, opera generally flourished in 1989. There were two competing productions of Wagner's complete "Ring" cycle in the spring. One was the Metropolitan Opera's cycle. Installments had been unveiled gradually, with *Walküre* in 1986, *Rheingold* in 1987, *Siegfried* in 1988, and *Götterdämmerung* in the 1988 and 1989 seasons. Then, for the first time in half a century, the Met mounted the tetralogy on consecutive evenings (and also on Saturday afternoons).

The Met lately has favored a production style that is glitzy and expensive, but essentially bound to the 19th-century tradition, and its "Ring" operas were no exception. Critical opinion is split on this approach, not only with regard to the "Ring," but to opera in general, with some supporting this link with past tradition and others arguing that for opera to remain a vital theatrical form, directors must be free to explore new staging approaches, whether allegorical, updated, or radically stylized.

For those subscribing to the latter view, the Deutsche Oper Berlin came to Washington's Kennedy Center with a staging of the "Ring" that did away with the traditional forests and mountaintops, and put the cycle into something like a subway tunnel. Wagnerians also were served by an enthusiastically received new production of *Die Meistersinger* at the Seattle Opera, a company that also has a highly regarded "Ring."

If Wagner sometimes seemed to tower over the opera world, he did not dominate it entirely. There were a few premieres that attracted considerable interest, but elicited mixed responses. Anthony Davis, a composer who works in both classical music and avant-garde jazz, unveiled his second opera, a science-fiction tale called *Under the Double Moon,* at the Opera Theater of St. Louis. Davis, whose *X* put the story of Malcolm X on the opera stage, has an ear for drama and for orchestral writing, but it generally was agreed that his vocal writing still lacks a natural flow.

The Cleveland Opera stepped into the spotlight in 1989 with *Holy Blood and Crescent Moon,* an opera set in the Middle East at the time of the Crusades, composed by the rock musician Stewart Copeland (best known as the drummer of the rock group Police). Presented in the hope that it would bring a new audience and new musical notions into the opera house, the work succeeded on the first point, but failed on the second. Copeland had come to the task of composing the work without having heard an opera. After immersing himself in recordings for a while, he came up with a work that parroted certain of the genre's conventions in a way that critics regarded as ultimately little more than a student exercise.

Early opera remains an acquired taste for many operagoers, but it has made great inroads in recent years, and in 1989 it seemed to flourish, often with support from orchestras that perform on early instruments. The Paris Opera production of Lully's *Atys,* accompanied by William Christie's Les Arts Florissants ensemble, crossed the Atlantic for a successful run at the Brooklyn Academy of Music (BAM). The production was part of a new series at BAM that offers both newly staged presentations and performances by foreign companies whose work rarely is seen in the United States. Although not an early opera, Verdi's *Falstaff,* presented by the Welsh National Opera, was another notable BAM offering.

The operatic centerpiece of the Boston Early Music Festival was Mozart's *Idomeneo,* heard in a re-creation of the version presented at its premiere in 1781. Roger Norrington, a British conductor who has emerged in recent years as a star of the early instrument world, presided over the production. By contrast, a staging of Monteverdi's *Incoronazione di Poppea,* at the Théâtre de la Monie in Brussels, set aside the notion of historical re-creation (musical and theatrical) and was played in a new orchestration by Philippe Boesmans.

Instrumental Music. In the orchestral and chamber music world, there was greater volatility than usual, and musical politics seemed to be in the news more than music itself. In the spring, Herbert von Karajan resigned as director of the Berlin Philharmonic after several years of rocky relations with the orchestra. Karajan had taken over the philharmonic in 1955 and had molded it into a polished, streamlined ensemble that many considered the world's finest orchestra. In July, three months after his

Claudio Abbado, 56-year-old Italian-born conductor of the Vienna Philharmonic, was named music director of the renowned Berlin Philharmonic in the fall.

Vladimir Horowitz (1904–89)

AP/Wide World

The Russian-born virtuoso pianist, Vladimir Horowitz, died suddenly at his home in New York City of an apparent heart attack on November 5. Noted for his outstanding technical control of the piano, he enthralled audiences over a period of 60 years. In a grand gesture, he returned to Moscow and Leningrad in 1986 after an absence of 61 years for a concert tour that became a major media event (*photo right*). It was said that he "knew all the repertory and could play pieces he hadn't done in 20 years," but he was noted especially for Tchaikovsky's Piano Concerto no. 1 and Rachmaninoff's Piano Concerto no. 3, a composition that he played in 1978 at Carnegie Hall in a memorable performance with the New York Philharmonic under Eugene Ormandy on the occasion of the 50th anniversary of his American debut. A man known for fragile nerves, Horowitz quit playing in public on four occasions, but his absences seemed only to enlarge his mystique.

Horowitz also made recordings and helped to establish a new audience for the composer Muzio Clementi and with popularizing the sonatas of Domenico Scarlatti.

Background. Vladimir Gorowitz was born on Oct. 1, 1904, into a prosperous family in Kiev. He studied both the piano and composition at the Kiev Conservatory and began performing to support the family after the Bolshevik Revolution of 1917. With his Berlin debut in 1926, he changed his name to Horowitz. In 1928 he made his U.S. debut, and following some years in the 1930s when he lived in Europe, he settled permanently in the United States in 1940. Earlier (in 1933) he had married Wanda Toscanini, the daughter of conductor Arturo Toscanini. They had one daughter who died in 1975.

resignation, he died, leaving a legacy of some 800 recordings and a sizable collection of filmed and videotaped performances.

The search for Karajan's successor took six months, with a half dozen of the world's most established conductors among the candidates. In October, Claudio Abbado was named to the post. Abbado had been a principal contender for the directorship of the New York Philharmonic, which had not yet found a successor to Zubin Mehta, who is to leave in 1991. Before he came to New York, Mehta was director of the Los Angeles Philharmonic, which also had its upheavals during the year, as André Previn walked away from the Los Angeles podium. He was succeeded by Esa-Pekka Salonen, a young Finn who was the principal conductor of the Swedish Radio Symphony and who had made a strong impression in recent years both on recordings and in the concert hall.

Early instrument orchestras continued their march into the Romantic literature, with Roger Norrington and his London Classical Players venturing as far as Berlioz, and two other London groups—the Orchestra of the Age of Enlightenment and the Hanover Band—beginning an exploration of Schubert and Mendelssohn. Norrington brought his group to the United States for its American debut as the final event of Pepsico Summerfare, presenting what he called a "Beethoven Experience," a full weekend devoted to Beethoven's Ninth Symphony, with lectures, chamber music, dance events, and open rehearsals, all culminating in a performance of the Ninth and the Choral Fantasy.

Although the United States still lags behind in period instrument orchestras, there are the Mozartean Players in New York, the Smithsonian Chamber Orchestra in Washington, the Handel and Haydn Society of Boston, and the Philharmonia Baroque Orchestra in San Francisco. In 1989 another New York-based group joined the ranks, formed by Trevor Pinnock, one of England's early music stars. Its May debut concert, with works of Mozart, Haydn, and Beethoven, drew scathing reviews. Even so, on the strength of Pinnock's reputation, Deutsche Grammophon gave the group a six-year recording contract, and several conductors who heretofore have not evinced an interest in early instruments have been mentioned as possible guest conductors, among them Leonard Bernstein.

ALLAN KOZINN, *"The New York Times"*

Popular and Jazz

The year 1989 in popular music was characterized by an infusion of fresh young talent and by high-profile reunions of superstar bands of the past. Both trends came together in October when the Rolling Stones, whose first U.S. tour in eight years dominated the fall season, invited Guns N' Roses, the year's most popular new band, to open its series of Los Angeles concerts.

The pop marketplace continued to be fragmented into a number of genres, although that did not stop a host of hits from emerging from the realms of rap, dance music, and so-called "postmodern" music. The year saw a number of such performers break from underground status to mainstream success.

Déjà Rock. Among a number of former rock stars who returned to the concert stage in 1989 were such bona fide legends of the 1960s as the Rolling Stones, The Who, Paul McCartney, Ringo Starr, and the reunited Jefferson Airplane.

The Who did not even release a new album to promote their summer tour of outdoor stadiums, but attracted much attention for two performances of their rock opera *Tommy,* with the Los Angeles performance including cameo appearances by such other stars as Phil Collins and Steve Winwood. Though the tour proved a financial windfall, it was a minor one compared with the fall tour by the Rolling Stones.

Rock legends The Who (with Roger Daltrey, below*) and the Rolling Stones (featuring Mick Jagger,* right*) reunited for highly profitable concert tours during 1989.*

© Mark Sluder/Picture Group

The Stones, who released a solid new album called *Steel Wheels,* were guaranteed more than $65 million for a North American tour of more than 30 concerts. But the group was expected to earn closer to $90 million, less expenses, estimated to be about half of that. The concerts, generally well-received by critics, also were seen widely as the ultimate expression of the mercantile nature of modern rock and roll. There was no small irony in the fact that Mick Jagger and Keith Richards, the former bad boys of rock, were pictured on the cover of *Forbes.*

McCartney also released a fine album in 1989, *Flowers in the Dirt,* which included four songs written with Elvis Costello. However, the LP was not nearly as much of a commercial success as his first concert tour since 1976.

Sadly, the Dec. 6, 1988, death of Roy Orbison robbed a veteran rock star of the chance to enjoy a career revived by his induction into the Rock and Roll Hall of Fame and his participation in the hit album *The Traveling Wilburys.*

Bob Dylan had played more concerts in the past few years than at almost any point in his career, so he could not be considered a revivalist as much as a perennial. Critics cheered his latest album, *Oh Mercy,* with some calling it his best in 15 years.

© Dimo Safari/Sygma

© Larry Busacca/Retna Ltd.

Rapper Tone-Lōc, who scored the biggest-selling single in years with "Wild Thing," performed at Madison Square Garden in February 1989 as the opening act for singer Bobby Brown.

Genre Stars. With eclectic album-oriented radio stations increasingly a thing of the past, most pop acts generate sales by landing songs on a format called "contemporary hits radio" (CHR), a latter-day variation of Top 40 radio. Stations skew their playlist toward different audiences, but the biggest hits eventually appear on the playlist of almost all CHR outlets.

The year saw such hits emerge from the worlds of rap, dance music, heavy metal, and from a wide variety of acts grouped under the rubric of "postmodern" music. Music video, particularly the cable channel MTV, continued to be a highly valuable method for promoting new records. With a restructured programming format, MTV made waves with individual programs that featured these different musical styles.

Rap, which many mistakenly pegged as a fad, continued to spawn new stars, though some of the genre's veterans seemed to be losing their commercial potency. De La Soul was the most highly regarded new rap act of the year, with a playful lyrical and musical style that expanded a genre typically concerned with steely beats and masculine bravado. Public Enemy, a politically oriented rap group, garnered sales and critical praise, but also was mired in controversy when a member made public statements deemed by many to be anti-Semitic.

The rap single of the year by far was "Wild Thing," a ribald romp by a Los Angeles performer named Tone-Lōc. The song exemplified a style of rap, identified more with the West Coast, that mirrors the lyrical concerns of more benign pop music. Fans of all types of music could relate to "Wild Thing," which was why it became the biggest-selling single since "We Are the World."

The big noise in rap music, however, came from acts that incorporated rap beats with the vocal and lyrical seasoning of more traditional soul music. Bobby Brown, with hit singles like "My Prerogative" and "Don't Be Cruel," was the year's new high-profile black star, spearheading a style critics dubbed "new-jack soul."

Neneh Cherry, the stepdaughter of jazz trumpeter Don Cherry, was the most highly regarded new artist in the world of dance music, largely through her song "Buffalo Stance" and the fact that she brought a refreshingly feminine perspective to rap-like dance music. Commercially, however, the dance star of the year was Paula Abdul, whose *Forever Your Girl* spawned numerous hit singles and major video support from MTV. It was significant that Abdul's professional background was as a choreographer. In the realm of dance music, high-kicking style is a proven path to the top of the charts.

Prince, whose popularity had waned since 1984's *Purple Rain,* rebounded with an album inspired by the film *Batman*. Though only a couple of his funk-rock tunes were used in the movie, association with the box-office blockbuster helped put him back at the top of the charts.

Hard rock and heavy metal continued to hold sway with younger fans. Guns N' Roses, a volatile band that vaguely mirrored the Rolling Stones, was the hottest new group of the year, with its *Appetite for Destruction* both a runaway best-seller and a flash point for parental protests over objectionable lyrics. Bon Jovi's *New Jersey* was a major seller with a gentler style of hard rock, while Metallica's *. . . And Justice for All* grafted more substantial lyrics onto frenetic heavy-metal music.

Living Colour had a heavy-metal hit with its album *Vivid,* but what was most significant was that the group is a quartet of black musicians in an almost totally white genre. Touring as the opening act for the Rolling Stones was the appropriate cap to an intriguing breakthrough.

Postmodern. Pundits struggled for a term to describe a wide-ranging group of artists whose

The Return of Ballroom Dancing

© Mario Ruiz/Picture Group

For a few decades, the wrecking ball seemed to be waiting outside the ballrooms of the United States. After Chubby Checker got Americans to twist, touch dancing fell from favor. Rock and roll and disco did not help; they encouraged an improvisatory style of dance. But in truth, ballroom dancing never really could die. In fact, as the 1980s ended, it even was making a comeback and becoming a trend again.

In recent years, more than 500,000 people have been signing up annually for dancing lessons. Dance classes also are offered on college campuses, from Yale to University of California at Berkeley. Others book passage on cruise ships offering dance instructions and big bands. The U.S. Amateur Ballroom Dancers Association, with chapters in 24 states, has doubled its membership since the mid-1980s. Compiling a list of more than 1,000 dance halls, the publisher of *Ballroom Dancing USA* found that the greatest concentration of ballrooms was in the Midwest.

Nightclubs have responded to the demand. After a $20 million renovation, the Rainbow Room, perched high above midtown Manhattan, has become once more a fixture of New York nightlife. Roseland Ballroom opened in 1919 and remains a New York landmark. Rock clubs have found new business by setting nights aside for a whole new clientele who want to dress up and waltz, tango, mambo, and generally look good in sophisticated surroundings.

Explaining the trend, Larry Schulz of the Sandra Cameron Dance Center believes that the basic motivation is contact. According to Schulz, "that's always been why people have danced. We're dealing with a generation . . . that never touched on the dance floor, and it's a very startling experience for them."

The theatrical world also has contributed to the popularity of more formal dancing. The American Ballroom Theater Company, which is devoted to bringing dance steps to the stage, presented *Rendezvous With Romance* in New York City in 1989. It featured a company of seven dancing couples. Conversely, the stage can provoke interest in the dance floor. The 1985 Broadway success of *Tango Argentino,* for instance, revived that South American style.

Dancing even has become something of a competitive sport. There are dozens of dance competitions held annually throughout the United States. Major competitions can draw more than 2,000 participants. Ballroom dancing also is seen as a great way to get low-impact aerobic exercise. The U.S. Olympic Committee already has judged ballroom dancing a bona fide sport.

Touch dancing, pop sociologists contend, reflects a nostalgic desire for a simpler world. Others, especially those romantics who just remember dancing as a good time, will beg the question. They'll just face the music and dance.

JOHN MILWARD

popularity often sprouted from trendsetters in college radio and the music press. While "modern rock" fit the bill for many, the term "postmodern" had the fitting panache for artists who often had roots in the punk/new wave trends of the past decade. The huge success of bands like U2, REM, and the Cure were indicative that what starts out small can become big indeed. The Cure, the biggest surprise of the three, released a moody album called *Disintegration* and played select summer dates in baseball stadiums.

Other bands who flourished in this format included the English new wave veterans, XTC, who released a dense collection of pop-rock, *Oranges and Lemons,* and a spindly young rock band called the Pixies who made a critically acclaimed major-label debut with *Doolittle.* Lou Reed, a father figure to young musicians due to his participation in the seminal 1960s group the Velvet Underground, received positive notices for his lucid depiction of his hometown, *New York.*

Edie Brickell and the New Bohemians achieved mass success with a debut album, *Shooting Rubber Bands at the Stars,* that favored a loose, folk-rock style. 10,000 Maniacs scored with a more socially conscious style of folk-rock. Other artists making a mark in this genre were Cowboy Junkies, Robyn Hitchcock, and Love & Rockets.

Fine Young Cannibals, a British group, bridged the stylistic gap between postmodern music and the regimented beats of dance music; the group's *The Raw and the Cooked* sold in the millions, and singer/actor Roland Gift was one of the pop faces of the year.

As for teenage girls, they continued to support such young role models as Debbie Gibson and Tiffany, but also made the teenage boy group New Kids on the Block one of the year's top pop phenomena, with its *Hangin' Tough* LP selling more than 6 million copies.

Country. How much has country music changed in the 17 years since the Nitty Gritty Dirt Band released its monumental three-record set, *Will the Circle Be Unbroken?* That album placed a host of young players seasoned in rock and folk alongside established country stars. By 1989, when the Dirt Band revived the concept for a second volume, the young upstarts had become the lifeblood of modern country music. Album guests like John Hiatt, Roseanne Cash, John Prine, and Emmylou Harris showed how much country music has been open to intriguing hybrid performers.

Singers Randy Travis and George Strait continued to thrive with traditional country styles. Working in much the same vein, Clint Black had the country debut of the year, with his *Killin' Time* album revealing him to be a succinct songwriting talent.

Jazz. The year in jazz was one of consolidation, with many top names shaking out their styles and reaching new levels of critical regard. For instance, even those who had dismissed the recent pop-funk music of trumpeter Miles Davis conceded that his *Amandla* album was his best execution of the style. Davis also published an outspoken autobiography, *Miles.*

A young trumpet player, Wynton Marsalis, also won over many critics who had considered him more of a technician than a truly soulful player. He made a highly regarded album exploring his New Orleans roots, *The Majesty of the Blues,* and played a series of concerts at New York's Lincoln Center celebrating the music of Jellyroll Morton, Duke Ellington, and bebop pianist Bud Powell. Wynton's brother Branford also spent the year further establishing himself as a major tenor saxophonist.

The Marsalis brothers are hardly the only jazz artists from New Orleans. The Dirty Dozen Brass Band put a twist on tradition with its album *Voodoo,* and attracted some interest from the pop audience through its work with Elvis Costello. Young pianist Harry Connick, Jr., made a big stir when he brought his Crescent City stylings to the cabaret atmosphere of New York's Algonquin Hotel and recorded the soundtrack for the 1989 film *When Harry Met Sally.*

Veteran players also emerged as bandleaders, including drummer Paul Motian and pianist Don Pullen. Young players whose stars were on the rise included pianist Geoff Keezer, tenor saxophonist Ralph Moore, and drummer Ralph Peterson.

Vintage jazz continued to be reissued in vast quantities, with two sets garnering particular praise: *Duke Ellington: Braggin' in Brass, The Immortal 1938 Year,* and *Charlie Parker: The Complete Verve Years.* A film about pianist Thelonious Monk, *Straight No Chaser,* also spurred interest in the seminal stylist.

The jazz world mourned the deaths of trumpeter Woody Shaw and Max Gordon, the proprietor of one of New York's best-kown jazz clubs, the Village Vanguard. But 1989 also saw the rise of another influential Manhattan club, the Knitting Factory, which pursued a booking policy that put a spotlight on all sorts of young players from the worlds of jazz, rock, and the avant garde.

Broadway. Theatergoers looking for the future of Broadway musicals were content with productions that celebrated the past. The Tony Award for best musical went to *Jerome Robbins' Broadway,* while Ruth Brown, a rhythm and blues hitmaker of the 1950s, won a Tony for her performance in the hit musical *Black and Blue,* which packaged tap and other dance routines with a score composed of vintage blues songs.

JOHN MILWARD, *Free-lance Writer and Critic*

MYANMAR. *See* BURMA, page 151.

© Tony Pupkewitz/Black Star

More than 700,000 Namibians, 90% of them blacks, registered to vote in elections for an assembly that would draft a constitution for Africa's last colony. Approximately 96% of those eligible cast ballots in November.

NAMIBIA

With the arrival in Namibia (South-West Africa) on March 31, 1989, of United Nations Special Envoy Martti Ahtisaari, Namibia took a decisive step toward independence. At midnight on March 31, on behalf of the UN, Ahtisaari assumed joint control of Namibia with South African Administrator-General Louis Pienaar. The following day a formal cease-fire went into effect between South African forces and forces of the South West African People's Organization (SWAPO), which had been waging a guerrilla war for more than 23 years. Ahtisaari's arrival marked the beginning of the process toward the "free and fair" elections that were held in November to establish an assembly to frame the new nation's constitution.

Cease-fire Fighting. Ahtisaari no sooner had arrived to oversee the more than 4,650-member UN Transition Assistance Group (UNTAG) when heavy fighting broke out on the northern border between South African forces and SWAPO guerrillas who, the South Africans claimed, had infiltrated Namibia from Angola on March 31. The clashes took place the morning of April 1, just a few hours after the cease-fire had been agreed to. SWAPO denied initiating the fighting in which 276 guerrillas and more than 27 members of the South African security forces were killed.

After a meeting between the South African Administrator-General and UN officials, a restriction on the South African army against taking offensive action was lifted. This was a response in part to the threat from South Africa to expel the UN from Namibia, which would have undermined the independence process. A cease-fire session, attended by Soviet and U.S. observers, also rejected the position of UN Secretary-General Javier Pérez de Cuéllar that SWAPO guerrillas should be disarmed, but allowed to stay in UN-monitored camps within Namibia. By April 9, Angola, Cuba, and South Africa had agreed to terms under which SWAPO guerrillas would withdraw from Namibia. The UN supervised the assembly of the guerrillas in the bush and their transportation to points 90 mi (145 km) inside of Angola.

Namibian Elections. In a five-day election beginning on November 7, 96% of the eligible Namibians went to the polls to select the 72-member assembly that would draft a constitution leading to independence from South Africa. Ahtisaari declared that the election had been fair and free. SWAPO won 384,567 votes, or 57.3% of the total. There had been fears that if SWAPO had won less than 50% of the vote it would have challenged the election. Even in garnering a majority vote, however, SWAPO was not as successful as it had hoped. A two-thirds majority would have enabled it to draft the new constitution without the need for the support of any other group.

NAMIBIA • Information Highlights

Official Name: Namibia.
Location: Southwestern coast of Africa.
Area: 318,259 sq mi (824 290 km²).
Population (mid-1989 est.): 1,800,000.
Chief City (December 1988): Windhoek, the capital, 114,500.
Monetary Unit: South African rand (2.5625 rands equal U.S.$1, Dec. 12, 1989).
Gross National Product (1986 U.S.$): $1,250,000,000.

The election results created the need for compromise and the potential for broader multiparty democratic participation. The Democratic Turnhalle Alliance (DTA), a multiracial centrist coalition party, won 191,532 votes or 28.6% of the total. SWAPO will hold 41 seats in the assembly and the DTA 21; all assembly decisions will require a minimum of 48 votes. SWAPO, which has espoused a socialist orientation for a future Namibia, will have to vote with either the capitalist-oriented DTA or with one of the smaller parties, such as the United Democratic Front (holding four seats), with policies similar to its own but also with differences. Another group was the whites-only Action Christian National, a party seeking a return of apartheid, which won three seats in the assembly. The Namibia National Front and the Federal Convention of Namibia, the latter representing conservative mixed-race Namibians, each won one seat. It was estimated that Namibia's 80,000 white voters were split evenly in supporting the centrist DTA and the extreme Action Christian National parties; nine members elected to the assembly are whites. Under the terms of the UN Resolution on Namibia, final withdrawal of South African defense forces began almost immediately after the election.

Future Challenges. Once the elation over the relatively smooth transition to independence is over, Namibians will face many hard choices, including the resolution of strong differences over the redistribution of land and other resources, the future relations between a SWAPO-dominated government and multinational corporations operating in the country, and details of a proposed Bill of Rights.

PATRICK O'MEARA
AND N. BRIAN WINCHESTER
Indiana University

NEBRASKA

Water was the center of much attention, both politically and economically, in Nebraska in 1989. Politically, there was a dispute with neighboring Colorado over a controversial dam, and economically, the drought caused ongoing concern. In other news, P. J. Morgan, a real-estate manager, won Omaha's nonpartisan mayoral election in May.

Two Forks Dam. The dispute with Colorado involved plans of the Denver Water Board to build a dam and huge reservoir on the South Platte River. In March the Army Corps of Engineers announced its intent to authorize construction of the project despite opposition from environmental groups in Colorado and from Nebraskans who argued that it would destroy wildlife habitat along the Platte River.

Stating that the Two Forks Dam "could result in very serious adverse environmental impact," the head of the U.S. Environmental Protection Agency, William K. Reilly, ordered a thorough review of the project, and charges and countercharges were exchanged between government agencies and between Nebraska and Colorado officials. At year's end, the issue still was unresolved.

Drought. Of more immediate concern to many Nebraskans was a second year of severe drought. With subsoil moisture much depleted in 1988, crops were threatened by another year of below-normal rainfall. Fortunately, the rain that did occur was well timed for crop survival in large areas of the state. Although the wheat harvest was short, corn and soybean crops in much of Nebraska were near normal.

Another consequence of the drought occurred in July when lightning kindled the state's worst recorded forest fire, which swept over 48,000 acres (19 440 ha) of forest and rangeland in northwest Nebraska.

Economy. Despite water problems, Nebraska enjoyed restored prosperity after years of economic decline. Farm bankruptcies, which peaked at 566 in 1987, numbered only 64 by late October 1989. Bank profits hit an all-time high in 1988, and between January and mid-September 1989, there was only one bank failure.

One survey showed the average value of Nebraska farmland had increased by 32.4% in 1988, and other studies showed a comparable rise in farm income. Farm prosperity was reflected in sales-tax receipts in the cities as business boomed, and by August the unemployment rate stood at 3.1%, the third lowest among the states. Tax receipts were consistently ahead of forecasts, and although the percentage increase in state spending was the nation's largest (18.7%), so, too, was the budget reserve (28.9% of general-fund spending).

Legislature. In light of the budget surplus, the state legislature enacted a law to give Nebraska taxpayers $116 million in property and income-tax relief. Then, in July the state Su-

NEBRASKA • Information Highlights

Area: 77,355 sq mi (200 350 km²).
Population (July 1, 1988): 1,602,000.
Chief Cities (July 1, 1986 est.): Lincoln, the capital, 183,050; Omaha, 349,270; Grand Island (1980 census), 33,180.
Government (1989): *Chief Officers*—governor, Kay Orr (R); lt. gov., William E. Nichol (R). *Legislature* (unicameral)—49 members (nonpartisan).
State Finances (fiscal year 1988): *Revenue,* $2,624,000,000; *expenditure,* $2,347,000,000.
Personal Income (1988): $23,670,000,000; per capita, $14,774.
Labor Force (June 1989): *Civilian labor force,* 820,300; *unemployed,* 29,400 (3.6% of total force).
Education: *Enrollment* (fall 1987)—public elementary schools, 188,000; public secondary, 80,000; colleges and universities, 100,828. *Public school expenditures* (1987–88), $908,547,000 ($3,439 per pupil).

preme Court ruled in favor of a property-tax exemption for a gas-pipeline company, using as a precedent an exemption that the railroad had received. The resulting clamor on the part of other taxpayers for exemptions threatened, in effect, to subvert the state's property tax. To resolve the dilemma, Gov. Kay Orr called a special legislative session out of which came legislation defining personal and real property and putting the railroad in a special category with regard to a tax exemption.

WILLIAM E. CHRISTENSEN
Midland Lutheran College

NETHERLANDS, THE

As the Netherlands continued to confront its position as a small but highly developed country within a new unified European Community (EC), scheduled to go into effect at the end of 1992, a new Center-Left political coalition took over the reins of government in 1989.

Domestic Affairs. The core of the new cabinet, formed in November, remained the Christian Democratic Party (CDA), but its partner was no longer the Liberal (conservative) Party (VVD), but the Labor Party (PvdA). Christian Democratic Premier Rudolf (Ruud) F. M. Lubbers remained head of the government, with the new leader of the Labor Party, Wim Kok, as vice-premier and minister of finances.

The shift from a center-right to a center-left coalition was the result of the elections for a new Second Chamber of the parliament (States-General) on September 7. The Christian Democrats garnered about 35% of the vote, the Labor Party just under 32%, the Liberals 14.6%, the progressive party (called "Democrats '66") won almost 8%, and a far left coalition, the "Left-Greens," won just more than 4%. The principal loser in the vote was the Liberal Party, which retained only about two thirds of its seats. It had brought on the election, which came before the cabinet had finished its constitutional term of five years, by a resignation of its cabinet members in May over a relatively minor environmental issue. The estrangement between the Liberals and Christian Democrats had followed mounting disagreements about how to handle such problems as discontent among farmers and fishermen, the debacle over the introduction of a new, supposedly fraud-proof passport, and the Liberals' desire to reduce government expenditures more rigorously than the Christian Democrats advocate.

The principal beneficiary of the breakup of the cabinet, the second led by Lubbers since 1982, was the Labor Party, which divided the ministerial posts in the new cabinet evenly with the Christian Democrats. It maintained its position as the second-largest party although it lost slightly in the number of seats won. Under the leadership of Kok, who previously had been the head of the largest labor union federation, the party curtailed the influence of left-wing activists, who lost their principal issue with the abandonment of plans by the North Atlantic Treaty Organization (NATO) to install long-range cruise missiles in the wake of improved relations between the United States and the Soviet Union. Where the relations between the Liberals and the Christian Democrats had been exacerbated by differences over euthanasia and abortion, the new coalition partners compromised on these issues, even though the Labor position was similar to that of the Liberals. The legal status of both euthanasia and abortion was left deliberately ambiguous. In the negotiations for the formation of the new cabinet, which lasted almost two months, both parties seemed to avoid issues that would sharpen their differences.

Economic Affairs. Fishermen rioted over efforts to enforce quotas established by the EC. Farmers seeking to maintain high production levels protested efforts to protect water supplies by limiting use of fertilizers and pesticides. Economic activity continued to be generally prosperous, especially in the export business so important for the Netherlands. Nevertheless, there was concern about the failure of Dutch industry to develop high technology as rapidly as desired.

The level of unemployment remained moderately high, especially among immigrant workers from Turkey, Morocco, and Suriname, despite efforts to improve education and expand job training. Welfare payments, particularly to young persons, were restricted in order to discourage permanent dependence. Amsterdam and Arnhem, which had become notorious as centers for drug addicts, took steps to reduce the drug trade. Rowdyism, including violence against athletes, continued among supporters of professional soccer, leading to the exclusion of Amsterdam's team, Ajax, from competition for the Europe Cup.

HERBERT H. ROWEN, *Rutgers University*

NETHERLANDS • Information Highlights

Official Name: Kingdom of the Netherlands.
Location: Northwestern Europe.
Area: 16,023 sq mi (41 500 km²).
Population (mid-1989 est.): 14,900,000.
Chief Cities (Jan. 1, 1988 est.): Amsterdam, the capital, 691,738; Rotterdam, 574,299; The Hague, the seat of government, 444,313.
Government: *Head of state,* Beatrix, queen (acceded April 30, 1980). *Head of government,* Ruud Lubbers, prime minister (took office Nov. 1982). *Legislature*—States General: First Chamber and Second Chamber.
Monetary Unit: Guilder (2.0435 guilders equal U.S.$1, Nov. 24, 1989).
Economic Indexes (1988): *Consumer Prices* (1980 = 100), all items, 122.8; food, 115.4. *Industrial Production* (1980 = 100), 107.
Foreign Trade (1988 U.S.$): *Imports,* $99,802,000,000; *exports,* $103,559,000,000.

NEVADA

The longest legislative session in history, a vibrant economy, and continued opposition to the federal nuclear repository at Yucca Mountain were noteworthy in Nevada in 1989.

Taxes. The legislature, meeting in biennial session, did not pass a general tax increase despite pressure for a major overhaul of the tax system. Instead the legislators increased a patchwork of specialized taxes. The net profits tax on mining was increased from 2% to 5%, raising an additional $52 million over the biennium. This represented a defeat for Gov. Bob Miller, who had sought an additional $66 million for school class-size reductions. Property taxes were increased slightly and the cigarette tax was increased, as was the tax on insurance premiums. The average family's state tax bill was increased about $100.

The legislature failed to act on an initiative petition for a 10% corporate-income tax with proceeds earmarked for education. The measure would appear on the 1990 ballot instead.

Legislative Issues. During the record 167-day legislative session, Governor Miller's $1.6 billion budget, with 57% earmarked for public and higher education, was passed with only minor additions. Education was the dominant issue, with programs enacted to reduce elementary class size gradually over the next 11 years, and to establish tough state accreditation standards for schools.

Legislation was passed to hire a state drug czar, to create a children's resource bureau, to hire an ombudsman for seniors in nursing homes, and to start a seniors abuse hotline. Nevada's criminal justice system was reinforced with approval of a 500-bed addition for the new prison at Ely, and with funding to plan for another state prison to help house the highest per capita prison population in the nation. Penalties for selling drugs to minors also were increased, and funding was approved to fight a growing gang problem.

NEVADA • Information Highlights

Area: 110,561 sq mi (286 352 km²).
Population (July 1, 1988): 1,054,000.
Chief Cities (July 1, 1986 est.): Carson City, the capital (1980 census), 32,022; Las Vegas, 193,240; Reno, 111,420.
Government (1989): *Chief Officer*—governor, Robert J. Miller (D). *Legislature*—Senate, 21 members; Assembly, 42 members.
State Finances (fiscal year 1988): *Revenue,* $2,487,000,000; *expenditure,* $2,293,000,000.
Personal Income (1988): $18,461,000,000; per capita, $17,511.
Labor Force (June 1989): *Civilian labor force,* 605,500; *unemployed,* 31,900 (5.3% of total force).
Education: *Enrollment* (fall 1987)—public elementary schools, 119,000; public secondary, 49,000; colleges and universities, 48,063. *Public school expenditures* (1987–88), $581,573,000 ($3,520 per pupil).

Pension Increase. The legislature created a public uproar by overriding Governor Miller's veto and increasing their retirement pensions 300%. However, bowing to public pressure, the lawmakers unanimously repealed the increase in November at a special session convened by the governor.

The Economy. Despite efforts to make the state less dependent on gaming through economic diversification, gaming still dominated. The economy remained strong with state gaming revenue for fiscal year 1988–89 increasing 8.35% over the previous year. State sales tax revenue increased 14.1%. Nevada's nation-leading gold production grew despite a price drop to below $400 an ounce. In March the state's industrial employment grew at a national-high 7.6% with the unemployment rate dropping to 5.1%.

Nuclear Dump Opposition. The preliminary decision of the U.S. Department of Energy to place the nation's first high-level nuclear repository at Yucca Mountain galvanized Nevada residents and virtually every public official into vocal opposition. The legislature adopted two antirepository resolutions as well as a law prohibiting the federal government from placing the dump in Nevada.

TIMOTHY G. HALLER
University of Nevada, Reno

NEW BRUNSWICK

During 1989 a way was found to allow opposition questioning of New Brunswick's government; a French-language newspaper in the province branched out; and a New Brunswick member of the federal cabinet lost his job.

Questions Asked. Premier Frank McKenna's Liberal government fielded a barrage of opposition questions in the legislature, even though no opposition was there to ask them. Because the Liberals won all 58 seats in the 1987 election, only Liberal members were on hand to participate in the quizzing of cabinet ministers. So the government agreed to a system of oral answers to written questions from the Conservative and New Democratic parties. The experiment began March 23, when McKenna and four of his ministers responded to 16 questions read by the clerk of the House. The procedure was pronounced a success.

Off Welfare. The theme of putting people to work and slashing welfare rolls dominated the speech from the throne opening the legislature's spring session March 14. The speech, written by the Liberal government, offered incentives to business enterprises designed to spur industrial growth. They included grants for entrepreneurs and a stock-savings plan. The government also pledged to spend $10 million to employ as many as 2,000 welfare recipients on community work projects.

NEW BRUNSWICK • Information Highlights

Area: 28,355 sq mi (73 440 km²).
Population (June 1989): 717,600.
Chief Cities (1986 census): Fredericton, the capital, 44,352; Saint John, 76,381; Moncton, 55,468.
Government (1989): *Chief Officers*—lt. gov., Gilbert Finn; premier, Frank McKenna (Liberal). *Legislature*—Legislative Assembly, 58 members.
Provincial Finances (1989–90 fiscal year budget): *Revenues,* \$3,582,100,000; *expenditures,* \$3,846,-800,000.
Personal Income (average weekly earnings, June 1989): \$441.40.
Labor Force (August 1989, seasonally adjusted): *Employed* workers, 15 years of age and over, 286,000; *Unemployed*, 12.5%.
Education (1989–90): *Enrollment*—elementary and secondary schools, 136,450 pupils; postsecondary—universities, 16,060; community colleges, 2,900.
(All monetary figures are in Canadian dollars.)

Housing. A government task report released in February 1989 said that 30,000 New Brunswickers live in inadequate housing. As a result the government in April unveiled a multimillion-dollar program aimed at helping low-income families purchase their first homes and others improve their existing homes.

French Newspaper. *L'Acadie Nouvelle,* a French-language daily newspaper that had served only northeastern New Brunswick, went on sale across the province on September 5. The tabloid, based in Caraquet, fills a void left when the daily *Le Matin* folded in 1988. Its transition to a province-wide operation was described as "a historic occasion" by Michel Doucet, president of the New Brunswick Society of Acadians.

Federal Cabinet Minister. Bernard Valcourt, federal minister of consumer and corporate affairs, was involved in a motorcycle accident on July 4. Valcourt's motorcycle went out of control on a street in Edmundston, in his Madawaska-Victoria riding, and crashed through a wooden fence. The 37-year-old minister lost the sight of his right eye and had to have facial reconstruction surgery. He pleaded guilty to impaired driving and was fined C\$600, in addition to having his license suspended for six months. Later, Prime Minister Brian Mulroney accepted Valcourt's resignation. Valcourt, who was New Brunswick's foremost cabinet minister, had served on the cabinet's powerful priorities and planning committee.

New Party. The Confederation of Regions, noted for its strident advocacy of English-language rights, was registered as an official political party in Fredericton on September 28.

JOHN BEST, *"Canada World News"*

NEWFOUNDLAND

A provincial election held on April 20 resulted in the defeat of the Progressive Conservative (PC) government after 17 years. The Liberals, led by attorney Clyde Wells, elected 31 members (with 47% of the popular vote) while the PCs, led by new leader Tom Rideout, elected 21 members (with 48% of the vote). Rideout had replaced Brian Peckford in a March leadership convention. The two seats held by the New Democratic Party (NDP) (also led by a new man, Cle Newhook) were lost, and the party was unrepresented in any federal or provincial Newfoundland riding. The PC government perhaps had been hurt by a general dissatisfaction with a party too long in power and by the growing scandal surrounding the Sprung cucumber greenhouse affair, in which too much public money seemed spent unwisely.

Once in power the Liberals reduced the size of the cabinet to 20, rearranged the top levels of the civil service, and passed a tough budget. An election promise of an "Economic Recovery Commission" for the purpose of economic development in rural Newfoundland was fulfilled. The chairman of a similar 1987 royal commission, Professor Douglas House, was appointed chairman of the new group.

Economy. The perennial problems of the economy—fish and oil—remained. The final agreement on the production plans for the Hibernia oil field, promised for the spring of 1989, was delayed, as the principal company, Mobil Oil, suggested new production designs that had the advantage of being cheaper but the disadvantage of using much less Newfoundland labor in the construction of the production platform. As for the fishery, concern focused on the northern cod. Fishery biologists reported on new studies that suggested a serious decline in the stock that is the basic means of support for the province's northeast coast. A biologically necessary cut in the total harvest, suggested for both 1989 and 1990, would mean serious job losses among trawler crews, plant workers, and support workers. The federal government's response was the establishment of a cabinet-level committee to coordinate emergency responses. Both the federal and provincial governments were conscious, however, that help to the industry must not contravene the definition of subsidy under either the U.S.-Canada Free Trade Agreement or the General Agreement on Tariffs and Trade (GATT) rules.

Fishing Dispute. In the long-standing fishing dispute between Canada and France, it was left to Newfoundland's representative in the federal cabinet, Trade Minister John Crosbie, to present the argument to the European Community that overfishing on the "nose" and "tail" of the Grand Banks (beyond the 200-mi or 370-km limit) threatened the viability of the stock. The two countries agreed in 1989 to binding arbitration on their maritime boundary dispute.

Cleric Abuse. Since 1988, 18 priests, brothers, and other members of the Roman Catholic

NEWFOUNDLAND • Information Highlights

Area: 156,649 sq mi (405 720 km²).
Population (June 1989): 569,200.
Chief Cities (1986 census): St. John's, the capital, 96,216; Corner Brook, 22,719.
Government (1989): *Chief Officers*—lt. gov., James A. McGrath; premier, Clyde Wells (Liberal). *Legislature*—Legislative Assembly, 52 members.
Provincial Finances (1989–90 fiscal year budget): *Revenues,* $2,894,581,000; *expenditures,* $3,148,-019,000.
Personal Income (average weekly earnings, June 1989): $464.62.
Labor Force (August 1989, seasonally adjusted): *Employed* workers, 15 years of age and over, 202,000. *Unemployed,* 15.8%.
Education (1989–90): *Enrollment*—elementary and secondary schools, 128,830 pupils; postsecondary—universities, 11,550; community colleges, 3,500.
(All monetary figures are in Canadian dollars.)

community in Newfoundland have been charged or convicted of sexually abusing young boys, resulting in two investigations. The Winter Commission, formed by the church and chaired by former Newfoundland Lt.-Gov. Gordon Winter, investigated internal church concerns; and a provincial Royal Commission, chaired by Ontario Supreme Court Justice Samuel Hughes, looked into the administration of justice in the mid-1970s, when complaints of mistreatment in a Catholic-run orphanage appear to have been ignored.

SUSAN MCCORQUODALE
Memorial University of Newfoundland

NEW HAMPSHIRE

During 1989 residents of New Hampshire had to confront a new reality—the boom times were ending. Evidence of an economic slowdown appeared everywhere, with even nature playing a role in the downturn. A much lower-than-average snowfall hurt winter tourism.

At the beginning of 1989 news articles had documented the state's annual economic growth as 9.9% over the previous three years, the second-highest rate in the nation. But by the fall, a representative headline read: "N.H. joins regional doldrums; vibrant economy slams on brakes." Other indicators of the downturn included a slow-to-mediocre summer tourist season, increases in homeless and welfare costs, a poor construction outlook, layoffs, and plant closings. Particularly hard-hit were housing starts, off by 35% from 1988. By mid-1989 several construction firms had filed for bankruptcy, and the number of property auction notices in regional newspapers rose dramatically, especially for condominium developments. And the August unemployment rate of 3.6% was the highest since March 1986.

Base Closing. Another shock came early in the year with the announcement by the U.S. Department of Defense that Pease Air Force Base was one of 86 armed forces bases around the nation to be closed. Closing the base would have a major impact on the southeastern part of the state, since it has employed about 3,600 military and 1,000 civilian personnel. At mid-1989 the closing date was set for January 1991. Efforts were under way to decide the alternate use of the 4,300-acre (1 740-ha) facility.

State Cutbacks. The economy's impact on state government proved severe. Because of a decline in state revenues, Gov. Judd Gregg (R) imposed in February a 3% cut for all state agencies. In May the legislature approved a $3.3 billion biennial operating budget, but had to raise a variety of user fees and taxes on such things as cigarettes and property transactions to pay for the appropriation. Nonetheless, by early October tax revenues were falling behind estimates to such an extent that Governor Gregg issued an executive order freezing certain state expenditures.

Seabrook Saga. The saga of the Seabrook nuclear power plant continued in 1989. Public Service Co. of New Hampshire (PSNH) remained in receivership and several of its reorganization plans drew criticism. In May foes of nuclear power had a setback when the U.S. Nuclear Regulatory Commission granted permission for the plant to conduct low-power tests. On June 13 the first nuclear reaction took place. By year's end, the status of the plant and PSNH remained uncertain. No operating license had been granted and the reorganization process continued, causing supporters and foes alike anxiety over what effect the situation would have on electric rates.

Other News. Plans for a bypass route around North Conway, the state's leading outlet center, remained unresolved. Meanwhile, traffic jams in the area lasted as long as 12 hours over the summer weekends.

In July, Amtrak reestablished long-distance passenger service in New Hampshire for the first time since 1967 when the *Montrealer* stopped in Claremont.

WILLIAM L. TAYLOR
Plymouth State College

NEW HAMPSHIRE • Information Highlights

Area: 9,279 sq mi (24 032 km²).
Population (July 1, 1988): 1,085,000.
Chief Cities (1980 census): Concord, the capital, 30,400; Manchester, 90,936; Nashua, 67,865.
Government (1989): *Chief Officer*—governor, Judd Gregg (R). *General Court*—Senate, 24 members; House of Representatives, 400 members.
State Finances (fiscal year 1988): *Revenue,* $1,771,000,000; *expenditure,* $1,610,000,000.
Personal Income (1988): $21,090,000,000; per capita, $19,434.
Labor Force (June 1989): *Civilian labor force,* 634,500; *unemployed,* 21,300 (3.4% of total force).
Education: *Enrollment* (fall 1987)—public elementary schools, 114,000; public secondary, 52,000; colleges and universities, 56,163. *Public school expenditures* (1987–88), $620,626,000 ($3,909 per pupil).

NEW JERSEY

A gubernatorial election, fiscal problems, and further attempts at long-range regional planning were the dominant themes in New Jersey in 1989.

Fiscal Problems. After many years of budget surpluses, Gov. Thomas H. Kean announced in 1988 that there would be shortfalls in tax revenues in future years. Without cutbacks in government spending, New Jersey would face deficits that would impair the state's credit rating. The dimensions of the problem became clearer in 1989, as the governor's $12 billion budget represented only a 1.8% increase over 1988. Before the legislature approved the budget, there had been talk of a $300 million deficit, as well as large-scale layoffs of government employees. In early July, despite a court restraining order, 5,000 workers rallied in Trenton to demand that their contracts be honored.

In a broader context, politicians of both parties predicted tax increases, especially since the New Jersey Supreme Court was expected to declare the property tax unconstitutional as a means for support of public schools. Also at stake was the viability of Governor Kean's programs for ending no-fault automobile insurance, reducing local property taxes by having the state assume county welfare costs, and establishing an agency to regulate coastal development.

Regional Planning. In June the governor announced a $2.5 billion plan to build a 14-mi (22.5-km) system of rails, roads, and bus routes in order to coordinate the development of the Hudson County waterfront. The object was to lessen commuter dependence on private transportation and create 80,000 jobs and 50,000 new homes in one of the most rapidly changing areas of New Jersey. Simultaneously, Merrill Lynch declared plans to move 2,600 workers from New York to Jersey City by the early 1990s and to convert the Colgate-Palmolive factory into office space.

AP/Wide World

It was thumbs up for New Jersey's Democratic gubernatorial candidate James Florio and his wife Lucinda. He easily won the election to succeed Gov. Thomas H. Kean (R).

NEW JERSEY • Information Highlights
Area: 7,787 sq mi (20 169 km²).
Population (July 1, 1988): 7,721,000.
Chief Cities (July 1, 1984, est.): Trenton, the capital (1980 census), 92,124; Newark, 316,300; Jersey City, 219,480; Paterson, 139,160; Elizabeth, 106,560.
Government (1989): *Chief Officers*—governor, Thomas H. Kean (R); secretary of state, Jane Burgio (R). *Legislature*—Senate, 40 members; General Assembly, 80 members.
State Finances (fiscal year 1988): *Revenue,* $20,957,000,000; *expenditure,* $18,952,000,000.
Personal Income (1988): $168,810,000,000; per capita, $21,994.
Labor Force (June 1989): *Civilian labor force,* 4,037,700; *unemployed,* 166,200 (4.1% of total force).
Education: *Enrollment* (fall 1987)—public elementary schools, 747,000; public secondary, 346,000; colleges and universities, 294,433. *Public school expenditures* (1987–88), $6,993,500,000 ($6,441 per pupil).

The New Jersey Planning Commission was concerned especially with the potential for traffic congestion and suburban sprawl along Route 1 from New Brunswick to Trenton, and on the New Jersey Turnpike around Exit 8A. Future expansion, it was believed, should take into account the need for low-density housing and business construction.

Regional planning of a different sort occurred in the autumn, when a court order cleared the way for the state government to assume operation of the Jersey City school system, long judged one of the least effective in New Jersey. In a precedent-setting move, a state-appointed director, Elaine Scambio, was given power to fire the Jersey City school board and weed out politically appointed teachers and administrators. After five years, control would revert back to local authorities. No known action of this kind ever had been taken in the United States.

Gubernatorial Election. Since Governor Kean was constitutionally ineligible to run for a third term, the field in both parties was wide open. For Democrats, U.S. Congressman James Florio of Camden, who had opposed and almost beaten Kean in 1981, was the clear front-runner. In the June primary, Florio easily defeated Assemblyman Alan Karcher and Princeton Mayor Barbara Boggs Sigmund. The situation was more complex in the Republican ranks, as five candidates entered the race. All portrayed themselves as heirs of Kean, although only one, Sen. William L. Gormley, was a moderate. Kean himself did not endorse anyone, but appeared with each one separately in TV commercials. The two most prominent of the five were U.S. Congressman James Courter of Warren County and former Attorney General W. Cary Edwards. Courter won the nomination over Edwards by a narrow margin.

Courter and Florio adopted fundamentally different outlooks during the campaign. Courter presented himself as the heir to the Reagan tradition of laissez-faire. Florio emphasized a more active government role in dealing with urban and environmental problems.

Florio defeated Courter by a wide margin, gaining about two thirds of the vote. Margins were especially wide in the traditional Democratic strongholds of Essex and Hudson counties, but all counties except for Hunterdon and Morris went for Florio. Adding to the Democratic triumph was the capture of the Assembly, which had been under Republican control for four years.

HERMANN K. PLATT, *Saint Peter's College*

NEW MEXICO

The disposal of solid and nuclear waste was an encompassing issue in New Mexico in 1989, with citizens determined to stop government and private business from using the state as a national waste dump.

The Waste Isolation Pilot Plant (WIPP) continued to cause controversy after eight years as it tried and failed to open. The 2,150-ft-(665-m-)-deep manmade caverns southeast of Carlsbad are intended to store waste from federal nuclear projects. WIPP was scheduled to open in 1988, but a property transfer from the Department of the Interior to the Department of Energy pushed the opening date to September 1989. In early summer 1989, three days of public hearings saw several hundred New Mexicans testify against opening the facility, and in June, Energy Secretary James Watkins announced WIPP would not open until spring 1990 at the earliest.

On the solid-waste front, residents protested in January an inquiry from a Maryland company about opening a dump that would take in 20,000 tons of garbage per day. At the time, dump operators did not need permits and regulations were lax.

A legislative bill was introduced to beef up regulations and place a moratorium on the issuance of landfill permits. Gov. Garrey Carruthers vetoed the bill because of its technical flaws and issued an executive order to enforce the moratorium until the state Environmental Improvement Division (EID) could enact new landfill rules. In May counties statewide placed a moratorium on landfills not conforming to EID rules. Soon after, the state Association of Counties challenged the new regulations and the state Court of Appeals issued an order halting enforcement. By mid-October, a permanent solution to the question had not been found.

Legal Matters. In Las Cruces, Navy veteran Lee Bach was taken to court after a neighbor complained Bach's large nylon flag snapped loudly in the wind. A municipal court judge determined the noise was a public nuisance, and the case was appealed to state district court. It was dismissed after Bach replaced his flag with a quieter cotton one.

The Las Cruces police department removed a "Batman" logo from its Breath Alcohol Testing van after Warner Communications, which owns the Batman trademark, said the van violated trademark and copyright laws.

Isolation Experiment. As part of a scientific experiment to test the effects of solitude, an Italian woman spent 130 days in a cave 30 ft (9.14 m) underground near Carlsbad. The woman's biological cycles changed, but her concentration deepened. (*See* PEOPLE, PLACES, AND THINGS.)

Drug Trafficking. Concern increased for border issues such as drug trafficking between New Mexico and Mexico. U.S. Customs continued to use an areostat, a stationary radar blimp, on the U.S.-Mexico border. The blimp, one of six in use, scans airspace in a 260-mi (413.4-km) radius to detect low-flying aircraft. Border Patrol agents in the New Mexico-west Texas area seized $162 million in drugs from October 1988 to March 1989.

New Popularity. In 1989 the Southwest lured the nation as "Santa Fe chic" showed up in clothing and furnishings across the country. Desert colors and Mexican art became trendy as people rediscovered Santa Fe, which did its best to capitalize on its rosy-hued quaintness.

DORRAINE HARRIS
Free-lance Writer, Las Cruces, New Mexico

NEW MEXICO • Information Highlights

Area: 121,593 sq mi (314 925 km²).
Population (July 1, 1988): 1,507,000.
Chief Cities (1980 census): Santa Fe, the capital, 48,953; Albuquerque (July 1, 1986 est.): 366,750; Las Cruces, 45,086.
Government (1989): *Chief Officers*—governor, Garrey Carruthers (R); lt. gov., Jack L. Stahl (R). *Legislature*—Senate, 42 members; House of Representatives, 70 members.
State Finances (fiscal year 1988): *Revenue,* $4,138,000,000; *expenditure,* $3,504,000,000.
Personal Income (1988): $18,814,000,000; per capita, $12,488.
Labor Force (June 1989): *Civilian labor force,* 698,700; *unemployed,* 51,600 (7.4% of total force).
Education: *Enrollment* (fall 1987)—public elementary schools, 195,000; public secondary, 92,000; colleges and universities, 83,074. *Public school expenditures* (1987–88), $952,143,000 ($3,492 per pupil).

NEW YORK

New York's efforts in 1989 to solve such pressing problems as rising drug-related crime and a climbing school-dropout rate were stymied in part by a tight financial squeeze that gripped state and local governments.

Legislature. Declining federal aid and lower-than-anticipated state tax revenues prompted Gov. Mario Cuomo early in the year to warn leaders of the state legislature—divided between a Democrat-controlled Assembly and a Republican-led Senate—that the state faced a serious deficit. By cutting social programs, laying off some state workers, and increasing some fees and taxes, Cuomo's proposed $47 billion budget sought to prevent what fiscal experts eventually estimated as a potential $2.8 billion shortfall in revenue. The cuts led thousands of citizens to demonstrate in Albany and prompted the legislature to restore millions of dollars in proposed program cuts. To pay for the restorations, taxes and fees were raised on a host of products, including cigarettes and alcohol. But the legislative leaders and Cuomo left in place the third year of a multiyear phased-in state income-tax cut, arguing that New York could compete with other Northeastern states for business growth only by reducing the overall tax burden on citizens.

Despite the tight state financial picture, the state expanded prenatal care to an additional 70,000 poor women and their infants and provided additional funding for preschool handicapped services. Funding was authorized to build 6,400 additional prison cells to handle a tide of drug-related convictions, raising the capacity of state prisons beyond the 50,000 mark. Nearly 40% of the new space will be in drug-treatment units.

Cuomo forced the 64-campus state university system to step back from a plan to raise tuition by $200 a year, to $1,350, and cover the system's budget shortfall by administrative spending cuts instead. After 13 years of deliberations, the legislature finally approved legislation to ban smoking in most indoor public spaces, in one of the toughest antismoking bills in the nation. Lawmakers also increased unemployment benefits, set guidelines for courts to follow in setting child-support payments, and extended a law allowing cameras in courtrooms.

But the legislature did not act on the most controversial issue of the year: a push by advocates of the death penalty to reinstate capital punishment in the state. Governor Cuomo vetoed death-penalty legislation for the seventh straight year, prompting rallies on the Capitol steps by death-penalty proponents, including families of slain police officers. But despite early-year predictions of success by death-penalty sponsors, the legislature remained just short of the margin needed for override in both

AP/Wide World

In mid-November the flag was at half-mast at an elementary school near Newburgh, NY, after a small tornado knocked down a cafeteria wall, killing seven children.

NEW YORK • Information Highlights

Area: 49,108 sq mi (127 190 km²).
Population (July 1, 1988): 17,909,000.
Chief Cities (July 1, 1986 est.): Albany, the capital, 101,727 (1980 census); New York, 7,262,700; Buffalo, 324,820; Rochester, 235,970; Yonkers, 186,080; Syracuse, 160,750.
Government (1989): *Chief Officers*—governor, Mario M. Cuomo (D); lt. gov., Stan Lundine (D). *Legislature*—Senate, 61 members; Assembly, 150 members.
State Finances (fiscal year 1988): *Revenue,* $57,278,000,000; *expenditure,* $50,429,000,000.
Personal Income (1988): $345,741,000,000; per capita, $19,305.
Labor Force (June 1989): *Civilian labor force,* 8,771,500; *unemployed,* 411,100 (4.7% of total force).
Education: *Enrollment* (fall 1987)—public elementary schools, 1,736,000; public secondary, 859,000; colleges and universities, 992,544. *Public school expenditures* (1987–88), $15,755,000,000 ($6,257 per pupil).

houses. Neither house considered Cuomo's proposed alternative, a bill toughening the penalty for some murders to include life imprisonment without possibility of parole.

Other Headlines. The state also moved to take over and shut down the unpopular Shoreham nuclear-power plant on Long Island, which was completed but never operated commercially. Under the agreement between Cuomo and the Long Island Lighting Co. (LILCO), the utility would receive rate hikes to restore its fiscal stability and the state would pay $1 for the 809-megawatt reactor—marking the first time in U.S. history that a completed nuclear plant would be closed before operating. At year's end, the Bush administration was seeking to block the Cuomo-LILCO deal.

In a case watched closely by the gay community, the state Court of Appeals ruled 4-2 that longtime roommates could be considered a family unit under state housing law, entitling people to pass on rent-regulated housing to their companions.

The rising concern of New Yorkers about drug abuse was indicated in a statewide poll conducted in September by the Marist Institute of Public Opinion. More than 45% of those polled said that drugs were "the number one problem now facing New York State," almost double the percentage who considered it the state's top problem in a poll conducted earlier in the year. In a similar poll in June 1987, New Yorkers listed taxes as the state's top problem.

Responding to a high-school dropout rate of 30% in New York City, the state began to implement the Liberty Scholarship program, which promises all New York ninth graders that the state will assure them money to cover college tuition costs at state colleges when they graduate from high school.

The top Republican slot in state government, majority leader of the Senate, was taken over for the first time by a Long Islander, Sen. Ralph Marino of Muttontown. The election of Marino marked a continuing shift of GOP power from its traditional upstate base to the downstate suburbs.

REX SMITH, *"Newsday"*

NEW YORK CITY

New York City's government was overhauled dramatically in 1989. Not only were many of the faces of officials new; the governing bodies were, too. Politics dominated the headlines: the most contested mayoral election since 1969 and the toppling of the nation's most visible mayor, Edward I. Koch, after three terms; a referendum on the most fundamental revision of the city's charter since Greater New York was established in 1898; and the first test of the city's voluntary public campaign financing law.

New York was alone among the nation's ten largest cities in never having elected a black, a woman, or a Hispanic candidate as mayor. That the city's 106th mayor, David N. Dinkins (*see* BIOGRAPHY), is the first black elected to the post further heightened New York's historic undercurrent of racial consciousness in a year punctuated by two particularly heinous crimes. As the city headed toward another drug-driven record number of homicides, it was stunned by the rape and beating of a white jogger in Central Park, allegedly by black and Hispanic youths; and the murder of a black teenager, allegedly by a white gang, in the Bensonhurst section of Brooklyn. Moreover, the city's school system, normally in disarray, was disrupted further by the sudden death in May of Richard R. Green, the system's first black chancellor, and by the search for his successor. Joseph A. Fernandez, a native New Yorker and high-school dropout who was Miami's school superintendent, assumed the chancellorship Jan. 1, 1990, the same day Dinkins was inaugurated.

While the city sought to cope with the soaring social and financial consequences of the cocaine and AIDS epidemics and of a cooling local economy, it also paused in 1989 to reflect on past crises that it had survived and to commemorate other anniversaries. New York, the nation's first capital, celebrated with appropriate pomp the 200th anniversary of George Washington's inauguration at Federal Hall; less formally but perhaps more introspectively, the city marked the two decades since an experimental school decentralization plan rocked the education system.

Also, transit officials claimed victory in their war on graffiti vandals who had appropriated subway cars as their canvas, and the city rescinded severe restrictions on ornamental fountains and other nonessential water use when a drought was washed away by record rainfall.

The Election. The 1989 campaign began inauspiciously enough in the first month of the year: Ronald S. Lauder, the cosmetics heir and former U.S. ambassador to Austria, chose Albany, the state capital, as the place to declare his candidacy for the Republican mayoral nomination in New York City. Despite his political inexperience, Lauder made himself a force to be reckoned with by investing nearly $14 million of his own fortune in hopes of defeating another political novice, Rudolph W. Giuliani, who resigned in January as the United States attorney for New York's Southern District—a job in which he became known widely as a prosecutor of organized crime, corruption, and Wall Street insider trading cases. Yet Giuliani's difficult primary campaign demonstrated why nobody has been elected mayor of New York City since 1894 without having held prior elective office. He emerged from the September primary with the Republican nomination, but badly bruised by Lauder's unrelenting attacks.

In the Democratic primary, Mayor Koch's unprecedented campaign for a fourth four-year term was challenged by three opponents: Dinkins, the 62-year-old Manhattan borough president, who forged an effective coalition of labor leaders and liberals; Harrison J. Goldin, the four-term city controller; and Richard Ravitch, a businessman who had headed the Metropolitan Transportation Authority. Koch had spent a record $7 million on his 1985 reelection, but was constrained this time by the $3,000 limit on individual contributions and $3.6 million ceiling on expenditures for the primary (another $3.6 million could be spent on the general-election campaign). He also was hobbled by corruption scandals that shook his administration—but never touched him personally—and by 12 years of overexposure. Nonetheless, he appeared to be on the verge of vindication when, on August 23, the murder of Yusuf K. Hawkins, a black teenager, in Brooklyn became a grim reminder of the racial tension that Mayor Koch frequently had been accused of exacerbating. Indeed, his suggestion several days later that protest marches through the white neighborhood where the young man was murdered might be counterproductive merely reaffirmed his reputation for insensitivity. At a Labor Day parade, Gov. Mario M. Cuomo predicted that the next mayor would be the candidate best equipped to bring the city together. Dinkins, by dint of his race and his personality, fit the bill. He defeated Koch by nearly eight percentage points.

Dinkins began the eight-week general election campaign with a decided advantage: an unusually united Democratic Party in a city where enrolled Democrats outnumber Republicans by five to one. Moreover, Giuliani again demonstrated his political naïveté when his most visible bridge to the city's Jewish community, the comedian Jackie Mason, was quoted as having made racially charged remarks about blacks. But Dinkins was vulnerable, too. It was revealed that one campaign worker had read an anti-Semitic poem 20 years earlier. Another functionary who had been paid to corral votes on primary day later proclaimed himself to be antiwhite. Then questions arose about stock that Dinkins valued at more than $1 million in 1983 and which, two years later, he agreed to sell to his son for $58,000—a personal financial problem that resonated in Dinkins' failure nearly two decades before to file income tax returns, a lapse he blamed on negligence and later corrected.

Giuliani, also armed with the Liberal Party ballot line, expanded his alliterative message of crime, crack, and corruption to include competence and character. Dinkins, meanwhile, cloaked himself in the mantle of leading Democrats and painted his opponent as an untrustworthy handmaiden of antiurban Republican administrations in Washington. Lauder mounted a nominal campaign as the Conservative Party candidate. In the end, Dinkins, who had hailed the people of his city as a "gorgeous mosaic," fit enough of the pieces together to eke out a victory. His margin of less than three percentage points was the slimmest in a New York City mayoral race since 1905.

Voters also approved a revised City Charter, prompted by a federal court ruling, upheld in March by the U.S. Supreme Court, that the city's Board of Estimate, composed of the three citywide officials and five borough presidents, violated the constitutional principle of one person, one vote. The new framework, to be phased in during 1990, further empowers the mayor and transfers the board's responsibility over the budget to an expanded City Council.

Crime. The August killing of Yusuf Hawkins, who had ventured into a predominantly white neighborhood to answer an advertisement for a used car, evoked the 1986 murder in Howard Beach of Michael Griffith, who was chased to his death on a Queens highway. It apparently was motivated by race and territoriality, complicated by a case of mistaken identity. Six youths were charged with murder for "acting in concert with other persons" in the fatal shooting. Yet as much as the Hawkins case altered the dynamic of the primary campaign, the attack on the 28-year-old investment banker as she jogged through Central Park one April night startled a city seemingly numbed by gratuitous violence. Moreover, her accused assailants did not conform to the stereotype of drug-crazed products of the underclass. The victim became known publicly only as the "Central Park jogger." Her remarkable recovery was dramatized by her release in November from a Connecticut hospital and her return to work as pretrial hearings were being held against six youths accused in the attack.

Driven largely by addiction to crack, the cocaine derivative, the number of murders appeared to be surging past the 1988 record of 1,896 victims. Such was the revulsion to crime that all six of the major party candidates for mayor favored "boot camps" as one alternative to prison. Drug cases overwhelmed the court system and hospital emergency rooms, already overburdened by AIDS cases, and contributed to increased reports of child abuse and a flood of children into the foster-care system.

Other. The city launched a program that will require New Yorkers to separate recyclable waste from the rest of their garbage. Leona Helmsley, the hotel magnate, was convicted of evading $1.2 million in federal taxes after an investigation found she had charged personal expenses to corporate accounts. She was sentenced to four years in prison.

SAM ROBERTS, *"The New York Times"*

Courtesy, New Zealand Embassy

New Zealand's Deputy Prime Minister Geoffrey Palmer, a 47-year-old former law professor, took over the premiership following the resignation of David Lange in August.

NEW ZEALAND

Politics and economics, the traditional competitors for New Zealand's attention, were joined by the issue of race relations in 1989. Prime Minister David Lange, in a Labour Government divided by ideological discord, dramatically resigned in August. Inflation and unemployment rose steadily, then leveled off. Racial harmony looked increasingly fragile.

The Government. Early public-opinion polls gave the Labour Party little comfort. The April returns showed the National Party 33% ahead, the largest margin ever recorded. The same month, Jim Anderton, an outspoken member of Parliament (MP), defected and formed the New Labour Party. Polls revealed that Lange was losing popularity as prime minister. He survived two leadership challenges but the final blow occurred in August, when the Labour caucus reelected Roger Douglas to the Cabinet. Lange had sacked Douglas in 1988 as minister of finance. Lange then resigned, citing health reasons and a loss of confidence in him among colleagues. He was succeeded by his deputy, Geoffrey Palmer. Helen Clark became New Zealand's first woman deputy prime minister.

NEW ZEALAND • Information Highlights

Official Name: New Zealand.
Location: Southwest Pacific Ocean.
Area: 103,737 sq mi (268 680 km²).
Population (mid-1989 est.): 3,400,000.
Chief Cities (March 31, 1987 est.): Wellington, the capital, 351,400; Auckland, 899,200; Christchurch, 333,200; Hamilton, 169,000.
Government: *Head of state,* Elizabeth II, queen, represented by Archbishop Sir Paul Reeves, governor-general (took office Nov. 1985). *Head of government,* Geoffrey Palmer, prime minister (took office August 1989). *Legislature* (unicameral)—House of Representatives.
Monetary Unit: New Zealand dollar (1.70794 N.Z. dollars equal U.S.$1, Nov. 3, 1989).
Gross Domestic Product (1988 U.S. $): $27,900,000,000.
Economic Index (1988): *Consumer Prices* (1980 = 100), all items, 245.3; food, 222.0.
Foreign Trade (1988 U.S.$): *Imports,* $7,311,000,000; *exports,* $8,792,000,000.

Economy. With inflation running at 6.4% for 1988 and unemployment reaching a new peak of 13.5% of the work force, Minister of Finance David Caygill had few options. He slashed NZ$700 million (about U.S. $440 million) in expenditures and raised the goods and services tax from 10% to 12.5% by midyear. A major review of defense facilities recommended the selling of 13 bases and spending cuts amounting to 10% of the defense budget. By August the first signs of a recovery appeared. The unemployment level had dropped to 11% and foreign debt as a proportion of gross domestic product (GDP) plummeted from 82% to 59%. A survey noted that post-1984 reforms had created conditions for stronger, sustainable growth, predicted an annual GDP growth of 2%, and noted that for the first time since 1975 New Zealand's inflation rate was lower than expected.

The July budget was moderate, cautious, and orthodox. It imposed extra taxes on alcohol and tobacco and foreshadowed long-term restructuring of national pension plans. By contrast, there was a sharp increase in spending for education.

Foreign Policy. Relations with the United States remained strained. During an April visit to North America, Prime Minister Lange delivered a speech at Yale in which he declared the alliance between Australia, New Zealand, and the United States (ANZUS) formally dead and floated the idea of New Zealand's withdrawal. The change in leadership did not necessarily indicate any shift in policy, with polls showing an almost two-to-one opposition to visits by nuclear ships to New Zealand. In 1989 controversy simmered over a proposal to buy four frigates from Australia. There was overwhelming public antagonism, but eventually it was decided to purchase two at an approximate cost of NZ$1 billion (about U.S. $625 million).

Domestic Events. In April the government withdrew plans to hold a referendum on changing the system of parliamentary elections to proportional representation. The first elections for a radically reshaped local-government system in October generally favored conservative candidates. In August "wall of death" drift-net fishing was banned within the 200-mi (370-km) exclusive economic zone. Yachting egos were bruised when the New York State Court of Appeals overturned a lower court ruling that had awarded the America's Cup to New Zealand.

GRAHAM BUSH, *University of Auckland*

NIGERIA

Economic factors dominated Nigeria in the fourth year of Gen. Ibrahim Babangida's rule.

Economic Developments. Despite Babangida's plans for economic recovery, conditions continued to deteriorate. Per capita income was $1,000 in 1980 but fell to $370 in 1988, making Nigeria one of the world's poorest countries eligible for World Bank aid. Production of petroleum, the chief export, earned only $6.2 billion, down $1 billion from 1987. However, statistics indicated that Babangida's emphasis upon agriculture was working. Food production increased in 1988 by 3.5% over 1987 with wheat production up 35%, cassava 6.8%, and rice 3.4%. Nevertheless, food prices continued to rise largely because of the 1987 ban on imports.

Attempting to stimulate foreign investment, Babangida in January eased the 40% ceiling of foreign ownership of Nigerian ventures and now foreigners can own up to 100% of certain companies. Exceptions are in petroleum prospecting, mining, banking, and insurance where the 40% ceilings still apply. Agreements with AGIP, Shell, and Elf gave the three multinationals control of more than 20% of the southern oilfields. Profits from the sales are scheduled to complete Nigeria's $2.5 billion liquefied natural gas project. OPEC sanctioned increased oil production and by midyear Nigeria's fields were producing 1.5 million barrels per day.

Babangida successfully delayed the foreign debt problem. In March an agreement with Western creditors (Club of Paris) gave Nigeria a five-year grace period on debt payments of between $5 billion and $6 billion. In June an agreement with creditor banks (London Club) rescheduled $5.4 billion. An agreement with West Germany allowed Nigeria also to postpone repayment of that $4 billion debt until 1995, and a $6 billion World Bank debt was rescheduled.

Riots. Demonstrations by students against the austerity measures began on May 24 in Benin City and soon degenerated into looting. The High Court, former House of Assembly, and the federal prisons buildings were burned. The protest spread to nine states where there was also property damage, particularly in Lagos and Port Harcourt. Authorities closed the universities and gave the police orders to shoot rioters on sight. The government claimed 22 died but observers claimed more than 100 dead, with 50 bodies reported in Lagos alone. Decree number two of 1984 was invoked allowing the 1,500 arrested to be detained without trial up to six months. Babangida announced on June 18 some relaxation in his economic program, promising jobs for 62,000 and a salary increase for some government workers.

Constitutional Changes. The ban on political activity was lifted in May in preparation for a return to civilian rule. Deadline for application by the 13 political associations was July 19. From this number, two political parties will be selected to compete in the 1990–91 elections. All previous politicians and officeholders were banned from the elections. By August, the National Electoral Commission considered 7,000 individual applications and had turned down 600. Alhaji Balarbe Musa, former governor of Kaduna state and founder of the People's Liberation Party, was arrested as a security risk.

Foreign Affairs. Babangida's major efforts concentrated on convincing foreign creditors to restructure the heavy debt while continuing to supply more loans. His primary target was Britain, meeting briefly with Prime Minister Thatcher in Lagos on March 28 and then paying a state visit to London in early May. Babangida participated in the Gbadolite conference in Zaire moderating the civil war in Angola. He also represented Nigeria at Emperor Hirohito's funeral in Tokyo.

HARRY A. GAILEY, *San Jose State University*

NIGERIA • Information Highlights

Official Name: Federal Republic of Nigeria.
Location: West Africa.
Area: 356,668 sq mi (923 770 km²).
Population (mid-1989 est.): 115,300,000.
Chief City (1987 est.): Lagos, the capital, 1,213,000.
Government: *Head of state and government,* Maj. Gen. Ibrahim Babangida, president, federal military government (took office Aug. 27, 1985). *Legislature*—Armed Forces Ruling Council; National Council of Ministers and National Council of States.
Monetary Unit: Naira (7.199 naira equal U.S.$1, July 1989).
Economic Index (Jan. 1989): *Consumer Prices* (1980 = 100), all items, 454.9; food, 492.6.
Foreign Trade (1987 U.S.$): *Imports,* $3,917,000,000; *exports,* $7,383,000,000.

NORTH CAROLINA

The legislature, a hurricane, a television evangelist, college athletics, and hazardous waste held the attention of North Carolinians in 1989.

Legislature. In the longest session on record, an unruly General Assembly upset tradition. In the state House, Republicans and dissident Democrats replaced veteran speaker Liston Ramsey (D) with Joseph Mavretic (D), who had difficulty holding the coalition together. On the other hand, Senate Democrats stripped Jim Gardner—the first Republican lieutenant governor in this century—of his power to appoint committees. Despite confusion in their ranks, Democrats also rallied to blunt most of Gov. Jim Martin's proposals.

Taxes on gasoline and automobile sales were raised to pay for a long-range $9 billion highway program, and income taxes were

© Jerry L. Wolford

Members of GASP (Greensboro to Alleviate Smoking Pollution) anxiously awaited November election returns on the Greensboro ordinance to curb smoking in public places. The ordinance was passed by a slim margin.

pegged to federal returns to help pay for an $11 billion annual budget. Drug laws were tightened, and $150 million was appropriated for prison construction. The state's primary laws were amended to permit the nomination of the top candidate receiving more than 40% of the vote.

Election Day. An ordinance to curb smoking in public places was approved by a slim margin in Greensboro—deep in the heart of tobacco country. Meanwhile, Charlotte Mayor Sue Myrick (R) was reelected, and Durham and Hillsborough elected their first black mayors.

Education. In a year when North Carolina public school students scored lowest in the nation on the Scholastic Aptitude Test and demands for accountability grew louder, the teachers' lobbies again turned back a proposal for performance pay differentials. Teacher salaries were increased, nonetheless, and the basic education program was expanded. Tuition was raised by 20% for state residents attending North Carolina's public colleges. Friction continued between the appointed state board of education and the elected superintendent of public instruction.

At North Carolina State University, Chancellor Bruce Poulton resigned and basketball coach Jim Valvano lost his additional post as director of athletics because of reports of irregularities in the basketball program.

Hurricane *Hugo*. After devastating coastal South Carolina, Hurricane *Hugo* caused $1 billion in damage to North Carolina, nearly half of it in the Charlotte area. About two dozen counties were declared federal disaster areas, and electric power was interrupted in places for more than two weeks.

Waste Disposal. Hazardous-waste disposal vied with drugs and education as the state's most urgent problem. Pressure from "not-in-my-backyard" forces led the General Assembly to undermine the state Hazardous Waste Treatment Commission's efforts to select a site in North Carolina for a treatment facility. In response, South Carolina closed its landfill to North Carolina materials, and Alabama declined to negotiate with states without their own facilities. Governor Martin declared a "hazardous waste crisis" and urged a new commission to act quickly.

Names in the News. Former Gov. Jim Hunt stunned many Democrats by announcing that he would not challenge U.S. Sen. Jesse Helms (R) again in 1990. Michael Skube of the Raleigh *News and Observer* won a Pulitzer Prize for literary criticism. In federal court in Charlotte, Jim Bakker, the founder of the Praise the Lord (PTL) television ministry, was convicted on 24 counts of fraud and conspiracy, sentenced to 45 years in prison, and fined $500,000. Deaths included Albert Coates, founder of the Institute of Government, and Benjamin Swalin, longtime conductor of the North Carolina Symphony Orchestra.

H. G. JONES
University of North Carolina at Chapel Hill

NORTH CAROLINA • Information Highlights

Area: 52,669 sq mi (136 413 km^2).
Population (July 1, 1988): 6,489,000.
Chief Cities (July 1, 1986 est.): Raleigh, the capital, 180,430; Charlotte, 352,070; Greensboro, 176,650; Winston-Salem, 148,080; Durham, 113,890.
Government (1989): *Chief Officers*—governor, James G. Martin (R); lt. gov., Jim Gardner (R). *General Assembly*—Senate, 50 members; House of Representatives, 120 members.
State Finances (fiscal year 1988): *Revenue,* $12,806,000,000; *expenditure,* $11,022,000,000.
Personal Income (1988): $92,822,000,000; per capita, $14,304.
Labor Force (June 1989): *Civilian labor force,* 3,489,200; *unemployed,* 130,800 (3.7% of total force).
Education: *Enrollment* (fall 1987)—public elementary schools, 754,000; public secondary, 332,000; colleges and universities, 321,251. *Public school expenditures* (1987–88), $3,687,400,000 ($3,434 per pupil).

© Tom Stromme/"Bismarck Tribune"

Candles were lit on a huge styrofoam birthday cake as part of the celebrations during 1989 commemorating the 100th year of statehood for North Dakota. The state was admitted to the Union on Nov. 2, 1889.

NORTH DAKOTA

North Dakota marked its centennial in 1989 and state residents celebrated by defeating soundly a slate of referred legislative measures in a December special election. For a second straight year, drought shriveled the state's major crops.

Election. A record number of voters for a special election went to the polls on December 5 and voted "no" down the ballot. Three tax increases approved by lawmakers earlier in the year were among measures defeated, despite warnings from Gov. George Sinner and others that the loss of the funding would mean cuts in school aid, higher education, and human services. Revenue measures killed included an increase in sales-tax rates from 5% to 6%, defeated 55% to 45%; a three-cents-per-gallon gas tax hike, defeated 61% to 59%; and an increase in personal income-tax rates from 14% to 17% of federal-tax liability, defeated 62% to 38%.

Also rejected by the voters were measures that would have mandated the use of seat belts, required school districts to establish a health-care curriculum including sex education, allowed the state's charitable gambling operations to use electronic gaming machines, created a pension plan for lawmakers, and authorized the governor to appoint a commission to reorganize the state government.

Legislature. The December special election wrote the final chapter for the 1989 legislative session. Lawmakers met for 75 days early in the year, fashioning a $108 million tax package to bridge the gap between expected revenues and proposed spending for the 1989–91 biennium. Sinner also asked the legislature to begin reorganizing and consolidating local schools and the state's system of 11 colleges and universities. Both proposals were defeated by the legislature.

Drought. A lack of rain and high temperatures held North Dakota crop production well below average in 1989, although yields were about double those of 1988. State agriculture economists pegged direct crop losses at nearly $910 million, but farmers received an estimated $220 million in insurance payments and federal disaster aid to offset some losses. Reductions in related economic activity boosted total losses to an estimated $2.1 billion. Estimated grain production in the state in 1989 included: spring wheat, 162.8 million bushels, 14% below 1987; durum wheat, 63.8 million bushels, with per-acre yields 15% below 1987; barley, 87.5 million bushels, down 37% from 1987.

Centennial. North Dakota was one of six Western states celebrating centennials in 1989. The event was highlighted by a three-day party at Bismarck, the state capital, that drew approximately 120,000 participants over the July 4 weekend. President George Bush visited the state in April to join the celebration. Other observers found little to cheer, however. *Newsweek* magazine labeled the centennial states a "permanent outback" unable to support their populations. Two Rutgers University professors, meanwhile, suggested North Dakota be turned into a vast national park, called the Buffalo Commons, after the last farms had failed.

JIM NEUMANN, *Fargo, ND*

NORTH DAKOTA • Information Highlights

Area: 70,702 sq mi (183 119 km²).
Population (July 1, 1988): 667,000.
Chief Cities (1980 census): Bismarck, the capital, 44,485; Fargo, 61,383; Grand Forks, 43,765; Minot, 32,843.
Government (1989): *Chief Officers*—governor, George A. Sinner (D); lt. gov., Lloyd Omdahl (D). *Legislative Assembly*—Senate, 53 members; House of Representatives, 106 members.
State Finances (fiscal year 1988): *Revenue,* $1,615,000,000; *expenditure,* $1,597,000,000.
Personal Income (1988): $8,560,000,000; per capita, $12,833.
Labor Force (June 1989): *Civilian labor force,* 340,700; *unemployed,* 15,500 (4.6% of total force).
Education: *Enrollment* (fall 1987)—public elementary schools, 84,000; public secondary, 35,000; colleges and universities, 37,052. *Public school expenditures* (1987–88), $384,591,000 ($3,249 per pupil).

NORTHWEST TERRITORIES

The most significant event of 1989 in the Northwest Territories (NWT) occurred on December 8 when an agreement in principle on a land-claim settlement was reached between the government of Canada and the Inuit of the eastern and central Arctic regions, represented by the Tungavik Federation of Nunavut (TFN). The agreement granted the largest land-claims settlement in the history of Canada and included a cash settlement of C$580 million. The Inuit also would hold title to surface rights to about 138,000 sq mi (357 420 km²), and of that total area they would hold subsurface rights to 14,000 sq mi (36 260 km²). A ratification process was under way that all parties expected to be completed early in 1990, and the final land-claim agreement was anticipated from six months to a year after that. Concurrently, the TFN and the territorial government agreed to try to find a way to finance and establish "Nunavut" as an eastern territory, carved out of and separate from the NWT.

The Economy. In October a special committee of the legislative assembly of the NWT presented its report on the northern economy. The committee held extensive hearings in all 24 constituencies of the NWT and received wide public input into its work. Its recommendations included measures to provide improved educational services and enhance marketable work skills for NWT residents; implementation of a sustainable development strategy; and the establishment, in cooperation with the federal government, of an economic development agency.

New Commissioner. On October 2, Daniel L. Norris was appointed by the government of Canada as the new commissioner of the NWT, replacing John Parker, who had served as commissioner for ten years. Daniel Norris, from Inuvik, NWT, is of Métis heritage and is the first native-born commissioner of the territory. The commissioner's role in practice has evolved into one resembling that of a provincial lieutenant-governor.

ROSS M. HARVEY
Television Northern Canada

NORTHWEST TERRITORIES • Information Highlights

Area: 1,322,903 sq mi (3 426 320 km²).
Population (June 1989): 53,100.
Chief Cities (1986 census): Yellowknife, the capital, 11,753; Inuvik, 3,389; Hay River, 2,964.
Government (1988): *Chief Officers*—commissioner, Daniel L. Norris; government leader, Dennis Patterson. *Legislature*—Legislative Assembly, 24 elected members.
Public Finances (1987–88 fiscal year): *Revenues,* C$769,197,000; *expenditures,* C$797,653,000.
Education (1989–90): *Enrollment*—elementary and secondary schools, 13,580 pupils. *Public school expenditures* (1987–88), C$158,740,000.

NORWAY

Norway banned the illegal killing of baby seals in the Arctic Sea; a dispute with Great Britain over North Sea oil reserves broke out; and archaeologists uncovered an important Viking-age building in 1989.

Political Affairs. Norwegians went to the polls in September to elect a new Storting (parliament) for the next four years. No party obtained a majority, although the Labor Party remained the biggest party. Labor ended up with 34.3% of the vote, 6.5% less than in 1985, and held onto 63 seats in the 165-member Storting.

After weeks of negotiations, it was announced on October 16 that the Conservatives in coalition with the Center Party and the Christian People's Party would form a new cabinet, which was to contain a majority of Conservatives joined by members of the other two parties. Jan P. Syse, the leader of the Conservative Party, was appointed prime minister, and the new foreign minister was Kjell Magne Bondevik of the Christian People's Party. Of the 19 new ministers, eight were women.

Foreign Affairs. In the fall, Norway and the Soviet Union signed an agreement on space research. The agreement covered future observatories in space, land-based installations, astrophysics, space biology, medicine, and the outer layer of the earth's atmosphere, including the ozone.

A dispute developed between Britain and Norway over ownership of the oil reserves in the adjacent Norwegian-British areas in the North Sea. Norway claims 88.1% of the areas, while Great Britain insisted that Norway's share should be limited to 80%. The total area produces as much as 750,000 barrels of oil and gas daily. The new Oseberg Field was opened for production during the year and produces 340,000 barrels a day. Overall, Norwegian oil and gas fields in the North and Norwegian seas produce 1.1 million barrels a day, and there are

NORWAY • Information Highlights

Official Name: Kingdom of Norway.
Location: Northern Europe.
Area: 125,182 sq mi (324 220 km²).
Population (mid-1989 est.): 4,200,000.
Chief Cities (Oct. 1, 1988): Oslo, the capital, 453,730; Bergen, 210,422; Trondheim, 135,973.
Government: *Head of state,* Olav V, king (acceded Sept. 1957). *Head of government,* Jan P. Syse, prime minister (took office Oct. 16, 1989). *Legislature*—Storting: Lagting and Odelsting.
Monetary Unit: Krone (6.96 kroner equal U.S.$1, Nov. 13, 1989).
Gross Domestic Product (1987 U.S.$): $82,600,-000,000.
Economic Indexes (1988): *Consumer Prices* (1980 = 100), all items, 191.5; food, 205.2. *Industrial Production* (1980 = 100), 142.
Foreign Trade (1988 U.S.$): *Imports,* $23,222,-000,000; *exports,* $22,508,000,000.

proven gas reserves sufficient for the next 100 years.

Norwegian seal hunting in the Arctic Sea took the spotlight early in the year. Certain groups always have been opposed to it, but this opposition grew after the showing of a documentary by a former Norwegian sealing inspector, Odd Lindberg, on Swedish TV. Carl XVI Gustaf, the king of Sweden, as chairman of the Swedish section of the World Wildlife Fund, condemned illegal seal-slaughtering practices, and the Storting banned the killing of seal pups in February.

On June 1, Pope John Paul II arrived on a brief visit to Norway. He was received by King Olav V.

Domestic Affairs. Scandinavian archaeologists unearthed the remains of the largest known building from the Viking Age. It was found in an island in the Far North, and dates from the year 700 A.D. The building is no less than 275 ft (84 m) in length, had a ceiling height of 23 ft (7 m), and covered an area of 7,000 sq ft (650 m²).

The town of Lillehammer in central Norway was selected as the site of the 1994 Winter Olympics. This led to a flurry of construction, including hotels, sleeping facilities, and new downhill skiing courses, in the area.

Dag Solstad, a popular novelist, was the winner of the 1989 Nordic Council Literature Prize. His winning entry was *Roman 87* (*Novel 87*), the story of a generation of people in a small town.

ERIK J. FRIIS
The Scandinavian-American Bulletin

NOVA SCOTIA

Nova Scotians were preoccupied during 1989 with controversial legislation enacted by the government and were heartened by the resilience of the provincial economy during a cyclical downturn.

Legislation and Government. During the year the provincial government enacted 82 laws, including controversial measures to restrict the privatization of medical services and an unpopular amendment to the Public Utility Act. The former, by prohibiting the performance of several medical procedures, including abortion, outside a hospital, was perceived as a disguised response to Montreal doctor Henry Morgentaler's plan to open an abortion clinic in Halifax. The government met stiffer opposition when it proceeded to declaw the Public Utility Board by revoking its mandate to conduct public hearings on applications for all new power plants. Eventually it yielded to opposition pressure by limiting the application of the law only to the coal-fired Point Aconi power plant. The government was preoccupied with safeguarding the Cape Breton coal industry.

NOVA SCOTIA • Information Highlights

Area: 21,425 sq mi (55 491 km²).
Population (June 1989): 885,700.
Chief cities (1986 census): Halifax, the capital, 113,577; Dartmouth, 65,243; Sydney, 27,754.
Government (1989): *Chief Officers*—lt. gov., Lloyd R. Crouse; premier, John Buchanan (Progressive Conservative). *Legislature*—House of Assembly, 52 members.
Provincial Finances (1989–90 fiscal year budget): *Revenues,* $3,411,924,000; *expenditures,* $3,526,-635,000.
Personal Income (average weekly earnings, July 1989): $437.94.
Labor Force (September 1989, seasonally adjusted): *Employed* workers, 15 years of age and over, 373,000; *Unemployed,* 45,000 (10.3%).
Education (1989–90): *Enrollment*—elementary and secondary schools, 168,400 pupils; postsecondary—universities, 26,290; community colleges, 2,150.
(All monetary figures are in Canadian dollars.)

Legislation that demonstrated the government's commitment toward improving the socioeconomic welfare of Nova Scotians included enactments for assisting residents to save for the purchase of a first home, protecting the rights of victims of violent crimes, enforcing protective environmental measures, and imposing stiff penalties on motorists convicted of driving offenses.

Economy. The economy received a serious setback when the fish-processing industry, after the federal government announcement of reductions in fishing quotas, was plagued by plant closures and layoffs. A 12-week strike of railway workers at the Cape Breton Development Corporation and flooding problems in the Lingan Mine reduced coal production by more than 24% during the first half of 1989, compared with 1988 figures. Lower gold and tin prices further hindered the growth of the resource sector, although the sagging pace in that sector was countered by a 6.6% growth in manufacturing shipments, a 6.5% upturn in domestic exports, and a 5.7% upsurge in retail trade during the first six months of 1989. Similarly, the negative impact of a 15% reduction in residential housing starts in the first half of the year was eliminated by an increase in nonresidential construction, where permits were up by 21% during the first nine months of 1989. Overall, the provincial economy was expected to grow by about 2.5% in 1989.

Energy. Nova Scotians, after a lull of six years in electric-power rate increases, were hit by an average hike of 7.5%. On a more positive note was the announcement to drill an exploratory well on the Cohasset oil field, which signaled the end of Nova Scotia's offshore drilling drought. In the meantime, the Nova Scotia Power Corporation awarded a C$290 million contract to build a 165-megawatt, world-class coal-fired power plant in Point Aconi.

R. P. SETH
Mount Saint Vincent University, Halifax

HIROHITO

Emperor of Japan: b. Tokyo, Japan, April 29, 1901; d. Tokyo, Jan. 7, 1989.

The death of Hirohito, also known as the Shōwa (Enlightened Peace) Emperor, ended the 62-year reign of Japan's 124th emperor. His reign was the longest in recorded Japanese history.

Since 1926 the emperor had presided over not one, but several Japans. In the late 1920s, Japan actually was in the twilight of progressive change, known to Japanese as "Taishō democracy." It produced the oldest parliamentary tradition outside the West, civilian-led party cabinets, universal (male) suffrage, and the appearance of mass-urban style.

In the 1930s and 1940s, the emperor in uniform and astride his famous white horse, Shiroyuki, became the symbol of Japanese militarism, expansion, aggression, and, eventually, a disastrous defeat. On Sept. 26, 1945, in an interview with U.S. Gen. Douglas MacArthur, Hirohito stated that he "bore sole responsibility for every political and military decision made and taken by my people in the conduct of the war."

Under the new antiwar Constitution, adopted Nov. 3, 1946, the emperor assumed a more comfortable role as "symbol of the state and the unity of the people, deriving his position from the will of the people with whom resides sovereignty." As such, Hirohito, therefore, symbolized the remarkable reconstruction of the nation and its steady rise to become a major economic power.

Background. Born in 1901, Hirohito was the first son of Crown Prince Yoshihito (who became the Taishō Emperor) and Princess Sadako. His name meant "broad-minded" *(Hiro-)* "benevolence" (*-hito,* part of the personal name of every emperor). He was educated at the Gakushuin (peers' school) and by private tutors in a separate household. In 1921 as crown prince he traveled to London and other European capitals. At age 17 he was engaged to Princess Nagako. In 1923 their wedding ceremony was postponed for a year because of the Tokyo earthquake. The couple had five daughters and two sons, including Crown Prince Akihito (*see* BIOGRAPHY).

On Nov. 21, 1921, Hirohito became prince regent, serving in place of his ill father. The Taishō emperor died on Dec. 25, 1926, and Hirohito ascended the throne. The formal coronation was held in Kyoto on Nov. 10, 1928.

The weight of evidence shows that the emperor was neither emotionally nor politically trained to be a decision-maker. Rather, he served as a symbol, legitimizing secular policy decisions. Hirohito never, with one or two exceptions, directly expressed opinions. In 1941 he gave only oblique consent to the opening of hostilities, with the proviso that the United States should be given advance notice of war. (The declaration was delayed.) In an imperial conference held Aug. 10, 1945, on the invitation of Prime Minister Kantaro Suzuki, he did break a deadlock. Then and in the broadcast of Aug. 15, 1945, announcing Japan's surrender, Hirohito said that Japan must "bear the unbearable and endure the unendurable."

The emperor's status—in fact, his responsibility for the war—was debated. In August 1945 there were those who wanted him tried as a war criminal, but MacArthur argued successfully that it was essential to keep the emperor. On Jan. 1, 1946, Hirohito helped his cause by issuing an imperial rescript rejecting "mere legends and myths" of imperial divinity. Although in 1988, during Hirohito's long illness, the subject was officially taboo, many Japanese engaged in vigorous discussion of the emperor's wartime responsibility and the future of the imperial institution.

In 1971, Hirohito became the first reigning emperor to travel abroad, visiting Britain, Belgium, West Germany, the Netherlands, Denmark, France, and Switzerland. In returning to Japan, the imperial couple first set foot on U.S. soil in Anchorage, AK. In 1975 they made a full-scale visit to the United States.

From the time he was a young student, Hirohito showed a lively interest in marine biology. He regularly engaged in research at his laboratory in the Tokyo palace and in field work at a villa on Sagami Bay. He published several books and papers on his specialty, the hydrozoan, and on marine life and flora at his retreat in Nasu.

ARDATH W. BURKS

[1] Arranged chronologically by date of death.

LORENZ, Konrad Zacharias

Austrian zoologist: b. Vienna, Austria, Nov. 7, 1903; d. Altenburg, Austria, Feb. 27, 1989.

Konrad Lorenz was one of three scientists to share the 1973 Nobel Prize in medicine or physiology for their pioneer work in ethology, the study of animal behavior in the wild.

An enthusiastic and dedicated animal watcher, Lorenz popularized the term "imprinting," a process that occurs at a genetically predetermined time whereby an animal identifies with another individual, usually of its own species. A newly hatched duckling, for example, will follow the sounds of its mother's quacking and irreversibly become imprinted on her. If the baby animal first sees or hears a human, it will imprint on the person. Lorenz often was photographed leading a parade of goslings that he had imprinted on him. Lorenz' studies of the greylag goose and the jackdaw (a type of crow) led him to write *King Solomon's Ring* (1949), an entertaining book about animals for readers of all ages.

Lorenz probably will be remembered best, however, for his more-controversial *On Aggression* (1963), in which he theorized that evolution produced a killer instinct in man. Man undeniably has an aggressive nature but modern ethologists argue that such behavior is affected by environment and not predetermined genetically. They view humans as relatively peaceable.

Background. Lorenz' parents, both physicians, lived in Vienna but spent summers at their estate in Altenburg on the Danube River, where young Konrad developed his fascination with animals.

While his father was a visiting surgeon in New York, Lorenz enrolled as a medical student at Cornell University, but after a year he left for the University of Vienna, where he received a doctorate in zoology in 1933. From 1927 to 1935, he observed the social behavior of jackdaws and published many scientific papers. In 1940, he was appointed professor in psychology at the University of Königsberg (now Kaliningrad in the Soviet Union), but World War II interrupted his academic career. Drafted into the German Army, he served as a doctor on the Eastern front and was held prisoner by the Russians for four years.

After the war, he resumed his studies at Altenburg with the support of West Germany's Max Planck Society for the Advancement of Science. He became director of the Society's Institute for Behavioral Physiology in 1961—a position he held until 1973. He subsequently returned to Altenburg, where he continued studying animal behavior and writing until his death.

DEBORAH A. BEHLER

ROBINSON, Sugar Ray

U.S. boxer: b. Detroit, MI, May 3, 1921; d. Culver City, CA, April 12, 1989.

A six-time world champion in the welterweight and middleweight divisions, Sugar Ray Robinson was regarded by many boxing experts as "pound for pound, the greatest fighter of all time." In a 25-year professional career, from 1940 to 1965, he combined devastating punching power, dazzling footwork, and a unique "matador" style for a record 174 victories (109 by knockout), 19 defeats, and six draws. (Five losses came in the six months before he quit the ring at age 44.) Robinson was an idol to generations of boxers. Muhammad Ali copied his style, Sugar Ray Leonard (and many others) borrowed his nickname, but no one could match his greatness.

During his career, Robinson was known to spend money as fast as he earned it. A pink Cadillac was his trademark. He challenged the Internal Revenue Service in a back taxes case and won. The decision led to the regulation allowing income averaging.

Background. Born Walker Smith, Jr., the future champion moved with his mother from Detroit to Harlem at age 12. During the Depression, he earned money tap dancing on sidewalks and running errands for a grocery store. He also spent time at local gyms learning to box. As a young amateur, he borrowed the certificate of a boxer named Ray Robinson and decided to keep the name. "Sugar" was adopted later, after a sportswriter described his style as "sweet as sugar."

After winning all 89 of his amateur bouts, Robinson made his professional debut in October 1940. He won his first 40 pro fights, 29 by knockout, before dropping a decision to Jake La Motta in 1943; he would defeat La Motta in their four subsequent fights. Robinson won the vacant world welterweight title in 1946 with a decision over Tommy Bell. He held the title until February 1951, when he knocked out La Motta for the middleweight championship. By mid-1951, he had won 130 of 131 fights.

Robinson lost his middleweight crown to Randy Turpin in July 1951 but won it back two months later. After losing a light heavyweight title bout to Joey Maxim in 1952, he spent 22 months in show business as a tap dancer before regaining the middleweight belt with a knockout of Carl (Bobo) Olson in December 1955. In 1957–58, Robinson lost and regained the crown from both Gene Fullmer and Carmen Basilio. In 1960 he lost the title, and a rematch, to Paul Pender. He continued fighting for five more years, primarily out of financial necessity. He was elected to the Boxing Hall of Fame in 1967, and he founded the Sugar Ray Youth Foundation for inner-city children in 1969.

JEFFREY H. HACKER

AP/Wide World

BALL, Lucille

American entertainer: b. Jamestown, NY, Aug. 6, 1911; d. Los Angeles, CA, April 26, 1989.

An actress and comedienne whose career spanned five decades, Lucille Ball was known as the first lady of television comedy. As the star of the enormously popular *I Love Lucy* (1951–57), she became probably the most-recognized and best-loved woman in the history of show business. With the creation of her "Lucy" character, a zany housewife given to slapstick antics, Ball found the perfect showcase for her unique talent. Reruns of *I Love Lucy* still are shown daily worldwide.

As well as being a tremendously talented comedienne with wonderful timing and the ability to make the audience sympathetic to her character, Ball also was a pioneering business executive. Although many assumed she was much like her hapless, daffy character, she actually was a driven perfectionist who became the first woman to head a production studio, Desilu Productions, from 1962 to 1967. The company, founded by Ball and her husband, Desi Arnaz, became one of the most successful television production companies. After selling Desilu Productions to Gulf and Western Industries in 1967, she formed Lucille Ball Productions.

Background. Lucille Désirée Ball was the daughter of the former Désirée Hunt, a pianist, and Henry Dunnell Ball, a telephone lineman who died when she was very young. Raised mostly by her maternal grandparents, she longed to launch a career in show business. At 15 she went to Manhattan and enrolled in drama school, seeking roles in Broadway choruses and working occasionally as a model. Despite repeatedly being told she had no talent, as well as a setback caused by temporary paralysis from rheumatic fever, Ball reached Hollywood in 1933 in the musical *Roman Scandals*. During this first part of her career, she made scores of films; usually she was cast as the wisecracking sidekick of the leading lady. Although many of these films were forgettable, she often was hailed by critics as a talented actress.

In 1950, Ball and her husband, Cuban bandleader Desi Arnaz, whom she married in 1940, attempted to sell their idea for a television comedy to the networks. Repeatedly turned down, the Arnazes toured the United States with their act and made a pilot episode with their own money. Finally, the show got on the air—the rest is history. In the six years of its run, the program, which also featured William Frawley and Vivian Vance as the Ricardos' friends and landlords, never ranked below third in popularity. One episode in which Lucy Ricardo gave birth to Little Ricky (the same night Lucille Ball gave birth to a son in real life) garnered more viewers than the inauguration of President Dwight D. Eisenhower.

I Love Lucy was revolutionary in its production techniques as well as unprecedented in popularity. It was one of the first shows to be filmed rather than broadcast live and the first to film before an audience and to use three cameras simultaneously. These innovations influenced the shift from broadcasting TV shows live to taping them, and helped move the headquarters of U.S. television production to Hollywood from New York City.

After 179 episodes, *I Love Lucy* went off the air, although the Arnazes did occasional high-budget specials until 1960, when they were divorced. Ball married the comedian Gary Morton in 1961.

Ball kept the "Lucy" character alive as a widow in *The Lucy Show* (1962–68) and *Here's Lucy* (1968–74). She starred in several more movies, including *Yours, Mine and Ours* (1968) and *Mame* (1974), danced and sang in the Broadway musical *Wildcat* (1960), and made occasional appearances in TV movies. In 1986, Ball tried to revive Lucy in a new series called *Life with Lucy,* but the show was a popular failure.

Among Lucille Ball's many awards were four Emmys, induction into the Television Hall of Fame, and a citation for lifetime achievement from the Kennedy Center for the Performing Arts. She was awarded the Presidential Medal of Freedom posthumously in July 1989 by President Bush, who cited her as "a national treasure."

In addition to her husband and son, she was survived by a daughter, actress Lucie Arnaz.

MEGHAN O'REILLY

UPI/Bettmann Newsphotos

PEPPER, Claude Denson

U.S. politician: b. near Dudleyville, AL, Sept. 8, 1900; d. Washington, DC, May 30, 1989.

During a political career that spanned some 60 years, Claude Pepper fought hard for Americans in need of help. During his latter years especially, the Florida Democrat championed the causes of the elderly, becoming a protector of the Social Security System and an advocate of catastrophic health insurance. In the words of Rep. Martin Frost (D-TX), he was the "conscience of the Democratic Party."

Background. Claude Denson Pepper, an Alabama farm boy, was graduated from the University of Alabama in 1921 and Harvard Law School in 1924. He then practiced law in Florida, served one term in the Florida House of Representatives (1929–30), and was elected to

UPI/Bettmann Newsphotos

KHOMEINI, Ayatollah Ruhollah

Shiite religious leader, ruler of Iran: b. Khumain, Iran, May 17, 1900?; d. Tehran, Iran, June 3, 1989.

Early in 1979 the Ayatollah Khomeini brought to an end the 37-year reign of Shah Mohammed Reza Pahlavi. He himself then ruled Iran for a decade as head of a rigid theocracy.

Background. Khomeini was born, probably in 1900, in the small town of Khumain, south of Tehran. From that place he derived his surname, but the family name was Hendi. Ruhollah was very young when his father was murdered. The boy became known as a distinguished Islamic scholar. His patron was Abdul Karim Haeri, who in 1920 opened the Madresseh Faizieh, a center of Islamic studies in Qum.

AP/Wide World

GROMYKO, Andrei Andreyevich

Soviet statesman; b. Starye Gromyk, Byelorussia, USSR, July 18, 1909; d. Moscow, July 2, 1989.

The Soviet foreign minister from 1957 to 1985, Andrei Gromyko was a central figure in world politics for four decades, serving under six Soviet leaders, from Joseph Stalin to Mikhail Gorbachev. Only recently had Gromyko faded from the political stage. In October 1988 he retired from the ceremonial post of president which he had held for three years, and in April 1989 he was dropped from the Politburo in a sweeping purge by Gorbachev. In the age of rapid political reform, Gromyko, the epitome of the cautious old-liner, was an anomaly. It was Gromyko who nominated Gorbachev as the new Soviet leader after Konstantin Cher-

fill an unexpired term in the U.S. Senate in 1936. Once in Washington, Pepper became a New Deal liberal and a confidant of President Franklin Roosevelt. He supported the first federal minimum wage law and cosponsored legislation establishing the National Cancer Institute. He won reelection to the Senate in 1938 and 1944.

As a member of the Senate Foreign Relations Committee, he introduced legislation that led to the Lend-Lease Act. He also supported other war-preparedness measures, including the establishment of a military draft. Following World War II, he remained very much a liberal. The nation, including the state of Florida, however, was becoming more conservative. In 1950, Rep. George Smathers successfully challenged Pepper in a bitter primary campaign. The defeated senator returned to the practice of law.

After failing in a primary attempt to return to the Senate in 1958, he was elected to the U.S. House of Representatives in 1962 and reelected 13 times. The congressman backed the policies of Presidents Kennedy and Johnson, including Medicare, federal aid to education, and civil rights. During his 26 years in the House, he served as chairman of the Select Committee on Crime, the Select Committee on Aging, and the Rules Committee.

The recipient of many awards and honorary degrees, Congressman Pepper was presented with the Presidential Medal of Freedom by President Bush a few days before his death on May 30, 1989. That same day, his colleagues in the House voted 397-0 to allow his body to lie in state in the Capitol Rotunda—a rare honor.

The congressman's wife of 43 years had died in 1979.

JAMES E. CHURCHILL, JR.

Ruhollah studied and taught there for more than 40 years. In the 1950s he became an ayatollah by popular acclaim. In the early 1960s he began opposing the policies of the shah. His opposition to the reduction of church-owned landed estates and to the emancipation of women led to his imprisonment in 1963 and exile in 1964. He lived briefly in Turkey and then for 14 years in Iraq.

In 1978 the shah made the mistake of asking Iraq to expel Khomeini. The ayatollah moved to France and from his residence near Paris was able to manipulate the Western media with great skill, and successfully stimulate dissent in Iran. His calls for strikes in Iran in the fall of 1978 were heeded. Civilian violence spread throughout the country, and the shah and his family left "on vacation" in January 1979. On February 1, Khomeini made a triumphant return to Tehran from exile.

The Islamic state which he created and ruled undisputedly for ten years was a supreme combination of religious and secular power. Anti-American (as well as anti-Soviet), anti-Israeli, antifeminist, and antimodernist, Khomeini seemed to enunciate his hostilities more clearly than his positive precepts and policies. His regime maintained its supremacy by large-scale executions. The economy foundered. In the war which Iraq began in 1980, the ayatollah persisted in hostilities, causing the deaths of perhaps 900,000 young men before his enforced acceptance of a truce in 1988. He apparently did not instigate, but took no steps to end, the holding of 52 American hostages in the U.S. embassy from November 1979 to January 1981. Because of this and other actions Iran had become internationally isolated by the end of his time.

ARTHUR CAMPBELL TURNER

---

nenko's death in March 1985, yet he was replaced as foreign minister that July.

Cultured and well-read, Gromyko spoke English fluently and was said to have a good sense of humor. Even his adversaries admired his diplomatic skills.

Background. Andrei Andreyevich Gromyko was born July 18, 1909, in Starye Gromyk, Byelorussia. He was educated at the Minsk Institute of Agriculture and entered the Communist Party in 1931. He worked as an economist until entering the foreign ministry in 1939. Like many of his generation, he benefited from the Stalin purges of 1937–1939 and rose rapidly through the party ranks. In 1943 he became ambassador to the United States. He participated in the Dumbarton Oaks Conference, the Big Three meetings at Yalta and Potsdam, and the UN founding conference in San Francisco. In 1946, Gromyko became the permanent Soviet representative to the UN. He returned to Moscow two years later and was made first deputy foreign minister.

During the regime of Nikita Khrushchev, he was raised to the Central Committee of the party in 1956 and named foreign minister in 1957. A loyal functionary for the post-Stalin leadership, Gromyko was involved in the implementation of the coexistence and détente policies of the 1960s and 1970s. Under Leonid Brezhnev he was given membership in the Politburo (1973) and was involved in the negotiations for the SALT I and SALT II agreements. After the death of Yuri Andropov in February 1984 and his replacement by Konstantin Chernenko, responsibility for foreign policy decisions fell to Gromyko.

Despite his long service to the USSR, Gromyko was not given a state funeral.

RONALD GRIGOR SUNY

UPI/Bettmann Newsphotos

OLIVIER, Laurence Kerr

British actor, director, and producer: b. Dorking, Surrey, England, May 22, 1907; d. West Sussex, England, July 11, 1989.

Probably no other actor in the 20th century has been admired as widely for his protean theatrical gifts as Sir Laurence Olivier. One of the world's most powerful classical actors, he also became a noted film star and director. His screen adaptations of Shakespearean plays brought the Bard to mass audiences. As founder and first artistic director of the National Theatre of Britain (1963–73), he exercised a profound influence on the British theater.

Although Olivier gained laurels as a director and producer of both plays and films he was, at the core, an actor. His extraordinary attention to detail and ability to conceptualize every nuance of the characters he portrayed enabled him to master vastly different roles. In a remarkably diverse career that spanned more than 60 years, he became a living legend.

Viewed by his peers as a "born" actor, Olivier in actuality studied his craft assiduously—working hard to develop the mannerisms of the characters he depicted, perfecting their accents, and experimenting with makeup to define further his portrayals. A physically daring performer as well, he sought opportunities to take falls or leap from balconies, which he did with unusual agility.

Among the numerous awards he received were a best actor Oscar for his film *Hamlet* (1948), which he also directed and produced; Emmy Awards for *The Moon and Sixpence* (1960) and *Long Day's Journey Into Night* (1973); and an honorary Oscar for his lifelong contribution to the art of film (1979). Olivier was knighted in 1947, and was elevated to life peerage in 1970.

Background. Laurence Kerr Olivier was the son of the former Agnes Crookenden and Gerard Kerr, an Anglican clergyman. As a youngster, Olivier was mesmerized by his father's sense of drama in the pulpit.

His acting debut came at age 9 when he played Brutus in *Julius Caesar* at All Saints Choir School in London. Despite the praise he received for his acting ability in his early teen years, he was not yet serious about the stage. When Olivier was 17, his strict father surprisingly set his course in that direction, enrolling him at Elsie Fogerty's Central School of Speech Training and Dramatic Art in London.

After completing his training the young actor spent three years doing walk-ons and bit parts, followed by good notices in a half dozen flops. His luck turned with a part in Noel Coward's hit *Private Lives* (1930), where he also met his first wife, actress Jill Esmond. By the mid-1930s, Olivier had developed into a magnetic classical actor with London's revered Old Vic. In the mid-1940s he codirected the company with Ralph Richardson. His success at the Old Vic made him the choice for the job of first artistic director of the National Theatre, directing and acting in roles such as Astrov in *Uncle Vanya* and Shylock in *The Merchant of Venice*.

During this period Olivier also established himself as a leading film actor. His film debut was in *Murder for Sale* (1929), but he did not become a recognized star until his appearance in *Wuthering Heights* (1939). He added luster to this new crown with his role in *Rebecca* (1940).

Olivier met his second wife, actress Vivien Leigh, when they acted together in the film *Fire Over England* in 1937. The two later costarred in several plays, among them *Antony and Cleopatra* (1951) and *Sleeping Prince* (1953).

In 1957, Olivier directed and starred in the film version of *The Prince and the Showgirl* opposite Marilyn Monroe. He then tackled the role of Archie Rice, a seedy vaudevillian, in John Osborne's *The Entertainer* (play 1957–58; film 1960). It was a daring departure from his classic roles; some critics said it was his greatest performance. Joan Plowright, who later became his third wife, also appeared in the play.

Until his death at 82, Lord Olivier continued to act, focusing on films and television, since illness had forced his retirement from the stage in 1974. He found a niche as a character actor in films such as *Marathon Man* (1976). Several prominent television roles enabled another generation to enjoy his artistry.

Lord Olivier was survived by his wife and four children.

GLADYS HANDELMAN

BERLIN, Irving

American songwriter: b. Temun, Russia, May 11, 1888; d. New York, NY, Sept. 22, 1989.

Irving Berlin helped define the American popular song throughout the 20th century. His career spanned from his first published song in 1907 ("Marie from Sunny Italy"), to his last Broadway show (*Mr. President,* 1962). The range of his catalog of more than 1,000 songs strains the imagination: How could one person conjure everything from the World War I doughboy's lament, "Oh, How I Hate to Get Up in the Morning," to Ethel Merman's brassy signature tune from *Annie Get Your Gun,* "There's No Business Like Show Business"? "White Christmas," for one, defies the notion that it was written by a former singing waiter who required an assistant to translate the melody into notes. It entered the realm of folklore, a tune as bound to the holiday as Santa Claus.

The enduring popularity of Berlin's songs can be attributed to his primary philosophy: "Keep it simple." He believed that a tune's title should be placed prominently, and that the work must touch the heart.

Background. Israel Baline was born in Temun, Russia, the youngest of eight children. When he was 4, his family fled to the New World. Settled into New York's Lower East Side, he barely had begun school when his father died and he took to the streets to help his family survive.

He sold newspapers and sang in the street, leaving home at 14 to sing at a music hall and to work as a singing waiter. He learned to play the piano by ear, and began to compose harmonies by trial and error. (He became Irving Berlin when his first song was credited mistakenly to "I. Berlin," and he decided to change his first name as well.)

In 1909, Berlin got a job writing lyrics for a music publisher; he became an international celebrity two years later after writing "Alexander's Ragtime Band," which sparked a dance craze, introduced the mass audience to jazz, and sold more than 1 million copies of sheet music.

Berlin formed his own music publishing company—the Irving Berlin Music Company—in 1919. The 1920s saw the composer develop his touch for ballads, some of which reflected his courtship of Ellin MacKay, whom he married in 1926. In 1935 he wrote the first of many film scores, *Top Hat,* and in 1939 he produced one of his best-loved songs, "God Bless America."

His epithet was written by fellow songwriter Jerome Kern some years ago: "Irving Berlin has no place in American music. He is American music."

JOHN MILWARD

DAVIS, Bette

U.S. actress: b. Lowell, MA, April 5, 1908; d. Neuilly-sur-Seine, France, Oct. 6, 1989.

During the pre-World-War-II era that was to spawn legends of the silver screen, Bette Davis emerged as a star among stars. Sometimes considered difficult, she developed as an actress under a restrictive Hollywood film contract system, and her battles with Warner Brothers, the studio that for many years held her contract, were legendary. In the process, however, she became an artist of style and originality who cared deeply for her work and for her films. She won two Academy Awards—for *Dangerous* (1935) and *Jezebel* (1938)—and received ten nominations, the most any actress has been given.

In her nearly 100 feature films, she delivered some memorable one-liners, including "I'd love to kiss ya, but I just washed my hair" . . . and "Fasten your seat belts; it's going to be a bumpy night" . . . ; and she projected a distinctive acting style, with flamboyant mannerisms and staccato speech delivery.

Background. Bette Davis was born Ruth Elizabeth Davis in 1908. Her father, Harlow, an attorney, and her mother, Ruth, who became a photographer, were divorced when Bette was a child. Thereafter, Bette and her sister Barbara were reared by their mother in New England and New York City.

Davis became interested in an acting career after working in some regional stage productions. She made her first Broadway appearance in *Broken Dishes* (1929), and her next play, *Solid South* (1930), led to a film contract. She appeared in six lackluster movies before her first break came in *The Man Who Played God* (1932), with George Arliss. Subsequently, she was a featured player but failed to attract critical attention until she appeared in *Of Human Bondage* (1934), the film that made her a star. Then came many memorable films (*Dangerous, Jezebel, Dark Victory, The Letter, The Little Foxes, The Man Who Came to Dinner, Now, Voyager, A Stolen Life, Deception, June Bride,* and *All About Eve*) in which she created a gallery of strong, independent, modern women, some of them tough unsavory types.

She returned to Broadway in *Night of the Iguana* (1961) and took on character roles in the films *Pocketful of Miracles* (1961), *Whatever Happened to Baby Jane* (1962), and *The Whales of August* (1987). She also made several television movies. She received the Life Achievement Award of the American Film Institute (1977) and Kennedy Center Honors (1987).

She married four times and was the mother of three children. A 1985 memoir by her daughter B.D. was said to have caused her distress.

SAUNDRA FRANCE

Reuter/Bettmann Newsphotos

SAKHAROV, Andrei Dmitriyevich

Soviet physicist and dissident: b. Moscow, USSR, May 21, 1921; d. Moscow, Dec. 14, 1989.

Soviet nuclear physicist Andrei Sakharov was renowned in both arenas of war and peace. A principal designer of Soviet nuclear weapons in the 1940s and 1950s, Sakharov also was awarded the 1975 Nobel Peace Prize, granted in part for his efforts to rid the world of nuclear weapons. His criticism from within the Soviet system earned him the label *dissident* and eventually caused him to be exiled from Moscow for seven years.

Called the "conscience" of the Soviet Union by his own countrymen, Sakharov wielded a sharp pen and tongue as he championed a long list of causes. He addressed—both publicly and clandestinely—nuclear safety, human rights, free speech, freedom to travel, economic reform, environmentalism, and virtually every other issue touching Soviet life. In a famous essay smuggled out of the USSR in 1968, he wrote: "After 50 years of full control over the minds of the entire country, the leadership seems afraid of even a hint of debate. Yet the only guarantee of a scientific democratic approach to politics, economic development, and culture is intellectual freedom and debate."

Background. Son of a physics professor, Sakharov himself chose a career in physics. He distinguished himself not only in the field of nuclear weapons but also of nuclear reactors. By the mid-1950s he had received many of the USSR's top honors, including the Stalin Prize and the Order of Lenin, and he was named a Hero of Socialist Labor on three occasions. But Sakharov began his second career of dissension as early as 1957, when he criticized Soviet atmospheric nuclear tests. By the mid-1960s he was speaking out on issues ranging from government censorship to the revival of Stalin as a national hero.

His 1968 essay gave the world its first sustained view of the remarkable scientist's passions and concerns. It also caused him to be stripped of his security clearance and state honors. He never again would work as a nuclear physicist. His bravery in the face of a repressive state was admired by the world at large and by the 1975 Nobel Prize committee. The state would not let him travel to accept the award. His public stance against the Soviet invasion of Afghanistan resulted in his banishment to the city of Gorky in January 1980, where his health declined. Mikhail Gorbachev, in a widely hailed symbolic gesture affirming *glasnost,* brought him back in December 1986. He was allowed to travel freely and in April 1989 was elected to the Soviet Congress.

Sakharov died quietly at home after a day of freely criticizing Soviet policy in Congress. He was survived by his second wife, Yelena G. Bonner, and three children.

PHILIP STOREY

The following is a selected list of prominent persons who died during 1989. Articles on major figures appear in the preceding pages.

Abbey, Edward (62), naturalist, novelist, and former forest ranger; his 1956 novel, *The Brave Cowboy,* later was made into the film, *Lonely Are the Brave:* d. Oracle, AZ, March 14.

Adamson, George (83), India-born wildlife environmentalist of Kenya. He and his late wife (from whom he separated in 1970) had created the legend of Elsa, a lioness cub they had raised that was the basis of Mrs. Adamson's 1960 book *Born Free:* d. Kora Rock, Kenya, Aug. 20.

Aflag, Michel (79), Syrian-born founder and general secretary of Iraq's governing Arab Baath Socialist Party and a pioneer Arab nationalist: d. Paris, June 23.

Ahidjo, Ahmadou (65), president of Cameroon (1960–82): d. Dakar, Senegal, Nov. 30.

Ailey, Alvin (58), modern-dance choreographer, dancer, and director; founded the Alvin Ailey American Dance Theater in 1958. His most popular dance was *Revelations* (1960). In his choreography he drew upon classical ballet, jazz dance, Afro-Caribbean dance, and the dance idioms of Lester Horton and Martha Graham: d. New York City, Dec. 1.

George Adamson

AP/Wide World

Alvin Ailey

Kenn Duncan/The Alvin Ailey American Dance Theater

Allison, Fran (81), singer and entertainer, best known as the human star of the children's television series *Kukla, Fran, and Ollie* in the late 1940s and 1950s: d. Van Nuys, CA, June 13.

Allott, Gordon (82), U.S. senator (R-CO, 1955–73): d. Englewood, CO, Jan. 17.

Alsop, Joseph W., Jr. (78), syndicated political columnist; his column, first titled *Capital Parade* and then *Matter of Fact,* appeared in U.S. newspapers for five decades. He retired in 1974. He wrote several books: d. Washington, DC, Aug. 28.

Ashmore, Robert Thomas (85), U.S. representative (D-SC, 1953–69): d. Greenville, SC, Oct. 4.

Ayer, A. J. (Alfred Jules) (78), British philosopher of logical positivism; was influenced by the philosophers Bertrand Russell and Ludwig Wittgenstein. His book *Language, Truth, and Logic* (1936) came to be regarded as the basic English-language work on logical positivism. He was knighted in 1970: d. London, June 27.

Backus, Jim (James Gilmore) (76), actor; best known for his role as Thurston Howell III on the television series *Gilligan's Island,* which appeared on network television from 1964 to 1967 and since has been in syndication, and as the voice of the cartoon character Mr. Magoo: d. Santa Monica, CA, July 3.

Barthelme, Donald (58), novelist and short-story writer; his novels include *Snow White* (1967) and *The Slightly Irregular Fire Engine or the Hithering Thithering Djinn* (1971), a children's book for which he won a National Book Award. Among his short-story collections are the award-winning *Sixty Stories* (1981) and *40 Stories* (1987): d. Houston, TX, July 23.

Beadle, George W. (85), geneticist; shared the Nobel Prize in medicine or physiology in 1958 for his work in showing how genes control the basic chemistry of the living cell. He was president of the University of Chicago (1961–68): d. Pomona, CA, June 9.

Bechtel, Stephen (88), former head of one of the world's largest construction firms, which did work on the Hoover Dam, the San Francisco-Oakland Bay Bridge, and the first commercial nuclear-power plant: d. San Francisco, CA, March 14.

Beckett, Samuel (83), Nobel Prize-winning Irish-born writer of drama and fiction; through his works he altered the contemporary theater, encouraging experimentation and influencing many playwrights who followed. He is best known for his play *Waiting for Godot,* first performed in 1953 in Paris. A play about two tramps waiting for a salvation that does not come, *Waiting for Godot* became a cornerstone of the 20th-century theater. His novels, experimental and profound, include his trilogy *Molloy, Malone Dies,* and *The Unnamable.* Writing first in English and later in French, he received the Nobel Prize for literature in 1969. In all he wrote six novels, four long plays and many shorter ones, as well as short stories, poetry, and essays. A major theme in his work dealt with his exploration of man's relationship to God. Educated at Ireland's Trinity College, he taught there briefly before leaving Ireland in 1932. He settled in Paris permanently in 1937 and during World War II was active in the French Resistance, later receiving the Croix de Guerre and the Médaille de Résistance: d. Paris, Dec. 22.

Bernhard, Thomas (58), Austrian playwright, novelist, and poet: d. Gmunden, Austria, Feb. 12.

Beuve-Méry, Hubert (87), founder of the French newspaper *Le Monde* and its editor for 25 years until his retirement in 1969: d. Fountainebleau, France, Aug. 6.

Blaik, Earl (Red) (92), head football coach at the United States Military Academy (1941–58), where he had two national championship teams: d. Colorado Springs, CO, May 6.

Blake, Amanda (born Beverly Louise Neill) (60), actress; best known for her role as Miss Kitty, the saloonkeeper in the long-running television series *Gunsmoke* (1955–74): d. Los Angeles, CA, Aug. 16.

Blanc, Mel (Melvin Jerome) (81), actor who provided the voices for such cartoon characters as Bugs Bunny, Woody Woodpecker, Daffy Duck, Porky Pig, Tweety Pie, Sylvester, and the Road Runner. In a career spanning six decades, he provided voices for some 3,000 cartoons and helped develop nearly 400 characters. In the 1960s he was associated with *The Flintstones,* the first animated situation comedy created for television: d. Los Angeles, CA, July 10.

Brickwedde, Ferdinand (86), physicist; in 1931 was one of a three-member research team who produced the first measurable amounts of deuterium, or heavy hydrogen: d. Bellefonte, PA, March 29.

Brico, Antonia (87), orchestra conductor; led her own orchestras in New York in the 1930s and helped fight prejudice against women in the orchestral world: d. Denver, CO, Aug. 3.

Brodie, Bernard B. (81), drug-therapy researcher; he was a major figure in the field of drug metabolism and was the founder and former chief of the laboratory of chemical pharmacology at the National Heart Institute of the National Institutes of Health (1950–70): d. Charlottesville, VA, Feb. 27.

Brown, Irving (77), international-affairs specialist for the American labor movement: d. Paris, Feb. 10.

Brown, Sterling A. (87), poet and teacher of literature at Howard University (1926–69) who helped to establish Afro-American literary criticism. His poetry collections are *Southern Road, The Last Ride of Wild Bill,* and *The Collected Poems:* d. Takoma Park, MD, Jan. 13.

Browne, Dik (Richard Arthur Allan) (71), cartoonist; created the *Hagar the Horrible* strip: d. Sarasota, FL, June 4.

Brunner, Karl (73), Swiss-born economist; he was a leading member of the monetarist movement and known for his criticism of the U.S. Federal Reserve System: d. Rochester, NY, May 9.

Burns, Kenneth C. (Jethro) (69), mandolin player, part of the Homer and Jethro country music duo. The team won a Grammy for the best comedy performance in 1959 with *The Battle of Kookamonga:* d. Evanston, IL, Feb. 4.

Busch, August Anheuser, Jr. (90), former head of the St. Louis brewery concern, Anheuser-Busch, which was founded by his family in 1876. He became president of the company in 1946 and retired in 1975. The company bought the St. Louis Cardinals baseball club in 1953: d. St. Louis County, MO, Sept. 29.

Bustamante y Rivero, José (94), Peruvian president (1945–48); he was deposed in a military coup led by Manuel Odria. In 1961 he became a judge at the International Court of Justice in The Hague and was president of the court from 1967 until 1970: d. Lima, Peru, Jan. 11.

Cassavetes, John (59), actor, screenwriter, and director; involved in the U.S. cinema verité. As an actor he was nominated for a supporting actor Academy Award in 1967 for his role in *The Dirty Dozen.* In the late 1950s he had his own television series, *Johnny Staccato.* He first gained attention as a filmmaker with *Shadows* (1960) and went on to write and direct several films: d. Los Angeles, CA, Feb. 3.

Ceauşescu, Nicolae (71), president of Romania (1967–89) and secretary-general of the Communist Party since 1965; executed following the overthrow of his government in December. Known for his pursuit of an independent course for Romania in foreign affairs, he had denounced the USSR for its invasion of Afghanistan and refused to take part in the Warsaw Pact invasion of Czechoslovakia in 1968. He also allowed Romanian Jews to emigrate to Israel, although ransom fees were paid, and pursued independent economic trade policies with the West. But he demanded subservience on the domestic front, suppressing the people's discontent with his harsh economic policy; nepotism; ineffective agricultural schemes; architectural plans that saw the construction of huge and underused building projects and the destruction of several churches and other buildings to make room for government offices; and a cult of personality that also included his wife, Elena, deputy prime minister since 1980, who was executed with her husband. Ceauşescu had become a pro-

Donald Barthelme

Samuel Beckett

Amanda Blake

Mel Blanc

Photos, AP/Wide World

AP/Wide World

Malcolm Cowley

The Bettmann Archive

Daphne du Maurier

UPI/Bettmann Newsphotos

Minoru Genda

AP/Wide World

A. Bartlett Giamatti

tégé of Romania's first Communist chief of state, Gheorghe Gheorghiu-Dej, after meeting him when they shared a prison cell in 1937. He was inducted into the elite of the Romanian Communist Party, becoming a member of the Politburo in 1955 and later succeeding Gheorghiu-Dej: d. Romania, Dec. 25.

Chapman, Graham (48), British founder of the Monty Python Flying Circus comedy ensemble, a group that appeared on British television between 1969 and 1974 and who made several movies: d. England, Oct. 4.

Chappell, William, Jr. (67), U.S. representative (D-FL, 1969–89): d. Bethesda, MD, March 30.

Chatwin, Bruce (48), British author; his book *In Patagonia* (1977) established him as a prominent travel writer: d. Nice, France, Jan. 17.

Chen Boda (85), senior aide to former Chinese Communist leader Mao Zedong; he was convicted in 1981 of crimes during the Cultural Revolution but was released later in 1981: d. Beijing, China, Sept. 20.

Civil, Alan (59), British musician, regarded as one of the world's most accomplished French horn players: d. London, March 19.

Clubb, Oliver Edmund (88), foreign-service officer; became a major target of Sen. Joseph McCarthy's investigations of supposedly disloyal Americans in the U.S. State Department in the early 1950s: d. New York City, May 9.

Collins, James F. (83), U.S. Army four-star general; served in World War II. After retiring in 1964 he was president of the American Red Cross for more than six years: d. Washington, DC, Jan. 22.

Collins, James M. (73), U.S. representative (R-TX, 1968–83): d. Dallas, TX, July 21.

Cotton, Norris (88), U.S. senator (R-NH, 1954–75); he earlier had served in the House of Representatives (1947–54): d. Lebanon, NH, Feb. 24.

Cowley, Malcolm (90), literary critic, historian, editor, poet, and essayist; known for his writings on the post-World War I "Lost Generation" of American writers that included Ernest Hemingway and F. Scott Fitzgerald. He was also an editor of *The New Republic* from 1929 to 1944, worked at Viking Press from the mid-1940s until 1985, and was credited with reviving interest in the fiction of William Faulkner and discovering the writer John Cheever: d. New Milford, CT, March 27.

Cyrankiewicz, Josef (77), Polish premier (1947–52): d. Poland, Jan. 20.

Dali, Salvador. *See* page 116.

Davison, William (Wild Bill) (83), jazz cornetist: d. Santa Barbara, CA, Nov. 14.

de Hoffmann, Frederic (65), Austrian-born nuclear physicist; during World War II he worked on the Manhattan Project on the development of the hydrogen bomb; later he directed the Salk Institute of Biological Studies: d. La Jolla, CA, Oct. 4.

Deskey, Donald (94), industrial designer, best known for his 1932 design for the interiors of Radio City Music Hall in New York: d. Vero Beach, FL, April 29.

Diori, Hamani (72), president of Niger (1960–74): d. Rabat, Morocco, April 23.

du Maurier, Daphne (81), author, famous for *Rebecca* (1938), which later was made into a major motion picture, and for other Gothic and romantic novels. She also wrote plays and biography, history, and travel books: d. Par, Cornwall, England, April 19.

Eldridge, (David) Roy (78), jazz trumpet player: d. Valley Stream, NY, Feb. 26.

Evans, Maurice (87), British-born stage actor; began an association with London's Old Vic and was one of the best known Shakespearean actors of the 1930s and 1940s: d. Rottingdean, England, March 12.

Fain, Sammy (87), popular songwriter. His works include "I'll Be Seeing You," "That Old Feeling," and "Secret Love." He won Academy Awards for best song in the films *Calamity Jane* (1953) and *Love Is a Many-Splendored Thing* (1955): d. Los Angeles, Dec. 6.

Farley, Walter (74), author; created the "Black Stallion" series of children's novels: d. Sarasota, FL, Oct. 17.

Fine, Max (81), Polish-born ophthalmologist; performed the first corneal transplant in the West in 1939 and trained many leading corneal surgeons: d. San Francisco, CA, March 29.

Fitzgerald, Pegeen (78), radio talk-show hostess, along with her husband Edward, for 42 years on the program *The Fitzgeralds:* d. New York City, Jan. 30.

Prince Franz Josef II (83), head of state since 1938 of the principality of Liechtenstein. He had turned over his executive powers to his son in 1984: d. Vaduz, Liechtenstein, Nov. 13.

Furillo, Carl (66), baseball player, known as the "Reading Rifle," was a right fielder for the Dodgers in Brooklyn and Los Angeles for 15 years. He retired in 1960: d. Stony Creek Mills, PA, Jan. 21.

Gardner, Hy (80), former Broadway gossip columnist: d. Miami, FL, June 17.

Genda, Minoru (84), Japanese general who planned the Japanese attack on Pearl Harbor that brought the United States into World War II. After the war he was a general in the Air Force and served as chief of staff (1959–62); then he was elected to the upper house of parliament, where he served until 1986: d. Tokyo, Japan, Aug. 15.

Giamatti, A. Bartlett (51), Renaissance scholar, president of Yale University (1978–86), president of the National League baseball organization (1986–89), and baseball commissioner (1989). During his brief period as baseball commissioner, he banned Cincinnati's Pete Rose from the game: d. Oak Bluffs, Martha's Vineyard, MA, Sept. 1.

Glushko, Valentin (80), Soviet rocket scientist: d. USSR, reported Jan. 12.

Gomez, Vernon (Lefty) (80), pitcher; was with the New York Yankees (1929–42). In his 14 major-league seasons, he won 189 games and four times won more than 20 games in a season. He was elected to the Baseball Hall of Fame in 1972: d. Larkspur, CA, Feb. 17.

Guillen, Nicolas Batista (87), author; considered the national poet of Cuba: d. Cuba, July 16.

Harrington, Michael (61), American socialist leader; cochairman of the Democratic Socialists of America and author of *The Other America* (1962), which helped encourage the U.S. government's "War on Poverty": d. Larchmont, NY, July 31.

Haynsworth, Clement (77), federal judge; became a national figure when his nomination to the Supreme Court was rejected by the Senate in 1969: d. Greenville, SC, Nov. 22.

Hays, Wayne L. (77), U.S. representative (D-OH, 1949–76); he was forced to resign in 1976 following disclosure that he had put his mistress on his staff in a $14,000-a-year job: d. Wheeling, WV, Feb. 10.

Heywood, Eddie (73), jazz pianist, arranger, and composer: d. North Miami, FL, Jan. 2.

Hicks, John R. (85), British economist; was the 1972 Nobel Prize winner for economics, along with Kenneth J. Arrow, and was known especially for his general equilibrium theory work. The theory maintains that active forces cancel each other and produce a state of balance. Hicks' book *Value and Capital* (1939) created the groundwork for a renewal of the general equilibrium theory. He was knighted in 1964: d. Blockley, England, May 20.

Hillgruber, Andreas (64), West German historian involved in a controversy, known as the "historians' dispute," surrounding his 1986 book, *Two Kinds of Destruction: The Shattering of the German Reich and the End of European Jewry,* which seemed to some to suggest a connection between the collapse of the German Army's eastern front in World War II and the genocide against European Jews: d. Cologne, West Germany, May 8.

Hirsch, John (59), Hungarian-born Canadian theater, opera, and television director; best known as artistic director of the Stratford Festival in Ontario, Canada (1981–86): d. Toronto, Canada, Aug. 1.

Hoffman, Abbott (Abbie) (52), writer, antiwar protester, and radical activist, an organizer of the Youth International Party (Yippie movement) of the 1960s. He protested American involvement in the Vietnam War, rising to national prominence as part of the Chicago Seven, a group of radicals who stood trial on charges of conspiring to disrupt the 1968 Democratic National Convention in Chicago: d. New Hope, PA, April 12.

Hook, Sidney (86), philosopher; wrote many books on Marxism, public policy, and education and was best known for his anti-Communist stance and his defense of political and academic freedom: d. Stanford, CA, July 12.

Horowitz, Vladimir. *See* page 377.

Hufnagel, Charles A. (72), cardiac surgeon; in the early 1950s while he was director of the Georgetown University Medical Center's surgical research laboratory, he invented and implanted a plastic heart valve to replace faulty valves of the heart: d. Washington, DC, May 31.

Hu Yaobang (73), party chairman and general secretary of the Chinese Communist Party from 1981 to 1987, when he was forced to resign following student demonstrations and criticism from top level government officials who promoted a campaign against "bourgeois liberalization": d. Beijing, China, April 15.

Ibarruri, Dolores (93), president and a founder of the Spanish Communist Party, known as "La Pasionaria"; was a renowned orator during the Spanish Civil War: d. Madrid, Nov. 12.

Ivens, Joris (Georg Henri Anton) (90), Dutch filmmaker who specialized in documentaries and a founder of the Dutch film industry. His masterpiece was considered to be *The Spanish Earth* (1937): d. Paris, June 28.

James, C. L. R. (Cyril Lionel Robert) (88), Trinidad-born historian, cricket writer, literary critic, and philosopher; was a leader in the pan-African movement of the 1930s: d. London, May 31.

Johnson, William Julius (Judy) (89), baseball third baseman in the Negro Leagues; was the sixth black player from the Negro Leagues to be elected to the Baseball Hall of Fame: d. Wilmington, DE, June 14.

Jorgensen, Christine (born George) (62), the first recipient of a sex-change operation; George Jorgensen, Jr., underwent the procedure to be transformed into a woman in 1952 in Denmark: d. San Clemente, CA, May 3.

Kadar, Janos (77), Hungarian Communist Party leader (1956–88); rose to power replacing Imre Nagy, after initially supporting him, as the Soviet Army suppressed the liberal uprising in Hungary in 1956. (Mr. Nagy was hanged in 1958 but in 1989 was given a hero's burial.) After Kadar assumed power, he was viewed as a traitor to reformist hopes, but he quietly carried on with some of Nagy's policies. By the 1980s, however, he was perceived as blocking needed economic changes. In 1988 he was given a figurehead post as party president, and in 1989 was removed from that office and expelled from the Central Committee: d. Budapest, Hungary, July 6.

Kahn, Lord Richard Ferdinand (83), British economist; introduced the concept of the "multiplier": d. England, June 6.

Karajan, Herbert von (81), Austrian musical conductor; for many years he led the Berlin Philharmonic, having become its "conductor for life" in 1955. In recent years, however, there were publicized battles with the orchestra, and in April 1989, he resigned the post. One of the most powerful figures in classical music, he was the dominant personality at the famed Salzburg Festival for 25 years. He also made more than 800 phonograph recordings, more than any other conductor: d. Anif, Austria, July 16.

Kaufmann, Edgar, Jr. (79), architectural historian, curator, and philanthropist; he preserved his family's Frank Lloyd Wright-designed vacation home, Fallingwater, as a museum: d. New York City, July 31.

Keogh, Eugene J. (81), U.S. representative (D-NY, 1937–67); was the principal sponsor of the pension-plan legislation enacted in 1962 that carries his name: d. New York City, May 26.

Kirkwood, James (64), novelist, actor, and playwright; was coauthor of the book for the Broadway musical *A Chorus Line.* His books include *Hit Me with a Rainbow, Good Times-Bad Times, P.S. Your Cat Is Dead,* and *There Must Be a Pony:* d. New York City, April 21.

Kirst, Hans Helmut (74), West German novelist; among his 46 books were *The Night of the Generals* (1964) and the trilogy *Zero Eight Fifteen:* d. Bremen, West Germany, Feb. 23.

Laing, R. D. (61), British psychiatrist; he broke with traditional psychiatry and sought new treatments for schizophrenic patients based on concern for the rights of mental patients. With his 1960 book *The Divided Self,* he gained attention as a rebel against the status quo, and subsequently became the leader of the English "anti-psychiatry" movement: d. St. Tropez, France, Aug. 23.

Laroche, Guy (67), French couture designer; he founded his fashion house in 1957: d. Paris, Feb. 17.

Lattimore, Owen (88), scholar of the history, culture, and politics of the Far East and during the early 1950s a target of Sen. Joseph McCarthy in his crusade against alleged governmental Communist subversion. In 1941 he was the personal American adviser to Chiang Kai-shek: d. Providence, RI, May 31.

Leland, George Thomas (Mickey) (44), U.S. representative (D-TX, 1979–89). He died in a plane crash on a humanitarian mission in Ethiopia: d. Ethiopia, Aug. 13 (plane, lost on Aug. 7, was found).

Leone, Sergio (67), Italian film director; made Western films in the 1960s called spaghetti Westerns. His *Once Upon a Time in America* came out in 1984: d. Rome, Italy, April 30.

Liepa, Maris (52), Soviet ballet dancer and star of the Bolshoi Ballet (1960–81): d. Moscow, March 25.

Lillie, Beatrice (94), Canadian-born actress; considered by some as a comic genius. During a 50-year career she entertained on stage, screen, radio, television, and in vaudeville and supper clubs: d. Henley-on-Thames, England, Jan. 20.

Little, Royal (92), entrepreneur; known as the inventor of the modern conglomerate: d. Nassau, Bahamas, Jan. 12.

Magnuson, Warren G. (84), U.S. senator (D-WA, 1944–81); he earlier had served in the U.S. House of Representatives (1937–44): d. Seattle, WA, May 20.

Malula, Cardinal Joseph (71), leading Roman Catholic prelate in Africa: d. Louvain, Belgium, June 14.

Mangano, Silvana (59), Italian film actress; created a sensation in her role in *Bitter Rice* (1948); later appeared in *Ulysses* (1954) and in *Dark Eyes* (1987): d. Madrid, Spain, Dec. 16.

Manning, Cardinal Timothy (79), Roman Catholic archbishop of Los Angeles (1970–85); achieved the rank of cardinal in 1973: d. Los Angeles, CA, June 23.

Mapplethorpe, Robert (42), photographer; known for pictures that combined classicism with sometimes shocking subject matter; gained attention in the 1970s with his black and white photos of the male figure: d. Boston, MA, March 9.

Marcos, Ferdinand. See page 422.

Martin, Billy (Alfred Manuel) (61), baseball manager for the New York Yankees off and on between 1975 and 1988. He led the team to a World Series championship, but was fired five times from his position by the team's owner. In 16 seasons as a manager he had 1,258 victories and 1,018 losses with the Yankees, as well as the Minnesota Twins, Detroit Tigers, Texas Rangers, and Oakland Athletics. Earlier he was a second baseman for the Yankees (1950–57) and also played on other teams, ending his playing career after the 1961 season: d. near Fenton, NY, Dec. 25.

Abbie Hoffman

AP/Wide World

Janos Kadar

UPI/Bettmann Newsphotos

Herbert von Karajan

AP/Wide World

Billy Martin

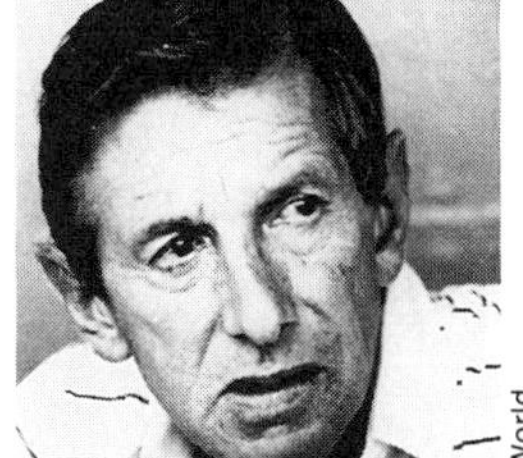

AP/Wide World

Matsushita, Konosuke (94), Japanese industrialist; founder of Matsushita Electric Industrial Company. His approach to business became a model emulated in Japan and studied in the West. He believed in the profit motive but also in motivation of his workers by inspiring total commitment to the company's goals, one means being through guaranteed lifetime employment: d. Osaka, Japan, April 27.

Matuszak, John (38), football defensive lineman for the Oakland (CA) Raiders (1976–81); played on two Super Bowl teams in 1976 and 1980: d. Los Angeles, June 17.

McCarthy, Mary (77), novelist, memoirist, critic, and journalist; was considered among America's major literary figures between the 1930s and the 1970s. She was probably best known for her 1963 novel *The Group.* She also wrote her memoirs, *Memories of a Catholic Girlhood* (1957) and the later *How I Grew* (1987). She provoked some celebrated altercations with other literary figures, including one in the 1980s with fellow writer Lillian Hellman: d. New York City, Oct. 25.

McCloy, John J. (93), lawyer and diplomat; was the U.S. High Commissioner in postwar Germany (1949–52). He practiced law in New York City, but from 1941 on, he usually was involved in public affairs, and in all he worked for seven presidents: d. Stamford, CT, March 11.

McMillan, Kenneth (56), character actor: d. Santa Monica, CA, Jan. 8.

Mellon, William L., Jr. (79), an heir to the Mellon banking and oil fortune who became engrossed with the work of Dr. Albert Schweitzer and became a physician who established a hospital in Haiti: d. Deschapelles, Haiti, Aug. 3.

Menen, Aubrey (76), Indian novelist, critic, and essayist: d. Trivandrum, India, Feb. 13.

Milanov, Zinka (83), Yugoslavian-born dramatic soprano of the Metropolitan Opera for nearly 30 years until her retirement in 1966: d. New York City, May 30.

Mills, Herbert (77), singer; member of the Mills Brothers group: d. Las Vegas, NV, April 12.

Moawad, René (64), president of Lebanon; elected on Nov. 5, 1989; assassinated in a car bombing: d. Beirut, Nov. 22.

Moore, Donnie (35), former major-league baseball pitcher for the California Angels: d. Anaheim, CA, July 18.

Morris, Richard B. (84), historian and former chairman of the history department of Columbia University, where he taught from 1946 to 1973: d. New York City, March 3.

Morrison, Joe (51), football player; with the New York Giants (1959–72). He also coached six seasons at the University of South Carolina: d. Columbia, SC, Feb. 5.

Newman, Lionel (73), composer; he composed, conducted, or supervised the scores of more than 250 motion pictures and, along with Lennie Hayton, won an Academy Award for musical adaptation of Jerry Herman's score for *Hello, Dolly!* (1969): d. Los Angeles, CA, Feb. 3.

Newton, Huey P. (47), cofounder of the Black Panther Party and a black activist of the 1960s: d. Oakland, CA, Aug. 22.

Norris, Clarence (76), last member of the "Scottsboro Boys" rape case that in the 1930s became a symbol of racial injustice in the American South: d. New York City, Jan. 23.

O'Dell, Scott (91), writer of more than 25 children's books, including *Island of the Blue Dolphins* (1960), which won the John Newbery prize in 1961: d. Mount Kisco, NY, Oct. 15.

Ogdon, John (52), British pianist; a champion of late Romantic-era and 20th-century musical scores, noted for his technique and unusual programming: d. London, Aug. 1.

O'Rourke, Frank (72), author of novels, short stories, Westerns, and mysteries; in all he wrote more than 60 books: d. Tucson, AZ, April 27.

O'Hara, James G. (63), U.S. representative (D-MI, 1959–77): d. Washington, DC, March 13.

Panchen Lama (50), second-ranking Tibetan spiritual leader after the Dalai Lama and the tenth holder of the title: d. Xigaze, Tibet, Jan. 28.

Mary McCarthy

Gilda Radner

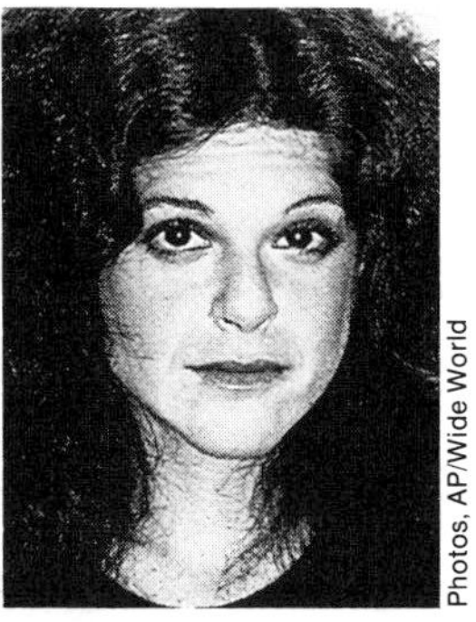

Photos, AP/Wide World

Payne, John (77), actor; appeared in nearly 50 films, including the Christmas classic *Miracle on 34th Street* (1947): d. Malibu, CA, Dec. 6.

Pechman, Joseph Aaron (71), economist and tax expert. Served as director of economic studies at the Brookings Institution: d. Potomac, MD, Aug. 19.

Pedersen, Charles (85), Nobel Prize-winning chemist; he shared the 1987 award for wide-ranging research, including the creation of artificial molecules that can mimic vital chemical reactions of the processes of life: d. Salem, NJ, Oct. 26.

Peli, Pinchas H. (59), Israeli rabbi, professor, and a popular Jewish scholar: d. Jerusalem, April 13.

Phat, Huynh Tan (76), theoretician of the Vietcong political movement during the Vietnam War: d. Ho Chi Minh City, Sept. 30.

Primeau, Joe (83), former Canadian hockey player and a coach with the National Hockey League's Toronto Maple Leafs; elected to the Hall of Fame in 1963: d. Toronto, May 15.

Quayle, Sir (John) Anthony (76), British stage, film, and television actor; received an Academy Award nomination for his role as Cardinal Wolsey in *Anne of the Thousand Days* (1970). On stage he performed a wide range of classical roles: d. London, Oct. 20.

Quine, Richard (68), film actor and director: d. Los Angeles, CA, June 10.

Radner, Gilda (42), Emmy award-winning television comedian, well known as a regular on *Saturday Night Live* (1975–80): d. Los Angeles, CA, May 20.

Roberts, Kenneth A. (76), U.S. representative (D-AL, 1951–65): d. Potomac, MD, May 9.

Rowicki, Witold (75), founder of the Warsaw National Philharmonic Orchestra in 1950 and its artistic director and conductor (1950–77), except for a three-year break during the 1950s: d. Poland, Oct. 1.

Rusk, Howard A. (88), medical doctor who was a pioneer in the rehabilitation of the physically disabled. Served as a medical columnist for *The New York Times* (1946–69): d. New York City, Nov. 4.

Russell, Francis (79), historian and biographer; in 1968 his biography of Warren G. Harding, *The Shadow of Blooming Grove,* caused the former president's relatives to act and succeed in preventing the publication of some of Harding's love letters. Russell also was involved in controversy over his contention that he had solved the Sacco-Vanzetti case: d. Falmouth, MA, March 21.

Sant'Angelo, Giorgio (56), fashion designer; noted for his avant-garde originality: d. New York City, Aug. 29.

Sauguet, Henri (88), French composer; important during the 1920s: d. Paris, June 22.

Schaffner, Franklin J. (69), film director; won an Academy Award for the 1970 film *Patton:* d. Santa Monica, CA, July 2.

Schiff, Dorothy (86), owner of *The New York Post* newspaper for 37 years from 1939 to 1976, when she sold it to Rupert Murdoch, who sold it in 1988: d. New York City, Aug. 30.

Scott, Charles S., Sr. (67), civil-rights attorney; involved in the Supreme Court case *Brown v. Topeka Board of Education* that produced the landmark ruling in 1954 that declared racial segregation in public schools unconstitutional: d. Topeka, KS, March 3.

Segre, Emilio G. (84), Italian-born physicist; shared the Nobel Prize in physics in 1959 with Dr. Owen Chamberlain for creating an antiproton that lent support to the theory that a mirror image of the universe exists in which atoms are made up of positively charged electrons and negatively charged nuclei: d. Lafayette, CA, April 22.

Sewell, Truett Banks (Rip) (82), baseball pitcher for the Pittsburgh Pirates, known for his "eephus ball," an arching blooper pitch that reached a height of 25 ft (8 m) before coming down toward the home plate: d. Plant City, FL, Sept. 3.

Shockley, William B. (79), physicist; shared the 1956 Nobel Prize in physics for the invention of the transistor. His ideas that intelligence capacity is a genetic trait and that blacks were genetically inferior to whites sparked great controversy: d. Stanford, CA, Aug. 12.

Simenon, Georges (86), Belgian-born novelist; created the Inspector Maigret mysteries. In all he wrote 84 Maigret mysteries and 136 other novels under his own name, as well as about 200 novels under 17 pseudonyms early in his career. His writing was praised for its psychological insights: d. Lausanne, Switzerland, Sept. 4.

Smith, Larkin (45), U.S. representative (R-MS, 1989); had been elected in November 1988; was killed in a plane crash: d. near New Augusta, MS, Aug. 13.

Sopwith, Sir Thomas (101), British pioneer aircraft designer: d. Winchester, England, Jan. 27.

Stephenson, Sir William (93), Canadian-born industrialist; he was Britain's chief of intelligence in the Western Hemisphere during World War II. His adventures were covered in the 1979 best seller *A Man Called Intrepid.* He was knighted in 1946: d. Paget, Bermuda, Jan. 31.

Steptoe, John (38), writer and illustrator of children's books: d. New York City, Aug. 28.

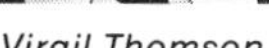
Virgil Thomson

Barbara Tuchman

Diana Vreeland

Robert Penn Warren

Photos, AP/Wide World

Stone, I. F. (born Isidor Feinstein) (81), journalist; in a career spanning 65 years he wrote for several mainly politically leftist publications and was the publisher of *I. F. Stone's Weekly* (1953–68) and *Bi-Weekly* (1969–71), both basically one-man pamphlets often critical of official Washington. His books include *Underground to Palestine* (1946), *This Is Israel* (1948), *The Hidden History of the Korean War* (1952), *The Killings at Kent State: How Murder Went Unpunished* (1971), and *The Trial of Socrates* (1988): d. Boston, MA, June 18.

Stone, Irving (born Irving Tennenbaum) (86), novelist and biographer; noted for his biographical novels on historic figures. In all he wrote more than 24 books, including two biographies, *Clarence Darrow for the Defense* (1941) and *Earl Warren* (1948). His biographical novels include *Lust for Life* (1934), based on the story of the artist Van Gogh, and *The Agony and the Ecstasy* (1961), based on the life of Michelangelo: d. Los Angeles, CA, Aug. 26.

Stone, Marshall Harvey (85), mathematician; known for synthesizing areas of abstract mathematics: d. Madras, India, Jan. 9.

Street, J. C. (Jabez Curry) (83), physicist; was the codiscoverer in 1937 of the subatomic muon particle. He also headed a group at the Massachusetts Institute of Technology's Radiation Laboratory that developed ground and ship radar systems in 1944: d. Charleston, SC, Nov. 7.

Taylor, Edward Plunket (88), Canadian brewer and industrialist; also was involved in thoroughbred horse racing and breeding: d. Bahamas, May 14.

Terry, William H. (Bill) (90), baseball player, the last player to bat .400 in the National League; his career batting average in 14 major league seasons with the New York Giants, beginning in 1927, was .341: d. Jacksonville, FL, Jan. 9.

Thayer, Walter (78), lawyer, partner in the Whitcom Investment Corporation, and former president of the *New York Herald Tribune* newspaper: d. New York City, March 4.

Thompson, Frank, Jr. (70), U.S. representative (D-NJ, 1955–81); his career ended when in 1980 he was convicted on charges coming out of the Abscam investigation: d. Baltimore, MD, July 22.

Thompson, Tommy (72), football quarterback for the Philadelphia Eagles; he led his team to National Football League championships in 1948 and 1949: d. Calico Rock, AR, April 21.

Thomson, Virgil (92), musical composer and critic; he was best known as a composer of two operas in collaboration with Gertrude Stein, who wrote the texts, *Four Saints in Three Acts* (1934) and *The Mother of Us All* (1947). Among his other compositions were the opera *Lord Byron* (1972), *Symphony on a Hymn Tune* (1928), and a collaborative effort with the documentary filmmaker Pare Lorentz on two acclaimed films—*The Plow that Broke the Plains* and *The River.* He received the only Pulitzer Prize ever given for a film score for *Louisiana Story* in 1948. His work as a music critic began in the 1920s, and from 1940 to 1954 he was a critic for the *New York Herald Tribune:* d. New York City, Sept. 30.

Tobey, Barney (82), cartoonist; his work appeared in *The New Yorker* for more than 50 years: d. New York City, March 27.

Toran, Stacey (27), pro-football defensive back for the Los Angeles Raiders: d. near Marina del Rey, CA, Aug. 5.

Tracy, Honor (75), British travel writer, columnist, and novelist; noted in her fiction for satirizing Irish and English society: d. Oxford, England, June 13.

Tuchman, Barbara (77), historian; noted for her popular histories on men at war or on the brink of war. She twice was awarded the Pulitzer Prize—for *The Guns of August* (1962) and for *Stillwell and the American Experience in China, 1911–45* (1971), which combined the biography of Gen. Joseph Stillwell with a history of modern China: d. Greenwich, CT, Feb. 6.

Tucker, Tommy (86), big-band leader of the 1940s: d. West Long Branch, NJ, July 11.

Valentina (born Valentina Nicholaevna Sanina Schlee) (90), Russian-born fashion designer: d. New York City, Sept. 14.

Vare, Glenna Collett (85), pioneer in American women's golf: d. Gulfstream, FL, Feb. 3.

Voorhees, Donald (85), conductor and musical director of the *Bell Telephone Hour.* He was on radio from 1940 to 1959 and on television from 1959 to 1968: d. Cape May Court House, NJ, Jan. 10.

Vreeland, Diana (86), French-born fashion editor and creator of fashion exhibitions at New York's Metropolitan Museum of Art. She was fashion editor of *Harper's Bazaar* magazine (1939–62) and editor-in-chief at *Vogue* magazine (1962–71): d. New York City, Aug. 22.

Walt, Lewis W. (76), four-star Marine Corps general; won combat decorations in World War II, Korea, and Vietnam; he later served as assistant commandant of the Marine Corps: d. Gulfport, MS, March 26.

Ward, Jay (69), cartoonist; with partner Bill Scott he created the character of the moose Bullwinkle and was best known for his television series about Bullwinkle and his companion Rocky, the flying squirrel: d. Los Angeles, CA, Oct. 12.

Warren, Robert Penn (84), author, literary critic, teacher, and the first U.S. poet laureate (1986–88). He was probably best known for his novel *All the King's Men* (1946), made into an Academy Award-winning 1949 film. He won two Pulitzer Prizes for poetry, in 1957 and 1979, and was coauthor of *Understanding Poetry* and *Understanding Fiction,* books of literary criticism that he wrote with critic Cleanth Brooks: d. Stratton, VT, Sept. 15.

Webber, Robert (64), character actor; appeared in many films and television dramas: d. Malibu, CA, May 19.

Weeks, Edward (91), author, essayist, and editor of *The Atlantic Monthly* (1938–66); had been an editor with the Atlantic Monthly Press (1928–37): d. Thompson, CT, March 11.

Weiss, Paul (91), Austrian-born biologist; professor emeritus of Rockefeller University; he won the National Medal of Science for his work in the theory of cellular development. He taught and conducted research for 21 years at the University of Chicago and from 1954 to 1964 was at Rockefeller University: d. White Plains, NY, Sept. 8.

Weston, Christine (85), novelist and short-story writer; her work was set primarily in India, where she was born and reared: d. Bangor, ME, May 3.

Wilde, Cornel (74), actor and film producer; often cast in swashbuckler roles and in action melodrama: d. Los Angeles, CA, Oct. 16.

Williams, Guy (born Armand Catalano) (65), television and film actor; best known for playing the title role in *Zorro,* a television series in the late 1950s. He later starred in the series *Lost in Space* (1965–68): d. Buenos Aires, Argentina, May 6 (reported).

Williams, Roy L. (74), president of the International Brotherhood of Teamsters (1981–83); served three years in prison for conspiring to commit bribery: d. Leeton, MO, April 28.

Yanovsky, V. S. (83), Soviet-born author and physician; he left the Soviet Union for Paris in 1927 and went to the United States in 1942. Of his 24 books, 20 are novels: d. New York City, July 20.

Zemach, Margot (57), children's book illustrator or author of more than 40 books, including *Duffy and the Devil,* for which she won the Caldecott Medal in 1974: d. Berkeley, CA, May 21.

Zhou Yang (81), former culture official in China; one of the Communist Party's leading arbiters of literature in China for 60 years: d. Beijing, China, July 31.

Zita, Empress of Austria-Hungary (96), the last empress of that empire; had been married to Karl I, who was crowned in 1916 after the death of Franz Josef. Karl I and Zita made two unsuccessful attempts in 1921 to be restored as monarchs in Hungary: d. Zizers, Switzerland, March 14.

OCEANOGRAPHY

In 1989 the Tropical Ocean-Global Atmosphere (TOGA) program continued to refine oceanic observation and satellite data in the quest to understand the mass distribution change in equatorial ocean currents that influences global weather. The TOGA program had some success in forecasting the 1986–87 El Niño—the current reversal and atmospheric pressure shift in the eastern Pacific. Scientists also collected the first clear evidence that the El Niño affects the equatorial undercurrent in the western Pacific. In a joint effort between the United States and the People's Republic of China, scientists used ocean current monitors moored in the western Pacific to measure the 1986–87 El Niño disruption. Although the forecast of the most recent El Niño was the first scientific prediction of the equatorial ocean events that influence the climate, the forecasting model needs much refining.

Scientific Drilling. The Ocean Drilling Program (ODP) in 1989 recovered rocks 220 million years old—the oldest ever recovered through scientific drilling—off the northwest continental margin of Australia. The rocks are particularly significant to marine geologists because they provide clues to the breakup of the supercontinent Pangaea in a period of massive continental rifting that began in the late Triassic period. In another cruise, rocks formed in the earth's mantle were recovered from the roots of an ancient volcano. There were 27 scientists from nine countries participating in the project, aboard the drill ship *Joides Resolution,* in waters near the arc-shaped volcanic chains of the Mariana and Izu Bonin islands, between Guam and Japan. Also recovered, near the deep trench north of Guam, were mantle rocks from a submarine mountain belt. The ODP has drilled more than 100 sites on the seafloor worldwide and some previously drilled holes were reentered successfully in 1989. Either a robot submersible or a manned deep-diving submarine was used to lower instruments to gather information on the ocean crust and on changes that have occurred over time. The added capabilities provided by the robot submersible and deep-diving submarine promise a significant expansion of future seafloor studies.

Mineral Deposits. Loihi, an active seamount, or mountain rising above the seafloor, is the next island to be formed as part of the Hawaiian chain, and the site of newly discovered hydrothermal mineral deposits. Discovered at a depth of 3,280 ft (1 000 m), the deposits also have a secondary enrichment of sulfides that are buried deeper. A new field of underwater hot springs, mineral deposits, and exotic animals also was found on the Gorda Ridge, about 100 mi (160 km) off the Oregon coast and within the Exclusive Economic Zone (EEZ) of the United States. This area, like Hawaii, may be the site of mineral formations of significant economic value.

The Global Ocean Flux Study (GOFS) seeks to understand better the processes by which ocean life and seawater chemistry interact on a global basis. A large-scale GOFS study of the spring phytoplankton bloom was undertaken in the North Atlantic, as British, French, German, Canadian, and Dutch scientists worked with ten American oceanographic laboratories and ships for periods of three to six months. Calibration of the sea-Wide Field Sensor (sea-WIFS) instruments on the Landsat 6 satellite was well under way in 1989. In addition to the GOFS data, the ocean color images from the satellite, scheduled for launch in 1991, may help to determine the effects of atmospheric carbon dioxide, which eventually could cause global heating and climate change. Continuing 35 years of observation, a station in Bermuda will be the primary Atlantic Ocean site for GOFS data collection. Monthly measurements from the surface to 13,780 ft (4 200 m) depth will include temperature, salinity, inorganic nutrients, plant pigment analyses, and plankton counts, as well as measurements of the rate of phytoplankton growth.

Sealife. The program for Biological Investigations of Marine Antarctic Systems and Stocks (BIOMASS), in 1989 reduced earlier estimates of the krill population and reported a dwindling of the fish resources of the Southern Ocean as well. The report was based on a ten-year study by hundreds of scientists. Overfishing of the protein-rich krill—a major organism in the food chain—would have a harmful effect on other resources. Conservation and future management of the shrimplike krill, and of other Antarctic resources, continued as the primary goals of the BIOMASS program.

Pollution. German scientists first reported increasing algal growth in the North Sea in 1988, producing plagues of "killer algae" and upsetting the normal balance of nature. A similar vast bloom of algae spread over more than 400 mi (644 km) of the Adriatic Sea in summer 1989, soiling many vacation beaches and killing marine life. The algae were most prevalent near the mouths of large rivers and the urban sewage outlets, pointing to land sources as a major cause of the problem. The situation was made worse by warmer than usual winter weather.

March 24, 1989, was a black day for Prince William Sound in Alaska, as the tanker *Exxon Valdez* grounded, dumping nearly 11 million gallons (41.6 million l) of oil into the sound. Effects of the spill on the food chain and the fisheries may last for a decade or more. Lesser oil spills in 1989 occurred near Newport, RI, in the Delaware River below Philadelphia, PA, and in the Houston, TX, ship channel. (*See* feature article, page 36.)

DAVID A. MCGILL
U.S. Coast Guard Academy

AP/Wide World

U.S. Rep. Donald Lukens (left) *of Middletown, OH, was found guilty in May of contributing to the unruliness of a minor. The House Ethics Committee later announced it would open preliminary inquiries into the matter to determine if congressional punishment was warranted.*

OHIO

Local government elections, a shipwreck treasure, pollution, and scandals captured Ohio's newspaper headlines in 1989.

Politics. Ohio state Sen. Michael R. White (D) and fellow Democrat George L. Forbes, Cleveland City Council president, eliminated three other candidates in a September nonpartisan primary, thus ensuring a second black Cleveland mayor. (The first was Carl B. Stokes, who served from 1967 to 1971.) White sidetracked Forbes by a 56% to 44% margin in the November election, attracting voters with promises of more police, rebuilding slum neighborhoods, and other improvements. In other mayoral races, Patrick J. Ungaro (D) of Youngstown and Clay Dixon (D) of Dayton were reelected, but Donna Owens (R), elected Toledo's mayor in 1983, was unseated by John McHugh, former Lucas County Democratic chairman and treasurer.

Republicans George V. Voinovich, Cleveland mayor since 1979, and Robert A. Taft II, great-grandson of U.S. President William Howard Taft, announced that they would seek Ohio's governorship in 1990, while Ohio Attorney General Anthony Celebrezze, Jr., was an early leader among Democratic entrants. Incumbent Gov. Richard F. Celeste cannot seek a third consecutive term.

A constitutional amendment assigning the governor the duty of nominating a lieutenant governor when the office is vacant was approved by the voters. The governor's choice, however, must have the approval of majorities in both houses of the state legislature.

Environment. A mock trial jury in Cincinnati's U.S. district court decided in a nonbinding verdict that the neighbors of a federal uranium treatment nuclear weapons plant in Fernald, 18 mi (29 km) northwest of Cincinnati, were entitled to $136 million in damages resulting from the possibly lethal amounts of waste released into the area's atmosphere over a long period of time. In September, however, a federal judge approved the U.S. Department of Energy's $78 million settlement offer.

Scandals. During the year three prominent Ohioans were touched by scandal. Cincinnati baseball star Pete Rose was banned from baseball as a result of betting allegations, and Donald E. (Buz) Lukens, Republican congressman from Middletown, was found guilty of having sex with a 16-year-old girl. In the fall, Ohio Sen. John Glenn (D) came under a preliminary inquiry conducted by the Senate Ethics Committee in connection with allegations that he had intervened improperly to stave

OHIO • Information Highlights

Area: 41,330 sq mi (107 044 km^2).
Population (July 1, 1988 est.): 10,855,000.
Chief Cities (July 1, 1986 est.): Columbus, the capital, 556,030; Cleveland, 535,830; Cincinnati, 369,750; Toledo, 340,680; Akron, 220,060; Dayton, 178,920.
Government (1989): *Chief Officers*—governor, Richard F. Celeste (D); lt. gov., Paul R. Leonard (D). *General Assembly*—Senate, 33 members; House of Representatives, 99 members.
State Finances (fiscal year 1988): *Revenue,* $25,642,000,000; *expenditure,* $21,395,000,000.
Personal Income (1988): $168,635,000,000; per capita, $15,536.
Labor Force (June 1989): *Civilian labor force,* 5,536,900; *unemployed,* 321,000 (5.8% of total force).
Education: *Enrollment* (fall 1987)—public elementary schools, 1,220,000; public secondary, 573,000; colleges and universities, 518,464. *Public school expenditures* (1987–88), $6,380,872,000 ($3,601 per pupil).

off regulators in the investigation of the now-failed Lincoln Savings and Loan Association in Irving, CA. Glenn had received a large campaign contribution from the bank's owner.

Other. Cleveland's main business district and its lakefront renaissance gained momentum with the demolition of old buildings to make room for hotels and office structures.

Homer, OH, honored Victoria Claflin Woodhull, the first woman to run for the U.S. presidency, in September. She had secured a few thousand votes in 1872.

In October a state Supreme Court disciplinary panel ordered judicial candidates and judges not to announce their abortion views. A 1973 code bans judges from voicing opinions on disputed political or legal issues.

After much research and underwater exploration, a side-wheeler that had sunk in an 1857 hurricane off South Carolina was located by Ohio Recovery Limited Partnership, under project leader Thomas Thompson. Gold from the San Francisco mint and the Alaska gold rush, worth an estimated $450 million to $1 billion, was recovered.

JOHN F. HUTH, JR., *Cleveland*

OKLAHOMA

The year 1989 in Oklahoma was highlighted by the centennial of the "Run of '89," denoting the federal government's opening of land for settlement on April 22, 1889. The state's nickname is derived from those settlers, "Sooners," who moved onto the new lands before the official opening date.

The Economy. The Oklahoma economy continued its sluggish performance well into the year. A U.S. Census Bureau report found that the state had lost 40,000 people from 1985 to 1988, and state employment data showed that there were 71,000 fewer people in the work force in May 1989 than in 1987. State nonfarm income grew at a meager 1% above inflation during the year ending March 30, 1989, a rate that placed Oklahoma 47th among U.S. states. According to the U.S. Department of Commerce's *Survey of Current Business*, the state's per capita income in 1988 ranked 37th. There were, however, indications that the state economy had stabilized and was diversifying.

OKLAHOMA • Information Highlights

Area: 69,956 sq mi (181 186 km²).
Population (July 1, 1988): 3,242,000.
Chief Cities (July 1, 1986 est.): Oklahoma City, the capital, 446,120; Tulsa, 373,750; Lawton (1980 census), 80,054.
Government (1989): *Chief Officers*—governor, Henry Bellmon (R); lt. gov., Robert S. Kerr III (D). *Legislature*—Senate, 48 members; House of Representatives, 101 members.
State Finances (fiscal year 1988): *Revenue*, $6,425,000,000; *expenditure*, $5,781,000,000.
Personal Income (1988): $43,192,000,000; per capita, $13,323.
Labor Force (June 1989): *Civilian labor force*, 1,546,600; *unemployed*, 87,400 (5.6% of total force).
Education: *Enrollment* (fall 1987)—public elementary schools, 411,000; public secondary, 173,000; colleges and universities, 172,730. *Public school expenditures* (1987–88), $1,711,000,000 ($2,960 per pupil).

Legislation. Education funding dominated the legislative news. Included were measures to encourage improvements in ad valorem property tax assessments and to aid in the voluntary consolidation of the state's many school districts. More than half of the new money went to elementary and secondary education, with 75% of the increase mandated for pay raises for teachers and staff. Higher education received a substantial appropriation for the operation of some 27 institutions. Endowed chairs at the University of Oklahoma and Oklahoma State University received $4 million, and other funding went for aid to students with exceptional academic records and to fund a special school for science and mathematics for outstanding high school seniors.

The perennial problem of prison overcrowding was addressed by tapping some $17 million from the state's so-called Rainy Day Fund to build additional cells. State employees, apart from teachers, got a small increase in pay, and their longevity pay was doubled.

The major political event of the session was the unprecedented vote on May 17 to oust the state speaker of the House, Jim Barker. The Democratic majority elected Representative Steve Lewis as the new speaker.

Republican Gov. Henry Bellmon later called a special session to tackle the "emergency state" of education funding. The governor proposed a phasing out of the property tax and its replacement with a 1.9% gross-receipts tax on goods and services. Democrats countered with a plan based heavily on income-tax increases. Each plan would raise approximately $300 million. The special session recessed without acting on either, but did create a commission to study education and set a further legislative session for November.

Athletic Scandals. Both of the state's major institutions of higher education, the University of Oklahoma and Oklahoma State University, came under National Collegiate Athletic Association (NCAA) sanctions for violations of the rules governing the football programs. The sanctions included the banning of television broadcasts of regular and bowl games.

Trouble continued for the University of Oklahoma when five football players were implicated in a variety of serious crimes; then in June football coach Barry Switzer abruptly resigned. Richard Van Horn became university president in July.

HARRY HOLLOWAY, *University of Oklahoma*

ONTARIO

Throughout 1989, Ontario's Liberal government of Premier David Peterson tried to shake off an image of drifting by pursuing a more vigorous approach, only to fall victim to a series of scandals.

Legislation. After securing passage of a controversial bill permitting Sunday shopping, the year's most intractable issue proved to be automobile insurance. In April, alarmed by new high rates proposed for auto insurance—largely caused by ending discrimination on the basis of age and sex—the government overruled its own commission, set a cap of 7.5% on rate increases, and began a study on the feasibility of a no-fault scheme.

On September 15 a no-fault scheme was announced, to go into effect in the spring of 1990. Only those permanently or seriously injured or the estates of the deceased would be able to sue for pain suffered and economic loss. There will be guaranteed payments of up to $450 a week for lost income and a maximum of $500,000 for medical and rehabilitation costs to be delivered within 10-30 days of an incident. To prevent further premium increases, possibly up to 30% in 1990, the government proposed stricter enforcement of traffic laws, the doubling of speeding fines, and checks on auto-repair shops for fraud.

The major proposal in the April throne speech was the extension of half-day kindergarten to four-year-olds throughout the province during the next five years. This was aimed at improving the provincial educational system and solving the growing day-care crisis. But many school boards were alarmed by the cost of the proposal.

Budget. The budget of May 17 reflected the government's more active role. Health-care costs were to rise by 10.7% (to C$13.9 billion or 33% of the total budget). Increased expenditures on welfare and social services and education also were proposed. Some C$2 billion was to be spent in the next five years on highways and public transit. Despite talk of a balanced budget, a deficit remained with higher taxes rather than spending cuts. A major feature was the elimination of health-insurance premiums, which would cost about C$1 billion, to be replaced by a payroll tax expected to net C$2.1 billion. Taxes were raised on beer and cigarettes; income tax was raised 1% in 1989 and 1% in 1990. A user payer approach was adopted by raising gasoline taxes, drivers' license and car registration fees, and imposing a progressive tax on "gas-guzzling" cars and a $5 tax on tires. Higher development fees were to be charged on commercial property and parking lots in the Toronto area, a major beneficiary of the increased spending on highways and transit.

Scandals. Despite the budget initiatives, the government was harmed by a series of scandals beginning when the opposition held up business in the legislature for two weeks to force the resignation of Solicitor General Joan Smith, who allegedly had intervened in a police case involving a friend.

Far more serious was the "Patricia Starr affair." This case involved allegations of the use of a charitable organization to channel funds (some C$80,000) originating with a major development company to Liberal politicians in contravention of the Income Tax Act. Some nine provincial cabinet ministers may have received questionable donations from charities managed by Starr. In June, Gordon Ashworth, executive director of Premier Peterson's office, resigned after receiving benefits from a development company. The premier was forced to set up a public inquiry into the affair, which began hearings in October.

To refurbish the government's image the premier reshuffled his cabinet in August. Eight ministers were replaced, including some implicated in the Starr affair. Ontario Hydro also had its share of embarrassment: In February there was uproar over proposed sales of tritium from its Darlington nuclear-power station to the United States and in September the same plant was refused a license to start up its new reactors because of fears over automated shutdown procedures.

PETER J. KING, *Carleton University*

ONTARIO • Information Highlights

Area: 412,580 sq mi (1 068 580 km²).
Population (June 1989): 9,546,200.
Chief Cities (1986 census): Toronto, the provincial capital, 612,289; Ottawa, the federal capital, 300,763; Scarborough, 484,676; Mississauga, 374,005; Hamilton, 306,728; London, 269,140.
Government (1989): *Chief Officers*—lt. gov., Lincoln Alexander; premier, David Peterson (Liberal). *Legislature*—Legislative Assembly, 130 members.
Provincial Finances (1989–90 fiscal year budget): *Revenues,* $40,700,000,000; *expenditures,* $41,300,000,000.
Personal Income (average weekly earnings, June 1989): $512.89.
Labor Force (August 1989, seasonally adjusted): *Employed* workers, 15 years of age and over, 4,960,000; *Unemployed,* 5.1%.
Education (1989–90): *Enrollment*—elementary and secondary schools, 1,977,700 pupils; postsecondary—universities, 209,600; community colleges, 94,100.
(All monetary figures are in Canadian dollars.)

OREGON

Personal income for Oregonians achieved a five-year high during the first quarter of 1989, with economists estimating the annual personal-income growth rate at 12.8%. Strong job growth based in part upon the attraction of new businesses, greater transfer payments, such as

It is getting more difficult to find new timber for a log stacker like this at a typical Oregon logging operation. A tightening in timber supplies had led to a loss of jobs and a projected economic slowdown in the state.

AP/Wide World

Social Security, and higher interest on investments were credited. A slowdown was projected, however, based largely on the loss of vigor in the wood-products industry as timber supplies tighten. The projected loss in timber —about 5,300 jobs over the next five years—was cited as a major factor in the predicted slowdown. Also cited was the state's failure to attract large firms and projects as five major projects went elsewhere during 1988–89 after having been wooed by Oregon.

Legislation. A hike in the state's minimum wage, toughened sentencing guidelines, stricter drug penalties, tougher handgun-purchase procedures, and the construction of more than 1,700 new prison beds were among actions taken by the legislature. Assured by the state's attorney general that economic development could be construed to include prison construction, the legislature tapped the state's lottery fund—dedicated to economic development projects—for $82 million for the construction of 1,721 new prison beds.

OREGON • Information Highlights

Area: 97,073 sq mi (251 419 km²).
Population (July 1, 1988): 2,767,000.
Chief Cities (July 1, 1984 est.): Salem, the capital (1980 census), 89,233; Portland, 387,870; Eugene, 105,410.
Government (1989): *Chief Officers*—governor, Neil Goldschmidt (D); secretary of state, Barbara Roberts (D); *Legislative Assembly*—Senate, 30 members; House of Representatives, 60 members.
State Finances (fiscal year 1988): *Revenue,* $6,266,000,000; *expenditure,* $5,255,000,000.
Personal Income (1988): $41,180,000,000; per capita, $14,885.
Labor Force (June 1989): *Civilian labor force,* 1,475,400; *unemployed,* 77,800 (5.3% of total force).
Education: *Enrollment* (fall 1987)—public elementary schools, 318,000; public secondary, 138,000; colleges and universities, 152,657. *Public school expenditures* (1987–88), $1,922,000,000 ($4,278 per pupil).

In other action the legislature raised taxes on gasoline, cigarettes, and fees for fishing licenses and auto registrations, and mandated registration of off-road vehicles for the first time. Considered by many the most bizarre of this session's legislative actions was the passage of a bill directing the state lottery to establish video poker games to finance salary increases for college professors and a sports-oriented game to finance college athletics.

Environment. The year's most serious environmental controversy dealt with the logging of old-growth timber, referred to as "ancient forests" by environmentalists. The controversy intensified when the spotted owl was found to require old-growth timber as habitat. Several groups sought endangered status for the owl. A compromise, tacked onto the U.S. Department of the Interior's appropriations bill, provided for the sale of federal old-growth timber for an added 12 months while directing the Bureau of Land Management and the Forest Service to begin protection of owl habitat in old-growth stands.

Other. Citizens defeated a school consolidation and finance reform proposal by the legislature, which responded by appropriating $2.1 billion and appointing an interim committee to bring solutions to the state's antiquated school finance system to the next session.

Once again migrant laborers arrived months ahead of schedule with the hope of getting first choice of diminishing numbers of jobs. As a result, many migrants, unable to secure employment, required food, clothing, and other charity as well as funds to return to Mexico.

Michael Francke, Oregon's administrator of corrections, was stabbed to death outside his Salem office. An intensive investigation continued at year's end and has revived questions of crime within the state penitentiary.

L. CARL AND JOANN C. BRANDHORST
Western Oregon State College

OTTAWA

For Ottawa, Canada's capital, 1989 was marked by perennial concerns about the impact of federal government policies on the region.

Reductions in the size of the public service as part of the Conservative federal government's budget deficit reduction policy led Ottawa voters to buck the national trend and defeat several sitting Conservative members in the area in October 1988 federal elections. Following the elections the federal government announced its delayed decision to establish the Canadian Space Agency near Montreal. With an abundance of high-tech firms in the capital area, it was felt that Ottawa was the logical choice. Some government scientists refused to relocate in Quebec. There were further fears that due to lobbying by Conservative members in the House of Commons, other research facilities would be moved out of the capital, especially to Quebec. The federal budget also dropped plans for a new headquarters for the federal Department of Transport, ending competition between local municipalities for its location.

Restraint by the provincial government affected the city too, forcing local area school boards to raise taxes drastically, as much as 17% in some cases. Ontario Premier David Peterson, however, promised that the start on the first phase of a major freeway linking Ottawa with Highway 401, the Montreal-Toronto Freeway, would begin. Completion is not expected until the late 1990s, however. Area officials led by Ottawa Mayor Jim Durrell began lobbying hard for earlier completion.

Moshe Safdie, designer of the National Gallery that opened in 1988, was chosen as architect for the new Ottawa city hall, also to be built on Sussex Drive. A dispute between Safdie and the city over extra fees to bring the design up to standards developed. The new Museum of Civilization opened in Hull during the summer. Designed by architect Douglas Cardinal, it provoked criticism because of its expense, its late completion, and by opening well before most of the exhibits actually were installed. (*See also* page 163.)

Attempts to attract a Triple A baseball franchise to the city pitted Mayor Durrell against federal authorities that own the proposed ballpark site in LeBreton Flats as well as against poverty groups who want it for low-cost housing. The Ottawa Rough Riders of the Canadian Football League, facing bankruptcy and having an appalling season, asked the city and region for financial assistance. After a heated public debate, the city council, by a close vote, agreed to let the club keep the profits from refreshment sales and parking at the city-owned stadium. A factor was the fear that a Rough Rider collapse would destroy the league.

PETER J. KING, *Carleton University*

AP/Wide World

Benazir Bhutto, the prime minister of Pakistan, was received warmly as she addressed a joint session of the U.S. Congress in June during a state visit to Washington, DC.

PAKISTAN

Benazir Bhutto, who took office as prime minister of Pakistan in late 1988, struggled throughout 1989 against several formidable legacies of the 11-year dictatorship of Gen. Zia ul-Haq: a strong opposition party which claimed to be Zia's rightful political heir; a president with extraordinary constitutional powers; a narrow parliamentary margin; and a range of pressing social, economic, and foreign-policy problems.

Political Developments. Bhutto's Pakistan People's Party (PPP) continued to hold power in Islamabad and in the provinces of Sind and Northwest Frontier (NWFP), but the other two provinces remained in opposition hands. Punjab, with 60% of the country's population, was led in 1989 by Chief Minister Mian Nawaz Sharif of the Islamic Democratic Alliance (IDA).

Nawaz Sharif's rivalry with Bhutto intensified in 1989, marked by unsuccessful attempts by each to topple the other through no-confidence votes. Both also used their respective governmental powers for political harassment. Disputes arose over several issues: transfer of provincial officials, arrests of national officials by provincial police, and alleged discriminatory restrictions on Nawaz Sharif's industrial interests. In midyear, an IDA-led Combined Opposition Party (COP) was created in the National Assembly, with Ghulam Mustafa Jatoi as its leader and defeat of the PPP government as its sole unifying objective.

Following the November 1988 national elections, Bhutto's parliamentary majority was built upon a coalition between her PPP and the Muhajir Qaumi Movement (MQM), an ethnic-based party of urban Sind. During 1989 the coalition broke down, in part because of IDA pressure, but more because of continuing conflict between the Muhajirs, predominantly Urdu-speaking immigrants from India, and the predominantly rural Sindhis, who are a mainstay of PPP support. The Bhutto government, nevertheless, survived a no-confidence motion in November by 12 votes.

Bhutto also clashed with President Ghulam Ishaq Khan over their respective powers and authority. Bhutto unsuccessfully attempted to repeal the eighth amendment to the constitution, which Zia had enacted in 1985 to legitimize the various actions of his martial-law regime. In effect, the amendment not only strengthened the president's authority vis-à-vis that of the prime minister, but also preserved several decrees which women's groups found objectionable.

One area of dispute has been military appointments. Bhutto removed Zia appointee Lt. Gen. Hamid Gul from the sensitive post of director of Inter-Services Intelligence (ISI), and replaced him with her own appointee. Her attempt in early August to force the retirement of Adm. Iftikhar Ahmed Sirohey as chairman of the Joint Chiefs of Staff Committee, however, led to a strong reaction from President Ishaq. The high-level dispute finally was resolved.

Narcotics continue to be a major problem, with Pakistan and Afghanistan second only to Southeast Asia as a source area for heroin.

The Economy. Pakistan's economy continued to grow, though at a slightly slower pace than the 6% annual average it has enjoyed for the past decade. Inflation rose to an official estimate of 12%, but unofficial estimates ranged as high as 22%. A growing debt burden includes an $833 million package from the International Monetary Fund (IMF). Bhutto reluctantly agreed to abide by the IMF's terms, which include pressure to restructure Pakistan's economy. The IMF conditions already have led to higher electricity and fertilizer prices and have helped to fuel the year's higher inflation rate.

The Bhutto government's first budget, issued in June, included higher, but generally quite moderate and cautious, expenditures for education and literacy programs. The allocation for debt servicing was larger than either the annual development plan or the defense budget. Pakistan continues to have one of the highest debt-service ratios in the world.

Despite its Socialist origins and image, the PPP government announced in September its decision to privatize seven public-sector enterprises, including two banks, two gas pipelines, Pakistan International Airlines, Pakistan National Shipping, and Pakistan Standard Oil. The four-year phased sale of shares in the public companies would help to raise capital for promised social programs.

Foreign Relations. The Soviet troop withdrawal from Afghanistan was completed in February, but the Pakistan-supported *mujahidin* failed to capture the city of Jalalabad or to overthrow the Najibullah government in Kabul. On her visit to Washington in June, Bhutto urged President Bush to give greater consideration to a negotiated settlement of the war.

Bhutto continued to seek better relations with India. Enthusiasm for closer bilateral relations waned later in the year, as domestic criticism grew within Pakistan and Indian general elections approached.

Relations with Bangladesh worsened during the year, both in response to Dhaka's decision to buy Thai rice at higher prices than Pakistan's and because of Pakistan's increasing reluctance to accept the immigration to Pakistan of the 250,000 Biharis still in Bangladesh. The Biharis, largely Urdu-speaking pro-Pakistani collaborators in the 1971 Bangladesh war, remained unwelcome in Bangladesh, but Bhutto feared that their migration to Pakistan might tip Sind's explosive ethnic balance too greatly toward the Muhajirs, with whom the Biharis most likely would assimilate. Bhutto visited Dhaka in October to discuss the Bihari issue, but without resolution.

Pakistan rejoined the Commonwealth after an absence of 17 years, and Benazir Bhutto attended the Commonwealth summit in Kuala Lumpur, Malaysia, in October.

See also BIOGRAPHY—*Bhutto, Benazir.*

WILLIAM L. RICHTER
Kansas State University

PAKISTAN • Information Highlights

Official Name: Islamic Republic of Pakistan.
Location: South Asia.
Area: 310,402 sq mi (803 940 km^2).
Population (mid-1989 est.): 110,400,000.
Chief Cities (1981 census): Islamabad, the capital, 204,364; Karachi, 5,180,562.
Government: *Head of state,* Ghulam Ishaq Khan, president (elected Dec. 12, 1988). *Head of government,* Benazir Bhutto, prime minister (took office Dec. 2, 1988). *Legislature*—Parliament: Senate and National Assembly.
Monetary Unit: Rupee (20.81 rupees equal U.S.$1, Nov. 17, 1989).
Gross National Product (1988 fiscal year U.S.$): $39,400,000,000.
Economic Index (1988): *Consumer Prices* (1982 = 100), all items, 140.5; food, 143.6.
Foreign Trade (1988 U.S.$): *Imports,* $6,590,000,000; *exports,* $4,497,000,000.

PARAGUAY

General Andrés Rodríguez became interim president on February 3, overthrowing the regime of 76-year-old Gen. Alfredo Stroessner, who had held the post for nearly 35 years. The following day, a cabinet was named and new elections were called. Rodríguez won that contest and was sworn in on May 16 to complete the four years remaining in Stroessner's eighth term. He took immediate action to reduce foreign debt and aligned his foreign policies with those of neighboring states.

Politics and Government. The coup by Rodríguez, the aging dictator's second-in-command, succeeded after a short-lived battle that took 300 lives. The fallen leader was exiled to Brazil. Once the ruling Colorado Party leadership had been replaced by a group loyal to Rodríguez, Colorados nominated the general as their candidate to complete the 1988–93 term of the deposed Stroessner. Upon accepting the nomination, Rodríguez indicated that he would not be a candidate for reelection. On May 1, Rodríguez won more than 74% of the popular vote with 20% going to Domingo Laíno of the Authentic Radical Liberal Party. The Colorados won 24 of 36 seats in the Senate and 48 of the 72 places in the lower chamber. Twelve parties fielded candidates in the 1989 electoral campaign; some of them had not been able to participate in elections held by the previous regime. Even so, only 23% of the electorate exercised its right to vote in a contest judged to be the freest since 1954.

At the end of the electoral campaign, Rodríguez reiterated that there would be no pardoning of either economic crimes or human-rights abuses committed by members of successive Stroessner governments. According to tallies divulged by congressmen, some 1,000 people were killed or disappeared between 1954 and 1989. Another 110,000 had been arrested and tortured. The new regime permitted the reopening of the daily *ABC Color,* a newspaper banned in 1984. With regard to one of the most pressing issues before his government—a need to redistribute the country's arable land—Rodríguez ordered a census of the landless peasants.

Economy. One of the initial problems attacked by the de facto president and his economic team was that of the $2 billion in foreign debt. While there was only $160 million available in foreign currency, arrears on the foreign debt had reached $300 million. Authorities rejected appeals by the International Monetary Fund (IMF) and World Bank, because of the harsh adjustments that would be required of Paraguayans. Instead, an arrangement was worked out under which Brazil would reduce the $440 million owed it by Paraguay, by 70%. Repayment would be made over 20 years, with an eight-year grace period.

A decision was announced on February 23 to devalue the guaraní by 60%. With a single, freely floating exchange rate implemented, the guaraní was expected to stabilize at about 1,000 to the dollar. Other fiscal reforms in Rodríguez' "free-market" approach to economic policy included the elimination of certain import and export taxes. Special treatment for imports from Argentina, Bolivia, and Brazil was announced in May; imports from the three countries would be subject to a single 10% tariff. Industrialists objected to the excessive opening of the Paraguayan market to foreign products and protested the lack of credit available to the domestic industry to meet the challenge of outside competition.

The incoming government began investigations of illicit enrichment of functionaries who had served under the now deposed President Stroessner. Among the first to be called by the judicial branch, in February, were Sabino Montonaro, former interior minister; Eugenio Jacquet, former minister of labor; and Mario Abdo Benítez, former private secretary to General Stroessner. Stroessner himself was accused in May by his successor of involvement in a $40 million fraud, involving the state-owned cement industry. Three generals offered in August to return millions in cash and property to the state, if charges of illicit enrichment against them were dropped.

Foreign Relations. In an address on April 14, opening the first session of the Inter-American Press Association ever held in Paraguay, interim President Rodríguez indicated that dissent and criticism no longer were forbidden in Paraguayan media. Presidents of Brazil, Argentina, and Uruguay attended Rodríguez' inauguration ceremonies held in Asuncíon on May 16. On that occasion, the incoming chief executive expressed his interest in joining a regional economic integration movement under way, embracing the neighboring states. At the United Nations on September 26, Rodríguez pledged his support in the suppression of narcotics trafficking.

LARRY L. PIPPIN
University of the Pacific

PARAGUAY • Information Highlights

Official Name: Republic of Paraguay.
Location: Central South America.
Area: 157,046 sq mi (406 750 km²).
Population (mid-1989 est.): 4,200,000.
Chief City (1982 census): Asunción, the capital, 455,517.
Government: *Head of state and government,* Gen. Andrés Rodríguez, president (took office 1989). *Legislature*—Congress: Senate and Chamber of Deputies.
Monetary Unit: Guaraní (1,147.0 guaraníes equal U.S.$1, July 1989).
Gross Domestic Product (1987 U.S.$): $7,400,-000,000.
Foreign Trade (1988 U.S.$): *Imports,* $555,000,000; *exports,* $607,000,000.

PENNSYLVANIA

No single event dominated the attention of Pennsylvanians in 1989. In the spring, public concern focused on a referendum proposing a change in the state's constitution that would have reformed Pennsylvania's system of local taxes. The current system limits local income-tax rates, placing the tax burden heavily upon property owners. Civic organizations and groups representing senior citizens, labor unions, and most industries urged voters to support the referendum so that, at the discretion of local elected officials, some of the local tax burden could shift from property owners to wage earners. Gov. Robert P. Casey (D) and other supporters said that the change probably would lower taxes for most citizens. Vocal opponents, primarily Republicans in the state Senate, the state's small Consumer Party, and some business groups, argued that lower taxes were not guaranteed and that the change would permit local officials to enact large raises in local wage taxes. In a referendum held on May 16 only 25.5% of the voters supported the change. Exit polls showed that the somewhat confusing nature of the referendum doomed the proposal.

Politics. Despite the voters' overwhelming rejection of his tax reform proposal, Democratic Governor Casey continued to maintain high popular support in the polls. Five prominent Republicans—U.S. Sen. John Heinz, Erie Congressman Tom Ridge, state Sen. Robert Jubelirer, former U.S. Secretary of Transportation Drew Lewis, and U.S. Attorney General and former Gov. Richard Thornburgh—declined to challenge Casey. Barbara Hafer, elected auditor general in 1988, won Republican leadership support to run against Casey and was scheduled to run in the spring 1990 primary election against former state Rep. John Kennedy.

PENNSYLVANIA • Information Highlights

Area: 45,308 sq mi (117 348 km²).
Population (July 1, 1988): 12,001,000.
Chief Cities (July 1, 1986 est.): Harrisburg, the capital (1980 census), 53,264; Philadelphia, 1,642,900; Pittsburgh, 387,490; Erie, 115,270; Allentown, 104,360.
Government (1989): *Chief Officers*—governor, Robert Casey (D); lt. gov., Mark Singel (D). *Legislature*—Senate, 50 members; House of Representatives, 203 members.
State Finances (fiscal year 1988): *Revenue,* $23,824,000,000; *expenditure,* $21,307,000,000.
Personal Income (1988): $194,819,000,000; per capita, $16,233.
Labor Force (June 1989): *Civilian labor force,* 5,981,000; *unemployed,* 272,200 (4.6% of total force).
Education: *Enrollment* (fall 1987)—public elementary schools, 1,078,000; public secondary, 591,000; colleges and universities, 554,370. *Public school expenditures* (1987–88), $7,749,819,000 ($4,742 per pupil).

In Pittsburgh, Mayor Sophie Masloff defeated county Controller Frank Lucchino and three other Democrats in a hotly contested primary to retain the office she acquired with the death of popular Mayor Richard Caliguiri in 1988. The Republicans failed to field a candidate for the fall general election.

Abortion. Pennsylvania responded to the July U.S. Supreme Court decision upholding a restrictive Missouri abortion law that gave states wider authority to limit abortions with the Abortion Control Act of 1989. The act prohibits abortions after a fetus is 24 weeks in most cases; outlaws all abortions at public hospitals, except in cases of rape or incest or to save the life of the mother; requires women contemplating abortions, in most cases, to notify husbands; mandates a 24-hour waiting period; and has other provisions that supporters argue discourage abortions. Opponents argued that the law interferes with a woman's constitutional right to abortion and asked the courts to enjoin its enforcement. Because the act includes provisions that the Supreme Court had ruled unconstitutional in other cases, the law challenges the Supreme Court to reverse or to narrow further the 1973 *Roe v. Wade* decision providing a constitutional right to abortion.

In other abortion-related news, the courts upheld the convictions of antiabortion protesters for violating the Racketeering Influenced and Corrupt Organizations Act (RICO). The protesters were ordered to pay $43,000 in damages and $65,000 in legal costs related to disruptive activities outside the Northwest Women's Center in Philadelphia. The defendants argued that RICO was organized to aid in combating organized crime, not thwart political protesters.

Economy. The state's economic news continued to be mixed. Unemployment in the late fall was 4.3%, lower than the national average of 5.2%. Nevertheless, declines in jobs in the retail sector and stagnation in the factory sector indicated a sluggish economy. Western Pennsylvania continued to face declining populations with higher than average unemployment; in contrast, the prosperous counties of southeastern Pennsylvania outside Philadelphia grew and experienced full employment.

Other. In Philadelphia on April 5, the trial of mobster Nicodermo Scarfo ended with his conviction, along with seven others, for murder. Judge Eugene Clark sentenced Scarfo to life in prison in ruling that the absence of "aggravating circumstances" ruled out the death penalty. In other judicial actions, Ashland Oil Inc. agreed to pay $4.6 million in costs and civil penalties for the 1988 spill that poured 715,000 gallons (2.7 million l) of diesel oil into the Monongahela and Ohio rivers. Ashland also paid $18 million in cleanup costs and claims.

ROBERT E. O'CONNOR
Pennsylvania State University

PERU

A recessive economy, a potent guerrilla insurrection, and a largely discredited government kept Peru tottering near chaos in 1989.

Domestic Affairs. The most serious threat to the government of President Alan García came from the Maoist *Sendero Luminoso* (Shining Path) guerrilla organization, which completed its ninth year of armed struggle. *Sendero* strengthened its hold on the south central highlands and the Upper Huallaga Valley, where it protected drug traffickers in exchange for money and sophisticated weaponry such as bazookas, machine guns, and explosives. Government officials, governors, and justices of the peace of different localities there either were forced to resign or were killed.

Political parties thereafter had difficulties finding candidates for the upcoming elections. Also successful were the "armed stoppages," in which workers were issued death threats to prevent them from challenging the strike. An estimated 70% of the area's public-works projects were stalled due to the stoppages and poor economic conditions. Despite a more visible urban presence, the group was unable to prevent municipal elections in November, although null voting and abstentions were very high in Ayacucho and other *Sendero* strongholds. It was unlikely that the group would be able to prevent the presidential elections scheduled for March 1990. Since the *Sendero* insurgency began in earnest in 1980, about 12,000 Peruvians have been killed due to political violence, and approximately 2,500 have "disappeared." An urban guerrilla group, the *Movimiento Revolucionario Tupac Amaru* (MRTA) extended its activities into the countryside, where it clashed not only with government troops but also with *Sendero Luminoso*.

President García responded in late July by turning over control of the counterinsurgency effort to the army. The new policy came after the May 7 assassination of American Popular Revolutionary Alliance (APRA) Congressman Pablo Ormeno by suspected *Sendero Luminoso* guerrillas. The next day, the entire third cabinet formed by the García administration resigned. Amnesty International reported in August that the military was responsible for routine murder, "disappearances," torture, assassination, and sabotage as it attacked the opposition with impunity. This included an alleged cover-up of the murders of 29 villagers from Cayara, a reprisal that followed an ambush of a military convoy by guerrillas. There were no convictions for any wrongdoings.

Economic Affairs. The Peruvian economy was in equal disarray. The rate of inflation for the 12-month period ending in July reached 5,548.9%. García provoked further inflation in August by pressuring the central bank to print $500 million to pay the July salaries of 880,000 state employees. As purchasing power continued to diminish and as the government raised the prices of basic goods and services, trade unions threatened and carried out lengthy strikes, especially in the mining, petroleum, health, and educational sectors. The government offered few concessions on the grounds that big wage increases would worsen inflation.

By June the country had entered a severe depression. The minister of economy predicted a possible 20% decline in gross domestic product (GDP). Industrial production suffered a 23.6% decline at the end of the first quarter compared to the first quarter in 1989. Industrialists estimated that up to 60% of industrial capacity was idle. Adding to the recession were a 35.5% productivity decrease in the manufacturing sector, a drop in food consumption which lowered foodstuffs production by 20%, and a decline in industrial and commercial sales.

Political uncertainty matched the economic adversity in the country. Both right- and left-wing factions struggled to hold together tenuous coalitions they hoped would win them the presidency in the spring of 1990. With support for the political center disintegrating due to the failure of the last two governments, the front-runner was prominent novelist Mario Vargas Llosa, the candidate of the right-wing coalition *Frente Democrático* (Fredemo). He was backed by former President Fernando Belaúnde Terry's *Acción Popular* and Luís Bedoya Reyes' *Partido Popular Cristiano.* Runner-up was the former mayor of Lima, Alfonso Barrantes, the candidate of a "moderate" faction of the divided *Izquierda Unida.*

MICHAEL COPPEDGE
Johns Hopkins University

PERU • Information Highlights

Official Name: Republic of Peru.
Location: West coast of South America.
Area: 496,224 sq mi (1 285 220 km^2).
Population (mid-1989 est.): 21,400,000.
Chief Cities (mid-1985 est.): Lima, the capital, 5,008,400; Arequipa, 531,829; Callao, 515,200.
Government: *Head of state,* Alan García Pérez, president (took office July 28, 1985). *Head of government,* Armando Villanueva del Campo, prime minister (took office May 1988). *Legislature*—Congress: Senate and Chamber of Deputies.
Monetary Unit: inti (2,942.5 intis equal U.S.$1, official rate, July 1989).
Gross Domestic Product (1988 est. U.S.$): $19,600,-000,000.
Economic Index (Lima, 1988): *Consumer Prices* (1980 = 100), all items, 85,780.9; food, 59,481.2.
Foreign Trade (1988 U.S.$): *Imports,* $2,556,000,000; *exports,* $2,672,000,000.

PHILIPPINES

Though Ferdinand Marcos lay critically ill in a Honolulu hospital early in 1989, he was considered a serious threat to Philippine stability and was not permitted to return from exile.

Even when he died in September (*see* sidebar), President Corazon Aquino refused him burial in his homeland and the Supreme Court subsequently upheld this ban. In December, Aquino survived the most serious of the six coup attempts that have been aimed at her government. The year also saw some economic improvement, the leftist insurgency seemed stalemated, and the government's tribulations included numerous charges of corruption.

Death of Marcos. President Aquino's refusal to permit the burial of Marcos in his native province of Ilocos Norte threatened to become —although it did not—an opportunity for political opponents to provoke the very turmoil it was intended to prevent. His wife, Imelda, against whom federal lawsuits for embezzlement and fraud continued in New York, had expected to accompany her husband's body home. In the absence of an extradition treaty, she then would be immune to U.S. charges. And although other indictments awaited her in Manila, she could have exploited the allegiance of Marcos loyalists and the sympathy of ordinary people for her reduced situation.

Others prepared to take advantage of the impasse included Vice-President Salvador Laurel and Sen. Juan Ponce Enrile, whose opposition party, Union for National Action (UNA), continued to grope for a cause to rally voters in the 1992 presidential election. They carefully monitored signs in early negotiations over the future of U.S. military bases in the Philippines—a contentious issue—that might indicate the Aquino administration's willingness to compromise Philippine nationalism.

Coup Attempt. On December 1, rebels in the armed forces occupied military installations in

Ferdinand E. Marcos (1917–1989)

The death of Ferdinand Marcos in Honolulu on Sept. 28, 1989, did not end the controversy that had surrounded the deposed Philippine president for years. His successor, President Corazon C. Aquino, refused to allow his body to be taken back to his homeland for fear that demonstrators would react in "widely and passionately conflicting ways." Marcos was buried in Honolulu, where he had spent nearly four years in exile.

Early Years. Ferdinand Edralin Marcos was born Sept. 11, 1917, in the town of Sarrat in Ilocos Norte province in northern Luzon. As a 22-year-old law student at the University of the Philippines, Marcos was convicted of murdering the man who defeated his father for Congress. Defending himself on appeal, however, he was acquitted by the Supreme Court.

Marcos became a trial lawyer. A guerrilla intelligence officer in World War II, he claimed 27 medals for acts of heroism whose validity later was challenged. In 1949 he was elected to the Philippine House of Representatives, serving there until 1959, when he was elected a senator. He was president of the Senate from 1963 to 1965.

Presidency. In 1965, Marcos was elected president; in 1969 he became the first Filipino president to be reelected. Marcos declared martial law in 1972, justifying this measure by proclaiming the need to combat Communist insurgency, Muslim separatism, and student unrest. He suspended Congress and declared himself absolute ruler; he also greatly enlarged the army. He was prime minister as well as president until 1981. In that year he lifted martial law (at the time of a papal visit) and won a presidential election under a new constitution that allowed him to continue to rule by decree.

Opposition to Marcos' rule mounted through the years as the economy deteriorated and the foreign debt burgeoned. Nonetheless, Marcos and his wife Imelda lived in sumptuous style, and many of Marcos' associates prospered. The United States supplied large amounts of military and economic aid to the Marcos regime, much of it to support campaigns against the Communist insurgency (and, it later was alleged, some of it went into Marcos' bank accounts and other holdings abroad). His political foes continued to clamor about corruption and dictatorial rule; their determination strengthened after the 1983 assassination of opposition leader Benigno S. Aquino, Jr.

To prove himself still popular, Marcos agreed to an early presidential election on Feb. 7, 1986. His opponent was Corazon Aquino, the widow of the slain opposition leader. Despite widespread charges of election fraud, the legislature declared Ferdinand Marcos the winner. The defense minister, Juan Ponce Enrile, and Gen. Fidel Ramos then defected to the Aquino camp and led a bloodless rebellion. They were protected against massed tanks by thousands of civilians practicing passive resistance. On Feb. 25, 1986, a U.S. Air Force plane flew the Marcoses and their entourage to exile in Hawaii.

Exile. Subsequently, details about the Marcoses' enormous wealth and regal way of life came to light. Both the Philippine and U.S. governments indicted Marcos (and his wife and others) on charges of embezzlement and conspiracy to defraud. Considered too ill to stand trial, Marcos spent most of his final year in a Honolulu hospital.

LEONARD CASPER

and around Manila, as well as two TV stations and the international airport. Surprised by the large-scale uprising, Aquino asked for, and received, U.S. military assistance. U.S. F-14 fighter planes provided cover for loyal troops and effectively grounded the rebels' aircraft. Rebels now were forced to withdraw from occupied installations, and within days they had surrendered. A principal rebel leader, Col. Gregorio Honasan, leader of the failed August 1987 coup, remained at large.

Many observers believed that Honasan and his comrades, who had been politicized during the Marcos years, were attempting to regain political power—although many mutineers contended that they were protesting continuing corruption and widespread poverty. For her part, Aquino, who reshuffled her cabinet following the coup attempt, proved that she has U.S. support, but domestic reactions to U.S. involvement could prove politically troublesome for her.

Economy and Foreign Aid. The clearest signs of Philippine recovery, beyond early political successes like the new constitution, have been economic. The growth in gross national product (GNP) rose from 2% in 1986 to approximately 7%. At a Tokyo conference sponsored by the World Bank in July, 19 nations pledged $3.5 billion in support of the Multilateral Assistance Initiative (or Philippine Aid Plan). The $14 billion anticipated over a four-year period is expected to create a favorable climate for private investors. Equally significant is the promised foreign-debt reduction under the Brady Plan, originating in the U.S. Treasury Department, which encourages repurchase of outstanding bank loans at substantial discount.

In August the respected director of the National Economic Development Agency, Solita Monsod, resigned because she advocated a moratorium on debt service, which consumes 40% of the national income. Monsod resented the fact that 80% of the $28 billion outstanding was borrowed by the Marcos regime, which also was responsible for the flight of capital overseas. But Aquino decided to honor all previous debts. To ease that burden, she visited Europe early in July and secured loans from West Germany ($55 million), France ($158 million), and the European Community ($19.4 million). In November, Aquino visited Washington seeking to encourage U.S. investment.

In addition, the government had privatized most of the 103 companies seized from Marcos associates. Although the Marcos properties in New York were sold for $400 million and his frozen assets abroad are subject to litigation (in Los Angeles alone, the Philippines has a $5 billion punitive lawsuit against the former president and his associates), Filipinos no longer were expecting quick court settlements.

Filipinos instead were finding satisfaction in the 23% drop in strikes, the rise in value of farm production, the drop in unemployment to near 8% (though underemployment remained at 30% in some rural areas), the 79% increase in tuna exports, the escalation of tourism in Cebu, and the successful shift from sugar plantations in Negros to prawn ponds. Half of all Filipino nurses were employed overseas; 250,000 men working in Saudi Arabia remitted $300 million each year. Still, 20% of Filipino children (in some areas, about 45%) suffer from malnutrition. Half the population remains below the poverty level, even as food prices rise sharply.

Insurgency and Civil Rights. Usually the leftist New People's Army (NPA) has flourished when little economic gain trickles down to the people. But in 1989, on its 20th anniversary, the NPA had little to celebrate. Its founder, Bernabe Buscayno, who had run unsuccessfully for public office in 1987, declared the movement dead. On July 27, Saturnino

AP/Wide World

During 1989, Philippine President Corazon Aquino had a strong ally in U.S. President George Bush. On November 9 she was accorded a formal welcome to the White House, left, *and three weeks later President Bush sent U.S. military assistance to the Philippines to help President Aquino suppress an attempted coup.*

Ocampo, former head of the NPA and a Communist Party central committeeman, was captured along with his wife, Carolina Malay. Ocampo, who had urged reconciliation with the government, complained that the insurgency movement, obsessed with armed revolution and taxation of people in its control, had committed "serious political errors." Middle-class and student support waned as a result of NPA massacres in Mindanao and Nueva Ecija. Regional cadres disagreed on policy; and "cleansing" themselves of alleged spies involved extensive torture and killing.

Still, the NPA claimed shadow governments in 100 towns in 25 provinces. In the *barangay* (a unit of administration of 50 to 100 families) elections, March 28, an estimated 18% of these local political units elected Communist heads. In April, Col. James Rowe, U.S. counterinsurgency adviser to the armed forces, was killed by gunmen near Manila; in September urban terrorists exploded grenades in the markets of Quiapo and Divisoria.

The government, however, seemed in equal disarray. Lt. Gen. Renato de Villa, chief of staff replacing Gen. Fidel Ramos (now defense secretary), continued to argue for the need of vigilante help. The Citizens Armed Forces Geographic Units (CAFGU), numbering more than 45,000, were the principal source of human-rights complaints. Anyone seeking social change, including the Base Christian Communities, was at risk from both CAFGU and army extremists, despite Aquino's order that there be dialogue between military commanders and the Association of Major Religious Superiors. Although 150 generals and colonels were under investigation, they were subject to military courts only. Soldiers of lesser rank were known to protect Manila crime syndicates.

In a plebiscite on November 19, voters rejected a limited autonomy proposal for parts of the southern Philippines with large Muslim populations.

PHILIPPINES • Information Highlights

Official Name: Republic of the Philippines.
Location: Southeast Asia.
Area: 115,830 sq mi (300 000 km²).
Population: (mid-1989 est.): 64,900,000.
Chief Cities (1984 est.): Manila, the capital, 1,728,441; Quezon City, 1,326,035; Davao, 552,155; Caloocan, 524,624.
Government: *Head of state and government,* Corazon C. Aquino, president (took office Feb. 25, 1986). *Legislature* (bicameral)—Senate and House of Representatives.
Monetary Unit: Peso (21.80 pesos equal U.S. $1, Dec. 15, 1989).
Gross National Product (1987 U.S.$): $33,600,-000,000.
Economic Index (1988): *Consumer Prices* (1980 = 100), all items, 288.7; food, 286.2.
Foreign Trade (1988 U.S.$): *Imports,* $8,731,-000,000; *exports,* $7,035,000,000.

Problems in Leadership. Little moral leadership was provided by Congress and its bureaucracy in 1989. The land-reform bill, enacted in 1988, was endangered by conspiracies between officials and landlords who inflated the value of their holdings so outrageously that Miriam Defensor Santiago, who as immigration commissioner had prevented graft in that branch, was shifted to the Department of Agrarian Reform. Elsewhere, it was assumed that half of the taxes collected nationally were pocketed by collectors and that widespread nepotism existed even in the Presidential Commission on Good Government. Ten cabinet members were accused of holding conflict-of-interest positions in government corporations. Rep. Nicanor de Guzman was charged with smuggling more than 300 weapons into the country for an arms syndicate. Gov. Mariano Ocampo III of Tarlac was accused of misusing more than $70 million of infrastructure funds.

In her July 24 State of the Nation address, President Aquino lamented that "corruption is again a way of public life." She had hoped to be seen not merely as reacting to inherited crises but also as leaving something of permanent value to the people who empowered her. She has denied any intention of running for office in 1992. Especially because she committed herself to a process (open, consultative, conservative) rather than to any specific program, and because she was identified only nominally with a political party, she had become increasingly vulnerable while others positioned themselves to succeed her. In 1986, through massive public demonstrations and closely defended ballot boxes, reform was managed from below. The question in late 1989 was whether reform now could be generated from above.

Ramón Mitra, speaker of the House and long Aquino's defender, distanced himself by resigning as head of the Laban ng Demokratikong Pilipino Party (LDP), which he cofounded with Aquino's brother, José Cojuangco. Mitra had become an advocate for strong and lean government through reducing the standing army and particularly by reducing bureaucratic overlap and supersaturation. Conceivably he was willing to forgo party diplomacy in an attempt at broad popular appeal.

Because the crisis in leadership had not been solved and the Philippine democracy remained fragile in 1989, President Aquino understandably was not eager for the return of any of the Marcoses or of the other 90 Filipinos currently on a "watch list." Together, such persons were capable of provoking both anti- and pro-Marcos demonstrations whose violence, for example, could cause investments to plummet—as they did, briefly, on May 19 after only the rumor of Marcos' death.

LEONARD CASPER, *Boston College*
GRETCHEN CASPER, *Texas A&M University*

PHOTOGRAPHY

In 1989 photography celebrated its sesquicentennial, a 150th birthday that featured, among other things, commemorative postage stamps issued by the United Nations and the Soviet Union; limited-edition reproductions of the first daguerreotype; and major exhibitions presenting historical overviews, as well as work of contemporary photographers. The year also was the 100th anniversary of the birth of the motion picture, marking the first time Thomas Edison put George Eastman's flexible, transparent film in the Kinetograph camera.

Innovation continued to change the face of photography in 1989. In hardware, five years after the introduction of the first autofocus (AF) single-lens-reflex camera (SLR), the emergence of the Canon EOS-1 for professionals heralded the dawning of a second-generation AF SLR. A slew of new autofocus 35mm point-and-shoot cameras, made of high-impact plastic, also captured the imagination and pocketbooks of amateurs, outselling SLRs by a 4:1 ratio (6 million:1.5 million).

Edward Weston's 1927 photograph "Shell" led the pack at the spring auction in New York City with a selling price of $115,000, the most ever paid for a single photograph at auction. By the time the gavel came down at Sotheby's, Christie's, and Swann Galleries, close to $5 million worth of photography had been sold.

Hardware and Software. For the professional, Canon's EOS-1 dispensed with conventional controls and displays, substituting push buttons and a top-deck, liquid-crystal display panel. A new cross-type, base-stored image sensor (CT-BASIS) system extended focus finesse to "predictive" autofocus, allowing the camera to adjust for a subject's movement.

For amateurs, a barrage of new autofocus point-and-shoot (P/S) 35mm cameras was introduced in zoom, dual-lens, and supercompact categories. Minolta's Freedom Zoom 90 sported a 38-90mm power-zoom lens and Nikon's Tele-Touch 300 was the first to tackle the problem of red eye. Unlike autofocus SLR cameras, point-and-shoot cameras do not focus continuously but in discrete steps. This zone system senses a range distance and zips there. While early P/S cameras had as few as four zones, some of the current models have 50 or more, with the Olympus Infinity Zoom 200 offering 116 zones.

Film wars continued between giants Fuji and Kodak, as each introduced new, improved, and, in some cases, revolutionary film products. Fuji introduced several films, including the revolutionary Fujicolor Reala ISO 100 with a fourth color layer that promises true color even under fluorescent light; the Super HG 200 and 400 with a new "reactivated inhibitor releasor;" and the revised and newly dubbed HG Fujicolor 1600. Kodak's entries included Ektar

Courtesy, The Art Institute of Chicago

August Sander's 1913 print "Young Peasants on Their Way to a Dance, Westerwald," was part of the "On the Art of Fixing a Shadow: 150 Years of Photography" exhibit in Washington, Chicago, and Los Angeles (as 1989 ended).

125 and 1000, touted to have the finest grain, sharpness, and color of any Kodak film ever produced; Kodacolor Gold 400; and super-speed Kodacolor Gold 1600. In April, Polaroid introduced OneFilm, which is intended for amateurs who prefer the simplicity of a single film type for different lighting conditions.

Legislation and the Courts. Photography was at the center of a legislative and artistic freedom controversy in 1989. Some members of Congress were incensed that Andres Serrano received a grant from the National Endowment for the Arts (NEA), in light of his exhibiting his photograph of a crucifix submerged in urine. In reaction to the controversy, the Corcoran Gallery of Art in Washington, DC, cancelled an exhibition of the photographs of the late Robert Mapplethorpe, which was financed partially by the NEA, and which included explicit homoerotic images. (The museum subsequently apologized to the arts community for canceling the show.) Meanwhile, Sen. Jesse Helms (R-NC) introduced an amendment to restrict federal funding for art exhibits found to be "obscene or indecent." Critics of the legislation said withholding government funds from controversial art projects could be viewed as a form of censorship. Although Congress rejected the Helms amendment, it did pass a less stringent bill denying federal funds for art deemed obscene.

The Disposable Camera

AP/Wide World

The saying, "the more things change, the more they stay the same," came clearly into focus with the introduction of two new throwaway cameras from Kodak. The Weekend 35 and Stretch 35 are disposable or "single-use" cameras with film that are mailed in for processing. Although these modern-day versions are for special-purpose use—underwater/all-weather shooting and panoramas, respectively—they echo Kodak's early cameras and slogan, "You press the button, we do the rest."

The Weekend 35 camera is sealed ultrasonically in a see-through plastic casing and is claimed to be submersible to 12 ft. (3.6 m). Essentially a Kodak Fling model with the special casing, it is a basic aim-and-shoot, single-element, 35mm camera with a plastic lens and one exposure setting, f/11 at 1/110 second. With its 24-exposure load of Kodacolor Gold 400 film, it is marketed toward casual snapshooters and those who do not want to risk pricey equipment with "wet" outdoor activities. Its list price is $13.95, not including processing.

The Stretch 35 (*photo above*) takes panoramic pictures through a 25mm lens, recording a 78-degree horizontal view on a 13.33 x 36.4 mm (.524 x 1.43 inch) band across the middle of a normal 35mm frame. It produces 3½ x 10 inch (89 x 255 mm) prints, which are exceptional, the result of the Stretch's plastic doublet ("duplet") lens that uses a different refractive-index plastic for each element. In between the two elements are the f/12 fixed aperture and 1/100-second shutter. Kodak loads the Stretch, designed for daylight use, with 12 exposures of Kodacolor Gold 200. Aimed at vacationers, realtors, and architects who want good-quality pictures of buildings and properties, its list price is $12.95, without processing.

These technological marvels have very limited exposure capability, a single shutter speed that eliminates fast action shots, no flash, and all the disadvantages of a fixed focus camera—working well only in bright light and only in sharp focus from 8 ft (2.4 m) on. But this impulse purchase is ideal for going places without concern that a camera is lost, stolen, or dropped at sea. Under the right conditions, both models can produce surprisingly good pictures.

BARBARA LOBRON

Photography issues also appeared on the court calendar in 1989. A landmark ruling by the U.S. Supreme Court found that freelancers retain the right to their work. Legal proceedings also got under way in another case involving slides lost by a major magazine and the value of such lost transparencies to the photographer.

Exhibitions and Publications. There was a wide diversity of photography shows celebrating the sesquicentennial year. In New York City, "Waller Evans: American Photographs" was seen at the Museum of Modern Art in conjunction with the 50th anniversary of the publication of his landmark book of the same title, which also was reissued. "Constructed Images: New Photography" was shown at the Studio Museum in Harlem, while "The Tell," a monumental photo mural on a foothill in Laguna Beach, CA, both called attention to the local countryside and stood in protest to a proposed highway project.

In book publishing, William Eggleston's color odyssey, *The Democratic Forest,* was released. *Epitaphs for the Living: Words and Images in the Time of AIDS* combined photographs with handwritten comments. *Yo Phos* (Young Photographers) was 16-year-old Bill Morong's answer to not being taken seriously; he started his own publishing company to distribute the photo work of his peers. Brian Lanker's *I Dream a World* combined photographs of leading black women with first-person accounts in a book that by late in the year was in its sixth printing.

In periodicals, 52-year-old *Modern Photography* magazine folded and the subscription list was acquired by *Popular Photography.*

BARBARA LOBRON
Editor, Photographer, Writer

PHYSICS

The reported observation of controlled thermonuclear fusion at room temperature captured worldwide attention in 1989. The enthusiasm for high-temperature superconductors moderated, while the first construction money was awarded for the giant Superconducting Super Collider. Also, two research groups announced that the universe may contain only three generations of fundamental particles.

Cold Fusion. What would have been the scientific breakthrough of a generation burst on the world scientific and media scene in March 1989, shone supernova-like for a brief time, then rapidly dimmed, but is not yet completely extinguished. On March 23, 1989, Martin Fleischmann and B. Stanley Pons, chemists at the University of Southampton, England and the University of Utah, respectively, announced the discovery of nuclear fusion at room temperature.

The idea of the experiment is simple. The element palladium has the capacity to absorb a large amount of hydrogen (H). Instead of ordinary hydrogen, Fleischmann and Pons used a heavy isotope of hydrogen—deuterium (D). The system consisted of a palladium cathode and an annular anode (platinum wire wound on a glass frame), all in a bath of heavy water (D_2O). A row of these cells, together with power supplies, constituted the experimental system. The cells then were charged (i.e., the deuterium was forced into the palladium rods). The claim was that when a voltage then was applied, the heat generated was much larger than the energy input. Since the excess energy was calculated to be too large to originate from chemical reactions, only nuclear processes were left. Fleischmann and Pons claim that fusion of the deuterium nuclei occurs.

The achievement of thermonuclear fusion at room temperature would revolutionize energy production and distribution on a scale beyond anything in recent generations. This explains the amazement displayed by the scientific community on hearing of the so-called "cold fusion." Controlled thermonuclear fusion is an appealing long-term solution to the energy problem. However, there are exceptionally difficult obstacles between the present conventional controlled fusion development and the fabrication of fusion-power plants.

Nuclear fusion takes place when two deuterium nuclei combine to form helium, while releasing a neutron plus extra energy. Since deuterium can be extracted easily from ocean water, the fuel supply is essentially limitless. The problem is to overcome electric repulsion and force the two nuclei together. The kinetic energy required to accomplish that corresponds to a temperature of millions of degrees. In nature, such temperatures are found only in the centers of stars.

The ultra-high temperature required for fusion leads to most of the technical problems. At such temperatures matter is a highly ionized gas—a plasma, which somehow must be contained. Since solid walls vaporize, indirect methods are utilized: magnetic confinement or inertial confinement. Confining a hot plasma in a magnetic field has proved extremely difficult. Only recently has magnetic fusion come close to producing as much energy as it consumes in fuel. An alternative is inertial confinement, where the fusion material is imploded either with particle or laser beams. Either method involves huge, complicated devices which cost hundreds of millions of dollars to build and require large research groups to operate.

These factors explain the almost universal skepticism with which the cold-fusion claims were greeted. The reported experiments seemed so inexpensive and simple that many groups tried to repeat the experiments. Although a few groups initially claimed some positive results, the vast majority of experimenters worldwide observed no effects. Attempts to verify the Utah results were complicated by the fact that the scientists did not make public the details of the experimental setup.

In the normal deuterium-deuterium (DD) fusion process, the deuterium nuclei fuse and are transformed to helium 3 and neutrons. If DD fusion occurred, then at least a billion times more neutrons should have been detected to explain the heat reported. If neutrons are released, they later should be captured by hydrogen atoms and emit gamma rays in the process. The initial reported observation of gamma rays (and therefore of confirmation of neutron production in the Fleischmann-Pons cells) later was withdrawn.

Efforts to repeat the experiments at many laboratories have failed. A large group of scientists from the California Institute of Technology—including electrochemist Nathan Lewis, and nuclear physicists Charles Barnes and Steven Koonin—performed extensive studies and found no evidence to support cold fusion. The leading British scientific journal *Nature* refused to publish a paper by Fleischmann and Pons without more detailed information on their laboratory procedures. The English national laboratory at Harwell mounted a large concerted effort by a group of ten researchers. The Harwell group tried the experiments more than 100 different ways, found no significant results, and canceled future efforts. Many other scientists reached the same conclusions.

By coincidence, another university research group, led by Steven Jones of Brigham Young University, also in Utah, performed similar experiments independently of the University of Utah group. They claim to have observed neutrons with the correct energy to originate from DD fusion. However, the rate of production was many, many orders of magnitude below the rate inferred from the heat production reported by Fleischmann and Pons. The rate observed by Jones is so small that it has no potential value as an energy source, but is of appreciable scientific interest.

There seems to be no reasonable theoretical explanation for the Fleischmann-Pons results, but there are a number of theories which may explain Jones' results. A conference on cold fusion at Santa Fe, NM, found few supporters of either form of cold fusion. Special panels evaluating cold fusion will try to collate all of the available evidence in 1990.

High-Temperature Superconductors. Recent results in the field of high-temperature superconductivity have been alternately exciting and frustrating. New results with critical temperatures as high as 122°K (−151°C or −247°F; 0°K, or absolute zero, is the hypothetical temperature at which all motion ceases) have been reported, but the large-scale application of high-temperature superconductors still seems remote.

The phenomenon of superconductivity (the complete disappearance of electrical resistance) first was observed in 1911 when mercury was cooled below 4°K. If an electrical current is set flowing in a superconducting ring, years later the current still will be flowing. The technological possibilities were and are enormous. Practical applications depend on the temperature at which the material becomes superconducting, called the critical temperature.

Materials with a critical temperature of 23°K had been developed before 1973, and there the temperature stood for many years. The major breakthrough came in 1986, when Karl Alexander Muller and Johannes Georg Bednorz at IBM-Zurich found a compound of lanthanum, barium, and copper oxide that superconducted above 23°K. By 1988 the critical temperature was up to 122°K. Several classes of compounds were found to superconduct, including yttrium barium copper oxide (at 95°K), bismuth strontium calcium copper oxide (at 90°K), and thallium barium calcium copper oxide (at 122° K). These finds were exceptionally encouraging, since temperatures of 77°K can be achieved rather simply and inexpensively with liquid nitrogen.

However, properties other than a high critical temperature are required for the practical utilization of these materials. The most important of these additional properties is the critical current (the maximum current a superconductor can carry before it loses superconductivity). Superconductors with high critical temperatures appear to have very low critical currents. The most success has been obtained for thin films, where the current-carrying capacity is large enough for most electronics applications. However, large-scale applications require bulk materials, and the best bulk superconductors have much lower critical currents. There are suggestions that this is an intrinsic property of high-temperature superconductors.

Meanwhile, some researchers have received tantalizing glimpses of materials that superconduct at temperatures above 200°K, but report that they fail to stabilize. When the materials are allowed to heat up and subsequently are recooled, superconductivity fails to reappear. In October, J. T. Chen of Wayne State University in Detroit claimed to have stabilized materials that superconduct at 250°K, and continue to show superconductivity after several heating and cooling cycles.

Superconducting Super Collider. A site for the proposed U.S. Superconducting Super Collider (SSC) was chosen and the U.S. Congress approved the first construction money to start building it in 1990. The SSC will be the largest particle accelerator ever built, with a 50 mi (80 km) tunnel and countercirculating proton beams of 20 TeV each (1 TeV = 10^{12} electron volts). After years of evaluation and discussion and many proposals, the possible sites were reduced to seven. Then in November 1988, the site around Waxahachie, TX, some 25 mi (40 km) south of Dallas, became the official location of the proposed SSC.

Essentially all scientists agreed that the physics would be interesting, that the standard model of particle physics is incomplete (in that gravity has not been reconciled with the other three basic forces) and that the SSC might provide key answers—such as finding the Holy Grail of particle physics, the Higgs boson (a theoretical particle with zero spin). However, significant concern remains about the monetary impact the $6 billion project may have on other physics and science projects which also seek federal funds.

The technical requirements for the SSC are impressive. For example, there will be 8,000 superconducting dipole magnets (each 17 m or 55.8 ft long) and 1,600 quadrupoles to guide the two beams along their racetrack-shaped paths. The construction schedule depends in large measure on funding: The most optimistic timetable has the SSC operating by 1996.

Fundamental Particles. The universe appears to be composed of only three generations or families of fundamental particles. Such was the import of two October announcements one day apart by research groups at the Stanford Linear Accelerator Center in California and at the European Laboratory for Particle Physics on the border of France and Switzerland. Each generation of quarks and leptons is predicted to have its own neutrino species. The standard model does not forbid more than the three generations already observed. The recently measured lifetimes of the neutral Z° particle indicates that there are only three types of neutrinos in nature.

GARY MITCHELL
North Carolina State University

AP/Wide World

Poland's Premier Tadeusz Mazowiecki (right) *welcomed East German Communist Party leader Egon Krenz to Poland in November; soon thereafter Krenz resigned his post.*

POLAND

The year 1989 was one of epochal significance in the life of modern Poland, when the nation began a transition from Communist Party rule to pluralistic democracy, and from Marxist-Leninist socialism to free-market capitalism.

In a historic appearance before the U.S. Congress in November, Lech Walesa, the founder of Solidarity, the union credited with helping bring these major transitions about, called for strong support of the nation's new political leaders from Western nations. Walesa called for a plan similar to one installed by the United States in Europe following World War II, known as the Marshall Plan, that helped Western European economies to rebuild. "And now it is the moment when Eastern Europe awaits an investment of this kind," Walesa said.

Round Table Talks and Accord. Early in the year, faced with worsening economic and political conditions, some of the Communist Party leaders—conspicuously led by Gen. Wojciech Jaruzelski—moved toward recognition of the Solidarity movement. At a meeting held on January 17 by the Communist Party's Central Committee, Jaruzelski and Premier Mieczyslaw Rakowski threatened to resign if the party failed to approve their plan for legalizing Solidarity subject to various conditions. The conditions, never fully publicized at the time, were believed to involve agreement by Solidarity not to seek to overthrow the Communist system but rather realize some form of coexistence with it.

The first meeting between Solidarity and government representatives took place on January 27 in Magdalenka, a Warsaw suburb. They agreed to begin more substantive and more inclusive discussions on February 6. The talks included representatives of Solidarity, the Roman Catholic Church, the party, the government, the party-dominated trade unions, and several smaller official organizations.

While negotiations continued, riots and demonstrations broke out in Krakow in late February, organized by groups who viewed Solidarity's talks with the regime as betrayal. At least 35 policemen were injured and 24 students were arrested. Similar, though smaller, demonstrations occurred in Warsaw, Gdansk, and Bialystok. In a televised speech on February 25, Premier Rakowski warned that violence threatened the foundations of the Polish state and would be dealt with immediately.

By early March, agreement was reached on the new election format, the creation of a new legislative body (the Senate), and also a restructured presidency. The accord provided for open and competitive elections for only 35% of the 460 seats in the Sejm, or lower chamber of parliament. The remaining 65% of the seats were to be filled by Communists and adjunct party candidates (Peasants and Democrats) subject to the usual Communist Party approval of the candidates. On the other hand, the new legislative chamber, the Senate, would have 100 seats—all open to competitive elections. The 560 members of the two chambers sitting as a National Assembly were given the power of electing the president of Poland by a simple majority. Solidarity leaders and regime representatives signed an accord on April 5 pledging restoration of legal status to Solidarity and outlining the electoral plan; the accord also committed both sides to moving Poland in the direction of a market-oriented economy.

Communist Concessions and Elections. The first step in implementing the agreement was taken on April 17 when a Warsaw court legalized Solidarity as an "independent, self-governing trade union." On May 8, the first politically independent daily newspaper in the Communist bloc was allowed in Poland as Solidarity began the publication of its *Gazeta Wyborcza* (Electoral Gazette) in Warsaw. Legally unshackled, Solidarity began a spirited electoral campaign throughout the month of May with a great outpouring of grass-roots volunteers. The electoral efforts of the Communists seemed to be characterized by a combination of lethargy and despair.

In the first round of balloting on June 4, Solidarity won 92 of the 100 Senate seats and

160 of the 161 Sejm seats which it contested. In the runoff balloting on June 18, Solidarity swept all but one seat in the Senate, thus winning 260 out of a possible 261 seats in the two chambers for a percentage of 99.6. The Communist Party's defeat was even more far-reaching than Solidarity's success. Among 35 party leaders who ran unopposed on a so-called national list, 33 (94%) failed to receive the necessary approval of at least 50% of those voting. Among those who went down to embarrassing defeat were Premier Rakowksi, Interior Minister Czeslaw Kiszczak, and six other Politburo members.

The party configuration of the new Sejm was: Communists 173, Solidarity 161, Peasants 76, Democrats 27, and 23 seats held by so-called independent Catholics historically allied with the Communists.

The Communist Party's immediate response to its election defeat was a suggestion by Premier Rakowski of a grand coalition, including Solidarity, to rule Poland. Walesa, seeing a token role for his movement, promptly rejected this initiative.

Although many Solidarity activists had opposed General Jaruzelski, Walesa and other leaders believed that he, at once the legitimate Communist leader but now also a reformer, would be useful in the presidency to deflect resentment from within the Soviet bloc and from domestic hard-liners. Initially unwilling to run, Jaruzelski changed his mind and on July 19, the National Assembly elected him to a six-year term as president, by the barest minimum required. Jaruzelski got 270 out of 537 valid votes cast. Some 30 Communist hard-liners did not vote for him. Invalid ballots by Solidarity deputies were crucially helpful to Jaruzelski—the seven invalid votes added to the abstainers or the opposition would have defeated him. On taking the oath of office, Jaruzelski declared that he wanted to be a "president of reconciliation, a representative of all Poles." Gen. Czeslaw Kiszczak took over as prime minister on August 2.

On August 7, Walesa proposed the formation of a government led by Solidarity but including the Democrats and the United Peasant Party. On August 12, Solidarity called a one-hour strike in Gdansk with some 200,000 workers participating. The strike had economic and political objectives—higher pay and an end to party meddling in economic management, but also an end to "rule of the generals."

New Government. With the defection of their Peasant and Democratic Party allies in early August, the Communists were unable to form a government with the minimal parliamentary support required. General Kiszczak gave up his mission of trying to form a cabinet and tendered his resignation to President Jaruzelski on August 17. After some negotiations involving the candicacy of Walesa (who declined) and others, Jaruzelski offered the premiership to Tadeusz Mazowiecki (*see* BIOGRAPHY).

On August 24, Mazowiecki, a 62-year-old Solidarity leader, was elected premier by the Sejm. The Communists' 45-year monopoly on power was broken. The new prime minister agreed to give the Communists at least two very sensitive Cabinet portfolios, defense and interior. All in all, Solidarity had, in addition to the premier, 12 ministers supportive of it. The Communists had four ministers, the Peasant Party four, and the Democrats three.

On December 30 parliament repealed the constitutional provision vesting monopolistic power in the Communist (PZPR) Party. It also changed the country's name from Polish People's Commonwealth *(Polska Rzeczpospolita Ludowa)* to the old Polish Commonwealth *(Rzeczpospolita Polska)* and restored the pre-1939 crown eagle as the national emblem.

Another meeting of the party's Central Committee and its parliamentary representatives took place in Warsaw on July 27 in the wake of the electoral disaster and mounting economic failure. There was considerable acrimony. One party report blamed the party's defeat in the elections on its lack of preparation for competitive voting and the unexpected amount of help by the Church to Solidarity.

On July 29—within ten days of his election to the presidency of the republic—General Jaruzelski resigned as first secretary of the Communist Party. He also resigned from the Politburo and Central Committee in an apparent effort to distance himself in his new role from partisan associations. The Central Committee elected Mieczyslaw Rakowski, the outgoing premier, to replace Jaruzelski as party leader. Four of 18 Politburo members and five of nine party secretaries also were replaced.

Economy. Inflation, low productivity, shortages, strikes, and deficits characterized the economy throughout the year. While inflation was projected early in the year at about 60%, by mid-1989 it was more than 1,000%. On August 1 the government had increased the prices of many state-supplied products at a single stroke by large amounts, e.g., sugar by 66%, tobacco products by 83%. It also froze state price supports and allowed food producers to demand whatever the market would allow. Meat rationing, in effect for the past seven years, was abolished. Prices on many basic foods tripled and quadrupled within 24 hours on August 1. As the year wore on, empty store shelves and interminable queues increasingly plagued consumers. Labor unrest persisted.

On October 6, Mazowiecki's new Council of Ministers revealed its plan for restructuring Poland's economy. The plan called for privatization of business by sale or lease of state enterprises; reform of the banking system; new wage restraints designed to stifle inflation; making the zloty into a convertible currency and balancing the government budget; and an end to price controls, subsidies, rationing, and centralized planning. The proposal envisioned tight money, bankruptcies, and unemployment in consequence of implementing the free-market formula. It also proposed the introduction of unemployment insurance to cushion the shock of change for many workers. The introduction of the plan as a legislative program in parliament on December 17 provoked considerable opposition, especially among farmers fearing loss of government subsidies.

Church and State. The year produced some important accomplishments for the Catholic Church. It achieved institutional recognition in the political process with the inauguration of round-table talks in February. It achieved legal recognition by the regime in May, and in July it was strengthened by the establishment of diplomatic ties between Poland and the Vatican. In August one of its lay leaders, Tadeusz Mazowiecki, became prime minister of the first non-Communist government in Poland in 50 years.

The Church also became involved in prolonged international controversy when on July 15 an American rabbi and six students staged a protest on the grounds of a Carmelite convent in Auschwitz (Oswiecim). The protesters demanded the removal of the convent, which they saw as an offensive intrusion of Christian symbols in an area where some 2.5 million Jews—out of about 4 million total victims—were killed by the Nazis. On September 19 the Vatican announced that, in its view, the Auschwitz convent should be relocated, and it offered to help defray the expense. On September 21, Poland's Cardinal Josef Glemp agreed in principle to relocation. (*See also* RELIGION—*Judaism*.)

Other Developments. In early January, Minister of Defense Gen. Florian Siwicki announced that substantial reductions in the defense budget and sharply decreased manpower levels for Poland's nearly 400,000-strong army were being planned due to decreasing East-West tensions.

On March 7, the government announced that in its view the 1940 murder of Polish officers in Katyn—the bodies had been discovered by the Nazis in 1943—was committed by the Soviet secret police. This was a surprising disclosure on the part of a Communist regime which always had denied any Soviet wrongdoing in a crime that had become a *cause célèbre* of Polish postwar politics.

Among more important public observances in 1989 were the 50th anniversaries of the Nazi invasion of Poland on September 1, but also the more controversial Sept. 17, 1939, invasion by the Red Army, in which thousands of Poles were killed and deported.

Foreign Relations. In late April, Walesa traveled to Rome for a four-day visit. He saw Pope John Paul II at the Vatican and also promoted the cause of Western economic aid to Poland. He expressed strong support for Mikhail Gorbachev's policies of *glasnost* and *perestroika,* significantly linking Soviet reforms to the prospects of future developments in Poland.

In early July, President Bush visited Poland and received a warm official and public welcome in Warsaw. He addressed the Polish Parliament on July 9 and voiced approval and encouragement of Poland's democratic reforms. The president linked U.S. and Western economic aid to further political liberalization and free-market reforms on the part of the Poles. Walesa, who met the president amid cheering crowds in Gdansk on July 11, called for a $10 billion, three-year Western aid package to Poland. In late December a substantial Western aid program, with a $725 million loan, was being made available to Poland under the auspices of the International Monetary Fund.

In early July, relations between Poland and West Germany became somewhat strained. A proposed visit to Poland by West German Chancellor Helmut Kohl to commemorate—in symbolic reconciliation—the anniversary of the beginning of World War II was cancelled. Negotiations between the two countries on a financial aid package to Poland in exchange for some recognition of the German legacy and minority populations of Poland's western territory also collapsed. The Communist Party paper *Trybuna Ludu* denounced German Finance Minister Theo Waigel for calling Poland's frontiers on the Oder-Neisse line an "unresolved issue" in postwar Europe. Relations improved, however, in early November as Chancellor Kohl visited Warsaw and the old German territories. Kohl brought with him $1 billion in investment proposals. He also sought to reassure the Poles on the border question.

On July 17, Poland established diplomatic ties with the Vatican, thus becoming the first

POLAND • Information Highlights

Official Name: Polish Commonwealth.
Location: Eastern Europe.
Area: 120,726 sq mi (312 680 km²).
Population (mid-1989 est.): 38,200,000.
Chief Cities (Dec. 31, 1987 est.): Warsaw, the capital, 1,671,400; Lodz, 844,900; Krakow, 744,900.
Government: *Head of state,* Gen. Wojciech Jaruzelski, president (elected July 19, 1989). *Head of government,* Tadeusz Mazowiecki, premier (took office August 24, 1989). First secretary of the Polish United Workers' Party, Mieczyslaw Rakowski (elected July 29, 1989). *Legislature* (bicameral)—Sejm and Senate.
Monetary Unit: Zloty (502.55 zlotys equal U.S.$1, Dec. 31, 1988).
Gross National Product (1988 U.S.$): $276,300,000,000.
Economic Indexes (1988): *Consumer Prices* (1980 = 100), all items, 927.5; food, 988.9. *Industrial Production* (1980 = 100), 112.
Foreign Trade (1988 U.S.$): *Imports,* $12,159,000,000; *exports,* $13,959,000,000.

Communist state to be so recognized and connected. Polish-Soviet relations continued in a generally friendly, though somewhat cautious tone. On August 26, Premier Mazowiecki received an important Soviet guest, Vladimir Kryuchkov, head of the KGB. Soviet Foreign Minister Eduard Shevardnadze visited Warsaw in late October, as did the new East German Party leader, Egon Krenz.

On November 24, Premier Mazowiecki visited Moscow for talks with President Gorbachev and other Soviet officials on security and economic issues. Mazowiecki reiterated Poland's adherence to the Warsaw Pact, and Gorbachev emphasized cooperation with the new Polish regime. Following the Bush-Gorbachev summit in Malta in December, Prime Minister Mazowiecki and President Jaruzelski attended a Warsaw Pact summit in Moscow.

In November, Lech Walesa visited the United States and made a historic address before the U.S. Congress. During his visit Walesa was awarded the Presidential Medal of Freedom at the White House and was received enthusiastically on his tour of several U.S. cities. He continued his trip on to Latin America. (*See* page 6.)

ALEXANDER J. GROTH
University of California, Davis

POLAR RESEARCH

Antarctic. In December 1988, researchers from the State University of New York at Stony Brook confirmed that chemical reactions involving chlorine dominate the ozone-destruction process, which occurs in the Antarctic atmosphere each spring. At altitudes of 9 and 12 mi (14.5 and 19.3 km), chlorine-monoxide (ClO) concentrations increased. This compound forms as chlorine from chlorofluorocarbons (CFCs) breaks down atmospheric ozone and combines with the oxygen. (Oxygen, under normal circumstances, forms diatomic molecules of O_2. In the ultraviolet bombardment of the upper atmosphere it forms triatomic molecules of O_3, or ozone, which, in turn, shield the Earth from the majority of the harmful ultraviolet rays.)

In high concentrations chlorine monoxide continues to combine with itself until solar ultraviolet radiation breaks down the compound into its constituent oxygen and chlorine elements. As the ozone-destroying chlorine regenerates, it begins the process again. According to scientists, the only source of chlorine at these altitudes is man-made CFCs.

During October 1989, the amount of ozone in the atmosphere above Antarctica unexpectedly dropped to 50% below normal in some areas—similar to the situation in 1987, when ozone concentrations reached the lowest levels ever.

On Jan. 28, 1989, the Argentine ship *Bahia Paraíso*, carrying 81 tourists, struck a rock and sank near the United States' research station Palmer. Although no one was injured, 200,000 gallons (757 000 l) of fuel spilled into the protected harbor. The long-term effects of the accident on the local environment are unknown, but initially about 30,000 birds were exposed to the fuel. To learn about how fuel spills behave in cold environments, U.S., Argentine, and Chilean researchers are monitoring the site.

Representatives of the 25 Antarctic Treaty nations met in Paris, France, in October 1989 for their 15th annual meeting. They discussed measuring environmental impacts, improving environmental protection, expanding international cooperation, and evaluating the repercussions of tourism and nongovernment expeditions. Besides adopting 12 recommendations, they agreed to meet in 1990 to discuss the Wellington Convention, an accord signed by 33 nations in 1988 to limit the development of Antarctic mineral resources. France and Australia dropped out of the accord during 1989, claiming that the convention did not go far enough to sufficiently protect the environment.

Arctic. Researchers recorded a 3% decrease in the overall levels of ozone above the Arctic during the 1989 winter. Although chemicals similar to those in the Antarctic stratosphere were present, these occurred at altitudes of 14 to 16 mi (22.5 to 25.7 km) where ozone levels normally are low. As yet, researchers are unsure whether they saw the beginning of a partially formed ozone hole or a normal phenomenon in the Arctic atmosphere.

On March 24, 1989, the *Exxon Valdez* supertanker ran aground in Prince William Sound, AK, spilling more than 10 million gallons (38 million l) of crude oil and affecting 368 mi (592 km) of shoreline. To aid cleanup efforts, the Environmental Protection Agency seeded six beaches with two experimental formulas to encourage the growth of petroleum-eating bacteria. If successful, the treatment will help improve the condition of the beaches. (*See* feature article, page 36.)

In June, 25 scientists and engineers began a five-year project to drill an ice core from the Greenland Ice Sheet. Their goal is to drill to bedrock—about 10,000 feet (3 048 m) below the surface—to obtain a core that will contain 200,000 years of environmental data.

In May 1989 the U.S. National Science Foundation and the Soviet Academy of Sciences signed an agreement for scientific cooperation in Arctic research. During the first year, the two countries will exchange information and hold meetings on global biogeochemical cycles, permafrost, and climate change.

See also ENVIRONMENT.

WINIFRED REUNING
National Science Foundation

PORTUGAL

The Portuguese version of *perestroika,* or economic restructuring, could become a victim of its own success: While privatization reforms ultimately may reduce the public debt, they also could contribute to an overheated economy.

Politics and Government. On June 1 the parliament approved reforms which removed Marxist phraseology from the 1976 constitution. Prime Minister Aníbal Cavaco Silva's Social Democratic Party (PSD) and the Socialist Party spearheaded such modifications as altering the goal of creating "a classless society" to "trying to construct a free, just and united society." Significantly, the Portuguese constitution now permits denationalization of industries and the sale of majority stakes in state-owned enterprises.

Privatization. The state previously could sell only minority shares, as it did when it offered to sell 49% of the Unicer brewery in April and a like percentage of the Banco Totta e Acores in July. Alianca Seguradora and Tranquilidade, two insurance companies, were targeted next for privatization. The government announced its aim to create a strong core of native shareholders to keep important companies, especially financial institutions, under Portuguese control. Robust foreign demand—despite a 10% cap on foreign ownership—has fanned fears about "the country being up for sale."

Cavaco Silva maintained that his reprivatization program is vital to the economy's competitiveness and efficiency. Plans called for 80% of the capital generated by privatizations to be used to reduce public debt. The public deficit—which represents 75% of the gross domestic product (GDP)—not only absorbs money that otherwise would be available for investment but also fuels inflation by requiring high levels of liquid assets for government spending.

The PSD lost a seat in the European Parliament when it received 33% of the vote for Portuguese representation on the continental parliament, down 4.7% from 1987. The opposition treated the election as a national referendum on Portuguese tax and labor reforms. Voter turnout fell to a disconcerting low of 51%. The drop in voter support for the PSD continued in December municipal elections as the Socialist Party posted a victory, resulting in a reshuffling of Cavaco Silva's cabinet.

Economy. Cavaco Silva continued to regard his July 1987 electoral success as a mandate to restructure the economy and to reduce the role of the state through selling off publicly owned companies. However, structural faults in his program remained daunting, and the economy showed signs of overheating. Private consumption outpaced growth in industrial output by 2%, swelling Portugal's deficit to $5.7 billion in 1988, a record high. By April 1989 the annual inflation rate reached a three-year high of 13.2%.

In March, Finance Minister Miguel Cadilhe announced strict new credit controls to slash the current account deficit and to curb inflation by restraining wage growth, restricting consumption, and forcing up interest rates to curb credit demand.

Foreign investment doubled in 1988 and was expected to more than double again by the end of 1989. The high rate of investment in industry stimulated capital goods purchases from abroad. This, combined with the strong influx of imported consumer goods, hurt the trade balance.

The government estimated the growth of the gross domestic product (GDP) in 1988 reached 4.1% and the 1989 budget deficit was estimated to be just under 8% of GDP. The strong growth rate cut unemployment from 6.7% in the last quarter of 1988 to 4.9% in October 1989. It was not certain, however, that this relatively low level could be maintained. About 90% of the Portuguese manufacturing industry is either small- or medium-sized and finds it difficult to compete with larger foreign firms.

Foreign Affairs. U.S. Secretary of State James A. Baker III visited Portugal during his tour of North Atlantic Treaty Organization (NATO) capitals in February. Baker pledged expanded economic aid—from the $150 million in military and economic aid approved for fiscal 1989. This increase was a result of Cavaco Silva's consultations in 1988 on compensation for U.S. use of the military base in the Azores. Washington also agreed to supply Portugal with 20 F16 fighter bombers, Hawk missiles, and other military equipment. The aid package strengthened Portugal's role in the defense of the mid-Atlantic.

GEORGE W. GRAYSON
College of William & Mary

PORTUGAL • Information Highlights

Official Name: Portuguese Republic.
Location: Southwestern Europe.
Area: 35,552 sq mi (92 080 km²).
Population (mid-1989 est.): 10,400,000.
Chief Cities (1981 census): Lisbon, the capital, 807,937; Oporto, 327,368; Amadora, 95,518.
Government: *Head of state,* Alberto Mário Soares, president (took office March 1986). *Head of government,* Aníbal Cavaco Silva, prime minister (took office November 1985). *Legislature* (unicameral)—Assembly of the Republic.
Monetary Unit: Escudo (157.0 escudos equal U.S.$1, Oct. 24, 1989).
Gross Domestic Product (1987 U.S.$): $33,500,000,000.
Economic Indexes (1988): *Consumer Prices* (1980 = 100), all items, 380.5. *Industrial Production* (1980 = 100), 136.
Foreign Trade (1988 U.S.$): *Imports,* $15,855,000,000; *exports,* $10,526,000,000.

POSTAL SERVICE

Anthony M. Frank, with 20 months of service as U.S. postmaster general by the end of 1989, has been in office longer than any of his three immediate predecessors. When appointed, he agreed to serve at least three years, long enough to help develop new plans for the future of the United States Postal Service (USPS).

Considerable planning by his two immediate predecessors, Albert Casey and Preston R. Tisch, was disrupted when Congress put the USPS "on budget" in late 1987 and subject to the anti-deficit Gramm-Rudman Act. This was done in light of recent postal surpluses (five of the previous eight years). In addition, Congress forced cuts in service and capital expenditures and ordered large contributions by USPS to the federal pension system.

To recoup, the USPS obtained a general rate increase on April 3, 1988. This allowed the service to end fiscal year 1988 (year ending Sept. 30, 1988) with a deficit of $597 million, much less than anticipated. For fiscal year 1989, Frank set himself four goals: to modernize the service, to cut costs, to improve labor relations, and to bring the system back off-budget and free from congressional controls.

In the spring of 1989 the USPS Board of Governors approved the allocation of up to $5 billion for new or modified automation equipment. Under an integrated automation plan the service is committed to bar-coding nearly all mail by 1995. A joint industry-postal task force was exploring work-sharing between independent mailers and the USPS to hold down costs. In May, Frank said that $500 million would be pared from headquarters and other operating expenses. In September, 37 Management Sectional Centers were closed, eliminating more than 1,000 positions. Frequently visiting postal workers on the job, Frank has insisted that the traditionally autocratic postal system treat its workers with more respect. However, his considerable success at fostering better labor relations was sure to be tested during contract negotiations in the summer and fall of 1990.

Nevertheless, by the fall of 1989 the USPS was facing a serious financial situation. In August, Frank said that productivity had fallen and that mail volume had leveled off. During fiscal year 1989 volume rose only from 160 billion pieces to under 164 billion, equal to half or less of the growth during each of the previous five fiscal years. Instead of showing the considerable fiscal year 1989 profit predicted in early 1989, the service was expected barely to break even when the accounts were closed on September 30. (A final tally revealed the service to be only $60 million in the black.) Moreover, increasing labor and health-care costs, plus congressionally mandated antideficit contributions to the U.S. Treasury, led to USPS predictions that it would face a deficit of up to $1.9 billion at the end of fiscal year 1990. With this prospect in mind, Congress proposed in late 1989 to take the service off-budget again, but at the price of contributing $406 million more to further help reduce the deficit.

Other developments of note included the appointment of two women as assistant postmasters general. The cost of Express Mail was reduced and volume was up. Seeking more volume, the service was expanding its contract offices in retail stores and malls, though the postal unions have been opposing strongly such measures. Finally, the anticipated fiscal year 1990 deficit indicates the probability of another rate increase during 1991.

Canada. While the USPS was struggling to break even, Canada Post (CPC), a federal Crown corporation created in 1981, reported a $96 million profit for its fiscal year 1989 (ending March 31). This was the first time the CPC ended a fiscal year in the black since 1957 and represented an improvement over fiscal year 1988 of $134 million.

Stressing long-run development, the CPC was seeking a new corporate identity under the name of *Mail Poste* and launched a $2.5 billion capital investment program over the next five years. The current profit was based on a volume of 8.3 billion pieces generating revenue of $3.4 billion. The system has 61,000 full- and part-time employees. Its products and services are marketed through more than 15,000 outlets, half in local businesses. The basic letter rate, at 38 cents (Canadian), is the second lowest among Western industrialized nations, after the United States.

PAUL P. VAN RIPER
Texas A&M University

PRINCE EDWARD ISLAND

Major news from Prince Edward Island in 1989 centered on the provincial election victory of the Liberal Party, which won its second majority mandate, and the announced closing in 1991 of the Summerside Canadian air force base, one of the Island's principal economic sources.

Liberal Landslide. The Liberals under Premier Joe Ghiz scored a landslide reelection victory on May 29, taking 30 of 32 seats in the provincial legislature. The Conservatives, who won only two seats, had paid dearly for what voters regarded as the sins of their Tory brethren in the federal government in Ottawa. The closing of the Summerside military base, employing about 1,300 people and infusing $50 million annually into the community, was decreed in the federal Conservative government's April 27 budget and dominated the campaign.

Ghiz, who had called the vote just days after the shutdown was announced, gambled

PRINCE EDWARD ISLAND
• Information Highlights

Area: 2,185 sq mi (5 660 km^2).
Population (June 1989): 130,000.
Chief Cities (1986 census): Charlottetown, the capital, 15,776; Summerside, 8,020.
Government (1989): *Chief Officers*—lt. gov., Lloyd G. MacPhail; premier, Joe Ghiz (Liberal). *Legislature*—Legislative Assembly, 32 members.
Provincial Finances (1989–90 fiscal year budget): *Revenues,* $638,415,900; *expenditures,* $636,117,700.
Personal Income (average weekly earnings, June 1989): $390.19.
Labor Force (August 1989, seasonally adjusted): *Employed* workers, 15 years of age and over, 54,000; *Unemployed,* 14.1%.
Education (1989–90): *Enrollment*—elementary and secondary schools, 24,830 pupils; postsecondary—universities, 2,320; community colleges, 990.
(All monetary figures are in Canadian dollars.)

correctly that Islanders would show their displeasure at the polls. He came out of the election with more than 60% of the vote.

Earlier Ghiz had set the stage for a 1989 election. The Throne speech opening the legislature in February contained a number of offerings, including low-interest loans for buyers and builders of homes in rural areas and cash-flow help for farmers. Then, in a March budget presentation, the Liberals increased spending on everything from health care to highways, but held the line on taxes.

A week after the election, on June 6, the premier shuffled his 11-member cabinet. Three members of the previous cabinet—Energy Minister Allison Ellis, Education Minister Betty Jean Brown, and Fisheries Minister Johnny Young—were dropped. Four newcomers were brought in: Paul Connolly to the education portfolio; Barry Hicken, energy and forestry; Nancy Guptill, tourism; and Roberta Hubley, labor. Ghiz took over the justice portfolio from Wayne Cheverie, who moved to health and social services. In July, Ghiz announced that the provincial government was preparing to take the federal government to court over the Summerside base closure.

Northumberland Strait Bridge. The federal government named a six-member environmental panel in April to assess the proposed 9-mi (14-km) fixed link between Prince Edward Island and New Brunswick. The panel is chaired by David Barnes, Atlantic regional assessment director. Three proposals from private developers for a bridge across the Northumberland Strait had survived an earlier examination, carried out by the federal public works department; however, fishermen and environmental groups have continued to oppose the project.

Other News. The death knell of rail service on Prince Edward Island sounded in July when the National Transportation Agency in Ottawa approved an application by Canadian National Rail to abandon all its freight lines on the Island. Rail passenger service on the Island was discontinued some years ago.

The federal government is to build a C$24 million animal and plant health laboratory near Charlottetown. A $2.4 million expenditure to complete the design phase was announced in July.

JOHN BEST, *Canada World News*

PRISONS

The steady and considerable increases in the number of Americans imprisoned continued a decade-long trend. Death-penalty issues were deemed newsworthy and continued to clog the courts with complex legal questions. Challenges to the overcrowded prison system ranged from economic concerns to medical, chiefly AIDS-related, difficulties.

Prison Population Explosion. While many Americans believe the United States is one of the most lenient nations in the world in punishing offenders, current trends suggest that the United States has surpassed the Soviet Union and South Africa as the nation with the highest imprisonment rate in the world. The number of people in federal and state prisons as of June 1989 reached 673,000, up more than 7% over 1988, while those in local jails on any given day, serving sentences of less than one year or awaiting trial, exceeded 300,000. With more than 2.4 million citizens under supervisory probation and parole, the number of Americans restricted under criminal laws was more than 3.3 million in 1989, double the number in 1980 and almost three times the number in 1970.

There are no indications that this increase can be halted in the 1990s. A study issued by the U.S. Justice Department in April on prisoners released in a number of states indicated that within three years of release 60% of those inmates were arrested for another serious crime and that more than 40% already had been sent back to jail. Although the number of women being arrested over the past ten years has not risen significantly, the number being sentenced to prison continued a sharp upswing. A majority of these women, almost 85%, were single mothers of at least two children. Provisions for the children separated from their mothers are often nonexistent and at best haphazard and some experts worry that another generation of offenders may be in the making.

In 1989 officials continued to call for stiffer sentencing. President Bush's crime package proposed increasing the minimum sentence from five to ten years for anyone using an assault weapon to commit a crime. In August, William J. Bennett, President Bush's director of the war on drugs, called for an even more expanded role for imprisonment in combating drug usage. The Bush administration also called for $1 billion in new prison construction.

Loudoun County Sheriff John Isom stands outside his new modular jail in Leesburg, VA. The prefab jail is an example of the many innovative experiments U.S. penal experts are trying in an effort to alleviate overcrowding in the nation's jails.

AP/Wide World

Some critics, however, expressed doubts that the money would be available for such proposals as prison expansion and the war on drugs. At the state level, prison costs increased faster than any other sector of state budgets.

Meanwhile, the steady stream of inmates continued to jam prisons. In 1989, 42 states were under court orders to relieve overcrowding. In Pennsylvania, overcrowding was one cause cited for two days of riots in October at the State Correctional Institute at Camp Hill. More than 100 inmates, guards, and police were injured in the rioting and prison buildings were burned down. Prisoners at another overcrowded facility—the Hudson County Jail in Jersey City, NJ—rioted December 7 when an inmate was not allowed to attend his mother's funeral; one prisoner was killed and six guards were injured. To deal with overcrowding, officials at some locations were forced to release inmates early. Texas experimented with hiring a private company to jail some of the state's inmates. Other officials turned to alternative sentencing programs or electronic monitoring of at-home detainees.

Death Penalty. The number of inmates on death row reached another record high during 1989, exceeding 2,200. In June the U.S. Supreme Court ruled in three separate 5-4 decisions that the U.S. Constitution's ban on "cruel and unusual punishment" did not apply to the execution of juveniles or mentally retarded murderers. In the cases involving 16 and 17 year olds, Justice Antonin Scalia, writing for the majority, argued that there was "neither a historical nor a modern societal consensus" against capital punishment of juveniles, since of the 37 states having death-penalty laws, only 12 did not permit persons under 18 to be executed. Justice William J. Brennan, Jr., in a dissenting opinion, noted the 12 states barring capital punishment for those under 18 years old, added to the 14 states not having death penalties at all, constituted a majority of states opposed to executing juveniles. Besides, Brennan went on to object, the Bill of Rights was not subject to political issues.

Theodore Bundy, a self-confessed murderer of a number of young women, was executed in January at the Florida State Prison in Starke as hundreds of spectators demonstrated outside the prison walls. Many waved banners emblazoned with such slogans as "Burn, Bundy, Burn." In Louisiana, on the other hand, Gov. Buddy Roemer commuted the death sentence of Ronald Monroe to life in prison without parole or probation because of information turned up by a new set of lawyers that suggested to the governor that another man may have committed the crime. During the 1980s the Supreme Court in a series of decisions narrowed the range of technical grounds for appealing a death sentence and in a number of cases lawyers now are raising questions about their clients' guilt. (*See also* CRIME.)

AIDS Issues. Medical treatment of prisoners long has been a concern of officials, but the national increase in AIDS cases has posed particularly difficult legal as well as medical problems for guards and inmates in the nation's prisons. In New York, which has more AIDS cases than any other state, both prison officials and their critics were concerned about the quality of medical care, and with balancing the competing claims for confidentiality against a right to information on possible risks. A New York Bar Association report issued in September estimated that 15% of the thousands of prisoners who enter New York state and city correctional facilities are infected with the AIDS virus. Relatively few prison systems conduct mass screening for HIV antibodies, and no probation or parole system in the nation administers the tests. In a number of court cases not decided in 1989 individuals testing positive for the virus have insisted on a right to privacy, while other inmates and correctional staff sued for public disclosure.

DONALD GOODMAN
John Jay College of Criminal Justice

PRIZES AND AWARDS

NOBEL PRIZES[1]

Chemistry: Thomas R. Cech, University of Colorado; Sidney Altman, Yale University; for discovering that RNA can aid chemical reactions in cells, a discovery that has "potential to create a new defense against viral infections."

Economics: Trygve Haavelmo, University of Oslo (Norway), for his pioneering work in methods for testing economic theories, which led to modern economic forecasting methods.

Literature: Camilio José Cela, Spanish novelist, for his "rich and intensive prose, which . . . forms a challenging vision of man's vulnerability." (*See* page 324.)

Peace Prize: Dalai Lama, exiled religious and political leader of Tibet, for advocating "peaceful solutions based upon tolerance and mutual respect in order to preserve the historical and cultural heritage of his people." (*See* page 82.)

Physics: Norman F. Ramsey, Harvard University; Hans G. Dehmelt, University of Washington; Wolfgang Paul, University of Bonn, West Germany; for development of exact methods of measurement that make it possible to "conduct experiments that might force us to reconsider some basic physical laws."

Physiology or Medicine: Dr. J. Michael Bishop and Dr. Harold E. Varmus, University of California Medical School; for discovering a group of normal genes that can cause cancer if they undergo alterations.

[1] About $455,000 in each category.

ART

American Academy and Institute of Arts and Letters Awards
- Academy-Institute Awards ($5,000 ea.): art—Rackstraw Downes, Willy Heeks, Henrietta Mantooth, Joseph Santore, Helen Miranda Wilson; music—John P. Corigliano, Michael Gandolfi, Karel Husa, Shulamit Ran
- Award for Distinguished Service to the Arts: Vartan Gregorian
- Arnold W. Brunner Memorial Prize in Architecture: Richard Rogers
- Gold Medal for Sculpture: Louise Bourgeois
- Walter Hinrichson Award: Ursula Mamlok
- Charles Ives Fellowship ($10,000): Susan Harding
- Charles Ives Scholarships ($5,000 ea.): Mark D. Johnson, John P. Russo, Michael Ruszczynski, Suzanne G. Sheppard, Augusta Read Thomas, Carolyn A. Yarnell
- Goddard Lieberson Fellowships ($10,000): Lori E. Dobbins, Steven Mackey
- Louise Nevelson Award in Art: Anne Arnold
- Richard and Hinda Rosenthal Foundation Award ($5,000): Michael Tompkins

Capezio Dance Award ($5,000): Edward Villella

Grawemeyer Award for musical composition ($150,000): Chinary Ung, *Inner Voices*

John F. Kennedy Center Honors for career achievement in the performing arts: Harry Belafonte, Claudette Colbert, Alexandra Danilova, Mary Martin, William Schuman

Edward MacDowell Medal: Stan Brakhage

National Academy of Recording Arts and Sciences Grammy Awards for excellence in phonograph records
- Album of the year: *Faith,* George Michael
- Classical album: *Requiem and Operatic Choruses,* Verdi; Robert Shaw conducting Atlanta Symphony Orchestra
- Country music song: *Hold Me,* K.T. Oslin
- Jazz vocal performance: (female) *Look What I Got,* Betty Carter; (male) *Brothers,* Bobby McFerrin
- New artist: Tracy Chapman
- Record of the year: *Don't Worry, Be Happy,* Bobby McFerrin
- Song of the year: *Don't Worry, Be Happy,* Bobby McFerrin

National Medal of Arts: Leopold Adler, The Dayton-Hudson Corporation, Katherine Dunham, Alfred Eisenstaedt, Martin Friedman, Leigh Gerdine, Dizzy Gillespie, Walker Kirkland Hancock, Vladimir Horowitz (posthumous), Czeslaw Milosz, Robert Motherwell, John Updike

Praemium Imperiale for lifetime achievement in the arts ($100,000 ea): Pierre Boulez (music), Marcel Carne (theater and film), David Hockney and Willem de Kooning (painting), Umberto Mastroianni (sculpture), I. M. Pei (architecture)

Pritzker Architecture Prize ($100,000): Frank O. Gehry

Pulitzer Prize for Music: Roger Reynolds, *Whispers Out of Time*

William Schuman Award for lifetime achievement in American musical composition ($50,000): Gunther Schuller

Samuel H. Scripps/American Dance Festival Award ($25,000): establishment of a fellowship in memory of Doris Humphrey, Charles Weidman, and José Limon

JOURNALISM

Maria Moors Cabot Prizes ($1,000 ea.): Felipe Lopez Caballero, editor and publisher, *Semana,* Bogota, Colombia; Humberto Rubin Schvartzman, director, Radio Nanduti, Asunción, Paraguay; Juan Vasquez, correspondent, CBS News, Miami, FL; Arturo Villar, publisher, *Vista,* Coral Gables, FL

National Magazine Awards
- Design: *Rolling Stone*
- Essays and criticism: *Harper's*
- Feature writing: *Esquire*
- Fiction: *The New Yorker*
- General excellence: *Sports Illustrated, Vanity Fair, American Heritage, The Sciences*
- Personal service: *Good Housekeeping*
- Photography: *National Geographic*
- Public-interest: *California*
- Reporting: *The New Yorker*
- Single-topic issue: *Hippocrates*
- Special-interest: *Traveler* (Condé Nast)

Overseas Press Club Awards
- Book on foreign affairs: Whitman Bassow, *The Moscow Correspondents: Reporting from the Revolution to Glasnost*
- Business or economic news reporting from abroad: (magazines)—John Curran, *Fortune,* "Tokyo's Stock Market: Stronger Than You Think"; (newspapers and wire services)—Philip Revzin, *The Wall Street Journal,* for articles on the European Common Market
- Cartoon on foreign affairs: Jim Morin, *The Miami Herald,* "Editorial Cartoons"
- Daily newspaper or wire-service interpretation on foreign affairs: Barry Newman, *The Wall Street Journal,* for articles on the Soviet Union and Eastern Europe
- Daily newspaper or wire-service reporting from abroad: The Associated Press Moscow Bureau correspondents, "Armenian Earthquake"
- Magazine article on foreign affairs: Karsten Prager, Murray J. Gart, Johanna McGeary, Michael Kramer, and Ed Magnuson, writers, and Dean Fischer and B. William Mader, reporters, *Time,* "Knowing the Enemy and Breakthrough"
- Magazine reporting from abroad: Richard M. Smith and *Newsweek* team, *Newsweek,* "His Game Plan: A Talk with Gorbachev"
- Photographic reporting from abroad: (magazines and books)—Maggie Steber, *U.S. News & World Report,* "Touching the Heart of the Matter"; (newspapers and wire services)—Boris Yurchenko, The Associated Press, "Armenia's Earthquake"
- Print reporting or interpretation by a foreign correspondent in the United States for publication abroad: Alex Brummer, *The Guardian* (London and Manchester), "Analytical Insights into American Politics"
- Radio interpretation of foreign affairs: Alex Chadwick, National Public Radio, "The New Vietnam"
- Radio spot-news reporting from abroad: David Ben-Arieah, WCBS News, AM Radio, "The Crash of Pan Am Flight 103"
- Television interpretation or documentary on foreign affairs: Ted Koppel and Richard Kaplan, *ABC Nightline,* "In the Holy Land"
- Television spot-news reporting from abroad: Dan Rather, Charles Kuralt, and Tom Bettag, *CBS Evening News with Dan Rather,* "Inside the Kremlin"
- Eric and Amy Burger Award (for best entry dealing with human rights): Colin Campbell and Deborah Scroggins, *Atlanta Journal and Constitution,* "The Famine Weapon in the Horn of Africa"
- Robert Capa Gold Medal (photographic reporting from abroad requiring exceptional courage and enterprise): Chris Steele-Perkins, *Time,* "Graveside Terror"
- Madeline Dane Ross Award (for foreign correspondent showing concern for the human condition): Harry Benson and Civia Tamarkin, *People,* "Celia Goldie: Dealing with the Aged, a Worldwide Problem"

George Polk Memorial Awards
- Career award: William Shawn, *The New Yorker*
- Cultural reporting: Lawrence Wechsler, *Shapinsky's Karma, Boggs's Bills* (essays)
- Economic reporting: Donald L. Barlett and James B. Steele, *The Philadelphia Inquirer*
- Environmental reporting: Mary Bishop, *Roanoke Times and World-News* (VA)
- Financial reporting: *National Thrift News*
- Foreign reporting: John Kifner, *The New York Times*
- Local reporting: David Gomez and Patricia Guthrie, *The Albuquerque Tribune* (NM)
- Local-television reporting: KING-TV, Seattle, WA
- National reporting: Keith Schneider, *The New York Times*
- Network television reporting: Brian Ross, correspondent, and Ira Silverman, producer, NBC News
- Photojournalism: Mary Ellen Mark, for still photographs of Seattle street children
- Radio reporting: Patricia Neighmond, National Public Radio

Pulitzer Prizes
- Commentary: Clarence Page, *Chicago Tribune*
- Criticism: Michael Skube, *The News and Observer* (Raleigh, NC)
- Editorial cartooning: Jack Higgins, *Chicago Sun-Times*
- Editorial writing: Lois Wille, *Chicago Tribune*
- Explanatory journalism: David Hanners, William Snyder, Karen Blessen, *The Dallas Morning News*
- Feature photography: Manny Crisostomo, *Detroit Free Press*
- Feature writing: David Zucchino, *The Philadelphia Inquirer*
- General-news reporting: *The* (Louisville) *Courier-Journal* staff
- International reporting (shared): Glenn Frankel, *The Washington Post;* Bill Keller, *The New York Times*
- Investigative reporting: Bill Dedman, *Atlanta Journal and Constitution*
- National reporting: Donald L. Barlett and James B. Steele, *The Philadelphia Inquirer*
- Public service: *Anchorage Daily News*
- Specialized reporting: Edward Humes, *The Orange County Register* (CA)
- Spot news photography: Ron Olshwanger, free-lance photographer, *St. Louis Post-Dispatch*

LITERATURE

American Academy and Institute of Arts and Letters Awards
- Academy-Institute Awards ($5,000 ea.): Richard Ford, Martin Greenberg, Ron Hansen, Herbert Morris, Gregory Rabassa, David R. Slavitt, Arturo Vivante, Joy Williams
- The American Academy in Rome Fellowship in Literature: Bob Shacochis
- Award of Merit Medal for Short Story: Doris Betts
- Michael Braude Award for Light Verse: X.J. Kennedy
- Witter Bynner Prize for Poetry ($1,500): Mary Jo Salter
- E.M. Forster Award: A.N. Wilson
- Gold Medal for Fiction: Isaac Bashevis Singer
- Sue Kaufman Prize for First Fiction ($2,500): Gary Krist
- Richard and Hinda Rosenthal Foundation Award ($5,000): James Robison
- Jean Stein Award ($5,000): Rodney Jones
- Harold D. Vursell Memorial Award ($5,000): Oliver Sacks
- Morton Dauwen Zabel Award ($2,500): C.K. Williams

Bancroft Prizes ($4,000 ea.): Eric Foner, *Reconstruction: America's Unfinished Revolution 1863–1877;* Edmund S. Morgan, *Inventing the People: The Rise of Popular Sovereignty in England and America*

Bollingen Prize in Poetry ($10,000): Edgar Bowers

Canada's Governor-General Literary Awards ($10,000 ea.):
- English-language awards
  - Drama—George F. Walker, *Nothing Sacred*
  - Fiction—David Adams Richards, *Nights Below Station Street*
  - Nonfiction—Anne Collins, *In the Sleep Room*
  - Poetry—Erin Mouré, *Furious*
- French-language awards
  - Drama—Jean Marc Dalpé, *Le Chien*
  - Fiction—Jacques Folch-Ribas, *Le Silence ou le Parfait Bonheur*
  - Nonfiction—Patricia Smart, *Écrire dans la maison du père*
  - Poetry—Marcel Labine, *Papiers d'épidémie*

International Fiction Prize ($54,000): Don DeLillo, *Libra*

Jerusalem Prize: Ernesto Sabato

Ruth Lilly Poetry Prize ($25,000): Mona Van Duyn

Mystery Writers of America/Edgar Allan Poe Awards
- Novel: Stuart M. Kaminsky, *A Cold Red Sunrise*
- Critical/biographical work: Francis M. Nevins, Jr., *Cornell Woolrich: First You Dream, Then You Die*
- Award for lifetime achievement: Joan Kahn

National Book Awards ($10,000 ea.):
- Fiction: John Casey, *Spartina*
- Nonfiction: Thomas L. Friedman, *From Beirut to Jerusalem*

National Book Critics Circle Awards
- Biography/autobiography: Richard Ellmann, *Oscar Wilde* (posthumous)
- Criticism: Clifford Geertz, *Works and Lives: The Anthropologist as Author*
- Fiction: Bharati Mukherjee, *The Middleman and Other Stories*
- Nonfiction: Taylor Branch, *Parting the Waters: America in the King Years, 1954–1963*
- Poetry: Donald Hall, *The One Day*

PEN/Faulkner Award ($7,500): James Salter, *Dusk and Other Stories*

Pulitzer Prizes
- Biography: Richard Ellmann, *Oscar Wilde* (posthumous)
- Fiction: Anne Tyler, *Breathing Lessons*
- General nonfiction: Neil Sheehan, *A Bright Shining Lie: John Paul Vann and America in Vietnam*
- History: Taylor Branch, *Parting the Waters: America in the King Years, 1954–1963;* James M. McPherson, *Battle Cry of Freedom: The Civil War Era*
- Poetry: Richard Wilbur, *New and Collected Poems*

Rea Award for the Short Story ($25,000): Tobias Wolff

MOTION PICTURES

Academy of Motion Picture Arts and Sciences ("Oscar") Awards
- Actor—leading: Dustin Hoffman, *Rain Man*
- Actor—supporting: Kevin Kline, *A Fish Called Wanda*
- Actress—leading: Jodie Foster, *The Accused*
- Actress—supporting: Geena Davis, *The Accidental Tourist*
- Cinematography: Peter Biziou, *Mississippi Burning*
- Costume design: James Acheson, *Dangerous Liaisons*
- Director: Barry Levinson, *Rain Man*
- Film: *Rain Man*
- Foreign-language film: *Pelle the Conqueror* (Denmark)
- Music—original score: David Grusin, *The Milagro Beanfield War*
- Music—original song: Carly Simon, *Let the River Run* (from *Working Girl*)
- Screenplay—original: Ronald Bass and Barry Morrow, *Rain Man*
- Screenplay—adaptation: Christopher Hampton, *Dangerous Liaisons*

American Film Institute's Life Achievement Award: David Lean

Cannes Film Festival Awards
- Golden Palm Award (best film): Steven Soderbergh, *sex, lies, and videotape* (United States)
- Special Grand Jury Prize (shared): Bertrand Blier, *Trop Belle Pour Toi* (Too Beautiful for You) (France); Giuseppe Tornatore, *New Cinema Paradise* (Italy)
- Best actor: James Spader, *sex, lies, and videotape*
- Best actress: Meryl Streep, *Cry in the Dark* (United States)
- Best director: Emir Kusturica, *Time of the Gypsies* (Yugoslavia)

National Society of Film Critics Awards
- Film: *The Unbearable Lightness of Being*
- Actor: Michael Keaton, *Beetlejuice* and *Clean and Sober*
- Actress: Judy Davis, *High Tide*
- Director: Philip Kaufman, *The Unbearable Lightness of Being*

PUBLIC SERVICE

Charles A. Dana Foundation Awards for pioneering achievements in health and higher education ($50,000 ea.): Susan P. Baker; Herbert L. Needleman; Colton Johnson and Janet Lieberman (shared); lifetime achievement awards: Franklin D. Murphy; Benno C. Schmidt, Sr.

General Foods World Food Prize ($200,000): Verghese Kurien, National Dairy Development Board, India

American Institute for Public Service Jefferson Awards
National Awards ($5,000 ea.): Marc Buoniconti, Leo Cherne, Kimi Gray, Paul H. Nitze

Philadelphia Liberty Medal ($100,000): Lech Walesa

Templeton Prize for Progress in Religion ($435,000 shared): Very Rev. Lord MacLeod, minister of the Church of Scotland and founder of the Iona Community; Professor Carl Friedrich Freiherr von Weizsaecker, nuclear physicist and philosopher

Harry S. Truman Public Service Award: Clara Hale

U.S. Presidential Citizens Medal: Robert Dole, Robert H. Michel, Strom Thurmond

U.S. Presidential Medal of Freedom (awarded by President Ronald Reagan on Jan. 19, 1989): Michael Mansfield, George P. Shultz; (awarded by President George Bush on July 6, 1989): Lucille Ball (posthumously), C. Douglas Dillon, James Doolittle, George Kennan, Margaret Chase Smith; (awarded by President George Bush on November 13, 1989): Lech Walesa

U.S. President's Award for Distinguished Federal Civilian Service: Frank Cavanaugh

SCIENCE

Bristol-Myers Award for distinguished achievement in cancer research ($50,000): Peter Vogt, University of Southern California

Enrico Fermi Award ($100,000 ea.): Richard B. Setlow, Brookhaven National Laboratory; Victor F. Weisskopf, Massachusetts Institute of Technology

General Motors Cancer Research Foundation Awards ($130,000 ea.): Mortimer Elkind, Colorado State University; Peter Nowell, University of Pennsylvania School of Medicine, and Janet Rowley, University of Chicago (shared); Donald Metcalf, Walter and Eliza Hall Institute of Medical Research, Australia, and Leo Sachs, Weizmann Institute of Science, Rehovot, Israel (shared)

Louisa Gross Horwitz Prize for research in biology or biochemistry ($22,000 shared); Alfred G. Gilman, University of Texas Southwestern Medical Center at Dallas; Edwin G. Krebs, Howard Hughes Medical Institute and University of Washington

Albert Lasker Medical Research Awards ($15,000 ea.): Etienne-Emile Baulieu, France; Michael J. Berridge, Trinity College, Cambridge, England; Alfred G. Gilman, University of Texas Southwestern Medical Center; Edwin G. Krebs, Howard Hughes Medical Institute, University of Washington School of Medicine; Yasutomi Nishizuka, Kobe University School of Medicine, Japan

TELEVISION AND RADIO

Academy of Television Arts and Sciences ("Emmy") Awards
Actor—comedy series: Richard Mulligan, *Empty Nest* (NBC)
Actor—drama series: Carroll O'Connor, *In the Heat of the Night* (NBC)
Actor—miniseries or a special: James Woods, "My Name Is Bill W.," *Hallmark Hall of Fame* (ABC)
Actress—comedy series: Candice Bergen, *Murphy Brown* (CBS)
Actress—drama series: Dana Delany, *China Beach* (ABC)
Actress—miniseries or a special: Holly Hunter, *Roe vs. Wade* (NBC)
Animated program: *Garfield: Babes and Bullets* (CBS)
Cinematography—miniseries or a special: Gayne Rescher, *Shooter* (NBC)
Cinematography—series: Roy H. Wagner, *Quantum Leap* (NBC)
Comedy series: *Cheers* (NBC)
Directing—comedy series: Peter Baldwin, "Our Miss White," *The Wonder Years* (ABC)
Directing—drama series: Robert Altman, "The Boiler Room," *Tanner '88* (HBO)
Directing—miniseries or a special: Simon Wincer, *Lonesome Dove* (CBS)
Directing—variety or music program: Jim Henson, "Dog City," *The Jim Henson Hour* (NBC)
Drama series: *L.A. Law* (NBC)
Drama/comedy special (tie): "Day One," *AT&T Presents* (CBS); *Roe vs. Wade* (NBC)
Miniseries: *War and Remembrance* (ABC)
Supporting actor—comedy series: Woody Harrelson, *Cheers* (NBC)
Supporting actor—drama series: Larry Drake, *L.A. Law* (NBC)
Supporting actor—miniseries or a special: Derek Jacobi, "The Tenth Man," *Hallmark Hall of Fame* (CBS)
Supporting actress—comedy series: Rhea Perlman, *Cheers* (NBC)
Supporting actress—drama series: Melanie Mayron, *thirtysomething* (ABC)
Supporting actress—miniseries or a special: Colleen Dewhurst, *Those She Left Behind* (NBC)
Variety, music, or comedy program: *The Tracy Ullman Show* (Fox)

George Foster Peabody Awards
Radio: WHAS Radio, Louisville, KY, *A Matter of Time: The Crisis in Kentucky Corrections;* WBUR Radio, Boston, *Speaking for Everyman: Ian McKellen Celebrates Shakespeare's Birthday;* KMOX Radio, St. Louis, MO, *Hate Crimes: America's Cancer;* National Public Radio, Washington, DC, *Cowboys on Everest;* The BBC World Service for Africa, London, *Nothing Political/Mandela at 70;* KTAR Radio, Phoenix, AZ, *The Impeachment of Evan Mecham*
Television: WPLG-TV, Miami, *Caution: Precious Cargo;* MacNeil/Lehrer Productions, New York, *The MacNeil/Lehrer Newshour: Election '88 Coverage;* Frontline, Boston, *Frontline: The Choice;* CBS News, New York, *48 Hours,* "Abortion Battle" and "On Runaway Street"; KCBS-TV, Los Angeles, *MCA and the Mob;* CBS Entertainment and Telecom Entertainment in association with Yorkshire Television, *The Attic: The Hiding of Anne Frank;* The BBC, London, and WNET/13, New York, *The Singing Detective;* NBC-TV, New York, *The Murder of Mary Phagan;* ABC Television, New York, and the Bedford Falls Company in association with MGM/UA Television, *thirtysomething;* The Children's Television Workshop, New York, *3-2-1 CONTACT Extra: I Have AIDS, A Teenager's Story;* The South Carolina ETV Network, Columbia, SC, *Children's Express NEWSMAGAZINE: Campaign '88;* The Christian Science Monitor Reports, New York, *Islam in Turmoil;* WTTW, Chicago, in association with Chloe Productions, Inc., *. . . And the Pursuit of Happiness;* HBO, New York, *Dear America: Letters Home From Vietnam;* HBO, New York, in association with Pro Image Productions, *Suzi's Story;* WBRZ-TV, Baton Rouge, LA, *The Best Insurance Commissioner Money Can Buy;* Turner Network Television, Atlanta, *The Making of a Legend: Gone With the Wind;* CBS News, *60 Minutes,* "Mr. Snow Goes to Washington"; WJLA-TV, Washington, DC, *The Radon Watch Campaign;* Public Affairs Television, New York, *Bill Moyers' World of Ideas*

THEATER

Susan Smith Blackburn Prize ($5,000): Wendy Wasserstein, *The Heidi Chronicles;* runner-up ($1,000): Timberlake Wertenbaker, *Our Country's Good*

New York Drama Critics Circle Awards
Best new play ($1,000): *The Heidi Chronicles,* by Wendy Wasserstein
Best foreign play: *Aristocrats,* by Brian Friel
Special citation: *Largely New York,* by Bill Irwin

Antoinette Perry ("Tony") Awards
Actor—play: Philip Bosco, *Lend Me a Tenor*
Actor—musical: Jason Alexander, *Jerome Robbins' Broadway*
Actress—play: Pauline Collins, *Shirley Valentine*
Actress—musical: Ruth Brown, *Black and Blue*
Choreography: Cholly Atkins, Henry LeTang, Frankie Manning, and Fayard Nicholas, *Black and Blue*
Director—play: Jerry Zaks, *Lend Me a Tenor*
Director—musical: Jerome Robbins, *Jerome Robbins' Broadway*
Featured actor—play: Boyd Gaines, *The Heidi Chronicles*
Featured actor—musical: Scott Wise, *Jerome Robbins' Broadway*
Featured actress—play: Christine Baranski, *Rumors*
Featured actress—musical: Debbie Shapiro, *Jerome Robbins' Broadway*
Musical: *Jerome Robbins' Broadway*
Play: *The Heidi Chronicles*

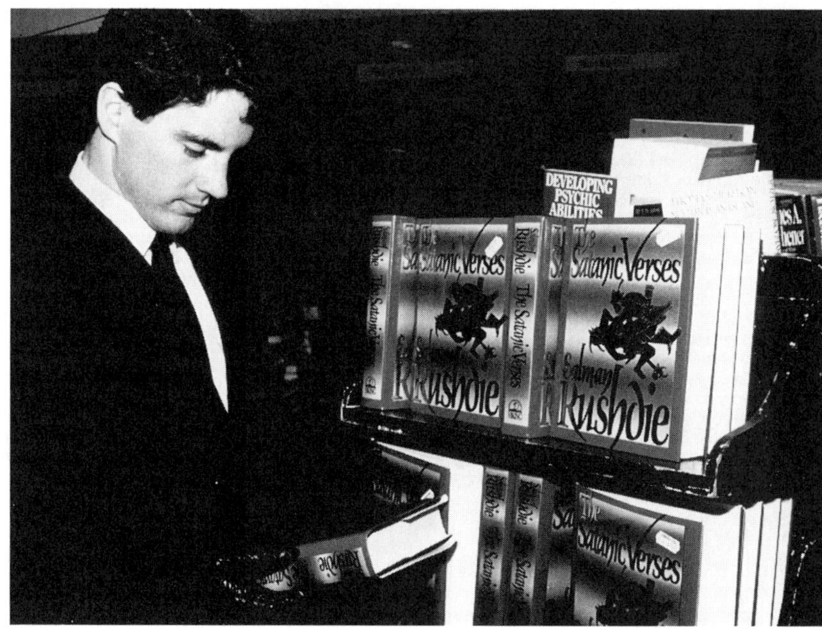

The controversy over the condemnation of Indian-born British author Salman Rushdie by Iran's Ayatollah Khomeini led Rushdie's novel "The Satanic Verses" to the best-sellers list.

©N. Berman/Sipa

PUBLISHING

After some disappointments during late 1988, many U.S. publishers approached 1989 with lowered expectations. As the year progressed, some economic bright spots appeared, especially in the magazine industry. Controversies concerning Salman Rushdie's best-selling book, *The Satanic Verses,* drew an unusual amount of public attention to publishing. The attempted hostile takeover of Time, Inc., and Time's subsequent merger with Warner Communications also drew widespread publicity. Finally, legal issues caused much concern within the industry, especially with a new configuration on the U.S. Supreme Court.

Books. For 1989, the U.S. Commerce Department predicted a rather modest increase in total U.S. sales to $14 billion. Final 1988 figures from the Association of American Publishers (AAP) indicated that sales reached $13.2 billion, an increase of 8.5% from 1987. Trade publishing showed an especially strong 11.9% gain from 1987. Output of book titles in 1988 declined 1% from 1987, to about 55,500. During 1988, U.S. book exports sharply exceeded imports for the first time in recent years.

In early 1989 the U.S. industry reacted sharply to a death threat from Iranian leader Ayatollah Ruhollah Khomeini against Rushdie, whose *The Satanic Verses* offended many Muslims. In February, Khomeini called on his followers to kill the author and publishers of the book. The AAP urged governments around the world to condemn the threat and to ensure that it was not carried out. Waldenbooks, the largest U.S. bookseller, briefly removed the novel from the shelves of its stores, but continued to sell it. Rushdie went into hiding, and bookstores that carried the work were bombed in Berkeley, CA, and elsewhere around the world. Evidently because of the controversy and not its literary merit, *The Satanic Verses* became a top seller. It spent almost six months on the *Publishers Weekly* list of 15 best-selling fiction hardcover titles, before falling off the list in August as the controversy faded. Despite Khomeini's death in June, Rushdie remained in hiding, and protests continued in some Muslim communities.

The rapid pace of mergers and acquisitions continued in 1989. In January, Rupert Murdoch's News International gained control of the British firm of William Collins, with which it had co-owned a U.S. company, Harper & Row. The worldwide book operations of Collins, Harper & Row, and News International then were combined into what could become the world's leading publisher of English-language books. A book publishing company of international significance also resulted from Time, Inc.'s merger with Warner Communications. Time Warner, Inc., combined Little, Brown & Co. with Warner Books to create Time Warner Trade Publishing. And in September, British publishing magnate Robert Maxwell's Macmillan, Inc. acquired Merrill, a major U.S. textbook publisher, from Bell & Howell for $260 million.

Magazines. The U.S. magazine industry opened 1989 with a mixed outlook. The pretax 1988 operating profits for 167 consumer magazines included in a Magazine Publishers of America (MPA)/Price Waterhouse annual survey averaged 12.4% of revenues, down from the record 13.5% for 1987. The decline reflected increases in paper costs and postal rates, and it followed several years of profit growth. Advertisers were concerned over a projection that industry ad rates would rise an average of 6.5% during 1989, in response to the increased costs. Nonetheless, the magazine industry appeared healthy. During the first three months of 1989, total magazine revenues increased 13% from the same period in 1988, according to Leading National Advertisers/Arbitron. Consumer ad revenues for 166 consumer titles were 12.4% greater during the first half of 1989 than during the same period in 1988. This is much larger than the increase registered in comparing the first half of 1988 with the same period in 1987. The number of advertising pages also increased 4.4% in the first six months of 1989, compared to the same months the previous year, according to the Publishers Information Bureau. In addition, the costs of the coated paper used by many magazines stopped increasing by late 1988 and remained generally steady through the first three quarters of 1989.

Modern Maturity, received by members of the American Association of Retired Persons, boosted its top-ranked circulation to about 20.3 million during the first half of 1989, a 13.3% increase from the same months in 1988. *Reader's Digest* and *TV Guide,* second and third with circulations of about 16.4 million each, lost between 3 and 4% of their total, however.

Observers viewed the Time, Inc., purchase of Warner Communications as an attempt to make it impossible for Paramount Communications, another media conglomerate, to acquire Time via a hostile takeover. In addition to its namesake, Time publishes *Sports Illustrated,* numerous other magazines, and Time-Life Books. In July the company completed its offer to purchase Warner after the Delaware Supreme Court upheld a lower court's rebuff of a hostile bid from Paramount for Time, Inc. Following the merger, Time Warner Inc. was expected to have estimated annual revenues of $10 billion, making it the largest communications conglomerate in the world. Time's Southern Progress Corp. also acquired *Southern Magazine,* a regional general interest title, during 1989. Finally, The Reader's Digest Association, a major magazine and book publisher, announced a public sale of nonvoting stock for the first time. The company long has been one of the last privately held media companies. Observers said the sales would discourage hostile takeover attempts.

The influence of new technology became increasingly apparent during late 1988 and into 1989. The December 1988 issue of *National Geographic,* ranked fourth in total circulation, included the most-ambitious hologram ever published in a large magazine. To celebrate its centennial, the magazine's cover featured a double-laser image of the Earth. Desktop publishing also continued to become an increasingly standard part of the industry.

Legal issues concerned many magazine publishers during 1989. Of special interest was a three-judge U.S. Court of Appeals panel decision to overturn a $9.4 million judgment against *Soldier of Fortune* magazine. A Houston jury had found the magazine liable for negligence after it carried what the appeals panel evidently saw as an ambiguously worded classified advertisement. A man responding to the ad hired the advertiser to kill his wife. The victim's mother and son sued, claiming the magazine was responsible for the murder. The magazine industry applauded the appeals court decision, which appeared to foreclose an appeal to the U.S. Supreme Court. Elsewhere, the industry faced the possibility of additional restriction and even an ultimate ban on advertisements for tobacco products. Bills were introduced in the U.S. Congress to limit tobacco advertising that could be seen or heard by children and to prohibit tobacco ads that contain human likenesses, models, or slogans. Meanwhile, evidence from Canada, which in 1988 banned tobacco ads in magazines, suggested that the industry could absorb the loss of these revenues. During the 1989 fiscal year, the ban resulted in only short-term revenue losses for Canadian titles. Finally, a decision of the U.S. Supreme Court in May concerned some magazine publishers who purchase material from free-lancers. The court ruled that free-lance workers who do not actually have a written agreement with a publisher retain the rights to a commissioned work.

Newspapers. The year 1989 opened on some sour notes for the U.S. newspaper industry. The previous year, which initially seemed favorable, turned flat toward the end. Instead of the hoped-for 8–9% growth in advertising revenues, an increase of only 6% occurred during 1988. Weekday newspaper circulation remained flat, but a 2% increase occurred in Sunday circulation. That all this occurred in the context of a healthy economy was a special concern.

The 1989 predictions reflected the disappointments of 1988. Forecasters initially projected only a 6% increase in advertising revenues, as well as unchanged or slightly declining daily circulation. Total Sunday circulation was expected to increase by 2%. Data from the early part of the year seemed to agree with the projections. From October 1988 through March 1989, daily circulations tended to decline and Sunday circulations to increase among the largest newspapers in the country. The data suggested that increasing segments of the population approach the newspaper as a Sunday reader. Daily circulation of *The Wall Street Journal,* the nation's leader, was especially hard-hit. It dropped by about 90,000 to 1.93 million. By midyear, the picture remained mixed. A majority of the publicly held newspaper companies reported increased net income during the first two quarters of 1989, reflecting cost containment programs, lower

In September, Ralph Ingersoll II, 43-year-old publisher of some 40 daily and 200 weekly newspapers, introduced the "St. Louis Sun," a color-splashed tabloid for "today's video world."

© Mark Katzman

newsprint prices, and moderate increases in advertising revenues. The reports contrasted with more-mixed income reports during the final quarter of 1988. On a downward note, in July the Newspaper Advertising Bureau lowered projected increases in 1989 advertising revenues to 5%.

By early 1989 newspaper chains owned about 76% of U.S. daily newspapers and accounted for 83% of total circulation. In April the imminent sale of the parent company of the *National Enquirer,* GP Group Inc., was announced. Mcfadden Holdings Inc., which is a major publisher of romance magazines, and the banking firm of Boston Ventures purchased it for $412.5 million. The new owners were considering publishing Hispanic and British versions of the *Enquirer,* as well as developing a television show patterned after it.

Major newspapers with new appearances during 1989 included *The Christian Science Monitor*. In January the *Monitor* unfolded its third redesign in 13 years. The new look featured widespread use of color in pictures and graphics, as well as a reduced, 20-page format. The *Monitor* attributed the new design to its needs to attract and retain younger readers. The *St. Louis Post-Dispatch,* faced with the late September birth of competition from the *St. Louis Sun,* also announced changes aimed at younger readers. The *Post-Dispatch* attempted to modify its image as a "serious" paper by becoming more reader-friendly. Finally, the *Boston Globe* introduced a new appearance, featuring larger type and additional graphics, in October.

Heavy capital expenditures and the influx of new technologies continued during late 1988 and 1989. For example, *The Christian Science Monitor* purchased $1.8 million in electronic color and communications equipment from Scitex America Corp. to achieve its new appearance. Advances were reported in using personal computers and high-quality pagination systems. Several newspapers experimented with improved no-rub inks, designed to reduce ink smears.

During 1989 a U.S. Supreme Court decision to consider the legality of the proposed merger of the noneditorial operations of Gannett Co. Inc.'s *Detroit News* and Knight-Ridder Inc.'s *Detroit Free Press,* two of the ten largest papers in the nation, surprised many observers. In late 1988 the U.S. Justice Department approved the deal, but a group of advertisers, citizens, and newspaper employees in Michigan challenged it. The case represented the first time the Supreme Court has scrutinized such joint-operating agreements since the 1970 Newspaper Preservation Act, which legalized them if one newspaper is failing. The court considered the case in November 1989 and reached a deadlock, 4–4, with one abstention. The deadlock allowed the joint-operating agreement between the two papers to take effect. By allowing the challenge from advertisers and the public, the court granted status to classes of individuals previously not recognized in joint-operating agreement negotiations. In another legal area, the free-speech leanings of the two newest members of the U.S. Supreme Court—Justices Anthony Kennedy and Antonin Scalia—reassured many in the industry during 1989. The two voted with the majority to declare unconstitutional a $100,000 jury award against a weekly newspaper in Florida that printed the name of a rape victim.

DAVID PERRY, *The University of Alabama*

PUERTO RICO

Hurricane *Hugo* visited Puerto Rico on Sept. 18, 1989, packing 140 mph (225 km/hr) winds that ripped roofs, toppled utility poles, and uprooted trees. Puerto Rican Gov. Rafael Hernández Colón also created a political whirlwind in 1989 by announcing it was time to begin a new political relationship between Puerto Rico and the United States.

Hurricane *Hugo*. Three people died in the hurricane and six utility linemen were electrocuted while trying to restore electricity after the storm. An estimated $1 billion in damage was recorded while authorities continued to assess the destruction. *Hugo* wrought its most fierce havoc on housing, destroying or damaging an estimated 25,000 homes with up to 80,000 people affected. Within a few days of the hurricane passage, massive relief was channeled into the island-commonwealth. The American Red Cross flew in beds and bedding, medicine, and hot meals for the homeless in public shelters. The U.S. military airlifted emergency generators and drinking water. Locally $12 million in donations was collected. On September 28, Congress passed $1.1 billion in relief aid for hurricane victims in South Carolina, Puerto Rico, and the U.S. Virgin Islands. Two thirds of Puerto Rico was declared a disaster area, qualifying residents and businesses for grants and low-interest loans.

Politics. At his swearing-in ceremony for a second consecutive term on January 4, Gov. Hernández Colón said it was time to seek a new relationship between Puerto Rico and the United States. A week later, leaders of the island's three main political parties drafted a letter to President Bush and the U.S. Congress asking that the will of the Puerto Rican people, expressed through a special election, be respected. A bill calling for a plebiscite in 1991 for Puerto Ricans to choose between statehood, an expanded commonwealth system, or independence was approved by the U.S. Senate Energy and Natural Resources Committee, but still had to be considered by the entire Senate membership. A similar measure was introduced in the House on October 26.

In local politics, San Juan City Hall continued to be the focus of a bitter battle between the procommonwealth Popular Democratic Party (PDP) and the prostatehood New Progressive Party (NPP). The PDP won control of the capital city in the November 1988 elections for the first time in 20 years. In January 1989, NPP contender José Granados Navedo filed a suit challenging a voting recount that declared PDP candidate Hector Luís Acevedo the winner by 29 votes. The suit maintains that 200 ballots never were counted. The case was still in court as the year drew to an end.

Also making headlines during 1989 was the acquittal of Filiberto Ojeda Rios by a federal jury on August 26 on charges of shooting at several Federal Bureau of Investigation (FBI) agents while he resisted arrest in 1985. A self-proclaimed leader of Los Macheteros, a violent Puerto Rican nationalist group, Ojeda claimed the FBI had planned to kill him. He still faced charges for his alleged role in the $7.1 million Wells Fargo robbery—the second-largest cash robbery in U.S. history, which occurred in West Hartford, CT, in September 1983.

Bank Merger. The largest bank merger ever recorded in Puerto Rico took place on October 19 with the uniting of Banco Popular and Banco de Ponce. The merger formed a $9 billion institution that will control two thirds of the banking business on the island.

DEBORAH RAMIREZ
"The San Juan Star"

PUERTO RICO • Information Highlights

Area: 3,515 sq mi (9 104 km²).
Population (mid-1989 est.): 3,300,000.
Chief Cities (1980 census): San Juan, the capital, 434,849; Bayamon, 196,206; Ponce, 189,046.
Government (1989): *Chief Officer*—governor, Rafael Hernández Colón (Popular Democratic Party). *Legislature*—Senate, 27 members; House of Representatives, 51 members.

QUEBEC

The Liberal Party was returned to office in Quebec with another decisive mandate in 1989, but the victory was not without some sobering side effects for Premier Robert Bourassa. The premier reorganized his cabinet, and the government took steps to improve Quebec's somber demographic outlook. A shooting tragedy occurred at the University of Montreal.

Liberals' Triumph. The Liberals easily retained control of the government in a provincial general election held on September 25. They won 92 seats in the 125-seat National Assembly, against 29 for the Parti Québecois (PQ) and four for the newly created Equality Party. The Liberals triumphed despite a serious outbreak of public-sector strikes in the weeks before the vote, and an embarrassing episode involving a wayward shipment of PCBs—polychlorinated biphenyls—a highly toxic chemical compound. The PCBs had to be stored at a Hydro-Quebec site near Baie Comeau after dockworkers at Liverpool refused to unload them from a ship that had taken them to Britain for incineration.

Despite the size of his victory margin, Bourassa had reason to feel troubled about some aspects of the election result. The share of the popular vote won by the PQ—which seeks Quebec's separation from Canada—rose to about 40% while the Liberal share went down. This could place the PQ in a strong position to contend for power in the next election, expected about 1993.

Then there was the surprisingly strong showing of the Equality Party, which came from nowhere to take four seats away from the Liberals in heavily Anglophone west-end Montreal. It meant that the long-standing Liberal hold on the important English-language vote in predominantly French-speaking Quebec may have melted away. The Equality Party campaigned almost exclusively on linguistic rights for English-speaking Quebecers.

Cabinet Shuffle. On October 11, two weeks after the election, Bourassa unveiled a new 30-member cabinet in which the Anglophone minority lost ground, while women and members of the ethnic community were given increased clout. Deputy Premier Lise Bacon, having managed to survive the PCB fiasco as environment minister, was elevated to the energy portfolio. She also was made regional development minister, emerging as the second most powerful person in the cabinet.

Prominent among eight newcomers was Sam Elkas, former mayor of the Montreal suburb of Kirkland, named to the transport and public security portfolios. In the cabinet he will represent west-island Montreal, where the Liberals lost those four seats to the Equality Party. John Ciaccia, the only Anglophone minister not to resign in protest against Bourassa's Bill 178—which provides that only French may be used on outdoor advertising signs in Quebec—was rewarded with the international relations portfolio. He also was named minister of state for native affairs.

Meech in Trouble. With the election out of the way, Bourassa had to confront the formidable question of how to rescue the Meech Lake accord, aimed at bringing Quebec into the Canadian constitutional fold. Support for the agreement, concluded by the federal government and all ten provinces in June 1987, had been eroding steadily among some of the English-speaking provinces. Bourassa, as well as Prime Minister Brian Mulroney, repeatedly warned that failure to ratify the accord by the June 1990 deadline would stoke the fires of separatism in Quebec. Among other things, the compact recognizes Quebec as a "distinct society" within the Canadian Confederation.

Baby Bonuses. The Liberal government's election-year budget, brought down May 16, increased the incentives offered for larger families. Couples who become parents for a third and any subsequent time receive $4,500 in cash, tax-free—a 50% hike. At 1.4 children per woman of childbearing age, Quebec has one of the lowest birth rates in the Western world. Some demographers have said the rate is so low that the province's 6.6 million population is in danger of slipping.

Immigration Policy. Two weeks after the budget, the ruling Liberal Party issued a policy program calling for a big jump—from 26,000 to 40,000—in Quebec's annual intake of immigrants. The program also would make it easier for those who do not speak French to take language courses. It warned that language laws were not enough to protect Quebec's French face.

The Demise of the Union Nationale. The Union Nationale (UN) party, which dominated Quebec politics in the 1940s and 1950s, folded in 1989. The province's chief electoral officer, Pierre Coté, announced on June 19 that he had withdrawn the UN's official party status because of nonpayment of debts. No UN candidate had won a seat in the National Assembly in more than 13 years.

University Tragedy. In a senseless rampage, a gunman killed 14 women and wounded 13 others at the University of Montreal engineering school on December 6. Marc Lepine opened fire with a semiautomatic rifle on the coeds before turning the gun on himself. He blamed "feminists" for his troubles and a list of prominent women was found on his body.

JOHN BEST, *"Canada World News"*

QUEBEC • Information Highlights

Area: 594,857 sq mi (1 540 680 km²).
Population (June 1989): 6,679,000.
Chief Cities (1986 census): Quebec, the capital, 164,580; Montreal, 1,015,420; Laval, 284,164.
Government (1989): *Chief Officers*—lt. gov., Gilles Lamontagne; premier, Robert Bourassa (Liberal). *Legislature*—National Assembly, 125 members.
Provincial Finances (1989–90 fiscal year budget): *Revenues,* $31,000,000,000; *expenditures,* $32,500,000,000.
Personal Income (average weekly earnings, June 1989): $472.06.
Labor Force (August 1989, seasonally adjusted): *Employed* workers, 15 years of age and over, 3,044,000; *Unemployed,* 8.8%.
Education (1989–90): *Enrollment*—elementary and secondary schools, 1,138,500 pupils; postsecondary—universities, 121,800; community colleges, 152,100.
(All monetary figures are in Canadian dollars.)

RECORDINGS

In the wake of the 1988 purchase of CBS Records by Sony, major labels went shopping to forestall unfriendly takeovers and further enlarge their market shares. Meanwhile, with the continuing popularity of the compact disc (CD), the industry took note of the decreasing sales of vinyl long-playing records (LPs) and sent distinct signs that their days were numbered.

Label Shopping. Mirroring acquisition activity throughout the business world, major record labels were bullish about expansion. Polygram bought Island Records, while Thorn-EMI purchased half of Chrysalis, with a future option to buy the rest. Thorn-EMI also bought a major song publishing company, SBK, and financed a new SBK record label. One of the largest remaining independent labels, A & M, also was rumored to be in play and was sold to Polygram for some $500 million.

The Warner-Elektra-Atlantic recording behemoth, itself part of the high-profile merger of Time Inc. and Warner Brothers, reactivated old labels instead of buying new ones. Atlantic relaunched its Atco label, while Warner's brought back Reprise.

Overall U.S. sales of recorded music hit an all-time high of $6.25 billion in 1988. Like the movie industry, part of the increase was due to higher prices, especially in the case of compact discs. Cassette tapes ($3.39 billion) and CDs ($2.09 billion) generated the lion's share of revenue, showing a shifting marketplace. CDs were up 31%, cassette sales rose 14%, and vinyl LPs were down 33% from 1987 figures.

Vinyl Death Watch. A harbinger of the extinction of major-label vinyl LPs was the downward sales spiral of 45 rpm records. Single sales were down 11%, generating only $180 million in revenue. Warners announced that it would phase them out in 1990. Though the recent rollout of cassette singles brought in $57 million, sales were up 300% over the previous year. Attempts to market 3-inch (7.6-cm) compact discs, the CD equivalent of a single, thus far have failed.

Numerous signals suggested the impending demise of the mass-market vinyl album. Some of the largest recorded music chains have dropped LPs altogether, since they generally accounted for only 3 to 5% of sales.

The compact disc boom has encouraged a number of labels to rerelease older music in the new format and many of these packages are not being marketed on LP. Sometime soon, some new releases may not make it to vinyl. Symbolically, the shift was reflected when Elektra Records changed its official name to Elektra Entertainment.

Digital Audio Tape (DAT). The digital audio tape recorder, seen by many as a companion to the CD player in much the same way as the analog recorder is to the vinyl LP, moved one step closer to the domestic marketplace. Though the machines have been available as imports, high prices and a lack of prerecorded tapes have slowed consumer acceptance. An agreement between electronic manufacturers and the Record Industry Association of America, however, moved the machines closer to general availability. The agreement states that, while the machines would be able to record compact discs on digital tape, they would be unable to generate second-generation copies from the recorded tapes. Many in the music industry still feel the machines are an invitation to violate copyrights, however, and still are calling for a conpensatory tax on blank tapes.

Consequently, the future is still cloudy for the DAT machine. Japanese manufacturers predict that the price will fall below $1,000 shortly after they are introduced, but the availability of prerecorded tapes remains a wild card. At present, there are no machines capable of high-speed duplication of DAT tapes. Such machines, expected shortly, will come with price tags that will be reflected by a high price of prerecorded tapes.

Personics System. Amid the new technologies, a quaint new product has popped up in many record stores. The Personics system permits consumers to customize their own cassette tapes from a library of available recordings, at a cost on a per-track basis. While some record companies have refused to permit use of their recordings, consumers have made it a popular new method of buying music.

JOHN MILWARD
Free-lance Writer and Critic

REFUGEES AND IMMIGRATION

The global refugee problem dominated much of the world's news during 1989. Political changes within the Communist bloc produced the largest surge of emigration from Central and Eastern Europe to the West and within Central and Eastern Europe since the late 1950s.

From East to West. During the first ten months of 1989, at least 167,000 East Germans emigrated with or without advance government permission. After Hungary took down the fence marking its border with Austria, tens of thousands of East Germans vacationing in Hungary during the summer months decided not to return to their country but to cross into Austria and seek settlement in the West. The exodus of East Germans through Hungary and Austria to West Germany was the most dramatic indication of the new East-West movements, but they followed significant increases in the number of East Germans asking for political asylum at the West German consulates in Central Europe. In October and November pressure built up at the West German embassy in Czechoslovakia as thousands more East Germans crowded into the embassy on their way to West Germany. By the end of the year it remained unclear how such refugee movements could be halted, particularly as they were occurring within what appeared to be an accelerating process of economic and political disintegration of East Germany.

In addition to East Germans, more than 300,000 ethnic Germans from Poland, the Soviet Union, and Romania arrived in West Germany during the year. The biggest flow of emigrants in recent years has been from Poland because of the combination of an economic crisis and a relaxation of travel restrictions. The number of Poles expected to move to West Germany during 1989 was expected to be about 200,000. Tens of thousands of Yugoslavs also emigrated to West Germany and other parts of

AP/Wide World

Vietnamese refugees continued to arrive in Hong Kong, even as the British colony initiated a tough forced-repatriation policy for most of the boat people.

Europe. The arrival of so many refugees and immigrants greatly strained housing, employment, and social services in West Germany and aroused strong resentment among working-class West Germans.

The movement from East to West is not simply a European issue. Given historic patterns of migration and family ties, many of those arriving from the East seek to settle in North America, Australia, and New Zealand, but particularly in the United States. For example, with the easing of Soviet exit controls, the number of Jews leaving the Soviet Union in 1989 exceeded 50,000, putting enormous strain on the system for processing their applications and causing huge backlogs. In order to control the number of arrivals, the United States required on October 1 that all applications would have to be processed at the U.S. embassy in Moscow.

From East to East. The political and social changes in Eastern Europe during 1989, along with rising ethnic demands for autonomy and economic improvements, created a volatile situation resulting in the mass movement of people in the region. For a few months during the summer more than 300,000 ethnic Turks arrived in Turkey from Bulgaria charging discrimination by Bulgarian authorities. Between 1987 and 1989, more than 40,000 ethnic Hungarians, claiming government efforts to suppress their culture, left Romania for Hungary. Economic unrest and ethnic conflicts within the Soviet Union caused increased movements of people during 1989. The exact numbers of people are undocumented, but reportedly more than 1 million Armenians arrived in Moscow during the year.

The Third World. The hope that the worldwide total of more than 14 million refugees would decrease during the year was dashed as renewed regional conflicts and internal wars in places as diverse as Central America, southern Africa and the Horn, Lebanon, Afghanistan, and Cambodia generated large numbers of refugees and displaced people. The needs of African refugees, who represented one third of the world's refugees, continued to be recognized inadequately. At the end of 1989, people in Eritrea, Tigre, and southern Sudan once again faced the threat of famine as a result of renewed fighting and droughts. Although refugees continued to flee violent conflicts in southern Africa, tentative moves toward peace raised some hope for an improvement in the situation there. Talks aimed at reaching peaceful accords in southern Africa and in other regions of the world (Central America, Cambodia, Lebanon, and the Sudan) included provisions for the repatriation of refugees and displaced people. The sudden return home of millions of refugees would require a major international response, but getting much-needed assistance for the returnees was made more difficult as the Office of the United Nations High Commissioner for Refugees (UNHCR) experienced a major funding crisis at the end of 1989.

Elsewhere, Vietnamese boat people were threatened repeatedly with forcible repatriation from Hong Kong, Malaysia, and other countries in Southeast Asia despite pledges made to the contrary at an international conference held in Geneva in June.

Asylum in the West. Political developments in Eastern Europe and the Third World resulted in a dramatic increase in applications for asylum in North America and Western Europe and led Western countries to make it increasingly difficult to file and pursue asylum claims. The U.S. Coast Guard continued to intercept Haitians at sea and return them to Haiti. Since the beginning of the program in 1981, more than 22,000 Haitians have been interdicted and only six persons have been allowed to enter the United States to have their claims heard. During the year, temporary safe haven bills for nationals of El Salvador, Nicaragua, China, and Lebanon were considered by Congress. Despite the Immigration Reform and Control Act of 1986, there were reports of continuing heavy illegal immigration into the United States. Further efforts also were made to strengthen the European Community's external border controls and to unify the policies and practices of West European governments toward asylum seekers by 1992.

GIL LOESCHER, *University of Notre Dame*

RELIGION

Overview

A controversy over the presence of a nun's convent outside the Auschwitz death camp in Poland, the issue of the ordination of women, the awarding of the Nobel Peace Prize to the Dalai Lama, the meeting of Pope John Paul II and Soviet President Gorbachev, and the trial of televangelist Jim Bakker were among the most prominent religious news stories of 1989.

Bakker Trial. The trial and conviction of televangelist Jim Bakker on 24 counts of fraud dominated headlines in the fall. Bakker and his wife Tammy had built the Praise The Lord (PTL) ministry into a multimillion-dollar industry that included a religious broadcasting network and a religious theme park. Federal prosecutors contended that Jim Bakker had cheated thousands of PTL followers out of $158 million through a lifetime vacation offer, and that he diverted much of the money to finance a lavish life-style. He was sentenced to 45 years in prison and fined $500,000. Bakker's problems over the previous 2½ years brought trouble for other televangelists as well, with viewership and revenue reported down by many.

Catholics and Anglicans. Reunification of the Catholic and Anglican Churches was set back by the latter's decision to ordain women priests and bishops. After a meeting in October, Pope John Paul II and the Most Rev. Robert Runcie, archbishop of Canterbury, pledged to continue seeking reunification, but acknowledged their division over the question of women clergy was almost insurmountable.

Templeton Prize. The John Templeton Prize —an international award for religious progress analogous to the Nobel Prize—was shared in 1989 by a Scottish clergyman and a German scientist. The Very Rev. Lord MacLeod was honored for founding an international ecumenical group; Professor Carl Friedrich von Weizsaecker was chosen for his work at reconciling the natural sciences with theology.

Far Eastern

The Panchen Lama, who ranked second to the Dalai Lama in the Tibetan Buddhist hierarchy, died in Xigaze, Tibet, after a heart attack Jan. 28, 1989, at the age of 50. Supporters of the Dalai Lama—who has lived in exile in India since 1959 and who won the Nobel Peace Prize in 1989 for his nonviolent protest against the Chinese domination of Tibet (*see* pages 82–83)—often charged that the Panchen Lama collaborated with the Chinese government. In reporting his death, the New China News Agency described the Panchen Lama as a "great patriot, noted statesman, devoted friend of the Communist Party of China, and outstanding leader of Tibetan Buddhism."

The Vajradhatu International Buddhist Church, a branch of Tibetan Buddhism with 3,500 to 5,000 followers in the United States, Canada, and Europe, was rocked by reports that its leader, Osel Tendzin, knowingly had transmitted AIDS through homosexual encounters. The group's board of directors asked Tendzin to give up his teaching and administrative duties in January, but he refused to comply. He remained in seclusion in California for most of the year while the board tried to decide what other action to take.

Phra Bodhirak, a former television personality who founded an unorthodox Buddhist sect in Thailand, was arrested in June on charges of violating laws governing both religious and political affairs. The Sangha, the mainstream Buddhist group in Thailand, charged that Bodhirak had ordained illegally at least 79 monks on his own authority. He also was accused of openly engaging in politics by influencing Chamlong Srimaung, the mayor of Bangkok. The cases had not been brought to court by the end of the year.

An estimated 30 million Hindu pilgrims gathered at the confluence of the Ganges and Yamuna rivers in Allahabad, India, between January and March, to take part in a religious festival known as the Kumbh Mela. The Kumbh is believed to have been a pitcher of divine nectar with the power of immortality which was spilled in 12 places during an ancient battle between gods and demons. Allahabad is one of the four sites of a Kumbh Mela that generally is celebrated every 12 years. The pilgrims bathed in the icy waters in a festival that enabled rich and poor, low and high caste to mingle as members of one faith.

A Japanese Buddhist, who started a movement to return to the original purity of the faith, visited New York in May to examine social action programs conducted by black clergy. Kiriyama Seiyu, leader of the Agon-Shu sect of Buddhism, said he was seeking the involvement of U.S. religious leaders in a foundation he was establishing to fund projects dealing with drug abuse, homelessness, and poverty.

DARRELL J. TURNER, *Religious News Service*

Islam

The publication of Salman Rushdie's novel *The Satanic Verses* outraged many Muslims who found the book offensive. In an ensuing international furor, Ayatollah Ruhollah Khomeini, Iran's spiritual leader, called for Rushdie's execution. Khomeini's own death in June removed from the world stage a Muslim leader who had a profound impact on international affairs during his decade of power in revolutionary Iran. The links between Islam and the political process that Khomeini had come to symbolize remained in evidence in many countries during 1989. (*See also* OBITUARIES—Khomeini.)

Demonstrations against *The Satanic Verses* began in January in Great Britain, where Rushdie's work first was published, but quickly spread throughout the world. Many Muslims, believing that the book's characterization of the Prophet Muhammad was insulting and blasphemous, demanded its suppression. Some nations with large Muslim populations banned the book and some booksellers in other countries discontinued its sale to avoid possible confrontations. (*See also* BIOGRAPHY.)

In Europe and the United States, advocates of free speech rallied in support of Rushdie. Many less-conservative Muslims denounced Khomeini's call for assassination although they, too, stressed the offensive nature of the book. The 45-member Islamic Conference Organization (ICO), at its annual meeting in Saudi Arabia in mid-March, refused to endorse Khomeini's position, but did condemn the book, labeling Rushdie, an Indian Muslim by birth, an apostate. A communiqué issued at the conclusion of the conference stated that freedom of expression should not extend to the toleration of blasphemy. The ICO urged its members to coordinate efforts to promote respect for Islam, and called upon all nations to adopt legislation that would safeguard the religious beliefs of citizens.

Palestinians. The ICO also expressed support for the Palestinian movement, officially recognizing the Palestine Liberation Organization's 1988 declaration of statehood.

In April, following Muslim protests against the Israeli occupation at the start of the Islamic holy month of Ramadan, Israeli authorities banned West Bank and Gazan Palestinians from worshipping at the al-Aqsa Mosque in Jerusalem, the third-most sacred site in Islam.

Tunisia. Religiously-based parties were prevented from participating in Tunisia's national elections in April, but many individuals affiliated with the Islamic Tendency Movement ran as independent candidates. Although the Islamists garnered about 14% of the national vote, and as much as 30% in some areas, none won a seat in the National Assembly because of the nature of the electoral system.

Afghanistan-Soviet Union. As Soviet forces completed their withdrawal from Afghanistan in 1989, Muslim resistance groups continued efforts to topple the Soviet-supported government in Kabul. In the USSR itself, rioting between Uzbek Sunni and Meskhetian Shi'i Muslims erupted in June allegedly over disagreements on whether to form a united front to oppose non-Muslims in the region. The 1989 census data revealed that Central Asia, the home of most of the Soviet Union's Muslims, had the nation's highest increase in the birthrate (34%) over the previous decade, underscoring the growing importance of the country's Muslims.

Bulgaria. During 1989, Bulgaria, another communist state that has a large Muslim minority, attempted to force the assimilation of its almost 1 million ethnic Turkish Muslims by punishing them for using the Turkish language and for engaging in certain Muslim practices.

Proponents of differing Muslim viewpoints competed for influence and occasionally clashed with each other in 1989. Shi'i Muslims in Iraq, a country with a mixed Sunni-Shi'i population ruled predominantly by Sunnis, accused the government of closing Shi'i schools and mosques. Continuing sectarian violence in Lebanon took the life of Shaikh Hassan Khaled, the leader of that country's Sunni Muslims, and police in Indonesia, Egypt, and Jordan clashed with religious extremists.

KENNETH J. PERKINS
University of South Carolina

Judaism

The overriding religious issue for world Jewry in 1989 was how to effect the removal of a Catholic convent from Auschwitz, which symbolically threatened Jewish perceptions of the Nazi Holocaust. Many American Jews worried about anti-Semitism and the implications of two U.S. Supreme Court decisions. And the Jewish world divided over two major religious questions: "Who is a Jew?" and the role of women in prayer.

The Auschwitz Convent. In 1987, Jewish leaders reached an agreement with Catholic officials for the removal, within two years, of a Carmelite convent on the site of the Nazi death camp in Auschwitz, Poland. Jewish leaders insisted on its removal on the grounds that a building set aside for Catholic prayer and contemplation was inappropriate at a place where millions of Jews were killed simply for being Jewish. Underlying Jewish apprehensions was the feeling that the Catholic Church was out to "appropriate" the Nazi Holocaust by making it appear that Catholics suffered as much as Jews. By February 1989, not only had no steps been taken to move the nuns out, but there was now a 23-ft- (7-m-) high cross on the site, symbolizing their determination to stay. When approached by concerned Jews, Vatican spokesmen asserted that local church officials had jurisdiction over such matters.

Tension escalated on July 14, when seven American Jews who entered the grounds of the convent without permission were attacked physically by Polish workers. Incensed at the incursion, the cardinal of Krakow announced that the convent would stay put, and Cardinal Jozef Glemp, the highest-ranking Catholic official in Poland, accused the allegedly Jewish-

© Peter Jordan/"Time" Magazine

A five-year-old Carmelite convent on the site of the Nazi death camp in Auschwitz, Poland, became a sore point in Jewish-Catholic relations. Following intervention by the Vatican, it was announced in the fall that the convent would be removed.

controlled media of an anti-Polish campaign. Adding fuel to the fire were three weekly homilies by Pope John Paul II, delivered in August, stating that God's covenant with the Jews had been superseded by the Christian "new covenant." But it was ultimately the Vatican—encouraged by Catholic leaders in Western Europe and the United States—that moved matters toward a resolution. On September 19 the Vatican publicly endorsed the 1987 agreement to remove the convent, and Cardinal Glemp acquiesced in the decision.

Concerns of American Jews. Jews in the United States expressed continuing concern about anti-Semitism. Particularly alarming were the victories—first in the Republican primary and then in the general election for a seat in the Louisiana state legislature—of David Duke, a former grand wizard of the Knights of the Ku Klux Klan. In June the Anti-Defamation League of B'nai B'rith issued a report on the growing threat posed by the "skinheads," a neo-Nazi group that teaches hostility toward minorities, and another on the danger of Holocaust revisionism.

On July 3 the U.S. Supreme Court issued two rulings that drew much Jewish attention. It decided, first, that a municipality could display religious symbols such as Christmas trees and Hanukkah menorahs on public property so long as they were part of a "seasonal display." The other decision upheld a Missouri law that denied public funds and facilities for counseling about or performing abortions. Since most American Jews—with the notable exception of the Orthodox—espouse a strict interpretation of the separation of church and state and support freedom of choice on abortion, both decisions evoked considerable Jewish displeasure.

Divisive Issues. The question of "who is a Jew," a bone of contention for years, emerged once again in 1989. The Orthodox parties in Israel, strengthened by their role as a potential balance of power between the two large political blocs, sought to enshrine their own definition of Jewishness into Israeli law. In January the Orthodox minister of the interior issued an order that no identity card designating the holder as a Jew would be issued to anyone who was not the child of a Jewish mother or who was not converted to Judaism according to Orthodox practice. But in July the Israeli Supreme Court countermanded this action, while reasserting the Orthodox monopoly over the performance of Jewish marriages.

Israel was also the scene of a dispute over the religious role of Jewish women. In March a number of women attempted to conduct services at the Western Wall in Jerusalem. Since strict Orthodox law does not allow women's prayer groups, ultra-Orthodox men threw chairs at the women, and police had to use tear gas to clear the area. Despite a court order protecting their right to pray as they wished, the women continued to be harassed. In several American communities, Jewish women held their own prayer services in solidarity with them.

LAWRENCE GROSSMAN
The American Jewish Committee

Orthodox Eastern

Within the Eastern Orthodox faith, 1989's most exciting developments resulted from Soviet leader Mikhail Gorbachev's policy of *perestroika,* which brought much encouraging change to the Russian Church, including the opening of more than 1,000 new parishes and new church construction. New seminaries also were being established, with two already in operation in Byelorussia and Siberia, and several monasteries—in addition to the famous Kievan Caves, were reopened partially during 1988's millennial celebrations—were restored.

The clergy and church affairs received greater media attention in the USSR. A newspaper referring to past religious persecution was available, as were articles written by priests and a few books on Orthodoxy. Some church services were televised. Nonetheless, the Russian Church, led by the ailing Patriarch Pimen and other hierarchs accustomed to subservience to the state, was criticized for lagging in "restructuring" activities and *glasnost.*

The process of rewriting Stalin's 1929 Law on Religious Associations continued with church involvement. When promulgated, the law will make the Orthodox Church a "legal person" with rights of ownership and of educational and social activities now denied it. An obstacle in writing the new law, the status of millions of Eastern Rite Catholics in the Ukraine, partly was resolved when the uniate churches won legal status in December 1989, but many related issues between the Orthodox Church and the Eastern Rite Catholics remained unresolved.

Europe. In Yugoslavia, Patriarch German of the Serbian Orthodox Church presided over celebrations of the 600th anniversary of the battle of Kosovo against the Turks. In the Kosovo region, conflicts persisted between the Muslim Albanian majority and the Serbian minority, whose rights in the province are defended by the Orthodox patriarchate. A cathedral dedicated to St. Sava, founder of Serbian Orthodoxy, was built in Belgrade.

In Romania many of the church's architectural landmarks were destroyed. Churches were razed in Bucharest, and church structures in the countryside were destroyed under government policy of "consolidating" villages.

Steps were taken in Greece to separate the Greek Orthodox Church from the government. Charges continued against high-handed measures by bishops, especially in financial matters.

North America. The Orthodox Church in America (OCA), held its triennial council in St. Louis. The OCA's declining membership and financial difficulties were debated, and the Standing Conference of Orthodox Bishops in America was criticized for failure to exercise effective leadership. A joint encyclical urged the establishment of administrative unity among the Orthodox in North America.

Canonizations. The Orthodox Church of Georgia (USSR) canonized Ilya Chavchavadze, the lay poet and political activist, and the Constantinople partiarchate canonized the Russian monk Silouan.

THOMAS HOPKO, *St. Vladimir's Seminary*

Protestantism

Disagreement over the leadership and structure of the National Council of Churches (NCC) came to a head in July when the Rev. Arie Brouwer resigned as general secretary of the ecumenical organization. Critics had accused Brouwer of treating the council staff in an authoritarian manner, and opposition grew when he accused critics of "character assassination" and a "lust for retribution," in a speech to the NCC's governing board in May.

The governing board of the NCC—which represents 32 denominations with more than 40 million members—adopted a plan for a massive overhaul and streamlining to help overcome the agency's financial problems. The Rev. Leonid Kishkovsky of the Orthodox

Courtesy, National Council of Churches

The Very Rev. Leonid Kishkovsky (far left) of the Orthodox Church of America was installed as president of the National Council of Churches in November and was to begin his two-year term in January 1990. NCC General Secretary James Hamilton, the Rev. Syngman Rhee, NCC president-elect, and the Rev. Patricia McClurg, outgoing NCC president, took part in the ceremony.

Church in America, president-elect of the National Council, was named head of a 22-member team overseeing the restructuring through May 1990.

The World Council of Churches' 150-member Central Committee met in Moscow in July, marking the first time that body had assembled in the Soviet Union. In May the World Council sponsored a conference on mission and evangelism in San Antonio where questions were raised about the uniqueness of the Christian message in a pluralistic world. A congress of evangelical Christians in Manila in July—a follow-up to a conference held in Lausanne, Switzerland, in 1974—brought together 4,000 people from 190 countries who drafted a manifesto affirming the uniqueness of Christ as the only way to salvation.

The Episcopalians. A seven-member commission, appointed by the Most Rev. Robert Runcie, the archbishop of Canterbury, issued a series of "pastoral guidelines" aimed at ending the battle in the worldwide Anglican Communion over female priests and bishops. One of the more controversial recommendations was that women bishops should perform ordination ceremonies only if a male bishop is present.

The Rev. Barbara C. Harris (*see* BIOGRAPHY) became a focus of the dispute when she was consecrated in Boston in February as the first female Episcopal bishop and the first woman bishop in the Anglican Communion. Traditionalists, who opposed that move and other liberal tendencies in the 2.5-million-member Episcopal Church, assembled in Fort Worth, TX, in early June to establish the Episcopal Synod of America. The new body set up a parallel structure to the Episcopal Church, including a house of bishops and a house of clergy, and lay deputies. The synod's organizers insisted that it would remain within the parent body, but critics in the Episcopal Church called it schismatic.

The Baptists. The battle between theological conservatives and moderates that has wracked the Southern Baptist Convention since 1979 was reflected in growing turmoil at Southeastern Baptist Theological Seminary in Wake Forest, NC. In December 1988 a regional accrediting agency criticized the seminary's trustees for making belief in biblical inerrancy a criterion for faculty hiring without regard for academic freedom. In June the American Association of University Professors (AAUP) censured the seminary based on similar charges. Throughout the year, the trustees and faculty blamed each other for the turmoil.

The Lutherans. The AAUP also censured the Lutheran Church-Missouri Synod's Concordia Seminary in Fort Wayne, IN, for violations of academic freedom. Among other things, the charges involved the June 1988 firing of tenured Professor Alvin J. Schmidt, who had advocated the ordination of women in opposition to the synod's official position. Concordia's board of regents voted in July to "honorably retire" President Robert D. Preus, against his will and after 15 years at the seminary, citing turmoil within the faculty and staff as a reason.

Financial matters dominated the first national assembly of the 5.2-million-member Evangelical Lutheran Church in America, which was formed by a three-way merger in 1988. Responding to a $15 million deficit, delegates to the meeting in suburban Chicago approved plans for staff layoffs and reductions in programs and services. In other matters, the assembly voted overwhelmingly to join the World and National Councils of Churches and directed that investments controlled by the church's pension board be removed from companies doing business in South Africa by September 1991.

The United Church of Christ. The 1.7-million-member United Church of Christ called for an "economic bill of rights" that would provide a guaranteed national minimum income, insuring food, clothing, and shelter for all citizens. At its General Synod in Fort Worth, the denomination also decided to relocate its national headquarters from New York to Cleveland and elected the Rev. Paul Sherry as president to succeed the Rev. Avery D. Post, who had served since 1977.

Ecumenism. The Christian Church (Disciples of Christ) made ecumenical history at its General Assembly in Indianapolis by electing a Roman Catholic priest as a full voting member of its Governing Board. The election of Msgr. Philip Morris of South Orange, NJ, to the Disciples board was the first time a U.S. Protestant body had taken such a step. The 1.1-million-member Disciples also voted to recognize the African National Congress in South Africa.

DARRELL J. TURNER

Roman Catholicism

On Dec. 1, 1989, Soviet President Mikhail Gorbachev and Pope John Paul II met at the Vatican, ending 70 years of spiritual and philosophical conflict. They agreed in principle to establish diplomatic ties between the Vatican and the Soviet Union, and the pope urged greater religious freedom in the USSR.

Disputes. Despite a papal document released in February condemning all forms of racism, a charismatic black priest from Washington, DC, declared that the Roman Catholic Church is itself racist. The Rev. George Stallings defied his superiors by creating the Imani Temple in June before being suspended by Cardinal James Hickey of the Washington archdiocese. Though he was not threatened with excommunication, Stallings kept imploring the hierarchy to form an African-American Catholic rite like the church's existing rites. Stallings based his new liturgy on a Mass used experimentally in Zaire. The new wing would let blacks lead spiritual lives not dominated by a "Euro-American, white-male hierarchy," he said.

In September, Cardinal Jozef Glemp of Poland delayed his planned visit to the United States in the midst of a conflict with Jewish groups over the presence of a Carmelite convent outside the Auschwitz death camp in Poland. Rome intervened and settled the conflict by asking the nuns to relocate, offering them aid. (*See* RELIGION—*Judaism.*)

Abortion Ruling. The Supreme Court's July 3 ruling in *Webster v. Reproductive Health Services* that upheld a state's right to regulate abortion delighted Catholic pro-life activists and the Catholic bishops of the United States. A statement by the U.S. Bishops' Committee on Pro-Life Activities called the decision a cause for hope, while conceding that the court stopped short of recognizing a right to life or overturning the landmark *Roe v. Wade* ruling of 1973. The prelates also challenged Catholics and all pro-life Americans to make their love for life after birth "so obvious it cannot be ignored." (*See* feature article, page 44.)

Theologians and Teaching. The teaching of Catholic doctrine and Catholic teaching generally were in the news in 1989. In January the Rev. Hans Kung and 162 other European theologians signed a Declaration of Cologne criticizing Pope John Paul II's stance on contraception and his use of authority in appointing bishops and theologians. In February the Vatican Congregation for the Doctrine of Faith published an oath of fidelity to all official Church teachings and a profession of faith that would be required of newly hired teachers of Catholic theology and church officials. Although church law already provided for a profession of faith, it never was applied. Some theologians expressed misgivings about the oath.

In March the Rev. Charles Curran, a theologian who sued the Catholic University of America after being dismissed at Rome's insistence, lost his suit and vowed not to appeal. And in June more than 800 American Jesuits gathered at Georgetown University to discuss what is distinctive today about a Jesuit education.

Other Developments. Pope John Paul II released an exhortation on the vocation and mission of the laity, which closely resembled the 1987 synod recommendations. His 1989 travels included trips to southern Africa, Scandinavia, and Southeast Asia. And for the price of $2, the pope began coming into U.S. homes by way of a recorded daily telephone message.

U.S. bishops met with the pope and top Vatican officials for an extended dialogue in Rome, March 8–11. Such topics as the American Catholic priesthood, family, and school were discussed. Archbishop Daniel Pilarczyk of Cincinnati, president of the American bishops' conference, noted that the conference was marked by "candor, conviction, and kindness." In a June meeting in South Orange, NJ, U.S. bishops approved guidelines aimed at resolving disputes between bishops and theologians and urged the U.S. government to "move beyond the legacy of war" and begin normalizing relations with Vietnam.

© Denise B. Walker

The Rev. William H. Keeler, 58, a native of San Antonio, TX, who is known as a theological centrist, was installed as archbishop of Baltimore in a May 23 ceremony.

The annual meeting of the National Conference of Catholic Bishops, held November 6–9 in Baltimore, MD, celebrated the bicentennial of the naming of the first American bishop. The 300 bishops attending the conference passed a resolution urging opposition to legal abortion by all Catholics, notably politicians.

U.S. pastoral changes included the Rev. William Keeler, head of the Harrisburg, PA, diocese, who replaced retired Archbishop William Borders of Baltimore. On the international scene, the pontiff named three resident bishops for Soviet Lithuania and the first Roman Catholic bishop in the Soviet republic of Byelorussia in six decades.

KEITH D. PICHER, *"The New World"*

AP/Wide World

To improve its profits picture, Sears, Roebuck lowered its prices by up to 50% on more than 50,000 items. Michael Bozic, left, *chairman of Sears' merchandising group, personally changed some price tags at a Chicago store.*

RETAILING

Although the important segment of women's apparel picked up in sales, American retailing in 1989 saw two financial crises that cast shadows over some of its best-known stores. Campeau Corporation, the Canadian developer which took on a large debt in buying Federated/Allied stores in 1988, announced in September its inability to pay. Two weeks earlier, Campeau had put its 17 Bloomingdale's stores up for sale, a decision that shocked many who regarded "Bloomie's" as the nation's most respected and imitated retailer. After a hectic week-long crisis, Olympia and York Developments, another large Canadian builder, bailed out Campeau Corporation with a $250 million loan and with Robert Campeau losing control of the company. All Federated/Allied's stores began receiving goods again but concern lingered.

Earlier, L. J. Hooker, the Australian developer that owns Bonwit Teller and B. Altman, also resolved a cash crunch by filing Chapter XI bankruptcy proceedings for those two chains. Six of the seven B. Altman stores were closed in November, however.

In 1989, Carson Pirie Scott, the old-line Chicago retailer, was acquired by the Swiss-based Maus family, which already owned the P. A. Bergner chain in the Midwest. And a possible change in ownership loomed over Saks Fifth Avenue and Marshall Field's as British financier James Goldsmith made a hostile bid for their parent company, B.A.T. Industries.

Strong women's clothing sales, coming after a 20-month drag, helped to bolster storewide business and gave specialty shop chains, such as The Limited and The Gap, some of the best results of the industry. Conversely, menswear sales began to slip. But the major slowdown was in big-ticket durables, such as furniture, appliances, and electronics, although camcorders and compact-disc players sold well.

A new intensity over pricing arose when the country's biggest retailer, Sears, Roebuck, cut prices between 20 and 50% on 50,000 items as part of a program to reverse an earnings slide. K Mart, the second-largest chain, which was having its own earnings problems, responded in kind but found Sears' thrust difficult to contain. Montgomery Ward, after a management buyout of the old Montgomery Ward company in June 1988 from Mobil Corporation, also entered the pricing fray with its own reductions, as did Newmark and Lewis, the New York appliance chain. But Sears, after several months of gains from the March launch of "everyday low prices," saw its sales trend slacken.

Amid the restructuring and pricing clamor, several big retailers continued to sail along seemingly undisturbed. Two such retailers were the May Department Stores Company—although it decided to sell its discount-store chain Caldor and to spin off its Venture unit, to concentrate on department stores—and Wal-Mart Stores, the nation's fastest-growing retailer which began to threaten K Mart's Number 2 spot while expanding northward from its southern base. The J. C. Penney Company, which had moved its main offices to the Dallas area from New York, also enjoyed increasingly improved results from its concentration on soft lines and its own store brands.

In food retailing, the Great Atlantic & Pacific Tea Company, known as A&P, bought the Borman's chain in the Midwest and after first trying to buy the British Gateway food chain became a large investor in it. Kroger Corporation, with its $19.1 billion sales, intensified its supermarket conversion into food-drug stores while trying to refinance its "public" leveraged buyout, in which employee ownership rose to 35% from 10%.

The hypermarket trend grew slowly, consisting of the French company Carrefour's establishment in the East, Wal-Mart's stores in the Southwest, K Mart's single American Fare in the South, and the Biggs' stores in the Midwest. These huge food and nonfood emporiums continued to create much interest and to worry the food chains.

ISADORE BARMASH
"The New York Times"

RHODE ISLAND

For a nonelection year, 1989 began on a strident political note in Rhode Island. As the new General Assembly convened to organize, the 22 Democratic state senators, who earlier had elected David R. Carlin, Jr., of Newport, majority leader, found themselves outvoted by the 19 other Democrats allied with seven of the nine Republicans. This gave control of the Senate to Democrat John J. Bevilacqua of Providence, who had lost to Carlin previously, and to his new ally, Minority Leader Robert D. Goldberg of South Kingstown.

Legislative Session. The split, together with difficult budget problems, did much to shape the rest of the 1989 session. The end result was the longest Assembly session since 1971, continuing 26 days beyond the 60 days for which members are paid by constitutional mandate.

Gov. Edward D. DiPrete (R) sent his proposed budget to the legislature amid growing concern about trends in revenue collections needed to support it, even though the budget proposed $52 million in new taxes. Democratic leaders demanded $30 million in cuts to avert the threat of a deficit. The spending plan finally approved by the Assembly on June 30 had changed little in total appropriations, but now had nearly $67 million in new taxes to pay for the appropriations.

Though hampered by delays in the divided Senate, the General Assembly passed legislation on home confinement of prisoners and landfill-siting regulations designed to override local objections. The General Assembly also increased the minimum wage and provided assistance for hospitals beset by deficits. A bill to ban assault rifles failed to pass. And bond issues on open space land acquisition and park improvement were slated for referendum.

Election Politics. Later in the year hopefuls began to position themselves for elections in 1990. A key question was whether U.S. Sen. Claiborne Pell (D) would seek a sixth term. Aspirants from both parties, including U.S. Rep. Claudine Schneider (R), eyed that contest. Several Democrats also laid plans to challenge Governor DiPrète.

The Economy. The state continued to prosper, although there were signs that growth was slowing, as reflected in the increasingly cautious tax-revenue estimates. Figures available in late summer showed that corporate and personal bankruptcies in Rhode Island were up 20% over 1988. The real-estate boom leveled off with demand slowing and prices stabilizing. New home construction was down, and the condominium market was saturated, forcing some developers into bankruptcy and others into cutting prices.

Unemployment remained low, although it rose from 3.2% in January to 3.9% in the fall. At the same time the service sector had trouble hiring. Manufacturing jobs continued to decline, however, down to 111,100 in 1989 from 121,800 in the peak year of 1984. In the first eight months of 1989, 2,000 manufacturing jobs were lost through plant closings. One of the last steel rolling mills in the state shut down in October, with the loss of up to 148 jobs.

Providence Development. Redevelopment in downtown Providence progressed rapidly in 1989. Two new office buildings were about complete, the Providence River was being relocated to become a scenic focal point for the city's core, and ambitious plans for a new convention center neared completion.

Oil Spill. Rhode Islanders were appalled June 23 when a tanker ripped its bottom open on Brenton Reef as it tried to enter Narragansett Bay, spilling several hundred thousand gallons of oil. Cleanup was quick and effective, and the state narrowly escaped an ecological disaster. (*See* feature article, page 36.)

ELMER E. CORNWELL, JR.
Brown University

RHODE ISLAND • Information Highlights

Area: 1,212 sq mi (3 140 km²).
Population (July 1, 1988): 993,000.
Chief Cities (1980 census): Providence, the capital (July 1, 1986 est.): 157,200; Warwick, 87,123.
Government (1989): *Chief Officers*—governor, Edward D. DiPrete (R); lt. gov., Roger N. Begin (D). *General Assembly*—Senate, 50 members; House of Representatives, 100 members.
State Finances (fiscal year 1988): *Revenue,* $2,719,000,000; *expenditure,* $2,480,000,000.
Personal Income (1988): $16,769,000,000; per capita, $16,892.
Labor Force (June 1989): *Civilian labor force,* 532,200; *unemployed,* 20,100 (3.8% of total force).
Education: *Enrollment* (fall 1987)—public elementary schools, 93,000; public secondary, 41,000; colleges and universities, 71,708. *Public school expenditures* (1987–88), $669,639,000 ($4,947 per pupil).

ROMANIA

The year 1989 was one of mounting crisis for Romania, climaxed in December by a series of bloody confrontations between government forces and opponents of Communist dictator Nicolae Ceauşescu, and the downfall of the 24-year-old Ceauşescu regime.

Domestic Affairs. Up to the time of his ouster, Ceauşescu resolutely continued the policies that made him so unpopular. At home, he pursued his radical plans of modernization. In Bucharest, many historic buildings were razed and some 50,000 inhabitants uprooted to make way for a huge complex of government buildings, boulevards, and blocks of prefabricated apartments, offices, and stores. Ceauşescu boasted that when the project was completed in 1991, 90% of the city's population would be housed in new quarters. He also an-

ROMANIA • Information Highlights

Official Name: Romania.
Location: Southeastern Europe.
Area: 91,699 sq mi (237 500 km^2).
Population (mid-1989 est.): 23,200,000.
Chief Cities (July 1, 1986 est.): Bucharest, the capital, 1,989,823; Braşov, 351,493; Constanta, 327,676.
Government: *Head of state,* Ion Iliescu, president (took office December 1989). *Head of government,* Petre Roman, prime minister (took office December 1989). *Legislature* (unicameral)—Grand National Assembly.
Monetary Unit: Leu (14.840 lei equal U.S.$1, July 1989).
Gross National Product (1988 U.S.$): $151,300,-000,000.
Foreign Trade (1986 U.S.$): *Imports,* $10,590,-000,000; *exports,* $12,543,000,000.

nounced the semicompletion of the planned destruction of about 13,000 rural villages, their inhabitants to be moved to large consolidated agro-industrial complexes. Such drastic measures, he claimed, would vacate much needed arable land and fulfill the socialist promise to provide equal living and working conditions for rural and urban dwellers.

Since a large proportion of the targeted villages were ethnic German or ethnic Hungarian settlements in Transylvania, both West Germany and Hungary labeled the rural relocation program an attempt to eradicate those minorities in Romania. In March, Hungary reported to the UN Commission on Human Rights that some 15,000–20,000 refugees from Romania already had sought asylum in Hungary, and the commission voted to investigate the case. Although Romania had closed its border with Hungary in 1988, in June 1989 it was reported to be erecting barbed-wire fences along its frontiers with Hungary and Yugoslavia, ostensibly to keep its people from fleeing abroad. In December, Nadia Comaneci, the former Olympic gymnast, defected to the United States.

In July a top-level Hungarian delegation led by Reszö Nyers, president of the presidium of the Hungarian Communist Party, met with Ceauşescu and his lieutenants in Romania to discuss the ethnic issue. Ceauşescu denied any persecution and allegedly threatened that Romania had developed the capability to produce nuclear weapons and medium-range missiles and might use them to annex additional territory in dispute between the two countries.

In March, Ceauşescu's blatant disregard for human rights and religious freedoms, together with his draconian domestic measures, provoked the most important challenge to his rule since the massive worker riots of 1987. Six prominent former state and party officials, led by Silviu Brucan, former Romanian ambassador to the United States and delegate to the UN, sent him an open letter denouncing his mismanaging of the economy, ignoring the constitutional rights of citizens, and violating the 1975 Helsinki accords. All reportedly were arrested. The incident, together with the arrest of about two dozen other dissidents, had severe repercussions abroad.

Foreign Affairs. In late 1988, Ceauşescu had proclaimed that the Romanian Communist Party "cannot share or relinquish its role." Allegedly, he had requested secretly a summit meeting of world Communist Party leaders that would void the elections that had brought the Solidarity union to political power in Poland, but without success.

In March, France withdrew its ambassador, and in April, West Germany did the same over the alleged human-rights violations. In April, Romania recalled its own ambassador to Great Britain, charging the British Foreign Office with pursuing an anti-Romanian policy. The European Common Market froze negotiations with Romania over trade cooperation. In July the leaders of the seven most industrialized nations of the world, meeting in Paris, also condemned Romania's repression of its domestic movement for democracy.

Already labeled the poorest country in Europe after Albania, Romania's economy was depressed further by Ceauşescu's continuing crash program to retire the country's foreign debt. In April, Romania completed the repayment of its remaining $3.2 billion debt to the World Bank and the International Monetary Fund ahead of schedule. It still owed $1.5 billion to the U.S. government and U.S. banks.

The Uprising. The final struggle between the regime and its opponents began in mid-December, when protesters in the western Romanian city of Timisoara tried to prevent the arrest of Rev. Laszlo Tokes, a Protestant clergyman and spokesman for the ethnic Hungarians. Security forces fired on the crowd, killing hundreds and perhaps thousands of the demonstrators. World opinion condemned the massacre and unrest spread to other parts of the country. Ceauşescu, returning from a trip to Iran on December 20, denounced the rebels as reactionaries and fascists. After further violence between troops and rioters in Cluj and Bucharest, army units joined the uprising on December 22. Ceauşescu and his wife Elena fled the capital, and a Council of National Salvation announced the formation of a new provisional government. The Ceauşescus were captured by the army and, after a quick trial, were executed on December 25 for crimes against the Romanian people.

Among the first acts of the country's new leaders were to remove the Communist Party symbol from the national flag, to legalize most abortions , which had been proscribed under Ceauşescu, and to repeal a law mandating the use of the term "comrade." A number of new political parties were formed in late December.

JOSEPH FREDERICK ZACEK
State University of New York at Albany

SASKATCHEWAN

Political turmoil and a shaky economy plagued Saskatchewan during most of 1989.

Politics. Premier Grant Devine's privatization plans provoked an uproar from opposition members of the provincial legislature. Though the Progressive Conservative government had privatized a growing number of government services and Crown corporations, when it moved to turn the natural gas distribution arm of the Saskatchewan Power Corporation into a public company, the New Democrats walked out of the assembly, halting the government's legislative work for 17 days. Devine claimed the opposition had hijacked the legislature. The New Democrats insisted the government had promised it never would privatize a utility.

As soon as the legislature reopened, the government passed a bill to privatize the Potash Corporation of Saskatchewan, formed in the mid-1970s by the then New Democratic government when it nationalized U.S.-owned potash mines.

Public-opinion polls in 1989 showed Devine's government far lower in popularity than the New Democrats. However, a provincial election was not necessary until 1991.

Budget. Finance Minister Gary Lane unveiled a 1989–90 budget totaling C$4.3 billion with a C$226 million deficit. Since the conservatives took power in 1982, there have been eight budget deficits in a row. The accumulated total now was C$3.8 billion. Lane's most controversial move was a 10% tax on lottery tickets and gambling. Lottery ticket sales fell by 20%, and, since proceeds go to fund sports and cultural activities, many organizations feared their grants would be cut. Lobby groups were created to fight the tax.

Agriculture. After three years of poor harvests, early summer pointed to a bumper crop for 1989. However, much-needed rain failed to arrive in time and much of the crop was scorched by the sun. Total production for the six major grains was estimated at 20.2 million tons (18.3 million metric tons).

Mining. Diamond fever swept Saskatchewan after it leaked out that a subsidiary of De Beers Mining of South Africa had found diamond-bearing ore near Prince Albert. Although company officials later said the diamonds were not of a commercial quality, the discovery, nonetheless, spurred prospecting.

Nuclear Power. A Regina-based company revealed it was studying the possibility of building a C$1 billion nuclear reactor in the province. The company would buy the plant from Atomic Energy of Canada Ltd., and sell the electricity to the Saskatchewan Power Corporation. The proposal was greeted with enthusiasm by businesses. Antinuclear groups, however, said that if the plan were approved, they would try to halt construction.

Rafferty Dam. One of the most ambitious construction projects of the current administration was brought to a temporary halt in April when the Federal Court of Canada granted an injunction to the Canadian Wildlife Federation, forcing the province to shut down work on the C$125 million Rafferty/Alameda dam project. The wildlife group claimed proper studies had not been done to ensure that the project would not damage the environment and endanger wildlife. With C$2 million per month being lost while work was stalled, the provincial government appealed to Federal Environment Minister Lucien Bouchard, and in September the ban was overturned.

Population. A lagging economy was blamed for a declining population. In 1989 it was estimated that more than 1,000 persons per month were leaving the province. After assessing births to longtime residents, it was estimated that 50,000 persons had left the province in the past several years.

PAUL JACKSON
"Star Phoenix," Saskatoon

SASKATCHEWAN • Information Highlights

Area: 251,865 sq mi (652 330 km²).
Population (June 1989): 1,007,100.
Chief Cities (1986 census): Regina, the capital, 175,064; Saskatoon, 177,641; Moose Jaw, 35,073.
Government (1989): *Chief Officers*—lt. gov., F. W. Johnson; premier, Grant Devine (Progressive Conservative). *Legislature*—Legislative Assembly, 64 members.
Provincial Finances (1989–90 fiscal year budget): *Revenues*, $4,074,000,000; *expenditures*, $4,300,000,000.
Personal Income (average weekly earnings, April 1989): $416.59.
Labor Force (June 1989, seasonally adjusted): *Employed* workers, 15 years of age and over, 445,000; *Unemployed*, 7.7%.
Education (1988–89): *Enrollment*—elementary and secondary schools, 216,100 pupils; postsecondary—universities, 21,000; community colleges, 2,830.
(All monetary figures are in Canadian dollars.)

SAUDI ARABIA

Saudi Arabia in 1989 received more government revenue as the world price of petroleum rose and Saudi foreign policy achieved success in improving relations with many countries.

Oil. In 1989, Saudi Arabia exported more oil than any other country in the world, while it produced about one quarter of all the oil coming from the Organization of Petroleum Exporting Countries (OPEC). As a result, the Saudis played a prominent role in making OPEC decisions on production quotas and price levels. Following the Iran-Iraq cease-fire in August 1988, both countries began to produce more oil and the Saudis proposed a compromise in October 1988 to bring the two former belligerents fully into the OPEC system. After Iran rejected

SAUDI ARABIA • Information Highlights

Official Name: Kingdom of Saudi Arabia.
Location: Arabian peninsula in southwest Asia.
Area: 829,996 sq mi (2 149 690 km²).
Population (mid-1989 est.): 14,700,000.
Capital (1981 est.): Riyadh, 1,000,000.
Government: *Head of state and government,* Fahd bin 'Abd al-'Aziz Al Sa'ud, king and prime minister (acceded June 1982).
Monetary Unit: Riyal (3.73 riyals equal U.S.$1, Nov. 10, 1989).
Gross National Product (1988 U.S.$): $74,000,000,000.
Economic Index (1988): *Consumer Prices* (1980 = 100), all items, 95.3; food, 100.0.
Foreign Trade (1988 U.S.$): *Imports,* $21,784,000,000; *exports,* $23,737,000,000.

that idea, Saudi Arabia increased production of oil, thereby helping to lower its price to about $10–$12 per barrel by November when OPEC met again to determine quotas and price "targets" or minimums. The Saudis suggested a target price of $15 per barrel; however, Algeria's President Chadli Benjedid called Saudi King Fahd and persuaded him to accept a target of $18. OPEC agreed to this new goal, set a production limit of 18.5 million barrels of oil per day effective January 1, and finally brought Iran and Iraq into accord with the organization.

New Saudi oil discoveries, announced Jan. 9, 1989, meant that Saudi Arabia, with 252 billion barrels of recoverable oil underground, had about one quarter of the world's oil. Despite the long-range implications of these discoveries, Saudis were concerned chiefly with the immediate issue of pricing, so they were delighted as rising world demand for oil and stricter OPEC adherence to production quotas led to prices going up to $18–$20 per barrel by March. King Fahd predicted on May 3 that by the end of 1989 the price would go up to as much as $26 per barrel, and he later condemned OPEC members who exceeded their quotas and thereby endangered the desired price increase. At the June OPEC meeting in Vienna, the Saudis supported the decision to increase total production to 19.5 million barrels per day while keeping the same distribution among countries. As a result, the Saudi quota increased from 4.5 to 4.76 million barrels per day. Actual Saudi production in 1989 was slightly above its quotas, but the surplus was stored and not sold. OPEC's success led it and Saudi Arabia to raise production levels yet again on September 23 as the OPEC total limit was set at 20.5 million barrels per day.

Foreign Affairs. Saudi Arabia tried in 1989 to improve relations with Iran, Iraq, Egypt, the Soviet Union, and China as well as to mediate the Lebanese civil conflict. On Oct. 19, 1988, King Fahd said that he wanted to avoid antagonizing Iran, but subsequently Iranian or pro-Iranian Lebanese groups attacked Saudi targets. A Saudi diplomat was killed in Thailand on Jan. 4, 1989, and another was wounded in Turkey on October 16. Iran again boycotted the Muslim pilgrimage to Mecca and diplomatic relations remained broken. On March 27 in Baghdad, King Fahd signed a treaty of nonaggression and mutual noninterference with Iraq, and Iraq later increased its export of crude oil through Saudi pipelines.

The king flew to Egypt for his first state visit since the Israeli-Egyptian peace treaty of 1979. Although Saudi Arabia had no formal diplomatic ties with the Soviet Union, the Saudis provided a location at Taif for talks on Dec. 3–5, 1988, between the Soviets and the Afghan *mujahidin* who opposed the Communist government of Afghanistan. Soviet Deputy Foreign Minister Yuli Vorontsov met with King Fahd on December 5. On March 9, 1989, Saudi Arabia became the first country to recognize the interim *mujahidin* Afghan government based in Pakistan. Saudi relations with China became clearer as the kingdom acquired Chinese weapons. In August the Saudis sent a commercial representative to China although they did not open formal diplomatic relations.

The May 23–26 Arab summit meeting at Casablanca appointed a committee consisting of the leaders of Saudi Arabia, Algeria, and Morocco to seek a cease-fire and national reconciliation in Lebanon. By August 1, Prince Saud ibn Faisal Al Saud, the Saudi foreign minister, admitted defeat in the task by saying the three countries had reached a "dead end." However, after three weeks of talks at Taif in October, 59 of the 62 members of the Lebanese Parliament accepted a Saudi-sponsored compromise plan for peace, foreign withdrawal, and political reforms. Saudi elation subsequently was curbed as Gen. Michel Aoun, leader of the Christian Lebanese government, rejected the plan.

Government. The king retained most of his political power in 1989 as no fundamental changes took place in the Saudi political system despite several challenges and some shuffling of administrative posts. Muslim condemnation of Salman Rushdie's novel *The Satanic Verses* was coordinated by the Saudi government as the 45 member nations of the Organization of the Islamic Conference met in Riyadh, March 13–16. The Saudis and King Fahd showed relative restraint by condemning Rushdie as an apostate from Islam but not calling for his death, and by emphasizing Islam's tolerance. A potential challenge to the Saudi royal family came from the Ayatollah Khomeini of Iran, who wrote in his deathbed statement that Fahd was a "traitor to God." Following an explosion that killed one pilgrim in Mecca on July 10, the Saudis on September 21 publicly beheaded 16 Kuwaitis, some of Iranian origin, for complicity in the attack.

In October the king named Muhammed ibn Ibrahim al-Jubairi minister of justice and Khalid ibn Muhammed al-Angari minister of municipal and rural affairs, while the government's attention was centered on the new five-year plan for economic development to be announced in January 1990. The plan was sure to include the expansion of the East-West Petroline's capacity by one third, since contracts for that project were signed in October.

Military. Saudi Arabia continued to diversify its sources of armaments while remaining pro-United States in its foreign policy. Launching pads for Chinese medium-range missiles were constructed in late 1988, but Saudi Arabia in April 1988 said it would sign the Nuclear Nonproliferation Treaty as a signal that it did not plan to acquire nuclear weapons to use in conjunction with the missiles. Two new arms deals with France in June 1989 were worth about \$2.7 billion, and in October the United States announced a planned sale to Saudi Arabia of as many as 315 M1-A1 tanks.

WILLIAM OCHSENWALD
Virginia Polytechnic Institute and State University

SINGAPORE

Slower yet still healthy economic growth, measures to control immigration, and murmurs of change in domestic politics and foreign affairs marked a postelection year in Singapore.

Economy. After a record growth rate of 11% in 1988, Singapore's economy was expected to grow by 7% in 1989. A decline in non-oil exports, especially manufacturing goods to the United States, was offset partially by a boom in the construction sector. Singapore managed to maintain strong economic growth while keeping inflation and interest rates low. Consumer prices were expected to rise less than 2% in 1989; the prime interest rate remained 5.5% for much of the year, then saw modest increases. In March the government announced hefty pay raises for civil servants, politicians, and the armed forces. The increases ranged from about 30% for cabinet ministers and bureaucrats to 60% for Prime Minister Lee Kuan Yew. Singapore's most serious economic problem was a shortage of labor, aggravated by government efforts to hold back the entry of foreign laborers.

Immigration. In mid-March, Singapore joined with the five other members of the Association of Southeast Asian Nations (ASEAN) in adopting restrictions on Vietnamese refugees seeking asylum. Then on April 1, a strict new immigration law passed by Parliament took effect. Under the measure, any foreigner found to be in Singapore illegally was subject to caning and imprisonment. During a two-week amnesty period prior to imposition of the law, some 10,000 illegal aliens, mostly Thais, fled the country. A negative reaction by Bangkok led to high-level talks, and by early May Singapore agreed to let some 9,800 of the Thai laborers return legally to work.

In mid-July, the government announced that it would allow some 25,000 Hong Kong Chinese and their families (concerned over their future under Beijing rule, beginning in 1997) to immigrate over the next five years. The regime stressed that the influx would not be allowed to upset the nation's "multiracial character"—about 76% Chinese, 15% Malays, and 9% Indians and other minorities.

Politics and Government. Prime Minister Lee marked his 30th year as the leader of Singapore, turned 66 in September, and looked toward retirement in 1990. First Deputy Prime Minister Goh Chok Tong (also assistant secretary-general of the Political Action Party, or PAP) remained the heir apparent, but Trade and Industry Minister Lee Hsien Loong, the prime minister's son, further consolidated his political, military, and administrative powers. Within the PAP, he moved up to the position of second assistant secretary-general, behind Goh.

In mid-May the government released Chia Thye Poh, a former member of Parliament who had been arrested in 1966 for his alleged ties with the Communist Party of Malaysia.

Foreign Affairs. Singapore in 1989 took steps to shore up its security through closer military cooperation with neighboring Indonesia and Malaysia. In March it signed an agreement with Indonesia on joint land-forces training, followed by an official visit to Jakarta by First Deputy Prime Minister Goh. Earlier it had reached an understanding with Malaysia on joint military exercises.

Prime Minister Lee took a major step toward improved U.S. relations by offering to let the United States base some of its military forces in Singapore. The offer was timely, as Washington was negotiating with the Philippines over the future of U.S. military bases in that country. The prime minister also favored a role for the Khmer Rouge in an interim government in Cambodia, following the withdrawal of Vietnamese from that country in September.

JEFFREY H. HACKER, *Free-lance Writer*

SINGAPORE • Information Highlights

Official Name: Republic of Singapore.
Location: Southeast Asia.
Area: 244 sq mi (632.6 km²).
Population (mid-1989 est.): 2,700,000.
Capital: Singapore City.
Government: *Head of state,* Wee Kim Wee, president (took office September 1985). *Head of government,* Lee Kuan Yew, prime minister (took office 1959). *Legislature* (unicameral)—Parliament.
Monetary Unit: Singapore dollar (1.9505 S. dollars equal U.S. \$1, Nov. 29, 1989).
Gross Domestic Product (1988 est. U.S.\$): \$23,700,000,000.
Economic Index (1988): *Consumer Prices* (1980 = 100), all items, 118.1; food, 115.4.
Foreign Trade (1988 U.S.\$): *Imports,* \$43,862,000,000; *exports,* \$39,305,000,000.

© Gamma-Liaison

The homeless, government officials, and celebrities joined together in the U.S. capital on October 7 for a "Housing Now!" march. Responding to the homeless problem, the Bush administration later proposed a $7 billion housing plan.

SOCIAL WELFARE

The decade of the 1980s will be remembered as one in which the U.S. economy survived a recession and then enjoyed a healthy pattern of steady growth combined with low rates of inflation and unemployment. This good economic news continued in 1989. However, as was the case throughout most of the decade, the nation's general economic prosperity in 1989 had little or no positive impact on large numbers of Americans mired in poverty.

The Extent of Poverty. The annual Census Bureau report on family income released in October 1989 found that in 1988 nearly 32 million Americans—about 13.1% of the population—lived below the poverty line, defined as a total cash income of $12,091 for a family of four. The national poverty rate dropped by about three tenths of one percent compared to 1987. The poverty rate among blacks decreased slightly to 31.6%; for whites the figure for 1987 was 10.1%; and for Hispanics, 26.8%. Despite those decreases, the figures strongly indicated that poverty remained a significant problem throughout the nation. The poverty rate, noted Robert Greenstein, director of the Center on Budget and Policy Priorities, "remains higher than in any year of the 1970s, including the most severe recession years of that decade."

A series of reports released throughout the year gave a fuller picture of the nation's social welfare. The National Urban League's annual report, "State of Black America," issued in January, contended that social policies instituted by the Reagan administration had hit particularly hard at black Americans. "In 1988, blacks were three times as likely as whites to be poor, two-and-a-half times as likely to be jobless," said John Jacob, the league's president. "Housing segregation increased. For the second straight year, black life expectancy declined."

More than 45% of all black children in the United States were living in poverty in the late 1980s—a 5% increase compared to a decade earlier, according to a report issued in late January by the Children's Defense Fund. The report, which used Census Bureau and U.S. Department of Labor data, also said that from 1979 to 1987 the number of Hispanic children living in poverty increased from about 28% to nearly 40%. The report called for expanding a range of social programs that were cut back in the 1980s, including the federal nutrition program for pregnant women and education programs for disadvantaged children.

An October report by the House Select Committee on Children, Youth and Families concurred with the Children's Defense Fund findings, pointing out that half the nation's black children lived in households headed by their mothers, and that nearly 70% of those children were living below the poverty line. For Hispanic children in single-parent poverty homes, the figure was slightly higher.

Not unexpectedly, the majority of impoverished Americans lived in urban areas. A report issued in March by the National League of Cities found that some 70% of the nation's poor lived in metropolitan areas, compared with about 62% in 1979. But poverty was by no means confined to the large cities. Analysts believed that about 500 of the nation's some 6,500 suburbs—once viewed as middle-class enclaves—also faced severe poverty problems. These problems included high unemployment and crime rates and growing homelessness.

"Poor suburbs range from old bedroom towns in the East to new barrios in the West," said Pierre deVise, an urbanologist at Roosevelt University in Chicago. "They are at an increasingly huge disadvantage." The nation's poorest suburb was Ford Heights, IL, near Chicago, where per capita income was less than $5,000, according to a survey deVise released in June. Four Los Angeles suburbs (Cudahy, Bell Gardens, Huntington Park, and Coachella) were among the nation's ten poorest, as were three Illinois suburbs of St. Louis (Alorton, East St. Louis, and Centreville); others were Camden, NJ, and Florida City, FL.

There was also evidence put forward in 1989 that those on the bottom rung of the economic ladder were worse off economically than in previous years. One example was the House Ways and Means Committee's annual report on federal assistance programs, released in March. The report, using data from the Congressional Budget Office and the Census Bureau, found that the average family income of the poorest one fifth of the population decreased from just more than $5,500 a year in 1973 to about $5,100 in 1987.

Census Bureau statistics released in June agreed with the Ways and Means Committee's findings. According to a report written by Mark Littman, a Census Bureau poverty expert, the number of poor families whose incomes were less than half the poverty level increased by nearly 6% from 1980 to 1986. "It would appear that the poor are no better off in the 1980s than they were in the 1960s and 1970s," Littman said.

The Homeless. The group of poor Americans that received the most public attention in 1989 was the homeless. As in the past, there was disagreement over the extent of the homeless problem. Because of the extremely transient nature of the homeless population, it was virtually impossible to determine exactly how many persons were without homes, although the Census Bureau would attempt for the first time to count the homeless in 1990. Federal government and some academic studies generally estimated the number of homeless Amer-

Voluntarism

It was too early to speak of a return to the New Deal or the Great Society, but 1989 may have marked the beginning of a resurgence of interest in public service. As the 1980s ended, there were signs of rekindled support for volunteer efforts to protect the environment and lend a helping hand to Americans who have fallen through the welfare system's safety net.

Support for "voluntarism" or "national service," as public-spiritedness now is called, has its roots in similar movements of the 1960s. That period produced the Peace Corps, which sent more than 15,500 U.S. volunteers to serve in developing countries at its peak in 1966. Domestic programs, including VISTA (Volunteers Service to America), were created as part of President Johnson's war on poverty and now are part of ACTION, an umbrella agency that oversees the main federal volunteer programs.

The Gallup Organization has tracked a recent surge in the number of Americans who say they devote time to charity or public-service activities. Reflecting this renewed interest in public service, George Bush called on the nation to create "a thousand points of light"—a new corps of volunteers—during the 1988 presidential campaign. Upon taking office, Bush created the new Office of National Service to draw up legislation reflecting the president's interest in fostering the "gentler, kinder nation" he envisioned in his inauguration speech. Although Bush had not presented the details of his program by mid-November, he announced on June 22 his intention to ask Congress to provide $25 million a year to set up and run a special foundation that would encourage Americans, especially young people, to provide public service without pay. The encouragement would come in the form of special awards for outstanding service.

Congress was quick to come up with its own initiatives and in 1989 produced more than 20 bills promoting national service. But unlike Bush's reliance on voluntarism as its own reward, most congressional proposals would offer financial incentives such as post-service education or housing benefits. The most radical of these would have required student-aid recipients to earn their federal benefits by serving as volunteers in civilian or military service. Sponsored by Sen. Sam Nunn (D-GA) and Rep. Dave McCurdy (D-OK), the proposal drew criticism for discriminating against the poor by forcing them to interrupt their education while imposing no such penalty on students who do not need student aid.

Although it discarded the Nunn-McCurdy plan, Congress passed a number of other initiatives to fund national service programs. Both chambers agreed to reauthorize funding through 1993 for the main domestic volunteer programs, such as ACTION, which includes VISTA, the Foster Grandparents, the Retired Senior Volunteer Program (RSVP), and the Senior Companion Program (SCP). Both chambers would require ACTION to spend more money to recruit volunteers.

As 1989 ended, it remained uncertain what form of legislation in support of voluntarism would emerge. Many Republicans, including the president, remained opposed to the financial incentives included in several congressional measures. But the new bipartisan support of voluntarism appeared certain to produce some form of national service legislation in the early 1990s.

MARY H. COOPER

icans at about 600,000. Homeless advocacy groups, on the other hand, estimated the number as high as 4 million and contended that the problem was growing worse. Homeless advocates believed there were some 30,000 homeless persons in New York City, which spent more than $300 million in services for the homeless in fiscal year 1989.

The California Office of Emergency Service estimated that more than 13,000 persons joined the ranks of the homeless, at least temporarily, due to the October 17 earthquake that jolted the San Francisco Bay area. Homeless advocates said the earthquake doubled or perhaps tripled the number of homeless in the area.

The U.S. Department of Education issued a report in February that estimated there were 220,000 homeless school-age children across the country, and that more than 65,000 of those children did not attend school regularly. Homeless advocates believed the numbers were much larger. Maria Foscarinis, Washington counsel for the National Coalition for the Homeless, said that there were between 500,000 and 700,000 homeless children in the country and that a higher percentage of them were not enrolled in schools.

Homelessness also appeared to be growing worse in rural areas, where increasing numbers of farm families and others were forced out of their homes and living in shelters either in rural areas or in nearby cities such as Minneapolis, Chicago, Des Moines, and Omaha.

A report released in August by the American Affordable Housing Institute at Rutgers University warned that in addition to the current homeless population, there was a large group of "near homeless" Americans. Between 4 million and 14 million U.S. families, the report said, were "living on the knife edge of homelessness; they are doubled and tripled up in the apartments of friends and family; they are one paycheck, one domestic argument from the streets."

Positive News for the Disabled. No one knows what percentage of the homeless population is made up of disabled persons. But it is agreed generally that altogether some 43 million Americans have some type of physical, mental, or emotional problem that severely limits their abilities. Beginning in the early 1970s, advocacy groups fought for and won the passage of scores of federal, state, and local laws making buildings, education, and employment more accessible to the disabled. Still, according to Census Bureau data released in August 1989, only about 23% of disabled men and some 11% of disabled women were able to work full-time.

There was good news for disabled Americans in 1989. The U.S. Senate, in a 76-8 vote in September, passed the Americans With Disabilities Act, a measure that Sen. Tom Harkin (D-IA) called "the emancipation proclamation for disabled Americans." The Senate bill—a similar version of which was expected to be approved by the House early in 1990 and signed by President Bush—for the first time prohibited private employers from denying jobs on the basis of disability. The bill also obligated companies with more than 14 employees to make their facilities accessible to the disabled.

The Catastrophic Coverage Act. The 1988 Medicare Catastrophic Coverage Act, designed to help elderly Americans avoid astronomical health-care bills, was repealed by Congress during the final hours of its 1989 session. Better-off seniors, who would have been required to pay a surcharge to help pay for the plan, led a virtual citizens' revolt against the law. (*See* TAXATION.)

The International Situation. The social problems of Americans, as severe as they were, once again were dwarfed by those of hundreds of millions of others in Third World nations faced with hunger, disease, and starvation. About 20% of the world's population—some 1.3 billion people—suffered from serious illness or malnutrition, according to a report issued in September by the World Health Organization (WHO). The problems were most severe in developing countries in south and east Asia and in sub-Saharan Africa. The most common diseases were malaria, measles, diarrhea, respiratory illnesses, and AIDS. Prospects for improving the lives of the impoverished worldwide were dim, even though most of the widespread diseases were preventable and treatable. WHO officials estimated that the cost of implementing an effective immunization and treatment program for the most prevalent diseases was about $2.8 billion per year.

Another potentially catastrophic problem throughout most of the Third World involved declining world food production and stocks beginning in the 1986–87 growing season. Poor harvests in the past three years (including widespread 1988 droughts in the United States, Canada, and China) could mean a steep increase in hunger and starvation, according to the United Nations Food and Agriculture Organization (FAO). The global food situation was "a cause for serious concern," said Edouard Saouma, FAO's director. A FAO report said that in 1989 "exceptional" or "emergency" food-assistance conditions existed in 15 countries: Angola, Bangladesh, Ethiopia, Haiti, Jamaica, Laos, Lebanon, Mozambique, Nicaragua, Peru, Sierra Leone, Somalia, Sri Lanka, the Sudan, and Vietnam.

The problems of hunger and disease were particularly devastating among children. Severe poverty in developing nations directly accounted for the deaths of about 500,000 children in 1988, according to statistics compiled by the United Nations Children's Fund.

MARC LEEPSON, *Free-lance Writer*

In mid-October eight of South Africa's most prominent political prisoners, including African National Congress associate Elias Motsoaledi (center) were released by President de Klerk.

© Kuus/Sipa

SOUTH AFRICA

No year in recent memory has been so uncertain yet so critical for the future direction of South Africa. In 1989 advocates of reform, retrenchment, and of revolutionary change confronted each other in the diplomatic arena as well as in the streets. For the first time, whites in power acknowledged the need for a negotiated settlement with blacks, but were circumspect about what such a settlement would entail and the pace at which change should occur. The African National Congress (ANC) emerged as the principal representative of black opposition. Support for the ANC at the annual meetings of the Organization of African Unity (OAU), the non-aligned states, and Commonwealth ministers contributed to its bargaining power at home.

Early in April a new political organization, the Democratic Party, was formed. It aimed to establish "a true democracy which rejects race as its basis and protects the human dignity and liberty of all of its citizens." The new party was a merger of three white groups—the Progressive Federal Party (PFP) led by Zach J. de Beer, Wynand G. Malan's National Democratic Movement, and the Independent Party under Denis J. Worrall, the former South African ambassador to Britain. Moderate black supporters of the Democratic Party included Oscar Dhlomo, an official in Chief Mangosuthu Gatsha Buthelezi's *Inkatha* movement.

At the end of the parliamentary session in June, PFP member Helen Suzman retired from active politics after 36 years in office. From 1961 to 1974 she was the only liberal opposition party member in the Parliament. During her tenure, Suzman fought against racial segregation and discrimination, called for an investigation of the death of Black Consciousness leader Steven Biko while he was in police custody, communicated with ANC leader Nelson Mandela, and was an ardent advocate for blacks held without trial. She also called for fundamental reforms such as an end to the oppressive pass laws.

Notwithstanding official talk of reform, the legislative foundation of apartheid remained, the state of emergency continued, and the struggle over desegregation was far from resolved. Given this uncertainty, international corporations such as Mobil Oil and Goodyear Tire and Rubber disinvested, bringing to 190 the number of U.S. corporations which have withdrawn since 1985. Despite an increase in the price of gold toward the end of the year, South Africa's economy was beset by high inflation and lack of investor confidence; its currency, the rand, remained at an all-time low.

Some evidence suggested that a combination of domestic and international pressures finally forced many whites to concede the need to dismantle apartheid, but it was equally clear that the government intended for the extent and pace of change to be dictated by the white minority. During the September 1989 national election, the ruling National Party (NP) maintained that it would take between five and ten years to bring blacks into the political process. Even then, participation would be based on the protection of "group rights," and thus the ultimate determinant of policy would continue to be based on race classification, conditions that were unacceptable to the majority of blacks.

Botha's Waning Days. After suffering a mild stroke in January, President P. W. Botha relinquished the leadership of the National Party the following month. He was succeeded by the Minister of National Education, F. W. de

Klerk, who had been leader of the National Party in the Transvaal province since 1982. On August 14, Botha resigned as president after ten years in power, claiming that the cabinet had ignored his wishes. The crisis revolved around a dispute over de Klerk's right to travel to Zambia to meet with President Kenneth Kaunda, a longtime supporter of the ANC. Botha said that he would not give de Klerk permission because the time was not opportune and because of Kaunda's ANC sympathies. Ironically, Botha himself had met with Kaunda in April 1982. Botha resigned because the cabinet unanimously supported de Klerk. Despite the fact that there was to be a national election within a few weeks, it was believed generally that if de Klerk had stepped down in this confrontation his legitimacy as leader of the party and as future president of South Africa would have been threatened.

On September 14, de Klerk was elected president and was sworn in at a church ceremony in Pretoria six days later. While he was chosen by the electoral college representing all three houses of the tricameral Parliament, in actual fact, the NP majority in the white Assembly made the choice. Most white South African politicians saw de Klerk as a pragmatist and expected him to expand the limited reforms that had been instituted by Botha.

September Election. Early in May, President P. W. Botha announced that there would be a general election on September 6. This was the first time that ballots for the three segregated branches of Parliament were cast on the same day. A total of 763 candidates contested 166 seats in the all-white House of Assembly, 80 seats in the so-called Coloured House of Representatives, and 40 seats in the Indian House of Delegates. None of the country's 28 million blacks were entitled to vote in the national elections. In the campaign, the National Party's "Plan of Action" proposed to bring blacks into the political system on a limited basis, while the opposition Conservative Party (CP) called for strengthening segregation laws and opposed widening political rights for blacks. The Democratic Party advocated the abolition of all segregation laws and universal political rights with entrenched protection for whites and other minority groups. The National Party won the election, as it had done in every election since 1948, even though it suffered substantial losses. After the election the NP representation was reduced from 123 seats to 93 seats, the CP increased its number from 22 to 39, and the DP increased from 21 to 33 seats. The contest for the seat in Fauresmith in the Orange Free State resulted in a tie, which would be decided in a by-election in 1990. (Twelve additional seats were filled by nomination after the election based on the number of votes cast for each party.) While the Nationalists won only 47% of all the votes cast, the Conservatives 28%, and the Democrats 25%, de Klerk maintained that white voters had endorsed a change of direction.

SOUTH AFRICA • Information highlights

Official Name: Republic of South Africa.
Location: Southern tip of Africa.
Area: 471,444 sq mi (1 221 040 km²).
Population (mid-1989 est.): 38,500,000.
Chief Cities (1985 census, city proper): Pretoria, the administrative capital, 443,059; Cape Town, the legislative capital, 776,617; Durban, 634,301; Johannesburg, 632,369.
Government: *Head of state and government,* Frederik W. de Klerk, state president (took office Sept. 1989). *Legislature*—Parliament (tricameral): House of Assembly, House of Representatives (Coloured), and House of Delegates (Indians).
Monetary Unit: Rand (2.59 rands equal U.S. $1, Dec. 11, 1988).
Gross Domestic Product (1987 U.S.$): $81,000,000,000.
Economic Index (1988): *Consumer Prices* (1980 = 100), all items, 299.0; food, 322.1.
Foreign Trade (1988 U.S.$): *Imports,* $17,355,000,000; *exports,* excluding exports of gold, $13,060,000,000.

Reforms Implemented by de Klerk. One week after the election, in an unprecedented move, de Klerk permitted a multiracial crowd of nearly 20,000 to march against apartheid in Cape Town. This was considered significant because immediately prior to the election such political gatherings had been banned officially and there had been police harassment of blacks demonstrating against the election. A few days later, the South African government permitted an equally large protest meeting in Johannesburg. On October 11, Archbishop Desmond M. Tutu and other church leaders met with President de Klerk for more than three hours in what were described as "talks about talks." In a move interpreted by some as an attempt to deflect continuing international demands for sanctions, de Klerk ordered the release of eight of South Africa's most prominent black political prisoners, including Walter Sisulu, former secretary-general of the ANC and a close friend and business partner of Nelson Mandela. Seven of the eight released were over the age of 60. This was regarded widely as a prelude to the release of Nelson Mandela and a test of the political climate for the eventual unbanning of the ANC. In mid-November, de Klerk announced that South Africa's beaches and some other public facilities such as libraries and parks would be desegregated officially as soon as Parliament reconvened in February 1990. Schools, hospitals, and most neighborhoods would remain segregated legally. De Klerk also acted to shift control of the national security system away from the security establishment into the hands of politicians, and indicated that the three and a half year state of emergency soon might be lifted.

Nelson and Winnie Mandela. Despite his continued imprisonment for more than 25

On August 28, Frederik W. de Klerk, then South Africa's acting president, met with Zambia's President Kenneth Kaunda (right) in a Zambian resort town. The planned meeting had led to the crisis causing the resignation of P. W. Botha as president.

© Peter Magubane/Gamma-Liaison

years, Nelson Mandela had become the single most important symbol of opposition to apartheid domestically and internationally. Early in June the first meeting ever to take place between President P. W. Botha and Nelson Mandela occurred at the presidential residence, Tuynhuis, in Cape Town. The South African president and the jailed leader, according to an official statement, confirmed their support "for peaceful development in South Africa." While this historic meeting ultimately might have been an early signal for the release of Mandela, the Conservative Party, as expected, was highly critical of the meeting. Even some members of the ruling National Party expressed concern that it might seem to be a formal recognition of the exiled ANC. Calling President P. W. Botha and Justice Minister Kobie Coetsee the most senior of Nelson Mandela's captors, Winnie Mandela accused the government of exploiting the situation. However, after a meeting with her husband at the prison farm near Paarl, she said the official statement on the meeting was "fairly accurate."

For 54-year-old Winnie Mandela, 1989 was a year of controversy and criticism. In February critics alleged that she had taken part in the December 1988 beating of four black youths, one of whom, a 14-year-old youth named Stompie Moeketsi, had died at her home. The Mandela United Football Club, an organization of between 20 and 30 young blacks who acted as Mrs. Mandela's bodyguards, was implicated in the murder and beatings and the abduction of two other young blacks. According to some reports, the club and Winnie Mandela had developed a reputation in Soweto for being highhanded and a "law unto themselves" and were seen as becoming an embarrassment to the antiapartheid movement. Many had called for the football club to disband; the South African police began an investigation of the club and later arrested four of its members.

Corporations Withdraw. In April the Mobil Corporation, the largest remaining U.S. corporation in South Africa, decided to sell its South African holdings because of economic difficulties. Allen E. Murray, chairman and chief executive officer of Mobil, maintained that U.S. regulations and legislation had made it more difficult for the company to be competitive in South Africa. In particular, a 1987 change in the U.S. tax law prohibited American companies from claiming tax benefits from taxes paid in South Africa. He emphasized that Mobil, an employer of nearly 3,000 South Africans with more than $400 million in assets, was not withdrawing from South Africa in response to pressures from antiapartheid groups or from shareholders but for purely economic reasons. In June the Goodyear Tire and Rubber Company announced that it too was leaving South Africa after operating there for more than 42 years. The Hewlett-Packard Company and National Cash Register also withdrew in 1989.

Death Squads. Within months of assuming the presidency, de Klerk was faced with one of the most important tests of his political career. Capt. Dirk Coetzee, a white former security policeman, alleged in an interview with *Vrye Weekblad,* a liberal Afrikaans newspaper, that over the past 12 years police death squads had assassinated a number of antiapartheid activists including Ruth First, the wife of Joe Slovo, secretary-general of the South African Communist Party. It was alleged that they were also responsible for such actions as the bombing of the ANC offices in London as well as assassinations in adjacent South African states. Coetzee's claims were corroborated by Bufana Almond Nofomela, who was awaiting execution for the 1981 killing of Griffiths Mxenge, a human-rights lawyer. A few hours before he was to be executed Nofomela was granted a temporary reprieve when he claimed that Coetzee was his superior officer. President de Klerk now might be forced to take decisive action to purge the police force of senior officers involved in these death squads should the allegations prove true, or suffer a loss of credibility at a crucial stage in his attempts at reform.

PATRICK O'MEARA AND
N. BRIAN WINCHESTER
Indiana University

SOUTH CAROLINA

At midnight on Sept. 21, 1989, Hurricane *Hugo* slammed into Charleston and nearby sea islands with a storm force that occurs only once every 200 years. Surprisingly, many of the state's interior communities had winds and resulting damage equal to, or higher than, the coastal areas. Beaches south of Charleston escaped serious harm. Elsewhere in the state, private property and public facilities sustained extensive damage. Of the 46 counties in South Carolina, 24 were declared disaster areas.

Storm Aftermath. While the death toll directly attributable to the hurricane was held to 18, largely thanks to ordered evacuations and advanced planning, the total monetary loss was among the highest of any disaster in history.

Despite heavy damage, all of Charleston's historic buildings survived, as well as the city's Port Authority facilities and hospitals. Monetary damage to schools was estimated at $55 million, with 40% of the damage in Charleston County.

The disaster brought quick response from all levels of government, disaster-relief agencies, and individuals. Looting and price gouging were held in check. Within three weeks of the storm, all of the state's students were back in school, most electric power had been restored, and many tourist facilities were reopened. Restoration efforts, however, were expected to continue well into 1990.

Regulations protecting the tidal zone disallowed repair or reconstruction of 159 buildings and many seawalls adjacent to the shore. Fearing ten-year-high tides would cause additional damage, Gov. Carroll A. Campbell, Jr. (R) ordered the restoration of sand dunes along many miles of shoreline. Further erosion did not occur.

Politics and Legislation. The state budget was increased by 11%. New legislation reduced automobile-insurance premiums for safe drivers, required the use of seat belts, added 1,500 medicaid beds to health-care facilities in the state, and made hazardous-waste disposal regulations more stringent. Employers offering child care also were offered tax credits. On the political front, four Democrats in the state House of Representatives and one Democratic senator switched to the Republican Party.

Education. The legislature provided $15 million for reducing the state's dropout rate, improving early childhood education, and meeting other educational goals by the year 2000. On basic skill tests, South Carolina students in grades four, five, and seven scored higher than the national median. In 1989 the number of students qualifying for advanced placement tripled over those who qualified in 1983–84. A total of 63% of tenth-grade students passed all sections of the high school exit examination.

Economy. Industrial growth was slower than the record pace of 1988. However, foreign investment grew for the 22d year. While higher crop yields than normal had been expected, the results were reduced greatly by the hurricane. The state's forestry industry lost an estimated

SOUTH CAROLINA • Information Highlights

Area: 31,113 sq mi (80 582 km^2).
Population (July 1, 1988): 3,470,000.
Chief Cities (1980 census): Columbia, the capital (July 1, 1982 est.), 101,457; Charleston, 69,510; Greenville, 58,242.
Government (1989): *Chief Officers*—governor, Carroll A. Campbell, Jr. (R); lt. gov., Nick A. Theodore (D). *General Assembly*—Senate, 46 members; House of Representatives, 124 members.
State Finances (fiscal year 1988): *Revenue,* $7,344,000,000; *expenditure,* $6,383,000,000.
Personal Income (1988): $44,855,000,000; per capita, $12,926.
Labor Force (June 1989): *Civilian labor force,* 1,759,400; *unemployed,* 87,700 (5.0% of total force).
Education: *Enrollment* (fall 1987)—public elementary schools, 432,000; public secondary, 241,000; colleges and universities, 140,841. *Public school expenditures* (1987–88), $1,891,470,000 ($3,198 per pupil).

AP/Wide World

Hurricane "Hugo," considered the costliest storm ever to hit the U.S. mainland, struck South Carolina at midnight, September 21. The state's small barrier islands off Charleston were particularly hard hit. Damage to the city's historic district, left, *was limited to flooding.*

$1 billion in revenue because of the hurricane. Tobacco continued as the leading cash crop, but the poultry industry brought in more income. Governor Campbell suspended intrastate imports of hazardous waste for burial in South Carolina. New site suitability standards were set for burying the state's own waste. The start-up of the reactor at the Savannah River power plant was scheduled for 1990.

PTL. The expected sale of the Heritage USA religious theme park at Fort Mill, SC, fell through and the park closed. Heritage USA was a central part of the Praise the Lord (PTL) ministry founded by Jim and Tammy Bakker. Jim Bakker was found guilty by a federal jury on 23 counts of fraud and one count of conspiracy in October and sentenced to 45 years in prison for overselling lifetime membership plans to a religious retreat at the park.

ROBERT H. STOUDEMIRE
University of South Carolina

SOUTH DAKOTA

Celebrations went on year-round as South Dakota observed the centennial of its statehood. Wagon trains visited all of the state's 66 counties, demonstrating to more than 40,000 youngsters the pioneer drive that led to statehood in 1889.

Legislation. By proposing a constitutional amendment that would establish a four-year term in the U.S. House of Representatives and a 12-year maximum tenure in both houses of the U.S. Congress, members of the state's U.S. congressional delegation hoped that federal officials would become more concerned about public issues and less with their own reelection. Meanwhile the state legislature passed a law requiring compliance with U.S. Environmental Protection Agency standards for solid-waste disposal in the state. State legislators authorized greater diversity in gambling activities at Deadwood on approval by at least 60% of the town's voters, reorganized the state departments of social services and corrections in response to recent reports of corruption, and revised the human services administration to help fight drug abuse.

SOUTH DAKOTA • Information Highlights

Area: 77,116 sq mi (199 730 km²).
Population (July 1, 1988): 713,000.
Chief Cities (1980 census): Pierre, the capital, 11,973; Sioux Falls, 81,343; Rapid City, 46,492.
Government (1989): *Chief Officers*—governor, George S. Mickelson (R); lt. gov., Walter D. Miller (R). *Legislature*—Senate, 35 members; House of Representatives, 70 members.
State Finances (fiscal year 1988): *Revenue,* $1,303,000,000; *expenditure,* $1,133,000,000.
Personal Income (1988): $9,095,000,000; per capita, $12,755.
Labor Force (June 1989): *Civilian labor force,* 373,800; *unemployed,* 15,800 (4.2% of total force).
Education: *Enrollment* (fall 1987)—public elementary schools, 91,000; public secondary, 35,000; colleges and universities, 31,755. *Public school expenditures* (1987–88), $379,475,000 ($3,038 per pupil).

Economy. Average personal income rose about 3.5%. Unemployment approximated 4% for the entire eligible work force but remained in excess of 70% on some Indian reservations. Scattered drought in the growing season prevented banner production of corn and grain, but in most instances the loss was offset by rising prices. A recent trend of gradual increase in the gross state product continued, but the growth rate for South Dakota fell below those of neighboring states. Protracted recession in farming and ranching coupled with insufficient diversity of occupations were the main causes.

Diminished springtime snowmelt and summer rainfall through the late 1980s brought power production from the Missouri River mainstem system to a record low of 8.1 billion (compared with an average of 10 billion) kilowatt hours. Six massive reservoirs (four in South Dakota) with a capacity of 73.4 million acre-feet contained only 45.3 million. Recreational opportunities and Missouri-Mississippi River navigation also were affected. To conserve water, the U.S. Army Corps of Engineers announced an early closing for barge transportation to Sioux City.

New Institutions. There were a number of new institutions that opened in 1989, including the Cultural Heritage Center near the capitol at Pierre, that was designed to house the State Historical Society as well as public records and cultural archives. The opening of a hot-air balloon museum at Tyndall generated worldwide interest because of the ballooning records held by South Dakotans. A new Roman Catholic archive opened at the Sioux Falls Cathedral. The University of South Dakota Press came into existence in 1989 with the publication of *South Dakota Leaders,* a look at state history through the lives of 51 past leaders.

The Sioux Agreement of 1889. The centennial observation was a reminder of the sacrifices made by the Sioux people, who gave up about 58 million acres (23.5 million ha) of land in treaties with the United States in 1858, 1877, and 1889. Their growing populations eventually surrendered nearly half of their remaining 14 million acres (5.7 million ha), and in 1989 many of those who stayed on the reservation suffered the need for basic services, adequate health care, and understanding from non-Indians around them. But for all South Dakotans there was gratification in the evidence of cultural survival. More than 25 Sun Dance ceremonies in 1989 and the emergence of tribally controlled colleges signaled a growing commitment by the Indian people to their legacy.

HERBERT T. HOOVER
University of South Dakota

SPACE EXPLORATION

The year 1989 marked the 20th anniversary of Neil Armstrong's "one small step for man," the first manned moon landing. During anniversary celebrations, President Bush mapped out the course for future American space exploration, directing NASA to establish a manned lunar outpost during the first decade of the new millennium and to plan a manned mission to Mars by 2016 (*see* page 78). In August, *Voyager 2* flew past Neptune and its large moon, Triton, in the final planetary encounter of a mission that began in 1977 (*see* page 469).

Two new U.S. planetary explorers were launched in 1989: *Magellan,* which will use radar to map the surface of Venus; and *Galileo,* which will investigate Jupiter's atmosphere and its largest moons. Two Soviet spacecraft launched in 1988 to investigate the Martian satellite, Phobos, experienced technical difficulties and returned only limited data.

Shuttle Program. There were five U.S. shuttle flights during 1989. By the close of the year the launch rate was back to pre-*Challenger* safety margins even though the replacement for *Challenger*—named *Endeavor,* following a nationwide competition among schoolchildren—would not join the fleet until 1991. *Columbia,* the first shuttle launched into orbit in 1981, rejoined the fleet after a three-and-one-half-year stand-down for a major refit. During its five-day mission in March, the *Discovery* crew—Navy Capt. Michael Coats, USAF Col. John Blaha, Marine Col. James Buchli, civilian physician James Bagian, and Marine Col. Robert Springer—deployed a third Tracking and Data Relay Satellite, completing the worldwide network for orbiter and spacecraft communications.

Two shuttle missions, STS-30 in May and STS-34 in October, carried two planetary probes into orbit. The STS-30 crew—Navy Capt. David Walker, USAF Col. Ron Grabe, Mary Cleave, Norman Thagard, and USAF Major Mark Lee—deployed the *Magellan* spacecraft to Venus in May. STS-34 was launched from the Kennedy Space Center October 18 with a crew of five—Navy Capt. Donald Williams, Navy Cdr. Michael McCulley with mission specialists Franklin Chang-Diaz, Shannon Lucid, and Ellen Baker. During the first day in orbit the *Atlantis* crew deployed the *Galileo* spacecraft to begin its five-year journey to Jupiter.

Two missions, in August and November, deployed military intelligence satellites. STS-28, launched on August 8, was commanded by USAF Col. Brewster Shaw. The pilot was Navy Cdr. Richard Richards and mission specialists were Navy Cdr. David Leestma, Army Lt. Col. James Adamson, and USAF Maj. Mark Brown. A KH11 digital imaging satellite deployed by the *Columbia* crew malfunctioned

McDonnell Douglas Space Systems Co.

The U.S. Air Force launched the fourth of a series of navigation satellites from Cape Canaveral on October 21. The booster rocket used was a McDonnell Douglas Delta 2.

initially. Course correction commands were relayed from the ground.

STS-33 launched on November 22 at 7:23 P.M. (only the third night launch in 32 shuttle missions), and landed on November 27. STS-33 was commanded by Col. Fred Gregory and piloted by Air Force Col. John Blaha. Mission specialists were Navy Capt. Manley Carter, Story Musgrave, and Kathryn Thornton. The crew deployed a secret Defense Department signal intelligence satellite.

A mission of the *Columbia* shuttle, set to boost a communications satellite into orbit and retrieve the Long Duration Exposure Facility (LDEF) in late December, had to be postponed until January 1990 due to a freak storm that blanketed much of the coastal South with snow. The LDEF, which included 57 scientific, technical, and applications experiments, was launched in 1984 and was designed for a ten-month duration in the environment of space. Its retrieval is necessary before a fiery reentry destroys it.

Soviet Space Program. Soviet cosmonauts Alexander Volkov, Sergey Krikalev, and Valery Polyakov returned to Earth April 27, ending two years of continuous occupation of the *Mir* space station. On September 6, Col. Alexander Viktorenko and Alexander Serebrov aboard *Soyuz* TM-8 were launched from Baikonur Cosmodrome to restaff the *Mir* space station from September 8. *Kvant 2,* the first of four building-block modules, was docked with the *Mir* space station December 6. The Soviet

NASA

The Space Shuttle Mission STS-34 crew consisted of: (front, l-r) *Franklin Chang-Diaz, Donald Williams, Michael McCulley;* (back) *Shannon Lucid and Ellen Baker.*

space shuttle *Buran* had its maiden unmanned flight in November 1988. A second unmanned mission for *Buran* is not anticipated before late 1990 or early 1991.

Space Science. Dr. Lennard A. Fisk, associate administrator for the NASA Office of Space Science and Applications, called NASA's deployment of an impressive array of major scientific missions—with similarly ambitious flights planned through 2010—the "second golden age" of exploration. The *Magellan,* a sophisticated radar mapping probe, will use radar signals to penetrate the thick carbon dioxide atmosphere of Venus and map the topography of its rocky surface in 1990–91. Existing radar data indicate highland and lowland regions somewhat similar in extent to Earth's continents and ocean basins, but not, respectively, as high or deep. Volcanic and impact structures, and features suggestive of Earth's mid-oceanic ridge spreading systems, as well as other potential plate tectonic features and evidence of preexisting oceans, will be explored at higher resolution. *Magellan* will provide denser, higher quality data, covering a greater area of Venus' surface than previous studies. Venus' greenhouse effect and gravity will be studied further.

Galileo will probe the atmosphere of Jupiter and fly by the Jovian satellites in 1995 to 1997. In its indirect trajectory to Jupiter, *Galileo* will "slingshot" around Venus (utilizing that planet's gravity for a boost in speed), hurtle back toward Earth, and receive another "gravity assist" from its home planet before it flies off toward Jupiter. New data from Earth's moon will be collected during the flybys.

Galileo carries both a spin-stabilized section for imaging and a slowly spinning section for the measurement of particles and fields. It will provide close-up data from the four large satellites of Jupiter during its nearly two-year orbiting study and will deploy a parachute probe to collect physical and chemical information downward into the Jovian atmosphere.

Shuttle crews during the year continued to collect natural color photographs of Earth. These photographs have proven a valuable resource, supplying perspectives of Earth quite different from aircraft or from geostationary satellites. They will provide significant documentation of some short-term events and processes.

Full development funding was provided late in the year for two major innovative flight programs, the CRAF (Comet Rendezvous-Asteroid Flyby) and *Cassini* missions. These sophisticated missions, both using the versatile Mariner Mark II spacecraft, are designed to augment our understanding of important but poorly known solar system objects—comets, asteroids, and the Saturnian moon, Titan.

CRAF, scheduled for launch in 1995, will study closely an asteroid and a comet (respectively, Hamburga and Kopff). It will release a sophisticated penetrator that will pierce the comet's surface, relaying physical and chemical information to the orbiting spacecraft, then to Earth.

Cassini, scheduled for launch in early 1996, will conduct detailed studies of Saturn's rings, atmosphere, and magnetosphere over a four-year period. A probe designed by the European Space Agency (ESA) will descend into and characterize Titan's atmosphere, shown by *Voyager* data to contain organic chemistry perhaps similar to that of early life on Earth.

On August 8, ESA launched its first space astronomy mission, Hipparcos (acronym for High-Precision Parallax-Collecting Satellite). The main objective of the satellite is to provide precise positional measurements on about 120,000 stars. Unfortunately, the spacecraft has failed to achieve geostationary orbit, limiting its useful lifetime.

COBE, the Cosmic Background Explorer satellite, was launched November 18 by NASA on a Delta rocket. COBE's objective is a one-year study of the background radiation many scientists believe is a relic of the Big Bang, the primeval explosion that began the expansion of the universe some 15 billion years ago. Instruments will map the sky at 100 different wavelengths, yielding data that is hoped to contribute answers to such questions as the origin of galaxies, their spatial relations, and whether there is an "edge" to the universe.

COBE data may provide a timely piece of the puzzle created by two major discoveries late in the year, the most distant quasar and the "great wall of galaxies." These discoveries raise the possibility that the Big Bang ("standard") theory may require significant revision.

Failure to reestablish contact with the USSR spacecraft *Phobos 2* prior to its major

Voyager 2 at Neptune

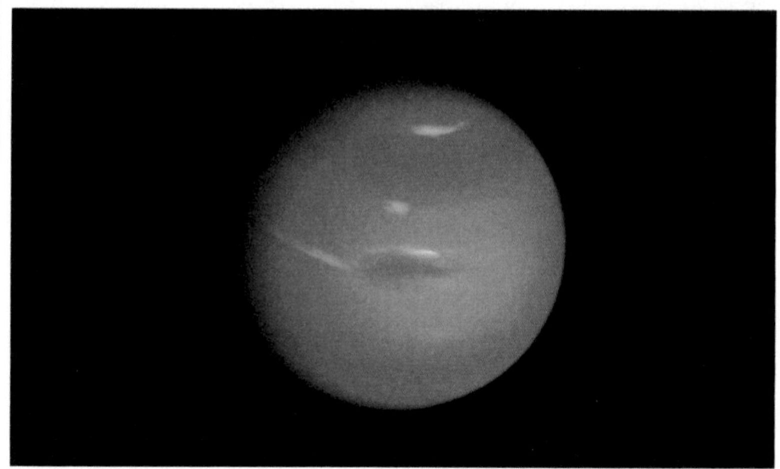

NASA

Neptune's beautiful blue-green atmosphere is rendered in greater detail than ever before in this image captured from 10 million mi (16 million km) away by "Voyager 2" as it approached the gas giant. The Great Dark Spot at its center measures about 8,100 by 4,100 mi (13 000 by 6 600 km). The "cirrus-type" clouds surrounding it are at a higher altitude. "Voyager 2" images revealed that Neptune's dynamic weather patterns change significantly even on the scale of one rotation (18 hours).

After completing a spectacular tour of the giant outer planets with its Neptune flyby in August, *Voyager 2*—like *Pioneer 10, Pioneer 11,* and *Voyager 1* before it—has left the solar system. *Voyager 2* has provided mankind with awesome discoveries and yet more intriguing questions. Designed for the exploration of Jupiter and Saturn, *Voyager 2*'s mission was augmented magnificently with the exploration of Uranus and Neptune. The mission extension was made possible by sending new instructions to the spacecraft's computers and by upgrading receiving equipment on Earth.

Unresolved questions include: Neptune's rotation rate and its consequences for the planet's atmospheric heat flow and winds; its steeply tilted magnetic field, off-center poles, and exceptional variability of surface magnetic field strength; the origin and evolution of its rings; and the fascinating geology of Neptune's largest moon, Triton, including ongoing volcanism.

Though much further from the sun, Neptune is no colder than Uranus, indicating an internal source of heat of an origin and distribution that only can be guessed at. Neptune has high cirrus clouds composed of methane ice and strong (about 700 mph, or 1127 km/h) jet streams. Neptune's principal riddle, however, concerns its magnetic properties. Theories for the origin and evolution of planetary magnetic fields, including Earth's, remain unproven. Unexpectedly, Neptune's magnetic field is much like that of Uranus, though without Uranus' topsy-turvy attitude. These two gas giants are unique in having magnetic fields so steeply tilted from their rotational axes. Whereas Uranus' tilt seems explicable in terms of a cataclysmic hit early in its formation, there is no ready explanation for the attitude of Neptune's magnetic field.

Neptune's rings yield fresh information on planetary ring systems in general. Earth-based telescope data had suggested that the planet had incomplete rings or "ring arcs." But *Voyager 2* images show complete rings with boudinage structure—shapes like sausages on a string—indicative of an aging ring system. Planetary rings apparently are ephemeral, having come and gone repeatedly during their hosts' 4.5-billion-year existences.

Voyager 2 discovered six new moons around Neptune which, including the already known Triton and Nereid, brings that planet's count to eight. Neptune's biggest surprise, however, was furnished by the wrong-way orbiting Triton. This surprisingly colorful, remelted/refrozen body has a geologic history unique in the solar system, even compared to exotic cousins like Hyperion, Iapetus, Io, and Titan. Like Io and Titan, Triton has an atmosphere. It has a huge pinkish-white southern polar cap comprised of frozen nitrogen and methane. Geologists are awed at its terrain—mainly white and organically colored ices, rather than rock. Pockmarked with irregular features about 19 to 31 mi (30 to 50 km) across delimited by long ridges and grooves, the surface is much less scarred by meteorite bombardment than other satellite surfaces.

Triton also has large plains that look volcanic; however, the "lava" is largely ice (though the satellite probably has a silicate core perhaps 620 mi, or 1 000 km, in diameter). Triton, like Earth and Io, apparently has active volcanism. A plume of material, darkish compared with the frozen surface underneath, rises straight up to about 5 mi (8 km), then is bent by upper winds to form a long, horizontal plume of material, probably gaseous nitrogen, downwind.

E. JULIUS DASCH AND PAT JONES

scientific mission to the tiny moon of Mars disappointed the scientific community early in the year. Some gas, dust, and imaging data from Mars was collected prior to the loss, however. Valery L. Barsukov, director of the Vernadsky Institute in Moscow, said that Mars would continue as a Soviet focus until 2000. The USSR has elaborate plans for a Mars orbiter/lander in 1994 and a rover/sample return mission four years later. Plans for joint space activity with the United States continued to be discussed. A collection of U.S. crystal growth experiments was launched to the *Mir* space station December 20, marking the first U.S. commercial cargo on the Soviet space station.

Intercosmos-24, a Soviet spacecraft designed to study how radio waves propagate through Earth's atmosphere, was launched September 28 on board a Cyclone booster; the large "Activny" spacecraft includes a Czechoslovakia-built satellite that will fly in formation with the larger vehicle and deploy a 66 ft- (20 m-) wide antenna. The Soviet GRANAT gamma-ray astrophysics satellite was launched on a Proton booster from Baikonur Cosmodrome on December 1.

Applications Satellites. The January 21 failure of the imager on the GOES-West weather satellite reduced weather-monitoring capability in the United States until the GOES-East satellite was moved to a more central station. The first of the next generation of GOES satellites is scheduled to be launched in 1990. GOES-West had outlasted its design life by five years and had tracked 34 hurricanes in the Atlantic and more than 100 in the Pacific since its launch in April 1983. (*See also* METEOROLOGY.)

The U.S. Air Force plan for 1989 called for 12 Delta, six Titan, and one Atlas Centaur launches with provision for four commercial launches. The first in a planned Air Force network of 18 Navstar Global Positioning Satellites was placed in orbit February 14 by the first McDonnell Douglas Delta 2 booster. The Air Force planned to launch five of the network of Navstar satellites during 1989. The fifth was launched, again on a Delta 2 booster, on December 11, marking the eighth Delta launch of the year. The SDI Delta Star satellite was launched in March. It will test on-board sensors by observing a variety of launches.

An intelligence signal-gathering satellite was launched successfully on a USAF/Martin Marietta Titan 34D launch vehicle on May 10. Also in May, the United States launched the 12th NOAA weather satellite. The first Titan 4 launch on June 14 carried a missile warning satellite into orbit. A faulty valve caused the first rocket designed and built with commercial funds to topple in flames at the first launch attempt at Vandenburg Air Force Base, October 5. Three military intelligence satellites were deployed by shuttle missions 28 and 33 in August and November.

During 1989 the Soviets launched more than 30 reconnaissance satellites, one of which was in orbit for six months. Seven Soviet navigational spacecraft and three scientific satellites were launched. Two Soviet weather satellites were launched during 1989. The Soviets also launched two new military ocean surveillance satellites and a missile early-warning satellite. *Intercosmos 24,* launched September 28 on a Cyclone booster, will study the Earth's magnetosphere. *Cosmos 2030,* launched July 12, was exploded deliberately when ground controllers lost control of the advanced reconnaissance spacecraft. On July 28 the Soviets commanded the *Cosmos 1870* Earth resources Radarsat into a destructive reentry because it was beginning to fail. The satellite, the size of a school bus, was one of the most advanced satellites ever built in the USSR.

Communications Satellites. Great advances in the commercial satellite launch industry occurred in 1989. The successful Ariane V34 launch on October 27 employed the Ariane 44L, the most powerful launcher of the Ariane 4 class, to place the first *Intel-6* series communications satellite into geostationary orbit. The *Intelsat 6F2* is one of the heaviest telecommunications satellites yet launched and will provide telephone, television, and data relay services. This launch marked the sixth Ariane launch of 1989 and the 16th consecutive successful mission for Ariane since the May 1986 launch failure that destroyed an *Intelsat* spacecraft. A planned seventh Ariane launch in 1989, to put two Japanese telecommunications satellites into orbit, was postponed.

The *Discovery* shuttle mission, March 13–18, deployed the third and final satellite in the Tracking and Data Relay Satellite communications network for shuttle orbiters and spacecraft, resulting in the closure of five more ground tracking stations in 1989: Guam; Santiago, Chile; Ascension Island; Dakar, Senegal; and Hawaii.

The launch of *Consort 1* from White Sands, NM, on March 29, marked the first in a series of spaceflights sponsored by the Consortium for Materials Development in Space. Launch services were provided by Space Services Inc. (SSI). The SSI *Starfire 1* mission was paid for by NASA. On August 27, McDonnell Douglas achieved the first satellite mission launched by a private company when a Delta 1 vehicle launched *Marcopolo 1,* a British direct broadcast relay satellite. December 31 witnessed the first commercial launch of the Martin Marietta Titan 3 carrying two communications satellites, the British military *Skynet 4* and a Japanese *JCSat.* The Soviet Union had 12 dedicated communications satellite launches during the year. Each launch carried several communications satellites.

E. JULIUS DASCH, *NASA*
PAT JONES, *Science Applications Int. Corp.*

SPAIN

The Socialist Workers' Party (PSOE) claimed victory in 1989 parliamentary elections, but court challenges cast doubt over the party's ability to retain its legislative majority. While Prime Minister Felipe González' longevity increased his stature abroad as he formed his third government, the uncertainty surrounding the electoral contest reinforced unrest focused on economic conditions.

Politics and Government. On October 29 the PSOE captured only 165 seats in the 350-member lower house of parliament—a decline of 25 deputies. Complicating the political picture as 1990 began were legal disputes involving 17 seats in three districts (Ponte Vedra, Murcía, and Melilla). Failure of the Socialists to obtain at least 11 of these disputed seats would deprive them of a working majority and imperil the status of González. On December 4 he won reelection as prime minister by a one-vote margin, supplied by a deputy from the Canary Islands. The electoral outcome signaled voter discontent with the PSOE as the Communist-led United Left more than doubled its seven-seat parliamentary delegation.

For the first time, the General Workers Union, the PSOE's labor affiliate, refused to campaign for González. Resentment lingered from the Dec. 14, 1988, general strike when two thirds of Spain's workers stayed home to inflict on the government "an extraparliamentary vote of no confidence." A major dispute during the campaign was over the Spanish military, and especially conscription, with some parties in support of shortening the length of a term in the military service.

Earlier, in the June elections for the European Community's European Parliament, the Socialists suffered a similar setback when they received 1 million fewer votes than in 1987. Amid the lowest voter turnout (55%) in 12 years, the ruling party lost one seat, capturing only 39.6% of the ballots.

SPAIN • Information Highlights

Official Name: Spanish State.
Location: Iberian Peninsula in southwestern Europe.
Area: 194,884 sq mi (504 750 km²).
Population (mid-1989 est.): 39,200,000.
Chief Cities (Jan. 1987 est.): Madrid, the capital, 3,100,507; Barcelona, 1,703,744; Valencia, 732,491.
Government: *Head of state,* Juan Carlos I, king (took office Nov. 1975). *Head of government,* Felipe González Márquez, prime minister (took office Dec. 1982). *Legislature*—Cortés Generales: Senate and Congress of Deputies.
Monetary Unit: Peseta (116.15 pesetas equal U.S.$1, Nov. 24,1989).
Gross National Product (1987 U.S.$): $288,300,000,000.
Economic Indexes (1988): *Consumer Prices* (1980 = 100), all items, 213.7; food, 214.5. *Industrial Production* (1980 = 100), 115.
Foreign Trade (1988 U.S.$): *Imports,* $60,576,000,000; *exports,* $40,067,000,000.

Also in June the conservative Popular Party and the centrist Social and Democratic Center (CDS) forged an alliance in the Madrid city council. This partnership succeeded in replacing Socialist Mayor Juan Barranco with CDS stalwart Agustín Rodríguez Sahagun. The two parties earlier announced their intent to oust Socialist mayors governing with minorities.

Economy. González chaired the semiannual summit meeting of heads of European Community (EC) nations held in Madrid on June 27. As the EC president for the first six months of 1989, González gave impetus to an economic and monetary union scheduled to take effect at the end of 1992. Also in June, the Spanish peseta fully entered the European Monetary System with its inclusion in the exchange rate mechanism.

For the third year in a row, overall growth remained above 5%—faster than that registered by any other European state. At the same time, however, unemployment stood at 16.6% in August, down 3.2% from the year before. Although the lowest rate during González' tenure, this figure, which meant that more than 2 million Spaniards were jobless, was the highest in Western Europe.

The expanding economy showed signs of overheating. By the first quarter of 1989, Spain's trade deficit widened to $6.04 billion, up from the level posted during 1988. Inflation rose to a 6.8% annual rate in October, well above the 5.8% rate for 1988. The Socialist government continued to cross swords with trade unions because of its unwillingness to increase wages lest prices soar and unemployment rise.

Foreign Affairs. Despite the expulsion of 72 U.S. F-16 fighters from the Torrejón Air Base in 1988, González expressed the belief that Madrid and Washington now are entering a "stage of normality in relations." Evidence of increased consultation between the two countries occurred on October 19 when González and U.S. President George Bush met in Washington. Bush praised Spain's transition from dictatorship to democracy as a possible model for Eastern European countries attempting similar transformations. U.S.-Spanish concerns, East-West relations, and Latin American affairs dominated the agenda.

Spain began negotiations with separate North Atlantic Treaty Organization (NATO) commands on detailed accords concerning the Iberian nation's role in a military crisis. This move represented a desire on González' part for his country to be a full partner in a unified Western Europe. For the first time, units of the Spanish navy placed themselves under the tactical command of NATO's Northwood Headquarters to participate in exercises held in September.

GEORGE W. GRAYSON
College of William and Mary

SPORTS

© Rick Stewart/Allsport

Toronto's new SkyDome, featuring a retractable roof, opened with a big gala in June. With a seating capacity exceeding 52,000, the stadium is the home of baseball's Blue Jays and the Argonauts of the Canadian Football League.

Overview

As the 1980s drew to a close, followers of professional, collegiate, and world-class amateur sports looked back on a decade marred by drug scandals, strikes, recruiting violations, court cases, and other unsavory—sometimes tragic—off-the-field developments. Not entirely without justification, many of the incidents were blamed on the growth of organized athletic competition from mere "big business" into a multibillion-dollar, mass media industry. Victory was no longer its own reward. Exorbitant long-term contracts, performance bonuses, endorsement fees, and TV revenues at every level became the spoils and, for many, the spoilers.

Developments in 1989 did little to alter the decade's legacy or to dispute the easy explanation. Pete Rose, one of baseball's immortals, was banned from the game for life for gambling. Canadian sprinter Ben Johnson, whose 1988 Olympic gold medal for the 100-meter dash was stripped from him after a postrace test revealed steroid use, finally admitted his wrongdoing and had all of his world records erased from the books. Even the America's Cup, yachting's most coveted prize, became grist for the legal mill.

At the collegiate level, the year's major controversy actually grew out of efforts to make student-athletes real students again. Under a rule passed by the National Collegiate Athletic Association (NCAA) in January, dubbed Proposition 42, athletic scholarships for incoming freshmen would be tied to high school grade-point average and scores on standardized tests. Critics of Proposition 42, led by Georgetown University basketball coach John Thompson, argued that it unfairly would deprive underprivileged minority students—mostly black—of a chance to attend college.

The NCAA later agreed to postpone enactment pending further review, and a number of college officials said they had misunderstood the original proposal and would vote against it the next time around.

The embarrassing condition of college sports in the United States was underscored by the results of a federal study released in September: At one third of colleges and universities with major men's basketball programs, fewer than 20% of players ever graduate; the rate for football players was only slightly higher. The study was done at the request of Senate sponsors of a bill that would require colleges to disclose the graduation rates of their student-athletes.

The signs of the big-buck times also took a more benign—even spectacular—form. In June the city of Toronto, Canada, unveiled a stadium complex featuring the world's first retractable stadium roof. Within 20 minutes of the first drop of rain, three giant concrete panels are swung automatically into place to form a dome over the entire field and stands. Billed as a "higher form of entertainment," the facility also includes the world's largest TV screen, the world's longest bar, a 350-room hotel, a shopping mall, a health club, and other facilities. Other cities, including Atlanta, GA, Baltimore, MD, and San Antonio, TX, went ahead with plans for new stadiums.

More signs of the times: With the blessings of the Kremlin, some of the Soviet Union's top basketball and hockey players made their way west to share in the riches of professional sports in North America. Total 1989 prize money for the Association of Surfing Professionals and the Association of Volleyball Professionals (beach volleyball, that is) both exceeded $2 million. The Major Indoor Lacrosse League provided an outlet—and a modest supplementary income—to some yuppie stockbrokers. And polo, the sport of millionaires, was booming.

By way of perspective, the tragic earthquake that rocked San Francisco just prior to Game 3 of the World Series left a message for the 1990s: It's all just a game.

JEFFREY H. HACKER

Auto Racing

France's Alain Prost won his third Formula One driving championship, wrapping up the world title in the Japanese Grand Prix when his closest challenger, Brazil's Ayrton Senna, was disqualified.

Senna was involved in a car crash that knocked Prost out of the Japanese race with six laps to go. Senna's car was disqualified for taking a shortcut to the pits following the accident. The Brazilian could have captured the Formula One crown with victories in the Japanese race and the season's final event, the Australian Grand Prix. Thierry Boutsen of Belgium won the latter. Prost also took the Formula One championship in 1985 and 1986 and his 39 Grand Prix victories are a record.

Emerson Fittipaldi, a two-time Formula One champion in the 1970s, reached the pinnacle of his new career in CART-PPG Indy Cars by winning the season driving championship and the Indianapolis 500. Fittipaldi and Al Unser, Jr., had less than three laps to go at Indianapolis when they contested for a one-lane groove in the third turn. Their wheels touched and Unser's car backed into the wall at some 200 mph (320 km/hr) as Fittipaldi straightened his wobbling car and continued to the win.

Fittipaldi, a native of Brazil now living in Miami, finished the season with five victories and $1,712,578 in earnings. He outpointed runner-up Rick Mears, 196-186, in the CART-PPG points race.

Rusty Wallace of Fenton, MO, won his first Winston Cup stock-car championship by outpointing Dale Earnhardt, 4,176-4,164, for the second-closest finish in Winston Cup history. Wallace lost the 1988 title to Bill Elliott by 24 points.

Darrell Waltrip of Franklin, TN, won his first Daytona 500 in 17 attempts and finished 7.64 seconds ahead of runner-up Ken Schrader. Waltrip's bid to win a $1 million bonus—promised to anyone who could win three of four designated superspeedway events—failed when Earnhardt won the Southern 500 at Darlington, SC. Waltrip also had won the Coca-Cola 600 at Concord, NC.

STAN SUTTON
"Louisville Courier-Journal"

AUTO RACING

Major Race Winners, 1989

Indianapolis 500: Emerson Fittipaldi, Brazil
Marlboro 500: Michael Andretti, United States
Quaker State 500: Danny Sullivan, United States
Daytona 500: Darrell Waltrip, United States

1989 Champions

World Championship: Alain Prost, France
CART: Fittipaldi
NASCAR: Rusty Wallace, United States

Grand Prix for Formula One Cars, 1989

Brazilian: Nigel Mansell, Great Britain
San Marino: Ayrton Senna, Brazil
Monaco: Senna
Mexican: Senna
U.S.: Prost
Canadian: Thierry Boutsen, Belgium
French: Prost
British: Prost
West German: Senna
Hungarian: Mansell
Belgian: Senna
Italian: Prost
Portuguese: Gerhard Berger, Austria
Spanish: Senna
Japanese: Alessandro Nannini, Italy
Australian: Boutsen

Baseball

Almost from the beginning, misfortune marred the 1989 major league baseball season. Pete Rose, manager of the Cincinnati Reds and the game's career leader in hits, was suspended for life on August 24 after six months of investigation and legal maneuvers. The man who made that decision, Commissioner A. Bartlett Giamatti, suffered a fatal heart attack on September 1, after only five months on the job, and was replaced by Deputy Commissioner Francis T. (Fay) Vincent, Jr. And the World Series was delayed ten days when an earthquake that registered 7.1 on the Richter scale struck the Oakland-San Francisco Bay area as the Athletics and Giants were warming up for Game 3.

Play-Offs and World Series. Oakland advanced to postseason play for the second straight year by winning 99 games, the most in the majors, and outlasting the Kansas City Royals and California Angels in a race that remained tight beyond Labor Day. Potent pitching plus skillful maneuvering by manager Tony LaRussa enabled the Athletics to survive prolonged absences by slugger José Canseco, who missed the first half with a wrist injury, and star reliever Dennis Eckersley, who was out six weeks with a strained rotator cuff.

Though Oakland had been expected to win in the West, the script was decidedly different in the American League East. The Baltimore Orioles, fortified by rookies, rebounded from a 107-loss season in 1988 to season-long contention. The team spent 97 days at the top of the division before the Toronto Blue Jays caught up. The Jays overcame a 12-24 start after batting coach Clarence (Cito) Gaston replaced Jimy Williams as manager. They eventually won the division by two games when they beat Baltimore twice in a three-game, season-ending series at their new SkyDome.

Like the Orioles, the Chicago Cubs had not been considered contenders when the season began. But the additions of rookie outfielders Jerome Walton and Dwight Smith and relief specialist Mitch Williams helped the Cubs outlast the New York Mets, St. Louis Cardinals, and Montreal Expos in a race that was close into September. The San Francisco Giants, winning their second NL West crown in three seasons, also jumped from fourth to first—thanks in part to the 70 homers and 236 runs batted in (RBIs) produced by Kevin Mitchell and Will Clark. San Francisco took first on June 17 and held on, surviving challenges from the San Diego Padres and the Houston Astros.

Both the Giants and the Athletics won their respective League Championship Series (LCS) in five games. Clark was named the series' most valuable player (MVP) for San Francisco after hitting .650 (13-for-20) with eight runs batted in, a 1.200 slugging percentage, and 24 total bases, an NLCS record. The MVP of the Oakland series was Rickey Henderson, a June trade acquisition from the New York Yankees, whose ALCS statistics included a .400 batting average, .609 on-base percentage, eight runs, seven walks, and eight stolen bases (a play-off record).

The success of the Bay Area teams gave baseball its first same-city World Series since 1956. But festivities were curtailed when Candlestick Park was shaken by the October 17 earthquake that struck northern California at 5:04 P.M. PDT, less than one-half hour before

The Hall of Fame at 50

When the Baseball Hall of Fame was dedicated on June 12, 1939, 5,000 fans made the difficult journey to the tiny upstate New York hamlet of Cooperstown for the first induction of members. Twenty-six baseball immortals had been elected by then and all of the 11 still alive, including Babe Ruth and Ty Cobb, attended. The hall had a handful of exhibits in a single room, an adjacent one-room library, and three full-time employees. Attendance in 1940 was 7,648.

Things changed substantially during the following 50 years. The fifth major expansion, timed to coincide with the 50th anniversary celebration in 1989, cost $6 million and brought total display space to 60,000 sq ft (5 574 m²). Included in the expansion was a 200-seat theater where visitors are entertained by a multimedia show utilizing state-of-the-art technology.

The $3 million generated by the Hall of Fame each year covers operating expenses. Annual attendance has climbed to 300,000—with induction weekend remaining the busiest of the year. A record 25,000 fans swamped the sleepy hamlet on July 23, 1989, to see the inductions of Johnny Bench, Carl Yastrzemski, Red Schoendienst, and umpire Al Barlick. Those inductions brought the number of bronze plaques in the Hall of Fame gallery to 204. More than 6,000 artifacts, accompanied by detailed explanations, are on display.

Plans for the immediate future include a $1 million modernization of the Hall of Fame's extensive baseball library, repository for more than 125,000 autographs and a file of newspapers and magazines estimated to contain more than 5 million items.

DAN SCHLOSSBERG

© V. J. Lovero/"Sports Illustrated"

Oakland's Dave Stewart capped a 21-9 season with two victories against Toronto in the Championship Series and two wins against San Francisco in the World Series.

starting time. Oakland had won the two previous games on its home turf, 5-0 and 5-1, before the series shifted to San Francisco for Game 3. By the time the series resumed on October 27, the hitters had taken over. Oakland won, 13-7, as the teams combined for seven home runs and 24 hits, both World Series records, in the highest-scoring Series game since 1956. The Athletics completed a sweep—the first since 1976—with a 9-6 win the next day. Pitcher Dave Stewart, winner of the first and third games, was named World Series MVP.

Regular Season. For the second straight season, power production was down in the major leagues. There were 3,083 home runs, a drop of 3.1% from the 1988 figure and 44.5% below the record of 4,458 home runs produced in 1987. The percentage of balks fell even more sharply—70.1% in the American League, where a record 558 were recorded during the strict enforcement year of 1988. There were 239 in the NL, down 34.7% from the 1988 total of 366.

Total attendance of 55,173,597 was a record high for the fifth straight year. Toronto, with its new SkyDome drawing curiosity seekers, led the majors with an AL record of 3,375,573.

The fans got to see a number of spectacular performances. Pitcher Bret Saberhagen of the Kansas City Royals led both leagues with 23 victories and a 2.16 earned run average, figures that helped him win the American League's Cy Young Memorial Award for a second time. But Houston's Mike Scott, the lone 20-game win-

BASEBALL

Professional—Major Leagues

Final Standings, 1989

AMERICAN LEAGUE

Eastern Division	W	L	Pct.	Western Division	W	L	Pct.
Toronto	89	73	.549	Oakland	99	63	.611
Baltimore	87	75	.537	Kansas City	92	70	.568
Boston	83	79	.512	California	91	71	.562
Milwaukee	81	81	.500	Texas	83	79	.512
New York	74	87	.460	Minnesota	80	82	.494
Cleveland	73	89	.451	Seattle	73	89	.451
Detroit	59	103	.364	Chicago	69	92	.429

NATIONAL LEAGUE

Eastern Division	W	L	Pct.	Western Division	W	L	Pct.
Chicago	93	69	.574	San Francisco	92	70	.568
New York	87	75	.537	San Diego	89	73	.549
St. Louis	86	76	.531	Houston	86	76	.531
Montreal	81	81	.500	Los Angeles	77	83	.481
Pittsburgh	74	88	.457	Cincinnati	75	87	.463
Philadelphia	67	95	.414	Atlanta	63	97	.394

Play-offs—American League: Oakland defeated Toronto, 4 games to 1; San Francisco defeated Chicago, 4 games to 1.

World Series—Oakland defeated San Francisco, 4 games to 0. First Game (Oakland Coliseum, Oct. 14, attendance 49,385): Oakland 5, San Francisco 0; Second Game (Oakland Coliseum, Oct. 15, attendance 49,388): Oakland 5, San Francisco 1; Third Game (San Francisco's Candlestick Park, Oct. 27, attendance 62,038): Oakland 13, San Francisco 7; Fourth Game (Candlestick Park, Oct. 28, attendance 62,032): Oakland 9, San Francisco 6.

All-Star Game (Anaheim Stadium, Anaheim, CA, July 11, attendance 64,036): American League 5, National League 3.

Most Valuable Players—American League: Robin Yount, Milwaukee; National League: Kevin Mitchell, San Francisco.

Cy Young Memorial Awards (outstanding pitchers)—American League: Bret Saberhagen, Kansas City; National League: Mark Davis, San Diego.

Managers of the Year—American League: Frank Robinson, Baltimore; National League: Don Zimmer, Chicago.

Rookies of the Year—American League: Greg Olson, Baltimore; National League: Jerome Walton, Chicago.

Leading Hitters—(Percentage) American League: Kirby Puckett, Minnesota, .339; National League: Tony Gwynn, San Diego, .336. (Runs Batted In) American League: Ruben Sierra, Texas, 119; National League: Kevin Mitchell, San Francisco, 125. (Home Runs) American League: Fred McGriff, Toronto, 36; National League: Mitchell, 47. (Hits) American League: Puckett, 215; National League: Gwynn, 203. (Runs) American League: Wade Boggs, Boston, Rickey Henderson, Oakland, 113; National League: Will Clark, San Francisco, Howard Johnson, New York, Ryne Sandberg, Chicago, 104. (Slugging Percentage) American League: Sierra, .543; National League: Mitchell, .635.

Leading Pitchers—(Earned Run Average) American League: Bret Saberhagen, Kansas City, 2.16; National League: Scott Garrelts, San Francisco, 2.28. (Victories) American League: Saberhagen, 23; National League: Mike Scott, Houston, 20. (Strikeouts) American League: Nolan Ryan, Texas, 301; National League: José DeLeon, St. Louis, 201. (Shutouts) American League: Bert Blyleven, California, 5; National League: Tim Bleicher, Los Angeles, 8. (Saves) American League: Jeff Russell, Texas, 38; National League: Mark Davis, San Diego, 44.

Professional—Minor Leagues, Class AAA

American Association: Indianapolis
International League: Richmond
Pacific Coast League: Vancouver

Amateur

NCAA: Wichita State
Little League World Series: Trumbull, CT

AP/Wide World

The Banning of Pete Rose

The baseball world was saddened Aug. 24, 1989, when Pete Rose, manager of the Cincinnati Reds and the all-time leader in career hits, was suspended from the game for life by Commissioner A. Bartlett Giamatti for violations of Major League Rule 21. Giamatti's decision—the result of a negotiated settlement initiated by Rose's representative Reuven Katz—ended six months of investigations and court rulings regarding allegations that Rose had bet on baseball games, including those involving his own team. The legal tug-of-war between Rose and the commissioner's office dominated the entire term of Giamatti, who succeeded Peter V. Ueberroth on April 1 and died of a sudden heart attack on September 1.

The agreement placed Rose on the ineligible list—barring him from employment in any baseball capacity or participation in such baseball functions as old-timers' games—but did not include an admission by Rose that he had bet on baseball. After the settlement, Rose apologized for the controversy. "I made some mistakes and I think I'm being punished for those mistakes," he said. "The settlement is fair and especially the wording that says they have no finding that I bet on baseball."

Giamatti had attempted to resolve the matter in May after special counsel John Dowd had submitted a 225-page report accompanied by seven volumes of exhibits. On May 11, two days after Dowd's data was given to Giamatti, the commissioner sent copies to Rose and ordered him to appear at a hearing on May 25. After Giamatti granted a Rose request for a one-month postponement of the hearing date, the courts took over. Rose filed a lawsuit against Giamatti on June 19 and won a temporary restraining order, preventing the hearing, six days later. But Giamatti managed to move the case from Hamilton County (OH) Common Pleas Court to U.S. District Court in Columbus, OH, where Rose realized his chances of winning were not good.

On August 18, Katz agreed to accept the three conditions mandated by Giamatti as part of any settlement:

- No set period of time for the suspension.
- An agreement never again to challenge the commissioner in court.
- Rose could not deny betting on baseball in the agreement.

Five days later, the five-page, 862-word statement was signed by Rose and Giamatti. The agreement gave Giamatti unchallenged authority to rule on any Rose application for reinstatement. That authority later was passed to new Commissioner Francis T. (Fay) Vincent, Jr., Giamatti's deputy commissioner and chief representative during the Rose proceedings.

Rose still faced other difficulties, including an investigation by a Cincinnati-based federal grand jury regarding possible tax evasion on income from gambling and promotional appearances. His name also was mentioned in the drug and tax-evasion trial of former friend Tommy Gioiosa.

Because he holds 19 major league records, Rose would have been considered a certain first-ballot selection for the Baseball Hall of Fame when he becomes eligible in 1992. But election rules stipulate that character, as well as on-the-field accomplishment, is an important criterion for consideration. Regarding the issue of Rose's enshrinement in the Hall of Fame, Giamatti said that "it is the baseball writers' responsibility to decide" the issue.

DAN SCHLOSSBERG

ner in the NL, was runner-up in the NL's Cy Young Award voting to San Diego reliever Mark Davis, who saved 44 games in 48 opportunities. The only other pitcher to win 20 games was Oakland's Dave Stewart, who reached that plateau for the third straight season. In his first season with the Texas Rangers, 42-year-old Nolan Ryan became the oldest pitcher to record a 300-strikeout season (301) and the first man to record 5,000 career strikeouts. In winning his tenth strikeout crown, Ryan threw a pair of one-hitters for a career total of 16 games in which he has allowed one or fewer hits. (Bob Feller had held the record at 15.) Toronto's Dave Stieb also threw two one-hitters; there were no no-hit games during 1989. National League strikeout leader José DeLeon fanned 201 for the St. Louis Cardinals, while Scott

© Joe Patronite/Allsport

In 1989, Texas' Nolan Ryan led the majors with 301 strikeouts. He also made baseball history by becoming the first pitcher to record 5,000 career strikeouts.

Garrelts of the San Francisco Giants led the NL with a 2.28 ERA. Another NL hurler, Tim Belcher of the Los Angeles Dodgers, led both leagues with eight shutouts.

The best relief pitchers were Davis, who finished one short of the NL record and two short of the major league record for saves, and Jeff Russell, who led the AL with 38 saves for Texas. Minnesota's Jeff Reardon became the first reliever to record five straight 30-save seasons, while Oakland's Dennis Eckersley became the first pitcher to post more saves (33) than hits allowed (32).

Both batting champions won their titles on the last day of the season. Minnesota's Kirby Puckett, a first-time winner, went two for five at Seattle to finish at .339, while Oakland's Carney Lansford went zero for three at Kansas City to finish at .336. With a total of 215 hits, Puckett became the first right-handed hitter to lead the majors in that department for two straight seasons. Boston's Wade Boggs had 205 hits to become the first player of the century to produce seven straight 200-hit seasons. He finished with a .330 average, third in the league, to end a string of four straight batting crowns.

A streak of batting titles remained alive, however. Tony Gwynn of the San Diego Padres became the first National Leaguer to win three straight since Stan Musial did it for St. Louis (1950–52). Gwynn finished at .336, three points ahead of San Francisco's Will Clark, when he went three for four against the Giants in both of the season's final two games. Clark, who had taken a three-point lead over Gwynn with two games left, went one for four in each game. Gwynn also led the NL with 203 hits.

Clark's teammate, Kevin Mitchell, was named the National League's MVP after leading the majors with 47 homers, 125 runs batted in, 345 total bases, and a .635 slugging percentage. Ruben Sierra of Texas led the AL with 119 RBIs, 344 total bases, and a .543 slugging percentage, but finished second in the MVP voting to Milwaukee's Robin Yount, who won for the second time. Yount batted .318, with 21 home runs and 103 RBIs. Toronto's Fred McGriff led the AL with 36 home runs. Leaders in stolen bases were Oakland's Rickey Henderson, who swiped 77 to lead the AL, and Vince Coleman, who stole 65 for St. Louis.

Rookies of the year were Jerome Walton, a superb defensive center fielder who hit .293 with 24 stolen bases for the Chicago Cubs, and Gregg Olson, who had a 5-2 record, 27 saves, and 1.69 ERA while helping the Baltimore Orioles engineer a 32½-game improvement—third best in this century—over the previous season. Walton had the year's longest hitting streak, 30 games.

Comeback of the year awards went to Lonnie Smith of the Atlanta Braves in the National League and Bert Blyleven of the California Angels in the American. Smith, a veteran outfielder who spent much of 1988 in the minors, joined Will Clark as the only players in the majors to post a .300 batting average, .400 on-base percentage, and .500 slugging percentage. Blyleven, in his first year with the Angels, went 17-5 with a 2.73 ERA one year after posting a 10-17 mark for Minnesota.

The selections of the managers of the year were no surprise. Winners were the pilots of the two Cinderella clubs, Don Zimmer of the National League Cubs and Frank Robinson of the American League Orioles. Oakland's Tony LaRussa, who trailed Robinson in the AL voting, came up as the winning All-Star manager when the American League took a 5-3 decision at Anaheim on July 11. The game's highlight was a leadoff 448-ft (137-m) home run by Kansas City's Bo Jackson against San Francisco's Rick Reuschel. Jackson, later named All-Star MVP, also had a single, a stolen base, a run scored, and two RBIs in the game.

During the 50th-anniversary year of Little League baseball, an underdog team from Trumbull, CT, captured the World Series, becoming the first U.S. team in six years to win the crown. They defeated Kaohsiung, Taiwan, 5-2. (*See* page 81).

DAN SCHLOSSBERG, *Baseball Writer*

Basketball

The Detroit Pistons won the 1989 National Basketball Association (NBA) championship by becoming only the fifth team in NBA history to sweep the championship round series. The Pistons defeated the injury-hindered Los Angeles Lakers in four straight games to capture the first pro-basketball title in Detroit history. The previous year, the Pistons had lost to the Lakers in the final round. In a game matching overachieving teams, the University of Michigan defeated Seton Hall, 80–79, in overtime to win the National Collegiate Athletic Association (NCAA) men's tournament. It was Michigan's first NCAA basketball title. St. John's won the National Invitation Tournament (NIT) and Tennessee captured the women's NCAA title.

In April the international basketball federation voted to permit professional basketball players to participate in the Olympic Games.

© Andrew Bernstein/NBA 1989

Joe Dumars tries for two as he leads his Pistons to their first NBA title. Detroit swept the L.A. Lakers in four straight in the play-off finals. Dumars was voted MVP.

The Professional Season

This was a season of change for the NBA. The Boston Celtics, long a traditional power, lost star Larry Bird for most of the schedule because of a foot injury. The Lakers once again won the Pacific Division but lost out to Detroit (63–19) in pursuit of the league's best record. Indeed, the Lakers had to finish strongly in order to tie the Cleveland Cavaliers for the second best mark (57–25), while also holding off Phoenix (55–27) for the division title.

That was not the only close division race. The Cavaliers led in the Central Division for most of the season before slumping the final month and losing out to the Pistons. Still, the Cavaliers, along with Phoenix, stood as one of the most improved teams in the league. The Suns improved by 27 games over the previous year, the third best turnaround in NBA history. The Golden State Warriors, who were picked to be among the NBA's worst teams, made it to the play-offs behind the play of Chris Mullin, who had missed part of the 1987–88 season while going through alcoholic rehabilitation. The New York Knicks, another quickly improving squad, beat out the Philadelphia 76ers for the Eastern Division championship, their first since 1971, while the Utah Jazz held off Houston in the Midwest Division. Atlanta had been expected to challenge the elite teams but got off to a slow start and never recovered, and Dallas was nagged by injuries and failed to make the play-offs. Two expansion teams, the Miami Heat and the Charlotte Hornets, made their debuts. Charlotte led the league in attendance, and Miami set a record by losing its first 17 games.

It was another spectacular season for Chicago star Michael Jordan and Lakers' guard Earvin "Magic" Johnson. Jordan won his third straight scoring title with a 32.5 points-per-game average. Only five others have been the scoring leader three straight seasons. Johnson led the league in free throw percentage (.911) for the first time and was selected as the NBA's most valuable player. He also joined Bird as one of only two players in NBA history to shoot at least 50% from the field and 90% from the foul line in the same season. Jordan also made the league's all-defensive team, along with Dennis Rodman of Detroit, Larry Nance of Cleveland, Mark Eaton of Utah, and Joe Dumars of Detroit. Eaton, Utah's massive center, was named defensive player of the year.

Jordan and Johnson both were named to the All-NBA team, as were Karl Malone of Utah, Charles Barkley of Philadelphia, and Akeem Olajuwon of Houston. Utah's John Stockton led the league in assists, becoming the first player ever to have 1,000 assists in two straight seasons. Olajuwon led in rebounding (13.5 per game), while Rodman was the field-goal percentage leader (.595).

The 1988–89 season marked the 20th and last for Laker center Kareem Abdul-Jabbar, who was honored during a retirement tour. He left the NBA holding numerous records, and is considered one of the all-time best players. For the seventh straight season, the NBA set a record for attendance. The league drew 15.5 million fans, averaging 15,088 per game. Two more teams, the Orlando Magic and the Minnesota Timberwolves, were to be added for the 1989–90 season.

Play-offs. Based on their regular-season records, Detroit and Los Angeles were favorites to meet in the finals. But the Lakers were expected to receive stiff challenges from both Utah and Phoenix, while Detroit was expected to have a much easier time. However, just the opposite proved true.

PROFESSIONAL BASKETBALL

National Basketball Association
(Final Standings, 1988–89)

Eastern Conference

Atlantic Division	W	L	Pct.
*New York	52	30	.634
*Philadelphia	46	36	.561
*Boston	42	40	.512
Washington	40	42	.488
New Jersey	26	56	.317
Charlotte	20	62	.244
Central Division			
*Detroit	63	19	.768
*Cleveland	57	25	.695
*Atlanta	52	30	.634
*Milwaukee	49	33	.598
*Chicago	47	35	.573
Indiana	28	54	.341

Western Conference

Midwestern Division	W	L	Pct.
*Utah	51	31	.622
*Houston	45	37	.549
*Denver	44	38	.537
Dallas	38	44	.463
San Antonio	21	61	.256
Miami	15	67	.183
Pacific Division			
*L.A. Lakers	57	25	.695
*Phoenix	55	27	.671
*Seattle	47	35	.573
*Golden State	43	39	.524
*Portland	39	43	.476
Sacramento	27	55	.329
L.A. Clippers	21	61	.256

*Made play-offs

Play-Offs

Eastern Conference

Round	Winner		Loser	
First Round	Chicago	3 games	Cleveland	2
	Detroit	3 games	Boston	0
	Milwaukee	3 games	Atlanta	2
	New York	3 games	Philadelphia	0
Second Round	Chicago	4 games	New York	2
	Detroit	4 games	Milwaukee	0
Finals	Detroit	4 games	Chicago	2

Western Conference

Round	Winner		Loser	
First Round	Golden State	3 games	Utah	0
	L.A. Lakers	3 games	Portland	0
	Phoenix	3 games	Denver	0
	Seattle	3 games	Houston	1
Second Round	L.A. Lakers	4 games	Seattle	0
	Phoenix	4 games	Golden State	1
Finals	L.A. Lakers	4 games	Phoenix	0
Championship	Detroit	4 games	L.A. Lakers	0
All-Star Game	West 143, East 134			

Individual Honors

Most Valuable Player: Magic Johnson, L.A. Lakers
Most Valuable Player (championship play-offs): Joe Dumars, Detroit
Most Valuable Player (All-Star Game): Karl Malone, Utah
Rookie of the Year: Mitch Richmond, Golden State
Coach of the Year: Lowell (Cotton) Fitzsimmons, Phoenix
Leading Scorer: Michael Jordan, Chicago, 32.5 points per game
Leader in Assists: John Stockton, Utah, 13.6 per game
Leading Rebounder: Akeem Olajuwon, Houston, 13.5 per game
Leader in Field Goal Percentage: Dennis Rodman, Detroit, .595

© Andy Hayt/"Sports Illustrated"

Farewell, Kareem

Kareem Abdul-Jabbar, the NBA's all-time highest scorer (38,387 points), retired as a player in 1989. Famous for his skyhook shot, the 7′2″ (2.18-m) center had set several other NBA records, including games played (1,560), field goals made (15,837), and blocked shots (3,189). A member of the Milwaukee Bucks (1969–75) and the Los Angeles Lakers (1975–89), he played on six NBA championship teams and was the league's MVP a record six times.

Born Lewis Alcindor, Jr., in New York City in 1947, he led UCLA to three NCAA crowns in the late 1960s. In 1971 he changed his name after converting to the Muslim faith.

The Lakers won 11 straight play-off games, setting a league record, as they swept past Portland, Seattle, and Phoenix en route to the final round. Los Angeles played so well that the Lakers suddenly were considered the equal of the Pistons, who still enjoyed home-court advantage in the championship series. To get that far, the Pistons beat the Celtics, then had a few rough moments against the Bucks before taking that series. Then they lost the opening game of the Eastern Conference finals to Chicago and Michael Jordan. The Pistons eventually beat Chicago in six games, but not until Jordan continued his play-off-long sensational performances, which included three game-winning, final-moment shots.

Los Angeles, which was trying to win its third straight title, received a jolt prior to the start of the final round when guard Byron Scott pulled a hamstring and could not play. Detroit won the opening game, 109–97, on its home floor, the Palace at Auburn Hills. Guards Joe Dumars (22), Isiah Thomas (24), and Vinnie Johnson (19) combined for 65 points. In game two, Magic Johnson pulled a hamstring late in the third quarter, leaving the Lakers without their starting backcourt. Despite those injuries, Los Angeles led by eight points going into the last period. But forward James Worthy missed a foul shot with two seconds left, and Detroit won, 108–105.

The teams moved to Los Angeles for game three, which the Lakers played without both Scott and Johnson, who limped through the opening four minutes before leaving for good. Once again, it was the Pistons' backcourt that made the difference as Detroit won, 114–110. Vinnie Johnson, Thomas, and Dumars combined for 74 points, with Dumars scoring 21 in the third period. Abdul-Jabbar had his finest game of the play-offs, scoring 24 points. The Lakers had a chance to win the game but Dumars blocked a David Rivers shot in the final seconds. In game four, Detroit wrapped up the series with a 105–97 victory. The Pistons' reserve center James Edwards scored 13 points in the final period and Dumars added 23 for the game. Dumars was a unanimous selection as most valuable player in the series. The Pistons held opponents to less than 100 points in all but two play-off games and their defensive average was the lowest since the 24-second clock was instituted in the early 1950s.

The College Season

Three remarkable players—Danny Ferry of Duke, Sean Elliott of Arizona, and Stacey King of Oklahoma—dominated the 1988–89 college regular season. There was no clear-cut choice among the three for best player in the United States, and they ultimately wound up dividing most of the major player-of-the-year awards. During the 1988–89 campaign, King was a thin center with a deft shooting touch around the basket; Ferry was a versatile big forward who led his team in assists and scoring; and Elliott was a smooth small forward with the ball-handling skills of a guard. Other standouts included center Pervis Ellison of Louisville, guard Mookie Blaylock of Oklahoma, forward Glen Rice of Michigan, forward Lionel Simmons of La Salle, guard Charles Smith of Georgetown, guard Sherman Douglas of Syracuse, guard Jay Edwards of Indiana, guard Jay Burson of Ohio State, forward Todd Lichti of Stanford, center Hank Gathers of Loyola Marymount, and center Alonzo Mourning of Georgetown. Louisiana State guard Chris Jackson, only a freshman, made some All-America teams on the strength of his outside shooting.

Oklahoma and Arizona were considered the two strongest teams during the regular season, even after the Sooners squeezed out a home-court victory over Arizona in February. But Oklahoma slumped in the late season and Georgetown closed strongly to move ahead of the Sooners in the rankings. Even though Indiana won the Big Ten championship, Illinois was viewed as the better team and received one of the four top seeds in the NCAA tournament.

But the great parity in college basketball continued, with a number of teams considered good enough to win the national title when the tournament began. Duke, Georgetown, Michigan, North Carolina, and Louisville had been

COLLEGE BASKETBALL

Conference Champions*

American South: Louisiana Tech
Association of Mid-Continent: Southwest Missouri State
Atlantic Coast: North Carolina
Atlantic-10: Rutgers
Big East: Georgetown
Big Eight: Missouri
Big Sky: Idaho
Big Ten: Indiana
Big West: UNLV
Colonial Athletic: George Mason
East Coast: Bucknell
ECAC North Atlantic: Siena
Ivy League: Princeton
Metro Athletic: Louisville
Metro Atlantic Athletic: LaSalle
Mid-American: Ball State
Mid-Eastern Athletic: South Carolina State
Midwestern Collegiate: Xavier
Missouri Valley: Creighton
Northeast: Robert Morris
Ohio Valley: Middle Tennessee
Pacific-10: Arizona
Southeastern: Alabama
Southern: Eastern Tennessee State
Southland: McNeese State
Southwest: Arkansas
Southwestern Athletic: Southern U.
Sun Belt: South Alabama
Trans America Athletic: Arkansas-Little Rock
West Coast Athletic: Loyola-Marymount
Western Athletic: Texas-El Paso

* Based on postseason conference tournaments, where applicable

Tournaments

NCAA: Michigan
NIT: St. John's
NCAA Div. II: North Carolina Central
NCAA Div. III: University of Wisconsin at Whitewater
NAIA: St. Mary's of Texas
NCAA (women's): Tennessee

chosen the top teams in the nation prior to the season, and only Louisville failed to live up to its ratings. Duke (24–7), Georgetown (26–4), Michigan (24–7), and North Carolina (27–7) all qualified for the NCAA, as did such other strong schools as Missouri (27–7), Syracuse (27–7), Iowa (22–9), Stanford (26–6), Seton Hall (26–6), Nevada-Las Vegas (26–7), and North Carolina State (20–8). The strongest conferences were the Big Eight, the Big Ten, and the Atlantic Coast, while the Big East slipped a bit from previous years. The season was marred by an ongoing investigation of traditional power Kentucky, which ultimately was placed on probation for three years by the NCAA. Coach Eddie Sutton resigned and was replaced by New York Knicks coach Rick Pitino.

The Tournaments. This was the year of the unexpected in the NCAA tournament. Underdog teams pulled off upset after upset, throwing off tournament seedings and leaving most of the favorite teams on the sidelines by the last few rounds. The only top-seeded team to survive until the Final Four was Illinois, which squeezed past Syracuse, 89–86, in the Midwest Regional final. In the Southeast, Virginia upset top-seeded Oklahoma, 86–80, only to lose to unsung Michigan, 102–65, in the regional final. Georgetown struggled in the early rounds, then was defeated by an efficient Duke team, 85–77, in the East Regional final. Another unsung team, Seton Hall, won the West Regional, defeating Indiana in the semifinals, 78–65, and then beating Nevada-Las Vegas, 84–61, in the final. Las Vegas had upset Arizona, 68–67, in the semifinals.

In the Final Four at Seattle's Kingdome, Seton Hall played Duke in one game and Michigan met Illinois in the other. Seton Hall was magnificent against the Blue Devils, who got off to a fast opening-half start to lead by as many as 18 points. But Seton Hall shot 71% in the second half to pull away to a 95–78 win. In the matchup of Big Ten teams, Rice scored 28 for Michigan and teammate Sean Higgins made a six-foot jumper in the final seconds as the Wolverines beat Illinois, 83–81. That set up a final between Seton Hall, which was considered the third best team in the Big East, and Michigan, which finished fourth in the Big Ten. Prior to the start of the tournament, Michigan coach Bill Frieder was released after he accepted a job with Arizona State. Steve Fisher, who had been an assistant, was named interim coach.

Fisher ultimately guided the Wolverines to the NCAA championship, the school's first. In an exciting title game, the teams wound up going into overtime tied at 71 after Rice missed a jump shot at the buzzer. In the extra period, Seton Hall led by three with three minutes to play, but Michigan rallied and wound up winning, 80–79, on two Rumeal Robinson free throws with three seconds to go. Rice scored 31 points and was named the tournament's most valuable player. With 184 points for the tournament, he also broke Bill Bradley's NCAA scoring record of 177. Fisher later was named Michigan's full-time coach.

AP/Wide World

In an unusually exciting NCAA final, Michigan forward Glen Rice (41), the star of the tournament, grabs a rebound as the Wolverines defeat Seton Hall, 80–79, in overtime.

In the NIT, St. John's of the Big East shook off a disappointing regular season and beat St. Louis, 73–65, in the title game. It was the Redmen's fifth NIT crown, a record. Center Jayson Williams scored 28 points and had 17 rebounds for the winners. He was named the tournament's most valuable player.

In the women's NCAA tournament, Tennessee's Bridgette Gordon performed marvelously, leading her team to its second national title in three years. Gordon made 11 of 21 shots in the title game against Auburn and scored 27 points in the 76–60 triumph. The teams had beaten each other during the regular season. Auburn's Vicki Orr scored 16 points. In a semifinal victory over Louisiana Tech, 76–71, Orr had 18 points, avenging her team's 1988 loss in the final game. In the other semifinal, Gordon scored 24 points as Tennessee beat Maryland, 77–65.

PAUL ATTNER, *"The Sporting News"*

Boxing

Professional boxing was alive and well in 1989 and once again its dominant figure was the heavyweight champion Mike Tyson, who reeled off two quick knockouts and raised his unbeaten record to 36 bouts. While Tyson was continuing to win, some of the lighterweight and older boxers, especially Sugar Ray Leonard, Thomas (Hit Man) Kearns, and Roberto Duran, made exciting and lucrative returns to the ring and won the plaudits of the fans.

The Heavyweight Champ. Mike Tyson continued to keep a profile outside the ring as large as the one he had in it. He managed to slug a television cameraman, get ticketed for speeding, win a divorce from Robin Givens, vow to win a college diploma, and fall sick with a lung infection that forced him to cancel a scheduled third defense of his title in 1989.

He made his first defense of the year in February against an Englishman named Frank Bruno, a game lumbering fighter who lasted into the fifth round and even seemed to shake Tyson several times before Tyson stopped him on a technical knockout at the Hilton Center in Las Vegas, NV. Tyson dropped Bruno, a heavy-muscled 6′3½″ (1.92 m), 228-pounder (103 kg), 12 seconds into the bout, and the fans thought this was another first-round exit for another inept Tyson opponent. However, Bruno, dazed but stouthearted, got up from the canvas, an act that seemed to surprise Tyson. Later in the round Bruno sent a hook to Tyson's jaw that seemed to stop the champion in his tracks. Tyson, who had not fought for eight months, appeared rusty. But the 22-year-old champion caught up with the 27-year-old Bruno and the bout was stopped at 2:55 of the fifth round. Bruno, a 10-1 underdog, earned the fans' respect, especially the 2,000 Britons who went to the United States to see him fight.

In July, Tyson took only 93 seconds to dispose of Carl (the Truth) Williams in an Atlantic City ring and appeared to give credence to the fans' appraisal that there is no fighter around who can dent his armor. Despite that appraisal, there were several contenders standing in the wings hoping for the chance. Among them were the former heavyweight champion George Foreman, who was making a noticeable comeback at age 42, and Evander Holyfield, ranked as the Number 1 heavyweight contender. One contender, Donovan (Razor) Ruddock, who already had been booked to fight Tyson in November, lost out when Tyson's lung infection forced cancellation of the bout.

Other Fights. Perhaps the fight fans' most rewarding bout of the year was the rematch between 33-year-old Sugar Ray Leonard and 30-year-old Thomas Hearns, fighters whose ages normally would designate them for the over-the-hill mob. But on June 12, eight years after their first donnybrook in which Leonard stopped the overconfident Hit Man in the 14th round, they came together again in the same ring at Las Vegas and waged a 12-round war that ended in a draw.

The bout was for Leonard's World Boxing Council (WBC) super middleweight title, which he had relinquished, then reclaimed, in 1988. Hearns floored Leonard twice—in the third and 11th rounds—and seemed to have an edge. But in the 12th round, Leonard mustered all his skills and showered a perpetual barrage of blows at Hearns, who barely was able to stand at the end. For the work, Leonard was guaranteed $14 million; Hearns, $12 million.

At age 37, the remarkable Roberto Duran of Panama, who already had held three different world titles, came out swinging and scored a split 12-round decision over Iran Barkley to capture the WBC middleweight crown at Convention Center in Atlantic City in February. He immediately embarked on a campaign to set up a rematch with Leonard. Such a rematch occurred on December 7 in Las Vegas, with Leonard winning a unanimous 12-round decision. Leonard thereby retained his WBC super middleweight crown.

GEORGE DE GREGORIO
"The New York Times"

World Boxing Champions*

Heavyweight: World Boxing Council (WBC)—Mike Tyson, United States, 1986; World Boxing Association (WBA)—Tyson, 1987; International Boxing Federation (IBF)—Tyson, 1987.
Cruiserweight: WBC—Carlos De Leon, Puerto Rico, 1989; WBA—vacant; IBF—Glenn McCrory, Britain, 1989.
Light Heavyweight: WBC—Jeff Harding, Australia, 1989; WBA—Virgil Hill, United States, 1987; IBF—Charles Williams, United States, 1987.
Super Middleweight: WBC—Sugar Ray Leonard, United States, 1989; WBA—Inchul Baek, South Korea, 1989; IBF—vacant.
Middleweight: WBC—Roberto Durán, Panama, 1989; WBA—Mike McCallum, Jamaica, 1989; IBF—Michael Nunn, United States, 1988.
Junior Middleweight: WBC—John Mugabi, Uganda, 1989; WBA—Julian Jackson, Virgin Islands, 1987; IBF—Gianfranco Rosi, Italy, 1989.
Welterweight: WBC—Marlon Starling, United States, 1989; WBA—Mark Breland, United States, 1989; IBF—Simon Brown, United States, 1988.
Junior Welterweight: WBC—Julio César Chavez, Mexico, 1989; WBA—Juan Coggi, Argentina, 1987; IBF—Meldrick Taylor, United States, 1988.
Lightweight: WBC—Pernell Whitaker, United States, 1989; WBA—Edwin Rosario, Puerto Rico, 1989; IBF—Whitaker, 1989.
Junior Lightweight: WBC—Azumah Nelson, Ghana, 1988; WBA—Brian Mitchell, South Africa, 1986; IBF—Juan Molina, Puerto Rico, 1989.
Featherweight: WBC—Jeff Fenech, Australia, 1988; WBA—Antonio Esparragoza, Venezuela, 1987; IBF—Jorge Paez, Mexico, 1988.
Junior Featherweight: WBC—Daniel Zaragoza, Mexico, 1988; WBA—Jesus Salud, United States, 1989; IBF—Fabrice Benichou, France, 1989.
Bantamweight: WBC—Raul Pérez, Mexico, 1988; WBA—Lusita Espinosa, Philippines, 1989; IBF—Orlando Canizales, United States, 1988.
Junior Bantamweight: WBC—Gilberto Roman, Mexico, 1988; WBA—Kaosai Galaxy, Thailand, 1984; IBF—Juan Polo, Colombia, 1989.
Flyweight: WBC—Sot Chitalada, Thailand, 1989; WBA—Jesus Rojas, Venezuela, 1989; IBF—Dave McCauley, England, 1989.
Junior Flyweight: WBC—Humberto Gonzalez, Mexico, 1989; WBA—Woo-Yuh Myung, South Korea, 1985; IBF—Muangshai Kittikasem, Thailand, 1989.
Strawweight: WBC—Napa Katwanchai, Thailand, 1989; WBA—Bong-jun-Kim, South Korea, 1989; IBF—Eric Chavez, Philippines, 1989.

*As of Dec. 31, 1989; date indicates year title was won.

Football

For the National Football League (NFL), the 1989–90 season was highlighted both by dramatic change and familiar occurrences. The change came at the top, where Pete Rozelle retired as commissioner after 29 years and was replaced by Paul Tagliabue, who, as outside counsel, had helped direct many of the league's lawsuits under the Rozelle regime. The familiar was the dominance of the San Francisco 49ers, who already had won three Super Bowls during the 1980s and ended this season with the best record (14-2) in the league. Their Super Bowl opponent also was quite familiar. The Denver Broncos (11-5), winners of the American Football Conference (AFC) title, made their third appearance in that game since 1987.

In the Louisiana Superdome in New Orleans on Jan. 28, 1990, the 49ers played nearly perfect football—offensively and defensively—and overwhelmed the Broncos, 55–10, in Super Bowl XXIV. San Francisco was led by quarterback Joe Montana, who completed 22 of 29 passes for 297 yards. Three of Montana's record five touchdown passes were caught by Jerry Rice, also a Super Bowl record. The victory was the 49ers' fourth Super Bowl win, tying the Pittsburgh Steelers' accomplishment, and the loss was the Broncos' fourth in the big game, tying them with the Minnesota Vikings for the most Super Bowl defeats.

With a last-minute 35-yard field goal by David Ridgway, the Saskatchewan Roughriders defeated the Hamilton Tiger-Cats, 43-40, for Canada's Grey Cup.

In college competition, the Miami Hurricanes won the national championship after beating Alabama in the Sugar Bowl, while Number 1-ranked Colorado was losing to Notre Dame in the Orange Bowl. Houston quarterback Andre Ware, who set numerous National Collegiate Athletic Association (NCAA) single-season passing and total offense records, won the Heisman Trophy as the nation's best college football player. At the beginning of the season, Ware had not even been considered a contender for the trophy.

National Football League

The decision by Pete Rozelle to retire as NFL commissioner ended a golden era for the league. Rozelle had been responsible largely for making the NFL one of the most successful sports organizations in history. He was especially influential in obtaining large television contracts and in promoting the league so well that sellouts for many teams were common every week. League owners had a difficult time deciding on a replacement for him. The final candidates were Jim Finks, president of the New Orleans Saints, and Paul Tagliabue, a partner in the Washington, DC, law firm of Covington & Burling and a legal adviser to the NFL. Finally, in October, Tagliabue was selected, a victory for the so-called "New Guard," a group of new team owners who wanted more say in how the NFL was being run.

Things were much more stable on the field. The 49ers' longtime head coach, Bill Walsh,

Two fine quarterbacks, San Francisco's Joe Montana (16) and Denver's John Elway (7), led their teams to Super Bowl XXIV. On Jan. 28, 1990, the 49ers crushed the Broncos, 55–10, as Montana picked up his third Super Bowl MVP award.

Photos, AP/Wide World

PROFESSIONAL FOOTBALL

National Football League

Final Standings

NATIONAL CONFERENCE

Eastern Division	W	L	T	Pct.	Points For	Points Against
N.Y. Giants	12	4	0	.750	348	252
Philadelphia	11	5	0	.688	342	274
Washington	10	6	0	.625	386	308
Phoenix	5	11	0	.313	258	377
Dallas	1	15	0	.063	204	393
Central Division						
Minnesota	10	6	0	.625	351	275
Green Bay	10	6	0	.625	362	356
Detroit	7	9	0	.438	312	364
Chicago	6	10	0	.375	358	377
Tampa Bay	5	11	0	.313	320	419
Western Division						
San Francisco	14	2	0	.875	442	253
L.A. Rams	11	5	0	.688	426	344
New Orleans	9	7	0	.563	386	301
Atlanta	3	13	0	.188	279	437

PLAY-OFFS
Los Angeles 21, Philadelphia 7
San Francisco 41, Minnesota 13
Los Angeles 19, N.Y. Giants 13
San Francisco 30, Los Angeles 3

AMERICAN CONFERENCE

Eastern Division	W	L	T	Pct.	Points For	Points Against
Buffalo	9	7	0	.563	409	317
Indianapolis	8	8	0	.500	298	301
Miami	8	8	0	.500	331	379
New England	5	11	0	.313	297	391
N.Y. Jets	4	12	0	.250	253	411
Central Division						
Cleveland	9	6	1	.594	334	254
Houston	9	7	0	.563	365	412
Pittsburgh	9	7	0	.563	265	326
Cincinnati	8	8	0	.500	404	285
Western Division						
Denver	11	5	0	.688	362	226
Kansas City	8	7	1	.531	318	286
L.A. Raiders	8	8	0	.500	315	297
Seattle	7	9	0	.438	241	327
San Diego	6	10	0	.375	266	290

PLAY-OFFS
Pittsburgh 26, Houston 23
Cleveland 34, Buffalo 30
Denver 24, Pittsburgh 23
Denver 37, Cleveland 21

SUPER BOWL XXIV: San Francisco 55, Denver 10

retired and eventually became a color commentator on pro-football telecasts. His replacement, George Seifert, who had been the team's defensive coordinator, did a superb job, guiding San Francisco to the National Football Conference (NFC) Western Division title. His quarterback, Joe Montana, enjoyed the best year of an already magnificent career. He was the league's most valuable player and he established the highest single-season quarterback rating in league history. The best team in the AFC, the Denver Broncos, was more surprising. The Broncos had finished 8-8 the year before but had remade their defensive team and coaching staff and finished with an 11-5 record to win the Western Division.

The New York Giants also played better than anticipated and captured the NFC Eastern title behind the play of quarterback Phil Simms and running back Ottis Anderson. The Minnesota Vikings obtained running back Herschel Walker from the Dallas Cowboys in midseason and went on to win the NFC Central, as longtime division rival Chicago (6-10) had a miserable season. Philadelphia, which had been expected to be a dominant team with quarterback Randall Cunningham, and the Los Angeles Rams were the other NFC play-off qualifiers. But the most improved NFC team was Green Bay, which finished 10-6 to barely miss out on a play-off spot. It was a significant showing for the Packers, who had been struggling ever since the end of the Vince Lombardi era in the 1960s.

In the AFC, Cleveland, which had a new coach, Bud Carson, beat Houston on the last day of the regular season to become Central Division champs, while Buffalo overcame a disappointing season from quarterback Jim Kelly to win the Eastern crown. Other AFC qualifiers were Houston and Pittsburgh. Kansas City was one of the most improved teams in the AFC, ending with an 8-7-1 record under new coach Marty Schottenheimer, who had been fired at Cleveland. Cincinnati, which went to the Super Bowl in 1989, did not make the play-offs.

Pittsburgh, the conference's most surprising team, beat the Oilers in overtime in the AFC wild-card game, while the Rams, behind a strong defense, upset Philadelphia in the NFC wild-card contest. In the semifinal games, the Rams toppled the Giants in overtime, 19-13, with quarterback Jim Everett throwing for 315 yards. The 49ers demolished the Vikings, 41-13, as San Francisco gained 403 yards against the league's best defense. Cleveland survived a late rally and beat Buffalo, 34-30, while Denver came back to defeat Pittsburgh, 24-23, after trailing most of the game.

Denver was a slight favorite to beat Cleveland in the AFC championship game, mainly because of home-field advantage. But quarterback John Elway had a wonderful game, throwing for 385 yards and three touchdowns, and the Broncos wound up winning, 37-21. Cleveland was hindered by a sub-par performance from quarterback Bernie Kosar, who had hand and elbow injuries.

San Francisco had an even easier time beating the Rams, 30-3, in the NFC title game. Montana passed for 262 yards and two touchdowns and the 49er defense held the Rams to 156 total yards. Everett could complete just 16 of 36 passes and was intercepted three times. The Rams had split two games with San Francisco during the regular season, giving them hope of being able to upset the 49ers. Instead, the 49ers made their fourth trip to the Super Bowl in nine years.

Regular Season and Off the Field. Christian Okoye of Kansas City won the league rushing title (1,480) with rookie Barry Sanders of Detroit (1,470), a former Heisman Trophy winner from Oklahoma State, finishing second. Defending champion Eric Dickerson of Indianapolis (1,311) was third. Dalton Hillard had a league-high 18 touchdowns. Montana was the most accurate passer, with Cincinnati's Boomer Esiason second and Everett third. Everett (4,310) finished behind Green Bay's Don Majkowski (4,318) for top passing yardage, while Sterling Sharpe of Green Bay (90) and Andre Reed of Buffalo (88) were one-two in receptions. Jerry Rice of San Francisco (1,483) had the most pass-receiving yards. Mike Cofer of San Francisco (136 points) won the scoring title, with Chip Lohmiller of Washington (128) finishing second. Standout defensive players included ends Reggie White of Philadelphia, Chris Doleman of Minnesota, and Bruce Smith of Buffalo, tackle Keith Millard of Minnesota, and linebacker Lawrence Taylor of the Giants. Seattle receiver Steve Largent retired as the league's all-time leader in touchdown passes and overall catches.

A number of players, most notably defensive end Dexter Manley of Washington, were suspended for violations of the league's drug-use policy. A significant coaching change occurred in midseason when the Los Angeles Raiders fired Mike Shanahan and hired former Raider offensive line great Art Shell, who became the league's first black head coach. Earlier, Tom Landry, longtime head coach of the Dallas Cowboys, was fired.

In August four players—Pittsburgh quarterback Terry Bradshaw, defensive back Mel Blount, also of the Steelers, defensive back Willie Wood of the Green Bay Packers, and Shell of the Raiders—were inducted into the Pro Football Hall of Fame in Canton, OH.

The College Season

The muddled race for the national championship cleared up on New Year's Day when Number 4-ranked Notre Dame upset previously undefeated and Number 1-ranked Colorado in the Orange Bowl, while second-ranked Miami defeated seventh-ranked Alabama in the Sugar Bowl. Miami then was voted Number 1 in the final Associated Press (AP) poll.

Notre Dame coach Lou Holtz thought his team should have won the championship. The Irish played what was considered the most difficult schedule in the country and lost just once in 13 games, to Miami, 27-10, on November 25. That defeat ended Notre Dame's 23-game winning streak and knocked the Irish from the Number-1 ranking. But Holtz believed his team redeemed itself by overcoming Colorado, which enjoyed the best season in school history. Instead, the Irish wound up Number 2.

AP/Wide World

With the balloting close, Houston's Andre Ware took the 1989 Heisman Trophy. The quarterback had set 13 NCAA records, including most passing yards in a season.

The Buffaloes, who were the first Big Eight Conference team other than Nebraska and Oklahoma to play in the Orange Bowl since 1977, could not capitalize on three scoring opportunities in the first half against Notre Dame and then could not stop tailback Raghib (Rocket) Ismail in the second half. Ismail, normally a wide receiver, gained a career-high 108 yards in the game, scoring on a 35-yard run in the third quarter. Teammate Anthony Johnson scored twice, on two- and seven-yard runs. Colorado had played the season in honor of quarterback Sal Aunese, who had been a starter but died of cancer in September 1989. The Buffaloes finished the year with an 11-1 record and ranked fourth.

Miami had lost the 1988 national title when Notre Dame beat the Hurricanes during the regular season. Entering the Sugar Bowl, Miami had lost only to Florida State but had climbed to Number 2 after the November triumph over Notre Dame. In the bowl, quarterback Craig Erickson passed for three touchdowns and 250 yards and Miami gained 477 total yards to beat Alabama, which fell to ninth in the final poll. Miami finished with an 11-1 record and Alabama was 10-2.

Florida State felt it might be the best team around. The Seminoles, after losing their first two games, won their last ten contests, includ-

In what turned out to be the most important game of the 1989 college season, the Miami Hurricanes ended Notre Dame's 23-game winning streak on November 25. The win plus a victory in the Sugar Bowl helped Miami capture their third national title of the 1980s. They also took the crown in 1983 and 1987.

AP/Wide World

ing a 24-10 triumph over Miami. Florida State ended the year ranked Number 3 after a 41-17 trouncing of Nebraska in the Fiesta Bowl. Quarterback Peter Tom Willis passed for 422 yards and five touchdowns. Nebraska finished 10-2 and ranked eleventh.

In the 76th Rose Bowl, Michigan, the Big Ten champion, lost to USC, the Pac Ten champion, 17-10, when Ricky Ervins scored on a 14-yard run with 70 seconds left. It was the final game for Michigan coach Bo Schembechler, who ended his 27-year coaching career (21 at Michigan). Schembechler's teams became dominant in the Big Ten but never won a national championship. He finished with a 234-65-8 career record, the fifth-winningest in Division I-A history. In the Cotton Bowl, tailback Chuck Webb gained 250 yards and scored twice as Tennessee beat Arkansas, 31-27.

In the fourth-closest race in Heisman Trophy history, Houston quarterback Andre Ware won the award, becoming the first black quarterback to be so honored. Ware set 13 NCAA records, including most passing yards (4,699) in a season. He also became the first player from a team on probation to capture the award. Indiana running back Anthony Thompson was second in the voting. Third was West Virginia quarterback Major Harris, fourth was Notre Dame quarterback Tony Rice, and fifth was Colorado quarterback Darian Hagan.

Michigan State linebacker Percy Snow won two of the top linemen awards. He was named recipient of the Butkus Award, given annually to the nation's best linebacker, and the Lombardi Award, honoring the top linebacker or lineman. Brigham Young offensive guard Mohammed Elewonibi was chosen as the Outland Trophy winner, honoring the nation's outstanding interior lineman. Other top players included Florida running back Emmitt Smith, nose tackle Chris Zorich of Notre Dame, and linebacker Keith McCants of Alabama.

Georgia Southern won its third NCAA Division I-AA title in five years by beating Stephen F. Austin, 37-34. Mississippi College defeated Jacksonville State, 3-0, in the Division II championship game, while Dayton downed Union, 17-7, in the Division III final.

PAUL ATTNER
National Correspondent, "Sporting News"

COLLEGE FOOTBALL

Conference Champions	Atlantic Coast—(tie) Virginia and Duke Big Eight—Colorado Big Ten—Michigan Big West—Fresno State Ivy League—(tie) Princeton and Yale Mid-American—Ball State Pacific Ten—Southern California Southeastern—(tie) Alabama, Tennessee, Auburn Southwest—Arkansas Western Athletic—Brigham Young
NCAA Champions	Division I-AA—Georgia Southern Division II—Mississippi College Division III—Dayton
NAIA Champions	Division I—Carson-Newman Division II—Westminster
Individual Honors	Heisman Trophy—Andre Ware, Houston Lombardi Award—Percy Snow, Michigan State Outland Trophy—Mohammed Elewonibi, Brigham Young

Major Bowl Games

All-American Bowl (Birmingham, AL, Dec. 28)—Texas Tech 49, Duke 21
Aloha Bowl (Honolulu, HI, Dec. 25)—Michigan State 33, Hawaii 13
California Bowl (Fresno, CA, Dec. 9)—Fresno State 27, Ball State 6
Copper Bowl (Tucson, AZ, Dec. 31)—Arizona 17, North Carolina State 10
Cotton Bowl (Dallas, Jan. 1)—Tennessee 31, Arkansas 27
Fiesta Bowl (Tempe, AZ, Jan. 1)—Florida State 41, Nebraska 17
Florida Citrus Bowl (Orlando, FL, Jan. 1)—Illinois 31, Virginia 21
Freedom Bowl (Anaheim, CA, Dec. 30)—Washington 34, Florida 7
Gator Bowl (Jacksonville, FL, Dec. 30)—Clemson 27, West Virginia 7
Hall of Fame Bowl (Tampa, FL, Jan. 1)—Auburn 31, Ohio State 14
John Hancock Bowl (El Paso, TX, Dec. 30)—Pittsburgh 31, Texas A&M 28
Holiday Bowl (San Diego, CA, Dec. 29)—Penn State 50, Brigham Young 39
Independence Bowl (Shreveport, LA, Dec. 16)—Oregon 27, Tulsa 24
Liberty Bowl (Memphis, TN, Dec. 28)—Mississippi 42, Air Force 29
Orange Bowl (Miami, Jan. 1)—Notre Dame 21, Colorado 6
Peach Bowl (Atlanta, Dec. 30)—Syracuse 19, Georgia 18
Rose Bowl (Pasadena, CA, Jan. 1)—Southern California 17, Michigan 10
Sugar Bowl (New Orleans, Jan. 1)—Miami 33, Alabama 25

Golf

The U.S. golf scene featured a curious mixture of highs and lows in 1989, especially on the PGA Tour and the attendant major championships. All of the latter were lost rather than won, which is usually the case.

Scott Hoch missed a two-foot putt on the first playoff hole of the Masters to let England's Nick Faldo tie him and win on the next hole. Tom Kite collapsed in the final round of the U.S. Open and Curtis Strange won his second straight championship. Greg Norman faltered in the British Open playoff and Mark Calcavecchia won with a strong finish. Finally, Mike Reid went three over par on the finishing holes of the PGA's final round and yielded to Payne Stewart's closing 65.

Kite had won two tournaments early in the year, including the prestigious Players Championship, and he partially atoned for his U.S. Open tragedy by winning the season-ending Nabisco Championship. The victory, worth $625,000, made Kite the season's leading money winner with a record $1,395,278 and the PGA player of the year. He also became golf's all-time leading money winner with $5,600,691. Stewart also went over the million mark with $1,201,301.

Norman won the Vardon Trophy with a 69.49 scoring average and the Jack Nicklaus Performance Average award given by *Golf Digest*. Tim Simpson, with two victories, was named most improved player by *Golf Digest,* and Bob Estes, who won $135,628, was the magazine's rookie of the year. Bob Charles, the New Zealand left-hander, won five times on the Senior PGA Tour and finished as the leading money winner with a record $725,889. Charles also had the low scoring average at 69.78. Close behind on the senior money list was Orville Moody, the U.S. Senior Open winner, with $647,985.

Betsy King dominated the Ladies Professional Golf Association (LPGA) Tour. She won six events, including the U.S. Women's Open, earned a record $654,132, and was the player of the year. Beth Daniel, coming back from illness and injury, won four tournaments and $504,851. She also won the Vare Trophy with a low scoring average of 70.38 and the *Golf Digest* Mickey Wright Performance Average

Golf's Upswing

Golf, which has been knocking around for some 500 years, 200 of them in the United States, suddenly has become the hottest game in town.

The National Golf Foundation (NGF) reported 23.4 million golfers in the United States in 1988, up from 15.1 million in 1980. The golfing population had increased by 30% since 1985 and was growing at better than a 7% annual rate. Two million players are joining the ranks each year. For the first time ever, the golf participation rate climbed above 10% of the population, reaching 10.4% in the latest report. Dr. Gordon Benson, NGF vice-president of research, estimated that there could be 40, maybe 50 million golfers by the year 2000.

Not only are more Americans playing, they are playing more. Total rounds played swelled from 434 million in 1987 to 487 million in 1988. The surge is being fueled by a dramatic increase in the number of frequent golfers—those who play 25 rounds or more a year. Their total jumped from 4.8 million to 5.6 million in 1988, a 16% rise compared with a zero increase the previous year. And an NGF survey indicated the annual average number of rounds per player was expected to rise almost 50% in 1989, from 19.4 to 29.1.

Golf once was considered a game for rich, older, white males. No more. Today half of the country's golfers are in their 20s and 30s. More and more blacks and Hispanics are taking up the game, and 41% of the new golfers are women, who now make up 23% of the golfing population. Still, while only 25% of golfers are over 50, they play more than half the rounds. The over-50 golfer averages 43 rounds each year, three times the pace of younger golfers.

The growth in popularity of the game has spawned a huge peripheral business. Golf is now a $20 billion industry, $5 billion of which is in merchandise sales that grew 8% annually in 1987 and 1988. Golfers on the Professional Golf Association (PGA) Tour, Ladies Professional Golf Association (LPGA) Tour, and the burgeoning Senior PGA Tour played for more than $70 million in 1989—more than double the total of four years earlier. Nearly $8 billion was spent on golf travel alone in 1988.

The boom is not without peril. The NGF estimates 400 new courses a year will be needed over the next decade. Because of rocketing land and development costs, only about half that number are opening at the moment, although the percentage is growing. So courses are becoming overcrowded. Rounds that should take four hours often stretch to ordeals of five hours or more. Etiquette and course care are slipping as more newcomers show up. The cost to play the game also is escalating, with club memberships going for $50,000 and up in some areas, and annual dues sometimes reaching upward of $4,000. All this eventually might quiet the boom, but at the moment, nothing seems to be standing in its way.

LARRY DENNIS

GOLF

PGA TOUR

MONY Tournament of Champions: Steve Jones (279)
Bob Hope Chrysler Classic: Steve Jones (343)
Phoenix Open: Mark Calcavecchia (263)
AT&T Pebble Beach National Pro-Am: Mark O'Meara (277)
Los Angeles Open Presented by Nissan: Mark Calcavecchia (272)
Hawaiian Open: Gene Sauers (197)
Shearson Lehman Hutton Andy Williams Open: Greg Twiggs (271)
Doral Ryder Open: Bill Glasson (275)
Honda Classic: Blaine McCallister (266)
The Nestle Invitational: Tom Kite (278)
THE PLAYERS Championship: Tom Kite (279)
USF&G Classic: Tim Simpson (274)
Independent Insurance Agent Open: Mike Sullivan (280)
The Masters: Nick Faldo (283)
Deposit Guaranty Classic: Jim Booros (199)
MCI Heritage Classic: Payne Stewart (268)
K Mart Greater Greensboro Open: Ken Green (277)
Las Vegas Invitational: Scott Hoch (336)
GTE Byron Nelson Classic: Jodie Mudd (265)
Memorial Tournament: Bob Tway (277)
Southwestern Bell Colonial: Ian Baker-Finch (270)
Bell South Atlanta Classic: Scott Simpson (278)
Kemper Open: Tom Byrum (268)
Manufacturers Hanover Westchester Classic: Wayne Grady (277)
U.S. Open: Curtis Strange (278)
Canadian Open: Steve Jones (271)
Beatrice Western Open: Mark McCumber (275)
Canon Greater Hartford Open: Paul Azinger (267)
Anheuser-Busch Classic: Mike Donald (268)
Hardee's Golf Classic and British Open: Curt Byrum (268)
Buick Open: Leonard Thompson (273)
Federal Express St. Jude Classic: John Mahaffey (272)
PGA Championship: Payne Stewart (276)
The International: Greg Norman (+13)
NEC World Series of Golf: David Frost (276)
Chattanooga Classic: Stan Utley (263)
Greater Milwaukee Open: Greg Norman (269)
B.C. Open: Mike Hulbert (268)
Bank of Boston Classic: Blaine McCallister (271)
Southern Open: Ted Schulz (266)
Centel Classic: Bill Britton (200)
Texas Open Presented by Nabisco: Donnie Hammond (258)
Walt Disney World/Oldsmobile Classic: Tim Simpson (272)
Nabisco Golf Championships: Tom Kite (276)

LPGA

The Jamaica Classic: Betsy King (202)
Oldsmobile LPGA Classic: Dottie Mochrie (279)
Orix Hawaiian Ladies Open: Sherri Turner (205)
Women's Kemper Open: Betsy King (202)
Circle K LPGA Tucson Open: Lori Garbacz (274)
Standard Register Turquoise Classic: Allison Finney (282)
Nabisco Dinah Shore: Juli Inkster (279)
Red Robin Kyocera Inamori Classic: Patti Rizzo (277)
Al Star/Centinela Hospital Classic: Pat Bradley (208)
USX Golf Classic: Betsy King (275)
Sara Lee Classic: Kathy Postlewait (203)
Crestar Classic: Juli Inkster (210)
Chrysler-Plymouth Classic: Cindy Rarick (214)
Mazda LPGA Championship: Nancy Lopez (274)
LPGA Corning Classic: Ayako Okamoto (272)
Rochester International: Patty Sheehan (278)
Planters Pat Bradley International: Robin Hood (16 points)
Lady Keystone Open: Laura Davies (207)
McDonald's Championship: Betsy King (272)
du Maurier Classic: Tammie Green (279)
Jamie Farr Toledo Classic: Penny Hammel (206)
U.S. Women's Open Championship: Betsy King (278)
Boston Five Classic: Amy Alcott (272)
Atlantic City Classic: Nancy Lopez (206)
Greater Washington Open: Beth Daniel (205)
Nestle World Championship: Betsy King (275)
Mitsubishi Motors Ocean State Open: Tina Barrett (210)
Rail Charity Golf Classic: Beth Daniel (203)
Cellular One-Ping Golf Championship: Muffin Spencer-Devlin (214)
Safeco Classic: Beth Daniel (273)
Nippon Travel-MBS Classic: Nancy Lopez (277)
Konica San Jose Classic: Beth Daniel (205)
Nichirei International, Japan-WUS LPGA: Colleen Walker (210)
Mazda Japan Classic: Elaine Crosby (205)

Senior PGA Tour

MONY Senior Tournament of Champions: Miller Barber (280)
Senior Skins Game: Chi Chi Rodriguez
General Foods PGA Seniors Championship: Larry Mowry (281)
GTE Suncoast Classic: Bob Charles (207)
Aetna Challenge: Gene Littler (209)
Vintage Chrysler Invitational: Miller Barber (281)
MONY Arizona Classic: Bruce Crampton (200)
FUJI Electric Grand Slam: Bob Charles (207)
Murata Seniors Reunion: Don Bies (208)
The TRADITION at Desert Mtn: Don Bies (275)
Chrysler Cup: United States (71)
Liberty Mutual Legends of Golf: Al Geiberger/Harold Henning (251)
RJR at the Dominion: Larry Mowry (201)
Bell Atlantic St. Christopher's Classic: Dave Hill (206)
NYNEX/Golf Digest Commemorative: Bob Charles (193)
Southwestern Bell Classic: Bobby Nichols (209)
Doug Sanders Kingwood Celebrity Classic: Homero Blancas (208)

AP/Wide World

Nick Faldo captured the 1989 Masters with a birdie on the second hole of a play-off against Scott Hoch. He later was named world player of the year by "Golf Digest."

Mazda Senior TPC: Orville Moody (271)
Northville Long Island Classic: Butch Baird (183)
MONY Syracuse Senior Classic: Jim Dent (201)
USGA Senior Open: Orville Moody (279)
Digital Seniors Classic: Bob Charles (200)
Greater Grand Rapids Open: John Paul Cain (203)
Ameritech Senior Open: Bruce Crampton (205)
The Newport Cup: Jim Dent (206)
U.S. West Showdown Classic: Tom Shaw (207)
Rancho Murieta Senior Gold Rush: Dave Hill (207)
GTE Northwest Classic: Al Geiberger (204)
Sunwest Bank/Charley Pride Senior Golf Classic: Bob Charles (203)
RJR Bank One Classic: Rives McBee (202)
GTE North Classic: Gary Player (135)
Crestar Classic: Chi Chi Rodriguez (203)
PaineWebber Invitational: canceled
Fairfield Barnett Space Coast Classic: Bob Charles (203)
RJR Classics Champion: Gardner Dickinson (146)
Gatlin Brothers Southwest Golf Classic: George Archer (209)
TransAmerica Seniors Championship: Billy Casper (207)
RJR Championship: Gary Player (207)
General Tire Classic: Charles Coody (205)
GTE West Classic: Walt Zembriski (197)
GTE Kaanapali Classic: Don Bies (132)

Other Tournaments

British Open: Mark Calcavecchia (275)
World Match Play: Nick Faldo
Ryder Cup: United States 14, Europe 14
Walker Cup: Britain—Ireland 12½, United States 11½
World Cup: Individual—Peter Fowler, Australia (137); Team—Australia
U.S. Men's Amateur: Chris Patton
U.S. Women's Amateur: Vicky Goetze
U.S. Men's Public Links: Tim Hobby
U.S. Women's Public Links: Pearl Sinn
U.S. Mid-Amateur: James Taylor
U.S. Women's Mid-Amateur: Robin Weiss
U.S. Senior Men's Amateur: R. S. (Bo) Williams
U.S. Senior Women's Amateur: Anne Sander
U.S. Junior Boys: David Duval
U.S. Junior Girls: Brandie Burton
NCAA Men: Individual—Phil Mickelson; Team—Oklahoma
NCAA Women: Individual—Pat Hurst; Team—San Jose State

award. Hall of Famer Nancy Lopez won three tournaments, inluding the LPGA Championship, and finished third on the money list. Tammie Green was named most improved player by *Golf Digest* and Pamela Wright was the rookie of the year.

In international competition, Europe and the United States tied in Ryder Cup competition at the Belfry in England, and Britain-Ireland defeated the United States in the Walker Cup.

Faldo was named the world player of the year by *Golf Digest*.

LARRY DENNIS, *Free-lance Golf Writer*

Horse Racing

Sunday Silence capped off a season-long duel with Easy Goer by winning the $3 million Breeders' Cup Classic by a neck in a record 2:00 1/5 for 1.25 mi (2 km) at Gulfstream Park. The victory gave Sunday Silence, trained by 76-year-old Charlie Whittingham, a three-to-one edge on Easy Goer, whose eight-length victory in the Belmont Stakes had cost Sunday Silence the Triple Crown.

Sunday Silence was raced lightly coming into the November 4 Classic and his last outing before the Breeders' Cup had come six weeks earlier when he won the Louisiana Super Derby. He had followed his defeat in the Belmont with an upset loss to Prized in the Swaps Stakes. Easy Goer had won five straight Grade I races heading into the Breeders' Cup. Sunday Silence won seven of nine in 1989, including the Kentucky Derby and Preakness Stakes, and Easy Goer captured eight of 11 starts including an eight-length victory in the Belmont. The two three-year-olds were one-two in each of their four meetings.

Open Mind became the first three-year-old filly to win New York's filly triple crown, the Kentucky Oaks at Churchill Downs, and the Alabama at Saratoga. Bayakoa, a five-year-old Argentine-bred mare, completed an impressive season by winning the Breeders' Cup Distaff.

Secretariat, one of the best and most popular horses in history, was destroyed humanely on October 4 at Claiborne Farm in Paris, KY. The 19-year-old son of Bold Ruler had been the first Triple Crown winner in 25 years in 1973. Secretariat set the current Kentucky Derby record of 1:59⅖ and won the Belmont by an incredible 31 lengths.

Kent Desormeaux, a 19-year-old Louisiana jockey, broke Chris McCarron's 15-year-old record of 546 wins in a year on November 30. Pat Day became the first to ride eight winners in a nine-race card on September 13 at Arlington Park.

Harness Racing. The 64th Hambletonian required a third heat in which Park Avenue Joe and Probe finished in a dead heat with both horses being timed in 2:02 ⅖ on the 1-mi (1.6-km) Meadowlands track. Park Avenue Joe was declared the champion based on overall finishes in the three heats.

The Breeders Crown, a series of eight races emulating thoroughbred racing's Breeders' Cup, was staged in a single program at Pompano Park with a total purse of $3.2 million. Peace Corps' victory in the three-year-old Filly Trot, her 24th consecutive victory against fillies, was a highlight.

STAN SUTTON

HORSE RACING

Major North American Thoroughbred Races

Alabama: Open Mind, $232,400 (money distributed)
Belmont Stakes: Easy Goer, $689,200
Breeders' Cup Classic: Sunday Silence, $3 million
Breeders' Cup Distaff: Bayakoa, $1 million
Breeders' Cup Juvenile: Rhythm, $1 million
Breeders' Cup Juvenile Fillies: Go For Wand, $1 million
Breeders' Cup Mile: Steinlen, $1 milllon
Breeders' Cup Sprint: Dancing Spree, $1 million
Breeders' Cup Turf: Prized, $2 million
Budweiser-Arlington Million: Steinlen, $1 million
Budweiser International: Caltech, $750,000
Florida Derby: Mercedes Won, $500,000
Gotham Stakes: Easy Goer, $280,500
Haskell Invitational Handicap: King Glorious, $500,000
Hollywood Invitational: Great Communicator, $500,000
Iselin Handicap: Proper Reality, $250,000
Jockey Club Gold Cup: Easy Goer, $1,099,000
Kentucky Derby: Sunday Silence, $749,000
Kentucky Oaks: Open Mind, $231,600
Man o' War Stakes: Yankee Affair, $470,400
Metropolitan Handicap: Proper Reality, $589,000
Mother Goose: Open Mind, $227,200
Pimlico Special: Blushing John, $700,000
Preakness Stakes: Sunday Silence, $674,200
Rothmans International: Hodges Bay, $959,000
Ruffian Handicap: Bayakoa, $226,400
Santa Anita Derby: Sunday Silence, $500,000
Santa Anita Handicap: Martial Law, $1 million
Spinster Stakes: Bayakoa, $262,250
Strub Stakes: Nasr El Arab, $500,000
Suburban Handicap: Dancing Spree, $431,200
Super Derby: Sunday Silence, $1 million
Travers Stakes: Easy Goer, $1,088,500
Turf Classic: Yankee Affair, $654,300
Wood Memorial: Easy Goer, $568,000
Whitney Handicap: Easy Goer, $287,500
Woodward Handicap: Easy Goer, $809,000

Major North American Harness Races

Breeders Crown 3-year-old Filly Trot: Peace Corps, $335,701
Breeders Crown 2-year-old Colt and Gelding Pace: Till We Meet Again, $567,213
Breeders Crown 3-year-old Colt and Gelding Trot: Esquire Spur, $322,276
Breeders Crown 3-year-old Filly Pace: Cheery Hello, $285,701
Breeders Crown 2-year-old Filly Pace: Town Pro, $438,213
Breeders Crown 2-year-old Colt and Gelding Trot: Royal Troubador, $356,410
Breeders Crown 2-year-old Filly Trot: Delphi's Lobell, $445,213
Breeders Crown 3-year-old Colt and Gelding Pace: Goalie Jeff, $377,701
Cane Pace: Dancing Master, $621,210
Diamond Stake: Choice Yankee, $429,550
Hambletonian: Park Avenue Joe, $1,131,000
Hambletonian Oaks: Park Avenue Kathy, $423,000
Kentucky Futurity: Peace Corps, $177,230
Kentucky Pacing Derby: Jake And Elwood, $329,913
Little Brown Jug: Goalie Jeff, $500,200
Meadowlands Pace: Dexter Nukes, $852,000
Merrie Annabelle: Cayster, $433,750
Messenger Stake: Sandman Hanover, $315,749
Peter Haughton Memorial: Backstreet Guy, $669,000
Sweetheart Pace: Before Hours, $669,000
Woodrow Wilson Pace: San Francisco Ben, $907,000
World Trotting Derby: Peace Corps, $600,000

The Calgary Flames defeated the Montreal Canadiens, four games to two, for their first Stanley Cup. The Flames' Al MacInnis (right, #2) was the first defenseman to lead the play-offs in scoring, making at least one point in 17 straight games. He was judged the most valuable player of the play-offs.

Ice Hockey

Prior to the 1989 Stanley Cup play-offs, the Calgary Flames had looked with envy at the Edmonton Oilers' amazing run of four Stanley Cup titles in their first nine years in the National Hockey League (NHL). With the Oilers' shocking trade of Wayne Gretzky to the Los Angeles Kings in August 1988, the door was opened for Calgary, however, and they went on to win their first NHL crown in 1989. In a battle between the two teams with the best records over 80 regular-season games, the Flames avenged their 1986 loss to the Montreal Canadiens in the 1989 play-off finals. This time they defeated the Canadiens, four games to two.

Regular Season. The Flames squeezed past the Canadiens in a battle for the overall points title of the regular season. Calgary had 117 points, two more than Montreal. The Washington Capitals were a distant third (92 points). The 1988 champion Oilers fell to seventh (84). Calgary had the second best offense (354 goals) and also finished Number 2 in defense (226 goals allowed), a dramatic improvement from 305 in 1987–88. The Flames and the Detroit Red Wings repeated as winners of the Smythe and Norris Divisions, respectively. The Canadiens, who had the league's stingiest defense (218 goals allowed), won the Adams Division. The Washington Capitals took their first Patrick Division crown.

Pittsburgh center Mario Lemieux (*see* BIOGRAPHY) won his second straight Ross (scoring) Trophy, falling one point short of joining Wayne Gretzky as the only players to hit the 200-point plateau in a season. Lemieux had 199 points, including 85 goals. Only Gretzky ever scored more (92 in 1981–82 and 87 in 1983–84). Gretzky was second in points with 168, with Detroit's Steve Yzerman third at 155. Gretzky's Los Angeles teammate Bernie Nicholls was next at 150. He had 70 goals, joining Gretzky, Lemieux, Juri Kurri, and Phil Esposito as the only players ever to score 70 or more in one season. In all, nine players had at least 100 points in 1988–89, including Calgary's Joe Mullen, who became the highest American-born scorer with 110.

Gretzky's 168 points moved him into second place on the all-time scoring list, only 13 points behind Gordie Howe. While Lemieux captured the scoring title, Gretzky was a surprisingly easy winner of the Hart Trophy as the league's most valuable player (MVP). He became the first player to win an NHL award nine times.

Play-offs. The Edmonton Oilers' reign as NHL champions ended after seven games in the first round of the Smythe Division play-offs. Gretzky spearheaded his new Los Angeles team past his former team, scoring two goals in the clinching seventh game. Calgary survived an overtime scare in the seventh game of their test with Vancouver, a team that was 43 points worse in the league standings. In the Smythe finals, Calgary crushed Los Angeles four straight. In the Norris Division, Chicago shocked the Red Wings, taking them four games to two. The Blackhawks had made the play-offs on the last day of the season. St. Louis beat Minnesota, 4–1, in the other series but could not stop the surging Hawks in the division finals. Chicago won in five games.

In the Adams Division, Montreal got past the fourth-place Hartford Whalers in four games, and Boston beat Buffalo in five in their matchup. The Canadiens had no trouble beating Boston in five games in the next round. Philadelphia pulled off a surprise in the Patrick Division. The fourth-place team beat the Capitals in six games. In the other series, Pittsburgh swept the New York Rangers in four straight. In the finals, the Flyers shaded Pittsburgh, four games to three.

In the conference finals, there were no sudden twists. Calgary bounced the Hawks, four games to one, to take the Campbell title. The Canadiens needed six games to subdue the injury-ridden Flyers. In the final game, Philadelphia goalie Ron Hextall attacked Montreal's Chris Chelios, who took the Norris Trophy as best defenseman, and received a 12-game suspension to start the 1989–90 season.

ICE HOCKEY

National Hockey League
(Final Standings, 1988–89)

Wales Conference

Patrick Division	W	L	T	Pts.	Goals For	Goals Against
*Washington	41	29	10	92	305	259
*Pittsburgh	40	33	7	87	347	349
*N.Y. Rangers	37	35	8	82	310	307
*Philadelphia	36	36	8	80	307	285
New Jersey	27	41	12	66	281	325
N.Y. Islanders	28	47	5	61	265	325
Adams Division						
*Montreal	53	18	9	115	315	218
*Boston	37	29	14	88	289	256
*Buffalo	38	35	7	83	291	299
*Hartford	37	38	5	79	299	290
Quebec	27	46	7	61	269	342

Campbell Conference

Norris Division	W	L	T	Pts.	Goals For	Goals Against
*Detroit	34	34	12	80	313	316
*St. Louis	33	35	12	78	275	285
*Minnesota	27	37	16	70	258	278
*Chicago	27	41	12	66	297	335
Toronto	28	46	6	62	259	342
Smythe Division						
*Calgary	54	17	9	117	354	226
*Los Angeles	42	31	7	91	376	335
*Edmonton	38	34	8	84	325	306
*Vancouver	33	39	8	74	251	253
Winnipeg	26	42	12	64	300	355

*In play-offs

Stanley Cup Play-Offs
Wales Conference

First Round	Boston	4 games	Buffalo	1
	Montreal	4 games	Hartford	0
	Philadelphia	4 games	Washington	2
	Pittsburgh	4 games	N.Y. Rangers	0
Semifinals	Montreal	4 games	Boston	1
	Philadelphia	4 games	Pittsburgh	3
Finals	Montreal	4 games	Philadelphia	2

Campbell Conference

First Round	Calgary	4 games	Vancouver	3
	Chicago	4 games	Detroit	2
	Los Angeles	4 games	Edmonton	3
	St. Louis	4 games	Minnesota	1
Semifinals	Calgary	4 games	Los Angeles	0
	Chicago	4 games	St. Louis	1
Finals	Calgary	4 games	Chicago	1

Championship

Calgary	4 games	Montreal	2

Individual Honors

Hart Trophy (most valuable player): Wayne Gretzky, Los Angeles
Ross Trophy (leading scorer): Mario Lemieux, Pittsburgh
Vezina Trophy (top goaltender): Patrick Roy, Montreal
Norris Trophy (best defenseman): Chris Chelios, Montreal
Selke Trophy (best defensive forward): Guy Carbonneau, Montreal
Calder Trophy (rookie of the year): Brian Leetch, N.Y. Rangers
Lady Byng Trophy (sportsmanship): Joe Mullen, Calgary
Conn Smythe Trophy (most valuable in play-offs): Al MacInnis, Calgary
Adams Trophy (coach of the year): Pat Burns, Montreal
King Clancy Trophy (humanitarian service): Bryan Trottier, N.Y. Islanders

NCAA: Harvard

The final series was not as compelling as the Oiler-Philadelphia seven-game affair in 1987 but it was a battle between two excellent teams. Calgary played without their best defenseman, Gary Suter, who had broken his jaw in the opening Vancouver series, but got great work from Al MacInnis, who was chosen the play-offs' MVP. He became the first defenseman to lead the play-offs in scoring.

The NHL's smallest player, Theoren Fleury (5′5″, 150 lbs—1.7 m, 68 kg), scored the winner in game one in Calgary as the Flames squeezed past Montreal, 3–2. Montreal bounced back in the second game with Chelios scoring once and adding two assists in a 4–2 victory.

In Montreal for game three, Calgary was 41 seconds from a 3–2 win but the Canadiens' Mats Naslund tied it. With less than two minutes left in the second overtime, Ryan Walter gave Montreal a 4–3 win. The Flames refused to feel sorry for themselves, however, and got two goals from Mullen to take game four, 4–2, to tie the series.

Back in Calgary for game five, MacInnis ripped a 55-ft (17-m) shot past Patrick Roy late in the first period for a 3–2 game winner. In game six, Doug Gilmour had two goals in a 4–2 Calgary win at the Montreal Forum. It was the first time that the Canadiens had lost the Cup on their home ice.

Other. On April 29 the Soviet Union defeated Canada, 5–3, to clinch the World Championships. Canada and Czechoslovakia captured the silver and bronze medals, respectively. On the collegiate level, Harvard won its first NCAA title with a win over Minnesota.

JIM MATHESON, *"The Edmonton Journal"*

Ice Skating

Japan won its first gold medal in the history of the world figure skating championships in 1989 when Midori Ito, a 19-year-old, 4′9″ (1.45-m), 97-lb (44.3-kg) spitfire, put on an amazing display of athleticism and upset favored Jill Trenary, the U.S. national champion, at the Bercy Arena in Paris in March. The 20-year-old Trenary, who had won the national title in Baltimore in February, faltered in the long program and was unable to maintain her lead as Ito swept past her with a superb display that included the first triple-axel jump ever accomplished by a woman in the world championships. Claudia Leistner of West Germany rallied to finish second and Trenary was a disappointing third.

The men's world championship went to 22-year-old Kurt Browning of Canada, who scored an upset by dazzling the 7,000 spectators with a routine that included seven triple jumps. Browning became only the fourth Canadian in 78 years to win the men's world title. Christopher Bowman of Los Angeles, the U.S. national champion who went into the world event as a favorite, finished second; third place went to Grzegorz Filipowski of Poland.

Soviet skaters captured the pairs and ice dancing crowns: Sergei Grinkov and Yekaterina Gordeyeva won in pairs, and Sergei Ponomarenko and Marina Klimova won in ice dancing.

© Allsport USA/Vandystadt

Japan's Midori Ito, 19, became the new world figure skating champion. In her four previous appearances for the world title, she finished no better than sixth.

In the U.S. nationals, Trenary and Bowman took different stylistic approaches on their way to titles. Trenary skated a conservative program, while the 21-year-old Bowman opened with a triple axel in his long program, then reeled off six of his seven triple jumps.

Trenary was able to win her second national title in three years, but not before she got a scare from 17-year-old Kristi Yamaguchi of Fremont, CA, who became the first U.S. woman since Margaret Graham competed in singles and pairs in 1954 to qualify for the world championships in two disciplines. Yamaguchi, who had won the national pairs with Rudi Galindo 18 hours earlier, skated a sensational freestyle program, beating Trenary in that phase and earning enough points to finish second overall. Trenary's first-place finishes in the compulsory and original programs, however, enabled her to gain the margin of victory. Yamaguchi went on to finish a strong sixth in the world event. In the nationals, Tonya Harding finished third for the women, and Daniel Doran and Paul Wylie finished second and third, respectively, in the men's competition. Susan Wynne and Joseph Druar won the ice dancing.

Speed Skating. In the world speed-skating sprint championships in Heerenveen, the Netherlands, Bonnie Blair of the United States captured the women's title with a world-record total of 159.435 points, with victories in both 500-meter races and second- and third-place finishes in the 1,000-meter events. The men's title went to Igor Zhelezovski of the Soviet Union, who also set a world mark with 145.945 points.

Leo Visser of the Netherlands and Constanze Moser of East Germany took the overall crowns at the world championships.

GEORGE DE GREGORIO

Skiing

One of the most eye-catching of many remarkable skiing performances in 1989 came from Vreni Schneider of Switzerland, who ended the season with 14 World Cup victories to break the 11-year-old one-season record held by the legendary Ingemar Stenmark of Sweden.

Schneider turned in her achievement in the closing meet of the season at Shiga Kogen, Japan, where she won a giant slalom and a slalom event to surpass Stenmark's record of 13 triumphs set in 1979. Her 12th victory, in a slalom at Furano, Japan, broke the women's record of 11 cup victories held by Annemarie Moser-Proell. En route to the record, Schneider easily captured the World Cup overall title.

After the men's slalom event at Shiga Kogen, Stenmark, who during the season lifted his World Cup victory total to 86, more than three times as many as his nearest rival, retired from the sport.

Another star who broke new ground was Marc Girardelli of Luxembourg, who became the first skier to win at least once in all four disciplines—slalom, giant slalom, super giant slalom, and downhill—during the 1989 campaign.

Thrilling and bizarre events took place at Vail, CO, site of the world Alpine championships in late January and early February. The United States was host for the first time since 1950, and the event attracted a virtual Olympic field of talent.

Tamara McKinney, a 26-year-old, 11-year veteran of the skiing circuit who has 18 World Cup victories in her career, gave the United States a gold medal in the women's combined, the first gold for an American in the world-class skiing event since January 1987.

Girardelli added another laurel by winning the men's combined. Rudolf Nierlich of Austria won both the slalom and giant slalom, and Martin Hangl of Switzerland took the super giant slalom. Among the women, Schneider won the giant slalom, Mateja Svet of Yugoslavia, the slalom, and Ulrike Maier of Austria, the super giant slalom. The downhill went to Maria Walliser of Switzerland and Hansjörg Tauscher of West Germany.

The world meet took a bizarre turn with numerous mishaps and one fatality. Don Alfonso de Borbón y Dampierre, 52-year-old cousin of King Juan Carlos of Spain and a veteran member of the Fédèration Internationale de Ski Council, was killed when he skied into a cable suspended several feet over the snow at the finish of the men's downhill course at nearby Beaver Creek. Only two days later, Pirmin Zurbriggen of Switzerland, the 1988 World Cup overall champion, was injured when he was swept by a gust of wind and was blown off the course during a workout on the same hill.

GEORGE DE GREGORIO

Soccer

The United States in late 1989 joined 23 other nations in qualifying for the 1990 World Cup finals.

World. Qualifying matches for the 14th quadrennial World Cup finals, to be held in Italy during June 1990, were played on five continents from April to November 1989. With a crucial 1-0 victory over Trinidad and Tobago on November 19, the United States advanced to the finals for the first time since 1950. The hero was Paul Caligiuri, a defender, who tallied the game's lone goal in the 31st minute of play. In addition to Italy and Argentina, which received automatic berths as the host country and the defending champion, respectively, the other qualifiers were: Austria, Belgium, Brazil, Cameroon, Colombia, Costa Rica, Czechoslovakia, Egypt, England, Ireland, the Netherlands, Romania, Scotland, South Korea, the Soviet Union, Spain, Sweden, the United Arab Emirates, Uruguay, West Germany, and Yugoslavia.

British soccer was marred by tragedy once again in April, as 95 fans were crushed or suffocated to death at an overcrowded Hillsborough Stadium in Sheffield. The disaster occurred when police admitted thousands of fans into an already packed section of the stadium. Many of those inside were pinned against a wire fence or trampled by the onrushing mob. In addition to the 95 fatalities, there were a reported 170 injuries. Following other violent incidents in recent years, the April tragedy led to a variety of proposals to make soccer matches safer for fans. Among these were the issuance of identity cards for all spectators, eliminating standing-room sections, and removing barriers between grandstands.

A.C. Milan won the 1989 European Champions' Cup with a 4-0 victory over Steaua Bucharest on May 24 in Barcelona, Spain. The Milan club got two goals each from Dutch internationals Ruud Gullit and Marco Van Basten.

United States. In Major Indoor Soccer League (MISL) competition, the San Diego Sockers successfully defended their league crown with a four-games-to-three triumph over the Baltimore Blast in the best-of-seven championship series. Led by midfielder Branko Segota's two goals, the Sockers defeated the Blast on the latter's home field, 6-5, in the deciding seventh game. For San Diego, it was the fifth MISL title in seven years.

The final of the NCAA Division I national championship tournament ended in a 1-1 tie between Virginia and Santa Clara.

With the U.S. national team earning a spot in the 1990 World Cup finals and the United States playing host to the 1994 tournament, America's interest in soccer was rising.

JEFF HACKER

Swimming

For 13 years a U.S. swimmer had not been able to break through for a world record in the 200-m breaststroke. Mike Barrowman of Rockville, MD, achieved that distinction in the U.S. national long-course championships in August 1989, but it appeared for a brief period that he might not hold the record by himself for long.

Barrowman, a 20-year-old junior at the University of Michigan, lowered the record of 2:13.34 held by Victor Davis of Canada with a clocking of 2:12.90 at Los Angeles on August 3. But soon another swimmer edged his way into the record books and Barrowman had to share the record with Great Britain's Nick Gillingham, who equaled 2:12.90 in the European championships in Bonn, West Germany, on August 18. Barrowman, disappointed over his fourth-place finish in the event in the 1988 Olympics at Seoul, had been eager to return the mark to the United States. On August 20, in the star-studded Pan Pacific championships in Tokyo, he broke the tie with Gillingham, reclaiming the record with 2:12.89. Before Barrowman, the last American to hold the world record in this event had been John Hencken, who set it in 1974. Davis had held the record since the 1984 Olympics at Los Angeles.

Barrowman's effort was one of four world marks netted by U.S. swimmers in one day at Tokyo, where Americans took 25 of a possible 36 medals in the meet. Among those smashing a world mark was 17-year-old Janet Evans. She sent her winning streak to 22 races by clipping .90 of a second off her 1988 record in the 800-m freestyle, with a clocking of 8:16.22.

Other contributors to the American show of record prowess in Tokyo were Tom Jager in the 50-m freestyle and David Wharton in the 200-m individual medley. Jager had missed a chance in the long-course nationals when he was disqualified in the final for moving on the starting block. His chief rival then was Matt Biondi, the world-record holder Jager hoped to dethrone. Biondi went on to win the final easily. In the 1988 Olympics, Biondi had beaten Jager with his world-record time of 22.14 seconds in the 50-m. But at the Pan Pacific meet, Jager atoned for his mishap in the nationals and swam a 22.12 to break Biondi's mark. Wharton, a University of Southern California sophomore, broke the 2:00.17 record set by Tamás Darnyi of Hungary with a time of 2:00.11 in the 200-m individual medley.

The European championships produced two other records. The 100-m men's breaststroke record fell to Adrian Moorhouse of Britain, who swam 1:01.49 and broke a five-year-old standard of 1:01.65 held by Steve Lundquist of the United States. Giorgio Lamberti of Italy broke Australian Duncan Armstrong's 1:47.25 in the 200-m freestyle with 1:46.69.

GEORGE DE GREGORIO

Tennis

A young West German pair, Steffi Graf, 20, and Boris Becker, 21, made a great impact on the world tennis scene, racking up five of the eight major singles championships between them in 1989. But the year's most astounding tennis deeds were achieved by two 17-year-olds, Spain's Arantxa Sanchez Vicario and American Michael Chang, in winning the French Open.

Sanchez Vicario's stunning 7-6, 3-6, 7-5 final-round victory in Paris canceled Graf's designs on a second successive Grand Slam, but the West German took the other three Slam tournaments: the Australian Open, Wimbledon, and the U.S. Open. Chang, the youngest male ever to win a major tournament, scored an astonishing fourth-round victory over Number 1 Ivan Lendl and continued on to beat Sweden's Stefan Edberg in the final, 6-1, 3-6, 4-6, 6-4, 6-2. Chang, exhibiting extraordinary mental and physical toughness, was the first American male since Tony Trabert in 1955 to win the foremost clay-court title. More outgoing, yet just as strong, Sanchez Vicario was not only the youngest female winner of the French but the first Spanish female to win a major.

© Roland Garrow/Vandystadt from Allsport

Michael Chang scored a dazzling win in the French Open. The 17-year-old American defeated Stefan Edberg in the finals after crushing Ivan Lendl in an earlier match.

Thunderous server Becker impressively regained Wimbledon from Edberg, reigning there for a third time, 6-0, 7-6, 6-4. Becker also became the first German male to win the U.S. title, overpowering three-time king, Lendl, 7-6, 1-6, 6-3, 7-6. Becker had come from behind, 2-1 in sets, to beat Lendl in a Wimbledon semifinal.

Graf's victories over American Martina Navratilova, 6-2, 6-7, 6-1, at Wimbledon, and 3-6, 7-5, 6-1, at the U.S. Open, left no doubt of her position at the top of the women's game for a second year running. West Germany rejoiced in the Graf-Becker success. It had been 20 years since two players from the same country accounted for so many majors. Australians Rod Laver and Margaret Court won four and three, respectively, in 1969.

Lendl, the Czechoslovakian-born defector who resides in the United States and had ranked Number 1 (1985–88), quickly regained the pinnacle he had lost to Sweden's Mats Wilander in the 1988 U.S Open final. Lendl won the Australian for the first time, 6-2, 6-2, 6-2, over Czechoslovak Miloslav Mecir, while defending champ Wilander commenced a year-long slump, falling from the top ten.

Graf's victim in her second Australian championship was Czechoslovak Helena Sukova, 6-4, 6-4. She lost merely two matches while winning 14 tournaments, including the season-closing Virginia Slims Championship,

TENNIS

Davis Cup: West Germany
Federation Cup: United States
Wrightman Cup: United States

Major Tournaments

Australian Open—men's singles: Ivan Lendl (Czechoslovakia); men's doubles: Jim Pugh and Rick Leach; women's singles: Steffi Graf (West Germany); women's doubles: Martina Navratilova and Pam Shriver; mixed doubles: Jim Pugh and Jana Novotna (Czechoslovakia).
World Championship Tennis—John McEnroe.
Italian Open—men's singles: Alberto Mancini (Argentina); men's doubles: Jim Courier and Pete Sampras; women's singles: Gabriela Sabatini (Argentina); women's doubles: Elizabeth Smylie (Australia) and Janine Thompson (Australia).
U.S. Clay Courts—Jay Berger.
French Open—men's singles: Michael Chang; men's doubles: Patrick McEnroe and Jim Grabb; women's singles: Arantxa Sanchez Vicario (Spain); women's doubles: Natalia Zvereva (USSR) and Larissa Savchenko (USSR); mixed doubles: Manon Bollegraf (Netherlands) and Tom Nijssen (Netherlands).
Wimbledon—men's singles: Boris Becker (West Germany); men's doubles: John Fitzgerald (Australia) and Anders Jarryd (Sweden); women's singles: Steffi Graf (West Germany); women's doubles: Jana Novotna (Czechoslovakia) and Helena Sukova (Czechoslovakia); mixed doubles: Jana Novotna (Czechoslovakia) and Jim Pugh.
Player's International Canadian Open—singles: Ivan Lendl (Czechoslovakia); doubles: Kelly Evernden (New Zealand) and Todd Witsken.
Canadian Player's Challenge—singles: Martina Navratilova; doubles: Gigi Fernandez and Robin White.
U.S. Open—men's singles: Boris Becker (West Germany); men's doubles: John McEnroe and Mark Woodforde (Australia); women's singles: Steffi Graf (West Germany); women's doubles: Hana Mandlikova (Czechoslovakia) and Martina Navratilova; mixed doubles: Robin White and Shelby Cannon; senior men's singles: Hank Pfister; senior men's doubles: Tom Gulikson and Dick Stockton; senior women's doubles: Wendy Turnbull (Australia) and Virginia Wade (Great Britain); boys' singles: Jonathan Stark; boys' doubles: Wayne Ferreira (South Africa) and Grant Stafford (South Africa); girls' singles: Jennifer Capriati; girls' doubles: Jennifer Capriati and Meredith McGrath.
Virginia Slims Championships—singles: Steffi Graf (West Germany); doubles: Martina Navratilova and Pam Shriver.
Nabisco Grand Prix Masters—singles: Stefan Edberg (Sweden).
NCAA (Division I)—men's singles: Donni Leaycraft, Louisiana State University; men's team: Stanford; women's singles: Sandra Birch, Stanford; women's team: Stanford.

N.B. All Players are from the United States unless otherwise noted.

for a second time, over Martina Navratilova, 6-4, 7-5, 2-6, 6-2, at New York's Madison Square Garden.

One of the greatest of all careers wound down as 34-year-old Chris Evert announced her retirement. After an unsurpassed 19 consecutive years of winning professional tournaments, amounting to a record 157, she failed to win one in 1989. She did attain the Wimbledon semis for a record 17th time, losing to Graf, and the U.S. quarters also for a record 17th time, losing to countrywoman Zina Garrison. Evert concluded by winning all five singles matches to help the U.S. capture the Federation Cup for the 13th time, in Tokyo. Navratilova won all her singles, and Garrison and Pam Shriver their doubles.

Navratilova won eight titles in singles for a lifetime total of 146. Graf's singles career total is 44. Lendl won ten singles tournaments for a career total of 85, Becker five for 29, and American John McEnroe two for 60. But it was the zestful 37-year-old American Jimmy Connors who may have been more amazing, winning two tournaments to lengthen his male record for titles to 109. He was a quarter-finalist at the U.S. Open for a male record 16th time.

As the men's season concluded in December, Stefan Edberg won the Masters at Madison Square Garden, and Becker, the runner-up at the latter event, spearheaded West Germany's second consecutive Davis Cup triumph, 3-2, over Sweden, at Stuttgart.

(*See also* BIOGRAPHY—*Graf, Stephanie*.)

BUD COLLINS, *"The Boston Globe"*

Track and Field

In track and field in 1989, an off-track event achieved headlines when Ben Johnson of Canada was stripped of his world record of 9.83 seconds in the 100-meter dash and his 6.41 indoor record in the 60-meter event after he admitted to the use of performance-enhancing drugs.

The ruling was made by the International Amateur Athletic Federation, the world governing body in track, in September. It followed a long inquiry conducted by the Canadian government, during which Johnson admitted that he used drugs since 1981 and at the time his records were achieved. Johnson set the 100-meter record of 9.83 seconds at the world championships in Rome in 1987, and the 60-meter mark at the indoor championships in 1987 in Indianapolis.

Carl Lewis in the 100-meter and Lee McRae in the 60-meter, both Americans, replaced Johnson as the new holders of the records in those events. Lewis' mark of 9.92 seconds became the new standard on the strength of his finish in the event in the 1988 Olympics at Seoul. Lewis was second in the event; Johnson finished first in 9.79. But when Johnson tested positive after the race for an anabolic steroid he was disqualified from the Olympics and his gold medal was taken from him, with Lewis being declared winner of the event. McRae's time of 6.50 in the 60-meter became the new record, although it ranked sixth-fastest on record. Johnson had the other five times, all clocked when he said he had used drugs.

On August 16 at Zurich's Letzigrund Stadium, Roger Kingdom, a 26-year-old American, lowered the world record in the 110-meter hurdles to 12.92. Fellow American Renaldo Nehemiah had set the old mark (12.93) in 1981.

Florence Griffith Joyner, who won three gold medals and set two world records at the 1988 Olympics in Seoul, announced her retirement in February.

On The Field. World records tumbled legitimately. A historic barrier was broken in the high jump when Javier Sotomayor of Cuba went 8′ (2.44 m) on July 29 in the Caribbean championships in San Juan, Puerto Rico. The 21-year-old Sotomayor broke his previous record of 7′11½″ (2.42 m), set in Spain in 1988.

The women's mile record, held by Mary Decker Slaney and unbroken since 1985, went by the wayside when Paula Ivan of Romania shaved 1.10 seconds off Slaney's mark with a time of 4:15.61 at Nice, France, in July.

The eight-year-old mark of 12.93 seconds held by Renaldo Nehemiah in the 110-meter hurdles was erased by Roger Kingdom of the United States with a clocking of 12.92. And Said Aouita of Morocco brought down the 11-year-old record of Henry Rono of Kenya in the 3,000-meter run, erasing Rono's 7:32.1 with 7:29.45.

Aouita and Ivan won the Grand Prix titles in Monte Carlo. Each won for the second year in a row, the first time any athlete has repeated, and Aouita for the third time in four seasons. Kingdom trailed him by six points.

In the 10,000-meter run a 25-year-old Mexican, Arturo Barrios, clipped 5.58 seconds off the five-year-old record with a time of 27:08.23 at West Berlin on August 18.

Lewis anchored a U.S. team in the 800-meter relay to a world record. Lewis, Danny Everett, LeRoy Burrell, and Floyd Heard clocked 1:19.38 at Koblenz, West Germany, on August 23, bettering by .88 of a second the 1978 mark set by another U.S. team.

The women's triple jump record fell to Galina Chistyakova of the USSR in July at Stockholm. She jumped 47′7¾″ (14.53 m) to erase the 46′5½″ (14.16 m) registered in 1988 by Li Huirong of China. Chistyakova wound up as runner-up to Ivan in the Grand Prix standings.

Winning the Boston Marathon were Abebe Mekonnen of Ethiopia and Ingrid Kristiansen of Norway. New York City Marathon winners were Juma Ikangaa of Tanzania and Kristiansen.

GEORGE DEGREGORIO

Yachting

The America's Cup, a symbol of yachting supremacy since it first was contested in 1851 and which had bounded over water and through the courts for the previous two years, finally found a place to rest in 1989.

A New York appeals court overturned a lower court decision on Sept. 19, 1989, and ruled that the San Diego Yacht Club could keep the cup, which it had won in races against New Zealand in 1988 and then lost in court. San Diego won its appeal after a five-judge panel of the Appellate Division of the New York State Supreme Court voted, 4 to 1, to overturn a decision handed down on March 28, 1989, by Justice Carmen Beauchamp Ciparick of the state Supreme Court. Judge Ciparick had disqualified the California yacht and awarded the cup by forfeit to the Mercury Bay Boating Club of Auckland, New Zealand, after *Stars & Stripes,* a U.S. multihull catamaran skippered by Dennis Conner, had scored an overwhelming two-race sweep over *New Zealand,* a 132-ft (40-m) monohull, in the summer of 1988 in waters off San Diego.

In September 1983, Conner, then sailing for the New York Yacht Club, lost the cup to Australia. But in February 1987, sailing for San Diego, he won it back. He had planned to defend it in 1990 in the traditional 12-meter sloop. Michael Fay, an investment banker and chairman of the syndicate that backed New Zealand, entered the picture in the summer of 1987, challenging the San Diego club to a race for the cup in 1988 with boats larger than 12 meters. Conner refused the challenge, and Fay won a suit in New York Supreme Court on Nov. 25, 1987, when Judge Ciparick ordered Conner to accept Fay's challenge and defend the cup. The judge said she would leave a decision on the sizes of the boats to be determined after the races.

After the contest, Fay contended that the Deed of Gift, the document written in 1887 that governs the competition, prescribed that competing boats must be similar and that the Americans, by using a catamaran, had an unfair advantage over his monohull yacht. The Americans contended that under the existing interpretation of the rules, the use of any type yacht was permissible. Judge Ciparick had upheld the New Zealanders' argument in her March 1989 decision.

The legal wrangle seemed to have no end, even in the face of what appeared to be a definitive recovery of the cup by San Diego. Fay called the ruling "a disgrace" and filed an appeal. The cup, meanwhile, was in a bank vault in New York under the custodianship of the New York Yacht Club. The San Diego club said it was ready to go forward with plans for an America's Cup regatta in May 1992.

In on-the-water yachting competition in 1989, New Zealand did salvage a prestigious award by taking the Liberty Cup regatta in New York Harbor. Great Britain won its ninth Admiral's Cup by defeating Denmark by 17½ points in a two-week series of races off Plymouth, England. The 82d Chicago-to-Mackinac Island, MI, race was won by *Renegade* of Detroit, guided by Kenneth Meade, and the Port Huron-to-Mackinac Island event went to *Pied Piper* of Chicago, skippered by Dick Jennings.

GEORGE DE GREGORIO

SPORTS SUMMARIES[1]

ARCHERY—World Champions: men: Stanislav Zabrodsky, Soviet Union; men's team: Soviet Union; women: Kim Soo Nyung, South Korea; women's team: South Korea.

BADMINTON—U.S. Champions: men's singles: Tariq Wadood, Redondo Beach, CA; women's singles: Linda Safarik-Tong, Berkeley, CA. **World Champions:** men's singles: Yang Yang, China; women's singles: Li Lingwei, China.

BIATHLON—U.S. Champions: men: 10k: Josh Thompson, Gunnison, CO; 20k: Josh Thompson; women: 7.5k: Anna Sonnerup, Hanover, NH; 15k: Anna Sonnerup.

BILLIARDS—World Champions: men's 9-ball: Nick Varner, Owensboro, KY; women's 9-ball: Mary Kenniston, Las Vegas, NV.

BOBSLEDDING—World Champions: world 2-man: Switzerland; world 4-man: Switzerland; World Cup 2-man: Switzerland; World Cup 4-man: Austria.

BOWLING—Professional Bowlers Association Tour: Firestone Tournament of Champions: Del Ballard, Jr., Richardson, TX; National Championship: Pete Weber, St. Louis; Seagram's Coolers U.S. Open: Mike Auldy, Indianapolis; Touring Players Championship: Amleto Monacelli, Venezuela. **American Bowling Congress:** singles: Paul Tetreault, Claremont, NH; doubles: Gus Yannaras and Gary Daroszewski, Oak Creek, WI; events: George Hall, Mundelein, IL; team all-events: Browning Pontiac, No. 2, Cincinnati; regular team: Chilton Vending, Wichita, KS; Masters Tournament: Mike Auldy.

CANOEING—U.S. Champions: canoe: 1,000 m: Jim Terrell, Costa Mesa, CA; men's kayak: 1,000 m: Mike Harbold, Honolulu; women's kayak: 500 m: Traci Philips, Honolulu.

COURT TENNIS—World: Wayne Davis, New York. U.S. Open: Wayne Davis.

CRICKET—World Champion: The Ashes, Australia.

CROSS-COUNTRY—World Champions: men: John Ngugi, Kenya; women: Annette Sergent, France. **U.S. Athletics Congress:** men: Pat Porter, Alamosa, CO; women: Lynn Jennings, Newmarket, NH.

CURLING—World Champions: men: Pat Ryan, Kelowna, British Columbia; women: Heather Houston, Thunder Bay, Ont.

CYCLING—Tour de France: men: Greg LeMond, Wayzata, MN; women: Jeannie Longo, France.

DOG SHOWS—Westminster: best-in-show: Ch. Royal Tudor's Wild as the Wind, C.D., Doberman pinscher, owned by Arthur and Susan Korp, Beth Wilhite, and Richard and Carolyn Vida.

FENCING—U.S. Fencing Association: men's foil: Peter Lewison, New York City; men's épée: Robert Stull, San Antonio; men's saber: Peter Westbrook, New York City; women's foil: Caty Bilodeaux, Concord, MA; women's épée: Cathy McClellan, Marblehead, MA.

FIELD HOCKEY—NCAA Division 1: women: University of North Carolina.

GYMNASTICS—U.S. Champions: men's all-around: Tim Ryan, Palo Alto, CA; women's all-around: Brandy Johnson, Altamonte Springs, FL.

HANDBALL—U.S. Handball Association: men's one-wall: Joe Durso, Brooklyn, NY; men's four-wall: Poncho Monreal, El Paso.

HANG GLIDING—World Champions: Robbie Whittall, Great Britain; team: Great Britain.

HORSESHOE PITCHING—World Champions: men: Alan Francis, Blytheville, MO; women: Phyllis Negaard, St. Joseph, MN.

HORSE SHOWS—U.S. Equestrian Team: dressage: Robert Dover, Lebanon, NJ, riding Walzertakt; three-day event: Bruce Davidson, Unionville, PA, riding Dr. Peaches (spring) and Karen Lende, Upperville, VA, riding Nos Ecus (fall); show jumping: Michael Matz, Collegeville, PA, riding Schnapps.

JUDO—U.S. Senior Champions: men: 56 kg: Clifton Sunada, Honolulu; 60 kg: Edward Liddie, Colorado Springs; 65 kg: James Pedro, Daners, MA; 71 kg: Dan Hotano, Rio Palos Verdes, CA; 78 kg: Jason Morris, Scotia, NY; 86 kg: Rene Capo, Minneapolis; 95 kg: Lee White, Fort Carson, CO; plus 95 kg: Dewey Mitchell, New Port Richey, FL; open: Damon Keeve, San Francisco; Women: 45 kg: Dennisse Vidal, Colorado Springs; 48 kg: Valerie Lafon, San Diego; 52 kg: Hannelore Brown, Dallas; 56 kg: Kate Donahoo, Colorado Springs; 61 kg: Lynn Roethke, West Bend, WI; 66 kg: Grace Gividen, Colorado Springs; 72 kg: Belinda Binkley, Seattle; plus 72 kg: Juanita Cardwell, Tallahassee; open: Sharon Seibel, Sacramento.

KARATE—U.S. Champions: men: International Kata: Ferdie Allas, California; 18-21: Kevin Suzuki, California; Advanced Free Kata: Kent Kim, Oregon; 35 and over Free Kata: Douglas Dennis, Illinois; 45 and over Free Kata: Carl Felling, California; 35 and over Advanced Weapons: Roy Center, California; 45 and over Advanced Weapons: Ronald Donahue, Ohio; Women: International Kata: Debbie Tang, Washington; 18-21: Mimi Tang, Washington; Advanced Free Kata: Debbie Tang; 35 and over Free Kata: Hiroyo Ringler, Ohio; 45 and over Free Kata: Elizabeth Tellow, Los Angeles; 35 and over Advanced Weapons: Hiroyo Ringler; 45 and over Advanced Weapons: Patricia Wright, Ohio.

LACROSSE—NCAA Division I: men: Syracuse; women: Penn State.

LUGE—U.S. Champions: men: Duncan Kennedy, Lake Placid, NY; women: Cammy Myler, Lake Placid.

MODERN PENTATHLON—World Champions: men: Laszlo Fabian, Hungary; women: Lori Norwood, Bryan, TX.

PADDLE TENNIS—U.S. Champions: men's singles: Javier Sartorius, Spain; men's doubles: Scott Freedman, Santa Monica, CA, and Sol Hauptman, Culver City, CA; women's singles: Denise Yogi, Glendale, CA.

PLATFORM TENNIS—U.S. Champions: men's singles: Jack Kleinert, Franklin Lakes, NJ; men's doubles: Rich Maier, Scarsdale, NY, and Steve Baird, Harrison, NY; women's singles: none; women's doubles: Bobo Mangan, Chatham, NJ, and Sarah Krieger, Summit, NJ.

POLO—World Champion: United States.

RACQUETBALL—U.S. Champions: men: Mike Ray, Marietta, GA; women: Caryn McKinney, Atlanta.

RACQUETS—U.S. Open: singles: James Male, England; doubles: James Male and Nicholas Barham, England.

ROWING—U.S. Collegiate Champions: men: Harvard; women: Cornell.

SHOOTING—U.S. Champions: men's small-bore rifle, prone: David Weaver, Oil City, PA; men's small-bore rifle, three position: Thomas Tamas, Columbus, GA; men's high-power rifle: Patrick McCann, Staunton, IL; men's all-round pistol: Darius Young, Calgary, Alta.

SOFTBALL—U.S. Champions: men's fast pitch: Penn Corporation, Sioux City, IA; women's fast pitch: Whittier (CA) Raiders; men's major-slow pitch: Ritch's Salvage, Harrisburg, NC; women's major-slow pitch: Canaan's Illusions, Houston.

SQUASH TENNIS—U.S. Champion: men: Gary Squires, Darien, CT.

TEAM HANDBALL—U.S. Division I: men: Garden City, L.I.; women: University of Minnesota.

TRIATHLON—World Champions: men: Mark Allen, Cardiff, CA; women: Erin Baker, New Zealand.

TUMBLING—U.S. Tumbling: men: Aaron Wilkens, Newark, NJ; women: Michelle Mara, Rockford, IL. **U.S. Trampoline:** men: Jeremy Spehar, Mission Viejo, CA; women: Cali Shulman, Colts Neck, NJ.

VOLLEYBALL—U.S. Open Champions: men: Kenneth Allen Volleyball Club, Chicago; women: Burmy, Long Beach, CA. **NCAA:** men: UCLA; women: Long Beach State.

WATER POLO—World Cup Champions: men: Yugoslavia; women: The Netherlands.

WATER SKIING—U.S. Overall: men: Kreg Llewellyn, Innisfail, Alberta; women: Deena Brush Mapple, Windermere, FL.

WRESTLING—U.S. Open (freestyle): 48 kg: Tim Vanni, Tempe, AZ; 52 kg: Zeke Jones, Tempe; 57 kg: Brad Penrith, Iowa City, IA; 62 kg: John Smith, Stillwater, OK; 68 kg: Nate Carr, Morgantown, WV; 74 kg: Rob Koll, Ithaca, NY; 82 kg: Rico Chiapparelli, Iowa City; 90 kg: Jim Scherr, Chicago; 100 kg: Bill Scherr, Bloomington, IN; 130 kg: Bruce Baumgartner, Cambridge Springs, PA; (Greco-Roman): 48 kg: Lew Dorrance, Quantico, VA; 52 kg: Mark Fuller, Provo, UT; 57 kg: Gogi Parseghian, San Clemente, CA; 62 kg: Ike Anderson, Albany, NY; 68 kg: Andy Seras, Albany, NY; 74 kg: Andy Butler, San Diego, CA; 82 kg: John Morgan, Minneapolis, MN; 90 kg: Michael Foy, Brooklyn Park, MN; 100 kg: Steve Lawson, Bakersfield, CA; 130 kg: Craig Pittman, Dumfried, VA. **U.S. Champions** (freestyle): super heavyweight: Bruce Baumgartner; (Greco-Roman): super heavyweight: Craig Pittman.

[1]Sports for which articles do not appear in pages 472-96.

SRI LANKA

Another year of violence and economic and social deterioration brought Sri Lanka to "the edge of anarchy" in 1989. In February, in the first parliamentary elections since 1977, the ruling United National Party (UNP), led by Ranasinghe Premadasa, won a majority of the seats in the National Assembly. Relations with India were highlighted by the signing of an agreement in September for the withdrawal of the Indian Peace Keeping Force (IPKF) from the island by the end of the year.

Political Affairs. On January 2, Premadasa was inaugurated as president of Sri Lanka. One of his first major acts, on January 12, was to lift the state of emergency that had been in force since May 1983. On February 12, 63% of the 9.4 million eligible voters went to the polls to choose the 225 members of the National Assembly, from a list of some 1,400 candidates. The campaign was described as "the worst and bloodiest in Sri Lanka's history." More than 1,000 persons, including 14 candidates, were killed, mostly by members of a militant Sinhalese group, the Janatha Vimukthi Peramuna (JVP), or People's Liberation Front (PLF). The UNP won 125 of the 225 seats, while the main opposition party, the Sri Lanka Freedom Party (SLFP), led by former Prime Minister Sirimavo Bandaranaike, won 67 seats.

Immediately after the elections Premadasa appointed a 22-member cabinet. He postponed naming a prime minister until March 3, when he announced the selection of D. B. Wijetunga.

In its efforts to curb the civil strife, the government tried to reach agreements for a cease-fire and negotiations with both the major radical Tamil group, the Liberation Tigers of Tamil Eelam (LTTE), and the JVP. In June, after several weeks of intermittent discussions, the LTTE agreed to a cease-fire but the JVP spurned all feelers from the government and escalated their violent attacks.

On June 20 a state of emergency was reimposed. In midsummer government security forces launched a systematic campaign in the south against the JVP, which soon became a campaign of terrorism and counterterrorism.

On October 12 an "All-Party Conference" began a monthlong search for some kind of political formula that would save the country from the growing anarchy. In mid-November, Rohana Wijeweera, leader of the antigovernment PLF, was killed. The foreign minister said he was shot while in government custody.

The Economy. After the February 15 elections, it was hoped that the sagging economy at last would begin to improve. The first budget of the new administration, presented to the National Assembly on March 16 by the new prime minister, who continued to be finance minister as well, seemed to indicate that the government was determined to focus on economic development, featuring a new "poverty alleviation program" (PAP). Effective implementation of the PAP, sometimes referred to as the Janasaviya program, did not begin until the end of September, and only limited assistance was given to a few thousand poor families. About one third of the budget still was spent on efforts to restore law and order. Foreign donors pledged continuing assistance of more than $500 million; but some of this was held up because of Sri Lanka's failures or delays in meeting some of the conditions stipulated by the lenders. Income from the three major exports —tea, textiles, and rubber—increased slightly, but the rate of growth continued to be low.

Foreign Policy. Sri Lanka continued to pursue an active foreign policy, with extensive contacts with international donors and loan institutions. It also participated in the 20th summit meeting of the nonaligned countries, held in Belgrade, Yugoslavia, in September, and in the Commonwealth summit in Kuala Lumpur, Malaysia, in October. But its main foreign policy preoccupation continued to be its relations with India, and specifically the withdrawal of the IPKF, which had been operating in the northern part of Sri Lanka under the terms of the India-Sri Lanka accord of July 1987.

On June 1, President Premadasa demanded that all Indian troops—then numbering about 45,000—be withdrawn from Sri Lanka by July 30, the second anniversary of the 1987 accord. India's Prime Minister Rajiv Gandhi said Indian troops were in Sri Lanka under the bilateral agreement of 1987, and that their withdrawal could not be decided upon unilaterally. Premadasa was forced to abandon his "deadline," but he did persuade Gandhi to withdraw a token force of some 600 troops on July 30. Protracted and often tense negotiations followed. On August 18 a compromise agreement was announced. India agreed to an unconditional cease-fire within a few days, and to a withdrawal of all its forces by year's end.

NORMAN D. PALMER, *Professor Emeritus*
University of Pennsylvania

SRI LANKA • Information Highlights

Official Name: Democratic Socialist Republic of Sri Lanka.
Location: South Asia.
Area: 25,332 sq mi (65 610 km^2).
Population (mid-1989 est.): 16,900,000.
Chief Cities (mid-1986 est.): Colombo, the capital, 683,000; Dehiwala-Mount Lavinia, 191,000.
Government: *Head of state,* R. Premadasa, president (took office Jan. 1989). *Head of government,* D. B. Wijetunga, prime minister (appointed March 3, 1989). *Legislature* (unicameral)—Parliament.
Monetary Unit: Rupee (35.1 rupees equal U.S.$1, July 1989).
Gross Domestic Product (1987 U.S.$): $6,040,-000,000.
Economic Index (Colombo, 1988): *Consumer Prices* (1980 = 100), all items, 233.8; food, 236.1.
Foreign Trade (1988 U.S.$): *Imports,* $2,227,000,000; *exports,* $1,466,000,000.

STAMPS AND STAMP COLLECTING

U.S. Postal Service

"America the Beautiful" was the theme of a continuing series of postal cards issued by the U.S. Postal Service (USPS) in 1989. Depicted on the cards were beautiful landscapes and historic sites in various parts of the country, incorporating scenes of the desert, wetlands, mountains, woodlands, and seashores.

Two branches of the U.S. government—legislative and executive—were honored on three stamps. The legislative branch—the House and the Senate—had two. (A fourth stamp, honoring the judicial branch, was expected in 1990.) These were part of the Constitutional Series. Added to the series was an adhesive hailing the drafting of the Bill of Rights.

A tribute to the 200th anniversary of the French Revolution, which was marked in 1989, resulted in a joint issue with France; the U.S. tripartite design displayed "Equality, Fraternity, and Liberty."

Statehood commemoratives honored Montana, North Carolina, North Dakota, South Dakota, Oklahoma, and Washington. Another important commemorative in 1989 was a $2.40 Priority Mail stamp celebrating the 20th anniversary of the moon landing. It featured two men planting the Stars and Stripes on the lunar surface.

A block of four airmail stamps honoring the 20th Universal Postal Congress was released during World Stamp Expo '89 to commemorate this international meeting, held in Washington, DC, in November 1989. It was the first time in 92 years that the United States had hosted the congress. A 25¢ stamp also was issued for World Stamp Expo '89.

At year's end a series of issues were released over a two-week period to complete the Universal Postal Congress testimonial. The items included postal cards depicting Washington, DC, and other U.S. cities, a World Stamp Expo '89 stamped envelope, and numerous other stamps and cards.

The USPS honored its own with the issuance of a stamp picturing three postal workers. The slogan "Letter Carriers: We Deliver" appeared atop the stamp.

In the Historic Preservation Series, stamps were dedicated to Healy Hall at Georgetown University in Washington, DC, and Hull House in Chicago. Honorees in other series were: Arturo Toscanini in the Performing Arts Series, Lou Gehrig in the American Sports Series, A. Philip Randolph in the Black Heritage Series, Johns Hopkins and Sitting Bull in the Great Americans Series, and Ernest Hemingway in the Literary Arts Series.

A booklet of five designs featured steamboats famous in U.S. history. A quartet of prehistoric dinosaurs was illustrated in a block of four stamps: pteranodon, stegosaurus, brontosaurus, and tyrannosaurus rex.

SYD KRONISH
Stamp Editor, The Associated Press

Selected U.S. Commemorative Stamps, 1989

Subject	Denomination	Date	Subject	Denomination	Date	Subject	Denomination	Date
Desert (card)	15¢	Jan. 12	U.S. House of Representatives	25¢	April 4	Moon Landing Priority Mail	$2.40	July 20
Montana Statehood	25¢	Jan. 15	U.S. Senate	25¢	April 6	Ernest Hemingway	25¢	July 21
Healy Hall (card)	15¢	Jan. 23	U.S. Executive Branch	25¢	April 16	North Carolina Statehood	25¢	Aug. 22
A. Philip Randolph	25¢	Feb. 3	Inauguration of George Washington	25¢	April 16	Woodlands (card)	15¢	Aug. 26
Flag Over Yosemite (coil)	25¢	Feb. 14	Settling of Oklahoma (card)	15¢	April 22	Letter Carriers	25¢	Aug. 30
North Dakota Statehood	25¢	Feb. 21	South Dakota Statehood	25¢	May 3	Sitting Bull	28¢	Sept. 14
Washington Statehood	25¢	Feb. 22	Mountains (card)	21¢	May 5	Hull House (card)	15¢	Sept. 18
Steamboats (five)	25¢	March 3	Johns Hopkins	$1.00	June 7	Drafting of Bill of Rights	25¢	Sept. 25
World Stamp Expo '89	25¢	March 16	Lou Gehrig	25¢	June 10	Prehistoric Animals (four)	25¢	Oct. 1
Wetlands (card)	15¢	March 17	Seashore (card)	15¢	June 17	Christmas (contemporary)	25¢	Oct. 19
Arturo Toscanini	25¢	March 25	French Revolution Airmail	45¢	July 14	Christmas (traditional)	25¢	Oct. 19
						UPU Congress (11 issues)	varied	Nov. 17–Dec. 3

STOCKS AND BONDS

The U.S. stock market climbed to record highs in 1989, in a style that typified an exuberant but stormy decade on Wall Street. Stock prices had just completed their recovery from the crash of 1987 when they were hit with a new and jarring decline on Friday, October 13. But even after suffering those shocks, the bull market that traced its origins to the summer of 1982 still seemed full of vitality as the decade drew to a close.

The American economy kept growing as well, extending a seven-year expansion that repeatedly defied its many doubters. When the pace of business and corporate profits showed signs of flagging as the years passed, the Federal Reserve Board (Fed) began to relax its previously tight credit policy, fostering a decline in interest rates and a rise in the prices of U.S. Treasury securities and other high-quality interest-bearing investments.

The Dow Jones average of 30 industrial stocks, the oldest and best known gauge of market trends, finished the year at 2,753.20, up 584.63 points, or 26.96%, from its 1988 close, having more than tripled from 838.74 at the end of 1979. At mid-December, yields on long-term Treasury bonds hovered slightly below 8%, down from about 9% a year earlier.

Market Weaknesses. All was hardly sunshine in the financial world. The market for high-yielding, lower-quality "junk bonds" took a severe pounding as investors grew increasingly leery of the debt burden incurred through the wave of corporate takeovers and buyouts that made many an individual fortune (and lost more than a few) during the 1980s. In part because of the waning of the takeover boom, profits and payrolls shrank in the securities industry, leaving many of Wall Street's most prominent firms groping for a new course.

Bitter controversy revived over the practice known as program trading, involving computer-driven transactions by professional traders, and its purported role in volatile swings in stock prices that were said widely to have scared the individual investor away from the market. Critics both on Wall Street and in Washington charged that the industry had failed to correct structural flaws in its markets that had been exposed by the 1987 debacle. In a telling commentary on the state of the business, a seat, or membership, on the New York Stock Exchange sold for $420,000 in late 1989, down from a peak level of $1,150,000 just two and one-half years earlier.

Such worries contrasted sharply with the misgivings that prevailed at the start of 1989, when the economy appeared to be growing too strongly, forcing the Federal Reserve Board to raise interest rates to restrain inflation and keep business conditions from overheating. As evidence began to accumulate month by month that growth was slowing, stock analysts hailed it as a portent of a "soft landing" for the economy and the markets—a successful and relatively painless slowdown that could set the stage for future expansion without the need for a recession.

Doubts about this bright prospect began to stir in late summer and early fall, however, when the Toronto-based Campeau Corp. disclosed that it was having trouble keeping up with the debts of its huge U.S. retailing empire, embracing such stalwart names as Federated Department Stores and Allied Stores. That helped put the stock and junk-bond markets in a vulnerable state for a bigger and nastier surprise. On October 13 an employee-management group that was readying a buyout bid for UAL Corp., parent of United Airlines, announced that financing for the deal was not readily available. A wave of selling immediately sent stocks into a free-fall decline, leaving the Dow Jones industrial average with a 190.58-point loss for the day. In points, although not in proportion, it was the second-biggest drop ever recorded, exceeded only by the 508-point fall the average took on Black Monday, Oct. 19, 1987.

The next week, stocks rebounded almost as swiftly as they had dropped, producing a 119.88-point recovery in the Dow. Investors who recalled the profitable opportunities they had missed in the 1987 crash bid eagerly for stocks, acting on the hope that whatever damage arose from takeover-debt problems could be kept isolated from the rest of corporate America. But a revival of confidence in the junk-bond market was slower in coming. Near year's end, an index of yields on junk bonds calculated by First Boston Corp. stood at about 15.5%, its highest level in more than five years and nearly double the yields available at the same time on Treasury bonds.

Mutual Fund Popularity. Whether stocks were up or down, their unpredictable behavior appeared to be driving many individual investors to less chancy alternatives—including the diversified portfolios of mutual funds, a business whose runaway growth seemed only to have been interrupted temporarily by the 1987 crash. At the end of the 1980s mutual-fund assets under management, as reported by the Investment Company Institute trade group, soared past $950 billion, ten times the comparable amount a decade before. At the beginning of the 1980s the institute counted 524 funds with slightly fewer than 10 million shareholder accounts. By the end of 1988, there were 2,718 funds with more than 50 million accounts.

A large measure of that expansion stemmed from the funds' move away from their traditional bread-and-butter stocks into such other vehicles as municipal bonds and short-term money-market securities. In 1989 stock funds, with assets of roughly $250 billion, remained a significant part of the industry. But they were

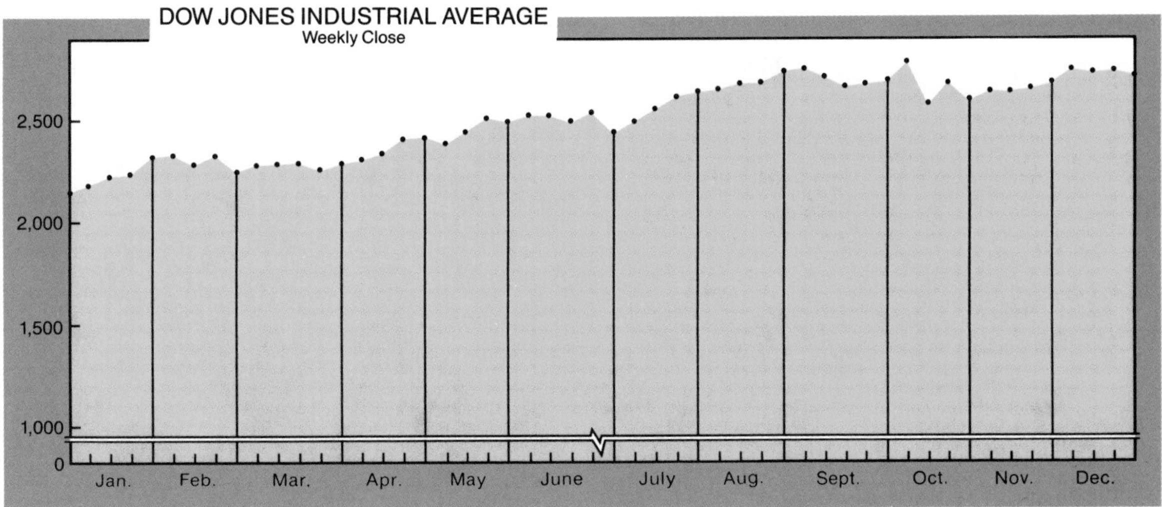

outranked by both money-market and short-term municipal funds, at about $400 billion, and bond and income funds, at about $300 billion. In the course of what the experts labeled "the decade of financial assets," millions of American investors evidently concluded that they wanted or needed specialized, professional help in managing their finances. When demand for that kind of service increased, mutual-fund managers were in the right place at the right time to meet it.

Investment Business Competition. Even though the outlook looked spotty at best for the investment business going into 1990, plenty of competition persisted for a share of the action. Banks, even while coping with their own problems of Third World debt, takeover debt, and real-estate debt, kept up pressure to break down barriers erected by the Glass-Steagall Act of 1933 to keep them out of such activities as underwriting corporations' offers of new stocks and bonds. Securities brokers already had made substantial inroads into the banking business by providing products such as central assets accounts, which, although not legally defined or insured as bank deposits, offered such traditional banking services as check-writing and credit cards.

In early December, Wall Street firms, acting through the Securities Industry Association, announced an abrupt change of tactics in this long-fought turf battle. They declared that they no longer would fight to defend Glass-Steagall, but instead would support new legislation permitting separate subsidiaries of banking organizations to enter the stocks-and-bonds business. In return, the brokers said they wanted access to the consumer banking market and the right to participate with banks in the Federal Reserve payments system. In some future time of need, like the 1987 crash, brokers then could turn directly to the Fed for credit, rather than having to depend on the favor of bankers. Many details of such a new approach remained to be worked out. Still, the proposal helped shape a new and prominent item on the financial agenda for regulators and Congress to consider in the 1990s.

Opportunities in Eastern Europe. International events in 1989 were working to inject other new variables into the business and financial equation of the new decade. As country after country in Eastern Europe won new freedoms from long dominance by communism, financial analysts scrambled to sort out the fresh opportunities and problems that might arise. The European Common Market, already planning to embark on a new economic alliance in 1992, in particular seemed to have struck a rich lode of potential customers and labor supplies. U.S. multinational corporations, too, hurried to capitalize on new room for growth. Complex international trade relationships seemed headed for a thorough shake-up.

The changes helped give fresh impetus to stock markets around the world that, for the most part, had joined in Wall Street's rising trend through the 1980s. The West German market enjoyed a powerful rally in the autumn as wide cracks opened in the Berlin Wall. For the 11 months through November 30, all 13 world markets tracked by the firm of Datastream International, as published in *The Wall Street Journal,* showed gains for the year. In terms of local currency, Singapore ranked first, up 35.88%, followed by Britain, up 26.98%; France, up 26.40%; the United States, up 24.80%; and Japan, up 23.57% to cap off the 1980s as the undisputed standout of the decade in the global performance race. Behind the five leaders came West Germany, up 19.85%; the Netherlands, up 19.30%; Switzerland, up 18.95%; Canada, up 16.31%; Italy, up 12.68%; Spain, up 10.71%; Australia, up 8.42%; and Hong Kong, up 2.27%.

CHET CURRIER, *The Associated Press*

© E.C.P.A./Sygma

A French transport plane delivers relief supplies in southern Sudan as part of the international effort to save lives in an area ravaged by civil war. An estimated 2.2 million Sudanese were malnourished and needed food.

SUDAN

A coup d'état ended a three-year-old regime in Sudan in 1989. Civil war and a decrepit economy dragged on. Relations with the Sudan's critical neighbors—Egypt, Libya, and Ethiopia—were improving.

Domestic Issues. On June 30, 1989, Prime Minister Sadiq al-Mahdi was ousted in a military coup, known as the "June Revolution." The coup was the work of junior military officers headed by Lt. Gen. Omar Hassan Ahmed al-Bashir. Shortly after the takeover, Bashir promoted himself to brigadier general. Within days, Bashir arrested more than 100 Mahdi supporters, including the former prime minister, and dismissed 28 generals. A 15-member Revolutionary Command Council of National Salvation was appointed to handle the affairs of the nation. A state of emergency was declared; all parliamentary, political party, and trade union activities were halted; and the nation's free press was shut down. The costly stalemate in the six-year civil war and deteriorating economic conditions were believed to be the major reasons for the coup. Egypt was the first country to recognize the new government.

Civil War. Growing military pressure on the Mahdi government forced the latter to open up a dialogue with the rebels, the Sudanese People's Liberation Army (SPLA). In February the army delivered an ultimatum to the Mahdi regime demanding political and economic reforms as well as an increase in military spending. The army acted because of the deplorable fighting conditions it faced in the war. The lack of guns, ammunition, uniforms, and other important supplies irritated an already war-weary army. Since February, the army lost 12 garrison towns to the rebels. In early March, Prime Minister Mahdi offered to make fundamental constitutional changes in exchange for a rebel cease-fire. John Garang, the SPLA leader, vowed to continue the struggle, however, until Islamic *sharia* law was abolished, all foreign military agreements abrogated, and the state of emergency rescinded.

In April government officials and SPLA rebel leaders met in the Ethiopian capital of Addis Ababa to elaborate further the necessary conditions for peace. In a surprise initiative on May 1, the SPLA declared a unilateral cease-fire in order to facilitate a massive United Nations shipment of food and supplies to the poverty-stricken war zones of the southern Sudan. The UN operation ("Lifeline Sudan") began in April to feed about 2.2 million people. By late 1989, 100,000 tons of relief supplies had been delivered. It was estimated that 100,000 would have died without it.

SUDAN • Information Highlights

Official Name: Republic of the Sudan.
Location: Northeast Africa.
Area: 967,494 sq mi (2 505 810 km²).
Population (mid-1989 est.): 24,500,000.
Chief Cities (1983 census): Khartoum, the capital, 476,218; Omdurman, 526,287; Khartoum North, 341,146.
Government: *Head of government,* Omar Hassan Ahmed al-Bashir, prime minister (took over June 30, 1989). A 15-member Revolutionary Command Council of National Salvation serves as the supreme executive, legislative, and judicial body.
Monetary Unit: Pound (4.5 pounds equal U.S.$1, May 1989).
Foreign Trade (1987 U.S.$): *Imports,* $929,000,000; exports, $504,000,000.

In June, Garang met with U.S. officials, including former President Jimmy Carter, to help bring an end to the civil war. Garang also extended the May 1 cease-fire to June 15. Shortly after seizing power, Bashir declared a government cease-fire, promising amnesty to the rebels and vowing to send the *sharia* law debate to a national referendum if negotiations collapsed.

Economy. The festering civil war continued to block economic development, taxing the national budget by $1 million per day. A struggling industrial sector and a crippled agricultural sector has forced the government to borrow heavily from central banks and international lenders. Borrowing has triggered an 80% annual inflation rate, while Sudan's foreign debt climbed to $14 billion by August. The country owed $1 billion to the International Monetary Fund (IMF), more than any other nation. Negotiations between the IMF and the Sudan government continued despite the military coup although future loans would depend on Sudan's ability to handle its back payments.

Further exacerbating Sudan's dismal economy was the growing black market. According to officials, $5 million per day is smuggled out of the Sudan despite government attempts to curb black marketeering. In May, 50 dealers were detained on currency smuggling charges.

Foreign Relations. Despite Mahdi's attempt to maintain a balanced foreign policy, Sudan had developed close relations with Libya and Iran. Moderate Arab states like Egypt, Jordan, and Saudi Arabia were among the first nations to congratulate the new military government. For its part, the United States, as the largest provider of military and financial aid to the Sudan, threatened to invoke a little-used amendment to the Foreign Assistance Act, which states that a democracy that is swept away by a military dictatorship is cut off immediately from U.S. economic and military assistance. A special presidential waiver is needed for the aid to be continued.

JOHN P. ENTELIS, *Fordham University*
OMER K. ALPTEKIN, *Columbia University*

SWEDEN

Economists predicted a decline in Sweden's growth despite a healthy surge in exports in 1989, and the government signed a series of agreements with Poland during the year aimed at settling fishing disputes, the extradition of criminals, and battling pollution in the Baltic.

Political Affairs. The centenary of Sweden's Social Democratic Party was celebrated in April with a conference in Stockholm. The Riksdag (parliament) opened its 1989–90 session in October. In his statement on government policy, Prime Minister Ingvar Carlsson said the nation faced serious labor shortages, higher consumer prices, and a growing deficit in the balance of payments. The parliament was prepared to consider extensive tax changes.

SWEDEN • Information Highlights

Official Name: Kingdom of Sweden.
Location: Northern Europe.
Area: 173,730 sq mi (449 960 km²).
Population (mid-1989 est.): 8,500,000.
Chief Cities (Dec. 31, 1988 est.): Stockholm, the capital, 669,485; Göteborg, 430,763; Malmö, 231,575; Uppsala, 161,828.
Government: *Head of state,* Carl XVI Gustaf, king (acceded Sept. 1973). *Head of government,* Ingvar Carlsson, prime minister (elected March 12, 1986). *Legislature* (unicameral)—Riksdag.
Monetary Unit: Krona (6.435 kronor equal U.S.$1, Nov. 15, 1989).
Gross National Product (1987 U.S.$): $116,500,-000,000.
Economic Indexes (1988): *Consumer Prices* (1980 = 100), all items, 176.7; food, 201.6. *Industrial Production* (1980 = 100), 118.
Foreign Trade (1988 U.S.$): *Imports,* $45,818,-000,000; *exports,* $49,979,000,000.

Economic Affairs. The Federation of Swedish industries emphasized the healthy growth of the export industries in a midyear report, but the Swedish economy nevertheless would enter a period of declining growth. It was predicted that the gross domestic product (GDP) growth would drop from 1.7% in 1989 to 0.5% in 1990. The rate of growth of industrial production would parallel the GDP, while investment activity should remain high—4% in 1989 after a growth of 5.3% in 1988.

Foreign Affairs and Papal Visit. Sweden joined the European Columbus Space Project, sponsored by the European Space Agency (ESA). The project will include a manned laboratory module to be connected with the U.S. international space station. Sweden also is involved in other European space programs for the development of manned space flights, including the Ariane 5 rocket and the space shuttle *Hermes*.

Sweden and Poland signed three agreements in February that would serve to mitigate their future relations. In the first treaty, Sweden obtained 75% of a previously disputed fishing area in the Baltic Sea. A second treaty dealt with the countries' respective responsibility for combating pollution in the Baltic, while a third agreement dealt with such legal topics as documents, the questioning of witnesses, and transfers of criminal proceedings.

Pope John Paul II visited Sweden in June. He was received by King Carl XVI Gustaf and Queen Silvia at the Royal Palace and officiated at Mass at the new Globe, the world's largest spherical building.

Domestic Affairs. After the biggest police investigation ever launched in Sweden, the murder case of Prime Minister Olof Palme took two unexpected turns during the year. Christer Pettersson, a drifter, had been arrested and was found guilty of the prime minister's murder by the City Court of Stockholm in July after an eight-week trial. The lay members of the court voted for conviction while the two professional judges thought the evidence not very convincing. The suspect had been identified by the prime minister's wife, Lisbeth Palme, who was injured during the attack. The case went to the Court of Appeals, which in mid-October found that there was a lack of solid evidence for conviction. Pettersson, who had spent almost a year in jail, was released.

The fate of Raoul Wallenberg, the Swede credited with saving thousands of Hungarian Jews in 1944–45 from death in Nazi concentration camps, became clearer in 1989. Wallenberg disappeared in 1945 after he was arrested by the Soviets and taken to Budapest. In the fall of 1989, both his half-brother and half-sister were invited to Moscow to inspect some of the evidence that up until then had been unavailable, Wallenberg's diplomatic passport and an identification card. Soviet officials still maintain that Wallenberg died in Russia in 1947, but rumors and claims that he still is alive are believed widely.

ERIK J. FRIIS
The Scandinavian-American Bulletin

SWITZERLAND

Major banking and government scandals, plus a referendum on abolishing Switzerland's armed forces, dominated Swiss concerns during 1989.

Criminal Investigations. On January 12, Minister of Justice and Federal Vice-President Designate Elisabeth Kopp resigned from the government. In December, Kopp had admitted having warned her husband to resign as deputy chairman of Shakarchi Trading Co., which was about to be investigated on charges of laundering drug profits deposited with it by Lebanese drug merchants. However, she denied giving her husband any official information about the investigation. Originally, Minister Kopp had planned to leave office at the end of February; her early resignation was prompted by government allegations that her secretary, with Minister Kopp's knowledge, indeed had provided copies of classified government documents concerning the investigation to Mr. Kopp.

On February 7 the Swiss Banking Commission announced it was investigating allegations that *Credit Suisse,* one of the largest and most respected Swiss banking establishments, was engaging in improper money-laundering activities. On March 6 the government dismissed Attorney General Rudolf Gerber and ordered a formal investigation of charges that he had been lax in combating the laundering of drug-trafficking profits.

On April 18, Swiss police arrested Saudi Arabian Adnan Khashoggi, a longtime Swiss resident, in his hotel suite in Bern. Khashoggi, an international arms dealer and financier, first had come to public attention as the middleman in negotiating arrangements for the Iran-contra U.S. arms deals of the mid-1980s. He now was charged by American officials with having aided Philippines former President Ferdinand Marcos in laundering funds stolen from the Philippines treasury, as well as having helped conceal Marcos' ownership of a collection of valuable paintings. On July 19, Khashoggi was extradited to the United States to await trial.

Women's Suffrage. On April 30, by a show of hands at the annual meeting of the traditional open-air, all-male *Landsgemeinde* (cantonal parliament), men of the half-canton of Appenzell-Ausserrhoden voted to enfranchise women at the cantonal level. This action leaves the half-canton of Appenzell-Innerrhoden as the only Swiss canton in which women are not allowed to participate in politics. Women were granted voting rights on federal matters in 1971.

The Armed Forces. On November 27, voters rejected a proposal to abolish Switzerland's armed forces, and retain only a militia suitable for dealing with domestic crises. Currently, every able-bodied Swiss male must undergo military training and serve in the reserves until age 50. The annual military budget vastly exceeds that of any other Western European nation in per capita spending.

The 68.6% voter turnout was the largest for any national referendum in 15 years, and the 35.6% pro-abolition vote shocked the political-military establishment. Termed an "idiocy" by President Jean-Pascal Delamuraz, the proposition, nonetheless, had gained the clear, if cautious, support of both Swiss Evangelical and Roman Catholic leadership. On November 26, Defense Minister Kaspar Villiger stated that if more than one third voted in favor it would be a "catastrophe." In the aftermath, analysts and government officials agreed on the need for a reassessment of Swiss military policy.

PAUL C. HELMREICH, *Wheaton College, MA*

SWITZERLAND • Information Highlights

Official Name: Swiss Confederation.
Location: Central Europe.
Area: 15,942 sq mi (41 290 km²).
Population (mid-1989 est.): 6,600,000.
Chief Cities (Dec. 31, 1987 est.): Bern, the capital, 136,292; Zurich, 346,879; Basel, 171,574.
Government: *Head of state,* Arnold Koller, president (took office Jan. 1990). *Legislature*—Council of States and National Council.
Monetary Unit: Franc (1.6040 francs equal U.S.$1, Dec. 4, 1989).
Gross National Product (1988 U.S.$): $111,300,-000,000.
Economic Indexes (1988): *Consumer Prices* (1980 = 100), all items, 128.4; food, 135.3. *Industrial Production* (1980 = 100), 115.
Foreign Trade (1988 U.S.$): *Imports,* $56,384,-000,000; *exports,* $50,733,000,000.

SYRIA

Syria continued in 1989 to be firmly in the grasp of the Baath Party regime headed by President Hafiz al-Assad. In power since early 1971, Assad is a remarkably astute, adroit, and when necessary, ruthless ruler who has weathered innumerable storms. His grip on power has seemed to strengthen rather than weaken with time. While past years have been marked by plots or uprisings, this did not seem to be the case in 1989.

Assad's regime, however, is not in calm waters. The country's economy is in very bad shape, showing only modest signs of improvement in 1989. And external relations continued to be hampered by Syria's marked isolation.

Economic Issues. Viewing Syria today, it is hard to believe the area once was noted for its bustling prosperity. The reduced private sector and the inefficient public sector both were working at less than half capacity in 1989. Capital was scarce and new investment minimal. The country's foreign exchange reserves were inadequate for the scale of the economy. Foreign exchange operations were controlled tightly, and there were at least three different official exchange rates for different kinds of transactions—in addition to the black-market rate. Syria's external debt was mounting and payments were chronically late or in default.

Much of this is intrinsic to the nature of an avowedly socialist regime, but the situation has been worsened by several factors. The first and most overwhelming factor is the immense drain on Syrian resources in maintaining perhaps 40,000 troops in neighboring Lebanon. Agreements made by richer Arab states in 1978 to subsidize the Syrian occupation have not been honored fully. Syria's food subsidies and the cost of heavy arms purchases, mostly from the USSR, also are drains on the economy.

The year, however, saw some modest signs of economic improvement and developments holding promise for the future. Arab countries resumed payment of promised subsidies. By far the greatest boost to Syria's economy, however, was a sharp increase in oil production. Other favorable influences included an excellent harvest in 1988; new economic agreements and joint projects with some Arab and European countries; and an expansion of tourism, aided by construction of several new hotels in Damascus, with about 1.5 million foreign tourists traveling annually to Syria.

Foreign Relations. Syria is increasingly the odd man out in the Arab world, and is not a member of any of the three regional Arab groups. As Iran's sole ally among Arab states, Syria professed to be a useful bridge as long as the Iraqi-Iranian war lasted, but the war ended in 1988. The great prop of Syria's foreign policy has been a client-patron relationship with the Soviet Union. This relationship, however, is not as reliable as it once was. There were signs that the USSR was becoming increasingly disenchanted with Syria's intransigence toward Israel, at a time when Soviet-Israeli rapprochement clearly was under way. Syria's continued diplomatic isolation also makes it of less use to the Soviets in the Middle East. Soviet arms shipments to Syria have been scaled down (though ten fighter planes were promised in April), and Syria has turned to China for some supplies. It generally is believed that when Soviet Foreign Minister Eduard Shevardnadze visited Damascus in February, he urged moderation on three issues: Assad's uncompromising hostility with Israel's very existence; his feud with Yasir Arafat and the Palestinian Liberation Organization (PLO); and his hostility to Egypt because of its peace treaty with Israel.

A slightly restrained Assad took part in the four-day emergency summit meeting of the Arab League at Casablanca in May. He did not oppose Egypt's return to the fold of the Arab world, nor increased aid for the PLO. In a gesture of conciliation in June, Syria released 140 Arafat followers who had been jailed for six years. In December, Syria and Egypt agreed to reopen air links. The move was seen as a step toward restoring Syrian-Egyptian diplomatic relations, which occurred as 1989 ended.

At the Arab League summit, Assad was also able to avoid the threat of concerted Arab pressure on Syria to withdraw its troops from Lebanon in the interest of peace. Assad could not gain what he wants in Lebanon—total control—but any settlement remained dependent on his concurrence.

The steady improvement in Syrian-U.S. relations was interrupted on March 3 when two members of the Popular Front for the Liberation of Palestine (PFLP) held two U.S. defense attachés in Damascus hostage for eight hours. The United States requested Syria to end all PFLP activity on its soil.

ARTHUR CAMPBELL TURNER
University of California, Riverside

SYRIA • Information Highlights

Official Name: Syrian Arab Republic.
Location: Southwest Asia.
Area: 71,498 sq mi (185 180 km^2).
Population (mid-1989 est.): 12,100,000.
Chief Cities (1986 est.): Damascus, the capital, 1,219,448; Aleppo, 1,191,151; Homs, 427,500.
Government: *Head of state,* Gen. Hafiz al-Assad, president (took office officially March 1971). *Head of government,* Mahmoud Zubi, prime minister (took office Nov. 1987). *Legislature* (unicameral)—People's Council.
Monetary Unit: Pound (11.225 pounds equal U.S.$1, July 1989).
Gross Domestic Product (1985 U.S.$): $20,300,-000,000.
Economic Index (1988): *Consumer Prices* (1980 = 100), all items, 537.9; food, 583.2.
Foreign Trade (1988 U.S.$): *Imports,* $2,231,000,000; *exports,* $1,345,000,000.

TAIWAN

During 1989, Taiwan took significant steps toward democratizing its political system, and further increased its ties with mainland China.

Politics and Government. For the first time since the Kuomintang (KMT) or Nationalist Party took control of Taiwan from the Japanese following World War II, an election was held in December in which more than one political party legally contended for positions at every level of government. Although the KMT won sufficient support to allow it to maintain its control of the political system, opposition parties made significant inroads in both national and local contests.

Final results in the December 2 parliamentary election showed the KMT with 60% of the vote, the Democratic Progressive Party (DPP) with 31%; the remaining 9% went to independent opposition candidates. Having won 21 seats, the DPP now had a sufficient presence to introduce legislative proposals under new procedures adopted by the Legislative Yuan in July.

The three-year-old opposition party succeeded in weathering preelection factional disputes that threatened to divide it on the very eve of its first legal electoral contest. A major issue was the question of Taiwan independence, advocacy of which by opposition parties is still an infraction of the national constitution.

The DPP devoted significant attention to local elections, where its candidates won six of 16 contests for county magistrate and strengthened the party's representation on city councils in Taiwan's three largest municipalities.

Putting as good a face as possible on the KMT's losses, government spokesman Shaw Yu-ming described the election as "a victory for democracy . . . [that] may prove to be a healthy thing for the government." It was not so clear whether it would prove to be a healthy thing for the presidency of Lee Teng-hui, who faced an election in March 1990. Some speculated that the legislative elections could be seen as a kind of presidential primary, and that a poor showing for the KMT might be used as a reason for the party's choosing a new candidate to replace Lee.

Ties with the Mainland. Taiwan's informal relationships with the mainland continued to proliferate during 1989. In response to the democracy movement in April and May, direct telephone and mail links were reestablished with the mainland and reporters for the Taiwan press were stationed in Beijing. In the wake of the suppression of the movement in June, response by authorities on Taiwan was muted in order to thwart Beijing's efforts to blame Taiwan agents for fomenting the "counter-revolutionary rebellion," as the hard-liners characterized the student prodemocracy demonstrations.

AP/Wide World

Supporters of Taiwan's ruling Nationalist Party campaign prior to December 2 elections, the first in which opposition candidates were allowed to participate.

By the end of 1989 more than 600,000 Taiwan residents had taken advantage of relaxed travel restrictions to visit the mainland. Although members of the government and armed forces were prevented from taking advantage of this new rule, an exception was made in the case of Finance Minister Shirley Kuo, who visited Beijing in May as Taiwan's representative to the Asian Development Bank. She was the first KMT official to visit the mainland since 1949. Though she avoided any direct interaction with mainland officials, her visit was opposed by Premier Yu Kwo-hua, who resigned his office shortly after her return. He was re-

TAIWAN • Information Highlights

Official Name: Taiwan.
Location: Island off the southeastern coast of mainland China.
Area: 13,892 sq mi (35 980 km²).
Population (mid-1989 est.): 20,000,000.
Chief Cities (Dec. 31, 1986): Taipei, the capital, 2,575,180; Kaohsiung, 1,320,552; Taichung, 695,562; Tainan, 646,298.
Government: *Head of state,* Lee Teng-hui, president (installed Jan. 1988). *Head of government* Lee Huan, president, executive yuan (premier) (appointed May 24, 1989). *Legislature* (unicameral)—Legislative Yuan.
Monetary Unit: New Taiwan dollar (25.96 NT dollars equal U.S.$1, Dec. 29, 1989).
Gross National Product (1988 U.S.$): $91,700,000,000.

placed by Lee Huan, a party official whose views were said to be more in line with those of the president.

Taiwan's investments on the mainland now exceeded $1 billion in value including some 200 manufacturing enterprises in Guangdong and Fujian. Two-way trade was likely to exceed $3 billion by year's end. Mainland imports of goods from Taiwan far outstripped its exports to Taiwan, but the deficit was compensated for partially by revenue earned from tourism and from the smuggling of goods directly across the Taiwan Strait.

Foreign Relations. Speaking to a KMT plenum in June, President Lee told his colleagues, "We must have the courage to face the fact that we do not now exercise effective control over the Chinese mainland." This simple statement of fact marked a significant departure from earlier KMT pronouncements and opened the way for a discussion on the concept of "one country, two governments." The concept responds to the mainland's proposal of "one government, two systems" as a basis for reunification.

Pursuing this concept as a basis for a new "flexible diplomacy," Taiwan representatives abroad abandoned their insistence that foreign governments recognize either Taipei or Beijing. As a result, they were successful in reopening diplomatic ties with Liberia, Grenada, the Bahamas, and Belize. Beijing responded by suspending its relations with Liberia and Grenada (it had no ties with the Bahamas and Belize) and accused Taiwan of "buying friends" with its new $1.2 billion Overseas Economic Cooperation Fund. The United States government actively encouraged Taiwan to play a more prominent role in the world economy, enlisting Taipei's participation in Treasury Secretary Nicholas Brady's plan to reduce Third World debt. It was well positioned to do so, with more than $75 billion in foreign currency reserves—second only to those of Japan.

Responding to Washington's pressure to take steps to reduce its very substantial trade surplus with the United States, the government on Taiwan changed currency regulations and allowed the value of the New Taiwan dollar to be determined by foreign-exchange transactions. The move made Taiwan products more expensive for foreign buyers and some 10% of Taiwan's smaller manufacturing firms were driven into bankruptcy as a result.

JOHN BRYAN STARR
Yale-China Association

TANZANIA

Zanzibar and the reform program of the International Monetary Fund (IMF) continued to dominate the attention of Tanzania's President Ali Hassan Mwinyi's government in 1989 and to strain relations between the government and the ruling Chama Cha Mapinduzi (CCM) Party.

TANZANIA • Information Highlights

Official Name: United Republic of Tanzania.
Location: East coast of Africa.
Area: 364,900 sq mi (945 090 km²).
Population (mid-1989 est.): 26,300,000.
Chief City (1985 est.): Dar es Salaam, the capital, 1,096,000.
Government: *Head of state,* Ali Hassan Mwinyi, president (took office Nov. 1985). *Head of government,* Joseph S. Warioba, prime minister (took office Nov. 1985). *Legislature* (unicameral)—National Assembly, 233 members.
Monetary Unit: Tanzanian shilling (145.0 shillings equal U.S.$1, July 1989).
Gross Domestic Product (fiscal year 1987 U.S.$): $4,960,000,000.
Foreign Trade (1988 U.S.$): *Imports,* $823,000,000; *exports,* $276,000,000.

Relations with Zanzibar. The relationship between Zanzibar and the mainland continued to deteriorate. Zanzibar residents, led by the extremely popular former Chief Minister Seif Sharif Hamad, demanded a UN-supervised referendum on the island's future relations with the mainland, while the former president and current chairman of the CCM, Julius K. Nyerere, remained committed to Zanzibar's complete integration with the mainland before his retirement in 1992. In March, Nyerere called for the detention of all those who expressed antiunion views and in May, Hamad, who had been ousted from the party in 1988, was arrested.

Domestic Affairs. Zanzibar's economy also continued to deteriorate. The gross domestic product of the island declined by 26% during the 1980s, while real wages dropped by 50%.

President Mwinyi remained one of the chief advocates of economic reform. After initial disagreements, Mwinyi completed negotiations with the IMF for an enhanced structural adjustment facility, which included a 25% currency devaluation and decontrol of prices, both for the consumer and for farmers. Nevertheless, farmers continued to shift production away from traditional export crops, such as tobacco and cotton, toward food crops, which could be marketed without government interference.

In spite of an impressive 4% growth rate during 1988–89, conditions in Tanzania remained very difficult. Wages remained depressed. In the face of rapidly rising food prices, the monthly milk production of one cow was worth more than the monthly salary of a teacher.

In a March cabinet reshuffle, Mwinyi strengthened the reform package by removing hard-line CCM opponents. Rather than attend the executive meeting at which the CCM was to approve the reforms, Nyerere, a vocal opponent of the IMF, left the country to attend to foreign relations duties.

WILLIAM CYRUS REED, *Wabash College*

TAXATION

In 1989 the Bush administration pressed to deliver on a campaign promise of a cut in the capital-gains tax, while Congress struggled to reduce the U.S. budget deficit in accordance with the mandate of the Gramm-Rudman-Hollings Act. These seemingly inconsistent objectives of the executive and legislative branches created a political stalemate, in which Congress failed to include a proposal to cut the capital-gains tax in its revenue bill and budget resolution. Japan saw major tax-reform legislation become effective in 1989, and Canada proposed a new goods and services tax.

United States

Federal. Since the mid-1970s, the distribution of U.S. federal tax receipts has shifted markedly away from taxes on business and in the direction of personal taxes. Moreover, within the category of personal taxes the relative importance of payroll taxes, in the form of contributions for Social Security and unemployment insurance, has continued to grow. In fiscal year (FY) 1989, ending September 30, receipts from the personal income tax comprised an estimated 43.6% of total federal tax receipts, while payroll taxes comprised 37.3%, and corporate income taxes represented 11%. Receipts from all other taxes, including excise, estate and gift taxes, and customs duties, comprised only 8.1% of the total.

The share of revenues coming from payroll taxes has risen from 30.8% in 1975. More than half of all U.S. households now pay more in payroll taxes than in individual income taxes. This increasing importance of the payroll tax has contributed to a decline in the progressivity of the overall federal tax system. (A *progressive* tax imposes higher rates on larger incomes and a *regressive* tax, lower rates.) The individual income tax is the most progressive federal tax, while payroll taxes are, on balance, regressive (since income is taxed at a flat rate up to a cutoff point, after which no tax is imposed).

Tax collections by the U.S. federal government during FY 1989 were estimated to be $975.5 billion—including an estimated $425.2 billion in individual income taxes (up 6%) and $107 billion in corporate income taxes (up 13.2%). Despite a 7.3% increase over FY 1988 collections, the government budget deficit increased by $6.4 billion, standing at $161.5 billion for FY 1989. The Gramm-Rudman-Hollings Act mandates that the deficit be brought to $100 billion by FY 1990.

Faced with a formidable gap between the actual deficit and the legislative target, Congress struggled in 1989 for ways to raise revenues and reduce government expenditures. President Bush's continued opposition to a tax increase and his insistence on a reduction in the tax on capital gains meant that congressional leaders would require a two-thirds majority support for tax-increase legislation in order to override a likely presidential veto. Thus it was not surprising that after six months of effort, Congress made only minor changes in tax legislation. It postponed consideration of the capital-gains tax reduction and voted to repeal both the taxes and the benefits contained in the Medicare Catastrophic Coverage Act of 1988.

Capital Gains. Historically, taxes on gains or losses that occur when assets such as stocks and bonds are sold have been assessed at lower rates than taxes on other income. Only "long-term" capital gains have been eligible for this preferential treatment, a definition which involves a specified holding period before an asset can be sold. Capital gains (or losses) also can arise from sales of real estate, although capital losses for sales of a personal residence are not tax-deductible as are capital losses from investment property.

One rationale for preferential treatment of capital gains is that some of a long-term gain normally reflects inflationary increases in the overall price level, and is not a real increase in wealth. Another, more controversial, rationale is that capital gains should have preferred status in order to encourage saving. Opposition to preferential treatment generally centers on the argument that all income, regardless of its source, should be taxed at the same rate and, further, that since capital-gains income is realized disproportionately by the well-to-do, favored treatment of capital gains makes the tax structure less progressive.

The Tax Reform Act of 1986 eliminated favored treatment of capital gains along with a large number of so-called "loopholes" or exemptions in the tax system, while at the same time reducing marginal tax rates and creating essentially a flat rate structure for most taxpayers. To compensate for the elimination of the capital-gains exemption, the rate on incomes in the highest bracket was set at 28%, five percentage points below the 33% rate imposed on middle and upper-middle incomes.

In his FY 1990 budget proposal, President Bush called for a decrease in the capital-gains tax rate to a maximum of 15%. He argued that reducing the capital-gains tax actually would increase revenue, as asset holders would have an incentive to sell assets to take advantage of the lower rate. Opponents maintained that this revenue gain would be only temporary, and would be offset by lower revenues in later years. Moreover, they contended that preferred treatment of capital gains violates the spirit and intent of tax reform and has undesirable distributional consequences. After considerable debate, Congress postponed a vote on the capital-gains tax and failed to include the president's proposal in the congressional budget resolution.

Medicare. Intense lobbying by the elderly resulted in repeal of a surtax enacted in 1988 to pay for expanded health benefits under Medicare. The associated benefits also were discontinued. The Medicare Catastrophic Coverage Act of 1988 placed a limit on fees that Medicare patients paid for hospitals and doctors, expanded nursing-home coverage, and added coverage for prescription drugs. At the same time, a surtax of $22.50 was imposed for each $150 in taxes paid by the elderly in 1989, up to a maximum of $800 per person or $1,600 per couple. The surtax would be increased gradually to $42 in 1993, with a maximum of $1,050 per person or $2,100 per couple. In 1989 only about 5% of Medicare beneficiaries paid the maximum. In addition to the surtax, there was a flat monthly premium of $4 deducted from Social Security checks. Despite the fact that the 1988 act had the strong support of organizations representing senior citizens, repeal came in response to a barrage of protests from seniors, especially the more affluent, who resented paying the surtax. Elderly people who were less well off, however, would be affected adversely by the repeal.

State and Local. States and municipalities levy taxes to support the provision of state and local services such as schools, highways and related infrastructure, and social services. The bulk of state revenues are from sales and income taxes, while local taxes are primarily on property and, to a lesser extent, on income. State and local governments also impose taxes on business enterprises as well as a myriad of business licensing and other fees.

There is considerable variation among states in the average tax burden (that is, the overall rate of taxation from all sources as a percentage of state income). However, because individuals and business firms can move from state to state to avoid high taxes and to receive state services, state budgets must be set to create balances between the tax base and the demands on public services. Imposition of high taxes to finance expanded services for the poor may create an outflow of the more affluent and an inflow of low-income individuals. The outcome will be an erosion of the tax base, making it inadequate to support planned expenditures. On the other hand, low taxes coupled with a low rate of expenditure on highways and other amenities could create an inflow of resources that would generate environmental problems with an inadequate infrastructure to support expanded economic activity.

Taxation also is used by states as a way to enforce antidrug laws. Eleven states tax illegal drug sales, with nine of these requiring the purchase of tax stamps similar to those on cigarettes. These controversial laws enable states to charge drug dealers with tax evasion and freeze their assets so they cannot dispose of them while in jail. The money from taxes paid usually is divided among state law-enforcement agencies.

In FY 1988 state and local tax revenues, including receipts from business licensing and other fees, amounted to $656.6 billion, an increase of 7.4% over the previous year. In 1989 several states debated tax-reform legislation, and in some states, including Louisiana and Michigan, voters rejected reconstruction packages which would have resulted in tax increases. Although there was a general trend to increase sales taxes, these hikes often were tempered with tax breaks on property or decreased licensing fees.

International

Japan. The Japanese government enacted major tax-reform legislation in 1988 which took effect in April 1989. One component of the measure, a 3% sales/consumption tax, came under attack by Japanese consumer groups. Because of rampant evasion of direct income taxes, especially among small business owners and professionals, the new tax will be a major source of revenue in Japan. It would bring in roughly $40 billion in revenue, or about 10% of the national budget annually. Japan also finances a much larger part of its budget by borrowing than does the United States, with debt service running about 20% of the budget.

While the new tax has been criticized as regressive and as a conspicuous burden on consumers, the government sees few alternatives for expanding the tax base. Deterioration of the tax base will become increasingly problematic in the future, due to Japan's rapidly aging population.

Canada. In 1989, Canada proposed a wide-ranging federal goods and services tax (GST), essentially a version of the value-added tax used extensively throughout Europe. The GST, scheduled to take effect in 1991, would replace a 13.5% tax on manufactured goods presently in effect. However, although the new rate is lower, thousands of previously untaxed goods would be covered, and services would be taxed for the first time.

The measure was unpopular among Canadians; critics claimed it was inherently regressive and would burden the poor disproportionately. The Mulroney government did not agree, and pointed out it planned to reduce income tax rates from their present high level. A campaign was in place to convince the government to alter or drop the GST. Six weeks of public hearings regarding the GST were opened in late September. The committee conducting the hearings recommended 86 changes in the GST. By December the government was undecided as to which of these changes, if any, it would incorporate into the tax.

NANCY S. BARRETT
Fairleigh Dickinson University

In the 1989 television movie "My Name Is Bill W.," veteran actor James Garner (right) *provided outstanding support for James Woods* (left), *who received an Emmy Award for his performance in the title role. The two actors previously had teamed in the Emmy Award-winning "Promise" (1986).*

Courtesy of Hallmark Hall of Fame

TELEVISION AND RADIO

The year 1989 was a special one in television history, the 50th anniversary of television's first public broadcast at the 1939 New York World's Fair. The event was celebrated during the year with television specials and with a yearlong exhibition at the Smithsonian Institution. (*See* page 56.)

The year also was one in which Roseanne Barr, star of *Roseanne,* became the triumphant video role model for yet two more oppressed constituencies: working-class women and the corpulent. Indeed it was the year of corpulence: Talk-show host Oprah Winfrey and *Designing Women* star Delta Burke created a tabloid headline frenzy with their weight loss and gain, respectively.

And, too, it was the year of coinage for a new verb, "to Norville"—that is, to usurp a senior colleague's position, following Deborah Norville's ascent to Jane Pauley's anchor seat on the *Today* show.

It also was the season that the people spoke, and television listened. Because of the campaign of a Michigan housewife, mighty corporations backed away from advertising on some of the more shameless new television fare. Smarting from press ridicule, the networks backed off from their attempts to spice up news with dramatic "reenactments."

Sleaze seemed to be the people's choice in the ratings, and yet widespread community backlash against it suggested otherwise. "I believe there are some changes going on in the society," National Broadcasting Company (NBC) Entertainment President Brandon Tartikoff said. "People are saying they want a different texture in their programming."

Network Programming. Taking the number one ratings crown away from the perennial NBC series king *Cosby* six out of 25 weeks in its inaugural season, *Roseanne* led a resurgent American Broadcasting Companies (ABC) to second place in the ratings for the 1988–89 season. NBC scored a 15.7 season rating (percentage of American households with television sets tuned to NBC), ABC had a 12.9, and the Columbia Broadcasting System (CBS) had a 12.7. CBS' astounding payment of $300 million for the broadcast rights to the 1994 Winter Olympics was described by *Variety* as "a plan to bring the network back into contention in the ratings race—at any cost."

Critics gauged the public's lack of enthusiasm by noting that an unusually low number of new shows (three) for 1988–89 were popular enough to break into the list of the top ten rated shows. Aside from *Roseanne,* they were *Empty Nest* and *Anything But Love* (with Jamie Lee Curtis and comedian Richard Lewis successfully transferring his quirky style from *Late Night with David Letterman*), joining such favorites as CBS' *60 Minutes,* ABC's *Who's the Boss?,* and NBC's *Cheers.*

With titillating crime dramas and potboilers making up so much of the made-for-television film stock, *Lonesome Dove,* adapted for CBS from Larry McMurtry's Western epic and starring Robert Duvall, stood out like a beacon.

There were also kudos for David Straithairn as atom-bomb mastermind Robert Oppenheimer in CBS' *Day One*.

The canceled shows of 1989, perhaps even more than the unexceptional new entries, mirrored a transition in American society. In *The New York Times,* commentator Stephanie Brush wrote that with the end of the series *Moonlighting, Miami Vice,* and *Family Ties,* "it's almost as if the 1980s have been purged in one fell swoop."

The sensitivity of such ABC series as *Thirtysomething* and *Life Goes On* (a 1989 entry about a family whose son has Down's syndrome), held out hope for the 1990s, along with the stylish intelligence of such CBS crime dramas as *Wise Guy* and new entry *Wolf.* But the overall ratings momentum seemed to favor the rise of so-called "trash TV"—tabloid-style reality-based programs such as *The Reporters, America's Most Wanted,* and *A Current Affair* on the Fox Network.

The Content Issue. Under pressure to stem the exodus of viewers to such tabloid-style programs and to cable television, the big three networks stooped lower than ever in program taste. NBC's *Nightingales,* highlighting the scantily clad forms of its nurse heroines, came in for special contempt from critics and women's groups, and was short-lived. Geraldo Rivera also came under criticism following an incident on his morning talk show in which he received a bloodied nose during a racial melee. Even so, his ratings went up, and his picture made the cover of a national magazine.

Even New York's Cardinal John O'Connor joined the fray over television tastes, responding to a risqué joke by Robin Williams on WNBC-TV's *Live at Five* with blasts from the pulpit of St. Patrick's Cathedral. Grant Tinker, the former NBC chairman and current program producer, was quoted as saying, "What's changed in scheduling is its white-hot competition. It's war."

Mrs. Terry Rakolta of the wealthy Detroit suburb of Bloomfield Hills became the banner carrier of the citizen movement against sleaze. Her lobbying resulted in four major corporations, including Procter & Gamble, pulling their ads from Fox's explicitly titillating *Married . . . With Children.* In the wake of Mrs. Rakolta's campaign, ABC canceled its sensationalistic special, *Crimes of Passion II,* because it could attract no advertisers. It was skittish advertisers, too, that brought the cancellation of the syndicated *Morton Downey Jr. Show* after its 15-month lifetime of coarse, luridly confrontational "debate."

News. Two foreign stories—in China and Eastern Europe—required resourcefulness from the network-news departments and drew their chief anchors to report from the scene. There were reports that during the antigovernment uprisings in China, crews from CBS, NBC, and CNN were chased or assaulted by soldiers but were unswerving in their coverage from Beijing. In a milestone move, black staffers at ABC were given editorial control over the documentary *Black in White America.* A journalistic power transfer occurred late in the year as ABC News established a steady dominance over the traditional news king, CBS.

A heated and—for the networks, embarrassing—debate over news "reenactments" was touched off when ABC simulated a scene in which American diplomat Felix Bloch handed over government secrets to a Soviet agent before there was any solid confirmation that Bloch had committed such an act. CBS launched an investigation into charges that it had "staged" scenes in 1984 news footage from Afghanistan. After criticism for reenactments was focused on its new magazine show, *Yesterday, Today & Tomorrow,* NBC discontinued the practice.

ABC teamed Diane Sawyer, its pricey new recruit from CBS, with Sam Donaldson for a new magazine program, *Prime Time Live. Variety* noted that the format, combining live and taped segments, gave the show some of the spontaneous "newsy-ness" of the network's respected *Nightline.*

Public Television. Losing bids for new programming with competitive, commercial cable channels—principally Arts and Entertainment and Discovery—public television found itself at a critical crossroads.

John Wicklein of the Working Group for Public Broadcasting declared, "Public broadcasting is broke, and it ought to be fixed." He outlined his plan to present to Congress a proposal for a new public broadcasting act that will "guarantee increased, stable financing for the

ABC newsman Sam Donaldson and recent ABC recruit Diane Sawyer, formerly of CBS' "60 Minutes," were cohosts of the new magazine program, "Prime Time Live."

© Harry Benson/"Time" Magazine

© Tony Esparza/CBS

Robert Duvall (left) *and Tommy Lee Jones, heading a stellar cast in the miniseries "Lonesome Dove," portrayed two former Texas rangers who make a cattle drive to Montana.*

TELEVISION | 1989

Some Sample Programs

Arab and Jew—Report on the Arab-Israeli conflict, PBS, May 29.

Around the World in Eighty Days—Three-part miniseries adapted from Jules Verne's 1873 novel. With Pierce Brosnan, Eric Idle, John Hillerman. NBC, April 16.

The Aspern Papers—A *Great Performances* telecast of the Dallas Opera's world premiere production of Dominick Argento's adaptation of the Henry James novella. With Neil Rosenshein, Elisabeth Soederstroem, Frederica von Stade, Richard Stilwell. PBS, June 9.

Black in White America—An *ABC News Special* dealing with racism, the way blacks view themselves, and negative media messages. ABC, Aug. 29.

Bridge to Silence—A 1989 TV movie about the struggle between a mother and her deaf daughter over the mother's desire to raise her granddaughter after her daughter has been in a car accident. With Lee Remick, Marlee Matlin, Josef Sommer. CBS, April 9.

Can't Afford to Grow Old—A report on exploring the burdens on senior citizens who require long-term health care. With Walter Cronkite. PBS, Oct. 4.

The Case of the Hillside Stranglers—A 1989 fact-based TV movie about the hunt for two serial killers. With Richard Crenna, Dennis Farina. NBC, April 2.

Color of Honor—A documentary focusing on Japanese-American soldiers in World War II. PBS, Jan. 12.

Cross of Fire—A two-part 1989 TV movie about the Ku Klux Klan in the 1920s. With John Heard, Mel Harris, Donald Moffat, Kim Hunter. NBC, Nov. 5.

Dark Holiday—A 1989 TV movie about an American tourist jailed in Turkey for possession of national antiquities. With Lee Remick, Norma Aleandro, Roy Thinnes. NBC, May 1.

Day One—A 1989 TV movie about the Manhattan Project and the men who developed the atom bomb. With Brian Dennehy, David Strathairn, Michael Tucker. CBS, March 5.

50 Years of Television—A comprehensive documentary celebrating the 50th anniversary of the first public-television broadcast. Hosts include Walter Cronkite and Carl Reiner. CBS, Nov. 26.

The Final Days—A 1989 TV movie about the last days of the Richard Nixon presidency, based on the book by Bob Woodward and Carl Bernstein. With Lane Smith. ABC, Oct. 29.

First Born—Three-part miniseries about the life and loves of a first born of a species. With Charles Dance, Philip Madoc. Arts and Entertainment, June 17.

A Fool for You—A *Live from Lincoln Center* telecast of the ballet, choreographed by Peter Martins. With Ray Charles and his orchestra and the New York City Ballet Company. PBS, May 12.

Halftime—A documentary exploring the male mid-life transition as seen from the points of view of five 1963 Yale University graduates. PBS, July 26.

Intifada: The Palestinians and Israel—A documentary on the Palestinian uprising in the Israeli-occupied West Bank and Gaza Strip. PBS, Sept. 6.

Learning in America—The Education Race—A five-part series on U.S. schools. PBS, March 27.

---

system and insulate its programs from improper influences from politicians and corporate executives."

Cable Television. *The New York Times* reported that, only six years after there had been only one cable programming service in the black financially—Superstation TBS—12 of the 15 largest advertising-supported services were making money. The most successful were Turner Entertainment Networks' TBS and all-sports ESPN with $95 million in operating cash flow, followed in order by all-news CNN, music-video MTV, children-oriented Nickelodeon, general-interest USA Network, country-music Nashville Network, health and fitness Lifetime, and the religious CBN Family Channel with $13 million cash flow.

Another successful Turner Entertainment venture was TNT, specializing in vintage films and National Basketball Association cable broadcasts, which celebrated its first anniversary with *Variety* dubbing it "the benchmark for successful launches." NBC started an all-business cable news channel, CNBC, and HBO took a gamble on 24-hour mirth with its new comedy channel.

People. NBC's *Today* provided practically a solid year's grist for gossip columns. First, a confidential memo from anchor Bryant Gumbel, containing harsh criticism of several on-air colleagues, particularly clowning weatherman Willard Scott, was leaked and gleefully quoted in the news media. But the studio rancor was barely visible to the eager scrutiny of commentators and home viewers. Then, in a kind of epic showdown of journalistic queen bees, *Today* anchor Jane Pauley let her dismay be known when news reader Deborah Norville swiftly was promoted to co-anchor at a salary comparable to her own. Having achieved the longest *Today* tenure at 13 years, Pauley soon had an emotional leave-taking from the show,

Live from Lincoln Center—The New York Philharmonic Orchestra opens its season with a program of Wagner, Mahler, and Mozart. With Jessye Norman and conductor Zubin Mehta. PBS, Sept. 20.
Lonesome Dove—Four-part miniseries based on the novel by Larry McMurtry about two Texas rangers who decide to make a cattle drive to Montana. With Robert Duvall, Tommy Lee Jones, Robert Urich, Diane Lane, Anjelica Huston, Danny Glover, Frederic Forrest, Ricky Schroeder. CBS, Feb. 5.
Mr. Burns Goes to Washington—Documentarian Ken Burns uses interviews and archival materials to tell his story of the U.S. Congress in its bicentennial year. PBS, March 20.
The Moon Above, the Earth Below—A *CBS News Special* reporting on the July 20, 1969, moon landing by U.S. astronauts on the occasion of the 20th anniversary. With Dan Rather, Charles Kuralt, CBS, July 13.
My Name is Bill W.—A 1989 fact-based TV movie about the founding of Alcoholics Anonymous. With James Woods, James Garner. ABC, April 30.
A Night at the Joffrey—Three works from the ballet company's repertory by Frederick Ashton, William Forsythe, and Gerald Arpino. PBS, April 28.
Our Town—A *Great Performances* telecast of Thornton Wilder's classic play. With Eric Stoltz, Penelope Ann Miller. PBS, Nov. 3.
Paris Live!—A six-hour telecast from Paris on the occasion of the 200th anniversary of the French Revolution. Arts and Entertainment, July 14.
Peter Pan—A repeat of the 1960 production of the musical version of the James M. Barrie play. With Mary Martin, Cyril Ritchard. NBC, March 24.
Polly—A musical remake of the Walt Disney classic *Pollyanna.* With Keshia Knight Pulliam, Phylicia Rashad, Brandon Adams, Celeste Holm. NBC, Nov. 12.
The Rainbow—A three-part adaptation of the D.H. Lawrence novel. With Imogen Stubbs, Martin Wenner. Arts and Entertainment, Aug. 5.
Return to Crack Street—A *48 Hours* report on America's drug epidemic. With Dan Rather. CBS, Sept. 14.
Roe vs. Wade—A 1989 TV movie about the Texas woman whose unwanted pregnancy led to the 1973 abortion ruling by the U.S. Supreme Court. With Holly Hunter, Amy Madigan. NBC, May 15.
Show Boat—A *Great Performances* telecast of the Jerome Kern-Oscar Hammerstein musical based on the Edna Ferber novel about life on the Mississippi. With Eddie Bracken, Rebecca Baxter, Richard White, Shelly Burch, Robert Jensen, P.L. Brown, Lee Roy Reams. PBS, Oct. 27.
Small Sacrifices—A two-part 1989 fact-based TV movie about the mysterious shootings of three children whose mother comes under increasing suspicion. With Farrah Fawcett, John Shea, Ryan O'Neal. ABC, Nov. 12.
Struggle for Democracy—A ten-part series exploring the origins and the nature of democracy. With Patrick Watson. PBS, July 13.
Sweet Bird of Youth—A 1989 TV movie based on the Tennessee Williams play about an aging actress and a younger drifter. With Elizabeth Taylor, Mark Harmon, Cheryl Paris, Rip Torn. NBC, Oct. 1.
A Tale of Two Cities—A four-part adaptation of Charles Dickens' classic novel of the French Revolution. With Jean-Pierre Aumont, Serena Gordon, Gerard Klein, Kathie Kriegel, John Mills, Xavier Deluc, James Wilby. PBS, Nov. 19.
A Television Story—Documentary reporting on 50 years of television. NBC, May 31.
Till We Meet Again—Two-part miniseries based on the Judith Krantz best-seller. With Bruce Boxleitner, Michael York, Barry Bostwick, Mia Sara, Lucy Gutteridge, Courteney Cox, Maxwell Caulfield. CBS, Nov. 19.
Tommy—The Who rock group celebrates the 20th anniversary of their famous rock opera with Patti LaBelle, Phil Collins, Elton John, Billy Idol, Steve Winwood. Fox Network, Sept. 13.
A Tribute to Lucille Ball—A Bob Hope special in which the comedian offers a tribute to the late Lucille Ball. With George Burns, Danny Thomas, Betty White, Kirk Cameron. NBC, Sept. 23.
The Triumph of Charlie Parker—An *American Masters* telecast profiling the famed saxophonist. PBS, July 17.
Twist of Fate—Two-part 1989 TV movie about a Nazi officer who foresees the fall of the Third Reich and to save himself has plastic surgery and passes himself off as a Jew. With Ben Cross, John Glover, Ian Richardson. NBC, Jan. 8.
A Visit to the White House—A *Primetime Live* telecast in which President and Mrs. Bush provide a tour of the White House living quarters. With Sam Donaldson, Diane Sawyer. ABC, Sept. 21.
War and Remembrance—TV miniseries that presents the final 11½ hours of the 46-hour saga (including 1983's *Winds of War*) that presents events of World War II through the adventures of the Henry family. With Robert Mitchum, Jane Seymour, John Gielgud, Victoria Tennant, Hart Bochner, Barry Bostwick, Polly Bergen. ABC, May 7.
The Women of Brewster Place—Two-part 1989 TV movie about seven women in the ghetto who find the strength to survive. With Cicely Tyson, Oprah Winfrey, Mary Alice, Barbara Montgomery, Paula Kelly, Olivia Cole, Robin Givens, Jackée, Lynn Whitfield, Lonette McKee, Paul Winfield, Eugene Lee, Samm Art Williams. ABC, March 19.

---

announcing plans to appear in a new NBC prime-time magazine vehicle.

Although a great comeback story, comedian Jackie Mason could not make ABC's *Chicken Soup* fly. There was speculation that his popularity was hurt by remarks in the New York mayoral campaign that were considered racist.

Lucille Ball, the beloved TV institution (particularly on CBS' *I Love Lucy,* 1951–57), died at age 77 and was mourned by the nation and the world. (*See also* OBITUARIES.)

Radio. Despite reports of rising industry revenues—$7.9 billion in 1988, an 8.2% increase over 1987—radio mounted a $100 million public-relations drive to disprove reports of its widespread creative decline. Ten thousand radio stations went silent for 30 seconds at 7:42 A.M. on May 26, to dramatize the slogan: "Radio: What would life be without it?"

Garrison Keillor, the gentle and witty bard of mythical Lake Wobegon, MN, whose 1987 departure from National Public Radio (NPR) was mourned widely, returned to NPR. His new vehicle, *American Radio Company of the Air,* was billed as a similar, but not identical, music-and-humor format to his beloved and defunct *Prairie Home Companion.*

NBC, the company that originated radio network broadcasting in 1926, quietly shut down its radio network. *Variety* offered a full-page "Fond Farewell" to the network that once ruled the airwaves with Chet Huntley, Jimmy Durante, George Burns and Gracie Allen, and Edgar Bergen with his favorite dummy, Charlie McCarthy. Having reached its financial zenith in 1964, when it had a 36% share of national radio billing, the NBC radio network had been in a long decline, and the sale of its assets earned $253 million for NBC parent company General Electric.

DAN HULBERT
"The Atlanta Journal and Constitution"

Workers demonstrate against union representation at the Nissan Motor Manufacturing Corporation in Smyrna, TN. By a two-to-one margin, the United Auto Workers (UAW) lost a key representation vote on July 27.

© P. Casey Daley

TENNESSEE

In a nonelection year, political interest in Tennessee centered chiefly on legislative action and Gov. Ned Ray McWherter's announcement that he would seek a second term in 1990. The 59-year-old chief executive was elected in June as vice-chair of the National Governors' Association.

Legislature. To help provide for a record-breaking $7.7 billion budget, lawmakers in 1989 added almost $200 million in higher taxes and special fee increases—the highest since 1984. New taxes included a 4¢ increase on gasoline, making the state's levy on the fuel the highest in the nation. Increased funds are designed to build prisons to relieve crowded conditions, continue road building and road improvement at an accelerated pace, improve teachers' salaries, and meet spiraling education costs. Teachers, nevertheless, were unhappy with the amount of their pay raises; more than 1,600 marched on the state Capitol to present McWherter with a copy of their written grievances.

In other new laws, legislators completely rewrote the state's criminal code, eliminated certain loopholes in the state's lobbying and disclosure laws, established a Department of Youth Development to administer all juvenile correction programs, tightened drug-abuse laws, and established a statewide public-defender program. By early September, the 21 public-defender posts had been filled by gubernatorial appointment.

Corruption. The legislative session was marred by accusations that several lawmakers had taken bribes or otherwise might be indicted for wrongdoing. In July prominent Knoxville Democrat, state Rep. Ted Ray Miller, committed suicide a few days before he was scheduled to face federal charges of bribe taking. By the end of the year, another official had admitted to embezzlement and was granted immunity from prosecution in return for cooperation in the ongoing probe of public corruption. At the same time, McWherter and prominent Democrats called for the resignation of State Election Commission Chair Thomas Powell of Memphis, because of a federal indictment charging tax evasion, mail fraud, and other crimes.

New Prisons. The first of six new prisons became operational. The new prison near Nashville has a capacity for 652 people. Another new prison, 100 mi (160 km) north of Memphis, in Lauderdale County, was scheduled for opening early in 1990, while the remaining four would open in 1991 and 1992.

Economy. Industry continued to develop primarily in the urban and suburban areas of central and eastern Tennessee. Nissan Motor Manufacturing Corporation, located near Nashville, announced a $490 million expansion which, when completed, would add 2,000 more workers to its 3,215 employees. Production was expected to increase from a current 220,000 annual units to nearly twice that number by 1990. Other industry expansions have helped keep the state's unemployment rate below the national average.

While 1988's drought conditions curtailed crop production, heavy rains throughout the spring and early summer in 1989 caused farm-

TENNESSEE • Information Highlights

Area: 42,144 sq mi (109 152 km^2).
Population (July 1, 1988): 4,895,000.
Chief Cities (July 1, 1986 est.): Nashville-Davidson, the capital, 473,670; Memphis, 652,640; Knoxville, 173,210; Chattanooga, 162,170; Clarksville (1980 census), 54,777.
Government (1989): *Chief Officer*—governor, Ned McWherter (D); *General Assembly*—Senate, 33 members; House of Representatives, 99 members.
State Finances (fiscal year 1988): *Revenue,* $7,798,000,000; *expenditure,* $7,082,000,000.
Personal Income (1988): $67,909,000,000; per capita, $13,873.
Labor Force (June 1989): *Civilian labor force,* 2,364,700; *unemployed,* 130,900 (5.5% of total force).
Education: *Enrollment* (fall 1987)—public elementary schools, 582,000; public secondary, 241,000; colleges and universities, 202,006. *Public school expenditures* (1987–88), $2,370,392,000 ($2,902 per pupil).

ers to fall behind in spring plantings. Thousands of acres normally devoted to soybeans went unplanted, but corn, drilled in just before the spring rains became heavy, yielded well, as did hay. Cotton, wheat, and tobacco production was down.

Legal Precedent. In a bizarre custody case heard at Maryville and watched across the nation, Judge W. Dale Young, ruling that life begins at conception, awarded custody of seven fertilized frozen eggs to a divorced woman who had produced the eggs.

ROBERT E. CORLEW
Middle Tennessee State University

TERRORISM

From Islamic extremists in Lebanon to drug traffickers in Colombia, terrorism continued to be a major problem for governments and societies throughout the world in 1989.

Hostage Killing. The first major terrorist-related crisis for the Bush administration unfolded during the summer when Hezbollah, the Islamic fundamentalist terrorist group based in Lebanon, claimed that they had killed American Lt. Col. William Higgins in retaliation for Israel's abduction of a Hezbollah leader, Sheik Abdul Karim Obeid. Higgins had been kidnapped early in 1988 while serving as chief of staff of the UN Truce Supervision Organization in Lebanon.

Although Hezbollah produced a videotape of Higgins hanging from a post, it was not certain at what point in time he actually had been murdered. Following the news of his death and a subsequent threat by the terrorists to kill another American hostage, Joseph Cicippio, if Israel did not release Obeid, the U.S.S. *Coral Sea* headed for the coast of Lebanon for a possible retaliatory strike. The crisis subsided when Hezbollah "suspended" the death sentence against Cicippio.

Rushdie Affair. Perhaps the most unusual terrorist incident in 1989 was the highly publicized death threat issued by Iran's leader Ayatollah Khomeini against Salman Rushdie, the author of a controversial book, *The Satanic Verses,* that many Muslims found blasphemous. Bookstores in many countries that carried Rushdie's novel were firebombed, and a Muslim leader in Belgium was assassinated after criticizing Khomeini for issuing the death sentence. (*See also* BIOGRAPHY—*Rushdie;* LITERATURE—*Overview*.)

Airplane Bombings. As 1989 drew to a close, there was still no official confirmation that the Popular Front for the Liberation of Palestine-General Command (PFLP-GC) was responsible for the December 1988 bombing of Pan Am flight 103 over Lockerbie, Scotland, which claimed the lives of 270 people, including several Americans. There is, nevertheless, strong circumstantial evidence pointing to the PFLP-GC and its leader, Ahmed Jabril, as the perpetrators of the midair bombing. A few months prior to the tragedy, West German police arrested several PFLP-GC members and found in their possession a plastic explosive hidden in a radio-cassette player, the same type of device used to blow up the Pan Am flight.

A DC-10 en route from Chad to France blew up over Nigeria on September 19, killing all 171 people aboard. French investigators said a bomb probably caused the explosion. One pro-Iranian group claimed credit for the act, but the case was still open at year's end.

The United States. In San Diego, the van of Sharon Rogers, wife of the U.S. Navy captain whose ship in July of 1988 mistakenly shot down an Iranian civilian airliner in the Persian Gulf, was the target of a pipe-bombing on March 10. It was not clear, however, whether the attack was in retaliation for the accidental downing of the Iranian plane.

Among the legal victories over terrorism in 1989 was the U.S. conviction of Fawaz Younis on charges of air piracy and seizure of hostages. The Lebanese terrorist had been involved in the hijacking of a Royal Jordanian airliner in 1985 in which two Americans were on board. U.S. courts in February sentenced Yu Kikumura to 30 years in jail. Kikumura, a Japanese nationalist, had been convicted of plotting bombings in the United States.

Latin America. Among the major terrorist incidents in Latin America in 1989 were the assassination of El Salvador's Attorney General Roberto Garciá Alvarado—the highest-ranking government official ever to be killed by leftist guerrillas in El Salvador—and the assassination of a leading presidential candidate in Colombia who was advocating a tough stand on drugs. That killing led to a new declaration of "war" on drugs by the Colombian government and to an influx of $65 million in military aid from the United States. "Narcoterrorism," though, continued to plague Colombia throughout the remainder of the year as the drug lords set off bombings and killed judges in order to intimidate the Colombian government.

IRA. Terrorist incidents in the United Kingdom included the killing of two senior leaders of the Royal Ulster Constabulary by the Irish Republican Army (IRA) in March, and the bombing of the Royal Marines School of Music in a southeastern English village in September, which killed ten people and wounded 22 others. The IRA in 1989 attacked British targets in Northern Ireland, within England, and in several countries on the European continent.

Other Events. The Red Army Faction assassinated a leading West German banker on November 20, while on November 22 the new president of Lebanon, Rene Moawad, was killed in a bombing.

JEFFREY D. SIMON, *The RAND Corporation*

TEXAS

By late 1989 indications were that the Texas economy had bottomed out and that a gradual upturn had begun. Oil and gas prices stabilized and a greater national demand for gas was viewed as a favorable omen. Oil reserves had been depleted nationwide, and an anticipated beneficial tax climate would mean renewed drilling in Texas. Real-estate prices tended upward and mercantile sales were brisk. At one time among the highest in the nation, the Texas jobless rate was down to about 7% at midyear.

Texas was hard-hit by banking's savings and loan (S&L) scandal but the federally financed bailout restored confidence in that area (*see* special report, page 130). Galveston was hurt by Hurricane Jenny in October.

Politics. On the state gubernatorial level, Gov. William ("Bill") Clements (R) indicated he would not seek reelection in 1990. Kent Hance, a former member of the U.S. House of Representatives from Lubbock, and Clayton Williams, an independent oilman, became candidates for the Republican nomination in the primaries. Both oppose a state income tax and endorse a "law and order" antidrug platform. For the Democrats, the candidates seemed to be state Treasurer Ann Richards and Attorney General Jim Mattox. Both favor an increase in corporate income taxes and greater funding for education and prison reform. Former Gov. Mark White (D) also entered the race.

Texas was the scene of two special elections for seats to the U.S. House of Representatives in 1989. Following the resignation of House Speaker Jim Wright (D) in the 12th District, Preston M. (Pete) Geren, a 37-year-old Democratic lawyer, was elected to fill the vacancy. Wright, who had been a member of the House since 1955 and speaker since 1987, resigned from Congress in the midst of an extensive ethics investigation (*see* special report, page 540). Another Texas Democrat, Rep. Mickey Leland of the 18th District (Houston), was killed in a plane crash during a humanitarian mission to Ethiopia in August. He was succeeded by Craig Washington, a 48-year-old state senator.

El Paso City Councilwoman Suzie Azar scored a landslide victory in the city's runoff mayoralty race on May 27. Dallas Mayor Annette Strauss was reelected, as was Houston's Mayor Kathryn Whitmire, who won a fifth consecutive term. San Antonio's former Mayor Lila Cockrell was returned to the post. Six major Texas cities now have women mayors. In Fort Worth, Mayor Bob Bolen was returned for a fourth two-year term. On the November ballot were 21 propositions, including an approved $500 million water measure for Texas border towns and an approved $400 million measure for new prisons. A proposal to raise state legislators' salaries was defeated.

Funding and Education. In a 1989 unanimous decision, the Texas Supreme Court held that the legislature must provide for "equal funding" of local public school systems throughout the state. In the words of Associate Justice Oscar Mauzy, a "band-aid" solution to the problem would not suffice. "Equalization" of school funds has been hailed as long overdue by black and Hispanic activists. However, implementing the court's mandate would require a massive infusion of state funds.

Texas also was under a federal court order to build more prisons and improve existing conditions. Governor Clements promised to call a special meeting of the legislature to deal with financing these reforms. Although a lottery proposal failed to pass in previous sessions, partisans of a state-sponsored lottery were encouraged by the present situation. Organized religious groups, particularly Baptists and Methodists, still opposed a lottery. However, public-opinion polls suggested that a majority of Texans find that solution preferable to a state income tax.

On the level of higher education, college enrollments were up throughout Texas. The University of Texas at Austin (52,000) and the University of Houston (35,000) attained record highs. Despite the fact that admission standards had been tightened, officials at Texas A & M University also reported a moderate increase. *U.S. News and World Report* ranked Trinity, a private school in San Antonio, among the best "regional colleges and universities" in the United States.

Sports. After an absence of some 40 years, thoroughbred racing returned to Texas on a local option basis. A track was in operation at Brady, TX, and sites were contemplated for the Houston and Dallas areas. San Antonio approved plans to build a 65,000-seat domed stadium.

STANLEY E. SIEGEL, *University of Houston*

TEXAS • Information Highlights

Area: 266,807 sq mi (691 030 km²).
Population (July 1, 1988): 16,841,000.
Chief Cities (July 1, 1986 est.): Austin, the capital, 466,550; Houston, 1,728,910; Dallas, 1,003,520; San Antonio, 914,350; El Paso, 491,800; Fort Worth, 429,550; Corpus Christi, 263,900.
Government (1989): *Chief Officers*—governor, William Clements (R); lt. gov., William P. Hobby (D). *Legislature*—Senate, 31 members; House of Representatives, 150 members.
State Finances (fiscal year 1988): *Revenue,* $26,650,000,000; *expenditure,* $22,790,000,000.
Personal Income (1988): $245,647,000,000; per capita, $14,586.
Labor Force (June 1989): *Civilian labor force,* 8,332,900; *unemployed,* 587,700 (7.1% of total force).
Education: *Enrollment* (fall 1987)—public elementary schools, 2,351,000; public secondary, 886,000; colleges and universities, 802,226. *Public school expenditures* (1987–88), $11,132,002,000 ($3,722 per pupil).

THAILAND

Thailand's economy grew by nearly 10% in 1989, helping to make the reform government of Prime Minister Chatichai Choonhavan increasingly popular at home, and likely increasing Thailand's stature abroad.

Politics. Chatichai's government, which took office in August 1988, was the first in Thai history to be composed entirely of civilians who had been elected to parliament. Democracy was the keynote agenda item of Chatichai's administration. He held "mobile" cabinet meetings in some of the more depressed regions of the country to allow the people of these areas a voice in development plans. An amnesty was granted to persons who had been jailed as alleged Communists.

In addition to being democratic, Chatichai's government was pro-business. During its first year in office, it invested enormous sums of money in economic development projects and still managed to produce a budget surplus.

Although Chatichai was a former military officer, his relations with the powerful Thai Army commander, Gen. Chaovalit Yongchaiyut, were somewhat rocky. Chaovalit, who made no secret of his desire to be prime minister, accused the government of corruption and criticized the active role of Chatichai's young academic advisers. One of them, Sukhumbhand Paribatra, was forced to resign after charging the military with being too political. But Chatichai avoided an open split with the military by providing them with a generous budget while deftly limiting their voice in politics.

With decreasing tension on the Laotian border and the withdrawal of Vietnamese troops from Cambodia, Thailand faced less of an external security threat. The fighting in Cambodia remained a worry, as did the chronic instability in Burma, but the Thai people seemed to like Chatichai's policy of trying to make Indochina a "marketplace instead of a battleground."

THAILAND • Information Highlights

Official Name: Kingdom of Thailand (conventional); Prathet Thai (Thai).
Location: Southeast Asia.
Area: 198,456 sq mi (514 000 km²).
Population (mid-1989 est.): 55,600,000.
Chief City (Dec. 31, 1986 est.): Bangkok, the capital, 5,468,915.
Government: *Head of state,* Bhumibol Adulyadej, king (acceded June 1946). *Head of government,* Chatichai Choonhavan, prime minister (took office August 1988).
Monetary Unit: Baht (25.74 baht equal U.S.$1, July 1989).
Gross National Product (1988 est. U.S.$): $52,200,-000,000.
Economic Index (Bangkok, 1988): *Consumer Prices* (1980 = 100), all items, 139.0; food, 124.5.
Foreign Trade (1988 U.S.$): *Imports,* $18,559,-000,000; *exports,* $15,384,000,000.

Economics. Thai economic growth continued to be led by the export sector, and the United States was again the leading customer. With prices fairly strong for many Thai commodities, exports were up 27% compared with 1988. This helped to produce a budget surplus as well as a current accounts surplus. And the government was in the happy position of being able to buy popularity by raising the salaries of civil servants and by twice raising the minimum wage. Nevertheless, the minimum wage in Thailand remained one of the lowest in the region. Efforts to increase the strength of labor unions and to introduce welfare legislation in parliament produced no immediate results. Meanwhile, rising inflation ate up some of the workers' gains, especially in Bangkok and other urban areas.

In anticipation of greater stability in Indochina, the Thai government was making plans to develop the chronically poor northeast region as an industrial and commercial hub for trade with Indochina. The plans included upgrading the airport at Ubon to international status.

Thailand's increasing economic maturity was demonstrated by a successful bond issue which was floated in the United States. The Thai government planned to use the proceeds to pay back a World Bank loan which had a less predictable interest rate. Two Japanese auto manufacturers, Toyota and Nissan, were planning to use diesel engines manufactured in Thailand in cars that would be assembled from parts made in Thailand and other Association of Southeast Asian Nations (ASEAN) countries.

Foreign Affairs. Although Thailand welcomed the withdrawal of Vietnamese forces from Cambodia, there was increasing public disagreement among Thai leaders over Indochina policy. One of Chatichai's most publicized feuds was with his foreign minister, Siddhi Savetsila. As a former foreign minister, Chatichai seemed quite willing to take the lead in shaping foreign policy—as when he invited Cambodian leader Hun Sen to Bangkok. This was an open challenge to the foreign ministry's policy of pursuing a coalition of all four Cambodian factions. Foreign Minister Siddhi demonstrated his own independence by traveling to Hanoi to meet with the Vietnamese foreign minister. Siddhi and Chatichai also made separate visits to Washington to meet with U.S. leaders.

For the past decade, the Cambodian conflict had held together the ASEAN, and Thailand played a leading role in the organization as the "front-line state" nearest Cambodia. Vietnam's military withdrawal from Cambodia challenged Thailand to find a way to use its economic strength to help stabilize Indochina.

PETER A. POOLE
Author, "The Vietnamese in Thailand"

THEATER

The 1989 year was one of double messages in the American theater, when even the best news contained the sobering reminders of the bad. It began with *Jerome Robbins' Broadway,* the magnificent tour of the golden age of American musicals by way of their Robbins' dances, from *On the Town* (1944) to *West Side Story* (1957) to *Fiddler on the Roof* (1964). But while the musical swept the Tony Awards (including a trophy for the grand director-choreographer himself) against the pipsqueak competition typical of the 1980s, it could not help but also be a ringing reproach to the lackluster musicals of the post-*Fiddler* era. It was a bittersweet reminder of an art form that still could impersonate skillfully the greatness of its past, but seemed to have no future. The death of Irving Berlin at 101 only seemed to underline the transition.

The year ended, however, on a note that seemed to confirm the promising ascendancy of America's nonprofit resident theaters. Rhapsodic notices greeted the Guthrie Theatre of Minneapolis and director JoAnne Akalaitis following the rare staging of Jean Genet's 1961 visionary drama, *The Screens. Newsweek* critic Jack Kroll concluded that "A healthy American theater would find the money to enable this landmark production to tour the country." Few would dispute that overall diagnosis of the American theater's condition, but scattered success stories like the Guthrie's continued to unfold across the country.

Broadway. As a commercial institution, Broadway measures its success in terms of box-office sales, and by that gauge the 1988–89 season, which officially closed May 28, was a mixed affair. Box-office receipts set a record level of $262 million, but so did ticket prices, finally jumping the controversial $50 barrier for a $55 "top" at *Jerome Robbins' Broadway.* The season set an all-time low mark for new productions—30. Meanwhile, the 8 million attendance, while slightly off the previous season's pace, still represented a comeback from the severe doldrums of the mid-1980s.

But the numbers again were deceptive. A great proportion of the sales went to previously entrenched British import musicals (*Cats, Les Misérables, Phantom of the Opera*), and the season provided only *Jerome Robbins' Broadway* as a major reinforcement hit.

Black and Blue, a jazz revue that won a best actress/musical Tony Award for veteran Ruth Brown, and the lighthearted comic-book adventure musical, *Starmites,* were the only other new 1988–89 musical entries that garnered any critical respectability. One of the bombs, a musical about alimony jail called *Welcome to the Club,* was newsworthy because its composer was Cy Coleman of *Sweet Charity* fame and its author was Ernest Hemingway biographer A. E. Hotchner. The crop of musicals was so weak, in fact, that the Tony nominating committee decided not to give awards in the best book and best score categories, and debate flared anew over whether to make off-Broadway productions eligible.

The Heidi Chronicles was one fully scripted, new American play to enjoy both serious critical acclaim and major box-office success on Broadway. Wendy Wasserstein's witty

One of the high points of the Broadway musical year was the acclaimed production of "Jerome Robbins' Broadway," presenting the dances of director-choreographer Robbins from past Broadway musicals with which he was associated.

© Martha Swope

and poignant comedy-drama, tracing a young woman's coming of age through the 1960s, 1970s, and 1980s, and featuring an exquisite performance by Joan Allen in the title role, won both the Pulitzer Prize and the Tony for best play.

Tony Awards for best actress and best actor both went to performers in more popular, crowd-pleasing plays that happened to originate in London with Andrew Lloyd Webber's production firm. The winning actress was Pauline Collins, whose utterly lovable and authentic solo performance as a yearning British housewife elevated *Shirley Valentine,* and the actor was New York veteran Philip Bosco, whose apoplectic opera impresario similarly redeemed the so-so 1930s-style farce, *Lend Me a Tenor.* Madeline Kahn was also a best actress nominee in the role made famous by Judy Holliday in *Born Yesterday,* an otherwise lackluster and short-lived revival that also starred Ed Asner.

Another farce, *Rumors* (1988), was an automatic hit on the strength of Neil Simon's name, although many critics found it a little crass and retrograde after the playwright's fine seriocomic trilogy of the mid-1980s that culminated in *Broadway Bound.* On the other hand, Richard Greenberg's scathing comedy of Yuppie social conscience, *Eastern Standard* (1988), and Michael Weller's resonant family drama, *Spoils of War* (1988), featuring a stunning performance by Kate Nelligan, were fine plays that deserved better success.

Athleticism was the Broadway calling card for Mikhail Baryshnikov and Bill Irwin. But the great Russian-born dancer made his Broadway debut vigorously mimicking a man-insect in an ill-conceived dramatization of Franz Kafka's *Metamorphosis,* while the brilliant vaudevillian

BROADWAY OPENINGS 1989

MUSICALS

Black and Blue, written and directed by Claudio Segovia and Hector Orezzoli; with Ruth Brown; Jan. 26–.

Chu Chem, music by Mitch Leigh; lyrics by Jim Haines and Jack Wohl; book by Ted Allan; directed by Albert Marre; with Mark Zeller, Irving Burton; April 7–May 14.

City of Angels, music by Cy Coleman; lyrics by David Zippel; book by Larry Gelbart; directed by Michael Blakemore; with James Naughton; Dec. 11–.

Dangerous Games, music by Astor Piazzolla; lyrics by William Finn; book by Jim Lewis and Graciela Daniele; directed by Ms. Daniele; with Gregory Mitchell and Rene Ceballos; Oct. 19–21.

Grand Hotel, music and lyrics by Robert Wright and George Forrest; book by Luther Davis; directed by Tommy Tune; with Karen Akers; Nov. 12–.

Gypsy!, music by Jule Styne; lyrics by Stephen Sondheim; book by Arthur Laurents; directed by Mr. Laurents; with Tyne Daly, Jonathan Hadary; Nov. 16–.

Jerome Robbins' Broadway, conceived, choreographed, and directed by Jerome Robbins; with Jason Alexander, Charlotte D'Amboise; Feb. 26–.

Meet Me In St. Louis, music and lyrics by Hugh Martin and Ralph Blane; book by Hugh Wheeler; directed by Louis Burke; with George Hearn, Milo O'Shea; Nov. 2–.

Prince of Central Park, music by Don Sebesky; lyrics by Gloria Nissenson; book by Evan H. Rhodes; directed by Tony Tanner; with Jo Anne Worley; Nov. 9–11.

Shenandoah, music by Gary Geld; lyrics by Peter Udell; book by James Lee Barrett, Mr. Udell, and Philip Rose; directed by Rose; with John Cullum; Aug. 8–Sept. 2.

Starmites, music and lyrics by Barry Keating; book by Stuart Ross and Mr. Keating; directed by Larry Carpenter; with Gabriel Barre; April 27–June 18.

Sweeney Todd, music and lyrics by Stephen Sondheim; book by Hugh Wheeler; adaptation by Christopher Bond; directed by Susan H. Schulman; with Bob Gunton, Beth Fowler; Sept. 14–.

Threepenny Opera, music by Kurt Weill; book and lyrics by Bertolt Brecht; directed by John Dexter; with Sting, Nancy Ringham, Georgia Brown; Nov. 5–Dec. 31.

Welcome to the Club, music by Cy Coleman; lyrics by Mr. Coleman and A. E. Hotchner; book by Mr. Hotchner; directed by Peter Mark Schifter; with Avery Schreiber, Marilyn Sokol; April 13–22.

PLAYS

Artist Descending a Staircase, by Tom Stoppard; directed by Tim Luscombe; with Harold Gould, John McMartin, Paxton Whitehead; Nov. 30–Dec. 31.

Born Yesterday, by Garson Kanin; directed by Josephine R. Abady; with Edward Asner, Madeline Kahn; Jan. 29–June 11.

Café Crown, by Hy Kraft; directed by Martin Charnin; with Eli Wallach, Anne Jackson; Feb. 18–March 26.

The Circle, by W. Somerset Maugham; directed by Brian Murray; with Rex Harrison, Glynis Johns; Nov. 20–.

Eastern Standard, by Richard Greenberg; directed by Michael Engler; with Dylan Baker, Patricia Clarkson, Keven Conroy, Anne Meara; Jan. 5–March 25.

A Few Good Men, by Aaron Sorkin; directed by Don Scardino; with Tom Hulce; Nov. 15–.

Ghetto, by Joshua Sobol; directed by Gedalia Besser; with Avner Eisenberg, George Hearn; April 30–May 28.

The Heidi Chronicles, by Wendy Wasserstein; directed by Daniel Sullivan; with Joan Allen (March 9–Sept. 4), Christine Lahti (Sept. 5–); March 9–.

Hizzoner, by Paul Shyre; directed by John Going; with Tony LoBianco; Feb. 23–March 5.

Largely New York, written and directed by Bill Irwin; with Mr. Irwin, Margaret Eginton; May 1–Sept. 2.

Lend Me a Tenor, by Ken Ludwig; directed by Jerry Zaks; with Victor Garber, Tovah Feldshuh; March 2–.

Love Letters, by A. R. Gurney; directed by John Tillinger; Oct. 31–.

Mastergate, by Larry Gelbart; directed by Michael Engler; with Jerome Kilty; Oct. 12–Dec. 10.

The Merchant of Venice, by William Shakespeare; directed by Peter Hall; with Dustin Hoffman; Dec. 19–.

Metamorphosis, adapted by Steven Berkoff from Franz Kafka's story; directed by Mr. Berkoff; with Mikhail Baryshnikov; March 6–July 1.

Orpheus Descending, by Tennessee Williams; directed by Peter Hall; with Vanessa Redgrave; Sept. 24–Dec. 17.

Run for Your Wife, written and directed by Ray Cooney; with Mr. Cooney, Paxton Whitehead; March 7–April 9.

The Secret Rapture, written and directed by David Hare; with Blair Brown, Mary Beth Hurt; Oct. 26–Nov. 4.

Shirley Valentine, by Willy Russell; directed by Simon Callow; with Pauline Collins (Feb. 16–July 1), Patricia Kilgarriff (July 2–16), Ellen Burstyn (July 17–Nov. 25); Feb. 16–Nov. 25.

The Tenth Man, by Paddy Chayefsky; directed by Ulu Grosbard; Dec. 10–.

Tru, written and directed by Jay Presson Allen; with Robert Morse; Dec. 14–.

OTHER ENTERTAINMENT

Sid Caesar and Company, a comedy revue with music; with Sid Caesar; Nov. 1–Nov. 5.

Mandy Patinkin in Concert: Dress Casual, a concert; July 25–Sept. 16.

Irwin earned high acclaim for his evening of inventive, witty clowning and pantomime in *Largely New York.*

As the 1989–90 season began to warm up in the fall, rock star Sting took a noisy tumble in his Broadway debut, a panned production of the Brecht/Weill classic of 1928, *The Threepenny Opera.* But the musical scene was kept simmering with acclaimed revivals of the 1959 hit *Gypsy* (starring Tyne Daly of television's *Cagney and Lacey,* a surprisingly effective heir to Ethel Merman as Mama Rose) and the 1979 epic *Sweeney Todd.* Both revivals reaffirmed the durable mastery of Stephen Sondheim, lyricist of the former and composer-lyricist of the latter.

Tommy Tune, conspicuously absent from Broadway since 1984's *My One and Only,* brought some of his signature stylishness back to Broadway as director-choreographer of the musical *Grand Hotel,* adapted from the Greta Garbo film. Honing in on the ripe and absurd possibilities of the 1987 Iran-contra hearings that starred Col. Oliver North, Larry Gelbart *(Tootsie)* brought witty political satire back to Broadway with his new fall entry, *Mastergate.*

Vanessa Redgrave delivered what some described as the performance of her life as a love-starved Southerner in the London import *Orpheus Descending,* with the almost operatic style of director Peter Hall (*Amadeus*) encouraging a new assessment of this previously belittled 1957 Tennessee Williams drama. As 1989 drew to a close, the other eagerly awaited Hall production from London was *The Merchant of Venice,* with Dustin Hoffman in his Shakespearean debut in the role of Shylock.

Joan Allen was a hit in "The Heidi Chronicles," Wendy Wasserstein's popular comedy-drama that won both the Pulitzer Prize and the Tony Award for best play.

© Peter Cunningham

Off-Broadway. The 1988–89 theater season was not a particularly strong one for artistic discovery, overall, for the principal off-Broadway resident theaters that specialize in new works—Manhattan Theatre Club (MTC), Playwrights Horizons, Circle Repertory Company, and the New York Shakespeare Festival. Still, individual productions shone.

A case in point was Christopher Walken's scalding title-role performance in Steven Berkoff's fierce, dark production of *Coriolanus,* which began early in the 1988–89 season at the Shakesfest. Another memorable production was MTC's beautifully played *Aristocrats,* an almost Chekhovian saga of a disintegrating, once-affluent Irish clan by Brian Friel.

The mores of the well-heeled also were lampooned, although more gently, in the popular commercial production of A.R. Gurney's *The Cocktail Hour,* which opened in late 1988 with old pros Nancy Marchand and Keene Curtis in the highly civilized comedy. Another popular mainstream comedy was Larry L. King's *The Night Hank Williams Died,* providing a nostalgic view of an aspiring country singer in a tiny Texas town of the early 1950s.

One of the exceedingly scarce promising musicals on the off-Broadway circuit came from the trenchant composer-lyricist Randy Newman, whose various songs were strung together by author Kim Friedman with the device of assembling a cross-section of travelers in a Southern bus station in the 1960s. There were high hopes for *The Warrior Ant,* the multicultural musical extravaganza by composer Bob Telson and avant-garde director-playwright Lee Breuer (who earlier had teamed for *Gospel at Colonus*), but the sprawling epic at the Brooklyn Academy of Music generally was deemed a disappointment.

Three provocative new plays dealt with the ethical void of the 1980s' business landscape. In 1988–89, they were *Other People's Money,* Jerry Sterner's study of a corporate takeover featuring a blistering performance by Kevin Conway, and *Emerald City,* David Williamson's homegrown critique of the show-business game in Australia. Early in the 1989–90 season, playwright David Mamet continued his famed skewering of capitalism with the one-act *Bobby Gould in Hell,* in which the unscrupulous Hollywood producer-hero of Mamet's *Speed-the-Plow* (1988) gets his comeuppance in the nether regions.

The glamour event of the off-Broadway season was the Lincoln Center production of Samuel Beckett's *Waiting for Godot* (1988), with Mike Nichols directing F. Murray Abraham, Bill Irwin, and superstar comedians Steve Martin and Robin Williams. The production received mixed reviews, and its claim to fame may have been the controversy it generated when even Lincoln-Center subscribers could not get tickets.

Resident Theaters. In *The New York Times,* writer Hilary De Vries assessed the nation's 320 nonprofit, resident theaters as "at a crossroads" and expressed concern that "their ability to nurture pioneering works may decline." With federal funding having shrunk to less than half of the 10% of theater budgets it accounted for in the 1960s and with much of the best talent —including playwrights—defecting to the better-paying worlds of film and television, the resident theaters were responding with economically safer and more popular fare, shortened production calendars, and shared production with other theaters.

Production sharing, when two or more theaters combine resources to mount a production that can visit all the participating theaters, was more frequent, but that did not always mean an artistic deficit. A striking example was *The Misanthrope,* a coproduction of the La Jolla (CA) Playhouse and the Goodman Theatre of Chicago, in which Goodman artistic director Robert Falls set Molière's posturing sycophants in an apt milieu: 1989 Hollywood.

The resident theaters also were quick and passionate to exploit the new theatrical possibilities of *glasnost,* with many theaters suddenly able to contact their Soviet counterparts directly and bypass the old, censorious machinery of the Soviet Ministry of Culture. The landmark event of the U.S.-Soviet exchanges was the performance of the Maly Theatre of Leningrad at the Old Globe Theatre of San Diego (as part of the citywide arts festival, "Treasures of the Soviet Union") in its legendary epic *Brothers and Sisters.* Based on three novels by Fyodor Abramov, the play chronicled the immense hardships endured by northern Russian peasants in the years following World War II. With its harsh, implicit condemnation of the Soviet political system, the export represented a stunning example of the new "openness."

Other Soviet guest companies included the Theatre Mussoviet, which brought to the Alliance Theatre of Atlanta *My Dear Helena Sergevnya,* its once-banned study of cynical Soviet youth scheming to cheat on their exams and avoid being drafted for the conflict in Afghanistan. (The Alliance sent to Moscow's Mussoviet *Driving Miss Daisy,* Alfred Uhry's Pulitzer Prize-winning comedy that distills 25 years of American race relations into the complex relationship between an Atlanta matron and her black chauffeur.) Also, the expatriate Soviet director Jonas Jursas staged Dostoyevsky's *The Idiot* at the Dallas Theater Center, and the fabled Moscow Art Theatre was in residence at the annual "Classics in Context" festival of the Actors Theatre of Louisville (ATL).

Meanwhile, ATL's other major annual festival, the Humana Festival of New Plays, continued its drought of good new works despite some commissions from well-known writers. Seasoned dramatist Arthur Kopit submitted an easy spoof of David Mamet, *Bone-the-Fish.* William F. Buckley, Jr., was criticized not only for his cold-war suspense drama, *Stained Glass,* but also for receiving a relatively generous fee.

© Martha Swope

British actress Vanessa Redgrave received new critical accolades for her performance in Peter Hall's production of the Tennessee Williams drama "Orpheus Descending."

San Diego's Old Globe continued to be a dependable developer of new scripts for New York (*The Cocktail Hour*) as well as a tryout venue for New York-bound commercial productions (*Rumors*), but the Seattle Repertory Theatre may have originated the most intelligent brace of plays to be on Broadway during 1989—the stylish comedies *Eastern Standard* and *The Heidi Chronicles.* American Repertory Theatre of Cambridge, MA, premiered *Mastergate* and propelled it to New York, and the Goodman sent its landmark *Grapes of Wrath* to Great Britain and prepared for a Broadway mounting in 1990.

The Hartford Stage Company received the 1989 special Tony Award for achievement by a resident theater, and artistic director Mark Lamos' proficiency for stylish classics was validated further when he was invited to stage Shakespeare's *Measure for Measure* at Lincoln Center.

DAN HULBERT
"The Atlanta Journal and Constitution"

TRANSPORTATION

Downtrends in traffic and earnings affected many North American freight and passenger carriers in 1989, as overall economic growth slackened and some key industries such as automobile manufacturing suffered declines in sales.

Airlines. Air-passenger traffic showed strength early in the year, but softened following fare increases of 16% each in February and March. The 261.8 million passengers carried by major U.S.-based airlines from January through July 1989 matched traffic levels for the same period in 1988. A general decline in travel from July through September, together with rising fuel costs and promotional fare cuts intended to increase traffic, caused several major carriers' net income to decline in the third quarter. Of particular surprise was the $77.7 million net loss reported by USAir, which had been among the industry's best performers.

U.S.-based regional and commuter airlines outperformed the majors, with a 20.3% increase in passengers carried between January and August over the same period in 1988. NWA, Inc., the parent of Northwest Airlines, was bought by an investor group including KLM Royal Dutch Airlines. Following expressions of concern over foreign control of U.S.-domiciled air carriers by Secretary of Transportation Samuel Skinner, KLM's stake in the buyout was cut from $400 million to $175 million. United Airlines (UAL) also became the object of two buyout offers, but neither was completed. On October 5 real-estate investor Donald J. Trump bid $7.5 billion for AMR Corporation, the parent of American Airlines. Trump soon withdrew his bid. Debt-heavy Braniff, Inc., filed for bankruptcy on September 28.

A realignment in European air transport occurred on December 13, when KLM and British Airways agreed to acquire a 20% shareholding each in Sabena Belgian World Airlines and rename the company Sabena World Airlines. In the Pacific Rim area, Delta and Singapore Airlines signed a joint marketing agreement.

Aviation officials in the Soviet Union began efforts to form a private enterprise airline that would compete with Aeroflot Soviet Airlines on long-haul domestic and international routes. Delegations of Soviet aviation officials visited Boeing Commercial Airplane Company and McDonnell Douglas Corporation to explore ways for equipping the proposed new line with U.S.-built aircraft. Separately, Aeroflot held talks about possible acquisition of Boeing 747-400 and McDonnell Douglas MD-11 aircraft.

Corporate changes occurred in the cargo sector of air transport. On January 31, Federal Express Corporation, famed for its express package delivery service, purchased Tiger International, Inc., the world's largest general freight air carrier. On April 17, CF AirFreight and Emery Air Freight merged their operations under the name Emery Worldwide.

Airline pricing and other competitive practices drew rising criticism during the year. The Justice Department's Antitrust Division began an investigation to determine whether some airlines might have used their computer networks to coordinate fare increases illegally.

Bus. Greyhound Lines, Inc., the largest U.S. intercity bus operator, reduced fares at three different times during the year, in an effort to continue the growth in passenger traffic that it experienced in 1988 (up 10% over 1987). Success was achieved in the first quarter, with a 20% rise in the number of passengers carried over the same period in 1988.

Minneapolis-based Jefferson Transportation Company, a large regional operator of scheduled, charter, and tour bus services, filed for bankruptcy on October 27, but continued to operate.

Rail. Amtrak's intercity passenger traffic remained almost static during the company's 1989 fiscal year (Oct. 1, 1988-Sept. 30, 1989). Passengers carried declined by 0.5% over the previous year, while passenger miles increased 3.2%, indicating a shift toward higher average distances per passenger trip.

On October 5, Canadian Transport Minister Benoit Bouchard announced that the level of service operated by VIA Rail Canada would be reduced by approximately 50%, effective Jan. 15, 1990. The number of trains operated per week would drop from 405 to 190, and the number of routes served would fall from 35 to 20.

Rail passenger developments in Europe were more positive. A new world railway speed record was set on December 5 when a French National Railways (SNCF) TGV (*Train à Grande Vitesse,* or train of very high speed) train reached 299.7 mph (482.4 km/hr) on a test run over a section of new line linking Paris with LeMans. Trains in regular service on the new line, which opened September 24, operate at a maximum speed of 186 mph (300 km/hr), compared with 168 mph (270 km/hr) on the TGV Southeast line opened to Lyon in 1981.

In the freight sector, carloadings on U.S. Class 1 railroads declined 1.3% between November 1988 and November 1989, while ton-mileage was 0.2% lower. Strength in grain and coal traffic was offset by weakness in movements of various manufactured items such as automobiles and motor-vehicle parts.

Innovations in freight service included a self-unloading conveyer train placed in service during the fall by the Consolidated Rail Corporation (Conrail). The train is designed for short-haul movements of bulk materials, such as stone, aggregates, and coal.

On March 22 the Interstate Commerce Commission (ICC) decided that railroads must

© Christian Vioujard/Gamma-Liaison

Plans are going forward for a new high-speed railroad network in Europe. Accordingly, the French National Railways TGV ("Train à Grande Vitesse," or "very high-speed train") began a new run from Paris to LeMans in 1989. Featuring electronic circuitry, the TGV "Atlantique" averages 186 mph (300 km/hr).

pass on to shippers the economic gains that they obtain from increases in productivity. In November the ICC issued a report indicating that as many as four Class 1 railroads may have achieved revenue adequacy in 1988—that is, earning a rate of return on their assets equal to or greater than their cost of capital. However, the ICC also found that the earnings of most rail carriers remained highly inadequate.

The leveraged buyout phenomenon affected rail as well as air carriers. On January 20, three weeks after attaining independence from a conglomerate parent, the Illinois Central became the target of a $440 million stock purchase offer. The bidders succeeded.

CNW Corporation, parent of Chicago & North Western Transportation Company, was confronted by a hostile bid of $44 per share, or $747 million, from Japonica Partners, a New York investment concern. CNW then sought and obtained a bid of $50 per share, or $950 million, from an investor group which included Union Pacific Corporation, parent of Union Pacific Railroad. The total amount of the transaction, including assumption of CNW's previously existing debt, was $1.6 billion. Completion of the transaction more than doubled CNW's debt and interest-payment burden.

On September 29 the ICC approved purchase of the Chicago-St. Louis line of the bankrupt Chicago, Missouri & Western Railway by Rio Grande Industries, Inc. Rio Grande is the parent of Southern Pacific, which took over operation of the line. In December, Canadian Pacific Ltd. (CP) reached an agreement to acquire about 44% of the outstanding shares of the Soo Line Railroad. CP has owned the remaining 56% of Soo Line's stock for many years. CP also became a bidder for the bankrupt Delaware & Hudson Railway, which services New York and Pennsylvania with 1,200 miles (1 931 km) of line.

Legislation signed by President Bush on December 11 revived the Local Rail Assistance Program, which had expired in 1988. The bill authorizes $10 million per year to fund small rail rehabilitation projects. The same bill also contained a provision lifting dividend payment limits and stock buy-back restrictions for Conrail, which were seen as necessary to permit Conrail to defend itself from possible hostile takeover bids.

Efforts to negotiate new national rail labor contracts produced no results as the year ended. Some carriers which chose to bargain independently succeeded in reaching agreements that provided changes in long-standing obsolete work rules and crew sizes.

On December 11 the Federal Railroad Administration (FRA) proposed federal rules establishing minimum qualifications and federal licensing for locomotive operators. In doing so, the FRA acted to fulfill a provision contained in the Rail Safety Improvement Act of 1988. That act, in turn, had been precipitated by a multiple fatality in a Jan. 4, 1987, collision caused by a locomotive engineer's gross violation of rail-company operating rules.

Shipping. Freight traffic on the Ohio and Mississippi Rivers and tributaries changed little from 1988, as measured by barge and tonnage movements through key locks. On the Great Lakes, iron ore, coal, and stone shipments through October rose 2.7% above 1988 levels.

Intense competition depressed earnings of liner containership operators and increased pressures for cost savings. Lykes Brothers Steamship Company moved to acquire Farrell Lines, Inc. Completion of the merger would reduce to only six the number of major U.S.-flag ocean carriers offering liner service on international shipping lanes. Topgallant Lines, a small U.S.-flag trans-Atlantic containership operator, entered bankruptcy on December 13 and ceased operation.

Trucking. TL carriers (specializing in movement of full truckload-sized shipments of 10,000 lbs (4 536 kg) and above) and LTL carriers (focusing on consignments below 10,000 lbs) experienced trying conditions.

For TL carriers 1989 marked the end of almost ten years of continuing increases in traffic and net income. A number of them suffered deficits. In addition to revenue reductions

The Story of Eastern Airlines

Turmoil engulfed Eastern Airlines in 1989. At its core was labor unrest, followed by entry into bankruptcy, service disruptions, loss of traffic to other air carriers, cuts in routes operated, and efforts to sell portions of the company's network.

The turbulence is deep-rooted. Eastern's average profit margin has been below that of the airline industry for more than 20 years. Before airline deregulation in 1978, Eastern was a North-South carrier, heavily dependent on seasonal tourist traffic. It later tried unsuccessfully to create a more balanced network by adding East-West routes. Other long-standing weaknesses included uneven service quality, excessive layers of management, inefficient labor contracts, and hostility in union-management relations.

Former astronaut Frank Borman attempted to overcome these problems after becoming head of Eastern in 1975. He did succeed in getting Eastern's union employees to accept a wage freeze in 1976, in return for participation in a profit-sharing program. But deregulation in 1978 increased competition on Eastern's major routes and depressed its earnings.

Increasing losses drove Eastern to obtain additional wage and benefit concessions from its unions in 1983–84. Eastern unilaterally extended wage concessions into 1985. Unions representing pilots and flight attendants subsequently accepted additional cuts. However, Charles E. Bryan, president of Eastern's chapter of the International Association of Machinists (IAM)—representing mechanics and baggage handlers—indicated that he would accept the wage reduction only if Borman resigned. Borman refused. Eastern's board of directors subsequently accepted an offer of purchase from Texas Air Corporation. The sale was finalized on Nov. 25, 1986.

Texas Air Corporation is a holding company controlled by Frank Lorenzo. Shortly after acquiring Eastern, Lorenzo forced Charles Bryan and other union representatives to resign from Eastern's board of directors.

Eastern relentlessly pressed its unions for additional wage and work-rule concessions from 1987 onward. Rancor between labor and management escalated, contributing to declines in service quality and drops in passenger traffic and revenue. System size shrank, and Eastern sold its computerized reservation system to Texas Air Corporation. Terminations and layoffs reduced employment from 43,300 in 1986 to 29,500 in 1988.

© Dan Helms/Compix

February 1989 ended without progress in the negotiation of a new labor agreement between Eastern and the IAM to replace the contract which had expired on Dec. 31, 1987. Eastern's contracts with the Airline Pilots' Association (ALPA) and the Transport Workers Union (TWU) also had expired. Citing net losses of $181.7 million in 1987, and $335.3 million in 1988, Eastern steadfastly sought $150 million in wage and work-rule concessions from the IAM. These demands were softened somewhat at the beginning of March, but the IAM remained negative; on March 4 it struck against Eastern.

Most Eastern ALPA and TWU members honored IAM picket lines. The three unions came to agree on the viewpoint that Lorenzo intended to liquidate Eastern and transfer its assets and traffic to his Texas Air's nonunion subsidiary, Continental Airlines. This show of solidarity crippled service. Eastern operated only about 10% of its 1,040 prestrike scheduled flights between March and early June.

Claiming heavy strike-caused losses, Eastern filed for bankruptcy on March 9. Shortly thereafter, presiding Judge Burton R. Lifland began exhorting Eastern, its unions, and its creditors to work out a way for restoring full service.

A possibility for doing so appeared in April, when an investment group led by former baseball commissioner Peter V. Ueberroth proposed to buy Eastern for $464 million. But the offer failed. Other investor groups looked at Eastern in May and June, but none progressed beyond the proposal stage. Simultaneously, Eastern acted to raise cash through sales of selected assets, and to increase flight operations.

On May 25, Judge Lifland approved real-estate developer Donald Trump's $365 million bid for Eastern's famous Shuttle, linking New York, Boston, and Washington, D.C. And on June 19, Eastern agreed to sell 16 DC9-30 aircraft and eight gates at Philadelphia International Airport to Midway Airlines for $206.5 million. Service at Eastern's Atlanta hub, a skeletal four daily flights since the start of the strike, began increasing in June toward a planned total of 82 per day to 26 cities by July 2. Systemwide daily flights reached approximately 225 on that date and 350 one month later.

To operate its reinstated services, Eastern drew upon a growing number of returning pilots who crossed picket lines, and upon newly hired and trained pilots. Maintenance forces were built up by new hires and by some returnees. ALPA and IAM alleged that the large number of new hires among pilots and mechanics, together with the limits of their proficiency, had compromised airline and passenger safety. The Federal Aviation Administration investigated and in August issued a report refuting the allegations.

On July 21, Eastern filed a formal reorganization plan—to be carried out by December—with the bankruptcy court. The plan called for the sale of $1.8 billion in assets and the profitable operation of an airline two thirds of its prestrike size. However, in October the plan was discovered to be flawed. Eastern confirmed in November that it has been unable to find means for fully satisfying claims against it, and that it would seek extension of the deadline for completion of its reorganization.

Meanwhile, Eastern renewed negotiations to sell its South American routes to American Airlines. Proceeds could be as much as $500 million, and boost Eastern's reorganization.

On November 21, President Bush vetoed legislation establishing a special commission to investigate Eastern's labor dispute. The pilots and flight attendants had viewed the proposed commission as their last hope for winning against Eastern and thus ending their 264-day strike. But the machinists' union's Eastern chapter vowed to continue its strike.

As 1989 drew to a close, Eastern was emerging as a greatly changed airline with a higher hope for long-run survival. Operations had risen to about 800 daily flights, approximately 75% of the prestrike level. The unions' long struggle seemed in vain. Employment had reached 20,000, two thirds of the prestrike count, including about 800 pilots and 200 mechanics who crossed picket lines.

JOHN C. SPYCHALSKI

stemming from slackening national economic activity and competition from double-stack rail container services, TL carriers faced higher fuel and personnel recruitment costs as the supply of qualified drivers tightened.

LTL carriers' profits declined steeply in the last three quarters of the year as large national carriers cut rates in efforts to either increase market share by wresting traffic from competitors, or keep existing major customers from defecting. Another competitive thrust came as United Parcel Service (UPS) moved beyond its traditional niche of small package transport by introducing two marketing programs aimed at portions of the traditional LTL business. Also, Federal Express Corporation lifted its 150 lb. (68 kg) weight limit on all packages moving within the United States.

On December 7, Transcon Lines announced plans to purchase ANR Freight Systems. If completed, the merger would create the United States' fourth-largest LTL carrier.

Urban Transit. Ground was broken on May 10 for the first 22.4-mi (36-km) segment of Baltimore's Central Corridor Light Rail Line. On June 27 test runs began on the new Long Beach-Los Angeles light rail line. Seattle Metro began testing new dual-powered diesel and electric buses specially designed for operation on both surface roads and in a downtown transit tunnel scheduled to open in 1990.

Mass-transit facilities escaped the October 17 northern California earthquake with minimal damage and provided valuable alternatives to blockages in the San Francisco Bay Area highway system. The Bay Area Rapid Transit District (BART) expanded service to fill the gap caused by closure of the Bay Bridge. BART's rush-hour ridership increased 100% over pre-quake levels. Legislation (PL 101-164) enacted on November 21 appropriated $3.048 billion in federal funds during fiscal year 1990 for Urban Mass Transportation Administration programs.

Drug Testing. Federally mandated drug-testing began in December for those in safety and security-related positions in urban transit, aviation, maritime transport, and trucking (except for random testing and some forms of postaccident testing of truck drivers, which were delayed in court actions by opponents).

JOHN C. SPYCHALSKI
The Pennsylvania State University

The luxury train arrived in 1989. Service on the American-European Express, a top-quality hotel and restaurant on wheels, began between Chicago and Washington, DC, in November. The concept features five specially fitted cars pulled by a standard Amtrak train. Accommodations include the club car (right) *with its black granite bar and baby grand piano. The cost of a one-way, single-occupancy ticket on the Chicago-Washington route was $695 in 1989. More routes may be added in the future.*

© Carol Highsmith

TRAVEL

Americans continued to travel in record numbers in 1989. While they shied away from regional trouble spots, they did not stop traveling, they merely changed course temporarily. Oil spills, political turmoil, hurricanes, and earthquakes may have led to cancellations and even some bankruptcies, but they did not seem to make an appreciable dent in the overall travel industry.

Altogether, Americans in 1989 were estimated to have made some 1.3 billion trips of 100 mi (161 km) or more, according to the U.S. Travel Data Center. That was a gain of 6% over the previous year. Inbound travel was again a particularly bright spot, with 38.5 million foreign visitors coming to America, up 13% over 1988.

Most foreign guests continued to come from Canada, with 15.6 million arrivals for a 12% annual increase—the third year of double-digit growth. Mexico, reflecting its improved economic picture, sent 9 million visitors to the United States, up 14% over the previous year. The 13.9 million overseas arrivals, too, showed impressive growth of 11%. Of the overseas' total, Europe accounted for 6.3 million (up 10%); Asia and the Middle East 4.2 million (up 14%); South America 1.13 million (up 12%), and the Caribbean 1.1 million (up 11%). Oceania, including Australia, accounted for 610,000 visitors, an 18% rise.

Heading Abroad. Outbound travel by U.S. citizens—to Mexico, Canada, and overseas—increased by 2% with 42 million Americans heading for foreign destinations in 1989. The modest growth rate was held down by a 3% drop of U.S. visitors to Canada, to 12.9 million, for no clear reason. Mexico had 13.7 million U.S. visitors for a 2% increase, but travel by Americans overseas showed a more substantial 7% growth with 15.5 million departures.

Europe, made more attractive by a somewhat strengthened U.S. dollar and by the French Revolution Bicentennial festivities, drew more than 7 million U.S. visitors, up from 6.5 million in 1988—and an all-time record. American travel to the Pacific/Asia region kept pace with the previous year, despite a dramatic drop in visits to China following the political violence there in the spring; travelers seemed to be substituting other Asian destinations rather than staying at home.

Cruising. In what has come to be a standard yearly performance, cruising chalked up a 12% growth for 1989, attracting some 3.5 million North American passengers. The year was marked by the return of cruise ships to the Mediterranean in full strength for the first time since 1986, when political terrorism nearly cleared the region's waters of cruise vessels. Recent trends in the cruise industry were solidified further, including shorter cruises, younger passengers, and ever more exotic destinations.

The pace of cruise line consolidation set in motion during 1988 slowed after Carnival Cruise Lines' purchase of Holland America Line and its Windstar Sail Cruises subsidiary was finalized in January 1989, but nobody expected that to be the final merger. Though the breakneck expansion of 1988 abated, several cruise companies also added either newly built vessels or refurbished ships previously owned by other lines.

Trends. The year marked the continued strengthening of a number of travel trends. Shorter and more frequent vacations became ever more popular, with trips of a few days supplanting or supplementing the more traditional long vacation. And the line between peak and off-peak travel seasons was blurred increasingly, with every season a peak travel period somewhere for Americans.

Consolidation continued to shape the travel industry. Giant travel agency chains took ever bigger shares of the market—a trend helped along by increasingly sophisticated technology. As a counterpoint, specialization also became more and more important. Tours were tailored to suit almost every imaginable group of travelers, from cooks to cyclists.

PHYLLIS ELVING, *Free-lance Writer*

TUNISIA

The personal stature of President Zine El Abidine Ben Ali and his political reforms remained unchallenged in 1989, but the promises of sweeping change made by the president were being viewed with increased skepticism. Tensions with fundamentalist groups and a stagnant economy have led to a sense of pessimism over the country's future. As a result, Ben Ali replaced his first prime minister on September 27.

In foreign affairs, Tunisia joined its four North African neighbors in February to create the Arab Maghreb Union, aimed at enhancing socioeconomic cooperation. French President François Mitterrand visited Tunisia in June, sealing the renewed warmth in relations between the two countries.

Domestic Affairs. Parliamentary and presidential elections were held on April 2 under new electoral laws. Seven legalized parties were allowed to run candidates; the Islamic-oriented Renewal or Renaissance Party (*An-Nahda*) was not. Formerly known as the Islamic Tendency Movement, the Nahda had changed its name specifically to qualify under the new law which forbids parties from having Islam in their names.

Election turnout was relatively low (70%). The ruling Constitutional Democratic Rally won all 141 seats in the parliament. Ben Ali received nearly 100% of the popular vote in his uncontested presidential election. The mainstream opposition party, the Movement of Social Democrats (MDS), fared poorly. Four moderate or leftist parties fared even worse. Only An-Nahda could demonstrate grass-roots support as independent candidates known to be Nahda sympathizers received between 14% and 30% of the national vote in some constituencies.

On April 11 a new cabinet was formed with a majority being young technocrats. Only four of the 32-member cabinet had any previous government experience.

Economic Affairs. Economic problems continued to plague the country. In his speeches to the Chamber of Deputies in April and again on July 25, President Ben Ali warned the nation to work harder and show greater rigor to confront various economic challenges. The privatization of state-owned enterprises remained a key element in the government's economic strategy, in line with the recommendations of the International Monetary Fund (IMF) and the 1986 World Bank reform package. About 25% of the nearly 400 public-sector companies employing close to 200,000 people were likely to be sold off.

Agriculture remained the economy's Achilles' heel given the country's continued dependence on food imports. A second year of drought dashed hopes for recovery in that crucial sector. Price increases were announced on August 11 affecting a wide range of basic foodstuffs such as bread, flour, sugar, milk, meat, and coffee. Feeling that Prime Minister Hedi Baccouche was not pushing these and other liberalization measures quickly enough, Ben Ali dismissed him on September 27 and appointed Justice Minister Hamed Karoui as the new prime minister. President Ben Ali assigned the new premier specific objectives: Streamline democratic processes and promote a policy of national reconciliation and dialogue with different social and political groups. Most importantly, Ben Ali sought to invigorate the economy by encouraging individual initiative in all public and private sectors.

Foreign Affairs. Relations with Libya have improved significantly since Ben Ali's accession to power in 1987. Colonel Qaddafi of Libya visited Tunisia in December 1988 and in February 1989 in the company of Algerian President Chadli Benjedid shortly before all three leaders left for the Maghreb summit meeting in Morocco on February 17–19. President Ben Ali was in Libya in late May for talks with Qaddafi and heads of state from Syria and Algeria.

The creation of the Arab Maghreb Union capped the successful effort of both Ben Ali and Benjedid to overcome regional differences.

JOHN P. ENTELIS, *Fordham University*

TUNISIA • Information Highlights

Official Name: Republic of Tunisia.
Location: North Africa.
Area: 63,170 sq mi (163 610 km^2).
Population (mid-1989 est.): 7,900,000.
Chief City (1987 est.): Tunis, the capital, 1,600,000, district population.
Government: *Head of state,* Zine El Abidine Ben Ali, president (took office Nov. 7, 1987). *Head of government,* Hamed Karoui, prime minister (took office Sept. 27, 1989). *Legislature* (unicameral)—National Assembly.
Monetary Unit: Dinar (0.975 dinar equals U.S.$1, June 1989).
Gross Domestic Product (1987 est. U.S.$): $9,600,000,000.
Economic Indexes (1988): *Consumer Prices* (1980 = 100), all items, 190.5; food, 194.5.
Foreign Trade (1988 U.S.$): *Imports,* $3,688,000,000; *exports,* $2,395,000,000.

© ABC Ajansi/Gamma-Liaison

Turkey's new president, Turgut Ozal, leads an inauguration day procession. Ozal, 62, had been serving as prime minister and Motherland Party leader.

TURKEY

A new president and prime minister, local elections, the economy, and a flood of refugees from Bulgaria were among the things that commanded public attention in Turkey in 1989.

Internal Developments. On October 31, Prime Minister and Motherland Party (MP) leader Turgut Ozal was elected as Turkey's eighth president by the National Assembly, succeeding Kenan Evren, who was not eligible for reelection. Ozal was opposed strongly by the opposition parties, partly on the grounds that election of someone closely identified with a political party would make the presidency into a partisan office. They also maintained, however, that Ozal no longer had the confidence of the country, based on the results of local elections held in March in which the MP ran behind both the Social Democratic Populist Party and the right-wing True Path Party. Yildirim Akbulut, former speaker of the National Assembly, succeeded Ozal as prime minister and has the unenviable task of rebuilding MP strength before the next scheduled parliamentary elections in 1992.

The main reason for the MP's poor showing, and the single issue that was on the minds of most Turks, was again the economy. The 1989 inflation rate was about 75%, as it had been for the previous several years, so that the government's repeated promises to reduce it met with increasing disbelief. Ozal and the MP vowed to continue their policy of economic recovery through rapid development and decreased protectionism through the end of their mandate in 1992. Positive developments included increased exports, strong interest by Japanese and European investors, a large increase in tourism, advances in the program of expanding energy generation, and some progress toward privatization. Less encouraging was the gross national product (GNP) growth rate, which in 1988 was only 3.4%, significantly down from previous years. Also, the value of the lira against other currencies continued to erode rapidly, and serious fund shortages were anticipated for export and manufacturing incentives. The sixth Five-Year Development Plan, envisioning a growth rate of 7%, was considered by many to be overly optimistic.

On a related matter, Turkey complained increasingly in 1989 about the lack of progress toward association with the European Community, to which Turkey had applied for full membership in 1987. Talks continued in only preliminary stages, and the Turks expressed concern that unless there were greater momentum, the planned 1992 consolidation of European economies would shut them out. Implications of developments in Eastern Europe also began to cause concern.

Among social issues, the role of Islam was again a matter of controversy. In March the Constitutional Court annulled an Assembly bill that allowed women to wear head-scarves on university campuses, on the grounds that it violated the secular nature of the state. A move in the conservative province of Konya to provide segregated buses for male and female students also was rejected. In April, Turkey also recalled its ambassador to Iran, accusing that country of abetting fundamentalist Turkish Muslims. Despite some demonstrations over these issues, a poll by the newspaper *Hurriyet* showed overwhelming support for secularism.

Human-rights issues also continued to plague Turkey. An Amnesty International re-

TURKEY • Information Highlights

Official Name: Republic of Turkey.
Location: Southeastern Europe and southwestern Asia.
Area: 301,382 sq mi (780 580 km²).
Population (mid-1989 est.): 55,400,000.
Chief Cities (1985 census): Ankara, the capital, 2,235,035; Istanbul, 5,475,982; Izmir, 1,489,772.
Government: *Head of state,* Turgut Ozal, president (took office November 1989). *Head of government,* Yildirim Akbulut, prime minister (took office November 1989). *Legislature*—Grand National Assembly.
Monetary Unit: Lira (2,288 liras equal U.S. $1, Nov. 20, 1989).
Gross Domestic Product (1987 est. U.S.$): $62,600,-000,000.
Economic Index (1988): *Consumer Prices* (1982 = 100), all items, 926.4; food, 869.0.
Foreign Trade (1988 U.S.$): *Imports,* $14,380,-000,000; *exports,* $11,608,000,000.

port found numerous instances of mistreatment of prisoners. The government repeated its insistence that they were isolated cases, but as a result of a hunger strike in Turkish prisons it announced that a number of policies of severely disciplining recalcitrant prisoners would be ended.

Foreign Affairs. The long-simmering dispute with Bulgaria over the treatment of ethnic Turks in that country boiled over in early summer, and by August some 300,000 of an estimated 1.5 million had fled to Turkey, causing severe strains on Turkey's resources to absorb them. The Bulgarian government's policy of forced assimilation drew a large volume of condemnation around the world, which by the end of the year appeared to have had little effect. Its impact also was lessened when some observers compared the Bulgarian actions with Turkey's treatment of its own Kurdish minority.

There was little improvement in regard to ongoing disputes with Greece. Talks between Greek and Turkish Cypriots were held but made no progress, and the United Nations extended the mandate of its peacekeeping force on Cyprus. Toward the end of the year UN Secretary-General Pérez de Cuéllar declared that he saw little prospect for new talks in the foreseeable future. Ankara also continued to complain of Greek discrimination against Turks in western Thrace.

In January, Turkey moved to open its national archives to wider use by scholars, assuming that investigation of Turkish treatment of the Armenians during World War I would confirm Turkey's position.

WALTER F. WEIKER, *Rutgers University*

UGANDA

After three years in office, President Yoweri Museveni restored order to most of Uganda in 1989. But without a constitution and with a development policy that relies almost entirely on the International Monetary Fund (IMF), he came under increasing criticism for not having a vision for Uganda's future.

UGANDA • Information Highlights

Official Name: Republic of Uganda.
Location: Interior of East Africa.
Area: 91,135 sq mi (236 040 km^2).
Population: (mid-1989 est.): 17,000,000.
Chief Cities (1980 census): Kampala, the capital, 458,423; Jinja, 45,060.
Government: *Head of state,* Yoweri Museveni, president (Jan. 29, 1986). *Head of government,* Samson Kisekka, prime minister (Jan. 30, 1986). *Legislature* (unicameral)—National Assembly.
Monetary Unit: Uganda shilling (200 shillings equal U.S. $1, July 1989).
Foreign Trade (1987 est. U.S.$): *Imports,* $319,400,000; *exports,* $605,500,000.

Internal Affairs. Uganda experienced its first free, if not altogether democratic, elections since 1962. Polling was not secret, as voters stood in queues to indicate their preferences. No parties were allowed to organize nor were any candidates permitted to campaign. Local Resistance Committees (RCs) were the only bodies directly elected. Higher level RCs were elected indirectly, with lower level RCs serving as electoral colleges for those above. In the National Resistance Committee (NRC), 210 seats were elected indirectly. Of the remaining 68 seats, 38 were reserved for members of the original NRC, ten were reserved for the military, and 20 were nominated by Museveni.

Elections in the northern district of Gulu were delayed due to disturbances caused by Joseph Kony's Holy Spirit rebels. Kony claims to communicate directly with eight major spirits in Africa, China, and the United States. Following a major government offensive, the National Resistance Army (NRA) was accused of sectarian violence against the Acholi people near Gulu. The NRA burned buildings in an attempt to isolate the rebels from the rural population. The size of Kony's army fell from 5,000 in 1987 to less than 300 in 1989. In the process, more than 124,000 people were displaced, crops were not planted, and a major shortage of food was expected in the area. As a result, the army came under harsh criticism for human-rights violations and the government changed its tactics. Local RCs were permitted to investigate human-rights violations, which in one case resulted in the execution of three NRA soldiers for rape.

In the Bakonjo area of western Uganda, rebels headquartered in Zaire and led by former President Milton Obote's former deputy minister of lands, Amon Bazira, attacked a local RC, killing one member and kidnapping two others. Following the disturbances, Finance Minister Crispus Kiyonga, thought to be the most influential member of Museveni's cabinet, campaigned extensively to build support for the government among his fellow Bakonjo.

The Economy. Uganda continued to adhere to the conditions of an IMF austerity program. Wages remained depressed, access to credit restricted, and public expenditures for social services were low. Government-imposed price controls had little impact on inflation and simply drove commodities into the black market, where the cost of basic necessities, including food, was well beyond the purchasing power of most Ugandans.

In spite of a 33% devaluation in May, the U.S. dollar brought more than double its official value on the black market. Uganda also turned increasingly to barter trade, expected to rise in value from $50–$70 million in 1988 to more than $450 million in the coming years.

WILLIAM CYRUS REED, *Wabash College*

© Blanche/Gamma-Liaison

Mikhail Gorbachev relaxes with his wife, Raisa, and his mother in his village birthplace, Privolnoye. As 1989 ended, the Soviet president faced severe national economic problems and calls for more freedom from the Soviet republics.

USSR

The year 1989 began auspiciously for *perestroika,* General Secretary Mikhail Gorbachev's slogan for restructuring the Soviet system, but ended amidst recrimination and retrenchment, and with the Soviet internal and external empires in increasing disarray. The buoyant optimism of the first six months progressively gave way to dark pessimism as economic progress continued to elude the Soviet consumer, and as Gorbachev steadily lost patience with the political and social forces he had unleashed, but no longer could control. Even Soviet foreign policy presented a mixed picture rather than the usual unqualified success. While Gorbachev's foreign policy toward the West continued to win him accolades for statesmanship, his actions in the Communist world were marked by hesitation, ambivalence, and, ultimately, in East Europe, a necessity of basing policy on the inevitable. Although chosen by *Time* magazine as the "Man of the Decade," Gorbachev by year's end seemed battered by intractable problems and besieged by the unwanted consequences of his rhetoric and policies.

Domestic Affairs

On the home front, the year was characterized both by political euphoria over the new-style parliamentary election campaign of the winter-spring and the restructured legislative system it brought forth, and by growing social despair over the seeming insolubility of some of the country's myriad problems. The future may show 1989 to be a turning point in Gorbachev's attitude toward his policies of *glasnost* and democratization, as first the fruits of the former began to erode his civility and then the latter boomeranged to threaten the unitary system led by the Communist Party.

Political Developments. The main political event of 1989 was the campaign in the first half of the year to elect the new grand parliament, dubbed the Congress of People's Deputies. The Congress was the result of constitutional amendments which Gorbachev pushed through the preceding, compliant legislature in the fall of 1988. Although the nomination process was very complicated to ensure the Communist Party's hegemony in the new institution, the election itself was the Soviet Union's freest since 1918. Many of the 2,250 seats were contested, a novelty in Soviet politics. And a new category of vocal *glasnost* emerged as campaigners and voters alike said nearly anything they wanted to in public.

The party as an institution lost, as numerous party stalwarts were trounced in contested races, and failed to win a majority through "safe" seats in which they ran unopposed. However, most candidates were at least low-level party members, thereby ensuring a party majority in the new Congress. There were exceptions, such as the Baltic delegations, which were dominated by members of the popular fronts in the Latvian, Estonian, and Lithuanian union republics. Among the new deputies were the party maverick Boris Yeltsin, a critic of Gorbachev from the left, and erstwhile dissidents Andrei Sakharov and Roy Medvedev.

The first ten-day session of the Congress in the spring was televised live, and the nation watched spellbound.

The main business of the first session was to elect from congressional ranks the smaller, day-to-day legislature, the 450-member, restructured Supreme Soviet. The chairman of the Supreme Soviet's Presidium, who is referred to in the West as the Soviet president, also was to be chosen. Gorbachev, predictably, was elected to this post. Unlike its predecessor of the same name, the new Supreme Soviet scheduled longer sessions, set up standing committees which actually drafted legislation, carried out investigations, and engaged in often sharp debate. By the end of the year, however, the fledgling legislators had neither offices nor staff to assist them. Gorbachev presided over both the Congress and the Supreme Soviet masterfully, but as the second session proceeded in November-December, his patience with critics began to wear thin and his parliamentary style became more abrupt. As a Western journalist observed, Gorbachev seemed to like democracy, so long as he got his way.

The legislative business of the first session was more symbolic than substantive as both bodies of parliament organized themselves and established procedural rules. Larger and longer-term issues received attention, such as the launch of an investigation of the penal system that included Brezhnev-era political justice, and a mandate to draft a new constitution. Perhaps the most significant outcome was the creation of a legislative agenda which included economic policy, restructuring of federal-republic relations, and a number of legislative projects which long had been mired in the drafting stage.

By the second session in the fall-winter of 1989, the post-Stalin split between reformers and conservatives had expanded leftward with the reform camp dividing into extreme (*e.g.*, ethnic-loyalists), radical (*e.g.*, immediate pluralism), and moderate reformers (*e.g.*, Gorbachev the centrist), and with the conservatives to the right. The extreme and radical factions merged into an unofficial opposition bloc, including Sakharov's Interregional Group, while Gorbachev and the moderates dominated the government. The conservatives—whose stronghold remained in the political and economic bureaucracies—were relegated to a reactive position. It was apparent, however, that the social turmoil accompanying *perestroika* was generating gradually more support for the extra-parliamentary conservative opposition. If anything, the dramatic events in East Europe intensified this trend.

The second session of the parliament indicated that the earlier euphoria was waning as harsh economic and political realities hit the legislators. One disheartening example was the Supreme Soviet's decision to terminate Moscow's special administration of the contested, violence-ridden Nagorno-Karabakh region with its Armenian majority on Azerbaijan territory, thereby reaffirming the integrity of internal borders. The decision neither satisfied the Armenians, who resumed large-scale strikes, nor the Azeris, who were affronted that the central government continued to maintain an observer in the region. On the larger issues of pluralism and economic reform, the parliament degenerated into rancorous controversy while an increasingly nettled Gorbachev arbitrarily cut off critical speakers. Article 6 of the Soviet Constitution, which guarantees the leading role of the Communist Party, was an issue brought to the fore by the dethronement of Communism in several East European client states during the fall. While Gorbachev had little choice but to countenance the East European changes, he was adamant about not raising the question of Soviet pluralism in 1989, arguing that the party was the only institution which could guide the multinational USSR through the difficulties of *perestroika*. He prevailed on the issue, as he and Prime Minister Nikolai Ryzhkov did on the government's retrenched economic program as well. At the same time, other promised legislation, such as the long-awaited statute codifying *glasnost,* remained stalled in the pipeline.

The Economic Situation. The economic situation in the USSR, especially as regards consumer goods, the barometer of the public mood, worsened during 1989. More goods were rationed in wider areas of the country while political and economic strikes took a further toll. Of 1,200 items that shape the standard of living, 1,000 were in short supply. The situation was aggravated further by large-scale strikes during the summer, principally among coal miners from Siberia to the Ukraine. The scarcity of consumer goods in the mining towns and poor working conditions in the pits, rather than wages, were the principal grievances. The demands were for such items as shoes and detergent. Fearing the spread of strike fever to the railways and steel centers, the government agreed to improve living conditions in the regions hit by strikes with promises of huge deliveries of consumer goods. The strikes, however, already had left urban power plants dangerously low on coal for the coming winter. The government responded by proposing in the Supreme Soviet a moratorium on strikes. A compromise was reached banning strikes in such crucial industries as defense, transportation, and energy. This was to no avail as the Siberian miners went out again in the fall in defiance of the new law, protesting the government's failure to fulfill promises made in the summer. The new rash of strikes was brought to an end, but not without unconfirmed rumors that pressure and even force may have been used against strike leaders.

The limited success of "perestroika" is demonstrated by the continuing long lines the Soviets must endure to buy meat and other consumer items.

© White/Sygma

Even before these labor problems arose, radical and mainstream economists were predicting that the party had little time left to deliver on economic reform to avoid economic collapse. Estimates ranged from one to three years until a catastrophic collapse. Fueling the pessimism was an official survey revealing that the vast majority of citizens no longer had much confidence in the success of economic *perestroika*—more than half saying that it never would work while the remainder allowed it would take at least ten years to work. To complicate matters, even the lifeline of foreign economic aid was not working that well. A Western study indicated that the USSR was having difficulty both putting foreign capital to work at a reasonable tempo and in absorbing new technologies into the still hidebound economy.

Gorbachev was caught between radical economic advisers urgently recommending breaking the bottlenecks by deepening economic reform, and political advisers who feared the possible consequences of uncontrolled inflation. Once again East Europe cast its shadow over the Soviet policy arena with the specter of Polish inflation surging toward 500% annually while inflation in Yugoslavia soared upward toward 2,000%. Political fears of inflation prevailed as Prime Minister Ryzhkov pushed through in the December session of the Congress a moderately conservative, reform-shy economic program, deferring further into the 1990s such steps as decontrol of prices. By the latter part of the year, Gorbachev had conceded publicly that the economic situation was very serious and that the fate of *perestroika* depended upon resolving it.

Ethnic Unrest and Social Change. During 1989, various ethnic groups in the USSR continued to see in Gorbachev's policy of democratization an opportunity to rectify historic wrongs (*e.g.*, the Baltics), to redefine internal boundaries (*e.g.*, Armenia), and to settle scores with minorities (Uzbekistan, Georgia). Accompanying the growing ethnic ferment was a rising curve of communal violence. Outbreaks in Uzbekistan, Georgia, and the Nagorno-Karabakh section of Azerbaijan required the dispatch of, or the continued presence of, riot troops. The killings in Nagorno-Karabakh between Armenians and Azeris continued with no end in sight. The conflict might be termed a sporadic, guerrilla-style civil war. Adding to the hatred, the Azeri Popular Front in 1989 imposed a railway blockade on neighboring Armenia, which receives 80% of its supplies from Azerbaijan. So effective was the blockade that work on rebuilding from the 1988 earthquake had to be suspended; even general ambulance service had to be cut back due to the shortage of gasoline. Moscow seemed powerless to lift the blockade. When it was suggested that the southern railroads might be run by troops, the Azeri Popular Front responded that its members would retaliate by sabotaging the tracks. Political negotiations finally succeeded in lifting the blockade but not until after significant damage to the Armenian economy. The Nagorno-Karabakh area well could become the Soviet Union's Belfast or Beirut.

In June large-scale violence also broke out in Uzbekistan as well-armed gangs of Uzbeks,

USSR • Information Highlights

Official Name: Union of Soviet Socialist Republics.
Location: Eastern Europe and northern Asia.
Area: 8,649,498 sq mi (22 402 200 km²).
Population (mid-1989 est.): 289,000,000.
Chief Cities (Jan. 1, 1989 est.): Moscow, the capital, 8,967,000; Leningrad, 5,020,000; Kiev, 2,587,000.
Government: *Head of government,* Nikolai I. Ryzhkov, chairman of the USSR Council of Ministers (took office Sept. 1985). *Head of state,* Mikhail S. Gorbachev, chairman of the Supreme Soviet's Presidium (president) (elected May 1989). *Legislature* (bicameral)—Supreme Soviet and Congress of People's Deputies.
Monetary Unit: Ruble (0.638 ruble equals U.S. $1, July 1989—noncommercial rate).
Gross National Product (1988 U.S. $): $2,500,000,000,000.
Economic Indexes (1987): *Consumer Prices* (1980 = 100), all items, 106.5; food 114.2. *Industrial Production* (1980 = 100), 130.
Foreign Trade (1988 U.S.$): *Imports,* $107,229,000,000; *exports,* $110,559,000,000.

including white-collar professionals as well as riffraff, massacred many members of an ethnic Turkish minority living among them. Unemployment as a consequence of economic reform, ranging from 20% to 30% in the southern Soviet Union, was a contributing factor to the violence, but the roots of ethnic rage in the region run much deeper. Similar, but less extensive, ethnic violence took place in Soviet Georgia. In Soviet Moldavia, the violence was aimed in a different direction. A counter-parade in the republic capital on November 7, the anniversary of the Bolshevik Revolution, was suppressed by the police and a number of demonstrators were arrested. Several days later an immense crowd attacked police headquarters, trying to free the prisoners. Order was restored in the city only with great difficulty.

Elsewhere, ethnic activism was peaceful in 1989, but nonetheless fraught with potential for violence. The hard-line party leader of the Ukraine was replaced by a reformer, and the Ukrainian Popular Front, *Ruk,* grew rapidly, especially in the western section of the area where relegalization of the Ukrainian Roman Catholic Church was also an issue. In the Baltic region, the first local elections under the new 1988 electoral law confirmed the control of the Popular Fronts over the political life of the republics in Latvia and Estonia, with the exception of those cities with very large Russian concentrations. By far, the most dramatic developments (and ominous from Gorbachev's perspective) took place in Lithuania. Echoing similar moves in East Europe, Article 6 on the party's leading role in governing was repealed from the republic's constitution, opening the possibility for a multiparty system. To add to the precedent and Gorbachev's woes, the Lithuanian Communist Party split from the Communist Party of the Soviet Union in December with the Lithuanian party leader signaling that the next step may be secession from the USSR.

Gorbachev's reaction to the Lithuanian initiatives at a special Central Committee meeting was one of controlled fury. Fearing the precedent would lead to "the disintegration of the Soviet Union," Gorbachev lashed out at "anti-Soviet and left-wing forces" in Lithuania. With the Central Committee stalemated on how to respond and the party ideology secretary not ruling out force, Gorbachev prepared to rush to Lithuania, to try to find a way out of the dilemma, as December drew to a close. Paradoxically, while Gorbachev has suspended, and even apologized for the past use of the Brezhnev Doctrine of military intervention in East Europe, he and his lieutenants apparently have not ruled out its use inside the Soviet Union.

The situation on the civil-rights front was uneven during 1989. While *de facto* freedom of conscience was implemented by the reopening of hundreds of churches, the new statute on religious rights was still not in final form. As Jewish emigration achieved a new all-time high of approximately 62,000 emigrants and Jewish culture was being revived, open anti-Semitism also continued to spread in the USSR. Journalistic *glasnost* pushed on to ever new and startling revelations, but high-level party criticism of aggressive editors became more strident, with Gorbachev even calling for the resignation of one major editor, who refused. Similarly, while the laws on political crime finally were revised in April, the new versions contained fresh ambiguities which could be exploited by a repressive administration. Last, with the number of independent groups in the thousands and demonstrations in the tens of thousands, the police were equally energetic in using the law on demonstrations to enforce selectively the limits of democratization.

Striking up some new notes of détente, several American and European hard-rock groups, including Mötley Crüe and Bon Jovi, performed before 100,000 Muscovites at the two-day Music Peace Festival in Lenin Stadium in August.

© Laski/Sipa

© Vlastimir Shone/Gamma-Liaison

Religious tolerance increases in the USSR. In October the Orthodox Eucharist was celebrated in Assumption Cathedral, inside the Kremlin, for the first time since 1918.

Sakharov's Legacy. The most notable loss in the field of human rights was the death of Andrei Sakharov on December 14 during the second session of the Congress of People's Deputies. He died at home while writing a speech on the need for an opposition to the party, the final act of a consummate human-rights campaigner. In many ways Sakharov's personal journey paralleled the journey of Soviet society from Brezhnev's "stagnation" to Gorbachev's *perestroika*. (*See* OBITUARIES.)

Foreign Affairs

Gorbachev's long consecutive streak of successes in foreign policy was broken in 1989 by some qualified outcomes. His first summit with U.S. President George Bush at Malta and his historic meeting with Pope John Paul II can be scored as successes. From Malta, Gorbachev came away with the American endorsement of *perestroika*. From his meeting with the pope, Gorbachev garnered increased respectability as a statesman. As a *quid pro quo,* he began the process leading to the reestablishment of the Uniate Church, the Roman Catholic Church of the Ukraine which was dismantled by Stalin in 1946.

In the qualified column would go his visits to China and Cuba. In China in the spring, as a symbol of reform, Gorbachev drew thousands of students who called upon their own leaders for political reforms. Inhibited by Gorbachev's presence and his international press entourage as well, the Chinese leaders could not take immediate action to rein in the students, and the demonstrations grew out of control from their point of view. After Gorbachev's departure, troops finally retook the central square of Beijing, inflicting several thousand casualties on students and workers. Gorbachev returned home with normalized trade and military relations with China, but the political and ideological relationship soured as the Chinese leadership now regarded him as the betrayer of Communism in the USSR and East Europe. Similarly, Soviet-Cuban relations have been strained since Gorbachev's visit to Havana in early April when he presumably told Castro of the USSR's need to cut back on its expensive financial commitments to Third World, left-wing client states. Castro commented dryly in Gorbachev's presence that if a socialist country wants to go down the road of capitalism, that is its business, implicitly labeling the Soviet leader an espouser of capitalism—a grave ideological insult.

In mid-February the Soviet Union announced that it had completed the withdrawal of its military forces from Afghanistan following nine years of fighting. At the height of the intervention some 115,000 were reported to be stationed in Afghanistan. From a Soviet viewpoint, its actions in Afghanistan—not a Gorbachev initiative—must receive a negative review. Some 15,000 Soviet troops were killed in the fighting, another 35,000 were injured, and millions of dollars that could have been spent on the Soviet economy were devoted to the fighting, including supplies and weapons. In addition, the primary purpose of the encounter—the subjugation of the rebels, the *mujahidin,* fighting the Soviet-backed government in Afghanistan—was not accomplished. On the other side, the Soviet-backed government in Afghanistan confounded many predictions and remained in power following the Soviet pullout and throughout 1989.

Finally, there is the case of East Europe, which would have to go in the loss column as it spun out of Soviet control in the last few months of 1989. Gorbachev himself played a key role in destabilizing Communist rule in East Germany and Czechoslovakia, and in encouraging the ouster of the longtime Bulgarian leader. As a result, as 1989 ended, President Gorbachev faced the possible demise of the Warsaw Pact as an effective military alliance, while the North Atlantic Treaty Organization (NATO) remained intact; the possible reunification of Germany; and the immediate reciprocal influence of the rapid changes in Hungary, Poland, and elsewhere on his own restive republics (*e.g.,* Lithuania), as well as the dissatisfaction of the Soviet public in general.

See also feature article, COMMUNISM IN FLUX, page 24.

ROBERT SHARLET, *Union College*

UNITED NATIONS

For the United Nations, 1989 began on a harmonious chord but ended on a sour note struck by U.S. financial delinquency and its invasion of Panama. However, optimism dominated, fueled by unprecedented U.S.-Soviet cooperation both outside and within the UN.

A potentially damaging year-end crisis stemmed from a face-off between Washington and the Palestine Liberation Organization's (PLO's) supporters, who were demanding that the PLO be recognized as the UN nonmember "state" of Palestine instead of merely as a nonmember "organization." The Arab side blinked first and shelved the demand, and the United States withdrew a threat to withhold further financial contributions to the UN—an action that would have bankrupted the organization. With only hours of the year remaining, the General Assembly also adopted a resolution condemning the U.S. military invasion of Panama. Otherwise, peacemaking topped the UN's 1989 activities.

Peacekeeping Missions. The advance party of a new UN Transition Assistance Group (UNTAG) was fielded in February to guide Namibia toward independence from South Africa. The planned multinational force of 6,000 military, 1,000 police, and 1,700 civilians represented the largest UN peace undertaking since the Congo operation in the 1960s. UNTAG soldiers began monitoring the withdrawal from Namibia into Angola of the South West Africa People's Organization (SWAPO) guerrillas on April 11. Under UNTAG supervision, a 97% Namibian voter turnout elected a SWAPO-dominated constituent assembly in November to draft a charter for the territory's scheduled independence in the spring of 1990.

In a related peacekeeping mission, the UN Angola Verification Mission (UNAVEM) of 70 military observers had been in Angola since early January, monitoring the withdrawal of 50,000 Cuban troops there. The United States and South Africa had linked agreement on Namibia to the withdrawal of the Cubans, who had been supporting Angola's Marxist government in its civil war against insurgents led by Jonas Savimbi. The UN observers are to remain on duty through August 1991, one month after the last Cuban is scheduled to leave.

In Central America, the UN established a series of interlocking peace operations—the organization's first such involvement in the Western Hemisphere—at the request of the region's governments. The UN Observer Group for the Verification of Elections in Nicaragua (ONUVEN) monitored the registration and campaigning for elections, scheduled for Feb. 25, 1990.

Another contingent, the UN Observer Group in Central America (ONUCA), was mandated to conduct on-site verification of the cutoff of outside aid to Central American insurrectionists—principally the Nicaraguan and Salvadoran rebels—and to assure that guerrillas are denied bases in one country for strikes against another. Simultaneously, the International Commission of Support and Verification (CIAV) was deployed to oversee the demobilization, disarming, and repatriation or resettlement of the Nicaraguan rebels encamped in Honduras.

General Assembly. The 44th General Assembly opened on Sept. 19, 1989, with the election by acclamation of Nigeria's Maj. Gen. Joseph N. Garba to the regionally rotated presidency to succeed Dante Caputo of Argentina. The nearly 160 items on the agenda included such perennial issues as the Mideast, disarmament, apartheid, and the Third World debt crisis. Environment and illicit drugs, previously relatively low in priority, also were spotlighted.

In what Garba called a "major achievement," the Assembly adopted by consensus a declaration proposing negotiations with South Africa to end apartheid, or racial separation. The text marked a departure from previous antiapartheid measures, which routinely emphasized a solution through armed struggle.

The withdrawal of Soviet troops from Afghanistan in February under the UN-brokered Geneva accords failed to halt the war. In November the Assembly called on all parties to abide by the accords—an allusive condemnation of the continuing military aid provided by the United States to the Afghan rebels and by the USSR to the Soviet-installed regime.

Similarly, the Hanoi-announced withdrawal of Vietnamese forces from Cambodia in September merely triggered an upsurge in fighting between indigenous Cambodian factions: the Hanoi-installed Hun Sen regime in Phnom Penh and the UN-recognized tripartite coalition headed by Prince Norodom Sihanouk. In October the General Assembly adopted by a 124-to-17 vote a resolution demanding UN verification of the troop withdrawal and opposing the return to power of the coalition's Khmer Rouge faction, heir to the Pol Pot regime.

In the Iran-Iraq conflict, peace talks were deadlocked despite UN mediation. Nevertheless, the 15-month-old cease-fire was holding with the help of the UN Iran-Iraq Military Observer Group (UNIIMOG).

President Virgilio Barco Vargas of Colombia reported to the Assembly on his embattled country's "frontline war" against drug traffickers. Emphasizing that the scourge is of global proportions, he called for international action to curb demand, stop the illegal trade in chemicals used to process drugs, and control arms sales to "narco-terrorists." The Assembly later called a special session on drugs, to convene in February 1990.

The Assembly's main ecological action was a call for a World Conference on the Environment and Development, to be held in June 1992 in Brazil. The session would mark the 20th anniversary of the Stockholm conference that initiated UN involvement in environmental issues and that led to the creation of the UN Environment Program (UNEP), headquartered in Kenya. The Assembly also called for action to preserve Antarctica's ecosystem and urged a moratorium on drift-net fishing on the high seas, beginning June 30, 1992.

UN proceedings during 1989 were characterized widely as exercises in "cooperation, not confrontation"—a spinoff of the East-West détente. The development was highlighted by two superpower speakers, who addressed the Assembly: U.S. President George Bush and Soviet Foreign Minister Eduard Shevardnadze. Both speeches were free of the vituperation of past addresses. Shevardnadze was quick to welcome Bush's reiteration that the United States was ready to move toward a treaty to eliminate all chemical weapons over ten years.

In the first such action in UN history, the United States and the USSR joined in drafting a resolution reaffirming their dedication to the UN Charter and calling on all other countries to use its provisions to settle disputes by peaceful means. The Assembly adopted the draft without a vote.

Events largely external to the UN also resonated in the world organization. Within hours of the Tiananmen Square massacre on June 3-4, Secretary-General Javier Pérez de Cuéllar said he was "greatly saddened" by the Chinese army's resort to massive force against the prodemocracy demonstrators. Later that month, he appealed to Beijing for clemency for protesters under sentence of execution. Rumblings about bringing the Tiananmen affair to the Security Council, however, were silenced at the outset. Even delegations outraged by Beijing's action argued—given China's veto-wielding power as one of the Security Council's five permanent members—there was little of substance the UN could do.

Similarly, China's veto threat forestalled attempts by Austria, West Germany, and Hungary to bring the "oppressive actions" of Nicolae Ceauşescu's then-moribund dictatorship in Romania before the Security Council.

Following Ceauşescu's ouster in December, Austria initiated a General Assembly resolution calling for international emergency humanitarian aid to the new Romanian government. The measure—with 40 cosponsors—was adopted by consensus.

The Panama invasion and the overthrow of Ceauşescu kept the General Assembly, normally adjourned before Christmas, in session until almost New Year's Eve. When the United States, British, and French triple-vetoed Security Council efforts to condemn the U.S. invasion, the issue was taken to the 159-nation Assembly. By a vote of 75 to 20, with 40 abstentions, the Assembly branded the military intervention "a flagrant violation of international law" and demanded the immediate withdrawal of U.S. troops.

Security Council. The Middle East dominated the Security Council's schedule in 1989, with 26 of its 69 meetings dealing with such issues as the Israeli-occupied territories, Israel's deportation of Palestinians, and the Lebanon crisis. Eleven of the year's meetings were devoted to Namibia, and ten dealt with Central American regional peace efforts. The rest concerned Afghanistan, UN peace operations, and the U.S. downing of two Libyan fighter planes. In Security Council changes for 1990–91, the Ivory Coast, Cuba, Democratic Yemen, Romania, and Zaire were named to replace Algeria, Brazil, Nepal, Senegal, and Yugoslavia as nonpermanent members.

UN Agencies. In agency activities, former Foreign Minister Thorvald Stoltenberg of Norway was named UN High Commissioner for Refugees (UNHCR) to replace Jean-Pierre Hocké of Switzerland, amid accusations that Hocké had misspent agency funds.

In his report to the General Assembly on the International Atomic Energy Agency, Director General Hans Blix noted a 4% increase in the world's nuclear-power-generating capacity during 1988.

Edouard Saouma, director general of the Food and Agriculture Organization, warned that "famine looms again" in Africa, especially in Ethiopia, Sudan, Mozambique, and Angola.

On December 1, designated as World AIDS Day, the World Health Organization (WHO) reported 600,000 AIDS cases in 152 countries, plus 5 million to 10 million victims believed to be infected with the virus that causes the lethal disease. WHO added that nearly half of the victims are under the age of 25.

Also in December the executive board of the UN Children's Fund (UNICEF) voted to convene a World Summit for Children during the forthcoming 45th General Assembly session.

Financial Crisis. Financially, the UN ended the year with a short-term deficit of about $315 million and what the secretary-general called "very grim" prospects for 1990. U.S. Vice-President Dan Quayle had handed over a $65 million check as a partial U.S. payment of assessed-contributions arrears but suggested that continuing payments would be affected by compliance with the U.S. demand for the repeal of the Assembly's 1975 resolution equating Zionism with racism. As of Jan. 1, 1990, the United States owed some $600 million to the regular budget and an additional $160 million in peacekeeping contributions. The 44th Assembly voted a budget of $1,910,448,600 for the 1990–91 biennium.

TED MORELLO, *UN Correspondent*
"The Christian Science Monitor"

ORGANIZATION OF THE UNITED NATIONS

THE SECRETARIAT

Secretary-General: Javier Pérez de Cuéllar (until Dec. 31, 1991)

THE GENERAL ASSEMBLY (1989)

President: Joseph Nanven Garba, Nigeria
The 159 member nations were as follows:

Afghanistan
Albania
Algeria
Angola
Antigua and Barbuda
Argentina
Australia
Austria
Bahamas
Bahrain
Bangladesh
Barbados
Belgium
Belize
Belorussian SSR
Benin
Bhutan
Bolivia
Botswana
Brazil
Brunei Darussalam
Bulgaria
Burkina Faso
Burundi
Cambodia
Cameroon
Canada
Cape Verde
Central African Republic
Chad
Chile
China, People's Republic of
Colombia
Comoros
Congo
Costa Rica
Cuba
Cyprus
Czechoslovakia
Denmark
Djibouti
Dominica
Dominican Republic
Ecuador
Egypt
El Salvador
Equatorial Guinea
Ethiopia
Fiji
Finland
France
Gabon
Gambia
German Democratic Republic
Germany, Federal Republic of
Ghana
Greece
Grenada
Guatemala
Guinea
Guinea-Bissau
Guyana
Haiti
Honduras
Hungary
Iceland
India
Indonesia
Iran
Iraq
Ireland
Israel
Italy
Ivory Coast
Jamaica
Japan
Jordan
Kenya
Kuwait
Laos
Lebanon
Lesotho
Liberia
Libya
Luxembourg
Madagascar
Malawi
Malaysia
Maldives
Mali
Malta
Mauritania
Mauritius
Mexico
Mongolia
Morocco
Mozambique
Nepal
Netherlands
New Zealand
Nicaragua
Niger
Nigeria
Norway
Oman
Pakistan
Panama
Papua New Guinea
Paraguay
Peru
Philippines
Poland
Portugal
Qatar
Romania
Rwanda
Saint Christopher and Nevis
Saint Lucia
Saint Vincent and The Grenadines
São Tomé and Principe
Saudi Arabia
Senegal
Seychelles
Sierra Leone
Singapore
Solomon Islands
Somalia
South Africa
Spain
Sri Lanka
Sudan
Suriname
Swaziland
Sweden
Syria
Tanzania
Thailand
Togo
Trinidad and Tobago
Tunisia
Turkey
Uganda
Ukrainian SSR
Union of Myanmar (Burma)
USSR
United Arab Emirates
United Kingdom
United States
Uruguay
Vanuatu
Venezuela
Vietnam
Western Samoa
Yemen
Yemen, Democratic
Yugoslavia
Zaire
Zambia
Zimbabwe

COMMITTEES

General. Composed of 29 members as follows: The General Assembly president; the 21 General Assembly vice-presidents (heads of delegations or their deputies of Antigua and Barbuda, Bolivia, Brunei Darussalam, China, Congo, Costa Rica, France, Gambia, Iran, Iraq, Kuwait, Luxembourg, Morocco, Norway, Papua New Guinea, Poland, Sudan, Union of Soviet Socialist Republics, United Kingdom of Great Britain and Northern Ireland, United States, Zimbabwe); and the chairmen of the main committees at right, which are composed of all 159 member countries.

First (Political and Security): Adolfo Taylhardat (Venezuela)
Special Political: Guennadi I. Oudovenko (Ukrainian SSR)
Second (Economic and Financial): Ahmed Ghezal (Tunisia)
Third (Social, Humanitarian and Cultural): Paul Désiré Kaboré (Burkina Faso)
Fourth (Decolonization): Robert F. Van Lierop (Vanuatu)
Fifth (Administrative and Budgetary): Ahmad Fathi Al-Masri (Syria)
Sixth (Legal): Helmut Turk (Austria)

THE SECURITY COUNCIL

Membership ends on December 31 of the year noted; asterisks indicate permanent membership.

Canada (1990)
China*
Colombia (1990)
Cuba (1991)
Ethiopia (1990)
Finland (1990)
France*
Ivory Coast (1991)
Malaysia (1990)
Romania (1991)
USSR*
United Kingdom*
United States*
Yemen, Democratic (1991)
Zaire (1991)

THE ECONOMIC AND SOCIAL COUNCIL

President: Kjeld Mortensen (Denmark)
Membership ends on December 31 of the year noted.

Algeria (1992)
Bahamas (1991)
Bahrain (1992)
Brazil (1991)
Bulgaria (1992)
Burkina Faso (1992)
Cameroon (1991)
Canada (1992)
China (1992)
Colombia (1990)
Cuba (1990)
Czechoslovakia (1991)
Ecuador (1992)
Finland (1992)
France (1990)
German Democratic Republic (1992)
Germany, Federal Republic of (1990)
Ghana (1990)
Greece (1990)
Guinea (1990)
India (1990)
Indonesia (1991)
Iran (1992)
Iraq (1991)
Ireland (1990)
Italy (1991)
Jamaica (1992)
Japan (1990)
Jordan (1991)
Kenya (1991)
Lesotho (1990)
Liberia (1990)
Libya (1990)
Mexico (1992)
Netherlands (1991)
New Zealand (1991)
Nicaragua (1991)
Niger (1991)
Pakistan (1992)
Portugal (1990)
Saudi Arabia (1990)
Sweden (1992)
Thailand (1991)
Trinidad and Tobago (1990)
Tunisia (1991)
Ukrainian Soviet Socialist Republic (1991)
USSR (1992)
United Kingdom (1992)
United States (1991)
Venezuela (1990)
Yugoslavia (1990)
Zaire (1992)
Zambia (1991)

THE TRUSTEESHIP COUNCIL

President: John Birch (United Kingdom)

China[2] France[2] USSR[2] United Kingdom[2] United States[1]

[1] Administers Trust Territory. [2] Permanent member of Security Council not administering Trust Territory.

THE INTERNATIONAL COURT OF JUSTICE

Membership ends on February 5 of the year noted.

President: José María Ruda (Argentina, 1991)
Vice-President: Kéba Mbaye (Senegal, 1991)

Roberto Ago (Italy, 1997)
Mohammed Bedjaoui (Algeria, 1997)
Taslim O. Elias (Nigeria, 1994)
Jens Evensen (Norway, 1994)
Gilbert Guillaume (France, 1991)
Robert Y. Jennings (United Kingdom, 1991)
Manfred Lachs (Poland, 1994)
Kéba Mbaye (Senegal, 1991)
Ni Zhengyu (China, 1994)
Shigeru Oda (Japan, 1994)
Raghunandan Swarup Pathak (India, 1991)
Stephen Schwebel (United States, 1997)
Mohamed Shahabuddeen (Guyana, 1997)
Nikolai Konstantinovich Tarassov (USSR, 1997)

INTERGOVERNMENTAL AGENCIES

Food and Agricultural Organization (FAO); General Agreement on Tariffs and Trade (GATT); International Atomic Energy Agency (IAEA); International Bank for Reconstruction and Development (World Bank); International Civil Aviation Organization (ICAO); International Fund for Agricultural Development (IFAD); International Labor Organization (ILO); International Maritime Organization (IMO); International Monetary Fund (IMF); International Telecommunication Union (ITU); United Nations Educational, Scientific and Cultural Organization (UNESCO); United Nations Industrial Development Organization (UNIDO); Universal Postal Union (UPU); World Health Organization (WHO); World Intellectual Property Organization (WIPO); World Meteorological Organization (WMO).

© Barthelmey/Sipa

The new 41st chief executive of the United States enjoys a favorite retreat, Kennebunkport, ME. After serving as President Reagan's loyal vice-president, George Bush began putting his own stamp on the presidency in 1989.

UNITED STATES

Domestic Affairs

"A president is neither prince nor pope," George Bush told his fellow citizens Jan. 20, 1989, in his first public utterance as president. Discarding the traditional high-flown rhetoric of inaugural addresses along with his topcoat, the new president made clear on a bright and blustery Washington day that his view of his new job was far from grandiose or imperious. Also clear was that his approach to the presidency differed from that of his predecessor, Ronald Reagan, whom he had served loyally as vice-president for eight years. Bush presented himself to the nation as unpretentious, well-intentioned, and determined to achieve harmony rather than the divisions that often had marked the Reagan years.

In what was probably the most striking moment of his address he turned to Democratic congressional leaders seated at the platform and promised them "the offered hand" of bipartisan cooperation. "The American people await action," he asserted. "They didn't send us here to bicker. They ask us to rise above the merely partisan." And echoing one of the themes of his campaign for the White House, he proclaimed a national purpose "to make kinder the face of the nation and gentler the face of the world."

The Presidency. These lofty and conciliatory themes generated an early aura of good feeling around Bush's presidency and contributed to the new chief executive's favorable poll ratings, which he maintained throughout his first year in office. But as was only to be expected given the partisanship inherent in the political process, Bush's commitment to kindness and gentleness did not still the voices of his detractors.

On January 12, Bush had completed the cabinet selection process he had begun right after his election by naming retired Adm. James D. Watkins to be secretary of energy and William J. Bennett to the new position of director of the Office of National Drug Control Policy. Critics pointed out that both Watkins, who had headed a Reagan presidential commission on dealing with AIDS, and Bennett, who had been Reagan's secretary of education, were like most of the rest of his high-ranking appointees Washington insiders and unlikely to generate the fresh ideas that Bush had promised as a candidate.

Complaints that Bush was lacking in forcefulness and focus as the nation's leader mounted before his first winter in the White House was over. Republicans as well as Democrats also grumbled that he had been too slow to fill important slots in his administration. But Bush shrugged off these charges in a March 7 press conference.

If the Bush presidency at times seemed bogged down, it may have been because Bush still had to deal with problems left over from his predecessor's administration. One such difficulty was what to do about the financially beleaguered savings and loan industry. On February 6, Bush proposed a plan that would close or sell 350 ailing savings and loans, revamp the federal system for regulating the industry, and split the $126.2 billion cost between taxpayers and the thrift industry. A few weeks later the estimated cost of the rescue plan was raised to $157.6 billion, or more than $30 billion over the original estimate. The extra funds would be needed, it was explained, to bail out thrift institutions expected to run into financial trouble between 1992 and 1999 while the rescue plan was going into effect. Despite the cost, Congress agreed to a resolution of the problem which closely resembled Bush's proposal and which the president signed into law on August 9.

A more fundamental problem left over from the Reagan era was the budget deficit. The president's plan, outlined in a televised address to a joint session of Congress on February 9, called for holding military spending increases to the inflation rate while cutting taxes on capital gains. Total spending would be $1.16 trillion with a projected deficit of $91.1 billion. Bush promised new proposals for dealing with education, child care, environmental cleanup, drug abuse, and homelessness.

On April 14 the president announced an agreement with congressional leaders on the general outlines of a budget that would meet the 1990 deficit target mandated by the Gramm-Rudman law. But differences between Bush and the Democratic-controlled Congress turned out to be hard to resolve. Congress was unable to meet the October 15 deadline set by Gramm-Rudman for agreement on a reconciliation bill that would reduce the deficit to at least $110 billion. As a result, in compliance with that law, Bush on October 16 signed an order imposing $16.1 billion in automatic across-the-board spending cuts.

Still another leftover Reagan problem that plagued Bush was the revelation of a far-reaching scandal in the Department of Housing and Urban Development (HUD). This came to light on April 26 with the release of an internal audit by the department showing that former department officials and well-connected Republican politicians had received millions of dollars in consulting fees from developers seeking approval from HUD for federally subsidized housing projects. Abuses were centered in the Moderate Rehabilitation Program under which the government gave financial incentives to developers to renovate existing housing for low- and moderate-income families.

Following release of the report, HUD Secretary Jack Kemp on April 26 suspended all funding for the program and several congressional committees began investigating the allegations. After hearing testimony from HUD Inspector General Paul A. Adams, Rep. Henry B. Gonzalez (D-TX), chairman of the House Banking Committee's subcommittee on housing and community development, criticized Adams for failing to probe the role of then HUD Secretary Samuel R. Pierce, Jr., in the operations of the program.

Testifying on May 25 before the House Government Operations subcommittee on employment and housing, chaired by Rep. Tom Lantos (D-CA), Pierce said that he turned much of the responsibility for decision-making on the grants over to aides, particularly his executive assistant, Deborah Gore Dean. Pierce admitted that he had asked his staff to give "careful consideration" to projects for which former Interior Secretary James G. Watt and other prominent Republicans had sought HUD support, but denied that such persons had received special treatment. Watt himself testified that he had been paid more than $400,000 between 1984 and 1986 as a consultant to various housing projects. He said his own actions had been "legal, moral, ethical, and effective," contending that the large fees he had collected showed that "the system is flawed." Paul Manafort, a former campaign aide to both Bush and Reagan, testified June 20 that he had engaged in "influence peddling" on behalf of a developer seeking funding for an apartment rehabilitation project. Manafort's firm had been paid $326,000 in 1986 for his services.

Subsequent testimony from other witnesses and documents from Pierce's files tended to contradict the former secretary's earlier claim that he had played only a limited part in project funding, and interest in his role intensified. Scheduled to testify September 15 before Lantos' subcommittee, Pierce refused to appear, saying his recently hired lawyers had not had sufficient time to prepare him. When he finally did appear before the committee on September 26, Pierce refused to answer questions, citing the 5th Amendment's protections against self-incrimination. After Pierce appeared before the committee October 27 and again took the 5th Amendment, 19 Democratic members of the House Judiciary Committee formally called on the Justice Department to act. On December 4 the department announced that it had opened a formal criminal inquiry to decide whether a special prosecutor should investigate allegations of perjury and conspiracy against Pierce.

To prevent recurrence of such abuses, Congress approved most provisions of a reform plan proposed by Secretary Kemp. The new law will tighten internal and external inspections of HUD operations and limit its discretion in handing out money.

Meanwhile, Bush sought to push ahead with his promised new initiatives in several areas:

• *Education*. Following up on his campaign promise to be the "education president," on April 5 he proposed to Congress a $441 million plan to improve education standards. The major components were a proposal for $250 million for cash awards to schools whose students raised their achievement levels, and another $100 million to help establish magnet schools. Democrats and some educators claimed that the funding was insufficient to have significant impact.

• *Drugs*. On September 5, in his first nationally televised speech from the White House, Bush outlined his program for combat-

(Continued on page 542.)

Government Ethics

One of George Bush's first acts as president was to appoint a special commission to "take a fresh look" at existing ethical standards for all three branches of the U.S. government and then to propose a brand new ethical code.

By highlighting ethics, President Bush appeared to be trying to use this issue to set his administration apart from that of his predecessor, Ronald Reagan, which critics charged had been blemished badly by insensitivity to propriety and outright wrongdoing by a number of its high officials. As such, the presidential stress on ethics was welcomed on Capitol Hill by Democrats and Republicans as a way of alleviating public cynicism toward government. As events developed though, both the president and the Congress got more than they bargained for from the new emphasis on ethics. The branches of government soon were embroiled in a series of ethical controversies.

The Tower Case. Apart from the president's rhetoric, intensified scrutiny by the media of public officials, inspired in part by the Watergate scandal, also contributed to the increased importance given ethics. At any rate, the Bush administration clearly was taken off guard when the first important victim of the new ethical climate that the president had helped to create was his own nominee for defense secretary, former Texas Sen. John Tower. Though as a former senator, Tower normally would have been assured of easy confirmation, he instead was subjected to intensive interrogation and criticism in two major groupings—possible conflicts of interest linked to the lucrative fees that Tower had accepted as a consultant to defense contractors, and his personal morality, concern over which stemmed from allegations of womanizing and insobriety.

In testimony before the Senate Armed Services Committee on January 26, Tower acknowledged receiving more than $750,000 from big defense firms between the time he left government service as arms-control negotiator in April 1986 and December 1988 when he resigned his consulting business because he was under consideration for the Pentagon post. "Being available at the end of the telephone for advice from someone who has some degree of experience and sophistication in a field is of value to people," Tower told the committee. But skeptical committee Democrats voiced their suspicions that the companies actually were paying Tower not for his advice but for favors rendered when he served in the Senate and for influence he would wield in the Pentagon.

Perhaps even more troublesome for Tower because it was more emotional was the morality issue, which first was given emphasis by conservative activist Paul M. Weyrich. He told the committee on January 31 that as a result of having on several occasions seen Tower drunk and making advances to women other than his wife, he had "serious reservations" about Tower's moral character. Because of Weyrich's credentials as a staunch conservative his criticism of Tower's behavior opened the way for critics from elsewhere on the political spectrum to pursue this subject, and Tower's personal life soon became the focus of a wide range of allegations, some of which his supporters contended had no basis in fact. Asked directly during the committee hearings if he had a drinking problem, Tower said flatly: "I have none. I am a man of some discipline." Nearly all Senate Republicans rallied behind him.

On February 23 the Armed Services Committee by an 11 to nine party line vote rejected the nomination. Tower and Bush refused to admit defeat and Tower sought to help his own cause by publicly pledging to abstain from alcohol in a television interview show February 26. But when the full Senate began to debate the nomination March 2, Tower's foes remained adamant.

On March 9 the full Senate voted to reject the nomination with 52 Democrats and only one Republican voting against confirmation while 44 Republicans and only three Democrats backed the nominee. Tower was the first presidential cabinet nominee in 30 years not to win Senate approval. Bush responded in a conciliatory fashion, saying that he respected the Senate's role in the nomination process. But Vice-President Dan Quayle accused Tower's Senate Democrat foes of waging a "McCarthyite mudslinging campaign," and the struggle over Tower's nomination left a residue of bitter partisan feelings on Capitol Hill as the next battle over ethics got under way.

House Speaker Wright. The central figure this time was a Democrat, House Speaker Jim Wright of Texas. He had been under investigation by the House Committee on Standards of Official Conduct, or Ethics Committee as it is known generally, since the previous June. The panel had been looking into the unusually high royalties Wright received from a published collection of his reflections, many copies of which were bought in bulk quantities by his political supporters, and other aspects of his political and financial dealings. The committee had acted on a complaint filed by Republican Congressman Newt Gingrich of Georgia, which was supported by Common Cause, the self-described public interest lobbying group. To demonstrate its objectivity the committee, made up of six Democrats and six Republicans, had hired an outside law firm, headed by Richard J. Phelan, to serve as special counsel for the probe.

On April 17 the committee issued a "statement of violations" against Wright in which he was charged with 69 specific instances of violating House rules dealing with the acceptance of gifts and outside income. The charges stemmed from sales of his book and his relationship with Texas businessman and friend George Mallick. The committee alleged that bulk sales of the book *Reflections of a Public Man* were designed as an "overall scheme to evade the House limits on outside earned income." As to Mallick, the committee's report contended that Wright and his wife Betty had received $145,000 in "apparent gifts" from Mallick over a ten-year period, including free and low-rent housing, use of an auto, and $18,000 in salary paid to Mrs. Wright while she purportedly was working for an investment company owned by Mallick.

As the committee began the process of deciding whether there was "clear and convincing proof" that Wright was guilty of the charges, the speaker fought back. "I know in my heart I have not violated any rules," he declared in a speech April 17. He then produced affidavits from Texas business people who contended that Mrs. Wright had been involved actively in her work for Mallick's firm, and that her compensation was thus no gift.

On May 23 his lawyers mounted a vigorous defense at committee hearings, demanding the dismissal of key charges against the speaker. But it soon became clear he was fighting a losing battle as his colleagues privately expressed concern that the charges against him were hurting his party and the Congress and as published reports of new allegations against him kept him on the defensive. His position also had been weakened when it was disclosed that one of his top aides, John Mack, had been convicted of a brutal assault on a young woman in 1973. Mack resigned May 11. Finally on May 31, Wright himself announced he would resign the speakership and his seat in Congress, becoming the first speaker to be forced from his post because of scandal.

Coelho and Other Cases. Wright's resignation was made even more dramatic because only a few days before he announced it, another top House Democrat, Tony Coelho of California, the majority whip, announced that he was going to quit to avoid a prolonged investigation of his financial dealings. Coelho had been in trouble because of published speculation that in 1986 he had used campaign contributions to purchase $100,000 in junk bonds. Coelho denied the use of campaign funds, but admitted that he had failed to report on his congressional disclosure form a $50,000 personal loan he had used to help make the purchase.

A few days after Coelho's announcement, *CBS News* reported that the Justice Department was probing the personnel practices of Rep. William H. Gray of Pennsylvania, the chairman of the House Democratic Caucus. Gray denied the charge and it ultimately turned out that the inquiry did not involve Gray directly. But the report, apparently leaked by the Justice Department, added to the crosscurrents of anger and resentment in the House which Wright referred to in a dramatic hour-long speech announcing his decision to resign. "It is intolerable that qualified members of the executive and legislative branches are resigning because of the ambiguities and the confusion surrounding the ethics laws and because of their own consequent vulnerability to personal attack," Wright said.

But Wright's words did not bring an end to ethics controversies in the Congress. Democratic Rep. Bill Alexander of Arkansas filed a complaint with the Ethics Committee asking it to look into allegations that Republican Congressman Gingrich, who had been the leading critic of Wright, himself had violated House rules through a book-promotion arrangement that some thought similar to the scheme that contributed to Wright's downfall. The committee once again retained the Phelan law firm that conducted the probe of Wright. But after a three-month investigation the firm reportedly informed the committee on October 20 that it had not found grounds to conduct a full-scale probe of Gingrich.

In addition to disputes over finances, the ethics committee also confronted a number of allegations of sexual misbehavior. On October 18, in its first decision in those cases, the committee issued a "letter of reproval" chastising Democratic Congressman Jim Bates of California for sexually harassing female members of his staff. Other cases before the committee involved the conviction in state court of Ohio Republican Donald E. (Buz) Lukens for having sexual relations with a minor, the charge that Democratic Rep. Gus Savage of Illinois had forced sexual attentions on a female Peace Corps volunteer while he was on a trip to Africa, and the admission by Democratic Rep. Barney Frank of Massachusetts, an acknowledged homosexual, that he had hired a male prostitute who, while serving as Frank's chauffeur and housekeeper, had run a male prostitution ring out of Frank's Washington apartment. The Frank case stirred the most controversy

controversy because of Frank's prominence as an advocate of liberal positions.

In a case involving not merely ethical misbehavior but a crime, Democratic Congressman Robert Garcia of New York and his wife, Jane Lee Garcia, were convicted on October 20 by a federal jury of extorting more than $170,000 in payoffs from Wedtech Corp., the scandal-ridden defense contractor. He later resigned his House seat. Meanwhile on the Senate side, five senators—Alan Cranston (D-CA), Dennis DeConcini (D-AZ), John Glenn (D-OH), John McCain (R-AZ), and Donald W. Riegel, Jr. (D-MI) were under fire late in the year in connection with receiving campaign contributions from the chairman of a failing savings and loan association. In addition the Senate Ethics Committee announced in December that it would investigate allegations that Sen. Alfonse D'Amato (R-NY) helped political donors receive grants from the Department of Housing and Urban Development. Sen. Dave Durenberger (R-MN) also was under committee scrutiny concerning questions on proceeds of his books. With such cases pending, it was apparent that the issue of how government officials should conduct themselves would remain into 1990.

ROBERT SHOGAN

ing drugs, as required under antidrug legislation enacted in 1988. The plan called for total spending of $7.9 billion, with the biggest single amount, $3.1 billion, going for law enforcement. Democrats pointed out that the spending Bush was asking for amounted to an increase of only $716 million over what already was contemplated in the next fiscal year and claimed that more money was needed, particularly for treatment and prevention. Eventually Congress approved about $8.8 billion for drug enforcement.

• *Housing.* In a November speech to the National Association of Realtors in Dallas, the president outlined a three-year, $4.2 billion package of proposals that he claimed would "bring basic shelter and affordable housing within reach of millions of Americans." Under the plan, which Bush called Homeownership and Opportunity for People Everywhere (HOPE), $2.15 billion would be available for grants to state and local governments and nonprofit groups to help rehabilitate public housing and assist low-income families in buying the refurbished property.

Congress. The first session of the 101st Congress was marked by internal fractiousness, as ethical controversies forced a shakeup in the Democratic leadership, and by bitter battles with President Bush. The first of these struggles, early in the year, over the nomination of John Tower to be defense secretary, ended in defeat for Tower and Bush. (*See* special report, page 540.) The final clash between the lawmakers and the chief executive was over the federal budget and resulted in a compromise that concluded the session.

In between these two battles, in addition to enacting a rescue plan for the savings and loan industry, Congress raised the minimum wage, revised the schedule for Medicare payments to physicians, and changed its own ethics rules. But many problems were put off until 1990. House Republican Whip Rep. Newt Gingrich of Georgia called the session "an unfinished Congress."

Despite the early hopes for accord on deficit reduction, this issue turned into the most prolonged controversy of the session. Democrats put the blame for collapse of the apparent compromise achieved in April on the president's insistence on pushing his proposed reduction in the rate of the capital-gains tax, an idea which they argued would have undercut attempts to reduce the deficit. Republicans accused the Democrats of excessive partisanship in resisting the capital-gains proposal, which had been a Bush campaign promise.

To reach the final compromise, which made it possible for Congress to adjourn just before the Thanksgiving holiday, Bush finally abandoned his drive for capital-gains reduction. On the other side, the Democrats gave up on a flock of varied and costly measures of their own, notably a proposal for child care. The result was a $14.7 billion reduction package, more than $6 billion of which came from such accounting gimmicks as accelerated collections of existing taxes and placing some agencies and programs "off budget" so their cost would not be counted in the deficit. Another $4.6 billion of the reduction was derived from extending through the first week in February the automatic spending cuts imposed under Gramm-Rudman in October.

Congress had a new Democratic leadership team in 1989. Thomas Foley (WA) became House speaker, while Maine's George Mitchell (r) *was the Senate majority leader.*

© Trippett/Sipa

With President Bush taking part, Dick Cheney (left), *former sixth term Republican congressman from Wyoming, was invested as the nation's 17th secretary of defense in the center courtyard of the Pentagon on March 21.*

Among other major action in various issue areas:

• *Defense.* President Reagan's 1990 budget proposal for spending $315 billion on defense programs was cut by about $10 billion. Economies included a slowdown in the production rate of the B-2 Stealth bomber and a reduction in spending on the so-called Star Wars antimissile system to $3.8 billion, nearly $300 million lower than had been appropriated in fiscal 1989 and $1.1 billion below the amount requested by Bush. Congress also continued the ban on tests of antimissile missiles which would violate the "traditional" interpretation of the 1972 antiballistic missile treaty with the Soviet Union.

• *Ethics.* Restrictions on outside income were tightened in exchange for pay raises for both House and Senate. House members, along with federal judges and high-ranking executive branch appointees, will get a nearly 40% increase over two years, raising the salary of House members from $89,500 to more than $120,000 by 1991. The Senate accepted a one-year raise of about 10%. Under the new income restrictions, honoraria will be banned outright in the House and phased out for the Senate.

• *Health.* In the face of furious protests from some senior citizens, Congress repealed almost the entire Medicare Catastrophic Coverage Act which it had passed in 1988 with bipartisan support. Though the law had been hailed widely as a boon for older people, middle- and upper-income seniors objected to having to pay a surtax to cover the cost of the added benefits the law provided. Congress scrapped the Medicare benefits along with the surtax, though it preserved expansions of the medicaid program for the indigent contained in the 1988 measure. Congress also established a new fee schedule for paying doctors, based on the time and skill required to provide services, designed to slow the soaring rate of Medicare costs.

Lawmakers acknowledged that the fundamental issue of providing health care for the elderly will have to be dealt with in the future, along with the federal deficit. Other areas in which serious problems were tabled but not solved include campaign financing, where a House task force was unable to agree on such questions as campaign cost limits and public financing; stock market regulation, where details of proposals to extend the authority of the Securities and Exchange Commission remain to be resolved; the environment, where differences over such issues as acid rain and alternative fuels prevented agreement on revision of the 1970 Clean Air Act; and child care, where legislation was blocked by ideological and jurisdictional disputes.

Politics. November 7 ballot results held unusual significance for an off-year campaign. Such elections ordinarily are dominated by local issues and personalities. But a number of 1989 contests cast light on voter attitudes on two issues—race and abortion—with far-reaching implications. The race issue was raised by the candidacies of black Democrats, most notably Virginia Lt. Gov. Douglas Wilder, who defeated Republican J. Marshall Coleman to become the first of his race in U.S. history to be elected governor, and David Dinkins, who defeated Republican Rudolph W. Giuliani, becoming New York City's first black mayor.

The success of Wilder, the grandson of slaves, seemed even more dramatic because it took place in a state that had been a bastion of the Old Confederacy and a stronghold of massive resistance to desegregation in the 1950s and 1960s. And Dinkins' victory took on added significance because he was one of four blacks to win mayoralty races in white majority cities.

A memorial to the civil-rights movement, designed by Maya Lin, who had done Washington's Vietnam War Memorial, was dedicated in Montgomery, AL, on November 5. The black granite memorial includes the names of 40 individuals who were killed as a result of racial conflict or because of their involvement in the civil-rights movement.

AP/Wide World

The others were Democrat John Daniels, who won in New Haven, CT, Democrat Norman Rice, who was elected mayor of Seattle, and Chester L. Jenkins, who won a nonpartisan election to become the first black mayor of Durham, NC. Another black, Coleman Young, was elected to a fifth mayoralty term in Detroit.

As for the abortion issue, it was pushed to the forefront by a Supreme Court decision handed down in the summer in the Webster case which upheld a state law restricting access to abortion. (*See* feature article, page 44.) The resultant controversy appeared to help Wilder and Dinkins, who supported the right to abortion, as well as another Democrat who took a similar position, Democratic Rep. James J. Florio, who was elected governor of New Jersey. Florio defeated Republican Rep. James Courter.

In an election-day press conference at the White House, President Bush sought to minimize the political importance of abortion, contending that most voters did not make up their minds over a "single issue." Nevertheless, Democrats said that the election results confirmed recent polling data indicating the Webster decision had galvanized supporters of abortion rights on an issue on which antiabortion forces hitherto had been the most active and effective. They contended that this trend, combined with the success of their black candidates in getting white votes, showed their party was staging a comeback after losing the last three presidential elections.

As further evidence of their renewed vitality Democrats pointed to their success in winning six of eight special House elections called in 1989 to fill vacancies. Democrats gained ground in two races. Democrat Jill Long won the Indiana seat that had been held by newly appointed Republican Sen. Daniel R. Coats and previously held by Vice-President Dan Quayle. And Democrat Gene Taylor won the Mississippi seat that had been held until his death by Republican Rep. Larkin Smith. Democrats lost only one seat they had held previously. This was in Florida, where Republican Ileana Ros-Lehtinen won the seat made vacant by the death of veteran Democrat lawmaker Claude Pepper. Republicans maintained their hold on the Wyoming seat formerly held by Dick Cheney, who resigned to become defense secretary, by electing state legislator Craig Thomas.

In the four other special elections the Democrats won in districts which they had controlled previously—in Alabama, where Glen Browder won the seat made vacant by the

UNITED STATES • Information Highlights

Official Name: United States of America.
Location: Central North America.
Area: 3,618,768 sq mi (9 372 610 km²).
Population (mid-1989 est.): 248,800,000.
Chief Cities (1988 est.): Washington, DC, the capital, 617,000; New York, 7,353,000; Los Angeles, 3,353,000; Chicago, 2,978,000; Houston, 1,698,000; Philadelphia, 1,647,000; San Diego, 1,070,000.
Government: *Head of state and government,* George Bush, president (took office Jan. 20, 1989). *Legislature*—Congress: Senate and House of Representatives.
Monetary Unit: Dollar.
Gross National Product (1988): $4,862,000,000,000.
Merchandise Trade (1988): *Imports,* $460,136,000,000; *exports,* $321,431,000,000.

death of Bill Nichols; in Texas, where Craig Washington took the seat that had been held until his death by Rep. Mickey Leland; in another Texas district where Pete Geren won the seat which former House Speaker Jim Wright had resigned; and in California, where Gary Condit won the seat which Tony Coelho had resigned.

Environment. National concern about damage to the environment was heightened during 1989 as a result of the largest oil spill in U.S. history. It happened March 24, in the Gulf of Alaska, when the oil tanker *Exxon Valdez,* loaded with 1.26 million barrels of crude oil, ran aground on Bligh Reef, located 25 mi (40 km) from Valdez, southern terminus of the Alyeska pipeline. Some 260,000 barrels of oil were spilled, extending over 2,600 sq mi (6 934 km^2). (*See* feature article, page 36.)

On another environmental front, the Bush administration announced May 12 that it would reverse its previous policy and work toward an international treaty to curb global warming.

Even amid increasing evidence of the damage done by man to nature, an earthquake in northern California served as a sobering reminder of the damage that nature could do to man. The quake struck on the evening of October 17 in the San Francisco Bay area. Casualties included 67 dead, 3,700 injured, and some 12,000 displaced from their homes. (*See* feature article, page 50.)

ROBERT SHOGAN
Washington Bureau, "Los Angeles Times"

The Economy

The U.S. economy plodded through its seventh straight year of expansion in 1989, a record for peacetime. Though it appeared winded at times, it continued to defy the forecasts of those who believed that age, if only that, would topple it into recession.

Early in the year, many economists were ready to write the obituary. Inflation seemed to be gaining a foothold and interest rates continued to rise. By summer, however, the worst of the price increases were over, interest rates were receding, and production was surprising everyone again. It was a repeat of what had become a familiar scenario during the previous few years, of an economy seemingly on the ropes and then getting its second wind. Economic strength was underestimated repeatedly. Commerce Department estimates of third-quarter growth, for example, had to be revised upward twice, eventually to 3% annually. After that the pace began receding into what, said the typically nervous forecasters once again, might be a recession in 1990.

Growth and Competition. Many people credited the Federal Reserve Board (the Fed) and its chairman, Alan Greenspan, for maintaining "sustainable" economic growth, albeit slight at times. From early 1988 until the spring of 1989 the Fed kept a lid on the money supply, forcing up interest rates to smother any little brushfires. Others criticized the Fed, saying it prevented the economy from reaching its potential, and that it was flirting with a downturn it might not be able to control.

More likely, the disinflation thrust was a team effort, involving not just the Federal Reserve but manufacturers who had learned how to be more efficient producers of goods, somewhat conservative consumptions on the part of everyone, a determination by the federal government to reduce the federal budget deficit—it was down slightly to $152.1 billion in fiscal year 1989—and restraint by labor in wage demands. Not to be forgotten, though, was the extreme level of competition. Several factors combined to produce the competitive situation, among them the desire of many producers to maintain market share even at the cost of short-term profits, and the growing pace of global trade. Automotive manufacturers were especially competitive with each other, vying for consumer attention with rebates that in some instances exceeded $1,000 and below-market interest rates that touched zero percentage. But they were not alone in competing. In some instances stock and real-estate brokers were compelled to cut their commissions, McDonald's ran 99¢ hamburger specials all year long, and Sears, the giant retailer, was forced to abandon its periodic discounts in favor of so-called everyday low prices.

The developing global competition also forced companies to restructure, in many instances by reducing their work forces, focusing their marketing efforts, and consolidating their manufacturing. Of the 40 companies deemed excellent in the early 1980s book *In Search of Excellence,* all but eight had restructured at least twice by the end of 1989.

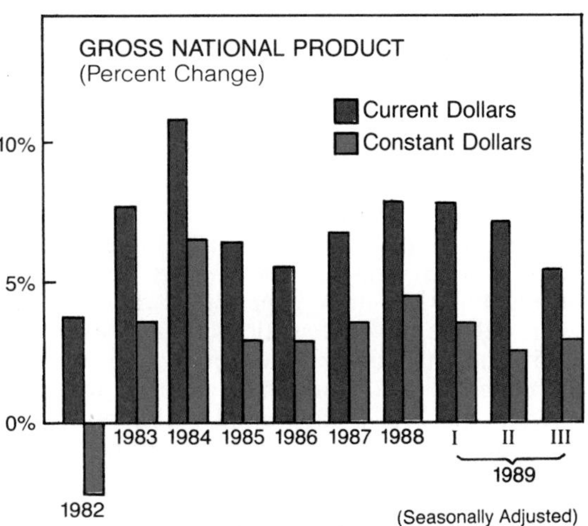

Inflation. The net result was continued talk of inflation—expansions always end that way, the pessimists said—but the rate of price increases declined as the year progressed. Irritated by repeated references in the media, the U.S. Chamber of Commerce commented in October that "a chorus of concern over the threat of accelerating inflation, led by the sopranos at the Federal Reserve, has been played over and over in daily news stories." But, it continued, "that tone rings discordantly." The evidence was overwhelming, it said, that general inflation had faded as the year wore on, perhaps disguised from statistical view because the consumer price index (CPI) was skewed by two great exceptions, the high and rising cost of medical-care services and continued price rises in business services. For the year, the increase in the CPI would average 4.6%. The first-quarter rate exceeded 5% and the final-quarter rate was 4.3%. While inflation watchers observed that this was but a modest improvement, the optimists observed that at least inflation was in the right direction.

Other Indicators. The price of lower inflation was a weakening economy. The operating rate of factories, mines, and utilities dropped from a ten-year high of 84.3% early in the year to just 82.7% near the end. The gross national product rose about 3% to an unofficial $4.15 trillion (in 1982 dollars, the official constant), but it had risen 4.4% the year before. Personal consumption rose 2.8% to $2.7 trillion (1982 dollars) but it had risen almost 3.5% in 1988. Automobile sales once again topped 10 million, but were about 350,000 lower than a year earlier. Housing starts reached 1.4 million but that represented a decline of about 100,000 from a year earlier.

By concentrating on such declines, as many economists and millions of Americans did throughout 1989, one inadvertently could overlook the many positive results turned in during the year. The savings rate, the low level of which had been a perennial irritant, rose to 5.3% from 4.2% a year earlier. While civilian employment grew only 2% to more than 117 million jobs, the civilian unemployment rate fell to 5.3% from 5.5% a year earlier. And worker productivity, after showing little improvement early in the year, rose sharply as the year ended.

The Finance Area. The Treasury long bond (30 years) dipped below 8%, and 30-year fixed home mortgage rates, which had risen sharply during the tight-money period earlier in the year, fell below 10% nationally and even to 9.25% in certain areas. The negative position of merchandise trade, an imbalance of imports over exports, fell from around $118.5 billion in 1988 to $109.5 billion in 1989. Exports increased, signifying a more competitive posture for American business, despite a 3.7% rise in the international exchange rate of the dollar.

On the tax front, President Bush was able to maintain his promise of no income-tax increase, a vow that many Americans thought would be impossible to fulfill. It cost him, however. During his campaign for the presidency, he had promised to seek a cut in the capital-gains tax rate, and immediately he set out to do so. The issue blew hot and cold during the year.

In all, the 1989 economic year was relatively bland, compared at least to some years of the preceding decade. The stock market was a big exception. As it did in 1987 and, said the chairman of the New York Stock Exchange, probably will do again, the stock market took a dive. Investors everywhere seemed to think the timing was ominous: Friday the 13th, almost two years to the day from the great crash of October 1987. One weekend cured such premonitions; on Monday, October 16, the market regained 88.12 of the 190.58 points lost from the Dow Jones industrial average, bringing it from 2569.26 to 2657.38. It was still rising, to record-high levels, as the year ended.

Why the stock market should continue to rise amid the prevailing uncertainties puzzled some analysts, especially since the growth rate of corporate profits had declined throughout the year. In the first quarter of the year the companies making up the Standard & Poor's 500-stock index reported total gains of 22% over the year-earlier figures. By the final quarter of the year the rate was far down into the single digits. Moreover, these analysts pointed out that companies burdened with heavy debt, as many were, faced problems paying bills in a weakening economy. In addition, the prime interest rate to the best corporate customers had ceased falling, puzzling even the Fed itself. After being as high as 11.5%, the prime fell a full percentage point and was forecast to fall again—and finally did so early in 1990. Critics said banks were reacting to the eased credit conditions because of a desire, in fact, a need, to conserve funds. Earlier in the year, many of the country's biggest banks had been forced to add hundreds of millions of dollars to reserves because of loans that increasingly appeared to be uncollectible. And as the year ended, banks in New England and some other parts of the Northeast, where economies had lost their strong momentum of the mid-1980s, struggled with large amounts of nonperforming real-estate loans.

Still, the economic recovery that began in the final month of 1982 remained on its feet. It had brought down interest rates and the rate of inflation, which had seemed almost beyond control a decade earlier. But it also was accompanied by an explosion of personal, business, and government debt that defied control. Those debts now became the burdensome inheritance of the 1990s.

JOHN CUNNIFF, *The Associated Press*

© Chip Hires/Gamma-Liaison

U.S. President George Bush and Soviet leader Mikhail Gorbachev meet aboard the cruise ship "Maxim Gorky" during their first summit, off Malta in December.

Foreign Affairs

In the area of foreign policy, observers gave President George Bush high marks as a policy manager in his first year in office, but the reviews were far more mixed on his ability as an innovator or alliance leader.

The administration was relatively slow in filling major foreign-policy posts and in responding to a number of Soviet and allied proposals and initiatives, slow at a time when Soviet President Mikhail Gorbachev appeared to need foreign-policy successes to strengthen his domestic position and reforms. Once under way, with a relatively businesslike approach to other countries and international organizations, the Bush administration appeared to downplay some of the Reagan priorities, such as contra aid in Nicaragua and the Strategic Defense Initiative (SDI). President Bush also was beset with a few near-crisis challenges, including Lebanese terrorism, Chinese repression, the drug cartel, trade frictions, abortive Philippine and Panamanian coups, and Eastern European uprisings. Many of these challenges were met diplomatically and cautiously, but U.S. military force was used in two major instances. Despite his campaign billing as an environmentalist, Bush for economic reasons also was cautious about supporting proposed global standards in such areas as fossil fuel emissions.

Washington at first appeared befuddled in responding to the peace and arms control overtures of the popular President Gorbachev. However, at the North Atlantic Treaty Organization (NATO) summit in June, Bush seemed to remove the last obstacles to an agreement on European conventional force (troops and aircraft as well as armor) reductions. While Soviet troops began withdrawals from Eastern Europe, NATO and Warsaw Pact states had yet to specify which countries' armaments would be reduced and in what proportions. The United States proposed ceilings of 275,000 troops on each side, and by year's end defense spending cuts appeared inevitable. Some U.S. cuts came as a result of congressional maneuvering and the Gramm-Rudman deficit reduction law, although Congress tended to reverse the Pentagon's preference for trimming conventional as opposed to nuclear forces.

Soviet-U.S. Relations. Presidents Bush and Gorbachev held their first summit meeting in December in the turbulent seas off Malta. The summit, however, resulted in a further calm in relations between the superpowers. Gorbachev denounced characteristics of the cold war. Bush promised to dismantle U.S. trade barriers that had been set up against the USSR in the mid-1970s and to help the Soviets join the world economic community. The two leaders also decided to press for agreements on nuclear weapon and conventional forces limitations in 1990, and a second summit was slated for June.

Prospects for a long-range nuclear weapons accord had improved earlier, when the Soviets agreed to separate other arms-control issues from the deemphasized, but still troubling, Strategic Defense Initiative ("Star Wars").

U.S. Secretary of State James Baker and Soviet Foreign Secretary Eduard Shevardnadze also had agreed to pursue major worldwide reductions of chemical weapons, although the United States insisted on retaining its latest stocks until other nations with chemical weapons, such as Iraq and Libya, also agreed to terms at ongoing talks in Geneva.

Despite obvious progress, only a few formal U.S.-Soviet agreements were reached in 1989, on such matters as preventing accidental mili-

© Dirck Halstead/"Time" Magazine

James A. Baker III, former White House chief of staff and treasury secretary, turned his attention to foreign affairs in 1989, becoming the 61st secretary of state.

tary confrontations, inspecting weapons facilities, and governing movement across the Bering Strait.

Communist Upheavals. The Bush administration was careful to adopt a watchful, nonprovocative approach to the domestic difficulties of the major Communist powers, China and the USSR. When Beijing violently repressed the Chinese prodemocracy movement in June, the United States was torn between desires for continued Chinese political and economic ties and the temptation to push for democracy. As the year neared an end, a high-level U.S. delegation, led by National Security Adviser Brent Scowcroft, went to China to seek an improvement in relations.

Western and southern Soviet ethnic republics also saw mass popular movements for reorganization and autonomy in 1989. Gorbachev struggled to control the pace of reform and prevent strikes, upheavals, and bloodshed. Bush emphasized the desire to see his Soviet counterpart succeed.

Washington cheered more openly for the development of opposition movements in Poland, Hungary, Czechoslovakia, and Romania. When 50,000 East Germans fled to the West in October and thousands more took to the streets in protest, the American response was relatively restrained, although Secretary of State Baker brought up the touchy subject of German reunification.

The Bush administration was challenged just to keep up with the number of changes in Eastern Europe. The amazing magnitude of the changes was demonstrated on November 9 when East Germany opened the Berlin Wall and allowed free access to the West. The opening also raised a number of questions, including the future roles of the NATO and Warsaw Pact military alliances and of Germany in a less threatening Europe.

Latin America. Hopes raised by peace talks between the El Salvador government and rebels were dashed when fierce fighting erupted in November. The offensive was the rebels' most extensive action in a decade. The United States continued aid to the rightist government, causing renewed protests from some Americans who cited alleged complicity in such atrocities as the murder of six Jesuit priests.

In neighboring Nicaragua, President Daniel Ortega unilaterally ended the government's cease-fire with the contras, claiming increased contra activity. U.S. congressional restrictions on contra aid, along with a joint United Nations and Central American peace initiative, meant at least grudging U.S. support for internationally observed elections to be held in 1990. In an attempt to defeat Ortega's Sandinista government, however, the United States moved to channel money to opposition candidates.

President Bush came to share former President Reagan's exasperation with Panama's military strongman and alleged international drug trafficker, Gen. Manuel Antonio Noriega, when an October coup attempt to oust him failed. The Bush administration was criticized because U.S. forces in Panama stood by, offering little, if any, support for the coup. The president later resorted to large-scale U.S. military force to oust the dictator.

Latin drug cartels also preoccupied Washington as the cartels launched violent retaliatory attacks on government officials in Colombia. In addition to such issues as development, debt, and democracy, drug traffic was also a topic of discussion between Bush and Latin American leaders in 1989. In a seeming confusion of priorities, however, the United States withdrew from the International Coffee Agreement, which is crucial to Colombia's main legal export, over price disputes.

The Philippines and Cambodia. The United States played a role in turning back an early December coup attempt to oust Philippine President Corazon Aquino. U.S. fighter jets flew cover for loyalist troops fighting a rebel faction of the Philippine Army. Opposition leaders criticized Aquino for requesting the U.S. intervention, contending she surrendered the country's sovereignty to stay in power.

No agreement was reached among participants in Paris peace talks in August to end the civil war in Cambodia. The Vietnamese unilaterally pulled out of the country in 1989, after a ten-year occupation. But the United States continued to support non-Communist rebels over the Vietnamese-installed government.

Middle East and Afghanistan. Exasperation was also the Bush administration's reaction when Lebanese terrorists announced their execution in July of U.S. hostage Col. William Higgins, in response to an Israeli abduction of a prominent Shiite Muslim cleric. Washington could do little to retaliate since the terrorists and hostages were out of reach. Diplomatic pressure against Iran and some U.S. congressional criticism of Israel led to the postponement of threatened executions of additional Western hostages.

In conjunction with Egyptian President Hosni Mubarak, U.S. Secretary of State Baker attempted in 1989 to renew Arab-Israeli peace talks on the Palestinian question. Israel rejected Mubarak's proposed talks in October, but terms acceptable to Egypt, the Palestine Liberation Organization (PLO), and Israel were reached in December, and talks on Prime Minister Yitzhak Shamir's proposals for limited Arab elections in Israeli-held territory were expected in early 1990. Israel's cooperation with South Africa on military matters and nuclear technology also concerned Washington in 1989, as did Iraq's announcement of ballistic-missile technology.

In Afghanistan, the predicted collapse of the Soviet-backed government did not occur when the last Soviet troops left the country in 1989. The opposition *mujahidin* forces lacked unity and were subject to corruption. A stalemate set in as the United States continued assistance to the *mujahidin* through Pakistan.

Africa. The Angolan cease-fire accords appeared to unravel in 1989. But in light of Cuba's apparent willingness to withdraw from the country, U.S. congressional critics pressed the Bush administration to drop support for Jonas Savimbi's Angolan rebel faction.

The election to set up a framework for Namibian independence from South Africa went smoothly in November, and was judged free and fair by international observers. The South West Africa People's Organization (SWAPO), the guerrilla group that has fought South Africa for Namibian independence since the mid-1960s, garnered the most votes. However, SWAPO failed to win the two-thirds majority that would have enabled it to control the writing of the new country's constitution.

Meanwhile, the U.S. Department of State sought in 1989 to promote a consensus in Washington on how to bring appropriate pressure to bear on South Africa against apartheid.

Economic Relations. On the economic front, the new administration scored modest successes, while international frictions and mounting American and foreign debts persisted. The U.S. economy still was subject to the uncertainties of large foreign capital investments, mainly from Japan, since the new administration stood firm against raising taxes to pay for the budget deficit. This complicated other economic problems, such as trade.

With trade deficits generally mounting, in May, Japan was designated as an "unfair" trade partner for some of its practices. The issue was taken up at the summer Association of Southeast Asian Nations (ASEAN) summit and at a subsequent meeting in Australia. Japan blamed U.S. trade deficits on low domestic investment and savings, and Australia criticized U.S. agricultural export subsidies. Sanctions could be imposed if U.S.-Japanese trade talks fail, but both sides seemed anxious to resolve the dispute. The United States applied similar trade pressures to South Korea, despite the turbulent Korean domestic situation over reunification and U.S. troop commitments. (The latter also was controversial in Washington.)

At the midsummer economic summit of the seven major democracies in Paris, diverse Third World debt relief strategies were discussed. Japan, which displaced the United States as the largest development aid donor, proposed agreements to erase debts. Going beyond the plan of Treasury Secretary Nicholas Brady on restructuring commercial debts, Washington also moved for debt forgiveness for the most impoverished African nations if they adopted economic reforms. Although a beginning, this left the bulk of the Third World debt load unremedied.

Military weapons continued to be a major American export to the Third World, increasing by 66% in 1988, and the Bush administration broached the possibility of selling the most advanced U.S. tanks to Saudi Arabia, as well as others. Although much of the arms trade went to relatively rich Middle Eastern states, the high cost of such exports tended to aggravate debt problems for less wealthy customers, such as Egypt and Pakistan.

Partners in Leadership. The new administration's key foreign-policy challenges concerned responses to changing threat perception in Europe and Asia, Third World instability, and the difficulties of managing the international economy. While papering over disagreements in 1989, President Bush and important European leaders, such as West Germany's Helmut Kohl, had yet to harmonize their views of the Soviet Union and the future of East-West relations and nuclear weapons in Europe. President Bush coined the phrase, "partners in leadership," during a 1989 visit to Bonn, and this status became appropriate for the major European states as well as for Japan in security and economic policy. In an era in which people began to speak of dismantling the two major cold war alliances, it would be difficult to maintain the old premises of U.S. foreign policy.

FREDERIC S. PEARSON
University of Missouri—St. Louis

URUGUAY

An April referendum and a November presidential election dominated 1989 events in Uruguay.

Politics and Government. A referendum held on April 16 let stand a 20-year-old law granting amnesty to the nation's military and police officers, accused of about 200 deaths and thousands of cases of torture during a period of military rule, from 1973 to 1985. Those favoring amnesty won the vote, 57% to 43%. Nearly 84% of those eligible to vote did so.

In an open Colorado Party primary on May 28, Sen. Jorge Batlle beat out Vice-President Enrique Tarigo for the presidential nomination of the party's "Batllism" faction. By August, eight contenders had entered the presidential contest. In a regrouping of the political left, an Integration Movement appeared, with Sen. Hugo Batalla as its presidential candidate. That left-of-center coalition embraced the People's Government Party, Christian Democrats (PDC), and the Civic Union, a splinter from the PDC. Consequently, the Broad Front (FA) was reduced to Communist and Socialist activists, who chose retired Gen. Liber Seregni as FA standard-bearer. Batlle, however, lost the November 26 presidential contest to centrist Luis Alberto Lacalle, a 48-year-old senator of the Nationalist Party. Lacalle's votes and those of two other candidates from the Nationalist Party added up to 37.4%, or a plurality of the two million votes cast.

Sen. Francisco Forteza entered the cabinet of President Julio Sanguinetti on July 29. He replaced Interior Minister Antonio Marchesano, who had been censured by congress for the death of a young Communist bricklayer who died while in police custody on a minor charge. Marchesano also was under fire for an outbreak of violence in Uruguay.

Economy. The economy remained stable in 1989, due in part to additional foreign aid. Italy announced in March that it would lend $100 million in soft loans during the next three years. A $257 million road and port improvement project was funded partially in March by an outlay of nearly $81 million from the World Bank and an unsecured loan of about $74 million from Japan. A structural adjustment loan of $140 million was made available in July by the World Bank for the purpose of export promotion, reduction of unemployment, and promotion of domestic savings. Inflation had reached 38% at midyear. An Argentine company announced in July that it would invest $40 million in the construction of a pulp factory at Nueva Palmira, east of Montevideo.

Foreign Relations. A British ferryboat arrived at Montevideo on January 16 with passengers and cargo and was allowed into port, over the objections of a group of Argentine nationalists. It was the first vessel from the Falkland Islands to dock at Montevideo since an armed confrontation in 1982 between Argentine and British forces over the island's sovereignty. The British had hoped to initiate regular freight and passenger service between its 156-year-old colony and Uruguay. The foreign ministry in Montevideo reminded Buenos Aires of its policy of free access to Uruguayan ports and promised the Argentines that it would prevent the de facto establishment of a regularly scheduled service to the islands, for which authorization had not and would not be granted.

Raúl Sendic. Some 15,000 persons attended the burial of Raúl Sendic, founder of the National Liberation Movement (MLN), who died in Paris on April 28. His death was attributed to an illness resulting from the torture to which he had been submitted during imprisonment under a repressive military regime (1973–85). Sendic led a guerrilla war (1967–72).

LARRY L. PIPPIN
University of the Pacific

URUGUAY • Information Highlights

Official Name: Oriental Republic of Uruguay.
Location: Southeastern coast of South America.
Area: 68,039 sq mi (176 220 km²).
Population (mid-1989 est.): 3,000,000.
Capital (1985 census): Montevideo, 1,246,500.
Government: *Head of state,* Julio María Sanguinetti, president (took office March 2, 1985). *Legislature* —National Congress: Senate and House of Deputies.
Monetary Unit: Peso (641.5 pesos equal U.S.$1, Dec. 6, 1989).
Gross Domestic Product (1988 est. U.S.$): $7,500,000,000.
Foreign Trade (1988 U.S.$): *Imports,* $1,177,000,000; *exports,* $1,405,000,000.

UTAH

The scientific quest for cold fusion in a University of Utah laboratory and the level of the state's commitment to education were major issues in 1989.

Cold Fusion. A scientific controversy erupted in March when an electrochemist at the University of Utah and a colleague in England announced they had achieved fusion at room temperature—a possible limitless source of energy. University of Utah researcher B. Stanley Pons and Martin Fleischmann of the University of Southampton reported that their experiments had produced up to 50 times as much energy as they consumed, concluding that the unusual reaction must be nuclear fusion.

Although the experiment received various degrees of verification from researchers at Stanford University, Texas A & M, and Ohio's Case Western Reserve, other researchers at such institutions as the Massachusetts Institute of Technology (MIT), Caltech, and the University of Michigan reported negative results.

UTAH • Information Highlights

Area 84,899 sq mi (219 889 km²).
Population (July 1, 1988): 1,690,000.
Chief Cities (1980 census): Salt Lake City, the capital (July 1, 1986 est.), 158,440; Provo, 74,108; Ogden, 64,407.
Government (1989): *Chief Officers*—governor, Norman H. Bangerter (R); lt. gov., W. Val Oveson (R). *Legislature*—Senate, 29 members; House of Representatives, 75 members.
State Finances (fiscal year 1988): *Revenue,* $3,601,000,000; *expenditure,* $3,224,000,000.
Personal Income (1988): $20,604,000,000; per capita, $12,193.
Labor Force (June 1989): *Civilian labor force,* 779,900; *unemployed,* 31,300 (4.0% of total force).
Education: *Enrollment* (fall 1987)—public elementary schools, 314,000; public secondary, 109,000; colleges and universities, 106,792. *Public school expenditures* (1987–88), $1,045,439,000 ($2,490 per pupil).

There was open skepticism in the scientific community over claims of cold fusion. And most of the scientists attending the spring meeting of the American Physical Society found that "the purported" breakthrough was actually a widely publicized mistake.

Despite the skepticism, the Utah legislature allocated $5 million for further fusion research; the state attorney general retained a Salt Lake City law firm to represent Utah's and the university's interests in protecting patent rights; and more than 200 businesses interested in the ramifications of the experiment contacted the university. (*See also* PHYSICS.)

Education Funding. A special session of the legislature, convened by Gov. Norm Bangerter to address a projected budget surplus, approved a $38.4 million tax reduction. This triggered a wildcat strike by teachers at Davis High School in Kaysville in protest of the tax cut at the expense of education. In support of the protests, teachers from 39 of the state's 40 school districts staged a one-day "symbolic" walkout, closing nearly every elementary and secondary school in Utah.

Educators argued that budget surpluses should be used for education. They pointed out that Utah's class sizes are the largest in the nation, with 1988 U.S. Department of Education statistics showing a pupil-teacher ratio of 24.7 compared with a national average of 17.6. Utah's per pupil expenditure of $2,415 in 1988, according to the federal data, was less than any other state except Mississippi, and it compared poorly to a national average of $3,977. Utah's average teacher salary of $22,572 also was well below the $28,008 national average, and in 43d place.

Republican leaders in the legislature and Governor Bangerter responded by noting that the $38.4 million tax reduction was only a portion of the estimated surplus and that 75% of the total still was intact. Legislators pledged that the educational needs would be addressed in the general session beginning in January 1990. House Speaker Nolan Karras (R) said: "Our commitment . . . has always been to appropriate the majority of the surplus and ongoing revenues for the use of education and the other critical needs facing Utah."

LORENZO K. KIMBALL, *University of Utah*

VENEZUELA

Carlos Andrés Pérez began his second term as president of Venezuela in 1989. In the oil boom that coincided with his first term in office (1974–79), Pérez had earned a reputation as a free spender with a grandiose vision of state-led development. Many Venezuelans who voted him back into office therefore were disillusioned when the new president announced a package of tough economic measures on February 16 designed to restore the confidence of the international financial community by reducing the state's role in regulating the economy. These measures included the replacement of the dual exchange rate with a single devalued floating rate, the freeing of bank interest rates, higher taxes, and budget cuts, including subsidy reductions that nearly doubled the price of gasoline.

Popular disillusionment with Pérez, unauthorized increases in bus fares, and shortages resulting from hoarding in anticipation of further price increases combined to spark three days of vandalism and looting at the end of February. The riots, which caught the government by surprise, began around Caracas and spread to all the major cities, destroying 45% of the country's supermarkets. Order was restored by the police and National Guard, whose brutal efforts left an official total of 350 dead.

The Economy and the Labor Movement. The president's popularity, already severely eroded by the riots and the government's response, was undermined further by disappointing eco-

VENEZUELA • Information Highlights

Official Name: Republic of Venezuela.
Location: Northern coast of South America.
Area: 352,143 sq mi (912 050 km²).
Population (mid-1989 est.): 19,100,000.
Chief Cities (1987 est., incl. suburbs): Caracas, the capital, 3,310,236; Maracaibo, 1,330,215; Valencia, 1,180,820.
Government: *Head of state and government,* Carlos Andrés Pérez, president (took office February 1989). *Legislature*—National Congress: Senate and Chamber of Deputies.
Monetary Unit: Bolívar (42.80 bolívares equal U.S.$1, Nov. 7, 1989).
Gross Domestic Product (1988 U.S.$): $47,300,-000,000.
Economic Index (1988): *Consumer Prices* (1984 = 100), all items, 206.1; food, 288.8.
Foreign Trade (1988 U.S.$): *Imports,* $11,461,-000,000; *exports,* $9,629,000,000.

© Rob Crandall/Picture Group

Martial law was declared February 28 in Venezuela, after urban riots—caused by price increases—had broken out the day before. About 350 people died in the week-long rioting. Soldiers (above) *stand guard in the city of Mérida.*

nomic performance. Inflation reached 21% in March alone and even though it slowed considerably in subsequent months, it seemed possible that Pérez would have to fulfill his campaign promise to resign if inflation reached 80% for the year. By June, unemployment had risen to 9.7%, with 582,000 Venezuelans out of work. Furthermore, an estimated 43% of the population was living below the official poverty level.

The fall in demand and the rising cost of foreign exchange made survival difficult for many businesses, and foreign investment fell to an estimated $300 million to $400 million, reflecting waning confidence in the economy. The private sector also was discouraged by a wave of prosecutions of prominent multinational executives for their alleged fraudulent acquisition of subsidized foreign exchange from the scandal-ridden Office of Differential Exchange Rate Controls (RECADI). Two former finance ministers and the personal secretary to former President Jaime Lusinchi, Blanca Ibáñez, also were implicated in the scandal. Executives from dozens of multinational corporations fled Venezuela in July, fearing prosecution.

Pérez began his term enjoying good relations with the labor movement dating from his nomination in 1987. During 1989, he attempted to maintain those ties by decreeing a 30% across-the-board wage increase following the riots, committing $657 million to the creation of 150,000 jobs in August, and supporting legislation to permit the organization of industry-wide unions. In spite of these gestures, union leaders took an increasingly militant stance, culminating in a general strike in May. The strike was of little immediate consequence, but the unions were later able to condition their support for an anti-inflation pact with government and business on the inclusion of several nonwage concessions to workers such as subsidies for housing and food. Governing party officials feared that ties of party loyalty would not guarantee the support of organized labor for governments led by the *Acción Democrática* party much longer.

Debt and Politics. While not completely satisfied, the financial world was encouraged by the Pérez administration's economic policies, and extended more than $5 billion in new credit to help the nation service its $33 billion debt. United States concern over Venezuela's political stability following the February riots probably influenced the World Bank and the International Monetary Fund (IMF) to favor these loans, as did the country's flexible approach to debt reduction in response to the plan of U.S. Treasury Secretary Nicholas Brady.

Significant political reforms also went into effect in 1989: On December 4, governors and mayors were elected directly for the first time in the country's history. Of the 20 governorships, Pérez' Democratic Action Party (AD) won 13, the Social Christian Party (COPEI) took five, while the leftist *Movimiento al Socialismo* (MAS) and an opposition coalition took one each. Despite the AD's strong showing, the trend favored the opposition parties, who formerly would have had little power.

MICHAEL COPPEDGE
Johns Hopkins University

VERMONT

Although the Burlington-Montpelier area ranked in the top 50 U.S. metropolitan areas in the rate of business expansion in 1989, Vermont felt the slowdown in New England's economic growth, and fiscal considerations inhibited major state government initiatives.

Politics and Legislation. The state House of Representatives retained its Democratic speaker despite a narrow Republican majority, while the state Senate remained under firm Democratic control. The legislature rejected a tax cut and exceeded the budget limit of nearly $600 million recommended by Gov. Madeleine Kunin. Subsequently, declining revenue estimates led Governor Kunin to order a 2% spending cut in almost all programs. Earlier, cost considerations had prompted her to withdraw a proposal to provide state-sponsored health insurance for all Vermonters and substitute a prenatal and child-health program. A fiscal crisis in the Vermont Blue Cross/Blue Shield organization, culminating in the resignation of its top officers, lent added urgency to the health-insurance situation.

The legislature approved a ban on new cars with air conditioning using chlorofluorocarbons, effective in 1993. Amid vocal protests against recent legislation encouraging town and regional planning, and public objections to hydroelectric projects and a gas pipeline, Governor Kunin proposed a long-term program to promote better environmental protection and energy conservation.

The city of Burlington continued its maverick political course when retiring Mayor Bernard Sanders, a self-styled socialist, was succeeded by his director of economic development, Peter Clavelle. Running in March as an independent with progressive coalition support, Clavelle trounced the Democratic candidate (tacitly supported by the Republicans) by a 54 to 42% margin in a low turnout election. A coalition of Democrats and Republicans retained narrow control of the Board of Aldermen.

Education. Rising educational costs threatened a funding crisis. Special education drew strong criticism, while the cost of higher education at the University of Vermont and in the state college system prompted studies by various state commissions. In the midst of these inquiries, and faced with a faculty unionization drive, University of Vermont president Lattie F. Coor resigned to accept the presidency of Arizona State University. In October, Middlebury College President Olin Robison resigned. Teacher strikes in Barre and Winooski were settled with relative ease, but school budgets were voted down with regularity.

Governor Kunin and influential legislators set in motion a new initiative in international education, and the governor concluded a sister-state exchange agreement with the Karelian Autonomous Republic in the Soviet Union.

Tribal Recognition. Abenaki Indian efforts to achieve tribal recognition gained momentum from a state court ruling that they retained aboriginal rights to fish without a state license. The court, however, upheld the state's right to prosecute criminal infractions that occurred in "Indian country." The Abenakis voted to give their elective chief life tenure.

Law. The state Supreme Court publicly reprimanded retired Justice William C. Hill for violating the judicial code of conduct, and suspended him from sitting on the bench again. Justice Louis Peck successfully challenged a state constitutional mandate that judges must retire after reaching 70.

SAMUEL B. HAND AND ROBERT V. DANIELS
University of Vermont

VERMONT • Information Highlights

Area: 9,614 sq mi (24 900 km²).
Population (July 1, 1988): 557,000.
Chief Cities (1980 census): Montpelier, the capital, 8,241; Burlington, 37,712; Rutland, 18,436.
Government (1989): *Chief Officers*—governor, Madeleine M. Kunin (D); lt. gov., Howard Dean (D). *General Assembly*—Senate, 30 members; House of Representatives, 150 members.
State Finances (fiscal year 1988): *Revenue*, $1,401,000,000; *expenditure*, $1,268,000,000.
Personal Income (1988): $8,530,000,000; per capita, $15,302.
Labor Force (June 1989): *Civilian labor force*, 312,600; *unemployed*, 11,900 (3.8% of total force).
Education: *Enrollment* (fall 1987)—public elementary schools, 65,000; public secondary, 28,000; colleges and universities, 33,242. *Public school expenditures* (1987–88), $412,000,000 ($4,532 per pupil).

VIETNAM

The economic crisis in Vietnam eased slightly in 1989, and foreign investors were courted actively. But Communist party hardliners resisted political change and even rolled back some of the reforms enacted by the 1986 party congress. Meanwhile, the withdrawal of Vietnamese forces from Cambodia added to instability there, at least in the short term, and also added to the massive unemployment in Vietnam. Yet the withdrawal also opened up the prospect that Vietnam would be able to renew its ties with the world economy.

Politics. A harsh statement rejecting "bourgeois liberalism" and political pluralism was issued by the Vietnamese Communist Party's Central Committee in August. This policy statement was even stronger than one issued by the same body in March (in which they stressed the need for economic reform while rejecting political reform). A number of outspoken journalists and intellectuals lost their jobs as a result of the new policy.

© J. Langevin/Sygma

An enthusiastic Cambodian crowd cheers a Vietnamese military convoy as it departs. After a ten-year occupation of Cambodia, officials in Vietnam claimed all troops had been pulled out by the end of September.

According to press reports, the party's new policy was supported fully by Gen. Sec. Nguyen Van Linh, who once had been regarded as an advocate of political as well as economic reform. It appeared that party hard-liners were becoming more convinced of the need for economic reform, while party liberals such as Linh were more fearful that political change could destabilize the country.

Despite these pressures, a number of prominent liberals and retired party leaders tried to exert what influence they could on behalf of political reform. The group, known as the Club of Former Resistance Fighters, described itself as a pressure group within the Communist Party rather than an opposition movement.

Economics. As a result of economic reforms which were recommended in many cases by the International Monetary Fund (IMF), Vietnam's inflation rate is believed to have dropped considerably in 1989 from about 700% annually for the previous few years. The closing of unprofitable state enterprises and the abolition of certain subsidies that distorted the markets helped to account for this improvement. Yet the same factors added to already high rates of unemployment and underemployment. The Vietnamese were learning that economic reform, though essential for the future of the country, was painful in the short term.

By the summer of 1989, Vietnam's new laws designed to attract private foreign investors had been in place for only one year, but the government already had granted 48 investment licenses involving $450 million worth of desperately needed foreign capital. The bulk of the licenses, 43, were for investment in the southern half of the country, and about half of the investment was in offshore oil and gas exploration. Thai and Japanese businessmen were among the investors.

Foreign Affairs. Vietnam claimed that all of its military forces were out of Cambodia by the end of September. One of the main purposes of the withdrawal was an attempt to make Vietnam eligible for foreign aid from Western nations, which had boycotted Vietnam during the ten-year occupation. Western donors reportedly were poised to provide large sums needed by Vietnam, but first they wanted some assurance that Vietnam would cooperate in helping to create a neutral and independent Cambodian government.

PETER A. POOLE
Author, "The Vietnamese In Thailand"

VIETNAM • Information Highlights

Official Name: Socialist Republic of Vietnam.
Location: Southeast Asia.
Area: 127,243 sq mi (329 560 km²).
Population (mid-1989 est.): 66,800,000.
Chief Cities (1985 est.): Hanoi, the capital, 2,000,000; Ho Chi Minh City (1986 est.), 4,000,000.
Government: Communist Party secretary, Nguyen Van Linh.
Monetary Unit: Dong (4,200 dongs equal U.S.$1, July 1989).
Gross National Product (1987 U.S.$): $12,600,-000,000.

VIRGINIA

Lawrence Douglas Wilder, the 58-year-old grandson of slaves, became the United States' first elected black governor. Though his victory margin in the Virginia election was only about 6,800 votes out of the almost 1.8 million cast, it was an epochal event in the former capital of the Confederacy, of which blacks make up only 20% of the population. Wilder's pro-choice position on abortion was given major credit for his defeat of Republican J. Marshall Coleman. A former state attorney general, Coleman narrowly had won the right to take on Wilder, the lieutenant governor, by coming from well behind in the first Republican gubernatorial primary ever held in Virginia.

The November statewide election gave Virginia another new political star—Donald S. Beyer, Jr., who beat out state Sen. Edwina Dalton, widow of the state's last Republican governor, for the lieutenant governorship. It was the first try for elective office for Beyer, a 38-year-old northern Virginia car dealer.

Mary Sue Terry, who in 1985 had become the first woman ever elected to statewide office in Virginia, handily won reelection to the state's attorney general post. In the House of Delegates the Republicans picked up five seats, but still were outnumbered. The most stunning triumph went to Jackie Stump as an outgrowth of the bitter coal strike in southwest Virginia. Running as a write-in, Stump, district president of the United Mine Workers Union (UMW), defeated a 20-year incumbent by a greater than two to one margin. The incumbent's son, a circuit judge, had levied more than $30 million in fines against the union.

Coal Strike. The longest coal strike in state history began on April 5 against Pittston Coal Group Inc. and resulted in more than 2,500 arrests, as the UMW adopted nonviolent protest tactics redolent of the civil-rights movement.

© Cynthia Johnson/"Time" Magazine

In a close race, Virginia's Lt. Gov. L. Douglas Wilder, 58, was elected to the governorship, becoming the first black to be elected governor of a U.S. state.

The huge fines were levied against the camouflage-dressed union sympathizers for actions such as blocking roads.

Explosion. Norfolk, home of the country's largest naval base, was rocked emotionally by an explosion on the battleship *Iowa* that killed 47 sailors. The Norfolk-based ship was engaged in gunnery exercises near Puerto Rico when an explosion of the powder bags in one of the 16-inch (40.6-cm) guns immolated all but 11 of the sailors in the gun turret.

Riot. A Labor Day weekend gathering of about 100,000 young people in Virginia Beach ended violently in two days of rioting. The gathering was centered around an informal celebration of black fraternities and sororities known as Greekfest. Some charged police with brutality in combating the unrest.

Legislature. The 1989 General Assembly passed a gun-control measure that set up a toll-free number for police to check the criminal records of gun buyers. The legislature also passed a law revoking driving privileges for minors convicted of drug or alcohol use, outlawed corporal punishment in the schools, and raised the mandatory school attendance age from 17 to 18.

Education Summit. In an unprecedented gathering, President Bush met with the nation's governors at the University of Virginia in Charlottesville, September 27–28, to devise national education goals that would touch every child in the United States. Specific details on the way to achieve the goals remained to be worked out by the administration and the governors prior to the National Governors' Association meeting in February 1990.

ED NEWLAND
"Richmond Times-Dispatch"

VIRGINIA • Information Highlights

Area: 40,767 sq mi (105 586 km²).
Population (July 1, 1988): 6,015,000.
Chief Cities (July 1, 1986 est.): Richmond, the capital, 217,700; Virginia Beach, 333,400; Norfolk, 274,800; Newport News, 161,700; Chesapeake, 134,400.
Government (1989): *Chief Officers*—governor, Gerald L. Baliles (D); lt. gov., L. Douglas Wilder (D). *General Assembly*—Senate, 40 members; House of Delegates, 100 members.
State Finances (fiscal year 1988): *Revenue,* $11,835,000,000; *expenditure,* $10,004,000,000.
Personal Income (1988): $106,315,000,000; per capita, $17,675.
Labor Force (June 1989): *Civilian labor force,* 3,176,400; *unemployed,* 115,000 (3.6% of total force).
Education: *Enrollment* (fall 1987)—public elementary schools, 685,000; public secondary, 294,000; colleges and universities, 319,026. *Public school expenditures* (1987–88), $4,056,036,000 ($4,177 per pupil).

Norm Rice, the Democratic candidate for mayor of Seattle, beams on election night while his campaign managers Charles Holland and Terry Wittman hug. Rice is the first black to be elected mayor of Seattle, winning easily in a city with a black population of about 10%.

© Alan Berner/"Seattle Times"

WASHINGTON

Fireworks and a laser light show lit up the skies in Olympia and bells rang across the state on Nov. 11, 1989, marking Washington's centennial as a state. Washington's economy grew throughout the year as unemployment dropped to just above 5% in late 1989.

Elections and Politics. State voters turned down a sales-tax increase backed by Gov. Booth Gardner which would have raised $360 million for education and children's programs, but passed measures to reform the state's judicial-conduct system and to strengthen the rights of crime victims.

In Seattle the city's first black mayor, Norm Rice, was elected. At the time of the election, he held the post of city councilman. Seattle voters also passed initiatives to curtail school busing and to limit building height and density in the downtown area.

During the year, state legislators passed a multifaceted attack on drugs and revamped the state's mental-health care system. In June, U.S. Rep. Thomas Foley (D-Spokane) became the speaker of the U.S. House of Representatives after the resignation of Rep. Jim Wright of Texas. And the state's most prominent senior statesman, former Sen. Warren G. Magnuson, died in May at the age of 84.

Economy. The Boeing Co., the state's largest private employer, set a record for commercial airplane sales in 1989, taking orders for 882 jets valued at more than $46 billion by late in the year. But production was disrupted by a 48-day strike by 58,700 machinists, including 43,000 in Washington. In addition, a federal probe into illegal possession and use of government documents resulted in charges against Boeing, which pleaded guilty and paid $5.22 million in fines, and a former Boeing executive, Richard Fowler, who was convicted of 39 felony counts.

The Boeing strike capped a year that saw the state's largest rash of labor disputes since the 1970s. Other major strikes and lockouts involved carpenters, shipbuilders, grocery workers, and nurses for Group Health Cooperative.

Apple sales plunged more than 50% and prices dropped sharply when a consumer group reported that the growth regulator Alar posed a cancer risk for children. Government agencies said the risk was overstated and that most Washington growers had stopped using Alar in recent years. By late 1989 sales had rebounded, due in part to a federal government commitment to buy $9.5 million worth of apples for the poor.

City News. Two national publications rated Seattle as the nation's most livable city in 1989

WASHINGTON • Information Highlights

Area: 68,139 sq mi (176 479 km²).
Population (July 1, 1988): 4,648,000.
Chief Cities (July 1, 1986 est.): Olympia, the capital (1980 census), 27,447; Seattle, 486,200; Spokane, 172,890; Tacoma, 158,950.
Government (1989): *Chief Officers*—governor, Booth Gardner (D); lt. gov., Joel Pritchard (R). *Legislature*—Senate, 49 members; House of Representatives, 98 members.
State Finances (fiscal year 1988): *Revenue,* $12,465,000,000; *expenditure,* $11,404,000,000.
Personal Income (1988): $76,561,000,000; per capita, $16,473.
Labor Force (June 1989): *Civilian labor force,* 2,441,300; *unemployed,* 136,500 (5.6% of total force).
Education: *Enrollment* (fall 1987)—public elementary schools, 541,000; public secondary, 235,000; colleges and universities, 245,872. *Public school expenditures* (1987–88), $2,908,775,000 ($3,771 per pupil).

(*see also* feature article, page 66). And in Everett, dredging work began on a new Navy port which eventually was to accommodate an aircraft-carrier task force.

Environment. A federal-state agreement signed in May called for a 30-year, $50 billion cleanup program at the Hanford Nuclear Reservation in southeast Washington. The U.S. Department of Energy pledged to clean up radioactive and chemical wastes at the 560-sq-mi (1 450-km^2) site, starting with an investment of $2.8 billion in the first five years.

Crime. Three days before his January 24 execution in Florida, former Tacoma, WA, resident Theodore Bundy admitted he had killed at least eight young women in Washington in 1974. Bundy had been suspected of the Washington killings but never was charged. He was executed for the murder of a 12-year-old Florida girl.

In August, Seattle TV personality Larry Sturholm and a friend, Debra Sweiger, were stabbed fatally in Sweiger's home near a Seattle suburb. Sweiger's former boyfriend was charged with the killings. In December, Ron Burris of Spanway Pierce County fatally shot his two daughters, his former wife and her husband, and then himself.

JACK BROOM, *"The Seattle Times"*

WASHINGTON, DC

Illegal drug trafficking and related murders continued to plague the District of Columbia in 1989, with 391 homicides, many of them drug-related, recorded by early November—exceeding the 1988 total by 19. The escalating drug war left city leaders and police under siege and spilled into the political arena as 1990 mayoral candidates used the violence as campaign fodder to attack the administration of Mayor Marion Barry. The mayor himself was burdened by allegations of drug use, including court testimony from a convicted cocaine dealer that Barry had bought and smoked crack cocaine.

Since December 1988, when city police abruptly halted an undercover drug buy at a downtown hotel after learning Barry was visiting Charles Lewis, a former District government employee who later pleaded guilty in federal court to cocaine possession charges in connection with the incident, Barry's troubles deepened. His personal life and two federal investigations raised questions about his administration and life-style, but he continued to deny he ever used drugs.

Politics. Barry, who would seek a fourth term as mayor in 1990, faced early opposition for the Democratic nomination from three City Council members—John Ray, Charlene Drew Jarvis, and Council Chairman David A. Clarke, as well as from former utility company executive Sharon Pratt Dixon. Speculation also ran rampant that Barry's friend of 30 years, the Rev. Jesse Jackson, would seek to make the District's office of mayor his first elected post. Jackson moved his legal residency and political operations to the District in July. He repeatedly denied any interest in becoming mayor, but refused to state unequivocally that he did not want the job. Despite his disclaimers, Jackson launched a series of citywide back-to-school and antidrug rallies and renewed the district's three-year-old quest for statehood status.

Should Mayor Barry win the Democratic primary, he was expected to face his former police chief, Maurice Turner, a former Democrat who switched to the Republican Party when he retired in 1989 after 32 years on the force and eight years as police chief.

Politically, the Barry administration was burdened with a $14 million budget deficit, a burgeoning homeless population, and an ambulance service that frequently got lost on the way to emergencies, resulting in at least 11 patients dying subsequently. The mayor vowed to resolve lingering city problems before the primary election, hoping to preempt criticism from his challengers.

Other News. In September a District of Columbia judge ordered the release of Dr. Elizabeth Morgan, who had been imprisoned for 25 months for defying a court order to allow her former husband to see their young daughter. She alleged sexual abuse by the father and refused to reveal the whereabouts of the girl, who disappeared in 1987. The case earned widespread publicity and, to obtain Morgan's release, Congress passed a bill limiting the amount of time someone can be jailed on civil contempt charges in the District to 12 months.

VINCENT D. MCCRAW
"The Washington Times"

WEST VIRGINIA

In West Virginia, 1989 was marked by revelations of official wrongdoing, the defeat of a government reorganization plan, and a damaging coal strike.

The Governor's Program. Taking office in January, newly elected Gov. Gaston Caperton promised to make sweeping changes in the state's governmental structure and pay off the many debts he inherited from his predecessor, Arch A. Moore, Jr., including long-overdue Medicare payments and a nearly defunct Public Employees Insurance Program.

He immediately called a special session of the legislature, which gave him $392 million in new taxes (including a 6% sales tax on food and an additional five-cent tax on gasoline) and authorized him to move ahead with the drafting of ethics legislation and government reorganization. The governor also announced an im-

WEST VIRGINIA • Information Highlights

Area: 24,232 sq mi (62 760 km^2).
Population (July 1, 1988): 1,876,000.
Chief Cities (1980 census): Charleston, the capital, 63,968; Huntington, 63,684; Wheeling, 43,070.
Government (1989): *Chief Officers*—governor, Gaston Caperton (D); secy. of state, Ken Hechler (D). *Legislature*—Senate, 34 members; House of Delegates, 100 members.
State Finances (fiscal year 1988): *Revenue,* $3,701,000,000; *expenditure,* $3,809,000,000.
Personal Income (1988): $22,018,000,000; per capita, $11,735.
Labor Force (June 1989): *Civilian labor force,* 775,500; *unemployed,* 62,600 (8.1% of total force).
Education: *Enrollment* (fall 1987)—public elementary schools, 237,000; public secondary, 107,000; colleges and universities, 77,256. *Public school expenditures* (1987–88), $1,179,300,000 ($3,693 per pupil).

mediate 5% cut in expenditures, and received a recommendation from a Carnegie Foundation study group advising the merger of several of the state's institutions of higher education.

The regular session of the legislature authorized Caperton to borrow $135 million for overdue Public Employees Insurance payments to employees and health-care agencies.

The lawmakers approved a $1.7 billion budget and scheduled a September vote on three constitutional amendments that were the heart of the governor's reorganization plan—one allowing counties to change their form of administration, another revising the structure of the state Board of Education, and a third eliminating the elective offices of secretary of state, treasurer, and agriculture commissioner. All three were rejected by the voters.

Scandals. Caperton's call for a tougher set of ethics regulations was spurred partly by the revelation that more than $225 million had been "lost" in the 1987–88 State Investment pool. The pool was administered by former Governor Moore, state Treasurer A. James Manchin, Auditor Glen Gainer, and Assistant Treasurer Arnold Margolin. Gainer was "reprimanded" and Margolin resigned as Caperton's financial adviser. Manchin was urged to resign, and impeachment proceedings were authorized against him, with a trial set for midsummer. Shortly before the trial was to begin he announced his retirement.

In other developments, Senate President Dan Tonkovich—a gubernatorial candidate in the 1988 primary—resigned after being indicted for extortion and racketeering. State Senator Si Boettner, whose name also emerged in the Tonkovich hearings, later resigned after pleading guilty to tax evasion. In August a probe charged that State Attorney General Charlie Brown had changed his testimony during his divorce hearing, and he resigned. In September, Larry Tucker, who succeeded Dan Tonkovich as Senate president, also stepped down after pleading guilty to extortion.

Economy. West Virginia's shaky economy continued its 20-year decline, fueled by an unbroken population loss and tax revenues that somehow never came up to projections. The greatest blow of 1989 was the result of the United Mine Workers (UMW) strike against the Pittston Coal Company, which involved more than 16,000 miners.

DONOVAN H. BOND
West Virginia University

WISCONSIN

A yearlong tumultuous dispute over Indian treaty rights and a changing mood in the state capital highlighted the year in Wisconsin.

Treaty Rights. The dispute was more than a century in the making. In 1837 and 1842 the Chippewa Indians ceded roughly what is now the northern third of Wisconsin to the United States in exchange for hunting, fishing, and gathering rights in the territory. For more than a century, things were peaceful, but in 1974 a test case resulted from Indians spearing fish off their reservations in the area. The issue dragged on through the courts, and Indians were subject to harassment when they fished. In 1989 the harassment turned to violence; those claiming that the fish stock was being depleted, and the tourist industry therefore harmed, confronted the Indians. About 200 protestors were arrested during the spring spear-fishing season, and law enforcement costs topped $1 million.

In an effort to establish peace, Gov. Tommy G. Thompson and representatives of one of the six Chippewa bands, the Lac du Flambeau, proposed a compromise. For giving up nearly all spear-fishing and timber-cutting rights, the Indians would get $50 million in cash and program aid over ten years. On October 25, members of the band, led by a militant "Walleye Warrior" group, rejected the offer.

WISCONSIN • Information Highlights

Area: 56,153 sq mi (145 436 km^2).
Population (July 1, 1988): 4,855,000.
Chief Cities (July 1, 1986 est.): Madison, the capital, 175,850; Milwaukee, 605,090; Green Bay (1980 census), 87,899.
Government (1989): *Chief Officers*—governor, Tommy G. Thompson (R); lt. gov., Scott McCallum (R). *Legislature*—Senate, 33 members; Assembly, 99 members.
State Finances (fiscal year 1988): *Revenue,* $12,061,000,000; *expenditure,* $9,822,000,000.
Personal Income (1988): $75,362,000,000; per capita, $15,524.
Labor Force (June 1989): *Civilian labor force,* 2,683,700; *unemployed,* 121,200 (4.5% of total force).
Education: *Enrollment* (fall 1987)—public elementary schools, 522,000; public secondary, 251,000; colleges and universities, 281,717. *Public school expenditures* (1987–88), $3,430,900,000 ($4,665 per pupil).

They said they would not give their rights away. With no new settlement in sight, the Indians planned to continue exercising their treaty rights, opponents planned to confront them again, and the state prepared to spend more money on law enforcement.

State Government. Although Wisconsin had a Republican governor and a Democratic-controlled legislature in 1989, the mood of the state capital was one of compromise and togetherness at the start of the 1989–90 legislative session. The state enjoyed a healthy economy and state treasury, and the legislature approved a $23 billion budget bill that included a onetime property tax rebate check averaging about $138 for 1.2 million homeowners and renters. The budget also contained a "stewardship fund" of $250 million over ten years to buy and develop conservation and recreation land; it also included catch-up pay raises for University of Wisconsin faculty members. Lawmakers also strengthened the state law requiring advance notice of factory closings, extended the mandatory seat-belt bill for two years, and approved a tax-free college savings-bond plan.

By the end of the year the mood had changed, and Thompson was accusing Assembly Speaker Thomas Loftus of delaying his legislative agenda. Loftus was likely to seek the Democratic nomination for governor in 1990, and Thompson was expected to seek reelection. The governor's proposals to correct welfare fraud, to provide more money for education, and to deal with drug use and crime still were awaiting action.

Lottery Gains. Established after years of opposition, Wisconsin's lottery exceeded all predictions in its first year. The lottery began on Sept. 14, 1988, and a year later sales reached $267 million, with $93.5 million going for property-tax relief. About 75% of the net lottery profits go to schools.

Economy. The state's economy was performing well because of the manufacturing sector. More than 50,000 new wage and salary jobs were created in 1989 and the unemployment rate fell below the national average for 19 straight months. Personal income was expected to grow by 8.7% following a 6.1% growth in 1988.

PAUL SALSINI, *"The Milwaukee Journal"*

WOMEN

Abortion rights, equality on the job, and balancing the pressures of work and family were areas of concern to women in 1989.

Abortion. The landmark *Roe v. Wade* decision in 1973 that legalized abortion was challenged in July when the U.S. Supreme Court gave states the right to levy new limitations on abortion (*Webster v. Reproductive Health Services*). A volatile and divisive issue, abortion dominated both the judicial and political arenas. (*See* feature article, page 44.)

The Workplace. Women continued to enter the work force in greater numbers, with 56.2 million American women in the civilian work force. They currently make up 45% of working people, compared with 38% in 1970.

Pay parity with men slowly has increased, and women now earn a rate of 70¢ for every dollar that a man earns, up from 62¢ to every dollar in the late 1960s. More women also work in formerly all-male occupations. Women now comprise 20% of all U.S. doctors and lawyers and nearly 50% of all bus drivers and accountants are women, up from 29.7% and 23.3%, respectively, in 1970. However, fewer than 4% of women hold higher-paying unionized jobs such as pilots and mechanics.

A 1989 article in the *Harvard Business Review* by Felice Schwartz, president of Catalyst, a women's business research group, caused widespread comment in the media. Schwartz stated that it costs a corporation more to hire women than men because women resign to have children or will not work extra hours when they have children at home. She recommended that companies set up two broad categories for women managers, one for "career primary" women, who put work first, and an alternative career path, a career-and-family track, for women who need flexibility in their work in order to spend time with their children. Some feminists expressed the concern that women opting for the "mommy track" would forfeit career advancement and that it would reinforce corporate and social prejudices.

A series of U.S. Supreme Court decisions made it harder for women and minorities to win lawsuits to keep affirmative-action programs designed to compensate for past discrimination. In *Wards Cove Packing Co. Inc. v. Atonio,* the court freed employers of some of the burden of justifying biased practices.

Politics. In a hotly contested special election in August, Republican Ileana Ros-Lehtinen won the late Claude Pepper's Florida congressional seat; she is the first Cuban-American to be sent to Congress. Earlier in the year, Jill Long (D-IN) won the congressional seat vacated by Dan Coats (R) when he took over Vice-President Dan Quayle's Senate seat. Overall in 1989, there were 29 women in Congress—two in the Senate and 27 in the House. Three states—Arizona, Nebraska, and Vermont—had women governors, one more than in 1988.

Polls and Surveys. A *New York Times* poll in June indicated that U.S. women desired a movement working to further their goals of job equality and balancing the demands of work and family. Women at all socioeconomic levels stood behind more day-care options and stronger programs in prenatal and postnatal care.

A U.S. Census Bureau survey revealed that half of the married women interviewed who were 30–34 years old and without children planned to have a family compared with only one third of a similar group surveyed in 1975.

GLADYS HANDELMAN
Free-lance Writer and Editor

WYOMING

The opening session of Wyoming's 50th legislature, a special election for the state's only seat in the U.S. House, and the effects of a sluggish state economy shaped developments in Wyoming during 1989. National attention focused briefly on the state in June, when President George Bush toured fire-damaged Yellowstone Park, and in September when U.S. Secretary of State James Baker and Soviet Foreign Minister Eduard Shevardnadze flew to the resort town of Jackson for three days of presummit diplomacy.

Legislation. With solid majorities in both House and Senate, Republicans controlled all legislative committees but still worked smoothly with Gov. Mike Sullivan (D), approving almost exactly the $54 million he requested in his budget supplement for general operating expenses. In like fashion, the legislature passed a major omnibus bill designed to streamline state government, consolidating a host of state agencies into 12 cabinet-style departments administered directly by the governor. Lawmakers went beyond Sullivan's recommendation and increased by $19 million state funding for the public-school system. Signing the bill, the governor noted that it restored to school districts the 3.5% cut imposed by the 1987 legislature. The session granted state employees a pay increase of about 3%, and taxes on gasoline and cigarettes were increased slightly. Following a national trend, the session adopted a mandatory seat-belt law, although it includes no penalty for violators.

Special Election. Wyoming Congressman Dick Cheney's appointment as secretary of defense triggered a special election on April 26 to fill Wyoming's House seat. In accordance with a new state law, such a vacancy must be filled within 45 days, and the candidates are nominated by the state central committees (eliminating a primary election). In early March some 20 prospective nominees mounted minicampaigns within the party organizations, and on the last weekend in March the committees picked their candidates—Republican Craig Thomas, a state representative from Casper, and Democrat John Vinich, state senator from Hudson. Thomas campaigned on his own ideological resemblance to former Congressman Cheney, and worked to get out the Republican vote in a state which has about twice as many registered Republicans as Democrats. The strategy

WYOMING • Information Highlights

Area: 97,809 sq mi (253 326 km²).
Population (July 1, 1988): 479,000.
Chief Cities (1980 census): Cheyenne, the capital, 47,283; Casper, 51,016; Laramie, 24,410.
Government (1989): *Chief Officers*—governor, Mike Sullivan (D); secretary of state, Kathy Karpan (D). *Legislature*—Senate, 30 members; House of Representatives, 64 members.
State Finances (fiscal year 1988): *Revenue,* $1,691,000,000; *expenditure,* $1,509,000,000.
Personal Income (1988): $6,523,000,000; per capita, $13,609.
Labor Force (June 1989): *Civilian labor force,* 230,400; *unemployed,* 12,700 (5.5% of total force).
Education: *Enrollment* (fall 1987)—public elementary schools, 70,000; public secondary, 28,000; colleges and universities, 26,062. *Public school expenditures* (1987–88), $508,600,000 ($5,216 per pupil).

proved successful. He carried 18 of the state's 23 counties and polled a vote total of about 74,000 against his opponent's total of about 61,000. Seventy-two percent of the electorate cast ballots in the election.

Economy. Data for 1989 indicated little overall movement in the state's economic activity. Wyoming coal mines produced 165 million tons and its oil fields 116 million barrels of crude, both figures marginally higher than in 1988. In the next several years, however, oil production is expected to decrease slightly, while coal output will move gradually upward. Statewide unemployment hovered at about 5% of the work force, against the 6% that prevailed in 1988. But, in fact, the state had some 13,000 (5.6%) fewer jobs available than in the year preceding, suggesting some out-migration of job seekers.

H. R. DIETERICH
University of Wyoming

YUGOSLAVIA

In 1989, Yugoslavia continued to maintain a precarious existence in the face of economic chaos, increasingly widespread and violent ethnic antagonism, and a collectively led Communist Party and federal government unable to take resolute action.

Ethnic Tensions. The greatest danger to Yugoslavia's stability was the continuing and escalating armed violence between the rebellious 1.7 million ethnic Albanians of the autonomous province of Kosovo and the security forces sent there by the federal government. The government charged that separatist aspirations were being fueled among the ethnic Albanians by neighboring Albania. A more direct provocation was the desire of the Serbian Republic, led by its ambitious strongman Slobodan Milosevíc, to take direct control of the province. In early February, about 1,300 Albanian miners called an underground strike in the Trepca lead-zinc mine in Mitrovica, and some 10,000 Albanian students staged a sit-in at the University of Priština, both demanding guarantees of Kosovo's continuing autonomy.

In the largest show of force since 1981, the federal government sent more than 10,000 military troops to the province. In late March, there were new clashes after the Kosovo legislature approved a constitutional amendment that would give Serbia control of its police and civil-defense forces, courts, and officials, and surrender Kosovo's right to veto future changes. When masses of ethnic Albanians rose up to protest in Priština and other cities in Kosovo, the government ordered a curfew, closed public institutions, and forbade political gatherings. Claiming that it had evidence that Albanian intelligence agencies had recruited thousands to stage the uprising, it arrested dozens of business and political leaders, including Azem Vlasi, the outspokenly anti-Serbian former Communist chief of Kosovo, and 14 other provincial officials. Armed violence erupted again in November, when Vlasi and his codefendants were put on trial for counterrevolutionary activities.

Both the European Parliament and the U.S. Congress passed resolutions accusing Yugoslavia of repressing the human and national rights of its ethnic Albanians. At home, there were fears among other ethnic groups that Serbia would try to exploit the emergency to establish its dominance over the federal state and the Yugoslav League of Communists (Communist Party). The Slovenian Communist Party sent funds and expressions of support to the Kosovo Albanians, and similar sympathies were expressed in Croatia. In September, the Slovenian parliament overwhelmingly approved a constitutional amendment asserting Slovenia's right to bar federal intervention on Slovene soil, self-determination, and even secession from Yugoslavia. Tens of thousands of Serbs and Montenegrins denounced Slovenia and called for military intervention. An ominous warning came from Adm. Petar Simić, head of the Communist Party organization in the armed forces, that the military would confront individuals and groups "hungry for power and wanting to break up Yugoslavia."

Economy and Government. Ethnic tensions were played out against an equally alarming economic background of mass unemployment, waves of strikes and workers' demonstrations, and an annual inflation rate that had reached almost 1,200% by October. In Montenegro, where 25% of the population were unemployed, popular pressure forced the wholesale resignation of all top party and state leaders, the republic's representatives in the federal presidency and politburo, and leaders of many mass organizations, enterprises, and trade unions. In October, Yugoslavia asked the United States for help in securing $1 billion in financial aid to sustain its banking system and payments on its $21 billion foreign debt.

The Yugoslav League of Communists and federal government continued to act slowly and indecisively, and top officials continued to rotate at yearly intervals. Ante Marković, a Croat, became the new prime minister, and Janez Drnovsek, a Slovene, chairman of the collective federal presidency. Milan Pancevski, a Macedonian, took over the leadership of the League of Communists. In Serbia, Milosević was replaced as leader of the Serbian Communist Party by Bogdan Trifunović, and was himself elected president of the republic.

The most concrete political initiatives came from Serbia. In July the Serbian presidency circulated a draft proposal to change the federal constitution. It recommended that individual freedoms and civil rights, as well as direct, secret elections be guaranteed, and that the "monopolistic-political" position of the League of Communists be reduced and political pluralism legalized. Milosević himself was known to favor a noncollective, nonrotating federal presidency with strong executive powers. In the fall the Central Committee of the League absorbed much of this proposal into its own recommendations for a new party platform to be debated at the party congress in January 1990.

Royal Burial. Thousands of Montenegrins attended the September 30 ceremonies that marked the return of the remains of their last king, who died in exile in 1921. King Nicholas I fled what was the kingdom of Montenegro when Austria occupied the country during World War I. Montenegro later became part of Serbia and in 1944, the smallest of the six republics of Yugoslavia. The reinterment of Nicholas I, his wife Queen Milena, and their two daughters may represent the first time a Communist regime has allowed royal remains to be returned home.

JOSEPH FREDERICK ZACEK
State University of New York at Albany

YUGOSLAVIA • Information Highlights

Official Name: Socialist Federal Republic of Yugoslavia.
Location: Southeastern Europe.
Area: 98,764 sq mi (255 800 km²).
Population (mid-1989 est.): 23,700,000.
Chief Cities (1981 census): Belgrade, the capital, 1,470,073; Osijek, 867,646; Zagreb, 768,700.
Government: *Head of state,* collective state presidency, Slobodan Milosević, president (took office 1989). *Legislature*—Federal Assembly: Federal Chamber and Chamber of Republics and Provinces.
Monetary Unit: Dinar (55,548.0 dinars equal U.S.$1, Nov. 17, 1989).
Gross National Product (1988 U.S.$): $154,100,-000,000.
Economic Indexes (1988): *Consumer Prices* (1980 = 100), all items, 8,518. *Industrial Production* (June 1989, 1980 = 100), 146.
Foreign Trade (1988 U.S.$): *Imports,* $13,154,-000,000; *exports,* $12,597,000,000.

YUKON

Residents of the Yukon went to the polls in a general election in February 1989 and returned the socialist New Democratic Party (NDP) to power in the territorial legislature. The standings following the election were nine NDP and seven Progressive Conservative (PC) legislators. However, one seat was contested. The lone Liberal member for the mining town of Faro was defeated.

Economy. Yukon's mining economy leveled off somewhat during 1988 and early 1989, although the economy generally remained healthy. Total mineral production in 1988 was C$454.6 million, an increase of about $20 million from 1987, despite decreasing metal commodity prices. Gold values dropped from C$89 million in 1987 to C$74.5 million, due largely to a dramatic decrease in world gold prices. Silver and zinc values were also up. Lead values dropped by 17% over the same period.

Total value of retail trade in the Yukon was about $35 million in the first quarter of 1989, an increase of 6.5% compared with the C$33 million earned in the first quarter of 1988. Tourism dropped slightly. Travelers entering Yukon through Canada customs points of entry totaled 272,766 during 1988, down about 21,000 from 1987. Economic forecasts indicated that while Yukon's growth rate remained higher than the Canadian average, it would slow down.

Indian Land Claims. Band-by-band negotiations, ongoing over a 15-year period, continued under a "framework agreement-in-principle" that was signed earlier by the federal and territorial governments and the negotiators for Yukon's Indians. Talks deal with 24 specific areas, including land disposition, wildlife management, and Indian self-government. Indians may receive up to 16,000 sq mi (41 440 km^2) of land and more than $230 million.

Government. In the autumn the Yukon cabinet gave the government leader the title of premier, a matter under review by the federal office of Indian and Northern Affairs, which has the authority to reverse the decision.

DON SAWATSKY, *Whitehorse*

YUKON • Information Highlights

Area: 186,660 sq mi (483 450 km^2).
Population (Sept. 1988): 25,400.
Chief cities (1986 census): Whitehorse, the capital, 15,199.
Government (1989): *Chief Officers*—commissioner, J. Kenneth McKinnon; government leader, Tony Penikett (New Democratic Party). *Legislature*—16-member Legislative Assembly.
Public Finance (1989–90 fiscal year budget est.): *Revenues*, $329,695,000; *expenditures*, $329,000,000.
Personal Income (average weekly earnings, June 1989): $579.83.
Education (1989–90): *Enrollment*—elementary and secondary schools, 5,110 pupils.
(All dollar amounts expressed in Canadian currency)

ZAIRE

Zaire's economy was strengthened by the International Monetary Fund in mid-1989, but fiscal conditions continued to be precarious and unstable. President Mobutu Sese Seko replaced one third of his cabinet, changed prime ministers, and agreed to further restructuring of the economy. Nevertheless, inflation remained in double-digit figures, consumer goods were scarce, the currency continued to depreciate, and government corruption, while no longer blatant, remained a major factor.

Domestic Policy. Improvement in the diamond- and gold-mining sectors and in agriculture tended to mask the balance of payments problem and chronic shortages of vital goods. One deficient service is the bus system in the capital, Kinshasa, which had only 100 vehicles to serve a city of 4 million. This led to confrontations in February between students and government. Protesting an 80% rise in fares, students forced Mobutu to declare *de facto* martial law in the city. The confrontation left ten people dead and more than 125 protesters arrested. The unrest spread to Lubumbashi, where more than 1,000 students protested the death of one of their leaders. Two days of rioting followed and 52 persons were killed and approximately 300 were arrested. Mobutu closed all five universities.

Politically, Mobutu's MPR party continued dominant. Most opposition groups were forced to operate from exile. Etienne Tshiskedi wa Mulumba, leader of the rival UDPS party, was arrested and charged with complicity in the riots.

Foreign Policy. A major disagreement with Belgium over rescheduling a part of Zaire's $7 billion foreign debt was smoothed over in July (*see* BELGIUM). In January, Idi Amin, Uganda's former dictator, was apprehended in Kinshasa ostensibly attempting to return to Uganda and was forced to return to Saudi Arabia. Mobutu mounted a major public-relations offensive aimed primarily at the United States attempting to change foreign perception of Zaire and its alleged human-rights violations.

HARRY A. GAILEY
San José State University

ZAIRE • Information Highlights

Official Name: Republic of Zaire.
Location: Central equatorial Africa.
Area: 905,564 sq mi (2 345 410 km^2).
Population (mid-1989 est.): 34,900,000.
Chief City (1987 est.): Kinshasa, the capital, 2,500,000.
Government: *Head of state,* Mobutu Sese Seko, president (took office 1965). *Legislature* (unicameral)—National Legislative Council.
Monetary Unit: Zaire (396.0 zaires equal U.S.$1, July 1989).
Foreign Trade (1987 U.S.$): *Imports*, $756,000,000; *exports*, $970,000,000.

ZIMBABWE

During 1989, Zimbabwe's ninth year of independence, the country was at peace but it was troubled by increasing official corruption, unemployment, and student unrest.

"Willowgate Scandal." In January, President Robert Mugabe set up a three-member commission, headed by the judge-president of Zimbabwe, Wilson Sandura, to investigate the so-called "Willowgate Scandal" which implicated government officials in profiteering in the sale of new cars manufactured at Willowvale. This was a particularly significant government crisis because it took place at a time of high inflation and unemployment throughout Zimbabwe.

On April 21, Maurice Nyagumbo, a former senior cabinet minister who was implicated in the scandal, died of poisoning in what police said was a suicide. Earlier in April, Nyagumbo had resigned as senior minister for political affairs and as administrative secretary of the ruling Zimbabwe African National Union (ZANU). A presidential inquiry found that Nyagumbo had helped friends to buy cars directly from the state assembly plant instead of waiting nearly ten years like most buyers. Before his death, however, Nyagumbo denied that he had received bribes while in office. Four other government ministers and a provincial governor also quit as a result of the scandal. All had been accused by the judicial inquiry of profiteering from the sale of the cars.

Geoff Nyarota, the editor of the Bulawayo daily newspaper, *The Chronicle,* that investigated and publicized the scandal, was removed from his position in February and transferred to a public-relations job at the Harare headquarters of the state-controlled Zimbabwe newspapers. In an unexpected move which was highly criticized by opponents of ZANU, Mugabe pardoned former Minister of State for External Affairs Frederick Shava, who had been sentenced to nine months in prison for perjury. Shava acknowledged that he had lied about his involvement in the car scandals.

ZIMBABWE • Information Highlights

Official Name: Republic of Zimbabwe.
Location: Southern Africa.
Area: 150,803 sq mi (390 580 km²).
Population (mid-1989 est.): 10,100,000.
Chief Cities (1983 est.): Harare (formerly Salisbury), the capital, 681,000; Bulawayo, 429,000; Chitungwiza, 202,000.
Government: *Head of state and government,* Robert Mugabe, executive president (sworn in Dec. 31, 1987). *Legislature*—Parliament: Senate and House of Assembly.
Monetary Unit: Zimbabwe dollar (2.121 Z dollars equal U.S.$1, July 1989).
Economic Index (1988): *Industrial Production* (1980 = 100), 122.
Foreign Trade (1987 U.S.$): *Imports,* $1,044,000,000; *exports,* $1,419,000,000.

Student Unrest. Early in October the University of Zimbabwe was closed indefinitely and more than 40 people were arrested after students rioted and threw stones at police. Unrest began on the campus toward the end of September when students marked the first anniversary of anticorruption riots that led to the judicial investigation and the resignation of the five cabinet ministers. After publicly supporting the students and criticizing the government's use of emergency powers, the secretary general of the Zimbabwe Congress of Trade Unions, Morgan Tsvangirai, was arrested.

New Opposition Party. ZANU won an important by-election on July 6 against a new party, the Zimbabwe Unity Movement (ZUM), led by former ZANU cabinet minister Edgar Tekere. The election for a parliamentary representative from Harare, one of the townships near the capital city, had a low voter turnout. ZUM had campaigned on the theme that it was an anticorruption party but its activities were limited when the ZANU government prevented it from holding rallies and from placing advertising with the state-controlled television and radio stations and newspapers. Even though ZUM did not succeed in the October by-election it was clear that Tekere had developed a political following.

Foreign Investment. In May, Zimbabwe announced a new investment code that moved away from the government's stringent controls for the repatriation of profits earned by foreign investors. The government hoped the new code would attract much-needed foreign investment and lead to jobs for some of the country's nearly 1 million unemployed. Despite Zimbabwe's mineral wealth and sound agricultural sector, the nation only had been able to attract limited foreign investment since independence in 1980. While the government saw the need for changes, Finance Minister Bernard Chidzero emphasized that the government remained "dedicated to the transformation of the social system so that the poorest can be included." Chidzero said, "There is no inherent contradiction between socialism and market forces." It was anticipated that the new code would lead to a relaxation of wage and price controls and of some of the exchange control restrictions.

Constitutional Changes. The Zimbabwe government announced that it would introduce a bill in parliament to change some of the last remaining clauses of the 1979 independence constitution. It proposed to abolish the Zimbabwean Senate in April of 1990 and create a single parliamentary chamber with 140 members—120 elected and 20 nominated by the president. Twelve of the 20 were to be chosen to represent different racial groups. Charged with drafting a new constitution, the ruling party and the main opposition merged at the first national congress in mid-December.

PATRICK O'MEARA, *Indiana University*

Photo by Bill Meng/N.Y. Zoological Society

In 1989, Samuel R., a 1,300-lb (590-kg), 18-month-old elephant, took residence at the Bronx (NY) Zoo's renovated elephant house, the Keith W. Johnson Zoo Center.

ZOOS AND ZOOLOGY

Elephants were in the news often during 1989. Their numbers are declining drastically in the wild because of poaching for ivory. Since 1980, more than 500,000 have been slaughtered in Africa. In June 1989, consumer nations joined in a global ban on the ivory trade as a last-ditch effort to save the elephants. So it seemed fitting that in 1989 two major U.S. zoos opened exhibits featuring elephants and the efforts zoos are making to help ensure their survival.

Woodland Zoological Gardens, in Seattle, WA, replaced its 60-year-old elephant house with a lush Asian forest, where elephants enjoy bathing in a large pool, and a Thai logging camp, where visitors can watch the pachyderms demonstrate their skills in ancient Asian logging practices. The Bronx (NY) Zoo's magnificent 80-year-old Beaux Arts elephant house reopened in July as the Keith W. Johnson Zoo Center, a pachyderm palace for elephants, rhinos, and tapirs (relatives of horses and rhinos). Videos and graphics describe the battles to save elephants and rhinos from extinction.

The Bronx Zoo also unveiled the John Pierrepont Wildfowl Marsh, featuring a boardwalk meandering through shadblow trees and cattails, with wood ducks, chestnut-breasted teal, and other water birds. Similarly, the National Zoological Park in Washington, DC, opened its Wetlands Habitat in May for more than 40 species.

There's something for everyone in Louisville (KY) Zoo's new HerpAquarium, which displays more than 700 animals in 62 exhibits. The aquatic section features an Indo-Pacific reef with a variety of colorful fishes; the tropical rain forest hosts cottontop tamarins (small primates), Cuban crocodiles, and malachite swifts; and the arid region has bearded dragons, spiny-tailed skinks, and Aldabra tortoises.

Public education is a major goal of zoos, and during 1989 a number of institutions combined state-of-the-art technology and live animals to help visitors better understand nature. In The Living World—a $17 million facility at the St. Louis (MO) Zoo—you can use computers and look at animals to find the answers to questions such as What's the difference between an alligator and a crocodile? A stroll through the New York Aquarium's Discovery Cove immerses you in a dazzling array of aquatic habitats: from the sandy shore of periwinkles and hermit crabs to a tidal pool filled with sea urchins to a spectacular coral reef. At the Los Angeles (CA) Zoo, Adventure Island introduces youngsters to various creatures native to the Southwest. Celebrating its 70th birthday in 1989, the Jackson (MS) Zoological Park opened Discovery Zoo, where children can pet domestic animals, climb inside a turtle shell in the Turtle Crawl, and discover how animals become endangered in ZooArk.

Zoos across the United States are engaged in updating their facilities to provide better displays for both visitors and animals. As part of its multimillion-dollar redevelopment, Zoo Atlanta (GA) opened Masai Mara, a re-creation of the savannas of East Africa, in 1989. The San Diego (CA) Zoo's Sun Bear Forest is the third exhibit in that zoo's plan to reorganize displays into ten climate zones. The smallest of the world's bears, Malayan sun bears, are expert climbers and love honey, so the zoo constructed a huge artificial fig tree with heated branches for sleeping and an automatic honey dispenser that releases the treat several times a day. Other inhabitants of Sun Bear Forest include lion-tailed macaques (arboreal monkeys) and colorful tropical birds.

The Houston (TX) Zoo unveiled two new exhibits in 1989: The McGovern Mammal Marina re-creates the Pacific Northwest coast, with California sea lions and harbor seals. The refurbished Reptile House features a Temper-

Photos by Max Guiterrez/Metro Washington Park Zoo

The Metro Washington Park Zoo in Portland, OR, has undergone a remodeling. Its new Africa exhibit—including a grazing area for Hartmann's mountain zebras, a spacious land and water home for Freddy the Hippo, and the Howard Vollum Aviary (building above)*—is a major attraction.*

ate Forest with pine snakes and box turtles, a Tropical Forest inhabited by Gaboon vipers and iguanas, a Grasslands habitat for prairie rattlers, and a Desert with sidewinders and Gila monsters.

Endangered Species. California condors and black-footed ferrets, two critically endangered North American species, were also in the news in 1989—good news, this time. Four condor chicks hatched at San Diego Zoo, bringing to 32 the number of condors in the world. And the ferret population rose to 124 with the addition of 67 captive-born babies during the year. Officials plan to reintroduce captive-bred black-footed ferrets in 1991 into their natural habitat in the West.

Herpetologists at Seattle's Woodland Park were up to their ears in Solomon Island leaf frogs. Hundreds of the amphibians hatched there in 1989, marking the first time the species has bred in captivity. In addition, zoo staff members discovered that the females dig holes in the soil, lay their eggs, and then cover them up—an egg-laying procedure never before reported in frogs.

At Washington's National Zoo, a cub was born to the giant panda Ling-Ling on September 1, but died of infection two days later. Zoo officials feared that the panda and her mate, Hsing-Hsing, were nearing the end of their fertile years.

Scientific Findings. Biologist Bernard J. Crespi, at the University of Michigan's Museum of Zoology, discovered that the thrips, a tiny sucking insect, can either lay eggs or bear live young—the first known animal that can switch between the two reproductive methods. He also found that all the larvae from egg-laying females were female and that all the young from live-bearers were male. Crespi hopes to find out how the thrips makes the switch.

Scientists at the University of Alaska at Fairbanks recorded temperatures of 12 hibernating Arctic ground squirrels and found that they can survive, without freezing, at temperatures as low as 26.8°F (-2.9°C). Some fish can live at temperatures that low, and there are a number of turtles and frogs that can pass the winter between 26.6°F (-3°C) and 19.4°F (-7°C). These ectothermic vertebrates rely on antifreeze properties in their blood for survival. Because the scientists found no antifreeze molecules in the squirrels' blood, they hypothesize that the squirrels use supercooling, by which a fluid somehow is prevented from freezing below its normal freezing point.

Glue is the secret to the stretch in a spiderweb, according to Oxford University researchers. They studied the garden cross spider and discovered that the radial supporting strands of its web are dry and can stretch only about 20%. The capture strands, however, are coated with a gluelike substance and can stretch four times their original length, recovering with no obvious sag. The glue helps the silk give when an insect struggles to escape.

DEBORAH A. BEHLER
Senior Editor, "Animal Kingdom"

THE 1980S—A LOOK BACK

Although in the annals of history a decade is an insignificant period of time, the end of such a span offers an appropriate opportunity to look back and not only review but also consider the significance of the events just past. Accordingly, a chronological summary of some of the highlights and trends of the decade of the 1980s follows.

1980

February 26: Egypt and Israel exchanged diplomatic ambassadors for the first time.
April 18: The British colony of Rhodesia officially became the independent nation of Zimbabwe.
April 30: Princess Beatrix was invested as queen of the Netherlands, following the abdication of her mother, Queen Juliana.
May 4: The U.S. Department of Education came into existence as the nation's 13th cabinet-level office.
May 21: A state of emergency was declared at Love Canal in Niagara Falls, NY, as a new study revealed that 30% of the residents in the area, which had been used as a chemical dump site, had suffered chromosomal damage.
July 19–August 3: The United States and other Western nations, including Canada, Japan, and West Germany, boycotted the Summer Olympic Games in Moscow. The action was in retaliation for the Soviet invasion of Afghanistan in late 1979.
September 22: War broke out between Iran and Iraq.
November 4: Former California Gov. Ronald Reagan (R) was elected president, defeating President Jimmy Carter and third-party candidate John Anderson.
December 8: Former Beatle John Lennon was shot and killed in New York City.

THE YEAR ALSO SAW thousands of refugees from Cuba and Haiti arriving on U.S. shores; young American men again required to register for the draft; volcanic eruptions at Mount St. Helens in southwestern Washington; Ab-

scam, the latest scandal involving members of the U.S. Congress and state and local officials in Pennsylvania and New Jersey; the bacterial production of interferon, a virus-fighting substance; the birth of the new Pacific nation of Vanuatu; the death of the former shah of Iran, President Tito of Yugoslavia, and labor leader George Meany; the U.S. population reaching 226,504,825 persons.

1981

January 1: Greece joined the European Community.
January 20: Fifty-two Americans, who had been held hostage in Iran since November 1979, were released and flown to a U.S. Air Force base in West Germany. Moments later, Ronald Reagan was inaugurated as the 40th president of the United States.
March 30: President Reagan was wounded seriously in an assassination attempt in Washington, DC. He returned to the White House on April 11, following 12 days in the hospital.
April 14: The space shuttle *Columbia* completed its maiden mission.
April 24: Ronald Reagan lifted a 15-month-old embargo on grain sales to the USSR.
May 10: François Mitterrand, a socialist, was elected president of France.
May 13: Pope John Paul II was shot and wounded in St. Peter's Square.
July 29: Britain's Prince Charles and Lady Diana Spencer were married in St. Paul's Cathedral in London.
September 25: Sandra Day O'Connor officially became the 102d—and first woman—justice of the U.S. Supreme Court.
October 6: Egypt's President Anwar el-Sadat was assassinated during a military parade in Cairo.
October 22: Representatives of 22 nations gathered in Cancún, Mexico, for a two-day North-South summit meeting.
December 11: Javier Pérez de Cuellar, a Peruvian diplomat, was elected secretary-general of the United Nations.
December 13: Martial law was declared in Poland, and the operations of the independent trade union Solidarity were suspended.

THE YEAR ALSO SAW the emergence of supply-side economics as major tax- and budget-reduction legislation was enacted in the United States; a seven-week strike by major-league baseball players; some 13,000 air-traffic controllers on the picket lines across the United States; independence for the former British dependencies of Belize in Central America and Antigua and Barbuda in the Caribbean; the birth of the first American test-tube baby; wide distribution for the latest form of video technology, the videodisc; and the latest fad, the Rubik's Cube.

1982

April 17: In Ottawa, Britain's Queen Elizabeth II signed the Constitution Act, 1982, giving Canada complete legal and statutory independence from the United Kingdom.
April 25: Israel returned the final portions of the Sinai peninsula to Egypt in accord with the Israeli-Egyptian peace treaty of 1979.

Page 566: *The 1980s opened with former actor Ronald Reagan staging a successful campaign for the White House and beginning a new political era, with the U.S. Congress approving a $1.6 billion superfund to help clean up toxic chemical wastes in such areas as the Love Canal near Niagara Falls, NY, and with Misha the Bear serving as the official mascot for the XXII Summer Olympics in Moscow. Although 5,687 athletes from 81 nations participated, some 55 nations, including the United States, boycotted the games.*
Above: *In 1981, Britain's Prince Charles and Lady Diana Spencer were married in a glittering London ceremony, the Rubik's Cube was the latest fad, and Iran and Iraq were in the midst of a devastating war. In 1982, Iran captured thousands of Iraqi troops and forced them to display photos of Iran's leader, the Ayatollah Khomeini.*

May 1: Open warfare broke out between Britain and Argentina over the Falkland Islands and surrounding South Atlantic waters. Fighting continued until the Argentine forces surrendered and a cease-fire was reached on June 14.
June 6: Israeli troops invaded southern Lebanon with the purpose of destroying military bases of the Palestine Liberation Organization.
June 30: The date for ratification of the Equal Rights Amendment to the U.S. Constitution passed with only 35 of the required 38 state legislatures having approved.
July 23: The International Whaling Commission voted to ban commercial whaling, effective by 1986.
September 14: Lebanon's President-elect Bashir Gemayel was killed in a bomb blast in east Beirut.
November 12: Following the death of Leonid Brezhnev on November 10, former Soviet KGB chief Yuri Andropov was chosen general secretary of the Communist Party of the Soviet Union.

THE YEAR ALSO SAW the implantation of an artificial heart into a 61-year-old American dentist; the settlement of an eight-year-old antitrust suit against American Telephone and Telegraph Company; the dedication of the Vietnam Veterans Memorial in Washington, DC; the opening of Epcot Center at Walt Disney World, near Orlando, FL; the National Football League on strike; increasing popularity for Pacmen, Smurfs, and home computers; the introduction of a new savings plan, the Certificate of Deposit (CD); and movieland's E.T. being urged to "please, call home."

Below: *In Ottawa, April 17, 1982, Queen Elizabeth II signed the Constitution Act, 1982, granting Canada complete independence from Great Britain. In 1983, Pope John Paul II returned to his native Poland and encouraged the government to recognize the Solidarity trade union, and fighting between the USSR and the Afghan resistance was in its fourth year. Captured Soviet equipment remained a cherished prize for the Afghan freedom fighter.*

1983

April 12: Harold Washington (D) became the first black to be elected mayor of Chicago.
April 20: President Reagan signed into law a bill to ensure the solvency of the Social Security system.
June 9: Britain's Conservative Party of Prime Minister Margaret Thatcher increased its parliamentary majority in national elections.
July 21: Martial law was ended in Poland.
August 21: Philippine opposition leader Benigno S. Aquino, Jr., was assassinated at Manila Airport minutes after returning from self-imposed exile in the United States.
September 1: A Korean Air Lines Boeing 747, flight 007 from New York to Seoul, was downed by a Soviet missile after crossing into Soviet airspace. All 240 passengers and 29 crewmen were killed.
September 19: The Caribbean islands of St. Kitts-Nevis became independent.
October 5: Lech Walesa, the founder of Poland's outlawed trade union Solidarity, was named winner of the Nobel Peace Prize.
October 10: Yitzhak Shamir succeeded Menahem Begin as prime minister of Israel.
October 23: A truck loaded with explosives barreled into a U.S. Marine headquarters building at Lebanon's Beirut International Airport, killing 241 Americans. A simultaneous attack occurred at a nearby French compound.

October 25: U.S. forces, with troops from six Caribbean nations, invaded the Caribbean island of Grenada in "a joint effort to restore order and democracy."
October 31: Raúl Alfonsín emerged as winner of Argentina's October 30 presidential elections.
November 2: President Reagan signed legislation establishing a federal holiday in honor of the late civil-rights leader Dr. Martin Luther King, Jr.

THE YEAR ALSO SAW the U.S. economy recover from recession; Australia II *become the first non-U.S. yacht to capture the America's Cup; the release of the report "A Nation at Risk: The Imperatives for Educational Reform;" the 100th birthday of New York's Metropolitan Opera and the Brooklyn Bridge; the bicentennial of air and space flight; the final episode of the TV hit* M*A*S*H *and* Chorus Line *becoming the longest-running show in Broadway history; Chrysler Corporation repaying the last two thirds of its federally guaranteed loans; and the arrival of Cabbage Patch Kids dolls.*

1984

January 1: Brunei, a small Islamic sultanate on Borneo's northeast coast, was granted independence.
January 10: The United States and the Vatican restored diplomatic relations, broken for more than a century.
January 11: The National Bipartisan Commission on Central America, chaired by Henry Kissinger, issued its report, recommending a five-year, $8 billion economic-aid plan for the region.
February 13: Konstantin U. Chernenko succeeded Yuri V. Andropov, who died February 9, as general secretary of the Soviet Communist Party.
February 18: Italy and the Vatican signed a concordat under which Roman Catholicism ceased to be the state religion.
May 1: President Reagan concluded an official visit to China.
June 6: Indian troops attacked the holiest Sikh shrine, the Golden Temple in Amritsar, the Punjab, to end escalating violence by Sikh separatists.
July 19: Rep. Geraldine A. Ferraro was nominated as vice-president at the Democratic National Convention, becoming the first woman to serve on the presidential ticket of a major party.
July 28–August 12: The USSR and various Soviet-bloc nations boycotted the XXIII Summer Olympic Games in Los Angeles.
August 1: In accord with a newly announced Chinese-British agreement, China would assume control of Hong Kong after Britain's lease on the colony expires in 1997.
September 20: The U.S. Embassy annex outside Beirut, Lebanon, was bombed in a suicide car attack.
October 16: Bishop Desmond Tutu, a leader of the antiapartheid movement in South Africa, was named winner of the 1984 Nobel Peace Prize.
October 18: Representatives of Chile and Argentina initialed a treaty settling a long-standing dispute over the Beagle Channel.
October 31: Rajiv Gandhi became prime minister of India, following the assassination of his mother, Prime Minister Indira Gandhi.
November 6: President Reagan and Vice-President George Bush were reelected to a second term.
December 3: In Bhopal, India, a poisonous gas leak from a pesticide plant, owned jointly by Union Carbide and Indian investors, left more than 2,000 persons dead.

THE YEAR ALSO SAW the George Orwell novel 1984 *at the top of the bestsellers list; the end of the Pierre Trudeau era in Canada; a new awareness of*

Above: *In 1984 the increasingly militant campaign of Sikh separatist extremists in the state of Punjab moved the Indian government to harsh countermeasures; U.S. track star Carl Lewis dominated the Summer Olympics, winning four gold medals; and the Democratic presidential ticket of former Vice-President Walter Mondale and U.S. Rep. Geraldine Ferraro was defeated in a landslide. The 49-year-old congresswoman made history, however, by being the first woman to be on the national ticket of a major U.S. political party.*

Above: *In 1985, Nicaraguan contra leader Enrique Bermúdez rallied new recruits as efforts to bring down the Sandinista regime continued, and Desmond M. Tutu, the winner of the 1984 Nobel Peace Prize for his nonviolent campaign to end apartheid in South Africa, was enthroned as the first black Anglican bishop of Johannesburg. In 1986, in the Philippines, Corazon Aquino, the wife of the assassinated opposition leader Benigno Aquino, led a peaceful "people's revolution" that ousted President Ferdinand Marcos after 20 years in power.*

the plight of the U.S. homeless; the rise of Michael Jackson as the latest pop-music sensation; the election of a new paramount ruler in Malaysia; long lines to buy lottery tickets throughout the United States; Trivial Pursuit and break-dancing as the latest pastime diversions; and the 50th birthday of Donald Duck.

1985

January 20: President Reagan and Vice-President Bush were sworn in for a second term.
February 5: Spain fully reopened its border with Gibraltar, which had been closed since June 1969.
March 11: Mikhail Gorbachev was named chairman of the Soviet Communist Party following the March 10 death of Konstantin Chernenko.
April 26: Leaders of the Warsaw Pact nations ratified a 20-year extension of the Soviet-led military alliance.
May 1: President Reagan ordered a trade embargo against Nicaragua, saying that Nicaraguan actions were a threat to U.S. security.
June 10: Israel completed the final phase of its military withdrawal from Lebanon.
September 1: A team of U.S. and French researchers located the SS *Titanic*, the ocean liner lost in 1912.
September 19: A major earthquake rocked southwestern Mexico, devastating portions of Mexico City.
November 21: President Reagan and Soviet General Secretary Gorbachev concluded a summit meeting in Geneva; no major breakthroughs occurred.
December 8: The Organization of the Petroleum Exporting Countries (OPEC) abandoned its price structure to concentrate on capturing a "fair" share of the market.
December 28: Warring militias in Lebanon signed an agreement, mediated by Syria, to end ten years of civil war. Violence continued to plague the nation, however.

THE YEAR ALSO SAW Live Aid, a rock music telethon, which raised $70 million for African famine victims, and the Farm Aid concert, which raised $10 million to benefit the American farmer, heavily burdened by debt; increased international terrorism; violence and unrest in South Africa; protest over the introduction of a new formula for Coca-Cola and the reintroduction of the old formula; a new pro football celebrity, Chicago's William "the Refrigerator" Perry; Wrestlemania; continued fighting in Central America, where El Salvador's government has been battling leftist guerrillas and Nicaragua's Sandinista junta has been fighting guerrillas supported by the United States; and the New York City case of Bernhard Goetz, who claimed self-defense in a December 1984 subway shooting.

1986

January 1: Spain and Portugal officially joined the European Community.
January 7: The United States severed all economic ties with Libya, accusing it of supporting terrorist acts, and ordered all Americans out of Libya.
January 28: The U.S. space shuttle *Challenger* exploded shortly after takeoff from Cape Canaveral. All seven crew members were killed.

February 7: Haiti's President-for-Life Jean-Claude Duvalier fled to exile in France. A military-civilian council took power.
February 26: Following February 7 elections, Philippine President Ferdinand Marcos left the country, ending 20 years in power; Corazon Aquino was inaugurated as president.
February 28: Sweden's Prime Minister Olof Palme was murdered in Stockholm.
April 14: U.S. fighter planes bombed "terrorist centers" in Tripoli and Benghazi, Libya, in retaliation for Libya's role in the April 5 bombing of a West Berlin discotheque in which a U.S. serviceman was killed.
April 28: The USSR confirmed that a serious accident had taken place at the Chernobyl nuclear power plant north of Kiev, releasing radiation into the atmosphere.
June 17: William H. Rehnquist was named chief justice of the U.S. Supreme Court, replacing the retiring Warren E. Burger. Antonin Scalia was appointed to the vacant seat.
October 12: President Reagan and Soviet General Secretary Gorbachev concluded two days of arms control talks in Reykjavik, Iceland; disagreement occurred over the U.S. Strategic Defense Initiative ("Star Wars").
November 13: President Reagan confirmed reports that the United States had sent shipments of arms and military parts to Iran "to effect the safe return" of American hostages.

THE YEAR ALSO SAW the appearance of Halley's Comet; Expo 86, a world's fair held in Vancouver, B.C.; "Hands Across America," a human chain across the United States organized to raise money for the poor and homeless; the 100th birthday celebration of the Statue of Liberty; the marriage of Great Britain's Prince Andrew and Sarah Ferguson; the continuing reduction of oil prices worldwide; a sweeping reform of the U.S. tax code; the first nonstop around-the-world flight on a single load of fuel, made by Voyager.

Below: *At 11:38 A.M. on Jan. 28, 1986, the U.S. space shuttle "Challenger" was launched from Cape Canaveral, FL, with a crew of seven on board. Seconds later the shuttle was engulfed in a cloud of fire and smoke; the seven astronauts were believed to have died instantly. On Monday, Oct. 19, 1987, the New York Stock Exchange's Dow Jones industrial average dropped a record 508.32 points. By 1987, Oliver North, a decorated Marine and member of the National Security Council staff in the Reagan administration, had become a central figure in the Iran-contra affair.*

1987

January 20: Anglican Church envoy Terry Waite disappeared during a mission to Lebanon to seek the release of Western hostages.
May 5: Under the 1986 Immigration Reform and Control Act, undocumented residents of the United States were given one year to apply for legal status.
May 17: The U.S.S. *Stark,* a Navy frigate on patrol in the Persian Gulf, was struck by Iraqi missiles, killing 37 sailors. Iraq apologized, calling the attack an accident.
June 11: Great Britain's Conservative Prime Minister Margaret Thatcher became the nation's first prime minister since 1827 to be elected to a third consecutive term.
July 22: U.S. Navy warships began escorting Kuwaiti oil tankers, sailing under U.S. flags, into the Persian Gulf.
August 7: The presidents of five Central American countries signed a preliminary agreement calling for a regional cease-fire and other steps toward lasting peace.
October 3: Canada and the United States reached a comprehensive trade pact on the elimination of all bilateral tariffs over ten years.
October 19: The Dow Jones industrial stock average plunged 508.32 points, by far the largest one-day drop to date.

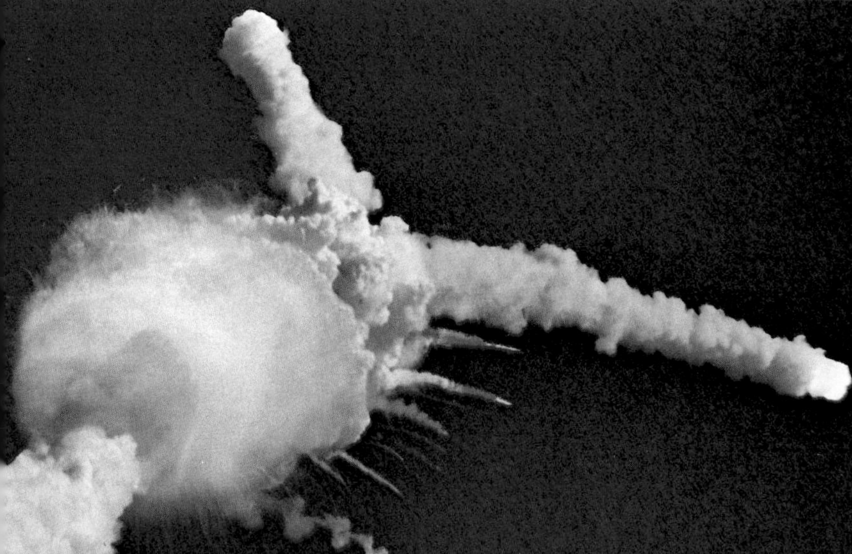

Above: *On June 11, 1987, Margaret Thatcher of Great Britain became the nation's first prime minister since 1827 to be elected to a third term, as her Conservative Party scored a major victory at the polls. From May 29 to June 2, 1988, President Reagan was in the USSR to confer with Mikhail Gorbachev and other Muscovites. In 1987 the U.S. yacht "Stars & Stripes" defeated Australia's "Kookaburra III" to return the America's Cup to U.S. shores. One year later it also turned back a New Zealand challenge. A court battle resulted, however, and in 1989 a New York judge ordered the cup forfeited to New Zealand. An appeals court overturned that decision.*

November 18: The U.S. House and Senate committees investigating the Iran-contra affair issued their final report, blaming the scandal on White House "secrecy, deception, and disdain for the law." A minority report rejected the panels' "hysterical conclusions."
December 8: In Washington, President Reagan and Soviet leader Gorbachev signed a treaty on the global elimination of intermediate-range nuclear forces.

THE YEAR ALSO SAW the death of Andy Warhol; a "televangelism" scandal involving Jim and Tammy Faye Bakker and the PTL; the "Baby M" surrogate motherhood case; the flight of West German Mathias Rust into Moscow's Red Square; the bicentennial of the U.S. Constitution; the beginnings of perestroika *(restructuring) and* glasnost *(openness) in the USSR; the capture of the last wild California condor; the return of yachting's America's Cup to U.S. shores; and the unification of the world's heavyweight boxing title by Mike Tyson.*

1988

January 13: Following the death of Chiang Ching-kuo, the 77-year-old son of the late Chiang Kai-shek, Taiwan's Vice-President Lee Teng-hui succeeded to the presidency.
February 18: Anthony M. Kennedy was sworn in as an associate justice of the U.S. Supreme Court.
February 26: Panama's President Eric Arturo Delvalle was ousted after moving to fire de facto leader Gen. Manuel Noriega, a suspected drug trafficker.
May 15: The USSR officially began withdrawing its troops from Afghanistan.
June 2: President Reagan concluded a five-day summit in Moscow.
July 3: A U.S. cruiser in the Persian Gulf shot down an Iranian commercial airliner after mistaking it for an attack plane; all 290 persons aboard the plane were killed.
July 6: In Mexico's first truly competitive elections in more than a century, Carlos Salinas de Gortari was chosen president.
August 20: A UN-negotiated cease-fire between Iran and Iraq took effect.
October 3: Libya and Chad resumed diplomatic relations and formally ended their border war.
November 8: Republican Vice-President George Bush and Sen. Dan Quayle (IN) defeated the Democratic ticket of Massachusetts Gov. Michael Dukakis and Sen. Lloyd Bentsen (TX) in the U.S. presidential election.
November 15: The Palestine Liberation Organization (PLO) declared an independent Palestinian state and agreed to recognize Israel. The USSR launched its first space shuttle, *Buran.*
December 2: Benazir Bhutto took office as Pakistan's prime minister, becoming the first woman leader of a Muslim nation.
December 22: Representatives of Angola, Cuba, and South Africa signed final accords on Namibia's independence and the withdrawal of Cuban troops from Angola.

THE YEAR ALSO SAW the bicentennial of Australia's settlement; a 22-week-long strike by television and movie writers; severe drought and forest fires in parts of the United States; Steffi Graf as the first tennis player in 18 years to win the Grand Slam; the XXIV Summer Olympic Games, marred by a drug

scandal; the reelection of Canada's Conservative Party, led by Prime Minister M. Brian Mulroney; the return of the United States to space with the flight of the space shuttle Discovery; *the rescue of three whales trapped in ice in Barrow, AK; sweeping changes in the Soviet political system; the spread of computer viruses; Kohlberg Kravis and Roberts take over RJR Nabisco; uprisings by Palestinians against Israeli occupation in the West Bank and Gaza; a massive Soviet earthquake; enactment of catastrophic health insurance and the establishment of a cabinet-level Department of Veterans Affairs in the United States; and continuing political unrest in the Caribbean nation of Haiti.*

Above: *In October 1988, international attention was focused on three gray whales trapped in an Arctic ice pack at Point Barrow, AK. After 19 days, a Soviet icebreaker cut a path to open water, freeing two of the whales. The third was lost. For many, the incident was a diversion from the U.S. presidential campaign then in full swing. Vice-President George Bush was elected as the 41st president, capturing the electoral votes of 40 states.* Below: *Although world communism was in a state of flux as the decade came to an end, a massive, springtime 1989, prodemocracy movement in China was squelched by the government.*

1989

January 7: Hirohito, emperor of Japan since 1926, died at the age of 87.
January 22: George Herbert Walker Bush was inaugurated as 41st president of the United States.
February 3: Alfredo Stroessner, the president of Ecuador for 34 years, was ousted in a military coup.
March 24: The Exxon oil tanker *Valdez* ran aground in the Gulf of Alaska, causing a major oil spill.
May 4: Former U.S. National Security Council staff member Oliver North was convicted of three of 12 counts for his role in the Iran-contra affair.
May 15–18: Massive prodemocracy demonstrations by Chinese students overshadowed President Gorbachev's visit to China, during which Sino-Soviet relations were restored.
July 28: Ali Akbar Hashemi Rafsanjani was elected president of Iran, succeeding the late Ayatollah Khomeini.
August 18: Colombia presidential candidate Luís Carlos Galán was assassinated by drug traffickers, prompting a government crackdown.
September 21: Hurricane *Hugo* slammed into the U.S. mainland.
October 17: A major earthquake rumbled through northern California.
November 9: East Germany opened up the notorious Berlin Wall.
December 20: U.S. troops arrived in Panama to depose Gen. Manuel Antonio Noriega.
December 25: Romania's Nicolae Ceauşescu was overthrown and executed.

THE YEAR ALSO SAW the bicentennial of the French Revolution; the climax of 12 years of space exploration for Voyager II; *the 50th anniversary of television and* Gone With the Wind; *multicandidate elections in the USSR and Poland; Nintendo; death threat against Salman Rushdie; the cold fusion controversy; a major Andy Warhol retrospective; Batmania;* Jerome Robbins' Broadway; *the resignation of U.S. House Speaker Jim Wright; Pete Rose's agreement to leave baseball for alleged gambling.*

Photo Credits: *page 566,* the 1980 Olympics—© Bevilacqua/Sygma; Ronald Reagan—© Larry Downing/"Newsweek;" Love Canal—© Joe Traver/Gamma-Liaison; *Page 567,* royal wedding—© David Burnett/Contact; Iraqi troops—© Kalari/Sygma; Rubik's Cube—courtesy, Ideal. *Page 568,* Canada's constitution—© John deVisser/Black Star; Pope John Paul II —© David Burnett/Contact; Afghanistan—© Roland Neveu/Gamma-Liaison. *Page 569,* Sikh separatists—© Santosh Basak/Gamma-Liaison; Mondale-Ferraro—© Mario Ruiz/Picture Group; Carl Lewis—© David Madison/Duomo. *Page 570,* Nicaragua—© Claude Urraca/Sygma; Desmond Tutu—© Mark Peters/Black Star; Corazon Aquino—© A. Hernandez/Sygma. *Page 571,* Oliver North—Terry Ashe/"Time" Magazine; "Challenger" disaster—AP/Wide World; stock market crash —© Owen Franken/Picture Group. *Page 572,* Reagan-Gorbachev—© Tass from Sovfoto; Margaret Thatcher—© Cavendish-Reflex/Picture Group; America's Cup—AP/Wide World. *Page 573,* the whales—© Charles Mason/Black Star; George Bush—© J. L. Atlan/Sygma; China—© Peter Turnley/Black Star.

Statistical and Tabular Data

Table of Contents

NATIONS OF THE WORLD

A Profile and Synopsis of Major 1989 Developments

Nation, Region	Population in millions	Capital	Area Sq mi (km²)	Head of State/Government
Antigua and Barbuda, Caribbean	0.1	St. John's	170 (440)	Sir Wilfred E. Jacobs, governor-general Vere C. Bird, prime minister

Prime Minister Vere C. Bird, Sr., was reelected March 9. In July, Antigua and Barbuda joined together with ten other Caribbean nations in agreeing to participate in common-market arrangements which were scheduled to begin by mid-1993. Gross Domestic Product (GDP) (1987 est.): $215 million. Foreign Trade (1987): Imports, $278.9 million; exports, $30.8 million.

Nation, Region	Population in millions	Capital	Area Sq mi (km²)	Head of State/Government
Bahamas, Caribbean	0.2	Nassau	5,382 (13 940)	Sir Henry Taylor, governor-general Lynden O. Pindling, prime minister

At a meeting of Caribbean leaders in July, the Bahamas announced it would remain within the Caribbean Community, but would not enter a common market until definitive trading rules are established. GDP (1987): $2.3 billion. Foreign Trade (1987): Imports, $3.2 billion; exports, $2.5 billion.

Nation, Region	Population in millions	Capital	Area Sq mi (km²)	Head of State/Government
Bahrain, W. Asia	0.5	Manama	239 (620)	Isa bin Sulman Al Khalifa, emir Khalifa bin Salman Al Khalifa, prime minister

Bahrain became one of the first nations to recognize the Afghan government established in February 1989 by a coalition of rebel groups based in Pakistan. GDP (1987): $3.5 billion. Foreign Trade (1988 est.): Imports, $2.5 billion; exports, $2.4 billion.

Nation, Region	Population in millions	Capital	Area Sq mi (km²)	Head of State/Government
Barbados, Caribbean	0.3	Bridgetown	166 (430)	Sir Hugh Springer, governor-general L. Erskine Sandiford, prime minister

Barbados' foreign minister, James Tudor, resigned March 31 amid charges that members of the Barbados diplomatic staff based in Venezuela had smuggled drugs into Barbados. GDP (1987 est.): $1.4 billion. Foreign Trade (1987): Imports, $515 million; exports, $156 million.

Nation, Region	Population in millions	Capital	Area Sq mi (km²)	Head of State/Government
Benin, W. Africa	4.7	Porto Novo	43,483 (112 620)	Mathieu Kérékou, president

Popular discontent in Benin went on throughout 1989 as the nation's economic crisis and resultant austerity measures continued. On December 11, 20,000 protesters demanding the resignation of President Mathieu Kérékou were dispersed by police using tear gas and guns fired into the air. Two protesters were killed by police in the city of Cotonou. The protests were quieted after troops were ordered to prevent public gatherings.The government officially had renounced Marxism-Leninism and promised economic liberalization one week earlier, but opposition to Kérékou only had intensified after the announcement. GDP (1986): $1.4 billion. Foreign Trade (1986): Imports, $338 million; exports, $108 million.

Nation, Region	Population in millions	Capital	Area Sq mi (km²)	Head of State/Government
Bhutan, S. Asia	1.5	Thimphu	18,147 (47 000)	Jigme Singye Wangchuck, king

GDP (1987): $252 million. Foreign Trade (1988): Imports, $105.1 million; exports, $60.8 million.

Nation, Region	Population in millions	Capital	Area Sq mi (km²)	Head of State/Government
Botswana, S. Africa	1.2	Gaborone	231,803 (600 370)	Quett Masire, president

University students demanding higher grants and better conditions staged a four-day boycott of classes in January 1989; the university was closed indefinitely after the boycott. GDP (1987): $1.5 billion. Foreign Trade (1988): Imports, $1.1 billion; exports, $1.3 billion.

Nation, Region	Population in millions	Capital	Area Sq mi (km^2)	Head of State/Government
Brunei, S.E. Asia	0.3	Bandar Seri Begawan	2,288 (5 770)	Sir Muda Hassanal Bolkiah, sultan and prime minister

Along with the five other member nations of the Association of Southeast Asian Nations (ASEAN), Brunei agreed on March 13 to adopt new restrictions on Vietnamese refugees. They would have to prove they faced religious or political persecution to qualify for asylum. GDP (1987): $3.1 billion. Foreign Trade (1987): Imports, $800 million; exports, $2.07 billion.

Nation, Region	Population in millions	Capital	Area Sq mi (km^2)	Head of State/Government
Burkina Faso, W. Africa	8.7	Ouagadougou	105,869 (274 200)	Blaise Compaoré, president

In October, President Compaoré's chief advisers and principal rivals, Capt. Henri Zongo and Maj. Jean-Baptiste Boukari Lengani, were accused of conspiring in a coup attempt and were executed. The government reported at Christmastime that it had foiled another coup attempt. GDP (1986 est.): $1.32 billion. Foreign Trade (1986): Imports, $405 million; exports, $83 million.

Nation, Region	Population in millions	Capital	Area Sq mi (km^2)	Head of State/Government
Burundi, E. Africa	5.5	Bujumbura	10,745 (27 830)	Pierre Buyoya, president Adrien Sibomana, prime minister

Burundi joined with Zaire and Rwanda in January 1989 to form a tripartite security commission. Also in January former Burundi President Bagaza obtained political asylum in Libya. In early April all Libyan diplomats were expelled from Burundi. GDP (1986): $1.3 billion. Foreign Trade (1987): Imports, $212 million; exports, $84 million.

Nation, Region	Population in millions	Capital	Area Sq mi (km^2)	Head of State/Government
Cameroon, Cen. Africa	10.8	Yaoundé	183,568 (475 440)	Paul Biya, president

Work began on a new international airport in Cameroon as part of a plan to modernize and expand the nation's air traffic sector. On November 30 former President Ahmadou Ahidjo died in exile in Senegal at age 65. He had led Cameroon for 22 years. GDP (1987): $12.3 billion. Foreign Trade (1987): Imports, $1.7 billion; exports, $2.2 billion.

Nation, Region	Population in millions	Capital	Area Sq mi (km^2)	Head of State/Government
Cape Verde, W. Africa	0.4	Praia	1,556 (4 030)	Aristides Pereira, president Pedro Pires, prime minister

Cape Verde's economy continued to progress and develop, aided by the highest per capita aid of any West African nation in the 1980s. The government hoped to continue its economic development in the 1990s with the help of private foreign investment. GDP (1987 est.): $136 million. Foreign Trade (1987): Imports, $82 million; exports, $5.6 million.

Nation, Region	Population in millions	Capital	Area Sq mi (km^2)	Head of State/Government
Central African Republic, Cen. Africa	2.8	Bangui	240,533 (622 980)	André-Dieudonne Kolingba, president

On January 16, Central African Republic resumed diplomatic relations with Israel, which had been broken off in 1973 over the Yom Kippur War. GDP (1987): $1.1 billion. Foreign Trade (1987): Imports, $269 million; exports, $131 million.

Nation, Region	Population in millions	Capital	Area Sq mi (km^2)	Head of State/Government
Chad, Cen. Africa	4.9	Ndjamena	495,753 (1 284 000)	Hissein Habré, president

Libya and Chad signed an agreement in August to end 16 years of hostility between the two nations. They agreed to withdraw troops from the contested Aouzou strip, and to try to seek a political settlement of the dispute. A Chadian coup attempt was crushed April 1. GDP (1986): $818 million. Foreign Trade (1986): Imports, $206 million; exports, $98.6 million.

Nation, Region	Population in millions	Capital	Area Sq mi (km^2)	Head of State/Government
Comoros, E. Africa	0.4	Moroni	838 (2 170)	Mohammed Djohar, interim president

Members of the presidential guard, led by Col. Bob Denard, assassinated President Ahmed Abdallah Abderemane on November 26. Denard, a French mercenary, took control of the nation, triggering widespread protesting. France and South Africa cut off financial aid to the country until Denard left Comoros. After three weeks, the French government sent naval forces into the waters off Comoros' largest island. He and 21 other mercenaries were sent to France. GDP (1986 est.): $163 million. Foreign Trade (1986): Imports, $41 million; exports, $39 million.

Nation, Region	Population in millions	Capital	Area Sq mi (km^2)	Head of State/Government
Congo, Cen. Africa	2.2	Brazzaville	132,046 (342 000)	Denis Sassou-Nguesso, president Ange Edouard Poungui, prime minister

On January 14 the African Anti-Apartheid Committee was formed. It was to be based in Brazzaville. It was founded at a meeting held under the auspices of the Organization for African Unity (OAU). With Gabon and Zaire, at a summit of African leaders held in June in Zaire, Congo was named to be a member of a national reconciliation committee to work for peace in Angola, following the declaration of a cease-fire there. GDP (1987): $2.2 billion. Foreign Trade (1987): Imports, $494.4 million; exports, $912 million.

Nation, Region	Population in millions	Capital	Area Sq mi (km^2)	Head of State/Government
Djibouti, E. Africa	0.4	Djibouti	8,494 (22 000)	Hassan Gouled Aptidon, president Barkat Gourad Hamadou, premier

Several strong earthquakes, centered in Ethiopia, caused some damage in Djibouti in August. GDP (1986): $333 million. Foreign Trade (1986): Imports, $198 million; exports, $128 million.

Nation, Region	Population in millions	Capital	Area Sq mi (km^2)	Head of State/Government
Dominica, Caribbean	0.1	Roseau	290 (750)	Clarence A. Seignoret, president Mary Eugenia Charles, prime minister

Hurricane Hugo struck Dominica in September, causing widespread damage. GDP (1987): $124.5 million. Foreign Trade (1987): Imports, $66 million; exports, $46 million.

Nation, Region	Population in millions	Capital	Area Sq mi (km^2)	Head of State/Government
Dominican Republic, Caribbean	7.0	Santo Domingo	18,815 (48 730)	Joaquín Balaguer Ricardo, president

A 48-hour general strike nationwide took place June 19–20 to protest the government's new, harsher austerity measures. GDP (1987 est.): $5.6 billion. Foreign Trade (1987): Imports, $1.8 billion; exports, $711 million.

Nation, Region	Population in millions	Capital	Area Sq mi (km^2)	Head of State/Government
Equatorial Guinea, Cen. Africa	0.4	Malabo	10,830 (28 050)	Obiang Nguema Mbasogo, president Cristino Seriche Bioko, prime minister

President Mbasogo pardoned the secretary-general of the opposition Progress Party in January 1989. In September 1988 he had been sentenced to 17 years in prison for plotting against security. Gross National Product (GNP) (1986): $75 million. Foreign Trade (1986): Imports, $41 million; exports, $39 million.

Nation, Region	Population in millions	Capital	Area Sq mi (km^2)	Head of State/Government
Fiji, Oceania	0.7	Suva	7,054 (18 270)	Sir Penaia Ganilau, president Sir Kamisese Mara, prime minister

Prime Minister Mara on April 12 announced that he would retire in December, when his current term in office was to expire. GDP (1987): $1.12 billion. Foreign Trade (1987): Imports, $385 million; exports, $328 million.

Nation, Region	Population in millions	Capital	Area Sq mi (km²)	Head of State/Government

Gabon, Cen. Africa | 1.1 | Libreville | 103,348 (267 670) | El Hadj Omar Bongo, president
Léon Mébiame, premier

Gabon's economy profited from the sharp rise in oil prices in early 1989. The Rabi-Kounga oilfield, opened in March, was expected to pump 120,000 barrels of oil daily. At a June summit of African leaders held in Zaire, Gabon was named as a member of a national reconciliation committee to work for peace in Angola. GNP (1986): $3.4 billion. Foreign Trade (1986 est.): Imports, $0.95 billion; exports, $1.95 billion.

Gambia, W. Africa | 0.8 | Banjul | 4,363 (11 300) | Sir Dawda Kairaba Jawara, president

In January, Gambia made a formal complaint to China about the treatment of its students there, charging discrimination and racism against black African students. GDP (1988): $145 million. Foreign Trade (1987): Imports, $117.5 million; exports, $70.1 million.

Ghana, W. Africa | 14.6 | Accra | 92,100 (238 540) | Jerry Rawlings, chairman of the Provisional National Defense Council

In February district assembly elections, the first elections of any kind in Ghana for ten years, were held. Widespread corruption and fraud in Ghana's timber industry was discovered, some of it thought to be in collusion with Ghanaian officials and World Bank agents. A cleanup campaign was launched. GNP (1986): $5.73 billion. Foreign Trade (1986): Imports, $783 million; exports, $863 million.

Grenada, Caribbean | 0.1 | St. George's | 131 (340) | Sir Paul Scoon, governor-general
Ben Jones, acting prime minister

In January 24 elections, Prime Minister Herbert Blaize was ousted as leader of the New National Party, but was to remain as head of government. Blaize, a longtime Caribbean political figure, died December 19. Ben Jones was named acting prime minister. GDP (1987 est.): $118.7 million. Foreign Trade (1987): Imports, $88 million; exports, $31.6 million.

Guinea, W. Africa | 7.1 | Conakry | 94,927 (245 860) | Lansana Conté, president

President Lansana Conté announced in October that the military leadership would allow competing political parties to form, and that a new constitution, regular elections, an independent judiciary, and a bill of rights all would be included in a five-year transition to constitutional rule. Gross domestic product grew by 5% in 1988. GDP (1987 est.): $1.7 billion. Foreign Trade (1987): Imports, $560 million; exports, $571 million.

Guinea-Bissau, W. Africa | 1.0 | Bissau | 13,946 (36 120) | João Bernardo Vieira, president

Guinea-Bissau in August announced its intention not to abide by an international arbitration panel's decision that a disputed piece of territory along the border with Senegal belonged to the latter. If Senegal refused to negotiate, Guinea-Bissau threatened to increase its military presence in the disputed area. GDP (1986 est.): $168 million. Foreign Trade (1987): Imports, $48.8 million; exports, $16.5 million.

Guyana, N.E. South America | 0.8 | Georgetown | 83,000 (214 970) | Hugh Desmond Hoyte, president
Hamilton Green, prime minister

With the other members of the eight-nation Amazon Pact, Guyana in 1989 denounced foreign interference in Amazonia, and condemned "meddling" on the issue of preserving the Amazon rain forest. GDP (1987): $344 million. Foreign Trade (1987): Imports, $254 million; exports, $240 million.

Ivory Coast, W. Africa | 12.1 | Yamoussoukro | 124,502 (322 460) | Félix Houphouët-Boigny, president

Due to several years of falling commodity prices, the economy of Ivory Coast was plunged into a recession. However, the largest Christian church in the world, a Roman Catholic basilica in Yamoussoukro, was completed in 1989. It cost at least $130 million to build. GDP (1987): $10.3 billion. Foreign Trade (1987): Imports, $2.7 billion; exports, $3.4 billion.

Kiribati, Oceania | 0.06 | Tarawa | 277 (717) | Ieremia Tabai, president

GDP (1987): $24.7 million. Foreign Trade (1987 est.): Imports, $17.5 million; exports, $2.3 million.

Kuwait, S.W. Asia | 2.1 | Kuwait | 6,800 (17 820) | Jabir al-Ahmad Al Sabah, emir

In February the Kuwaiti government released two of 17 jailed Shiite Muslim terrorists whose release had been demanded by kidnappers holding U.S. hostages in Lebanon. Kuwait said the release had nothing to do with the demands. GDP (1988): $19.1 billion. Foreign Trade (1988): Imports, $4.9 billion; exports, $8.7 billion.

Lesotho, S. Africa | 1.7 | Maseru | 11,718 (30 350) | Moshoeshoe II, king
Justin Lekhanya, chairman, military council

King Moshoeshoe II addressed the United Nations General Assembly in October and proposed talks among leaders of all southern African nations to discuss South Africa's political future after the abolishment of apartheid. If the meeting were to occur, the king said, it would be necessary for South Africa to cooperate actively. An epidemic of cutworm severely affected output of the nation's chief grain crops, forcing the government to appeal to the UN for food aid. During the year, Justin Lekhanya, chairman of the military council, faced demands that he resign following a published report implicating him in a corruption scandal and in the fatal shooting of a college student. GDP (1988 est.): $408 million. Foreign Trade (1986): Imports, $343 million; exports, $25 million.

Liberia, W. Africa | 2.5 | Monrovia | 43,000 (111 370) | Samuel K. Doe, president

Eleven persons, among them Liberia's defense minister, were charged in June with the ritual killing of a policeman as part of a plot to overthrow the government. GDP (1987): $973 million. Foreign Trade: Imports (1986), $259 million; exports (1987), $458 million.

Liechtenstein, Cen. Europe | 0.03 | Vaduz | 62 (160) | Hans Adam, prince
Hans Brunhart, prime minister

After reigning 51 years, Prince Franz Josef II died in 1989, and Crown Prince Hans Adam assumed his title. In November, Liechtenstein announced its intent to seek full membership in the United Nations in 1990. It already belongs to several UN agencies.

Luxembourg, W. Europe | 0.4 | Luxembourg | 998 (2 586) | Jean, grand duke
Jacques Santer, prime minister

In April, Luxembourg celebrated its 150th year as a nation. Several prominent European leaders attended the festivities. In summer elections, Prime Minister Santer retained his office, as his Christian Social Party won a majority of parliament seats. GDP (1988 est.): $4.9 billion. (Luxembourg's foreign trade is recorded with Belgium's.)

Nation, Region	Population in millions	Capital	Area Sq mi (km²)	Head of State/Government
Madagascar, E. Africa	11.6	Antananarivo	226,656 (587 040)	Didier Ratsiraka, president Victor Ramahatra, prime minister

On March 12 presidential elections were held in Madagascar, and President Ratsiraka was reelected to a third seven-year term. Antigovernment rallies in mid-April, organized by opposition parties to coincide with Ratsiraka's inauguration, ended in five deaths, 70 injuries, and 64 arrests. The protesters claimed that the election results were fraudulent and vowed to continue their opposition in hopes of forcing the president's resignation. Pope John Paul II visited Madagascar in late April. GDP (1987): $2.1 billion. Foreign Trade (1987): Imports, $315 million; exports, $310 million.

Malawi, E. Africa	8.7	Lilongwe	45,745 (118 480)	Hastings Kamuzu Banda, president

President-for-Life Banda began a harsh crackdown on residents of northern Malawi. During a nationwide crop inspection tour in February, Banda accused northern civil servants of regionalism and teachers from the area of supporting a plot to secede from Malawi. Several northerners later were arrested and teachers were prohibited from working outside their own regions. Banda's actions were thought to be related to an incident at the University of Malawi, where the entire student body had boycotted classes for two days following the suspension of four northern pupils who had criticized a new selection system based on regional quotas. GDP (1986): $1.2 billion. Foreign Trade (1987): Imports, $296 million; exports, $277 million.

Maldives, S. Asia	0.2	Male	116 (300)	Maumoon Abdul Gayoom, president

It was reported August 14 that 16 people had been sentenced to death and 59 had received jail sentences for their role in an unsuccessful 1988 coup attempt. GDP (1987 est.): $69.7 million. Foreign Trade (1987): Imports, $73.9 million; exports, $31.2 million.

Mali, W. Africa	8.9	Bamako	478,764 (1 240 000)	Moussa Traoré, president

A notorious desert prison at Taoudénit was closed down by the government in 1989. The prison, known as a "special reeducation center," allegedly was used to detain political opponents of President Traoré. Many prisoners detained there later died. GDP (1986): $1.7 billion. Foreign Trade (1987): Imports, $493 million; exports, $260 million.

Malta, S. Europe	0.4	Valletta	124 (320)	Vincent Tabone, president Edward Fenech Adami, prime minister

On April 4, Vincent (Censu) Tabone was sworn in as the island nation's fourth president. In early December, Malta's harbor was the site of a shipboard summit meeting between U.S. President George Bush and Soviet President Mikhail Gorbachev. The preceding weekend, Malta formally had ended its military cooperation agreement with Libya. It had had close ties with Libya for more than 20 years. GDP (1987): $1.6 billion. Foreign Trade (1987): Imports, $1.13 billion; exports, $600 million.

Mauritania, W. Africa	2.0	Nouakchott	397,954 (1 030 700)	Maaouiya Ould Sid Ahmed Taya, president

At a North African summit on February 17, Mauritania, Algeria, Libya, Morocco, and Tunisia formed a common market called the Arab Maghreb Union (UMA). In the worst ethnic violence in several years, more than 400 Senegalese reportedly were killed in Nouakchott in April when a border shooting over disputed grazing rights between Mauritania and Senegal set off rioting in both nations. By mid-July, nearly 40,000 blacks had been forced out of Mauritania in what relief workers and Senegalese officials claimed were racially motivated expulsions. GDP (1988): $843 million. Foreign Trade (1986): Imports, $329 million; exports, $428 million.

Mauritius, E. Africa	1.1	Port Louis	718 (1 860)	Sir Veerasamy Ringadoo, governor-general Anerood Jugnauth, prime minister

Prime Minister Anerood Jugnauth was uninjured during an assassination attempt on March 3, 1989. This was the second attempt against him in less than a year. In May, Mauritius received its first offshore banking license application, five months after announcing its plan to become Africa's first offshore banking center. The nation was positioning itself as a tax haven for foreign banks and hoped to become a regional financial center. Critics feared, however, that the plan could lead to Mauritius becoming a center for laundering drug and organized crime money. In mid-October, Pope John Paul II visited the country and spoke against excessive materialism in this increasingly prosperous nation. GDP (1987 est.): $1.3 billion. Foreign Trade (1986): Imports, $684 million; exports, $676 million.

Monaco, S. Europe	0.03	Monaco-Ville	0.7 (1.9)	Rainier III, prince M. Jean Ausseil, minister of state

Prince Rainier III marked the 40th year of his reign in 1989 with a range of festivities.

Mongolia, E. Asia	2.1	Ulan Bator	604,247 (1 565 000)	Jambyn Batmonh, chairman of the Presidium Dumaagiyn Sodnom, chairman, Council of Ministers

The Soviet Union announced on March 7 that it planned to withdraw 75% of the estimated 50,000 troops stationed in Mongolia. Mongolia itself decided to reduce its own military forces by 13,000 and reduce defense spending by 11%. GDP (1985 est.): $1.7 billion. Foreign Trade (1985): Imports, $1.0 billion; exports, $388 million.

Nauru, Oceania	0.008	Nauru	8 (20)	Kenas Aroi, president

Nauru began a suit at the International Court of Justice at The Hague, Netherlands, in May, against Australia. It charged Australia with exploitation and neglect for its removal of Nauruan phosphates earlier in the century, when Nauru was a colony administered by Australia. The nation demanded compensation for the land, the low price it received for the mineral, and an award for "aggravated or moral damages." Australia claimed a contract reached with Nauru in 1968 nullified prior claims. GNP (1985): $160 million. Foreign Trade (1984): Imports, $73 million; exports, $93 million.

Nepal, S. Asia	18.7	Katmandu	54,363 (140 800)	Birendra Bir Bikram, king Marich Man Singh Shrestha, prime minister

India closed most of the roads to Nepal, which serve as Nepal's only trade links to the outside world, in March because of a trade dispute. India also objected to Nepal's growing political and economic links to China. The nation also was shaken by student demonstrations on April 3 and 4. Universities were closed temporarily until the riots were quelled. GDP (1988): $3.1 billion. Foreign Trade (1987): Imports, $507 million; exports, $139 million.

Niger, W. Africa	7.4	Niamey	489,189 (1 267 000)	Ali Saibou, president Oumarou Mamane, prime minister

Niger's new constitution was approved by referendum on September 24. The first presidential and legislative elections since independence was gained from France in 1960 took place on December 10. President Ali Saibou faced no opposition in the election. On April 23, Niger's first president after independence, Diori Hamani, died. He was ousted in a coup in 1974. GDP (1987 est.): $2.2 billion. Foreign Trade (1988 est.): Imports, $441 million; exports, $371 million.

Nation, Region	Population in millions	Capital	Area Sq mi (km²)	Head of State/Government
Oman, W. Asia	1.4	Muscat	82,031 (212 460)	Qaboos bin Said, sultan and prime minister

GDP (1987 est.): $7.5 billion. Foreign Trade (1988 est.): Imports, $1.9 billion; exports, $3.6 billion.

Papua New Guinea, Oceania	3.9	Port Moresby	178,259 (461 690)	Sir Kingsford Dibela, governor-general Rabbie Namaliu, prime minister

Riot police and government troops were sent to the island of Bougainville, the site of one of the world's largest copper mines, after violence broke out in March. Several persons were killed in the ongoing conflict. Employee strikes and the closure of the mine by rebel landowners in May tested the government and resulted in reduced revenues. GDP (1987 est.): $2.93 billion. Foreign Trade (1987): Imports, $1.1 billion; exports, $1.17 billion.

Qatar, W. Asia	0.4	Doha	4,247 (11 000)	Khalifa bin Hamad Al Thani, emir and prime minister

GDP (1987): $5.4 billion. Foreign Trade (1988 est.): Imports, $1 billion; exports, $2.2 billion.

Rwanda, E. Africa	7.0	Kigali	10,170 (26 340)	Juvénal Habyarimana, president

In January, Rwanda joined with Burundi and Zaire to form a tripartite security commission. GNP (1987): $2.3 billion. Foreign Trade (1987): Imports, $352 million; exports, $113 million.

Saint Christopher and Nevis, Caribbean	0.04	Basseterre	139 (360)	Clement A. Arrindell, governor-general Kennedy A. Simmonds, prime minister

In elections on March 21, Prime Minister Kennedy Simmonds was reelected to a third straight term. In September damage was reported to be moderate from Hurricane Hugo. *GDP (1986): $83 million. Foreign Trade (1987): Imports, $79.5 million; exports, $27.2 million.*

Saint Lucia, Caribbean	0.2	Castries	239 (620)	Sir Stanislaus A. James, governor-general John Compton, prime minister

GDP (1987): $166.1 million. Foreign Trade (1987): Imports, $178.1 million; exports, $76.8 million.

Saint Vincent and the Grenadines, Caribbean	0.1	Kingstown	131 (340)	Jack David, acting governor-general James F. Mitchell, prime minister

Prime minister James Mitchell's ruling New Democratic Party won in national elections held on May 16, with Mitchell being elected to his second five-year term. GDP (1986): $94.6 million. Foreign Trade (1986): Imports, $87.3 million; exports, $63.8 million.

San Marino, S. Europe	0.023	San Marino	23 (60)	Co-regents appointed semi-annually
São Tomé and Principe, W. Africa	0.1	São Tomé	371 (960)	Manuel Pinto da Costa, president Celestino Rocha da Costa, prime minister

GDP (1986): $37.9 million. Foreign Trade (1987 est.): Imports, $2.6 million; exports, $9.8 million.

Senegal, W. Africa	7.2	Dakar	75,749 (196 190)	Abdou Diouf, president

On February 1, Senegal and Iran restored diplomatic relations. In early April, rioting set off by a shooting at the Mauritania-Senegal border over disputed grazing rights led to at least 50 deaths in Dakar and its environs, as Senegalese mobs attacked shops and businesses owned by Mauritanians. The government was forced to declare a state of emergency in the capital to stop the riots. More than 400 Senegalese reportedly were killed during the same period in rioting in the Mauritanian capital. By midsummer nearly 40,000 blacks had been forced out of Mauritania into Senegal in what were claimed by Senegalese officials to be racially motivated expulsions. The United Nations High Commissioner for Refugees agreed to help Senegal resettle the expelled Mauritanians. GDP (1987): $2 billion. Foreign Trade (1987): Imports, $983 million; exports, $749 million.

Seychelles, E. Africa	0.1	Victoria	176 (455)	France Albert René, president

GDP (1986): $192 million. Foreign Trade (1986): Imports, $106 million; exports, $19 million.

Sierra Leone, W. Africa	4.1	Freetown	27,699 (71 740)	Joseph Momoh, president

A new policy designed to improve government control over Sierra Leone's key mining sector, which supplies almost 85% of the nation's foreign exchange earnings, was introduced early in the year. The measures would regulate the mining and marketing of diamonds and gold; widespread smuggling of these minerals had cut severely into earnings from their mining in recent years. GDP (1987): $965 million. Foreign Trade (1987): Imports, $137 million; exports, $129 million.

Solomon Islands, Oceania	0.3	Honiara	10,985 (28 450)	Sir George Lepping, governor-general Solomon Mamaloni, prime minister

The leader of the People's Alliance Party (PAP), Solomon Mamaloni, was installed as prime minister on March 28. PAP had emerged as the nation's largest single party in national elections on February 22. GDP (1987): $141.3 million. Foreign Trade (1987): Imports, $67.4 million; exports, $64.5 million.

Somalia, E. Africa	8.2	Mogadishu	246,200 (637 660)	Mohammed Siad Barre, president Mohammed Ali Samantar, premier

All political prisoners were granted amnesty by the government on January 25. On February 6, four Somalian football players tried unsuccessfully to defect to Kenya. Rioting erupted in Mogadishu after the assassination of a Roman Catholic bishop and the subsequent arrests of Muslim religious leaders in mid-July. Approximately 400 were killed in the riots, it was estimated by human-rights groups, although the government set the death toll at 23. Somalia's military then allegedly rounded up thousands of people and executed 46 it named as "troublemakers." In September a report commissioned by the U.S. State Department said the Somali army had killed at least 5,000 unarmed civilians in various raids since March 1988. Foreign journalists were not allowed in Somalia. GDP (1987): $1.5 billion. Foreign Trade (1987): Imports, $418 million; exports, $95 million.

Nation, Region	Population in millions	Capital	Area Sq mi (km^2)	Head of State/Government
Suriname, S. America	0.4	Paramaribo	63,039 (163 270)	Ramsewak Shankar, president

In March foreign interference on the issue of the Amazon rain forests was criticized by the eight-nation Amazon Pact, of which Suriname is a member. Army Commander Desi Bouterse on July 25 rejected a peace accord that had been signed by both the civilian government and by the leaders of a three-year-old guerrilla insurgency which called for a cease-fire and amnesty for the rebels. Under the pact, the guerrillas would have been allowed to remain armed and patrol the jungle interior of the nation. Bouterse claimed the terms of the agreement violated the Surinamese constitution and refused to withdraw his troops. It was the most serious crisis in Suriname since Bouterse had ceded his power to a civilian government in 1988. GDP (1987): $1.19 billion. Foreign Trade (1987): Imports, $274.3 million; exports, $338.8 million.

Nation, Region	Population in millions	Capital	Area Sq mi (km^2)	Head of State/Government
Swaziland, S. Africa	0.8	Mbabane	6,703 (17 360)	Mswati III, king Prince Sotsha Dlamini, premier

GNP (1987 est.): $539 million. Foreign Trade (1987): Imports, $381 million; exports, $300 million.

Nation, Region	Population in millions	Capital	Area Sq mi (km^2)	Head of State/Government
Togo, W. Africa	3.4	Lomé	21,927 (56 790)	Gnassingbé Eyadéma, president

On March 7, Justice Minister Kpotivi Tevi Djidjogbe Laclé was dismissed from his post and charged with corruption over the running of a lottery scheme. GDP (1987 est.): $1.3 billion. Foreign Trade (1987): Imports, $358.0 million; exports, $296.1 million.

Nation, Region	Population in millions	Capital	Area Sq mi (km^2)	Head of State/Government
Tonga, Oceania	0.1	Nuku'alofa	270 (700)	Taufa'ahau Tupou IV, king Prince Fatafehi Tu'ipelehake, prime minister

GDP (1987): $65.8 million. Foreign Trade (1987): Imports, $46.2 million; exports, $5.9 million.

Nation, Region	Population in millions	Capital	Area Sq mi (km^2)	Head of State/Government
Trinidad and Tobago, Caribbean	1.2	Port-of-Spain	1,981 (5 130)	Noor Hassanali, president Arthur Robinson, prime minister

Prime Minister Robinson shuffled his cabinet on February 28, expanding it to 18 members and giving up the finance portfolio to Selby Wilson. In early March workers in Trinidad staged a general strike to protest an economic austerity program put in place in order to meet requirements for a $128 million loan from the International Monetary Fund. Sporadic violence occurred during the strike. GDP (1987): $4.2 billion. Foreign Trade (1987): Imports, $1.2 billion; exports, $1.4 billion.

Nation, Region	Population in millions	Capital	Area Sq mi (km^2)	Head of State/Government
Tuvalu, Oceania	0.008	Funafuti	10 (26)	Sir Tupua Leupena, governor-general Tomasi Puapua, prime minister

GNP (1984 est.): $4 million. Foreign Trade (1983 est.): Imports, $2.8 million; exports, $1 million.

Nation, Region	Population in millions	Capital	Area Sq mi (km^2)	Head of State/Government
United Arab Emirates, W. Asia	1.7	Abu Dhabi	32,278 (83 600)	Zayid bin Sultan Al Nuhayyan, president Rashid bin Said Al Maktum, prime minister

The United States in July announced an offer to pay $100,000 to $250,000 to the families of each of the 290 victims of the accidental shooting down of an Iranian Airbus by a U.S. Navy warship on July 3, 1988. Seventeen of those killed were natives of the United Arab Emirates. GDP (1987 est.): $22 billion. Foreign Trade (1988 est.): Imports, $6.4 billion; exports, $11.6 billion.

Nation, Region	Population in millions	Capital	Area Sq mi (km^2)	Head of State/Government
Vanuatu, Oceania	0.2	Port-Vila	5,699 (14 760)	Fred Timakata, president Walter Lini, prime minister

Ati George Sokomanu, who was dismissed as president in January, was convicted March 7 of incitement to mutiny and was sentenced to six years in prison. He had been arrested in December 1988 after an unsuccessful attempt to unseat Prime Minister Lini and dissolve parliament. Sokomanu was released from prison on April 14 after an appeals court overturned the conviction. Minister of Health Fred Timakata succeeded Sokomanu as president. GDP (1986): $84 million. Foreign Trade (1987): Imports, $68 million; exports, $17 million.

Nation, Region	Population in millions	Capital	Area Sq mi (km^2)	Head of State/Government
Vatican City, S. Europe	0.001	Vatican City	0.17 (0.438)	John Paul II, pope

Soviet President Mikhail Gorbachev met with Pope John Paul II on December 1, ending more than 70 years of conflict and estrangement. The two agreed in principle to establish diplomatic ties between the Vatican and the USSR, but full political relations between the two governments were expected to be a long time in coming. The Vatican enjoyed a vastly improved relationship with the nations of Eastern Europe throughout 1989. It established diplomatic relations with Poland in August, the first with a Warsaw Pact nation.

Nation, Region	Population in millions	Capital	Area Sq mi (km^2)	Head of State/Government
Western Samoa, Oceania	0.2	Apia	1,104 (2 860)	Tanumafili II Malietoa, head of state Tofilau Eti, prime minister

GDP (1987 est.): $100 million. Foreign Trade (1987): Imports, $47.3 million; exports, $8.4 million.

Nation, Region	Population in millions	Capital	Area Sq mi (km^2)	Head of State/Government
Yemen, North, S. Asia	6.9	San'a	75,290 (195 000)	Ali Abdallah Salih, president Abd al-Aziz Abd al-Ghani, prime minister

North and South Yemen in 1989 set up a joint oil-exploration consortium along their common border and established a demilitarized zone in that area. The border between the two nations was opened to travelers, and visa restrictions were canceled. In December the two nations agreed to merge. GDP (1987): $4.5 billion. Foreign Trade (1987): Imports, $1.4 billion; exports, $51.1 million.

Nation, Region	Population in millions	Capital	Area Sq mi (km^2)	Head of State/Government
Yemen, South, S. Asia	2.5	Aden	128,560 (332 970)	Haydar Abu Bakr al-Attas, chairman of the Presidium

The political tensions between North and South Yemen eased, and an economic loosening took place in South Yemen in 1989. It was thought that the government was easing its orthodox Marxist principles slightly. GDP (1986): $1.01 billion. Foreign Trade (1987 est.): Imports, $497 million; exports, $54 million.

Nation, Region	Population in millions	Capital	Area Sq mi (km^2)	Head of State/Government
Zambia, E. Africa	8.1	Lusaka	290,583 (752 610)	Kenneth David Kaunda, president Malimba Masheke, prime minister

President Kaunda shuffled his cabinet early in 1989, replacing Prime Minister Kebby Musokotwane with Home Affairs Minister Malimba Masheke. Musokotwane was transferred to the foreign service; it was thought that he had been questioned concerning his connection to a plot to overthrow Kaunda in October 1988. On August 28, South African acting President F. W. de Klerk met with President Kaunda in Livingston, Zambia. The two leaders discussed South Africa's internal situation as well as the situation in Angola. GDP (1987): $2 billion. Foreign Trade (1987): Imports, $765 million; exports, $866 million.

WORLD MINERAL AND METAL PRODUCTION

	1987	1988
ALUMINUM, primary smelter (thousand metric tons)		
United States	3,343	3,944
USSR[e]	2,400	2,400
Canada	1,540	1,534
Australia	1,004	1,141
Brazil	843	874
Norway	806	827
China[e]	615	800
West Germany	738	744
Venezuela	440	443
India	267	334
France	323	325
Spain	341	323
United Kingdom	294	300
Netherlands	276	278
Other countries[a]	3,168	3,080
Total	16,398	17,347

	1987	1988
ANTIMONY, mine[b] (metric tons)		
China[e]	27,000	32,000
Bolivia	10,635	9,943
USSR[e]	9,600	9,600
South Africa[e]	6,800	6,900
Canada	3,706	2,977
Mexico	2,839	2,304
Guatemala	1,575	1,335
Australia	1,231	1,200[e]
Turkey	1,488	1,000[e]
Czechoslovakia[e]	1,000	1,000
Yugoslavia	830	650
Other countries[a]	2,105	2,287
Total	68,809	71,196

	1987	1988
ASBESTOS[c] (thousand metric tons)		
USSR	2,554	2,600[e]
Canada	665	705
Brazil	213	230[e]
Zimbabwe	194	190[e]
China[e]	150	150
South Africa	135	145
Italy	101	120[e]
Other countries[a]	244	221
Total	4,256	4,361

	1987	1988
BARITE[e] (thousand metric tons)		
China[e]	1,250	1,500
USSR[e]	540	540
Mexico	401	529
United States	406	404
Turkey[e]	294	388
Morocco	144	322
India	212	240[e]
West Germany	173	167
Brazil	110	125[e]
Other countries[a]	1,184	1,090
Total	4,714	5,305

	1987	1988
BAUXITE[d] (thousand metric tons)		
Australia	34,102	36,192
Guinea	13,500	15,600
Brazil	6,567	7,728
Jamaica	7,660	7,408
USSR[e]	5,725	5,731
India	2,736	3,829
Suriname	2,581	3,434
China[e]	2,400	3,200
Yugoslavia	3,394	3,034
Hungary	3,101	2,906
Greece	2,472	2,440
Guyana	2,785	1,774
Sierra Leone	1,390	1,379
France	1,271	878
Other countries[a]	3,227	3,453
Total	92,911	98,986

	1987	1988
CEMENT[c] (thousand metric tons)		
China	186,252	204,144
USSR	137,404	138,036
Japan	71,551	77,554
United States	72,122	70,989
India	36,980	40,716
Italy	35,748	37,257
West Germany	25,268	31,010
South Korea	25,662	28,995
Brazil	25,470	25,328
France	23,560	25,272
Spain	23,016	24,372
Mexico	22,749	22,872
Turkey	21,980	22,668
Other countries[a]	341,878	351,834
Total	1,049,640	1,101,047

	1987	1988
CHROMITE[c] (thousand metric tons)		
South Africa	3,789	4,200
USSR[e]	3,150	3,240
Albania	830	750
India	624	700[e]
Finland	543	700[e]
Turkey	600	625
Zimbabwe[e]	570	600
Brazil	225	230
Philippines	188	190
Other countries[a]	398	431
Total	10,917	11,666

	1987	1988
COAL, anthracite and bituminous[c] (million metric tons)		
China	920	969
United States	762	792[e]
USSR	595	600
India	186	195[e]
Poland	193	193
Australia	176	180[e]
South Africa	175	176
United Kingdom	104	104
West Germany	82	79
Canada	60	69
North Korea[e]	55	55
Other countries	187	192
Total	3,495	3,604

	1987	1988
COAL, lignite[c f] (million metric tons)		
East Germany	309	310
USSR	165	172[e]
West Germany	109	109
Czechoslovakia	102	101
Poland	73	73
United States	71	70[e]
Yugoslavia	60	59
Australia	38	43
Other countries	234	235
Total	1,161	1,172

	1987	1988
COPPER, mine[b] (thousand metric tons)		
Chile	1,413	1,472
United States	1,244	1,420
Canada	794	756
USSR[e]	630	640
Zaire	525	530[e]
Poland	438	440[e]
Zambia	463	400[e]
Peru	406	298
China[e]	250	300
Mexico	254	280
Australia	233	246
Papua New Guinea	218	219
Philippines	216	218
South Africa	188	170
Other countries[a]	1,056	1,064
Total	8,328	8,453

	1987	1988
COPPER, refined, primary and secondary (thousand metric tons)		
United States	1,542	1,859
Chile	970	1,013
USSR	987	999
Japan	980	955
Canada	525	566
Zambia	496	445
Belgium	476	435[e]
West Germany	400	426
Poland	390	401
China[e]	400	400
Australia	208	218
Zaire	210	203
Peru	225	179
South Korea	158	169
Spain	151	159
South Africa	153	148[e]
Other countries[a]	1,544	1,545
Total	9,815	10,120

	1987	1988
DIAMOND, natural (thousand carats)		
Australia	30,333	35,034
Zaire	19,425	19,000[e]
Botswana	13,207	13,229
USSR[e]	10,800	11,000
South Africa	9,053	8,382
China[e]	1,000	1,000
Namibia	1,037	938
Brazil	522	610[e]
Other countries[a]	2,238	4,806
Total	87,615	93,999

	1987	1988
FLUORSPAR[g] (thousand metric tons)		
China[e]	1,000	1,100
Mongolia	780	790
Mexico	724	774
USSR[e]	560	560
South Africa	317	335
Spain	255	266
France[e]	200	200
Italy	147	145[e]
Other countries[a]	982	975
Total	4,965	5,145

	1987	1988
GAS, natural[h] (billion cubic feet)		
USSR	25,700	28,900[e]
United States	17,349	17,457
Canada	2,803	2,885
Netherlands	2,587	2,773
United Kingdom	1,418	1,364
Algeria[e]	1,320	1,338
Indonesia	1,188	1,190[e]
Mexico	1,194	1,185[e]
Romania[e]	1,120	1,120
Other countries[a]	11,800	12,517
Total	66,479	70,729

	1987	1988
GOLD, mine[b] (thousand troy ounces)		
South Africa	19,177	19,881
USSR[e]	8,850	9,000
United States	4,947	6,460
Australia	3,559	4,887
Canada	3,724	4,110
Brazil[e]	2,690	3,220
China[e]	2,300	2,500
Papua New Guinea	1,069	1,226
Philippines	1,048	1,135
Poland[e]	1,000	1,000
Colombia	854	933
Other countries[a]	4,816	5,102
Total	54,034	59,454

	1987	1988
GYPSUM[c] (thousand metric tons)		
United States	14,163	14,869
Canada	9,054	8,522
Iran[e]	8,400	8,400
China[e]	7,200	8,100
Japan	6,000	6,300[e]
Spain[e]	5,500	5,500
France	5,409	5,400[e]
USSR	4,781	4,800[e]
Thailand	3,031	4,549
Mexico	4,575	4,500[e]
United Kingdom[e]	3,200	3,500
West Germany	1,707	1,700[e]
Other countries[a]	16,630	19,069
Total	89,650	95,209

	1987	1988
IRON ORE[c] (thousand metric tons)		
USSR	250,874	251,000
Brazil	134,105	145,040
China[e]	100,000	106,000
Australia	101,748	97,000
United States	47,568	57,515
India	51,018	52,322
Canada	37,702	38,742
South Africa	22,008	24,676
Sweden	19,627	20,940
Venezuela	17,780	18,789
Liberia	13,742	12,767
France	10,852	10,650
Other countries[a]	81,013	81,095
Total	888,037	916,536

	1987	1988
IRON, steel ingots and equivalent forms (thousand metric tons)		
USSR	161,887	163,000
Japan	98,513	105,681
United States	80,877	90,650
China	56,000	59,000
West Germany	36,248	41,023
Brazil	22,231	24,536
Italy	22,847	23,668
South Korea	16,782	19,113
United Kingdom	17,425	19,013
France	17,726	19,003
Poland	17,148	16,872
Czechoslovakia	15,415	15,384
Canada	14,736	15,175
India	12,883	14,198
Romania	13,885	14,000[e]
Spain	11,691	11,628
Belgium	9,787	11,196
South Africa	9,156	9,108
East Germany	8,243	8,400[e]
Mexico	7,571	7,794
Other countries[a]	82,940	89,734
Total	733,991	778,176

	1987	1988
LEAD, mine[b] (thousand metric tons)		
Australia	489	475
USSR[e]	440	440
United States	319	394
Canada	414	368
China	252	255
Mexico	177	170
Peru	204	149
North Korea[e]	110	110
Yugoslavia	107	100
Other countries[a]	917	920
Total	3,429	3,381

	1987	1988
LEAD, refined, primary and secondary[i] (thousand metric tons)		
United States	1,084	1,129
USSR[e]	780	785
United Kingdom	338	374
West Germany	341	345
Japan	338	340
Canada	231	269
France	246	256
China[e]	240	245
Mexico	209	200
Australia	217	178
Other countries[a]	1,703	1,734
Total	5,727	5,855

	1987	1988
MAGNESIUM, primary (thousand metric tons)		
United States	124	142
USSR[e]	90	91
Norway	57	52
France	14	14
Japan	8	10
Canada	9	8
China[e]	7	7
Italy	9	5
Other countries[a]	10	9
Total	328	338
MANGANESE ORES[c] (thousand metric tons)		
USSR	9,400	9,200
South Africa	2,892	3,440
China[e]	2,750	2,750
Gabon	2,403	2,250
Australia	1,853	1,985
Brazil	2,070	1,900[e]
India	1,303	1,324
Other countries[a]	1,055	1,078
Total	23,726	23,927
MERCURY (76-pound flasks)		
USSR[e]	67,000	67,000
Spain	43,000[e]	43,483
Algeria[e]	22,000	20,000
China[e]	20,000	20,000
Mexico	3,597	2,901
Other countries[a]	16,493	13,520
Total	172,090	166,904
MOLYBDENUM, mine[b] (metric tons)		
United States	34,073	43,051
Chile	16,941	17,000[e]
Canada	14,771	12,388
USSR[e]	11,500	11,500
Mexico	4,400	4,296
Peru	3,353	2,400
Other countries[a]	4,140	4,115
Total	89,178	94,750
NATURAL GAS LIQUIDS (million barrels)		
United States[e]	578	545
USSR[e]	190	210
Saudi Arabia[e]	150	160
Mexico[e]	132	130
Algeria[e]	125	127
Canada	117	120[e]
Other countries[a]	385	390
Total	1,677	1,682
NICKEL, mine[b] (thousand metric tons)		
Canada	189	199
USSR[e]	185	190
New Caledonia	57	68
Australia	75	62
Indonesia	58	53
Cuba[e]	36	44
South Africa[e]	34	35
China[e]	25	27
Other countries[a]	153	157
Total	812	835
NITROGEN, content of ammonia (thousand metric tons)		
USSR[e]	20,000	20,500
China[e]	14,500	16,200
United States	12,002	12,637
India	5,300	6,205
Canada	2,887	3,297
Netherlands	2,828	2,956
Romania	2,788	2,800[e]
Indonesia	2,364	2,367
Poland	2,177	2,200
Mexico	1,744	2,067
Other countries[a]	27,684	27,719
Total	94,274	98,948
PETROLEUM, crude (million barrels)		
USSR	4,590	4,640[e]
United States	3,047	2,979
Saudi Arabia	1,544	1,866
Iraq	785	979
China	978	946
Mexico	946	940[e]
Iran	849	830[e]
United Kingdom	861	811
Venezuela	664	673[e]
United Arab Emirates	547	582

	1987	1988
PETROLEUM, crude (cont'd)		
Kuwait	497	581
Canada	547	563
Indonesia	509	510[e]
Nigeria	455	509
Libya	368	351
Other countries[a]	3,234	3,341
Total	20,421	21,101
PHOSPHATE ROCK[c] (thousand metric tons)		
United States	40,954	45,389
USSR[e]	34,100	38,820
Morocco	20,955	24,783
China[e]	9,000	15,000
Tunisia	6,390	6,103
Jordan	6,800	5,666
Brazil	4,777	4,672
Israel	3,798	3,479
Togo	2,644	3,464
South Africa	2,623	2,850
Other countries[a]	13,142	13,447
Total	145,183	163,673
POTASH, K_2O equivalent basis (thousand metric tons)		
USSR	10,888	11,000[e]
Canada	7,668	8,070
East Germany[e]	3,500	3,510
West Germany	2,199	2,290
United States	1,262	1,521
France	1,539	1,502
Israel	1,253	1,244
Other countries[a]	2,161	2,292
Total	30,470	31,429
SALT[c] (thousand metric tons)		
United States	33,142	34,506
China[e]	18,000	22,000
USSR	15,400	15,500[e]
West Germany	13,466	13,605
Canada	10,129	10,647
India	9,902	8,402
France	7,836	7,925
United Kingdom[e]	7,000	7,000
Mexico	6,199	6,965
Australia	6,486	6,500[e]
Poland	6,168	5,700[e]
Romania	5,395	5,400[e]
Brazil	4,550	4,600[e]
Other countries[a]	28,963	35,236
Total	172,636	183,986
SILVER, mine[b] (thousand troy ounces)		
Mexico	77,643	75,841
United States	39,790	53,416
Peru	66,052	49,885
USSR[e]	48,200	48,000
Canada	44,207	44,094
Australia	35,986	35,848
Poland[e]	26,500	26,500
Chile	16,068	16,700[e]
Japan	9,035	8,085
Bolivia	4,565	7,459
Spain	5,709	7,395
Sweden	6,912	6,800
South Africa	6,691	5,759
Other countries[a]	45,929	48,707
Total	433,287	434,489
SULFUR, all forms[j] (thousand metric tons)		
United States	10,538	10,746
USSR[e]	10,100	10,700
Canada	6,588	6,907
Poland	5,324	5,090
China[e]	4,500	4,750
Japan	2,316	2,447
Mexico	2,484	2,393
West Germany	1,825	1,795
Saudi Arabia	1,432	1,450[e]
Spain	1,195	1,340
France	1,252	1,142
Other countries[a]	9,386	9,638
Total	56,940	58,398
TIN, mine[b] (metric tons)		
Brazil	27,364	43,700
Indonesia	26,217	30,590
Malaysia	30,388	28,866
China[e]	20,000	25,000
USSR[e]	16,000	16,000
Thailand	15,006	14,225

	1987	1988
TIN, mine (cont'd)		
Bolivia	8,128	10,504
Australia	7,691	7,247
Other countries[a]	26,411	24,666
Total	177,205	200,798
TITANIUM MINERALS[k] (thousand metric tons)		
ILMENITE		
Australia	1,509	1,622
Norway	852	875
Malaysia	509	460
USSR[e]	455	460
China[e]	145	150
India[e]	140	140
Other countries[a]	274	235
Total	3,884	3,942
RUTILE		
Australia	246	231
Sierra Leone	113	126
South Africa[e]	55	55
Other countries[a]	25	23
Total	439	435
TITANIFEROUS SLAG		
Canada	925	1,025
South Africa[e]	650	700
Total	1,575	1,725
TUNGSTEN, mine[b] (metric tons)		
China[e]	21,000	21,000
USSR	9,200	9,200
Mongolia[e]	1,500	2,000
South Korea	2,375	1,906
Austria	1,250	1,507
Portugal	1,150	1,370
Australia	1,150	1,261
Bolivia	638	950
Brazil	672	700[e]
Thailand	705	700[e]
Peru	259	545
North Korea[e]	500	500
Other countries[a]	1,737	1,551
Total	42,136	43,190
URANIUM OXIDE (U_3O_8)[l] (metric tons)		
Canada	14,696	14,606
United States[e]	5,900	5,900
South Africa	4,627	4,600[e]
Australia	4,445	4,264
France	3,800	3,810
Namibia	3,810	3,800[e]
Niger	3,447	3,450[e]
Other countries[a]	1,805	1,690
Total	42,530	42,120
ZINC, mine[b] (thousand metric tons)		
Canada	1,504	1,352
USSR[e]	810	810
Australia	778	766
China	458	527
Peru	613	489
Mexico	272	262
Spain	266	256
United States	233	256
North Korea	220	225
Sweden	219	187
Poland	184	184[e]
Ireland	177	177
Other countries[a]	1,508	1,486
Total	7,242	6,977
ZINC, smelter, primary and secondary (thousand metric tons)		
USSR[e]	1,000	963
Canada	610	703
Japan	666	678
China	383	425
West Germany	378	352
United States	343	330
Belgium	309	325
Australia	312	307
France	249	274
Spain	224	256
Italy	242	242
Netherlands	207	211
Mexico	185	193
Poland	177	180
Other countries[a]	1,729	1,755
Total	7,014	7,194

[a] Estimated in part. [b] Content of concentrates. [c] Gross weight. [d] Includes calculated bauxite equivalent of estimated output of aluminum ores other than bauxite (nepheline concentrate and alunite ore) for the USSR, the only producer of such materials. [e] Estimate. [f] Includes coal classified in some countries as brown coal. [g] Gross weight of marketable product. [h] Marketed production (includes gas sold or used by producers; excludes gas reinjected into reservoirs for pressure maintenance, as well as that flared or vented to the atmosphere, which is not used as fuel or industrial raw material, and which thus has no economic value). [i] Excludes bullion produced for refining elsewhere. [j] Includes Frasch process sulfur, elemental sulfur mined by conventional means, by-product recovered elemental sulfur, and the elemental sulfur equivalent of sulfuric acid produced directly from pyrite, sulfide metal ores, and other materials. [k] Excludes output in the United States, which cannot be disclosed because it is company proprietary information. [l] Excludes output (if any) by Albania, Bulgaria, China, Czechoslovakia, East Germany, Hungary, North Korea, Mongolia, Poland, Romania, USSR, and Vietnam.

Compiled by Charles L. Kimbell primarily from data collected by the U.S. Bureau of Mines, but includes some modifications and revisions from other sources regarded as more correctly representing actual output levels at the time of compilation.

THE UNITED STATES GOVERNMENT

EXECUTIVE BRANCH

(selected listing, as of Dec. 31, 1989)

President: George Bush

Vice-President: Dan Quayle

Executive Office of the President

The White House

Chief of Staff to the President: John H. Sununu
Assistant to the President and Deputy to the Chief of Staff: Andrew H. Card, Jr., and James W. Cicconi
Assistant to the President and Secretary to the Cabinet: David Q. Bates, Jr.
Assistant to the President for Issues Analysis: Richard C. Breeden
Assistant to the President for Communications: David F. Demarest, Jr.
Assistant to the President and Press Secretary: Max Marlin Fitzwater
Counsel to the President: C. Boyden Gray
Assistant to the President for Legislative Affairs: Frederick D. McClure
Assistant to the President for Management and Administration: J. Bonnie Newman
Assistant to the President for Economic and Domestic Policy: Roger B. Porter
Assistant to the President for National Security Affairs: Gen. Brent Scowcroft, USAF (Ret.)
Assistant to the President for Special Acitivities and Initiatives: Stephen M. Studdert
Assistant to the President and Director of Presidential Personnel: Charles G. Untermeyer
Office of Management and Budget, Director: Richard G. Darman
Council of Economic Advisers, Chairman: Michael J. Boskin
Office of Policy Development, Deputy Assistant to the President for Domestic Policy and Director: William L. Roper
Office of United States Trade Representative, United States Trade Representative: Carla A. Hills
Council on Environmental Quality, Chairman: A. Alan Hill
Office of Science and Technology Policy, Science Advisor to the President and Director: William R. Graham, Jr.
Office of National Drug Control Policy, Director: William J. Bennett
National Critical Materials Council, Chairman: (vacancy)
Office of Administration, Deputy Assistant to the President for Management and Director: Paul W. Bateman

The Cabinet

Department of Agriculture
Secretary: Clayton K. Yeutter
Deputy Secretary: Jack C. Parnell

Department of Commerce
Secretary: Robert A. Mosbacher
Deputy Secretary: Thomas J. Murrin
Bureau of the Census, Director: Barbara E. Bryant

Department of Defense
Secretary: Richard Cheney
Deputy Secretary: Donald J. Atwood
Joint Chiefs of Staff
Chairman: Gen. Colin L. Powell, USA
Chief of Staff, Army: Gen. Carl E. Vuono, USA
Chief of Staff, Air Force: Gen. Larry D. Welsh, USAF
Chief of Naval Operations: Adm. C. A. H. Trost, USN
Commandant, Marine Corps: Gen. A. M. Gray, Jr., USMC
Secretary of the Air Force: Donald B. Rice
Secretary of the Army: Michael P. W. Stone
Secretary of the Navy: H. Lawrence Garrett III

Department of Education
Secretary: Lauro F. Cavazos

Department of Energy
Secretary: James D. Watkins
Deputy Secretary: W. Henson Moore

Department of Health and Human Services
Secretary: Louis W. Sullivan, M.D.
Undersecretary: Constance Horner
Surgeon General: Antonia Coello Novello
Centers for Disease Control, Director: Walter R. Dowdle, acting
National Institutes of Health, Director: James B. Wyngaarden
Social Security Administration, Commissioner: Gwendolyn S. King

Department of Housing and Urban Development
Secretary: Jack Kemp
Undersecretary: Alfred Dellibovi

Department of Interior
Secretary: Manuel Lujan, Jr.
Undersecretary: Frank A. Bracken
Assistant Secretary for Indian Affairs: Eddie F. Brown
National Park Service, Director: James M. Ridenour
Bureau of Mines, Director: T. S. Ary

Department of Justice
Attorney General: Richard Thornburgh
Deputy Attorney General: Donald B. Ayer
Solicitor General: Kenneth W. Starr
Federal Bureau of Investigation, Director: William S. Sessions
Drug Enforcement Administrator: John C. Lawn
Immigration and Naturalization Service, Commissioner: Gene McNary
Bureau of Prisons, Director: J. Michael Quinlan

Department of Labor
Secretary: Elizabeth Dole
Deputy Secretary: Roderick DeArment
Women's Bureau, Director: Jill Houghton Emery
Commissioner of Labor Statistics: Janet L. Norwood

Department of State
Secretary: James A. Baker III
Chief of Protocol: Joseph V. Reed, Jr.
Undersecretary for Political Affairs: R. M. Kimmitt
Assistant Secretary for Human Rights and Humanitarian Affairs: Richard Schifter
Assistant Secretary for African Affairs: Herman J. Cohen
Assistant Secretary for East Asian and Pacific Affairs: Richard Solomon
Assistant Secretary for European and Canadian Affairs: Raymond G. H. Seitz
Assistant Secretary for Inter-American Affairs: Bernard W. Aronson
Assistant Secretary for Near Eastern and South Asian Affairs: John H. Kelly
United Nations Representative: Thomas R. Pickering

Department of Transportation
Secretary: Samuel K. Skinner
U. S. Coast Guard, Commandant: Adm. Paul A. Yost, Jr.
Federal Aviation Administrator: James B. Busey IV
Federal Highway Administrator: Thomas D. Larson
Federal Railroad Administrator: Gilbert E. Carmichael

Department of the Treasury
Secretary: Nicholas F. Brady
Deputy Secretary: John E. Robson
Comptroller of the Currency: Robert L. Clarke
Internal Revenue Service, Commissioner: Fred T. Goldberg, Jr.

Department of Veterans Affairs
Secretary: Edward J. Derwinski
Deputy Secretary: Anthony J. Principi

Independent Agencies (selected listing)

ACTION, Director: Jane A. Kenny
Appalachian Regional Commission, Federal cochairman: Jacqueline L. Phillips
Central Intelligence Agency, Director: William H. Webster
Commission on Civil Rights, Chairman: (vacant)
Commission of Fine Arts, Chairman: J. Carter Brown
Consumer Product Safety Commission, Chairman: Jacqueline Jones-Smith
Environmental Protection Agency, Administrator: William K. Reilly
Equal Employment Opportunity Commission, Chairman: Evan J. Kemp, Jr.
Export-Import Bank, President: John D. Macomber
Farm Credit Administration, Chairman: Harold B. Steele
Federal Communications Commission, Chairman: Alfred C. Sikes
Federal Deposit Insurance Corporation, Chairman: L. William Seidman
Federal Election Commission, Chairman: Danny L. McDonald
Federal Emergency Management Agency, Director: Robert Morris, acting
Federal Labor Relations Authority, Chairman: Jean McKee
Federal Maritime Commission, Chairman: James J. Carey, acting
Federal Mediation and Conciliation Service, Director: Bernard E. DeLury
Federal Reserve System, Chairman: Alan Greenspan
Federal Trade Commission, Commissioner and Chairman: Janet D. Steiger
General Services Administrator: Richard G. Austin
Interstate Commerce Commission, Chairman: Edward J. Philbin
National Aeronautics and Space Administration, Administrator: Richard H. Truly
National Foundation on the Arts and Humanities
National Endowment for the Arts, Chairman: John E. Frohnmayer
National Endowment for the Humanities, Chairman: Lynne V. Cheney
National Labor Relations Board, Chairman: James M. Stephens
National Science Foundation, Chairman: Mary L. Good
National Transportation Safety Board, Chairman: James L. Kolstad, acting
Nuclear Regulatory Commission, Chairman: Kenneth Carr
Peace Corps, Director: Paul D. Coverdell
Postal Rate Commission, Chairman: George W. Haley
Securities and Exchange Commission, Chairman: Edward H. Fleischman
Selective Service System, Director: Samuel K. Lessey, Jr.
Small Business Administrator: Susan S. Engeleiter
Tennessee Valley Authority, Chairman: Marvin Runyon
U.S. Arms Control and Disarmament Agency, Director: Ronald F. Lehman II
U.S. Information Agency, Director: Bruce S. Gelb
U.S. International Development Cooperation Agency, Director: Mark L. Edelman, acting
U.S. International Trade Commission, Chairman: Anne E. Brunsdale
U.S. Postal Service, Postmaster General: Anthony M. Frank

THE SUPREME COURT

William H. Rehnquist, chief justice
William J. Brennan, Jr.
Byron R. White
Thurgood Marshall
Harry A. Blackmun
John Paul Stevens
Sandra Day O'Connor
Antonin Scalia
Anthony M. Kennedy

THE 101ST CONGRESS

Senate Committee Chairmen

Agriculture, Nutrition, and Forestry: Patrick J. Leahy (VT)
Appropriations: Robert C. Byrd (WV)
Armed Services: Sam Nunn (GA)
Banking, Housing, and Urban Affairs: Donald W. Riegle, Jr. (MI)
Budget: Jim Sasser (TN)
Commerce, Science, and Transportation: Ernest F. Hollings (SC)
Energy and Natural Resources: J. Bennett Johnston (LA)
Environment and Public Works: Quentin N. Burdick (ND)
Finance: Lloyd Bentsen (TX)
Foreign Relations: Claiborne Pell (RI)
Governmental Affairs: John Glenn (OH)
Judiciary: Joseph R. Biden, Jr. (DE)
Labor and Human Resources: Edward Kennedy (MA)
Rules and Administration: Wendell H. Ford (KY)
Small Business: Dale Bumpers (AR)
Special Aging: David Pryor (AR)
Veterans' Affairs: Alan Cranston (CA)

Select Senate Committee Chairmen

Ethics: Howell T. Heflin (AL)
Indian Affairs: Daniel K. Inouye (HI)
Intelligence: David L. Boren (OK)

House Committee Chairmen

Agriculture: E. (Kika) de la Garza (TX)
Appropriations: Jamie L. Whitten (MS)
Armed Services: Les Aspin (WI)
Banking, Finance, and Urban Affairs: Henry B. Gonzalez (TX)
Budget: Leon E. Panetta (CA)
District of Columbia: Ronald V. Dellums (CA)
Education and Labor: Augustus F. Hawkins (CA)
Energy and Commerce: John D. Dingell (MI)
Foreign Affairs: Dante B. Fascell (FL)
Government Operations: John Conyers, Jr. (MI)
House Administration: Frank Annunzio (IL)
Interior and Insular Affairs: Morris K. Udall (AZ)
Judiciary: Jack Brooks (TX)
Merchant Marine and Fisheries: Walter B. Jones (NC)
Post Office and Civil Service: William D. Ford (MI)
Public Works and Transportation: Glenn M. Anderson (CA)
Rules: Joe Moakley (MA)
Science, Space, and Technology: Robert A. Roe (NJ)
Small Business: John J. LaFalce (NY)
Standards of Official Conduct: Julian C. Dixon (CA)
Veterans' Affairs: G. V. (Sonny) Montgomery (MS)
Ways and Means: Dan Rostenkowski (IL)

Select House Committees

Aging: Edward R. Roybal (CA)
Children, Youth, and Families: George Miller (CA)
Hunger: Tony P. Hall (OH)
Intelligence: Anthony C. Beilenson (CA)
Narcotics Abuse and Control: Charles B. Rangel (NY)

UNITED STATES: 101st CONGRESS
Second Session

SENATE MEMBERSHIP

(As of January 1990: 55 Democrats, 45 Republicans). Letters after senators' names refer to party affiliation—D for Democrat, R for Republican. Single asterisk (*) denotes term expiring in January 1991; double asterisk (**), term expiring in January 1993; triple asterisk (***), term expiring in January 1995.

Alabama
* H. Heflin, D
** R. C. Shelby, D

Alaska
* T. Stevens, R
** F. H. Murkowski, R

Arizona
*** D. DeConcini, D
*** J. S. McCain III, R

Arkansas
** D. Bumpers, D
* D. H. Pryor, D

California
** A. Cranston, D
*** P. Wilson, R

Colorado
* W. L. Armstrong, R
** T. E. Wirth, D

Connecticut
** C. J. Dodd, D
*** J. I. Lieberman, D

Delaware
*** W. V. Roth, Jr., R
* J. R. Biden, Jr., D

Florida
** B. Graham, D
*** C. Mack, R

Georgia
* S. Nunn, D
** W. Fowler, Jr., D

Hawaii
** D. K. Inouye, D
*** S. M. Matsunaga, D

Idaho
* J. A. McClure, R
** S. Symms, R

Illinois
** A. J. Dixon, D
* P. Simon, D

Indiana
*** R. G. Lugar, R
** D. Coats, R

Iowa
** C. E. Grassley, R
* T. R. Harkin, D

Kansas
** R. J. Dole, R
* N. L. Kassebaum, R

Kentucky
** W. H. Ford, D
* M. McConnell, R

Louisiana
* J. B. Johnston, D
** J. B. Breaux, D

Maine
* W. Cohen, R
*** G. J. Mitchell, D

Maryland
*** P. S. Sarbanes, D
** B. A. Mikulski, D

Massachusetts
*** E. M. Kennedy, D
* J. F. Kerry, D

Michigan
*** D. W. Riegle, Jr., D
* C. Levin, D

Minnesota
*** D. F. Durenberger, R
* R. Boschwitz, R

Mississippi
* T. Cochran, R
*** T. Lott, R

Missouri
*** J. C. Danforth, R
** C. S. Bond, R

Montana
* M. Baucus, D
*** C. Burns, R

Nebraska
* J. J. Exon, Jr., D
*** J. R. Kerrey, D

Nevada
** H. Reid, D
*** R. H. Bryan, D

New Hampshire
* G. J. Humphrey, R
** W. B. Rudman, R

New Jersey
* B. Bradley, D
*** F. R. Lautenberg, D

New Mexico
* P. V. Domenici, R
*** J. Bingaman, D

New York
*** D. P. Moynihan, D
** A. M D'Amato, R

North Carolina
* J. Helms, R
** T. Sanford, D

North Dakota
*** Q. N. Burdick, D
** K. Conrad, D

Ohio
** J. H. Glenn, Jr., D
*** H. M. Metzenbaum, D

Oklahoma
* D. L. Boren, D
** D. L. Nickles, R

Oregon
* M. O. Hatfield, R
** B. Packwood, R

Pennsylvania
*** J. Heinz, R
** A. Specter, R

Rhode Island
* C. Pell, D
*** J. H. Chafee, R

South Carolina
* S. Thurmond, R
** E. F. Hollings, D

South Dakota
* L. Pressler, R
** T. A. Daschle, D

Tennessee
*** J. R. Sasser, D
* A. Gore, Jr., D

Texas
*** L. Bentsen, D
* W. Gramm, R

Utah
** J. Garn, R
*** O. G. Hatch, R

Vermont
** P. J. Leahy, D
*** J. M. Jeffords, R

Virginia
* J. W. Warner, R
*** C. S. Robb, D

Washington
** B. Adams, D
*** S. Gorton, R

West Virginia
*** R. C. Byrd, D
* J. D. Rockefeller IV, D

Wisconsin
** R. W. Kasten, Jr., R
*** H. Kohl, D

Wyoming
*** M. Wallop, R
* A. K. Simpson, R

HOUSE MEMBERSHIP

(As of January 1990, 257 Democrats, 175 Republicans, 3 vacancies). "At-L." in place of congressional district number means "representative at large." * Indicates elected in special 1989 election.

Alabama
1. H. L. Callahan, R
2. W. L. Dickinson, R
3. G. Browder, D*
4. T. Bevill, D
5. R. G. Flippo, D
6. B. Erdreich, D
7. C. Harris, Jr., D

Alaska
At-L. D. Young, R

Arizona
1. J. J. Rhodes, III, R
2. M. K. Udall, D
3. B. Stump, R
4. J. L. Kyl, R
5. J. Kolbe, R

Arkansas
1. W. V. Alexander, Jr., D
2. T. F. Robinson, R
3. J. P. Hammerschmidt, R
4. B. F. Anthony, Jr., D

California
1. D. H. Bosco, D
2. W. W. Herger, R
3. R. T. Matsui, D
4. V. Fazio, D
5. N. Pelosi, D
6. B. Boxer, D
7. G. Miller, D
8. R. V. Dellums, D
9. F. H. Stark, Jr., D
10. D. Edwards, D
11. T. P. Lantos, D
12. T. Campbell, R
13. N. Y. Mineta, D
14. N. D. Shumway, R
15. G. Condit, D*
16. L. E. Panetta, D
17. C. J. Pashayan, Jr., R
18. R. H. Lehman, D
19. R. J. Lagomarsino, R
20. W. M. Thomas, R
21. E. W. Gallegly, R
22. C. J. Moorhead, R
23. A, C. Beilenson, D
24. H. A. Waxman, D
25. E. R. Roybal, D
26. H. L. Berman, D
27. M. Levine, D
28. J. C. Dixon, D
29. A. F. Hawkins, D
30. M. G. Martinez, Jr., D
31. M. W. Dymally, D
32. G. M. Anderson, D
33. D. Dreier, R
34. E. E. Torres, D
35. J. Lewis, R
36. G. E. Brown, Jr., D
37. A. A. McCandless, R
38. R. K. Dornan, R
39. W. E. Dannemeyer, R
40. C. C. Cox, R
41. W. D. Lowery, R
42. D. Rohrabacher, R
43. R. Packard, R
44. J. Bates, D
45. D. L. Hunter, R

Colorado
1. P. Schroeder, D
2. D. Skaggs, D
3. B. N. Campbell, D
4. H. Brown, R
5. J. M. Hefley, R
6. D. Schaefer, R

Connecticut
1. B. B. Kennelly, D
2. S. Gejdenson, D
3. B. A. Morrison, D
4. C. Shays, R
5. J. G. Rowland, R
6. N. L. Johnson, R

Delaware
At-L. T. R. Carper, D

Florida
1. E. Hutto, D
2. B. Grant, R
3. C. E. Bennett, D
4. C. T. James, R
5. B. McCollum, Jr., R
6. C. B. Stearns, R
7. S. M. Gibbons, D
8. C. W. B. Young, R
9. M. Bilirakis, R
10. A. Ireland, R
11. B. Nelson, D
12. T. Lewis, R
13. P. J. Goss, R
14. H. A. Johnston, D
15. E. C. Shaw, Jr., R
16. L. J. Smith, D
17. W. Lehman, D
18. I. Ros-Lehtinen, R*
19. D. B. Fascell, D

Georgia
1. R. L. Thomas, D
2. C. F. Hatcher, D
3. R. B. Ray, D
4. B. Jones, D
5. J. R. Lewis, D
6. N. Gingrich, R
7. G. Darden, D
8. J. R. Rowland, D
9. E. L. Jenkins, D
10. D. Barnard, Jr., D

Hawaii
1. P. F. Saiki, R
2. D. K. Akaka, D

Idaho
1. L. Craig, R
2. R. H. Stallings, D

Illinois
1. C. A. Hayes, D
2. G. Savage, D
3. M. Russo, D
4. G. E. Sangmeister, D
5. W. O. Lipinski, D
6. H. J. Hyde, R
7. C. Collins, D
8. D. Rostenkowski, D
9. S. R. Yates, D
10. J. E. Porter, R
11. F. Annunzio, D
12. P. M. Crane, R
13. H. W. Fawell, R
14. J. D. Hastert, R
15. E. R. Madigan, R
16. L. M. Martin, R
17. L. Evans, D

18. R. H. Michel, R
19. T. L. Bruce, D
20. R. Durbin, D
21. J. F. Costello, D
22. G. Poshard, D

Indiana
1. P. J. Visclosky, D
2. P. R. Sharp, D
3. J. P. Hiler, R
4. J. Long, D*
5. J. P. Jontz, D
6. D. L. Burton, R
7. J. T. Myers, R
8. F. McCloskey, D
9. L. H. Hamilton, D
10. A. Jacobs, Jr., D

Iowa
1. J. Leach, R
2. T. J. Tauke, R
3. D. R. Nagle, D
4. N. Smith, D
5. J. R. Lightfoot, R
6. F. L. Grandy, R

Kansas
1. C. P. Roberts, R
2. J. C. Slattery, D
3. J. Meyers, R
4. D. Glickman, D
5. B. Whittaker, R

Kentucky
1. C. Hubbard, Jr., D
2. W. H. Natcher, D
3. R. L. Mazzoli, D
4. J. Bunning, R
5. H. D. Rogers, R
6. L. J. Hopkins, R
7. C. C. Perkins, D

Louisiana
1. R. L. Livingston, Jr., R
2. C. C. Boggs, D
3. W. J. Tauzin, D
4. J. McCrery, R
5. T. J. Huckaby, D
6. R. H. Baker, R
7. J. A. Hayes, D
8. C. C. Holloway, R

Maine
1. J. E. Brennan, D
2. O. J. Snowe, R

Maryland
1. R. P. Dyson, D
2. H. D. Bentley, R
3. B. L. Cardin, D
4. C. T. McMillen, D
5. S. H. Hoyer, D
6. B. B. Byron, D
7. K. Mfume, D
8. C. A. Morella, R

Massachusetts
1. S. O. Conte, R
2. R. E. Neal, D
3. J. D. Early, D
4. B. Frank, D
5. C. G. Atkins, D
6. N. Mavroules, D
7. E. J. Markey, D
8. J. P. Kennedy II, D
9. J. J. Moakley, D
10. G. E. Studds, D
11. B. J. Donnelly, D

Michigan
1. J. Conyers, Jr., D
2. C. D. Pursell, R
3. H. E. Wolpe, D
4. F. S. Upton, R
5. P. B. Henry, R
6. B. Carr, D
7. D. E. Kildee, D
8. B. Traxler, D
9. G. Vander Jagt, R
10. B. Schuette, R
11. R. W. Davis, R
12. D. E. Bonior, D
13. G. W. Crockett, Jr., D
14. D. M. Hertel, D
15. W. D. Ford, D
16. J. D. Dingell, D
17. S. M. Levin, D
18. W. S. Broomfield, R

Minnesota
1. T. J. Penny, D
2. V. Weber, R
3. B. Frenzel, R
4. B. F. Vento, D
5. M. O. Sabo, D
6. G. Sikorski, D
7. A. Stangeland, R
8. J. L. Oberstar, D

Mississippi
1. J. L. Whitten, D
2. M. Espy, D
3. G. V. Montgomery, D
4. M. Parker, D
5. Gene Taylor, D*

Missouri
1. W. L. Clay, D
2. J. W. Buechner, R
3. R. A. Gephardt, D
4. I. Skelton, D
5. A. D. Wheat, D
6. E. T. Coleman, R
7. M. D. Hancock, R
8. W. Emerson, R
9. H. L. Volkmer, D

Montana
1. P. Williams, D
2. R. C. Marlenee, R

Nebraska
1. D. Bereuter, R
2. P. Hoagland, D
3. V. Smith, R

Nevada
1. J. H. Bilbray, D
2. B. F. Vucanovich, R

New Hampshire
1. R. C. Smith, R
2. C. Douglas, R

New Jersey
1. vacant
2. W. J. Hughes, D
3. F. Pallone, Jr., D
4. C. H. Smith, R
5. M. S. Roukema, R
6. B. J. Dwyer, D
7. M. J. Rinaldo, R
8. R. A. Roe, D
9. R. G. Torricelli, D
10. D. M. Payne, D
11. D. A. Gallo, R
12. J. Courter, R
13. H. J. Saxton, R
14. F. J. Guarini, D

New Mexico
1. S. Schiff, R
2. J. R. Skeen, R
3. W. B. Richardson, D

New York
1. G. J. Hochbrueckner, D
2. T. J. Downey, D
3. R. J. Mrazek, D
4. N. F. Lent, R
5. R. J. McGrath, R
6. F. H. Flake, D
7. G. L. Ackerman, D
8. J. H. Scheuer, D
9. T. J. Manton, D
10. C. E. Schumer, D
11. E. Towns, D
12. M. R. Owens, D
13. S. J. Solarz, D
14. vacant
15. B. Green, R
16. C. B. Rangel, D
17. T. Weiss, D
18. vacant
19. E. L. Engel, D
20. N. Lowey, D
21. H. Fish, Jr., R
22. B. A. Gilman, R
23. M. R. McNulty, D
24. G. B. Solomon, R
25. S. L. Boehlert, R
26. D. O'B. Martin, R
27. J. T. Walsh, R
28. M. F. McHugh, D
29. F. Horton, R
30. L. M. Slaughter, D
31. B. Paxon, R
32. J. J. LaFalce, D
33. H. J. Nowak, D
34. A. Houghton, R

North Carolina
1. W. B. Jones, D
2. T. Valentine, D
3. H. M. Lancaster, D
4. D. E. Price, D
5. S. L. Neal, D
6. H. Coble, R
7. C. Rose, D
8. W. G. Hefner, D
9. J. A. McMillan, R
10. C. Ballenger, R
11. J. McC. Clarke, D

North Dakota
At-L. B. L. Dorgan, D

Ohio
1. T. A. Luken, D
2. W. D. Gradison, Jr., R
3. T. P. Hall, D
4. M. G. Oxley, R
5. P. E. Gillmor, R
6. B. McEwen, R
7. M. DeWine, R
8. D. E. Lukens, R
9. M. C. Kaptur, D
10. C. E. Miller, R
11. D. E. Eckart, D
12. J. R. Kasich, R
13. D. J. Pease, D
14. T. C. Sawyer, D
15. C. P. Wylie, R
16. R. Regula, R
17. J. A. Traficant, Jr., D
18. D. Applegate, D
19. E. F. Feighan, D
20. M. R. Oakar, D
21. L. Stokes, D

Oklahoma
1. J. M. Inhofe, R
2. M. Synar, D
3. W. W. Watkins, D
4. D. McCurdy, D
5. M. Edwards, R
6. G. English, D

Oregon
1. L. AuCoin, D
2. R. F. Smith, R
3. R. Wyden, D
4. P. A. DeFazio, D
5. D. Smith, R

Pennsylvania
1. T. M. Foglietta, D
2. W. H. Gray, III, D
3. R. A. Borski, Jr., D
4. J. P. Kolter, D
5. R. T. Schulze, R
6. G. Yatron, D
7. W. C. Weldon, R
8. P. H. Kostmayer, D
9. B. Shuster, R
10. J. M. McDade, R
11. P. E. Kanjorski, D
12. J. P. Murtha, D
13. L. Coughlin, R
14. W. J. Coyne, D
15. D. L. Ritter, R
16. R. S. Walker, R
17. G. W. Gekas, R
18. D. Walgren, D
19. W. F. Goodling, R
20. J. M. Gaydos, D
21. T. J. Ridge, R
22. A. J. Murphy, D
23. W. F. Clinger, Jr., R

Rhode Island
1. R. K. Machtley, R
2. C. Schneider, R

South Carolina
1. A. Ravenel, Jr., R
2. F. D. Spence, R
3. B. C. Derrick, Jr., D
4. E. J. Patterson, D
5. J. M. Spratt, Jr., D
6. R. M. Tallon, Jr., D

South Dakota
At-L. T. Johnson, D

Tennessee
1. J. H. Quillen, R
2. J. J. Duncan, R
3. M. Lloyd, D
4. J. Cooper, D
5. B. Clement, D
6. B. J. Gordon, D
7. D. K. Sundquist, R
8. J. S. Tanner, D
9. H. E. Ford, D

Texas
1. J. Chapman, D
2. C. Wilson, D
3. S. Bartlett, R
4. R. M. Hall, D
5. J. W. Bryant, D
6. J. L. Barton, R
7. B. Archer, R
8. J. M. Fields, R
9. J. Brooks, D
10. J. J. Pickle, D
11. J. M. Leath, D
12. P. Geren, D*
13. B. Sarpalius, D
14. G. Laughlin, D
15. E. de la Garza, D
16. R. D. Coleman, D
17. C. W. Stenholm, D
18. C. Washington, D*
19. L. E. Combest, R
20. H. B. Gonzalez, D
21. L. S. Smith, R
22. T. D. DeLay, R
23. A. G. Bustamante, D
24. M. Frost, D
25. M. A. Andrews, D
26. R. K. Armey, R
27. S. P. Ortiz, D

Utah
1. J. V. Hansen, R
2. D. W. Owens, D
3. H. C. Nielson, R

Vermont
At-L. P. Smith, R

Virginia
1. H. H. Bateman, R
2. O. B. Pickett, D
3. T. J. Bliley, Jr., R
4. N. Sisisky, D
5. L. F. Payne, Jr., D
6. J. R. Olin, D
7. D. F. Slaughter, Jr., R
8. S. Parris, R
9. F. C. Boucher, D
10. F. R. Wolf, R

Washington
1. J. R. Miller, R
2. A. Swift, D
3. J. Unsoeld, D
4. S. W. Morrison, R
5. T. S. Foley, D
6. N. D. Dicks, D
7. J. McDermott, D
8. R. Chandler, R

West Virginia
1. A. B. Mollohan, D
2. H. O. Staggers, Jr., D
3. R. E. Wise, Jr., D
4. N. J. Rahall, II, D

Wisconsin
1. L. Aspin, D
2. R. W. Kastenmeier, D
3. S. C. Gunderson, R
4. G. D. Kleczka, D
5. J. Moody, D
6. T. E. Petri, R
7. D. R. Obey, D
8. T. Roth, R
9. F. J. Sensenbrenner, Jr., R

Wyoming
At-L. C. Thomas, R*

AMERICAN SAMOA
Delegate, E. F. H. Faleomavaega, D

DISTRICT OF COLUMBIA
Delegate, W. E. Fauntroy, D

GUAM
Delegate, Ben Blaz, R

PUERTO RICO
Resident Commissioner
J. B. Fuster, D

VIRGIN ISLANDS
Delegate, Ron de Lugo, D

AMBASSADORS AND ENVOYS[1]

From U.S.	Countries	To U.S.
Jon D. Glassman*	AFGHANISTAN	Mr. Miagol*
Christopher W. S. Ross	ALGERIA	Abderrahmane Bensid
Reginald J. McHugh*	ANTIGUA AND BARBUDA	Edmund Hawkins Lake
Terence A. Todman	ARGENTINA	Guido DiTella
Melvin F. Sembler	AUSTRALIA	Michael John Cook
H. A. Grunwald	AUSTRIA	Friedrich Hoess
Chic Hecht	BAHAMAS	Margaret E. McDonald
Charles W. Hostler	BAHRAIN	G. M. Algosaibi
Willard Ames DePree	BANGLADESH	A. H. S. Ataul Karim
(vacant)	BARBADOS	William Douglas
Maynard W. Glitman	BELGIUM	Herman Dehennin
Robert G. Rich, Jr.	BELIZE	Edward A. Laing
Harriet W. Isom	BENIN	Theophile Nata
Robert S. Gelbard	BOLIVIA	Carlos E. Deluis
John F. Kordek	BOTSWANA	Botsweletse K. Sebele
Richard H. Melton	BRAZIL	M. M. Moreira
Christopher H. Phillips	BRUNEI DARUSSALAM	D. P. H. Mohammad Suni bin Haji Idris
Sol Polansky	BULGARIA	Velichko F. Velichkov
David H. Shinn	BURKINA FASO	Paul-Desiré Kaboré
Cynthia S. Perry	BURUNDI	Edouard Kadigiri
Frances D. Cook	CAMEROON	Paul Pondi
Edward Ney	CANADA	Derek H. Burney
Francis T. McNamara	CAPE VERDE	J. Fernandes Lopes
Daniel H. Simpson	CENTRAL AFR. REP.	C. Lingama-Toleque
Robert L. Pugh	CHAD	Mahamat Ali Adoum
Charles A. Gillespie	CHILE	Octavio Errazuriz
James Lilley	CHINA	Han Xu
Thomas E. McNamara	COLOMBIA	Victor Mosquera
Howard K. Walker	COMOROS	Amini Ali Moumin
Leonard G. Shurtleff	CONGO	Benjamin Bounkoulou
Deane Roesch Hinton	COSTA RICA	Danilo Jiminez
Bill K. Perrin	CYPRUS	Michael E. Sherifis
Shirley Temple Black	CZECHOSLOVAKIA	Miroslav Houstecky
Keith L. Brown	DENMARK	Peter P. Dyvig
Robert S. Barrett, Jr.	DJIBOUTI	Roble Olhaye
(vacant)	DOMINICA	McDonald P. Benjamin
Paul D. Taylor	DOMINICAN REP.	Eduardo Leon
Richard N. Holwill	ECUADOR	Jaime Moncayo
Frank G. Wisner	EGYPT	El Sayed A.R. El Reedy
William J. Walker	EL SALVADOR	Miguel Angel Salaverria
Chester E. Norris, Jr.	EQUATORIAL GUINEA	Damaso O. Ndong
Robert G. Houdek	ETHIOPIA	Girma Amare*
Evelyn I. H. Teegen	FIJI	Abdul H. Yusuf*
(vacant)	FINLAND	Jukka Valtasaari
Walter J. P. Curley	FRANCE	Emmanuel de Margerie
Keith L. Wauchope	GABON	Jean Robert Odzaga
Ruth V. Washington	GAMBIA	Ousman A. Sallah
Richard C. Barkley	GERMANY (E)	Gerhard Herder
Vernon A. Walters	GERMANY (W)	Juergen Ruhfus
Raymond C. Ewing	GHANA	Eric K. Otoo
Henry Catto	GREAT BRITAIN	Antony Acland
Michael G. Sotirhos	GREECE	Christos Zacharakis
John Ford Cooper*	GRENADA	A. O. Xavier
Thomas F. Stroock	GUATEMALA	Rodolfo Rohrmoser V
Samuel Eldred Lupo	GUINEA	Kekoura Camara
W. L. Jacobsen, Jr.	GUINEA-BISSAU	Alfredo Lopes Cabral
Theresa A. Tulle	GUYANA	Cedric Hilburn Grant
Alvin P. Adams, Jr.	HAITI	Pierre F. Benoit
Thomas P. Melady	HOLY SEE	The Most Rev. Pio Laghi
Cresencio S. Arcos, Jr.	HONDURAS	Jorge R. Hernandez-Alcerro
Robie M. H. Palmer	HUNGARY	Peter Varkonyi
Charles E. Cobb, Jr.	ICELAND	Ingvi S. Ingvarsson
William Clark, Jr.	INDIA	Karan Singh
John C. Monjo	INDONESIA	Abdul Rachman Ramly
April C. Glaspie	IRAQ	M. S. Al-Mashat
Richard A. Moore	IRELAND	Padraic N. MacKernan
William Brown	ISRAEL	Moshe Arad
Peter F. Secchia	ITALY	Rinaldo Petrignani
Kenneth L. Brown	IVORY COAST	Charles Gomis
Glen Holden	JAMAICA	Keith Johnson
Michael Armacost	JAPAN	Nobuo Matsunaga
Roscoe S. Suddarth	JORDAN	Hussein A. Hammani
Smith Hempstone, Jr.	KENYA	Denis D. Afande
Evelyn I. H. Teegen	KIRIBATI	(vacant)
Donald Gregg	KOREA (S)	Tong-Jin Park
W. Nathaniel Howell	KUWAIT	S. S. N. Al-Sabah
(vacant)	LAOS	Done Somvorachit
John T. McCarthy	LEBANON	Abdallah Bouhabib
(vacant)	LESOTHO	W. T. Van Tonder
James K. Bishop	LIBERIA	Eugenia A. Wordsworth-Stevenson
Jean B. S. Gerard	LUXEMBOURG	Andre Philippe
Howard K. Walker	MADAGASCAR	Leon M. Rajaobelina
George A. Trail III	MALAWI	Robert Mbaya
Paul M. Cleveland	MALAYSIA	Albert S. Talalla
Marion V. Creekmore	MALDIVE IS.	(vacant)
R. M. Pringle	MALI	Nouhoum Samassekou
Sally Novetzke	MALTA	Salv J. Stellini
William H. Twaddell	MAURITANIA	Abdellah Ould Daddah
Penne Percy Korth	MAURITIUS	C. Jesseramsing
John D. Negroponte	MEXICO	G. P. Iturbide
Michael Ussery	MOROCCO	Ali Bengelloun
Melissa F. Wells	MOZAMBIQUE	Valeriano Ferrao
Burton Levin	MYANMAR	U Myo Aung
Melvin F. Sembler	NAURU	(vacant)
Julia Chang Bloch	NEPAL	Mohan Man Sainju
C. Howard Wilkins	NETHERLANDS	Richard H. Fein
Della Newman	NEW ZEALAND	Harold Huyton Francis
(vacant)	NICARAGUA	Leonor de Huper*
Carl C. Cundiff	NIGER	Moumouni A. Djemakoye
Lannon Walker	NIGERIA	Hamzat Ahmadu
Loret Ruppe	NORWAY	Kjeld Vibe
Richard Wood Boehm	OMAN	Awadh Bader Al-Shanfari
Robert B. Oakley	PAKISTAN	Zulfiqar Ali Khan
Arthur H. Davis	PANAMA	Juan B. Sosa
Robert W. Farrand	PAPUA NEW GUINEA	Margaret Taylor
Timothy L. Towell	PARAGUAY	M. Martinez Mendieta
A. C. E. Quainton	PERU	Cesar G. Atala
Nicholas Platt	PHILIPPINES	Emmanuel Palaez
John R. Davis, Jr.	POLAND	Jan Kinkast
Everett E. Briggs	PORTUGAL	J. E. M. Pereira Bastos
Mark G. Hambley	QATAR	A. A. Z. Al-Mahmoud
Alan Green, Jr.	ROMANIA	Ion Stoichici
L. H. Spearman, Sr.	RWANDA	Aloys Uwimana
Reginald J. McHugh*	ST. CHRISTOPHER AND NEVIS	Erstein M. Edwards
(vacant)	ST. LUCIA	Joseph Edsel Edmunds
(vacant)	ST. VINCENT	(vacant)
Keith L. Wauchope	SÃO TOMÉ AND PRINCIPE	Joaquim Rafael Branco
Charles W. Freeman	SAUDI ARABIA	Bandar Bin Sultan
George E. Moose	SENEGAL	Ibra Deguene Ka
James B. Moran	SEYCHELLES	Marc R. Marengo*
Johnny Young	SIERRA LEONE	George Carew
Robert D. Orr	SINGAPORE	Tommy T. B. Koh
Robert W. Farrand	SOLOMON ISLANDS	Francis Saemala
Trusten Frank Crigler	SOMALIA	Abdi Awale Jama*
William L. Swing	SOUTH AFRICA	Piet G. J. Koornhof
Joseph Zappala	SPAIN	Julian Saiha Maria
Marion V. Creekmore	SRI LANKA	W. Susanta De Alwis
James R. Cheek	SUDAN	Hassan Elamin El-Bashir
Richard C. Howland	SURINAME	Willem A. Udenhout
Mary A. Ryan	SWAZILAND	Absalom V. Mamba
Charles Redman	SWEDEN	Anders I. Thunborg
Joseph B. Gildenhorn	SWITZERLAND	Edouard Brunner
Edward P. Djerejian	SYRIA	Bushra Kanafani*
E. DeJarnette, Jr.	TANZANIA	Asterius M. Hyera
Daniel A. O'Donohue	THAILAND	Vitthya Vejjajiva
Rush Walker Taylor, Jr.	TOGO	Ellom-Kodjo Schuppius
Evelyn I. H. Teegen	TONGA	Siosaia Ma'Ulupekotofa Tuita
Charles A. Gargano	TRINIDAD AND TOBAGO	Angus A. Khan
R. H. Pelletreau, Jr.	TUNISIA	Abdelaziz Hamzaoui
Morton Abramowitz	TURKEY	Nuzhet Kandemir
Evelyn I. H. Teegen	TUVALU	(vacant)
John A. Burroughs, Jr.	UGANDA	Stephen K. Katenta-Apuli
Jack F. Matlock	USSR	Yuriy V. Dubinin
Edward S. Walker, Jr.	UNITED ARAB EMIRATES	Abdulla bin Zayed Al-Nahayyan
Malcolm R. Wilkey	URUGUAY	Hector Luisi
Eric M. Javits	VENEZUELA	Simon A. Consalvi
(vacant)	WESTERN SAMOA	Maiava I. Toma
Charles F. Dunbar	YEMEN	Mohsin A. Alaini
Warren Zimmermann	YUGOSLAVIA	Zivorad Kovacevic
William C. Harrop	ZAIRE	Mushobekwa Kalimba wa Katana
Jeffrey Davidow	ZAMBIA	Paul J. F. Lusaka
J. Steven Rhodes	ZIMBABWE	S. G. Chigwedere

[1]As of Dec. 31, 1989. *Chargé d'Affaires.

UNITED STATES: Major Legislation Enacted During the First Session of the 101st Congress

SUBJECT	PURPOSE
"Whistleblowers"	Establishes the Office of the Special Council, now an arm of the Merit Systems Protection Board (MSPB), as an independent agency responsible for looking into allegations that a federal worker has been mistreated after reporting waste, fraud, or abuse within an agency. Signed April 10. Public Law 101-12.
Contra Aid	Extends previous nonmilitary aid to the contra guerrillas in Nicaragua through February 1990 by appropriating $49.75 million. Signed April 18. Public Law 101-14.
Indians Settlement	Resolves long-standing land, fishing, and jurisdictional dispute between the Puyallup Indians and the local non-Indian community in the area of Tacoma, WA. Signed June 21. Public Law 101-41.
National Children's Day	Designates the second Sunday in October 1989 as National Children's Day. Signed July 6. Public Law 101-52.
Natural Gas Decontrol	Eliminates the remaining natural gas wellhead price controls by Jan. 1, 1993. Signed July 26. Public Law 101-60.
Marshall Islands and Micronesia	Approves diplomatic-relations agreements with the Republic of the Marshall Islands and the Federated States of Micronesia. Signed July 26. Public Law 101-62.
Savings and Loan Reform	Restructures and refinances the savings and loan industry's deposit-insurance system. Signed August 9. Public Law 101-73. *See* special report, page 130.
Farm Aid	Approves $900 million in disaster-relief aid to farmers who lost from 35% to 50% of their crops. Signed August 14. Public Law 101-82.
Ulysses S. Grant Historic Site	Establishes the Ulysses S. Grant National Historic Site in the state of Missouri. Signed September 30. Public Law 101-106.
Nicaraguan Elections	Provides $9 million to ensure free and fair elections in Nicaragua in 1990. Signed October 21. Public Law 101-119.
Lobbying Restrictions	A part of the Department of Interior appropriations bill, requires recipients of federal grants, loans, or contracts to file information on the names of, and fees paid to, lobbyists hired in pursuit of those funds. Signed October 23. Public Law 101-121.
Flag Desecration	Bans defacement of the U.S. flag. Bill became law without presidential signature, October 28. Public Law 101-131. *See* page 315.
Debt Limit	Extends federal borrowing authority to $3.12 trillion through calendar year 1990. Signed November 8. Public Law 101-140.
The Leland Building	Redesignates the Concorde Tower federal building in Houston, TX, as the George Thomas (Mickey) Leland Federal Building, honoring the Texas congressman who was killed during a humanitarian mission in Ethiopia. Signed November 15. Public Law 101-152.
Minimum Wage	Increases the federal minimum wage from $3.35 per hour to $4.25 per hour over two years and allows a temporary training wage equal to 85% of the minimum for those aged 16 to 19. Signed November 17. Public Law 101-157. *See* page 308.
Smoking Ban	A part of the fiscal 1990 spending bill for transportation, bans smoking on virtually all domestic airplane flights. Signed November 21. Public Law 101-164.
Foreign Nationals	A part of the foreign-aid appropriations bill, declares that Soviet Jews, Evangelical Christians, other potential targets of persecution in the USSR, and certain nationals of Vietnam, Laos, and Cambodia would have a well-founded fear of persecution, a condition for refugee status. Signed November 21. Public Law 101-167.
Poland-Hungary Aid	Authorizes a three-year aid program of $938 million for Hungary and Poland. Signed November 28. Public Law 101-179.
Civil Rights	Extends the U.S. Commission on Civil Rights until Sept. 30, 1991. Signed November 28. Public Law 101-180.
South Dakota-Nebraska Boundary	Grants the consent of Congress to a boundary change between South Dakota and Nebraska. Signed November 28. Public Law 101-183.
Indian Museum	Establishes a museum of American Indian history and culture as part of the Smithsonian Institution. Signed November 28. Public Law 101-185.
Women's Vietnam Memorial	Approves the location of a memorial to women who served in the Vietnam war. Signed November 28. Public Law 101-187.
Congressional Pay	Increases the pay of members of the House of Representatives and top federal officials by 40% and the pay of senators by 10%. Bans House members from keeping honoraria beginning in 1990. Signed November 30. Public Law 101-194.
Catastrophic Health Cost	Repeals virtually the entire Medicare Catastrophic Coverage Act of 1988. Signed December 13. Public Law 101-234. *See* page 509.
HUD Reform	Subjects the Department of Housing and Urban Development (HUD) to more internal and external scrutiny. Signed December 15. Public Law 101-235.
Physician Payment Reform	As part of a $14.7 billion deficit-reduction "reconciliation" bill, overhauls the way Medicare pays doctors. Payments will be based on a "resource-based relative value scale." Signed December 19. Public Law 101-239.

SOCIETIES AND ORGANIZATIONS

This listing includes some of the most noteworthy associations, societies, foundations, and trusts of the United States and Canada. The information was verified by the organization concerned.

Academy of Motion Picture Arts & Sciences. Membership: 5,000. Executive director, James M. Roberts. Headquarters: 8949 Wilshire Blvd., Beverly Hills, CA 90211.

Alcoholics Anonymous (The General Service Board of A.A., Inc.). Membership: more than 1,700,000 in more than 85,000 groups worldwide in 135 countries. Chairman, Michael Alexander. Headquarters: 468 Park Ave. S., New York, NY. Mailing address: Box 459, Grand Central Station, New York, NY 10163.

American Academy and Institute of Arts and Letters. Membership: 250. Executive director, Margaret M. Mills. Headquarters: 633 W. 155th St., New York, NY 10032.

American Academy of Political and Social Science. Membership: 10,500, including 5,500 libraries. President, Marvin E. Wolfgang. Headquarters: 3937 Chestnut St., Philadelphia, PA 19104.

American Anthropological Association. Membership: 10,529. Executive director, Eugene Sterud. Headquarters: 1703 New Hampshire Ave. NW, Washington, DC 20009.

American Association for the Advancement of Science. Membership: 132,000 and 285 affiliated scientific and engineering societies and academies of science. Meeting: New Orleans, LA, Feb. 15–20, 1990. President, Richard Atkinson; executive officer, Richard S. Nicholson. Headquarters: 1333 H. Street NW, Washington, DC 20005.

American Association of Museums. Membership: 10,000. Meeting: Chicago, IL, May 9–13, 1990. Director, Edward H. Able. Headquarters: 1225 Eye St. NW, Suite 200, Washington, DC 20005.

American Association of Retired Persons. Membership: 28,000,000. Biennial convention: Orlando, FL, June 12–14, 1990. Executive director, Horace B. Deets. Headquarters: 1909 K St., NW, Washington, DC 20049.

American Association of University Professors. Membership: 41,000. President, Carol Simpson Stern. Headquarters: 1012 14th St. NW, Washington, DC 20005.

American Association of University Women. Membership: 140,000. President, Sharon Schuster. Headquarters: 2401 Virginia Ave. NW, Washington, DC 20037.

American Astronomical Society. Membership: 4,700. Meetings: Washington, DC, Jan. 9–13, 1990; Albuquerque, NM, June 10–14, 1990. Executive officer, Peter B. Boyce. Headquarters: 2000 Florida Ave. NW, Suite 300, Washington, DC 20009.

American Automobile Association. Membership: 30,000,000 in 154 affiliated clubs. President, James B. Creal. Headquarters: 8111 Gatehouse Rd., Falls Church, VA 22047.

American Bankers Association (ABA). Membership: nearly 13,000. President, Charles H. Pistor. Headquarters: 1120 Connecticut Ave. NW, Washington, DC 20036.

American Bar Association. Membership: 350,000. Annual meeting: Chicago, IL, Aug. 1–8, 1990; Midyear meeting: Los Angeles, CA, Feb. 1–8, 1990. President, Robert Raven; president-elect, L. Stanley Chauvin; executive director and chief operating officer, Jill Wine-Banks. Headquarters: 750 North Lake Shore Drive, Chicago, IL 60611.

American Bible Society. Distribution: U.S. 93,299,951; overseas, 215,678,146. Annual meeting, New York City, May 10, 1990. President, James Wood; vice-president, Mrs. Norman Vincent Peale; general officers, John D. Erickson, Maria I. Martinez, Daniel K. Scarberry. Headquarters: 1865 Broadway, New York, NY 10023.

American Booksellers Association, Inc. Membership: 7,300. Convention: Las Vegas, NV, June 2–5, 1990. President, Edward Morrow; executive director, Bernard Rath. Headquarters: 137 W. 25th St., New York, NY 10001.

American Cancer Society, Inc. Membership: 124 voting members; 57 chartered divisions. Executive vice-president, William A. Tipping. Headquarters: 1599 Clifton Rd. NE, Atlanta, GA 30329.

American Chemical Society. Membership: 138,000. National meetings, 1990: Boston, MA, April 22–27; Washington, DC, Aug. 26–31. President, Clayton F. Callis. Headquarters: 1155 16th St. NW, Washington, DC 20036.

American Civil Liberties Union. Membership: 280,000. President, Norman Dorsen; executive director, Ira Glasser. Headquarters: 132 W. 43rd St., New York, NY 10036.

American Correctional Association. Membership: 24,000. Executive director, Anthony P. Travisono. Headquarters: 8025 Laurel Lakes Court, Laurel, MD 20707.

American Council on Education. Membership: 1,452 institutional members, 75 national associates, 74 regional associates, 15 affiliates, 56 international associates, and 29 corporate associates. Annual meeting: Washington, DC, January 1990. President, Robert H. Atwell. Headquarters: One Dupont Circle NW, Washington, DC 20036.

American Council of Learned Societies. Membership: 46 professional societies concerned with the humanities and the humanistic aspects of the social sciences. President, Stanley N. Katz. Headquarters: 228 East 45th St., New York, NY 10017.

American Dental Association. Membership: 148,048. Annual session: Boston, MA, Oct. 13–18, 1990. President, R. Malcolm Overbey, D.D.S.; executive director, Thomas J. Ginley, Ph.D. Headquarters: 211 E. Chicago Ave., Chicago, IL 60611.

American Economic Association. Membership: 20,000 and 6,000 subscribers. President, Joseph A. Pechman. Headquarters: 1313 21st Avenue South, Nashville, TN 37212.

American Farm Bureau Federation. Membership: 3,600,000 families. President, Dean R. Kleckner. Headquarters: 225 Touhy Ave., Park Ridge, IL 60068.

American Geographical Society. Fellows and subscribers: 8,500. President, John E. Gould; director, Mary Lynne Bird. Headquarters: 156 Fifth Ave., Suite 600, New York, NY 10010.

American Geophysical Union. Membership: about 20,000 individuals. Meetings: spring—Baltimore, MD, May 7–11, 1990; fall—San Francisco, CA, Dec. 3–7, 1990. President, Don L. Anderson. Headquarters: 2000 Florida Ave. NW, Washington, DC 20009.

American Heart Association. Membership: 2,000,000 medical and lay volunteers in 56 affiliates and more than 1,800 local divisions. 1989–90 president, Myron L. Weisfeldt, M.D. Headquarters: 7320 Greenville Ave., Dallas, TX 75231.

American Historical Association. Membership: 13,000. Annual meeting: New York, NY, Dec. 27–30, 1990. President: Louis R. Harlan; executive director, Samuel Gammon. Headquarters: 400 A St. SE, Washington, DC 20003.

American Horticultural Society. Membership: 20,000. Annual meeting: Seattle, WA, July 18–22, 1990. President, Carolyn Marsh Lindsay. Headquarters: 7931 East Blvd. Dr., Alexandria, VA 22308.

American Hospital Association. Membership: 48,357 persons; 5,500 institutions. Annual meeting: Washington, DC, Jan. 28–30, 1990. Convention: Washington, DC, July 30–Aug. 1, 1990. Chairman of the board, Edward J. Connors. Headquarters: 840 North Lake Shore Drive, Chicago, IL 60611.

American Hotel & Motel Association. Membership: 10,000. Annual convention: Nashville, TN, April 4–8, 1990. Chief executive officer, Kenneth F. Hine. Headquarters: 1201 New York Avenue NW, Washington, DC 20005.

American Institute of Aeronautics and Astronautics. Membership: 34,849 plus 7,406 student members. Annual meeting: Crystal City, VA, May 1–3, 1990. Executive director, Cort Durocher. Headquarters: 370 L'Enfant Promenade SW, Washington, DC 20024-2518.

American Institute of Architects. Membership: 56,400. Convention: Houston, TX, May 19–22, 1990. President, Benjamin E. Brewer, Jr., FAIA. Headquarters: 1735 New York Avenue NW, Washington, DC 20006.

American Institute of Biological Sciences. Membership: 8,000 with 35 societies and 6 affiliate organizations. Annual meeting: Richmond, VA, Aug. 5–9, 1990. President, Paul R. Ehrlich. Headquarters: 730 11th St. NW, Washington, DC 20001.

American Institute of Certified Public Accountants. Membership: 285,000. Annual meeting: Baltimore, MD, Oct. 21–23, 1990. Chairman, Robert L. May; president, Philip B. Chenok. Headquarters: 1211 Avenue of the Americas, New York, NY 10036-8775.

American Institute of Chemical Engineers. Membership: 50,000. President, E. R. H. McDowell. Headquarters: 345 E. 47th Street, New York, NY 10017.

American Institute of Graphic Arts. Membership: 5,000. President, Nancye Green; executive director, Caroline Hightower. Headquarters: 1059 Third Ave., New York, NY 10021.

American Institute of Mining, Metallurgical and Petroleum Engineers, Inc. 4 member societies: Society for Mining & Exploration Engineers; The Minerals, Metals & Materials Society; Iron & Steel Society; Society of Petroleum Engineers. Annual meeting: Salt Lake City, UT, Feb. 26–March 2, 1990. President, Howard N. Hubbard. Headquarters: 345 E. 47th St., New York, NY 10017.

American Institute of Nutrition. Membership: 2,774. Annual meeting: Washington, DC, April 1–5, 1990. Executive officer, R. G. Allison, Ph.D. Headquarters: 9650 Rockville Pike, Bethesda, MD 20814.

American Legion, The. Membership: 2,900,000. National Executive Committee is chief administrative body between national conventions. National convention: Indianapolis, IN, Aug. 24–30, 1990. Headquarters: 700 N. Pennsylvania St., Indianapolis, IN 46204.

American Library Association. Membership: 47,000. Meetings, 1990: Midwinter—Chicago, IL, Jan. 13–18; Annual conference—Chicago, IL, June 23–28. Executive director, Linda F. Crismond. Headquarters: 50 E. Huron, Chicago, IL 60611.

American Lung Association. Membership: 135 affiliated groups. Annual meeting: Boston, MA, May 20–24, 1990. President, Anne L. Davis, M.D. Headquarters: 1740 Broadway, New York, NY 10019-4374.

American Management Association. Membership: 75,000. Chairman of the board, Robert C. Stites; president, Thomas R. Horton. Headquarters: 135 W. 50th St., New York, NY 10020.

American Mathematical Society. Membership: 22,607. President, William Browder. Headquarters: P.O. Box 6248, Providence, RI 02940.

American Medical Association. Membership: 250,361. President, Alan R. Nelson, M.D.; president-elect, C. John Tupper, M.D. Headquarters: 535 N. Dearborn St., Chicago, IL 60610.

American Meteorological Society. Membership: 10,000 including 128 corporate members. Executive director, Dr. Richard E. Hallgren. Headquarters: 45 Beacon St., Boston, MA 02108.

American Newspaper Publishers Association. Membership: 1,425. Annual convention: Los Angeles, CA, April 23–25, 1990. Chairman, William H. Cowles 3rd, *The Spokesman-Review,* Spokane, WA; president, Jerry W. Friedheim. Executive offices: The Newspaper Center, 11600 Sunrise Valley Dr., Reston, VA 22091. Mailing Address: The Newspaper Center, Box 17407, Dulles International Airport, Washington, DC 20041.

American Nurses' Association. Membership: 190,000 in 53 state and territorial associations. National convention: Boston, MA, June 15–21, 1990. President, Lucille Joel. Headquarters: 2420 Pershing Road, Kansas City, MO 64108.

American Physical Society. Membership: 38,000 American and foreign. President, James A. Krumhansl; executive secretary, W. W. Havens, Jr. Headquarters: 335 E. 45th St., New York, NY 10017.

American Psychiatric Association. Membership: 35,000. Annual meeting: New York, NY, May 12–17, 1990. President, Herbert Pardes, M.D. Headquarters: 1400 K Street NW, Washington, DC 20005.

American Psychological Association. Membership: 70,000. Annual meeting: Boston, MA, Aug. 10–14, 1990. President, Joseph D. Matarazzo. Headquarters: 1200 17th Street NW, Washington, DC 20036.

American Red Cross. Chapters: 2,889. National convention: Orlando, FL, May 20–23, 1990. Chairman, George F. Moody; president, Richard F. Schubert. Headquarters: 17th and D Sts. NW, Washington, DC 20006.

American Society of Civil Engineers. Membership: 108,000. Executive director, Edward O. Pfrang. Headquarters: 345 E. 47th St., New York, NY 10017-2398.

American Society of Composers, Authors, and Publishers. Membership: 29,900 writer members; 1,540 associate members; 12,500 publisher members. President, Morton Gould; secretary, Arthur Hamilton. Headquarters: One Lincoln Plaza, New York, NY 10023.

American Society of Mechanical Engineers. Membership: 117,000. President, C. O. Velzy. Headquarters: 345 E. 47th St., New York, NY 10017.

American Sociological Association. Membership: 13,000. Meeting: Washington, DC, Aug. 11–15, 1990. President, Joan Huber. Executive office: 1722 N St. NW, Washington, DC 20036.

American Statistical Association. Membership: 15,500. President, Janet Norwood. Meeting: Anaheim, CA, Aug. 6–9, 1990. Headquarters: 1429 Duke Street, Alexandria, VA 22314.

American Youth Hostels, Inc. Membership: 100,000; 39 councils in the United States. Executive director, Richard Martyr. Headquarters: P. O. Box 37613, Washington, DC 20013-7613.

Archaeological Institute of America. Membership: 8,000. President, Martha S. Joukowsky; director, Joan C. Bowlen. Annual meeting: San Francisco, CA, Dec. 27–30, 1990. Headquarters: 675 Commonwealth Ave., Boston, MA 02215.

Arthritis Foundation. Membership: 70 chapters. Annual scientific meeting: Seattle, WA, Oct. 20–Nov. 3, 1990. Chairman, Betsey B. Case; president, Clifford M. Clarke. Headquarters: 1314 Spring St. NW, Atlanta, GA 30309.

Association of American Publishers. Membership: approximately 350. Annual meeting: Washington, DC, March 28–30, 1990. Chairman of the board, Jeremiah Kaplan; president, Ambassador Veliotes; vice-president, Thomas McKee. Addresses: 220 E. 23rd St., New York, NY 10010; and 2005 Massachusetts Ave. NW, Washington, DC 20036.

Association of Junior Leagues, Inc. Membership: 273 member leagues in U.S., Canada, Mexico, and the United Kingdom. Annual conference: Toronto, Ontario, May 5-9, 1990. President, Maridel M. Moulton. Headquarters: 660 First Ave., New York, NY 10016.

Association of Operating Room Nurses, Inc. Membership: 41,000 with 363 local chapters. Convention: Houston, TX, March 18–23, 1990. President, Carol Applegeet; executive director, Clifford H. Jordan. Headquarters: 10170 East Mississippi Avenue, Denver, CO 80231.

Benevolent and Protective Order of Elks. Membership: 1,500,000 in 2,300 lodges. Convention: Las Vegas, NV, July 1–5, 1990. Grand exalted ruler, Robert J. Sabin; grand secretary, S. F. Kocur. Headquarters: 2750 Lake View Ave., Chicago, IL 60614.

Bide-A-Wee Home Association, Inc. Executive director, Ursula Goetz. Headquarters: 410 E. 38th St., New York, NY 10016.

Big Brothers/Big Sisters of America. Membership: 460+ local affiliated agencies. National conference: Dallas-Fort Worth, TX, June 20–22, 1990. President, Joyce Black. Headquarters: 230 North 13th St., Philadelphia, PA 19107.

B'nai B'rith International. Membership: 500,000 in approximately 3,000 lodges, chapters, and units. President, Seymour D. Reich; executive vice-president, Thomas Neumann. Headquarters: 1640 Rhode Island Ave. NW, Washington, DC 20036.

Boat Owners Association of the United States. Membership: 300,000. President, Richard Schwartz. Headquarters: 880 S. Pickett St., Alexandria, VA 22304.

Boys Club of America. Youth served: 1,300,000 in 1,100 affiliated Boys Clubs and Boys and Girls Clubs. National conference: Houston, TX, May 10–13, 1990. Chairman, Jeremiah Milbank; national director, Thomas G. Garth. Headquarters: 771 First Ave., New York, NY 10017.

Boy Scouts of America. Membership: total youth members and leaders, 5,377,493 in 408 local councils. Biennial meeting: Baltimore, MD, May 22–25, 1990. President, Harold S. Hook; chief scout executive, Ben H. Love. National office: 1325 Walnut Hill Lane, P.O. Box 152079, Irving, TX 75015-2079.

Camp Fire, Inc. Membership: 550,000 boys and girls in more than 35,000 communities. President, Chuck Heinrich. Headquarters: 4601 Madison Ave., Kansas City, MO 64112.

Canadian Library Association. Membership: 3,500 personal, 800 institutional, 4,300 total. 1990 annual conference: Ottawa, Ont. Executive director, Sharon Henry. Headquarters: 200 Elgin Street, #602, Ottawa, Ont. K2P 1L5.

Canadian Medical Association. Membership: 44,000. Annual meeting, Regina, Sask., Aug. 19–24, 1990. Secretary general, Leo Paul Landry, M.D. Address: 1867 Alta Vista Drive, Ottawa, Ont. K1G 3Y6.

Chamber of Commerce, U.S. Membership: approximately 4,200 associations and state and local chambers; approximately 180,000 business members. Annual meeting: Washington, DC, April 29–May 1, 1990. President, Richard L. Lesher; chairman, John L. Clendenin. Headquarters: 1615 H Street NW, Washington, DC 20062.

Common Cause. Membership: 275,000. Chairman, Archibald Cox. Headquarters: 2030 M St. NW, Washington, DC 20036.

Consumers Union of United States, Inc. Executive director, Rhoda H. Karpatkin. Headquarters: 256 Washington St., Mount Vernon, NY 10553.

Council of Better Business Bureaus. Membership: 2,000. Headquarters: 1515 Wilson Blvd., Suite 300, Arlington, VA 22209.

Council on Foreign Relations, Inc. Membership: 2,510. Annual meeting: New York City, fall 1990. President, Peter Tarnoff. Headquarters: 58 E. 68th St., New York, NY 10021.

Daughters of the American Revolution (National Society). Membership: 204,000 in 3,011 chapters. Continental congress: Washington, DC, April 16–20, 1990. President general, Mrs. Eldred Martin Yochim. Headquarters: 1776 D St. NW, Washington, DC 20006.

Esperanto League for North America, Inc. Membership: 850. President, Ken Thompson. Headquarters: P.O. Box 1129, El Cerrito, CA 94530.

Foreign Policy Association. President, John W. Kiermaier. Headquarters: 729 Seventh Ave., New York, NY 10019.

Freemasonry, Ancient Accepted Scottish Rite of (Northern Masonic Jurisdiction): Supreme Council, 33°. Membership: 435,497 in 110 valleys. Sovereign grand commander, Francis G. Paul. Headquarters: 33 Marrett Rd., Lexington, MA 02173.

Freemasonry, Ancient and Accepted Scottish Rite of (Southern Jurisdiction): Supreme Council, 33°. Membership: 590,000 in 221 affiliated groups. Sovereign grand commander, Fred Kleinknecht. Headquarters: 1733 16th Street NW, Washington, DC 20009.

Gamblers Anonymous. Groups worldwide: 900. Headquarters: 3255 Wilshire Blvd., Suite 610, Los Angeles, CA 90010.

Garden Club of America, The. Membership: 15,000 in 187 clubs. Annual meeting: New York City, April 29–May 2, 1990. President, Mrs. Charles G. Ward, Jr. Headquarters: 598 Madison Ave., New York, NY 10022.

General Federation of Women's Clubs. Membership: 500,000 in 11,000 U.S. clubs and 10,000,000 worldwide. International president, Alice C. Donahue. Headquarters: 1734 N St. NW, Washington, DC 20036.

Geological Society of America. Membership: 17,000. President, Randolph W. Bromery; vice-president, Raymond A. Price; executive director, F. Michael Wahl. Headquarters: 3300 Penrose Place, P.O. Box 9140, Boulder, CO 80301.

Girl Scouts of the U.S.A. Membership: 3,051,956. National president, Betty F. Pilsbury; national executive director, Frances R. Hesselbein. Headquarters: 830 Third Ave., New York, NY 10022.

Humane Society of the United States. Membership: approximately 930,000. Annual convention: San Francisco, CA, October 1990. President, John A. Hoyt. Headquarters: 2100 L St. NW, Washington, DC 20037.

Institute of Electrical and Electronics Engineers, Inc. Membership: 282,700. President, Carleton A. Bayless. Headquarters: 345 E. 47th St., New York, NY 10017.

Jewish War Veterans of the U.S.A. Membership: 100,000 in 450 units. Annual national convention: San Diego, CA, Aug. 12–18, 1990. National commander, Herbert D. Greff; executive director, Steve Shaw. Headquarters: 1811 R St. NW, Washington, DC 20009.

Kiwanis International. Membership: 315,000 in 8,500 clubs in U.S. and abroad. President, Noris A. Lusche. Headquarters: 3636 Woodview Trace, Indianapolis, IN 46268.

Knights of Columbus. Membership: 1,470,598. Supreme knight, Virgil C. Dechant. Headquarters: Columbus Plaza, New Haven, CT 06507.

Knights of Pythias, Supreme Lodge International. Membership: 89,305 in 888 subordinate lodges. Supreme chancellor, Harold D. Burke; supreme secretary, Jack R. Klai. Executive office: 2785 East Desert Inn Rd., #150, Las Vegas, NV 89121.

League of Women Voters of the U.S. Membership: 105,000. President, Nancy M. Neuman. Headquarters: 1730 M Street NW, Washington, DC 20036.

Lions Clubs International. Membership: 1,360,709 in 39,227 clubs in 164 countries and areas. Annual convention: St. Louis, MO, July 11–14, 1990. President, William L. Woolard. Headquarters: 300 22nd St., Oak Brook, IL 60570-0001.

March of Dimes Birth Defects Foundation. Membership: 133 chapters. President, Charles L. Massey. Headquarters: 1275 Mamaroneck Ave., White Plains, NY 10605.

Mental Health Association, Membership: 650 state and local chapters. Headquarters: 1021 Prince St., Alexandria, VA 22314-2971.

Modern Language Association of America. Membership: 27,000. Annual convention: Chicago, IL, Dec. 27–30, 1990. President, Victor Brombert. Headquarters: 10 Astor Place, New York, NY 10003.

National Academy of Sciences. Membership: 1,913. Annual meeting: Washington, DC, April 1990. President, Frank Press. Headquarters: 2101 Constitution Ave. NW, Washington, DC 20418.

National Association for the Advancement of Colored People. Membership: 450,000 in 1,700 branches and 500 youth and college chapters. National convention: Los Angeles, CA, July 7–12, 1990. President, Enolia McMillan; board chairman, William S. Gibson; executive director, Benjamin Hooks. Headquarters: 4805 Mt. Hope Dr., Baltimore, MD 21215-3297.

National Association of Manufacturers. Membership: 13,500. President, Jerry J. Jasinowski. Headquarters: 1331 Pennsylvania Ave. NW, Suite 1500 North Lobby, Washington, DC 20004-1703.

National Audubon Society. Membership: 550,000 in 500 local groups. President, Peter A. A. Berle. Headquarters: 950 Third Ave., New York, NY 10022.

National Committee for Prevention of Child Abuse. Executive director, Anne H. Cohn. Headquarters: 332 S. Michigan Ave., Suite 1600, Chicago, IL 60604.

National Conference of Christians and Jews, Inc. Membership: 75 regional offices. President, Jacqueline G. Wexler. Headquarters: 71 Fifth Ave., Suite 1100, New York, NY 10003.

National Council of the Churches of Christ in the U.S.A. Membership: 32 Protestant, Anglican, and Orthodox denominations. Headquarters: 475 Riverside Dr., New York, NY 10115.

National Council on the Aging, Inc. Membership: 6,000. President, Dr. Daniel Thursz. Annual conference: Washington, DC, April 25–28, 1990. Headquarters: 600 Maryland Ave. SW, West Wing 100, Washington, DC 20024.

National Easter Seal Society. Annual conference: Baltimore, MD, Nov. 14–17, 1990. Chairman of the board, Walter Spencer. Headquarters: 70 East Lake St., Chicago, IL 60601.

National Education Association of the U.S. Membership: 1,900,000. Annual convention: Kansas City, KS, July 3–8, 1990. President, Keith Geiger. Headquarters: 1201 16th St. NW, Washington, DC 20036.

National Federation of Business and Professional Women's Clubs, Inc. (BPW/USA). Membership: 130,000 in 3,400 clubs. President, LaVerne Collins. Headquarters: 2012 Massachusetts Ave. NW, Washington , DC 20036.

National Federation of Independent Business, Inc. Membership: 560,000. President, John Sloan, Jr. Administrative office: 150 W. 20th Ave., San Mateo, CA 94403. Legislative and research office: 600 Maryland Ave. SW, Suite 700, Washington, DC 20024.

National Federation of Music Clubs. Membership: 500,000 in 4,500 clubs and 12 national affiliates. President, Mrs. Glenn L. Brown. Headquarters: 1336 North Delaware St., Indianapolis, IN 46202.

National FFA Organization. Membership: 397,115 in 53 state associations. National convention: Kansas City, MO, Nov. 8–10, 1990. Executive secretary, Coleman Harris. Headquarters: 5632 Mt. Vernon Memorial Hwy., P.O. Box 15160, Alexandria, VA 22309.

National Fire Protection Association. Membership: 48,500. Annual meeting: San Antonio, TX, May 20–24, 1990; fall meeting: Miami, FL, Nov. 12–15, 1990. President, Robert W. Grant. Headquarters: Batterymarch Park, Quincy, MA 02269.

National Organization for Women. Membership: 200,000 in 750 local groups. President, Molly Yard. Headquarters: 1000 16th St. NW, Suite 700, Washington, DC 20036.

National PTA (National Parent-Teacher Association). Membership: 6,466,312 in 26,300 local units. National convention: Indianapolis, IN, June 13–16, 1990. President, Ann Lynch. Headquarters: 700 N. Rush St., Chicago, IL 60611.

National Safety Council. Membership: 12,500. President, T. C. Gilchrest. Headquarters: 444 N. Michigan Ave., Chicago, IL 60611.

National Urban League, Inc. President and chief executive officer, John E. Jacob. Annual conference: New York, NY, July 29–Aug. 1, 1990. Headquarters: 500 East 62nd St., New York, NY 10021.

National Woman's Christian Temperance Union. Membership: approximately 100,000 in 5,000 local unions. National convention: Beckley, WV, August 1990. President, Mrs. Rachel B. Kelly. Headquarters: 1730 Chicago Ave., Evanston, IL 60201.

Parents Without Partners, Inc. International membership: 120,000. International convention: Winnipeg, Manitoba, July 2–7, 1990. Executive director, Maurine McKinley. International office: 8807 Colesville Rd., Silver Spring, MD 20910.

Phi Beta Kappa. Membership: 440,000. Headquarters: 1811 Q St., NW, Washington, DC 20009.

Photographic Society of America. Membership: 12,000. President, Ralph E. Venk. Headquarters: 3000 United Founders Blvd., Suite 103, Oklahoma City, OK 73120.

Planned Parenthood Federation of America, Inc. (Planned Parenthood-World Population). Membership: 177 U.S. affiliates. President, Faye Wattleton; chairperson of the Federation, Anne Saunier. Headquarters: 810 Seventh Ave., New York, NY 10019.

Rotary International. Membership: 1,066,850 in 24,050 clubs functioning in 165 countries and geographical regions. International convention: Portland, OR, May 27–30, 1990. General secretary, Philip H. Lindsey. Headquarters: 1560 Sherman Ave., Evanston, IL 60201-3698.

Salvation Army, The. Membership: 432,893. National commander, James Osborne. National headquarters: 799 Bloomfield Ave., Verona, NJ 07044.

Special Libraries Association. Membership: 12,500. Annual conference: Pittsburgh, PA, June 1990. President, Muriel Regan. Headquarters: 1700 18th St. NW, Washington, DC 20009.

United Dairy Industry Association. Annual convention: Salt Lake City, UT, Sept. 12–13, 1990. Chief executive officer: M. F. Brink. Headquarters: Dairy Center, 6300 N. River Rd., Rosemont, IL 60618.

United States Jaycees. Membership: 240,000 in 5,000 affiliated chapters. Annual meeting: Louisville, KY, June 11–14, 1990. President, Robby Dawkins. Headquarters: P.O. Box 7, 4 W. 21st St.,Tulsa, OK 74145.

U.S. Metric Association. Membership: 2,500. Executive director, Valerie Antoine. Headquarters: 10245 Andasol Ave., Northridge, CA 91325.

United Way of America. Service organization for more than 2,300 autonomous local United Ways. 1990 volunteer leaders conference: Miami Beach, FL, Feb, 24-27, 1990. Chairman of the board of governors, Edward A. Brennan, chairman and CEO, Sears, Roebuck and Co. Address: 701 N. Fairfax St., Alexandria, VA 22314.

Veterans of Foreign Wars of the United States. Membership: VFW and Auxiliary 2,800,000. Commander-in-chief, Larry W. Rivers. Headquarters: VFW Building, Broadway at 34th St., Kansas City, MO 64111.

World Council of Churches (U.S. Conference). Membership: 31 churches or denominations in U.S. Moderator, Dr. Sylvia Talbot. Headquarters: 150 route de Ferney, 1211 Geneva 20, Switzerland. New York office: 475 Riverside Dr., Room 1062, New York, NY 10115.

YMCA of the USA. Membership: 13,000,000 in some 2,000 associations. Board chairman, Harold Davis. Headquarters: 101 North Wacker Dr., Chicago, IL 60606.

YWCA of the USA. Members and participants: approximately 2,000,000. President, Glendora M. Putnam. Headquarters: 726 Broadway, New York, NY 10003.

Zionist Organization of America. Membership: 130,000 in 600 districts. President, Milton S. Shapiro; executive vice-president, Paul Flacks. Headquarters: ZOA House, 4 East 34th St., New York, NY 10016.

Contributors

ADRIAN, CHARLES R., Professor of Political Science, University of California at Riverside; Author, *A History of City Government: The Emergence of the Metropolis 1920–1945;* Coauthor, *A History of American City Government: The Formation of Traditions, 1775–1870, Governing Urban America:* California; Los Angeles

ALPTEKIN, OMER, Columbia University: Sudan

ALTER, STEWART, Editor, *Adweek:* Advertising

AMBRE, AGO, Economist, Office of Economic Affairs, U.S. Department of Commerce: Industrial Production

ARNOLD, ANTHONY, Visiting Scholar, Hoover Institution, Stanford, CA; Author, *Afghanistan: The Soviet Invasion in Perspective, Afghanistan's Two-Party Communism: Parcham and Khalq:* Afghanistan

ATTNER, PAUL, National Correspondent, *The Sporting News:* Sports—*Basketball, Football*

BARMASH, ISADORE, Business-Financial Writer, *The New York Times;* Author, *Always Live Better Than Your Clients, More Than They Bargained For, The Chief Executives:* Retailing

BARRETT, NANCY S., Dean, College of Business Administration, Fairleigh Dickinson University; Author, *The Theory of Macroeconomic Policy, The Theory of Microeconomic Policy, Prices and Wages in U.S. Manufacturing:* Taxation

BASCOM, LIONEL, Free-lance Writer and Editor; Western Connecticut State University: Biography—*David N. Dinkins;* Law—*International*

BATRA, PREM P., Professor of Biochemistry, Wright State University: Biochemistry

BECK, KAY, School of Urban Life, Georgia State University: Georgia

BEHLER, DEBORAH A., Senior Editor, *Animal Kingdom* magazine: Obituaries—*Konrad Lorenz;* Zoos and Zoology

BEST, JOHN, Chief, *Canada World News,* Ottawa: New Brunswick; Prince Edward Island; Quebec

BLANCHARD, PAUL, Professor of Political Science, Eastern Kentucky University; Author, *Kentucky State and Local Government, New School Board Members: A Portrait:* Kentucky

BOND, DONOVAN H., Professor Emeritus of Journalism, West Virginia University: West Virginia

BOULAY, HARVEY, Director of Development, Rogerson House; Author, *The Twilight Cities:* Massachusetts

BOWER, BRUCE, Behavioral Sciences Editor, *Science News:* Anthropology; Archaeology

BRAMMER, DANA B., Director, Public Policy Research Center, University of Mississippi: Mississippi

BRANDHORST, L. CARL, and JoANN C., Department of Geography, Western Oregon State College: Oregon

BROOM, JACK, Reporter, *The Seattle Times:* Washington

BURANELLI, VINCENT, Free-lance Writer and Editor; Author, *Thomas Edison, The Trial of Peter Zenger, Louis XIV;* Coauthor, *Spy/Counterspy: An Encyclopedia of Espionage:* Espionage

BURKS, ARDATH W., Professor Emeritus Asian Studies, Rutgers University; Author, *Japan: A Postindustrial Power:* Biography—*Akihito, Toshiki Kaifu;* Japan; Japan—*The Economic Superpower;* Obituaries—*Hirohito*

BUSH, GRAHAM W. A., Associate Professor of Political Studies, University of Auckland; Author, *Local Government & Politics in New Zealand;* Editor, *New Zealand—A Nation Divided?:* New Zealand

BUTTRY, STEPHEN, National/Mid-America Editor, *The Kansas City Times:* Missouri

CASPER, GRETCHEN, Department of Political Science, Texas A&M: Philippines

CASPER, LEONARD, Professor of English, Boston College; Past Recipient of Fulbright grants to lecture in the Philippines: Philippines; Philippines—*Ferdinand E. Marcos*

CASSIDY, SUZANNE, Free-lance Writer; Researcher, London Bureau, *The New York Times:* Great Britain; Great Britain—*The Arts*

CASTAGNO, ANTHONY J., Energy Consultant; Manager, Nuclear Information, Northeast Utilities: Energy

CHALMERS, JOHN W., Historical Society of Alberta; Editor, *Alberta Diamond Jubilee* Anthology: Alberta

CHRISTENSEN, WILLIAM E., Professor of History, Midland Lutheran College; Author, *In Such Harmony: A History of the Federated Church of Columbus, Nebraska:* Nebraska

COLE, JOHN N., Founder, *Maine Times;* Author, *Fishing Came First, In Maine, Striper, Salmon, House Building:* Maine

COLLINS, BUD, Sports Columnist, *The Boston Globe;* Author, *My Life With The Pros:* Sports—*Tennis*

COLTON, KENT W., Executive Vice-President and Chief Executive Officer, National Association of Home Builders, Washington, DC: Housing

CONRADT, DAVID P., Professor of Political Science, University of Florida; Author, *The German Polity, Comparative Politics, The Civic Culture Revisited, The West German Party System:* Germany

COOPER, MARY H., Staff Writer, *Editorial Research Reports:* Abortion: The Continuing Controversy; Insurance, Liability; Social Welfare—*Voluntarism*

COPPEDGE, MICHAEL, Assistant Professor, Paul H. Nitze School of Advanced International Studies, Johns Hopkins University: Ecuador; Peru; Venezuela

CORLEW, ROBERT E., Dean, School of Liberal Arts, Middle Tennessee State University: Tennessee

CORNWELL, ELMER E., JR., Professor of Political Science, Brown University: Rhode Island

CUNNIFF, JOHN, Business News Analyst, The Associated Press; Author, *How to Stretch Your Dollar:* Business and Corporate Affairs; United States—*The Economy*

CUNNINGHAM, PEGGY, *The Evening Sun,* Baltimore, MD: Maryland

CURRIER, CHET, Financial Writer, The Associated Press; Author, *The Investor's Encyclopedia, The 15-Minute Investor;* Coauthor, *No-Cost/Low-Cost Investing:* Stocks and Bonds

CURTIS, L. PERRY, JR., Professor of History, Brown University: Ireland

DANIELS, ROBERT V., Professor of History, University of

Vermont; former Vermont state senator; Author, *Russia: The Roots of Confrontation:* VERMONT

DARBY, JOSEPH W., III, Reporter, *The Times-Picayune,* New Orleans: LOUISIANA

DASCH, E. JULIUS, NRC/NASA Headquarters; Author of more than 100 papers and abstracts in geology and geochemistry: SPACE EXPLORATION

De GREGORIO, GEORGE, Sports Department, *The New York Times;* Author, *Joe DiMaggio, An Informal Biography:* SPORTS—*Boxing, Ice Skating, Skiing, Swimming, Track and Field, Yachting*

DELZELL, CHARLES F., Professor of History, Vanderbilt University; Author, *Italy in the Twentieth Century, Mediterranean Fascism, Mussolini's Enemies:* ITALY

DENNIS, LARRY, Golf Writer, Creative Communications: SPORTS—*Golf, Golf's Upswing*

DIETERICH, H.R., Professor of History, University of Wyoming: WYOMING

DOSSEY, JOHN A., Distinguished Professor of Mathematics, Illinois State University; Chairman, Standards Commission, National Council of Teachers of Mathematics: EDUCATION—*A New Focus on Mathematics*

DUFF, ERNEST A., Professor of Politics, Randolph-Macon Woman's College; Author, *Agrarian Reform in Colombia, Violence and Repression in Latin America:* COLOMBIA

DUIKER, WILLIAM J., Professor of East Asian History, The Pennsylvania State University; Author, *The Communist Road to Power in Vietnam, Vietnam Since the Fall of Saigon, China and Vietnam: The Roots of Conflict:* ASIA

ELKINS, ANN M., Fashion Director, *Good Housekeeping Magazine:* FASHION

ELVING, PHYLLIS, Free-lance Travel Writer: TRAVEL

ENSTAD, ROBERT H., Writer, *Chicago Tribune:* BIOGRAPHY—*Richard M. Daley;* CHICAGO; ILLINOIS

ENTELIS, JOHN P., Professor, Department of Political Science, Fordham University: MOROCCO; SUDAN; TUNISIA

ENTER, JACK E., Assistant Professor of Criminal Justice, Georgia State University: CRIME

EWEGEN, ROBERT D., Editorial Writer, *The Denver Post:* COLORADO

FAGEN, MORTON D., AT&T Bell Laboratories (retired); Editor, *A History of Engineering and Science in the Bell System,* Vol. 1, *The Early Years, 1875–1925,* and Vol. II, *National Service in War and Peace, 1925–1975:* COMMUNICATION TECHNOLOGY

FISHER, JIM, Editorial Writer, *Lewiston Morning Tribune:* IDAHO

FRANCIS, DAVID R., Economic Columnist, *The Christian Science Monitor:* INTERNATIONAL TRADE AND FINANCE

FRIIS, ERIK J., Editor and Publisher, *The Scandinavian-American Bulletin:* DENMARK; FINLAND; NORWAY; SWEDEN

GAILEY, HARRY A., Professor of History, San Jose State University; Author, *History of the Gambia, History of Africa, Road to Aba:* MOZAMBIQUE; NIGERIA; ZAIRE

GIBSON, ROBERT C., Regional Editor, *The Billings Gazette:* MONTANA

GOODMAN, DONALD, Associate Professor of Sociology, John Jay College of Criminal Justice, City University of New York: PRISONS

GORDON, MAYNARD M., Detroit Editor, *Auto Age;* Author, *The Iacocca Management Technique:* AUTOMOBILES

GOUDINOFF, PETER, Member, House of Representatives, Arizona; Professor, Department of Political Science, University of Arizona; Author, *People's Guide to National Defense:* ARIZONA

GRAYSON, GEORGE W., John Marshall Professor of Government and Citizenship, College of William and Mary; Author, *The Politics of Mexican Oil, The United States and Mexico: Patterns of Influence, Oil and Mexican Foreign Policy:* BRAZIL; PORTUGAL; SPAIN

GREEN, MAUREEN, Writer and Publisher, London: LITERATURE—*English*

GREENE, ELAINE, Free-lance Design Reporter: INTERIOR DESIGN

GROSSMAN, LAWRENCE, Director of Publications, The American Jewish Committee: RELIGION—*Judaism*

GROTH, ALEXANDER J., Professor of Political Science, University of California, Davis; Author, *People's Poland;* Coauthor, *Contemporary Politics: Europe, Comparative Resource Allocation, Public Policy Across Nations:* BIOGRAPHY—*Tadeusz Mazowiecki;* POLAND

HACKER, JEFFREY H., Free-lance Writer and Editor; Author, *Government Subsidy to Industry, Franklin D. Roosevelt, Carl Sandburg, The New China:* 50 YEARS OF TELEVISION; BIOGRAPHY—*Salman Rushdie;* INDONESIA; MALAYSIA; OBITUARIES—*Sugar Ray Robinson;* SINGAPORE; SPORTS—*Overview, Soccer*

HADWIGER, DON F., Professor of Political Science, Iowa State University; Coauthor, *World Food Policies: Toward Agricultural Interdependence:* AGRICULTURE; FOOD

HALLER, TIMOTHY G., Assistant Professor, Department of Political Science, University of Nevada, Reno: NEVADA

HALSEY, MARGARET BROWN, Professor, New York City Technical College: ART

HAND, SAMUEL B., Professor of History, University of Vermont: VERMONT

HANDELMAN, GLADYS, Free-lance Writer and Editor: BIOGRAPHY—*Jerome Robbins;* FAMILY; OBITUARIES—*Laurence Olivier;* WOMEN

HARMON, CHARLES, American Library Association: LIBRARIES

HARRIS, DORRAINE, Free-lance Writer, Las Cruces, NM: NEW MEXICO

HARVEY, ROSS M., Executive Director, Television Northern Canada: NORTHWEST TERRITORIES

HELMREICH, ERNST C., Professor Emeritus of History, Bowdoin College; Author, *The German Churches under Hitler: Background, Struggle, and Epilogue:* AUSTRIA

HELMREICH, JONATHAN E., Professor of History, Allegheny College; Author, *Belgium and Europe: A Study in Small Power Diplomacy, Gathering Rare Ores: The Diplomacy of Uranium Acquisition, 1943–54:* BELGIUM

HELMREICH, PAUL C., Professor of History, Wheaton College; Author, *Wheaton College: The Seminary Years, 1834–1912; From Paris to Sèvres: The Partition of the Ottoman Empire at the Peace Conference of 1919–1920:* SWITZERLAND

HINTON, HAROLD C., Professor of Political Science and International Affairs, The George Washington University; Author, *Korea under New Leadership: The Fifth Republic, Communist China in World Politics, The China Sea: The American Stake in Its Future:* KOREA

HOLLOWAY, HARRY, Professor of Political Science, University of Oklahoma; Coauthor, *Public Opinion: Coalitions, Elites, and Masses, Party and Factional Division in Texas:* OKLAHOMA

HOOVER, HERBERT T., Professor of History, University of South Dakota; Author, *South Dakota Leaders, The Yankton Sioux, To Be an Indian:* SOUTH DAKOTA

HOPKO, THE REV. THOMAS, Assistant Professor, St. Vladimir's Orthodox Theological Seminary: RELIGION—*Orthodox Eastern*

HOYT, CHARLES K., Senior Editor, *Architectural Record;* Author, *More Places for People, Building for Commerce and Industry:* ARCHITECTURE

HUFFMAN, GEORGE J., Assistant Professor, Department of Meteorology, University of Maryland: METEOROLOGY

HULBERT, DAN, *Atlanta Journal & Constitution:* TELEVISION AND RADIO; THEATER

HUTH, JOHN F., JR., Reporter (retired), *The Plain Dealer,* Cleveland: OHIO

JACKSON, PAUL CONRAD, Journalist, *Saskatoon Star-Phoenix:* SASKATCHEWAN

JONES, H.G., Curator, North Carolina Collection, University of North Carolina at Chapel Hill; Author, *North Carolina Illustrated, 1524–1984:* NORTH CAROLINA

JONES, PAT, Science Applications International Corporation: SPACE EXPLORATION

JUDD, DENNIS R., Professor and Chair, Department of Political Science, University of Missouri; Author, *The Politics of Urban Planning, The Politics of American Cities, The Development of American Public Policy, Regenerating the Cities:* THE IDEAL CITY; CITIES AND URBAN AFFAIRS

JUDD, LEWIS L., Director, National Institute of Mental Health: MEDICINE AND HEALTH—*Mental Health*

KARNES, THOMAS L., Professor of History Emeritus, Arizona State University; Author, *Latin American Policy of the United States, Failure of Union: Central America 1824–1960:* CENTRAL AMERICA

KIMBALL, LORENZO K., Professor Emeritus, Department of Political Science, University of Utah: UTAH

KIMBELL, CHARLES L., Senior Foreign Mineral Specialist, U.S. Bureau of Mines: STATISTICAL AND TABULAR DATA—*Mineral and Metal Production*

KING, PETER J., Professor of History, Carleton University, Ottawa; Author, *Utilitarian Jurisprudence in America:* ONTARIO; OTTAWA

KINLOCH, GRAHAM C., Professor of Sociology, Florida State University; Author, *The Sociology of Minority Group Relations:* ETHNIC GROUPS

KINNEAR, MICHAEL, Professor of History, University of Manitoba; Author, *The Fall of Lloyd George, The British Voter:* MANITOBA

KISSELGOFF, ANNA, Chief Dance Critic, *The New York Times:* DANCE

KOZINN, ALLAN, Music Critic, *The New York Times;* Author, *Mischa Elman and the Romantic Style, The Guitar: The History, The Music, The Players:* MUSIC—*Classical*

KRONISH, SYD, Stamp Editor, The Associated Press: STAMPS AND STAMP COLLECTING

KUNZ, KENEVA, BBC Foreign Correspondent, Reykjavik: ICELAND

LaFRANCHI, HOWARD, Reporter, Paris Bureau, *The Christian Science Monitor:* FRANCE; FRANCE—*The French Revolution Bicentennial*

LAI, DAVID CHUENYAN, Professor of Geography, University of Victoria, British Columbia; Author, *Chinatowns: Towns Within Cities in Canada:* HONG KONG

LANCASTER, CAROL, Director, African Studies Program, Georgetown University; Coeditor, *African Debt and Financing:* AFRICA

LAWRENCE, ROBERT M., Professor of Political Science, Colorado State University; Author, *Strategic Defense Initiative: Bibliography and Research Guide:* ARMS CONTROL AND DISARMAMENT; MILITARY AFFAIRS

LEE, STEWART M., Chairman, Department of Economics and Business Administration, Geneva College; Coauthor, *Personal Finance for Consumers, Consumer Economics:* CONSUMER AFFAIRS

LEEPSON, MARC, Free-lance Writer: DRUGS AND ALCOHOL; SOCIAL WELFARE

LEVINE, LOUIS, Professor, Department of Biology, City College of New York; Author, *Biology of the Gene, Biology for a Modern Society:* BIOTECHNOLOGY; GENETICS; MICROBIOLOGY

LEWIS, ANNE C., Education Policy Writer: EDUCATION

LEWIS, JEROME R., Director for Public Administration, College of Urban Affairs and Public Policy, University of Delaware: DELAWARE

LOBRON, BARBARA L., Writer, Editor, Photographer: PHOTOGRAPHY; PHOTOGRAPHY—*The Disposable Camera*

LOESCHER, GIL, Associate Professor of International Relations, University of Notre Dame; Author, *Calculated Kindness: Refugees and America's Half-Open Door, Refugees and International Relations, The Moral Nation: Humanitarianism and U.S. Foreign Policy:* REFUGEES AND IMMIGRATION

MABRY, DONALD J., Professor of History, Mississippi State University; Author, *Mexico's Acción Nacional, The Mexican University and the State;* Coauthor, *Neighbors—Mexico and the United States:* MEXICO

MARCOPOULOS, GEORGE J., Associate Professor of History, Tufts University: CYPRUS; GREECE

MATHESON, JIM, Sportswriter, *Edmonton Journal:* BIOGRAPHY—*Mario Lemieux;* SPORTS—*Ice Hockey*

MATTHEWS, WILLIAM H., III, Professor of Geology, Lamar University; Author, *Fossils: An Introduction to Prehistoric Life, Exploring the World of Fossils:* GEOLOGY

McCORQUODALE, SUSAN, Professor of Political Science, Memorial University of Newfoundland: NEWFOUNDLAND

McCRAW, VINCENT D., *The Washington Times:* WASHINGTON, DC

McGILL, DAVID A., Professor of Marine Science, U.S. Coast Guard Academy: OCEANOGRAPHY

MELIKOV, GREG, Editor, State Desk, *The Miami Herald:* FLORIDA

MICHAELIS, PATRICIA A., Curator of Manuscripts, Kansas State Historical Society: KANSAS

MICHIE, ARUNA NAYYAR, Associate Professor of Political Science, Kansas State University: BANGLADESH

MILWARD, JOHN, Free-lance Writer and Critic: MUSIC—*The Return of Ballroom Dancing, Popular and Jazz;* OBITUARIES—*Irving Berlin;* RECORDINGS

MITCHELL, GARY, Professor of Physics, North Carolina State University: PHYSICS

MORELLO, TED, United Nations Correspondent, *The Christian Science Monitor;* Author, *Official Handbook of the Hall of Fame:* UNITED NATIONS

MORTIMER, ROBERT A., Professor, Department of Political Science, Haverford College; Author, *The Third World Coalition in International Politics:* ALGERIA

MORTON, DESMOND, Professor of History and Principal, Erindale College, University of Toronto; Author, *A Short History of Canada, Bloody Victory: Canadians and the D-Day Campaign, Working People: An Illustrated History of the Canadian Labour Movement, A Military History of Canada, Winning the Second Battle: Canadian Veterans and the Return to Civilian Life, 1915–1930;* Coauthor, *Marching to Armageddon: Canadians in the First World War, 1914–1919:* CANADA

MURPHY, ROBERT F., Reporter, *The Hartford Courant:* CONNECTICUT

NAFTALIN, ARTHUR, Professor Emeritus of Public Affairs, University of Minnesota: MINNESOTA

NASH, NATHANIEL C., Economics Reporter, Washington Bureau, *The New York Times:* BANKING AND FINANCE; BANKING AND FINANCE—*The Savings and Loan Crisis*

NEUMANN, JIM, Free-lance Writer, Fargo, ND: NORTH DAKOTA

NEWLAND, ED, Assistant State Editor, *Richmond Times-Dispatch:* VIRGINIA

OCHSENWALD, WILLIAM, Professor of History, Virginia Polytechnic Institute; Author, *The Middle East: A History, The Hijaz Railroad, Religion, Society, and the State in Arabia:* SAUDI ARABIA

O'CONNOR, ROBERT E., Associate Professor of Political Science, The Pennsylvania State University; Author, *Politics and Structure: Essentials of American National Government:* PENNSYLVANIA

O'MEARA, PATRICK, Director, African Studies Program, Indiana University; Coeditor, *Africa, International Politics in Southern Africa, Southern Africa, The Continuing Crisis:* ANGOLA; NAMIBIA; SOUTH AFRICA; ZIMBABWE

O'SHAUGHNESSY, ANNE E., Assistant Editor, *The Numismatist:* COINS AND COIN COLLECTING

PALMER, NORMAN D., Professor Emeritus of Political Science and South Asian Studies, University of Pennsylvania; Author, *Westward Watch: The United States and the Changing Western Pacific, The United States and India: The Dimensions of Influence, Elections and Political Development: The South Asian Experience:* INDIA; SRI LANKA

PEARSON, FREDERIC S., Professor of Political Science and Fellow, Center for International Studies, University of Missouri-St. Louis; Author, *International Relations: The Global Condition in the Late Twentieth Century; The Weak State in International Crisis:* UNITED STATES—*Foreign Affairs*

PERETZ, DON, Professor of Political Science, State University of New York at Binghamton; Author, *The West Bank—History, Politics, Society & Economy, Government and Politics of Israel, The Middle East Today:* EGYPT; ISRAEL

PERKINS, KENNETH J., Assistant Professor of History, University of South Carolina: LIBYA; RELIGION—*Islam*

PERRY, DAVID K., Associate Professor, Department of Journalism, The University of Alabama: PUBLISHING

PICHER, KEITH D., Staff Writer, *The New World:* RELIGION—*Roman Catholicism*

PIPPIN, LARRY L., Professor of Political Science, University of the Pacific; Author, *The Remón Era:* ARGENTINA; BIOGRAPHY—*Carlos Saúl Menem;* PARAGUAY; URUGUAY

PLATT, HERMAN K., Professor of History, Saint Peter's College: NEW JERSEY

POOLE, PETER A., Author, *The Vietnamese in Thailand, Eight Presidents and Indochina:* CAMBODIA; LAOS; THAILAND; VIETNAM

PREZIOSI, DOMINIC, Free-lance Writer: ENGINEERING, CIVIL

RALOFF, JANET, Environment/Policy Editor, *Science News:* ENVIRONMENT

RAMIREZ, DEBORAH, Reporter, *San Juan Star:* PUERTO RICO

REED, WILLIAM CYRUS, Professor, Department of Political Science, Wabash College: KENYA; TANZANIA; UGANDA

REUNING, WINIFRED, Writer, Polar Program, National Science Foundation: POLAR RESEARCH

RICHTER, LINDA K., Associate Professor, Department of Political Science, Kansas State University; Author, *Land Reform and Tourism Development: Policy-Making in the Philippines, The Politics of Tourism in Asia:* BURMA

RICHTER, WILLIAM L., Professor and Head, Department of Political Science, Kansas State University: BIOGRAPHY—*Benazir Bhutto;* PAKISTAN

RIGGAN, WILLIAM, Associate Editor, *World Literature Today,* University of Oklahoma; Author, *Picaros, Madmen, Naïfs, and Clowns, Comparative Literature and Literary Theory:* LITERATURE—*World*

ROBERTS, SAM, Urban Affairs Columnist, *The New York Times;* Editor, *The New York Times Reader;* Coauthor, *I Never Wanted To Be Vice-President of Anything:* NEW YORK CITY

ROBINSON, LEIF J., Editor, *Sky & Telescope:* ASTRONOMY

ROSS, RUSSELL M., Professor of Political Science, University of Iowa; Author, *State and Local Government and Administration, Iowa Government and Administration:* IOWA

ROVIN, JEFF, Free-lance Writer; Author, *A Pictorial History of Science Fiction Films, The Fabulous Fantasy Films, The Films of Charlton Heston, From Jules Verne to Star Trek:* BIOGRAPHY—*Jodie Foster, Dustin Hoffman*

ROWEN, HERBERT H., Professor Emeritus, Rutgers University, New Brunswick; Author, *The Princes of Orange, John de Witt: Statesman of the "True Freedom", The King's State, John de Witt: Grand Pensionary of Holland:* NETHERLANDS

RUBIN, JIM, Supreme Court Correspondent, The Associated Press: LAW

RUFF, NORMAN J., Assistant Professor, Department of Political Science, University of Victoria, B.C.; Coauthor, *The Reins of Power: Governing British Columbia:* BRITISH COLUMBIA

SALSINI, PAUL, Staff Development Director, *The Milwaukee Journal:* WISCONSIN

SAVAGE, DAVID, Free-lance Writer: CANADA—*The Arts, The National Film Board at 50;* LITERATURE—*Canadian*

SAWATSKY, DON, Free-lance Writer/Broadcaster; Author, *Ghost Town Trails of the Yukon:* YUKON

SCHLOSSBERG, DAN, Baseball Writer; Author, *The Baseball IQ Challenge, The Baseball Catalog, The Baseball Book of Why:* BIOGRAPHY—*Orel Hershiser;* SPORTS—*Baseball, The Banning of Peter Rose, The Hall of Fame at 50*

SCHROEDER, RICHARD, Syndicated Writer, various U.S. newspapers; Consultant to Organization of American States: BOLIVIA; CARIBBEAN; CHILE; HAITI; JAMAICA; LATIN AMERICA

SCHWAB, PETER, Professor of Political Science, State University of New York at Purchase; Author, *Ethiopia: Politics, Economics, and Society, Toward a Human Rights Framework:* ETHIOPIA

SEIDERS, DAVID F., Chief Economist and Senior Staff Vice-President, National Association of Home Builders, Washington, DC: HOUSING

SENSER, ROBERT A., Free-lance Writer, Washington, DC: COMMUNISM IN FLUX: THE DEMOCRATIC REVOLUTION; LABOR

SETH, R.P., Professor of Economics, Mount Saint Vincent University, Halifax: CANADA—*The Economy;* NOVA SCOTIA

SEYBOLD, PAUL G., Professor, Department of Chemistry, Wright State University: CHEMISTRY

SHARLET, ROBERT, Professor of Political Science, Union College; Coeditor, *P.I. Stuchka: Selected Writings on Soviet Law and Marxism, The Soviet Union Since Stalin, Pashukanis: Selected Writings on Marxism and Law:* USSR

SHEPRO, CARL E., Professor, University of Alaska-Anchorage: ALASKA

SHOGAN, ROBERT, National Political Correspondent, Washington Bureau, *Los Angeles Times;* Author, *A Question of Judgment, Promises to Keep:* BIOGRAPHY—*Richard Bruce Cheney, Thomas S. Foley, William H. Gray III, George Mitchell;* UNITED STATES—*Domestic Affairs, Government Ethics*

SIEGEL, STANLEY E., Professor of History, University of Houston; Author, *A Political History of the Texas Republic, 1836–1845, Houston: Portrait of the Supercity on Buffalo Bayou:* TEXAS

SIMON, JEFFREY D., The RAND Corporation, Santa Monica, CA: TERRORISM

SMITH, REX, Albany Bureau Chief, *Newsday:* NEW YORK

SNIDER, LEWIS W., Associate Professor of International Relations and Government, Center for Politics and Policy, Claremont Graduate School; Author, *The Political Economy of Military Production and Arms Exports: The Industrialized vs. the Developing World;* Coauthor, *Middle East Foreign Policy:* LEBANON

SNODSMITH, RALPH L., Garden Editor, "Good Morning America", ABC-TV; Host, "Garden Hotline"; Author, *Ralph Snodsmith's Tips from the Garden Hotline, Garden Calendar and Record Keeper 1985–1988:* GARDENING AND HORTICULTURE

SPYCHALSKI, JOHN C., Chairman, Department of Business Logistics, College of Business Administration, The Pennsylvania State University; Editor, *Transportation Journal:* TRANSPORTATION; TRANSPORTATION—*The Story of Eastern Airlines*

STARR, JOHN BRYAN, Executive Director, Yale-China Association; Author, *Continuing the Revolution: The Political Thought of Mao;* Editor, *The Future of U.S.-China Relations:* BIOGRAPHY—*Jiang Zemin, Li Peng;* CHINA; TAIWAN

STERN, JEROME H., Associate Professor of English, Florida State University; Editor, *Studies in Popular Culture:* LITERATURE—*American*

STEWART, WILLIAM H., Associate Professor of Political Science, The University of Alabama; Coauthor, *Alabama Government and Politics:* ALABAMA

STOUDEMIRE, ROBERT H., Distinguished Professor Emeritus, University of South Carolina: SOUTH CAROLINA

SUNY, RONALD GRIGOR, Alex Manoogian Professor of Modern Armenian History, University of Michigan; Author, *The Baku Commune, 1917–18: Class and Nationality in the Russian Revolution, Armenia in the Twentieth Century:* OBITUARIES—*Andrei A. Gromyko*

SUTTON, STAN, Sportswriter, *The Courier-Journal,* Louisville, KY: SPORTS—*Auto Racing, Horse Racing*

SYLVESTER, LORNA LUTES, Associate Editor, *Indiana Magazine of History,* Indiana University: INDIANA

TABORSKY, EDWARD, Professor of Government, University of Texas at Austin; Author, *Communism in Czechoslovakia, 1948–1960, Communist Penetration of the Third World:* CZECHOSLOVAKIA

TAYLOR, WILLIAM L., Professor of History, Plymouth State College: NEW HAMPSHIRE

TESAR, JENNY, Science and Medicine Writer; Author, *Parents as Teachers:* COMPUTERS; MEDICINE AND HEALTH; MEDICINE AND HEALTH—*Allergies: Nothing to Sneeze At, Recent Advances in Ophthalmology*

THEISEN, CHARLES W., Assistant News Editor, *The Detroit News:* MICHIGAN

TURNER, ARTHUR CAMPBELL, Professor of Political Science, University of California, Riverside; Coauthor, *Ideology and Power in the Middle East:* BIOGRAPHY—*Ali Akbar Hashemi Rafsanjani;* IRAN; IRAQ; JORDAN; MIDDLE EAST; OBITUARIES—*Ayatollah Ruhollah Khomeini;* SYRIA

TURNER, CHARLES H., Free-lance Writer: HAWAII

TURNER, DARRELL J., Associate Editor, Religious News Service: BIOGRAPHY—*Barbara C. Harris;* RELIGION—*Far Eastern, Protestantism*

VAN RIPER, PAUL P., Professor Emeritus and Head, Department of Political Science, Texas A&M University: POSTAL SERVICE

VOLSKY, GEORGE, Center for Advanced International Studies, University of Miami: CUBA

WEIKER, WALTER F., Professor of Political Science, Rutgers University: TURKEY

WEISBERGER, BERNARD A., Author, *Many People, One Nation, The Statue of Liberty: The First 100 Years, The American Heritage History of the American People:* 200 YEARS OF PRESIDENTIAL INAUGURATIONS

WILLIAMS, C. FRED, Associate Vice Chancellor for Educational Programs, University of Arkansas at Little Rock; Author, *Arkansas: An Illustrated History of the Land of Opportunity, Arkansas: A Documentary History:* ARKANSAS

WILLIS, F. ROY, Professor of History, University of California, Davis; Author, *France, Germany and the New Europe, 1945–1968, Italy Chooses Europe, The French Paradox:* EUROPE

WILMS, DENISE MURCKO, Assistant Editor, *Booklist Magazine,* American Library Association: LITERATURE—*Children's*

WINCHESTER, N. BRIAN, Associate Director, African Studies Program, Indiana University: ANGOLA; NAMIBIA; SOUTH AFRICA

WITTEMAN, PAUL A., San Francisco Bureau Chief, *Time* magazine: THE EXXON VALDEZ: THE LARGEST OIL SPILL IN U.S. HISTORY; THE BAY AREA EARTHQUAKE

WOLF, WILLIAM, New York University; Author, *The Marx Brothers, The Landmark Films, The Cinema and Our Century:* MOTION PICTURES

YOUNGER, R.M., Journalist and Author; Author, *Australia and the Australians, Australia! Australia! A Bicentennial Record:* AUSTRALIA

ZACEK, JOSEPH FREDERICK, Professor of History, State University of New York, Albany; Author, *Palacky: The Historian as Scholar and Nationalist;* Coauthor, *Frantisek Palacky, 1798–1876: A Centennial Appreciation, The Enlightenment and the National Revivals in Eastern Europe:* ALBANIA; BULGARIA; HUNGARY; ROMANIA; YUGOSLAVIA

Index

Main article headings appear in this index as bold-faced capitals; subjects within articles appear as lower-case entries. Both the general references and the subentries should be consulted for maximum usefulness of this index. Illustrations are indexed herein. Cross references are to the entries in this index.

A

B

C

D

E

F

G

H

I

J

N

O

P

Q

R

S

T

U

V

W

Y

Z